is an online assessment and preparation

Management

Twelfth Edition

Stephen P. Robbins
San Diego State University

Mary Coulter
Missouri State University

PEARSON

Boston Columbus Indianapolis New York San Francisco Upper Saddle River
Amsterdam Cape Town Dubai London Madrid Milan Munich Paris Montréal Toronto
Delhi Mexico City São Paulo Sydney Hong Kong Seoul Singapore Taipei Tokyo

Editor in Chief: Stephanie Wall
Senior Acquisitions Editor: April Cole
Director of Editorial Services: Ashley Santora
Editorial Project Manager: Claudia Fernandes
Editorial Assistant: Bernard Ollila
Director of Marketing: Maggie Moylan
Senior Marketing Manager: Nikki Ayana Jones
Marketing Assistant: Gianna Sandri
Senior Managing Editor: Judy Leale
Production Project Manager: Kelly Warsak
Operations Specialist: Cathleen Petersen
Creative Director: Blair Brown
Senior Art Director: Kenny Beck
Interior Designer: Ray Cruz
Cover Designer: Ray Cruz
Permission Specialist: Brooks Hill-Whilton
Media Project Manager, Production: Lisa Rinaldi
Media Project Manager, Editorial: Denise Vaughn
Full-Service Project Management and Composition: Integra
Printer/Binder: Courier/Kendallville
Cover Printer: Lehigh-Phoenix Color/Hagerstown
Text Font: Times New Roman MT Std

Credits and acknowledgments borrowed from other sources and reproduced, with permission, in this textbook appear on appropriate page within text.

Many of the designations by manufacturers and seller to distinguish their products are claimed as trademarks. Where those designations appear in this book, and the publisher was aware of a trademark claim, the designations have been printed in initial caps or all caps.

Library of Congress Cataloging-in-Publication Data

CIP data for this title is available on file at the Library of Congress.

10 9 8 7 6 5
V011

ISBN 10:   0-13-304360-6
ISBN 13: 978-0-13-304360-0

To my wife, Laura

Steve

———————————

To My Sweet Babies:
Brooklynn and Blake

Mary

About *the* Authors

STEPHEN P. ROBBINS (Ph.D., University of Arizona) is professor emeritus of management at San Diego State University and the world's best-selling textbook author in the areas of both management and organizational behavior. His books have sold more than 5 million copies and have been translated into 20 languages. His books are currently used at more than 1,500 U.S. colleges and universities as well as hundreds of schools throughout Canada, Latin America, Australia, New Zealand, Asia, and Europe. Dr. Robbins is also the author of the best-selling *The Truth About Managing People,* 2nd ed. (Financial Times/Prentice Hall, 2008) and *Decide & Conquer* (Financial Times/Prentice Hall, 2004).

Dr. Robbins actively participates in masters' track competitions. Since turning 50 in 1993, he's won 23 national championships and 14 world titles. He was inducted into the U.S. Masters' Track & Field Hall of Fame in 2005 and is currently the world record holder at 100m (12.37) and 200m (25.20) for men 65 and over.

MARY COULTER (Ph.D., University of Arkansas) is professor emeritus of management at Missouri State University. Dr. Coulter has published other books with Prentice Hall, including *Strategic Management in Action,* now in its sixth edition, and *Entrepreneurship in Action,* which is in its second edition. When she's not busy writing, Dr. Coulter enjoys puttering around in her flower garden, trying new recipes on family members (usually successful!), reading a variety of books, and enjoying many different activities with family: Ron, Sarah and James, Katie and Matt, and granddaughter, Brooklynn, and grandson, Blake. Love my sweet babies!

Brief Contents

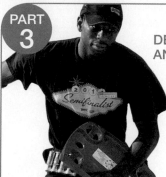

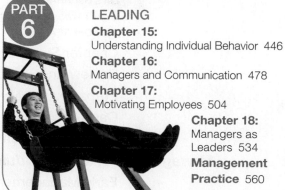
v

Contents

Preface

You've made a good decision! You're taking a college course ... maybe more than one. Although you may sometimes feel like you're wasting your time being in college, you're not. Yes, it's expensive. Yes, it's even sometimes hard. But what you're doing now will pay off in the long run. In a survey of job seekers, a whopping 92 percent said that a major disadvantage in competing for jobs was not having taken college courses. But that's not what you'll face because you *are* enrolled in a college course—the course for which you've purchased this book.

Key Changes to the 12th Edition

Between the two of us, we've taught for more than 50 years, so we personally understand the challenges of getting a classroom of students engaged and enthusiastic about coming to class! What worked exceptionally well for us was showing students that management isn't just some dry, boring subject that you learn about in a book but something vital that real people do in organizations every day. That's why we've always incorporated "real" managers into our textbook. Students can see how managers actually use the theories and approaches discussed in the chapters. And it's the only principles textbook that presents management from the perspective of the people who actually *do* management. Our real-world approach has been so popular that we gave it a "different spin" this time by asking our real managers to comment on realistic manager scenarios specifically written for each chapter. We think these will help get students excited about studying management and provide many avenues for class discussion. After many discussions about how we could make our book better reflect the realities of today's environment, here are some of the main changes we've made in the 12th edition:

- Chapter opener spotlighting a real manager at work in a real organization
- End-of-part Management Practice designed to give students a chance to "practice" management using:
  - A Manager's Dilemma—a realistic dilemma a manager might face for which students must decide how to resolve the dilemma
  - Global Sense—additional material on global issues that face managers and for which students research and discuss the implications
  - Continuing Case on Starbucks—a comprehensive case that addresses important aspects from each part in the text and for which students have several questions to answer
- Developed realistic chapter topic-relevant scenarios that our "real" managers address
- Set up decision making and change as a separate part
- Moved control material to planning part
- Placed the managing operations material in a module

Chapter-by-Chapter Changes

Chapter 1 Management and Organizations

- new chapter opener
- new "Leader Who Made a Difference"
- new discussion on social media and its importance to manager's job
- "real" manager scenarios
- updated examples
- new ethics dilemma
- new end-of-chapter cases

Chapter 2 Understanding Management: Constraints and Challenges

- new chapter opener
- new discussion on economic inequality
- "real" manager scenarios
- new "Leader Who Made a Difference"

- updated examples
- new end-of-chapter cases

Chapter 3 Managing in a Global Environment

- new chapter opener
- new material on problems in European Union and eurozone
- "real" manager scenario
- updated "Leader Who Made a Difference"
- several new examples
- new ethics dilemma
- one new and one updated end-of-chapter case

Chapter 4 Managing Diversity

- new chapter opener
- "real" manager scenarios
- updated statistics
- new "Leader Who Made a Difference"
- several new examples
- new ethics dilemma
- one new and one updated end-of-chapter case

Chapter 5 Managing Social Responsibility and Ethics

- new chapter opener
- "real" manager scenarios
- updated statistics
- new examples
- new ethics dilemma
- one new and one updated end-of-chapter case

Chapter 6 Managers as Decision Makers

- new chapter opener
- new examples
- "real" manager scenario
- updated "Future Vision" box
- updated "Leader Who Made a Difference"
- updated statistics
- new material on design thinking
- new ethics dilemma
- one new and one updated end-of-chapter case

Chapter 7 Managing Change and Innovation

- totally revised chapter opener
- new examples
- "real" manager scenarios
- updated "Future Vision" box
- updated "Leader Who Made a Difference"
- new data points box
- new material on design thinking
- revised ethics dilemma
- updated team exercise
- one new and one updated end-of-chapter case

Chapter 8 Foundations of Planning

- new chapter opener
- "real" manager scenarios
- new ethics dilemma
- one new end-of-chapter case

Chapter 9 Strategic Management

- new chapter opener
- new and updated examples
- "real" manager scenarios
- new "Leader Who Made a Difference"
- new material on design thinking as a competitive advantage
- new ethics dilemma
- two new end-of-chapter cases

Chapter 10 Managerial Controls

- new chapter opener
- new and updated examples
- "real" manager scenarios
- new material on controlling for employee performance
- new material on global turmoil
- updated statistics
- updated end-of-chapter cases

Chapter 11 Basic Organizational Design

- updated chapter opener
- "real" manager scenarios
- updated statistics
- new "Leader Who Made a Difference"
- new ethics dilemma
- updated end-of-chapter cases

Chapter 12 Adaptive Organizational Design

- new chapter opener
- some new examples
- "real" manager scenarios
- new statistics
- one new and one updated end-of-chapter case

Chapter 13 Managing Human Resources

- new chapter opener
- several new examples
- new statistics
- new "Leader Who Made a Difference"
- "real" manager scenarios
- new ethics dilemma
- one new and one updated end-of-chapter case

Chapter 14 Managing Teams

- new chapter opener
- some new statistics
- new "Leader Who Made a Difference"
- "real" manager scenarios
- two new end-of-chapter cases

Chapter 15 Understanding Individual Behavior

- updated chapter opener
- new statistics
- new "Leader Who Made a Difference"
- "real" manager scenarios
- one new end-of-chapter case

Chapter 16 Managers and Communication
- totally revised and updated chapter opener
- several new examples throughout chapter
- new "Leader Who Made a Difference"
- new statistics
- "real" manager scenarios
- new discussion of town hall meetings
- one new end-of-chapter case

Chapter 17 Motivating Employees
- new chapter opener
- new examples throughout chapter
- new statistics
- "real" manager scenarios
- new information on cross-cultural top motivators
- new ethics dilemma
- one new end-of-chapter case

Chapter 18 Managers as Leaders
- new chapter opener
- some new examples throughout chapter
- new statistics
- "real" manager scenarios
- new ethics dilemma
- one new end-of-chapter case

What This Course Is About and Why It's Important

This course and this book are about management and managers. Managers are the one thing that all organizations—no matter the size, kind, or location—need. And there's no doubt that the world managers face has changed, is changing, and will continue to change. The dynamic nature of today's organizations means both rewards *and* challenges for the individuals who will be managing those organizations. Management is a dynamic subject, and a textbook on it should reflect those changes to help prepare you to manage under the current conditions. We've written this 12th edition of *Management* to provide you with the best possible understanding of what it means to be a manager confronting change.

Our Approach

Our approach to management is simple: Management is about people. Managers manage people. Thus, we introduce you to real managers, real people who manage people. We've talked with these real managers and asked them to share their experiences with you. You get to see what being a manager is all about—the problems these real managers have faced and how they have resolved those problems. Not only do you have the benefit of your professor's wisdom and knowledge, you also have access to your very own team of advisors and mentors.

What's Expected of You in This Course

It's simple. Come to class. Read the book. Do your assignments. And...study for your exams. If you want to get the most out of the money you've spent for this course and this textbook, that's what you need to do. In addition to writing this book, we have taught management classes, and that's what we expected of the students we taught.

User's Guide

Your management course may be described as a "survey" course because a lot of topics are covered very quickly, and none of the topics are covered in great depth. It can be overwhelming at times! Your classroom professor is your primary source of information and will provide you with an outline of what you're expected to do during the course. That's also the person who will be evaluating your work and assigning you a grade, so pay attention to what is expected of you! View us, your textbook authors, as your supplementary professors. As your partners in this endeavor, we've provided you the best information possible both in the textbook and in the materials on MyManagementLab® to help you succeed in this course. Now it's up to you to use them!

Getting the Most Out of Your Textbook: Getting a Good Grade in This Course

Professors use a textbook because it provides a compact source of information that you need to know about the course's subject material. Professors like this particular textbook because it presents management from the perspective of the people who actually *do* management—real managers. So take advantage of that and read what these real managers have to say. See how they've handled managerial problems. Learn about their management styles and think about how you might manage.

In addition to what you can learn from these real managers, we provide several ways to help you get a good grade in this course. Use the review and discussion questions at the end of the chapter. They provide a great way to see if you understand the material you've just read.

Finally, we include a wide variety of useful learning experiences both in the textbook and on MyManagementLab. From ethical dilemmas and skill-building exercises to case analyses and hands-on management tasks, we've provided a lot of things to make your management course fun and worthwhile. Your professor will tell you what assignments you will be expected to do. But you don't need to limit your learning experiences to those. Try out some of the other activities, even if they aren't assigned. We know you won't be disappointed!

Student Resources

CourseSmart eTextbook

CourseSmart eTextbooks were developed for students looking to save on required or recommended textbooks. Students simply select their eText by title or author and purchase immediate access to the content for the duration of the course using any major credit card. With a CourseSmart eText, students can search for specific keywords or page numbers, take notes online, print out reading assignments that incorporate lecture notes, and bookmark important passages for later review. For more information or to purchase a CourseSmart eTextbook, visit www.coursesmart.com.

MyManagementLab

MyManagementLab® is an easy-to-use online tool that personalizes course content and provides robust assessment and reporting to measure individual and class performance. All of the resources students need for course success are in one place—flexible and easily adapted for students' course experience.

Self-Assessment Library (S.A.L.)

If you are interested in additional self-assessments, this valuable tool includes 67 individual self-assessment exercises that allow students to assess their knowledge, beliefs, feelings, and actions in regard to a wide range of personal skills, abilities, and interests. Provided scoring keys allow for immediate, individual analysis. S.A.L. is available as a printed workbook, a CD-ROM, and by an access code, so students have a choice of how they want to complete the assessments. S.A.L. ISBN 0-13-608376-5.

Acknowledgments

Every author relies on the comments of reviewers, and ours have been very helpful. We want to thank the following people for their insightful comments and suggestions for the 12th edition and previous editions of *Management:*

Suhail Abboushi, *Duquesne State*

Cheryl Adkins, *Longwood College*

Aline Arnold, *Eastern Illinois University*

Joseph Atallah, *DeVry Institute of Technology*

Jayanta Bandyopadhyay, *Central Michigan University*

Robb Bay, *Community College of Southern Nevada*

Henry C. Bohleke, *San Juan College*

Ernest Bourgeois, *Castleton State College*

Jenell Bramlage, *University of Northwestern Ohio*

Jacqueline H. Bull, *Immaculata University*

James F. Cashman, *The University of Alabama*

Rick Castaldi, *San Francisco State University*

Casey G. Cegielski, *Auburn University*

Bobbic Chan, *Open University of Hong Kong*

Jim Chimenti, *Jamestown Community College*

Jay Christensen-Szalanski, *University of Iowa*

Thomas Clark, *Xavier University*

Sharon Clinebell, *University of Northern Colorado*

Daniel Cochran, *Mississippi State University*

Augustus B. Colangelo, *Penn State*

Jason Coleman, *Wesley College*

Donald Conlon, *University of Delaware*

Roy Cook, *Fort Lewis College*

Anne C. Cowden, *California State University, Sacramento*

Claudia Daumer, *California State University, Chico*

H. Kristl Davison, *University of Mississippi*

Thomas Deckleman, *Owens Community College*

R. Dortch, *Austin Peay State University*

Mary Ann Edwards, *College of Mount St. Joseph*

Ronald Eggers, *Barton College*

Tan Eng, *Ngee Ann Polytechnic*

Allen D. Engle, Sr., *Eastern Kentucky University*

Judson C. Faurer, *Metro State College*

Dale M. Feinauer, *University of Wisconsin, Oshkosh*

Janice Feldbauer, *Austin Community College*

Diane L. Ferry, *University of Delaware*

Louis Firenze, *Northwood University*

Bruce Fischer, *Elmhurst College*

Phillip Flamm, *Angelo State University*

Robert Foley, *College of St. Joseph*

Barbara Foltz, *Clemson University*

June Freund, *Pittsburgh State University*

Michele Fritz, *DeAnza College*

Charles V. Goodman, *Texas A&M University*

H. Gregg Hamby, *University of Houston*

Frank Hamilton, *University of South Florida*

Robert W. Hanna, *California State University, Northridge*

James C. Hayton, *Utah State University*

Wei He, *Indiana State University*

Phyllis G. Holland, *Valdosta State College*

Phil Holleran, *Mitchell Community College*

Henry Jackson, *Delaware County Community College*

Matrecia James, *Jacksonville University*

Jim Jones, *University of Nebraska, Omaha*

Kathleen Jones, *University of North Dakota*

Rusty Juban, *Southeastern Louisiana University*

Ahmad Karim, *Indiana Purdue University*

Marvin Karlins, *University of South Florida*

Andy Kein, *Keller Graduate School of Management*

David Kennedy, *Berkeley School of Business*

Russell Kent, *Georgia Southern University*

William H. Kirchman, *Fayetteville Technical Community College*

John L. Kmetz, *University of Delaware*

Gary Kohut, *University of North Carolina at Charlotte*

William Laing, *Anderson College*

Gary M. Lande, *Montana State University*

Ellis L. Langston, *Texas Tech University*

Les Ledger, *Central Texas College*

David Linthicum, *Cecil College*

W. L. Loh, *Mohawk Valley Community College*

Susan D. Looney, *Delaware Technical and Community College*

James Mazza, *Middlesex Community College*

Lisa McCormick, *Community College of Allegheny*

James McElroy, *Iowa State University*

Carrie Blair Messal, *College of Charleston*

Joseph F. Michlitsch, *Southern Illinois University–Edwardsville*

Sandy J. Miles, *Murray State University*

Lavelle Mills, *West Texas A&M University*

Corey Moore, *Angelo State University*

Rick Moron, *University of California, Berkeley*

Jennifer Morton, *Ivy Tech Community College*

Don C. Mosley, Jr., *University of South Alabama*

Anne M. O'Leary-Kelly, *Texas A&M University*

Rhonda Palladi, *Georgia State University*

Shelia Pechinski, *University of Maine*

Anthony Plunkett, *Harrison College*

Victor Preisser, *Golden Gate University*

Michelle Reavis, *University of Alabama, Huntsville*

Clint Relyea, *Arkansas State University, University of Arkansas*

James Robinson, *The College of New Jersey*

Patrick Rogers, *North Carolina A&T University*

James Salvucci, *Curry College*

Elliot M. Ser, *Barry University*

Tracy Huneycutt Sigler, *Western Washington University*

Eva Smith, *Spartanburg Technical College*

James Spee, *The Claremont Graduate School*

Roger R. Stanton, *California State University*

Dena M. Stephenson, *Calhoun Community College*

Charles Stubbart, *Southern Illinois University*

Ram Subramanian, *Grand Valley State University*

Thomas G. Thompson, *University of Maryland, University College*

Frank Tomassi, *Johnson & Wales University*

Isaiah O. Ugboro, *North Carolina A&T State University*

Philip M. VanAuken, *Baylor University*

Donna Vassallo, *Atlantic Cape Community College*

Carolyn Waits, *Cincinnati State University*

Bill Walsh, *University of Illinois*

Richard C. Warner, *Lehigh Carbon Community College*

Michael Wayland, *Methodist University*

Emilia S. Westney, *Texas Tech University*

Gary L. Whaley, *Norfolk State University*

Bobbie Williams, *Georgia Southern University*

Bob Willis, *Rogers State University*

Lucia Worthington, *University of Maryland University College*

Wendy Wysocki, *Monroe Community College*

Our team at Prentice Hall has been amazing to work with! This team of editors, production experts, technology gurus, designers, marketing specialists, sales representatives, and warehouse employees works hard to turn our digital files into a bound textbook and to see that it gets to faculty and students. We couldn't do this without all of you! Our sincere thanks to the people who made this book "ready to go" include April Cole, Nikki Jones, Stephanie Wall, Judy Leale, Claudia Fernandes, Kelly Warsak, Kenny Beck, Nancy Moudry, Solange Binef, and Allison Campbell. All of you are consummate professionals who truly are committed to publishing the best textbooks! We're glad to have you on our team!

Finally, Steve would like to thank his wife, Laura, for her encouragement and support. Mary would like to thank her husband and family for being supportive and understanding and for patiently enduring her many hours at the computer! And Mary would like to acknowledge her Wednesday night Bible study class…you ladies have been so supportive of me and you continue to be an important part of my life. Thank you!

Management

1 Management and Organizations

SPOTLIGHT: *Manager at Work*

Farmville. Cityville. Words with Friends. Mafia Wars 2. These are some of the more popular online games created by Zynga that are available for free on Facebook, Myspace, and Yahoo!, as apps on iPads and iPhones, and on Zynga's own Web site.[1] Founded by CEO Mark Pincus (see photo) in 2007, Zynga (named after his late dog, Zinga) is one of the world's leading social game developers and one of the tech industry's most interesting companies. The company's goal is to "connect a billion people around the world through play." But how do you build a viable business getting people "to buy a bunch of things that don't exist?" You do it with highly skilled and talented employees who are guided by highly skilled and talented managers.

Although Zynga's employees are exceptionally creative in developing virtual games, in a completely different twist, they're also good at analyzing data. While sifting through data Zynga collects when people play its online games, product managers for a game called FishVille discovered something quite interesting. Players were buying "a translucent anglerfish at six times the rate of other sea creatures, using an imaginary currency people get by playing the game." So they quickly had company artists create "a set of similar imaginary sea creatures with translucent fins and other distinctive features." One difference—this time they charged real money for the virtual fish. Players snapped them up at $3 to $4 each. Although the vast majority of Zynga's game players never spend any real money on its games, some players—Zynga calls them "whales," the same name used for casino high rollers—spend hundreds or even thousands of dollars a month. Zynga's revenues in 2010 were nearly $600 million, with profits of

Source: Karsten Lemm/Picture Alliance/ Photoshot

$91 million; however, as global economic uncertainties persist, the company's revenues in 2011 reached more than $1 billion but with a net loss of $404 million.

Recently, Zynga's employees moved into their new San Francisco headquarters

The company's goal is to

"connect a billion people around the world through play."

building (nicknamed The Dog House), which is designed to look like one of its online games come to life. In the lobby is a Western facade reminiscent of its FrontierVille virtual world. Parked across from the receptionist's desk is a "Zyngabago, a white 1970s Winnebago emblazoned with a giant Z." And then there's the "time travel tube, a tunnel of 20,000 programmable LED lights." Like most other Silicon Valley startups, Zynga's home office employees

get to enjoy amenities such as a sports bar, Zen tea garden, wellness center, and coffee station. Such surroundings are needed to lure and retain talented employees who have their pick of companies to work at. So far, Zynga's attrition rate (a measure of how many employees leave a company) runs a little over 3 percent, while the "average Silicon Valley rate is 14 percent." Pincus believes it's a good sign that employees like the company and the culture. And it's

---

MyManagementLab®

⭐ **Improve Your Grade!**

Over 10 million students improved their results using the Pearson MyLabs.
Visit **mymanagementlab.com** for simulations, tutorials, and end-of-chapter problems.

LEARNING OUTCOMES

1.1	**Explain** why managers are important to organizations.
1.2	**Tell** who managers are and where they work.
1.3	**Describe** the functions, roles, and skills of managers.
1.4	**Describe** the factors that are reshaping and redefining the manager's job.
1.5	**Explain** the value of studying management.

a competitive culture. Employees who thrive under that pressure find many career opportunities for mobility. **What do you think it would take to successfully manage such talented and ambitious employees?**

How would you like to work at a business like Zynga? How about being a manager in a company like Zynga? This interesting company is a good example of what managing in today's world can be: challenging, yet fun!

Like many students, you've probably worked at some time or another while working on your degree. And your work experiences, regardless of where you've worked, are likely to have been influenced by the skills and abilities of your manager. With a low employee attrition rate, Zynga's managers seem to be good examples of what today's successful managers are like and the skills they must have in dealing with the problems and challenges of managing in the twenty-first century. This text is about the important managerial work that managers do. The reality facing today's managers—and that might include you in the near future—is that the world is changing. In workplaces of all types—offices, retail stores, restaurants, factories, and the like—managers deal with changing expectations and new ways of managing employees and organizing work. In this chapter, we introduce you to managers and management by looking at why managers are important, who managers are and where they work, and what managers do. Finally, we wrap up the chapter by looking at the factors reshaping and redefining the manager's job and discussing why it's important to study management.

WHY **Are Managers Important?**

1.1 | *Explain* why managers are important to organizations.

"…A great boss can change your life, inspiring you to new heights both professionally and personally, and energizing you and your team to together overcome new challenges bigger than any one of you could tackle alone."[2] If you've worked with a manager like this, consider yourself lucky. Such a manager can make a job a lot more enjoyable and productive. However, even managers who don't live up to such lofty ideals and expectations are important to organizations. Let's look at three reasons why.

The first reason why managers are important is because organizations need their managerial skills and abilities more than ever in uncertain, complex, and chaotic times. As organizations deal with today's challenges—the worldwide economic climate, changing technology, ever-increasing globalization, and so forth—managers play an important role in identifying critical issues and crafting responses. For example, John Zapp, general manager of several car dealerships in Oklahoma City, struggled to keep his businesses afloat and profitable in the difficult economic environment, just as many other car dealers did.[3] However, after four decades in the car business, Zapp understands that he's the one calling the shots and his "call" was to focus on selling more used cars. How? By keeping inventory moving and by keeping his salespeople engaged through small cash payment rewards for hitting sales goals. His skills and abilities as a manager have been crucial in guiding his organization.

Another reason why managers are important to organizations is because they're critical to getting things done. For instance, in our chapter-opening story, Mark Pincus wasn't the person dreaming up the new virtual worlds, writing the necessary code, analyzing the customer usage data, or addressing customer issues, but he was the person creating and coordinating the workplace environment and work systems so that others could perform those tasks. Although he may weigh in on product development or data analysis, his job as manager is to ensure that all the employees are getting their jobs done so Zynga can do what it's in business to do. If work isn't getting done or isn't getting done as it should be, he's also the one who must find out why and get things back on track.

Finally, *managers do matter* to organizations! How do we know that? The Gallup Organization, which has polled millions of employees and tens of thousands of managers, has found that the single most important variable in employee productivity and loyalty isn't pay or benefits or workplace environment—it's the quality of the relationship between employees and their direct supervisors.[4] In addition, global consulting firm Towers Watson found that the way a company manages and engages its people can significantly affect its financial performance.[5] That's scary considering another study by Towers Watson that found only 42 percent of respondents think their leaders inspire and engage them.[6] In yet another study by different researchers, 44 percent of the respondents said their supervisors strongly increased engagement.[7] However, in this same study, 41 percent of respondents also said their supervisors strongly decreased engagement. So, as you can see, managers can and do have an impact—positive and negative. Finally, one more study of organizational performance recently found that managerial ability was important in creating organizational value.[8] Here's what we can conclude from such reports: Managers are important—and they *do* matter!

WHO Are Managers and Where Do They Work?

Managers may not be who or what you might expect! Managers can range in age from 18 to 80+. They run large corporations, medium-sized businesses, and entrepreneurial start-ups. They're found in government departments, hospitals, small businesses, not-for-profit agencies, museums, schools, and even such nontraditional organizations as political campaigns and music tours. Managers can also be found doing managerial work in every country on the globe. In addition, some managers are top-level managers while others are first-line managers. And today, managers are just as likely to be women as they are men; however, the number of women in top-level manager positions remains low—only 35 women were CEOs of major U.S. corporations in 2012.[10] But no matter where managers are found or what gender they are, managers have exciting and challenging jobs!

Who Is a Manager?

It used to be fairly simple to define who managers were: They were the organizational members who told others what to do and how to do it. It was easy to differentiate *managers* from *nonmanagerial employees*. Now, it isn't quite that simple. In many organizations, the changing nature of work has blurred the distinction between managers and nonmanagerial employees. Many traditional nonmanagerial jobs now include managerial activities.[11] For example, at General Cable Corporation's facility in Moose Jaw, Saskatchewan, Canada, managerial responsibilities are shared by managers and team members. Most of the employees at Moose Jaw are cross-trained and multi-skilled. Within a single shift, an employee can be a team leader, equipment operator, maintenance technician, quality inspector, or improvement planner.[12] Or consider an organization like Morning Star Company, the world's largest tomato processor, where no employees are called managers—just 400 full-time employees who do what needs to be done and who "manage" issues such as job responsibilities, compensation decisions, and budget decisions.[13] Sounds crazy, doesn't it? But it works—for this organization.

So, how *do* we define who managers are? A **manager** is someone who coordinates and oversees the work of other people so organizational goals can be accomplished. A manager's job is not about *personal* achievement—it's about helping *others* do their work. That may mean coordinating the work of a departmental group, or it might mean supervising a single person. It could involve coordinating the work activities of a team with people from different departments or even people outside the organization such as temporary employees or individuals who work for the organization's suppliers. Keep in mind that managers may also have work duties not related to coordinating and overseeing others' work. For example, an insurance claims supervisor might process claims in addition to coordinating the work activities of other claims clerks.

manager
Someone who coordinates and oversees the work of other people so organizational goals can be accomplished

Tell who managers are and where they work.   **1.2**

*data*points[9]

28 percent of workers surveyed said they could do a better job than their boss.

76 percent of workers surveyed said they would not like to have their manager's job.

27 percent of adults surveyed said working part time in a management position is possible.

45 percent of workers surveyed said their boss had taken credit for their work.

34 percent of workers surveyed said their boss had "thrown them under the bus" to save himself or herself.

27 percent of employees surveyed said their horrible boss was a know-it-all.

25 percent of employees surveyed said their horrible boss was a micromanager.

12 percent of employees surveyed said their employer genuinely listens to and cares about its employees.

Exhibit 1-1
Levels of Management

How can managers be classified in organizations? In traditionally structured organizations (often pictured as a pyramid because more employees are at lower organizational levels than at upper organizational levels), managers can be classified as first-line, middle, or top. (See Exhibit 1-1.) At the lowest level of management, **first-line managers** manage the work of nonmanagerial employees who typically are involved with producing the organization's products or servicing the organization's customers. First-line managers may be called *supervisors* or even *shift managers, district managers, department managers,* or *office managers.* **Middle managers** manage the work of first-line managers and can be found between the lowest and top levels of the organization. They may have titles such as *regional manager, project leader, store manager,* or *division manager.* At the upper levels of the organization are the **top managers**, who are responsible for making organization-wide decisions and establishing the plans and goals that affect the entire organization. These individuals typically have titles such as *executive vice president, president, managing director, chief operating officer,* or *chief executive officer.*

Andrea Schuch is the public programs manager of the education department at Lowry Park Zoo in Tampa, Florida. As a manager, she oversees all of the zoo's educational programs for children and adults including tours, camps, animal encounters, and sleepovers. In addition to overseeing and coordinating the activities of employees and volunteers, she performs duties not related to others' work. Shown in this photo, for example, Andrea shares her knowledge of the zoo's animals by discussing a prehensile-tailed porcupine during a news conference at the zoo's Wallaroo section, a family-oriented petting zoo featuring animals from Australia.
Source: ZUMA Press/Newscom

Not all organizations get work done with a traditional pyramidal form, however. Some organizations, for example, are more loosely configured with work done by ever-changing teams of employees who move from one project to another as work demands arise. Although it's not as easy to tell who the managers are in these organizations, we do know that someone must fulfill that role—that is, someone must coordinate and oversee the work of others, even if that "someone" changes as work tasks or projects change or that "someone" doesn't necessarily have the title of manager.

Where Do Managers Work?

It's obvious that managers do their work in organizations. But what is an **organization**? It's a deliberate arrangement of people to accomplish some specific purpose. Your college or university is an organization; so are fraternities and sororities, government departments, churches, Zynga, your neighborhood grocery store, the United Way, the St. Louis Cardinals baseball team, and the Mayo Clinic. All are considered organizations and have three common characteristics. (See Exhibit 1-2.)

Exhibit 1-2
Characteristics of Organizations

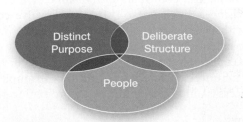

FUTURE VISION | The Working World in 2025

A noted inventor once said, "My interest is in the future because I'm going to spend the rest of my life there."[14] While this text presents a fairly accurate description of today's workplace, you're going to spend most of your worklife in the future. What will that worklife look like? How will it be different from today?

Although no one has a perfectly accurate window to the future, certain trends in place today offer insights into what tomorrow holds. Let's extrapolate from those trends to sneak a peek at the future. We've arbitrarily chosen to focus on the year 2025 because it's close enough that most of you will be actively in the workforce, yet far enough away that current managerial practices are likely to have changed because they've become irrelevant or even obsolete.

In his popular book *The Tipping Point,* Malcolm Gladwell looked at how major changes in our society occur. (Published more than 13 years ago, it's still fascinating to read, and we recommend it!) Many demographers predicted that 2010 could be a tipping point for the composition of the U.S. population as "the number of babies born to minorities outnumbers that of babies born to whites." This milestone would be yet another trend indicator in which minorities are expected to become the U.S. majority over the next 40 years—a demographic shift noted since the early 1990s. And guess what? The latest U.S. census figures from 2010 show that the "tipping point" has been reached![15] Although this reality has numerous societal implications, we're more interested in the implications for the work world that you'll be part of. Implications such as: What will employee hiring and selection processes be like? How will employee training programs change? How will employee reward programs be set up? Who will become the role models and business leaders who guide and shape our businesses? We look at these types of issues in our Future Vision boxes located in various chapters. So strap on your visionary goggles and enjoy this fascinating look at the future! After all, you're going to be spending the rest of your life there!

First, an organization has a distinct purpose typically expressed through goals the organization hopes to accomplish. Second, each organization is composed of people. It takes people to perform the work that's necessary for the organization to achieve its goals. Third, all organizations develop a deliberate structure within which members do their work. That structure may be open and flexible, with no specific job duties or strict adherence to explicit job arrangements. For instance, most big projects at Google (hundreds go on there simultaneously) are tackled by small, focused employee teams that set up in an instant and complete work just as quickly.[16] Or the structure may be more traditional—like that of Procter & Gamble or General Electric or any large corporation—with clearly defined rules, regulations, job descriptions, and some members identified as "bosses" who have authority over other members.

Many of today's organizations are structured more like Google, with flexible work arrangements, employee work teams, open communication systems, and supplier alliances. In these organizations, work is defined in terms of tasks to be done. And workdays have no time boundaries since work can—and is—done anywhere, anytime. However, no matter what type of approach an organization uses, some deliberate structure is needed so work can get done, with managers overseeing and coordinating that work.

first-line managers
Managers at the lowest level of management who manage the work of nonmanagerial employees

middle managers
Managers between the lowest level and top levels of the organization who manage the work of first-line managers

top managers
Managers at or near the upper levels of the organization structure who are responsible for making organization-wide decisions and establishing the goals and plans that affect the entire organization

organization
A deliberate arrangement of people to accomplish some specific purpose

WHAT Do Managers Do?

Describe the functions, roles, and skills of managers. **1.3**

Simply speaking, management is what managers do. But that simple statement doesn't tell us much, does it? Let's look first at what management is before discussing more specifically what managers do.

Management involves coordinating and overseeing the work activities of others so their activities are completed efficiently and effectively. We already know that coordinating and overseeing the work of others is what distinguishes a managerial position from a nonmanagerial one. However, this doesn't mean that managers can do what they want anytime, anywhere, or in any way. Instead, management involves

management
Coordinating and overseeing the work activities of others so their activities are completed efficiently and effectively

Exhibit 1-3
Efficiency and Effectiveness in
Management

ensuring that work activities are completed efficiently and effectively by the people responsible for doing them, or, at least that's what managers should be doing.

efficiency
Doing things right, or getting the most
output from the least amount of inputs

Efficiency refers to getting the most output from the least amount of inputs or resources. Managers deal with scarce resources—including people, money, and equipment—and want to use those resources efficiently. Efficiency is often referred to as "doing things right," that is, not wasting resources. For instance, at the HON Company plant in Cedartown, Georgia, where employees make and assemble office furniture, efficient manufacturing techniques were implemented by cutting inventory levels, decreasing the amount of time to manufacture products, and lowering product reject rates. These efficient work practices paid off as the plant reduced costs by more than $7 million in one year.[17]

effectiveness
Doing the right things, or doing those
work activities that will result in achieving
goals

It's not enough, however, just to be efficient. Management is also concerned with employee effectiveness. **Effectiveness** is often described as "doing the right things," that is, doing those work activities that will result in achieving goals. For instance, at the HON factory, goals included meeting customers' rigorous demands, executing world-class manufacturing strategies, and making employee jobs easier and safer. Through various employee work initiatives, these goals were pursued *and* achieved. Whereas efficiency is concerned with the *means* of getting things done, effectiveness is concerned with the *ends*, or attainment of organizational goals (see Exhibit 1-3).

let's
get **REAL**

The Scenario:

Micah, one of your best employees, was just promoted to a managerial position. You invited him to lunch to celebrate and to see what was on his mind about his new position. Waiting for your food to arrive, you asked him if he had any concerns or questions about being a manager. Looking straight at you, Micah said, "How is being a manager going to be different? What will I do as a manager?"

How would you respond?

I would let him know that being a manager comes with greater responsibility. You are now not only responsible for your success, but more importantly, of those that report to you. Their success is now your success. You will be seen as a leader, an expert, as someone to look up to, a model to further advance their own careers as you have for yourself. Although it may seem daunting at first, it is rewarding when you can help to shape the career and be an integral part of advancement of your direct reports.

Jennifer Jose
Manager, Product Safety & Facility SH&E

Exhibit 1-4
Four Functions of Management

Planning	Organizing	Leading	Controlling	
Setting goals, establishing strategies, and developing plans to coordinate activities	Determining what needs to be done, how it will be done, and who is to do it	Motivating, leading, and any other actions involved in dealing with people	Monitoring activities to ensure that they are accomplished as planned	*Lead to* → Achieving the organization's stated purposes

In successful organizations, high efficiency and high effectiveness typically go hand in hand. Poor management (which leads to poor performance) usually involves being inefficient and ineffective or being effective but inefficient.

Now let's take a more detailed look at what managers do. Describing what managers do isn't easy. Just as no two organizations are alike, no two managers' jobs are alike. In spite of this, management researchers have developed three approaches to describe what managers do: functions, roles, and skills.

Management Functions

According to the functions approach, managers perform certain activities or functions as they efficiently and effectively coordinate the work of others. What are these functions? Henri Fayol, a French businessman, first proposed in the early part of the twentieth century that all managers perform five functions: planning, organizing, commanding, coordinating, and controlling.[18] Today, these functions have been condensed to four: planning, organizing, leading, and controlling (see Exhibit 1-4). Let's briefly look at each function.

If you have no particular destination in mind, then any road will do. However, if you have someplace in particular you want to go, you've got to plan the best way to get there. Because organizations exist to achieve some particular purpose, someone must define that purpose and the means for its achievement. Managers are that someone. As managers engage in **planning**, they set goals, establish strategies for achieving those goals, and develop plans to integrate and coordinate activities.

Managers are also responsible for arranging and structuring work that employees do to accomplish the organization's goals. We call this function **organizing**. When managers organize, they determine what tasks are to be done, who is to do them, how the tasks are to be grouped, who reports to whom, and where decisions are to be made.

Every organization has people, and a manager's job is to work with and through people to accomplish goals. This is the **leading** function. When managers motivate subordinates, help resolve work group conflicts, influence individuals or teams as they work, select the most effective communication channel, or deal in any way with employee behavior issues, they're leading.

The final management function is **controlling**. After goals and plans are set (planning); tasks and structural arrangements put in place (organizing); and people are hired, trained, and motivated (leading)—there has to be an evaluation of whether things are going as planned. To ensure goals are met and work is done as it should be, managers monitor and evaluate performance. Actual performance is compared with the set goals. If those goals aren't achieved, it's the manager's job to get work back on track. This process of monitoring, comparing, and correcting is the controlling function.

Just how well does the functions approach describe what managers do? Do managers always plan, organize, lead, and then control? Not necessarily. What a manager does

planning
Management function that involves setting goals, establishing strategies for achieving those goals, and developing plans to integrate and coordinate activities

organizing
Management function that involves arranging and structuring work to accomplish the organization's goals

leading
Management function that involves working with and through people to accomplish organizational goals

controlling
Management function that involves monitoring, comparing, and correcting work performance

Elon Musk (center), CEO of Tesla Motors, raised his hand at the NASDAQ Stock Exchange opening-bell ceremony to celebrate the electric automaker's initial public offering. Musk decided to go public as part of a massive expansion plan to augment the firm's line of electric cars with more affordable models. Musk launched Tesla with the goal of creating mass-market electric vehicles and devised a three-phase plan to achieve it. First he introduced the high-priced, low-volume Roadster sports car, and then he developed the mid-priced, mid-volume Model S. The IPO helped Tesla transition to the third phase of the plan by providing funds for research, development, tooling, and production of lower-priced electric vehicles.
Source: Mark Lennihan/Associated Press

may not always happen in this sequence. However, regardless of the "order" in which these functions are performed, managers do plan, organize, lead, and control as they manage. To illustrate, review the chapter-opening story. When Mark is trying to keep his employees motivated and engaged, he's leading. He was planning as he made decisions about the company's new headquarters. When he is trying to cut costs and make his company more efficient, those actions involve controlling. And as new games are developed, that's likely to involve planning, organizing, leading, and maybe even controlling.

Although the functions approach is a popular way to describe what managers do, some have argued that it isn't relevant.[19] So let's look at another perspective.

Mintzberg's Managerial Roles and a Contemporary Model of Managing

Henry Mintzberg, a well-known management researcher, studied actual managers at work. In his first comprehensive study, Mintzberg concluded that what managers do can best be described by looking at the managerial roles they engage in at work.[20] The term **managerial roles** refers to specific actions or behaviors expected of and exhibited by a manager. (Think of the different roles you play—student, employee, student organization member, volunteer, sibling, and so forth—and the different things you're expected to do in these roles.) When describing what managers do from a roles perspective, we're not looking at a specific person per se, but at the expectations and responsibilities associated with the person in that role—the role of a manager.[21] As shown in Exhibit 1-5, these 10 roles are grouped around interpersonal relationships, the transfer of information, and decision making.

The **interpersonal roles** involve people (subordinates and persons outside the organization) and other ceremonial and symbolic duties. The three interpersonal roles include figurehead, leader, and liaison. The **informational roles** involve collecting, receiving, and disseminating information. The three informational roles include

managerial roles
Specific actions or behaviors expected of and exhibited by a manager

interpersonal roles
Managerial roles that involve people and other duties that are ceremonial and symbolic in nature

informational roles
Managerial roles that involve collecting, receiving, and disseminating information

Exhibit 1-5
Mintzberg's Managerial Roles

Interpersonal Roles

- Figurehead
- Leader
- Liaison

Informational Roles

- Monitor
- Disseminator
- Spokesperson

Decisional Roles

- Entrepreneur
- Disturbance handler
- Resource allocator
- Negotiator

Source: Based on *The Nature of Managerial Work* by Henry Mintzberg.

monitor, disseminator, and spokesperson. Finally, the **decisional roles** entail making decisions or choices and include entrepreneur, disturbance handler, resource allocator, and negotiator.

decisional roles
Managerial roles that revolve around making choices

As managers perform these roles, Mintzberg proposed that their activities included both reflection (thinking) and action (doing).[22] Our manager in the chapter opener would do both as he manages. For instance, reflection would occur as Mark listens to his management team's problems and ideas, while action would occur when he resolves those problems or acts on the ideas.

A number of follow-up studies have tested the validity of Mintzberg's role categories, and the evidence generally supports the idea that managers—regardless of the type of organization or level in the organization—perform similar roles.[23] However, the emphasis that managers give to the various roles seems to change with organizational level.[24] At higher levels of the organization, the roles of disseminator, figurehead, negotiator, liaison, and spokesperson are more important; while the leader role (as Mintzberg defined it) is more important for lower-level managers than it is for either middle or top-level managers.

From another hands-on and up-close study of managers at work, Mintzberg concluded that, "Basically, managing is about influencing action. It's about helping organizations and units to get things done, which means action."[25] Based on his observations, he went on to explain that a manager does this in three ways: (1) by managing actions directly (for instance, negotiating contracts, managing projects, etc.); (2) by managing people who take action (for example, motivating them, building teams, enhancing the organization's culture, etc.); or (3) by managing information that propels people to take action (using budgets, goals, task delegation, etc.). It's an interesting perspective on the manager's job and one that adds to our understanding of what it is that managers do.

So which approach is better—managerial functions or Mintzberg's propositions? Although each does a good job of depicting what managers do, the functions approach still seems to be the generally accepted way of describing the manager's job. "The classical functions provide clear and discrete methods of classifying the thousands of activities managers carry out and the techniques they use in terms of the functions they perform for the achievement of goals."[26] However, Mintzberg's role approach and additional model of managing do offer us other insights into managers' work.

LEADER *who made a* DIFFERENCE

Source: Jemal Countess/Getty Images Entertainment/Gettyimages.com

Ursula Burns *is the first African American woman to lead a company the size of Xerox.[27] Appointed to the CEO's position in 2009, Burns is known for her courage to "tell the truth in ugly times." Having grown up in the projects on the Lower East Side of New York, Burns understands what it takes to get through those uncertainties. With her aptitude for math, Burns went on to earn a mechanical engineering degree from Polytechnic Institute of New York. After a summer engineering internship at Xerox, she was hooked. At Xerox, Burns was mentored by individuals who saw her potential. Throughout her more than 30-year career at Xerox, Burns had a reputation for being bold. As a mechanical engineer, she got noticed because she wasn't afraid to speak up bluntly in a culture that's known more for being polite, courteous, and discreet than for being outspoken. Although Burns is still radically honest and direct, she has become more of a listener, calling herself a "listener-in-chief." What can you learn from this leader who made a difference?*

Management Skills

Dell Inc. is a company that understands the importance of management skills.[28] It started an intensive five-day offsite skills training program for first-line managers as a way to improve its operations. One of Dell's directors of learning and development thought this was the best way to develop "leaders who can build that strong relationship with their front-line employees." What have the supervisors learned from the skills training? Some things they mentioned were how to communicate more effectively and how to refrain from jumping to conclusions when discussing a problem with a worker.

What types of skills do managers need? Robert L. Katz proposed that managers need three critical skills in managing: technical, human, and conceptual.[29]

Exhibit 1-6

Skills Needed at Different
Managerial Levels

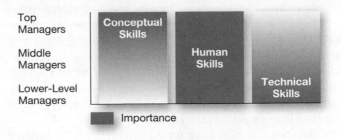

technical skills

Job-specific knowledge and techniques needed to proficiently perform work tasks

human skills

The ability to work well with other people individually and in a group

conceptual skills

The ability to think and to conceptualize about abstract and complex situations

(Exhibit 1-6 shows the relationships of these skills to managerial levels.) **Technical skills** are the job-specific knowledge and techniques needed to proficiently perform work tasks. These skills tend to be more important for first-line managers because they typically manage employees who use tools and techniques to produce the organization's products or service the organization's customers. Often, employees with excellent technical skills get promoted to first-line manager. For example, Dean White, a production supervisor at Springfield Remanufacturing, started as a parts cleaner. Now, White manages 25 people in six departments. He said at first it was difficult to get people to listen, especially his former peers. "I learned I had to gain respect before I could lead." He credits mentors—other supervisors whose examples he followed—with helping him become the type of manager he is today.[30] Dean is a manager who has technical skills, but also recognizes the importance of **human skills**, which involve the ability to work well with other people both individually and in a group. Because all managers deal with people, these skills are equally important to all levels of management. Managers with good human skills get the best out of their people. They know how to communicate, motivate, lead, and inspire enthusiasm and trust. Finally, **conceptual skills** are the skills managers use to think and to conceptualize about abstract and complex situations. Using these skills, managers see the organization as a whole, understand the relationships among various subunits, and visualize how the organization fits into its broader environment. These skills are most important to top managers.

Other important managerial skills that have been identified are listed in Exhibit 1-7. In today's demanding and dynamic workplace, employees who want to be valuable assets must constantly upgrade their skills, and developing management skills can be particularly beneficial in today's workplace. We feel that understanding and developing management skills is so important that we've included a skills feature at the end of each chapter. (The one in

Exhibit 1-7

Important Managerial Skills

- Managing human capital
- Inspiring commitment
- Managing change
- Structuring work and getting things done
- Facilitating the psychological and social contexts of work
- Using purposeful networking
- Managing decision-making processes
- Managing strategy and innovation
- Managing logistics and technology

Source: Based on *Workforce Online*; J. R. Ryan, *Bloomberg BusinessWeek Online*; In-Sue Oh and C. M. Berry; and R. S. Rubin and E. C. Dierdorff.

let's get REAL

The Scenario:

Recently, one of your employees, Ryan, was moved from team member to team leader. Walking down the hallway, you overhear this conversation, "I don't understand what's up with Ryan these days. Just Tuesday, he went out with us for a while after work, laughing and joking like always. Then today he calls me in to tell me I need to put more effort in on the Langley project and to stop wasting time. One minute he wants to be my friend, and the next he acts all boss-like. I never thought he'd turn on us like that when he got promoted to team leader."

Source: Braeden Rogers

Braeden Rogers
Emerging Solutions
Manager

What advice would you give Ryan?

Ryan, just because you were promoted from team member to team leader doesn't mean that you flip a switch and instantly go from sociable co-worker to hard driving manager. The relationships you have built with the team over time as their co-worker are invaluable. You have to find a way to properly motivate your team without alienating them.

this chapter looks at developing your political skills.) In addition, you'll find other material on skill building as well as several interactive skills exercises in our mymanagementlab. As you study the four management functions throughout the rest of the book, you'll be able to start developing some key management skills. Although a simple skill-building exercise won't make you an instant expert, it can provide you an introductory understanding of some of the skills you'll need to master to be an effective manager.

HOW Is the Manager's Job Changing?

Describe the factors that are reshaping and redefining the manager's job. **1.4**

A radical work experiment at Best Buy's headquarters involves a flexible work program called ROWE, which stands for Results-Only Work Environment. What does this mean? Well, a majority of Best Buy's employees are now judged only on tasks or results, not on how long they work. The bottom line for Best Buy? Employee productivity jumped 41 percent and voluntary turnover fell to 8 percent from 12 percent. (The Case Application at the end of Chapter 17 provides more information on this unique approach.)[31] Welcome to the new world of managing!

In today's world, managers are dealing with global economic and political uncertainties, changing workplaces, ethical issues, security threats, and changing technology. For example, Dave Maney, the top manager of Headwaters MB, a Denver-based investment bank, had to fashion a new game plan during the recession. When the company's board of directors gave senior management complete freedom to ensure the company's survival, they made a bold move. All but seven key employees were laid off. Although this doesn't sound very responsible or resourceful, it invited those laid-off employees to form independent member firms. Now, Headwaters steers investment transactions to those firms, while keeping a small percentage for itself. The "restructuring drastically reduced fixed costs and also freed management to do more marketing, rather than day-to-day investment banking transactions." As Maney said, "It was a good strategy for us and positioned us for the future."[32] It's likely that more managers *will* have to manage under such demanding circumstances, and the fact is

Exhibit 1-8
Changes Facing Managers

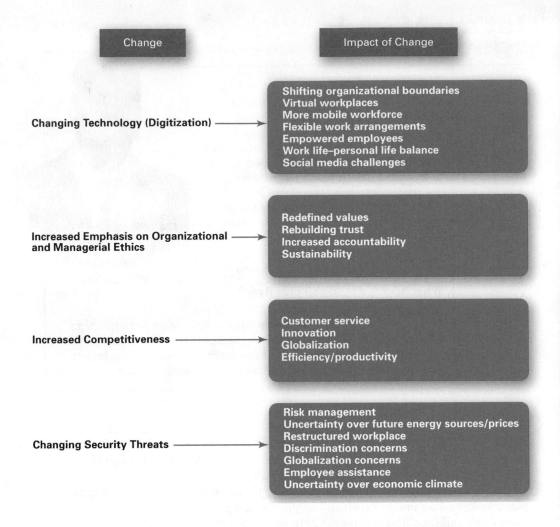

that *how* managers manage is changing. Exhibit 1-8 shows some of the most important changes facing managers. Throughout the rest of this text, we'll discuss these and other changes and how they affect the way managers plan, organize, lead, and control. We want to highlight four of these changes: the increasing importance of customers, social media, innovation, and sustainability.

Importance of Customers to the Manager's Job

John Chambers, CEO of Cisco Systems, likes to listen to voice mails forwarded to him from dissatisfied customers. He says, "E-mail would be more efficient, but I want to hear the emotion, I want to hear the frustration, I want to hear the caller's level of comfort with the strategy we're employing. I can't get that through e-mail."[33] This manager understands the importance of customers. You need customers. Without them, most organizations would cease to exist. Yet, focusing on the customer has long been thought to be the responsibility of marketing types. "Let the marketers worry about the customers" is how many managers felt. We're discovering, however, that employee attitudes and behaviors play a big role in customer satisfaction. For instance, passengers of Qantas Airways were asked to rate their "essential needs" in air travel. Almost every factor listed was one directly influenced by the actions of company employees—from prompt baggage delivery, to courteous and efficient cabin crews, to assistance with connections, to quick and friendly check-ins.[34]

Today, the majority of employees in developed countries work in service jobs. For instance, almost 77 percent of the U.S. labor force is employed in service industries.

In Australia, 70 percent work in service industries. In the United Kingdom, Germany, and Japan, the percentages are 78, 74, and 75, respectively. Even in developing countries like India, Russia, and China, we find 56 percent, 59 percent, and 43 percent of the labor force employed in service jobs.[35] Examples of service jobs include technical support representatives, food servers or fast-food counter workers, sales clerks, teachers, nurses, computer repair technicians, front desk clerks, consultants, purchasing agents, credit representatives, financial planners, and bank tellers. The odds are pretty good that when you graduate, you'll go to work for a company that's in a service industry, not in manufacturing or agriculture.

Managers are recognizing that delivering consistent, high-quality customer service is essential for survival and success in today's competitive environment and that employees are an important part of that equation.[36] The implication is clear—managers must create a customer-responsive organization where employees are friendly and courteous, accessible, knowledgeable, prompt in responding to customer needs and willing to do what's necessary to please the customer.[37] We'll look at customer service management in several chapters. Before we leave this topic, though, we want to share one more story that illustrates why it's important for today's managers (all managers, not just those in marketing) to understand what it takes to serve customers. During a broadcasted Stanley Cup playoff game, Comcast subscribers suddenly found themselves staring at a blank screen. Many of those customers got on Twitter to find out why. And it was there, not on a phone system, that they discovered a lightning strike in Atlanta had caused the power outage and that transmission would be restored as quickly as possible. Managers at Comcast understood how to exploit popular communications technology, and the company's smart use of Twitter "underscores what is becoming a staple in modern-day customer service…beefing up communications with customers through social-media tools."[38]

social media
Forms of electronic communication through which users create online communities to share ideas, information, personal messages, and other content

Importance of Social Media to the Manager's Job

You probably can't imagine a time when employees did their work without e-mail or Internet access. Yet, 15 years ago, as these communication tools were becoming more common in workplaces, managers struggled with the challenges of providing guidelines for using the Internet and e-mail in their organizations. Today, the new frontier is **social media**, forms of electronic communication through which users create online communities to share ideas, information, personal messages, and other content. "More than a billion people use social platforms such as Facebook, Twitter, YouTube, LinkedIn, and others."[39] And employees don't just use these on their personal time, but also for work purposes. That's why managers need to understand and manage the power and peril of social media. For instance, at grocery chain SuperValu, managers realized that keeping 135,000 plus employees connected and engaged was imperative to continued success.[40] They decided to adopt an internal social media tool to foster cooperation and collaboration among its 10 distinct store brands operating in 44 states. And they're not alone. More and more businesses are turning to social media not just as a way to connect with customers but also as a way to manage their human resources and tap into their innovation and talent. That's the potential power of social media. But the potential peril is in how it's used. When the social media platform becomes a way for boastful employees to brag about their accomplishments, for managers to publish one-way messages to employees, or for employees to argue or gripe about something or someone they don't like at work, then it's lost its usefulness. To avoid this, managers need to remember that social media is a tool that needs to be managed to be beneficial. At SuperValu, about 9,000 store managers and assistant managers use the social media system. Although sources say it's too early to

This young woman in Switzerland competing in a worldwide paper airplane event created by Red Bull Media House illustrates the importance of innovation for Red Bull, the Austrian-based energy-drink firm. Rather than just sponsoring an event or developing an ad campaign to promote its brand, Red Bull launched its own global media company that produces, publishes, and distributes print, multimedia, and audiovisual material in the fields of sports, culture, and entertainment. The innovative marketing approach with its core message of "Gives You Wings" has created a strong bond between Red Bull and its young target audience and has helped the company capture close to half of the energy-drink market.
Source: Maurin Bisig/ZUMA Press/Newscom

draw any conclusions, it appears that managers who actively make use of the system are having better store sales revenues than those who don't. In the remainder of the book, we'll look at how social media is impacting how managers manage, especially in the areas of human resource management, communication, teams, and strategy.

Importance of Innovation to the Manager's Job

"Nothing is more risky than not innovating."[41] Innovation means doing things differently, exploring new territory, and taking risks. And innovation isn't just for high-tech or other technologically sophisticated organizations. Innovative efforts can be found in all types of organizations. For instance, the manager of the Best Buy store in Manchester, Connecticut, clearly understood the importance of getting employees to be innovative, a task made particularly challenging because the average Best Buy store is often staffed by young adults in their first or second jobs. "The complexity of the products demands a high level of training, but the many distractions that tempt college-aged employees keep the turnover potential high." However, the store manager tackled the problem by getting employees to suggest new ideas. One idea—a "team close," in which employees scheduled to work at the store's closing time, closed the store together and walked out together as a team—has had a remarkable impact on employee attitudes and commitment.[42] As you'll see throughout the book, innovation is critical throughout all levels and parts of an organization. For example, the top manager of India's Tata Group, chairman Ratan Tata, told his employees during the global economic downturn to "Cut costs. Think out of the box. Even if the world around you is collapsing, be bold, be daring, think big."[43] And his employees obviously got the message. The company's $2,000 minicar, the Nano, was the talk of the global automotive industry. As these stories illustrate, innovation is critical. It's so critical to today's organizations and managers that we also address this topic in several later chapters.

Importance of Sustainability to the Manager's Job

It's the world's largest retailer with nearly $447 billion in annual sales, 2.2 million employees, and 8,700 stores. Yes, we're talking about Walmart. And Walmart is probably the last company that you'd think about in a section describing sustainability. However, Walmart announced at the beginning of this decade that it would "cut some 20 million metric tons of greenhouse gas emissions from its supply chain by the end of 2015—the equivalent of removing more than 3.8 million cars from the road for a year."[44] The company recently announced that it now reuses or recycles more than 80 percent of the waste produced in its domestic stores and in other U.S. operations.[45] This corporate action affirms that sustainability and green management have become mainstream issues for managers.

What's emerging in the twenty-first century is the concept of managing in a sustainable way, which has had the effect of widening corporate responsibility not only to managing in an efficient and effective way, but also to responding strategically to a wide range of environmental and societal challenges.[46] Although "sustainability" means different things to different people, in essence, according to the World Business Council for Sustainable Development (2005), it is concerned with "meeting the needs of people today without compromising the ability of future generations to meet their own needs." From a business perspective, **sustainability** has been defined as a company's ability to achieve its business goals and increase long-term shareholder value by integrating economic, environmental, and social opportunities into its business strategies.[47] Sustainability issues are now moving up the agenda of business leaders and the boards of thousands of companies. Like the managers at Walmart are discovering, running an organization in a more sustainable way will mean that managers have to make informed business decisions based on thorough communication with various stakeholders; understanding their requirements; and starting to factor economic, environmental, and social aspects into how they pursue their business goals. We'll examine managing for sustainability and its importance to planning, organizing, leading, and controlling in other places throughout the book.

sustainability
A company's ability to achieve its business goals and increase long-term shareholder value by integrating economic, environmental, and social opportunities into its business strategies

WHY **Study Management?**

You may be wondering why you need to study management. If you're majoring in accounting or marketing or any field other than management, you may not understand how studying management is going to help your career. We can explain the value of studying management by looking at three things: the universality of management, the reality of work, and the rewards and challenges of being a manager.

The Universality of Management

Just how universal is the need for management in organizations? We can say with absolute certainty that management is needed in all types and sizes of organizations, at all organizational levels and in all organizational work areas, and in all organizations, no matter where they're located. This is known as the **universality of management**. (See Exhibit 1-9.) In all these organizations, managers must plan, organize, lead, and control. However, that's not to say that management is done the same way. What a supervisor in a software applications testing group at Microsoft does versus what the CEO of Microsoft does is a matter of degree and emphasis, not function. Because both are managers, both will plan, organize, lead, and control. How much and how they do so will differ, however.

Management is universally needed in all organizations, so we want to find ways to improve the way organizations are managed. Why? Because we interact with organizations every single day. Are you frustrated when you have to spend two hours in a state government office to get your driver's license renewed? Are you irritated when none of the salespeople in a retail store seem interested in helping you? Is it annoying when you call an airline three times and customer sales representatives quote you three different prices for the same trip? These examples show problems created by poor management. Organizations that are well managed—and we'll share many examples of these throughout the text—develop a loyal customer base, grow, and prosper, even during challenging times. Those that are poorly managed find themselves losing customers and revenues. By studying management, you'll be able to recognize poor management and work to get it corrected. In addition, you'll be able to recognize and support good management, whether it's in an organization with which you're simply interacting or whether it's in an organization in which you're employed.

The Reality of Work

Another reason for studying management is the reality that for most of you, once you graduate from college and begin your career, you will either manage or be managed. For those who plan to be managers, an understanding of management forms the foundation upon which to build your management knowledge and skills. For those of you who don't see yourself managing, you're still likely to have to work with

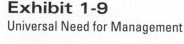

Explain the value of | **1.5**
studying management.

universality of management
The reality that management is needed in all types and sizes of organizations, at all organizational levels, in all organizational areas, and in organizations no matter where located

Exhibit 1-9
Universal Need for Management

managers. Also, assuming that you'll have to work for a living and recognizing that you're very likely to work in an organization, you'll probably have some managerial responsibilities even if you're not a manager. Our experience tells us that you can gain a great deal of insight into the way your boss (and fellow employees) behave and how organizations function by studying management. Our point is that you don't have to aspire to be a manager to gain something valuable from a course in management.

Rewards and Challenges of Being a Manager

We can't leave our discussion here without looking at the rewards and challenges of being a manager. (See Exhibit 1-10.) What *does* it mean to be a manager in today's workplace?

First, there are many challenges. It can be a tough and often thankless job. In addition, a portion of a manager's job (especially at lower organizational levels) may entail duties that are often more clerical (compiling and filing reports, dealing with bureaucratic procedures, or doing paperwork) than managerial.[48] Managers also spend significant amounts of time in meetings and dealing with interruptions, which can be time consuming and sometimes unproductive.[49] Managers often have to deal with a variety of personalities and have to make do with limited resources. It can be a challenge to motivate workers in the face of uncertainty and chaos, as this recession has illustrated time and time again. And managers may find it difficult to successfully blend the knowledge, skills, ambitions, and experiences of a diverse work group. Finally, as a manager, you're not in full control of your destiny. Your success typically is dependent on others' work performance.

Despite these challenges, being a manager *can* be rewarding. You're responsible for creating a work environment in which organizational members can do their work to the best of their ability and thus help the organization achieve its goals. You help others find meaning and fulfillment in their work. You get to support, coach, and nurture others and help them make good decisions. In addition, as a manager, you often have the opportunity to think creatively and use your imagination. You'll get to meet and work with a variety of people—both inside and outside the organization. Other rewards may include receiving recognition and status in your organization and in the community, playing a role in influencing organizational outcomes, and receiving attractive compensation in the form of salaries, bonuses, and stock options. Finally, as we said earlier in the chapter, organizations need good managers. It's through the combined efforts of motivated and passionate people working together that organizations accomplish their goals. As a manager, you can be assured that your efforts, skills, and abilities are needed.

Exhibit 1-10
Rewards and Challenges
of Being a Manager

Rewards	Challenges
• Create a work environment in which organizational members can work to the best of their ability	• Do hard work
• Have opportunities to think creatively and use imagination	• May have duties that are more clerical than managerial
• Help others find meaning and fulfillment in work	• Have to deal with a variety of personalities
• Support, coach, and nurture others	• Often have to make do with limited resources
• Work with a variety of people	• Motivate workers in chaotic and uncertain situations
• Receive recognition and status in organization and community	• Blend knowledge, skills, ambitions, and experiences of a diverse work group
• Play a role in influencing organizational outcomes	• Success depends on others' work performance
• Receive appropriate compensation in the form of salaries, bonuses, and stock options	
• Good managers are needed by organizations	

CHAPTER

PREPARING FOR: Exams/Quizzes
CHAPTER SUMMARY by Learning Outcomes

1.1 LEARNING OUTCOME

Explain why managers are important to organizations.
Managers are important to organizations for three reasons. First, organizations need their managerial skills and abilities in uncertain, complex, and chaotic times. Second, managers are critical to getting things done in organizations. Finally, managers contribute to employee productivity and loyalty; the way employees are managed can affect the organization's financial performance; and managerial ability has been shown to be important in creating organizational value.

1.2 LEARNING OUTCOME

Tell who managers are and where they work.
Managers coordinate and oversee the work of other people so that organizational goals can be accomplished. Nonmanagerial employees work directly on a job or task and have no one reporting to them. In traditionally structured organizations, managers can be first-line, middle, or top. In other more loosely configured organizations, the managers may not be as readily identifiable, although someone must fulfill that role.

Managers work in an organization, which is a deliberate arrangement of people to accomplish some specific purpose. Organizations have three characteristics: a distinctive purpose, composed of people, and a deliberate structure. Many of today's organizations are structured to be more open, flexible, and responsive to changes.

1.3 LEARNING OUTCOME

Describe the functions, roles, and skills of managers.
Broadly speaking, management is what managers do and involves coordinating and overseeing the efficient and effective completion of others' work activities. Efficiency means doing things right; effectiveness means doing the right things.

The four functions of management include planning (defining goals, establishing strategies, and developing plans), organizing (arranging and structuring work), leading (working with and through people), and controlling (monitoring, comparing, and correcting work performance).

Mintzberg's managerial roles include interpersonal, which involve people and other ceremonial/symbolic duties (figurehead, leader, and liaison); informational, which involve collecting, receiving, and disseminating information (monitor, disseminator, and spokesperson); and decisional, which involve making choices (entrepreneur, disturbance handler, resource allocator, and negotiator). Mintzberg's newest description of what managers do proposes that managing is about influencing action, which managers do in three ways: by managing actions directly, by managing people who take action, and by managing information that impels people to take action.

Katz's managerial skills include technical (job-specific knowledge and techniques), human (ability to work well with people), and conceptual (ability to think and express ideas). Technical skills are most important for lower-level managers while conceptual skills are most important for top managers. Human skills are equally important for all managers. Some other managerial skills also identified include managing human capital, inspiring commitment, managing change, using purposeful networking, and so forth.

1.4 [LEARNING OUTCOME]

Describe the factors that are reshaping and redefining the manager's job.

The changes impacting managers' jobs include global economic and political uncertainties, changing workplaces, ethical issues, security threats, and changing technology. Managers must be concerned with customer service because employee attitudes and behaviors play a big role in customer satisfaction. Managers must be concerned with social media because these forms of communication are becoming important and valuable tools in managing. Managers must also be concerned with innovation because it is important for organizations to be competitive. And finally, managers must be concerned with sustainability as business goals are developed.

1.5 [LEARNING OUTCOME]

Explain the value of studying management.

It's important to study management for three reasons: (1) the universality of management, which refers to the fact that managers are needed in all types and sizes of organizations, at all organizational levels and work areas, and in all global locations; (2) the reality of work—that is, you will either manage or be managed; and (3) the awareness of the significant rewards (such as creating work environments to help people work to the best of their ability, supporting and encouraging others, helping others find meaning and fulfillment in work, etc.) and challenges (such as it's hard work, may have more clerical than managerial duties, have to deal with a variety of personalities, etc.) in being a manager.

REVIEW AND DISCUSSION QUESTIONS ✪

1. How do managers differ from nonmanagerial employees?

2. Is your course instructor a manager? Discuss in terms of managerial functions, managerial roles, and skills.

3. "The manager's most basic responsibility is to focus people toward performance of work activities to achieve desired outcomes." What's your interpretation of this statement? Do you agree with it? Why or why not?

4. Explain the universality of management concept. Does it still hold true in today's world? Why or why not?

5. Is business management a profession? Why or why not? Do some external research in answering this question.

6. Does the way contemporary organizations are structured appeal to you? Why or why not?

7. In today's environment, which is more important to organizations—efficiency or effectiveness? Explain your choice.

8. "Management is undoubtedly one of humankind's most important inventions." Do you agree with this statement? Why or why not?

PREPARING FOR: My Career

ETHICS DILEMMA ✪

• 26 percent of new managers feel they are unprepared to transition into management roles • 58 percent of new managers don't receive any training to help them make the transition • 50 percent of first-time managers fail in that transition.[50]

Moving to a management position isn't easy as these statistics indicate. Does an organization have an ethical responsibility to assist its new managers in their new positions? Why or why not? What could organizations do to make this transition easier? Suppose you were a new manager; what support would you expect from your organization? From your manager?

SKILLS EXERCISE Developing Your Political Skill

About the Skill

Research has shown that people differ in their political skills.[51] Those who are politically skilled are more effective in their use of influence tactics. Political skill also appears to be more effective when the stakes are high. Finally, politically skilled individuals are able to exert their influence without others detecting it, which is important in being effective so that you're not labeled political. A person's political skill is determined by his or her networking ability, interpersonal influence, social astuteness, and apparent sincerity.

Steps in Practicing the Skill

1. *Develop your networking ability.* A good network can be a powerful tool. You can begin building a network by getting to know important people in your work area and the organization and then developing relationships with individuals in positions of power. Volunteer for committees or offer your help on projects that will be noticed by those in positions of power. Attend important organizational functions so that you can be seen as a team player and someone who's interested in the organization's success. Start a rolodex file of individuals that you meet, even if for a brief moment. Then, when you need advice on work, use your connections and network with others throughout the organization.

2. *Work on gaining interpersonal influence.* People will listen to you when they're comfortable and feel at ease around you. Work on your communication skills so that you can communicate easily and effectively with others. Work on developing good rapport with people in all areas and at all levels of your organization. Be open, friendly, and willing to pitch in. The amount of interpersonal influence you have will be affected by how well people like you.

3. *Develop your social astuteness.* Some people have an innate ability to understand people and sense what they're thinking. If you don't have that ability, you'll have to work at developing your social astuteness by doing things such as saying the right things at the right time, paying close attention to people's facial expressions, and trying to determine whether others have hidden agendas.

4. *Be sincere.* Sincerity is important to getting people to want to associate with you. Be genuine in what you say and do. And show a genuine interest in others and their situations.

Practicing the Skill

Select each of the components of political skill and spend one week working on it. Write a brief set of notes describing your experiences—good and bad. Were you able to begin developing a network of people throughout the organization or did you work at developing your social astuteness, maybe by starting to recognize and interpret people's facial expressions and the meaning behind those expressions? What could you have done differently to be more politically skilled? Once you begin to recognize what's involved with political skills, you should find yourself becoming more connected and politically adept.

WORKING TOGETHER Team Exercise

By this time in your life, all of you have had to work with individuals in managerial positions (or maybe *you* were the manager), either through work experiences or through other organizational experiences (social, hobby/interest, religious, and so forth). What do you think makes some managers better than others? Do certain characteristics distinguish good managers? Form small groups with 3–4 other class members. Discuss your experiences with managers—good and bad. Draw up a list of the characteristics of those individuals you felt were good managers. For each item, indicate which management function and which management skill you think it falls under. As a group, be prepared to share your list with the class and to explain your choice of management function and skill.

LEARNING TO BE A MANAGER

- Use the most current *Occupational Outlook Handbook* (U.S. Department of Labor, Bureau of Labor Statistics) to research three different categories of managers. For each, prepare a bulleted list that describes the following: the nature of the work, training and other qualifications needed, earnings, and job outlook and projections data.

- Get in the habit of reading at least one current business periodical (*Wall Street Journal, Bloomberg Business Week, Fortune, Fast Company, Forbes*, etc.). Keep a file with interesting information you find about managers or managing.

- Using current business periodicals, find five examples of managers you would describe as *Master Managers*. Write a paper describing these individuals as managers and why you feel they deserve this title.

- Steve's and Mary's suggested readings: Henry Mintzberg, *Managing* (Berrett-Koehler Publishers, 2009); Matthew Stewart, *The Management Myth* (W. W. Norton &

Company, 2009); Paul Osterman, *The Truth About Middle Managers: Who They Are, How They Work, and Why They Matter* (Harvard Business Press, 2008); Stephen P. Robbins, *The Truth About Managing People,* 2e (Financial Times/Prentice Hall, 2007); Gary Hamel, *The Future of Management* (Harvard Business School, 2007); Rod Wagner and James K. Harter, *12 Elements of Great Managing* (Gallup Press, 2006); Marcus Buckingham, *First Break All the Rules: What the World's Greatest Managers Do Differently* (Simon & Schuster, 1999); and Peter F. Drucker, *The Executive in Action* (Harper Business, 1985 and 1964).

- Interview two different managers and ask them the following questions: What are the best and worst parts about being a manager? What's the best management advice you ever received? Type up the questions and their answers to turn in to your professor.

- Accountants and other professionals have certification programs to verify their skills, knowledge, and professionalism. What about managers? Two certification programs for managers include the Certified Manager (Institute of Certified Professional Managers) and the Certified Business Manager (Association of Professional in Business Management). Research each of these programs. Prepare a bulleted list of what each involves.

- If you're involved in student organizations, volunteer for leadership roles or for projects where you can practice planning, organizing, leading, and controlling different projects and activities. You can also gain valuable managerial experience by taking a leadership role in class team projects.

- In your own words, write down three things you learned in this chapter about being a good manager.

- Self-knowledge can be a powerful learning tool. Go to mymanagementlab.com and complete any of these self-assessment exercises: How Motivated Am I to Manage? How Well Do I Handle Ambiguity? How Confident Am I in My Abilities to Succeed? or What's My Attitude Toward Achievement? Using the results of your assessments, identify personal strengths and weaknesses. What will you do to reinforce your strengths and improve your weaknesses?

MyManagementLab

Go to **mymanagementlab.com** for Auto-graded writing questions as well as the following Assisted-graded writing questions:

1-1. Is there one best "style" of management? Why or why not?

1-2. Researchers at Harvard Business School found that the most important managerial behaviors involve two fundamental things: enabling people to move forward in their work and treating them decently as human beings. What do you think of these two managerial behaviors? What are the implications for someone, like yourself, who is studying management?

1-3. Mymanagementlab Only – comprehensive writing assignment for this chapter.

CASE APPLICATION 1 Building a Better Boss

Google doesn't do anything halfway. So when it decided to "build a better boss," it did what it does best—look at data.[52] Using data from performance reviews, feedback surveys, and supporting papers turned in for individuals nominated for top-manager awards, Google correlated "phrases, words, praise, and complaints" trying to find what makes for a great boss. The project, dubbed Project Oxygen, examined some 100 variables and ultimately identified eight characteristics or habits of Google's most effective managers. Here are the "big eight":

- Have a clear vision and strategy for the team;
- Help your employees with career development;
- Express interest in your team members' success and well-being;
- Have technical skills so you can advise the team;
- Be a good communicator and listen to your team;
- Be a good coach;
- Be productive and results-oriented; and
- Empower your team and don't micromanage.

At first glance, you're probably thinking these eight attributes seem pretty simplistic and obvious, and you may be wondering why Google spent all this time and effort to uncover these. Even Google's vice president for people operations, Laszlo Bock, said, "My first reaction was, 'that's it?'" Another writer described it as "reading like a whiteboard gag from an episode of *The Office*." But, as the old saying goes, there *was* more to this list than meets the eye.

Through Google's Project Oxygen, Sundar Pichai, senior vice president of Chrome and Apps, and other managers are learning that in addition to being outstanding technical specialists, the best bosses share attributes such as being good coaches and good communicators.
Source: Marcio Jose Sanchez/Associated Press

When Bock and his team began looking closer and rank ordering the eight items by importance, Project Oxygen got interesting—a lot more interesting! And to understand this, you have to understand something about Google's approach to management since its founding in 1999. Plain and simple, managers were encouraged to "leave people alone. Let the engineers do their stuff. If they become stuck, they'll ask their bosses, whose deep technical expertise propelled them to management in the first place." It's not hard to see what Google wanted its managers to be—outstanding technical specialists. Mr. Bock explains, "In the Google context, we'd always believed that to be a manager, particularly on the engineering side, you need to be as deep or deeper a technical expert than the people who work for you." However, Project Oxygen revealed that technical expertise was ranked number eight (very last) on the list. So, here's the complete list from most important to least important, along with what each characteristic entails:

- *Be a good coach* (provide specific feedback and have regular one-on-one meetings with employees; offer solutions tailored to each employee's strengths)
- *Empower your team and don't micromanage* (give employees space to tackle problems themselves, but be available to offer advice)
- *Be interested in your team members' successes and well-being* (make new team members feel welcome and get to know your employees as people)
- *Be productive and results-oriented* (focus on helping the team achieve its goals by prioritizing work and getting rid of obstacles)
- *Be a good communicator and listen to your team* (learn to listen and to share information; encourage open dialogue and pay attention to the team's concerns)
- *Help your employees with career development* (notice employees' efforts so they can see how their hard work is furthering their careers; appreciate employees' efforts and make that appreciation known)

- *Have a clear vision and strategy for the team* (lead the team, but keep everyone involved in developing and working toward the team's vision)
- *Have technical skills so you can advise the team* (understand the challenges facing the team and be able to help team members solve problems)

Now, managers at Google aren't just encouraged to be great managers—they know what being a great manager involves. And the company is doing its part, as well. Using the list, Google started training managers as well as providing individual coaching and performance review sessions. You can say that Project Oxygen breathed new life into Google's managers. Bock says the company's efforts paid off quickly. "We were able to have a statistically significant improvement in manager quality for 75 percent of our worst-performing managers."

DISCUSSION QUESTIONS ✪

1. Describe the findings of Project Oxygen using the functions approach, Mintzberg's roles approach, and the skills approach.
2. Are you surprised at what Google found out about "building a better boss?" Explain your answer.
3. What's the difference between encouraging managers to be great managers and knowing what being a great manager involves?
4. What could other companies learn from Google's experiences?
5. Would you want to work for a company like Google? Why or why not?

CASE APPLICATION 2 Saving the World

Symantec managers understand how to use innovation in motivating virus hunters and security experts to detect and respond to security threats while working in a chaotic work environment characterized by quick changes in customer needs and new global competitors.
Source: Jonathan Alcorn/ZUMA Press/Newscom

You used to be able to tell who the bad guys were. But in our digital online world, those days are long gone.[53] Now, the bad guys are faceless and anonymous. And they can and do inflict all kinds of damage on individuals, businesses, governments, and other organizations. Surveys show that data breach attacks are happening with alarming regularity. And while your home and school PCs are hopefully well protected from data theft and viruses, don't think you're in the clear. The newest targets for data thieves are smart phones and other mobile devices. However, the good guys are fighting back. For instance, security technology company Symantec Corporation set up a recent sting called Operation HoneyStick in which it distributed 50 smart phones in Silicon Valley, Washington DC, New York, Los Angeles, and Ottawa, Canada. "The devices, loaded with a buffet of juicy, fake data, were left in restaurants, elevators, convenience stores, and student unions." Oh, and one other thing, the smart phones were equipped with monitoring software so the security experts could track where the devices were taken once found and what type of information was accessed by the finders. This is just one example of how Symantec's employees are trying to "save the world" one step at a time—not an easy thing to do.

"Imagine what life would be like if your product were never finished, if your work were never done, if your market shifted 30 times a day." Sounds pretty crazy, doesn't it? However, the computer-virus hunters and security experts at Symantec don't have to imagine—that's the reality of their daily work. For instance, at the company's well-obscured Dublin facility (one of three around the globe), operations manager Patrick Fitzgerald must keep his engineers and researchers focused 24/7 on identifying and combating what the bad guys are throwing out there. Right now, they're trying to stay ahead of a big virus threat, Stuxnet, which targets computer systems running the environmental controls in industrial facilities, such as temperature in power plants, pressure in pipelines, automated timing, and so forth. The consequences of someone intent on doing evil getting control over such critical functions could be disastrous.

Symantec, which designs content and network security software for both consumers and businesses, reflects the realities facing many organizations today—quickly shifting customer expectations and continuously emerging global competitors and global threats. Managing talented people in such an environment can be quite challenging.

Symantec's virus hunters around the world deal with some 20,000 virus samples each month, not all of which are unique, stand-alone viruses. To make the hunters' jobs even more interesting is that computer attacks are increasingly being spread by criminals around the world wanting to steal information, whether corporate data or personal user account information that can be used in fraud. Dealing with these critical and time-sensitive issues requires special talents. The response-center team is a diverse group whose members weren't easy to find. "It's not as if colleges are creating thousands of anti-malware or security experts every year that we can hire. If you find them in any part of the world, you just go after them." The response center team's makeup reflects that. For instance, one senior researcher is from Hungary; another is from Iceland; and another works out of her home in Melbourne, Florida. But they all share something in common: They're all motivated by solving problems.

The launch of the Blaster-B worm, a particularly nasty virus, in late summer 2003 changed the company's approach to dealing with viruses. The domino effect of Blaster-B and other viruses spawned by it meant that frontline software analysts were working around the clock for almost two weeks. The "employee burn-out" potential made the company realize that its virus-hunting team would now have to be much deeper talent-wise. Now, the response center's team numbers in the hundreds and managers can rotate people from the front lines, where they're responsible for responding to new security threats that crop up, into groups where they can help with new-product development. Others write internal research papers. Still others are assigned to develop new tools that will help their colleagues battle the next wave of threats. There's even an individual who tries to figure out what makes the virus writers tick—and the day never ends for these virus hunters. When Dublin's team finishes its day, colleagues in Santa Monica take over. When the U.S. team finishes its day, it hands off to the team in Tokyo, who then hands back to Dublin for the new day. It's a frenetic, chaotic, challenging work environment that spans the entire globe. But the goals for managing the virus hunters are to "try to take the chaos out, to make the exciting boring," to have a predictable and well-defined process for dealing with the virus threats, and to spread work evenly to the company's facilities around the world. It's a managerial challenge that company managers have embraced.

DISCUSSION QUESTIONS ✪

1. Keeping professionals excited about work that is routine and standardized *and* chaotic is a major challenge for Symantec's managers. How could they use technical, human, and conceptual skills to maintain an environment that encourages innovations and professionalism?

2. What management roles would operations manager Patrick Fitzgerald be playing as he (a) had weekly security briefing conference calls with coworkers around the globe, (b) assessed the feasibility of adding a new network consulting service, (c) kept employees focused on the company's commitment to customers?

3. Go to Symantec's Web site [www.symantec.com], and look up information about the company. What can you tell about its emphasis on customer service and innovation? In what ways does the organization support its employees in servicing customers and in being innovative?

4. What could other managers learn from Patrick Fitzgerald and Symantec's approach?

Management History Module

Henry Ford once said, "History is more or less bunk." Well, he was wrong! History is important because it can put current activities in perspective. In this module, we're going to take a trip back in time to see how the field of study called management has evolved. What you're going to see is that today's managers still use many elements of the historical approaches to management. Focus on the following learning outcomes as you read and study this module.

LEARNING OUTCOMES

MH 1 | *Describe* some early management examples.

MH 2 | *Explain* the various theories in the classical approach.

MH 3 | *Discuss* the development and uses of the behavioral approach.

MH 4 | *Describe* the quantitative approach.

MH 5 | *Explain* the various theories in the contemporary approach.

3000 BC – 1776	1911 – 1947	Late 1700s – 1950s	1940s – 1950s	1960s – present
Early Management	**Classical Approach**	**Behavioral Approach**	**Quantitative Approach**	**Contemporary Approaches**

MH 1 | *Describe* some early management examples.

EARLY **Management**

Management has been practiced a long time. Organized endeavors directed by people responsible for planning, organizing, leading, and controlling activities have existed for thousands of years. Let's look at some of the most interesting examples.

Source: Stephen Studd/Getty Images

The Egyptian pyramids and the Great Wall of China are proof that projects of tremendous scope, employing tens of thousands of people, were completed in ancient times.[1] It took more than 100,000 workers some 20 years to construct a single pyramid. Who told each worker what to do? Who ensured there would be enough stones at the site to keep workers busy? The answer is *managers*. Someone had to plan what was to be done, organize people and materials to do it, make sure those workers got the work done, and impose some controls to ensure that everything was done as planned.

Another example of early management can be found in the city of Venice, which was a major economic and trade center in the 1400s. The Venetians developed an early form of business enterprise and engaged in many activities common to today's organizations. For instance, at the arsenal of Venice, warships were floated along the canals, and at each stop, materials and riggings were added to the ship.[2] Sounds a lot like a car "floating" along an assembly line, doesn't it? In addition, the Venetians used warehouse and inventory systems to keep track of materials, human resource management functions to manage the labor force (including wine breaks), and an accounting system to keep track of revenues and costs.

Source: Antonio Natale/Bridgeman Art Library

In 1776, Adam Smith published *The Wealth of Nations*, in which he argued the economic advantages that organizations and society would gain from the **division of labor** (or **job specialization**)—that is, breaking down jobs into narrow and repetitive tasks. Using the pin industry as an example, Smith claimed that 10 individuals, each doing a specialized task, could produce about 48,000 pins a day among them. However, if each person worked alone performing each task separately, it would be quite an accomplishment to produce even 10 pins a day! Smith concluded that division of labor increased productivity by increasing each worker's skill and dexterity, saving time lost in changing tasks and creating labor-saving inventions and machinery. Job specialization continues to be popular. For example, think of the specialized tasks performed by members of a hospital surgery team, meal preparation tasks done by workers in restaurant kitchens, or positions played by players on a football team.

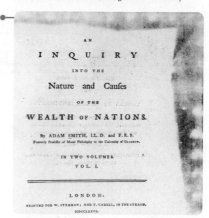

Source: Fotosearch/Stringer/Getty Images

Starting in the late eighteenth century when machine power was substituted for human power, a point in history known as the **industrial revolution**, it became more economical to manufacture goods in factories rather than at home. These large efficient factories needed someone to forecast demand, ensure that enough material was on hand to make products, assign tasks to people, direct daily activities, and so forth. That "someone" was a manager: These managers would need formal theories to guide them in running these large organizations. It wasn't until the early 1900s, however, that the first steps toward developing such theories were taken.

In this module, we'll look at four major approaches to management theory: classical, behavioral, quantitative, and contemporary. (See Exhibit MH-1.) Keep in

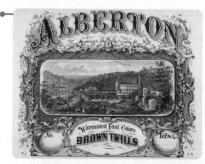

Source: Transcendental Graphics/Contributor/Getty Images

Exhibit MH-1
Major Approaches to Management

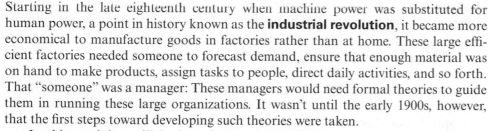

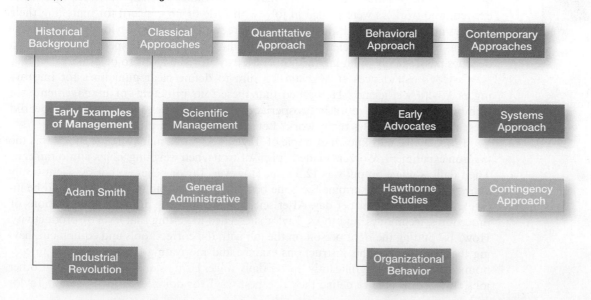

division of labor (job specialization)
The breakdown of jobs into narrow and repetitive tasks

industrial revolution
A period during the late eighteenth century when machine power was substituted for human power, making it more economical to manufacture goods in factories than at home

mind that each approach is concerned with trying to explain management from the perspective of what was important at that time in history and the backgrounds and interests of the researchers. Each of the four approaches contributes to our overall understanding of management, but each is also a limited view of what it is and how to best practice it.

3000 BC – 1776	1911 – 1947	Late 1700s – 1950s	1940s – 1950s	1960s – present
Early Management	Classical Approach	Behavioral Approach	Quantitative Approach	Contemporary Approaches

MH2 | ***Explain*** *the various theories in the classical approach.*

classical approach
First studies of management, which emphasized rationality and making organizations and workers as efficient as possible

CLASSICAL **Approach**

Although we've seen how management has been used in organized efforts since early history, the formal study of management didn't begin until early in the twentieth century. These first studies of management, often called the **classical approach**, emphasized rationality and making organizations and workers as efficient as possible. Two major theories comprise the classical approach: scientific management and general administrative theory. The two most important contributors to scientific management theory were Frederick W. Taylor and the husband-wife team of Frank and Lillian Gilbreth. The two most important contributors to general administrative theory were Henri Fayol and Max Weber. Let's take a look at each of these important figures in management history.

Scientific Management

Source: Jacques Boyer/The Image Works

scientific management
An approach that involves using the scientific method to find the "one best way" for a job to be done

If you had to pinpoint when modern management theory was born, 1911 might be a good choice. That was when Frederick Winslow Taylor's *Principles of Scientific Management* was published. Its contents were widely embraced by managers around the world. Taylor's book described the theory of **scientific management**: the use of scientific methods to define the "one best way" for a job to be done.

Taylor worked at the Midvale and Bethlehem Steel Companies in Pennsylvania. As a mechanical engineer with a Quaker and Puritan background, he was continually appalled by workers' inefficiencies. Employees used vastly different techniques to do the same job. They often "took it easy" on the job, and Taylor believed that worker output was only about one-third of what was possible. Virtually no work standards existed, and workers were placed in jobs with little or no concern for matching their abilities and aptitudes with the tasks they were required to do. Taylor set out to remedy that by applying the scientific method to shop-floor jobs. He spent more than two decades passionately pursuing the "one best way" for such jobs to be done.

Taylor's experiences at Midvale led him to define clear guidelines for improving production efficiency. He argued that these four principles of management (see Exhibit MH-2) would result in prosperity for both workers and managers.[3] How did these scientific principles really work? Let's look at an example.

Probably the best known example of Taylor's scientific management efforts was the pig iron experiment. Workers loaded "pigs" of iron (each weighing 92 lbs.) onto rail cars. Their daily average output was 12.5 tons. However, Taylor believed that by scientifically analyzing the job to determine the "one best way" to load pig iron, output could be increased to 47 or 48 tons per day. After scientifically applying different combinations of procedures, techniques, and tools, Taylor succeeded in getting that level of productivity. How? By putting the right person on the job with the correct tools and equipment, having the worker follow his instructions exactly, and motivating the worker with an economic incentive of a significantly higher daily wage. Using similar approaches for other jobs, Taylor was able to define the "one best way" for doing each job. Overall, Taylor

1. Develop a science for each element of an individual's work to replace the old rule-of-thumb method.

2. Scientifically select and then train, teach, and develop the worker.

3. Heartily cooperate with the workers to ensure that all work is done in accordance with the principles of the science that has been developed.

4. Divide work and responsibility almost equally between management and workers. Management does all work for which it is better suited than the workers.

Exhibit MH-2
Taylor's Scientific Management Principles

Source: *The Principles of Scientific Management* by Frederick Winslow Taylor. Published 1911.

achieved consistent productivity improvements in the range of 200 percent or more. Based on his groundbreaking studies of manual work using scientific principles, Taylor became known as the "father" of scientific management. His ideas spread in the United States and to other countries and inspired others to study and develop methods of scientific management. His most prominent followers were Frank and Lillian Gilbreth.

A construction contractor by trade, Frank Gilbreth gave up that career to study scientific management after hearing Taylor speak at a professional meeting. Frank and his wife Lillian, a psychologist, studied work to eliminate inefficient hand-and-body motions. The Gilbreths also experimented with the design and use of the proper tools and equipment for optimizing work performance.[4] Also, as parents of 12 children, the Gilbreths ran their household using scientific management principles and techniques. In fact, two of their children wrote a book, *Cheaper by the Dozen*, which described life with the two masters of efficiency.

Source: Bettmann/Corbis

Frank is probably best known for his bricklaying experiments. By carefully analyzing the bricklayer's job, he reduced the number of motions in laying exterior brick from 18 to about 5, and in laying interior brick from 18 to 2. Using Gilbreth's techniques, a bricklayer was more productive and less fatigued at the end of the day.

The Gilbreths invented a device called a microchronometer that recorded a worker's hand-and-body motions and the amount of time spent doing each motion. Wasted motions missed by the naked eye could be identified and eliminated. The Gilbreths also devised a classification scheme to label 17 basic hand motions (such as search, grasp, hold), which they called **therbligs** (Gilbreth spelled backward with the *th* transposed). This scheme gave the Gilbreths a more precise way of analyzing a worker's exact hand movements.

therbligs
A classification scheme for labeling basic hand motions

general administrative theory
An approach to management that focuses on describing what managers do and what constitutes good management practice

HOW TODAY'S MANAGERS USE SCIENTIFIC MANAGEMENT Many of the guidelines and techniques Taylor and the Gilbreths devised for improving production efficiency are still used in organizations today. When managers analyze the basic work tasks that must be performed, use time-and-motion study to eliminate wasted motions, hire the best-qualified workers for a job, or design incentive systems based on output, they're using the principles of scientific management.

General Administrative Theory

General administrative theory focused more on what managers do and what constituted good management practice. We introduced Henri Fayol in Chapter 1 because he first identified five functions that managers perform: planning, organizing, commanding, coordinating, and controlling.[5]

Fayol wrote during the same time period as Taylor. While Taylor was concerned with first-line managers and the scientific method, Fayol's attention was directed at the activities of *all* managers. He wrote from his personal experience as the managing director of a large French coal-mining firm.

Source: Jacques Boyer/The Image Works

principles of management
Fundamental rules of management that could be applied in all organizational situations and taught in schools

Source: Hulton Archive/Getty Images

bureaucracy
A form of organization characterized by division of labor, a clearly defined hierarchy, detailed rules and regulations, and impersonal relationships

Fayol described the practice of management as something distinct from accounting, finance, production, distribution, and other typical business functions. His belief that management was an activity common to all business endeavors, government, and even the home led him to develop 14 **principles of management**—fundamental rules of management that could be applied to all organizational situations and taught in schools. These principles are shown in Exhibit MH-3.

Weber (pronounced VAY-ber) was a German sociologist who studied organizations.[6] Writing in the early 1900s, he developed a theory of authority structures and relations based on an ideal type of organization he called a **bureaucracy**—a form of organization characterized by division of labor, a clearly defined hierarchy, detailed rules and regulations, and impersonal relationships. (See Exhibit MH-4.) Weber recognized that this "ideal bureaucracy" didn't exist in reality. Instead, he intended it as a basis for theorizing about how work could be done in large groups. His theory became the structural design for many of today's large organizations.

Bureaucracy, as described by Weber, is a lot like scientific management in its ideology. Both emphasized rationality, predictability, impersonality, technical competence, and authoritarianism. Although Weber's ideas were less practical than Taylor's, the fact that his "ideal type" still describes many contemporary organizations attests to their importance.

HOW TODAY'S MANAGERS USE GENERAL ADMINISTRATIVE THEORY   Several of our current management ideas and practices can be directly traced to the contributions of general administrative theory. For instance, the functional view of the manager's job can be attributed to Fayol. In addition, his 14 principles serve as a frame of reference from which many current management concepts—such as managerial authority, centralized decision making, reporting to only one boss, and so forth—have evolved.

Exhibit MH-3
Fayol's 14 Principles of Management

1. **Division of work.** Specialization increases output by making employees more efficient.
2. **Authority.** Managers must be able to give orders, and authority gives them this right.
3. **Discipline.** Employees must obey and respect the rules that govern the organization.
4. **Unity of command.** Every employee should receive orders from only one superior.
5. **Unity of direction.** The organization should have a single plan of action to guide managers and workers.
6. **Subordination of individual interests to the general interest.** The interests of any one employee or group of employees should not take precedence over the interests of the organization as a whole.
7. **Remuneration.** Workers must be paid a fair wage for their services.
8. **Centralization.** This term refers to the degree to which subordinates are involved in decision making.
9. **Scalar chain.** The line of authority from top management to the lowest ranks is the scalar chain.
10. **Order.** People and materials should be in the right place at the right time.
11. **Equity.** Managers should be kind and fair to their subordinates.
12. **Stability of tenure of personnel.** Management should provide orderly personnel planning and ensure that replacements are available to fill vacancies.
13. **Initiative.** Employees allowed to originate and carry out plans will exert high levels of effort.
14. **Esprit de corps.** Promoting team spirit will build harmony and unity within the organization.

Exhibit MH-4
Characteristics of Weber's Bureaucracy

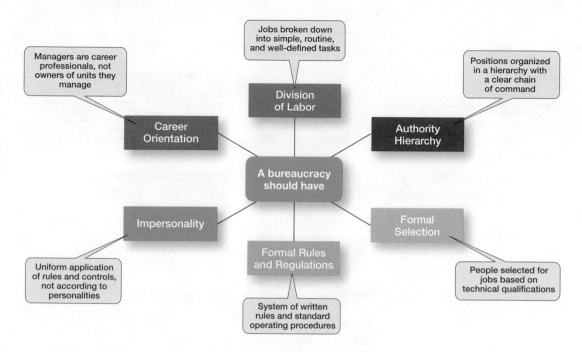

Weber's bureaucracy was an attempt to formulate an ideal prototype for organizations. Although many characteristics of Weber's bureaucracy are still evident in large organizations, his model isn't as popular today as it was in the twentieth century. Many managers feel that a bureaucratic structure hinders individual employees' creativity and limits an organization's ability to respond quickly to an increasingly dynamic environment. However, even in flexible organizations of creative professionals—such as Google, Samsung, General Electric, or Cisco Systems—bureaucratic mechanisms are necessary to ensure that resources are used efficiently and effectively.

3000 BC – 1776	1911 – 1947	Late 1700s – 1950s	1940s – 1950s	1960s – present
Early Management	Classical Approach	Behavioral Approach	Quantitative Approach	Contemporary Approaches

BEHAVIORAL Approach

As we know, managers get things done by working with people. This explains why some writers have chosen to look at management by focusing on the organization's people. The field of study that researches the actions (behavior) of people at work is called **organizational behavior (OB)**. Much of what managers do today when managing people—motivating, leading, building trust, working with a team, managing conflict, and so forth—has come out of OB research.

Although a number of individuals in the early twentieth century recognized the importance of people to an organization's success, four stand out as early advocates of the OB approach: Robert Owen, Hugo Munsterberg, Mary Parker Follett, and Chester Barnard. Their contributions were varied and distinct, yet all believed that people were the most important asset of the organization and should be managed accordingly. Their ideas provided the foundation for such management practices as employee selection procedures, motivation programs, and work teams. Exhibit MH-5 summarizes each individual's most important ideas.

***Discuss** the* **MH3**
development and uses of the behavioral approach.

organizational behavior (OB)
The study of the actions of people at work

Exhibit MH-5
Early OB Advocates

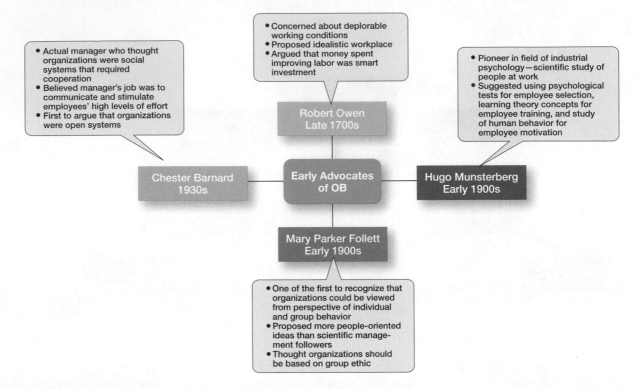

- Actual manager who thought organizations were social systems that required cooperation
- Believed manager's job was to communicate and stimulate employees' high levels of effort
- First to argue that organizations were open systems

- Concerned about deplorable working conditions
- Proposed idealistic workplace
- Argued that money spent improving labor was smart investment

- Pioneer in field of industrial psychology—scientific study of people at work
- Suggested using psychological tests for employee selection, learning theory concepts for employee training, and study of human behavior for employee motivation

Chester Barnard 1930s

Robert Owen Late 1700s

Early Advocates of OB

Hugo Munsterberg Early 1900s

Mary Parker Follett Early 1900s

- One of the first to recognize that organizations could be viewed from perspective of individual and group behavior
- Proposed more people-oriented ideas than scientific management followers
- Thought organizations should be based on group ethic

Source: Hawthorne Museum

Hawthorne Studies
A series of studies during the 1920s and 1930s that provided new insights into individual and group behavior

Without question, the most important contribution to the OB field came out of the **Hawthorne Studies**, a series of studies conducted at the Western Electric Company Works in Cicero, Illinois. These studies, which started in 1924, were initially designed by Western Electric industrial engineers as a scientific management experiment. They wanted to examine the effect of various lighting levels on worker productivity. Like any good scientific experiment, control and experimental groups were set up with the experimental group exposed to various lighting intensities, and the control group working under a constant intensity. If you were the industrial engineers in charge of this experiment, what would you have expected to happen? It's logical to think that individual output in the experimental group would be directly related to the intensity of the light. However, they found that as the level of light was increased in the experimental group, output for both groups increased. Then, much to the surprise of the engineers, as the light level was decreased in the experimental group, productivity continued to increase in both groups. In fact, a productivity decrease was observed in the experimental group *only* when the level of light was reduced to that of a moonlit night. What would explain these unexpected results? The engineers weren't sure, but concluded that lighting intensity was not directly related to group productivity and that something else must have contributed to the results. They weren't able to pinpoint what that "something else" was, though.

In 1927, the Western Electric engineers asked Harvard professor Elton Mayo and his associates to join the study as consultants. Thus began a relationship that would last through 1932 and encompass numerous experiments in the redesign of jobs, changes in workday and workweek length, introduction of rest periods, and individual versus group wage plans.[7] For example, one experiment was designed to evaluate the effect of a group piecework incentive pay system on group productivity. The results indicated that the incentive plan had less effect on a worker's output than group pressure, acceptance, and security. The researchers concluded that social norms or group standards were the key determinants of individual work behavior.

Scholars generally agree that the Hawthorne Studies had a game-changing impact on management beliefs about the role of people in organizations. Mayo concluded that people's behavior and attitudes are closely related, that group factors significantly affect individual behavior, that group standards establish individual worker output, and that money is less a factor in determining output than group standards, group attitudes, and security. These conclusions led to a new emphasis on the human behavior factor in the management of organizations.

Although critics attacked the research procedures, analyses of findings, and conclusions, it's of little importance from a historical perspective whether the Hawthorne Studies were academically sound or their conclusions justified.[8] What *is* important is that they stimulated an interest in human behavior in organizations.

HOW TODAY'S MANAGERS USE THE BEHAVIORAL APPROACH The behavioral approach has largely shaped how today's organizations are managed. From the way managers design jobs to the way they work with employee teams to the way they communicate, we see elements of the behavioral approach. Much of what the early OB advocates proposed and the conclusions from the Hawthorne studies have provided the foundation for our current theories of motivation, leadership, group behavior and development, and numerous other behavioral approaches.

3000 BC – 1776	1911 – 1947	Late 1700s – 1950s	1940s – 1950s	1960s – present
Early Management	Classical Approach	Behavioral Approach	Quantitative Approach	Contemporary Approaches

QUANTITATIVE Approach

Although passengers bumping into each other when trying to find their seats on an airplane can be a mild annoyance for them, it's a bigger problem for airlines because lines get backed up, slowing down how quickly the plane can get back in the air. Based on research in space-time geometry, one airline innovated a unique boarding process called "reverse pyramid" that has saved at least 2 minutes in boarding time.[9] This is an example of the **quantitative approach**, which is the use of quantitative techniques to improve decision making. This approach also is known as *management science*.

The quantitative approach evolved from mathematical and statistical solutions developed for military problems during World War II. After the war was over, many of these techniques used for military problems were applied to businesses. For example, one group of military officers, nicknamed the Whiz Kids, joined Ford Motor Company in the mid-1940s and immediately began using statistical methods and quantitative models to improve decision making.

What exactly does the quantitative approach do? It involves applying statistics, optimization models, information models, computer simulations, and other quantitative techniques to management activities. Linear programming, for instance, is a technique that managers use to improve resource allocation decisions. Work scheduling can be more efficient as a result of critical-path scheduling analysis. The economic order quantity model helps managers determine optimum inventory levels. Each of these is an example of quantitative techniques being applied to improve managerial decision making. Another area where quantitative techniques are used frequently is in total quality management.

A quality revolution swept through both the business and public sectors in the 1980s and 1990s.[10] It was inspired by a small group of quality experts; the most famous was W. Edwards Deming (pictured at right) and Joseph M. Juran. The ideas and techniques they advocated in the 1950s had few supporters in the United States but were enthusiastically embraced by Japanese organizations. As Japanese manufacturers began beating U.S. competitors in quality comparisons, however, Western managers soon took a more serious look at Deming's and Juran's ideas, which became the basis for today's quality management programs.

Describe the) **MH4**
quantitative approach.

quantitative approach
The use of quantitative techniques to improve decision making

Source: Bert Hardy/Hulton Archive/ Getty Images

Source: Richard Drew/AP Wide World Photos

Exhibit MH-6
What Is Quality Management?

1. **Intense focus on the customer.** The customer includes outsiders who buy the organization's products or services and internal customers who interact with and serve others in the organization.

2. **Concern for continual improvement.** Quality management is a commitment to never being satisfied. "Very good" is not good enough. Quality can always be improved.

3. **Process focused.** Quality management focuses on work processes as the quality of goods and services is continually improved.

4. **Improvement in the quality of everything the organization does.** This relates to the final product, how the organization handles deliveries, how rapidly it responds to complaints, how politely the phones are answered, and the like.

5. **Accurate measurement.** Quality management uses statistical techniques to measure every critical variable in the organization's operations. These are compared against standards to identify problems, trace them to their roots, and eliminate their causes.

6. **Empowerment of employees.** Quality management involves the people on the line in the improvement process. Teams are widely used in quality management programs as empowerment vehicles for finding and solving problems.

total quality management (TQM)
A philosophy of management that is driven by continuous improvement and responsiveness to customer needs and expectations

Total quality management, or **TQM**, is a management philosophy devoted to continual improvement and responding to customer needs and expectations. (See Exhibit MH-6.) The term *customer* includes anyone who interacts with the organization's product or services, internally or externally. It encompasses employees and suppliers as well as the people who purchase the organization's goods or services. *Continual improvement* isn't possible without accurate measurements, which require statistical techniques that measure every critical variable in the organization's work processes. These measurements are compared against standards to identify and correct problems.

HOW TODAY'S MANAGERS USE THE QUANTITATIVE APPROACH No one likes long lines, especially residents of New York City. If they see a long checkout line, they often go somewhere else. However, at Whole Foods' first gourmet supermarkets in Manhattan, customers found something different—that is, the longer the line, the shorter the wait. When ready to check out, customers are guided into serpentine single lines that feed into numerous checkout lanes. Whole Foods, widely known for its organic food selections, can charge premium prices, which allow it the luxury of staffing all those checkout lanes. And customers are finding that their wait times are shorter than expected.[11] The science of keeping lines moving is known as queue management. And for Whole Foods, this quantitative technique has translated into strong sales at its Manhattan stores.

The quantitative approach contributes directly to management decision making in the areas of planning and control. For instance, when managers make budgeting, queuing, scheduling, quality control, and similar decisions, they typically rely on quantitative techniques. Specialized software has made the use of these techniques less intimidating for managers, although many still feel anxious about using them.

3000 BC – 1776	1911 – 1947	Late 1700s – 1950s	1940s – 1950s	1960s – present
Early Management	Classical Approach	Behavioral Approach	Quantitative Approach	Contemporary Approaches

MH5 *Explain the various theories in the contemporary approach.*

CONTEMPORARY Approaches

As we've seen, many elements of the earlier approaches to management theory continue to influence how managers manage. Most of these earlier approaches focused on managers' concerns *inside* the organization. Starting in the 1960s, management researchers began to look at what was happening in the external environment *outside* the boundaries of the organization. Two contemporary management perspectives—systems and contingency—are part of this approach. Systems theory is a basic theory in the physical sciences, but had never been applied to organized human efforts. In 1938, Chester Barnard, a telephone company executive, first wrote in his book, *The Functions of an Executive,* that an organization functioned as a cooperative system. However, it wasn't until the 1960s that management researchers began to look more carefully at systems theory and how it related to organizations.

A **system** is a set of interrelated and interdependent parts arranged in a manner that produces a unified whole. The two basic types of systems are closed and open. **Closed systems** are not influenced by and do not interact with their environment. In contrast, **open systems** are influenced by and do interact with their environment. Today, when we describe organizations as systems, we mean open systems. Exhibit MH-7 shows a diagram of an organization from an open systems perspective. As you can see, an organization takes in inputs (resources) from the environment and transforms or processes these resources into outputs that are distributed into the environment. The organization is "open" to and interacts with its environment.

Source: AFP/Photo Frederic J. Brown/Newscom

system
A set of interrelated and interdependent parts arranged in a manner that produces a unified whole

closed systems
Systems that are not influenced by and do not interact with their environment

open systems
Systems that interact with their environment

How does the systems approach contribute to our understanding of management? Researchers envisioned an organization as made up of "interdependent factors, including individuals, groups, attitudes, motives, formal structure, interactions, goals, status, and authority."[12] What this means is that as managers coordinate work activities in the various parts of the organization, they ensure that all these parts are working together so the organization's goals can be achieved. For example, the systems approach recognizes that, no matter how efficient the production department, the marketing department must anticipate changes in customer tastes and work with the product development department in creating products customers want—or the organization's overall performance will suffer.

In addition, the systems approach implies that decisions and actions in one organizational area will affect other areas. For example, if the purchasing department doesn't acquire the right quantity and quality of inputs, the production department won't be able to do its job.

Finally, the systems approach recognizes that organizations are not self-contained. They rely on their environment for essential inputs and as outlets to absorb their outputs. No organization can survive for long if it ignores government regulations, supplier relations, or the varied external constituencies on which it depends.

How relevant is the systems approach to management? Quite relevant. Consider, for example, a shift manager at a Starbucks restaurant who must coordinate the work of employees filling customer orders at the front counter and the drive-through windows, direct the delivery and unloading of food supplies, and address any customer

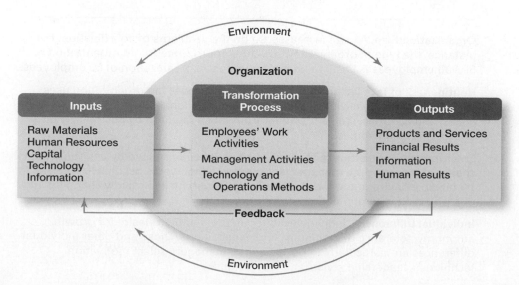

Exhibit MH-7
Organization as an
Open System

concerns that come up. This manager "manages" all parts of the "system" so that the restaurant meets its daily sales goals.

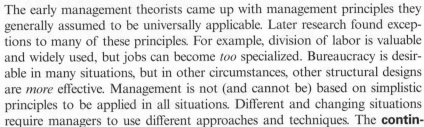

The early management theorists came up with management principles they generally assumed to be universally applicable. Later research found exceptions to many of these principles. For example, division of labor is valuable and widely used, but jobs can become *too* specialized. Bureaucracy is desirable in many situations, but in other circumstances, other structural designs are *more* effective. Management is not (and cannot be) based on simplistic principles to be applied in all situations. Different and changing situations require managers to use different approaches and techniques. The **contingency approach** (sometimes called the *situational approach*) says that organizations are different, face different situations (contingencies), and require different ways of managing.

contingency approach
A management approach that recognizes organizations as different, which means they face different situations (contingencies) and require different ways of managing

A good way to describe contingency is "if, then." *If* this is the way my situation is, *then* this is the best way for me to manage in this situation. It's intuitively logical because organizations and even units within the same organization differ—in size, goals, work activities, and the like. It would be surprising to find universally applicable management rules that would work in *all* situations. But, of course, it's one thing to say that the way to manage "depends on the situation" and another to say what the situation is. Management researchers continue working to identify these situational variables. Exhibit MH-8 describes four popular contingency variables. Although the list is by no means comprehensive—more than 100 different variables have been identified—it represents those most widely used and gives you an idea of what we mean by the term *contingency variable*. The primary value of the contingency approach is that it stresses there are no simplistic or universal rules for managers to follow.

Source: Newscom

So what do managers face today when managing? Although the dawn of the information age is said to have begun with Samuel Morse's telegraph in 1837, dramatic changes in information technology that occurred in the latter part of the twentieth century and continue through today directly affect the manager's job. Managers now may manage employees who are working from home or working halfway around the world. An organization's computing resources used to be mainframe computers locked away in temperature-controlled rooms and only accessed by the experts. Now, practically everyone in an organization is connected—wired or wireless—with devices no larger than the palm of the hand. Just like the impact of the Industrial Revolution in the 1700s on the emergence of management, the information age has brought dramatic changes that continue to influence the way organizations are managed.

Exhibit MH-8
Popular Contingency Variables

Organization Size. As size increases, so do the problems of coordination. For instance, the type of organization structure appropriate for an organization of 50,000 employees is likely to be inefficient for an organization of 50 employees.

Routineness of Task Technology. To achieve its purpose, an organization uses technology. Routine technologies require organizational structures, leadership styles, and control systems that differ from those required by customized or nonroutine technologies.

Environmental Uncertainty. The degree of uncertainty caused by environmental changes influences the management process. What works best in a stable and predictable environment may be totally inappropriate in a rapidly changing and unpredictable environment.

Individual Differences. Individuals differ in terms of their desire for growth, autonomy, tolerance of ambiguity, and expectations. These and other individual differences are particularly important when managers select motivation techniques, leadership styles, and job designs.

Management History *Module*

CHAPTER SUMMARY by Learning Outcomes

MH1 LEARNING OUTCOME

Describe some early management examples.

Studying history is important because it helps us see the origins of today's management practices and recognize what has and has not worked. We can see early examples of management practice in the construction of the Egyptian pyramids and in the arsenal of Venice. One important historical event was the publication of Adam Smith's *Wealth of Nations*, in which he argued the benefits of division of labor (job specialization). Another was the industrial revolution where it became more economical to manufacture in factories than at home. Managers were needed to manage these factories, and these managers needed formal management theories to guide them.

MH2 LEARNING OUTCOME

Explain the various theories in the classical approach.

Frederick W. Taylor, known as the "father" of scientific management, studied manual work using scientific principles—that is, guidelines for improving production efficiency—to find the one best way to do those jobs. The Gilbreths' primary contribution was finding efficient hand-and-body motions and designing proper tools and equipment for optimizing work performance. Fayol believed the functions of management were common to all business endeavors but also were distinct from other business functions. He developed 14 principles of management from which many current management concepts have evolved. Weber described an ideal type of organization he called a bureaucracy—characteristics that many of today's large organizations still have. Today's managers use the concepts of scientific management when they analyze basic work tasks to be performed, use time-and-motion study to eliminate wasted motions, hire the best qualified workers for a job, and design incentive systems based on output. They use general administrative theory when they perform the functions of management and structure their organizations so that resources are used efficiently and effectively.

MH3 LEARNING OUTCOME

Discuss the development and uses of the behavioral approach.

The early OB advocates (Robert Owen, Hugo Munsterberg, Mary Parker Follett, and Chester Barnard) contributed various ideas, but all believed that people were the most important asset of the organization and should be managed accordingly. The Hawthorne Studies dramatically affected management beliefs about the role of people in organizations, leading to a new emphasis on the human behavior factor in managing. The behavioral approach has largely shaped how today's organizations are managed. Many current theories of motivation, leadership, group behavior and development, and other behavioral issues can be traced to the early OB advocates and the conclusions from the Hawthorne Studies.

MH4 LEARNING OUTCOME

Describe the quantitative approach.

The quantitative approach involves applications of statistics, optimization models, information models, and computer simulations to management activities. Today's managers use the quantitative approach, especially when making decisions, as they plan and control work activities such as allocating resources, improving quality, scheduling work, or determining optimum inventory levels. Total quality management—a management philosophy devoted to continual improvement and responding to customer needs and expectations—also makes use of quantitative methods to meet its goals.

MH5 ⌐LEARNING OUTCOME⌐

Explain the various theories in the contemporary approach.

The systems approach says that an organization takes in inputs (resources) from the environment and transforms or processes these resources into outputs that are distributed into the environment. This approach provides a framework to help managers understand how all the interdependent units work together to achieve the organization's goals and that decisions and actions taken in one organizational area will affect others. In this way, managers can recognize that organizations are not self-contained, but instead rely on their environment for essential inputs and as outlets to absorb their outputs.

The contingency approach says that organizations are different, face different situations, and require different ways of managing. It helps us understand management because it stresses there are no simplistic or universal rules for managers to follow. Instead, managers must look at their situation and determine that *if* this is the way my situation is, *then* this is the best way for me to manage.

REVIEW AND DISCUSSION QUESTIONS

1. Explain why studying management history is important.

2. What early evidence of management practice can you describe?

3. Describe the important contributions made by the classical theorists.

4. What did the early advocates of OB contribute to our understanding of management?

5. Why were the Hawthorne Studies so critical to management history?

6. What kind of workplace would Henri Fayol create? How about Mary Parker Follett? How about Frederick W. Taylor?

7. Explain what the quantitative approach has contributed to the field of management.

8. Describe total quality management.

9. How do systems theory and the contingency approach make managers better at what they do?

10. How do societal trends influence the practice of management? What are the implications for someone studying management?

PREPARING FOR: My Career
MY TURN TO BE A MANAGER

• Choose two nonmanagement classes you are currently enrolled in or have taken previously. Describe three ideas and concepts from those subject areas that might help you be a better manager.

• Read at least one current business article from any popular business periodical each week for four weeks. Describe what each of the four articles is about and how each relates to any (or all) of the four approaches to management.

• Choose an organization with which you are familiar and describe the job specialization used there. Is it efficient and effective? Why or why not? How could it be improved?

• Can scientific management principles help you be more efficient? Choose a task you do regularly (such as laundry, fixing dinner, grocery shopping, studying for exams, etc.). Analyze it by writing down the steps involved in completing that task. See if any activities could be combined or eliminated. Find the "one best way" to do this task! And the next time you have to do the task, try the scientifically managed way! See if you become more efficient (keeping in mind that changing habits isn't easy to do).

• How do business organizations survive for 100+ years? Obviously, they've seen a lot of historical events come and go. Choose one of these companies and research their history: Coca-Cola, Procter & Gamble, Avon, or General Electric. How has it changed over the years? From your research on this company, what did you learn that could help you be a better manager?

- Find the current top five best-selling management books. Read a review of the book or the book covers (or even the book!). Write a short paragraph describing what each book is about. Also, write about which of the historical management approaches you think the book fits into and how you think it fits into that approach.

- Pick one historical event from this century and do some research on it. Write a paper describing the impact this event might be having or has had on how workplaces are managed.

- Steve's and Mary's suggested readings: Gary Hamel, *The Future of Management* (Harvard Business School Press, 2007); Malcolm Gladwell, *Blink* (Little, Brown and Company, 2005); James C. Collins, *Good to Great: Why Some Companies Make the Leap…and Others Don't* (Harper Business, 2001); Matthew J. Kiernan, *The Eleven Commandments of 21st Century Management* (Prentice Hall, 1996); and James C. Collins and Jerry I. Porras, *Built to Last: Successful Habits of Visionary Companies* (Harper Business, 1994).

- Come on, admit it. You multitask, don't you? And if not, you probably know people who do. Multitasking is also common in the workplace. But does it make employees more efficient and effective? Pretend you're the manager in charge of a loan-processing department. Describe how you would research this issue using each of the following management approaches or theories: scientific management, general administrative theory, quantitative approach, behavioral approach, systems theory, and contingency theory.

- In your own words, write down three things you learned in this module about being a good manager.

- Self-knowledge can be a powerful learning tool. Go to mymanagementlab.com and complete any of these self-assessment exercises: How Well Do I Respond to Turbulent Change? How Well Do I Handle Ambiguity? and What Do I Value? Using the results of your assessments, identify personal strengths and weaknesses. What will you do to reinforce your strengths and improve your weaknesses?

SPOTLIGHT: *Manager at Work*

Think of a job you've had. *Now suppose an unimaginable crisis happened while you were at work. How would you and your fellow employees respond? Mallika Jagad, the 24-year-old banquet manager at the Taj Mahal Palace in Mumbai, had that happen one terrifying work night. November 26, 2008, is a date she will not soon forget.[1] Jagad was managing a dinner event for an important group of clients from Unilever, which included senior executives, company directors, and their spouses. About the time the main course was being served to the guests, the unthinkable happened. Loud popping noises, which they first thought were fireworks from a nearby wedding, were actually the first gunshots fired by terrorists storming the hotel. The staff quickly realized that something was wrong. Jagad had the doors locked and the lights turned off. Then she asked everyone to lie down quietly under the tables and to not use cell phones. She also asked that husbands and wives be separated to reduce the potential risk of losing both family members. Throughout the night, the group crouched under the tables, listening to the violence taking place in the hotel outside the second-floor banquet room doors. As the terrified guests said later, the Taj staff was calm and continued to care for them by offering water and asking if there was anything else they needed. As morning*

Source: India Today Group/Getty Images

broke, another crisis erupted as a fire started in the hallway outside the room. The group had to climb out the windows with the staff evacuating the guests first. A fire crew spotted them and quickly helped the trapped people escape quickly with no casualties. As Jagad said later,

Source: Taj Mahal Palace and Tower Hotel/ AFP/Getty Images/Newscom

"It was my responsibility...

I may have been the youngest person in the room,

but I was still doing my job."

In the hotel's upscale restaurant, a hotel operator alerted the staff that terrorists in the building were headed that way. Thomas Varghese, the 48-year-old senior waiter immediately told his guests to get under the tables and directed employees to form a human barrier around them. After four anxious hours, security men called Varghese to see if he could get the guests out of the hotel. Using a spiral staircase near the restaurant, customers were evacuated first and then the staff. Varghese—a 30-year Taj employee—who insisted he would be the last to leave, never made it out. The terrorists shot him as he reached the bottom of the stairs.

Upon getting word of the crisis, hotel general manager Karambir Singh Kang (see photo), who was attending

---

MyManagementLab®
⭐ **Improve Your Grade!**
Over 10 million students improved their results using the Pearson MyLabs.
Visit **mymanagementlab.com** for simulations, tutorials, and end-of-chapter problems.

LEARNING OUTCOMES

2.1	**Contrast** the actions of managers according to the omnipotent and symbolic views.
2.2	**Describe** the constraints and challenges facing managers in today's external environment.
2.3	**Discuss** the characteristics and importance of organizational culture.
2.4	**Describe** current issues in organizational culture.

a conference at another Taj property, rushed to get to his hotel. Arriving at the chaotic scene, he immediately began supervising guest evacuation and coordinating the efforts of rescue personnel. Kang's own wife and two young children were in a sixth-floor suite where he thought they would be safe. But by midnight, the sixth floor was on fire with no hopes of anyone surviving. Kang continued to lead the rescue efforts, and it wasn't until the next day that he called his parents to tell them that the terrorists had killed his wife and children. "His father, a retired general told him, 'Son, do your duty. Do not desert your post,' to which Kang replied, "If it (the hotel) goes down, I will be the last man out." The day after the attack, hotel guests praised the hotel staff's "dedication to duty, their desire to protect guests without regard to personal safety, and their quick thinking." **How does an organization get such enduring attitudes and behaviors from employees?**

Here's an organization that recognizes how important culture is and has employees with complete dedication to that culture! The Taj Mahal Palace's extreme customer-centric culture is one in which employees are highly trained and are willing to go the extra mile to delight customers. Not surprisingly, the hotel is one of the world's finest, known for the highest levels of quality and customer service. Despite that catastrophic attack in 2008, the Taj continues to be a coveted destination for discerning travelers. Undoubtedly, its devoted employees and the organizational culture they embrace have played a key role in that accomplishment.

I n this chapter, we're going to look at culture and other important aspects of management's context. We'll examine the challenges in the external environment and discuss the characteristics of organizational culture. But before we address these topics, we first need to look at two perspectives on how much impact managers actually have on an organization's success or failure.

THE MANAGER: Omnipotent or Symbolic?

2.1 **Contrast** the actions of managers according to the omnipotent and symbolic views.

A slumping stock price and continued criticism by many Wall Street analysts about brand performance led to a top management shakeup at PepsiCo. Two top managers in the company's PepsiCo Americas Beverages unit were affected. One was reassigned to a position with lesser responsibility and the other "retired."[2] Such a move shuffling managers is not all that uncommon in the corporate world, but why?

How much difference *does* a manager make in how an organization performs? The dominant view in management theory and society in general is that managers are directly responsible for an organization's success or failure. We call this perspective the **omnipotent view of management**. In contrast, others have argued that much of an organization's success or failure is due to external forces outside managers' control. This perspective is called the **symbolic view of management**. Let's look at each perspective to try and clarify just how much credit or blame managers should get for their organization's performance.

omnipotent view of management
The view that managers are directly responsible for an organization's success or failure

symbolic view of management
The view that much of an organization's success or failure is due to external forces outside managers' control

The Omnipotent View

In Chapter 1, we stressed how important managers were to organizations. Differences in an organization's performance are assumed to be due to decisions and actions of its managers. Good managers anticipate change, exploit opportunities, correct poor performance, and lead their organizations. When profits are up, managers take the credit and are rewarded with bonuses, stock options, and the like. When profits are down, top managers are often fired in the belief that "new blood" will bring improved results. For instance, Yahoo's board of directors fired CEO Carol Bartz because the company's revenue growth had stalled and because a significant disagreement with important Chinese partner Alibaba had not been resolved.[3] In the omnipotent view, someone has to be held accountable when organizations perform poorly regardless of the reasons, and that "someone" is the manager. Of course, when things go well, managers also get the credit—even if they had little to do with achieving the positive outcomes.

This view of managers as omnipotent is consistent with the stereotypical picture of the take-charge business executive who overcomes any obstacle in seeing that the organization achieves its goals. And this view isn't limited to business organizations. It also explains turnover among college and professional sports coaches, who are considered the "managers" of their teams. Coaches who lose more games than they win are usually fired and replaced by new coaches who are expected to correct the poor performance.

The Symbolic View

In the 1990s, Cisco Systems was the picture of success. Growing rapidly, it was widely praised by analysts for its "brilliant strategy, masterful management of acquisitions and superb customer focus."[4] However, as Cisco's performance declined during the early part of the twenty-first century, analysts said its strategy was flawed, its acquisition approach was haphazard, and its customer service was poor. Was declining performance due to the managers' decisions and actions, or was it due to external circumstances beyond their control? The symbolic view would suggest the latter.

The symbolic view says that a manager's ability to affect performance outcomes is influenced and constrained by external factors.[5] According to this view, it's unreasonable to expect managers to significantly affect an organization's performance. Instead, performance is influenced by factors over which managers have little control such as the economy, customers, governmental policies, competitors' actions, industry conditions, and decisions made by previous managers.

This view is labeled "symbolic" because it's based on the belief that managers symbolize control and influence.[6] How? By developing plans, making decisions, and engaging in other managerial activities to make sense out of random, confusing, and ambiguous situations. However, the actual part that managers play in organizational success or failure is limited according to this view.

In reality, managers are neither all-powerful nor helpless. But their decisions and actions are constrained. As you can see in Exhibit 2-1, external constraints come from the organization's environment and internal constraints come from the organization's culture.

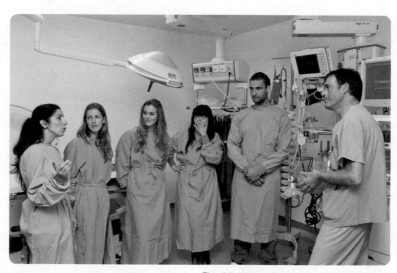

The global economic recession poses constraints and challenges for managers in the areas of jobs and employment. In this photo, Jens Schriewe (right), head of nursing services at University Hospital in Erlangen, Germany, talks with five young Spanish nurses who have joined his clinical staff. As Germany recovers from the global economic crisis, managers like Jens are faced with a shortage of skilled workers. To keep Germany's economy improving, they are drawing potential job candidates from Spain and other countries hardest hit by the economic crisis. With job creation stalling in Spain, where youth unemployment tops 40 percent, young job seekers look abroad for work in countries with better economic conditions.
Source: Daniel Karmann/EPA/Newscom

| Organizational Environment | Managerial Discretion | Organizational Culture |

Exhibit 2-1
Constraints on Managerial Discretion

2.2 ***Describe*** *the constraints and challenges facing managers in today's external environment.*

THE EXTERNAL ENVIRONMENT:
Constraints and Challenges

Digital technology has disrupted all types of industries—from financial services to recorded music. One industry in particular, the publishing industry, has been impacted significantly. As e-book sales skyrocketed, competition among e-book reader devices intensified. Amazon introduced the first device, the Kindle, in November 2007. As with any new product, customers had to adjust to the new technology, but once they did, the Kindles were on fire! Two years later, retailer Barnes & Noble introduced the Nook, a cheaper e-book device. Amazon responded by cutting the price of its cheapest Kindle. Three months later in January 2010, Apple introduced its iPad tablet. It was more expensive, but its functionality and options (and the Apple name) made it an instant hit with customers. In response, Barnes & Noble cut the price of its Nook, and Amazon again lowered the price of the Kindle. By September 2011, the basic Kindle's starting price had dropped to $79, and Amazon launched Kindle Fire. Then in November 2011, Barnes & Noble joined the tablet battle with its $249 Nook Tablet. And now Microsoft has invested $300 million in Barnes & Noble (which had been struggling) in an attempt to be more competitive with Amazon. Other e-book readers include Sony's Reader and Endless Ideas' BeBook Neo. As the popularity of e-books accelerates, the "reader wars" are likely to continue.[7] Anyone who doubts the impact the external environment has on managing just needs to look at what's happened in both the publishing industry and the e-book reader industry during the last few years.

external environment
Those factors and forces outside the organization that affect its performance

The term **external environment** refers to factors and forces outside the organization that affect its performance. As shown in Exhibit 2-2, it includes several different components. The economic component encompasses factors such as interest rates, inflation, changes in disposable income, stock market fluctuations, and business cycle stages. The demographic component is concerned with trends in population characteristics such as age, race, gender, education level, geographic location, income, and family composition. The political/legal component looks at federal, state, and local laws as well as global laws and laws of other countries. It also includes a country's political conditions and stability. The sociocultural component is concerned with societal and cultural factors such as values, attitudes, trends, traditions, lifestyles, beliefs, tastes, and patterns of behavior. The technological component is concerned with scientific or industrial innovations. And the global component encompasses those issues associated with globalization and a world economy. Although all these components pose potential constraints on managers' decisions and actions, we're going

Exhibit 2-2
Components of External Environment

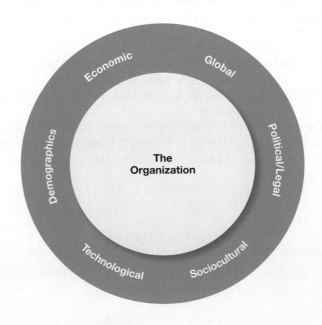

to take a closer look at two of them—the economic and demographic—by looking at how changes taking place in those components constrain managers and organizations. Then, we'll wrap up this section by examining environmental uncertainty and stakeholder relationships.

The Economic Environment

Like many global businesses, Nestlé faces increased commodity costs.[8] The maker of products from Crunch chocolate bars to Nescafé coffee to Purina pet food spends more than $30 billion a year on raw materials. To get a better feel for what that number reflects, think about this: annually, the company purchases about 10 percent of the world's coffee crop, 12 million metric tons of milk, and more than 300,000 tons of cocoa.

Commodity (raw materials) costs are just one of the many volatile economic factors facing organizations. The global economic recession, which continues to affect countries, consumers, businesses, and job seekers, also has been a significant economic factor. Let's look back at how this recession came about.

GLOBAL ECONOMIC RECESSION AND THE ECONOMIC CONTEXT   You knew the economic context had changed when a blue-ribbon company like General Motors declared bankruptcy; the Organization for Economic Cooperation and Development predicted some 25 million unemployed individuals globally; 8.4 million jobs in the United States vanished; and the economic vocabulary included terminology such as *toxic assets, collateralized debt obligations, TARP, bailouts, economic stabilization, wraparound mortgages,* and *stress tests.*[9]

The lingering economic crisis—called the "Great Recession" by some analysts— began with turmoil in home mortgage markets in the United States when many homeowners found themselves unable to make their payments. The problems soon affected businesses as credit markets collapsed. All of a sudden, credit was no longer readily available to fund business activities. It didn't take long for these economic troubles to spread worldwide.

FUTURE VISION | **More Diverse Than Ever**

Two of the largest changes that we see happening in the makeup of the workforce in 2025 in the United States will be a significant increase in Hispanic and senior-citizen participation.

Hispanic-Americans continue to be the fastest-growing segment of the U.S. population. They currently make up 16 percent of the population, although that number is forecasted to increase to 20 percent by 2025. In the southern part of the United States, the percentages will be higher. In cities such as Los Angeles, Phoenix, Tucson, El Paso, and Miami, more than a third of the population will be Hispanic. These general population percentages should translate equivalently to the labor force. The likelihood that you'll have a coworker whose first language is Spanish will be quite high.

You can also expect to see a graying of the workforce. By 2025, most employees will be working beyond normal retirement ages. People are living longer and enjoying good health well into their 70s. Those who enjoy being actively engaged in a job won't want to give that up. On the other hand, there also will be those senior citizens who can't afford to retire and have to continue working to avoid financial strains. In fact, we saw this happening in the most recent recession. Individuals who would like to have stepped away from their 8-to-5 jobs were happy to have a job and held onto that job. Now, envision that workplace where you'll also likely be working with many older (age 65+) coworkers. However, when those individuals *do* decide to retire, it could leave many organizations scrambling as these individuals take their institutional knowledge, communication skills, and professionalism gained from years of work experience.

Again, these two demographic changes foretell a workplace in which as a manager or as coworkers, you're going to be interacting and working with others who may not think or act or do things the way you would.

What caused these massive problems? Experts cited a long list of factors, including excessively low interest rates for a long period of time, fundamental flaws in the U.S. housing market, and massive global liquidity. Businesses and consumers became highly leveraged, which wasn't an issue when credit was easily available.[10] However, as liquidity dried up, the worldwide economic system sputtered and very nearly collapsed. Massive home foreclosures, a huge public debt burden in many countries, and continuing widespread social problems from job losses signaled clear changes in the U.S. and global economic environments. The slow recovery of global economies has continued to be a constraint on organizational decisions and actions. In addition, the World Economic Forum, identified two significant risks facing business leaders and policy makers over the next decade: "severe income disparity and chronic fiscal imbalances."[11] Let's take a quick look at the first of these risks, economic inequality since it reflects that it's not just the economic numbers, but also societal attitudes that can constrain managers.

ECONOMIC INEQUALITY AND THE ECONOMIC CONTEXT   A recent Harris Interactive Poll found that only 10 percent of adults think economic inequality is "not a problem at all." Most survey respondents believed it is either a major problem (57 percent) or a minor problem (23 percent).[12] Perhaps you saw news stories during late 2011 about a grassroots movement of protesters (Occupy) that started on Wall Street and soon spread to other cities in the United States and around the world. These protests focused on social and economic inequality, greed, corruption, and the undue influence of corporations on government. The protestors' slogan, *We are the 99%,* referred to the growing income and wealth gap between the wealthiest 1 percent and the rest of the population. Why has this issue become so sensitive? After all, those who worked hard and were rewarded because of their hard work or innovativeness have long been admired. And yes, an income gap has always existed. In the United States, that gap between the rich and the rest has been much wider than in other developed nations for decades and was accepted as part of our country's values and way of doing things. However, "our tolerance for a widening income gap may be ebbing."[13] As economic growth has languished and sputtered, and as people's belief that anyone could grab hold of an opportunity and have a decent shot at prosperity has wavered, social discontent over growing income gaps has increased. The bottom line is that business leaders need to recognize how societal attitudes in the economic context also may create constraints as they make decisions and manage their businesses.[14]

The Demographic Environment

"You can't understand the future without demographics. The composition of a society...shapes every aspect of civic life, from politics, economics, and culture to the kinds of products, services, and businesses that are likely to succeed or fail. Demographics isn't destiny, but it's close."[15] This quote should make it obvious why it's important to examine demographics.

Baby Boomers. Gen Y. Post-Millennials. Maybe you've heard or seen these terms before. Population researchers use these terms to refer to three of the more well-known age groups found in the U.S. population. Baby Boomers are those individuals born between 1946 and 1964. So much is written and reported about "boomers" because there are so many of them. The sheer number of people in that cohort means they've significantly affected every aspect of the external environment (from the educational system to entertainment/lifestyle choices to the Social Security system and so forth) as they cycle through the various life stages.

Gen Y (or the "Millennials") is typically considered to encompass those individuals born between 1978 and 1994. As the children of the Baby Boomers, this age group is also large in number and making its imprint on external environmental conditions as well. From technology to clothing styles to work attitudes, Gen Y is making their imprint on workplaces.

Then, we have the Post-Millennials—the youngest identified age group—basically teens and middle-schoolers.[16] This group has also been called the iGeneration, primarily because they've grown up with technology that customizes everything to the individual. Population experts say it's too early to tell whether elementary school-aged children and younger are part of this demographic group or whether the world they live in will be so different that they'll comprise a different demographic cohort.[17]

Demographic age cohorts are important to our study of management because, as we said earlier, large numbers of people at certain stages in the life cycle can constrain decisions and actions taken by businesses, governments, educational institutions, and other organizations. Demographics not only looks at current statistics, but also looks to the future. For instance, recent analysis of birth rates shows that more than 80 percent of babies born worldwide are from Africa and Asia.[18] And here's an interesting fact: India has one of the world's youngest populations with more males under the age of 5 than the entire population of France. And by 2050, it's predicted that China will have more people age 65 and older than the rest of the world combined.[19] Consider the impact of such population trends on future organizations and managers.

From technology to work attitudes, the Gen Y age group is making its imprint in the workplace. Gen Y is an important demographic at Facebook, where most employees are under 40. The company values the passion and pioneering spirit of its young employees who enjoy taking on the challenge of building ground-breaking technology and the excitement of working in a fast-paced environment with considerable change and ambiguity. Facebook has created a casual and fun-loving work environment where its young cohorts interact in a creative climate that encourages experimentation and tolerates conflict and risk.
Source: AP Photo/Paul Sakuma

How the External Environment Affects Managers

Knowing *what* the various components of the external environment are and examining certain aspects of that environment are important to managers. However, understanding *how* the environment affects managers is equally as important. We're going to look at three ways the environment constrains and challenges managers—first, through its impact on jobs and employment; next, through the environmental uncertainty that is present; and finally, through the various stakeholder relationships that exist between an organization and its external constituencies.

JOBS AND EMPLOYMENT As any or all external environmental conditions (economic, demographic, technological, globalization, etc.) change, one of the most powerful constraints managers face is the impact of such changes on jobs and employment—both in poor conditions and in good conditions. The power of this constraint became painfully obvious during the recent global recession as millions of jobs were eliminated and unemployment rates rose to levels not seen in many years. Economists now predict that about a quarter of the 8.4 million jobs eliminated in the United States during this most recent economic downturn won't be coming back and will instead be replaced by other types of work in growing industries.[20] Businesses have been slow to reinstate jobs, creating continued hardships for those individuals looking for work.[21] Other countries face the same issues. Although such readjustments aren't bad in and of themselves, they do create challenges for managers who must balance work demands and having enough of the right types of people with the right skills to do the organization's work.

Not only do changes in external conditions affect the types of jobs that are available, they affect how those jobs are created and managed. For instance, many employers use flexible work arrangements to meet work output demand.[22] For instance, work tasks may be done by freelancers hired to work on an as-needed basis or by temporary workers who work full-time but are not permanent employees or by individuals who share jobs. Keep in mind that such responses have come about because of the constraints from the external environment. As a manager, you'll need to recognize how these work arrangements affect the way you plan, organize, lead, and control.

let's get | REAL

The Scenario:

Kerri and Ralf co-own a full-line, full-service insurance agency. Their customers cover a wide range of ages from young professionals to families to retired seniors. They're considering using social media, especially Facebook and Twitter, for most communications with their customers. Before investing time, money, and other resources in this venture, they want to make sure the investment will benefit their business, especially given their broad customer base. Is the timing right?

What advice about external environmental trends would you give Kerri and Ralf?

Social media has had a profound impact on the insurance industry, and it's even more important today to leverage a social presence to build an avid community around marketing products, handling claims, and engaging customers. Taking a look at the pattern of behavior within the industry, adoption of social media has been slow, but its quick evolution shows positive results where the benefits, for both the insurer and customer, are savings of time and cost. With cost pressures on social marketing and a focus on younger consumers, eventual adoption will greatly improve interactive response, trust of provider, open communications, and sales conversions.

Paul Baranda
Marketing Executive Director

This whole issue of flexible work arrangements has become so prevalent and part of how work is done in organizations that we'll address it in other chapters as well.

ASSESSING ENVIRONMENTAL UNCERTAINTY   Another constraint posed by external environments is the amount of uncertainty found in that environment, which can affect organizational outcomes. **Environmental uncertainty** refers to the degree of change and complexity in an organization's environment. The matrix in Exhibit 2-3 shows these two aspects.

environmental uncertainty
The degree of change and complexity in an organization's environment

The first dimension of uncertainty is the degree of change. If the components in an organization's environment change frequently, it's a *dynamic* environment. If change is minimal, it's a *stable* one. A stable environment might be one with no new competitors, few technological breakthroughs by current competitors, little activity by pressure groups to influence the organization, and so forth. For instance, Zippo Manufacturing, best known for its Zippo lighters, faces a relatively stable environment, with few competitors and little technological change. The main external concern for the company is probably the declining numbers of tobacco smokers, although the company's lighters have other uses, and global markets remain attractive. In contrast, the recorded music industry faces a dynamic (highly uncertain and unpredictable) environment. Digital formats and music-downloading sites turned the industry upside down and brought high levels of uncertainty.

If change is predictable, is that considered dynamic? No. Think of department stores that typically make one-quarter to one-third of their sales in November and December. The drop-off from December to January is significant. But because the change is predictable, the environment isn't considered dynamic. When we talk about

Exhibit 2-3
Environmental Uncertainty
Matrix

	Stable	Dynamic
Simple	**Cell 1** Stable and predictable environment Few components in environment Components are somewhat similar and remain basically the same Minimal need for sophisticated knowledge of components	**Cell 2** Dynamic and unpredictable environment Few components in environment Components are somewhat similar but are continually changing Minimal need for sophisticated knowledge of components
Complex	**Cell 3** Stable and predictable environment Many components in environment Components are not similar to one another and remain basically the same High need for sophisticated knowledge of components	**Cell 4** Dynamic and unpredictable environment Many components in environment Components are not similar to one another and are continually changing High need for sophisticated knowledge of components

degree of change, we mean change that's unpredictable. If change can be accurately anticipated, it's not an uncertainty for managers.

The other dimension of uncertainty describes the degree of **environmental complexity**, which looks at the number of components in an organization's environment and the extent of the knowledge that the organization has about those components. An organization with fewer competitors, customers, suppliers, government agencies, and so forth faces a less complex and uncertain environment. Organizations deal with environmental complexity in various ways. For example, Hasbro Toy Company simplified its environment by acquiring many of its competitors.

Complexity is also measured in terms of the knowledge an organization needs about its environment. For instance, managers at Pinterest must know a great deal about their Internet service provider's operations if they want to ensure their Web site is available, reliable, and secure for their customers. On the other hand, managers of college bookstores have a minimal need for sophisticated knowledge about their suppliers.

How does the concept of environmental uncertainty influence managers? Looking again at Exhibit 2-3, each of the four cells represents different combinations of degree of complexity and degree of change. Cell 1 (stable and simple environment) represents the lowest level of environmental uncertainty and cell 4 (dynamic and complex environment) the highest. Not surprisingly, managers have the greatest influence on organizational outcomes in cell 1 and the least in cell 4. Because uncertainty poses a threat to an organization's effectiveness, managers try to minimize it. Given a choice, managers would prefer to operate in the

environmental complexity
The number of components in an organization's environment and the extent of the organization's knowledge about those components

LEADER *who made a* DIFFERENCE

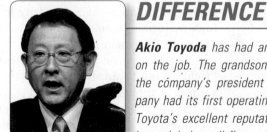

Source: AP Photo/Ahn Young-joon

Akio Toyoda *has had an interesting first three years on the job. The grandson of Toyota's founder became the company's president in 2009, the year the company had its first operating loss in 70 years.*[23] *In 2010, Toyota's excellent reputation for quality was damaged by a global recall fiasco. Then, on March 11, 2011, the devastating earthquake and tsunami and consequent nuclear crisis in Japan disrupted the company's global supply chain, forcing Toyota to slash production worldwide. What a set of challenges for the relatively new leader! However, Akio was not deterred. Instead, he looked at what he could do to bring Toyota through the crises to once again be the leader in the global car market. One thing he did was "dramatically change the way the company is managed." Most Japanese companies use a "bottom-up" management approach, which slows down decision making as ideas make their way through the organization for approval. Akio's management style is to "be fast" and to "be flexible." Such an approach was particularly crucial during the difficult aftermath of the earthquake and tsunami. Akio "took the unusual step of instructing the general managers of departments such as body engineering and powertrain to restore production and not waste time reporting upward." As Akio steers the company toward sustainable growth, he recognizes the importance of Toyota's different stakeholders including shareholders, employees, and customers. What can you learn from this leader who made a difference?*

least uncertain environments. However, they rarely control that choice. In addition, the nature of the external environment today is that most industries today are facing more dynamic change, making their environments more uncertain.

MANAGING STAKEHOLDER RELATIONSHIPS What makes MTV a popular cable channel for young adults year after year? One factor is its success in building relationships with its various stakeholders: viewers, celebrities and reality stars, advertisers, affiliate TV stations, public service groups, and others. The nature of stakeholder relationships is another way in which the environment influences managers. The more obvious and secure these relationships, the more influence managers will have over organizational outcomes.

stakeholders
Any constituencies in the organization's environment that are affected by an organization's decisions and actions

Stakeholders are any constituencies in the organization's environment affected by an organization's decisions and actions. These groups have a stake in or are significantly influenced by what the organization does. In turn, these groups can influence the organization. For example, think of the groups that might be affected by the decisions and actions of Starbucks—coffee bean farmers, employees, specialty coffee competitors, local communities, and so forth. Some of these stakeholders also, in turn, may influence decisions and actions of Starbucks' managers. The idea that organizations have stakeholders is now widely accepted by both management academics and practicing managers.[24]

Exhibit 2-4 identifies some of an organization's most common stakeholders. Note that these stakeholders include internal and external groups. Why? Because both can affect what an organization does and how it operates.

Why should managers even care about managing stakeholder relationships?[25] For one thing, it can lead to desirable organizational outcomes such as improved predictability of environmental changes, more successful innovations, greater degree of trust among stakeholders, and greater organizational flexibility to reduce the impact of change. But does it affect organizational performance? The answer is yes! Management researchers who have looked at this issue are finding that managers of high-performing companies tend to consider the interests of all major stakeholder groups as they make decisions.[26]

Another reason for managing external stakeholder relationships is that it's the "right" thing to do. Because an organization depends on these external groups as sources of inputs (resources) and as outlets for outputs (goods and services), managers need to consider their interests as they make decisions. We'll address this issue in more detail in the chapter on corporate social responsibility.

Exhibit 2-4
Organizational Stakeholders

ORGANIZATIONAL CULTURE:
Constraints and Challenges

Discuss the ⟩ 2.3
*characteristics
and importance of
organizational culture.*

Each of us has a unique personality—traits and characteristics that influence the way we act and interact with others. When we describe someone as warm, open, relaxed, shy, or aggressive, we're describing personality traits. An organization, too, has a personality, which we call its *culture*. And that culture influences the way employees act and interact with others.

What Is Organizational Culture?

Like the Taj Mahal Palace hotel in our chapter opener, W. L. Gore & Associates, a company known for its innovative and high-quality fabrics used in outdoor wear and other products, also understands the importance of organizational culture. Since its founding in 1958, Gore has used employee teams in a flexible, nonhierarchical organizational arrangement to develop its innovative products. Associates (employees) at Gore are committed to four basic principles articulated by company founder Bill Gore: (1) fairness to one another and everyone you come in contact with; (2) freedom to encourage, help, and allow other associates to grow in knowledge, skill, and scope of responsibility; (3) the ability to make your own commitments and keep them; and (4) consulting other associates before taking actions that could affect the company's reputation. After a visit to the company, one analyst reported that an associate told him, "If you tell anybody what to do here, they'll never work for you again." That's the type of independent, people-oriented culture Bill Gore wanted. And it works well for the company—it's earned a position on *Fortune*'s annual list of "100 Best Companies to Work For" every year since the list began in 1998, one of only three companies to achieve that distinction.[27]

Organizational culture has been described as the shared values, principles, traditions, and ways of doing things that influence the way organizational members act and that distinguish the organization from other organizations. In most organizations, these shared values and practices have evolved over time and determine, to a large extent, how "things are done around here."[28]

Our definition of culture implies three things. First, culture is a *perception*. It's not something that can be physically touched or seen, but employees perceive it on the basis of what they experience within the organization. Second, organizational culture is *descriptive*. It's concerned with how members perceive the culture and describe it, not with whether they like it. Finally, even though individuals may have different backgrounds or work at different organizational levels, they tend to describe the organization's culture in similar terms. That's the *shared* aspect of culture.

Research suggests seven dimensions that seem to capture the essence of an organization's culture.[29] These dimensions (shown in Exhibit 2-5) range from low to high, meaning it's not very typical of the culture (low) or is very typical of the culture (high). Describing an organization using these seven dimensions gives a composite picture of the organization's culture. In many organizations, one cultural dimension often is emphasized more than the others and essentially shapes the organization's personality and the way organizational members work. For instance, at Sony Corporation, the focus is product innovation (innovation and risk taking). The company "lives and breathes" new product development and employees' work behaviors support that goal. In contrast, Southwest Airlines has made its employees a central part of its culture (people orientation). Exhibit 2-6 describes how the dimensions can create significantly different cultures.

Strong Cultures

All organizations have cultures, but not all cultures equally influence employees' behaviors and actions. **Strong cultures**—those in which the key values are deeply held and widely shared—have a greater influence on employees than weaker cultures.

organizational culture
The shared values, principles, traditions, and ways of doing things that influence the way organizational members act and that distinguish the organization from other organizations

strong cultures
Organizational cultures in which the key values are intensely held and widely shared

Exhibit 2-5
Dimensions of Organizational Culture

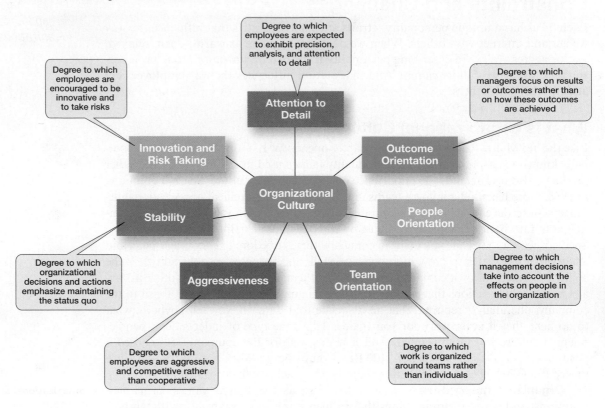

(Exhibit 2-7 on page 54 contrasts strong and weak cultures.) The more employees accept the organization's key values and the greater their commitment to those values, the stronger the culture. Most organizations have moderate to strong cultures, that is, there is relatively high agreement on what's important, what defines "good" employee behavior, what it takes to get ahead, and so forth. The stronger a culture becomes, the more it affects the way managers plan, organize, lead, and control.[30]

Why is having a strong culture important? For one thing, in organizations with strong cultures, employees are more loyal than employees in organizations with weak cultures.[31] Research also suggests that strong cultures are associated with high organizational performance.[32] And it's easy to understand why. After all, if values are clear and widely accepted, employees know what they're supposed to do and what's expected of them, so they can act quickly to take care of problems. However, the drawback is that a strong culture also might prevent employees from trying new approaches, especially when conditions change rapidly.[33]

Where Culture Comes From and How It Continues

Exhibit 2-8 illustrates how an organization's culture is established and maintained. The original source of the culture usually reflects the vision of the founders. For instance, as we described earlier, W. L. Gore's culture reflects the values of founder Bill Gore. Company founders are not constrained by previous customs or approaches and can establish the early culture by articulating a vision of what they want the organization to be. Also, the small size of most new organizations makes it easier to instill that vision with all organizational members.

Once the culture is in place, however, certain organizational practices help maintain it. For instance, during the employee selection process, managers typically judge job candidates not only on the job requirements, but also on how well they

Organization A

 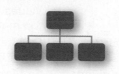

Exhibit 2-6
Contrasting Organizational
Cultures

This organization is a manufacturing firm. Managers are expected to fully document all decisions, and "good managers" are those who can provide detailed data to support their recommendations. Creative decisions that incur significant change or risk are not encouraged. Because managers of failed projects are openly criticized and penalized, managers try not to implement ideas that deviate much from the status quo. One lower-level manager quoted an often-used phrase in the company: "If it ain't broke, don't fix it."

Employees are required to follow extensive rules and regulations in this firm. Managers supervise employees closely to ensure there are no deviations. Management is concerned with high productivity, regardless of the impact on employee morale or turnover.

Work activities are designed around individuals. There are distinct departments and lines of authority, and employees are expected to minimize formal contact with other employees outside their functional area or line of command. Performance evaluations and rewards emphasize individual effort, although seniority tends to be the primary factor in the determination of pay raises and promotions.

Organization B

 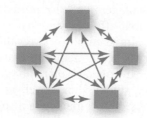 

This organization is also a manufacturing firm. Here, however, management encourages and rewards risk taking and change. Decisions based on intuition are valued as much as those that are well rationalized. Management prides itself on its history of experimenting with new technologies and its success in regularly introducing innovative products. Managers or employees who have a good idea are encouraged to "run with it," and failures are treated as "learning experiences." The company prides itself on being market driven and rapidly responsive to the changing needs of its customers.

There are few rules and regulations for employees to follow, and supervision is loose because management believes its employees are hardworking and trustworthy. Management is concerned with high productivity but believes this comes through treating its people right. The company is proud of its reputation as a good place to work.

Job activities are designed around work teams, and team members are encouraged to interact with people across functions and authority levels. Employees talk positively about the competition between teams. Individuals and teams have goals, and bonuses are based on achievement of outcomes. Employees are given considerable autonomy in choosing the means by which the goals are attained.

Exhibit 2-7
Strong Versus Weak Cultures

Strong Cultures	Weak Cultures
Values widely shared	Values limited to a few people—usually top management
Culture conveys consistent messages about what's important	Culture sends contradictory messages about what's important
Most employees can tell stories about company history or heroes	Employees have little knowledge of company history or heroes
Employees strongly identify with culture	Employees have little identification with culture
Strong connection between shared values and behaviors	Little connection between shared values and behaviors

might fit into the organization. At the same time, job candidates find out information about the organization and determine whether they are comfortable with what they see.

The actions of top managers also have a major impact on the organization's culture. For instance, at Best Buy, the company's chief marketing officer would take groups of employees for "regular tours of what the company called its retail hospital." Wearing white lab coats, employees would walk into a room with a row of real hospital beds and patient charts describing the ills affecting each of the company's major competitors. Now that each of those competitors has "succumbed to terminal illness" and is no longer in business, the room is darkened. Just think of the powerful message such a display would have on employees and their work.[34] Through what they say and how they behave, top managers establish norms that filter down through the organization and can have a positive effect on employees' behaviors. For instance, former IBM CEO Sam Palmisano wanted employees to value teamwork so he chose to take several million dollars from his yearly bonus and give it to his top executives based on their teamwork. He said, "If you say you're about a team, you have to be a team. You've got to walk the talk, right?"[35] However, as we've seen in numerous corporate ethics scandals, the actions of top managers also can lead to undesirable outcomes.

socialization
The process that helps employees adapt to the organization's culture

Finally, organizations help employees adapt to the culture through **socialization**, a process that helps new employees learn the organization's way of doing things. For instance, new employees at Starbucks stores go through 24 hours of intensive training that helps turn them into brewing consultants (baristas). They learn company philosophy, company jargon, and even how to assist customers with decisions about beans, grind, and espresso machines. One benefit of socialization is that employees understand the culture and are enthusiastic and knowledgeable with customers.[36] Another

Exhibit 2-8
Establishing and Maintaining Culture

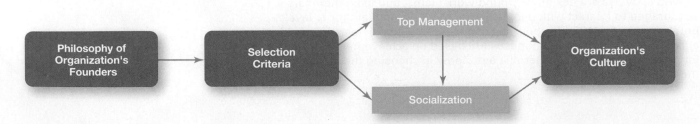

let's get REAL

Source: Sarah Saracino

The Scenario:

Paulo, the manager of a Web communications agency, is discovering that hiring employees can be frustrating. His last three hires are having trouble fitting in with the other 12 employees. For instance, one of the individuals—who's actually been there for six months now—doesn't want to jump in and help out the other team members when a deadline is fast approaching. And this same person doesn't say anything in team meetings and lets everyone else make decisions. And then there's the way they dress. "I don't expect them to 'suit up' or wear ties, but ripped cargo shorts and tattered flip-flops are a little too casual. Why don't these people 'get it'?"

Sarah Saracino
Human Resources Manager

What advice about organizational culture would you give Paulo?

During the interview process, the hiring manager must clearly communicate the company values and expectations of the organizational culture. Additionally, other team members should interview the prospective candidate to determine if s/he "fits" the established culture, ethics, and principles of the company. While performing reference checks, the hiring manager should ask questions that focus on the candidate's behavior, interaction with others, and dedication to the success of the company. Finally, once the newly hired employee is on board, the organization should partner him/her with a seasoned associate to serve as a mentor, thus fostering a seamless transition into the organizational culture.

benefit is that it minimizes the chance that new employees who are unfamiliar with the organization's culture might disrupt current beliefs and customs.

How Employees Learn Culture

Employees "learn" an organization's culture in a number of ways. The most common are stories, rituals, material symbols, and language.

STORIES Organizational "stories" typically contain a narrative of significant events or people, including such things as the organization's founders, rule breaking, reactions to past mistakes, and so forth.[37] Managers at Southwest Airlines tell stories celebrating employees who perform heroically for customers.[38] Such stories help convey what's important and provide examples that people can learn from. At 3M Company, the product innovation stories are legendary. There's the story about the 3M scientist who spilled chemicals on her tennis shoe and came up with Scotchgard. Then, there's the story about Art Fry, a 3M researcher, who wanted a better way to mark the pages of his church hymnal and invented the Post-It Note. These stories reflect what made 3M great and what it will take to continue that success.[39] To help employees learn the culture, organizational stories anchor the present in the past, provide explanations and legitimacy for current practices, exemplify what is important to the organization, and provide compelling pictures of an organization's goals.[40]

German automaker BMW helps employees learn its company's culture by repeating the "story of 1959." New employees learn that 1959 was a pivotal year for BMW because it almost went bankrupt after badly misjudging the market by producing a large expensive car few people could afford and a tiny two-seater that was too small to be practical. Management devised a turnaround plan for BMW that focused on producing a new class of sporty sedans and made a pact with employees that would help keep the company afloat. The "story of 1959" reflects the importance of employees in turning around BMW and steering it on the road to success. This photo shows BMW employees signing a new car model they helped produce, signifying the powerful role they continue to play in the company's performance.

Source: Andreas Gebert/EPA/Newscom

RITUALS In the early days of Facebook, founder Mark Zuckerberg had an artist paint a mural at company headquarters showing children taking over the world with laptops. Also, he would end employee meetings by pumping his fist in the air and leading employees in a chant of "domination." Although the cheering ritual was intended to be something simply fun, other company executives suggested he drop it because it made him seem silly, and they feared that competitors might cite it as evidence of monopolistic goals.[41] That's the power that rituals can have in shaping what employees believe is important. Corporate rituals are repetitive sequences of activities that express and reinforce the important values and goals of the organization. One of the best-known corporate rituals is Mary Kay Cosmetics' annual awards ceremony for its sales representatives. The company spends more than $50 million annually on rewards and prize incentives. Looking like a cross between a circus and a Miss America pageant, the ceremony takes place in a large auditorium, on a stage in front of a large, cheering audience, with all the participants dressed in glamorous evening clothes. Salespeople are rewarded for sales goal achievements with an array of expensive gifts, including big-screen televisions, diamond rings, trips, and pink Cadillacs. This "show" acts as a motivator by publicly acknowledging outstanding sales performance. In addition, the ritual aspect reinforces late founder Mary Kay's determination and optimism, which enabled her to overcome personal hardships, start her own company, and achieve material success. It conveys to her salespeople that reaching their sales goals is important and through hard work and encouragement, they too can achieve success. The contagious enthusiasm and excitement of Mary Kay sales representatives make it obvious that this annual "ritual" plays a significant role in establishing desired levels of motivation and behavioral expectations, which is, after all, what management hopes an organization's culture does.

MATERIAL ARTIFACTS AND SYMBOLS When you walk into different businesses, do you get a "feel" for what type of work environment it is—formal, casual, fun, serious, and so forth? These reactions demonstrate the power of material symbols or artifacts in creating an organization's personality.[42] The layout of an organization's facilities, how employees dress, the types of automobiles provided to top executives, and the availability of corporate aircraft are examples of material symbols. Others include the size of offices, the elegance of furnishings, executive "perks" (extra benefits provided to managers such as health club memberships, use of company-owned facilities, and so forth), employee fitness centers or on-site dining facilities, and reserved parking spaces for certain employees. At WorldNow, a business that helps local media companies develop new online distribution channels and revenue streams, an important material symbol is an old dented drill that the founders purchased for $2 at a thrift store. The drill symbolizes the company's culture of "drilling down to solve problems." When an employee is presented with the drill in recognition of outstanding work, he or she is expected to personalize the drill in some way and devise a new rule for caring for it. One employee installed a Bart Simpson trigger; another made the drill wireless by adding an antenna. The company's "icon" carries on the culture even as the organization evolves and changes.[43]

Material symbols convey to employees who is important and the kinds of behavior (for example, risk taking, conservative, authoritarian, participative, individualistic, and so forth) that are expected and appropriate.

LANGUAGE   Many organizations and units within organizations use language as a way to identify and unite members of a culture. By learning this language, members attest to their acceptance of the culture and their willingness to help preserve it. For instance, at Cranium, a Seattle board game company, "chiff" is used to remind employees of the need to be incessantly innovative in everything they do. "Chiff" stands for "clever, high-quality, innovative, friendly, fun."[44] At Build-A-Bear Workshop stores, employees are encouraged to use a sales technique called "Strive for Five," in which they work to sell each customer five items. The simple rhyming slogan is a powerful tool to drive sales.[45]

Over time, organizations often develop unique terms to describe equipment, key personnel, suppliers, customers, processes, or products related to its business. New employees are frequently overwhelmed with acronyms and jargon that, after a short period of time, become a natural part of their language. Once learned, this language acts as a common denominator that bonds members.

How Culture Affects Managers

Houston-based Apache Corp. has become one of the best performers in the independent oil drilling business because it has fashioned a culture that values risk taking and quick decision making. Potential hires are judged on how much initiative they've shown in getting projects done at other companies. And company employees are handsomely rewarded if they meet profit and production goals.[47] Because an organization's culture constrains what they can and cannot do and how they manage, it's particularly relevant to managers. Such constraints are rarely explicit. They're not written down. It's unlikely they'll even be spoken. But they're there, and all managers quickly learn what to do and not do in their organization. For instance, you won't find the following values written down, but each comes from a real organization.

- Look busy, even if you're not.
- If you take risks and fail around here, you'll pay dearly for it.
- Before you make a decision, run it by your boss so that he or she is never surprised.
- We make our product only as good as the competition forces us to.
- What made us successful in the past will make us successful in the future.
- If you want to get to the top here, you have to be a team player.

The link between values such as these and managerial behavior is fairly straightforward. Take, for example, a so-called "ready-aim-fire" culture. In such an organization, managers will study and analyze proposed projects endlessly before committing to them. However, in a "ready-*fire*-aim" culture, managers take action and then analyze what has been done. Or, say an organization's culture supports the belief that profits can be increased by cost cutting and that the company's best interests are served by achieving slow but steady increases in quarterly earnings. Managers are unlikely to pursue programs that are innovative, risky, long term, or expansionary. In an organization whose culture conveys a basic distrust of employees, managers are more likely to use an authoritarian leadership style than a democratic one. Why? The culture establishes for managers appropriate and expected behavior. For example, Banco Santander, whose headquarters are located 20 kilometers from downtown Madrid, has been described as a "risk-control freak." The company's managers adhered to "banking's stodgiest virtues—conservatism and patience." However, it's those values that triggered the company's growth from the sixth largest bank in Spain to the leading bank in the euro zone.[48]

As shown in Exhibit 2-9, a manager's decisions are influenced by the culture in which he or she operates. An organization's culture, especially a strong one, influences and constrains the way managers plan, organize, lead, and control.

***data*points**[46]

43 percent of workers surveyed would not recommend a job at their workplace to a friend or family member.

70 percent of large companies are likely to begin using digital-game-like reward and competitive tactics to motivate employee performance and encourage friendly competition.

61 percent of employees surveyed in Great Britain felt their boss was unapproachable.

8 percent of executives surveyed said fostering a shared understanding of values was an important capability.

32 percent of workers surveyed said acclimating to a different corporate culture could pose the greatest challenge when reentering the workforce.

67 percent of men surveyed never wear a tie to work.

45 percent of employees surveyed said their companies' ability to innovate was below average when it came to moving quickly from generating ideas to selling products.

45 percent of senior managers surveyed said their company's culture is clear about what motivates employees.

Exhibit 2-9
Types of Managerial Decisions
Affected by Culture

Planning
- The degree of risk that plans should contain
- Whether plans should be developed by individuals or teams
- The degree of environmental scanning in which management will engage

Organizing
- How much autonomy should be designed into employees' jobs
- Whether tasks should be done by individuals or in teams
- The degree to which department managers interact with each other

Leading
- The degree to which managers are concerned with increasing employee job satisfaction
- What leadership styles are appropriate
- Whether all disagreements—even constructive ones—should be eliminated

Controlling
- Whether to impose external controls or to allow employees to control their own actions
- What criteria should be emphasized in employee performance evaluations
- What repercussions will occur from exceeding one's budget

2.4 *Describe* current issues in organizational culture.

CURRENT ISSUES in Organizational Culture

Nordstrom, the specialty retail chain, is renowned for its attention to customers. Nike's innovations in athletic shoe and apparel technology are legendary. Tom's of Maine is known for its commitment to doing things ethically and spiritually. How have these organizations achieved such reputations? Their organizational cultures have played a crucial role. Let's look at three current cultural issues: creating an innovative culture, creating a customer-responsive culture, and nurturing workplace spirituality.

Creating an Innovative Culture

You may not recognize IDEO's name, but you've probably used a number of its products. As a product design firm, it takes the ideas that corporations bring it and turns those ideas into reality. Some of its creations range from the first commercial mouse (for Apple) to the first stand-up toothpaste tube (for Procter & Gamble) to the handheld personal organizer (for Palm) to the Contour USB glucose meter (for Bayer AG). It's critical that IDEO's culture support creativity and innovation.[49] And you might actually own and use products from another well-known innovative organization—Apple.[50] From its founding in 1976 to today, Apple has been on the forefront of product design and development. They've brought us Mac, iPod, iTunes, iPhone, and the iPad, which is changing the way you read materials such as this text. Although both these companies are in industries where innovation is critical to success, the fact is that any successful organization needs a culture that supports innovation. How important is culture to innovation? In a recent survey of senior executives, over half said that the most important driver of innovation for companies was a supportive corporate culture.[51]

What does an innovative culture look like? According to Swedish researcher Goran Ekvall, it would be characterized by the following:

- **Challenge and involvement**—Are employees involved in, motivated by, and committed to long-term goals and success of the organization?
- **Freedom**—Can employees independently define their work, exercise discretion, and take initiative in their day-to-day activities?
- **Trust and openness**—Are employees supportive and respectful to each other?

- **Idea time**—Do individuals have time to elaborate on new ideas before taking action?
- **Playfulness/humor**—Is the workplace spontaneous and fun?
- **Conflict resolution**—Do individuals make decisions and resolve issues based on the good of the organization versus personal interest?
- **Debates**—Are employees allowed to express opinions and put forth ideas for consideration and review?
- **Risk-taking**—Do managers tolerate uncertainty and ambiguity, and are employees rewarded for taking risks?[52]

Creating a Customer-Responsive Culture

Harrah's Entertainment, the world's largest gaming company, is fanatical about customer service—and for good reason. Company research showed that customers satisfied with the service they received at a Harrah's casino increased their gaming expenditures by 10 percent, and those extremely satisfied increased their gaming expenditures by 24 percent. When customer service translates into these types of results, of course managers would want to create a customer-responsive culture![53]

What does a customer-responsive culture look like?[54] Exhibit 2-10 describes five characteristics of customer-responsive cultures and offers suggestions as to what managers can do to create that type of culture.

Spirituality and Organizational Culture

What do Southwest Airlines, The Men's Wearhouse, Chick-fil-A, Ford, Xerox, Tyson Foods, and Hewlett-Packard have in common? They're among a growing number of organizations that have embraced workplace spirituality. What is **workplace spirituality**? It's a culture in which organizational values promote a sense of purpose through meaningful work taking place in the context of community.[55] Organizations with a spiritual culture recognize that people have a mind and a spirit, seek to find meaning and purpose in their work, and desire to connect with other human beings and be part of a community. And such desires aren't limited to workplaces, as a recent study showed that college students also are searching for meaning and purpose in life.[56]

Workplace spirituality seems to be important now for a number of reasons. Employees are looking for ways to cope with the stresses and pressures of a turbulent pace of life. Contemporary lifestyles—single-parent families, geographic mobility, temporary jobs, economic uncertainty, technologies that create distance between people—underscore the lack of community that many people feel. As humans, we crave

This jubilant customer jumps for joy to celebrate his purchase of an iPad tablet on the first day of its release at an Apple retail store in London. By creating an innovative and customer-responsive culture, Apple has achieved financial success and earned high customer satisfaction ratings and brand loyalty for its products and services. This culture fosters employee creativity, commitment to company goals, trust and openness, and risk taking. It involves hiring friendly and helpful employees and empowering them to make decisions about their jobs and what they can do to satisfy and delight customers.
Source: Carl Court/AFP/Getty Images/Newscom

workplace spirituality
A culture where organizational values promote a sense of purpose through meaningful work that takes place in the context of community

Characteristics of Customer-Responsive Culture	Suggestions for Managers
Type of employee	Hire people with personalities and attitudes consistent with customer service: friendly, attentive, enthusiastic, patient, good listening skills
Type of job environment	Design jobs so employees have as much control as possible to satisfy customers, without rigid rules and procedures
Empowerment	Give service-contact employees the discretion to make day-to-day decisions on job-related activities
Role clarity	Reduce uncertainty about what service-contact employees can and cannot do by continual training on product knowledge, listening, and other behavioral skills
Consistent desire to satisfy and delight customers	Clarify organization's commitment to doing whatever it takes, even if it's outside an employee's normal job requirements

Exhibit 2-10
Creating a Customer-Responsive Culture

involvement and connection. In addition, as baby boomers navigate mid-life issues, they're looking for something meaningful, something beyond the job. Others wish to integrate their personal life values with their professional lives. For others, formalized religion hasn't worked, and they continue to look for anchors to replace a lack of faith and to fill a growing sense of emptiness. What type of culture can do all these things? What differentiates spiritual organizations from their nonspiritual counterparts? Research shows that spiritual organizations tend to have five cultural characteristics.[57]

1. *Strong sense of purpose.* Spiritual organizations build their cultures around a meaningful purpose. While profits are important, they're not the primary values of the organization. For instance, Timberland's slogan is "Boots, Brand, Belief," which embodies the company's intent to use its "resources, energy, and profits as a publicly traded footwear-and-apparel company to combat social ills, help the environment, and improve conditions for laborers around the globe...and to create a more productive, efficient, loyal, and committed employee base."[58]
2. *Focus on individual development.* Spiritual organizations recognize the worth and value of individuals. They aren't just providing jobs; they seek to create cultures in which employees can continually grow and learn.
3. *Trust and openness.* Spiritual organizations are characterized by mutual trust, honesty, and openness. Managers aren't afraid to admit mistakes. And they tend to be extremely upfront with employees, customers, and suppliers.
4. *Employee empowerment.* Managers trust employees to make thoughtful and conscientious decisions. For instance, at Southwest Airlines, employees—including flight attendants, baggage handlers, gate agents, and customer service representatives—are encouraged to take whatever action they deem necessary to meet customer needs or help fellow workers, even if it means going against company policies.
5. *Tolerance of employee expression.* The final characteristic that differentiates spiritually based organizations is that they don't stifle employee emotions. They allow people to be themselves—to express their moods and feelings without guilt or fear of reprimand.

Using a different approach, a recent study suggests that the concept of spirituality in the workplace can best be captured by three factors: interconnection with a higher power, interconnection with human beings, and interconnection with nature and all living things.[59]

Critics of the spirituality movement have focused on two issues: legitimacy (Do organizations have the right to impose spiritual values on their employees?) and economics (Are spirituality and profits compatible?).

An emphasis on spirituality clearly has the potential to make some employees uneasy. Critics might argue that secular institutions, especially businesses, have no business imposing spiritual values on employees. This criticism is probably valid when spirituality is defined as bringing religion into the workplace.[60] However, it's less valid when the goal is helping employees find meaning in their work. If concerns about today's lifestyles and pressures truly characterize a growing number of workers, then maybe it is time for organizations to help employees find meaning and purpose in their work and to use the workplace to create a sense of community.

The issue of whether spirituality and profits are compatible is certainly important. Limited evidence suggests that the two may be compatible. One study found that companies that introduced spiritually based techniques improved productivity and significantly reduced turnover.[61] Another found that organizations that provided their employees with opportunities for spiritual development outperformed those that didn't.[62] Others reported that spirituality in organizations was positively related to creativity, ethics, employee satisfaction, job involvement, team performance, and organizational commitment.[63]

MyManagementLab

Go to **mymanagementlab.com** to complete the problems marked with this icon .

CHAPTER

PREPARING FOR: Exams/Quizzes

CHAPTER SUMMARY by Learning Outcomes

2.1 [LEARNING OUTCOME]

Contrast the actions of managers according to the omnipotent and symbolic views.

According to the omnipotent view, managers are directly responsible for an organization's success or failure. The symbolic view argues that much of an organization's success or failure is due to external forces outside managers' control. The two constraints on manager's discretion are the organization's culture (internal) and the environment (external). Managers aren't totally constrained by these two factors since they can and do influence their culture and environment.

2.2 [LEARNING OUTCOME]

Describe the constraints and challenges facing managers in today's external environment.

The external environment includes those factors and forces outside the organization that affect its performance. The main components include economic, demographic, political/legal, sociocultural, technological, and global. Managers face constraints and challenges from these components because of the impact they have on jobs and employment, environmental uncertainty, and stakeholder relationships.

2.3 [LEARNING OUTCOME]

Discuss the characteristics and importance of organizational culture.

The seven dimensions of culture are attention to detail, outcome orientation, people orientation, team orientation, aggressiveness, stability, and innovation and risk taking. In organizations with strong cultures, employees are more loyal and performance tends to be higher. The stronger a culture becomes, the more it affects the way managers plan, organize, lead, and control. The original source of a culture reflects the vision of organizational founders. A culture is maintained by employee selection practices, the actions of top managers, and socialization processes. Also, culture is transmitted to employees through stories, rituals, material symbols, and language. These elements help employees "learn" what values and behaviors are important as well as who exemplifies those values. The culture affects how managers plan, organize, lead, and control.

2.4 [LEARNING OUTCOME]

Describe current issues in organizational culture.

The characteristics of an innovative culture are challenge and involvement, freedom, trust and openness, idea time, playfulness/humor, conflict resolution, debates, and risk-taking. A customer-responsive culture has five characteristics: outgoing and friendly employees; jobs with few rigid rules, procedures, and regulations; empowerment; clear roles and expectations; and employees who are conscientious in their desire to please the customer. Workplace spirituality is important because employees are looking for a counterbalance to the stresses and pressures of a turbulent pace of life. Aging baby boomers and other workers are looking for something meaningful in their lives, an involvement and connection that they often don't find in contemporary lifestyles, and to meet the needs that organized religion is not meeting for some of them. Spiritual organizations tend to have five characteristics: strong sense of purpose, focus on individual development, trust and openness, employee empowerment, and toleration of employee expression.

REVIEW AND DISCUSSION QUESTIONS ✪

1. Describe the two perspectives on how much impact managers have on an organization's success or failure.

2. "Businesses are built on relationships." What do you think this statement means? What are the implications for managing the external environment?

3. Refer to Exhibit 2-6. How would a first-line manager's job differ in these two organizations? How about a top-level manager's job?

4. Classrooms have cultures. Describe your classroom culture using the seven dimensions of organizational culture. Does the culture constrain your instructor? How? Does it constrain you as a student? How?

5. Can culture be a liability to an organization? Explain.

6. Discuss the impact of a strong culture on organizations and managers.

7. Using Exhibit 2-8, explain how a culture is formed and maintained.

8. Explain why workplace spirituality seems to be an important concern.

PREPARING FOR: My Career
ETHICS DILEMMA ✪

In many ways, technology has made all of us more productive. However, ethical issues do arise in how and when technology is used. Take the sports arena. All kinds of technologically advanced sports equipment (swimsuits, golf clubs, ski suits, etc.) have been developed that can sometimes give competitors/players an edge over their opponents.[64] We saw it in swim meets at the summer Olympics and on the ski slopes at the winter Olympics. What do you think? Is this an ethical use of technology? What if your school (or country) was competing for a championship and couldn't afford to outfit athletes in such equipment and it affected your ability to compete? Would that make a difference? What ethical guidelines might you suggest for such situations?

SKILLS EXERCISE Developing Your Environmental Scanning Skill

About the Skill

Anticipating and interpreting changes that take place in the environment is an important skill managers need. Information that comes from scanning the environment can be used in making decisions and taking actions. And managers at all levels of an organization need to know how to scan the environment for important information and trends.

Steps in Practicing the Skill

You can be more effective at scanning the environment if you use the following suggestions:[65]

1. *Decide which type of environmental information is important to your work.* Perhaps you need to know changes in customers' needs and desires, or perhaps you need to know what your competitors are doing. Once you know the type of information you'd like to have, you can look at the best ways to get that information.

2. *Regularly read and monitor pertinent information.* There is no scarcity of information to scan, but what you need to do is read pertinent information sources. How do you know information sources are pertinent? They're pertinent if they provide you with the information you identified as important.

3. *Incorporate the information you get from your environmental scanning into your decisions and actions.* Unless you use the information you're getting, you're wasting your time getting it. Also, the more you use information from your environmental scanning, the more likely it is that you'll want to continue to invest time and other resources into gathering it. You'll see that this information is important to your ability to manage effectively and efficiently.

4. *Regularly review your environmental scanning activities.* If you're spending too much time getting nonuseful information, or if you're not using the pertinent information you've gathered, you need to make some adjustments.

5. *Encourage your subordinates to be alert to information that is important.* Your employees can be your "eyes and ears" as well. Emphasize to them the importance of gathering and sharing information that may affect your work unit's performance.

Practicing the Skill
The following suggestions are activities you can do to practice and reinforce the behaviors associated with scanning the environment.

1. Select an organization with which you're familiar either as an employee or perhaps as a frequent customer. Assume you're the top manager in this organization. What types of information from environmental scanning do you think would be important to you?

Where would you find this information? Now assume you're a first-level manager in this organization. Would the types of information you'd get from environmental scanning change? Explain.

2. Assume you're a regional manager for a large bookstore chain. Using the Internet, what types of environmental and competitive information were you able to identify? For each source, what information did you find that might help you do your job better?

WORKING TOGETHER Team Exercise

Although all organizations face environmental constraints, the components in their external environments differ. Get into a small group with three to four other class members and choose one organization from two different industries. Describe the external components for each organization. How are your descriptions different for the two organizations? How are they similar? Now, using the same two organizations, see if you can identify the important stakeholders for these organizations. As a group, be prepared to share your information with the class and to explain your choices.

LEARNING TO BE A MANAGER

- Find two current examples in any popular business periodicals of the omnipotent and symbolic views of management. Write a paper describing what you found and how the two examples you found represent these views of management.

- Choose an organization with which you're familiar or one you would like to know more about. Create a table identifying potential stakeholders of this organization. Then, indicate what particular interests or concerns these stakeholders might have.

- Pick two organizations you interact with frequently (as an employee or as a customer) and assess their cultures by looking at the following aspects:
  - *Physical Design* (buildings, furnishings, parking lot, office or store design): Where are they located and why? Where do customers and employees park? What does the office/store layout look like? What activities are encouraged or discouraged by the physical layout? What do these things say about what the organization values?
  - *Symbols* (logos, dress codes, slogans, philosophy statements): What values are highlighted? Where are logos displayed? Whose needs are emphasized? What concepts are emphasized? What actions are prohibited? Which are encouraged? Are any artifacts prominently displayed? What do those artifacts symbolize? What do these things say about what the organization values?
  - *Words* (stories, language, job titles): What stories are repeated? How are employees addressed? What do job

titles say about the organization? Are jokes/anecdotes used in conversation? What do these things say about what the organization values?
  - *Policies and Activities* (rituals, ceremonies, financial rewards, policies for how customers or employees are treated; note that you may be able to assess this one only if you're an employee or know the organization well): What activities are rewarded? Ignored? What kinds of people succeed? Fail? What rituals are important? Why? What events get commemorated? Why? What do these things say about what the organization values?

- If you belong to a student organization, evaluate its culture by answering the following: How would you describe the culture? How do new members learn the culture? How is the culture maintained? If you don't belong to a student organization, talk to another student who does and evaluate it using the same questions.

- Steve's and Mary's suggested readings: G. Barna, *Master Leaders* (Barna Books), 2009; Terrence E. Deal and Allan A. Kennedy, *Corporate Culture: The Rites and Rituals of Corporate Life* (Perseus Books Group, 2000); Edgar H. Schein, *The Corporate Culture Survival Guide* (Jossey-Bass, 1999); and Kim S. Cameron and Robert E. Quinn, *Diagnosing and Changing Organizational Culture* (Jossey-Bass, 2005).

- Find one example of a company that represents each of the current issues in organizational culture. Describe what the company is doing that reflects its commitment to this culture.

- In your own words, write down three things you learned in this chapter about being a good manager.
- Self-knowledge can be a powerful learning tool. Go to mymanagementlab.com and complete any of these self-assessment exercises: What's the Right Organizational Culture for Me? How Well Do I Respond to Turbulent Change? Am I Experiencing Work/Family Conflict? Using the results of your assessments, identify personal strengths and weaknesses. What will you do to reinforce your strengths and improve your weaknesses?

MyManagementLab

Go to **mymanagementlab.com** for Auto-graded writing questions as well as the following Assisted-graded writing questions:

2-1. Why is it important for managers to understand the external environmental components?

2-2. Describe an effective culture for (a) a relatively stable environment and (b) a dynamic environment. Explain your choices.

2-3. Mymanagementlab Only – comprehensive writing assignment for this chapter.

CASE APPLICATION 1 Going to Extremes

No. 1 best e-retailer. For those of you who have shopped on Zappos.com, that number one ranking probably isn't a surprise.[66] For those of you who haven't shopped on Zappos.com, it wouldn't take long for you to see why Zappos deserves that accolade. And it's more than the fact that Zappos has a great selection of products, super-fast shipping, and free returns. The real secret to its success is its people who make the Zappos shopping experience truly unique and outstanding. The company, which began selling shoes and other products online in 1999, has put "extraordinary effort into building a desirable organizational culture, which has provided a sure path to business success." As part of its culture, Zappos espouses 10 corporate values. At the top of that list is "Deliver WOW through service." And do they ever deliver the WOW! Even through the recent economic challenges, Zappos has continued to thrive—a sure sign its emphasis on organizational culture is paying off.

Zappos is not only the number 1 e-retailer but also the 11th best company to work for, according to a 2012 survey by *Fortune* magazine (which conducts this poll annually). Okay—so what is it really that makes Zappos' culture so great? Let's take a closer look.

Zappos began selling shoes and other products online in 1999. Four years later, it was profitable, and it reached more than $1 billion in sales by 2009. Also, in 2009, Zappos was named *Business Week*'s Customer Service Champ and was given an A+ rating by the Better Business Bureau. Also, that year, Amazon (yeah, that Amazon) purchased Zappos for 10 million Amazon shares, worth almost $928 million at the time. Zappos' employees divided up $40 million in cash and restricted stock and were assured that Zappos management would remain in place.

The person who was determined to "build a culture that applauds such things as weirdness and humility" was Tony Hsieh (pronounced *Shay*) who became CEO of Zappos in 2000. And Tony is the epitome of weirdness and humility. For instance, on April Fools' Day 2010, he issued a press release announcing that "Zappos was suing Walt Disney Company in a class action suit claiming that Disney was misleading the public by saying that Disneyland is 'the happiest place on earth' because clearly," Hsieh argued, Zappos is.

Before joining Zappos, Hsieh had been co-founder of the Internet advertising network LinkExchange and had seen firsthand the "dysfunction that can arise from building a company in which technical skill is all that matters." He was determined to do it differently at Zappos. Hsieh first invited Zappos' 300 employees to list the core values the culture should be based on. That process led to the 10 values that continue to drive the organization, which now employs about 1,400 people.

Another thing that distinguishes Zappos culture is the recognition that organizational culture is more than a list of written values. The culture has to be "lived." And Zappos does this by maintaining a "complex web of human interactions." At Zappos, social media is used liberally to link employees with one another and with the company's customers. For instance, one recent tweet said, "Hey. Did anyone bring a hairdryer to the office today?" This kind of camaraderie can maintain and sustain employee commitment to the company.

Also, at Zappos, the company's "pulse" or "health" of the culture is surveyed monthly. In these happiness surveys, employees answer such "unlikely questions as whether they believe that the company has a higher purpose than profits, whether their own role has meaning, whether they feel in control of their career path, whether they consider their co-workers to be like family and friends, and whether they are happy in their jobs." Survey results are broken down by department, and

Tony Hsieh, CEO of Zappos.com, believes that a powerful model for achieving business success is based on building and maintaining an organizational culture that matches corporate values with personal values.
Source: Bloomberg via Getty Images

opportunities for "development" are identified and acted on. For example, when one month's survey showed that a particular department had "veered off course and felt isolated from the rest of the organization," actions were taken to show employees how integral their work was to the rest of the company.

Oh, and one other thing about Zappos. Every year, to celebrate its accomplishments, it publishes a *Culture Book,* a testimonial to the power of its culture. "Zappos has a belief that the right culture with the right values will always produce the best organizational performance, and this belief trumps everything else."

DISCUSSION QUESTIONS ⊙

1. Find a list of all 10 of Zappos corporate values. Pick two of the values and explain how you think those values would influence the way employees do their work.

2. Using this list of corporate values and Exhibit 2-5, describe Zappos organizational culture. In which areas would you say that Zappos culture is very high (or typical)? Explain.

3. How did Zappos' corporate culture begin? How is Zappos' corporate culture maintained?

4. The right culture with the right values will always produce the best organizational performance. What do you think of this statement? Do you agree? Why or why not?

5. What could other companies learn from Tony Hsieh and Zappos' experiences?

CASE APPLICATION 2   Not Sold Out

Challenged by external factors including competition from home theaters and mobile devices, movie theater managers aim to attract customers by giving them the highest-quality fidelity experience and the social experience of watching films with other moviegoers.
Source: PhotoAlto/Alamy

After a couple of years of slight attendance increases, competitors in the movie theater industry had hoped the threats they faced were behind them.[67] Then along came the economic downturn. Ticket sales revenue in 2011 fell 4 percent from the previous year, and attendance was down 4.8 percent. The numbers of people going to see a movie were the smallest since 1995. The industry tried to pump up revenue with high-profile movies, higher ticket prices, and premium amenities. And 2012 ticket sales were forecasted to be flat, despite the successful debut of the much-anticipated *The Hunger Games.*

The number of movie screens in the United States totals a little more than 39,000. Together, the four largest movie theater chains in the United States have almost 19,000 screens—and a lot of seats to fill. The largest, Regal Entertainment Group (based in Knoxville, Tennessee), has more than 6,800 screens. AMC Entertainment (based in Kansas City, Missouri) has some 5,400 screens. The other two major competitors are Cinemark (based in Plano, Texas—about 3,800 screens) and Carmike Cinemas (based in Columbus, Georgia—about 2,300 screens). The challenge for these companies is getting people to watch movies on all those screens, a decision that encompasses many factors.

One important factor, according to industry analysts, is the uncertainty over how people want their movies delivered, which is largely a trade-off between convenience and quality (or what the experts call fidelity experience). Will consumers choose convenience over quality and use mobile devices such as iPads? Will they trade some quality for convenience and watch at home on surround-sound, flat-screen, high-definition home theater systems? Or will they go to a movie theater with wide screens, high-quality sound systems, and the social experience of being with other moviegoers and enjoy the highest fidelity experience—even with the inconveniences? Movie theater managers believe that mobile devices aren't much of a threat, even though they may be convenient. On the other hand, home theater systems may be more of a threat as they've become more affordable and have "acceptable" quality. Although not likely to replace any of these higher-quality offerings, drive-in theaters, analysts note, are experiencing a resurgence, especially in geographic locations where they can be open year-round.

Another factor managers need to wrestle with is the impression consumers have of the movie-going experience. A consumer lifestyle poll showed that the major dislike about going to the movies was the cost, a drawback cited by 36 percent of the respondents. Other factors noted included the noise, uncomfortable seats, the inconvenience, the crowds, and too many previews/commercials before the movie.

A final question facing the movie theater industry *and* the major film studios is how to be proactive in avoiding the problems that the recorded music industry faced with the illegal downloading of songs. The amount of entertainment sold online (which includes both music and video) continues to experience double digit growth. The biggest threat so far has been YouTube, which has become a powerful force in the media world with owner Google's backing. To counter that threat, industry executives have asked for filtering mechanisms to keep unlawful material off the site and to develop some type of licensing arrangements whereby the industry has some protection over its copyrighted film content. As one theater executive said, "We're a little like the drug business. We are the pushers and our customers are the users. Even if business is good, you have to keep giving people more of what they want."

DISCUSSION QUESTIONS ✪

1. Using Exhibit 2-2, what external components might be most important for managers in movie theater chains to know about? Why?

2. According to the case, what external trends do managers at the movie theater chains have to deal with?

3. How do you think these trends might constrain decisions made by managers at the movie theater chains?

4. What stakeholders do you think might be most important to movie theater chains? What interests might these stakeholders might have?

PART **1** Management Practice

A Manager's Dilemma

Selina Lo loves her job as the manager of a toy store in San Francisco. She loves the chaos and the excitement of kids as they wander around the store searching for their favorite toys. Teddy bears pulled off the shelves and toy trucks left on the floor are part and parcel of managing a toy store. Yet, her biggest challenge, which is a problem faced by many retailers, is employee turnover. Many of her employees leave after just a few months on the job because of hectic schedules and long work hours. Selina is always looking for new ways to keep her employees committed to their jobs. She also takes care of customers' requests and complaints and tries to address them satisfactorily. This is what Selina's life as a manager is like. However, retailers are finding that people with Selina's skills and enthusiasm for store management are few and far between. Managing a retail store is not the career that most college graduates aspire to. Attracting and keeping talented managers continues to be a challenge for all kinds of retailers.

Suppose you're a recruiter for a large retail chain and want to get college graduates to consider store management as a career option. Using what you learned in Part 1, how would you do that?

Global Sense

Who holds more managerial positions worldwide: women or men? Statistics tell an interesting story. In the United States, women held 50 percent of all managerial positions, but only 2.4 percent of the Fortune 500 CEO spots. In the United Kingdom, only 1.8 percent of the FTSE 500 companies' top positions are held by women. In Germany, women hold 35.6 percent of all management positions, but only 3 percent of women are executive board members. Asian countries have a much higher percentage of women in CEO positions. In Thailand, 30 percent of female managers hold the title of CEO as do 18 percent in Taiwan. In China, 19 percent of China's female workforce are CEOs. Even in Japan, 8 percent of senior managers are women. A census of Australia's top 200 companies listed on the Australian Stock Exchange showed that 11 percent of company executive managers were women. Finally, in Arab countries, the percentage of women in management positions is less than 10 percent.

As you can see, companies across the globe have a large gender gap in leadership. Men far outnumber women in senior business leadership positions. These circumstances exist despite efforts and campaigns to improve equality in the workplace. One company—Deutsche Telekom—is tackling the problem head-on. It says it intends to "more than double the number of women who are managers within five years." In addition, it plans to increase the number of women in senior and middle management to 30 percent by the end of 2015. One action the company is taking is to improve and increase the recruiting of female university graduates. The company's goal: at least 30 percent of the places in executive development programs held by women. Other steps taken by the company revolve around the work environment and work-family issues. Deutsche's chief executive René Obermann said, "Taking on more women in management positions is not about the enforcement of misconstrued egalitarianism. Having a greater number of women at the top will quite simply enable us to operate better."

Discuss the following questions in light of what you learned in Part 1:

- *What issues might Deutsche Telekom face in recruiting female university graduates?*
- *How could they address those issues?*
- *What issues might it face in introducing changes in work-family programs, and how could they address those issues?*
- *What do you think of Obermann's statement that having a greater number of women at the top will enable the company to operate better?*
- *What could other organizations around the globe learn from Deutsche Telekom?*

Sources: J. Nerenberg, "*Nearly 20 percent of Female Chinese Managers Are CEOs,*" [www.fastcompany.com], *March 8, 2011;* S. Doughty, "*Cracking the Glass Ceiling: Female Staff Have the Same Chance As Men of Reaching the Top, Figures Reveal,*" [www.dailymail.co.uk], *March 4, 2011;* G. Toegel, "*Disappointing Statistics, Positive Outlook,*" Forbes.com, *February 18, 2011;* E. Butler, "*Wanted: Female Bosses for Germany,*" [www.bbc.co.uk], *February 10, 2011;* S. P. Robbins, M. Coulter, Y. Sidani, and D. Jamali, Management: Arab World Edition, *(London: Pearson Education Limited), 2011, p. 5;* "*Proportion of Executive Managers and Board Directors of ASX 200 Companies Who Are Women,*" *Australian Bureau of Statistics* [www.abs.gov.au], *September 15, 2010;* Stevens and J. Espinoza, "*Deutsche Telekom Sets Women-Manager Quota,*" Wall Street Journal Online, *March 22, 2010;* J. Blaue, "*Deutsche Telekom Launches Quota for Top Women Managers,*" www.german-info .com/business_shownews; *and* N. Clark, "*Goal at Deutsche Telekom: More Women as Managers,*" New York Times Online, *March 15, 2010.*

Continuing Case
Starbucks—Introduction

Community. Connection. Caring. Committed. Coffee. Five Cs that describe the essence of Starbucks Corporation— what it stands for and what it wants to be as a business. With more than 17,000 coffee shops in 55+ countries, Starbucks is the world's number one specialty coffee retailer. The company also owns Seattle's Best Coffee and Torrefazione Italia coffee brands. It's a company that truly

Beginning in 1971 as a coffee shop in Seattle's Pike's Place Market, Starbucks has grown to become the world's top specialty coffee retailer with shops in more than 40 countries and an expanded product line including merchandise, beverages and fresh food, and global consumer products. The first Starbucks store, shown here today, retains its original look with signs and other items bearing the company's first logo.
Source: © ZUMA Wire Service/Alamy

epitomizes the challenges facing managers in today's globally competitive environment. To help you better understand these challenges, we're going to take an in-depth look at Starbucks through these continuing cases, which you'll find at the end of every part in the textbook. Each of these six part-ending continuing cases will look at Starbucks from the perspective of the material presented in that part. Although each case "stands alone," you'll be able to see the progression of the management process as you work through each one.

The Beginning

"We aren't in the coffee business, serving people. We're in the people business, serving coffee." That's the philosophy of Howard Schultz, chairman and chief global strategist of Starbucks. It's a philosophy that has shaped—and continues to shape—the company.

The first Starbucks, which opened in Seattle's famous Pike Place Market in 1971, was founded by Gordon Bowker, Jerry Baldwin, and Zev Siegl. The company was named for the coffee-loving first mate in the book *Moby Dick,* which also influenced the design of Starbucks' distinctive two-tailed siren logo. Schultz, a successful New York City businessperson, first walked into Starbucks in 1981 as a sales representative for a Swedish kitchenware manufacturer. He was hooked immediately. He knew that he wanted to work for this company, but it took almost a year before he could persuade the owners to hire him. After all, he *was* from New York and he hadn't grown up with the values of the company. The owners thought Schultz's style and high energy would clash with the existing culture. But Schultz was quite persuasive and was able to allay the owners' fears. They asked him to join the company as director of retail operations and marketing, which he enthusiastically did. Schultz's passion for the coffee business

was obvious. Although some of the company's employees resented the fact that he was an "outsider," Schultz had found his niche and he had lots of ideas for the company. As he says, "I wanted to make a positive impact."

About a year after joining the company while on a business trip to Milan, Schultz walked into an espresso bar and right away knew that this concept could be successful in the United States. He said, "There was nothing like this in America. It was an extension of people's front porch. It was an emotional experience. I believed intuitively we could do it. I felt it in my bones." Schultz recognized that although Starbucks treated coffee as produce, something to be bagged and sent home with the groceries, the Italian coffee bars were more like an experience—a warm, community experience. That's what Schultz wanted to recreate in the United States. However, Starbucks' owners weren't really interested in making Starbucks big and didn't really want to give the idea a try. So Schultz left the company in 1985 to start his own small chain of espresso bars in Seattle and Vancouver called *Il Giornale*. Two years later when Starbucks' owners finally wanted to sell, Schultz raised $3.8 million from local investors to buy them out. That small investment has made him a very wealthy person indeed!

Company Facts

Starbucks' main product is coffee—more than 30 blends and single-origin coffees. In addition to fresh-brewed coffee, here's a sampling of other products the company also offers:

- **Handcrafted beverages:** Hot and iced espresso beverages, coffee and noncoffee blended beverages, Tazo® teas, and smoothies
- **Merchandise:** Home espresso machines, coffee brewers and grinders, premium chocolates, coffee mugs and coffee accessories, compact discs, and other assorted items
- **Fresh food:** Baked pastries, sandwiches, salads, hot breakfast items, and yogurt parfaits
- **Global consumer products:** Starbucks Frappuccino® coffee drinks, Starbucks Iced Coffee drinks, Starbucks Liqueurs, and a line of super-premium ice creams
- **Starbucks card and My Starbucks Rewards® program:** A reloadable stored-value card and a consumer rewards program
- **Brand portfolio:** Starbucks Entertainment, Ethos™ Water, Seattle's Best Coffee, and Tazo® Tea

At the end of 2011, the company had more than 149,000 full- and part-time partners (employees) around the world. Howard Schultz is the chairman, president, and CEO of Starbucks. Some of the other "interesting" top-level executive positions include chief administrative officer, senior vice president of logistics, executive vice president of global supply chain operations, senior vice president of coffee, executive vice president of partner resources, senior vice president of business technology, senior vice president of culture and leadership development, and vice president of corporate social responsibility.

Starbucks—Defining the Terrain

As managers manage, they must be aware of the terrain or broad environment within which they plan, organize, lead, and control. The characteristics and nature of this "terrain" will influence what managers and other employees do and how they do it. And more importantly, it will affect how efficiently and effectively managers do their job of coordinating and overseeing the work of other people so that goals—organizational and work-level or work unit—can be accomplished. What does Starbucks' terrain look like, and how is the company adapting to that terrain?

Starbucks Culture and Environment

An organization's culture is a mix of written and unwritten values, beliefs, and codes of behavior that influence the way work gets done and the way people behave in organizations. And the distinct flavor of Starbucks' culture can be traced to the original founders' philosophies and Howard Schultz's unique beliefs about how a company should be run. The three friends (Jerry Baldwin, Gordon Bowker, and Zev Siegl) who founded Starbucks in 1971 as a store in Seattle's historic Pike Place Market district did so for one reason: They loved coffee and tea and wanted Seattle to have access to the best. They had no intention of building a business empire. Their business philosophy, although never written down, was simple: "Every company must stand for something; don't just give customers what they ask for or what they think they want; and assume that your customers are intelligent and seekers of knowledge." The original Starbucks was a company passionately committed to world-class coffee and dedicated to educating its customers, one on one, about what great coffee can be. It was these qualities that ignited Howard Schultz's passion for the coffee business and inspired him to envision what Starbucks could become. Schultz continues to have that passion for his business—he is the visionary and soul behind Starbucks. He visits at least 30 to 40 stores a week, talking to partners (employees) and to customers. His ideas for running a business have been called "unconventional," but Schultz doesn't care. He says, "We can be extremely profitable and competitive, with a highly regarded brand, and also be respected for treating our people well." One member of the company's board of directors says about him, "Howard is consumed with his vision of Starbucks. That means showing the good that a corporation can do for its workers, shareholders, and customers."

The company's mission and guiding principles (which you can find at www.starbucks.com) are meant to guide the decisions and actions of company partners from top to bottom. They also have significantly influenced the organization's culture. Starbucks' culture emphasizes keeping employees motivated and content. One thing that's been important to Howard Schultz from day one is the relationship he has with his employees. He treasures those relationships and feels they're critically important to the way the company develops its relationships with its customers and the way it is viewed by the public. He says, "We know that our people are the heart and soul of our success." Starbucks' 149,000-plus employees worldwide serve millions of customers each week. That's a lot of opportunities to either satisfy or disappoint the customer. The experiences customers have in the stores ultimately affect the company's relationships with its customers. That's why Starbucks has created a unique relationship with its employees. Starbucks provides all employees who work more than 20 hours a week health care benefits and stock options. Schultz says, "The most important thing I ever did was give our partners (employees) bean stock (options to buy the company's stock). That's what sets us apart and gives us a higher-quality employee, an employee that cares more." And Starbucks does care about its employees. For instance, when three Starbucks' employees were murdered in a botched robbery attempt in Washington, D.C., Schultz immediately flew there to handle the situation. In addition, he decided that all future profits from that store would go to organizations working for victims' rights and violence prevention. It probably shouldn't come as a surprise that Starbucks has the lowest level of employee attrition (leaving) of any national retailer.

As a global company with revenues well over $11.7 billion, Starbucks' executives recognize they must be aware of the impact the environment has on their decisions and actions. It recently began lobbying legislators in Washington, D.C., on issues including lowering trade barriers, health care costs, and tax breaks. It's something that Schultz didn't really want to do, but he recognizes that such efforts could be important to the company's future.

So we're beginning to see how Starbucks epitomizes the five Cs—community, connection, caring, committed, and coffee. In this *Continuing Case* in the Management Practice section at the end of Parts 2–6, you'll discover more about Starbucks' unique and successful ways of managing. As you work on these remaining continuing cases, keep in mind that there may be information included in this introduction you might want to review.

Discussion Questions

1. What management skills do you think would be most important for Howard Schultz to have? Why? What skills do you think would be most important for a Starbucks store manager to have? Why?
2. How might the following management theories/approaches be useful to Starbucks: scientific management, organizational behavior, quantitative approach, systems approach?

3. Choose three of the current trends and issues facing managers and explain how Starbucks might be impacted. What might be the implications for first-line managers? Middle managers? Top managers?

4. Give examples of how Howard Schultz might perform the interpersonal roles, the informational roles, and the decisional roles.

5. Look at Howard Schultz's philosophy of Starbucks. How will this affect the way the company is managed?

6. Go to the company's Web site [www.starbucks.com], and find the list of senior officers. Pick one of those positions and describe what you think that job might involve. Try to envision what types of planning, organizing, leading, and controlling this person would have to do.

7. Look up the company's mission and guiding principles at the company's Web site. What do you think of the mission and guiding principles? Describe how these would influence how a barista at a local Starbucks store does his or her job. Describe how these would influence how one of the company's top executives does his or her job.

8. Do you think Howard Schultz views his role more from the omnipotent or from the symbolic perspective? Explain.

9. What has made Starbucks' culture what it is? How is that culture maintained?

10. Does Starbucks encourage a customer responsive culture? An ethical culture? Explain.

11. Describe some of the specific and general environmental components that are likely to impact Starbucks.

12. How would you classify the uncertainty of the environment in which Starbucks operates? Explain.

13. What stakeholders do you think Starbucks might be most concerned with? Why? What issue(s) might each of these stakeholders want Starbucks to address?

14. Why do you think Howard Schultz is uncomfortable with the idea of legislative lobbying? Do you think his discomfort is appropriate? Why or why not?

Notes for the Part 1 Continuing Case

Information from company Web site, www.starbucks.com, and Hoover's Online, www.hoovers.com, April 25, 2012; H. Schultz (with J. Gordon), *Onward: How Starbucks Fought for Its Life without Losing Its Soul* (New York: Rodale), 2011; J. Cummings, "Legislative Grind," *Wall Street Journal*, April 12, 2005, pp. A1+; A. Serwer and K. Bonamici, "Hot Starbucks to Go," *Fortune*, January 26, 2004, pp. 60–74; R. Gulati, Sarah Huffman, G. Neilson, "The Barista Principle," *Strategy and Business*, Third Quarter 2002, pp. 58–69; B. Horovitz, "Starbucks Nation," *USA Today*, May 29–21, 2006, pp. A1+; and H. Schultz and D. Jones Yang, *Pour Your Heart into It: How Starbucks Built a Company One Cup at a Time* (New York: Hyperion, 1997).

3 Managing in a Global Environment

SPOTLIGHT: *Manager at Work*

"In a global market, success flows from having ONE TEAM working on ONE PLAN with ONE GOAL in mind."[1] Alan Mulally, CEO and president of Ford Motor Company (Ford), long has realized the importance of managing globally and stated so in the company's 2012 Outlook. Mulally (see photo) joined Ford Motor in September 2006 from Boeing, where he led a successful turnaround effort. Although he recognized the massive problems facing Ford in being globally competitive and profitable, he was determined to take the dramatic, painful steps and to "plow through gut-wrenching change" to transform the company and return it to global prominence. Guiding his efforts was the Way Forward plan first announced in January 2006. This comprehensive plan addressed seven areas where organizational changes would be focused: bold leadership; customer focus; strong brands; bold, innovative products; great quality; clear pricing; and competitive costs and capacity. In addition to the Way Forward plan, Mulally fashioned a strategic effort dubbed ONE FORD in an attempt to "fully leverage the tremendous worldwide resources of Ford." In his remarks at an annual shareholders meeting, Mulally said: "We operate in a fiercely competitive global industry. To achieve profitable growth we have to make the best use of our human resources and take advantage of every potential economy of scale and best practice we can find. That means operating as one team around the world, with one plan and one goal...ONE FORD...profitable growth for all." In early 2011, Ford

Source: ChinaFotoPress/ZUMA Press/Newscom

introduced a worldwide line of compact cars under the Ford Focus name. Ford called the Focus its first truly global product—that is, designed to share as many parts as possible wherever it is built or sold. The company also introduced a new SUV, the 2012

Source: Manuel Bruque/Newscom

That means operating as one team around the world, with one plan and one goal...

Escape, that showcases the company's world car strategy. The car is made from a common set of parts and components that Ford will use to make its Focus compact car, two future minivans, and at least six other models. But the company is making its biggest global bet yet—in China, investing some $5 billion "in what it calls its largest industrial expansion in at least 50 years."

Ford has been late to the game in China, and its sales and production

ONE FORD...

capacity have lagged behind other auto manufacturers in this market. Now, with plans to double production capacity and sales outlets by 2015, Ford is spending big. When its expansion is complete, the company will be able to build 1.2 million passenger cars a year in China—a number that rivals what it built in North America in 2011. Ford's Asia chief, Joe Hinrichs, says, "Should we have done this five years ·

MyManagementLab®
⭐ Improve Your Grade!
Over 10 million students improved their results using the Pearson MyLabs.
Visit **mymanagementlab.com** for simulations, tutorials, and end-of-chapter problems.

LEARNING OUTCOMES

3.1	*Contrast* ethnocentric, polycentric, and geocentric attitudes toward global business.
3.2	*Discuss* the importance of regional trading alliances and global trade mechanisms.
3.3	*Describe* the structures and techniques organizations use as they go international.
3.4	*Explain* the relevance of the political/legal, economic, and cultural environments to global business.

ago? Sure. But we can't change that. We can only change the future."

China has long been an attractive target for U.S. companies, both for producing and for consuming. Second only to Canada, China is America's next largest trading partner. And experts predict that China will likely become the world's largest economy sometime in the next decade. Despite Ford's late push into the Chinese market, it anticipates bolstering its global sales. **What issues might local managers face as production ramps up at the company's newest facilities?**

Despite their vast experience in global markets, managers at Ford still face challenges as they enter new markets. Even large successful organizations with talented managers (such as Ford) don't always do it right. However, going global is something that most organizations want to do. A study of U.S. manufacturing firms found that companies operating in multiple countries had twice the sales growth and significantly higher profitability than strictly domestic firms.[2] However, if managers don't closely monitor changes in their global environment or don't consider specific location characteristics as they plan, organize, lead, and control, they may find limited global success. In this chapter, we're going to discuss the issues managers face as they manage in a global environment.

WHO **Owns What?**

One way to see how global the marketplace has become is to consider the country of ownership origin for some familiar products. You might be surprised to find that many products you thought were made by U.S. companies aren't! Take the following quiz[3] and then check your answers at the end of the chapter on page 97.

1. Tombstone and DiGiorno frozen pizzas are products of a company based in:
   a. Italy   **b.** United States   **c.** Canada   **d.** Switzerland

2. Lebedyansky juices are owned by a company based in:
   a. Japan   **b.** United Kingdom   **c.** United States   **d.** Russia

3. Rajah spices are products of a company based in:
   a. United States   **b.** Brazil   **c.** India   **d.** Switzerland

4. Tetley Tea is owned by a company located in:
   a. Great Britain   **b.** India   **c.** Japan   **d.** Spain

5. Hsu Fu Chi International Confectioners is controlled by a company based in:
   a. Switzerland   **b.** China   **c.** United States   **d.** Japan

6. Dos Equis, Tecate, and Sol beer products are owned by a company based in:
   a. The Netherlands   **b.** Mexico   **c.** United States   **d.** Colombia

7. The company that produces Boboli pizza crust is based in:
   a. United States   **b.** Mexico   **c.** Italy   **d.** Spain

8. Yoplait is owned by a company based in:
   a. Japan   **b.** France   **c.** United States   **d.** Germany

9. The company that owns Sephora Cosmetics retail stores is located in:
   a. Germany   **b.** Canada   **c.** France   **d.** United States

10. Jimmy Choo shoe brand is owned by a company based in:
    a. Japan   **b.** Germany   **c.** Spain   **d.** United States

11. Lean Cuisine frozen meals are products of a company based in:
    a. Germany   **b.** United States   **c.** Switzerland   **d.** Brazil

12. The British newspaper the *Independent* is owned by a company based in:
    a. Russia   **b.** United Kingdom   **c.** South Africa   **d.** Canada

13. The company that makes French's mustard is based in:
    a. China   **b.** United Kingdom   **c.** Japan   **d.** United States

14. Eight O'Clock Coffee is owned by a company located in:
    a. India   **b.** Costa Rica   **c.** United States   **d.** Canada

15. Frédérick Fekkai & Co. hair care products are marketed by a company based in:
    a. Switzerland   **b.** United States   **c.** France   **d.** Italy

How well did you do? Were you aware of how many products we use every day that are made by companies *not* based in the United States? Probably not! Most of us don't fully appreciate the truly global nature of today's marketplace.

WHAT'S **Your Global Perspective?**

It's not unusual for Germans, Italians, or Indonesians to speak three or four languages. "More than half of all primary school children in China now learn English and the number of English speakers in India and China—500 million—now exceeds the total number of mother-tongue English speakers elsewhere in the world." On the other hand, most U.S. children study only English in school—only 24,000 are studying Chinese. And only 22 percent of the population in the United States speaks a language other than English.[4] Americans tend to think of English as the only international business language and don't see a need to study other languages. This could lead to future problems as a major research report commissioned by the British Council says that the "competitiveness of both Britain and the United States is being undermined" by only speaking English.[5]

Monolingualism is one sign that a nation suffers from **parochialism**—viewing the world solely through one's own eyes and perspectives.[6] People with a parochial attitude do not recognize that others have different ways of living and working. They ignore others' values and customs and rigidly apply an attitude of "ours is better than theirs" to foreign cultures. This type of narrow, restricted attitude is one approach that managers might take, but isn't the only one.[7] In fact, there are three possible global attitudes. Let's look at each more closely.

First, an **ethnocentric attitude** is the parochialistic belief that the best work approaches and practices are those of the *home* country (the country in which the company's headquarters are located). Managers with an ethnocentric attitude believe that people in foreign countries don't have the needed skills, expertise, knowledge, or experience to make the best business decisions as people in the home country do. They don't trust foreign employees with key decisions or technology.

Next, a **polycentric attitude** is the view that employees in the *host* country (the foreign country in which the organization is doing business) know the best work approaches and practices for running their business. Managers with this attitude view every foreign operation as different and hard to understand. Thus, they're likely to let employees there figure out how best to do things.

The final type of global attitude managers might have is a **geocentric attitude,** a

---

Contrast ethnocentric, polycentric, and geocentric attitudes toward global business.   **3.1**

parochialism
Viewing the world solely through your own perspectives, leading to an inability to recognize differences between people

ethnocentric attitude
The parochialistic belief that the best work approaches and practices are those of the home country

polycentric attitude
The view that the managers in the host country know the best work approaches and practices for running their business

geocentric attitude
A world-oriented view that focuses on using the best approaches and people from around the globe

---

LEADER *who made a* DIFFERENCE

Source: WEF/Photoshot/Newscom

She has been on the Most Powerful Woman in Business list by Fortune *magazine for more than five years and was named one of the 100 most powerful women in the world by* Forbes *magazine.[8] "She" is Indra Nooyi, CEO of PepsiCo. Born in India, Ms. Nooyi joined PepsiCo as head of corporate strategy in 1994 and moved quickly up the ladder to become chief executive officer and chairman of PepsiCo's board of directors. As the CEO of a large American company, Nooyi recognizes the importance of her company's global business operations. On a recent trip to China, a critical market for PepsiCo, Nooyi didn't take the usual "CEO tour" of conference rooms, but spent 10 days immersing herself in China. She says, "I wanted to look at how people live, how they eat, what the growth possibilities are." Here's a leader who knows what it will take to succeed in today's global environment. What can you learn from this leader who made a difference?*

world-oriented view that focuses on using the best approaches and people from around the globe. Managers with this type of attitude have a global view and look for the best approaches and people regardless of origin. For instance, Carlos Ghosn, CEO of Nissan and Renault, was born in Brazil to Lebanese parents, educated in France, and speaks four languages fluently. He could very well be the "model of the modern major corporate leader in a globalized world bestraddled by multinational companies."[9] Ghosn's background and perspective have given him a much broader understanding of what it takes to manage in a global environment—something characteristic of the geocentric attitude. A geocentric attitude requires eliminating parochial attitudes and developing an understanding of cross-cultural differences. That's the type of approach successful managers will need in today's global environment.

3.2 ⌐ *Discuss* the importance of regional trading alliances and global trade mechanisms.

UNDERSTANDING the Global Environment

One important feature of today's global environment is global trade which, if you remember history class, isn't new. Countries and organizations have been trading with each other for centuries.[10] And it continues strong today, as we saw in the chapter-opening quiz. Global trade today is shaped by two forces: regional trading alliances and trade mechanisms that ensure that global trade can happen.

Regional Trading Alliances

Global competition once was considered country against country—the United States versus Japan, France versus Germany, Mexico versus Canada, and so on. Now, global competition and the global economy are shaped by regional trading agreements, including the European Union (EU), North American Free Trade Agreement (NAFTA), the Association of Southeast Asian Nations (ASEAN), and others.

European Union (EU)
A union of 27 European nations created as a unified economic and trade entity

THE EUROPEAN UNION   The **European Union (EU)** is an economic and political partnership of 27 democratic European countries. (See Exhibit 3-1.) Eight countries (Croatia, the former Yugoslav Republic of Macedonia, Turkey, Albania,

Exhibit 3-1
European Union
Map

Bosnia-Herzegovina, Iceland, Montenegro, and Serbia) are candidates to join the EU.[11] Before allowed to join, however, the countries must meet the criteria which include democracy, rule of law, a market economy, and adherence to the EU's goals of political and economic union. When the 12 original members formed the EU in 1992, the primary motivation was to reassert the region's economic position against the United States and Japan. Before then, each European nation had border controls, taxes, and subsidies; nationalistic policies; and protected industries. These barriers to travel, employment, investment, and trade prevented European companies from developing economic efficiencies. Now with these barriers removed, the economic power represented by the EU is considerable. Its current membership covers a population base of more than half a billion people (7 percent of the world population) and accounts for approximately 31 percent of the world's total economic output.[12]

Another step toward full unification occurred when the common European currency, the **euro,** was adopted. The euro is currently in use in 17 of the 27 member states, and all new member countries must adopt the euro. Only Denmark, the United Kingdom, and Sweden have been allowed to opt out of using the euro.[13] Another push in unification has been attempts to develop a unified European constitution. EU leaders struggled for nearly a decade to enact a treaty designed to strengthen the EU and give it a full-time president. The so-called Lisbon Treaty (or Reform Treaty), which was ratified by all 27 member states, provides the EU with a common legal framework and the tools to meet the challenges of a changing world, including climatic and demographic changes, globalization, security, and energy. And backers feel the new structure will help strengthen the EU's common foreign policy. Many believe that a more unified Europe could have more power and say in the global arena. As the former Italian prime minister and European Commission president said, "Europe has lost and lost and lost weight in the world."[14]

> **euro**
> A single common European currency

The last couple of years have been difficult economically for the EU and its members, like it was for many global regions. "The traditional concept of 'solidarity' is being undermined by protectionist pressures in some member countries and the rigors of maintaining a common currency for a region that has diverse economic needs."[15] Some analysts believe that the EU is at a pivotal point. "They can spur growth across the region by following through on long-overdue pledges to trim benefits and free up labor markets. Or they can face a decade of economic stagnation."[16] The European Commission—the executive body for the European union—faced with major economic issues of the 17 euro zone members, including the massive debt crisis in Greece, severe economic uncertainties in Spain and Italy, and bank uncertainties, has been given new powers to monitor national budgets.[17] Although European leaders came together and bridged sharp philosophical divides and joined forces with the International Monetary Fund to forge an agreement to bail out Greece when its debt troubles intensified, the region's economic crisis has worsened and the member disputes have intensified as much of Europe appears to be sliding into a new recession.[18]

The euro zone is a larger economic unit than the United States or China and is a major source of world demand for goods and services. As the economic crisis in the region intensifies, "a growing number of companies in the United States are warning investors that sales are slowing and could get much worse."[19] Therefore, the importance of this regional trading alliance will continue to evolve as EU members work together to resolve the region's economic issues and once again assert their economic power with successful European businesses continuing to play a crucial role in the global economy.

NORTH AMERICAN FREE TRADE AGREEMENT (NAFTA) AND OTHER LATIN AMERICAN AGREEMENTS When agreements in key issues covered by the **North American Free Trade Agreement (NAFTA)** were reached by the Mexican, Canadian, and U.S. governments in 1992, a vast economic bloc was created. As of 2012, it is the second largest trade bloc in the world in terms of combined GDP of its members.[20] Between 1994, when NAFTA went into effect, and 2007 (the most recent year for complete statistics), merchandise trade between the United States and Canada and Mexico has more than tripled while trade between Mexico and the

> **North American Free Trade Agreement (NAFTA)**
> An agreement among the Mexican, Canadian, and U.S. governments in which barriers to trade have been eliminated

Since NAFTA went into effect in 1994, the lifting of trade barriers has made it easier for Canadian-based aircraft maker Bombardier to operate across Canadian, United States, and Mexican borders. And because of NAFTA, Bombardier is boosting Mexico's aerospace industry by adding the country to its global manufacturing network. At its plant in Queretaro, Mexico, Bombardier employs more than 2,000 workers to produce electrical harnesses, fuselages (shown in this photo), and flight controls for all Bombardier aircraft in production. The plants in Mexico help Bombardier reduce production costs and put the company closer to the growing demand for its aircraft in the Latin American markets.
Source: Bloomberg via Getty Images

United States has more than quadrupled. Put into numbers, that translates to some $2.6 billion exchanged on a daily basis among NAFTA partners. [21] Eliminating the barriers to free trade (tariffs, import licensing requirements, customs user fees) has strengthened the economic power of all three countries. For instance, research into Mexican migration shows that "a mix of developments—expanding economic and educational opportunities, rising border crime and shrinking families" have suppressed the number of illegal immigrants coming to the United States in search of jobs and prosperity.[22] Despite early criticisms of the trade agreement, the North American trading bloc remains a powerful force in today's global economy.

Other Latin American nations have also become part of free trade blocs. Colombia, Mexico, and Venezuela led the way when all three signed an economic pact in 1994 eliminating import duties and tariffs. Another agreement, the U.S.–Central America Free Trade Agreement (CAFTA), promotes trade liberalization between the United States and five Central American countries: Costa Rica, El Salvador, Guatemala, Honduras, and Nicaragua. However, only El Salvador and Costa Rica have joined. The other countries have yet to change laws to be in line with the agreement.[23] The United States also signed a trade deal with Colombia that is said to be the "largest Washington has concluded with a Latin American country since signing" NAFTA.[24] Also, negotiators from 34 countries in the Western Hemisphere continue work on a Free Trade Area of the Americas (FTAA) agreement, which was to have been operational no later than 2005, a missed targeted deadline. Leaders of these nations have yet to reach any agreement, leaving the future of the FTAA up in the air.[25] However, another free trade bloc of 10 South American countries known as the Southern Common Market or Mercosur already exists. Some South Americans see Mercosur as an effective way to combine resources to better compete against other global economic powers, especially the EU and NAFTA. With the future of FTAA highly doubtful, this regional alliance could take on new importance.

Association of Southeast Asian Nations (ASEAN)

A trading alliance of 10 Southeast Asian nations

ASSOCIATION OF SOUTHEAST ASIAN NATIONS (ASEAN) The **Association of Southeast Asian Nations (ASEAN)** is a trading alliance of 10 Southeast Asian nations. (See Exhibit 3-2.) The ASEAN region has a population more than 591 million with a combined GDP of US$1.5 trillion.[26] In addition to these 10 nations, leaders from a group dubbed ASEAN+3, which include China, Japan, and South Korea, have met to discuss trade issues. Also, leaders from India, Australia, and New Zealand have participated in trade talks with ASEAN+3 as well. The main issue with creating a trade bloc of all 16 nations has been the lack of any push toward regional integration. Despite the Asian culture's emphasis on consensus building, "ASEAN's biggest problem is that individual members haven't been willing to sacrifice for the common good."[27] Although Southeast Asian leaders agree that closer regional integration would help economic growth, the large differences in wealth among ASEAN members have made it "difficult to create common standards because national standards remain so far apart."[28] However, the challenges brought on by the recent worldwide recession, which adversely affected many countries in this region, triggered greater interest in pushing for integration. In fact, on January 1, 2010, China and ASEAN launched an ambitious free trade agreement, making it the world's third largest trade bloc.[29] In addition to these free trade alliances, it's hoped that by 2015, an established ASEAN economic community will allow goods, skilled workers, and capital to move freely among member countries.

Despite the barriers and challenges, progress toward regional integration continues. This fast-growing region means ASEAN and other Asian trade alliances

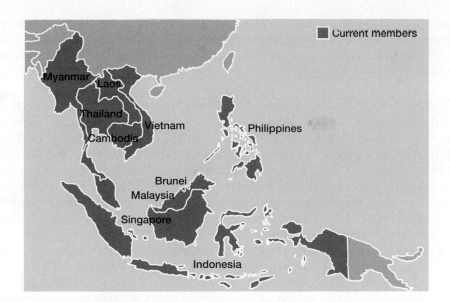

Exhibit 3-2
ASEAN Map

Source: Based on J. McClenahen and T. Clark, "ASEAN at Work," *IW*, May 19, 1997, p. 42.

will be increasingly important globally with an impact that eventually could rival that of both NAFTA and the EU.

OTHER TRADE ALLIANCES   Other regions around the world have also developed regional trading alliances. For instance, the 53-nation African Union (AU), which came into existence in 2002, has the vision of "building an integrated, prosperous and peaceful Africa."[30] Members of this alliance have created an economic development plan to achieve greater unity among Africa's nations. Like members of other trade alliances, these countries hope to gain economic, social, cultural, and trade benefits from their association. Such cooperation couldn't be more important as Africa's economic output is booming like never before. GDP growth rates have been averaging 4.8 percent, the highest rate outside Asia, with most of that growth coming domestically. In addition, Africa has been experiencing a "virtually unprecedented period of political stability with governments steadily deregulating industries and developing infrastructure."[31]

Five east African nations—Burundi, Kenya, Rwanda, Tanzania, and Uganda—have formed a common market called the East African Community (EAC).[32] Under this agreement, goods can be sold across borders without tariffs. The next step for the EAC will be monetary union, although that will take time to implement.

Finally, the South Asian Association for Regional Cooperation (SAARC) composed of eight member states (India, Pakistan, Sri Lanka, Bangladesh, Bhutan, Nepal, the Maldives, and Afghanistan) began eliminating tariffs in 2006.[33] Its aim, like all the other regional trading alliances, is to allow free flow of goods and services.

The preceding discussion indicates that global trade is alive and well. Regional trade alliances continue to be developed in areas where member countries believe it's in their best interest economically and globally to band together and strengthen their economic position.

Global Trade Mechanisms

Global trade among nations doesn't just happen on its own. As trade issues arise, global trade systems ensure that trade continues efficiently and effectively. Indeed, one of the realities of globalization is the interdependence of countries—that is, what happens in one can impact others, good or bad. For example, the financial crisis that started in the United States in 2008 threw the global economy into a tailspin. Although things spiraled precariously out of control, it didn't completely collapse. Why? Because governmental interventions and trade and financial mechanisms

World Trade Organization (WTO)
A global organization of 153 countries that deals with the rules of trade among nations

International Monetary Fund (IMF)
An organization of 185 countries that promotes international monetary cooperation and provides advice, loans, and technical assistance

*data*points[35]

75 percent of U.S. labor productivity growth has been attributed to MNCs.

61 percent of HR professionals say there will be a greater need for cross-cultural understanding and savvy in business settings.

63 percent of Americans say they can introduce themselves in a language they studied in school.

82 percent of global executives say they are willing to relocate to another region, state, or country.

58 percent of high-performing companies have some type of global leadership program in place.

93 percent of public middle and high schools in the United States offer Spanish; only 4 percent offer Chinese.

32 percent of college graduates see themselves using a language other than their first language at work.

70 percent of Americans aged 18 to 24 have not traveled outside the United States in the last three years.

54 percent of business travelers say they're more successful in their career because of global business travel experience.

helped avert a potential crisis. We're going to look at four important global trade mechanisms: the World Trade Organization, the International Monetary Fund, the World Bank Group, and the Organization for Economic Cooperation and Development.

WORLD TRADE ORGANIZATION The **World Trade Organization (WTO)** is a global organization of 155 countries that deals with the rules of trade among nations.[34] Formed in 1995, the WTO evolved from the General Agreement on Tariffs and Trade (GATT), a trade agreement in effect since the end of World War II. Today, the WTO is the only *global* organization that deals with trade rules among nations. Its membership consists of 155 member countries and 29 observer governments (which have a specific time frame within which they must apply to become members). The goal of the WTO is to help countries conduct trade through a system of rules. Although critics have staged vocal protests against the WTO, claiming that global trade destroys jobs and the natural environment, it appears to play an important role in monitoring, promoting, and protecting global trade. For instance, the WTO ruled that the European plane maker Airbus received improper European Union subsidies for the A380 super jumbo jet and several other airplanes, hurting its American rival, Boeing.[36] Airbus has the right to appeal the ruling, but even after appealing, any member ultimately found to have provided improper subsidies is obliged to bring its policies into compliance with global trade rules. Failure to comply could bring trade sanctions. In another news story, the U.S. government is weighing whether to file a WTO complaint against China's Internet censorship.[37] In addition, the WTO has played a pivotal role in keeping global trade active during the global economic crisis. WTO Director-General Pascal Lamy said, "During these difficult times, the multilateral trading system has once again proven its value. WTO rules and principles have assisted governments in keeping markets open and they now provide a platform from which trade can grow as the global economy improves."[38] These examples illustrate the types of trade issues with which the WTO deals. Such issues are best handled by an organization such as the WTO and it has played, without a doubt, an important role in promoting and protecting global trade.

INTERNATIONAL MONETARY FUND AND WORLD BANK GROUP Two other important and necessary global trade mechanisms include the International Monetary Fund and the World Bank Group. The **International Monetary Fund (IMF)** is an organization of 188 countries that promotes international monetary cooperation and provides member countries with policy advice, temporary loans, and technical assistance to establish and maintain financial stability and to strengthen economies.[39] During the global financial turmoil of the last few years, the IMF has been on the forefront of advising countries and governments in getting through the difficulties.[40] The **World Bank Group** is a group of five closely associated institutions, all owned by its member countries, that provides vital financial and technical assistance to developing countries around the world. The goal of the World Bank Group is to promote long-term economic development and poverty reduction by providing members with technical and financial support.[41] For instance, during the recent global recession, financial commitments by the World Bank Group reached $100 billion as it helped nations respond to and recover from the economic downturn.[42] Both entities have an important role in supporting and promoting global business.

ORGANIZATION FOR ECONOMIC COOPERATION AND DEVELOPMENT (OECD) The forerunner of the OECD, the Organization for European Economic Cooperation, was formed in 1947 to administer American and Canadian aid under the Marshall Plan for the reconstruction of Europe after World War II. Today, the **Organization for Economic Cooperation and Development (OECD)** is a Paris-based international economic organization whose mission is to help its 34 member countries achieve sustainable economic growth and employment and raise the standard of living in member countries while maintaining financial stability in order to contribute to the development of the world economy.[43] When needed, the OECD gets involved in negotiations with OECD countries so they can agree on "rules of the game" for international cooperation. One current focus is combating small-scale bribery in overseas commerce. The OECD says such "so-called facilitation payments are corrosive...particularly on sustainable economic development and the rule of law."[44] With a long history of facilitating economic growth around the globe, the OECD now shares its expertise and accumulated experiences with more than 70 developing and emerging market economies.

DOING **Business Globally**

Daimler, Nissan Motor, and Renault are part of a strategic partnership that shares small-car technology and power trains—an arrangement that all three automakers say will allow them to better compete in an environment where cutting costs is crucial. Convenience store operator 7-Eleven, a subsidiary of Japan-based Seven & iHoldings, has created a profitable niche in Jakarta by adapting its stores to Indonesian ways. Procter & Gamble Company relocated the top executives from its global skin, cosmetics, and personal-care unit from its Cincinnati headquarters to Singapore. Reckitt Benckiser, the U.K.-based maker of consumer products (Lysol, Woolite, and French's mustard are just a few of its products), has operations in more than 60 countries, and its top 400 managers represent 53 different nationalities. The Missouri State Employees' Retirement System pays retirement benefits to recipients in 20 countries outside the United States.[45] As these examples show, organizations in different industries and from different countries do business globally. But *how* do they do so?

Different Types of International Organizations

Companies doing business globally aren't new. DuPont started doing business in China in 1863. H.J. Heinz Company was manufacturing food products in the United Kingdom in 1905. Ford Motor Company set up its first overseas sales branch in France in 1908. By the 1920s, other companies, including Fiat, Unilever, and Royal Dutch/Shell, had gone international. But it wasn't until the mid-1960s that international companies became quite common. Today, few companies don't do business internationally. However, there's not a generally accepted approach to describe the different types of international companies; different authors call them different things. We use the terms *multinational, multidomestic, global,* and *transnational.*[46] A **multinational corporation (MNC)** is any type of international company that maintains operations in multiple countries.

One type of MNC is a **multidomestic corporation,** which decentralizes management and other decisions to the local country. This type of globalization reflects the polycentric attitude. A multidomestic corporation doesn't attempt to replicate its domestic successes by managing foreign operations from its home country. Instead, local employees typically are hired to manage the business and marketing strategies are tailored to that country's unique characteristics. For example, Switzerland-based Nestlé is a multidomestic corporation. With operations in almost every country on the globe, its managers match the company's products to its consumers. In parts of Europe, Nestlé sells products that are not available in the United States or Latin America. Another example is Frito-Lay, a division of PepsiCo, which markets a Dorito chip in the British market that differs in both taste and texture from the U.S. and Canadian version. Even the king of retailing, Walmart, has learned that it must "think locally to act globally" as it tailors its inventories and store formats to local tastes.[47] Many consumer product companies organize their global businesses using this approach because they must adapt their products to meet the needs of local markets.

World Bank Group
A group of five closely associated institutions that provides financial and technical assistance to developing countries

Organization for Economic Cooperation and Development (OECD)
An international economic organization that helps its 30 member countries achieve sustainable economic growth and employment

---

Describe *the structures* **3.3**
and techniques organizations use as they go international.

multinational corporation (MNC)
A broad term that refers to any and all types of international companies that maintain operations in multiple countries

multidomestic corporation
An MNC that decentralizes management and other decisions to the local country

global company
An MNC that centralizes management and other decisions in the home country

transnational or borderless organization
An MNC in which artificial geographical barriers are eliminated

global sourcing
Purchasing materials or labor from around the world wherever it is cheapest

exporting
Making products domestically and selling them abroad

importing
Acquiring products made abroad and selling them domestically

licensing
An organization gives another organization the right to make or sell its products using its technology or product specifications

franchising
An organization gives another organization the right to use its name and operating methods

strategic alliance
A partnership between an organization and a foreign company partner(s) in which both share resources and knowledge in developing new products or building production facilities

joint venture
A specific type of strategic alliance in which the partners agree to form a separate, independent organization for some business purpose

foreign subsidiary
Directly investing in a foreign country by setting up a separate and independent production facility or office

Another type of MNC is a **global company,** which centralizes its management and other decisions in the home country. This approach to globalization reflects the ethnocentric attitude. Global companies treat the world market as an integrated whole and focus on the need for global efficiency and cost savings. Although these companies may have considerable global holdings, management decisions with company-wide implications are made from headquarters in the home country. Some examples of global companies include Sony, Deutsche Bank AG, Starwood Hotels, and Merrill Lynch.

Other companies use an arrangement that eliminates artificial geographical barriers. This type of MNC is often called a **transnational, or borderless, organization** and reflects a geocentric attitude.[48] For example, IBM dropped its organizational structure based on country and reorganized into industry groups. As our chapter opener described, Ford Motor Company is pursuing what it calls the One Ford concept as it integrates its operations around the world. Another company, Thomson SA, which is legally based in France, has eight major locations around the globe. The CEO said, "We don't want people to think we're based anyplace."[49] Managers choose this approach to increase efficiency and effectiveness in a competitive global marketplace.[50]

How Organizations Go International

When organizations do go international, they often use different approaches. (See Exhibit 3-3.) Managers who want to get into a global market with minimal investment may start with **global sourcing** (also called global outsourcing), which is purchasing materials or labor from around the world wherever it is cheapest. The goal: take advantage of lower costs in order to be more competitive. For instance, Massachusetts General Hospital uses radiologists in India to interpret CT scans.[51] Although global sourcing may be the first step to going international for many companies, they often continue to use this approach because of the competitive advantages it offers. Each successive stage of going international beyond global sourcing, however, requires more investment and thus entails more risk for the organization.

The next step in going international may involve **exporting** the organization's products to other countries—that is, making products domestically and selling them abroad. In addition, an organization might do **importing**, which involves acquiring products made abroad and selling them domestically. Both usually entail minimal investment and risk, which is why many small businesses often use these approaches to doing business globally.

Managers also might use **licensing** or **franchising,** which are similar approaches involving one organization giving another organization the right to use its brand name, technology, or product specifications in return for a lump sum payment or a fee usually based on sales. The only difference is that licensing is primarily used by manufacturing organizations that make or sell another company's products and franchising is

Exhibit 3-3
How Organizations Go Global

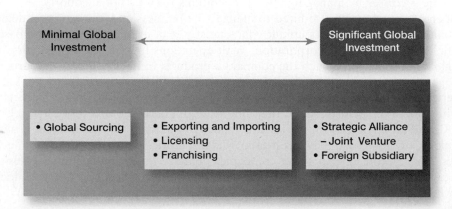

primarily used by service organizations that want to use another company's name and operating methods. For example, Chicago consumers can enjoy Guatemalan Pollo Campero fried chicken, South Koreans can indulge in Dunkin' Donuts coffee, Hong Kong residents can dine on Shakey's Pizza, and Malaysians can consume Schlotzsky's deli sandwiches—all because of *franchises* in these countries. On the other hand, Anheuser-Busch InBev has *licensed* the right to brew and market its Budweiser beer to brewers such as Kirin in Japan and Crown Beers in India.

When an organization has been doing business internationally for a while and has gained experience in international markets, managers may decide to make more of a direct foreign investment. One way to increase investment is through a **strategic alliance**, which is a partnership between an organization and a foreign company partner or partners in which both share resources and knowledge in developing new products or building production facilities. For example, Honda Motor and General Electric teamed up to produce a new jet engine. A specific type of strategic alliance in which the partners form a separate, independent organization for some business purpose is called a **joint venture**. For example, Hewlett-Packard has had numerous joint ventures with various suppliers around the globe to develop different components for its computer equipment. These partnerships provide a relatively easy way for companies to compete globally.

Finally, managers may choose to directly invest in a foreign country by setting up a **foreign subsidiary** as a separate and independent facility or office. This subsidiary can be managed as a multidomestic organization (local control) or as a global organization (centralized control). As you can probably guess, this arrangement involves the greatest commitment of resources and poses the greatest amount of risk. For instance, United Plastics Group of Westmont, Illinois, built two injection-molding facilities in Suzhou, China. The company's executive vice president for business development said that level of investment was necessary because "it fulfilled our mission of being a global supplier to our global accounts."[52]

China's Lenovo CEO Yang Yuanqing (left) raises hands with Japan's NEC Corporation President Nobuhiro Endo during a press conference in which the leading electronics firms announced a strategic alliance to create a new joint venture called NEC Lenovo Japan Group to sell personal computers in Japan. The joint venture gives both Lenovo and NEC the opportunity to expand their commercial and consumer personal computer businesses in Japan, the third largest PC market in the world. The alliance leverages each firm's strengths, such as NEC's product development capabilities. customer service, and knowledge of customer needs and Lenovo's technology expertise and global supply chain.
Source: Yoshikazu Tsuno/AFP/Getty Images/ Newscom

MANAGING in a Global Environment

Explain *the relevance* **3.4** *of the political/legal, economic, and cultural environments to global business.*

Assume for a moment that you're a manager going to work for a branch of a global organization in a foreign country. You know that your environment will differ from the one at home, but how? What should you look for?

Any manager who finds himself or herself in a new country faces challenges. In this section, we'll look at some of these challenges. Although our discussion is presented through the eyes of a U.S. manager, this framework could be used by any manager regardless of national origin who manages in a foreign environment.

The Political/Legal Environment

Managers of a company in New Hampshire who wanted to expand into Europe were stunned to discover that in some countries, by law, they would have to offer 36 days' holiday (vacation) pay to local workers who worked more than a 35-hour week.[53] The most vacation time awarded to U.S. workers was four weeks—and that was for the company's chief executive.

U.S. managers are accustomed to a stable legal and political system. Changes tend to be slow, and legal and political procedures are well established. Elections are held at regular intervals, and even when the political party in power changes after an election, it's unlikely that anything too radical will happen. The stability of laws allows for accurate predictions. However, this certainly isn't true for all countries.

Managers must stay informed of the specific laws in countries where they do business. For instance, the president of Zimbabwe is pushing ahead with plans to force foreign companies to sell majority stakes to locals.[54] Such a law would be a major barrier to foreign business investment. In China, foreign businesses are finding a less-than-welcoming climate as government policies are making it more difficult to do business there.[55] And Swedish retailer Ikea has halted further investment in Russia because of continual governmental red tape delays. Per Kaufmann, Ikea's Russia country manager, said the decision was "due to the unpredictability of the administrative processes in some regions."[56]

Also, some countries have risky political climates. For instance, BP could have warned Exxon about the challenges of doing business in Russia. During its long involvement in the country, BP has "had so many police run-ins that its stock price often nudges up or down in response to raids or the arrests of employees." However, almost a quarter of BP's output comes from Russian oil and natural gas so the company has learned to live with the disruptions. Recently, not long after Exxon formed a strategic alliance with Russia's state-owned oil company, armed commandos raided BP's offices in "one of the ritual armed searches of white-collar premises that are common here." These incidents are so common that they've been "given a nickname: masky shows (so-called because of the balaclavas—ski masks—the agents often wear)." The episode was sure to "send a signal that when it comes to dealing with the state-run business world of Prime Minister Vladimir V. Putin, Exxon wasn't in Texas anymore."[57] Chicago-based Aon Corporation does an annual political risk assessment, and its 2012 report found that businesses faced the highest level of risk in the following countries: Afghanistan, Belarus, Bissau, Democratic Republic of Congo, Iran, Iraq, North Korea, Pakistan, Somalia, South Sudan, Sudan, Syria, Venezuela, Yemen, and Zimbabwe. Company analysts said that political and financial instability remained a feature of the business landscape as a result of the global recession. They also said that "significant risks are shown for exchange transfer, sovereign non-payment, political interference, supply chain disruption, legal and regulatory risk, and political violence."[58] Managers of businesses in countries with higher risk levels face dramatically greater uncertainty. In addition, political interference is a fact of life in some regions, especially in some Asian countries such as China.[59]

Keep in mind that a country's political/legal environment doesn't have to be risky or unstable to be a concern to managers. Just the fact that it differs from that of the home country (United States or other) is important. Managers must recognize these differences if they hope to understand the constraints and opportunities that exist.

The Economic Environment

Strange as it may sound, 17,000 tons of Parmesan cheese, with an estimated value of $187 million, are being held in the vaults of Italian bank Credito Emiliano. The cheese is collateral from Italian cheese makers struggling through the recession.[60] Such an example of an economic factor of business may seem peculiar for those of us in the United States, but it's not all that unusual for Italian businesses.

A global manager must be aware of economic issues when doing business in other countries. First, it's important to understand a country's type of economic system. The two major types are a free market economy and a planned economy. A **free market economy** is one in which resources are primarily owned and controlled by the private sector. A **planned economy** is one in which economic decisions are planned by a central government. Actually, no economy is purely free market or planned. For instance, the United States and United Kingdom are toward the free market end of the spectrum but do have governmental intervention and controls. The economies of Vietnam and North Korea are more planned. China is also a more planned economy, but until recently had been moving toward being a more free market. Why would managers need to know about a country's economic system? Because it, too, has the potential to

free market economy
An economic system in which resources are primarily owned and controlled by the private sector

planned economy
An economic system in which economic decisions are planned by a central government

constrain decisions. Other economic issues managers need to understand include currency exchange rates, inflation rates, and diverse tax policies.

An MNC's profits can vary dramatically, depending on the strength of its home currency and the currencies of the countries in which it operates. For instance, prior to the overall global economic slowdown, the rising value of the euro against both the dollar and the yen had contributed to strong profits for German companies.[61] Any currency exchange revaluations can affect managers' decisions and the level of a company's profits.

Inflation means that prices for products and services are increasing, but it also affects interest rates, exchange rates, the cost of living, and the general confidence in a country's political and economic system. Country inflation rates can, and do, vary widely. The *World Factbook* shows rates ranging from a negative .80 percent in the Northern Mariana Islands to a positive 57.4 percent in Belarus.[62] Managers need to monitor inflation trends so they can anticipate possible changes in a country's monetary policies and make good business decisions regarding purchasing and pricing.

Finally, tax policies can be a major economic worry. Some countries' tax laws are more restrictive than those in an MNC's home country. Others are more lenient. About the only certainty is that they differ from country to country. Managers need accurate information on tax rules in countries in which they operate to minimize their business's overall tax obligation.

Understanding differences in values across cultures helps explain the behavior of employees from different countries. According to the GLOBE framework, one of the nine dimensions on which national cultures differ is gender differentiation. Like other Arab countries, the United Arab Emirates maximizes gender role differences, where schools and universities are segregated by gender, and only a small percentage of women choose to participate in the labor force. Conservative cultural values in Arab nations lead women to seek jobs that do not involve mixing with men. In this photo, a female taxi driver in Dubai, a city-state in the UAE, can only offer her services to female passengers.
Source. Reuters/Anwar Mirza

The Cultural Environment

For five weeks in June and July of 2011, the entire senior leadership team at Starwood Hotels relocated to Shanghai, China. Why? Because, clearly China is a huge growth market and "working closely with people from a different culture helps you to see pitfalls and opportunities in a very different way."[63]

Managing today's talented global workforce can be a challenge![64] A large multinational oil company found that employee productivity in one of its Mexican plants was off 20 percent and sent a U.S. manager to find out why. After talking to several employees, the manager discovered that the company used to have a monthly fiesta in the parking lot for all the employees and their families. Another U.S. manager had canceled the fiestas saying they were a waste of time and money. The message employees were getting was that the company didn't care about their families anymore. When the fiestas were reinstated, productivity and employee morale soared. At Hewlett-Packard, a cross-global team of U.S. and French engineers were assigned to work together on a software project. The U.S. engineers sent long, detailed e-mails to their counterparts in France. The French engineers viewed the lengthy e-mails as patronizing and replied with quick, concise e-mails. This made the U.S. engineers think that the French were hiding something from them. The situation spiraled out of control and negatively affected output until team members went through cultural training.[65]

As we know from Chapter 2, organizations have different cultures. Countries have cultures, too. **National culture** includes the values and attitudes shared by individuals from a specific country that shape their behavior and their beliefs about what is important.[66]

Which is more important to a manager—national culture or organizational culture? For example, is an IBM facility in Germany more likely to reflect German culture or IBM's corporate culture? Research indicates that national culture has a greater effect on employees than their organization's culture.[67] German employees at an IBM facility in Munich will be influenced more by German culture than by IBM's culture.

national culture
The values and attitudes shared by individuals from a specific country that shape their behavior and beliefs about what is important

Legal, political, and economic differences among countries are fairly obvious. The Japanese manager who works in the United States or his or her American counterpart who works in Japan can get information about laws or tax policies without too much effort. Getting information about cultural differences isn't quite that easy! The primary reason? It's difficult for natives to explain their country's unique cultural characteristics to someone else. For instance, if you were born and raised in the United States, how would you describe U.S. culture? In other words, what are Americans like? Think about it for a moment and see which characteristics in Exhibit 3-4 you identified.

HOFSTEDE'S FRAMEWORK FOR ASSESSING CULTURES   Geert Hofstede developed one of the most widely referenced approaches to helping managers better understand differences between national cultures. His research found that countries vary on five dimensions of national culture. [68] These dimensions are described in Exhibit 3-5, which also shows some of the countries characterized by those dimensions.

THE GLOBE FRAMEWORK FOR ASSESSING CULTURES   The **Global Leadership and Organizational Behavior Effectiveness (GLOBE)** is an ongoing research program that extended Hofstede's work by investigating cross-cultural leadership behaviors and giving managers additional information to help them identify and manage cultural differences. Using data from more than 18,000 managers in 62 countries, the GLOBE research team (led by Robert House) identified nine dimensions on which national cultures differ.[69] Two dimensions (power distance and uncertainty avoidance) fit directly with Hofstede's. Four are similar to Hofstede's (assertiveness, which is similar to achievement-nurturing; humane orientation, which is similar to the nurturing dimension; future orientation, which is similar to long-term and short-term orientation; and institutional collectivism, which is similar to individualism-collectivism). The remaining three (gender differentiation, in-group collectivism, and performance orientation) offer additional insights into a country's culture. Here are

Global Leadership and Organizational Behavior Effectiveness (GLOBE) program
The research program that studies cross-cultural leadership behaviors

Exhibit 3-4
What Are Americans Like?

- Americans are *very informal.* They tend to treat people alike even when great differences in age or social standing are evident.

- Americans are *direct.* They don't talk around things. To some foreigners, this may appear as abrupt or even rude behavior.

- Americans are *competitive.* Some foreigners may find Americans assertive or overbearing.

- Americans are *achievers.* They like to keep score, whether at work or at play. They emphasize accomplishments.

- Americans are *independent and individualistic.* They place a high value on freedom and believe that individuals can shape and control their own destiny.

- Americans are *questioners.* They ask a lot of questions, even of someone they have just met. Many may seem pointless ("How ya' doin'?") or personal ("What kind of work do you do?").

- Americans *dislike silence.* They would rather talk about the weather than deal with silence in a conversation.

- Americans *value punctuality.* They keep appointment calendars and live according to schedules and clocks.

- Americans *value cleanliness.* They often seem obsessed with bathing, eliminating body odors, and wearing clean clothes.

Sources: Based on M. Ernest (ed.), *Predeparture Orientation Handbook: For Foreign Students and Scholars Planning to Study in the United States* (Washington, DC: U.S. Information Agency, Bureau of Cultural Affairs, 1984), pp. 103–105; A. Bennett, "American Culture Is Often a Puzzle for Foreign Managers in the U.S.," *Wall Street Journal*, February 12, 1986, p. 29; "Don't Think Our Way's the Only Way," *The Pryor Report*, February 1988, p. 9; and B. J. Wattenberg, "The Attitudes Behind American Exceptionalism," *U.S. News & World Report*, August 7, 1989, p. 25.

Exhibit 3-5

Hofstede's Five Dimensions of National Culture

---

1. ***Individualistic***—People look after their own and family interests

   Collectivistic—People expect the group to look after and protect them

Individualistic	←——————————————→	*Collectivistic*
United States, Canada, Australia	Japan	Mexico, Thailand

2. ***High power distance***—Accepts wide differences in power; great deal of respect for those in authority

   Low power distance—Plays down inequalities: employees are not afraid to approach nor are in awe of the boss

High power distance	←——————————————→	*Low power distance*
Mexico, Singapore, France	Italy, Japan	United States, Sweden

3. ***High uncertainty avoidance***—Threatened with ambiguity and experience high levels of anxiety

   Low uncertainty avoidance—Comfortable with risks; tolerant of different behavior and opinions

High uncertainty avoidance	←——————————————→	*Low uncertainty avoidance*
Italy, Mexico, France	United Kingdom	Canada, United States, Singapore

4. ***Achievement***—Values such as assertiveness, acquiring money and goods, and competition prevail

   Nurturing—Values such as relationships and concern for others prevail

Achievement	←——————————————→	*Nurturing*
United States, Japan, Mexico	Canada, Greece	France, Sweden

5. ***Long-term orientation***—People look to the future and value thrift and persistence

   Short-term orientation—People value tradition and the past

Short-term orientation	←——————————————→	*Long-term orientation*
Germany, Australia, United States, Canada		China, Taiwan, Japan

---

descriptions of these nine dimensions. For each of these dimensions, we have indicated which countries rated high, which rated moderate, and which rated low.

- **Power distance:** the extent to which a society accepts that power in institutions and organizations is distributed unequally. (*High:* Russia, Spain, and Thailand. *Moderate:* England, France, and Brazil. *Low:* Denmark, the Netherlands, and South Africa.)
- **Uncertainty avoidance:** a society's reliance on social norms and procedures to alleviate the unpredictability of future events. (*High:* Austria, Denmark, and Germany. *Moderate:* Israel, United States, and Mexico. *Low:* Russia, Hungary, and Bolivia.)
- **Assertiveness:** the extent to which a society encourages people to be tough, confrontational, assertive, and competitive rather than modest and tender. (*High:* Spain, United States, and Greece. *Moderate:* Egypt, Ireland, and Philippines. *Low:* Sweden, New Zealand, and Switzerland.)
- **Humane orientation:** the degree to which a society encourages and rewards individuals for being fair, altruistic, generous, caring, and kind to others. (*High:* Indonesia, Egypt, and Malaysia. *Moderate:* Hong Kong, Sweden, and Taiwan. *Low:* Germany, Spain, and France.)

- **Future orientation:** the extent to which a society encourages and rewards future-oriented behaviors such as planning, investing in the future, and delaying gratification. (*High:* Denmark, Canada, and the Netherlands. *Moderate:* Slovenia, Egypt, and Ireland. *Low:* Russia, Argentina, and Poland.)
- **Institutional collectivism:** the degree to which individuals are encouraged by societal institutions to be integrated into groups within organizations and society. (*High:* Greece, Hungary, and Germany. *Moderate:* Hong Kong, United States, and Egypt. *Low:* Denmark, Singapore, and Japan.)
- **Gender differentiation:** the extent to which a society maximizes gender role differences as measured by how much status and decision-making responsibilities women have. (*High:* South Korea, Egypt, and Morocco. *Moderate:* Italy, Brazil, and Argentina. *Low:* Sweden, Denmark, and Slovenia.)
- **In-group collectivism:** the extent to which members of a society take pride in membership in small groups, such as their family and circle of close friends, and the organizations in which they're employed. (*High:* Egypt, China, and Morocco. *Moderate:* Japan, Israel, and Qatar. *Low:* Denmark, Sweden, and New Zealand.)
- **Performance orientation:** the degree to which a society encourages and rewards group members for performance improvement and excellence. (*High:* United States, Taiwan, and New Zealand. *Moderate:* Sweden, Israel, and Spain. *Low:* Russia, Argentina, and Greece.)

The GLOBE studies confirm that Hofstede's dimensions are still valid and extend his research rather than replace it. GLOBE's added dimensions provide an expanded and updated measure of countries' cultural differences. It's likely that cross-cultural studies of human behavior and organizational practices will increasingly use the GLOBE dimensions to assess differences between countries. [70]

let's get REAL

The Scenario:

Renata Zorzato, head of new product development for a global recruiting company, is preparing to move from Saõ Paulo to San Diego to head up a team of executive recruiters. Her newly formed team will include company employees from Berlin, London, Shanghai, Mexico City, Kuala Lumpur, New York, and San Diego. The team will be designing and launching an innovative new global executive recruiting tool. But first, Renata has to get the team members all working together, each bringing his or her unique strengths and perspectives to the project.

What's the best way for Renata to get this culturally diverse team up and running?

The first thing Renata should do is gather her team in an informal setting, such as a group dinner, so they can learn a little bit about each other. Since they are all from "out of town," they share a common link that should foster a sense of teamwork among them. Collaboration and communication will be key to their success, so Renata should set up regular team meetings where everyone is encouraged to share best practices and experiences. Since they will be working on a new global tool, it is critical for her to continuously reiterate that everyone's experience is equally valuable to the team's success.

Joe Binef
Director of Global
Process Development

Source: Joe Binef

Global Management in Today's World

Doing business globally today isn't easy! As we look at managing in today's global environment, we want to focus on two important issues. The first issue involves the challenges associated with globalization, especially in relation to the openness that's part of being global. The second issue revolves around the challenges of managing a global workforce.

THE CHALLENGE OF OPENNESS   The push to go global has been widespread. Advocates praise the economic and social benefits that come from globalization, but globalization also creates challenges because of the openness that's necessary for it to work. One challenge is the increased threat of terrorism by a truly global terror network. Globalization is meant to open up trade and to break down the geographical barriers separating countries. Yet, opening up means just that—being open to the bad as well as the good. In a wide range of countries, from the Philippines and the United Kingdom to Israel and Pakistan, organizations and employees face the risk of terrorist attacks. Another challenge from openness is the economic interdependence of trading countries. As we saw over the last couple of years, the faltering of one country's economy can have a domino effect on other countries with which it does business. So far, however, the world economy has proved to be resilient. And as we discussed earlier, structures that are currently in place, such as the World Trade Organization and the International Monetary Fund, help to isolate and address potential problems.

The far more serious challenge for managers in the openness required by globalization comes from intense underlying and fundamental cultural differences—differences that encompass traditions, history, religious beliefs, and deep-seated values. Managing in such an environment can be extremely complicated. Even though globalization has long been praised for its economic benefits, some individuals think that globalization is simply a euphemism for "Americanization"—that is, the way U.S. cultural values and U.S. business philosophy are said to be slowly taking over the world.[71] At its best, proponents of Americanization hope others will see how progressive, efficient, industrious, and free U.S. society and businesses are and want to emulate that way of doing things. However, critics claim that this attitude of the "almighty American dollar wanting to spread the American way to every single country" has created many problems.[72] Although history is filled with clashes between civilizations, what's unique now is the speed and ease with which misunderstandings and disagreements can erupt and escalate. The Internet, television and other media, and global air travel have brought the good and the bad of American entertainment, products, and behaviors to every corner of the globe. For those who don't like what Americans do, say, or believe, this exposure can lead to resentment, dislike, distrust, and even outright hatred.

Challenges of Managing a Global Workforce.

- "As more Americans go to mainland China to take jobs, more Chinese and Americans are working side by side. These cross-cultural partnerships, while beneficial in many ways, are also highlighting tensions that expose differences in work experience, pay levels, and communication."[73]
- Global companies with multicultural work teams are faced with the challenge of managing the cultural differences in work-family relationships. The work-family practices and programs appropriate and effective for employees in one country may not be the best solution for employees in other locations.[74]

These examples indicate challenges associated with managing a global workforce. As globalization continues to be important for businesses, it's obvious that managers need to understand how to best manage that global workforce. Some researchers have suggested that managers need **cultural intelligence** or cultural awareness and sensitivity skills.[75] Cultural intelligence encompasses three main dimensions: (1) knowledge of culture as a concept—how cultures vary and how they affect

cultural intelligence
Cultural awareness and sensitivity skills

behavior; (2) mindfulness—the ability to pay attention to signals and reactions in different cross-cultural situations; and (3) behavioral skills—using one's knowledge and mindfulness to choose appropriate behaviors in those situations.

Other researchers have said that what effective global leaders need is a **global mind-set,** attributes that allow a leader to be effective in cross-cultural environments.[76] Those attributes have three components as shown in Exhibit 3-6.

Leaders who possess such cross-cultural skills and abilities—whether cultural intelligence or a global mind-set—will be important assets to global organizations. Successfully managing in today's global environment will require incredible sensitivity and understanding. Managers from any country will need to be aware of how their decisions and actions will be viewed, not only by those who may agree, but more importantly, by those who may disagree. They will need to adjust their leadership styles and management approaches to accommodate these diverse views, and at the same time be as efficient and effective as possible in reaching the organization's goals.

global mind-set
Attributes that allow a leader to be effective in cross-cultural environments

Exhibit 3-6
A Global Mind-Set

Intellectual capital: Knowledge of international business and the capacity to understand how business works on a global scale

Psychological capital: Openness to new ideas and experiences

Social capital: Ability to form connections and build trusting relationships with people who are different from you

Source: Based on "Making It Overseas," by M. Javidan, M. Teagarden, and D. Bowen, from *Harvard Business Review,* April 2010; and "Testing Managers' Global IQ," by J. McGregor (ed.), from *Bloomberg BusinessWeek,* September 28, 2009.

MyManagementLab
Go to **mymanagementlab.com** to complete the problems marked with this icon

CHAPTER

PREPARING FOR: Exams/Quizzes
CHAPTER SUMMARY by Learning Outcomes

3.1 ⌐LEARNING OUTCOME¬

Contrast ethnocentric, polycentric, and geocentric attitudes toward global business.

Parochialism is viewing the world solely through your own eyes and perspectives and not recognizing that others have different ways of living and working. An ethnocentric attitude is the parochialistic belief that the best work approaches and practices are those of the home country. A polycentric attitude is the view that the managers in the host country know the best work approaches and practices for running their business. And a geocentric attitude is a world-oriented view that focuses on using the best approaches and people from around the globe.

3.2 ⌐LEARNING OUTCOME¬

Discuss the importance of regional trading alliances and global trade mechanisms.

The European Union consists of 27 democratic countries with eight countries having applied for membership. Seventeen countries have adopted the euro and all new member countries must adopt it. NAFTA continues to help Canada, Mexico, and the United States strengthen their global economic power. The U.S.–CAFTA alliance is still trying to get off the ground as is the proposed FTAA. Because of the delays for CAFTA and FTAA, Mercosur (Southern Common Market) will likely take on new importance. ASEAN is a trading alliance of 10 Southeast Asian nations—a region that remains important in the global economy. The African Union and SAARC are relatively new but will continue to see benefits from their alliances. To counteract some of the risks in global trade, the World Trade Organization (WTO) plays an important role in monitoring and promoting trade relationships. The International Monetary Fund (IMF) and the World Bank Group are two entities that provide monetary support and advice to their member countries. The Organization for Economic Cooperation and Development assists its member countries with financial support in achieving sustainable economic growth and employment.

3.3 ⌐LEARNING OUTCOME¬

Describe the structures and techniques organizations use as they go international.

A multinational corporation is an international company that maintains operations in multiple countries. A multidomestic organization is an MNC that decentralizes management and other decisions to the local country (the polycentric attitude). A global organization is an MNC that centralizes management and other decisions in the home country (the ethnocentric attitude). A transnational organization (the geocentric attitude) is an MNC that has eliminated artificial geographical barriers and uses the best work practices and approaches from wherever. Global sourcing is purchasing materials or labor from around the world wherever it is cheapest. Exporting is making products domestically and selling them abroad. Importing is acquiring products made abroad and selling them domestically. Licensing is used by manufacturing organizations that make or sell another company's products and gives that organization the right to use the company's brand name, technology, or product specifications. Franchising is similar but is usually used by service organizations that want to use another company's name and operating methods. A global strategic alliance is a partnership between an organization and foreign company partners in which they share resources and knowledge to develop new products or build facilities. A joint venture is a specific type of strategic alliance in which the partners agree to form a separate, independent organization for some business purpose. A foreign subsidiary is a direct investment in a foreign country that a company creates by establishing a separate and independent facility or office.

3.4 [LEARNING OUTCOME] **Explain** the relevance of the political/legal, economic, and cultural environments to global business.

The laws and political stability of a country are issues in the global political/legal environment with which managers must be familiar. Likewise, managers must be aware of a country's economic issues such as currency exchange rates, inflation rates, and tax policies. Geert Hofstede identified five dimensions for assessing a country's culture, including individualism-collectivism, power distance, uncertainty avoidance, achievement-nurturing, and long-term/short-term orientation. The GLOBE studies identified nine dimensions for assessing country cultures: power distance, uncertainty avoidance, assertiveness, humane orientation, future orientation, institutional collectivism, gender differentiation, in-group collectivism, and performance orientation. The main challenges of doing business globally in today's world include (1) the openness associated with globalization and the significant cultural differences between countries and (2) managing a global workforce, which requires cultural intelligence and a global mind-set.

REVIEW AND DISCUSSION QUESTIONS ✪

1. Contrast ethnocentric, polycentric, and geocentric attitudes toward global business.

2. Describe the current status of each of the various regional trading alliances.

3. Contrast multinational, multidomestic, global, and transnational organizations.

4. What are the managerial implications of a borderless organization?

5. Describe the different ways organizations can go international.

6. Can the GLOBE framework presented in this chapter be used to guide managers in a Russian hospital or a government agency in Egypt? Explain.

7. What challenges might confront a Mexican manager transferred to the United States to manage a manufacturing plant in Tucson, Arizona? Will these issues be the same for a U.S. manager transferred to Guadalajara? Explain.

8. How might the cultural differences in the GLOBE dimensions affect how managers (a) use work groups, (b) develop goals/plans, (c) reward outstanding employee performance, and (d) deal with employee conflict?

PREPARING FOR: My Career
ETHICS DILEMMA ✪

Workers' rights. It's not something we often think about when we're purchasing the latest tech gadget.[77] However, look at this list of some issues that investigations have uncovered: work shifts lasting up to 60 hours; factory explosion killing numerous workers that resulted from a build-up of combustible dust; repetitive motion injuries that are so bad workers lose the use of their hands. "According to recent press reports, that's what work is like for assembly workers in China who build Apple's iPhones, iPads, and iPods." In other locations where workers are assembling products for other tech companies, factory workers have committed suicide because of the pressure and stress. What do you think? Whose responsibility is it to ensure that workplaces are safe, especially when work is outsourced? Should managers even consider such issues as they navigate the global market? Why or why not? One analyst said, "It's a tricky dance between first-world brands and third-world production." What do you think this statement means? What are the implications for managers?

SKILLS EXERCISE Developing Your Collaboration Skill

About the Skill

Collaboration is the teamwork, synergy, and cooperation used by individuals when they seek a common goal. In many cross-cultural settings, the ability to collaborate is crucial. When all partners must work together to achieve goals, collaboration is critically important to the process.

Steps in Practicing the Skill

1. *Look for common points of interest.* The best way to start working together in a collaborative fashion is to seek commonalities that exist among the parties. Common points of interest enable communications to be more effective.

2. *Listen to others.* Collaboration is a team effort. Everyone has valid points to offer, and each individual should have an opportunity to express his or her ideas.

3. *Check for understanding.* Make sure you understand what the other person is saying. Use feedback when necessary.

4. *Accept diversity.* Not everything in a collaborative effort will "go your way." Be willing to accept different ideas and different ways of doing things. Be open to these ideas and the creativity that surrounds them.

5. *Seek additional information.* Ask individuals to provide additional information. Encourage others to talk and more fully explain suggestions. This brainstorming opportunity can assist in finding creative solutions.

6. *Don't become defensive.* Collaboration requires open communications. Discussions may focus on things you and others may not be doing or need to do better. Don't take the constructive feedback as personal criticism. Focus on the topic being discussed, not on the person delivering the message. Recognize that you cannot always be right!

Practicing the Skill

Interview managers from three different organizations about how they collaborate with others. What specific tips have they discovered for effectively collaborating with others? What problems have they encountered when collaborating? How have they dealt with these problems?

WORKING TOGETHER Team Exercise

Moving to a foreign country isn't easy, no matter how many times you've done it or how receptive you are to new experiences. Successful global organizations are able to identify the best candidates for global assignments, and one of the ways they do this is through individual assessments prior to assigning people to global facilities. Form groups of three to five individuals. Your newly formed team, the Global Assignment Task Force, has been given the responsibility for developing a global aptitude assessment form for Yum Brands (the largest food operator in the world whose units include Taco Bell, Pizza Hut, KFC, Long John Silver's, and A&W). Because Yum is expanding its global operations significantly, it wants to make sure it's sending the best possible people to the various global locations. Your team's assignment is to come up with a rough draft of a form to assess people's global aptitude. Think about the characteristics, skills, attitudes, and so on that you think a successful global employee would need. Your team's draft should be at least one-half page but not longer than one page. Be prepared to present your ideas to your classmates and professor.

MY TURN TO BE A MANAGER

- Find two current examples of each of the ways that organizations go international. Write a short paper describing what these companies are doing.

- The U.K.-based company Kwintessential has several cultural knowledge "quizzes" on its Web site [www.kwintessential.co.uk/resources/culture-tests.html]. Go to the Web site and try two or three of them. Were you surprised at your score? What does your score tell you about your cultural awareness?

- On this Web site, you'll also find Country Etiquette Guides. Pick two countries to study (from different regions), and compare them. How are they the same? Different? How would this information help a manager?

- Interview two or three professors or students at your school who are from other countries. Ask them to describe what the business world is like in their country. Write a short paper describing what you found out.

- Take advantage of opportunities you might have to travel to other countries, either on personal trips or on school-sponsored trips.

- Create a timeline illustrating the history of the European Union and a timeline illustrating the history of NAFTA.

- Suppose you were sent on an overseas assignment to another country (you decide which one). Research that country's economic, political/legal, and cultural environments. Write a report summarizing your findings.

- If you don't have your passport yet, go through the process to get one. (The current fee in the United States is $135.)

- Steve's and Mary's suggested readings: H. L. Sirkin, J. W. Hermerling, and A. K. Bhattacharya, *Globality: Competing with Everyone from Everywhere for Everything* (Boston Consulting Group, Inc., 2008); J. Zogby, *The Way We'll Be* (Random House, 2008); Nancy J. Adler, *International Dimensions of Organizational Behavior,* 5th ed. (South-Western Publishing, 2008); Kenichi Ohmae, *The Next Global Stage* (Wharton School Publishing, 2005); John Hooker, *Working Across Cultures* (Stanford Business Books, 2003); and Thomas L. Friedman, *The Lexus and the Olive Tree* (Anchor Books, 2000).

- If you want to better prepare yourself for working in an international setting, take additional classes in international management and international business.

- You've been put in charge of designing a program to prepare your company's managers to go on an overseas assignment. What should (and would) this program include? Be specific. Be thorough. Be creative.

- In your own words, write down three things you learned in this chapter about being a good manager.

- Self-knowledge can be a powerful learning tool. Go to mymanagementlab.com and complete these self-assessment exercises: Am I Well-Suited for a Career as a Global Manager? and What Are My Attitudes Toward Workplace Diversity? Using the results of your assessments, identify personal strengths and weaknesses. What will you do to reinforce your strengths and improve your weaknesses?

MyManagementLab

Go to **mymanagementlab.com** for Auto-graded writing questions as well as the following Assisted-graded writing questions:

3-1. Explain how the global political/legal and economic environments affect managers of global organizations.

3-2. Is globalization good for business? For consumers? Discuss.

3-3. Mymanagementlab Only – comprehensive writing assignment for this chapter.

CASE APPLICATION 1 Dirty Little Secret

Money. Secrecy. Foreign officials. "Greasing palms." Bribery. [78] That's the dirty little secret about doing business globally that managers at multinational companies don't want to talk about. It's illegal for U.S. companies to bribe foreign officials as the Foreign Corrupt Practices Act (FCPA) states. The FCPA resulted from Securities and Exchange Commission investigations in the 1970s in which more than 400 U.S. companies admitted to making questionable payments (some $300 million) to foreign government officials, politicians, and political parties. One major example: Lockheed officials who paid foreign officials to favor their company's products. "Congress enacted the FCPA to bring a halt to the bribery of foreign officials and to restore public confidence in the integrity of the American business system." With the passage of the FCPA, the United States became the first country to explicitly outlaw the practice of bribery.

Although it's illegal for U.S. firms to bribe foreign officials, politicians, and political parties, Walmart's subsidiary in Mexico allegedly paid bribes to local officials to obtain permits for opening new stores in an attempt to accelerate the retailer's expansion in the country.
Source: Daniel Aguilar/Stringer/Getty Images

Recently, however, managers at the world's largest retailer were sent reeling by allegations of bribery in Mexico to accelerate the company's expansion there. An investigation by a reporter for the *New York Times* claimed that Walmart's Mexican subsidiary paid $24 million in bribes to local officials to speed up the granting of permits to open new stores. The investigation also alleges that when evidence of the bribery's vast scope was presented to senior management in the United States, they shut down the probe. As the scenario unfolded, however, the company's board of directors reported that the audit committee was "examining possible violations of the Foreign Corrupt Practices Act and other alleged crimes or misconduct in connection with foreign subsidiaries...." This was the first public disclosure by Walmart that the internal inquiry could possibly involve additional subsidiaries.

DISCUSSION QUESTIONS

1. What's your reaction to these events? Are you surprised that bribery is illegal? Why do you think bribery takes place? Why do you think it needs to be outlawed?

2. Research whether other countries outlaw bribery. (Hint: look at the Organization for Economic Cooperation and Development.)

3. We've said it's important for managers to be aware of external environmental forces, especially in global settings. Discuss this statement in light of the events described.

4. What might Walmart's managers here in the United States and in foreign subsidiaries have done differently? Explain.

5. Walmart is not the only company to be linked to bribery. Find at least three other examples and describe those.

CASE APPLICATION 2 Global Stumble

Since Nomura acquired Lehman's international business as part of its global expansion strategy, Nomura's top managers learned that the cultural and business differences of the two firms in areas such as decision making and the treatment of women created tension among employees.
Source: Reuters/Toru Hanai

It's not always easy to do business globally, as executives at Japanese brokerage firm Nomura Holdings Inc. are discovering.[79] Nomura acquired Lehman's international operations in late 2008 after Lehman's parent company sought Chapter 11 bankruptcy protection—an action that added about 8,000 non-Japanese workers. For Nomura, the time seemed right to strengthen its global expansion strategy. However, since the acquisition, cultural and business differences between the two organizations have been a major stumbling block. Although blending two diverse cultures requires intentional efforts when different organizations merge or are acquired, it's particularly challenging when the key assets in the cross-border acquisition are the people employed by the organization being acquired.

Workplace tensions arose over executive compensation, how quickly decisions were made, and how women were treated. For instance, during Nomura's initial training session for new hires, the men and women were separated. The women—many of whom had earned prestigious degrees from the likes of Harvard—were taught how to wear their hair, serve tea, and choose their clothing according to the season. The company's dress code for women was also strictly interpreted. Women from Lehman were told to remove highlights from their hair, to wear sleeves no shorter than mid-bicep, and to avoid brightly colored clothing. Several women were sent home from the trading floor for dressing "inappropriately." One said, "I was sent home for wearing a short-sleeve dress, even though I was wearing a jacket." A Nomura spokesperson said, "The dress code is displayed on the company's intranet and is intended to ensure that clients and colleagues don't feel uncomfortable."

Lehman bankers also said they found the process for getting approval on deals was "slower and more difficult than it was at Lehman." Also, at Lehman, clients were categorized, in large part, by the fees they paid. At Nomura, more emphasis was placed on other factors, such as the length of the relationship. The bankers at Nomura said that "their new colleagues were too willing to dump loyal clients for a quick profit."

In its defense, Nomura has tried to blend the two cultures. In offices in Europe and in Asia outside of Japan, there's a mix of nationalities. Also, the company has promoted a handful of non-Japanese employees to high-ranking positions. "To reduce the Tokyo-centric nature of the company, Hiromi Yamaji, head of global investment banking, moved to London, and Naoki Matsuba, global head of equities, moved to New York." Until March 2010, Nomura's executive committee was all Japanese men. However, in an attempt to make the company more globally oriented, an ex-Lehman executive and foreigner, Jasjit "Jesse" Bhattal, a native of India, was promoted to the committee. Nomura's deputy president and chief operating officer, Takumi Shibata, said, "When your business is global, management needs to be global." Two years later, unable to garner support from Tokyo for an overhaul of the global wholesale-banking operations, however, Bhattal recently resigned as Nomura's highest-ranking foreign executive.

DISCUSSION QUESTIONS ✪

1. What obvious cultural differences between Nomura and Lehman do you see in this situation?

2. What global attitude do you think characterizes Nomura? Be specific in your description. Do you see any evidence of that changing?

3. Do some cultural research on Japan and the United States. Compare those cultural characteristics. What similarities and differences exist? How might these cultural differences be affecting the situation at Nomura?

4. What could Nomura managers do to support, promote, and encourage cultural awareness among employees? Explain.

5. What do you think the statement, "When your business is global, management needs to be global," is saying? In your opinion, is Nomura doing this? Explain.

ANSWERS TO "WHO OWNS WHAT" QUIZ

1. **d. Switzerland**
   Nestlé SA bought both the Tombstone and DiGiorno frozen-pizza brands from Kraft Foods in 2009.

2. **c. United States**
   The maker of Lebedyansky juices was acquired by PepsiCo Inc. and Pepsi Bottling Group Inc. in March 2008.

3. **a. United States**
   Rajah Spices are products of the Lea & Perrins sauce division, which the H.J. Heinz Company acquired in June of 2005.

4. **b. India**
   Tetley Tea is owned by the Tata Tea Group, a subsidiary of Indian conglomerate Tata Group.

5. **a. Switzerland**
   Nestlé bought control of China's biggest confectioner in 2011.

6. **a. The Netherlands**
   Mexico's second-largest beer producer was acquired by Heineken N.V. in January 2010.

7. **b. Mexico**
   Grupo Bimbo, one of the world's largest bakeries, bought the rights to make and distribute Boboli pizza crusts in 2002.

8. **c. United States**
   General Mills purchased the dairy product maker in 2011.

9. **c. France**
   LVMH Moët Hennessy Louis Vuitton SA, the world's largest luxury-goods group, owns Sephora.

10. **b. Germany**
    German luxury goods company Labelux bought the shoe brand in 2011.

11. **c. Switzerland**
    Nestlé SA purchased the maker of Lean Cuisine frozen meals in 2002.

12. **a. Russia**
    Russian tycoon Alexander Lebedev acquired the *Independent* in March 2010.

13. **b. United Kingdom**
    French's mustard is a product of Reckitt-Benckiser.

14. **a. India**
    Tata Coffee, a division of Indian conglomerate Tata Group, purchased Eight O'Clock Coffee in 2006.

15. **b. United States**
    Consumer products giant Procter & Gamble purchased the luxury hair-care brand from a private equity firm in 2008.

4 Managing Diversity

SPOTLIGHT: *Manager at Work*

Roll the calendar back to the year 2000. *The Coca-Cola Company has just agreed to a record settlement of $192.5 million for a class-action racial discrimination lawsuit.[1] Court documents describe a company atmosphere in which black employees "formed informal networks to provide 'sanity checks' and diversity efforts were not considered a high priority by senior management." Also, as the number of African American hires declined, a "number of highly educated and trained African Americans at the company noted receiving unfavorable treatment, thus creating the impression that Coke was a high-risk environment for high-potential and aggressive African Americans." Now, fast forward to 2012. The Coca-Cola Company is named by Diversity Inc. magazine as number 6 on the list of Top 10 Companies for Blacks and number 6 on the Top 10 Companies for Latinos. How did the company make such a drastic turnaround?*

Since being sued for racial discrimination, Coca-Cola has made considerable strides in its diversity efforts at all levels and in all areas. Commitment from top executives became and remains a cornerstone for managing diversity at the company. CEO Muhtar Kent (who was not CEO at the time of the discrimination problems) says, "Building a diverse and inclusive workforce is central to our 2020 Vision, which calls for us to 'achieve true diversity' throughout our business." Kent (see photo) also personally signs off on executive compensation tied to diversity goals and actions. Coca-Cola's chief diversity officer, Steve

Source: AP Photo/Ric Feld

Bucherati, has managed the company's diversity programs for years. He has been described as a strong and devoted advocate for inclusion and routinely provides Coke's board of directors with reports about diversity initiatives and outcomes.

Source: Manan Vatsyayana/Stringer/ Getty Images

"The real power of diversity is the synergies that are created when different people and cultures come together united behind a common goal..."

One diversity effort that Coca-Cola has encouraged is company-wide business resource groups. These groups—some of which include the Asian group, the African-American group, and the Latino group—provide employees opportunities to connect with colleagues who share similar backgrounds. In another show of top management support, a senior executive is a member of each group. These groups participate in recruiting events, bring experts in to speak on panel discussions of important diversity issues, and partner with customers in community events.

The company also addresses diversity from the legal aspect. Coca Cola's senior managing litigation counsel says its approach to diversity and inclusion

---

MyManagementLab®

⭐ **Improve Your Grade!**

Over 10 million students improved their results using the Pearson MyLabs.
Visit **mymanagementlab.com** for simulations, tutorials, and end-of-chapter problems.

LEARNING OUTCOMES

4.1 | **Define** workplace diversity and explain why managing it is so important.

4.2 | **Describe** the changing workplaces in the United States and around the world.

4.3 | **Explain** the different types of diversity found in workplaces.

4.4 | **Discuss** the challenges managers face in managing diversity.

4.5 | **Describe** various workplace diversity management initiatives.

has four dimensions: (1) internal recruitment, development, promotion, and retention of diverse employees; (2) supplier diversity; (3) surveying, comparing, measuring, and rewarding diversity practices against benchmarks; and (4) developing a "pipeline" of potential diverse applicants.

Besides the legal requirements of diversity, Coca-Cola has recognized that diversity can greatly benefit the company in many ways. CEO Kent says, "The real power of diversity is the synergies that are created when different people and cultures come together united behind a common goal of winning and creating shared value. Extraordinary things truly happen. **"How might**

Coca-Cola get all *its managers involved in diversity efforts?*

Although Coca-Cola's goal of cultivating a diverse workforce is admirable, there's still a lot of work to be done by corporate America. For instance, in the United States, women have been graduating with advanced professional degrees in record numbers, yet the number in senior leadership positions remains low—only 35 women were CEOs of major U.S. corporations in 2012.[2] Clearly, the issue of moving beyond a homogeneous workforce is one that is important for today's managers. In this chapter, we'll look closer at managing diversity of all kinds in the workplace.

4.1 **Define** workplace diversity and explain why managing it is so important.

DIVERSITY 101

Walking through the lobby of one of MGM Resorts International hotels, the company's director of diversity and leadership education notes, "It's amazing all the different languages I can hear.... Our guests come from all over the world, and it makes us realize the importance of reflecting that diversity in our workplace." And MGM's diversity efforts are all "about maximizing 100 percent inclusion of everyone in the organization."[3] Such diversity can be found in many organizational workplaces domestically and globally, and managers in those workplaces are looking for ways to value and develop that diversity, as you'll see through the various examples throughout this chapter. However, before we look at what it takes to manage diversity, we first have to know what workplace diversity is and why it's important.

What Is Workplace Diversity?

Look around your classroom (or your workplace). You're likely to see young/old, male/female, tall/short, blonde hair, blue-eyed/dark hair, brown-eyed, any number of races, and any variety of dress styles. You'll see people who speak up in class and others who are content to keep their attention on taking notes or daydreaming. Have you ever noticed your own little world of diversity where you are right now? Many of you may have grown up in an environment around diverse individuals, while others may not have had that experience. We want to focus on *workplace* diversity, so let's look at what it is. By looking at various ways that diversity has been defined, you'll gain a better understanding of it.

Diversity has been "one of the most popular business topics over the last two decades. It ranks with modern business disciplines such as quality, leadership, and ethics. Despite this popularity, it's also one of the most controversial and least understood topics."[4] With its basis in civil rights legislation and social justice, the word *diversity* often invokes a variety of attitudes and emotional responses in people. Diversity has traditionally been considered a term used by human resources departments, associated with fair hiring practices, discrimination, and inequality. But diversity today is considered to be so much more. Exhibit 4-1 illustrates an historical overview of how the concept and meaning of workforce diversity has evolved.

Let's take a look at some of the ways *diversity* has been defined. For instance, at State Farm, the number one provider of private auto insurance, diversity is viewed as

1960s to 1970s	**Focus on complying with laws and regulations:** Title VII of Civil Rights Act; Equal Employment Opportunity Commission; affirmative action policies and programs	**Exhibit 4-1** Timeline of the Evolution of Workforce Diversity
Early 1980s	**Focus on assimilating minorities and women into corporate setting:** Corporate programs developed to help improve self-confidence and qualifications of diverse individuals so they can "fit in"	
Late 1980s	**Concept of workforce diversity expanded from compliance to an issue of business survival:** Publication of *Workforce 2000* opened business leaders' eyes about the future composition of workforce—that is, more diverse; first use of term *workforce diversity*	
Late 1980s to Late 1990s	**Focus on fostering sensitivity:** Shift from compliance and focusing only on women and minorities to include everyone; making employees more aware and sensitive to the needs and differences of others	
New Millennium	**Focus on diversity and inclusion for business success:** Workforce diversity seen as core business issue; important to achieve business success, profitability, and growth	

Based on "The New Global Mindset: Driving Innovation Through Diversity" by Ernst & Young.

"the collective strength of experiences, skills, talents, perspectives, and cultures that each agent and employee brings to State Farm."[5] Dictionary definitions of diversity refer to variety, differences, multi-formity (instead of uniformity), or dissimilarities (instead of similarities). The Society for Human Resource Management, an association of human resource professionals, says that "diversity is often used to refer to differences based on ethnicity, gender, age, religion, disability, national origin and sexual orientation," but it also encompasses an "infinite range of unique characteristics and experiences, including communication styles, physical characteristics such as height and weight, and speed of learning and comprehension."[6] Another definition says that diversity is all the ways in which people differ.[7] One final definition of diversity is the "array of physical and cultural differences that constitute the spectrum of human differences."[8] One important thing to note about these diversity definitions is that they focus on *all* the ways in which people can differ. And that's significant because diversity is no longer viewed as simply specific categories like race, gender, age, or disability but has broadened to a more inclusive recognition of the spectrum of differences.

So, what's our definition of **workforce diversity**? We're defining it as the ways in which people in an organization are different from and similar to one another. Notice that our definition not only focuses on the differences, but the similarities, of employees. This reinforces our belief that managers and organizations should view employees as having qualities in common as well as differences that separate them. It doesn't mean that those differences are any less important, but that our focus as managers is in finding ways to develop strong relationships with and engage our entire workforce.

We want to point out one final thing about our description of "what" workforce diversity is:[9] The demographic characteristics that we tend to think of when we think of diversity—age, race, gender, ethnicity, and so on—are just the tip of the iceberg. These demographic differences reflect **surface-level diversity**, which are easily perceived differences that may trigger certain stereotypes but that do not necessarily

workforce diversity
The ways in which people in an organization are different from and similar to one another

surface-level diversity
Easily perceived differences that may trigger certain stereotypes, but that do not necessarily reflect the ways people think or feel

deep-level diversity
Differences in values, personality, and work preferences

reflect the ways people think or feel. Such surface-level differences in characteristics can affect the way people perceive others, especially when it comes to assumptions or stereotyping. However, as people get to know one another, these surface-level differences become less important and **deep-level diversity**—differences in values, personality, and work preferences—becomes more important. These deep-level differences can affect the way people view organizational work rewards, communicate, react to leaders, negotiate, and generally behave at work.

Why Is Managing Workforce Diversity So Important?

Ranked number 4 on *Diversity Inc.*'s list of top 50 companies for diversity, voice communications services company AT&T recognizes the powerful benefits of diversity. The company's chief diversity officer says, "We know that diverse, talented and dedicated people are critical to AT&T's success. Investing in a well-educated diverse workforce may be the single most important thing we can to do help America remain the leader in a digital, global economy."[10] BP, the British-owned energy company believes that "supplier diversity—that is, using minority or women suppliers—ensures that it gets the best products and services at the lowest price."[11] Many companies besides AT&T and BP are experiencing the benefits that diversity can bring. In this section, we want to look at *why* workforce diversity is so important to organizations. The benefits fall into three main categories: people management, organizational performance, and strategic. (See Exhibit 4-2.)

PEOPLE MANAGEMENT   When all is said and done, diversity *is*, after all, about people, both inside and outside the organization. The people management benefits that organizations get because of their workforce diversity efforts revolve around attracting and retaining a talented workforce. Organizations want a talented workforce

Exhibit 4-2
Benefits of Workforce Diversity

People Management
- Better use of employee talent
- Increased quality of team problem-solving efforts
- Ability to attract and retain employees of diverse backgrounds

Organizational Performance
- Reduced costs associated with high turnover, absenteeism, and lawsuits
- Enhanced problem-solving ability
- Improved system flexibility

Strategic
- Increased understanding of the marketplace, which improves ability to better market to diverse consumers
- Potential to improve sales growth and increase market share
- Potential source of competitive advantage because of improved innovation efforts
- Viewed as moral and ethical; the "right" thing to do

Sources: Based on Ernst &Young, "The New Global Mindset: Driving InnovationThrough Diversity," EYGM Limited, 2010; M. P. Bell, M. L. Connerley, and F. K. Cocchiara, "The Case for Mandatory Diversity Education," *Academy of Management Learning & Education*, December 2009, pp. 597–609; E. Kearney, D. Gebert, and S. C. Voelpel, "When and How Diversity BenefitsTeams: The Importance ofTeam Members' Need for Cognition," *Academy of Management Journal*, June 2009, pp. 581–598; J. A. Gonzalez and A. S. DeNisi, "Cross-Level Effects of Demography and Diversity Climate on Organizational Attachment and Firm Effectiveness," *Journal of Organizational Behavior*, January 2009, pp. 21–40; O. C. Richard, "Racial Diversity, Business Strategy, and Firm Performance: A Resource-Based View," *Academy of Management Journal*, April 2000, pp. 164–177; and G. Robinson and K. Dechant, "Building a Business Case for Diversity," *Academy of Management Executive*, August 1997, pp. 21–31.

because it's the people—their skills, abilities, and experiences—who make an organization successful. Positive and explicit workforce diversity efforts can help organizations attract and keep talented diverse people and make the best of the talents those individuals bring to the workplace. In addition, another important people management benefit is that as companies rely more on employee teams in the workplace, those work teams with diverse backgrounds often bring different and unique perspectives to discussions, which can result in more creative ideas and solutions. However, recent research has indicated that such benefits might be hard to come by in teams performing more interdependent tasks over a long period of time. Such situations also present more opportunities for conflicts and resentments to build.[12] But, as the researchers pointed out, that simply means that those teams may need stronger team training and coaching to facilitate group decision making and conflict resolution.

ORGANIZATIONAL PERFORMANCE   The performance benefits that organizations get from workforce diversity include cost savings and improvements in organizational functioning. The cost savings can be significant when organizations that cultivate a diverse workforce reduce employee turnover, absenteeism, and the chance of lawsuits. For instance, upscale retailer Abercrombie & Fitch paid $50 million to people who alleged in a lawsuit and two class-action suits that it discriminated against minorities and women.[13] That's an amount of money that can seriously affect an organization's bottom line. In 2011, the Equal Employment Opportunity Commission reported that 99,947 workplace discrimination claims were filed, the highest total number of claims ever. But more startling than the total number of claims filed was the monetary relief obtained for victims, which totaled more than $364 million.[14] Workforce diversity efforts can reduce the risk of such lawsuits. In

let's get REAL

The Scenario

Greg Martin is a mid-level manager at a specialty coffee retailer that's rapidly expanding by opening new stores around the country. He works closely with the new store managers in getting their facilities and operations up and running efficiently and effectively. One of the stumbling blocks he sees again and again revolves around diversity issues—managing a diverse workforce. He knows he could do a better job of training these new managers to welcome and promote diversity.

What advice would you give Greg?

I would advise Greg to research the customer demographics of each store and explain to each manager the percentage of customers and revenue brought in by each group. He must highlight the importance of hiring the right staff to service them properly. He should have all team members take diversity training, which will encourage mutual understanding and build trust among the team.

Shawn Linett
Sales Manager

Source: Shawn Linett

addition, a recent report by recruiting firm Korn/Ferry International found that U.S. companies waste $64 billion annually by losing and replacing employees who leave their jobs "solely due to failed diversity management."[15] That same report noted that 34 percent of those who left jobs because of diversity-related issues would have stayed if managers had recognized their abilities. Another study showed that when organizational biases manifest themselves in incivility toward those who are different, organizational performance is hindered.[16] However, from the positive side, organizational performance *can be* enhanced through workforce diversity because of improved problem-solving abilities and system flexibility. An organization with a diverse workforce can tap into the variety of skills and abilities represented and just the fact that its workforce is diverse requires that processes and procedures be more accommodative and inclusive.

STRATEGIC Organizations also benefit strategically from a diverse workforce. You have to look at managing workforce diversity as the key to extracting the best talent, performance, market share, and suppliers from a diverse country and world. One important strategic benefit is that with a diverse workforce, organizations can better anticipate and respond to changing consumer needs. Diverse employees bring a variety of points of view and approaches to opportunities, which can improve how the organization markets to diverse consumers. For instance, as the Hispanic population has grown, so have organizational efforts to market products and services to that demographic group. Organizations have found their Hispanic employees to be a fertile source of insights that would otherwise not have been available. Food service companies, retailers, financial services companies, and automobile manufacturers are just a few of the industries that have seen sales and market share increases because they paid attention to the needs of diverse consumers using information from employees.

A diverse workforce also can be a powerful source of competitive advantage, primarily because innovation thrives in such an environment. A recent report by Ernst & Young stated that, "Cultural diversity offers the flexibility and creativity we need to re-create the global economy for the twenty-first century."[17] Innovation is never easy, but in a globalized world, it's even more challenging. Tapping into differing voices and viewpoints can be powerful factors in steering innovation. Companies that want to lead their industries have to find ways to "stir the pot"—to generate the lively debate that can create those new ideas. And research shows that diverse viewpoints can do that. "Diversity powers innovation, helping businesses generate new products and services."[18]

Finally, from an ethical perspective, workforce diversity and effectively managing diversity is the right thing to do. Although many societies have laws that say it's illegal to treat diverse people unfairly, many cultures also exhibit a strong ethical belief that diverse people should have access to equal opportunities and be treated fairly and justly. Businesses do have an ethical imperative to build relationships that value and enable all employees to be successful. Managers need to view workforce diversity as a way to bring different voices to the table and to build an environment based on trusting relationships. If they can do that, good things can happen, as we've noted.

THE CHANGING Workplace

4.2 *Describe* the changing workplaces in the United States and around the world.

An African American as the chief executive of the United States. A woman heading up the State Department. A Latina sitting on the nation's highest court. Even at the highest levels of the political arena, we see a diverse workplace. In the business world, the once predominantly white male managerial workforce has given way to a more gender-balanced, multi-ethnic workforce. But it's a workforce still in transition as the overall population changes. In this section, we want to look at some of those changes, focusing on demographic trends by looking first at the characteristics of the U.S. population and then at global diversity trends. These trends will be reflected in a changing workplace, thus making this information important for managers to recognize and understand.

Characteristics of the U.S. Population

"For the first time in U.S. history, whites of European ancestry account for less than half of newborn children, marking a demographic tipping point that is already changing the nation's politics, economy, and workforce."[19] Statistics from the latest U.S. Census reports are reinforcing what we've already seen happening—America is changing.[20] We are an increasingly diverse society with some major readjustments occurring that will dramatically change the face of America by the year 2050. Let's look at some of the most dramatic of these changes.[21]

- **Total population of the United States:** The total population is projected to increase to 438 million by the year 2050, up from 296 million in 2005; 82 percent of that increase will be due to immigrants and their U.S.-born descendants. Nearly one in five Americans will be an immigrant in 2050, compared with one in eight in 2005.
- **Racial/ethnic groups:** In addition to total population changes, the components of that population are projected to change as well. Exhibit 4-3 provides the projected population breakdown. As the projections show, the main changes will be in the percentages of the Hispanic and white population. But the data also indicate that the Asian population will almost double.
- **An aging population.** As a nation, our population is aging. According to the CIA *World Factbook*, the median age of the U.S. population stands at 36.9 years, up from 36.2 years in 2001.[22] That's quite a change, although not unexpected. In the first half of the twentieth century, America was a relatively "young" country—the result of lots of babies born, declining infant and childhood mortality, and high rates of immigration. By 2050, however, one in every five persons will be aged 65 or over. The "oldest" of this group—those aged 80 and over—will be the most populous age group comprising 8 percent of the entire U.S. population. "Aging will continue to be one of the most important defining characteristics of the population."[23]

As you can probably imagine, such population trends are likely to have a major impact on U.S. workplaces. What workplace changes might we see?

According to the U.S. Bureau of Labor Statistics, by the year 2016, 47 percent of the labor force will be women and 37 percent will be Black, Latino, Asian/Pacific Islander, American Indian, or multiple racial categories.[24] In addition, by 2016, the average age of an employee will be 42.1 years.[25] The immigration issue is also likely to be a factor in a changing workplace. According to an analysis released by the U.S. Census Bureau, nearly one in six American workers is foreign-born, the

	2005	2050
Foreign-born	12%	19%
Racial/Ethnic Groups		
White*	67%	47%
Hispanic	14%	29%
Black*	13%	13%
Asian*	5%	9%

*= Non-Hispanic
American Indian/Alaska Native not included.

Exhibit 4-3
Changing Population Makeup of the United States

Source: Based on "U.S. Hispanic population to triple by 2050" by Haya El Nasser, from *USA Today*, February 12, 2008; and "U.S. Population Projections: 2005–2050" by Jeffrey Passel and D'Vera Cohn from Pew Research Center, February 11, 2008.

In this photo, young employees of Alibaba Group enjoy celebrating "Alibaba Day," a company event that allows employees to bring their children, parents, and pets to work. Based in Hangzhou, China, Alibaba Group is a fast-growing e-commerce firm that has become the world's largest online platform for trade between businesses. With a population that accounts for almost 20 percent of the world population, China is currently a developing nation that is experiencing the "demographic dividend" of a rising proportion of young people entering the workforce. Equipped with Internet-technology skills, these young workers are boosting Alibaba's productivity and China's economic growth.
Source: ChinaFotoPress/Newscom

highest proportion since the 1920s.[26] Despite the perception that the surge in immigration, especially over the last two decades, has flooded the United States with low-wage foreign labor, a new analysis of census data indicates that's not the reality. In 14 of the 25 largest metropolitan areas, more immigrants were employed in white-collar occupations than in lower-wage jobs like construction, cleaning, or manufacturing.[27] And now, with the total number of immigrants increasing dramatically, this, too, is likely to affect workplaces. Finally, people now entering the workforce are significantly younger, more ethnically diverse, and/or foreign-born. In fact, by the year 2016, it's forecasted that 68 percent of new entrants in the U.S. workforce will be women or people of color.[28] The reality of these trends for businesses is that they'll have to accommodate and embrace such workforce changes. Although America historically has been known as a "melting pot" where people of different nationalities, religions, races, and ethnicities have blended together to become one, that perspective is no longer relevant. Organizations must recognize that they can't expect employees to assimilate into the organization by adopting similar attitudes and values. Instead, there's value in the differences that people bring to the workplace. It's not been easy. The ability of managers and organizations to effectively manage diversity has not kept pace with these population changes, creating challenges for minorities, women, and older employees. But many businesses are excelling at managing diversity, and we'll discuss some of their workplace diversity initiatives in a later section of this chapter.

What About Global Workforce Changes?

Some significant worldwide population trends also are likely to affect global workforces. According to United Nations forecasts, "The world is in the midst of an epochal demographic shift that will reshape societies, economies, and markets over the next century."[29] Let's look at two of these trends.[30]

- **Total world population.** The total world population in 2012 is estimated at over almost 7.023 billion individuals.[31] However, that number is forecasted to hit 9 billion by 2050, at which point the United Nations predicts the total population will either stabilize or peak after growing for centuries at an ever-accelerating rate. The main reason for this major shift is the decline in birthrates as nations advance economically. However, in developing countries in Africa, Asia, Latin America, the Caribbean, and Oceania, birthrates remain high. One of the benefits is that many of these countries are likely to experience a "demographic dividend: a rising proportion of young people entering the workforce, driving productivity and economic growth."[32]
- **An aging population.** This demographic trend is one of critical importance for organizations. How critical? "The world's population is now aging at an *unprecedented rate.*"[33] How much do *you* know about global aging? (Our guess is . . . probably not much!) Take the quiz in Exhibit 4-4—no peeking at the answers beforehand—and see how well you scored. Were you surprised by some of the answers?

When we say the world's population is aging, some of the realities of this trend are hard to even fathom. For instance, people aged 65 and older will soon outnumber children under age 5 for the *first* time in history. Also, the world's population aged 80 and over is projected to increase 233 percent by 2040. The implications of these trends for societies and businesses are profound—from changing family structures to shifting patterns of work and retirement to emerging economic challenges based on increasing demands on social entitlement programs, dwindling labor supply, and

1. True or False: The world's children under age 5 outnumber people aged 65 and over.

2. The world's older population (65 and older) increased by approximately how many people each month in 2008?
   a. 75,000
   b. 350,000
   c. 600,000
   d. 870,000

3. Which of the world's developing regions has the highest percentage of older people?
   a. Africa
   b. Latin America
   c. The Caribbean
   d. Asia

4. True or False: More than half of the world's older people live in the industrialized nations of Europe, North America, Japan, and Australia.

5. Which country had the world's highest percentage of older people in 2008?
   a. Sweden
   b. Japan
   c. Spain
   d. Italy

Answers to quiz:

1. *True.* Although the world's population is aging, children still outnumber older people as of 2008. Projections indicate, however, that in fewer than 10 years, older people will outnumber children for the first time in history.

2. *d.* The estimated change in the total size of the world's older population between July 2007 and July 2008 was more than 10.4 million people, an average of 870,000 each month.

3. *c.* The Caribbean, with 7.8 percent of all people aged 65 and over in 2008. Numbers for the other regions: Latin America, 6.4 percent; Asia (excluding Japan), 6.2 percent; and Africa, 3.3 percent.

4. *False.* Although industrialized nations have higher percentages of older people than most developing countries, 62 percent of all people aged 65 and over now live in the developing regions of Africa, Asia, Latin America, the Caribbean, and Oceania.

5. *b.* Japan, with 22 percent of its population aged 65 or over, has supplanted Italy as the world's oldest major country.

Source: Based on "An Aging World: 2008," by K. Kinsella and W. He, from U.S. Census Bureau/International Population Reports, June 2009.

Exhibit 4-4
Global Aging: How Much Do You Know?

declining total global savings rates. Such demographic shifts will reshape the global workforce and organizational workplaces. Again, managers and organizations need to understand how such changes are likely to affect future workplace policies and practices.

TYPES of Workplace Diversity

Explain the different 4.3 types of diversity found in workplaces.

As we've seen so far, diversity is a big issue, and an important issue, in today's workplaces. What types of dissimilarities—that is, diversity—do we find in those workplaces? Exhibit 4-5 shows several types of workplace diversity. Let's work our way through the different types.

Exhibit 4-5
Types of Diversity Found
in Workplaces

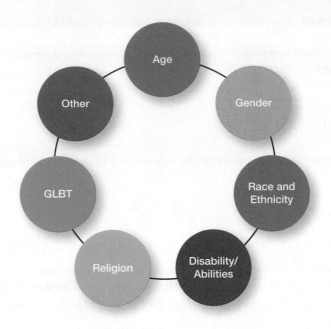

Age

The Marriott hotel group, headquartered in Bethesda, Maryland, employs more than 100,000 employees in the United States. What's interesting is that 43 percent of those employees are age 45 and older, and 18 percent are 55 and older.[34] Company managers are "finding ways for older workers to better handle tasks such as bending, stretching, lifting, pushing, and pulling." For instance, an older employee may be paired with a younger one, and tasks such as bending to clean under beds are shared.

As we saw in the last section, the aging population is a major critical shift taking place in the workforce. With many of the nearly 85 million baby boomers still employed and active in the workforce, managers must ensure that those employees are not discriminated against because of age. Both Title VII of the Civil Rights Act of 1964 and the Age Discrimination in Employment Act of 1967 prohibit age discrimination. And the Age Discrimination Act also restricts mandatory retirement at specific ages. In addition to complying with these laws, organizations need programs and policies in place that provide for fair and equal treatment of their older employees.

One issue with older workers is the perception that people have of those workers. Perceptions such as they're sick more often and they can't work as hard or as fast as younger employees—perceptions that are inaccurate. Employers have mixed feelings about older workers.[35] On the positive side, they believe that older workers bring a number of good qualities to the job including experience, judgment, a strong work ethic, and a commitment to doing quality work. However, they also view older workers as not being flexible or adaptable and being more resistant to new technology. The challenge for managers is overcoming those misperceptions of older workers and the widespread belief that work performance and work quality decline with age.

Another issue that also supports the need for effectively managing workplace age diversity is that when baby boomers do retire, experts point out that some industries will face severe shortages of qualified employees. "Many of today's growth industries require a higher level of technical competence in quantitative reasoning, problem solving, and communication skills...and the United States simply does not have enough students who are getting solid math and science education."[36] Organizations that do not plan for such a future may find themselves struggling to find a competent workforce, diverse or not. However, one "fly in the ointment" is that the lingering economic recession has altered the retirement plans of many older workers.[37] According to a survey by the Employee Benefit Research Institute, 1 in 5 workers say they aren't going to retire on time. In fact, these workers say they are more than twice as likely to work up to age 70 or older.[38]

Finally, the aging population is not the only age-related issue facing organizations. Some 50 million Generation Xers juggle work and family responsibilities. And now some 76 million members of Generation Y are either already in or poised to enter the workforce.[39] These Gen Yers will make up about 50 percent of the workforce by 2014 and 75 percent of the workforce by 2025.[40] Having grown up in a world where they've had the opportunity to experience many different things, Gen Y workers bring their own ideas and approaches to the workplace. Managers need to ensure that these workers, regardless of age, also are treated fairly and as valuable assets. Effectively managing an organization's diverse age groups can lead to their working well with each other, learning from each other, and taking advantage of the different perspectives and experiences that each has to offer. It can be a win-win situation for all.

Gender

Women (49.8%) and men (50.2%) now each make up almost half of the workforce.[41] Yet, gender diversity issues are still quite prevalent in organizations. Take the gender pay gap. The latest information on the ratio of women's to men's median weekly earnings showed the figure at 80.2; the ratio for median annual earnings stood at 77.1.[42] Other issues involve career start and progress. Recent research by Pew Research Center does show that young women now place more importance on having a high-paying career or profession than young men.[43] Yet, although 57 percent of today's college students are women, and women now collect nearly 60 percent of four-year degrees and are just as likely to have completed college and hold an advanced degree, inequities persist.[44] Research by Catalyst found that men start their careers at higher levels than women. And after starting out behind, women don't ever catch up. Men move further up the career ladder and faster as well.[45] Finally, misconceptions, mistaken beliefs, and unsupported opinions still exist about whether women perform their jobs as well as men do. You can see why gender diversity issues are important to attend to. So what *do* we know about differences between men and women in the workplace?

First of all, few, if any, important differences between men and women affect job performance.[46] No consistent male-female differences exist in problem-solving ability, analytical skills, competitive drive, motivation, sociability, or learning ability. Psychological research has found minor differences: Women tend to be more agreeable and willing to conform to authority while men are more aggressive and more likely to have expectations of success.

Another area where we also see differences between genders is in preference for work schedules, especially when the employee has preschool-age children. To accommodate their family responsibilities, working mothers are more likely to prefer part-time work, flexible work schedules, and telecommuting. They also prefer jobs that encourage work–life balance.

One question of much interest as it relates to gender is whether men and women are equally competent as managers. Research evidence indicates that a "good" manager is still perceived as predominantly masculine.[47] But the reality is that women tend to use a broader, more effective range of leadership styles to motivate and engage people. They usually blend traditional masculine styles—being directive, authoritative, and leading by example—with more feminine ones that

These employees of IBM India are listening to a speaker at a Winspiration leadership conference in Bangalore, India, that IBM organized to encourage its female employees in the workplace and to enhance their leadership and networking skills. The advancement of women is a key diversity initiative for IBM India, where the company is committed to recruit, retain, and promote the best female staff available and to ensure that women remain key to IBM's business success. IBM India relies heavily on mentoring and coaching programs for women to develop their careers and creates a work environment where they can balance their work, family, education, and other personal needs. *Source: AP Photo/Aijaz Rahi*

include being nurturing, inclusive, and collaborative. Men tend to rely primarily on masculine styles.[48] Another study showed that women managers were significantly more likely than their male counterparts to coach and develop others and to create more committed, collaborative, inclusive, and ultimately, more effective, teams. This study also found that women were more likely to foster genuine collaboration while males were far more likely to view negotiations and other business transactions as zero-sum games.[49]

What should you take away from this discussion? Not that either women or men are the superior employees, but a better appreciation for why it's important for organizations to explore the strengths that both women and men bring to an organization and the barriers they face in contributing fully to organizational efforts. And, it's important to note that many companies *are* "grooming more women for the corner office." The pool of highly qualified women continues to grow as those who have received advanced degrees and worked in the corporate world are moving up through the ranks. In fact, recent research by McKinsey & Co found that 24 percent of senior vice presidents at 58 big companies are women. [50]

Race and Ethnicity

Go back and re-read the chapter opener, especially the material that describes the "old" way of doing things at Coca-Cola. Many other companies have had similar racial issues. There's a long and controversial history in the United States and in other parts of the world over race and how people react to and treat others of a different race.[51] Race and ethnicity are important types of diversity in organizations. We're going to define **race** as the biological heritage (including physical characteristics such as one's skin color and associated traits) that people use to identify themselves. Most people identify themselves as part of a racial group. Such racial classifications are an integral part of a country's cultural, social, and legal environments. The racial choices on the 2010 Census included white, black, American Indian or Alaska Native, Asian, Native Hawaiian or other Pacific Islander, and some other race. This last choice, which was on the 2000 Census form for the first time, provided respondents the opportunity to identify themselves as multi-racial.[52] The Census Bureau's chief of the racial statistics branch says, "Multiracial Americans are one of the fastest-growing demographic groups in the country."[53] **Ethnicity** is related to race, but it refers to social traits—such as one's cultural background or allegiance—that are shared by a human population.

As we saw earlier in Exhibit 4-3, the racial and ethnic diversity of the U.S. population is increasing at an exponential rate. We're also seeing this same effect in the composition of the workforce. Most of the research on race and ethnicity as they relate to the workplace has looked at hiring decisions, performance evaluations, pay, and workplace discrimination.[54] However, much of that research has focused on the differences in attitudes and outcomes between Whites and African Americans. Minimal study has been done on issues relevant to Asian, Hispanic, and Native American populations. Let's look at a few key findings.

One finding is that individuals in workplaces tend to favor colleagues of their own race in performance evaluations, promotion decisions, and pay raises. Although such effects are small, they are consistent. Next, research shows substantial racial differences in attitudes toward affirmative action, with African Americans favoring such programs to a greater degree than Whites. Other research shows that African Americans generally do worse than Whites in decisions related to the workplace. For instance, in employment interviews, African Americans receive lower ratings. In the job setting, they receive lower job performance ratings, are paid less, and are promoted less frequently. However, no statistically significant differences between the two races are observed in absenteeism rates, applied social skills at work, or accident rates. As you can see, race and ethnicity issues are a key focus for managers in effectively managing workforce diversity.

race
The biological heritage (including skin color and associated traits) that people use to identify themselves

ethnicity
Social traits (such as cultural background or allegiance) that are shared by a human population

let's get REAL

The Scenario

Katie Harris is a manager in a branch office of a large insurance claims company. She manages a diverse team of 15 people. One of her team members stopped in to tell her that "several of them were upset that other team members were talking in their native language throughout the day." Their complaint? They felt it was "rude" for co-workers to speak another language at work, and it made the other team members feel excluded and uncomfortable.

What should Katie do to resolve this issue?

Katie should thank this team member for bringing "their concern" to her attention. Once she confirms that the complaint is in fact a group concern, she should create awareness by bringing up the subject during a branch meeting. Although it is not wrong for anyone to speak in their native language, it may be perceived as disrespectful. She should set ground rules to encourage common courtesy and respect among the team.

Kelly Osorio
Human Resources Manager

Disability/Abilities

According to the U.S. Census Bureau, people with disabilities are the largest minority in the United States. Estimates vary, but it's believed that there are some 19.8 million working-age Americans with disabilities. And that number continues to increase as military troops return from Iraq and Afghanistan.[55]

1990 was a watershed year for persons with disabilities. That was the year the Americans with Disabilities Act (ADA) became law. ADA prohibits discrimination against an individual who is "regarded as" having a disability and requires employers to make reasonable accommodations so their workplaces are accessible to people with physical or mental disabilities and enable them to effectively perform their jobs. With the law's enactment, individuals with disabilities became a more representative and integral part of the U.S. workforce.

One issue facing managers and organizations is that the definition of disability is quite broad. The U.S. Equal Employment Opportunity Commission classifies a person as disabled if he or she has any physical or mental impairment that substantially limits one or more major life activities. For instance, deafness, chronic back pain, AIDS, missing limbs, seizure disorder, schizophrenia, diabetes, and alcoholism would all qualify. However, since these conditions have almost no common features, it's been difficult to study how each condition affects employment. It's obvious that some jobs cannot be accommodated to a disability. For instance, the law recognizes that a visually impaired person could not be an airline pilot, a person with severe cerebral palsy could not be a surgeon, and a person with profound mobility constraints could not be a firefighter. However, computer technology and other adaptive devices have shattered many employment barriers for other employees with disabilities.

A recent survey by the Society for Human Resource Management found that 61 percent of the HR professionals responding said that their organizations now include disabilities in their diversity and inclusion plans. However, only 47 percent said that their organizations actively recruit individuals with disabilities. And 40 percent said that their senior managers demonstrate a strong commitment to do so.[56] Even after

Exhibit 4-6

Employers' Fears About
Disabled Workers

➤ *FEAR: Hiring people with disabilities leads to higher employment costs and lower profit margins*
  • **REALITY:** Absentee rates for sick time are virtually equal between employees with and without disabilities; workers' disabilities are not a factor in formulas calculating insurance costs for workers' compensation

➤ *FEAR: Workers with disabilities lack job skills and experience necessary to perform as well as their abled counterparts*
  • **REALITY:** Commonplace technologies such as the Internet and voice-recognition software have eliminated many of the obstacles for workers with disabilities; many individuals with disabilities have great problem-solving skills from finding creative ways to perform tasks that others may take for granted

➤ *FEAR: Uncertainty over how to take potential disciplinary action with a worker with disabilities*
  • **REALITY:** A person with a disability for whom workplace accommodations have been provided has the same obligations and rights as far as job performance

➤ *FEAR: High costs associated with accommodating disabled employees*
  • **REALITY:** Most workers with disabilities require *no* accommodation but for those who do, more than half of the workplace modifications cost $500 or less

Sources: Based on "Disabled Workers: Employer Fears Are Groundless," by R. Braum, from *Bloomberg BusinessWeek,* October 2, 2009; and "Survey of Employer Perspectives on the Employment of People with Disabilities" from U.S. Department of Labor/Office of Disability Employment Policy, November 2008.

20-plus years of the ADA, organizations and managers still have fears about employing disabled workers. A survey by the U.S. Department of Labor looked at these unfounded fears.[57] Exhibit 4-6 describes some of those fears as well as the reality, that is, what it's really like. Let's look at one company's experience. Walgreen has hired individuals with mental and physical disabilities to work at its distribution center in Anderson, South Carolina.[58] These employees work in one of three departments: case check-in (where merchandise initially comes in), de-trash (where merchandise is unpacked), or picking (where products are sorted into tubs based on individual store orders). Using an innovative approach that included job coaches, automated processes, and comprehensive training, Walgreens now has a capable and trusted workforce. The company's senior vice president of distribution said, "One thing we found is they (the disabled employees) can all do the job. What surprised us is the environment that it's created. It's a building where everybody helps each other out."

In effectively managing a workforce with disabled employees, managers need to create and maintain an environment in which employees feel comfortable disclosing their need for accommodation. Those accommodations, by law, need to enable individuals with disabilities to perform their jobs but they also need to be perceived as equitable by those not disabled. That's the balancing act that managers face.

Religion

In her sophomore year at college, Hani Khan worked for three months as a stock clerk at a Hollister clothing store in San Francisco.[59] One day, she was told by her supervisors to remove the head scarf that she wears in observance of Islam (known as a *hijab*) because it violated the company's "look policy" (which instructs employees on clothing, hair styles, makeup, and accessories they may wear to work). She refused on religious grounds and was fired one week later. Like a number of other Muslim women, she filed a federal job discrimination complaint. A spokesperson for Abercrombie & Fitch (Hollister's parent company) said, "If any Abercrombie associate identifies a religious conflict with an Abercrombie policy...the company will work with the associate in an attempt to find an accommodation." Although that's a step in the right direction, recently in Kansas City, Missouri, a Muslim woman won a $5 million discrimination lawsuit against AT&T for repeated harassment of her religious beliefs.[60]

Title VII of the Civil Rights Act prohibits discrimination on the basis of religion (as well as race/ethnicity, country of origin, and sex). Today, it seems that the greatest religious diversity issue in the United States revolves around Islam, especially after 9/11.[61] Islam is one of the world's most popular religions, and some 2 million Muslims live in the United States. For the most part, U.S. Muslims have attitudes similar to those of other U.S. citizens. However, there are real and perceived differences. For instance, nearly 4 in 10 U.S. adults admit they harbor negative feelings or prejudices toward U.S. Muslims, and 52 percent believe U.S. Muslims are not respectful of women.

Religious beliefs also can prohibit or encourage work behaviors. Many conservative Jews believe they should not work on Saturdays. Some Christians do not want to work on Sundays. Religious individuals may believe they have an obligation to express their beliefs in the workplace, making it uncomfortable for those who may not share those beliefs. Some pharmacists have refused to give out certain kinds of contraceptives on the basis of their beliefs.

As you can see, religion and religious beliefs can generate misperceptions and negative feelings. You'd probably not be surprised to find out that the number of religious discrimination claims has been growing in the United States.[62] The latest EEOC statistics showed that 4,151 religious-based complaints were filed in 2011.[63] In accommodating religious diversity, managers need to recognize and be aware of different religions and their beliefs, paying special attention to when certain religious holidays fall. Try to accommodate, when at all possible, employees who have special needs or requests, but do so in a way that other employees don't view it as "special treatment."

GLBT: Sexual Orientation and Gender Identity

The acronym GLBT—which refers to gay, lesbian, bisexual, and transgender people—is used more frequently and relates to the diversity of sexual orientation and gender identity.[64] There are an estimated 7 million GLBT employees in the U.S. private sector.[65] Sexual orientation has been called the "last acceptable bias."[66] We want to emphasize that we're not condoning this perspective, but what this comment refers to is that most people understand that racial and ethnic stereotypes are "off-limits," but it's not unusual to hear derogatory comments about gays or lesbians. U.S. federal law does not prohibit discrimination against employees on the basis of sexual orientation, although many states and municipalities do. In 29 states, in fact, workers can be fired for being gay.[67] However, in Europe, the Employment Equality Directive required all European Union member states to introduce legislation making it unlawful to discriminate on grounds of sexual orientation.[68] Despite the progress in making workplaces more accommodating of gays and lesbians, much more needs to be done. One study found more than 40 percent of gay and lesbian employees indicated they had been unfairly treated, denied a promotion, or pushed to quit their job because of their sexual orientation.[69] Another study found that "closeted" GLBTs who felt isolated at work were 73 percent more likely to leave their job within three years than "out" workers.[70]

Employers in the United States have taken differing approaches to their treatment of sexual orientation.[71] Many have adopted a variation of the "don't ask, don't tell" policy that the military used to have. Some just flat out do not hire any GLBT employees. However, according to a report from the Human Rights Campaign Foundation, 85 percent of the largest corporations in the United States now prohibit employment discrimination based on sexual orientation, and 35 percent prohibit bias based on gender identity.[72] An increasing number of large companies are implementing policies and practices to protect the rights of GLBT employees in the workplace. For instance, Ernst & Young, S. C. Johnson & Sons, Inc., and Kodak, among others,

---

*data*points[73]

45 percent of women and 61 percent of men have asked for a raise at work.

73 percent of CEOs say there is a business case for gender diversity.

57 percent of CEOs say that gender diversity is a top 10 strategic priority.

2 times the number of Blacks, Latinos, and Asians in management is what companies with executive diversity councils have.

79 percent of survey respondents believe that there is a definite generation gap.

75 percent of corporate executives believe that having minorities in senior executive positions is important.

78 percent of employees say their companies do not practice diversity in their workforces as much as they claim publicly.

all provide training to managers on ways to prevent sexual orientation discrimination. A diversity manager at IBM says, "We believe that having strong transgender and gender identification policies is a natural extension of IBM's corporate culture."[74] And more than 59 percent of the largest corporations in the United States now offer their employees health insurance benefits for domestic partners.[75] A recent study analyzed the effect of company GLBT nondiscrimination policies on that company's stock market value. The findings suggest that the stock prices of companies with more progressive GLBT policies outperform those of competitors in the same industry that don't have such policies.[76]

As with most of the types of diversity we've discussed in this section, managers need to look at how best to meet the needs of their GLBT employees. They need to respond to employees' concerns while also creating a safe and productive work environment for all.

Other Types of Diversity

As we said earlier, diversity refers to *any* dissimilarities or differences that might be present in a workplace. Other types of workplace diversity that managers might confront and have to deal with include socioeconomic background (social class and income-related factors), team members from different functional areas or organizational units, physical attractiveness, obesity/thinness, job seniority, or intellectual abilities. Each of these types of diversity also can affect how employees are treated in the workplace. Again, managers need to ensure that all employees—no matter the similarities or dissimilarities—are treated fairly and given the opportunity and support to do their jobs to the best of their abilities.

4.4 | ***Discuss*** *the challenges managers face in managing diversity.*

CHALLENGES in Managing Diversity

Nooses, racist graffiti, and Confederate battle flags should have been enough to warrant action. However, the discovery that he was paid less as a painter than white workers is what finally prompted an African American employee to complain to his employer, Texas-based Turner Industries Group LLC.[77] Soon after filing the complaint, he was fired. His complaints, along with those of seven other employees, "have led the federal government to conclude there was evidence of racial discrimination." Despite the benefits that we know workforce diversity brings to organizations, managers still face challenges in creating accommodating and safe work environments for diverse employees. In this section, we're going to look at two of those challenges: personal bias and the glass ceiling.

Personal Bias

Smokers. Working mothers. Football players. Blondes. Female president of the United States. Hispanic. What impressions come to mind when you read these words? Based on your background and experiences, you probably have pretty specific ideas and things you would say, maybe even to the point of characteristics you think that all smokers or all working mothers or all Hispanics share. Employees can and do bring such ideas about various groups of people with them into the workplace. Such ideas can lead to prejudice, discrimination, and stereotypes—all of which shape and influence our personal biases.

bias
A tendency or preference toward a particular perspective or ideology

Bias is a term that describes a tendency or preference toward a particular perspective or ideology. It's generally seen as a "one-sided" perspective. Our personal biases cause us to have preconceived opinions about people or things. Such preconceived opinions can create all kinds of inaccurate judgments and attitudes. Let's take a look at how our personal biases affect the way we view and respond to diversity.

prejudice
A preconceived belief, opinion, or judgment toward a person or a group of people

One outcome of our personal biases can be **prejudice**, a preconceived belief, opinion, or judgment toward a person or a group of people. Our prejudice can be based on all the types of diversity we discussed: race, gender, ethnicity, age, disability, religion, sexual orientation, or even other personal characteristics.

A major factor in prejudice is **stereotyping**, which is judging a person on the basis of one's perception of a group to which he or she belongs. For instance, "Married persons are more stable employees than single persons" is an example of stereotyping. Keep in mind, though, that not all stereotypes are inaccurate. For instance, asking someone in accounting about a budgeting problem you're having would be an appropriate assumption and action. However, many stereotypes—red-haired people have a bad temper, elderly drivers are the most dangerous, working mothers aren't as committed to their careers as men are, and so forth—aren't factual and distort our judgment.

Both prejudice and stereotyping can lead to someone treating others who are members of a particular group unequally. That's what we call **discrimination**, which is when someone acts out their prejudicial attitudes toward people who are the targets of their prejudice. You'll find in Exhibit 4-7 definitions and examples of

stereotyping
Judging a person based on a perception of a group to which that person belongs

discrimination
When someone acts out their prejudicial attitudes toward people who are the targets of their prejudice

Exhibit 4-7
Forms of Discrimination

Type of Discrimination	Definition	Examples from Organizations
Discriminatory policies or practices	Actions taken by representatives of the organization that deny equal opportunity to perform or unequal rewards for performance	Older workers may be targeted for layoffs because they are highly paid and have lucrative benefits.[a]
Sexual harassment	Unwanted sexual advances and other verbal or physical conduct of a sexual nature that create a hostile or offensive work environment	Salespeople at one company went on company-paid visits to strip clubs, brought strippers into the office to celebrate promotions, and fostered pervasive sexual rumors.[b]
Intimidation	Overt threats or bullying directed at members of specific groups of employees	African American employees at some companies have found nooses hanging over their work stations.[c]
Mockery and insults	Jokes or negative stereotypes; sometimes the result of jokes taken too far	Arab Americans have been asked at work whether they were carrying bombs or were members of terrorist organizations.[d]
Exclusion	Exclusion of certain people from job opportunities, social events, discussions, or informal mentoring; can occur unintentionally	Many women in finance claim they are assigned to marginal job roles or are given light workloads that don't lead to promotion.[e]
Incivility	Disrespectful treatment, including behaving in an aggressive manner, interrupting the person, or ignoring his or her opinions	Female lawyers note that male attorneys frequently cut them off or do not adequately address their comments.[f]

Notes:

a. J. Levitz and P. Shishkin, "More Workers Cite Age Bias After Layoffs," *Wall Street Journal,* March 11, 2009, pp. D1–D2.

b. W. M. Bulkeley, "A Data-Storage Titan Confronts Bias Claims," *Wall Street Journal*, September 12, 2007, pp. A1, A16.

c. D. Walker, "Incident with Noose Stirs Old Memories," *McClatchy-Tribune Business News,* June 29, 2008; and D. Solis, "Racial Horror Stories Keep EEOC Busy," *Knight-Ridder Tribune Business News,* July 30, 2005, p. 1.

d. H. Ibish and A. Stewart, *Report on Hate Crimes and Discrimination Against Arab Americans: The Post-September 11 Backlash, September 11, 2001–October 11, 2001* (Washington, DC: American-Arab Anti-Discrimination Committee, 2003).

e. A. Raghavan, "Wall Street's Disappearing Women," *Forbes,* March 16, 2009, pp. 72–78.

f. L. M. Cortina, "Unseen Injustice: Incivility as Modern Discrimination in Organizations."

Source: S. Robbins and T. Judge, *Organizational Behavior,* 15th ed., Prentice Hall, p. 43.

LEADER who made a DIFFERENCE

Dr. Rohini Anand, senior vice president and global chief diversity officer at Sodexo, says her job is to carry out the vision that "diversity and inclusion would result in Sodexo being able to identify and develop the best talent and create an environment where employees could thrive and deliver outstanding service solutions to clients and customers." [79] Anand, who grew up in India, was "surrounded by others who looked like me, but had variation by socioeconomic status or religion." It was when she moved to the United States that she was first perceived as a minority, which led her to the work she does today. After earning her PhD from the University of Michigan, Anand worked in various corporate and government positions and came to Sodexo in 2003. Under her intelligent and compassionate leadership, the company is consistently in the top two or three on DiversityInc.'s Top Companies for Diversity list. And it's easy to see why. From the CEO down, there is a strong commitment to integrating diversity and inclusion throughout the organization. What can you learn from this leader who made a difference?

different types of discrimination. Many of these actions are prohibited by law so you won't find them discussed in employee handbooks or organizational policy statements. However, you can still see these actions in workplaces. "As discrimination has increasingly come under both legal scrutiny and social disapproval, most overt forms have faded, which may have resulted in an increase in more covert forms like incivility or exclusion." [78]

Discrimination, whether intentional or not, can lead to serious negative consequences for employers as illustrated by the example we discussed at the beginning of this chapter and section. But it's not just the potential financial consequences organizations and managers face for discriminatory actions. It's the reduced employee productivity, negative and disruptive interpersonal conflicts, increased employee turnover, and overall negative climate that can lead to serious problems for managers. Even if an organization has never had an employment discrimination lawsuit filed against it, managers need to aggressively work to eliminate unfair discrimination.

Glass Ceiling

Pretend you've just finished your MBA degree. It's not been easy. Your graduate classes were challenging, but you feel well-prepared for and excited about that first post-MBA job. If you're female, that first job for 60 percent of you will be an entry-level position. However, if you're male, only 46 percent of you would start out in an entry-level position. [80] And 2 percent of women would make it to the CEO or senior executive position, although 6 percent of men would. "Although entry into occupations such as accounting, business, and law happens at about the same rate for men and women, evidence is mounting that women's and men's career paths begin to divide soon after." [81] This issue can be seen with minorities as well. Only a small percentage of both male and female Hispanics and African Americans have made it into management positions in the United States. What's going on here? After all these years of "equal opportunity," why do we still see statistics like these?

glass ceiling
The invisible barrier that separates women and minorities from top management positions

In the 1980s, the term **glass ceiling**, first used in a *Wall Street Journal* article, refers to the invisible barrier that separates women and minorities from top management positions. [82] The idea of a "ceiling" means something is blocking upward movement and the idea of "glass" is that whatever's blocking the way isn't immediately apparent.

Research on the glass ceiling has looked at identifying the organizational practices and interpersonal biases that have blocked women's advancement. Findings from those studies have ranged from lack of mentoring, sex stereotyping, views that associate masculine traits with leader effectiveness, and bosses' perceptions of family–work conflict. [83]

As others have said, it's time to shatter the glass ceiling for all employees. Every employee should have the opportunity to work in a career in which they can use their skills and abilities and to have a career path that allows them to progress as far as they want to go. Getting to that end, however, isn't going to be easy. As we'll see in the next section, there are a number of workplace diversity initiatives that organizations can implement to work toward that end.

WORKPLACE **Diversity Initiatives**

"Marriott International is the textbook definition of a great company for diversity."[84] Bill Marriott, the company's chairman and CEO, is a visible force and advocate for diversity both in the company and externally. He personally signs off on bonuses for his top staff, which are tied to diversity efforts and ability to meet diversity goals, an amount that can account for 13 percent of their compensation. The company also has mandatory diversity training every month and a number of employee resource groups that provide input and advice. Their diversity management efforts have earned the company the number 21 spot on the Top 50 Companies for Diversity list for 2012.

As the Marriott example shows, some businesses *are* effectively managing diversity. In this section, we look at various workplace diversity initiatives; however, before we start discussing these, we first look at the legal framework within which diversity efforts take place.

The Legal Aspect of Workplace Diversity

Would workplaces have evolved to the level of diversity that currently exists without federal legislation and mandates?[85] Although it's an interesting question, the fact is that federal laws *have* contributed to some of the social change we've seen over the last 50-plus years. Exhibit 4-8 describes the major equal employment opportunity laws with which organizations must comply. Failure to do so, as we have seen in some of the examples we've described, can be costly and damaging to an organization's bottom line and reputation. It's important that managers know what they can and cannot do legally and ensure that all employees understand as well.

Describe various **4.5** *workplace diversity management initiatives.*

Exhibit 4-8
Major Equal Employment Opportunity Laws

Year	Law or Ruling	Description
1963	Equal Pay Act	Prohibits pay differences for equal work based on gender
1964 (amended in 1972)	Civil Rights Act, Title VII	Prohibits discrimination based on race, color, religion, national origin, or gender
1967 (amended in 1978)	Age Discrimination in Employment Act	Prohibits discrimination against employees 40 years and older
1978	Pregnancy Discrimination Act	Prohibits discrimination against women in employment decisions on the basis of pregnancy, childbirth, and related medical decisions
1978	Mandatory Retirement Act	Prohibits the forced retirement of most employees
1990	Americans with Disabilities Act	Prohibits discrimination against individuals who have disabilities or chronic illnesses; also requires reasonable accommodations for these individuals
1991	Civil Rights Act of 1991	Reaffirms and tightens prohibition of discrimination and gives individuals right to sue for punitive damages
1993	Family and Medical Leave Act	Gives employees in organizations with 50 or more employees up to 12 weeks of unpaid leave each year for family or medical reasons
2009	Lilly Ledbetter Fair Pay Act	Changes the statute of limitations on pay discrimination to 180 days from each paycheck

However, effectively managing workplace diversity needs to be more than understanding and complying with federal laws. Organizations that are successful at managing diversity use additional diversity initiatives and programs. We're going to look at four of these, including top management commitment, mentoring, diversity skills training, and employee resource groups.

Top Management Commitment to Diversity

Today's increasingly competitive marketplace underscores the reality that creating a diverse workplace has never been more important. It's equally important to make diversity and inclusion an integral part of the organization's culture. "A sustainable diversity and inclusion strategy must play a central role in decision making at the highest leadership level and filter down to every level of the company."[86] How do organizational leaders do that?

One of the first things to do is make sure that diversity and inclusion are part of the organization's purpose, goals, and strategies. Look back at our chapter opener. That's one of the things that The Coca-Cola Company does. Even during economically challenging times, an organization needs a strong commitment to diversity and inclusion programs. Diversity needs to be integrated into every aspect of the business—from the workforce, customers, and suppliers to products, services, and the communities served. Policies and procedures must be in place to ensure that grievances and concerns are addressed immediately. Finally, the organizational culture needs to be one where diversity and inclusion are valued, even to the point where, like Marriott International, individual performance is measured and rewarded on diversity accomplishments.

mentoring
A process whereby an experienced organizational member (a mentor) provides advice and guidance to a less experienced member (a protégé)

A gospel choir affinity group at Nissan Motor Company's automotive plant in Canton, Mississippi, brings together a diverse group of employees from technicians to salaried workers who all share a love of singing. Directed by the plant's human resources director, the gospel choir performs for company executives, state officials, and community events. In addition to fishing clubs, basketball teams, and other affinity groups at the plant, the gospel choir builds relationships and respect among co-workers and inspires a team spirit. Nissan's top managers are committed to diversity initiatives that also include mentoring and skills training for employees and programs for dealers and suppliers.
Source: AP Photo/Rogelio V. Solis

Mentoring

One of the consequences of having few women and minorities in top corporate leadership positions is that lower-level diverse employees lack someone to turn to for support or advice. That's where a mentoring program can be beneficial. **Mentoring** is a process whereby an experienced organizational member (a mentor) provides advice and guidance to a less-experienced member (a protégé). Mentors usually provide two unique forms of mentoring functions: career development and social support.[87]

Andrea Jung, former CEO of Avon Products, the first woman to hold that job in the female-oriented products company, said her male mentor (previous CEO James Preston) had the most influence on her career.[88] A study by Catalyst of male mentors to women found that men who impeded or who were indifferent to the progress of women viewed the workplace as a zero-sum game where promotion of women came at the expense of men. However, one thing that stood out among males who championed women was a strong sense of fairness.[89]

A good mentoring program would be aimed at all diverse employees with high potential to move up the organization's career ladder. Exhibit 4-9 looks at what a good mentor does. If an organization is serious about its commitment to diversity, it needs to have a mentoring program in place.

Diversity Skills Training

"The only thing in human DNA is to discriminate. It's a part of normal human tribal behavior."[90] In a chapter on managing diversity, you might be surprised to find a statement like this. However, the reality is—it's reality. Our human nature is to not

- Provides instruction
- Offers advice
- Gives constructive criticism
- Helps build appropriate skills
- Shares technical expertise
- Develops a high-quality, close, and supportive relationship with protégé
- Keeps lines of communication open
- Knows when to "let go" and let the protégé prove what he/she can do

Sources: Based on J. Prime and C. A. Moss-Racusin, "Engaging Men in Gender Initiatives: What Change Agents Need to Know," *Catalyst* [www.catalyst.org], 2009; T. J. DeLong, J. J. Gabarro, and R. J. Lees, "Why Mentoring Matters in a Hypercompetitive World," *Harvard Business Review,* January 2008, pp. 115–121; S. N. Mehta, "Why Mentoring Works," *Fortune,* July 9, 2001, p. 119; and D. A. Thomas, "Race Matters: The Truth About Mentoring Minorities," *Harvard Business Review,* April 2001, pp. 99–107.

Exhibit 4-9
What a Good Mentor Does

accept or approach anything that's different from us. But it doesn't make discrimination of any type or form acceptable. And we live and work in a multicultural context. So the challenge for organizations is to find ways for employees to be effective in dealing with others who aren't like them. That's where **diversity skills training**—specialized training to educate employees about the importance of diversity and teach them skills for working in a diverse workplace—comes in. It's estimated that some $80 billion has been spent over the last 10 years on diversity programs, much of it on training.[91]

Most diversity skills training programs start with *diversity awareness training.* During this type of training, employees are made aware of the assumptions and biases they may have. Once we recognize that, we can look at increasing our sensitivity and openness to those who are different from us. Sounds simple, but it's not. However, if people can be taught to recognize that they're prejudging people and to consciously address that behavior, then the diversity awareness training has been successful. The next step is *diversity skills training*, in which people learn specific skills on how to communicate and work effectively in a diverse work environment. At Sodexo, the food services/facilities management company, employee diversity training is an important part of its diversity management program. The company's global chief diversity officer said, "As an organization, we have worked to implement the right policies, but more importantly, empower all our employees to understand issues of diversity and work to ensure change happens at every level of our company."[92]

diversity skills training
Specialized training to educate employees about the importance of diversity and teach them skills for working in a diverse workplace

Employee Resource Groups

Kellogg Company, the cereal corporation, is a pioneer in workplace diversity. More than 100 years ago, company founder W. K. Kellogg employed women in the workplace and reached across cultural boundaries. That commitment to diversity continues today. The company's CEO attributes much of the company's success to the wide variety of histories, experiences, ideas, and perspectives employees have brought to the business.[93] Kellogg's has been very supportive of its various **employee resource groups**, made up of employees connected by some common dimension of diversity. Such groups typically are formed by the employees themselves, not the organizations. However, it's important for organizations to recognize and support these groups.

Employee resource groups (also called employee networks or affinity groups) have become quite popular over the last 10 years.[94] Why are they so prevalent? The main reason is that diverse groups have the opportunity to see that their existence is acknowledged and that they have the support of people within and outside the group. Individuals in a minority often feel invisible and not important in

employee resource groups
Groups made up of employees connected by some common dimension of diversity

the overall organizational scheme of things. Employee resource groups provide an opportunity for those individuals to have a voice. For instance, at Kellogg, there's a WOK (Women of Kellogg) group, a KAARG (Kellogg African American Resource Group), !HOLA! (Kellogg's Latino Employee Resource Group), K-MERG (Kellogg Multinational Employee Resource Group), and YP (Kellogg Young Professionals Employee Resource Group). The description for WOK explains that this group of employees fosters the personal and professional growth and development of women at Kellogg Company. The statements about the other groups are similar in describing the commitment to empowering, leveraging, and fostering the development of the individual members of the resource group. Through these employee resource groups, those in a minority find they're not alone—and that can be a powerful means of embracing and including all employees, regardless of their differences.

MyManagementLab
Go to **mymanagementlab.com** to complete the problems marked with this icon .

PREPARING FOR: Exam/Quizzes
CHAPTER SUMMARY by Learning Outcomes

4.1 [LEARNING OUTCOME]

Define workplace diversity and explain why managing it is so important.

Workplace diversity is the ways in which people in an organization are different from and similar to one another. Managing workforce diversity is important for three reasons: (1) people management benefits—better use of employee talent, increased quality of team problem-solving efforts, and ability to attract and retain diverse employees; (2) organizational performance benefits—reduced costs, enhanced problem-solving ability, and improved system flexibility; and (3) strategic benefits—increased understanding of diverse marketplace, potential to improve sales and market share, competitive advantage because of improved innovation efforts, and viewed as moral and ethical.

4.2 [LEARNING OUTCOME]

Describe the changing workplaces in the United States and around the world.

The main changes in the workplace in the United States include the total increase in the population; the changing components of the population, especially in relation to racial/ethnic groups; and an aging population. The most important changes in the global population include the total world population and the aging of that population.

4.3 [LEARNING OUTCOME]

Explain the different types of diversity found in workplaces.

The different types of diversity found in workplaces include age (older workers and younger workers), gender (male and female), race and ethnicity (racial and ethnic classifications), disability/abilities (people with a disability that limits major life activities), religion (religious beliefs and religious practices), sexual orientation and gender identity (gay, lesbian, bisexual, and transgender), and other (for instance, socioeconomic background, team members from different functional areas, physical attractiveness, obesity, job seniority, and so forth).

4.4 [LEARNING OUTCOME]

Discuss the challenges managers face in managing diversity.

The two main challenges managers face are personal bias and the glass ceiling. Bias is a tendency or preference toward a particular perspective or ideology. Our biases can lead to prejudice, which is a preconceived belief, opinion, or judgment toward a person or a group of people; stereotyping, which is judging a person on the basis of one's perception of a group to which he or she belongs; and discrimination, which is when someone acts out their prejudicial attitudes toward people who are the targets of their prejudice. The glass ceiling refers to the invisible barrier that separates women and minorities from top management positions.

4.5 [LEARNING OUTCOME]

Describe various workplace diversity management initiatives.

It's important to understand the role of federal laws in diversity. Some of these laws include Title VII of the Civil Rights Act, the Americans with Disabilities Act, and Age Discrimination in Employment Act. Workplace diversity management initiatives include top management commitment to diversity; mentoring, which is a process whereby an experienced organizational member provides advice and guidance to a less experienced member; diversity skills training; and employee resource groups, which are groups made up of employees connected by some common dimension of diversity.

REVIEW AND DISCUSSION QUESTIONS ✪

1. Why is it important for an organization to have a clear definition of diversity?

2. Distinguish between surface-level diversity and deep-level diversity. Why is it important to understand the difference between the two?

3. What are the major trends in the changing populations of the United States and the world?

4. Distinguish between race and ethnicity.

5. What challenges do managers face in creating accommodating and safe work environments for employees?

6. Explain the relationship between bias, prejudice, stereotyping, and discrimination.

7. What U.S. federal laws are important to workplace diversity initiatives?

8. Why do you think the glass ceiling has proven to be a barrier to women and minorities?

PREPARING FOR: My Career
ETHICS DILEMMA ✪

Smokers. Overweight individuals. Two groups about whom a lot has been written and much discussion takes place, especially when it comes to workplaces. A recent Gallup poll found that most Americans said that if they were in a position to hire someone, it would make no difference to them if that person were overweight (79 percent) or smoked (74 percent.) However, the majority of Americans (60 percent) said it is justified to set higher health insurance rates for smokers. A majority (57 percent) also said it is *un*justified to set higher insurance rates because someone is very overweight. What do you think about these statistics? Do you think they reflect how people really feel? What biases, prejudices, and stereotypes do people have of smokers and overweight people? What ethical issues might arise in workplaces with individuals who fit into these two groups? As a manager, how might you handle such issues?

SKILLS EXERCISE   Developing Your Valuing Diversity Skill

About the Skill

Understanding and managing people who are similar to us are challenges—but understanding and managing people who are dissimilar from us and from each other can be even tougher.[95] The diversity issues a manager might face are many. They may include issues such as communicating with employees whose familiarity with the language may be limited; creating career development programs that fit the skills, needs, and values of a particular group; helping a diverse team cope with a conflict over goals or work assignments; or learning which rewards are valued by different groups.

Steps in Practicing the Skill

1. *Fully accept diversity.* Successfully valuing diversity starts with each individual accepting the principle of diversity. Accept the value of diversity for its own sake—not simply because it's the right thing to do. And

it's important that you reflect your acceptance in all you say and do.

2. *Recruit broadly.* When you have job openings, work to get a diverse applicant pool. Although referrals from current employees can be a good source of applicants, that source tends to produce candidates similar to the present workforce.

3. *Select fairly.* Make sure the selection process doesn't discriminate. One suggestion is to use job-specific tests rather than general aptitude or knowledge tests. Such tests measure specific skills, not subjective characteristics.

4. *Provide orientation and training for diverse employees.* Making the transition from outsider to insider can be particularly difficult for a diverse employee. Provide support either through a group or through a mentoring arrangement.

5. *Sensitize nondiverse employees.* Not only do you personally need to accept and value diversity, as a manager you need to encourage all your employees to do so. Many organizations do this through diversity training programs. In addition, employees can also be part of ongoing discussion groups whose members meet monthly to discuss stereotypes and ways of improving diversity relationships. The most important thing a manager can do is show by his or her actions that diversity is valued.

6. *Strive to be flexible.* Part of valuing diversity is recognizing that different groups have different needs and values. Be flexible in accommodating employee requests.

7. *Seek to motivate individually.* Motivating employees is an important skill for any manager; motivating a diverse workforce has its own special challenges. Managers must strive to be in tune with the background, cultures, and values of employees.

8. *Reinforce employee differences.* Encourage individuals to embrace and value diverse views. Create traditions and ceremonies that promote diversity. Celebrate diversity by accentuating its positive aspects. However, also be prepared to deal with the challenges of diversity such as mistrust, miscommunication, lack of cohesiveness, attitudinal differences, and stress.

Practicing the Skill

Read through the following scenario. Write down some notes about how you would handle the situation described. Be sure to refer to the eight behaviors described for valuing diversity.

Scenario

Read through the descriptions of the following employees who work for the same organization. After reading each description, write a short paragraph describing what you think the goals and priorities of each employee might be. With what types of employee issues might the manager of each employee have to deal? How could these managers show that they value the diversity represented by each?

Lester. Lester is 57 years old, a college graduate, and a vice president of the firm. His two children are married, and he is a grandparent of three beautiful grandchildren. He lives in a condo with his wife who does volunteer work and is active in their church. Lester is healthy and likes to stay active, both physically and mentally.

Sanjyot. Sanjyot is a 30-year-old clerical worker who came to the United States from Indonesia 10 years ago. She completed high school after moving to the United States and has begun to attend evening classes at a local community college. Sanjyot is a single parent with two children under the age of 8. Although her health is excellent, one of her children suffers from a severe learning disability.

Yuri. Yuri is a recent immigrant from one of the former Soviet republics. He is 42 and his English communication skills are quite limited. He has an engineering degree from his country but since he's not licensed to practice in the United States, he works as a parts clerk. He is unmarried and has no children but feels obligated to send much of his paycheck to relatives back in his home country.

WORKING TOGETHER Team Exercise

Employee resource groups continue to be popular. Form small groups with three or four other class members. Your task is to research how to form employee resource groups for staff members at your school. Come up with a written plan that discusses the benefits and challenges of employee resource groups, the steps to follow in creating these groups, and suggestions for maintaining the value of such groups for their members. Be prepared to turn in your written report to your professor or to present it in class.

MY TURN TO BE A MANAGER

- Describe your experiences with people from other backgrounds. What challenges have you faced? What have you learned that will help you in understanding the unique needs and challenges of a diverse workplace?

- Go to *DiversityInc.com* [www.diversityinc.com] and find the latest list of Top 50 Companies for Diversity. Select three companies from this list. Describe and evaluate what they're doing as far as workplace diversity.

- Think of times when you may have been treated unfairly because of stereotypical thinking. What stereotypes were being used? How did you respond to the treatment?

- Go to the website of Catalyst [www.catalyst.org] and find the Research & Knowledge tab. Click on "Browse Research & Knowledge." Search for the data on "Women in Management, Global Comparison." What surprised you the most about this data? Why?

- Find two examples of companies that are doing each of the four workplace diversity initiatives. Write a short description of what each is doing.

- Steve's and Mary's suggested readings: C. Harvey and M. J. Allard, *Understanding and Managing Diversity,* 5th ed. (Upper Saddle River, NJ: Pearson Prentice Hall,

2012); S. Thiederman, *Making Diversity Work: 7 Steps for Defeating Bias in the Workplace,* 2nd ed. (New York: Kaplan Publishing, 2008); A. M. Konrad, P. Prasad, and J. K. Pringle (eds.), *Handbook of Workplace Diversity* (Thousand Oaks, CA: Sage Publications, 2006); and G. N. Powell, *Managing a Diverse Workforce,* 2nd ed. (Thousand Oaks, CA: Sage Publications, 2004).

• Pick one of the laws listed in Exhibit 4-8. Research that law looking for these elements: Whom does the law cover? What does the law prohibit? What are the consequences for violating the law?

• Write down three things you learned in this chapter about being a good manager.

• Self-knowledge can be a powerful learning tool. Go to mymanagementlab.com and complete any of these self-assessment exercises: What Are My Attitudes Toward Workplace Diversity? Am I Well-Suited for a Career as a Global Manager? What's My Attitude Toward Older People? and What Are My Gender Role Perceptions? Using the results of your assessments, identify personal strengths and weaknesses. What will you do to reinforce your strengths and improve your weaknesses?

MyManagementLab

Go to **mymanagementlab.com** for Auto-graded writing questions as well as the following Assisted-graded writing questions:

4-1. What is workforce diversity, and why is managing it so important?

4-2. Describe the issues associated with each of the types of workforce diversity.

4-3. Mymanagementlab Only – comprehensive writing assignment for this chapter.

CASE APPLICATION 1 From Top to Bottom

Diversity management is the bottom line at PricewaterhouseCoopers (PwC), a professional services company. [96] And the company's commitment to diversity puts them at the top of the list for Top Companies for Diversity as determined by *DiversityInc*. So what does a company do to be recognized as the number one company for diversity management? Well, it starts at the top.

PwC's chairman and senior partner Bob Moritz is a vocal advocate of diversity and inclusion and says that "it's also the key to sustainable global growth for an organization." Moritz's commitment to diversity stems from his personal experiences. As a young professional, he lived in Japan for three years where he was a minority. He recalls, "If you're overseas or in a country where no one speaks your language—or the cab refuses to pick you up in the middle of the night because you're a foreigner—you get a different perspective." In addition, his work team included individuals from France, Australia, the United Kingdom, and Japan. He soon recognized that people from different cultures approach problems with differing perspectives and that his way wasn't necessarily the right way and certainly not the only way. That's why now as the company's top executive, he realizes that to help his company succeed in today's global economy, an inclusive culture that attracts and retains diverse talent is critical.

Finding, engaging, and promoting the best and brightest group of diverse employees such as the professionals shown here counting Oscar ballots for the Academy of Motion Picture Arts and Sciences is a top priority of PwC's commitment to diversity.
Source: Reuters/Jonathan Alcorn

PwC also has several diversity programs and initiatives in place. The company's first chief diversity officer (CDO) was appointed in 2003 and like at many organizations, was first "housed" in the human resources department. Now, however, the CDO reports directly to Moritz, giving the position credibility and more importantly, accountability. Another interesting thing about PwC's CDO position is that it is rotating—that is, partners are rotated in and out of the role every two years. Currently, that position belongs to Maria Castanón Moats, an audit partner.

Another diversity commitment that PwC has made is to talent development. Professional services companies like PwC prosper or fail because of their human talent. PwC has made it a priority to "find, engage, and promote the best and brightest employees, especially those from underrepresented groups." To attract such outstanding diverse talent, the company offers employees an enviable array of benefits. Because work at professional services companies can be arduous and demanding, PwC has looked for ways to offer its employees work–life flexibility to deal with personal and professional challenges. Some of the benefits it offers includes back-up childcare assistance, paid paternity leave, nanny resources and referrals, onsite religious accommodations, well-being rewards, and tax equalization for all domestic partners.

Finally, a major key to PwC's diversity management is its mentoring program, which has been described as "world class." A mentor is a senior employee who sponsors and supports a less experienced employee, called a protégé. Although half of the company's mentoring pairings are cross-cultural, Moritz has asked each of PwC's 2,500 partners to "consciously diversify their pool of protégés." A portion of the partners' evaluations will be based on their advocacy and investment in these individuals. But PwC doesn't just expect its employees to know what to do in mentoring. A toolkit for successful advocacy was created that includes guidelines, suggested readings, and other internal resources. And the most important part of that toolkit? Videos showing real-life examples of partners and staff members sharing their personal experiences with mentoring.

DISCUSSION QUESTIONS ⊘

1. How might population trends affect a professional services organization like PwC? What might it have to do to adapt to these trends?

2. What challenges might PwC face in adapting to a more diverse applicant pool of college graduates?

3. Businesses often face the dilemma of retaining diverse employees once they're trained. What can PwC do to retain its diverse employees?

4. What advantages do you think PwC's mentoring program provides? What potential drawbacks might there be?

5. PwC's "rotating" chief diversity officer is an unusual approach. What advantages do you see to such an arrangement? Drawbacks?

CASE APPLICATION 2 Women in Management at Deutsche Telekom

Believing that having more women in top leadership positions will help Deutsche Telekom to operate better, CEO Rene Obermann (center) has added two women to the firm's management board—Maria Schick (left), as head of human resources, and Claudia Nemat, as head of European operations.
Source: Michael Gottschalk/AP Images

Companies across Europe have a problem—a large gender gap in leadership.[97] Men far outnumber women in senior business leadership positions. This dismal picture of sexism in Europe exists despite efforts and campaigns to try and ensure equality in the workplace. But one European company is tackling the problem head-on.

Deutsche Telekom, Europe's largest telecommunication company, says it intends to "more than double the number of women who are managers within five years." In addition, it plans to increase the number of women in senior and middle management to 30 percent by the end of 2015. With this announcement, the company becomes the first member of the DAX 30 index of blue-chip German companies to introduce a gender quota. Deutsche's chief executive René Obermann said, "Taking on more women in management positions is not about the enforcement of misconstrued egalitarianism. Having a greater number of women at the top will quite simply enable us to operate better."

In addition to its plans to intensify recruiting of female university graduates, Deutsche Telekom will need to make changes in its corporate policies and practices to attract and keep women in management positions.

So what is Deutsche Telekom doing to achieve its goal of bringing more women into management positions? One action the company is taking is to increase and improve recruiting of female university graduates. In fact, the company has committed to having at least 30 percent of the places in executive development programs held by women.

Other steps being taken by the company revolve around the work environment and work–family issues. The company plans to expand its parental-leave programs and introduce more flexible working hours for managers. Right now, fewer than 1 percent of the company's managers work part time. In addition, the company plans to double the number of available places in company child-care programs. The company also has realized it needed to become more transparent in its selection and appointment processes and to monitor whether recruiting and retention goals had been reached. Despite its efforts, Deutsche Telekom has struggled with its gender goal. In 2011, only about 13 percent of senior executives in Germany were female, just a bit more than the pre-quota 12.5 percent. In other locations, however, the company has made progress. About 28 percent of Deutsche Telekom's leadership positions outside Germany are held by women, up from 24 percent in 2010.

DISCUSSION QUESTIONS ✪

1. What do you think of this "quota" approach that Deutsche Telekom is pursuing? What benefits and drawbacks does such an approach have?

2. What issues might Deutsche Telekom face in recruiting female university graduates? How could they address these issues?

3. What issues might the company face in introducing changes in work–family programs? Again, how could they address these issues?

4. What workplace diversity initiatives discussed in the chapter might be appropriate for Deutsche Telekom? What would be involved in implementing these initiatives?

5 Managing Social Responsibility and Ethics

SPOTLIGHT: *Manager at Work*

What started as a high-profile corporate espionage case turned into an enormously confusing, bewildering, and embarrassing mess for French car maker Renault SA and its top executives.[1] The story began in August 2010 when several top executives received an anonymous tip accusing a senior Renault executive of negotiating a bribe in return for information. The bribe was supposedly for information related to the cost of the company's electric car. According to CEO Carlos Ghosn (see photo on the next page), this information was critical economic data that could give competitors insight into the car's technology and its costs.

Renault's chief operating officer, Patrick Pélata (see photo below), launched a four-month internal investigation that led the company to conclude that "it was the target of a system organized to collect economic, technological and strategic information to serve interests

abroad." A company spokesperson also said that the company's compliance committee was alerted to possible unethical practices involving three employees. Renault then lodged a criminal complaint of "organized industrial espionage, corruption, breach of trust, theft and concealment" and

Source: Christophe Petit Tesson/ MAXPPP/Newscom

dismissed three executives who worked on its electric car program for allegedly leaking information in exchange for money. Ghosn said, "The action that has been taken by the company is designed to protect the company." He declared on a French evening

Source: Alexandre Marchi/PHOTOPQR/ L'Est REPUBLICAIN/Newscom

What started as a high-profile corporate espionage case turned into a confusing, bewildering, and embarrassing mess for Renault SA and its top executives.

news program on January 23, 2011, that Renault had "abundant proof and total certainty that the trio had been passing company secrets to outside sources." But the story takes an interesting twist here as these three men repeatedly denied any wrongdoing and asserted their innocence from the beginning.

Doubts began surfacing about the alleged spying when the Paris state prosecutor dismissed charges against the three fired executives for lack of evidence—the three were, in fact, innocent. Renault, for the first time, began suggesting the company may

---

MyManagementLab®
⭐ Improve Your Grade!
Over 10 million students improved their results using the Pearson MyLabs.
Visit **mymanagementlab.com** for simulations, tutorials, and end-of-chapter problems.

LEARNING OUTCOMES

5.1 | **Discuss** what it means to be socially responsible and what factors influence that decision.

5.2 | **Explain** green management and how organizations can go green.

5.3 | **Discuss** the factors that lead to ethical and unethical behavior.

5.4 | **Describe** management's role in encouraging ethical behavior.

5.5 | **Discuss** current social responsibility and ethics issues.

have been "tricked" into bringing the allegations against these men. Then, French prosecutors began trying to figure out whether someone had engineered the entire affair as a way to defraud the company. The French police had not found any foreign accounts into which the three executives were said to have deposited their spying proceeds, but they did find accounts in Spain and Dubai holding some of the money that Renault had given the head of its security division, who led the internal inquiry against his three colleagues.

Mr. Ghosn publicly apologized to the three fired managers and fully cleared them of any wrongdoing. He also promised full compensation, "taking into account the grave human prejudice that these three executives and their families suffered." Renault's board also had some things to say. Mr. Pélata stepped down as chief operating officer. Three other junior executives and three people in the company's security organization who handled the investigation of the bogus spying operations were fired. The board also demanded that the company create an ethics committee, restructure its compliance committee, and create a "world-class security organization." **How might Renault's managers have handled this situation more ethically and responsibly?**

What a story this was! (And who says management is boring?) Deciding when and how ethical and socially responsible an organization needs to be are examples of the complicated types of issues that managers, such as Carlos Ghosn and other Renault executives, may have to cope with as they plan, organize, lead, and control. As managers manage, these issues can and do influence their actions.

·5.1 *Discuss* what it means to be socially responsible and what factors influence that decision.

WHAT Is Social Responsibility?

Organizations profess their commitment to sustainability and package their products in non-recyclable materials. Companies have large pay inequities; however, the difference is often not linked to employee performance, but to entitlement and "custom." Large global corporations lower their costs by outsourcing to countries where human rights are not a high priority and justify it by saying they're bringing in jobs and helping to strengthen the local economies. Businesses facing a drastically changed economic environment offer employees reduced hours and early retirement packages. Are these companies being socially responsible? Managers regularly face decisions that have a dimension of social responsibility in areas such as employee relations, philanthropy, pricing, resource conservation, product quality and safety, and doing business in countries that devalue human rights. What does it mean to be socially responsible?

From Obligations to Responsiveness to Responsibility

The concept of *social responsibility* has been described in different ways. For instance, it's been called "profit making only," "going beyond profit making," "any discretionary corporate activity intended to further social welfare," and "improving social or environmental conditions."[2] We can understand it better if we first compare it to two similar concepts: social obligation and social responsiveness.[3] **Social obligation** is when a firm engages in social actions because of its obligation to meet certain economic and legal responsibilities. The organization does what it's obligated to do and nothing more. This idea reflects the **classical view** of social responsibility, which says that management's only social responsibility is to maximize profits. The most outspoken advocate of this approach is economist and Nobel laureate Milton Friedman. He argued that managers' primary responsibility is to operate the business in the best interests of the stockholders, whose primary concerns are financial.[4] He also argued that when managers decide to spend the organization's resources for "social good," they add to the costs of doing business, which

social obligation
When a firm engages in social actions because of its obligation to meet certain economic and legal responsibilities

classical view
The view that management's only social responsibility is to maximize profits

have to be passed on to consumers through higher prices or absorbed by stockholders through smaller dividends. Friedman doesn't say that organizations shouldn't be socially responsible, but his interpretation of social responsibility is to maximize profits for stockholders—a view still held by some today. An advisory firm that works with major corporations says, "Companies would achieve more social good by simply focusing on the bottom line rather than social responsibility programs."[5]

The other two concepts—social responsiveness and social responsibility—reflect the **socioeconomic view**, which says that managers' social responsibilities go beyond making profits to include protecting and improving society's welfare. This view is based on the belief that corporations are *not* independent entities responsible only to stockholders, but have an obligation to the larger society. Organizations around the world have embraced this view as shown by a survey of global executives in which 84 percent said that companies must balance obligations to shareholders with obligations to the public good.[6] But how do these two concepts differ?

Social responsiveness is when a company engages in social actions in response to some popular social need. Managers are guided by social norms and values and make practical, market-oriented decisions about their actions.[7] For instance, Ford Motor Company became the first automaker to endorse a federal ban on sending text messages while driving. A company spokesperson said: "The most complete and most recent research shows that activity that draws drivers' eyes away from the road for an extended period while driving, such as text messaging, substantially increases the risk of accidents."[8] By supporting this ban, company managers "responded" to what they felt was an important social need. When the disastrous earthquake and tsunami hit Japan in 2011, many tech companies responded with resources and support. For instance, social networking giant Facebook set up a Japan earthquake page for users to find information about disaster relief. After the Haiti earthquake in January 2010, many companies responded to the immense needs in that region. For instance, UPS has a company-wide policy that urges employees to volunteer during natural disasters and other crises. In support of this policy, UPS maintains a 20-person logistics emergency team in Asia, Europe, and the Americas that's trained in humanitarian relief.[9]

A socially *responsible* organization views things differently. It goes beyond what it's obligated to do or chooses to do because of some popular social need and does what it can to help improve society because it's the right thing to do. We define **social responsibility** as a business's intention, beyond its legal and economic obligations, to do the right things and act in ways that are good for society.[10] Our definition assumes that a business obeys the law and cares for its stockholders, but adds an ethical imperative to do those things that make society better and not to do those that make it worse. A socially responsible organization does what is right because it feels it has an ethical responsibility to do so. For example, according to our definition, Abt Electronics in Glenview, Illinois, would be described as socially responsible. As one of the largest single-store electronics retailers in the United States, Abt responded to soaring energy costs and environmental concerns by shutting off lights more frequently and reducing air conditioning and heating. However, an Abt family member said, "These actions weren't just about costs, but about doing the right thing. We don't do everything just because of money."[11]

So, how should we view an organization's social actions? A U.S. business that meets federal pollution control standards or that doesn't discriminate against employees over the age of 40 in job promotion decisions is meeting its social obligation because laws mandate these actions. However, when it provides on-site child-care facilities for employees or packages products using recycled paper, it's being socially responsive. Why? Working parents and environmentalists have voiced these social concerns and demanded such actions.

socioeconomic view
The view that management's social responsibility goes beyond making profits to include protecting and improving society's welfare

social responsiveness
When a firm engages in social actions in response to some popular social need

Little Caesars Pizza is both a socially responsive and a socially responsible company that feels a deep commitment to give back to the communities that sustain its business. The Detroit, Michigan-based pizza firm created a big-rig pizza kitchen on wheels called the Love Machine that travels across the United States and Canada providing food for the hungry at soup kitchens and homeless shelters and responding to the needs of survivors of floods, hurricanes, and other disasters. Little Caesars franchise owners and regional offices donate all the food and labor costs of serving meals to support the Love Machine in their local communities.
Source: Jim West/Alamy

social responsibility
A business's intention, beyond its legal and economic obligations, to do the right things and act in ways that are good for society

For many businesses, their social actions are better viewed as socially responsive than socially responsible (at least according to our definition). However, such actions are still good for society. For example, Walmart sponsored a program to address a serious social problem—hunger. Customers donated money to America's Second Harvest by purchasing puzzle pieces, and Walmart matched the first $5 million raised. As part of this program, the company ran advertisements in major newspapers showing the word H_NGER and the tag line, "The problem can't be solved without You."[12]

Should Organizations Be Socially Involved?

Other than meeting their social obligations (which they *must* do), should organizations be socially involved? One way to look at this question is by examining arguments for and against social involvement. Several points are outlined in Exhibit 5-1.[13]

Exhibit 5-1

Arguments For and Against Social Responsibility

For	Against
Public expectations Public opinion now supports businesses pursuing economic and social goals.	**Violation of profit maximization** Business is being socially responsible only when it pursues its economic interests.
Long-run profits Socially responsible companies tend to have more secure long-run profits.	**Dilution of purpose** Pursuing social goals dilutes business's primary purpose—economic productivity.
Ethical obligation Businesses should be socially responsible because responsible actions are the right thing to do.	**Costs** Many socially responsible actions do not cover their costs and someone must pay those costs.
Public image Businesses can create a favorable public image by pursuing social goals.	**Too much power** Businesses have a lot of power already; if they pursue social goals, they will have even more.
Better environment Business involvement can help solve difficult social problems.	**Lack of skills** Business leaders lack the necessary skills to address social issues.
Discouragement of further governmental regulation By becoming socially responsible, businesses can expect less government regulation.	**Lack of accountability** There are no direct lines of accountability for social actions.
Balance of responsibility and power Businesses have a lot of power and an equally large amount of responsibility is needed to balance against that power.	
Stockholder interests Social responsibility will improve a business's stock price in the long run.	
Possession of resources Businesses have the resources to support public and charitable projects that need assistance.	
Superiority of prevention over cures Businesses should address social problems before they become serious and costly to correct.	

Numerous studies have examined whether social involvement affects a company's economic performance.[14] Although most found a small positive relationship, no generalizable conclusions can be made because these studies have shown that relationship is affected by various contextual factors such as firm size, industry, economic conditions, and regulatory environment.[15] Another concern was causation. If a study showed that social involvement and economic performance were positively related, this correlation didn't necessarily mean that social involvement *caused* higher economic performance—it could simply mean that high profits afforded companies the "luxury" of being socially involved.[16] Such methodological concerns can't be taken lightly. In fact, one study found that if the flawed empirical analyses in these studies were "corrected," social responsibility had a neutral impact on a company's financial performance.[17] Another found that participating in social issues not related to the organization's primary stakeholders was negatively associated with shareholder value.[18] A re-analysis of several studies concluded that managers can afford to be (and should be) socially responsible.[19]

Another way to view social involvement and economic performance is by looking at socially responsible investing (SRI) funds, which provide a way for individual investors to support socially responsible companies. (You can find a list of SRI funds at [www.socialfunds.com].) Typically, these funds use some type of **social screening**; that is, they apply social and environmental criteria to investment decisions. For instance, SRI funds usually will not invest in companies involved in liquor, gambling, tobacco, nuclear power, weapons, price fixing, fraud, or in companies that have poor product safety, employee relations, and environmental track records. The number of socially screened mutual funds has grown from 55 to 260, and assets in these funds have grown to more than $2.7 trillion—about 11 percent of total assets in managed funds in the United States.[20] But more important than the total amount invested in these funds is that the Social Investment Forum reports that the performance of most SRI funds is comparable to that of non-SRI funds.[21]

> **social screening**
> Applying social criteria (screens) to investment decisions

So, what can we conclude about social involvement and economic performance? It appears that a company's social actions *don't hurt* its economic performance. Given political and societal pressures to be socially involved, managers probably need to take social issues and goals into consideration as they plan, organize, lead, and control.

GREEN Management and Sustainability

> *Explain* green | 5.2
> *management and how organizations can go green.*

Coca-Cola, the world's largest soft drink company, announced that 100 percent of its new vending machines and coolers would be hydrofluorocarbon-free (HFC-free) by 2015. This initiative alone would have the same effect on global carbon emissions as taking 11 million cars off the road for a single year.[22] The Fairmont Hotel chain has generated a lot of buzz over its decision to set up rooftop beehives to try and help strengthen the population of honeybees, which have been mysteriously abandoning their hives and dying off by the millions worldwide. This Colony Collapse Disorder could have potentially disastrous consequences since one-third of the food we eat comes from plants that depend on bee pollination. At Toronto's Fairmont Royal York, six hives are home to some 360,000 bees that forage in and around the city *and* produce a supply of award-winning honey.[23] Did you know that planning a driving route with more right-hand turns than left can save you money? UPS does. That's just one of many stats the global logistics leader can quote about how research-based changes in its delivery route design contribute to the sustainability of the planet.[24] Being green is in!

Until the late 1960s, few people (and organizations) paid attention to the environmental consequences of their decisions and actions. Although some groups were concerned with conserving natural resources, about the only reference to saving the environment was the ubiquitous printed request "Please Don't Litter." However, a number of environmental disasters brought a new spirit of environmentalism to

green management
Managers consider the impact of their organization on the natural environment

individuals, groups, and organizations. Increasingly, managers have begun to consider the impact of their organization on the natural environment, which we call **green management**. What do managers need to know about going green?

How Organizations Go Green

Managers and organizations can do many things to protect and preserve the natural environment.[25] Some do no more than what is required by law; that is, they fulfill their social obligation. However, others have radically changed their products and production processes. For instance, Fiji Water uses renewable energy sources, preserves forests, and conserves water. Carpet-maker Mohawk Industries uses recycled plastic containers to produce fiber used in its carpets. Google and Intel initiated an effort to get computer makers and customers to adopt technologies that reduce energy consumption. Paris-based TOTAL, SA, one of the world's largest integrated oil companies, is going green by implementing tough new rules on oil tanker safety and working with groups such as Global Witness and Greenpeace. UPS, the world's largest package delivery company, has done several things—from retrofitting its aircraft with advanced technology and fuel-efficient engines to developing a computer network that efficiently dispatches its fleet of brown trucks to using alternative fuel to run those trucks. Although interesting, these examples don't tell us much about how organizations go green. One model uses the terms *shades of green* to describe the different environmental approaches that organizations may take.[26] (See Exhibit 5-2.)

The first approach, the *legal (or light green) approach,* is simply doing what is required legally. In this approach, which illustrates social obligation, organizations exhibit little environmental sensitivity. They obey laws, rules, and regulations without legal challenge and that's the extent of their being green.

As an organization becomes more sensitive to environmental issues, it may adopt the *market approach* and respond to environmental preferences of customers. Whatever customers demand in terms of environmentally friendly products will be what the organization provides. For example, DuPont developed a new type of herbicide that helped farmers around the world reduce their annual use of chemicals by more than 45 million pounds. By developing this product, the company was responding to the demands of its customers (farmers) who wanted to minimize the use of chemicals on their crops. This is a good example of social responsiveness, as is the next approach.

In the *stakeholder approach*, an organization works to meet the environmental demands of multiple stakeholders such as

LEADER *who made a* DIFFERENCE

Source: Brad Barket/Stringer/Getty Images

Yvon Chouinard *is a self-taught blacksmith who, in 1957, started crafting mountain climbing pitons he and other climbing enthusiasts used as anchors on risky climbs.*[27] *His hardware became so popular that he would go on to found the outdoor-clothing company Patagonia. As his company grew, Chouinard realized that everything his company did had an effect—mostly negative—on the environment. Today, he defines the company's mission in eco-driven terms: "To use business to inspire and implement solutions to the environmental crisis." Chouinard has put environmental activism at the forefront of his company. Since 1985, Patagonia has donated 1 percent of its annual sales to grassroots environmental groups and has gotten more than 1,300 companies to follow its lead as part of its "1% for the Planet" group. He recognizes that "every product, no matter how much thought goes into it, has a destructive impact on Earth." But nonetheless, he keeps doing what he does because "it's the right thing to do." What can you learn from this leader who made a difference?*

Exhibit 5-2
Green Approaches

Source: Based on R. E. Freeman, J. Pierce, and R. Dodd, *Shades of Green: Business Ethics and the Environment* (New York: Oxford University Press, 1995).

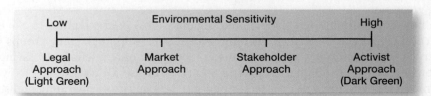

	Environmental Sensitivity		
Low			High
Legal Approach (Light Green)	Market Approach	Stakeholder Approach	Activist Approach (Dark Green)

employees, suppliers, or community. For instance, Hewlett-Packard has several corporate environmental programs in place for its supply chain (suppliers), product design and product recycling (customers and society), and work operations (employees and community).

Finally, if an organization pursues an *activist* (*or dark green*) *approach*, it looks for ways to protect the earth's natural resources. The activist approach reflects the highest degree of environmental sensitivity and illustrates social responsibility. For example, Belgian company Ecover produces ecological cleaning products in a near-zero-emissions factory. This factory (the world's first ecological one) is an engineering marvel with a huge grass roof that keeps things cool in summer and warm in winter and a water treatment system that runs on wind and solar energy. The company chose to build this facility because of its deep commitment to the environment.

Evaluating Green Management Actions

As businesses become "greener," they often release detailed reports on their environmental performance. More than 1,300 companies around the globe voluntarily report their efforts in promoting environmental sustainability using the guidelines developed by the Global Reporting Initiative (GRI). These reports, which can be found on the GRI Web site [www.globalreporting.org], describe the numerous green actions of these organizations.

Another way organizations show their commitment to being green is through pursuing standards developed by the nongovernmental International Organization for Standardization (ISO). Although ISO has developed more than 18,000 international standards, it's probably best known for its ISO 9000 (quality management) and ISO 14000 (environmental management) standards. Organizations that want to

let's get REAL

The Scenario:

Like many students, Sonjia Kresnik has to work part-time, mostly on the weekends, while taking classes at the local university. She likes her job as team leader for a popular restaurant in downtown Portland and has worked there for 3 years. She's also always had a strong interest in green issues and would like to see her weekend crew be more involved in sustainable practices. How can she get her employees involved in "greening" their workplace?

What do you suggest Sonjia do?

Sonjia should present her ideas on sustainable practices to her team and senior management with the intent to gain their consensus. Specifically, I recommend Sonjia present her long-term "going green" vision, any incremental costs, the very simple steps the team can take now (e.g. replacing current lights with compact fluorescent lights, etc.), which other restaurants/ companies have done, and, most importantly, the benefits to her employees of going "green." It would behoove Sonjia to tout benefits that involve not only saving the earth, but also saving the restaurant money, which would be a win-win for all parties involved.

Shanise King
Associate Director, Marketing

Source: Shanise King

become ISO 14000 compliant must develop a total management system for meeting environmental challenges. In other words, it must minimize the effects of its activities on the environment and continually improve its environmental performance. If an organization can meet these standards, it can state that it's ISO 14000 compliant—an accomplishment achieved by organizations in 155 countries.

One final way to evaluate a company's green actions is to use the Global 100 list of the most sustainable corporations in the world [www.global100.org].[28] To be named to this list— announced each year at the renowned World Economic Forum in Davos, Switzerland—a company has displayed a superior ability to effectively manage environmental and social factors. In 2012, the United Kingdom led the list with16 Global 100 companies. Japan followed with 12, and both France and the United States had 8 companies on the list. Some companies on the 2012 list included Novo Nordisk A/S (Denmark), NaturaCosmeticos SA (Brazil), Sims Metal Management Ltd. (Australia), Suncor Energy Inc. (Canada), and Intel Corp. (United States).

MANAGERS and Ethical Behavior

5.3 *Discuss* the factors that lead to ethical and unethical behavior.

One hundred fifty years. That was the maximum prison sentence handed to financier Bernard Madoff, who stole billions of dollars from his clients, by a U.S. district judge who called his crimes "evil." In Britain, which has been characterized by some critics as a "nanny state because of its purported high level of social control and surveillance," a controversy is brewing over the monitoring of garbage cans. Many local governments have installed monitoring chips in municipally distributed trash cans. These chips match cans with owners and can be used to track the weight of the bins, leading some critics to fear that the country is moving to a pay-as-you go system, which they believe will discriminate against large families. A government report says that Iceland, hit hard by both the global economic meltdown and a pesky volcano, was "victimized by politicians, bankers, and regulators who engaged in acts of extreme negligence."[29] When you hear about such behaviors—especially after the high-profile financial misconduct at companies such as Enron, WorldCom, Lehman Brothers, and others—you might conclude that businesses aren't ethical. Although that's not the case, managers—at all levels, in all areas, in all sizes, and in all kinds of organizations—do face ethical issues and dilemmas. For instance, is it ethical for a sales representative to bribe a purchasing agent as an inducement to buy? Would it make a difference if the bribe came out of the sales rep's commission? Is it ethical for someone to use a company car for private use? How about using company e-mail for personal correspondence or using the company phone to make personal phone calls? What if you managed an employee who worked all weekend on an emergency situation and you told him to take off two days sometime later and mark it down as "sick days" because your company had a clear policy that overtime would not be compensated for any reason?[30] Would that be okay? How will you handle such situations? As managers plan, organize, lead, and control, they must consider ethical dimensions.

ethics
Principles, values, and beliefs that define what is right and wrong behavior

What do we mean by **ethics**? We're defining it as the principles, values, and beliefs that define right and wrong decisions and behavior.[31] Many decisions managers make require them to consider both the process and who's affected by the result.[32] To better understand the ethical issues involved in such decisions, let's look at the factors that determine whether a person acts ethically or unethically.

Factors That Determine Ethical and Unethical Behavior

Whether someone behaves ethically or unethically when faced with an ethical dilemma is influenced by several things: his or her stage of moral development and other moderating variables, including individual characteristics, the organization's structural design, the organization's culture, and the intensity of the ethical issue. (See Exhibit 5-3.) People who lack a strong moral sense are much less likely to do the wrong things if they're constrained by rules, policies, job descriptions, or strong cultural norms that disapprove of such behaviors. Conversely, intensely moral

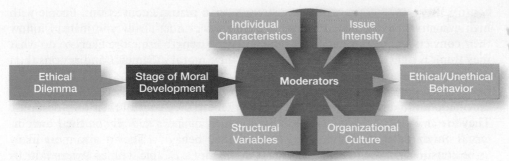

Exhibit 5-3
Factors That Determine Ethical and Unethical Behavior

individuals can be corrupted by an organizational structure and culture that permits or encourages unethical practices. Let's look more closely at these factors.

STAGE OF MORAL DEVELOPMENT Research divides moral development into three levels, each having two stages.[33] At each successive stage, an individual's moral judgment becomes less dependent on outside influences and more internalized.

At the first level, the *preconventional* level, a person's choice between right or wrong is based on personal consequences from outside sources, such as physical punishment, reward, or exchange of favors. At the second level, the *conventional* level, ethical decisions rely on maintaining expected standards and living up to the expectations of others. At the *principled* level, individuals define moral values apart from the authority of the groups to which they belong or society in general. The three levels and six stages are described in Exhibit 5-4.

What can we conclude about moral development?[34] First, people proceed through the six stages sequentially. Second, there is no guarantee of continued moral development. Third, the majority of adults are at Stage 4: They're limited to obeying the rules and will be inclined to behave ethically, although for different reasons. A manager at stage 3 is likely to make decisions based on peer approval; a manager at stage 4 will try to be a "good corporate citizen" by making decisions that respect the organization's rules and procedures; and a stage 5 manager is likely to challenge organizational practices that he or she believes to be wrong.

INDIVIDUAL CHARACTERISTICS Two individual characteristics—values and personality—play a role in determining whether a person behaves ethically. Each person comes to an organization with a relatively entrenched set of personal **values**, which represent basic convictions about what is right and wrong. Our values develop from a young age based on what we see and hear from parents, teachers, friends, and others. Thus, employees in the same organization often possess very different values.[35] Although *values* and *stage of moral development* may seem similar, they're not. Values are broad and cover a wide range of issues; the stage of moral development is a measure of independence from outside influences.

Two personality variables have been found to influence an individual's actions according to his or her beliefs about what is right or wrong: ego strength and locus of

values
Basic convictions about what is right and wrong

Level	Description of Stage
Principled	6. Following self-chosen ethical principles even if they violate the law
	5. Valuing rights of others and upholding absolute values and rights regardless of the majority's opinion
Conventional	4. Maintaining conventional order by fulfilling obligations to which you have agreed
	3. Living up to what is expected by people close to you
Preconventional	2. Following rules only when doing so is in your immediate interest
	1. Sticking to rules to avoid physical punishment

Exhibit 5-4
Stages of Moral Development

Source: Based on "Shades of Green: Business Ethics and the Environment" by R. Edward Freeman, Jessica Pierce, and Richard Dodd from *The Business of Consumption: Environmental Ethics and the Global Economy*, edited by Laura Westra and Patricia Hogue Werhane.

ego strength
A personality measure of the strength of a person's convictions

locus of control
A personality attribute that measures the degree to which people believe they control their own fate

control. **Ego strength** measures the strength of a person's convictions. People with high ego strength are likely to resist impulses to act unethically and instead follow their convictions. That is, individuals high in ego strength are more likely to do what they think is right and be more consistent in their moral judgments and actions than those with low ego strength.

Locus of control is the degree to which people believe they control their own fate. People with an *internal* locus of control believe they control their own destinies. They're more likely to take responsibility for consequences and rely on their own internal standards of right and wrong to guide their behavior. They're also more likely to be consistent in their moral judgments and actions. People with an *external* locus of control believe what happens to them is due to luck or chance. They're less likely to take personal responsibility for the consequences of their behavior and more likely to rely on external forces.[36]

STRUCTURAL VARIABLES An organization's structural design can influence whether employees behave ethically. Those structures that minimize ambiguity and uncertainty with formal rules and regulations and those that continuously remind employees of what is ethical are more likely to encourage ethical behavior. Other structural variables that influence ethical choices include goals, performance appraisal systems, and reward allocation procedures.

Although many organizations use goals to guide and motivate employees, those goals can create some unexpected problems. One study found that people who don't reach set goals are more likely to engage in unethical behavior, even if they do or don't have economic incentives to do so. The researchers concluded that "goal setting can lead to unethical behavior."[37] Examples of such behaviors abound—from companies shipping unfinished products just to reach sales goals or "managing earnings" to meet financial analysts' expectations, to schools excluding certain groups of students when reporting standardized test scores to make their "pass" rate look better.[38]

An organization's performance appraisal system also can influence ethical behavior. Some systems focus exclusively on outcomes, while others evaluate means as well as ends. When employees are evaluated only on outcomes, they may be pressured to do whatever is necessary to look good on the outcomes and not be concerned with how they got those results. Research suggests that "success may serve to excuse unethical behaviors."[39] The danger of such thinking is that if managers are more lenient in correcting unethical behaviors of successful employees, other employees will model their behavior on what they see.

Closely related to the organization's appraisal system is how rewards are allocated. The more that rewards or punishment depend on specific goal outcomes, the more employees are pressured to do whatever they must to reach those goals—perhaps to the point of compromising their ethical standards. Experts say that "It's a good idea to look at what you're encouraging employees to do. A sales goal of $147 an hour led auto mechanics at Sears to 'repair' things that weren't broken."[40]

At Microsoft Corporation, corporate values guide employees' behavior as they perform their jobs and interact with each other and with the company's stakeholders. Employees shown here at an annual employee meeting are some of the company's 90,000 workers who share Microsoft's values of "integrity and honesty; a passion for customers, partners, and technology; a willingness to take on big challenges and see them through; self-critical questioning and commitment to personal excellence and self-improvement; and accountability for commitments, results, and quality to customers, shareholders, partners, and employees." Microsoft's Standards of Business Conduct are an extension of these values and reflect employees' commitment to ethical practices and regulatory compliance.
Source: AP Photo/Ted S. Warren

ORGANIZATION'S CULTURE As Exhibit 5-3 showed, the content and strength of an organization's culture also influence ethical behavior.[41] We learned in Chapter 2 that an organization's culture consists of the shared organizational values. These values reflect what the organization stands for and what it believes in as well as create an environment that influences employee behavior ethically or unethically. When it comes to ethical behavior, a culture most likely to encourage high ethical standards is one that's high in risk tolerance, control, and conflict tolerance. Employees in such a culture are encouraged to be aggressive and innovative, are aware that unethical practices will be discovered, and feel free to openly challenge expectations they consider to be unrealistic or personally undesirable.

Because shared values can be powerful influences, many organizations are using **values-based management**, in which the organization's values guide employees in the way they do their jobs. For instance, Timberland is an example of a company using values-based management. With a simple statement, "Make It Better," employees at Timberland know what's expected and valued; that is, they find ways to "make it better"—whether it's creating quality products for customers, performing community service activities, designing employee training programs, or figuring out ways to make the company's packaging more environmentally friendly. As it says on the company's Web site, "Everything we do at Timberland grows out of our relentless pursuit to find a way to make it better." At Corning, one of the core values guiding employee behavior is integrity. Employees are expected to work in ways that are honest, decent, and fair. Timberland and Corning aren't alone in their use of values-based management. A survey of global companies found that a large number (more than 89%) said they had a written corporate values statement.[43] This survey also found that most of the companies believed their values influenced relationships and reputation, the top-performing companies consciously connected values with the way employees did their work, and top managers were important to reinforcing the importance of the values throughout the organization.

Thus, an organization's managers do play an important role here. They're responsible for creating an environment that encourages employees to embrace the culture and the desired values as they do their jobs. In fact, research shows that the behavior of managers is the single most important influence on an individual's decision to act ethically or unethically.[44] People look to see what those in authority are doing and use that as a benchmark for acceptable practices and expectations.

Finally, as we discussed in Chapter 2, a strong culture exerts more influence on employees than a weak one. If a culture is strong and supports high ethical standards, it has a powerful and positive influence on the decision to act ethically or unethically. For example, IBM has a strong culture that has long stressed ethical dealings with customers, employees, business partners, and communities.[45] To reinforce the importance of ethical behaviors, the company developed an explicitly detailed set of guidelines for business conduct and ethics. And the penalty for violating the guidelines: disciplinary actions, including dismissal. IBM's managers continually reinforce the importance of ethical behavior and reinforce the fact that a person's actions and decisions are important to the way the organization is viewed.

ISSUE INTENSITY A student who would never consider breaking into an instructor's office to steal an accounting exam doesn't think twice about asking a friend who took the same course from the same instructor last semester what questions were on an exam. Similarly, a manager might think nothing about taking home a few office supplies yet be highly concerned about the possible embezzlement of company funds. These examples illustrate the final factor that influences ethical behavior: the intensity of the ethical issue itself.[46]

As Exhibit 5-5 shows, six characteristics determine issue intensity or how important an ethical issue is to an individual: greatness of harm, consensus of wrong, probability of harm, immediacy of consequences, proximity to victim(s), and concentration of effect. These factors suggest that (a) the larger the number of people harmed, the more agreement that the action is wrong;(b) the greater the likelihood that the action will cause harm, the more immediately the consequences of the action will be felt; and (c) the closer the person feels to the victim(s) and the more concentrated the effect of the action on the victim(s), the greater the issue intensity or importance. When an ethical issue is important, employees are more likely to behave ethically.

Ethics in an International Context

Are ethical standards universal? Although some common moral beliefs exist, social and cultural differences between countries are important factors that determine ethical and unethical behavior.[47]

---

datapoints[42]

29 percent of employees said they don't feel guilty calling in sick when they aren't.

22 percent of employees who reported misconduct say they experienced some form of retaliation.

13 percent of employees perceived pressure to compromise standards in order to do their jobs.

42 percent of companies are believed to have weak ethics cultures according to their employees.

45 percent of employees witnessed misconduct at work.

49 percent of employees said, if granted access to a confidential document accidently, they would look at it.

14 percent of employees in an employee engagement survey said their company's leaders are ethical and honest.

values-based management
The organization's values guide employees in the way they do their jobs

Exhibit 5-5
Issue Intensity

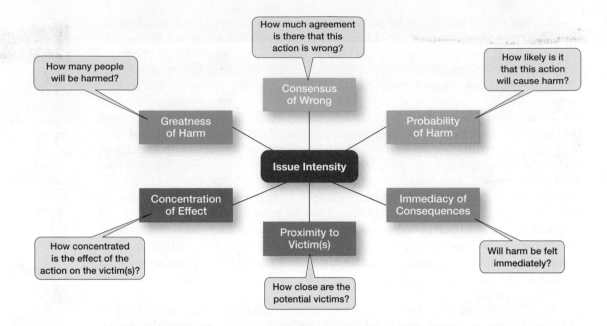

Should Coca-Cola employees in Saudi Arabia adhere to U.S. ethical standards, or should they follow local standards of acceptable behavior? If Airbus (a European company) pays a "broker's fee" to an intermediary to get a major contract with a Middle Eastern airline, should Boeing be restricted from doing the same because such practices are considered improper in the United States? (Note: In the United Kingdom, the Law Commission, a governmental advisory body, has said that bribing officials in foreign countries should be a criminal offense. It said that claims of "its local custom" should not be a reason for allowing it.[48]) British defense giant BAE, which has been the target of various bribery and corruption allegations, was ordered to "submit to the supervision of an ethics monitor and pay nearly $500 million to resolve the corruption allegations."[49]

In the case of payments to influence foreign officials or politicians, U.S. managers are guided by the Foreign Corrupt Practices Act (FCPA), which makes it illegal to knowingly corrupt a foreign official. However, even this law doesn't always reduce ethical dilemmas to black and white. In some countries, government bureaucrat salaries are low because custom dictates that they receive small payments from those they serve. Payoffs to these bureaucrats "grease the machinery" and ensure that things get done. The FCPA does not expressly prohibit small payoffs to foreign government employees whose duties are primarily administrative or clerical *when* such payoffs are an accepted part of doing business in that country. Any action other than this is illegal. In 2011, the U.S. Department of Justice brought 11 FCPA enforcement actions against corporations, collecting approximately $504 million in fines.[50]

It's important for individual managers working in foreign cultures to recognize the social, cultural, and political-legal influences on what is appropriate and acceptable behavior.[51] And international businesses must clarify their ethical guidelines so that employees know what's expected of them while working in a foreign location, which adds another dimension to making ethical judgments.

Another guide to being ethical in international business is the United Nations Global Compact, which is an initiative created by the United Nations outlining principles for doing business globally in the areas of human rights, labor, the environment, and anti-corruption (see Exhibit 5-6). More than 8,700 corporate participants and stakeholders from over 130 countries have committed to the UN Global Compact, making it the world's largest voluntary corporate citizenship initiative.[52] The goal of the UN Global Compact is a more sustainable and inclusive global economy. Organizations making this commitment do so because they believe that the world business community plays a significant role in improving economic and

The UN Global Compact asks companies to embrace, support, and enact, within their sphere of influence, a set of core values in the areas of human rights, labor standards, the environment, and anti-corruption:

Human Rights

Principle 1: Business should support and respect the protection of internationally-proclaimed human rights within their sphere of influence; and

Principle 2: Make sure they are not complicit in human rights abuses.

Labor Standards

Principle 3: Business should uphold the freedom of association and the effective recognition of the right to collective bargaining;

Principle 4: The elimination of all forms of forced and compulsory labor;

Principle 5: The effective abolition of child labor; and

Principle 6: The elimination of discrimination in respect to employment and occupation.

Environment

Principle 7: Business should support a precautionary approach to environmental challenges;

Principle 8: Undertake initiatives to promote greater environmental responsibility; and

Principle 9: Encourage the development and diffusion of environmentally friendly technologies.

Anti-Corruption

Principle 10: Business should work against corruption in all its forms, including extortion and bribery.

Source: Courtesy of United Nations Global Compact (www.unglobalcompact.org).

Exhibit 5-6
The Ten Principles of the United Nations Global Compact

social conditions. In addition, the Organization for Economic Co-operation and Development (OECD) has made fighting bribery and corruption in international business a high priority. The centerpiece of its efforts is the Anti-Bribery Convention (or set of rules and guidelines), which was the first global instrument to combat corruption in cross-border business deals. To date, significant gains have been made in fighting corruption in the 38 countries that have ratified it.[53]

ENCOURAGING Ethical Behavior

At a Senate hearing exploring the accusations that Wall Street firm Goldman Sachs deceived its clients during the housing-market meltdown, Arizona senator John McCain said, "I don't know if Goldman has done anything illegal, but there's no doubt their behavior was unethical."[54] You have to wonder what the firm's managers were thinking or doing while such ethically questionable decisions and actions were taking place.

Managers can do a number of things if they're serious about encouraging ethical behaviors—hire employees with high ethical standards, establish codes of ethics, lead by example, and so forth. By themselves, such actions won't have much of an impact. But if an organization has a comprehensive ethics program in place, it can potentially improve an organization's ethical climate. The key variable, however, is *potentially*. There are no guarantees that a well-designed ethics program will lead to the desired outcome. Sometimes corporate ethics programs are little more than public relations gestures that do little to influence managers and employees. For instance, Sears had a long history of encouraging ethical business practices through its corporate Office of Ethics and Business Practices. However, its ethics programs didn't stop managers from

Describe | **5.4**
management's role in encouraging ethical behavior.

let's get REAL

The Scenario:

All through university, Finlay Roberts wasn't sure what he really wanted to do. But now he had found what he thought was a great job, one where he could enhance his leadership skills in a competitive environment with teams of employees who sold security systems over the phone. What he soon discovered, though, was that competing to meet sales goals often led to unethical actions. After learning about ethics in pretty much every management class he took, Finlay wanted to show his employees that he was committed to an ethical workplace.

Patricia Ficco
Retail General Manager

What advice would you give Finlay?

Let's face it. No one likes criticism, and I have learned that employees respond better when you give them an opportunity to be part of the solution. I would advise Finlay to identify the core issues and then select a group of employees to generate ideas, implement strategies, and track results. The employees selected will feel valued and in turn work diligently toward achieving the goals.

illegally trying to collect payments from bankrupt charge account holders or from routinely deceiving automotive service center customers into thinking they needed unnecessary repairs. Even Enron, often referred to as the "poster child" of corporate wrongdoing, outlined values in its final annual report that most would consider ethical—communication, respect, integrity, and excellence. Yet the way top managers behaved didn't reflect those values at all.[55] Let's look at some specific ways that managers can encourage ethical behavior and create a comprehensive ethics program.

Employee Selection

Wanting to reduce workers' compensation claims, Hospitality Management Corp. did pre-employment integrity testing at one hotel to see if the tests could "weed out applicants likely to be dishonest, take dangerous risks or engage in other undesirable behaviors." After six months, claims were down among new hires.[56]

The selection process (interviews, tests, background checks, and so forth) should be viewed as an opportunity to learn about an individual's level of moral development, personal values, ego strength, and locus of control.[57] However, a carefully designed selection process isn't foolproof and, even under the best circumstances, individuals with questionable standards of right and wrong may be hired. That means having other ethics controls in place.

Codes of Ethics and Decision Rules

George David, former CEO and chairman of Hartford, Connecticut-based United Technologies Corporation (UTC), believed in the power of a code of ethics. That's why UTC has always had one that was quite explicit and detailed. Employees know the company's behavioral expectations, especially when it comes to ethics. UBS AG, the Swiss bank, also has an explicit employee code crafted by the CEO that bans staff from helping clients cheat on their taxes.[58] However, not all organizations have such explicit ethical guidelines.

Uncertainty about what is and is not ethical can be a problem for employees. A **code of ethics**, a formal statement of an organization's values and the ethical rules it

code of ethics
A formal statement of an organization's primary values and the ethical rules it expects its employees to follow

expects employees to follow, is a popular choice for reducing that ambiguity. Research shows that 97 percent of organizations with more than 10,000 employees have a written code of ethics. Even in smaller organizations, nearly 93 percent have one.[59] And codes of ethics are becoming more popular globally. Research by the Institute for Global Ethics says that shared values such as honesty, fairness, respect, responsibility, and caring are pretty much universally embraced.[60] In addition, a survey of businesses in 22 countries found that 78 percent have formally stated ethics standards and codes of ethics; and more than 85 percent of *Fortune* Global 200 companies have a business code of ethics.[61]

What should a code of ethics look like? It should be specific enough to show employees the spirit in which they're supposed to do things yet loose enough to allow for freedom of judgment. A survey of companies' codes of ethics found their content tended to fall into three categories as shown in Exhibit 5-7.[62]

Unfortunately, codes of ethics may not work as well as we think they should. A survey of employees in U.S. businesses found that 45 percent of those surveyed had observed ethical or legal violations in the previous 12 months, including such things as conflicts of interest, abusive or intimidating behavior, and lying to employees. And 35 percent of those employees didn't report observed misconduct.[63]

Exhibit 5-7
Codes of Ethics

Cluster 1. Be a Dependable Organizational Citizen

1. Comply with safety, health, and security regulations.
2. Demonstrate courtesy, respect, honesty, and fairness.
3. Illegal drugs and alcohol at work are prohibited.
4. Manage personal finances well.
5. Exhibit good attendance and punctuality.
6. Follow directives of supervisors.
7. Do not use abusive language.
8. Dress in business attire.
9. Firearms at work are prohibited.

Cluster 2. Do Not Do Anything Unlawful or Improper That Will Harm the Organization

1. Conduct business in compliance with all laws.
2. Payments for unlawful purposes are prohibited.
3. Bribes are prohibited.
4. Avoid outside activities that impair duties.
5. Maintain confidentiality of records.
6. Comply with all antitrust and trade regulations.
7. Comply with all accounting rules and controls.
8. Do not use company property for personal benefit.
9. Employees are personally accountable for company funds.
10. Do not propagate false or misleading information.
11. Make decisions without regard for personal gain.

Cluster 3. Be Good to Customers

1. Convey true claims in product advertisements.
2. Perform assigned duties to the best of your ability.
3. Provide products and services of the highest quality.

Source: F. R. David, "An Empirical Study of Codes of Business Ethics: A Strategic Perspective," paper presented at the 48th Annual Academy of Management Conference, Anaheim, California, August 1988. Used with permission of Fred David.

Exhibit 5-8

A Process for Addressing Ethical Dilemmas

Step 1: What is the **ethical dilemma**?

Step 2: Who are the **affected stakeholders**?

Step 3: Which **personal**, **organizational**, and **external factors** are important in this decision?

Step 4: What are possible **alternatives**?

Step 5: What is my **decision** and how will I act on it?

Does this mean that codes of ethics shouldn't be developed? No. However, in doing so, managers should use these suggestions:[64]

1. Organizational leaders should model appropriate behavior and reward those who act ethically.

2. All managers should continually reaffirm the importance of the ethics code and consistently discipline those who break it.

3. The organization's stakeholders (employees, customers, and so forth) should be considered as an ethics code is developed or improved.

4. Managers should communicate and reinforce the ethics code regularly.

5. Managers should use the five-step process (see Exhibit 5-8) to guide employees when faced with ethical dilemmas.

Leadership

In 2007, Peter Löescher was hired as CEO of German company Siemens to clean up a global bribery scandal that cost the company a record-setting $1.34 billion in fines. His approach: "Stick to your principles. Have a clear ethical north. Be trusted and be the role model of your company...true leaders have a set of core values they publicly commit to and live by in good times and bad."[65] Doing business ethically requires a commitment from top managers. Why? Because they're the ones who uphold the shared values and set the cultural tone. They're role models in terms of both words and actions, though what they *do* is far more important than what they *say.* If top managers, for example, take company resources for their personal use, inflate their expense accounts, or give favored treatment to friends, they imply that such behavior is acceptable for all employees.

Top managers also set the tone by their reward and punishment practices. The choices of whom and what are rewarded with pay increases and promotions send a strong signal to employees. As we said earlier, when an employee is rewarded for achieving impressive results in an ethically questionable manner, it indicates to others that those ways are acceptable. When an employee does something unethical, managers must punish the offender and publicize the fact by making the outcome visible to everyone in the organization. This practice sends a message that doing wrong has a price and it's not in employees' best interests to act unethically!

Job Goals and Performance Appraisal

Employees in three Internal Revenue Service offices were found in the bathrooms flushing tax returns and other related documents down the toilets. When questioned, they openly admitted doing it, but offered an interesting explanation for their behavior. The employees' supervisors had been pressuring them to complete more work in less time. If the piles of tax returns weren't processed and moved off their desks more quickly, they were told their performance reviews and salary raises would be adversely affected. Frustrated by few resources and an overworked computer system, the employees decided to "flush away" the paperwork on their desks. Although these employees knew what they did was wrong, it illustrates how powerful unrealistic goals and performance appraisals can be.[66] Under the stress of unrealistic goals, otherwise ethical employees may feel they have no choice but to do whatever is necessary to meet those goals. Also, goal achievement is usually a key issue in performance appraisal. If performance appraisals focus only on economic goals, ends will begin to justify means. To encourage ethical behavior, both ends *and* means should be evaluated. For example, a manager's annual review of employees might include a point-by-point evaluation of how their decisions measured up against the company's code of ethics as well as how well goals were met.

Ethics Training

More organizations are setting up seminars, workshops, and similar ethics training programs to encourage ethical behavior. Such training programs aren't without controversy as the primary concern is whether ethics can be taught. Critics stress that the effort is pointless because people establish their individual value systems when they're young. Proponents note, however, several studies have shown that values can be learned after early childhood. In addition, they cite evidence that shows that teaching ethical problem solving can make an actual difference in ethical behaviors;[67] that training has increased individuals' level of moral development;[68] and that, if nothing else, ethics training increases awareness of ethical issues in business.[69]

How can ethics be taught? Let's look at an example involving global defense contractor Lockheed Martin, one of the pioneers in the case-based approach to ethics training.[70] Lockheed Martin's employees take annual ethics training courses delivered by their managers. The main focus of these short courses is Lockheed Martin–specific case situations "chosen for their relevance to department or job-specific issues." In each department, employee teams review and discuss the cases and then apply an "Ethics Meter" to "rate whether the real-life decisions were ethical, unethical, or somewhere in between." For example, one of the possible ratings on the Ethics Meter, "On Thin Ice," is explained as "bordering on unethical and should raise a red flag." After the teams have applied their ratings, managers lead discussions about the ratings and examine "which of the company's core ethics principles were applied or ignored in the cases." In addition to its ethics training, Lockheed Martin has a widely used written code of ethics, an ethics helpline that employees can call for guidance on ethical issues, and ethics officers based in the company's various business units.

Independent Social Audits

The fear of being caught can be an important deterrent to unethical behavior. Independent social audits, which evaluate decisions and management practices in terms of the organization's code of ethics, increase that likelihood. Such audits can be regular evaluations or they can occur randomly with no prior announcement. An effective ethics program probably needs both. To maintain integrity, auditors should be responsible to the company's board of directors and present their findings directly to the board. This arrangement gives the auditors clout and lessens the opportunity for retaliation from those being audited. Because the Sarbanes-Oxley Act holds businesses to more rigorous standards of financial disclosure and corporate governance, more organizations are finding the idea of independent social audits appealing. As the publisher of *Business Ethics* magazine stated, "The debate has shifted from *whether* to be ethical to *how* to be ethical."[71]

Protective Mechanisms

Employees who face ethical dilemmas need protective mechanisms so they can do what's right without fear of reprimand. An organization might designate ethical counselors for employees facing an ethics dilemma. These advisors also might advocate the ethically "right" alternatives. Other organizations have appointed ethics officers who design, direct, and modify the organization's ethics programs as needed.[72]

To teach employees how to deal with ethical problems they encounter at work, Cisco Systems developed an innovative training program called "Ethics Idol." A parody of the *American Idol* TV show, the animated video training presents ethics scenarios that are evaluated by judges. Featured on Cisco's Intranet, the program shows cartoon contestants singing about various ethical scenarios included in the company's Code of Business Conduct and then poses questions to employees as to which judge's answer they agree with. Employees, such as those shown here working in a security operations room at Cisco headquarters, can provide feedback, see how other employees respond, and view the official Cisco answer to help them learn how to make good ethical decisions.
Source: AP Photo/Paul Sakuma

The Ethics and Compliance Officer Association is the world's largest group of ethics and compliance practitioners with a total membership topping 1,100 (including more than half of the *Fortune* 100 companies) and covering several countries including, among others, the United States, Germany, India, Japan, and Canada.[73]

5.5 | *Discuss* current social responsibility and ethics issues.

SOCIAL Responsibility and Ethics Issues in Today's World

Today's managers continue to face challenges in being socially responsible and ethical. Next, we examine three current issues: managing ethical lapses and social irresponsibility, social entrepreneurship, and promoting positive social change.

Managing Ethical Lapses and Social Irresponsibility

Even after public outrage over the Enron-era misdeeds, irresponsible and unethical practices by managers in all kinds of organizations haven't gone away, as you've observed with some of the questionable behaviors that took place at financial services firms such as Goldman Sachs and Lehman Brothers. But what's more alarming is what's going on "in the trenches" in offices, warehouses, and stores. One survey reported that among 5,000 employees: 45 percent admitted falling asleep at work; 22 percent said they spread a rumor about a coworker; 18 percent said they snooped after hours; and 2 percent said they took credit for someone else's work.[74] Some interesting recent research suggests that men are more likely to act unethically than women in situations where failure could harm their sense of masculinity.[75] The researchers suggest that the reason is that losing a "battle, particularly in contexts that are highly competitive and historically male oriented, presents a threat to masculine competency. To ensure victory, men will sacrifice moral standards if doing so means winning."

Unfortunately, it's not just at work that we see such behaviors. They're prevalent throughout society. Studies conducted by the Center for Academic Integrity showed that 26 percent of college and university business majors admitted to "serious cheating" on exams and 54 percent admitted to cheating on written assignments. But business students weren't the worst cheaters—that distinction belonged to journalism majors, of whom 27 percent said they had cheated.[76] And a survey by Students in Free Enterprise (SIFE) found that only 19 percent of students would report a classmate who cheated.[77] But even more frightening is what today's teenagers say is "acceptable." In a survey, 23 percent said they thought violence toward another person is acceptable on some level.[78] What do such statistics say about what managers may have to deal with in the future? It's not too far-fetched to say that organizations may have difficulty upholding high ethical standards when their future employees so readily accept unethical behavior.

What can managers do? Two actions seem particularly important: ethical leadership and protecting those who report wrongdoing.

ETHICAL LEADERSHIP Not long after Herb Baum took over as CEO of Dial Corporation, he got a call from Reuben Mark, the CEO of competitor Colgate-Palmolive, who told him he had a copy of Dial's strategic marketing plan that had come from a former Dial salesperson who recently had joined Colgate-Palmolive. Mark told Baum he had not looked at it, didn't intend to look at, and was returning it. In addition, he himself was going to deal appropriately with the new salesperson.[79] As this example illustrates, managers must provide ethical leadership. As we said earlier, what managers *do* has a strong influence on employees' decisions whether to behave ethically.[80] When managers cheat, lie, steal, manipulate, take advantage of situations or people, or treat others unfairly, what kind of signal are they sending to employees (or other stakeholders)? Probably not the one they want to send. Exhibit 5-9 gives some suggestions on how managers can provide ethical leadership.

- Be a good role model by being ethical and honest.
  - Tell the truth always.
  - Don't hide or manipulate information.
  - Be willing to admit your failures.
- Share your personal values by regularly communicating them to employees.
- Stress the organization's or team's important shared values.
- Use the reward system to hold everyone accountable to the values.

Exhibit 5-9
Being an Ethical Leader

PROTECTION OF EMPLOYEES WHO RAISE ETHICAL ISSUES   What would you do if you saw other employees doing something illegal, immoral, or unethical? Would you step forward? Many of us wouldn't because of the perceived risks. That's why it's important for managers to assure employees who raise ethical concerns or issues that they will face no personal or career risks. These individuals, often called **whistle-blowers**, can be a key part of any company's ethics program. For example, Sherron Watkins, who was a vice president at Enron, clearly outlined her concerns about the company's accounting practices in a letter to chairman Ken Lay. Her statement that, "I am incredibly nervous that we will implode in a wave of accounting scandals" couldn't have been more prophetic.[81] However, surveys show that most observers of wrongdoing don't report it and that's the attitude managers have to address.[82] How can they protect employees so they're willing to step up if they see unethical or illegal things occurring?

whistle-blower
Individual who raises ethical concerns or issues to others

One way is to set up toll-free ethics hotlines. For instance, Dell has an ethics hotline that employees can call anonymously to report infractions that the company will then investigate.[83] In addition, managers need to create a culture where bad news can be heard and acted on before it's too late. Michael Josephson, founder of the Josephson Institute of Ethics [www.josephsoninstitute.org] said, "It is absolutely and unequivocally important to establish a culture where it is possible for employees to complain and protest and to get heard."[84] Even if some whistle-blowers have a personal agenda they're pursuing, it's important to take them seriously. Finally, the federal legislation Sarbanes-Oxley offers some legal protection. Any manager who retaliates against an employee for reporting violations faces a stiff penalty: a 10-year jail sentence.[85] Unfortunately, despite this protection, hundreds of employees who have stepped forward and revealed wrongdoings at their companies have been fired or let go from their jobs.[86] So at the present time, it's not a perfect solution, but is a step in the right direction.

Catherine Rohr is a social entrepreneur with the vision of creating localized solutions that will impact urban communities throughout the United States. Rohr is the founder and CEO of Defy Ventures, an organization that provides carefully selected and ambitious men who have criminal histories with entrepreneurship training, intensive character development, and career opportunities that will help them transform their lives and succeed as income earners, entrepreneurs, fathers, and role models in their communities. Defy also offers the men mentoring, long-term housing, legal services, and family reunification counseling. In this photo, Rohr congratulates men who presented their ideas for startup businesses to a panel of judges in the hope of winning up to $150,000 in capital to launch their ventures.
Source: Christian Science Monitor/Getty Images

Social Entrepreneurship

The world's social problems are many and viable solutions are few. But numerous people and organizations are trying to do something. For instance, Reed Paget, founder and CEO of British bottled water company Belu, made his company the world's first to become carbon-neutral. Its bottles are made from corn and can be composted into soil. Also, Belu's profits go toward projects that bring clean water to parts of the world that lack access to it. Paget has chosen to pursue a purpose as well as a profit.[87] He is an example of a **social entrepreneur**, an individual or organization who seeks out opportunities to improve society by using practical, innovative, and sustainable approaches.[88] "What business entrepreneurs are to the economy, social entrepreneurs are to social change."[89] Social entrepreneurs want to make the world a better place and have a driving passion to make that happen. For example, AgSquared aims to help small farmers, who make up 90 percent of the farms in the

social entrepreneur
An individual or organization who seeks out opportunities to improve society by using practical, innovative, and sustainable approaches

United States, keep better track of critical information such as basic accounting of seeds, soil data and weather mapping, and even best practices from the farm community.[90] Also, social entrepreneurs use creativity and ingenuity to solve problems. For instance, Seattle-based PATH (Program for Appropriate Technology in Health) is an international nonprofit organization that uses low-cost technology to provide needed health-care solutions for poor, developing countries. By collaborating with public groups and for-profit businesses, PATH has developed simple life-saving solutions such as clean birthing kits, credit-card sized lab test kits, and disposable vaccination syringes that can't be reused. PATH has pioneered innovative approaches to solving global medical problems.[91]

What can we learn from these social entrepreneurs? Although many organizations have committed to doing business ethically and responsibly, perhaps there is more they can do, as these social entrepreneurs show. Maybe, as in the case of PATH, it's simply a matter of business organizations collaborating with public groups or nonprofit organizations to address a social issue. Or maybe, as in the case of AgSquared, it's providing expertise where needed. Or it may involve nurturing individuals who passionately and unwaveringly believe they have an idea that could make the world a better place and simply need the organizational support to pursue it.

Businesses Promoting Positive Social Change

Since 1946, Target has contributed 5 percent of its annual income to support community needs, an amount that adds up to more than $3 million a week. And it's not alone in those efforts. "Over the past two decades, a growing number of corporations, both within and beyond the United States, have been engaging in activities that promote positive social change."[92] Businesses can do this in a couple of ways: through corporate philanthropy and through employee volunteering efforts.

CORPORATE PHILANTHROPY Corporate philanthropy can be an effective way for companies to address societal problems.[93] For instance, the breast cancer "pink" campaign and the global AIDS Red campaign (started by Bono) are ways that companies support social causes.[94] Many organizations also donate money to various causes that employees and customers care about. In 2010 (latest numbers available), the sum of corporate giving totaled over $15.5 billion in cash and products.[95] Other corporations have funded their own foundations to support various social issues. For example, Google's foundation—called DotOrg by its employees—has about $2 billion in assets that it will use to support five areas: developing systems to help predict and prevent disease pandemics, empowering the poor with information about public services, creating jobs by investing in small and midsized businesses in the developing world, accelerating the commercialization of plug-in cars, and making renewable energy cheaper than coal.[96]

EMPLOYEE VOLUNTEERING EFFORTS Employee volunteering is another popular way for businesses to be involved in promoting social change. For instance, Dow Corning sent a small team of employees to rural India helping women "examine stitchery and figure out prices for garments to be sold in local markets."[97] Molson-Coors' eleven-member executive team spent a full day at their annual team-building retreat building a house in Las Vegas with Habitat for Humanity. PricewaterhouseCoopers employees renovated an abandoned school in Newark, New Jersey. Every Wachovia employee is given six paid days off from work each year to volunteer in his or her community. Other businesses are encouraging their employees to volunteer in various ways. The Committee to Encourage Corporate Philanthropy says that more than 90 percent of its members had volunteer programs and almost half encouraged volunteerism by providing paid time off or by creating volunteer events.[98] Many businesses have found that such efforts not only benefit communities, but enhance employees' work efforts and motivation.

MyManagementLab

Go to **mymanagementlab.com** to complete the problems marked with this icon .

CHAPTER

PREPARING FOR: Exams/Quizzes
CHAPTER SUMMARY by Learning Outcomes

5.1 | LEARNING OUTCOME |

Discuss what it means to be socially responsible and what factors influence that decision.

Social obligation, which reflects the classical view of social responsibility, is when a firm engages in social actions because of its obligation to meet certain economic and legal responsibilities. Social responsiveness is when a firm engages in social actions in response to some popular social need. Social responsibility is a business's intention, beyond its economic and legal obligations, to pursue long-term goals that are good for society. Both of these reflect the socioeconomic view of social responsibility. Determining whether organizations should be socially involved can be done by looking at arguments for and against it. Other ways are to assess the impact of social involvement on a company's economic performance and evaluate the performance of SRI funds versus non-SRI funds. We can conclude that a company's social responsibility doesn't appear to hurt its economic performance.

5.2 | LEARNING OUTCOME |

Explain green management and how organizations can go green.

Green management is when managers consider the impact of their organization on the natural environment. Organizations can "go green" in different ways. The light green approach is doing what is required legally, which is social obligation. Using the market approach, organizations respond to the environmental preferences of their customers. Using the stakeholder approach, organizations respond to the environmental demands of multiple stakeholders. Both the market and stakeholder approaches can be viewed as social responsiveness. With an activist or dark green approach, an organization looks for ways to respect and preserve the earth and its natural resources, which can be viewed as social responsibility.

Green actions can be evaluated by examining reports that companies compile about their environmental performance, by looking for compliance with global standards for environmental management (ISO 14000), and by using the Global 100 list of the most sustainable corporations in the world.

5.3 | LEARNING OUTCOME |

Discuss the factors that lead to ethical and unethical behavior.

Ethics refers to the principles, values, and beliefs that define right and wrong decisions and behavior. The factors that affect ethical and unethical behavior include an individual's level of moral development (preconventional, conventional, or principled), individual characteristics (values and personality variables—ego strength and locus of control), structural variables (structural design, use of goals, performance appraisal systems, and reward allocation procedures), organizational culture (shared values and cultural strength), and issue intensity (greatness of harm, consensus of wrong, probability of harm, immediacy of consequences, proximity to victims, and concentration of effect).

Since ethical standards aren't universal, managers should know what they can and cannot do legally as defined by the Foreign Corrupt Practices Act. It's also important to recognize any cultural differences and to clarify ethical guidelines for employees working in different global locations. Finally, managers should know about the principles of the Global Compact and the Anti-Bribery Convention.

5.4 [LEARNING OUTCOME] **Describe** management's role in encouraging ethical behavior.

The behavior of managers is the single most important influence on an individual's decision to act ethically or unethically. Some specific ways managers can encourage ethical behavior include paying attention to employee selection, having and using a code of ethics, recognizing the important ethical leadership role they play and how what they do is far more important than what they say, making sure that goals and the performance appraisal process don't reward goal achievement without taking into account how those goals were achieved, using ethics training and independent social audits, and establishing protective mechanisms.

5.5 [LEARNING OUTCOME] **Discuss** current social responsibility and ethics issues.

Managers can manage ethical lapses and social irresponsibility by being strong ethical leaders and by protecting employees who raise ethical issues. The example set by managers has a strong influence on whether employees behave ethically. Ethical leaders also are honest, share their values, stress important shared values, and use the reward system appropriately. Managers can protect whistle-blowers (employees who raise ethical issues or concerns) by encouraging them to come forward, by setting up toll-free ethics hotlines, and by establishing a culture in which employees can complain and be heard without fear of reprisal. Social entrepreneurs play an important role in solving social problems by seeking out opportunities to improve society by using practical, innovative, and sustainable approaches. Social entrepreneurs want to make the world a better place and have a driving passion to make that happen. Businesses can promote positive social change through corporate philanthropy and employee volunteering efforts.

REVIEW AND DISCUSSION QUESTIONS ✪

1. Differentiate between social obligation, social responsiveness, and social responsibility.

2. What does social responsibility mean to you personally? Do *you* think business organizations should be socially responsible? Explain.

3. What factors influence whether a person behaves ethically or unethically? Explain all relevant factors.

4. Do you think values-based management is just a "do-gooder" ploy? Explain your answer.

5. Internet file sharing programs are popular among college students. These programs work by allowing nonorganizational users to access any local network where desired files are located. Because these types of file sharing programs tend to clog bandwidth, local users' ability to access and use a local network is reduced. What ethical and social responsibilities does a university have in this situation? To whom do they have a responsibility? What guidelines might you suggest for university decision makers?

6. What are some problems that could be associated with employee whistle-blowing for (a) the whistle-blower and (b) the organization?

7. Describe the characteristics and behaviors of someone you consider to be an ethical person. How could the types of decisions and actions this person engages in be encouraged in a workplace?

8. Explain the ethical and social responsibility issues facing managers today.

PREPARING FOR: My Career
ETHICS DILEMMA ✪

Workers' rights. It's not something we often think about when we're purchasing the latest tech gadget. However, look at this list of some issues that investigations have uncovered: work shifts lasting up to 60 hours; factory explosion killing numerous workers that resulted from a build-up of combustible dust; repetitive motion injuries that are so bad workers lose the use of their hands. "According to recent press reports, that's what work is like for assembly workers in China who build Apple's iPhones, iPads, and iPods." In other locations where workers are assembling products for other tech companies, factory workers have committed suicide because of the pressure and stress.[99] • Whose responsibility is it to ensure that workplaces are safe, especially when work is outsourced? • "It's a tricky dance between first-world brands and third-world production." What do you think this statement means? • Should ethical/corporate responsibility issues be part of the international strategy decision-making process? Why or why not?

SKILLS EXERCISE   Developing Your Developing Trust Skill

About the Skill

Trust plays an important role in the manager's relationships with his or her employees.[100] Given the importance of trust in setting a good ethical example for employees, today's managers should actively seek to develop it within their work group.

Steps in Practicing the Skill

1. *Practice openness.* Mistrust comes as much from what people don't know as from what they do. Being open with employees leads to confidence and trust. Keep people informed. Make clear the criteria you use in making decisions. Explain the rationale for your decisions. Be forthright and candid about problems. Fully disclose all relevant information.

2. *Be fair.* Before making decisions or taking actions, consider how others will perceive them in terms of objectivity and fairness. Give credit where credit is due. Be objective and impartial in performance appraisals. Pay attention to equity perceptions in distributing rewards.

3. *Speak your feelings.* Managers who convey only hard facts come across as cold, distant, and unfeeling. When you share your feelings, others will see that you are real and human. They will know you for who you are and their respect for you is likely to increase.

4. *Tell the truth.* Being trustworthy means being credible. If honesty is critical to credibility, then you must be perceived as someone who tells the truth. Employees are more tolerant of hearing something "they don't want to hear" than of finding out that their manager lied to them.

5. *Be consistent.* People want predictability. Mistrust comes from not knowing what to expect. Take the time to think about your values and beliefs, and let those values and beliefs consistently guide your decisions. When you know what's important to you, your actions will follow, and you will project a consistency that earns trust.

6. *Fulfill your promises.* Trust requires that people believe that you are dependable. You need to ensure that you keep your word. Promises made must be promises kept.

7. *Maintain confidences.* You trust those whom you believe to be discreet and those on whom you can rely. If people open up to you and make themselves vulnerable by telling you something in confidence, they need to feel assured you won't discuss it with others or betray that confidence. If people perceive you as someone who leaks personal confidences or someone who can't be depended on, you've lost their trust.

8. *Demonstrate competence.* Develop the admiration and respect of others by demonstrating technical and professional ability. Pay particular attention to developing and displaying your communication, negotiation, and other interpersonal skills.

Practicing the Skill

Read through the following scenario. Write a paper describing how you would handle the situation. Be sure to refer to the eight behaviors described previouslyfor developing trust.

Scenario

Donna Romines is the shipping department manager at Tastefully Tempting, a gourmet candy company based in Phoenix. Orders for the company's candy come from around the world. Your six-member team processes these orders. Needless to say, the two months before Christmas are quite hectic. Everybody counts the days until December 24 when the phones finally stop ringing off the wall, at least for a couple of days. You and all of your team members breathe a sigh of relief as the last box of candy is sent on its way out the door.

When the company was first founded five years ago, after the holiday rush, the owners would shut down Tastefully Tempting for two weeks after Christmas. However, as the business has grown and moved into Internet sales, that practice has become too costly. There's too much business to be able to afford that luxury. And the rush for Valentine's Day orders start pouring in the week after Christmas. Although the two-week post-holiday company-wide shutdown has been phased out formally, some departments have found it difficult to get employees to gear up once again after the Christmas break. The employees who come to work after Christmas usually accomplish little. This year, though, things have got to change. You know that the cultural "tradition" won't be easy to overcome, but your shipping team needs to be ready to tackle the orders that have piled up. After all, Tastefully Tempting's customers want their orders filled promptly and correctly!

WORKING TOGETHER Team Exercise

In an effort to be (or at least appear to be) socially responsible, many organizations donate money to philanthropic and charitable causes. In addition, many organizations ask their employees to make individual donations to these causes. Suppose you're the manager of a work team, and you know that several of your employees can't afford to pledge money right now because of personal or financial problems. You've also been told by your supervisor that the CEO has been known to check the list of individual contributors to see who is and is not "supporting these very important causes." Working together in a small group of three or four, answer the following questions:

- How would you handle this situation?
- What ethical guidelines might you suggest for individual and organizational contributions in such a situation?
- Create a company policy statement that expresses your ethical guidelines.

MY TURN TO BE A MANAGER

- Find five different examples of organizational codes of ethics. Using Exhibit 5-7, describe what each contains. Compare and contrast the examples.

- Using the examples of codes of ethics you found, create what you feel would be an appropriate and effective organizational code of ethics. In addition, create your own *personal code of ethics* you can use as a guide to ethical dilemmas.

- Take advantage of volunteer opportunities. Be sure to include these on your résumé. If possible, try to do things in these volunteer positions that will improve your managerial skills in planning, organizing, leading, or controlling.

- Go to the Global Reporting Initiative Web site [www.globalreporting.org] and choose three businesses from the list that have filed reports. Look at those reports and describe/evaluate what's in them. In addition, identify the stakeholders that might be affected and how they might be affected by the company's actions.

- Make a list of what green management things your school is doing. If you're working, make a list of what green management things your employer is doing. Do some research on being green. Are there additional things your school or employer could be doing? Write a report to each describing any suggestions. (Look for ways you could use these suggestions to be more "green" in your personal life.)

- Over the course of two weeks, see what ethical "dilemmas" you observe. These could be ones you face personally or they could be ones that others (friends, colleagues, other students talking in the hallway or before class, and so forth) face. Write these dilemmas down and think about what you might do if faced with that dilemma.

- Interview two different managers about how they encourage their employees to be ethical. Write down their comments and discuss how these ideas might help you be a better manager.

- Steve's and Mary's suggested readings: Y. Chouinard and V. Stanley, *The Responsible Company* (Patagonia Inc., 2012); Bethany McLean and Peter Elkind, *The Smartest Guys in the Room: The Amazing Rise and Scandalous Fall of Enron* (Portfolio, 2003); Barbara Ley Toffler, *Final Accounting: Ambition, Greed, and the Fall of Arthur Andersen* (Broadway Books, 2003); Joseph L. Badaracco, Jr., *Leading Quietly: An Unorthodox Guide to Doing the Right Thing* (Harvard Business School Press, 2002); and Kenneth Blanchard and Norman Vincent Peale, *The Power of Ethical Management* (Morrow, 1988).

- If you have the opportunity, take a class on business or managerial ethics or on social responsibility—often called business and society—or both. Not only will this look good on your résumé, it could help you personally grapple with some of the tough issues managers face in being ethical and responsible.

- In your own words, write down three things you learned in this chapter about being a good manager.

- Self-knowledge can be a powerful learning tool. Go to mymanagementlab.com and complete these self-assessment exercises: What Do I Value? How Do My Ethics Rate? Do I Trust Others? and Do Others See Me as Trusting? Using the results of your assessments, identify personal strengths and weaknesses. What will you do to reinforce your strengths and improve your weaknesses?

MyManagementLab

Go to **mymanagementlab.com** for Auto-graded writing questions as well as the following Assisted-graded writing questions:

5-1. What is green management and how can organizations go green?

5-2. Discuss specific ways managers can encourage ethical behavior.

5-3. Mymanagementlab Only – comprehensive writing assignment for this chapter.

CASE APPLICATION 1 A Better Tomorrow

Building on his success of giving children a better tomorrow by providing them with a pair of shoes, TOMS founder Blake Mycoskie is giving more people a better tomorrow through a new venture that provides prescription eyeglasses, sight-saving surgery, and other medical treatment to people throughout the world who suffer from impaired vision.
Source: HANDOUT/MCT/Newscom

It's an incredibly simple but potentially world-changing idea.[101] For each pair of shoes sold, a pair is donated to a child in need. That's the business model followed by TOMS Shoes. During a visit to Argentina in 2006 as a contestant on the CBS reality show *The Amazing Race,* Blake Mycoskie, founder of TOMS, "saw lots of kids with no shoes who were suffering from injuries to their feet." Just think what it would be like to be barefoot, not by choice, but from lack of availability and ability to own a pair. He was so moved by the experience that he wanted to do something. That something is what TOMS does now by blending charity with commerce. (The name TOMS is actually short for "Shoes for a better tomorrow" which eventually became "Tomorrow's Shoes" which then became "Toms.") And a better tomorrow is what Blake wanted to provide to shoeless children around the world. Those shoe donations have been central to the success of the TOMS brand, which is popular among tweens, teens, and twenty-somethings. And TOMS has helped provide more than 1 million shoes to kids in need in the United States and abroad since its founding. Hoping to build on this success, the company recently launched its second one-for-one product—an eyewear line whose sales will help provide improved vision to those in need.

DISCUSSION QUESTIONS ✪

1. How can TOMS balance being socially responsible *and* being focused on profits?
2. Would you describe TOMS approach as social obligation, social responsiveness, or social responsibility? Explain.
3. It's time to think like a manager. TOMS' one-for-one approach is a wonderful idea, but what would be involved with making it work?
4. Do you think consumers are drawn to products with a charitable connection? Why or why not?

CASE APPLICATION 2 Lessons from Lehman Brothers: Will We Ever Learn?

On September 15, 2008, financial services firm Lehman Brothers filed for bankruptcy with the U.S. Bankruptcy Court in the Southern District of New York.[102] That action—the largest Chapter 11 filing in financial history—unleashed a "crisis of confidence that threw financial markets worldwide into turmoil, sparking the worst crisis since the Great Depression." The fall of this Wall Street icon is, unfortunately, not a new one, as we've seen in the stories of Enron, WorldCom, and others. In a report released by bankruptcy court-appointed examiner Anton Valukas, Lehman executives and the firm's auditor, Ernst & Young, were lambasted for actions that led to the firm's collapse. He said, "Lehman repeatedly exceeded its own internal risk limits and controls, and a wide range of bad calls by its management led to the bank's failure." Let's look behind the scenes at some of the issues.

One of the major problems at Lehman was its culture and reward structure. Excessive risk taking by employees was openly lauded and rewarded handsomely.

Individuals making questionable deals were hailed and treated as "conquering heroes." On the other hand, anyone who questioned decisions was often ignored or overruled. For instance, Oliver Budde, who served as an associate general counsel at Lehman for nine years, was responsible for preparing the firm's public filings on executive compensation. Infuriated by what he felt was the firm's "intentional under-representation of how much top executives were paid," Budde argued with his bosses for years about that matter, to no avail. Then, one time he objected to a tax deal that an outside accounting firm had proposed to lower medical insurance costs saying, "My gut feeling was that this was just reshuffling some papers to get an expense off the balance sheet. It was not the right thing, and I told them." However, Budde's bosses disagreed and okayed the deal.

A report examining actions leading to the collapse of Lehman Brothers cited top leadership errors of business judgment and balance sheet manipulation, but in testifying before a government hearing on the causes of the bankruptcy, Lehman's chief executive Richard Fuld said that he and other executives did everything they could to protect the bank.
Source: Shawn Thew/EPA/Newscom

Another problem at Lehman was the firm's top leadership. Valukas's report was highly critical of Lehman's executives who "should have done more, done better." He pointed out that the executives made the company's problems worse by their conduct, which ranged from "serious but nonculpable errors of business judgment to actionable balance sheet manipulation." Valukas went on to say that "former chief executive Richard Fuld was at least grossly negligent in causing Lehman to file misleading periodic reports." These reports were part of an accounting device called "Repo 105." Lehman used this device to get some $50 billion of undesirable assets off its balance sheet at the end of the first and second quarters of 2008, instead of selling those assets at a loss. The examiner's report "included e-mails from Lehman's global financial controller confirming that the only purpose or motive for Repo 105 transactions was reduction in the balance sheet, adding that there was no substance to the transactions." Lehman's auditor was aware of the use of Repo 105 but did not challenge or question it. Sufficient evidence indicated that Fuld knew about the use of it as well; however, he signed off on quarterly reports that made no mention of it. Fuld's attorney said, "Mr. Fuld did not know what these transactions were—he didn't structure or negotiate them, nor was he aware of their accounting treatment." A spokesperson from Ernst & Young (the auditor) said that, "Lehman's bankruptcy was the result of a series of unprecedented adverse events in the financial markets."

DISCUSSION QUESTIONS ✪

1. Describe the situation at Lehman Brothers from an ethics perspective. What's your opinion of what happened here?

2. What was the culture at Lehman Brothers like? How did this culture contribute to the company's downfall?

3. What role did Lehman's executives play in the company's collapse? Were they being responsible and ethical? Discuss.

4. Could anything have been done differently at Lehman Brothers to prevent what happened? Explain.

5. After all the public uproar over Enron and then the passage of the Sarbanes-Oxley Act to protect shareholders, why do you think we still continue to see these types of situations? Is it unreasonable to expect that businesses can and should act ethically?

PART 2 Management Practice

A Manager's Dilemma

One of the biggest fears of a food service company manager has to be the hepatitis A virus, a highly contagious virus transmitted by sharing food, utensils, cigarettes, or drug paraphernalia with an infected person. Food service workers aren't any more susceptible to the illness than anyone else, but an infected employee can easily spread the virus by handling food, especially cold foods. The virus, which is rarely fatal, can cause flulike illness for several weeks. There is no cure for hepatitis A, but a vaccine can prevent it. Jim Brady, manager of a restaurant, is facing a serious dilemma. He recently learned one of his cooks could have exposed as many as 350 people to hepatitis A during a five-day period when he was at work. The cook was thought to have contracted the virus through an infant living in his apartment complex. Because children usually show no symptoms of the disease, they can easily pass it on to adults. Jim has a decision to make. Should he go public with the information, or should he only report it to the local health department as required by law?

> *Using what you learned in Part 2, and especially in Chapter 5, what would you do in this situation?*

Global Sense

A vice president for engineering at a major chip-manufacturer who found one of his projects running more than a month late felt that perhaps the company's Indian engineers "didn't understand the sense of urgency" in getting the project completed. In the Scottish highlands, the general manager of O'Bryant's Kitchens is quite satisfied with his non-Scottish employees—cooks who are German, Swedish, and Slovak and waitresses who are mostly Polish. Other highland hotels and restaurants also have a large number of Eastern European staff. Despite the obvious language barriers, these Scottish employers are finding ways to help their foreign employees adapt and be successful. When the manager of a telecommunications company's developer forum gave a presentation to a Finnish audience and asked for feedback, he was told, "That was good." Based on his interpretation of that phrase, he assumed it must have been just an okay presentation—nothing spectacular. However, since Finns tend to be generally much quieter and more reserved than Americans, that response actually meant, "That was great, off the scale." And the owner of a Chicago-based manufacturing company, who now has two factories in Suzhou, China, is dealing with the challenges that many companies moving to China face: understanding the way their Chinese employees view work and nurturing Chinese managerial talent.

It's not easy being a successful global manager, especially when it comes to dealing with cultural differences. Those cultural differences have been described as an "iceberg," of which we only see the top 15 percent, mainly food, appearance, and language. Although these elements can be complicated, it's the other 85 percent of the "iceberg" that's not apparent initially that managers need to be especially concerned about. What does that include? Workplace issues such as communication styles, priorities, role expectations, work tempo, negotiation styles, nonverbal communication, attitudes toward planning, and so forth. Understanding these issues requires developing a global mindset and skill set. Many organizations are relying on cultural awareness training to help them do just that.

Discuss the following questions in light of what you learned in Part 2:

- *What global attitude do you think would most encourage, support, and promote cultural awareness? Explain.*
- *Would legal-political and economic differences play a role as companies design appropriate cultural awareness training for employees? Explain.*
- *Is diversity management related to cultural awareness? Discuss.*
- *Pick one of the countries mentioned above and do some cultural research on it. What did you find out about the culture of that country? How might this information affect the way a manager in that country plans, organizes, leads, and controls?*
- *What advice might you give to a manager who has little experience globally?*

Sources: P. Korkki, "More Courses Get You Ready to Face the World," New York Times Online, February 29, 2012; N. Bloom, C. Genakos, R. Sadun, and J. Van Reenen, "Management Practices Across Firms and Countries," Academy of Management Perspectives, February 2012, pp. 12–33; E. Spitznagel, "Impress Your Chinese Boss," Bloomberg Business Week, January 9–January 15, 2012, pp. 80–81; R. S. Vassolo, J. O. De Castro, and L. R. Gomez-Meija, "Managing in Latin America: Common Issues and A Research Agenda," Academy of Management Perspectives, November 2011, pp. 22–37; P. Thorby, "Great Expectations: Mastering Cultural Sensitivity in Business and HR," [www.workforce.com], August 17, 2011; K. Tyler, "Global Ease," HR Magazine, May 2011, pp. 41–48; J. S. Lublin, "Cultural Flexibility In Demand," Wall Street Journal, April 11, 2011, pp. B1+; and S. Russwurm, L. Hernandez, S. Chambers, and K. Chung, "Developing Your Global Know-How," Harvard Business Review, March 2011, pp. 70–75.

Continuing Case
Starbucks—Integrative Managerial Issues

As managers manage, they must be aware of some specific integrative issues that can affect the way they plan, organize, lead, and control. The characteristics and nature of

These customers are enjoying "the Starbucks experience" at a coffee shop in Guangzhou, China. Starbucks sees an enormous potential for growth in China, where 140 cities have a population exceeding one million people. While expanding in China and other global markets, Starbucks managers must take into account the cultural, economic, legal, and political aspects of different markets as they plan, organize, lead, and control.
Source: Imaginechina/Associated Press [Wide World Photos]

these integrative issues will influence what managers and other employees do and how they do it. And more importantly, it will affect how efficiently and effectively managers do their job of coordinating and overseeing the work of other people so that goals—organizational and work-level or work unit—can be accomplished. What are these integrative managerial issues, and how does Starbucks accommodate and respond to them? In this part of the Continuing Case, we're going to look at Starbucks' global, diversity, and social responsibility/ethical challenges.

Global Challenges

You could say that Starbucks has been a global business from day one. While on a business trip in 1983 to Milan, Howard Schultz (who worked in marketing for Starbucks' original founders and is now the company's CEO) experienced firsthand Italy's coffee culture and had an epiphany about how such an approach might work back home in the United States. Now, some 40 years later, Starbucks stores are found in 55 countries (as of 2012), including 600 in mainland China and its first stores in Finland and Costa Rica. Doing business globally, as Chapter 3 points out, can be challenging. Since much of the company's future growth prospects are global, the company has targeted some markets for additional global expansion, including China, Brazil, Vietnam, and China. Yes, we've listed China twice to make a point: Schultz is clear about the fact that his company sees China as the number one growth opportunity for Starbucks. During a visit in late 2011, a government official informed him that 140 cities in China now have a population exceeding one million people. That's a lot of potential coffee drinkers buying cups of Starbucks coffee and other Starbucks products! But in China and all of its global markets, Starbucks must be cognizant of the economic, legal-political, and cultural aspects that characterize those markets. For instance, in

Europe—the "birthplace of café and coffeehouse culture"—Starbucks is struggling, even after a decade of doing business there. Take France, where Starbucks has been since 2004 and has 63 stores. It has never made a profit. Of course, part of that could be attributed to the debt crisis and sluggish economy. And rents and labor costs are notoriously high. Yet, the biggest challenge for Starbucks may be trying to appeal to the vast array of European tastes. Michelle Gass, the company's new chief of Starbucks operations for Europe, the Middle East, and Africa, decided to take an "anthropological tour" to get a better feel for the varying wants and needs of coffee lovers in Europe. Although she initially thought the well-established coffeehouse culture in places like Paris or Vienna might be what customers wanted, she discovered instead that customers wanted the "Starbucks experience." But even that means different things in different markets. For instance, the British drink take-away (to-go) coffee, so Starbucks is planning for hundreds of drive-through locations there. In the rest of Europe, Starbucks plans to put many new sites in airports and railway stations on the continent. Although the growth potential seems real, cultural challenges still remain, not only in Europe but in Starbucks' other markets as well. The company is recognizing that not every customer wants a "watered-down Starbucks" experience. So, as Starbucks continues its global expansion, it's attempting to be respectful of the cultural differences, most especially in that important market, China.

Managing Diversity and Inclusion

Not only does Starbucks attempt to be respectful of global cultural differences, it is committed to being an organization that embraces and values diversity in how it does business. The company-wide diversity strategy encompasses four areas: customers, suppliers, partners (employees), and communities. Starbucks attempts to make the Starbucks Experience accessible to all customers and to respond to each customer's unique preferences and needs. Starbucks' supplier diversity program works to provide opportunities for developing a business relationship to women- and minority-owned suppliers. As far as its partners, the company is committed to a workplace that values and respects people from diverse backgrounds. And it aims to enable its partners to do their best work and to be successful in the Starbucks environment. The company does support partner networks (what we call employee resource groups in Chapter 4). Some of the current ones include Starbucks Access Alliance, a forum for partners with disabilities; Starbucks Armed Forces Support Network, which supports veterans and those currently in the armed forces and their families; and the Starbucks Black Partner Network, which strengthens relationships and connections among partners of African descent. Finally, Starbucks supports diversity in its local neighborhoods and global communities through programs and investments that deepen its ties in those areas. Although Starbucks is committed to practicing and valuing diversity, by no means is it perfect. For instance, an Americans with Disabilities Act case was filed against a specific Starbucks store by a job applicant who had short height because of the condition of dwarfism. The store management refused to hire her for a barista job even though she claimed she could do the job using a step stool. And they did not even offer to try this accommodation. Starbucks quickly settled the case and agreed to provide training to managers on proper ADA procedures. The company's response earned praise from the Equal Employment Opportunity Commission for its prompt resolution of the issue.

Social Responsibility and Ethics

Doing good coffee is important to Starbucks, but so is doing good. Starbucks takes its social responsibility and ethical commitments seriously. In 2001, the company began issuing an annual corporate social responsibility report, which addresses the company's decisions and actions in relation to its products, society, the environment, and the workplace. These reports aren't simply a way for Starbucks to brag about its socially responsible actions, but are intended to stress the importance of doing business in a responsible way and to hold employees and managers accountable for their actions.

Starbucks focuses its corporate responsibility efforts on three main areas: ethical sourcing (buying), environmental stewardship, and community involvement. Starbucks approaches ethical sourcing from the perspective of helping the farmers and suppliers who grow and produce their products use responsible growing methods and helping them be successful, thus promoting long-term sustainability of the supply of quality coffee. It's a win-win situation. The farmers have a better (and more secure) future and Starbucks is helping create a long-term supply of a commodity they depend on. Environmental stewardship has been one of the more challenging undertakings for Starbucks, especially when you think about the number of disposable containers generated weekly from nearly 60 million customers served. And front-of-the-store waste is only half the battle. Behind-the-counter waste is also generated in the form of cardboard boxes, milk jugs, syrup bottles, and, not surprisingly, coffee grounds. Even with recycling bins provided, one wrong item in a recycle bin can make the whole thing unrecyclable to a hauler. Despite this, the company has made significant strides in recycling. In a 2010 test program, 100,000 paper coffee cups were made into new ones. The company's goal by 2015 is to recycle all 4 billion cups sold annually. That's an ambitious goal, for sure. The progress it's made so far has been possible only through a cooperative effort with other companies in the materials value chain (even competitors) to find recycling solutions that work. But Starbucks is in it for the long haul. Finally, Starbucks has always strived

to be a good neighbor by providing a place for people to come together and by committing to supporting financially and in other ways the communities where its stores are located. Partners (and customers, for that matter) are encouraged to get involved in volunteering in their communities. In addition, the Starbucks Foundation, which started in 1997 with funding for literacy programs in the United States and Canada, now makes grants to a wide variety of community projects and service programs.

Starbucks is also very serious about doing business ethically. In fact, it was named to the 2012 list of World's Most Ethical Companies, as it has been for the last six years. From the executive level to the store level, individuals are expected and empowered to protect Starbucks' reputation through how they conduct business and how they treat others. And individuals are guided by the *Standards of Business Conduct,* a resource created for employees in doing business ethically, with integrity and honesty. These business conduct standards cover the workplace environment, business practices, intellectual property and proprietary information, and community involvement. A flow-chart model included in the standards document is used to illustrate an ethical decision-making framework for partners. Despite the thorough information in the standards, if partners face a situation where they're unsure how to respond or where they want to voice concerns, they're encouraged to seek out guidance from their manager, their partner resources representative, or even the corporate office of business ethics and compliance. The company also strongly states that it does not tolerate any retaliation against or victimization of any partner who raises concerns or questions.

Discussion Questions

1. What types of global economic and legal-political issues might Starbucks face as it does business globally?
2. You're responsible for developing a global cultural awareness program for Starbucks' executives who are leading the company's international expansion efforts. Describe what you think will be important for these executives to know.
3. Using information from the case and information you pull from Starbucks' Web site, what global attitude do you think Starbucks exhibits? Defend your choice.
4. Pick one of the countries mentioned as an important target for Starbucks. Make a bulleted list of economic, political-legal, and cultural characteristics of this country.
5. What workforce challenges might Starbucks face in global markets as far as its partners?
6. How does Starbucks manage diversity? What is Starbucks doing to manage diversity in each of the four areas: customers, suppliers, partners, and communities?

7. With more than 149,000 partners worldwide, what challenges would Starbucks face in making sure their diversity values are practiced and adhered to?

8. Starbucks defines diversity on its Web site in the form of an equation:

Diversity = Inclusion + Equity + Accessibility.

Explain what you think this means. What do you think of this definition of diversity?

9. What other workplace diversity initiatives discussed in Chapter 4 (besides employee resource groups) might be appropriate for an organization like Starbucks?

10. Go to the company's Web site [www.starbucks.com] and find the latest corporate social responsibility report. Choose one of the key areas in the report (or your professor may assign one of these areas). Describe and evaluate what the company has done in this key area.

11. What do you think of Starbucks' goal to recycle all 4 billion cups sold annually by 2015? What challenges does it face in meeting that goal?

12. Why is the concept of "empowering" employees important in doing business ethically?

13. Again, go to the company's Web site. Find the *Standards of Business Conduct* document. First, what's your impression of this document? Then, choose one topic from one of the main areas covered. Describe what advice is provided to partners.

14. What do you think the company's use of the term *partners* instead of employees implies? What's your reaction to this? Do you think it matters what companies call their employees? (For instance, Wal-Mart calls its employees *associates*.) Why or why not?

Notes for the Part 2 Continuing Case

Starbucks Corporation 2011 Annual Report, www.investor.starbucks.com, August 6, 2012; Starbucks Corporation Business Ethics and Compliance: Standards of Business Conduct," www.assets.starbucks.com, August 6, 2012; "2012 World's Most Ethical Companies," www.ethispere.com/wme/, August 6, 2012; Starbucks News Release, "Starbucks Reports Record Third Quarter Results," www.investor.starbucks.com, July 26, 2012; L. Alderman, "In Europe, Starbucks Adjusts to a Café Culture," *New York Times Online,* March 30, 2012; V. Varma and B. Packard, "Starbucks Global Responsibility Report Year in Review: Fiscal 2011," www.starbucks.com, March 16, 2012; B. Gregg, "Is Professor's 'Hi, Sweetie' Comment Sexual Harassment," www.diversityinc.com, March 12, 2012; S. Faris, "Grounds Zero," *Bloomberg BusinessWeek Online,* February 9, 2012; "Howard Schultz, on Getting a Second Shot," *Inc.,* April 2011, pp. 52–54; "A Shout Out to Starbucks," *Wholeliving.com,* April 2011, p. 111; and "Starbucks Quest for Healthy Growth: An Interview with Howard Schultz," *McKinsey Quarterly,* 2011, Issue 2, pp. 34–43.

Managers as Decision Makers

SPOTLIGHT: *Manager at Work*

Neon signs lighting up the night. *Sultry summer evenings. Pole speakers and roller-skating carhops. Hot and fresh food eaten in your car. When you think of a drive-in burger joint, is this what comes to mind? Sonic Corporation, headquartered in Oklahoma City, is top dog in this industry.[1] It operates the largest chain of quick-service drive-ins in the United States with a significant presence in the South. To stay alive in the competitive fast food industry, Sonic's managers have to continually look at new products and new promotions to draw in customers. That requires a lot of decision making!*

As the company's research and development team began the process of looking for what they hoped would be the chain's next product blockbuster, they didn't have far to look—the company's popular existing foot-long chili cheese Coney dog, which market research discovered was the product people most associated with Sonic. Using that initial data, it was a pretty easy decision to look for a natural extension of that product line. And even more so, since extending the line of hot dogs would also "capitalize on a confluence of culinary trends, including the growing interest in street food, comfort foods, and location-specific flavors." But even for an "easy" decision, the development team had their work cut out for them.

The first step sounds like the most fun—"hot dog dine arounds" in cities nationwide. (It's too bad that every decision can't start off like this!) The team went to Dallas, Chicago, Philadelphia, and Los Angeles and sampled all kinds of hot dogs and toppings. Each one was scrutinized

Source: ZUMA Press/Newscom

Source: © Jonathan Larsen/Diadem Images/Alamy

to find the right flavors, but also just as important, to find the vendors that could supply the logistical needs of the 3,600-unit chain. Matt Schein, the chain's senior director of brand marketing said, "As we went across the country, we saw that certain flavors—

To stay alive in the competitive fast food industry, Sonic's managers have to continually look at new products and new promotions to draw in customers.

sauerkraut, relish, chili—were everywhere. That made it pretty easy to narrow our choices down to four flavors." Once the team had identified those flavors, the challenge for the culinary team was replicating those beloved "hometown" flavors. What resulted was Sonic's new line of grilled 6-inch, all-beef hot dogs: the Chicago Dog (with a whole pickle, relish, tomatoes, hot pickled peppers

known as sport peppers, chopped onions, celery salt, and mustard all on a poppy-seed bun); the New York Dog (with spicy mustard, grilled onions, and sauerkraut); the All-American Dog (only the basics: ketchup, mustard, relish, and chopped onions); and, of course, the Chili Cheese Coney

MyManagementLab®
⭐ **Improve Your Grade!**
Over 10 million students improved their results using the Pearson MyLabs.
Visit **mymanagementlab.com** for simulations, tutorials, and end-of-chapter problems.

LEARNING OUTCOMES

6.1 | *Describe* the eight steps in the decision-making process.

6.2 | *Explain* the four ways managers make decisions.

6.3 | *Classify* decisions and decision-making conditions.

6.4 | *Describe* different decision-making styles and discuss how biases affect decision making.

6.5 | *Identify* effective decision-making techniques.

(with chili and melted, shredded Cheddar cheese).
Once the products were decided, it was time to
test in four different markets. After sailing through
testing, the products were ready for the menu line-
up. However, before the products could be rolled
out, new kitchen equipment had to be installed
and employees trained in all the company's various
locations. And now, the real test. Would the regional
flavors appeal to customers? Had the managers
made good decisions? **How might Matt Schein and**
other company managers evaluate whether their
decisions were good decisions?

Like managers everywhere, Matt Schein needs
to make decisions as he manages. Decision making
is the essence of management. It's what managers
do (or try to avoid). And all managers would like to
make good decisions because they're judged on
the outcomes of those decisions. For Matt Schein
and Sonic, the hot dog decision turned out to be a
winner. More than 70 million of the hot dogs have
been sold since their introduction in 2011. (That's
a lot of hot dogs!) In this chapter, we examine the
concept of decision making and how managers
make decisions.

THE DECISION-MAKING Process

6.1 | **Describe** the eight
steps in the decision-
making process.

It was the type of day that airline managers dread. A record-setting blizzard was
moving up the East Coast—covering roads, railroads, and airport runways with as
much as 27 inches of snow. One of the major airlines that would have to deal with
the storm, American Airlines, "has almost 80,000 employees who help make flights
possible and four who cancel them." Danny Burgin, who works at the company's
Fort Worth, Texas, control center, is one of those four. But fortunately for Danny,
snowstorms are fairly simple to deal with because they're usually "easier to predict
and airline crews can work around them quickly with de-icers and snowplows." But
still, even this doesn't mean that the decisions he has to make are easy, especially when
his decisions affect hundreds of flights and thousands of passengers![2] Although most
decisions managers make don't involve the weather, you can see that decisions play an
important role in what an organization has to do or is able to do.

Managers at all levels and in all areas of organizations make **decisions**. That
is, they make choices. For instance, top-level managers make decisions about their
organization's goals, where to locate manufacturing facilities, or what new markets
to move into. Middle- and lower-level managers make decisions about production
schedules, product quality problems, pay raises, and employee discipline. Making
decisions isn't something that just managers do; all organizational members make decisions that affect their jobs and the organization they work for. But our focus in this
chapter is on how *managers* make decisions.

Although decision making is typically described as choosing among alternatives,
this view is too simplistic. Why? Because decision making is (and should be) a process,
not just a simple act of choosing among alternatives.[3] Even for something as straightforward as deciding where to go for lunch, you do more than just choose burgers or
pizza or hot dogs. Granted, you may not spend a lot of time contemplating your lunch
decision, but you still go through the process when making that decision. Exhibit 6-1
shows the eight steps in the decision-making process. This process is as relevant to personal decisions as it is to corporate decisions. Let's use an example—a manager deciding what laptop computers to purchase—to illustrate the steps in the process.

Step 1: Identify a Problem

Your team is dysfunctional, your customers are leaving, or your plans are no longer
relevant.[4] Every decision starts with a **problem**, a discrepancy between an existing
and a desired condition.[5] Amanda is a sales manager whose reps need new laptops

decision
A choice among two or more alternatives

problem
An obstacle that makes it difficult to
achieve a desired goal or purpose

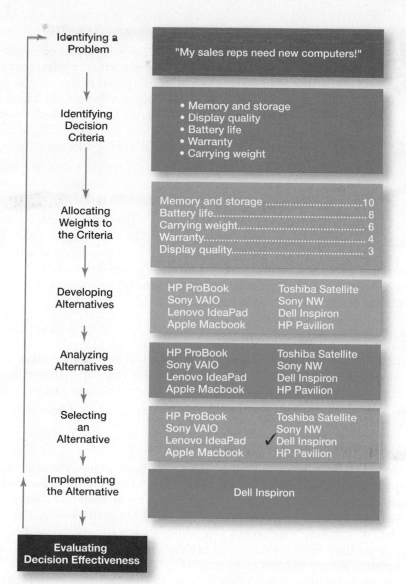

Exhibit 6-1
Decision-Making Process

because their old ones are outdated and inadequate for doing their job. To make it simple, assume it's not economical to add memory to the old computers and it's the company's policy to purchase, not lease. Now we have a problem—a disparity between the sales reps' current computers (existing condition) and their need to have more efficient ones (desired condition). Amanda has a decision to make.

How do managers identify problems? In the real world, most problems don't come with neon signs flashing "problem." When her reps started complaining about their computers, it was pretty clear to Amanda that something needed to be done, but few problems are that obvious. Managers also have to be cautious not to confuse problems with symptoms of the problem. Is a 5 percent drop in sales a problem? Or are declining sales merely a symptom of the real problem, such as poor-quality products, high prices, or bad advertising? Also, keep in mind that problem identification is subjective. What one manager considers a problem might not be considered a problem by another manager. In addition, a manager who resolves the wrong problem perfectly is likely to perform just as poorly as the manager who doesn't even recognize a problem and does nothing. As you can see, effectively identifying problems is important, but not easy.[6]

Decision making is an eight-step process that begins with identifying a problem and ends with evaluating the outcome of the decision. After problem identification, managers must determine the decision criteria that are relevant to solving the problem. For a manager looking for new laptops for her sales reps, the decision criteria may include price, display quality, memory and storage capabilities, battery life, and carrying weight. After the manager identifies the criteria, she must assign weights to the criteria if they aren't equally important.
Source: © Alex Segre/Alamy

decision criteria
Criteria that define what's important or relevant to resolving a problem

Step 2: Identify Decision Criteria

Once a manager has identified a problem, he or she must identify the **decision criteria** important or relevant to resolving the problem. Every decision maker has criteria guiding his or her decisions even if they're not explicitly stated. In our example, Amanda decides after careful consideration that memory and storage capabilities, display quality, battery life, warranty, and carrying weight are the relevant criteria in her decision.

Step 3: Allocate Weights to the Criteria

If the relevant criteria aren't equally important, the decision maker must weight the items in order to give them the correct priority in the decision. How? A simple way is to give the most important criterion a weight of 10 and then assign weights to the rest using that standard. Of course, you could use any number as the highest weight. The weighted criteria for our example are shown in Exhibit 6-2.

Step 4: Develop Alternatives

The fourth step in the decision-making process requires the decision maker to list viable alternatives that could resolve the problem. In this step, a decision maker needs to be creative, and the alternatives are only listed—not evaluated—just yet. Our sales manager, Amanda, identifies eight laptops as possible choices. (See Exhibit 6-3.)

Step 5: Analyze Alternatives

Once alternatives have been identified, a decision maker must evaluate each one. How? By using the criteria established in Step 2. Exhibit 6-3 shows the assessed values that Amanda gave each alternative after doing some research on them. Keep in mind that these data represent an assessment of the eight alternatives using the decision criteria, but *not* the weighting. When you multiply each alternative by the assigned weight, you get the weighted alternatives as shown in Exhibit 6-4. The total score for each alternative, then, is the sum of its weighted criteria.

Sometimes a decision maker might be able to skip this step. If one alternative scores highest on every criterion, you wouldn't need to consider the weights because that alternative would already be the top choice. Or if the weights were all equal, you could evaluate an alternative merely by summing up the assessed values for each one. (Look again at Exhibit 6-3.) For example, the score for the HP ProBook would be 36, and the score for the Sony NW would be 35.

Step 6: Select an Alternative

The sixth step in the decision-making process is choosing the best alternative or the one that generated the highest total in Step 5. In our example (Exhibit 6-4), Amanda would choose the Dell Inspiron because it scored higher than all other alternatives (249 total).

Exhibit 6-2
Important Decision Criteria

Memory and storage	10
Battery life	8
Carrying weight	6
Warranty	4
Display quality	3

	Memory and Storage	Battery Life	Carrying Weight	Warranty	Display Quality
HP ProBook	10	3	10	8	5
Sony VAIO	8	7	7	8	7
Lenovo IdeaPad	8	5	7	10	10
Apple Macbook	8	7	7	8	7
Toshiba Satellite	7	8	7	8	7
Sony NW	8	3	6	10	8
Dell Inspiron	10	7	8	6	7
HP Pavilion	4	10	4	8	10

Exhibit 6-3
Possible Alternatives

Step 7: Implement the Alternative

In Step 7 in the decision-making process, you put the decision into action by conveying it to those affected and getting their commitment to it. We know that if the people who must implement a decision participate in the process, they're more likely to support it than if you just tell them what to do. Another thing managers may need to do during implementation is reassess the environment for any changes, especially if it's a long-term decision. Are the criteria, alternatives, and choice still the best ones, or has the environment changed in such a way that we need to reevaluate?

Step 8: Evaluate Decision Effectiveness

The last step in the decision-making process involves evaluating the outcome or result of the decision to see whether the problem was resolved. If the evaluation shows that the problem still exists, then the manager needs to assess what went wrong. Was the problem incorrectly defined? Were errors made when evaluating alternatives? Was the right alternative selected but poorly implemented? The answers might lead you to redo an earlier step or might even require starting the whole process over.

MANAGERS Making Decisions

Although everyone in an organization makes decisions, decision making is particularly important to managers. As Exhibit 6-5 shows, it's part of all four managerial functions. In fact, that's why we say that decision making is the essence of management.[7] And that's why managers—when they plan, organize, lead, and control—are called *decision makers*.

Explain the four ways managers make decisions. **6.2**

	Memory and Storage	Battery Life	Carrying Weight	Warranty	Display Quality	Total
HP ProBook	100	24	60	32	15	231
Sony VAIO	80	56	42	32	21	231
Lenovo IdeaPad	80	40	42	40	30	232
Apple Macbook	80	56	42	32	21	231
Toshiba Satellite	70	64	42	32	21	229
Sony NW	80	24	36	40	24	204
Dell Inspiron	100	56	48	24	21	249
HP Pavilion	40	80	24	32	30	206

Exhibit 6-4
Evaluation of Alternatives

Exhibit 6-5

Decisions Managers May Make

Planning

- What are the organization's long-term objectives?
- What strategies will best achieve those objectives?
- What should the organization's short-term objectives be?
- How difficult should individual goals be?

Organizing

- How many employees should I have report directly to me?
- How much centralization should there be in the organization?
- How should jobs be designed?
- When should the organization implement a different structure?

Leading

- How do I handle employees who appear unmotivated?
- What is the most effective leadership style in a given situation?
- How will a specific change affect worker productivity?
- When is the right time to stimulate conflict?

Controlling

- What activities in the organization need to be controlled?
- How should those activities be controlled?
- When is a performance deviation significant?
- What type of management information system should the organization have?

The fact that almost everything a manager does involves making decisions doesn't mean that decisions are always time-consuming, complex, or evident to an outside observer. Most decision making is routine. For instance, every day of the year you make a decision about what to eat for dinner. It's no big deal. You've made the decision thousands of times before. It's a pretty simple decision and can usually be handled quickly. It's the type of decision you almost forget *is* a decision. And managers also make dozens of these routine decisions every day, such as, for example, which employee will work what shift next week, what information should be included in a report, or how to resolve a customer's complaint. Keep in mind that even though a decision seems easy or has been faced by a manager a number of times before, it still is a decision. Let's look at four perspectives on how managers make decisions.

Making Decisions: Rationality

When Hewlett-Packard (HP) acquired Compaq, the company did no research on how customers viewed Compaq products until "months after then-CEO Carly Fiorina publicly announced the deal and privately warned her top management team that she didn't want to hear any dissent pertaining to the acquisition."[8] By the time they discovered that customers perceived Compaq products as inferior—just the opposite of what customers felt about HP products—it was too late. HP's performance suffered and Fiorina lost her job.

rational decision making
Describes choices that are logical and consistent and maximize value

We assume that managers will use **rational decision making**; that is, they'll make logical and consistent choices to maximize value.[9] After all, managers have all sorts of tools and techniques to help them be rational decision makers. But as the HP example illustrates, managers aren't always rational. What does it mean to be a "rational" decision maker?

ASSUMPTIONS OF RATIONALITY A rational decision maker would be fully objective and logical. The problem faced would be clear and unambiguous, and the decision maker would have a clear and specific goal and know all possible alternatives and consequences. Finally, making decisions rationally would consistently lead to selecting the alternative that maximizes the likelihood of achieving that goal. These assumptions apply to any decision—personal or managerial. However, for managerial decision making, we need to add one additional assumption—decisions are made in the best interests of the organization. These assumptions of rationality aren't very realistic, but the next concept can help explain how most decisions get made in organizations.

Making Decisions: Bounded Rationality

Despite the unrealistic assumptions, managers *are* expected to be rational when making decisions.[10] They understand that "good" decision makers are supposed to do certain things and exhibit good decision-making behaviors as they identify problems, consider alternatives, gather information, and act decisively but prudently. When they do so, they show others that they're competent and that their decisions are the result of intelligent deliberation. However, a more realistic approach to describing how managers make decisions is the concept of **bounded rationality**, which says that managers make decisions rationally, but are limited (bounded) by their ability to process information.[11] Because they can't possibly analyze all information on all alternatives, managers **satisfice**, rather than maximize. That is, they accept solutions that are "good enough." They're being rational within the limits (bounds) of their ability to process information. Let's look at an example.

Suppose you're a finance major and upon graduation you want a job, preferably as a personal financial planner, with a minimum salary of $42,000 and within a hundred miles of your hometown. You accept a job offer as a business credit analyst—not exactly a personal financial planner but still in the finance field—at a bank 50 miles from home at a starting salary of $40,000. If you had done a more comprehensive job search, you would have discovered a job in personal financial planning at a trust company only 25 miles from your hometown and starting at a salary of $45,000. You weren't a perfectly rational decision maker because you didn't maximize your decision by searching all possible alternatives and then choosing the best. But because the first job offer was satisfactory (or "good enough"), you behaved in a bounded rationality manner by accepting it.

Most decisions that managers make don't fit the assumptions of perfect rationality, so they satisfice. However, keep in mind that their decision making is also likely influenced by the organization's culture, internal politics, power considerations, and by a phenomenon called **escalation of commitment**, an increased commitment to a previous decision despite evidence that it may have been wrong.[12] The *Challenger* space shuttle disaster is often used as an example of escalation of commitment. Decision makers chose to launch the shuttle that day even though the decision was questioned by several individuals who believed it was a bad one. Why would decision makers escalate commitment to a bad decision? Because they don't want to admit that their initial decision may have been flawed. Rather than search for new alternatives, they simply increase their commitment to the original solution.

Making Decisions: The Role of Intuition

When managers at stapler-maker Swingline saw the company's market share declining, they used a logical scientific approach to address the issue. For three years, they exhaustively researched stapler users before deciding what new products to develop. However, at Accentra, Inc., founder Todd Moses used a more intuitive decision approach to come up with his line of unique PaperPro staplers.[13]

"Trust your instincts" is one of the guiding principles for decision making advocated by Virgin Group founder Richard Branson. When Branson decided to enter the airline business, industry experts warned him that the competition was too fierce and the cost of entry was too high for him to succeed. Relying on his intuition, Branson decided to enter the market with the mission of running a profitable airline where people love to fly and where people love to work. He felt that by applying the right energy, focus, and flair his venture would succeed, and it did. Branson is shown here dressed up as a prize fighter determined to knock out his competitors while celebrating the launch of Virgin America's expanded service to Chicago with crew members.
Source: © *ZUMA Wire Service/Alamy*

bounded rationality
Decision making that's rational, but limited (bounded) by an individual's ability to process information

satisfice
Accept solutions that are "good enough"

escalation of commitment
An increased commitment to a previous decision despite evidence it may have been wrong

Exhibit 6-6
What Is Intuition?

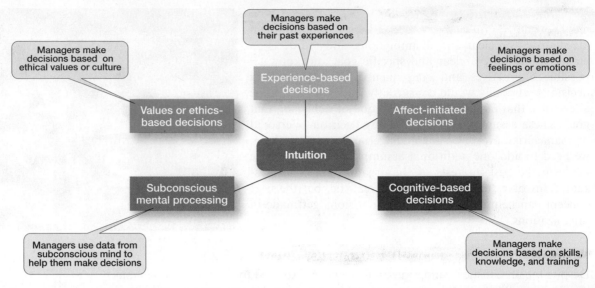

Source: Based on L. A. Burke and M. K. Miller, "Taking the Mystery Out of Intuitive Decision Making," *Academy of Management Executive,* October 1999, pp. 91–99.

intuitive decision making
Making decisions on the basis of experience, feelings, and accumulated judgment

Like Todd Moses, managers often use their intuition to help their decision making. What is **intuitive decision making**? It's making decisions on the basis of experience, feelings, and accumulated judgment. Researchers studying managers' use of intuitive decision making have identified five different aspects of intuition, which are described in Exhibit 6-6.[14] How common is intuitive decision making? One survey found that almost half of the executives surveyed "used intuition more often than formal analysis to run their companies."[15]

Intuitive decision making can complement both rational and bounded rational decision making.[16] First of all, a manager who has had experience with a similar type of problem or situation often can act quickly with what appears to be limited information because of that past experience. In addition, a recent study found that individuals who experienced intense feelings and emotions when making decisions actually achieved higher decision-making performance, especially when they understood their feelings as they were making decisions. The old belief that managers should ignore emotions when making decisions may not be the best advice.[17]

Making Decisions: The Role of Evidence-Based Management

Sales associates at the cosmetics counter at department store Bon-Ton Stores Inc. had the highest turnover of any store sales group. Using a data-driven decision approach, managers devised a more precise pre-employment assessment test. Now, not only do they have lower turnover, they actually have better hires.[18]

Suppose you were exhibiting some strange, puzzling physical symptoms. In order to make the best decisions about proper diagnosis and treatment, wouldn't you want your doctor to base her decisions on the best available evidence? Now suppose you're a manager faced with putting together an employee recognition program. Wouldn't you want those decisions also to be based on the best available evidence? "Any decision-making process is likely to be enhanced through the use of relevant and reliable evidence, whether it's buying someone a birthday present or wondering which new washing machine to buy."[19] That's the premise behind **evidence-based management (EBMgt)**, the "systematic use of the best available evidence to improve management practice."[20]

evidence-based management (EBMgt)
The systematic use of the best available evidence to improve management practice

EBMgt is quite relevant to managerial decision making. The four essential elements of EBMgt are the decision maker's expertise and judgment; external evidence

let's get REAL

that's been evaluated by the decision maker; opinions, preferences, and values of those who have a stake in the decision; and relevant organizational (internal) factors such as context, circumstances, and organizational members. The strength or influence of each of these elements on a decision will vary with each decision. Sometimes, the decision maker's intuition (judgment) might be given greater emphasis in the decision; other times it might be the opinions of stakeholders; and at other times, it might be ethical considerations (organizational context). The key for managers is to recognize and understand the mindful, conscious choice as to which element(s) are most important and should be emphasized in making a decision.

TYPES of Decisions and Decision-Making Conditions

Classify decisions and decision-making conditions. 6.3

Restaurant managers in Portland make routine decisions weekly about purchasing food supplies and scheduling employee work shifts. It's something they've done numerous times. But now they're facing a different kind of decision—one they've never encountered: how to adapt to a new law requiring that nutritional information be posted.

Types of Decisions

Such situations aren't all that unusual. Managers in all kinds of organizations face different types of problems and decisions as they do their jobs. Depending on the nature of the problem, a manager can use one of two different types of decisions.

structured problems
Straightforward, familiar, and easily defined problems

STRUCTURED PROBLEMS AND PROGRAMMED DECISIONS Some problems are straightforward. The decision maker's goal is clear, the problem is familiar, and information about the problem is easily defined and complete. Examples might include when a customer returns a purchase to a store, when a supplier is late with an important delivery, a news team's response to a fast-breaking event, or a college's handling of a student wanting to drop a class. Such situations are called **structured problems** because they're straightforward, familiar, and easily defined. For instance, a server spills a drink on a customer's coat. The customer is upset and the manager needs to do something. Because it's not an unusual occurrence, there's probably some standardized routine for handling it. For example, the manager offers to have the coat cleaned at the restaurant's expense. This is what we call a **programmed decision**, a repetitive decision that can be handled by a routine approach. Because the problem is structured, the manager doesn't have to go to the trouble and expense of going through an involved decision process. The "develop-the-alternatives" stage of the decision-making process either doesn't exist or is given little attention. Why? Because once the structured problem is defined, the solution is usually self-evident or at least reduced to a few alternatives that are familiar and have proved successful in the past. The spilled drink on the customer's coat doesn't require the restaurant manager to identify and weight decision criteria or to develop a long list of possible solutions. Instead, the manager relies on one of three types of programmed decisions: procedure, rule, or policy.

programmed decision
A repetitive decision that can be handled by a routine approach

A **procedure** is a series of sequential steps a manager uses to respond to a structured problem. The only difficulty is identifying the problem. Once it's clear, so is the procedure. For instance, a purchasing manager receives a request from a warehouse manager for 15 tablets for the inventory clerks. The purchasing manager knows how to make this decision by following the established purchasing procedure.

procedure
A series of sequential steps used to respond to a well-structured problem

A **rule** is an explicit statement that tells a manager what can or cannot be done. Rules are frequently used because they're simple to follow and ensure consistency. For example, rules about lateness and absenteeism permit supervisors to make disciplinary decisions rapidly and fairly.

rule
An explicit statement that tells managers what can or cannot be done

The third type of programmed decisions is a **policy**, a guideline for making a decision. In contrast to a rule, a policy establishes general parameters for the decision maker rather than specifically stating what should or should not be done. Policies typically contain an ambiguous term that leaves interpretation up to the decision maker. Here are some sample policy statements:

policy
A guideline for making decisions

- The customer always comes first and should always be *satisfied*.
- We promote from within, *whenever possible*.
- Employee wages shall be *competitive* within community standards.

Notice that the terms *satisfied, whenever possible,* and *competitive* require interpretation. For instance, the policy of paying competitive wages doesn't tell a company's human resources manager the exact amount he or she should pay, but it does guide them in making the decision.

UNSTRUCTURED PROBLEMS AND NONPROGRAMMED DECISIONS Not all the problems managers face can be solved using programmed decisions. Many organizational situations involve **unstructured problems**, new or unusual problems for which information is ambiguous or incomplete. Whether to build a new manufacturing facility in China is an example of an unstructured problem. So, too, is the problem facing restaurant managers in Portland who must decide how to modify their businesses to comply with the new law. When problems are unstructured, managers must rely on nonprogrammed decision making in order to develop unique solutions. **Nonprogrammed decisions** are unique and nonrecurring and involve custom-made solutions.

unstructured problems
Problems that are new or unusual and for which information is ambiguous or incomplete

Exhibit 6-7 describes the differences between programmed and nonprogrammed decisions. Lower-level managers mostly rely on programmed decisions (procedures,

nonprogrammed decisions
Unique and nonrecurring decisions that require a custom-made solution

Characteristic	Programmed Decisions	Nonprogrammed Decisions
Type of problem	Structured	Unstructured
Managerial level	Lower levels	Upper levels
Frequency	Repetitive, routine	New, unusual
Information	Readily available	Ambiguous or incomplete
Goals	Clear, specific	Vague
Time frame for solution	Short	Relatively long
Solution relies on...	Procedures, rules, policies	Judgment and creativity

Exhibit 6-7
Programmed Versus Nonprogrammed Decisions

rules, and policies) because they confront familiar and repetitive problems. As managers move up the organizational hierarchy, the problems they confront become more unstructured. Why? Because lower-level managers handle the routine decisions and let upper-level managers deal with the unusual or difficult decisions. Also, upper-level managers delegate routine decisions to their subordinates so they can deal with more difficult issues.[21] Thus, few managerial decisions in the real world are either fully programmed or nonprogrammed. Most fall somewhere in between.

Decision-Making Conditions

When making decisions, managers may face three different conditions: certainty, risk, and uncertainty. Let's look at the characteristics of each.

CERTAINTY The ideal situation for making decisions is one of **certainty**, a situation where a manager can make accurate decisions because the outcome of every alternative is known. For example, when Wyoming's state treasurer decides where to deposit excess state funds, he knows exactly the interest rate offered by each bank and the amount that will be earned on the funds. He is certain about the outcomes of each alternative. As you might expect, most managerial decisions aren't like this.

certainty
A situation in which a manager can make accurate decisions because all outcomes are known

---

FUTURE VISION | **Man or Machine?**

Do you have an E-book reader? You'd be surprised at what digital-book publishers and retailers now know about you. The major players in E-book publishing—Amazon, Apple, and Google—can "easily track how far readers are getting in books, how long they spend reading them and which search terms they use to find books." For instance, this passage from *Catching Fire,* the second book of the Hunger Games series—"Because sometimes things happen to people and they're not equipped to deal with them"—was the most highlighted among Kindle readers. And according to Nook data, science-fiction, romance, and crime-fiction fans often read more books more quickly than readers of literary fiction.[22]

The possibilities of technology as a tool for managerial decision making are endless and fascinating! Artificial intelligence software will be available to approach problems the way the human brain does—by trying to recognize patterns that underlie a complex set of data. Like people, this software will "learn" to pick out subtle patterns. In so doing, it will be able to perform a number of decision-making tasks.

Just as today's computers allow you to access information quickly from sources such as spreadsheets or search engines, most of the routine decisions that employees now do on the job are likely to be delegated to a software program. For instance, much of the diagnostic work now done by doctors will be done by software. Patients will describe their symptoms to a computer in a medical kiosk, possibly at their neighborhood drugstore; from answers the patient provides, the computer will render a decision. Similarly, many hiring decisions will be made by software programmed to simulate the successful decision processes used by recruiters and managers. Welcome to the future of decision making!

Exhibit 6-8
Expected Value

Event	Expected Revenues	×	Probability	=	Expected Value of Each Alternative
Heavy snowfall	$850,000		0.3		$255,000
Normal snowfall	725,000		0.5		362,500
Light snowfall	350,000		0.2		70,000
					$687,500

risk
A situation in which the decision maker is able to estimate the likelihood of certain outcomes

RISK A far more common situation is one of **risk**, conditions in which the decision maker is able to estimate the likelihood of certain outcomes. Under risk, managers have historical data from past personal experiences or secondary information that lets them assign probabilities to different alternatives. Let's do an example.

Suppose you manage a Colorado ski resort, and you're thinking about adding another lift. Obviously, your decision will be influenced by the additional revenue that the new lift would generate, which depends on snowfall. You have fairly reliable weather data from the last 10 years on snowfall levels in your area—three years of heavy snowfall, five years of normal snowfall, and two years of light snow. And you have good information on the amount of revenues generated during each level of snow. You can use this information to help you make your decision by calculating expected value—the expected return from each possible outcome—by multiplying expected revenues by snowfall probabilities. The result is the average revenue you can expect over time if the given probabilities hold. As Exhibit 6-8 shows, the expected revenue from adding a new ski lift is $687,500. Of course, whether that's enough to justify a decision to build depends on the costs involved in generating that revenue.

UNCERTAINTY What happens if you face a decision where you're not certain about the outcomes and can't even make reasonable probability estimates? We call this condition **uncertainty**. Managers face decision-making situations of uncertainty. Under these conditions, the choice of alternative is influenced by the limited amount of available information and by the psychological orientation of the decision maker. An optimistic manager will follow a *maximax* choice (maximizing the maximum possible payoff); a pessimist will follow a *maximin* choice (maximizing the minimum possible payoff); and a manager who desires to minimize his maximum "regret" will opt for a *minimax* choice. Let's look at these different choice approaches using an example.

uncertainty
A situation in which a decision maker has neither certainty nor reasonable probability estimates available

A marketing manager at Visa has determined four possible strategies (S_1, S_2, S_3, and S_4) for promoting the Visa card throughout the West Coast region of the United States. The marketing manager also knows that major competitor MasterCard has three competitive actions (CA_1, CA_2, and CA_3) it's using to promote its card in the same region. For this example, we'll assume that the Visa manager had no previous knowledge that would allow her to determine probabilities of success of any of the four strategies. She formulates the matrix shown in Exhibit 6-9 to show the various Visa strategies and the resulting profit, depending on the competitive action used by MasterCard.

Exhibit 6-9
Payoff Matrix

Visa Marketing Strategy (in millions of dollars)	MasterCard's Competitive Action		
	CA$_1$	CA$_2$	CA$_3$
S$_1$	13	14	11
S$_2$	9	15	18
S$_3$	24	21	15
S$_4$	18	14	28

Visa Marketing Strategy (in millions of dollars)	MasterCard's Competitive Action		
	CA$_1$	CA$_2$	CA$_3$
S$_1$	11	7	17
S$_2$	15	6	10
S$_3$	0	0	13
S$_4$	6	7	0

Exhibit 6-10
Regret Matrix

In this example, if our Visa manager is an optimist, she'll choose strategy 4 (S$_4$) because that could produce the largest possible gain: $28 million. Note that this choice maximizes the maximum possible gain (maximax choice).

If our manager is a pessimist, she'll assume that only the worst can occur. The worst outcome for each strategy is as follows: S$_1$ = $11 million; S$_2$ = $9 million; S$_3$ = $15 million; S$_4$ = $14 million. These are the most pessimistic outcomes from each strategy. Following the *maximin* choice, she would maximize the minimum pay-off; in other words, she'd select S$_3$ ($15 million is the largest of the minimum payoffs).

In the third approach, managers recognize that once a decision is made, it will not necessarily result in the most profitable payoff. There may be a "regret" of profits given up—*regret* referring to the amount of money that could have been made had a different strategy been used. Managers calculate regret by subtracting all possible payoffs in each category from the maximum possible payoff for each given event, in this case for each competitive action. For our Visa manager, the highest payoff—given that MasterCard engages in CA$_1$, CA$_2$, or CA$_3$— is $24 million, $21 million, or $28 million, respectively (the highest number in each column). Subtracting the payoffs in Exhibit 6-9 from those figures produces the results shown in Exhibit 6-10.

The maximum regrets are S$_1$ = $17 million, S$_2$ = $15 million, S$_3$ = $13 million, and S$_4$ = $7 million. The *minimax* choice minimizes the maximum regret, so our Visa manager would choose S$_4$. By making this choice, she'll never have a regret of profits given up of more than $7 million. This result contrasts, for example, with a regret of $15 million had she chosen S$_2$ and MasterCard had taken CA$_1$.

Although managers try to quantify a decision when possible by using payoff and regret matrices, uncertainty often forces them to rely more on intuition, creativity, hunches, and "gut feel."

LEADER who made a DIFFERENCE

Source: AP Photo/Misha Japaridze

As a business owner in Russia, Mikhail D. Prokhorov had to make a lot of risky decisions.[23] He's president of Onexim Group, a company with businesses in metal, gold, and real estate. And he's worth an estimated $13.2 billion. He says, "Doing business in Russia in the early 1990s was cowboy territory with no sheriff." That's an interesting and probably fairly accurate description of risk. And it's a good thing he's comfortable with risk because he's now made another risky decision, this time in the United States. He's become an NBA league owner. As the new majority owner of the newly-named Brooklyn Nets, he says, "I am real excited to take the worst team of the league and turn it into the best." Although the basketball-loving Russian billionaire's latest decision wasn't initially a slam dunk, Prokhorov is having a ball watching his team and their new arena take shape. Both can be considered in the building stage—a work in progress. And Prokhorov remains committed to doing what it takes to have his team win an NBA championship trophy. What can you learn from this leader who made a difference?

DECISION-MAKING Styles

Describe different decision-making styles and discuss how biases affect decision making. **6.4**

William D. Perez's tenure as Nike's CEO lasted a short and turbulent 13 months. Analysts attributed his abrupt dismissal to a difference in decision-making approaches between him and Nike co-founder Phil Knight. Perez tended to rely more on data and facts when making decisions, whereas Knight highly valued, and had always used, his

Nonlinear thinking characterizes the decision-making style of Hamdi Ulukaya, founder of the Chobani brand of yogurt. A native of Turkey, Hamdi says that people thought he was crazy when after reading a for-sale ad for a small yogurt factory he decided to buy it the next day based on a gut feeling that he could do something to introduce a quality, Greek-style yogurt in the United States without having any knowledge about how to do it. Hamdi also used nonlinear thinking in guiding his decisions involved in marketing and distributing Chobani. In this photo, Hamdi (center) and employees display yogurt creations at Chobani SoHo, a first-of-its kind Mediterranean yogurt bar, at its opening celebration in New York City.
Source: Photo by Diane Bondareff/Invision for Chobani/AP Images

linear thinking style
Decision style characterized by a person's preference for using external data and facts and processing this information through rational, logical thinking

judgment and feelings to make decisions.[24] As this example clearly shows, managers have different styles when it comes to making decisions.

Linear–Nonlinear Thinking Style Profile

Suppose you're a new manager. How will you make decisions? Recent research done with four distinct groups of people says the way a person approaches decision making is likely affected by his or her thinking style.[25] Your thinking style reflects two things: (1) the source of information you tend to use (external data and facts OR internal sources such as feelings and intuition), and (2) whether you process that information in a linear way (rational, logical, analytical) OR a nonlinear way (intuitive, creative, insightful). These four dimensions are collapsed into two styles. The first, **linear thinking style**, is characterized by a person's preference for using external data and facts and processing this information through rational, logical thinking to guide decisions and actions. The second, **nonlinear thinking style**, is characterized by a preference for internal sources of information (feelings and intuition) and processing this information with internal insights, feelings, and hunches to guide decisions and actions. Look back at the earlier Nike example and you'll see both styles described.

Managers need to recognize that their employees may use different decision-making styles. Some employees may take their time weighing alternatives and relying on how they feel about it while others rely on external data before logically making a decision. These differences don't make one person's approach better than the other. It just means their decision making styles are different.

Decision-Making Biases and Errors

When managers make decisions, they not only use their own particular style, they may use "rules of thumb," or **heuristics,** to simplify their decision making. Rules of thumb can be useful because they help make sense of complex, uncertain, and ambiguous information.[26] Even though managers may use rules of thumb, that doesn't mean those rules are reliable. Why? Because they may lead to errors and biases in processing and evaluating information. Exhibit 6-11 identifies 12 common decision errors and biases that managers make. Let's look at each.[27]

Exhibit 6-11
Common Decision-Making Biases

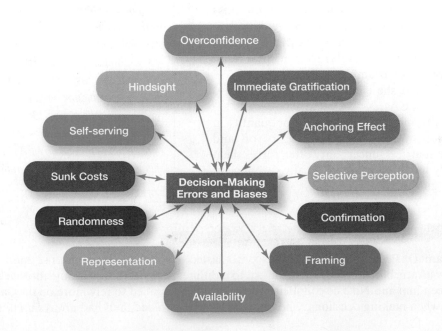

When decision makers tend to think they know more than they do or hold unrealistically positive views of themselves and their performance, they're exhibiting the *overconfidence bias*. The *immediate gratification bias* describes decision makers who tend to want immediate rewards and to avoid immediate costs. For these individuals, decision choices that provide quick payoffs are more appealing than those with payoffs in the future. The *anchoring effect* describes how decision makers fixate on initial information as a starting point and then, once set, fail to adequately adjust for subsequent information. First impressions, ideas, prices, and estimates carry unwarranted weight relative to information received later. When decision makers selectively organize and interpret events based on their biased perceptions, they're using the *selective perception bias*. This influences the information they pay attention to, the problems they identify, and the alternatives they develop. Decision makers who seek out information that reaffirms their past choices and discount information that contradicts past judgments exhibit the *confirmation bias*. These people tend to accept at face value information that confirms their preconceived views and are critical and skeptical of information that challenges these views. The *framing bias* is when decision makers select and highlight certain aspects of a situation while excluding others. By drawing attention to specific aspects of a situation and highlighting them, while at the same time downplaying or omitting other aspects, they distort what they see and create incorrect reference points. The *availability bias* happens when decisions makers tend to remember events that are the most recent and vivid in their memory. The result? It distorts their ability to recall events in an objective manner and results in distorted judgments and probability estimates. When decision makers assess the likelihood of an event based on how closely it resembles other events or sets of events, that's the *representation bias*. Managers exhibiting this bias draw analogies and see identical situations where they don't exist. The *randomness bias* describes the actions of decision makers who try to create meaning out of random events. They do this because most decision makers have difficulty dealing with chance even though random events happen to everyone, and there's nothing that can be done to predict them. The *sunk costs error* occurs when decision makers forget that current choices can't correct the past. They incorrectly fixate on past expenditures of time, money, or effort in assessing choices rather than on future consequences. Instead of ignoring sunk costs, they can't forget them. Decision makers who are quick to take credit for their successes and to blame failure on outside factors are exhibiting the *self-serving bias*. Finally, the *hindsight bias* is the tendency for decision makers to falsely believe that they would have accurately predicted the outcome of an event once that outcome is actually known.

Managers avoid the negative effects of these decision errors and biases by being aware of them and then not using them! Beyond that, managers also should pay attention to "how" they make decisions and try to identify the heuristics they typically use and critically evaluate the appropriateness of those heuristics. Finally, managers might want to ask trusted individuals to help them identify weaknesses in their decision-making style and try to improve on those weaknesses.

Overview of Managerial Decision Making

Exhibit 6-12 provides an overview of managerial decision making. Because it's in their best interests, managers *want* to make good decisions—that is, choose the "best" alternative, implement it, and determine whether it takes care of the problem, which is the reason the decision was needed in the first place. Their decision-making process is affected by four factors: the decision-making approach, the type of problem, decision-making conditions, and their decision-making style. In addition, certain decision-making errors and biases may impact the process. Each factor plays a role in determining how the manager makes a decision. So whether a decision involves addressing an employee's habitual tardiness, resolving a product

nonlinear thinking style
Decision style characterized by a person's preference for internal sources of information and processing this information with internal insights, feelings, and hunches

heuristics
Rules of thumb that managers use to simplify decision making

*data*points[28]

7 percentage points higher returns is what organizations gained when they reduced the effect of bias in their decision-making processes.

90 percent of people believe they are just a little more competent, smarter, or kinder than average.

91 percent of U.S. companies use teams and groups to solve specific problems.

40 percent more ideas are generated with electronic brainstorming than with individuals brainstorming alone.

59 percent of employees said a key obstacle to their job is that more attention is paid to placing blame than to solving problems.

77 percent of managers said the number of decisions they made during a typical workday had increased.

54 percent of managers said the amount of time given to each decision had decreased.

In Asia, RPS (rock, paper, scissors) is more recognized as a decision tiebreaker than it is in the United States.

20 percent of American adults said they think most creatively in their cars.

Exhibit 6-12
Overview of Managerial Decision Making

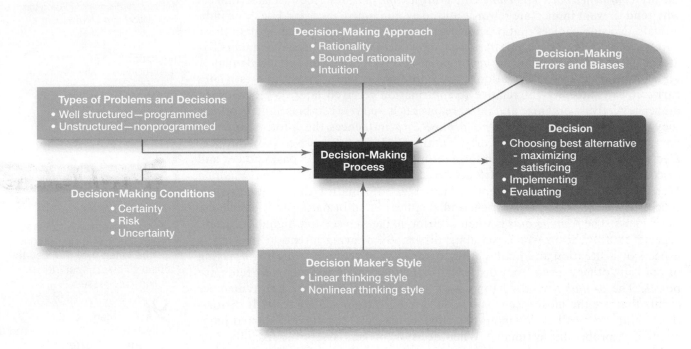

quality problem, or determining whether to enter a new market, it has been shaped by a number of factors.

6.5 | *Identify* effective decision-making techniques.

EFFECTIVE Decision Making in Today's World

Per Carlsson, a product development manager at IKEA, "spends his days creating Volvo-style kitchens at Yugo prices." His job is to take the "problems" identified by the company's product-strategy council (a group of globe-trotting senior managers that monitors consumer trends and establishes product priorities) and turn them into furniture that customers around the world want to buy. One "problem" identified by the council: the kitchen has replaced the living room as the social and entertaining center in the home. Customers are looking for kitchens that convey comfort and cleanliness while still allowing them to pursue their gourmet aspirations. Carlsson must take this information and make things happen. There are a lot of decisions to make—programmed and nonprogrammed—and the fact that IKEA is a global company makes it even more challenging. Comfort in Asia means small, cozy appliances and spaces, while North American customers want oversized glassware and giant refrigerators. His ability to make good decisions quickly has significant implications for IKEA's success.[29]

Today's business world revolves around making decisions, often risky ones, usually with incomplete or inadequate information, and under intense time pressure. Making good business decisions in today's rapid-paced and messy world isn't easy. Things happen too fast. Customers come and go in the click of a mouse or the swipe of a screen. Market landscapes can shift dramatically overnight along several dimensions. Competitors can enter a market and exit it just as quickly as they entered. Thriving and prospering under such conditions means managerial decision making must adapt to these realities. Most managers make one decision after another; and as if that weren't challenging enough, more is at stake than ever before. Bad decisions can cost millions. What do managers need to do to make effective decisions in today's fast-moving world? First, let's look at some suggested guidelines. Then, we'll discuss an interesting new line of thinking that has implications for making effective decisions—especially for business types—called design thinking.

Guidelines for Effective Decision Making

Decision making is serious business. Your abilities and track record as an effective decision maker will determine how your organizational work performance is evaluated and whether you'll be promoted to higher and higher positions of responsibility. Here are some guidelines to help you be a better decision maker.

- *Understand cultural differences.* Managers everywhere want to make good decisions. However, is there only one "best" way worldwide to make decisions? Or does the "best way depend on the values, beliefs, attitudes, and behavioral patterns of the people involved?"[30]

- *Create standards for good decision making.* Good decisions are forward-looking, use available information, consider all available and viable options, and do not create conflicts of interest.[31]

- *Know when it's time to call it quits.* When it's evident that a decision isn't working, don't be afraid to pull the plug. For instance, the CEO of L.L.Bean pulled the plug on building a new customer call center in Waterville, Maine—"literally stopping the bulldozers in their tracks"—after T-Mobile said it was building its own call center right next door. He was afraid that the city would not have enough qualified workers for both companies and so decided to build 55 miles away in Bangor.[32] He knew when it was time to call it quits. However, as we said earlier, many decision makers block or distort negative information because they don't want to believe their decision was bad. They become so attached to a decision that they refuse to recognize when it's time to move on. In today's dynamic environment, this type of thinking simply won't work.

- *Use an effective decision-making process.* Experts say an effective decision-making process has these six characteristics: (1) it focuses on what's important; (2) it's logical and consistent; (3) it acknowledges both subjective and objective thinking and blends analytical with intuitive thinking; (4) it requires only as much information and analysis as is necessary to resolve a particular dilemma; (5) it encourages and guides the gathering of relevant information and informed opinion; and (6) it's straightforward, reliable, easy to use, and flexible."[33]

- *Build an organization that can spot the unexpected and quickly adapt to the changed environment.* This suggestion comes from Karl Weick, an organizational psychologist, who has made a career of studying organizations and how people work.[34] He calls such organizations *highly reliable organizations* (HROs), and says they share five habits. (1) They're *not tricked by their success.* HROs are preoccupied with their failures. They're alert to the smallest deviations and react quickly to anything that doesn't fit with their expectations. He talks about Navy aviators who describe "leemers—a gut feeling that something isn't right." Typically, these leemers turn out to be accurate. Something, in fact, is wrong. Organizations need to create climates where people feel safe trusting their leemers. (2) They *defer to the experts on the front line.* Frontline workers—those who interact day in and day out with customers, products, suppliers, and so forth—have firsthand knowledge of what can and cannot be done, what will and will not work. Get their input. Let them make decisions. (3) They *let unexpected circumstances provide the solution.* One of Weick's better-known works is his study of the Mann Gulch fire in Montana that killed 13 smoke jumpers in 1949. The event was a massive, tragic organizational failure. However, the reaction of the foreman illustrates how effective decision makers respond to unexpected circumstances. When the fire was nearly on top of his men, he invented the escape fire—a small fire that consumed all the brush around the team, leaving an area where the larger fire couldn't burn.

His action was contrary to everything firefighters are taught (that is, you don't start fires—you extinguish them), but at the time it was the best decision. (4) They *embrace complexity.* Because business is complex, these organizations recognize that it "takes complexity to sense complexity." Rather than simplifying data, which we instinctively try to do when faced with complexity, these organizations aim for deeper understanding of the situation. They ask "why" and keep asking why as they probe more deeply into the causes of the problem and possible solutions. (5) Finally, they *anticipate, but also recognize their limits.* These organizations do try to anticipate as much as possible, but they recognize that they can't anticipate everything. As Weick says, they don't "think, then act. They think by acting. By actually doing things, you'll find out what works and what doesn't."

Design Thinking and Decision Making

The way managers approach decision making—using a rational and analytical mind-set in identifying problems, coming up with alternatives, evaluating alternatives, and choosing one of those alternatives—may not be best and certainly not the only choice in today's environment. That's where design thinking comes in. **Design thinking** has been described as "approaching management problems as designers approach design problems."[35] More organizations are beginning to recognize how design thinking can benefit them.[36] For instance, Apple has long been celebrated for its design thinking.

design thinking
Approaching management problems as designers approach design problems

The company's lead designer, Jonathan "Jony" Ive (who was behind some of Apple's most successful products, including the iPod and iPhone and was just knighted in the United Kingdom for services to design and enterprise) had this to say about Apple's design approach: "We try to develop products that seem somehow inevitable—that leave you with the sense that that's the only possible solution that makes sense."[37]

The design thinking approach to decision making is at the heart of Boeing's Concept Center, a developmental studio where engineers and designers create innovative concepts for airplane interiors through research, prototypes, mockups, and interactive workshops. The goal of the center is to help Boeing's airline customers provide their passengers and crew members with innovative products and services that enhance the flying experience. In this photo, Alan Anderson, director of the center, poses in a prototype of an inflatable crew rest module that features a sound system and adjustable recliner and that can be deflated to a fraction of its size for ease of installation and removal. Design thinking has helped underscore Boeing's reputation as a customer-focused and innovative company.
Source: © Dan Lamont/Alamy

While many managers don't deal specifically with product or process design decisions, they still make decisions about work issues that arise, and design thinking can help them be better decision makers. What can the design thinking approach teach managers about making better decisions? Well, it begins with the first step of identifying problems. Design thinking says that managers should look at problem identification collaboratively and integratively with the goal of gaining a deep understanding of the situation. They should look not only at the rational aspects, but also at the emotional elements. Then invariably, of course, design thinking would influence how managers identify and evaluate alternatives. "A traditional manager (educated in a business school, of course) would take the options that have been presented and analyze them based on deductive reasoning and then select the one with the highest net present value. However, using design thinking, a manager would say, "What is something completely new that would be lovely if it existed but doesn't now?"[38] Design thinking means opening up your perspective and gaining insights by using observation and inquiry skills and not relying simply on rational analysis. We're not saying that rational analysis isn't needed; we are saying that there's more needed in making effective decisions, especially in today's world. Just a heads up: Design thinking also has broad implications for managers in other areas, and we'll be looking in future chapters at its impact on innovation and strategies.

MyManagementLab
Go to **mymanagementlab.com** to complete the problems marked with this icon .

CHAPTER

PREPARING FOR: Exams/Quizzes
CHAPTER SUMMARY by Learning Outcomes

6.1 ⌐LEARNING OUTCOME⌐
Describe the eight steps in the decision-making process.
A decision is a choice. The decision-making process consists of eight steps: (1) identify problem; (2) identify decision criteria; (3) weight the criteria; (4) develop alternatives; (5) analyze alternatives; (6) select alternative; (7) mplement alternative; and (8) evaluate decision effectiveness.

6.2 ⌐LEARNING OUTCOME⌐
Explain the four ways managers make decisions.
The assumptions of rationality are as follows: the problem is clear and unambiguous; a single, well-defined goal is to be achieved; all alternatives and consequences are known; and the final choice will maximize the payoff. Bounded rationality says that managers make rational decisions but are bounded (limited) by their ability to process information. Satisficing happens when decision makers accept solutions that are good enough. With escalation of commitment, managers increase commitment to a decision even when they have evidence it may have been a wrong decision. Intuitive decision making means making decisions on the basis of experience, feelings, and accumulated judgment. Using evidence-based management, a manager makes decisions based on the best available evidence.

6.3 ⌐LEARNING OUTCOME⌐
Classify decisions and decision-making conditions.
Programmed decisions are repetitive decisions that can be handled by a routine approach and are used when the problem being resolved is straightforward, familiar, and easily defined (structured). Nonprogrammed decisions are unique decisions that require a custom-made solution and are used when the problems are new or unusual (unstructured) and for which information is ambiguous or incomplete. Certainty is a situation in which a manager can make accurate decisions because all outcomes are known. Risk is a situation in which a manager can estimate the likelihood of certain outcomes. Uncertainty is a situation in which a manager is not certain about the outcomes and can't even make reasonable probability estimates. When decision makers face uncertainty, their psychological orientation will determine whether they follow a maximax choice (maximizing the maximum possible payoff); a maximin choice (maximizing the minimum possible payoff); or a minimax choice (minimizing the maximum regret—amount of money that could have been made if a different decision had been made).

6.4 ⌐LEARNING OUTCOME⌐
Describe different decision-making styles and discuss how biases affect decision making.
A person's thinking style reflects two things: the source of information you tend to use (external or internal) and how you process that information (linear or nonlinear). These four dimensions were collapsed into two styles. The linear thinking style is characterized by a person's preference for using external data and processing this information through rational, logical thinking. The nonlinear thinking style is characterized by a preference for internal sources of information and processing this information with internal insights, feelings, and hunches. The 12 common decision-making errors and biases include overconfidence, immediate

gratification, anchoring, selective perception, confirmation, framing, availability, representation, randomness, sunk costs, self-serving bias, and hindsight. The managerial decision making model helps explain how the decision-making process is used to choose the best alternative(s), either through maximizing or satisficing and then implement and evaluate the alternative. It also helps explain what factors affect the decision-making process, including the decision-making approach (rationality, bounded rationality, intuition), the types of problems and decisions (well structured and programmed or unstructured and nonprogrammed), the decision-making conditions (certainty, risk, uncertainty), and the decision maker's style (linear or nonlinear).

6.5 (LEARNING OUTCOME) **Identify** effective decision-making techniques.

Managers can make effective decisions by understanding cultural differences in decision making, knowing when it's time to call it quits, using an effective decision-making process, and building an organization that can spot the unexpected and quickly adapt to the changed environment. An effective decision-making process (1) focuses on what's important; (2) is logical and consistent; (3) acknowledges both subjective and objective thinking and blends both analytical and intuitive approaches; (4) requires only "enough" information as is necessary to resolve a problem; (5) encourages and guides gathering relevant information and informed opinions; and (6) is straightforward, reliable, easy to use, and flexible. The five habits of highly reliable organizations are (1) not being tricked by their successes; (2) deferring to experts on the front line; (3) letting unexpected circumstances provide the solution; (4) embracing complexity; and (5) anticipating, but also recognizing, limits.

Design thinking is "approaching management problems as designers approach design problems." It can be useful when identifying problems and when identifying and evaluating alternatives.

REVIEW AND DISCUSSION QUESTIONS ✪

1. Why is decision making often described as the essence of a manager's job?
2. Describe the eight steps in the decision-making process.
3. Compare and contrast the four ways managers make decisions.
4. Explain the two types of problems and decisions. Contrast the three decision-making conditions.
5. Would you call yourself a linear or nonlinear thinker? What are the decision-making implications of these labels? What are the implications for choosing where you want to work?
6. "As managers use computers and software tools more often, they'll be able to make more rational decisions." Do you agree or disagree with this statement? Why?
7. How can managers blend the guidelines for making effective decisions in today's world with the rationality and bounded rationality models of decision making, or can they? Explain.
8. Is there a difference between wrong decisions and bad decisions? Why do good managers sometimes make wrong decisions? Bad decisions? How can managers improve their decision-making skills?

PREPARING FOR: My Career
ETHICS DILEMMA ✪

We opened the chapter with a story about Sonic's decision making as they were developing a new product line. Well, hot dogs weren't the only new thing on Sonic's menu. Sonic along with Burger King, White Castle, and Starbucks are test marketing beer and wine at their restaurants.[39] When evaluating this decision, companies have to look at the added revenue from the sales of these products as compared to the costs incurred when serving alcoholic beverages, primarily the new equipment required and the liquor law regulations governing the age of employees who are allowed to serve alcohol. What do you think? What potential ethical issues do you see here? What stakeholders would be impacted and how? Should ethical considerations be part of a decision-making process? Why or why not?

SKILLS EXERCISE Developing Your Creativity Skill

About the Skill
Creativity is a frame of mind. You need to open your mind to new ideas. Every individual has the ability to be creative, but many people simply don't try to develop that ability. In contemporary organizations, such people may have difficulty achieving success. Dynamic environments and managerial chaos require that managers look for new and innovative ways to attain their goals as well as those of the organization.[40]

Steps in Practicing the Skill
1. *Think of yourself as creative.* Although it's a simple suggestion, research shows that if you think you can't be creative, you won't be. Believing in yourself is the first step in becoming more creative.

2. *Pay attention to your intuition.* Every individual's subconscious mind works well. Sometimes answers come to you when least expected. For example, when you are about to go to sleep, your relaxed mind sometimes whispers a solution to a problem you're facing. Listen to that voice. In fact, most creative people keep a notepad near their bed and write down those great ideas when they occur. That way, they don't forget them.

3. *Move away from your comfort zone.* Every individual has a comfort zone in which certainty exists. But creativity and the known often do not mix. To be creative, you need to move away from the status quo and focus your mind on something new.

4. *Engage in activities that put you outside your comfort zone.* You not only must think differently; you need to do things differently and thus challenge yourself. Learning to play a musical instrument or learning a foreign language, for example, opens your mind to a new challenge.

5. *Seek a change of scenery.* People are often creatures of habit. Creative people force themselves out of their habits by changing their scenery, which may mean going into a quiet and serene area where you can be alone with your thoughts.

6. *Find several right answers.* In the discussion of bounded rationality, we said that people seek solutions that are good enough. Being creative means continuing to look for other solutions even when you think you have solved the problem. A better, more creative solution just might be found.

7. *Play your own devil's advocate.* Challenging yourself to defend your solutions helps you to develop confidence in your creative efforts. Second-guessing yourself may also help you find more creative solutions.

8. *Believe in finding a workable solution.* Like believing in yourself, you also need to believe in your ideas. If you don't think you can find a solution, you probably won't.

9. *Brainstorm with others.* Being creative is not a solitary activity. Bouncing ideas off others creates a synergistic effect.

10. *Turn creative ideas into action.* Coming up with ideas is only half the process. Once the ideas are generated, they must be implemented. Keeping great ideas in your mind or on paper that no one will read does little to expand your creative abilities.

Practicing the Skill
How many words can you make using the letters in the word *brainstorm*? There are at least 95.

WORKING TOGETHER Team Exercise

Being effective in decision making is something that managers obviously want. What's involved with being a good decision maker? Form groups of three to four students. Discuss your experiences making decisions—for example, buying a car or some other purchase, choosing classes and professors, making summer or spring break plans, and so forth. Each of you should share times when you felt you made good decisions. Analyze what happened during that decision-making process that contributed to it being a good decision. Then, consider some decisions that you felt were bad. What happened to make them bad? What common characteristics, if any, did you identify among the good decisions? The bad decisions? Come up with a bulleted list of practical suggestions for making good decisions. As a group, be prepared to share your list with the class.

MY TURN TO BE A MANAGER

- For one week, pay close attention to the decisions you make and how you make them. Write a description of five of those decisions using the steps in the decision-making process as your guide. Also, describe whether you relied on external or internal sources of information to help you make the decision and whether you think you were more linear or nonlinear in how you processed that information.

- When you feel you haven't made a good decision, assess how you could have made a better decision.

- Find two examples of a procedure, a rule, and a policy. Bring a description of these examples to class and be prepared to share them.

- Write a procedure, a rule, and a policy for your instructor to use in your class. Be sure that each one is clear and understandable. And be sure to explain how it fits the characteristics of a procedure, a rule, or a policy.

- Find three examples of managerial decisions described in any of the popular business periodicals (*Wall Street Journal, BusinessWeek, Fortune,* etc.). Write a paper describing each decision and any other information such as what led to the decision, what happened as a result of the decision, etc. What did you learn about decision making from these examples?

- Interview two managers and ask them for suggestions on what it takes to be a good decision maker. Write down their suggestions and be prepared to present them in class.

- Steve's and Mary's suggested readings: Jeanne Liedtka and Tim Ogilvie, *Designing for Growth: A Design Thinking Toolkit for Managers* (Columbia Business School Publishing, 2011); Roger Martin, *The Design of Business: Why Design Thinking Is the Next Competitive Advantage,* (Harvard Business School Press, 2009); Noel M. Tichy and Warren G. Bennis, *Judgment: How Winning Leaders Make Great Calls* (Portfolio, 2007); Gerd Gigerenzer, *Gut Feelings: The Intelligence of the Unconscious* (Viking, 2007); Stephen P. Robbins, *Decide & Conquer: Make Winning Decisions and Take Control of Your Life* (Financial Times Press, 2004); and John S. Hammond, Ralph L. Keeney, and Howard Raiffa, *Smart Choices: A Practical Guide to Making Better Decisions* (Harvard Business School Press, 1999).

- Do a Web search on the phrase "101 dumbest moments in business." Get the most current version of this end-of-year list. Pick three of the examples and describe what happened. What's your reaction to the examples? How could the managers have made better decisions?

- In your own words, write down three things you learned in this chapter about being a good manager.

- Self-knowledge can be a powerful learning tool. Go to mymanagementlab.com and complete these self-assessment exercises: How Well Do I Handle Ambiguity? How Well Do I Respond to Turbulent Change? and What's My Decision-Making Style? Using the results of your assessments, identify personal strengths and weaknesses. What will you do to reinforce your strengths and improve your weaknesses?

MyManagementLab

Go to **mymanagementlab.com** for Auto-graded writing questions as well as the following Assisted-graded writing questions:

6-1. How might an organization's culture influence the way managers make decisions?

6-2. All of us bring biases to the decisions we make. What would be the drawbacks of having biases? Could there be any advantages to having biases? Explain. What are the implications for managerial decision making?

6-3. Mymanagementlab Only – comprehensive writing assignment for this chapter.

CASE APPLICATION 1 The Business of Baseball

Baseball has long been called "America's national pastime" (although according to a Harris Interactive survey, the NFL has been, hands down, the favorite sport of Americans).[41] Now, the game of baseball can probably be better described as America's number crunchers. Take, for instance, Sandy Alderson, the general manager of the New York Mets. He explained the team's decision to let batting champion and free agent shortstop Jose Reyes go to the Miami Marlins. "I'm happy with the analysis we used and the strategy we pursued." As he made this announcement, three members of his baseball operations staff stood by with their laptops open and ready to provide any needed data. A baseball writer has described the sport's move to data analysis this way, "Don't overlook the increasing value of facts, figures, and other data ... and the people who interpret them."

For the managers and operational staff of baseball teams such as the Oakland Athletics executives shown here, the analysis of facts, figures, and other data has become an important tool in evaluating a player's ability, performance, and potential that helps them decide how to make the best use of their financial resources in building a winning team.
Source: Michael Zagaris/Getty Images

As the 2011 film *Moneyball* (based on an earlier book by the same name) emphasizes, statistics—the "right" statistics—are crucial aspects of effective decision making in the sport of baseball. The central premise of *Moneyball* was that the collected wisdom of baseball insiders (players, managers, coaches, scouts, and the front office) had pretty much been flawed almost from the onset of the game. Commonly-used statistics—such as stolen bases, runs batted in, and batting averages—that were typically used to evaluate players' abilities and performances were inadequate and poor gauges of potential. Rigorous statistical analysis showed that on-base percentages and slugging percentages were better indicators of a player's offensive potential. The goal of all this number crunching? To make better decisions. Team managers want to allocate their limited payroll in the best way possible to help the team be a winner.

The move to more systematic data usage can also be seen in college baseball. At this level, coaches have long used their faces (touching their ears, noses, and chins at a "dizzying speed") to communicate pitch selection to the catcher. Now, however, hundreds of college teams at all levels have abandoned these body signals and are using a system in which the coach yells out a series of numbers. "The catcher decodes the sequence by looking at a chart tucked into a wristband—the kind football quarterbacks have worn since 1965—and then relays the information to the pitcher the way he always has." Coaches say this approach is not only faster and more efficient, it's not decipherable by "dugout spies" wanting to steal the signs. Since the method allows for many combinations that can mean many different pitches, the same number sequence won't be used for the rest of the game—and maybe not even for the rest of the season.

DISCUSSION QUESTIONS ✪

1. In a general sense, what kinds of decisions are made in baseball? Would you characterize these decisions as structured or unstructured problems? Explain. What type(s) of decision-making condition would you consider this to be? Explain.

2. Is it appropriate for baseball managers to use only quantitative, objective criteria in evaluating their players? What do you think? Why?

3. Do some research on Sabermetrics. What is it? What does it have to do with decision making?

4. Describe how baseball front office executives and college coaches could use each of the following to make better decisions: (a) rationality, (b) bounded rationality, (c) intuition, and (d) evidence-based management.

5. Can there be too much information in managing the business of baseball? Discuss.

CASE APPLICATION 2 Underwater Chaos

Poor decision making by managers of Eurostar and the operator of Eurotunnel created chaos for thousands of passengers who were trapped beneath the channel tunnel and for travelers shown here at St. Pancras train station in London whose train service was suspended following the breakdown of the tunnel trains.
Source: AP Photo/Akira Suemori

It would be a claustrophobe's worst nightmare— trapped subsea in the 31-mile Eurotunnel beneath the English Channel on the Eurostar train that travels between Britain and the European mainland.[42] The first time it happened was after a series of breakdowns on five London-bound trains from Brussels, which began December 18, 2009, left more than 2,000 passengers stranded for up to 16 hours. Many of those passengers trapped in the dark and overheated tunnel endured serious distress. The acutely uncomfortable temperatures led parents to remove their children's outer clothing. Other passengers felt ill, with some suffering "stress and panic attacks." Was this just an unfortunate incident for the unlucky passengers who happened to be on those trains, or did poor managerial decision making about the operation of both the train and the channel tunnel also play a role?

An independent review of the incident blamed Eurostar and the operator of the tunnel for being unprepared for severe winter weather. The report said that Eurostar had failed to adequately maintain and winterize its high-speed trains to protect sensitive components from malfunctioning due to excessive snow and moisture build-up. At the time of the Eurostar train breakdowns, severe winter weather had been wreaking havoc in Europe. Airlines, car and truck drivers, and rail operators across Europe were also suffering from a winter that was on course to be the coldest in more than 30 years. Freezing weather and snow had caused travel problems for days in Northern Europe. In addition, the report criticized Eurotunnel (the operator of the channel tunnel) for having unsatisfactory communications systems in place inside the tunnel, which could have given its employees direct contact with train drivers and other Eurostar staff. "If a train breaks down and passengers have to be rescued and evacuated, this must be done with greater speed and consideration. In an emergency, passengers need to have prompt information and regular updates." Although the severe weather conditions undoubtedly played a role in this fiasco, there's no doubt that managers could have done a better job of making decisions in preparing for such scenarios.

The second disruption was in March 2012. Thousands of travelers, including Sir Paul McCartney and his family, were delayed by a faulty power cable. One passenger said, "There was absolute chaos at Gare du Nord and there was no information about possible delays. Eurostar staff were extremely unhelpful." However, another passenger said that despite the nine-hour wait with the train standing still and lack of information, the staff were helpful and supportive. As London prepared to host the 2012 Summer Olympics, car and coach traffic was expected to increase, lending even more urgency to prevent a repeat of the troubles.

DISCUSSION QUESTIONS ✪

1. What's your reaction to this story? What does it illustrate about decision making?

2. How could the decision-making process have helped in both the response to the crisis situations and in preventing them from happening?

3. Could procedures, policies, and rules play any role in future crisis situations like this one? If so, how? If not, why not?

4. What could other organizations learn from this incident?

7 Managing Change and Innovation

SPOTLIGHT: *Manager at Work*

After 30 years, 135 missions, and 542 million miles traveled in space, NASA's space shuttle program ended in 2011.[1] Over that time span, we've seen highs and lows, triumphs and tragedies—from the launches of the Magellan Venus probe and the Hubble telescope with their fantastic photos from outer space to the catastrophic endings of Challenger and Columbia. Needless to say, dismantling a program of this magnitude involves massive changes for managers and employees.

The major change facing Charles Bolden (see photo), NASA's administrator, is how the agency will be structured to carry on the space program—a decision that's not his to make. Because NASA is a governmental agency, lawmakers will make the decision. And the reputation of the United States as a leader in space exploration—the only country to put people on the moon—is at stake. But there are also national security and industrial consequences to be considered.

With the final space shuttle launch and landing, NASA is no longer in the manned space flight business. NASA now relies on foreign governments and commercial enterprises for space transportation. Astronauts still need to be shuttled to the International Space Station, and in November 2011, U.S. astronauts took their first trip on a Russian Soyuz spacecraft, at a cost of $47 million. NASA soon hopes to contract with companies such as Space Exploration Technologies (SpaceX, for short), Blue Origin (founded by Amazon. com's Jeff

Source: AP Photo/Damian Dovarganes

Source: Scott J. Ferrell/Congressional Quarterly/Newscom

Bezos), Sierra Nevada, Orbital Sciences Corporation, or even aerospace industry stalwart Boeing for spacecraft. One expert said, "Things that used to only be accessible to a few carefully selected highly qualified right-stuff government employees are

As NASA adjusts to a "new" normal, the uncertainty about funding, jobs, roles, and expectations can be a challenge for managers and employees.

finally coming within reach of researchers, businesspeople, and explorers." Private companies are even rushing in to fill the astronaut gap, training those professional workers who will eventually be needed in commercial space ventures serving researchers, tourists, and the businesses. "The result could be a relationship between NASA and private space-hands much like

the Department of Defense has with private soldiers."

The most critical change facing NASA's managers is what to do with its workforce of highly trained and skilled individuals while the future of its space exploration and other programs are debated and decided. Although

---

MyManagementLab®

⭐ **Improve Your Grade!**

Over 10 million students improved their results using the Pearson MyLabs.
Visit **mymanagementlab.com** for simulations, tutorials, and end-of-chapter problems.

LEARNING OUTCOMES

7.1	**Compare** and contrast views on the change process.
7.2	**Classify** types of organizational change.
7.3	**Explain** how to manage resistance to change.
7.4	**Discuss** contemporary issues in managing change.
7.5	**Describe** techniques for stimulating innovation.

the shuttle has landed permanently and NASA's manned space flights are currently dependent on others, the agency still has a "robust program of exploration, technology development, and scientific research" that will keep employees busy for years. The successful landing of Mars rover Curiosity on August 6, 2012, is evidence of NASA's skilled employees. However, as the organization adjusts to a "new" normal, the uncertainty about funding, jobs, roles, and expectations can be a challenge for managers and employees. Still, NASA doesn't want to lose its innovative, forward-thinking culture or heritage. **How might NASA's managers keep employees focused during these changes?**

The managerial challenges facing NASA's leaders in encouraging continued innovative efforts among all the agency's employees during uncertain times is certainly not unique. Big companies and small businesses, universities and colleges, state and city governments, and even the military are forced to be innovative. Although innovation has always been a part of the manager's job, it has become even more important in recent years. We'll describe why innovation is important and how managers can manage innovation in this chapter. Because innovation is often closely tied to an organization's change efforts, we'll start by looking at change and how managers manage change.

THE CHANGE Process

7.1 *Compare and contrast views on the change process.*

When John Lechleiter assumed the CEO's job at Eli Lilly, he sent each of his senior executives a gift—"a digital clock counting down, second by second, to October 23, 2011. That's the day Lilly's $5 billion-a-year schizophrenia pill, Zyprexa, was no longer under patent." Between now and the end of 2016, Lilly stands to lose $10 billion in annual revenues as patents on three of its key drugs expire. Needless to say, the company has been making some organizational changes as it picks up the pace of drug development.[2] Lilly's managers have had to do what managers everywhere must do—implement change!

If it weren't for change, a manager's job would be relatively easy. Planning would be simple because tomorrow would be no different from today. The issue of effective organizational design would also be resolved because the environment would not be uncertain and there would be no need to redesign the structure. Similarly, decision making would be dramatically streamlined because the outcome of each alternative could be predicted with almost certain accuracy. But that's not the way it is. Change is an organizational reality.[3] Organizations face change because external and internal factors create the need for change (see Exhibit 7-1). When managers recognize that change is needed, then what? How do they respond?

Exhibit 7-1

External and Internal Forces for Change

External
- Changing consumer needs and wants
- New governmental laws
- Changing technology
- Economic changes

Internal
- New organizational strategy
- Change in composition of workforce
- New equipment
- Changing employee attitudes

Two Views of the Change Process

Two very different metaphors can be used to describe the change process.[4] One metaphor envisions the organization as a large ship crossing a calm sea. The ship's captain and crew know exactly where they're going because they've made the trip many times before. Change comes in the form of an occasional storm, a brief distraction in an otherwise calm and predictable trip. In the calm waters metaphor, change is seen as an occasional disruption in the normal flow of events. In the other metaphor, the organization is seen as a small raft navigating a raging river with uninterrupted white-water rapids. Aboard the raft are half-a-dozen people who have never worked together before, who are totally unfamiliar with the river, who are unsure of their eventual destination, and who, as if things weren't bad enough, are traveling at night. In the white-water rapids metaphor, change is normal and expected and managing it is a continual process. These two metaphors present very different approaches to understanding and responding to change. Let's take a closer look at each one.

THE CALM WATERS METAPHOR   At one time, the calm waters metaphor was fairly descriptive of the situation managers faced. It's best discussed using Kurt Lewin's three-step change process.[5] (See Exhibit 7-2.)

According to Lewin, successful change can be planned and requires *unfreezing* the status quo, *changing* to a new state, and *refreezing* to make the change permanent. The status quo is considered equilibrium. To move away from this equilibrium, unfreezing is necessary. Unfreezing can be thought of as preparing for the needed change. It can be done by increasing the *driving forces,* which are forces pushing for change; by decreasing the *restraining forces*, which are forces that resist change; or by combining the two approaches.

Once unfreezing is done, the change itself can be implemented. However, merely introducing change doesn't ensure that it will take hold. The new situation needs to be *refrozen* so that it can be sustained over time. Unless this last step is done, there's a strong chance that employees will revert back to the old equilibrium state—that is, the old ways of doing things. The objective of refreezing, then, is to stabilize the new situation by reinforcing the new behaviors.

Lewin's three-step process treats change as a move away from the organization's current equilibrium state. It's a calm waters scenario where an occasional disruption (a "storm") means planning change to deal with the disruption. Once the disruption has been dealt with, however, things can continue on under the new changed situation. This type of environment isn't what most managers face today.

WHITE-WATER RAPIDS METAPHOR   DJ Patil, an expert in chaos theory, first made his name as a researcher on weather patterns at the University of Maryland. He says, "There are some times when you can predict weather well for the next 15 days.

Samsung Electronics, the world's largest maker of mobile phones, competes in the wireless communications industry, a white-water rapids environment where significant change is the status quo. Changes include ongoing improvements in the capacity and quality of digital technology, the development of new wireless data services, shorter new-product development cycles, and shifts in end-user requirements and preferences. To maintain its competitive position, Samsung must anticipate or adapt to these changes and continue to develop products that meet customer demands. This photo shows shoppers in Seoul, South Korea, trying out a new Galaxy smart phone, a product Samsung launched in 145 countries and that emerged as the biggest competitor to Apple's iPhone.
Source: AP Photo/Ahn Young-joon

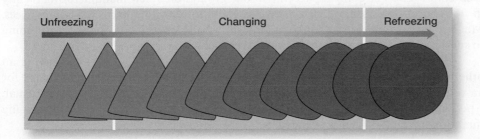

Unfreezing   Changing   Refreezing

Exhibit 7-2
The Three-Step Change Process

Other times, you can only really forecast a couple of days. Sometimes you can't predict the next two hours." The business climate is turning out to be a lot like the two-hour weather scenario. "The pace of change in our economy and our culture is accelerating and our visibility about the future is declining."[6]

Laura Ipsen is senior vice president and general manager of Connected Energy, a unit of Cisco. Her company works on developing energy ecosystems for the smart-grid market. She describes her job as follows, "My job is like having to put together a 1,000-piece puzzle but I don't have the box top with the picture of what it looks like, and some of the pieces are missing."[7] Susan Whiting is chairman of Nielsen Media Research, the company best known for its television ratings, which are frequently used to determine how much advertisers pay for TV commercials. The media research business isn't what it used to be, however, as the Internet, video on demand, cell phones, iPods, digital video recorders, and other changing technologies have made data collection much more challenging. Whiting says, "If you look at a typical week I have, it's a combination of trying to lead a company in change in an industry in change."[8] These are pretty accurate descriptions of what change is like in our second change metaphor—white-water rapids. It's also consistent with a world that's increasingly dominated by information, ideas, and knowledge.[9]

Here's what managing change might be like for you in a white-water rapids environment: The college you're attending has the following rules: Courses vary in length. When you sign up, you don't know how long a course will run. It might go for 2 weeks or 15 weeks. Furthermore, the instructor can end a course at any time with no prior warning. If that isn't challenging enough, the length of the class changes each time it meets: Sometimes the class lasts 20 minutes; other times it runs for 3 hours. And the time of the next class meeting is set by the instructor during this class. There's one more thing: All exams are unannounced, so you have to be ready for a test at any time. To succeed in this type of environment, you'd have to respond quickly to changing conditions. Students who are overly structured or uncomfortable with change wouldn't succeed.

Increasingly, managers are realizing that their job is much like what a student would face in such a college. The stability and predictability of the calm waters metaphor don't exist. Disruptions in the status quo are not occasional and temporary, and they are not followed by a return to calm waters. Many managers never get out of the rapids. Like DJ Patil, Laura Ipsen, and Susan Whiting, they face constant change.

Is the white-water rapids metaphor an exaggeration? Probably not! Although you'd expect a chaotic and dynamic environment in high-tech industries, even organizations in non-high-tech industries are faced with constant change. Take the case of Swedish home appliance company Electrolux. You might think the home appliances industry couldn't be all that difficult—after all, most households need the products, which are fairly uncomplicated—but that impression would be wrong. Electrolux's chief executive Keith McLoughlin has had several challenges to confront.[10] First, there's the challenge of developing products that will appeal to a wide range of global customers. For instance, only four in 10 adults in the United Kingdom own a dishwasher. On the other hand, about 78 percent of U.S. homeowners have a dishwasher. Then, there's the challenge of cheaper alternatives flooding the market. Electrolux faces intense competition in the United States, and during the economic slowdown, the global appliance market tumbled on stubbornly weak demand. In addition, with a unionized labor force in Sweden, Electrolux faces expectations as far as how they treat their employees. The company recently broke ground on a new manufacturing facility in Memphis, Tennessee, which when fully operational will employ 1,200 employees. McLoughlin recognizes that his company will have to continue to change if it's going to survive and prosper in the white-water rapids environment in which it operates.

Today, any organization that treats change as the occasional disturbance in an otherwise calm and stable world runs a great risk. Too much is changing too fast for an organization or its managers to be complacent. It's no longer business as usual. And managers must be ready to efficiently and effectively manage the changes facing their organization or their work area.

TYPES of Organizational Change

Managers at Verizon Wireless know what change is all about. "Even in an industry where rapid change is the status quo, it takes a special kind of company to handle the challenges posed by a major corporate acquisition and massive product rollout."[11] Verizon was up for the challenges and focused its change efforts on its people and processes.

Classify types of | **7.2**
organizational change.

What Is Organizational Change?

Most managers, at one point or another, will have to change some things in their workplace. We classify these changes as **organizational change**, which is any alteration of people, structure, or technology. Organizational changes often need someone to act as a catalyst and assume the responsibility for managing the change process—that is, a **change agent.** Change agents can be a manager within the organization, but could be a nonmanager—for example, a change specialist from the HR department or even an outside consultant.[12] For major changes, an organization often hires outside consultants to provide advice and assistance. Because they're from the outside, they have an objective perspective that insiders may lack. But outside consultants have a limited understanding of the organization's history, culture, operating procedures, and people. They're also more likely to initiate drastic change than insiders would because they don't have to live with the repercussions after the change is implemented. In contrast, internal managers may be more thoughtful, but possibly overcautious, because they must live with the consequences of their decisions.

organizational change
Any alteration of people, structure, or technology in an organization

change agent
Someone who acts as a catalyst and assumes the responsibility for managing the change process

Types of Change

Managers face three main types of change: structure, technology, and people (see Exhibit 7-3). Changing *structure* includes any change in structural variables such as reporting relationships, coordination mechanisms, employee empowerment, or job redesign. Changing *technology* encompasses modifications in the way work is performed or the methods and equipment that are used. Changing *people* refers to changes in attitudes, expectations, perceptions, and behavior of individuals or groups.

CHANGING STRUCTURE Jin Zhiguo, chairman of Tsingtao Brewery understands how important structural change can be. When the company shifted from a government-run company to a market-led company, many changes had to take place. He says, "Having worked for a state-owned enterprise, our people weren't used to competing for jobs or to being replaced for performance."[13] The change

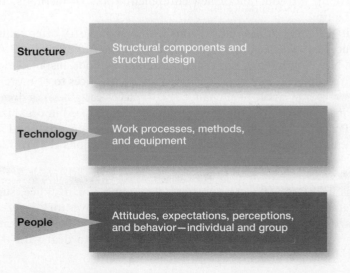

Exhibit 7-3
Three Types of Change

Structure → Structural components and structural design

Technology → Work processes, methods, and equipment

People → Attitudes, expectations, perceptions, and behavior—individual and group

FUTURE VISION | Life-Long Learning

By 2025, the line between school and work will have blurred. The life span of most skills will be less than 10 years, requiring people to continuously update their skills. Under these types of conditions, you'll have to be able to adapt to change.

Technology will allow life-long learning to proceed without going to formal classes. Instead, training will take place via online learning. You'll take courses adapted to your specific needs and time schedule. In the same way that you brush your teeth daily, you'll spend time each day online, learning new skills that will allow you to maintain currency in your field.

Lisa Brown, CEO of Tallahassee-Leon Federal Credit Union says, "I'm a huge proponent of life-long learning. The moment you think you know everything and stop listening is the minute you set yourself up to fail. What you're learning or who you're learning from is not as important as being open to the experience, listening, and constantly pushing yourself to be better tomorrow than today."[14] Do you have the vision to make yourself better every day?

from a bureaucratic and risk averse company to one that could compete in a global market required structural change.

Changes in the external environment or in organizational strategies often lead to changes in the organizational structure. Because an organization's structure is defined by how work gets done and who does it, managers can alter one or both of these *structural components*. For instance, departmental responsibilities could be combined, organizational levels eliminated, or the number of persons a manager supervises could be increased. More rules and procedures could be implemented to increase standardization. Or employees could be empowered to make decisions so decision making could be faster.

Another option would be to make major changes in the actual *structural design*. For instance, when Hewlett-Packard acquired Compaq Computer, product divisions were dropped, merged, or expanded. Structural design changes also might include, for instance, a shift from a functional to a product structure or the creation of a project structure design. Avery-Dennis Corporation, for example, revamped its structure to a new design that arranges work around teams.

CHANGING TECHNOLOGY Managers can also change the technology used to convert inputs into outputs. Most early management studies dealt with changing technology. For instance, scientific management techniques involved implementing changes that would increase production efficiency. Today, technological changes usually involve the introduction of new equipment, tools, or methods; automation; or computerization.

Competitive factors or new innovations within an industry often require managers to introduce *new equipment, tools,* or *operating methods*. For example, coal mining companies in New South Wales updated operational methods, installed more efficient coal handling equipment, and made changes in work practices to be more productive.

Automation is a technological change that replaces certain tasks done by people with tasks done by machines. Automation has been introduced in organizations such as the U.S. Postal Service where automatic mail sorters are used, and in automobile assembly lines, where robots are programmed to do jobs that workers used to perform.

The most visible technological changes have come from *computerization*. Most organizations have sophisticated information systems. For instance, supermarkets and other retailers use scanners that provide instant inventory information and many are starting to accept mobile payments. Also, most offices are computerized. At BP p.l.c., for example, employees had to learn how to deal with the personal visibility and accountability brought about by an enterprise-wide information system. The integrative nature of this system meant that what any employee did on his or her computer automatically affected other computer systems on the internal network.[15] At the Benetton Group SpA, computers link its manufacturing plants outside Treviso, Italy, with the company's various sales outlets and a highly automated warehouse. Now, product information can be transmitted and shared instantaneously, a real plus in today's environment.[16]

CHANGING PEOPLE Changing people involves changing attitudes, expectations, perceptions, and behaviors—something that's not easy to do. **Organizational development (OD)** is the term used to describe change methods that focus on people and the nature and quality of interpersonal work relationships.[17] The most popular OD techniques are described in Exhibit 7-4. Each seeks to bring about changes in the organization's people and make them work together better. For example, executives at Scotiabank, one of Canada's Big Five banks, knew that the success of a new customer sales and service strategy depended on changing employee attitudes and behaviors. Managers used different OD techniques during the strategic change, including team building, survey feedback, and intergroup development. One indicator of how well these techniques worked in getting people to change was that every branch in Canada implemented the new strategy on or ahead of schedule.[18]

Much of what we know about OD practices has come from North American research. However, managers need to recognize that some techniques that work for U.S. organizations may not be appropriate for organizations or organizational divisions based in other countries.[19] For instance, a study of OD interventions showed that "multirater [survey] feedback as practiced in the United States is not embraced in Taiwan" because the cultural value of "saving face is simply more powerful

Hiking four round-trip miles together serves as a healthy team-building exercise for the employees of Wellness Corporate Solutions, a company that provides customized wellness programs and health screening services to organizations throughout the United States. Taking these long walks together helps Wellness employees learn how other employees think and work. Team-building is one organizational development method managers use to bring about changes in employees that improve the quality of interpersonal work relationships.
Source: The Washington Post/Getty Images

organizational development (OD)
Change methods that focus on people and the nature and quality of interpersonal work relationships

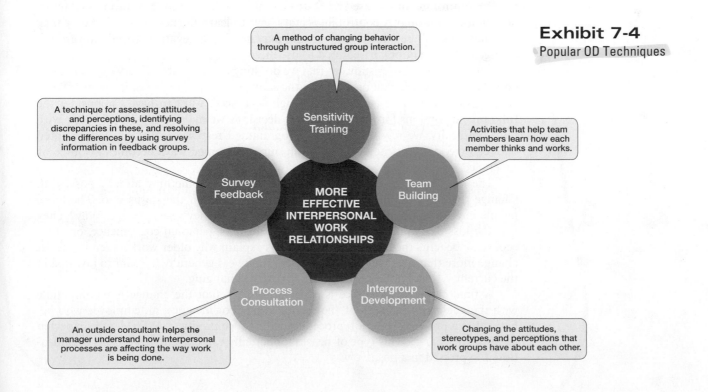

Exhibit 7-4
Popular OD Techniques

A method of changing behavior through unstructured group interaction.

A technique for assessing attitudes and perceptions, identifying discrepancies in these, and resolving the differences by using survey information in feedback groups.

Activities that help team members learn how each member thinks and works.

An outside consultant helps the manager understand how interpersonal processes are affecting the way work is being done.

Changing the attitudes, stereotypes, and perceptions that work groups have about each other.

Sensitivity Training

Survey Feedback

Team Building

MORE EFFECTIVE INTERPERSONAL WORK RELATIONSHIPS

Process Consultation

Intergroup Development

than the value of receiving feedback from subordinates."[20] What's the lesson for managers? Before using the same OD techniques to implement behavioral changes, especially across different countries, managers need to be sure they've taken into account cultural characteristics and whether the techniques "make sense for the local culture."

7.3 *Explain* how to manage resistance to change.

MANAGING Resistance to Change

We know it's better for us to eat healthy and to be active, yet few of us follow that advice. We resist making changes in our lifestyle. Volkswagen Sweden and ad agency DDB Stockholm did an experiment to see if they could get people to change their behavior and take the healthier option of using the stairs instead of riding an escalator.[21] How? They put a working piano keyboard on a stairway in a Stockholm subway station (you can see a video of it on YouTube) to see if commuters would use it. The experiment was a resounding success as stair traffic rose 66 percent. The lesson—people can change if you make the change appealing.

Change can be a threat to people in an organization. Organizations can build up inertia that motivates people to resist changing their status quo, even though change might be beneficial. Why do people resist change, and what can be done to minimize their resistance?

Why Do People Resist Change?

It's often said that most people hate any change that doesn't jingle in their pockets. This resistance to change is well documented.[22] Why *do* people resist change? The main reasons include uncertainty, habit, concern over personal loss, and the belief that the change is not in the organization's best interest.[23]

Change replaces the known with uncertainty. No matter how much you may dislike attending college, at least you know what's expected of you. When you leave college for the world of full-time employment, you'll trade the known for the unknown. Employees in organizations are faced with similar uncertainty. For example, when quality control methods based on statistical models are introduced into manufacturing plants, many quality control inspectors have to learn the new methods. Some may fear that they will be unable to do so and may develop a negative attitude toward the change or behave poorly if required to use them.

Another cause of resistance is that we do things out of habit. Every day when you go to school or work, you probably go the same way, if you're like most people. We're creatures of habit. Life is complex enough—we don't want to have to consider the full range of options for the hundreds of decisions we make every day. To cope with this complexity, we rely on habits or programmed responses. But when confronted with change, our tendency to respond in our accustomed ways becomes a source of resistance.

The third cause of resistance is the fear of losing something already possessed. Change threatens the investment you've already made in the status quo. The more people have invested in the current system, the more they resist change. Why? They fear the loss of status, money, authority, friendships, personal convenience, or other economic benefits they value. This fear helps explain why older workers tend to resist change more than younger workers. Older employees generally have more invested in the current system and thus have more to lose by changing.

A final cause of resistance is a person's belief that the change is incompatible with the goals and interests of the organization. For instance, an employee who believes that a proposed new job procedure will reduce product quality can be expected to resist the change. This type of resistance actually can be beneficial to the organization if expressed in a positive way.

let's get REAL

The Scenario:

After the National Transportation Safety Board recommended that states ban the use of cell phones while driving because of safety concerns, many companies are changing their policy on employee cell phone use. Jeff Turner, owner of an appliance repair service company in Toledo, Ohio, has told his employees that the company's new policy is "No cell phone use while driving." However, he's having a difficult time enforcing the policy.

What suggestions would you give Jeff about getting his employees to change their behavior?

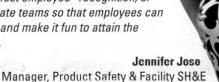

I have tried various ways to have employees comply with safety policies, which can be quite difficult. The most successful method is positive reinforcement using incentives, such as a driving performance bonus or an extra vacation day. By providing employees with additional beneficial goals for adhering to safety policies, it gives them something extra to strive for. Employees can further race to achieve "safest employee" recognition, or you can create teams so that employees can collaborate and make it fun to attain the overall goal.

Jennifer Jose
Manager, Product Safety & Facility SH&E

Source: Jennifer Jose

Techniques for Reducing Resistance to Change

When managers see resistance to change as dysfunctional, what can they do? Several strategies have been suggested in dealing with resistance to change. These approaches include education and communication, participation, facilitation and support, negotiation, manipulation and co-optation, and coercion. These tactics are summarized here and described in Exhibit 7-5. Managers should view these techniques as tools and use the most appropriate one, depending on the type and source of the resistance.

Education and communication can help reduce resistance to change by helping employees see the logic of the change effort. This technique, of course, assumes that much of the resistance lies in misinformation or poor communication.

Participation involves bringing those individuals directly affected by the proposed change into the decision-making process. Their participation allows these individuals to express their feelings, increase the quality of the process, and increase employee commitment to the final decision.

Facilitation and support involve helping employees deal with the fear and anxiety associated with the change effort. This help may include employee counseling, therapy, new skills training, or a short paid leave of absence.

Negotiation involves exchanging something of value for an agreement to lessen the resistance to the change effort. This resistance technique may be quite useful when the resistance comes from a powerful source.

Manipulation and co-optation refer to covert attempts to influence others about the change. It may involve distorting facts to make the change appear more attractive.

Finally, *coercion* can be used to deal with resistance to change. Coercion involves the use of direct threats or force against the resisters.

Exhibit 7-5

Techniques for Reducing
Resistance to Change

Technique	When Used	Advantage	Disadvantage
Education and communication	When resistance is due to misinformation	Clear up misunderstandings	May not work when mutual trust and credibility are lacking
Participation	When resisters have the expertise to make a contribution	Increase involvement and acceptance	Time-consuming; has potential for a poor solution
Facilitation and support	When resisters are fearful and anxiety ridden	Can facilitate needed adjustments	Expensive; no guarantee of success
Negotiation	When resistance comes from a powerful group	Can "buy" commitment	Potentially high cost; opens doors for others to apply pressure too
Manipulation and co-optation	When a powerful group's endorsement is needed	Inexpensive, easy way to gain support	Can backfire, causing change agent to lose credibility
Coercion	When a powerful group's endorsement is needed	Inexpensive, easy way to gain support	May be illegal; may undermine change agent's credibility

7.4 *Discuss* contemporary issues in managing change.

CONTEMPORARY Issues in Managing Change

When CEO David Gray joined Daxko, a small software vendor based in Birmingham, Alabama, he wanted a more collegial workplace and he wanted to relieve employee stress. Now with a Wii console and a 52-inch plasma TV in the work/play lounge and an open-office layout, the company's "casual but driven environment now resembles Silicon Valley more than the Deep South." One employee said, "It's pretty intense here. Expectations for what I need to accomplish are clearly set. And if I can play the Wii while doing it, that's even better."[24] Employee stress is one of the major critical concerns for managers today. In this section, we're going to discuss stress and two other critical concerns—changing organizational culture and making change happen successfully. Let's look first at changing culture.

Changing Organizational Culture

Korean Air CEO Cho Yang-Ho had a challenging change situation facing him. He wanted to transform his airline's image of an accident-prone airline from a developing country to that of a strong international competitor.[25] His main focus was on improving safety above all else, which meant making significant changes to the organization's culture. What made his task even more challenging was Korea's hierarchical culture that teaches Koreans to be deferential toward their elders and superiors. Cho says, "It (the hierarchical culture) exists in all Oriental culture." His approach to changing his company's culture involved implementing a "systems approach aimed at minimizing the personality-driven, top-down culture that is a legacy of Korean business managers who place emphasis on intuition and responding to orders." The cultural change must have worked. Korean Air is now the world's largest commercial cargo carrier, and it has earned a four-star rating (out of five possible stars) from a London aviation firm that rates airlines on quality.

The fact that an organization's culture is made up of relatively stable and permanent characteristics tends to make it very resistant to change.[26] A culture takes a long time to form, and once established it tends to become entrenched. Strong cultures are particularly resistant to change because employees have become so committed to them. For instance, it didn't take long for Lou Gerstner, who was CEO of IBM from 1993 to 2002, to discover the power of a strong culture. Gerstner, the first outsider to lead IBM, needed to overhaul the ailing, tradition-bound company if it was going to regain its role as the dominant player in the computer industry. However, accomplishing that feat in an organization that prided itself on its long-standing culture was Gerstner's biggest challenge. He said, "I came to see in my decade at IBM that culture isn't just one aspect of the game—it *is* the game."[27] Over time, if a certain culture becomes a handicap, a manager might be able to do little to change it, especially in the short run. Even under the most favorable conditions, cultural changes have to be viewed in years, not weeks or even months.

UNDERSTANDING THE SITUATIONAL FACTORS What "favorable conditions" facilitate cultural change? One is that *a dramatic crisis occurs,* such as an unexpected financial setback, the loss of a major customer, or a dramatic technological innovation by a competitor. Such a shock can weaken the status quo and make people start thinking about the relevance of the current culture. Another condition may be that *leadership changes hands.* New top leadership can provide an alternative set of key values and may be perceived as more capable of responding to the crisis than the old leaders were. Another is that *the organization is young and small.* The younger the organization, the less entrenched its culture. It's easier for managers to communicate new values in a small organization than in a large one. Finally, the *culture is weak.* Weak cultures are more receptive to change than strong ones.[28]

These stock traders working on the floor of the BM&F Bovespa stock exchange in Sao Paulo, Brazil, have highly stressful jobs. As stock traders, they buy and sell stocks on behalf of investors who may be individuals or companies. The role and task demands of traders contribute to the stress of their jobs because they make instantaneous buy and sell decisions that affect others' finances and wealth. Their challenging career requires that traders study business news and economic statistics, analyze companies and investment opportunities, devise trading strategies, and continually monitor stock market developments on a daily basis.
Source: Reuters/Paulo Whitaker

MAKING CHANGES IN CULTURE If conditions are right, how do managers change culture? No single action is likely to have the impact necessary to change something ingrained and highly valued. Managers need a strategy for managing cultural change, as described in Exhibit 7-6. These suggestions focus on specific actions that managers can take. Following them, however, is no guarantee that the cultural change efforts will succeed. Organizational members don't quickly let go of values that they understand and that have worked well for them in the past. Change, if it comes, will be slow. Also, managers must stay alert to protect against any return to old, familiar traditions.

- *Set the tone through management behavior;* top managers, particularly, need to be positive role models.
- Create *new stories, symbols, and rituals* to replace those currently in use.
- Select, promote, and support employees who *adopt the new values.*
- *Redesign socialization processes* to align with the new values.
- To encourage acceptance of the new values, *change the reward system.*
- Replace unwritten norms with *clearly specified expectations.*
- *Shake up current subcultures* through job transfers, job rotation, and/or terminations.
- Work to get consensus through *employee participation* and creating a *climate with a high level of trust.*

Exhibit 7-6
Changing Culture

stress
The adverse reaction people have to excessive pressure placed on them from extraordinary demands, constraints, or opportunities

stressors
Factors that cause stress

*data*points[37]

41 percent lower health costs is what companies achieve when they help employees with well-being initiatives.

63 percent of Americans are working more than 40 hours per week.

41 percent of Americans feel they have significantly more responsibilities at work today than when the recession started.

70 percent of Americans say they're stressed about work.

52 percent of employees say that colleagues are the more stress-inducing aspect of their jobs.

70 percent of change initiatives fail to deliver intended outcomes.

8 percent of executives whose organizations went through a redesign said the efforts added value.

43 percent of companies have a chief innovation officer.

66 percent of top managers say that creativity/innovation skills are important for advancement.

Employee Stress

"Most weekdays at 5:30 p.m., after putting in eight hours as an insurance agent in Lawrenceville, Georgia, April Hamby scurries about 100 yards to the Kroger supermarket two doors away. She's not there to pick up some milk and bread, but instead to work an additional six hours as a cashier before driving home 35 miles and slipping into bed by 2 a.m. so she can get up at 7 a.m. and begin the grind anew."[29] And April's situation isn't all that unusual. During the economic downturn, many people found themselves working two or more jobs and battling stress.[30]

As a student, you've probably experienced stress—class projects, exams, even juggling a job and school. Then, there's the stress associated with getting a decent job after graduation. But even after you've landed that job, stress isn't likely to stop. For many employees, organizational change creates stress. An uncertain environment characterized by time pressures, increasing workloads, mergers, and restructuring has created a large number of employees who are overworked and stressed.[31] In fact, depending on which survey you look at, the number of employees experiencing job stress in the United States ranges anywhere from 40 percent to 80 percent.[32] However, workplace stress isn't just an American problem. Global studies indicate that some 50 percent of workers surveyed in 16 European countries reported that stress and job responsibility have risen significantly over a five-year period; 35 percent of Canadian workers surveyed said they are under high job stress; in Australia, cases of occupational stress jumped 21 percent in a one-year period; more than 57 percent of Japanese employees suffer from work-related stress; some 83 percent of call-center workers in India suffer from sleeping disorders; and a study of stress in China showed that managers are experiencing more stress.[33] Another interesting study found that stress was the leading cause of people quitting their jobs. Surprisingly, however, employers were clueless. They said that stress wasn't even among the top five reasons why people leave and instead wrongly believed that insufficient pay was the main reason.[34]

WHAT IS STRESS? **Stress** is the adverse reaction people have to excessive pressure placed on them from extraordinary demands, constraints, or opportunities.[35] Stress isn't always bad. Although it's often discussed in a negative context, stress can be positive, especially when it offers a potential gain. For instance, functional stress allows an athlete, stage performer, or employee to perform at his or her highest level at crucial times.

However, stress is more often associated with constraints and demands. A constraint prevents you from doing what you desire; demands refer to the loss of something desired. When you take a test at school or have your annual performance review at work, you feel stress because you confront opportunity, constraints, and demands. A good performance review may lead to a promotion, greater responsibilities, and a higher salary. But a poor review may keep you from getting the promotion. An extremely poor review might lead to your being fired.

One other thing to understand about stress is that just because the conditions are right for stress to surface doesn't always mean it will. Two conditions are necessary for *potential* stress to become *actual* stress.[36] First, there must be uncertainty over the outcome, and second, the outcome must be important.

WHAT CAUSES STRESS? Stress can be caused by personal factors and by job-related factors called **stressors**. Clearly, change of any kind—personal or job-related—has the potential to cause stress because it can involve demands, constraints, or opportunities. Organizations have no shortage of factors that can cause stress. Pressures to avoid errors or complete tasks in a limited time period, changes in the way reports are filed, a demanding supervisor, and unpleasant coworkers are a few examples. Let's look at five categories of organizational stressors: task demands, role demands, interpersonal demands, organization structure, and organizational leadership.

Task demands are factors related to an employee's job. They include the design of a person's job (autonomy, task variety, degree of automation), working conditions, and the physical work layout. Work quotas can put pressure on employees when their "outcomes" are perceived as excessive.[38] The more interdependence between an employee's tasks and the tasks of others, the greater the potential for stress. *Autonomy*, on the other hand, tends to lessen stress. Jobs in which temperatures, noise, or other working conditions are dangerous or undesirable can increase anxiety. So, too, can working in an overcrowded room or in a visible location where interruptions are constant.

Role demands relate to pressures placed on an employee as a function of the particular role he or she plays in the organization. **Role conflicts** create expectations that may be hard to reconcile or satisfy. **Role overload** is experienced when the employee is expected to do more than time permits. **Role ambiguity** is created when role expectations are not clearly understood and the employee is not sure what he or she is to do.

Interpersonal demands are pressures created by other employees. Lack of social support from colleagues and poor interpersonal relationships can cause considerable stress, especially among employees with a high social need.

Organization structure can increase stress. Excessive rules and an employee's lack of opportunity to participate in decisions that affect him or her are examples of structural variables that might be potential sources of stress.

Organizational leadership represents the supervisory style of the organization's managers. Some managers create a culture characterized by tension, fear, and anxiety. They establish unrealistic pressures to perform in the short run, impose excessively tight controls, and routinely fire employees who don't measure up. This style of leadership filters down through the organization and affects all employees.

Personal factors that can create stress include family issues, personal economic problems, and inherent personality characteristics. Because employees bring their personal problems to work with them, a full understanding of employee stress requires a manager to be understanding of these personal factors.[39] Evidence also indicates that employees' personalities have an effect on how susceptible they are to stress. The most commonly used labels for these personality traits are Type A and Type B.

Type A personality is characterized by chronic feelings of a sense of time urgency, an excessive competitive drive, and difficulty accepting and enjoying leisure time. The opposite of Type A is **Type B personality**. Type Bs don't suffer from time urgency or impatience. Until quite recently, it was believed that Type As were more likely to experience stress on and off the job. A closer analysis of the evidence, however, has produced new conclusions. Studies show that only the hostility and anger associated with Type A behavior are actually associated with the negative effects of stress. And Type Bs are just as susceptible to the same anxiety-producing elements. For managers, it is important to recognize that Type A employees are more likely to show symptoms of stress, even if organizational and personal stressors are low.

WHAT ARE THE SYMPTOMS OF STRESS? We see stress in a number of ways. For instance, an employee who is experiencing high stress may become depressed, accident prone, or argumentative; may have difficulty making routine decisions; may be easily distracted, and so on. As Exhibit 7-7 shows, stress symptoms can be grouped

role conflicts
Work expectations that are hard to satisfy

role overload
Having more work to accomplish than time permits

role ambiguity
When role expectations are not clearly understood

Type A personality
People who have a chronic sense of urgency and an excessive competitive drive

Type B personality
People who are relaxed and easygoing and accept change easily

Exhibit 7-7
Symptoms of Stress

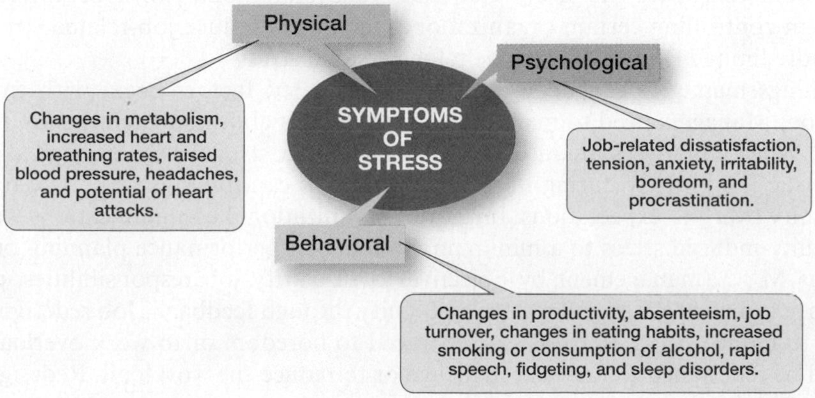

let's get REAL

The Scenario:

Sondra Chan manages a team of 12 researchers at an organics-based cosmetics company. Like many companies during the past few years, she's asked her employees to take on greater responsibility since budgets are tight and no new hires have been brought onboard. Although she wants her team members to view these added responsibilities as furthering their own personal development, she also doesn't want to stretch them too far, causing out-of-control workplace stress and burnout.

What can Sondra do so her team doesn't get too stressed?

Sondra is in a common situation where payroll is not seemingly meeting the needs of the business. The positive effect of this situation is greatly assisting in the realization and achievement of each member's potential, including hers. She must first ensure that the perception and atmosphere is clear of any negative connotations by devoting personal time to each team member to discuss and execute their respective developmental plans and how these added tasks will help them achieve their goals. Through motivational observations and consistent follow-up, Sondra will be able to see which team members are able to take on more responsibilities and which team members are showing signs of stress, then shifting tasks and creating a well-balanced team, leveraged by utilizing each employee's full potential.

Mina Nematalla
Business Owner and Manager

Source: Mina Nematalla

under three general categories: physical, psychological, and behavioral. All of these can significantly affect an employee's work.

In Japan, there's a stress phenomenon called *karoshi* (pronounced kah-roe-she), which is translated literally as "death from overwork." During the late 1980s, "several high-ranking Japanese executives still in their prime years suddenly died without any previous sign of illness."[40] As Japanese multinational companies expand operations to China, Korea, and Taiwan, it's feared that the karoshi culture may follow.

HOW CAN STRESS BE REDUCED? As mentioned earlier, not all stress is dysfunctional. Because stress can never be totally eliminated from a person's life, managers want to reduce the stress that leads to dysfunctional work behavior. How? Through controlling certain organizational factors to reduce job-related stress, and to a more limited extent, offering help for personal stress.

Things managers can do in terms of job-related factors begin with employee selection. Managers need to make sure an employee's abilities match the job requirements. When employees are in over their heads, their stress levels are typically high. A realistic job preview during the selection process can minimize stress by reducing ambiguity over job expectations. Improved organizational communications will keep ambiguity-induced stress to a minimum. Similarly, a performance planning program such as **MBO** (management by objectives) will clarify job responsibilities, provide clear performance goals, and reduce ambiguity through feedback. Job redesign is also a way to reduce stress. If stress can be traced to boredom or to work overload, jobs should be redesigned to increase challenge or to reduce the workload. Redesigns that increase opportunities for employees to participate in decisions and to gain social support also have been found to reduce stress.[41] For instance, at U.K. pharmaceutical maker GlaxoSmithKline, a team-resilience program in which employees can shift assignments, depending on people's workload and deadlines, has helped reduce work-related stress by 60 percent.[42]

Stress from an employee's personal life raises two problems. First, it's difficult for the manager to control directly. Second, ethical considerations include whether the manager has the right to intrude—even in the most subtle ways—in an employee's personal life. If a manager believes it's ethical and the employee is receptive, the manager might consider several approaches. Employee *counseling* can provide stress relief. Employees often want to talk to someone about their problems, and the organization—through its managers, in-house human resource counselors, or free or low-cost outside professional help—can meet that need. Companies such as Citicorp, AT&T, and Johnson & Johnson provide extensive counseling services for their employees. A *time management program* can help employees whose personal lives suffer from a lack of planning to sort out their priorities.[43] Still another approach is organizationally sponsored *wellness programs.* For example, Wellmark Blue Cross Blue Shield of Des Moines, Iowa, offers employees an onsite health and fitness facility that is open six days a week. Employees at Cianbro, a general contracting company located in the northeastern United States, are provided a wellness program tailored to the unique demands of the construction environment.[44]

Making Change Happen Successfully

Organizational change is an ongoing daily challenge facing managers in the United States and around the globe. In a global study of organizational changes in more than 2,000 organizations in Europe, Japan, the United States, and the United Kingdom, 82 percent of the respondents had implemented major information systems changes, 74 percent had created horizontal sharing of services and information, 65 percent had implemented flexible human resource practices, and 62 percent had decentralized operational decisions.[45] Each of these major changes entailed numerous other changes in structure, technology, and people. When changes are needed, who makes them happen? Who manages them? Although you may think it's just top-level managers, actually managers at *all* organizational levels are involved in the change process.

Even with the involvement of all levels of managers, change efforts don't always work the way they should. In fact, a global study of organizational change concluded that "Hundreds of managers from scores of U.S. and European companies [are] satisfied with their operating prowess...[but] dissatisfied with their ability to implement change."[46] How can managers make change happen successfully? They can (1) make the organization change capable, (2) understand their own role in the process, and (3) give individual employees a role in the change process. Let's look at each of these suggestions.

In an industry where growth is slowing and competitors are becoming stronger, United Parcel Service (UPS) prospers. How? By embracing change! Managers spent a decade creating new worldwide logistics businesses because they anticipated slowing domestic shipping demand. They continue change efforts in order to exploit new opportunities.[47] UPS is what we call a change-capable organization. What does it take to be a change-capable organization? Exhibit 7-8 summarizes the characteristics.

The second component of making change happen successfully is for managers to recognize their own important role in the process. Managers can, and do, act as change agents. But their role in the change process includes more than being catalysts for change; they must also be change leaders. When organizational members resist change, it's the manager's responsibility to lead the change effort. But even when there's no resistance to the change, someone has to assume leadership. That someone is managers.

The final aspect of making change happen successfully revolves around getting all organizational members involved. Successful organizational change is not a

Exhibit 7-8

Change-Capable Organizations

- *Link the present and the future.* Think of work as more than an extension of the past; think about future opportunities and issues and factor them into today's decisions.
- *Make learning a way of life.* Change-friendly organizations excel at knowledge sharing and management.
- *Actively support and encourage day-to-day improvements and changes.* Successful change can come from the small changes as well as the big ones.
- *Ensure diverse teams.* Diversity ensures that things won't be done like they've always been done.
- *Encourage mavericks.* Because their ideas and approaches are outside the mainstream, mavericks can help bring about radical change.
- *Shelter breakthroughs.* Change-friendly organizations have found ways to protect those breakthrough ideas.
- *Integrate technology.* Use technology to implement changes.
- *Build and deepen trust.* People are more likely to support changes when the organization's culture is trusting and managers have credibility and integrity.
- *Couple permanence with perpetual change.* Because change is the only constant, companies need to figure out how to protect their core strengths during times of change.
- *Support an entrepreneurial mindset.* Many younger employees bring a more entrepreneurial mindset to organizations and can serve as catalysts for radical change.

Sources: Based on S. Ante, "Change Is Good—So Get Used to It," *BusinessWeek,* June 22, 2009, pp. 69–70; and P. A. McLagan, "The Change-Capable Organization," *T&D,* January 2003, pp. 50–59.

one-person job. Individual employees are a powerful resource in identifying and addressing change issues. "If you develop a program for change and simply hand it to your people, saying, 'Here, implement this,' it's unlikely to work. But when people help to build something, they will support it and make it work."[48] Managers need to encourage employees to be change agents—to look for those day-to-day improvements and changes that individuals and teams can make. For instance, a study of organizational change found that 77 percent of changes at the work group level were reactions to a specific, current problem or to a suggestion from someone outside the work group; and 68 percent of those changes occurred in the course of employees' day-to-day work.[49]

7.5 *Describe* techniques for stimulating innovation.

STIMULATING Innovation

"Innovation is the key to continued success." "We innovate today to secure the future."[50] These two quotes (the first by Ajay Banga, the CEO of MasterCard, and the second by Sophie Vandebroek, chief technology officer of Xerox Innovation Group) reflect how important innovation is to organizations. Success in business today demands innovation. In the dynamic, chaotic world of global competition, organizations must create new products and services and adopt state-of-the-art technology if they're going to compete successfully.[51]

What companies come to mind when you think of successful innovators? Maybe it's Apple with its iPad, iPhone, iPod, and wide array of computers. Maybe it's Google with its continually evolving web platform. And Google is a good example of the new, faster pace of innovation. The company runs 50 to 200 online search experiments with users at any given time. In one instance, Google asked selected users how many search results they'd like to see on a single screen. The reply from the users was more, many more. So Google ran an experiment that tripled the number of search results per screen to 30. The result: traffic declined because "it took about a third of a second longer for search results to appear—a seemingly insignificant delay that nonetheless upset many of the users."[52] Google tried something new and quickly found out it wasn't something they wanted to pursue. Even Procter & Gamble, the global household and personal products giant, is doing the "vast majority of our concept testing online, which has created truly substantial savings in money and time," according to the company's global consumer and market knowledge officer.[53] What's the secret to the success of these and other innovator champions? What can other managers do to make their organizations more innovative? In the following sections, we'll try to answer those questions as we discuss the factors behind innovation.

Intel fosters innovation by including creative people within its organization. The company hired will.i.am—music artist, producer, and front man for The Black Eyed Peas—as its Director of Creative Innovation. In this position, will.i.am is collaborating with Intel scientists, researchers, and computer programmers in developing creative and technology initiatives that will communicate with people in new ways. According to Intel, will.i.am's creativity will help stimulate innovation for products including laptops, smart phones, and tablets aimed at "the global youth culture that embraces new devices and new forms of communication and entertainment."
Source: Bloomberg via Getty Images

Creativity Versus Innovation

The definition of innovation varies widely, depending on who you ask. For instance, the Merriam-Webster dictionary defines innovation as "the introduction of something new" and "a new idea, method, or device; novelty." The CEO of the company that makes Bubble Wrap says, "It means inventing a product that has never existed." To the CEO of Ocean Spray Cranberries, it means "turning an overlooked commodity, such as leftover cranberry skins into a consumer snack like Craisins."[54] We're going to define it by first looking at the concept of creativity. **Creativity** refers to the ability to combine ideas in a unique way or to make unusual associations between ideas.[55] A creative organization develops unique ways of working or novel solutions to problems. But creativity by itself isn't enough. The outcomes of the creative process need to be turned into useful products or work methods, which is defined as **innovation**. Thus, the innovative organization is characterized by its ability to generate new ideas that are implemented into new products, processes, and procedures designed to be useful—that is, to channel creativity into useful outcomes. When managers talk about changing an organization to make it more creative, they usually mean they want to stimulate and nurture innovation.

creativity
The ability to combine ideas in a unique way or to make unusual associations between ideas

innovation
Taking creative ideas and turning them into useful products or work methods

Stimulating and Nurturing Innovation

The systems model (see Management History Module, p. 35) can help us understand how organizations become more innovative.[56] Getting the desired outputs (innovative products and work methods) involves transforming inputs. These inputs include creative people and groups within the organization. But having creative people isn't enough. It takes the right environment to help transform those inputs into innovative products or work methods. This "right" environment—that is, an environment that stimulates innovation—includes three variables: the organization's structure, culture, and human resource practices. (See Exhibit 7-9.)

Structural Variables

An organization's structure can have a huge impact on innovativeness. Research into the effect of structural variables on innovation shows five things.[57] First, an organic-type structure positively influences innovation. Because this structure is low in formalization, centralization, and work specialization, it facilitates the flexibility and sharing of ideas that are critical to innovation. Second, the availability of plentiful resources provides a key building block for innovation. With an abundance of resources, managers can afford to purchase innovations, can afford the cost of instituting innovations, and can absorb failures. For example, at Smart Balance Inc., the heart-healthy food developer uses its resources efficiently by focusing on product development and outsourcing almost everything else, including manufacturing, product distribution, and sales. The company's CEO says this approach allows them to be "a pretty aggressive innovator" even during economic downturns.[58] Third, frequent communication between organizational units helps break down barriers

Exhibit 7-9
Innovation Variables

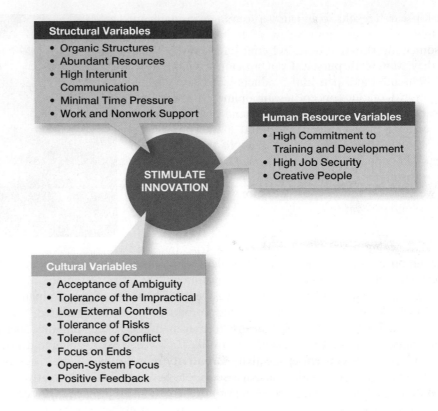

Structural Variables
- Organic Structures
- Abundant Resources
- High Interunit Communication
- Minimal Time Pressure
- Work and Nonwork Support

Human Resource Variables
- High Commitment to Training and Development
- High Job Security
- Creative People

STIMULATE INNOVATION

Cultural Variables
- Acceptance of Ambiguity
- Tolerance of the Impractical
- Low External Controls
- Tolerance of Risks
- Tolerance of Conflict
- Focus on Ends
- Open-System Focus
- Positive Feedback

to innovation.[59] Cross-functional teams, task forces, and other such organizational designs facilitate interaction across departmental lines and are widely used in innovative organizations. For instance, Pitney Bowes, the mail and documents company, uses an electronic meeting place called IdeaNet where its employees can collaborate and provide comments and input on any idea they think will help create new sources of revenue, improve profitability, or add new value for customers. IdeaNet isn't just an electronic suggestion box or open forum; employees are presented with specific idea challenges. A recent one involved how to expand its mail service business into new segments. Hundreds of employees from multiple functions and business units weighed in with ideas, and eight promising ideas were generated.[60] Fourth, innovative organizations try to minimize extreme time pressures on creative activities despite the demands of white-water rapids environments. Although time pressures may spur people to work harder and may make them feel more creative, studies show that it actually causes them to be less creative.[61] Companies such as Google, 3M, and Hewlett-Packard actually urge staff researchers to spend a chunk of their work-week on self-initiated projects, even if those projects are outside the individual's work area of expertise.[62] Finally, studies have shown that an employee's creative performance was enhanced when an organization's structure explicitly supported creativity. Beneficial kinds of support included things like encouragement, open communication, readiness to listen, and useful feedback.[63]

LEADER who made a DIFFERENCE

Ratan Tata, *former chairman of Tata Sons, built one of the world's largest conglomerates.[64] When India's long-protected economy was opened in 1981, Tata decided that for his myriad companies to survive and thrive in a global economy, he had to "make innovation a priority and build it into the DNA of the Tata Group so that every employee at every company might think and act like an innovator." One unique way innovation is encouraged at Tata is an internal innovation competition. Teams from units of the Indian conglomerate are presented with a challenge and prepare projects that are presented at the global finals at headquarters in Mumbai. Employee teams register for the competition and the winners get no cash, only awards such as the Tata's Promising Innovation Award or the Dare to Try Award. The real prize for employees is the respect and recognition of Tata's leadership. However, the biggest winner is probably the company itself. What can you learn from this leader who made a difference?*

CULTURAL VARIABLES   "Throw the bunny" is part of the lingo used by a product development team at toy company Mattel. It refers to a juggling lesson where team members learn to juggle two balls and a stuffed bunny. Most people easily learn to juggle two balls but can't let go of that third object. Creativity, like juggling, is learning to let go—that is, to "throw the bunny." And for Mattel, having a culture where people are encouraged to "throw the bunny" is important to its continued product innovations.[65]

Innovative organizations tend to have similar cultures.[66] They encourage experimentation, set creativity goals, reward both successes and failures, and celebrate mistakes. An innovative organization is likely to have the following characteristics.

- *Accept ambiguity.* Too much emphasis on objectivity and specificity constrains creativity.
- *Tolerate the impractical.* Individuals who offer impractical, even foolish, answers to what-if questions are not stifled. What at first seems impractical might lead to innovative solutions. Encourage entrepreneurial thinking.[67]
- *Keep external controls minimal.* Rules, regulations, policies, and similar organizational controls are kept to a minimum.
- *Tolerate risk.* Employees are encouraged to experiment without fear of consequences should they fail.[68] "Failure, and how companies deal with failure, is a very big part of innovation."[69] Treat mistakes as learning opportunities. You don't want your employees to fear putting forth new ideas. In an uncertain economic environment, it's especially important that employees don't feel they have to avoid innovation and initiative because it's unsafe for them to do so. A recent study found that one fear employees have is that their coworkers will think negatively of them if they try to come up with better ways of doing things. Another fear is that they'll "provoke anger among others who are comfortable with the status quo."[70] In an innovative culture, such fears are not an issue.
- *Tolerate conflict.* Diversity of opinions is encouraged. Harmony and agreement between individuals or units are *not* assumed to be evidence of high performance.
- *Focus on ends rather than means.* Goals are made clear, and individuals are encouraged to consider alternative routes toward meeting the goals. Focusing on ends suggests that several right answers might be possible for any given problem.[71]
- *Use an open-system focus.* Managers closely monitor the environment and respond to changes as they occur. For example, at Starbucks, product development depends on "inspiration field trips to view customers and trends." When Michelle Gass was the company's senior vice president of global strategy (she's now the president of Starbucks Europe, Middle East, and Africa), she "took her team to Paris, Düsseldorf, and London to visit local Starbucks and other restaurants to get a better sense of local cultures, behaviors, and fashions." She says, "You come back just full of different ideas and different ways to think about things than you would had you read about it in a magazine or e-mail."[72]
- *Provide positive feedback.* Managers provide positive feedback, encouragement, and support so employees feel that their creative ideas receive attention.
- *Exhibit empowering leadership.* Be a leader who lets organizational members know that the work they do is significant. Provide organizational members the opportunity to participate in decision making. Show them you're confident they can achieve high performance levels and outcomes. Being this type of leader will have a positive influence on creativity.[73]

HUMAN RESOURCE VARIABLES   In this category, we find that innovative organizations actively promote the training and development of their members so their knowledge remains current; offer their employees high job security to reduce the fear of getting fired for making mistakes; and encourage individuals to become **idea champions**, actively and enthusiastically supporting new ideas, building support, overcoming resistance, and ensuring that innovations are implemented. Research

idea champion
Individuals who actively and enthusiastically support new ideas, build support, overcome resistance, and ensure that innovations are implemented

finds that idea champions have common personality characteristics: extremely high self-confidence, persistence, energy, and a tendency toward risk taking. They also display characteristics associated with dynamic leadership. They inspire and energize others with their vision of the potential of an innovation and through their strong personal conviction in their mission. They're also good at gaining the commitment of others to support their mission. In addition, idea champions have jobs that provide considerable decision-making discretion. This autonomy helps them introduce and implement innovations in organizations.[74]

Innovation and Design Thinking

We introduced you to the concept of design thinking in the previous chapter on decision making. Well, undoubtedly, a strong connection exists between design thinking and innovation. "Design thinking can do for innovation what TQM did for quality."[75] Just as TQM provides a process for improving quality throughout an organization, design thinking can provide a process for coming up with things that don't exist. When a business approaches innovation with a design thinking mentality, the emphasis is on getting a deeper understanding of what customers need and want. It entails knowing customers as real people with real problems—not just as sales targets or demographic statistics. But it also entails being able to convert those customer insights into real and usable products. For instance, at Intuit, the company behind TurboTax software, founder Scott Cook felt "the company wasn't innovating fast enough."[76] So he decided to apply design thinking. He called the initiative "Design for Delight" and it involved customer field research to understand their "pain points"—that is, what most frustrated them as they worked in the office and at home. Then, Intuit staffers brainstormed (they nicknamed it "painstorm") a "variety of solutions to address the problems and experiment with customers to find the best ones." For example, one pain point uncovered by an Intuit team was how customers could take pictures of tax forms to reduce typing errors. Some younger customers, used to taking photos with their smartphones, were frustrated that they couldn't just complete their taxes on their mobiles. To address this, Intuit developed a mobile app called SnapTax, which the company says has been downloaded more than a million times since it was introduced in 2010. That's how design thinking works in innovation.

MyManagementLab

Go to **mymanagementlab.com** to complete the problems marked with this icon .

CHAPTER

PREPARING FOR: Exams/Quizzes

CHAPTER SUMMARY by Learning Outcomes

7.1 [LEARNING OUTCOME]

Compare and contrast views on the change process.

The calm waters metaphor suggests that change is an occasional disruption in the normal flow of events and can be planned and managed as it happens. In the white-water rapids metaphor, change is ongoing and managing it is a continual process.

Lewin's three-step model says change can be managed by unfreezing the status quo (old behaviors), changing to a new state, and refreezing the new behaviors.

7.2 [LEARNING OUTCOME]

Classify types of organizational change.

Organizational change is any alteration of people, structure, or technology. Making changes often requires a change agent to act as a catalyst and guide the change process.

Changing structure involves any changes in structural components or structural design. Changing technology involves introducing new equipment, tools, or methods; automation; or computerization. Changing people involves changing attitudes, expectations, perceptions, and behaviors.

7.3 [LEARNING OUTCOME]

Explain how to manage resistance to change.

People resist change because of uncertainty, habit, concern over personal loss, and the belief that the change is not in the organization's best interest.

The techniques for reducing resistance to change include education and communication (educating employees about and communicating to them the need for the change), participation (allowing employees to participate in the change process), facilitation and support (giving employees the support they need to implement the change), negotiation (exchanging something of value to reduce resistance), manipulation and co-optation (using negative actions to influence), and coercion (using direct threats or force).

7.4 [LEARNING OUTCOME]

Discuss contemporary issues in managing change.

The shared values that comprise an organization's culture are relatively stable, which makes it difficult to change. Managers can do so by being positive role models; creating new stories, symbols, and rituals; selecting, promoting, and supporting employees who adopt the new values; redesigning socialization processes; changing the reward system, clearly specifying expectations; shaking up current subcultures; and getting employees to participate in change.

Stress is the adverse reaction people have to excessive pressure placed on them from extraordinary demands, constraints, or opportunities. To help employees deal with stress, managers can address job-related factors by making sure an employee's abilities match the job requirements, improve organizational communications, use a performance planning program, or redesign jobs. Addressing personal stress factors is trickier, but managers could offer employee counseling, time management programs, and wellness programs.

Making change happen successfully involves focusing on making the organization change capable, making sure managers understand their own role in the process, and giving individual employees a role in the process.

7.5 LEARNING OUTCOME **Describe** techniques for stimulating innovation.
Creativity is the ability to combine ideas in a unique way or to make unusual associations between ideas. Innovation is turning the outcomes of the creative process into useful products or work methods.

Important structural variables include an organic-type structure, abundant resources, frequent communication between organizational units, minimal time pressure, and support. Important cultural variables include accepting ambiguity, tolerating the impractical, keeping external controls minimal, tolerating risk, tolerating conflict, focusing on ends not means, using an open-system focus, providing positive feedback, and being an empowering leader. Important human resource variables include high commitment to training and development, high job security, and encouraging individuals to be idea champions.

A close and strong connection exists between design thinking and innovation. It involves knowing customers as real people with real problems and converting those insights into usable and real products.

REVIEW AND DISCUSSION QUESTIONS ✪

1. Contrast the calm waters and white-water rapids metaphors of change.

2. Explain Lewin's three-step model of the change process.

3. Describe how managers might change structure, technology, and people.

4. Can a low-level employee be a change agent? Explain your answer.

5. How are opportunities, constraints, and demands related to stress? Give an example of each.

6. Planned change is often thought to be the best approach to take in organizations. Can unplanned change ever be effective? Explain.

7. Organizations typically have limits to how much change they can absorb. As a manager, what signs would you look for that might suggest your organization has exceeded its capacity to change?

8. Innovation requires allowing people to make mistakes. However, being wrong too many times can be disastrous to your career. Do you agree? Why or why not? What are the implications for nurturing innovation?

PREPARING FOR: My Career
ETHICS DILEMMA ✪

Half of all Americans say they've taken on major new roles and duties at work since the recession ended, often without extra pay. One in five companies offers some form of stress management program.[77] Although employee assistance programs (EAPs) are available, many employees may choose not to participate. Why? Many employees are reluctant to ask for help, especially if a major source of that stress is job overload or job insecurity. After all, there's still a stigma associated with stress. Employees don't want to be perceived as being unable to handle the demands of their job. Although they may need stress management now more than ever, few employees want to admit they're stressed. What can be done about this paradox? Do organizations even *have* an ethical responsibility to help employees deal with stress?

SKILLS EXERCISE Developing Your Change Management Skill

About the Skill
Managers play an important role in organizational change. That is, they often serve as a catalyst for the change—a change agent. However, managers may find that change is resisted by employees. After all, change represents ambiguity and uncertainty, or it threatens the status quo. How can this resistance to change be effectively managed? Here are some suggestions.[78]

Steps in Practicing the Skill

1. *Assess the climate for change.* One major factor in why some changes succeed while others fail is the readiness for change. Assessing the climate for change involves asking several questions. The more affirmative answers you get, the more likely it is that change efforts will succeed. Here are some guiding questions:
   a. Is the sponsor of the change high enough in the organization to have power to effectively deal with resistance?
   b. Is senior management supportive of the change and committed to it?
   c. Do senior managers convey the need for change, and is this feeling shared by others in the organization?
   d. Do managers have a clear vision of how the future will look after the change?
   e. Are objective measures in place to evaluate the change effort, and have reward systems been explicitly designed to reinforce them?
   f. Is the specific change effort consistent with other changes going on in the organization?
   g. Are managers willing to sacrifice their personal self-interests for the good of the organization as a whole?
   h. Do managers pride themselves on closely monitoring changes and actions by competitors?
   i. Are managers and employees rewarded for taking risks, being innovative, and looking for new and better solutions?
   j. Is the organizational structure flexible?
   k. Does communication flow both down and up in the organization?
   l. Has the organization successfully implemented changes in the past?
   m. Are employees satisfied with, and do they trust, management?
   n. Is a high degree of interaction and cooperation typical between organizational work units?
   o. Are decisions made quickly, and do they take into account a wide variety of suggestions?

2. *Choose an appropriate approach for managing the resistance to change.* In this chapter, six strategies have been suggested for dealing with resistance to change—education and communication, participation, facilitation and support, negotiation, manipulation and co-optation, and coercion. Review Exhibit 7-5 (p. 196) for the advantages and disadvantages and when it is best to use each approach.

3. *During the time the change is implemented and after the change is completed, communicate with employees regarding what support you may be able to provide.* Your employees need to know you are there to support them during change efforts. Be prepared to offer the assistance that may be necessary to help them enact the change.

Practicing the Skill

Read through the following scenario. Write down some notes about how you would handle the situation described. Be sure to refer to the three suggestions for managing resistance to change.

You're the nursing supervisor at a community hospital employing both emergency room and floor nurses. Each of these teams of nurses tends to work almost exclusively with others doing the same job. In your professional reading, you've come across the concept of cross-training nursing teams and giving them more varied responsibilities, which in turn has been shown to improve patient care while lowering costs. You call the two team leaders, Sue and Scott, into your office to discuss your plan to have the nursing teams move to this approach. To your surprise, they're both opposed to the idea. Sue says she and the other emergency room nurses feel they're needed in the ER, where they fill the most vital role in the hospital. They work special hours when needed, do whatever tasks are required, and often work in difficult and stressful circumstances. They think the floor nurses have relatively easy jobs for the pay they receive. Scott, leader of the floor nurses team, tells you that his group believes the ER nurses lack the special training and extra experience that the floor nurses bring to the hospital. The floor nurses claim they have the heaviest responsibilities and do the most exacting work. Because they have ongoing contact with the patients and their families, they believe they shouldn't be pulled away from vital floor duties to help ER nurses complete their tasks. Now—what would you do?

WORKING TOGETHER Team Exercise

Almost every country around the world already is using or in the process of changing to International Financial Reporting Standards, also known as IFRS.[79] (See map at [http://www.pwc.com/us/en/issues/ifrs-reporting/country-adoption/index.jhtml].) In the United States where Generally Accepted Accounting Principles (GAAP) have been the standard for decades, the move to IFRS will involve significant changes at both accounting services firms and other business firms who must now adhere to the new standards.

Form teams of 3–4 people. Your team is responsible for planning how to proceed with this change at your accounting firm. What will need to be done to ensure this conversion goes as smoothly as possible? Use the following two topic areas to guide you in planning this change for your professional CPA staff: (1) using communication channels to engage and inform employees, and (2) building needed skills and capabilities. Come up with a change plan that addresses each of these issues.

MY TURN TO BE A MANAGER

- Take responsibility for your own future career path. Don't depend on your employer to provide you with career development and training opportunities. Right now, sign up for things that will help you enhance your skills—workshops, seminars, continuing education courses, etc.

- Pay attention to how you handle change. Try to figure out why you resist certain changes and not others.

- Pay attention to how others around you handle change. When friends or family resist change, practice using different approaches to managing this resistance to change.

- When you find yourself experiencing dysfunctional stress, write down what's causing the stress, what stress symptoms you're exhibiting, and how you're dealing with the stress. Keep this information in a journal and evaluate how well your stress reducers are working and how you could handle stress better. Your goal is to get to a point where you recognize that you're stressed and can take positive actions to deal with the stress.

- Research information on how to be a more creative person. Write down suggestions in a bulleted-list format and be prepared to present your information in class.

- Is innovation more about (1) stopping something old, or (2) starting something new? Prepare arguments supporting or challenging each view.

- Choose two organizations you're familiar with and assess whether these organizations face a calm waters or white-water rapids environment. Write a short report describing these organizations and your assessment of the change environment each faces. Be sure to explain your choice of change environment.

- Steve's and Mary's recommended readings: C. S. Dawson, *Leading Culture Change: What Every CEO Needs to Know* (Stanford University Press, 2010); C. Heath and D. Heath, *Switch: How to Change When Change Is Hard* (Broadway Books, 2010); T. Brown, *Change by Design: How Design Thinking Transforms Organizations and Inspires Creativity* (HarperBusiness, 2009); D. K. Murray, *Borrowing Brilliance: The Six Steps to Business Innovation by Building on the Ideas of Others* (Gotham, 2009); Malcolm Gladwell, *Blink* (Little, Brown, 2005); Peter Senge et al., *Presence* (Doubleday, 2004); Tom Peters, *Re-Imagine!* (Dorling Kindersely, 2003); John P. Kotter and Dan S. Cohen, *The Heart of Change* (Harvard Business School Press, 2002); Malcolm Gladwell, *The Tipping Point* (Back Bay Books, 2002); Tom Kelley, *The Art of Innovation* (Doubleday, 2001); and Ian Morrison, *The Second Curve* (Ballantine Books, 1996).

- Choose an organization with which you're familiar (employer, student organization, family business, etc.). Describe its culture (shared values and beliefs). Select two of those values/beliefs and describe how you would go about changing them. Put this information in a report.

- In your own words, write down three things you learned in this chapter about being a good manager.

- Self-knowledge can be a powerful learning tool. Go to mymanagementlab.com and complete these self-assessment exercises: How Well Do I Handle Ambiguity? How Creative Am I? How Well Do I Respond to Turbulent Change? How Stressed Is My Life? Am I Burned Out? Using the results of your assessments, identify personal strengths and weaknesses. What will you do to reinforce your strengths and improve your weaknesses?

MyManagementLab

Go to **mymanagementlab.com** for Auto-graded writing questions as well as the following Assisted-graded writing questions:

7-1. Why do people resist change? How can resistance to change be reduced?

7-2. Describe the structural, cultural, and human resources variables that are necessary for innovation.

7-3. Mymanagementlab Only – comprehensive writing assignment for this chapter.

In Search of the Next Big Thing

It all started with a simple plan to make a superior T-shirt. As special teams captain during the mid-1990s for the University of Maryland football team, Kevin Plank hated having to repeatedly change the cotton T-shirt he wore under his jersey as it became wet and heavy during the course of a game.[80] He knew there had to be a better alternative and set out to make it. After a year of fabric and product testing, Plank introduced the first Under Armour compression product— a synthetic shirt worn like a second skin under a uniform or jersey. And it was an immediate hit! The silky fabric was light and made athletes feel faster and fresher, giving them, according to Plank, an important psychological edge. Today, Under Armour continues to passionately strive to make all athletes better by relentlessly pursuing

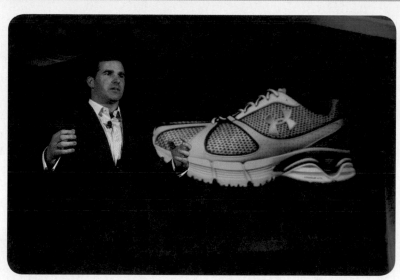

Kevin Plank, founder and chief executive of Under Armour, has grown his company from a T-shirt startup to a challenging competitor in the athletic apparel industry by pursuing innovation and design in developing products that make athletes better. Plank is shown here at the launch event for Under Armour's entry into the footwear market with an innovative running shoe designed to improve athletic performance.
Source: AP Photo/Rick Maiman

innovation and design. A telling sign of the company's philosophy is found over the door of its product design studios: "We have not yet built our defining product."

Today, Baltimore-based Under Armour (UA) is a $1.4 billion company. In 16 years, it has grown from a college start-up to a "formidable competitor of the Beaverton, Oregon behemoth" (better known as Nike, a $21 billion company). The company has nearly 3 percent of the fragmented U.S. sports apparel market and sells products from shirts, shorts, and cleats to underwear. In addition, more than 100 universities wear UA uniforms. The company's logo—an interlocking U and A—is becoming almost as recognizable as the Nike swoosh.

Starting out, Plank sold his shirts using the only advantage he had—his athletic connections. "Among his teams from high school, military school, and the University of Maryland, he knew at least 40 NFL players well enough to call and offer them the shirt." He was soon joined by another Maryland player, Kip Fulks, who played lacrosse. Fulks used the same "six-degrees strategy" in the lacrosse world. (Today, Fulks is the company's COO.) Believe it or not, the strategy worked. UA sales quickly gained momentum. However, selling products to teams and schools would take a business only so far. That's when Plank began to look at the mass market. In 2000, he made his first deal with a big-box store, Galyan's (which was eventually bought by Dick's Sporting Goods). Today, almost 30 percent of UA's sales come from Dick's and the Sports Authority. But they haven't forgotten where they started, either. The company has all-school deals with 10 Division 1 schools. "Although these deals don't bring in big bucks, they deliver brand visibility. . . ."

Despite their marketing successes, innovation continues to be the name of the game at UA. How important is innovation to the company's heart and soul? Consider what you have to do to enter its new products lab. "Place your hands inside a state-of-the-art scanner that reads—and calculates—the exact pattern of the veins on the back. If it recognizes the pattern, which it does for only 20 out of 5,000 employees, you're in. If it doesn't, the vault-like door won't budge." In the unmarked lab at the company's headquarters campus in Baltimore, products being developed include a shirt that can monitor an athlete's heart rate, a running shoe designed like your back spine, and a sweatshirt that repels water almost as well as a duck's feathers. There's also work being done on a shirt that may help air condition your body by reading your vital signs.

So what's next for Under Armour? With a motto that refers to protecting this house, innovation will continue to be important. Building a business beyond what it's known for—that is, what athletes wear next to their skin— is going to be challenging. However, Plank is "utterly determined to conquer that next layer, and the layer after that." He says, "There's not a product we can't build."

DISCUSSION QUESTIONS ✪

1. What do you think of UA's approach to innovation? Would you expect to see this type of innovation in an athletic wear company? Explain.

2. What do you think UA's culture might be like in regards to innovation? (Hint: refer to the list on p. 204.)

3. Could design thinking help UA improve its innovation efforts? Discuss.

4. What's your interpretation of the company's philosophy posted prominently over the door of its design studio? What does it say about innovation?

4. What could other companies learn from the way UA innovates?

CASE APPLICATION 2 Workplace Stress Can Kill

Protestors representing Students and Scholars Against Corporate Misbehavior demonstrated outside Foxconn's annual general meeting in Hong Kong by displaying a long list of labor abuses and stressful working conditions that contributed to the suicides of 13 young employees. To reduce employee stress, Foxconn improved its workplace environment by establishing new safety procedures and hiring additional employees that reduced overtime hours.
Source: Mike Clarke/AFP/Getty Images/ Newscom

We know that too much stress can be bad for our health and well-being. That connection has proved itself painfully and tragically in two high-profile situations at France Télécom and at China's Foxconn Technology Group.[81]

Between 2008 and 2011, more than 50 people at France Télécom committed suicide. The situation captured the attention of the worldwide media, the public, and the French government because many of the suicides and more than a dozen failed suicide attempts were attributed to work-related problems. Although France has a higher suicide rate than any other large Western country, this scenario is particularly troublesome. So much so, that the Paris prosecutor's office opened an investigation of the company over accusations of psychological harassment. The judicial inquiry began with a complaint by the union Solidares Unitaires Démocratiques against France Télécom's former chief executive and two members of his top management team. The complaint accused management of conducting a "pathogenic restructuring." Excerpts of the inspector's report, although not public, were published in the French media and described a situation in which the company used various forms of psychological pressure in an effort to eliminate 22,000 jobs from 2006 to 2008. Company doctors alerted management about the possible psychological dangers of the stress that could accompany such drastic change. "The spate of suicides highlighted a quirk at the heart of French society: Even with robust labor protection, workers see themselves as profoundly insecure in the face of globalization, with many complaining about being pushed beyond their limits." A company lawyer denied that France Télécom had systematically pressured employees to leave.

Company executives realized they needed to take drastic measures to address the issue. One of the first changes was a new CEO, Stéphane Richard, who said his priority "would be to rebuild the morale of staff who have been through trauma, suffering and much worse." The company halted some workplace practices identified as particularly disruptive, like involuntary transfers, and began encouraging more supportive practices, including working from home. A company spokesperson says the company has completed two of six agreements with unions that cover a wide range of workplace issues such as mobility, work-life balance, and stress. Yet, France isn't the only country dealing with worker suicides.

Workplace conditions at China's Foxconn Technology Group—the world's largest maker of electronic components, which employs over a million workers—were strongly criticized after a series of suicides among young workers. In what was described as sweatshop conditions, employees often worked 76-hour weeks for low wages. Some workers said they had to stand so long, their legs swelled until they could barely walk. Other complaints revolved around child labor and hazardous waste. One worker said, "The assembly line ran very fast and after just one morning we all had blisters and the skin on our hand was black. The factory was also really choked with dust and no one could bear it." In March 2012, Apple and Foxconn reached an agreement to improve conditions for the workers assembling iPhones and iPads. According to the agreement, Foxconn would hire thousands of new workers to reduce overtime work, improve safety protocols, and upgrade housing and other amenities. It's also reported that the company has launched a $224 million project to build one million robots in the next three years to use in its factories. This "empire of robots" will replace half a million Foxconn employees and move them "higher up the value chain."

DISCUSSION QUESTIONS ✪

1. What is your reaction to the situations described in this case? What factors, both inside the companies and externally, appear to have contributed to this situation?

2. What appeared to be happening in the France Télécom's workplace? What stress symptoms might have alerted managers to a problem?

3. Should managers be free to make decisions that are in the best interests of the company without worrying about employee reactions? Discuss. What are the implications for managing change?

4. What are France Télécom's and Foxconn's executives doing to address the situation? Do you think it's enough? Are there other actions they might take? If so, describe those actions. If not, why not?

5. What could other companies and managers learn from this situation?

PART 3 Management Practice

A Manager's Dilemma

As global health leaders look at statistics on what's killing us, they used to focus on diseases that can spread from person to person—AIDS, tuberculosis, and new and odd flu bugs. To combat these, they've pushed for better vaccines, treatments, and other ways to control germs that could multiply quickly via air travel patterns and start an outbreak anywhere in the world. Now, these experts are looking at a whole new set of culprits that are contributing to an international public health emergency. But this time, it's not germs, but we humans and our bad habits who are the target. Bad habits like smoking, overeating, and too little exercise. These habits have been linked to chronic diseases, including cancer, diabetes, and heart and lung disease, which together account for nearly two-thirds of deaths worldwide. The sad part is many of these are preventable. So, global leaders are changing direction. Now, they're looking at ways to get people to change their bad habits.

> Based on what you've read in Part 3 of the text, especially when it comes to change, what suggestions would you make to these leaders in getting people to change? Be creative!

Global Sense

True or false: The workplace can be stressful. You probably said true, and it's especially true as the economic recession has gone on and on. During the recession, work teams have shrunk and workloads and pressures have grown. Businesses have asked their employees to be more innovative and creative, but at the same time to be more efficient. It's a recipe for stress, for sure! One stress reliever is taking a break from work—a vacation. And most advanced countries have a national vacation policy requiring companies to give their workers time off. In Germany, for instance, workers are guaranteed a month of vacation. In the United Kingdom, they're guaranteed more than five weeks of paid vacation. In Switzerland, employees get at least 20 work days or four weeks. However, in the United States, there is no guarantee. The U.S. is practically the only developed country in the world that doesn't require companies to give their workers time off. Yet, although many companies in the U.S. *do* give their employees vacation days, employees aren't using them. A recent survey found that the average American worker has accumulated more than a week's worth of unused vacation days. Why? The most-cited reasons employees give is lack of money and no time to plan a vacation. However, some management experts say the unwillingness to claim unused vacation time is more likely based on fears related to the economy.

Discuss the following questions in light of what you learned in Part 3:

- *Why is a vacation from work a good remedy for stress?*
- *What's your opinion? Are American workers not using up all their vacation time because of money or is it because of fear? Or maybe both? Discuss.*
- *As a manager, what could you do to "encourage" your employees to use their vacation time?*
- *Do some research. What other countries suffer from "vacation deprivation?"*
- *Why do you think European and other countries are more supportive of the concept of taking a vacation from work?*
- *Does the United States need a national vacation policy? Support your argument. Would this be good for businesses? Why or why not?*

Sources: D. Thompson, "The Only Advanced Country Without a National Vacation Policy? It's the U.S.," www.theatlantic.com, July 2, 2012; P. Korkki, "Drive to Worry, and to Procrastinate," New York Times Online, February 25, 2012; "Expedia 2011 Vacation Deprivation Study Reveals Work-Life Disparity Across Five Continents," finance.yahoo.com/news/, November 30, 2011; "Overworked, Older Americans Not Using Up Allotted Vacation Days," www.huffingtonpost.com, November 26, 2011; and P. Korkki, "Working at Making the Most of Your Vacation," New York Times Online, August 13, 2011.

Continuing Case

Starbucks—Decision Making and Change

Decisions, Decisions

One thing you may not realize is that after running the show for 15 years at Starbucks, Howard Schultz at age 46 stepped out of the CEO job in 2000 (he remained as chairman of the company) because he was "a bit bored." By stepping down as CEO—which he had planned to do, had prepared for, and had no intention of returning to—essentially he was saying that he agreed to trust the decisions of others. At first the company thrived, but then the perils of rapid mass-market expansion began to set in and customer traffic began to fall for the first time ever. As he watched what was happening, there were times when he felt the decisions being made were not good ones. Schultz couldn't shake his gut feeling that Starbucks had lost its way. In fact, in a memo dubbed the "espresso shot heard round the world," he wrote to his top managers explaining in detail how the company's unprecedented growth had led to many minor compromises that when added up led to a "watering down of the Starbucks experience." Among his complaints: sterile "cookie cutter" store layouts, automatic espresso machines that robbed the "barista theater" of roasting and brewing a cup of coffee, and flavor-locked

Starbucks Chairman and CEO Howard Schultz displays the company's new instant coffee "VIA" during a launching ceremony at Tokyo's Haneda airport on April 14, 2010.
Source: YOSHIKAZU TSUNO/AFP/Getty Images/Newscom

packaging that didn't allow customers to inhale and savor that distinctive coffee aroma. Starbucks had lost its "cool" factor, and Schultz's criticism of the state of the company's stores was blunt and bold. There was no longer a focus on coffee but only on making the cash register ring. Within a year of the memo (and eight years after he left the CEO gig), Schultz was back in charge and working to restore the Starbucks experience. His goals were to fix the troubled stores, to reawaken the emotional attachment with customers, and to make long-term changes like reorganizing the company and revamping the supply chain. The first thing he did, however, was to apologize to the staff for the decisions that had brought the company to this point. In fact, his intention to restore quality control led him to a decision to close all (at that time) 7,100 U.S. stores for one evening to retrain 135,000 baristas on the coffee experience… what it meant, what it was. It was a bold decision, and one that many "experts" felt would be a public relations and financial disaster. But Schultz felt doing so was absolutely necessary to revive and reenergize Starbucks. Another controversial decision was to hold a leadership conference with

all store managers (some 8,000 of them) and 2,000 other partners—all at one time and all in one location. Why? To energize and galvanize these employees around what Starbucks stands for and what needed to be done for the company to survive and prosper. Schultz was unsure about how Wall Street would react to the cost, which was around $30 million total (air fare, meals, hotels, etc.), but again he didn't care because he felt doing so was absolutely necessary and critical. And rather than gathering together in Seattle, where Starbucks is headquartered, Schultz chose New Orleans as the site for the conference. Here was a city still recovering from Hurricane Katrina, which had totally devastated it five years earlier in 2005. Talk about a logistical nightmare—and it was. But, the decision was a symbolic choice. New Orleans was in the process of rebuilding itself and succeeding, and Starbucks was in the process of rebuilding itself and could succeed, too. While there, Starbucks partners volunteered some 50,000 hours of time, reinforcing to Schultz and to all the managers that despite all the problems, Starbucks had not lost its values. Other decisions, like closing 800 stores and laying off 4,000 partners, were more difficult. Since that transition time, Schultz has made lots of decisions. Starbucks has again come back even stronger in what it stands for, achieving in 2011 record financial results and on track to continue those record results.

Innovation, Innovation

Starbucks has always thought "outside the box." From the beginning, it took the concept of the corner coffee shop and totally revamped the coffee experience. And the company has always had the ability to roll out new products relatively quickly. The company's R&D (research and development) teams are responsible for innovating food and beverage products and new equipment. In 2011, the company spent nearly $15 million on technical R&D, product testing, and product and process improvements in all areas of the business. That was a 67 percent increase over 2010 expenditures and a 114 percent increase over 2009 expenditures.

A glimpse of Starbucks innovation process can be seen in how it approaches the all-important Christmas season since "Starbucks has Christmas down to a science." It takes many months of meetings and tastings before rolling out the flavors and aromas. For the 2011 season, the process started in October 2010 when customers had the opportunity to fill out in-store and online surveys used to gauge their "mindset." In mid-December 2010, Schultz—who has final approval on all new products and themes—reviewed the 2011 theme. And things better be "Christmas-perfect." In March 2011, the 2011 theme (Let's Merry) was approved. By mid-March, the "core holiday team" started to meet weekly. On June 1, production cranked up on the company's seasonal red cups (which were introduced in 1997 and remain very popular). By the end of June, the holiday team has assembled a mock-up of a Starbucks café for Schultz to review and approve. By mid-August, all of the in-store signs, menu boards, and window decals are on their way to the printer. All of these pieces come together for the full holiday rollout on November 15, 2011. It's important to get everything right for this season. Want proof? The company had revenues of almost $3 billion during the holiday quarter. That's a lot of Christmas cheer!

The company's product innovation process must be doing something right as many of its Christmas products have been popular for years. For instance, the company's Christmas Blend debuted in 1985. The Gingerbread Latte was a Christmas 2000 innovation. The Caramel Brulée Latte came out during the 2009 holiday season. During the Christmas 2011 season, customers got their first taste of the Skinny Peppermint Mocha—a nod to the trend of healthier, but still tasty products—and the line of petite desserts, which were introduced to commemorate the company's 40th birthday. But obviously, given Starbucks' outcomes, it's not only the Christmas products that have been successful. One of Starbucks' latest creations is a line of light-roasted coffee beans and brews. And the popularity of energy drinks led the company to create a line of "natural" energy drinks called Refreshers. The new fruity, carbonated drink that's high in antioxidants will get its energy boost from unroasted green coffee extract. Schultz told shareholders that the company is continuing to create lots of Starbucks products that "live outside of our stores." Starbucks Refreshers are sold at 160,000 grocery stores and made-to-order versions in Starbucks stores.

Starbucks doesn't always get new products through in-house development. There are times when it "buys" the product. For instance, it purchased Evolution Fresh Inc. in late 2011. Evolution Fresh juice is sold in grocery stores on the West Coast, but Starbucks intends to expand the brand to more retailers, including its own cafés. It also plans on opening juice bars that will sell the juice products as well as health foods.

Discussion Questions

1. Starbucks has some pretty specific goals it wants to achieve (look ahead to Part 4 on p. 325 for these company goals). Given this, do you think managers would be more likely to make rational decisions, bounded rationality decisions, or intuitive decisions? Explain.

2. Give examples of decisions that Starbucks managers might made under conditions of certainty. Under conditions of risk. Under conditions of uncertainty.

3. What kind of decision maker does Howard Schultz appear to be? Explain your answer.

4. How might biases and errors affect the decision making done by Starbucks executives? By Starbucks store managers? By Starbucks partners?

5. How might design thinking be important to a company like Starbucks? Do you see any indication that Starbucks uses design thinking? Explain.

6. Howard Schultz is adamant about providing the best "Starbucks experience" to each and every customer. As a store manager, how would you keep your employees from experiencing high levels of stress when lines are out the door and customers want their Starbucks now?

7. Would you classify Starbucks' environment as more calm waters or white-water rapids? Explain. How does the company manage change in this type of environment?

8. Using Exhibit 7-9, describe Starbucks' innovation environment.

9. Review the company's mission and guiding principles (at www.starbucks.com). Explain how these affect managerial decision making; how they affect change and innovation issues.

Notes for the Part 3 Continuing Case

Sources: Starbucks News Release, "Starbucks Reports Record Third Quarter Results," www.investor.starbucks.com, July 26, 2012; B. Horovitz, "Starbucks Rolling Out Pop with Pep," *USA Today,* March 22, 2012, p. 1B; K. McLaughlin, "The Hot Blonde in the Coffee Shop: A Lighter Roast," *Wall Street Journal,* February 1, 2012, p. D1+; L. Patton, "Starbucks's 12 Months of Christmas," *Bloomberg BusinessWeek,* December 12–December 18, 2011, pp. 34–35; "2011 Leader of the Year: Howard Schultz. Strong Coffee," *Fortune,* December 12, 2011, pp. 100–116; J. Jargon, "Latest Starbucks Concoction: Juice," *Wall Street Journal,* November 11, 2011, pp. B1+; "Howard Schultz, On Getting a Second Shot," *Inc.,* April 2011, pp. 52–54; D. Brady, "Hard Choices," *Bloomberg BusinessWeek,* April 4–April 10, 2011, p. 102; H. Schultz, "How Starbucks Got Mojo Back," *Newsweek,* March 21, 2011, pp. 50–51; C. Cain Miller, "A Changed Starbucks. A Changed CEO," *New York Times Online,* March 12, 2011; A. Ignatious, "We Had To Own Our Mistakes," *Harvard Business Review,* July-August, 2010, pp. 108–115; "Training 135,000 Employees In One Day—Starbucks Closes Stores To Do It," www.thecareerrevolution.com, February 27, 2008; and "Howard Schultz's Starbucks Memo," www.ft.com, February 23, 2007.

8 Foundations of Planning

SPOTLIGHT: *Manager at Work*

You know what delicious is? *A bag of hot and fresh McDonald's fries drizzled with salt. You know how many fries McDonald's sells daily worldwide? 9 million. That's a lot of deliciousness! How does this company with over 33,500 restaurants in 119 countries serving nearly 68 million customers every day do what it does it well and do it consistently?*[1] *The key to McDonald's doing what it does well and consistently is its Plan to Win . . . . And here a decade later, the basics of the plan still guide the company's activities.*

The Plan to Win was built on three components. The first is operational excellence. The company implements this through a consistent restaurant-specific review and measurement process. The second component is retaining the lead in marketing, which McDonald's does by continually connecting with customers through a hip and contemporary global marketing direction. The third component in the Plan to Win is innovation. The company is continually innovating. Its goal is to provide a variety of value, premium, and wholesome product options and to deliver the right products at the right price to customers. The Plan to Win remains the cornerstone of McDonald's business today. A recent annual report stated that, "Our success remains global, with all areas of the world contributing significantly to our results. We achieved all of this through our Plan to Win, which has served as our blueprint." Newly appointed CEO Don Thompson reaffirms the Plan to Win, and together with his leadership team has identified three global growth goals: to optimize its menu, to modernize the customer experience, and to broaden restaurant

Source: Time & Life Pictures/Getty Images

Source: Antonio Perez/MCT/Newscom

accessibility. Now what does all this have to do with those delicious fries?

Barbara Booth (see photo), McDonald's director of sensory science, is responsible for monitoring and evaluating all the products found on the company's menu.

The key to McDonald's doing

what it does well and consistently is its Plan to Win...

However, during its semiannual French fry evaluation, she's focused on the pursuit of the perfect French fry. (You can see a video at http://www.businessweek. com/videos/2012-04-09/mcdonalds-fries-undergo-rigorous-sensory-tests.) She wants those fries to be like "walking on freshly fallen snow." And taste, consistency, and appearance are crucial to achieving that. During this contest, the chain's top suppliers of potatoes bring in samples from their facilities which are then prepared

according to McDonald's precise operational guidelines—down to the exact amount of salt to be added (which, by the way, is automatically measured and controlled by the salt shaker used). Crowded around a large rectangular table, the testers sniff, sample, and spit fries in order to evaluate and score the products. But this is more than a taste test and taste contest—it's an opportunity for Booth and her team to interact with suppliers and teach them about quality characteristics. All in the

LEARNING OUTCOMES

8.1 | *Define* the nature and purposes of planning.

8.2 | *Classify* the types of goals organizations might have and the plans they use.

8.3 | *Compare* and contrast approaches to goal-setting and planning.

8.4 | *Discuss* contemporary issues in planning.

pursuit of French fry perfection! All made possible by goals and plans. **Why is planning so important to successful companies like McDonald's?**

You may think "planning" is relevant to large companies like McDonald's, but not something that's relevant to you right now. But when you figure out your class schedule for the next term or when you decide what you need to do to

finish a class project on time, you're planning. And planning is something that all managers, such as Barbara Booth and others throughout the McDonald's worldwide organization, need to do. Although what they plan and how they plan may differ, it's still important that they do plan. In this chapter, we present the basics: what planning is, why managers plan, and how they plan.

8.1 **Define** the nature and purposes of planning.

THE WHAT AND WHY of Planning

Boeing called its new 787 aircraft the Dreamliner, but the project turned into more of a nightmare for managers. The new plane was the company's most popular product ever, mostly because of its innovations, especially in fuel efficiency. However, the plane was three years behind schedule. The first airplanes were delivered to ANA (All Nippon Airways) in late September 2011. Boeing admitted the project's timeline was way too ambitious, even though every detail had been meticulously planned.[2] Some customers (the airlines who ordered the jets)—around 60 in total—got tired of waiting or responded to the changing economic environment and canceled their orders. Could Boeing's managers have planned better?

What Is Planning?

planning
Defining the organization's goals, establishing strategies for achieving those goals, and developing plans to integrate and coordinate work activities

As we stated in Chapter 1, **planning** involves defining the organization's goals, establishing strategies for achieving those goals, and developing plans to integrate and coordinate work activities. It's concerned with both ends (what) and means (how).

When we use the term *planning*, we mean *formal* planning. In formal planning, specific goals covering a specific time period are defined. These goals are written and shared with organizational members to reduce ambiguity and create a common understanding about what needs to be done. Finally, specific plans exist for achieving these goals.

Why Do Managers Plan?

Planning seems to take a lot of effort. So why should managers plan? We can give you at least four reasons. First, planning *provides direction* to managers and nonmanagers alike. When employees know what their organization or work unit is trying to accomplish and what they must contribute to reach goals, they can coordinate their activities, cooperate with each other, and do what it takes to accomplish those goals. Without planning, departments and individuals might work at cross-purposes and prevent the organization from efficiently achieving its goals.

Next, planning *reduces uncertainty* by forcing managers to look ahead, anticipate change, consider the impact of change, and develop appropriate responses. Although planning won't eliminate uncertainty, managers plan so they can respond effectively.

In addition, planning *minimizes waste and redundancy.* When work activities are coordinated around plans, inefficiencies become obvious and can be corrected or eliminated.

Finally, planning *establishes the goals or standards used in controlling*. When managers plan, they develop goals and plans. When they control, they see whether the plans have been carried out and the goals met. Without planning, there would be no goals against which to measure work effort.

Planning and Performance

Is planning worthwhile? Numerous studies have looked at the relationship between planning and performance.[3] Although most showed generally positive relationships, we can't say that organizations that formally plan *always* outperform those that don't plan. What *can* we conclude?

First, generally speaking, formal planning is associated with positive financial results—higher profits, higher return on assets, and so forth. Second, it seems that doing a good job planning and implementing those plans play a bigger part in high performance than how much planning is done. Next, in those studies where formal planning didn't lead to higher performance, the external environment often was the culprit. When external forces—think governmental regulations or powerful labor unions—constrain managers' options, it reduces the impact planning has on an organization's performance. Finally, the planning-performance relationship seems to be influenced by the planning time frame. It seems that at least four years of formal planning is required before it begins to affect performance.

Planning continues to contribute to the profitable performance of Recreational Equipment, Inc. By implementing its formal expansion plans, REI has grown from a one-store enterprise in 1944 to a major retailer of outdoor recreational gear and clothing with more than 120 stores, over 10,000 employees, and sales that top $1 billion. In addition to products for outdoor enthusiasts, REI also offers global adventure vacations and day outings and educational programs at the local level. In this photo, employees celebrate the opening of a new REI store in New York City's SoHo shopping district. Measured by employees, REI ranks high in performance, as the company has appeared on the list of "100 Best Companies to Work For" since *Fortune* magazine began compiling the list in 1998. *Source: Matt Peyton/AP Images for REI*

GOALS and Plans

Planning is often called the primary management function because it establishes the basis for all the other things managers do as they organize, lead, and control. It involves two important aspects: goals and plans.

Goals (objectives) are desired outcomes or targets.[4] They guide management decisions and form the criterion against which work results are measured. That's why they're often described as the essential elements of planning. You have to know the desired target or outcome before you can establish plans for reaching it. **Plans** are documents that outline how goals are going to be met. They usually include resource allocations, schedules, and other necessary actions to accomplish the goals. As managers plan, they develop both goals and plans.

Types of Goals

It might seem that organizations have a single goal. Businesses want to make a profit and not-for-profit organizations want to meet the needs of some constituent group(s). However, a single goal can't adequately define an organization's success. And if managers emphasize only one goal, other goals essential for long-term success are ignored. Also, as we discussed in Chapter 5, using a single goal such as profit may result in unethical behaviors because managers and employees will ignore other aspects of their jobs in order to look good on that one measure.[5] In reality, all organizations have multiple goals. For instance, businesses may want to increase market share, keep employees enthused about working for the organization, and work toward more environmentally sustainable practices. And a church provides a place for religious practices, but also assists economically disadvantaged individuals in its community and acts as a social gathering place for church members.

We can classify most company's goals as either strategic or financial. Financial goals are related to the financial performance of the organization, while strategic

---

Classify the types of goals organizations might have and the plans they use. **8.2**

goals (objectives)
Desired outcomes or targets

plans
Documents that outline how goals are going to be met

stated goals
Official statements of what an organization says, and what it wants its various stakeholders to believe, its goals are

goals are related to all other areas of an organization's performance. For instance, McDonald's states that its financial targets are 3 to 5 percent average annual sales and revenue growth, 6 to 7 percent average annual operating income growth, and returns on invested capital in the high teens.[6] Here's an example of a strategic goal from Bloomberg L.P.: "We want to be the world's most influential news organization."[7]

The goals just described are **stated goals**—official statements of what an organization says, and what it wants its stakeholders to believe, its goals are. However, stated goals—which can be found in an organization's charter, annual report, public relations announcements, or in public statements made by managers—are often conflicting and influenced by what various stakeholders think organizations should do. For instance, Nike's goal is "delivering inspiration and innovation to every athlete." Canadian company EnCana's vision is to "be the world's high performance benchmark independent oil and gas company." Deutsche Bank's goal is "to be the leading global provider of financial solutions, creating lasting value for our clients, our shareholders and people and the communities in which we operate."[8] Such statements are vague and probably better represent management's public relations skills than being meaningful guides to what the organization is actually trying to accomplish. It shouldn't be surprising then to find that an organization's stated goals are often irrelevant to what actually goes on.[9]

real goals
Goals that an organization actually pursues, as defined by the actions of its members

If you want to know an organization's **real goals**—those goals an organization actually pursues—observe what organizational members are doing. Actions define priorities. For example, universities may say their goal is limiting class sizes, facilitating close student-faculty relations, and actively involving students in the learning process, but then they put students into 300+ student lecture classes! Knowing that real and stated goals may differ is important for recognizing what you might otherwise think are inconsistencies.

Types of Plans

The most popular ways to describe organizational plans are breadth (strategic versus operational), time frame (short term versus long term), specificity (directional versus specific), and frequency of use (single use versus standing). As Exhibit 8-1 shows,

let's get **REAL**

Source: Braeden Rogers

The Scenario:

Tommy and Kate Larkin recently started a restaurant and specialty food store in Northern California. The store also sells wine and locally made crafts. Although the business does well during the summer tourist months, things get pretty lean from October to April when visitor numbers dwindle. The Larkins felt that the potential opportunities in this location were good.

What types of plans do the Larkins need to survive the off-season?

Tommy and Kate need to find ways to drive their business in the off season. They can try establishing a stronger online e-commerce business, selling wines and crafts, so that they won't be solely dependent on foot traffic for business. Tommy and Kate could also increase their advertising and restaurant/ shop offers to increase the business from the locals during their down time.

Braeden Rogers
Emerging Solutions
Manager

Exhibit 8-1
Types of Plans

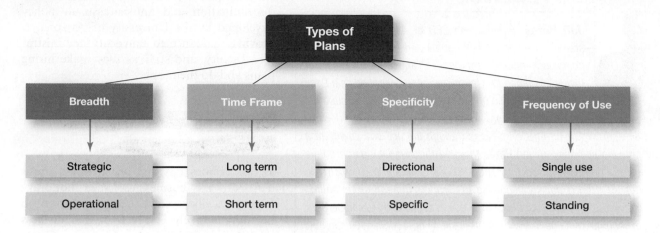

these types of plans aren't independent. That is, strategic plans are usually long term, directional, and single use whereas operational plans are usually short term, specific, and standing. What does each include?

Strategic plans are plans that apply to the entire organization and establish the organization's overall goals. Plans that encompass a particular operational area of the organization are called **operational plans**. These two types of plans differ because strategic plans are broad while operational plans are narrow.

The number of years used to define short-term and long-term plans has declined considerably because of environmental uncertainty. Long-term used to mean anything over seven years. Try to imagine what you're likely to be doing in seven years, and you can begin to appreciate how difficult it would be for managers to establish plans that far in the future. We define **long-term plans** as those with a time frame beyond three years.[10] **Short-term plans** cover one year or less. Any time period in between would be an intermediate plan. Although these time classifications are fairly common, an organization can use any planning time frame it wants.

Intuitively, it would seem that specific plans would be preferable to directional, or loosely guided, plans. **Specific plans** are clearly defined and leave no room for interpretation. A specific plan states its objectives in a way that eliminates ambiguity and problems with misunderstanding. For example, a manager who seeks to increase his or her unit's work output by 8 percent over a given 12-month period might establish specific procedures, budget allocations, and schedules of activities to reach that goal.

However, when uncertainty is high and managers must be flexible in order to respond to unexpected changes, directional plans are preferable. **Directional plans** are flexible plans that set out general guidelines. They provide focus but don't lock managers into specific goals or courses of action. For example, Sylvia Rhone, president of Motown Records, said she has a simple goal—to "sign great artists."[12] So instead of creating a specific plan to produce and market 10 albums from new artists this year, she might formulate a directional plan to use a network of people around the world to alert her to new and promising talent so she can increase the number of new artists she has under contract. Keep in mind, however, that the flexibility of directional plans must be weighed against the lack of clarity of specific plans.

Some plans that managers develop are ongoing while others are used only once. A **single-use plan** is a one-time plan specifically designed to meet the needs of a unique situation. For instance, when Walmart wanted to expand the number of its stores in China, top-level executives formulated a single-use plan as a guide. In contrast, **standing plans** are ongoing plans that provide guidance for activities performed

strategic plans
Plans that apply to the entire organization and establish the organization's overall goals

operational plans
Plans that encompass a particular operational area of the organization

long-term plans
Plans with a time frame beyond three years

short-term plans
Plans covering one year or less

specific plans
Plans that are clearly defined and leave no room for interpretation

directional plans
Plans that are flexible and set out general guidelines

single-use plan
A one-time plan specifically designed to meet the needs of a unique situation

standing plans
Ongoing plans that provide guidance for activities performed repeatedly

LEADER *who made a* DIFFERENCE

***Jeff Bezos**, founder and CEO of Amazon.com, understands the importance of goals and plans. As a leader, he exudes energy, enthusiasm, and drive.[11] He's fun loving (his legendary laugh has been described as a flock of Canadian geese on nitrous oxide) but has pursued his vision for Amazon with serious intensity and has demonstrated an ability to inspire his employees through the ups and downs of a rapidly growing company. When Bezos founded the company as an online bookstore, his goal was to be the leader in online retailing. Now fifteen years later, Amazon is quickly becoming the world's general store, selling not only books, CDs, and DVDs, but LEGOs, power drills, and Jackalope Buck taxidermy mounts, to name a few of the thousands of products you can buy. What can you learn from this leader who made a difference?*

repeatedly. Standing plans include policies, rules, and procedures, which we defined in Chapter 6. An example of a standing plan is the non-discrimination and anti-harassment policy developed by the University of Arizona. It provides guidance to university administrators, faculty, and staff as they make hiring plans and do their jobs.

SETTING Goals and Developing Plans

Taylor Haines has just been elected president of her business school's honorary fraternity. She wants the organization to be more actively involved in the business school than it has been. Francisco Garza graduated from Tecnologico de Monterrey with a degree in marketing and computers three years ago and went to work for a regional consulting services firm. He recently was promoted to manager of an eight-person e-business development team and hopes to strengthen the team's financial contributions to the firm. What should Taylor and Francisco do now? Their first step should be to set goals.

8.3 | ***Compare** and contrast approaches to goal-setting and planning.*

Approaches to Setting Goals

As we stated earlier, goals provide the direction for all management decisions and actions and form the criterion against which actual accomplishments are measured. Everything organizational members do should be oriented toward achieving goals. These goals can be set either through a traditional process or by using management by objectives.

traditional goal-setting
An approach to setting goals in which top managers set goals that then flow down through the organization and become subgoals for each organizational area

In **traditional goal-setting**, goals set by top managers flow down through the organization and become subgoals for each organizational area. This traditional perspective assumes that top managers know what's best because they see the "big picture." And the goals passed down to each succeeding level guide individual employees as they work to achieve those assigned goals. If Taylor were to use this approach, she would see what goals the dean or director of the school of business had set and develop goals for her group that would contribute to achieving those goals. Or take a manufacturing business, for example. The president tells the vice president of production what he expects manufacturing costs to be for the coming year and tells the marketing vice president what level he expects sales to reach for the year. These goals are passed to the next organizational level and written to reflect the responsibilities of that level, passed to the next level, and so forth. Then, at some later time, performance is evaluated to determine whether the assigned goals have been achieved. Although the process is supposed to happen in this way, in reality it doesn't always do so. Turning broad strategic goals into departmental, team, and individual goals can be a difficult and frustrating process.

Another problem with traditional goal-setting is that when top managers define the organization's goals in broad terms—such as achieving "sufficient" profits or increasing "market leadership"—these ambiguous goals have to be made more specific as they flow down through the organization. Managers at each level define the goals and apply their own interpretations and biases as they make them more specific. However, what often happens is that clarity is lost as the goals make their way down from the top of the organization to lower levels. Exhibit 8-2 illustrates what can happen. But it doesn't have to be that way. For example, at the Carrier-Carlyle Compressor Facility in Stone Mountain, Georgia, employees and managers focus their work efforts around goals. Those goals encompass meeting and exceeding

"We need to improve the company's performance."

"I want to see a significant improvement in this division's profits."

Top Management's Objective

"Increase profits regardless of the means."

Division Manager's Objective

"Don't worry about quality; just work fast."

Department Manager's Objective

Individual Employee's Objective

Exhibit 8-2
The Downside of Traditional Goal-Setting

customer needs, concentrating on continuous improvement efforts, and engaging the workforce. To keep everyone focused on those goals, a "thermostat"—a 3-foot-by-4-foot metric indicator—found at the employee entrance communicates what factory performance is at any given time and where attention is needed. "The thermostat outlines plant goals across a range of metrics as well as monthly performance against those goals." Company executives state, "We have found that well-executed pre-planning drives improved results." Does their goal approach work? In the past three years, the facility has experienced a nearly 76 percent reduction in customer reject rates and a 54.5 percent reduction in OSHA-recordable injury and illness cases.[13]

When the hierarchy of organizational goals *is* clearly defined, as it is at Carrier-Carlyle Compressor, it forms an integrated network of goals, or a **means-ends chain**. Higher-level goals (or ends) are linked to lower-level goals, which serve as the means for their accomplishment. In other words, the goals achieved at lower levels become the

means-ends chain
An integrated network of goals in which the accomplishment of goals at one level serves as the means for achieving the goals, or ends, at the next level

let's get REAL

The Scenario:

Geoff Vuleta, the CEO of Fahrenheit 212, an innovation consulting firm, has an interesting approach to planning. Every 100 days, the employees get together as a group and draw up a list of all the things they want to get done in the next 100 days. Then, each individual makes a list of commitments to how he or she is going to contribute to that list and sits down with the CEO and the company president to discuss the plan. The sum of everybody's plan becomes the focus of action.

What do you think of this approach—good and bad?

In small organizations, this approach will ensure that a corporate culture is truly pervasive, with everyone aware of the same values and overarching goals. It runs the risk of stifling individual creativity in favor of a collective view—some employees in the group will tend to align their commitments with those of their peers. Nevertheless, this is a great way to ensure that everyone is a stakeholder in the company's fortunes.

Susan Mathew
Program Manager

Source: Susan Mathew

Exhibit 8-3
Steps in MBO

1. The organization's *overall objectives and strategies* are formulated.
2. Major objectives are allocated among *divisional and departmental units*.
3. Unit managers *collaboratively set specific objectives* for their units with their managers.
4. Specific objectives are collaboratively set with *all department members*.
5. *Action plans*, defining how objectives are to be achieved, are specified and agreed upon by managers and employees.
6. The action plans are *implemented*.
7. Progress toward objectives is *periodically reviewed*, and *feedback is provided*.
8. Successful achievement of objectives is reinforced by *performance-based rewards*.

management by objectives (MBO)
A process of setting mutually agreed-upon goals and using those goals to evaluate employee performance

means to reach the goals (ends) at the next level. And the accomplishment of goals at that level becomes the means to achieve the goals (ends) at the next level and on up through the different organizational levels. That's how traditional goal-setting is supposed to work.

Instead of using traditional goal-setting, many organizations use **management by objectives (MBO)**, a process of setting mutually agreed-upon goals and using those goals to evaluate employee performance. If Francisco were to use this approach, he would sit down with each member of his team and set goals and periodically review whether progress was being made toward achieving those goals. MBO programs have four elements: goal specificity, participative decision making, an explicit time period, and performance feedback.[14] Instead of using goals to make sure employees are doing what they're supposed to be doing, MBO uses goals to motivate them as well. The appeal is that it focuses on employees working to accomplish goals they've had a hand in setting. Exhibit 8-3 lists the steps in a typical MBO program.

Does MBO work? Studies have shown that it can increase employee performance and organizational productivity. For example, one review of MBO programs found productivity gains in almost all of them.[15] But is MBO relevant for today's organizations? If it's viewed as a way of setting goals, then yes, because research shows that goal-setting can be an effective approach to motivating employees.[16]

CHARACTERISTICS OF WELL-WRITTEN GOALS Goals aren't all written the same way. Some are better than others at making the desired outcomes clear. For instance, the CEO of Procter & Gamble said that he wants to see the company add close to 548,000 new customers a day, every day, for the next five years.[17] It's an ambitious but specific goal. Managers should be able to write well-written goals. What makes a "well-written" goal?[18] Exhibit 8-4 lists the characteristics.

STEPS IN GOAL-SETTING Managers should follow five steps when setting goals.

mission
The purpose of an organization

1. *Review the organization's* **mission**, *or purpose.* A mission is a broad statement of an organization's purpose that provides an overall guide to what organizational members think is important. Managers should review the mission before writing goals because goals should reflect that mission.

Exhibit 8-4
Well-Written Goals

- Written in terms of outcomes rather than actions
- Measurable and quantifiable
- Clear as to a time frame
- Challenging yet attainable
- Written down
- Communicated to all necessary organizational members

2. *Evaluate available resources.* You don't want to set goals that are impossible to achieve given your available resources. Even though goals should be challenging, they should be realistic. After all, if the resources you have to work with won't allow you to achieve a goal no matter how hard you try or how much effort is exerted, you shouldn't set that goal. That would be like the person with a $50,000 annual income and no other financial resources setting a goal of building an investment portfolio worth $1 million in three years. No matter how hard he or she works at it, it's not going to happen.

3. *Determine the goals individually or with input from others.* The goals reflect desired outcomes and should be congruent with the organizational mission and goals in other organizational areas. These goals should be measurable, specific, and include a time frame for accomplishment.

4. *Write down the goals and communicate them to all who need to know.* Writing down and communicating goals forces people to think them through. The written goals also become visible evidence of the importance of working toward something.

5. *Review results and whether goals are being met.* If goals aren't being met, change them as needed.

Once the goals have been established, written down, and communicated, a manager is ready to develop plans for pursuing the goals.

Developing Plans

The process of developing plans is influenced by three contingency factors and by the planning approach followed.

CONTINGENCY FACTORS IN PLANNING Three contingency factors affect the choice of plans: organizational level, degree of environmental uncertainty, and length of future commitments.[20]

Exhibit 8-5 shows the relationship between a manager's level in the organization and the type of planning done. For the most part, lower-level managers do operational planning while upper-level managers do strategic planning.

The second contingency factor is environmental uncertainty. When uncertainty is high, plans should be specific, but flexible. Managers must be prepared to change or amend plans as they're implemented. At times, they may even have to abandon the plans.[21] For example, prior to Continental Airlines' merger with United Airlines, the former CEO and his management team established a specific goal of focusing on what customers wanted most—on-time flights—to help the company become more competitive in the highly uncertain airline industry. Because of the high level of uncertainty, the management team identified a "destination, but not a flight plan," and changed plans as necessary to achieve that goal of on-time service.

The last contingency factor also is related to the time frame of plans. The **commitment concept** says that plans should extend far enough to meet those commitments made when the plans were developed. Planning for too long or too short a time

commitment concept
Plans should extend far enough to meet those commitments made when the plans were developed

Exhibit 8-5
Planning and Organizational Level

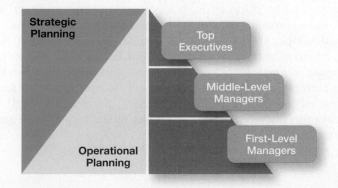

Strategic Planning

Top Executives

Middle-Level Managers

First-Level Managers

Operational Planning

Michael Dell, founder and chief executive of Dell, Inc., uses an approach to the planning process that actively involves employees from different levels and functional areas throughout the company. Work teams, for example, develop their own daily schedules, track their progress, and develop alternate plans when they miss their daily goals. And each week, Dell's functional department leaders from production, supply management, and channel management meet to make plans based on product demand and supply. An advantage of this planning approach is that employees can actually see the plans that are used in directing and coordinating their work.
Source: Grzegorz Michalowski/EPA/Newscom

formal planning department
A group of planning specialists whose sole responsibility is helping to write organizational plans

period is inefficient and ineffective. What happened at AT&T with the iPhone is a good example of why it's important to understand the commitment concept. When it secured exclusive rights to support the iPhone on its wireless network in June 2007, both Apple and AT&T vastly underestimated the phone's popularity—some 21.8 million alone have been sold from 2011 through the first quarter of 2012.[22] And then there's all those apps—at least 500,000 different ones that have been downloaded over 15 billion times—many of which consume bandwidth. AT&T's network "simply can't handle the traffic." AT&T's chief strategy officer John Stankey said, "We missed on our usage estimates." As the company discovered, the bandwidth-hungry super-phone has created serious challenges.[23] How does this illustrate the commitment concept? In becoming the primary provider of the iPhone, AT&T "committed" to whatever future expenses are generated by that planned decision. And they have to live with the decision and its consequences—good and bad.

Approaches to Planning

Federal, state, and local government officials are working together on a plan to boost populations of wild salmon in the northwestern United States. Managers in the Global Fleet Graphics division of the 3M Company are developing detailed plans to satisfy increasingly demanding customers and to battle more aggressive competitors. Emilio Azcárraga Jean, chairman, president, and CEO of Grupo Televisa, gets input from many different people before setting company goals and then turns over the planning for achieving the goals to various executives. In each of these situations, planning is done a little differently. *How* an organization plans can best be understood by looking at *who* does the planning.

In the traditional approach, planning is done entirely by top-level managers who often are assisted by a **formal planning department**, a group of planning specialists whose sole responsibility is to help write the various organizational plans. Under this approach, plans developed by top-level managers flow down through other organizational levels, much like the traditional approach to goal-setting. As they flow down through the organization, the plans are tailored to the particular needs of each level. Although this approach makes managerial planning thorough, systematic, and coordinated, all too often the focus is on developing "the plan"—a thick binder (or binders) full of meaningless information that's stuck on a shelf and never used by anyone for guiding or coordinating work efforts. In fact, in a survey of managers about formal top-down organizational planning processes, more than 75 percent said their company's planning approach was unsatisfactory.[24] A common complaint was that, "plans are documents that you prepare for the corporate planning staff and later forget." Although this traditional top-down approach to planning is used by many organizations, it can be effective only if managers understand the importance of creating documents that organizational members actually use, not documents that look impressive but are ignored.

Another approach to planning is to involve more organizational members in the process. In this approach, plans aren't handed down from one level to the next, but instead are developed by organizational members at the various levels and in the various work units to meet their specific needs. For instance, at Dell, employees from production, supply management, and channel management meet weekly to make plans based on current product demand and supply. In addition, work teams set their own daily schedules and track their progress against those schedules. If a team falls behind, team members develop "recovery" plans to try to get back on schedule.[25] When organizational members are more actively involved in planning, they see that the plans are more than just something written down on paper. They can actually see that the plans are used in directing and coordinating work.

CONTEMPORARY Issues in Planning

Discuss contemporary issues in planning. **8.4**

The second floor of the 21-story Hyundai Motor headquarters buzzes with data 24 hours a day. That's where you'd find the company's Global Command and Control Center (GCCC), which is modeled after the CNN newsroom with "dozens of computer screens relaying video and data keeping watch on Hyundai operations around the world." Managers get information on parts shipments from suppliers to factories. Cameras watch assembly lines and "keep a close watch on Hyundai's giant Ulsan, Korea, plant, the world's largest integrated auto factory" looking for competitors' spies and any hints of labor unrest. The GCCC also keeps tabs on the company's R&D activities in Europe, Japan, and North America. Hyundai can identify problems in an instant and react quickly. The company is all about aggressiveness and speed and is representative of how a successful twenty-first-century company approaches planning.[26]

We conclude this chapter by addressing two contemporary issues in planning. Specifically, we're going to look at planning effectively in dynamic environments and then at how managers can use environmental scanning, especially competitive intelligence.

How Can Managers Plan Effectively in Dynamic Environments?

As we saw in Chapter 2, the external environment is continually changing. For instance, cloud computing storage is revolutionizing all kinds of industries from financial services to health care to engineering.[27] Social networking sites are used by companies to connect with customers, employees, and potential employees. Amounts spent on eating out instead of cooking at home are predicted to decline. And experts believe that China and India are transforming the twenty-first-century global economy.

How can managers effectively plan when the external environment is continually changing? We already discussed uncertain environments as one of the contingency factors that affect the types of plans managers develop. Because dynamic environments are more the norm than the exception, let's look at how managers can effectively plan in such environments.

In an uncertain environment, managers should develop plans that are specific, but flexible. Although this may seem contradictory, it's not. To be useful, plans need some specificity, but the plans should not be set in stone. Managers need to recognize that planning is an ongoing process. The plans serve as a road map although the destination may change due to dynamic market conditions. They should be ready to change directions if environmental conditions warrant. This flexibility is particularly important as plans are implemented. Managers need to stay alert to environmental changes that may impact implementation and respond as needed. Keep in mind, also, that even when the environment is highly uncertain, it's important to continue formal planning in order to see any effect on organizational performance. It's the persistence in planning that contributes to significant performance improvement. Why? It seems that, as with most activities, managers "learn to plan" and the quality of their planning improves when they continue to do it.[28] Finally, make the organizational hierarchy flatter to effectively plan in dynamic environments. This means allowing lower organizational levels to set goals and develop plans because there's little time for goals and plans to flow down from the top. Managers should teach their employees how to set goals and to plan and then trust them to do it. And you need look no further than Bangalore, India, to find a company that effectively understands this. Just a decade ago, Wipro Limited was "an anonymous conglomerate selling cooking oil and personal computers, mostly in India." Today, it's a $7.5 billion-a-year global company with much of its business coming from information-technology services.[29] Accenture, Hewlett-Packard, IBM, and the big U.S. accounting firms know all too well the competitive threat Wipro represents. Not only are Wipro's employees economical, they're knowledgeable and skilled. And they play an important role in the company's planning. Because the information services industry is continually changing, employees are taught to analyze situations and to define the scale and scope of a client's problems in order to offer the

Knowledgeable and skilled employees play an important role in planning at Wipro, a global information technology services company serving more than 800 clients including governments, educational institutions, and businesses. Wipro has become successful while operating in a dynamic environment by teaching employees how to set goals and make plans and then trusting them to do it. Wipro gives employees responsibility to analyze customers' ever-changing business needs and then devise solutions that help them function faster and more efficiently. Shown here are Wipro software employees at company headquarters in Bangalore, India.
Source: Jagadeesh Nv/EPA/Newscom

environmental scanning
Screening information to detect emerging trends

competitor intelligence
Gathering information about competitors that allows managers to anticipate competitors' actions rather than merely react to them

best solutions. These employees are on the front line with the clients, and it's their responsibility to establish what to do and how to do it. It's an approach that positions Wipro for success—no matter how the industry changes.

How Can Managers Use Environmental Scanning?

Crammed into a small Shanghai apartment that houses four generations of a Chinese family, Indra Nooyi, Chairman and CEO of PepsiCo Inc., asked the inhabitants several questions about "China's rapid development, their shopping habits, and how they feel about Western brands." This visit was part of an "immersion" tour of China for Ms. Nooyi, who hopes to strengthen PepsiCo's business in emerging markets. She said, "I wanted to look at how people live, how they eat, what the growth possibilities are."[30] The information gleaned from her research—a prime example of environmental scanning up close and personal—will help in establishing PepsiCo's future goals and plans.

A manager's analysis of the external environment may be improved by **environmental scanning**, which involves screening information to detect emerging trends. One of the fastest-growing forms of environmental scanning is **competitor intelligence**, gathering information about competitors that allows managers to anticipate competitors' actions rather than merely react to them.[31] It seeks basic information about competitors: Who are they? What are they doing? How will what they're doing affect us?

Many who study competitive intelligence suggest that much of the competitor-related information managers need to make crucial strategic decisions is available and accessible to the public.[32] In other words, competitive intelligence isn't corporate espionage. Advertisements, promotional materials, press releases, reports filed with government agencies, annual reports, want ads, newspaper reports, information on the Internet, and industry studies are readily accessible sources of information. Specific information on an industry and associated organizations is increasingly available through electronic databases. Managers can literally tap into this wealth of competitive information by purchasing access to databases. Attending trade shows and debriefing your own sales staff also can be good sources of information on competitors. In addition, many organizations even regularly buy competitors' products and ask their own employees to evaluate them to learn about new technical innovations.[33]

In a changing global business environment, environmental scanning and obtaining competitive intelligence can be quite complex, especially since information must be gathered from around the world. However, one thing managers could do is subscribe to news services that review newspapers and magazines from around the globe and provide summaries to client companies.

Managers do need to be careful about the way information, especially competitive intelligence, is gathered to prevent any concerns about whether it's legal or ethical.[34] For instance, Starwood Hotels sued Hilton Hotels, alleging that two former employees stole trade secrets and helped Hilton develop a new line of luxury, trendy hotels designed to appeal to a young demographic.[35] The court filing said, "This is the clearest imaginable case of corporate espionage, theft of trade secrets, unfair competition, and computer fraud." Competitive intelligence becomes illegal corporate spying when it involves the theft of proprietary materials or trade secrets by any means. The Economic Espionage Act makes it a crime in the United States to engage in economic espionage or to steal a trade secret. Difficult decisions about competitive intelligence arise because often there's a fine line between what's considered *legal and ethical* and what's considered *legal but unethical.* Although the top manager at one competitive intelligence firm contends that 99.9 percent of intelligence gathering is legal, there's no question that some people or companies will go to any lengths—some unethical—to get information about competitors.[36]

CHAPTER

PREPARING FOR: Exams/Quizzes
CHAPTER SUMMARY by Learning Outcomes

8.1

Define the nature and purposes of planning.

Planning involves defining the organization's goals, establishing an overall strategy for achieving those goals, and developing plans for organizational work activities. The four purposes of planning include providing direction, reducing uncertainty, minimizing waste and redundancy, and establishing the goals or standards used in controlling. Studies of the planning-performance relationship have concluded that formal planning is associated with positive financial performance, for the most part; it's more important to do a good job of planning and implementing the plans than doing more extensive planning; the external environment is usually the reason why companies that plan don't achieve high levels of performance; and the planning-performance relationship seems to be influenced by the planning time frame.

8.2 [LEARNING OUTCOME]

Classify the types of goals organizations might have and the plans they use.

Goals are desired outcomes. Plans are documents that outline how goals are going to be met. Goals might be strategic or financial and they might be stated or real. Strategic plans apply to the entire organization while operational plans encompass a particular functional area. Long-term plans are those with a time frame beyond three years. Short-term plans cover one year or less. Specific plans are clearly defined and leave no room for interpretation. Directional plans are flexible and set out general guidelines. A single-use plan is a one-time plan designed to meet the needs of a unique situation. Standing plans are ongoing plans that provide guidance for activities performed repeatedly.

8.3 [LEARNING OUTCOME]

Compare and contrast approaches to goal-setting and planning.

In traditional goal-setting, goals are set at the top of the organization and then become subgoals for each organizational area. MBO (management by objectives) is a process of setting mutually agreed-upon goals and using those goals to evaluate employee performance. Well-written goals have six characteristics: (1) written in terms of outcomes, (2) measurable and quantifiable, (3) clear as to time frame, (4) challenging but attainable, (5) written down, and (6) communicated to all organizational members who need to know them. Goal-setting involves these steps: review the organization's mission; evaluate available resources; determine the goals individually or with input from others; write down the goals and communicate them to all who need to know them; and review results and change goals as needed. The contingency factors that affect planning include the manager's level in the organization, the degree of environmental uncertainty, and the length of future commitments. The two main approaches to planning include the traditional approach, which has plans developed by top managers that flow down through other organizational levels and which may use a formal planning department. The other approach is to involve more organizational members in the planning process.

8.4 LEARNING OUTCOME

Discuss contemporary issues in planning.
One contemporary planning issue is planning in dynamic environments, which usually means developing plans that are specific but flexible. Also, it's important to continue planning, even when the environment is highly uncertain. Finally, because there's little time in a dynamic environment for goals and plans to flow down from the top, lower organizational levels should be allowed to set goals and develop plans. Another contemporary planning issue involves using environmental scanning to help do a better analysis of the external environment. One form of environmental scanning, competitive intelligence, can be especially helpful in finding out what competitors are doing.

REVIEW AND DISCUSSION QUESTIONS ✪

1. Explain what studies have shown about the relationship between planning and performance.

2. Discuss the contingency factors that affect planning.

3. Will planning become more or less important to managers in the future? Why?

4. If planning is so crucial, why do some managers choose not to do it? What would you tell these managers?

5. Explain how planning involves making decisions today that will have an impact later.

6. How might planning in a not-for-profit organization such as the American Cancer Society differ from

planning in a for-profit organization such as Coca-Cola?

7. What types of planning do you do in your personal life? Describe these plans in terms of being (a) strategic or operational, (b) short term or long term, and (c) specific or directional.

8. Many companies have a goal of becoming more environmentally sustainable. One of the most important steps they can take is controlling paper waste. Choose a company—any type, any size. You've been put in charge of creating a program to do this for your company. Set goals and develop plans. Prepare a report for your boss (that is, your professor) outlining these goals and plans.

PREPARING FOR: My Career
ETHICS DILEMMA ✪

Rules are rules. Or are they? An incident at a Safeway store in Hawaii made international headlines after cops were called on a couple who failed to pay for two $2.50 sandwiches.[37] The couple had bought $50 worth of groceries and said they intended to pay for the sandwiches, which they'd eaten while shopping. The couple was with their 2-year-old daughter and the mother was about 8 months pregnant and said she had felt lightheaded before eating one of the sandwiches. Despite the couple's request to just let them pay for the sandwiches, the store manager, trying

to follow company policy, called the police, leading to the arrest of both parents and their separation from their young daughter for more than 18 hours. Safeway did ultimately drop the shoplifting charges and apologized to the couple. But "by rigidly following a rule, the store may have turned a $5 theft into a much bigger dent in its reputation and bottom line." What do you think? Was this a good business decision for Safeway? What potential ethical issues do you see here? If you were the store manager, what would you have done in this situation?

SKILLS EXERCISE   Developing Your Goal-Setting Skill

About the Skill
Employees should have a clear understanding of what they're attempting to accomplish. In addition, managers have the responsibility for seeing that this is done by helping employees set work goals. Setting goals is a skill every manager needs to develop.

Steps in Practicing the Skill
You can be more effective at setting goals if you use the following eight suggestions.

1. *Identify an employee's key job tasks.* Goal-setting begins by defining what you want your employees

to accomplish. The best source for this information is each employee's job description.

2. *Establish specific and challenging goals for each key task.* Identify the level of performance expected of each employee. Specify the target toward which the employee is working.

3. *Specify the deadlines for each goal.* Putting deadlines on each goal reduces ambiguity. Deadlines, however, should not be set arbitrarily. Rather, they need to be realistic given the tasks to be completed.

4. *Allow the employee to actively participate.* When employees participate in goal-setting, they're more likely to accept the goals. However, it must be sincere participation. That is, employees must perceive that you are truly seeking their input, not just going through the motions.

5. *Prioritize goals.* When you give someone more than one goal, it's important for you to rank the goals in order of importance. The purpose of prioritizing is to encourage the employee to take action and expend effort on each goal in proportion to its importance.

6. *Rate goals for difficulty and importance.* Goal-setting should not encourage people to choose easy goals.

Instead, goals should be rated for their difficulty and importance. When goals are rated, individuals can be given credit for trying difficult goals, even if they don't fully achieve them.

7. *Build in feedback mechanisms to assess goal progress.* Feedback lets employees know whether their level of effort is sufficient to attain the goal. Feedback should be both self- and supervisor-generated. In either case, feedback should be frequent and recurring.

8. *Link rewards to goal attainment.* It's natural for employees to ask, "What's in it for me?" Linking rewards to the achievement of goals will help answer that question.

Practicing the Skill

1. Where do you want to be in five years? Do you have specific five-year goals? Establish three goals you want to achieve in five years. Make sure these goals are specific, challenging, and measurable.

2. Set personal and academic goals you want to achieve by the end of this college term. Prioritize and rate them for difficulty.

WORKING TOGETHER Team Exercise

Form small groups of three to four individuals and read through the following scenario. Complete the work that's called for. Be sure your goals are well designed and your plans are descriptive.

Scenario
Facing dire budget predictions, many school districts are moving to a four-day week. Of nearly 15,000-plus districts nationwide, more than 100 in at least 17 states have moved

to the four-day system.[38] Suppose you are employed by a school district in San Antonio, Texas, that is going to move to a four-day week by the start of the next school year. What type of planning would need to be done as your school district embarked on this process? Identify three or four primary goals for accomplishing this action. Then, describe what plans would be needed to ensure that those goals are met.

MY TURN TO BE A MANAGER

- Practice setting goals for various aspects of your personal life such as academics, career preparation, family, hobbies, and so forth. Set at least two short-term goals and at least two long-term goals for each area.

- For these goals that you have set, write out plans for achieving those goals. Think in terms of what you will have to do to accomplish each. For instance, if one of your academic goals is to improve your grade-point average, what will you have to do to reach it?

- Write a personal mission statement. Although this may sound simple to do, it's not going to be simple or easy.

Our hope is that it will be something you'll want to keep, use, and revise when necessary and that it will help you be the person you'd like to be and live the life you'd like to live. Start by doing some research on personal mission statements. There are some wonderful Web resources that can guide you. Good luck!

- Interview three managers about the types of planning they do. Ask them for suggestions on how to be a better planner. Write a report describing and comparing your findings.

- Choose two companies, preferably in different industries. Research the companies' Web sites and find examples of goals they have stated. (Hint: A company's annual report is often a good place to start.) Evaluate these goals. Are they well-written? Rewrite those that don't exhibit the characteristics of well-written goals so that they do.

- Steve's and Mary's suggested readings: Atul Gawande, *The Checklist Manifesto: How to Get Things Right* (Metropolitan Books, 2009); Peter F. Drucker, *Management: Tasks, Responsibilities, Practices* (Harper Business, 1974); Peter F. Drucker, *The Executive in Action; Managing for Results* (Harper Business, 1967); and Peter F. Drucker, *The Practice of Management* (HarperCollins, 1954).

- What does it take to be a good planner? Do some research on this issue. As part of your research, talk to professors and other professionals. Make a bulleted list of suggestions. Be sure to cite your sources.

- Write down three things you learned in this chapter about being a good manager.

- Self-knowledge can be a powerful learning tool. Go to mymanagementlab.com and complete these self-assessment exercises: What's My Attitude Toward Achievement? What Are My Course Performance Goals? What Time of Day Am I Most Productive? and How Good Am I at Personal Planning? Using the results of your assessments, identify personal strengths and weaknesses. What will you do to reinforce your strengths and improve your weaknesses?

MyManagementLab

Go to **mymanagementlab.com** for Auto-graded writing questions as well as the following Assisted-graded writing questions:

8-1. Describe how managers can effectively plan in today's dynamic environment.

8-2. The late Peter Drucker, an eminent management author, coined the SMART format for setting goals back in 1954: S (specific), M (measurable), A (attainable), R (relevant), and T (time-bound). Are these still relevant today? Discuss.

8-3. Mymanagementlab Only – comprehensive writing assignment for this chapter.

1 Funny Name— Not-So-Funny Effect

This volcano has a funny name—Eyjafjallajokull—but its impact was not so funny to global businesses, both large and small.[39] When it erupted in April 2010, the plume of volcanic ash that spread across thousands of miles disrupted air travel and global commerce for a number of days.

As thousands of flights were canceled across Europe, tens of thousands of air travelers couldn't get to their destinations. For example, Marthin De Beer, vice president of emerging technologies at Cisco Systems, was headed to Oslo to discuss the final aspects of its acquisition of Tandberg, a Norwegian teleconferencing company. However, when his flight was canceled, he and Tandberg's CEO, Fredrik Halvorsen, used their merged companies' equipment to hold a virtual press conference. Other businesses weren't as lucky, especially

The eruption of the Icelandic volcano Eyjafjallajokull that produced a huge drifting ash cloud throughout Europe resulted in flight cancellations that disrupted global commerce. The halting of air travel for several days impacted managers' plans for the production and distribution of goods and services and many other scheduled business operations.
Source: Reuters/Lucas Jackson

those with high-value, highly perishable products such as berries, fresh fish and flowers, and medicines and pharmaceuticals. African farmers, European fresh-produce importers, and flower traders from Kenya to the Netherlands found their businesses threatened by the air traffic shutdown. Even manufacturers were affected. For instance, BMW had to scale back work hours and had even prepared for possibly shutting down production at its Spartanburg, South Carolina, plant because it depended on trans-Atlantic flights to bring transmissions and other components from German factories by air. A spokesperson at another automobile company, Mercedes-Benz, said, "There has been disruption in our parts supply. We expect that there may be shortages of some parts or delays in some instances."

DISCUSSION QUESTIONS ✪

1. Could a company even plan for this type of situation? If yes, how? If not, why not?

2. Would goals be useful in this type of situation? What types of goals might a manufacturing company like BMW have in such a situation? How about a global airline? How about a small flower grower in Kenya?

3. What types of plans could companies use in this type of situation? Explain why you think these plans would be important.

4. What lessons about planning can managers learn from this crisis?

CASE APPLICATION 2 Shifting Direction

With more people using their smart phones for directions and maps, sales for Garmin's dashboard-mounted navigation systems have declined. Garmin plans to boost sales by partnering with automakers to embed its GPS systems in dashboard command centers and by improving the design and adding features to its dedicated navigation systems that will add value for consumers like those shown here trying out new Garmin models at a consumer electronics show.
Source: AP Photo/Paul Sakuma

As the global leader in satellite navigation equipment, Garmin Ltd. recently hit a milestone number. It has sold more than 100 million of its products to customers—from motorists to runners to geocachers and more—who depend on the company's equipment to "help show them the way." Despite this milestone, the company's core business is in decline due to changing circumstances.[40] In response, managers at Garmin, the biggest maker of personal navigation devices, are shifting direction. Many of you probably have a dashboard-mounted navigation device in your car and chances are it might be a Garmin. However, a number of cars now have "dashboard command centers which combine smartphone docking stations with navigation systems." Sales of Garmin devices have declined as consumers increasingly use their smartphones for directions and maps. However, have you ever tried to use your smartphone navigation system while holding a phone to look at its display? It's dangerous to hold a phone and steer. Also, GPS apps can "crash" if multiple apps are running. That's why the Olathe, Kansas-based company is taking action to "aggressively partner" with automakers to embed its GPS systems in car dashboards. Right now, its biggest in-dash contract is with Chrysler and its Uconnect dashboard system found in several models of Jeep, Dodge, and Chrysler vehicles. Garmin also is working with Honda and Toyota for dashboard systems in the Asian market.

Despite these new market shifts, customers have gotten used to the GPS devices and it's become an essential part of their lives. That's why Garmin's executive team still believes there's a market for dedicated navigation systems. It's trying to breathe some life into the product with new features, better designs, and more value for the consumer's money. For instance, some of the new features include faster searching for addresses or points of interest, voice-activated navigation, and highlighting exit services such as gas stations and restaurants.

DISCUSSION QUESTIONS ✪

1. What role do you think goals would play in planning the change in direction for the company? List some goals you think might be important. (Make sure these goals have the characteristics of well-written goals.)

2. What types of plans would be needed in an industry such as this one? (For instance, long-term or short-term, or both?) Explain why you think these plans would be important.

3. What contingency factors might affect the planning Garmin executives have to do? How might those contingency factors affect the planning?

4. What planning challenges do you think Garmin executives face with continuing to be the global market leader? How should they cope with those challenges?

9 Strategic Management

SPOTLIGHT: *Manager at Work*

Did you ever use a Nokia cell phone? *Nokia, the Finnish company, was once positioned as one of the leading mobile phone makers.[1] In 1998, Nokia sold more than 40 million mobile phones to surpass Motorola as the world's number one mobile phone company. During this time period, Nokia was light years ahead of its rivals with digital phones. However, "Nokia was caught sleeping in 2007 when Apple Inc.'s iPhone redefined the cell phone as a PC-like device with a touch screen and sleek software." Since that crucial time, Nokia has lost 75 percent of its market value and is struggling to catch up to Apple and Google Inc.'s Android.*

Despite its failure to recognize the market-changing characteristics of Apple's iPhone, Nokia is still the world's largest handset manufacturer by volume. Europe is the company's largest combined market, with about a third of sales. Somewhat surprisingly, China is Nokia's largest single-country market, accounting for nearly 20 percent of sales. The United States accounts for only 4 percent of sales, and India (another important target) accounts for only 7 percent of sales. The company has been crafting strategies it hopes will help position it as a dominant force once again in this industry. New CEO Stephen Elop (see photo), the first non-Finnish leader and a former top Microsoft executive, has pledged to turn around the struggling company.

Elop's initial plans were aimed at streamlining its smart phone operations costs and speeding delivery of new products. He said, "Nokia has been characterized as an organization where it is too hard to get things done. More than anything else, the changing market dynamics demand that we must improve our ability to aggressively lead through changes in our environment." Getting

Source: Reuters/Mike Blake

its products to market faster would be a key failing that would have to be improved. In addition to the first round of 1,800 jobs cut, Elop eliminated several senior officials on the company's group executive board. He also sent a memo to Nokia employees that compared the company's predicament

Source: AP Photo/Alastair Grant

Now, it's do-or-die time for Nokia.

in catching up to Apple and Google in smart phones to "that of a man who was standing on a burning oil rig at sea. Standing there, he needed to make a choice and he decided to jump." He went on to say that "Nokia, too, had to jump metaphorically—to take bold action to make up for lost ground." And bold actions it has taken.

In February 2011, the company announced that it would partner with Microsoft to produce their first phone using the Windows operating system by the end of the year—a pace two to three times faster than Nokia's past product introductions. Getting that done would "require an accelerated, effective collaboration with a completely different corporate culture in a creative endeavor so intimate that both would have to discard mutual distrust to make it work." By mid-2011, Nokia had unveiled a new smart phone and three lower-priced handsets as

---

MyManagementLab®

⭐ **Improve Your Grade!**

Over 10 million students improved their results using the Pearson MyLabs.
Visit **mymanagementlab.com** for simulations, tutorials, and end-of-chapter problems.

LEARNING OUTCOMES

9.1 | *Define* strategic management and explain why it's important.

9.2 | *Explain* what managers do during the six steps of the strategic management process.

9.3 | *Describe* the three types of corporate strategies.

9.4 | *Describe* competitive advantage and the competitive strategies organizations use to get it.

9.5 | *Discuss* current strategic management issues.

initial steps in its transition to Microsoft software. Elop said, "We are seeing solid progress against our strategy, and with these planned changes we will emerge as a more dynamic, nimble and efficient challenger." Now, it's do-or-die time for Nokia. **How will managers keep employees focused on the company's strategic goals?**

The importance of having good strategies can be seen by what Stephen Elop is attempting

to accomplish with Nokia. By recognizing market opportunities to exploit and his own company's weaknesses to be corrected, he was able to formulate new, and hopefully more effective, strategies to once again become a strong competitor. Strategic management will continue to play an important role in the company's ability to reach its goals. An underlying theme in this chapter is that effective strategies can result in high organizational performance.

STRATEGIC Management

9.1 *Define strategic management and explain why it's important.*

- Swedish furniture giant IKEA Group says it's planning to set up 25 stores in India in coming years, a move made possible by a change in Indian government policy that says some retailers can now own 100 percent of their Indian units.
- Airbus, a unit of European Aeronautics & Space Co., has released information detailing its plans for building a $600 million factory in Alabama—its first in the United States.
- Applebee's, the casual restaurant chain, is remaking its food and atmosphere. The company's CEO said the company recognized that it had an opportunity to revitalize itself—and it's pursuing that opportunity in a big way.
- In a fierce battle over tablet computers, Apple announced it's building a miniature iPad to rival Amazon's Kindle Fire, Google's Nexus 7, and Barnes & Noble's Nook Color. The race to build book-size tablets is driven by consumer desire for greater portability.[2]

These are just a few of the business news stories from a single week, and each one is about a company's strategies. Strategic management is very much a part of what managers do. In this section, we want to look at what strategic management is and why it's important.

What Is Strategic Management?

The discount retail industry is a good place to see what strategic management is all about. Walmart and Kmart Corporation (now part of Sears Holdings) have battled for market dominance since 1962, the year both companies were founded. The two chains have other similarities: store atmosphere, names, markets served, and organizational purpose. Yet, Walmart's performance (financial and otherwise) has far surpassed that of Kmart. Walmart is the world's largest retailer and Kmart was the largest retailer ever to seek Chapter 11 bankruptcy protection. Why the difference in performance? Because of different strategies and competitive abilities.[3] Walmart has excelled by using strategic management effectively while Kmart has struggled by failing to use strategic management effectively.

Strategic management is what managers do to develop the organization's strategies. It's an important task involving all the basic management functions—planning, organizing, leading, and controlling. What are an organization's **strategies**? They're the plans for how the organization will do whatever it's in business to do, how it will compete successfully, and how it will attract and satisfy its customers in order to achieve its goals.[4]

One term often used in strategic management is **business model**, which simply is how a company is going to make money. It focuses on two things: (1) whether

strategic management
What managers do to develop the organization's strategies

strategies
The plans for how the organization will do what it's in business to do, how it will compete successfully, and how it will attract and satisfy its customers in order to achieve its goals

business model
How a company is going to make money

customers will value what the company is providing and (2) whether the company can make any money doing that.[5] For instance, Jeff Bezos pioneered a new business model for selling books to consumers directly online instead of selling through bookstores. Did customers "value" that? Absolutely! Did Amazon make money doing it that way? Not at first, but now, absolutely! What began as the world's biggest bookstore is now the world's biggest everything store. As managers think about strategies, they need to think about the economic viability of their company's business model.

Why Is Strategic Management Important?

In the summer of 2002, a British television show spin-off called *American Idol* became one of the biggest shows in American television history. Twelve seasons later, it's still one of the most-watched shows on television, although its audience has declined. However, the show's executive producer said, "If we're smart about it, there's no reason why 'Idol' wouldn't keep going. Just look at 'Price is Right.' It's been on for over 35 years."[6] The managers behind *Idol* seem to understand the importance of strategic management as they've developed and exploited every aspect of the *Idol* business—the television show, the music, the concerts, and all the other associated licensed products. Now, their challenge is to keep the franchise a strong presence in the market by making strategic changes.

Why is strategic management so important? There are three reasons. The most significant one is that it can make a difference in how well an organization performs. Why do some businesses succeed and others fail, even when faced with the same environmental conditions? (Remember our Walmart and Kmart example.) Research has found a generally positive relationship between strategic planning and performance.[7] In other words, it appears that organizations that use strategic management do have higher levels of performance. And that fact makes it pretty important for managers!

Another reason it's important has to do with the fact that managers in organizations of all types and sizes face continually changing situations (as we discussed in Chapter 7). They cope with this uncertainty by using the strategic management process to examine relevant factors and decide what actions to take. For instance, as business executives across a wide spectrum of industries coped with the global recession, they focused on making their strategies more flexible. At Office Depot, for example, store managers throughout the company told CEO Steve Odland that cash-strapped consumers no longer wanted to buy pens or printer paper in bulk. So the company created special displays promoting single Sharpie pens and introduced five-ream packages of paper, half the size of the normal big box of paper.[8]

Finally, strategic management is important because organizations are complex and diverse. Each part needs to work together toward achieving the organization's goals; strategic management helps do this. For example, with more than 2.2 million employees worldwide working in various departments, functional areas, and stores, Walmart Stores, Inc., uses strategic management to help coordinate and focus employees' efforts on what's important as determined by its goals.

Today, both business organizations and not-for-profit organizations use strategic management. For instance, the U.S. Postal Service (USPS) is locked in competitive battles with overnight package delivery companies, telecommunications companies' e-mail and text messaging services, and private mailing facilities. In 2006, 213 billion pieces of mail were handled by the postal service. By 2011, that total had dropped to 168 billion, a decline of more than 21 percent. Patrick Donahoe, USPS's

Since introducing "Mr. Potato Head" in 1950, Hasbro has used strategic management to achieve high organizational performance in the toy and game industry. A major part of Hasbro's strategy is focused on innovation in developing new toys and in growing its core brands to meet the ever changing demands of all age groups worldwide. Vital to Hasbro's continued success is the development of core brands such as Milton Bradley with new zAPPed editions of *The Game of Life* and other classic games that combine digital gaming with the traditional board game. Toy demonstrators shown here at an international toy fair use an iPad to play *The Game of Life zAPPed*, Hasbro's first app-enhanced version of a core brand.
Source: AP Photo/Hasbro, Ray Stubblebine

CEO (the U.S. Postmaster General), is using strategic management to come up with a response. One possible action plan, which many critics consider drastic, is discontinuing Saturday mail delivery. Others include shutting down some postal facilities and consolidating others. However, strategic changes are needed as the USPS faces losses of $238 billion over the next decade.[9] Strategic management will continue to be important to its operation. Check out the organization's *Vision 2013,* which outlines its internal plan for the future.[10] Although strategic management in not-for-profits hasn't been as well researched as it has in for-profit organizations, we know it's important for these organizations as well.

THE STRATEGIC Management Process

The **strategic management process** (see Exhibit 9-1) is a six-step process that encompasses strategy planning, implementation, and evaluation. Although the first four steps describe the planning that must take place, implementation and evaluation are just as important! Even the best strategies can fail if management doesn't implement or evaluate them properly.

Step 1: Identifying the Organization's Current Mission, Goals, and Strategies

Every organization needs a **mission**—a statement of its purpose. Defining the mission forces managers to identify what it's in business to do. But sometimes that mission statement can be too limiting. For example, the co-founder of the leading Internet search engine Google says that while the company's purpose of "organizing the world's information and making it universally accessible and useful" has served them well, they failed to see the whole social side of the Internet and have been playing catch-up.[11] What *should* a mission statement include? Exhibit 9-2 describes some typical components.

Step 2: Doing an External Analysis

What impact might the following trends have for businesses?

- With the passage of the national health care legislation, every big restaurant chain must now post calorie information on their menus and drive-through signs.
- Cell phones are now used by customers more for data transmittal and retrieval than for phone calls and the number of smart phones and tablet computers continues to soar.
- More young adults are earning college degrees according to data released from the U.S. Department of Education.[12]

9.2 | *Explain* what managers do during the six steps of the strategic management process.

strategic management process
A six-step process that encompasses strategic planning, implementation, and evaluation

mission
A statement of an organization's purpose

Exhibit 9-1
Strategic Management Process

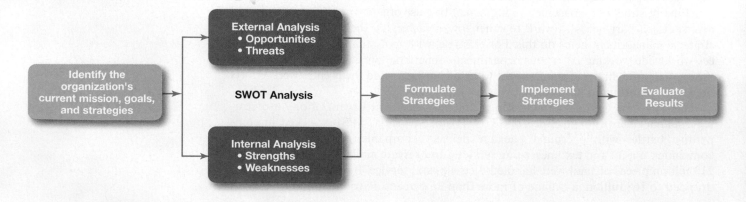

Customers: Who are the firm's customers?

Markets: Where does the firm compete geographically?

Concern for survival, growth, and profitability: Is the firm committed to growth and financial stability?

Philosophy: What are the firm's basic beliefs, values, and ethical priorities?

Concern for public image: How responsive is the firm to societal and environmental concerns?

Products or services: What are the firm's major products or services?

Technology: Is the firm technologically current?

Self-concept: What are the firm's major competitive advantage and core competencies?

Concern for employees: Are employees a valuable asset of the firm?

Source: Based on *Strategic Management*, 13th edition, by F. David. Published by Pearson Education, Inc.

Exhibit 9-2
Components of a
Mission Statement

We described the external environment in Chapter 2 as an important constraint on a manager's actions. Analyzing that environment is a critical step in the strategic management process. Managers do an external analysis so they know, for instance, what the competition is doing, what pending legislation might affect the organization, or what the labor supply is like in locations where it operates. In an external analysis, managers should examine the economic, demographic, political/legal, sociocultural, technological, and global components to see the trends and changes.

Once they've analyzed the environment, managers need to pinpoint opportunities that the organization can exploit and threats that it must counteract or buffer against. **Opportunities** are positive trends in the external environment; **threats** are negative trends.

Step 3: Doing an Internal Analysis

Now we move to the internal analysis, which provides important information about an organization's specific resources and capabilities. An organization's **resources** are its assets—financial, physical, human, and intangible—that it uses to develop, manufacture, and deliver products to its customers. They're "what" the organization has. On the other hand, its **capabilities** are its skills and abilities in doing the work activities needed in its business—"how" it does its work. The major value-creating capabilities of the organization are known as its **core competencies**.[13] Both resources and core competencies determine the organization's competitive weapons.

After completing an internal analysis, managers should be able to identify organizational strengths and weaknesses. Any activities the organization does well or any unique resources that it has are called **strengths**. **Weaknesses** are activities the organization doesn't do well or resources it needs but doesn't possess.

The combined external and internal analyses are called the **SWOT analysis**, an analysis of the organization's *s*trengths, *w*eaknesses, *o*pportunities, and *t*hreats. After completing the SWOT analysis, managers are ready to formulate appropriate strategies—that is, strategies that (1) exploit an organization's strengths and external opportunities, (2) buffer or protect the organization from external threats, or (3) correct critical weaknesses.

Step 4: Formulating Strategies

As managers formulate strategies, they should consider the realities of the external environment and their available resources and capabilities in order to design strategies that will help an organization achieve its goals. The three main types of

opportunities
Positive trends in the external environment

threats
Negative trends in the external environment

resources
An organization's assets that are used to develop, manufacture, and deliver products to its customers

capabilities
An organization's skills and abilities in doing the work activities needed in its business

core competencies
The organization's major value-creating capabilities that determine its competitive weapons

strengths
Any activities the organization does well or its unique resources

weaknesses
Activities the organization does not do well or resources it needs but does not possess

SWOT analysis
An analysis of the organization's strengths, weaknesses, opportunities, and threats

let's get REAL

The Scenario:

Johan Nilsson started his architectural firm in Stockholm more than 15 years ago. His business has grown to where he now employs 8 architects in addition to himself and an office staff of 4. Like many other companies, Johan's business suffered through the global economic downturn. However, now that things are starting to turn around, he feels it's important to re-establish his company's strategic direction. And he also believes that his job as a leader is to make sure his employees understand the strategic goals of the company.

Joe Binef
Director of Global
Process Development

What advice might you give Johan about sharing his organization's strategy and getting his employees to "buy into" the company's future?

I would advise Johan to schedule a meeting in order to bring the team together and state what his vision and goals are for the company. He should explain the company's strategy, define clear goals and objectives, and promote training and development. This will reassure his team that as they succeed in achieving his strategic direction, his success will ultimately be their success as well.

strategies managers will formulate include corporate, competitive, and functional. We'll describe each shortly.

Step 5: Implementing Strategies

Once strategies are formulated, they must be implemented. No matter how effectively an organization has planned its strategies, performance will suffer if the strategies aren't implemented properly.

Step 6: Evaluating Results

The final step in the strategic management process is evaluating results. How effective have the strategies been at helping the organization reach its goals? What adjustments are necessary? For example, after assessing the results of previous strategies and determining that changes were needed, Xerox CEO Ursula Burns made strategic adjustments to regain market share and improve her company's bottom line. The company cut jobs, sold assets, and reorganized management.

9.3 *Describe the three types of corporate strategies.*

CORPORATE Strategies

As we said earlier, organizations use three types of strategies: corporate, competitive, and functional. (See Exhibit 9-3.) Top-level managers typically are responsible for corporate strategies, middle-level managers for competitive strategies, and lower-level managers for the functional strategies. In this section, we'll look at corporate strategies.

Corporate

Competitive

Functional

Exhibit 9-3
Types of
Organizational
Strategies

What Is Corporate Strategy?

A **corporate strategy** is one that determines what businesses a company is in or wants to be in and what it wants to do with those businesses. It's based on the mission and goals of the organization and the roles that each business unit of the organization will play. We can see both of these aspects with PepsiCo, for instance. Its mission: To be the world's premier consumer products company focused on convenient foods and beverages. It pursues that mission with a corporate strategy that has put it in different businesses, including its Pepsico Americas Beverage (beverage business), Frito Lay North America (snack food business), Quaker Oats North America (prepared foods business), and then its global businesses—Latin America Foods, Europe, Asia/Middle East/Africa. The other part of corporate strategy is when top managers decide what to do with those businesses: grow them, keep them the same, or renew them.

corporate strategy
An organizational strategy that determines what businesses a company is in or wants to be in, and what it wants to do with those businesses

What Are the Types of Corporate Strategy?

The three main types of corporate strategies are growth, stability, and renewal. Let's look at each type.

GROWTH   Even though Walmart Stores is the world's largest retailer, it continues to grow internationally and in the United States. A **growth strategy** is when an organization expands the number of markets served or products offered, either through its current business(es) or through new business(es). Because of its growth strategy, an organization may increase revenues, number of employees, or market share. Organizations grow by using concentration, vertical integration, horizontal integration, or diversification.

growth strategy
A corporate strategy that's used when an organization wants to expand the number of markets served or products offered, either through its current business(es) or through new business(es)

An organization that grows using *concentration* focuses on its primary line of business and increases the number of products offered or markets served in this primary business. For instance, Beckman Coulter, Inc., a Fullerton, California-based organization with annual revenues of almost $4 billion, has used concentration to become one of the world's largest medical diagnostics and research equipment companies. (It was acquired by Danaher Corporation in 2011.) Another example of a company using concentration is Bose Corporation of Framingham, Massachusetts, which focuses on developing innovative audio products and has become one of the world's leading manufacturers of speakers for home entertainment, automotive, and pro audio markets with sales of more than $773 million.

A company also might choose to grow by *vertical integration*, either backward, forward, or both. In backward vertical integration, the organization becomes its own supplier so it can control its inputs. For instance, eBay owns an online payment business that helps it provide more secure transactions and control one of its most critical processes. In forward vertical integration, the organization becomes its own distributor and is able to control its outputs. For example, Apple has more than 360 retail stores worldwide to distribute its product.

LEADER who made a DIFFERENCE

She's known as Home Depot's own "fix-it lady!"[14] Chief Financial Officer Carol Tomé joined the company in 1992 and has worked her way up to the corporate suite. She's been CFO since 2001 and has advanced, according to colleagues, because of her "sharp intelligence with a zeal to learn the business from the hammers and nails on up." Tomé has been instrumental in recognizing and solving the retailer's technology problems. She says, "We were ... like that Kevin Costner movie: Build a store and they will come. That's no longer the case. We need to look at what we're doing inside the company to grow." And what they're doing inside the company is becoming very focused on improving its information technology capabilities. One of the company's goals is not to have any customer waiting in line to check out. So they're outfitting their stores with some different options. One is that they're outfitting every Home Depot associate with a "First Phone"—a combination phone/walkie-talkie/scanner. When the merchandise is in a remote location or the store is extremely busy (as they tend to be on weekends), the unit can be set up with a card reader and receipt printer so it can accept credit and debit payments. Another option is that Home Depot became PayPal's first retail partner and checkout registers now offer a PayPal Wallet button, which enables consumers to pay with any funding source that's linked to their PayPal account. Here's a leader who knows about formulating and implementing strategy. What can you learn from this leader who made a difference?

In *horizontal integration*, a company grows by combining with competitors. For instance, French cosmetics giant L'Oreal acquired The Body Shop. Another example is Live Nation, the largest concert promoter in the United States, which combined operations with competitor HOB Entertainment, the operator of the House of Blues Clubs. Horizontal integration has been used in a number of industries in the last few years—financial services, consumer products, airlines, department stores, and software, among others. The U.S. Federal Trade Commission usually scrutinizes these combinations closely to see if consumers might be harmed by decreased competition. Other countries may have similar restrictions. For instance, the European Commission, the "watchdog" for the European Union, conducted an in-depth investigation into Unilever's acquisition of the body and laundry care units of Sara Lee.

Finally, an organization can grow through *diversification*, either related or unrelated. Related diversification happens when a company combines with other companies in different, but related, industries. For example, American Standard Cos., based in Piscataway, New Jersey, is in a variety of businesses, including bathroom fixtures, air conditioning and heating units, plumbing parts, and pneumatic brakes for trucks. Although this mix of businesses seems odd, the company's "strategic fit" is the efficiency-oriented manufacturing techniques developed in its primary business of bathroom fixtures, which it has transferred to all its other businesses. Unrelated diversification is when a company combines with firms in different and unrelated industries. For instance, the Tata Group of India has businesses in chemicals, communications and IT, consumer products, energy, engineering, materials, and services. Again, an odd mix. But in this case, there's no strategic fit among the businesses.

STABILITY As the global recession dragged on and U.S. sales of candy and chocolate slowed down, Cadbury Schweppes—with almost half of its confectionary sales coming from chocolate—is maintaining things as they are. A **stability strategy** is a corporate strategy in which an organization continues to do what it is currently doing. Examples of this strategy include continuing to serve the same clients by offering the same product or service, maintaining market share, and sustaining the organization's current business operations. The organization doesn't grow, but doesn't fall behind, either.

stability strategy
A corporate strategy in which an organization continues to do what it is currently doing

RENEWAL In 2011, AMR (American Airlines' parent) lost almost $2 billion. Fannie Mae lost $16.8 billion, Panasonic lost over $9.7 billion, and many financial services and real-estate-related companies faced serious financial issues with huge losses. When an organization is in trouble, something needs to be done. Managers need to develop strategies, called **renewal strategies**, that address declining performance. The two main types of renewal strategies are retrenchment and turnaround strategies. A *retrenchment strategy* is a short-run renewal strategy used for minor performance problems. This strategy helps an organization stabilize operations, revitalize

renewal strategy
A corporate strategy designed to address declining performance

organizational resources and capabilities, and prepare to compete once again. When an organization's problems are more serious, more drastic action—the *turnaround strategy*—is needed. Managers do two things for both renewal strategies: cut costs and restructure organizational operations. However, in a turnaround strategy, these measures are more extensive than in a retrenchment strategy.

How Are Corporate Strategies Managed?

When an organization's corporate strategy encompasses a number of businesses, managers can manage this collection, or portfolio, of businesses using a tool called a corporate portfolio matrix. This matrix provides a framework for understanding diverse businesses and helps managers establish priorities for allocating resources.[15] The first portfolio matrix—the **BCG matrix**—was developed by the Boston Consulting Group and introduced the idea that an organization's various businesses could be evaluated and plotted using a 2 × 2 matrix to identify which ones offered high potential and which were a drain on organizational resources.[16] The horizontal axis represents market share (low or high), and the vertical axis indicates anticipated market growth (low or high). A business unit is evaluated using a SWOT analysis and placed in one of the four categories, which are as follows:

- **Stars:** High market share/High anticipated growth rate
- **Cash Cows:** High market share/Low anticipated growth rate
- **Question Marks:** Low market share/High anticipated growth rate
- **Dogs:** Low market share/Low anticipated growth rate

What are the strategic implications of the BCG matrix? The dogs should be sold off or liquidated as they have low market share in markets with low growth potential. Managers should "milk" cash cows for as much as they can, limit any new investment in them, and use the large amounts of cash generated to invest in stars and question marks with strong potential to improve market share. Heavy investment in stars will help take advantage of the market's growth and help maintain high market share. The stars, of course, will eventually develop into cash cows as their markets mature and sales growth slows. The hardest decision for managers relates to the question marks. After careful analysis, some will be sold off and others strategically nurtured into stars.

Procter & Gamble, which markets products in 180 countries, continues to grow internationally. P&G's mission is to "provide branded products and services of superior quality and value that improve the lives of the world's consumers." Based on this mission, P&G developed its Purpose Inspired Growth Strategy with the goal of "touching and improving the lives of more consumers in more parts of the world more completely." The company's expansion plans include entering more markets and offering more products to increase its global revenues and market share. Shown here is Deb Henretta, president of P&G's Asia Group, a region where P&G expects robust and accelerated growth in China, India, and other fast-growing developing nations.
Source: AP Photo/David Kohl

BCG matrix
A strategy tool that guides resource allocation decisions on the basis of market share and growth rate of SBUs

COMPETITIVE Strategies

Describe competitive advantage and the competitive strategies organizations use to get it. | **9.4**

A **competitive strategy** is a strategy for how an organization will compete in its business(es). For a small organization in only one line of business or a large organization that has not diversified into different products or markets, its competitive strategy describes how it will compete in its primary or main market. For organizations in multiple businesses, however, each business will have its own competitive strategy that defines its competitive advantage, the products or services it will offer, the customers it wants to reach, and the like. For example, French company LVMH-Moët Hennessy Louis Vuitton SA has different competitive strategies for its businesses, which include Donna Karan fashions, Louis Vuitton leather goods, Guerlain perfume, TAG Heuer watches, Dom Perignon champagne, and other luxury products. When an

competitive strategy
An organizational strategy for how an organization will compete in its business(es)

strategic business unit (SBU)
The single independent businesses of
an organization that formulate their own
competitive strategies

competitive advantage
What sets an organization apart; its
distinctive edge

organization is in several different businesses, those single businesses that are independent and that have their own competitive strategies are referred to as **strategic business units (SBUs)**.

The Role of Competitive Advantage

Michelin has mastered a complex technological process for making superior radial tires. Coca-Cola has created the world's best and most powerful brand using specialized marketing and merchandising capabilities.[17] The Ritz Carlton hotels have a unique ability to deliver personalized customer service. Each of these companies has created a competitive advantage.

Developing an effective competitive strategy requires an understanding of **competitive advantage**, which is what sets an organization apart—that is, its distinctive edge.[18] That distinctive edge can come from the organization's core competencies by doing something that others cannot do or doing it better than others can do it. For example, Southwest Airlines has a competitive advantage because of its skills at giving passengers what they want—convenient and inexpensive air passenger service. Or competitive advantage can come from the company's resources because the organization has something its competitors do not have. For instance, Walmart's state-of-the-art information system allows it to monitor and control inventories and supplier relations more efficiently than its competitors, which Walmart has turned into a cost advantage.

QUALITY AS A COMPETITIVE ADVANTAGE   When W. K. Kellogg started manufacturing his cornflake cereal in 1906, his goal was to provide his customers with a high-quality, nutritious product that was enjoyable to eat. That emphasis on quality is still important today. Every employee has a responsibility to maintain the high quality of Kellogg products. If implemented properly, quality can be a way for an organization to create a sustainable competitive advantage.[19] That's why many organizations apply quality management concepts in an attempt to set themselves apart from competitors. If a business is able to continuously improve the quality and reliability of its products, it may have a competitive advantage that can't be taken away.[20]

DESIGN THINKING AS A COMPETITIVE ADVANTAGE   In today's world, consumers can find just about anything they want online. And those consumers also expect a greater variety of choices and faster service when ordering online than ever before. One company that recognized the opportunities—and challenges—of this is Kiva Systems.[21] Kiva makes autonomous robots used in flexible automation systems that are critical to companies' strategic e-commerce efforts. Kiva's CEO says that, "We transform inventory atoms into bits of information and run algorithms on that data and organize it in much the same way that Google sorts web pages." By doing this efficiently, the company's robots can gather goods within minutes of an order and deliver them to warehouse pickworkers who can then ship up to four times more packages in an hour. Kiva (which was recently acquired by Amazon) also has "taught" its robots to move cardboard boxes to the trash compactor and to assist in gift-wrapping.

Here's a company that understands the power of design thinking—defined in Chapter 6 as approaching management problems the way designers approach design problems. Using design thinking means thinking in unusual ways about what the business is and how it's doing what it's in business to do—or as one person said, "solving wicked problems with creative resolutions by thinking outside existing alternatives and creating new alternatives."[22] After all, who would have thought to "teach" robots to help wrap gifts so that e-commerce warehouse fulfillment could be made even more efficient? However, as important as design thinking is to the design of amazing products, it also means recognizing that "design" isn't just for products or processes but for any organizational work problems that can arise. That's why a company's ability to use design thinking in the way its employees and managers strategically manage can be a powerful competitive tool.

SUSTAINING COMPETITIVE ADVANTAGE   Every organization has resources (assets) and capabilities (how work gets done). So what makes some organizations more successful than others? Why do some professional baseball teams consistently win championships or draw large crowds? Why do some organizations have consistent and continuous growth in revenues and profits? Why do some colleges, universities, or departments experience continually increasing enrollments? Why do some companies consistently appear at the top of lists ranking the "best," or the "most admired," or the "most profitable"? The answer is that not every organization is able to effectively exploit its resources and to develop the core competencies that can provide it with a competitive advantage. And it's not enough simply to create a competitive advantage. The organization must be able to sustain that advantage; that is, to keep its edge despite competitors' actions or evolutionary changes in the industry. But that's not easy to do! Market instabilities, new technology, and other changes can challenge managers' attempts at creating a long-term, sustainable competitive advantage. However, by using strategic management, managers can better position their organizations to get a sustainable competitive advantage.

Many important ideas in strategic management have come from the work of Michael Porter.[23] One of his major contributions was explaining how managers can create a sustainable competitive advantage. An important part of doing this is an industry analysis, which is done using the five forces model.

FIVE FORCES MODEL   In any industry, five competitive forces dictate the rules of competition. Together, these five forces determine industry attractiveness and profitability, which managers assess using these five factors:

1. *Threat of new entrants.* How likely is it that new competitors will come into the industry?
2. *Threat of substitutes.* How likely is it that other industries' products can be substituted for our industry's products?
3. *Bargaining power of buyers.* How much bargaining power do buyers (customers) have?
4. *Bargaining power of suppliers.* How much bargaining power do suppliers have?
5. *Current rivalry.* How intense is the rivalry among current industry competitors?

Choosing a Competitive Strategy

Once managers have assessed the five forces and done a SWOT analysis, they're ready to select an appropriate competitive strategy—that is, one that fits the competitive strengths (resources and capabilities) of the organization and the industry it's in. According to Porter, no firm can be successful by trying to be all things to all people. He proposed that managers select a strategy that will give the organization a competitive advantage, either from having lower costs than all other industry competitors or by being significantly different from competitors.

When an organization competes on the basis of having the lowest costs (costs or expenses, not prices) in its industry, it's following a *cost leadership strategy*. A low-cost leader is highly efficient. Overhead is kept to a minimum, and the firm does everything it can to cut costs. You won't find expensive art or interior décor at offices of low-cost leaders. For example, at Walmart's headquarters in Bentonville, Arkansas, office furnishings are functional, not elaborate, maybe not what you'd expect for the world's largest retailer. Although a low-cost leader doesn't place a lot of emphasis

*data*points[25]

21 percent more profitable—what studies have shown about companies that are information-technology-savvy.

25 percent of allegedly high-performing companies are actually remarkable performers.

29 percent of respondents said losing their job was their biggest concern during a corporate merger or acquisition.

46 percent of executives at smaller companies are likely to take a collaborative approach to developing strategy.

29 percent of executives at larger companies are likely to take a collaborative approach to developing strategy.

60 percent of executives believe their employees are not prepared for future company growth.

functional strategy
The strategies used by an organization's various functional departments to support the competitive strategy

on "frills," its product must be perceived as comparable in quality to that offered by rivals or at least be acceptable to buyers.

A company that competes by offering unique products that are widely valued by customers is following a *differentiation strategy*. Product differences might come from exceptionally high quality, extraordinary service, innovative design, technological capability, or an unusually positive brand image. Practically any successful consumer product or service can be identified as an example of the differentiation strategy; for instance, Nordstrom (customer service); 3M Corporation (product quality and innovative design); Coach (design and brand image); and Apple (product design).

Although these two competitive strategies are aimed at the broad market, the final type of competitive strategy—the *focus strategy*—involves a cost advantage (cost focus) or a differentiation advantage (differentiation focus) in a narrow segment or niche. Segments can be based on product variety, customer type, distribution channel, or geographical location. For example, Denmark's Bang & Olufsen, whose revenues exceed $549 million, focuses on high-end audio equipment sales. Whether a focus strategy is feasible depends on the size of the segment and whether the organization can make money serving that segment.

What happens if an organization can't develop a cost or a differentiation advantage? Porter called that being *stuck in the middle* and warned that's not a good place to be. An organization becomes stuck in the middle when its costs are too high to compete with the low-cost leader or when its products and services aren't differentiated enough to compete with the differentiator. Getting unstuck means choosing which competitive advantage to pursue and then doing so by aligning resource, capabilities, and core competencies.

Although Porter said you had to pursue either the low cost or the differentiation advantage to prevent being stuck in the middle, more recent research has shown that organizations *can* successfully pursue both a low cost and a differentiation advantage and achieve high performance.[24] Needless to say, it's not easy to pull off! You have to keep costs low *and* be truly differentiated. But companies such as FedEx, Southwest Airlines, Google, and Coca-Cola have been able to do it.

Before we leave this section, we want to point out the final type of organizational strategy, the **functional strategies**, which are the strategies used by an organization's various functional departments to support the competitive strategy. For example, when R. R. Donnelley & Sons Company, a Chicago-based printer, wanted to become more competitive and invested in high-tech digital printing methods, its marketing department had to develop new sales plans and promotional pieces, the production department had to incorporate the digital equipment in the printing plants, and the human resources department had to update its employee selection and training programs. We don't cover specific functional strategies in this book because you'll cover them in other business courses you take.

9.5 | ***Discuss*** *current strategic management issues.*

CURRENT **Strategic Management Issues**

There's no better example of the strategic challenges faced by managers in today's environment than the recorded music industry. Overall, sales of CDs have plummeted in the last decade and are down about 50 percent from their peak. Not only has this trend impacted the music companies, but it's affected music retailers as well. "Retailers have been forced to adjust, often by devoting some shelf space to other products." For instance, Best Buy, the national electronics retailer, decided to experiment with selling musical instruments. Other major music retailers, such as Walmart, have shifted selling space used for CDs to other departments. "At music specialty stores, however, diversification has become a matter of survival." Managers are struggling to find strategies that will help their organizations succeed in such an environment. Many have had to shift into whole new areas of business.[26] But it isn't just the music industry that's dealing with strategic challenges. Managers everywhere face increasingly intense global competition and high performance expectations by investors and customers. How have they responded to these new realities? In this section, we look at three current strategic management issues, including the need for strategic leadership, the need for strategic flexibility, and how managers design strategies to emphasize e-business, customer service, and innovation.

The Need for Strategic Leadership

"Amazon is so serious about its next big thing that it hired three women to do nothing but try on size 8 shoes for its Web reviews. Full time." Hmmmm...now that sounds like a fun job! What exactly is Amazon's CEO Jeff Bezos thinking? Having conquered the book publishing, electronics, and toy industries (among others), his next target is high-end clothing. And he's doing it in its "typical way: go big and spare no expense."[27]

An organization's strategies are usually developed and overseen by its top managers. An organization's top manager is typically the CEO (chief executive officer). This individual usually works with a top management team that includes other executive or senior managers such as a COO (chief operating officer), CFO (chief financial officer), CIO (chief information officer), and other individuals who may have various titles. Traditional descriptions of the CEO's role in strategic management include being the "chief" strategist, structural architect, and developer of the organization's information/control systems.[28] Other descriptions of the strategic role of the "chief executive" include key decision maker, visionary leader, political actor, monitor and interpreter of environment changes, and strategy designer.[29]

Whole Foods Market uses a differentiation strategy for competing in the retail food industry by offering unique products that are widely valued by customers. The retailer is committed to buying fruits and vegetables from local farmers who are dedicated to sustainable agriculture and appreciated by shoppers like those shown here in the produce department of a market in Pasadena, California. Since its inception, Whole Foods has focused on selling the highest quality natural and organic products that benefit customers' health and on following environment-friendly operating practices. This competitive strategy reflects the company's motto of "Whole Foods—Whole People—Whole Planet."
Source: AP Photo/Damian Dovarganes

let's get REAL

The Scenario:

Caroline Fulmer was just promoted to executive director of a municipal art museum in a medium-sized city in the Midwest. Although she's very excited about her new position and what she hopes to accomplish there, she knows the museum's board is adamant about solidifying the organization's strategic future. Although she knows they feel she's capable of doing so since they hired her for the position, she wants to be an effective strategic leader.

What skills do you think Caroline will need to be an effective strategic leader?

To be a strategic leader, Caroline must be focused and determined to meet the museum's short- and long-term objectives. She must influence and lead her team with an innovative approach, drawn from her prior experiences and applied to the new environment—all the while demonstrating strong communication skills and the ability to embrace change with ease.

Source: Sarah Saracino

Sarah Saracino
Human Resources Manager

Exhibit 9-4
Effective Strategic Leadership

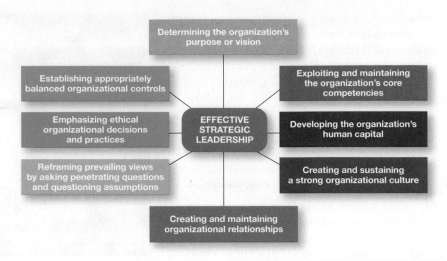

Sources: Based on J. P. Wallman, "Strategic Transactions and Managing the Future: A Druckerian Perspective," *Management Decision,* vol. 48, no. 4, 2010, pp. 485–499; D. E. Zand, "Drucker's Strategic Thinking Process: Three Key Techniques," *Strategy & Leadership,* vol. 38, no. 3, 2010, pp. 23–28; and R. D. Ireland and M. A. Hitt, "Achieving and Maintaining Strategic Competitiveness in the 21st Century: The Role of Strategic Leadership," *Academy of Management Executive,* February 1999, pp. 43–57.

strategic leadership
The ability to anticipate, envision, maintain flexibility, think strategically, and work with others in the organization to initiate changes that will create a viable and valuable future for the organization

No matter how top management's job is described, you can be certain that from their perspective at the organization's upper levels, it's like no other job in the organization. By definition, top managers are ultimately responsible for every decision and action of every organizational employee. One important role that top managers play is that of strategic leader. Organizational researchers study leadership in relation to strategic management because an organization's top managers must provide effective strategic leadership. What is **strategic leadership**? It's the ability to anticipate, envision, maintain flexibility, think strategically, and work with others in the organization to initiate changes that will create a viable and valuable future for the organization.[30] How can top managers provide effective strategic leadership? Eight key dimensions have been identified.[31] (See Exhibit 9-4.) These dimensions include determining the organization's purpose or vision, exploiting and maintaining the organization's core competencies, developing the organization's human capital, creating and sustaining a strong organizational culture, creating and maintaining organizational relationships, reframing prevailing views by asking penetrating questions and questioning assumptions, emphasizing ethical organizational decisions and practices, and establishing appropriately balanced organizational controls. Each dimension encompasses an important part of the strategic management process.

The Need for Strategic Flexibility

Not surprisingly, the economic recession changed the way that many companies approached strategic planning.[32] For instance, at Spartan Motors, a maker of specialty vehicles, managers used to draft a one-year strategic plan and a three-year financial plan, reviewing each one every financial quarter. However, CEO John Sztykiel said, "that relatively inflexible method bears some of the blame for Spartan's sharp drop in sales and gross profit." He also said that the company didn't "respond quickly enough to shifting demand." Now, the company uses a three-year strategic plan that the top management team updates every month. And at J.C. Penney Company, an ambitious five-year strategic growth plan rolled out in 2007 was put on hold as the economy floundered.[33] In its place, the CEO crafted a tentative "bridge" plan to guide the company. This plan worked as the company improved its profit margins and did not have to lay off any employees.

Jürgen Schrempp, former CEO of Daimler AG, stated, "My principle always was...move as fast as you can and [if] you indeed make mistakes, you have to correct

- *Encourage leadership unity* by making sure everyone is on the same page.
- *Keep resources fluid* and move them as circumstances warrant.
- *Have the right mindset* to explore and understand issues and challenges.
- Know what's happening with strategies currently being used by *monitoring and measuring results*.
- Encourage employees to *be open about disclosing and sharing negative information*.
- *Get new ideas and perspectives from outside* the organization.
- Have *multiple alternatives* when making strategic decisions.
- *Learn from mistakes*.

Exhibit 9-5
Developing Strategic Flexibility

Sources: Based on Y. L. Doz and M. Kosonen, "Embedding Strategic Agility: A Leadership Agenda for Accelerating Business Model Renewal," *Long Range Planning*, April 2010, pp. 370–382; E. Lewis, D. Romanaggi, and A. Chapple, "Successfully Managing Change During Uncertain Times," *Strategic HR Review*, vol. 9, no. 2, 2010, pp. 12–18; and K. Shimizu and M. Hitt, "Strategic Flexibility: Organizational Preparedness to Reverse Ineffective Strategic Decisions," *Academy of Management Executive*, November 2004, pp. 44–59.

them.... It's much better to move fast, and make mistakes occasionally, than move too slowly."[34] You wouldn't think that smart individuals who are paid lots of money to manage organizations would make mistakes when it comes to strategic decisions. But even when managers use the strategic management process, there's no guarantee that the chosen strategies will lead to positive outcomes. Reading any of the current business periodicals would certainly support this assertion! But the key is responding quickly when it's obvious the strategy isn't working. In other words, they need **strategic flexibility**—that is, the ability to recognize major external changes, to quickly commit resources, and to recognize when a strategic decision isn't working. Given the highly uncertain environment that managers face today, strategic flexibility seems absolutely necessary! Exhibit 9-5 provides suggestions for developing such strategic flexibility.

strategic flexibility
The ability to recognize major external changes, to quickly commit resources, and to recognize when a strategic decision was a mistake

Important Organizational Strategies for Today's Environment

ESPN.com gets more than 16 million unique users a month. Sixteen million! That's almost twice the population of New York City. And its popular online business is just one of many of ESPN's businesses. Originally founded as a television channel, ESPN is now into original programming, radio, online, publishing, gaming, X games, ESPY awards, ESPN Zones, global, and is looking to move into more local sports coverage.[35] Company president John Skipper "runs one of the most successful and envied franchises in entertainment" and obviously understands how to successfully manage its various strategies in today's environment! We think three strategies are important in today's environment: e-business, customer service, and innovation.

E-BUSINESS STRATEGIES Managers use e-business strategies to develop a sustainable competitive advantage.[36] A cost leader can use e-business to lower costs in a variety of ways. For instance, it might use online bidding and order processing to eliminate the need for sales calls and to decrease sales force expenses; it could use Web-based inventory control systems that reduce storage costs; or it might use online testing and evaluation of job applicants.

A differentiator needs to offer products or services that customers perceive and value as unique. For instance, a business might use Internet-based knowledge systems to shorten customer response times, provide rapid online responses to service requests, or automate purchasing and payment systems so that customers have detailed status reports and purchasing histories.

At a press conference, Marc Benioff, CEO of Salesforce.com, announced the formation of a strategic alliance with Toyota Motors to build "Toyota Friend," a private social network for the automaker's customers. Offered first in Japan with Toyota's electric vehicles and plug-in hybrids, Toyota Friend is a customer communication system that is an important part of the automaker's customer service strategy. Accessible through smart phones, tablet PCs, and other mobile devices, the network gives Toyota customers the ability to connect with their cars, dealership, and Toyota. And it enables Toyota to communicate with customers by giving them product and service data and real-time information such as the battery level of their cars and locations of charging stations.
Source: ZUMA Wire Service/Alamy

Finally, because the focuser targets a narrow market segment with customized products, it might provide chat rooms or discussion boards for customers to interact with others who have common interests, design niche Web sites that target specific groups with specific interests, or use Web sites to perform standardized office functions such as payroll or budgeting.

Research also has shown that an important e-business strategy might be a clicks-and-bricks strategy. A clicks-and-bricks firm is one that uses both online (clicks) and traditional stand-alone locations (bricks).[37] For example, Walgreen's established an online site for ordering prescriptions, but some 90 percent of its customers who placed orders on the Web preferred to pick up their prescriptions at a nearby store rather than have them shipped to their home. So its "clicks-and-bricks" strategy has worked well! Other retailers, such as Best Buy, The Container Store, and Walmart, are transforming their stores into extensions of their online operations by adding Web return centers, pickup locations, free shipping outlets, and payment booths.[38]

CUSTOMER SERVICE STRATEGIES Companies emphasizing excellent customer service need strategies that cultivate that atmosphere from top to bottom. Such strategies involve giving customers what they want, communicating effectively with them, and providing employees with customer service training. Let's look first at the strategy of giving customers what they want.

It shouldn't surprise you that an important customer service strategy is giving customers what they want, which is a major aspect of an organization's overall marketing strategy. For instance, New Balance Athletic Shoes gives customers a truly unique product: shoes in varying widths. No other athletic shoe manufacturer has shoes for narrow or wide feet and in practically any size.[39]

Having an effective customer communication system is an important customer service strategy. Managers should know what's going on with customers. They need to find out what customers liked and didn't like about their purchase encounter—from their interactions with employees to their experience with the actual product or service. It's also important to let customers know if something is going on with the company that might affect future purchase decisions. Finally, an organization's culture is important to providing excellent customer service. This typically requires that employees be trained to provide exceptional customer service. For example, Singapore Airlines is well-known for its customer treatment. "On everything facing the customer, they do not scrimp," says an analyst based in Singapore.[40] Employees are expected to "get service right," leaving employees with no doubt about the expectations as far as how to treat customers.

INNOVATION STRATEGIES When Procter & Gamble purchased the Iams pet food business, it did what it always does—used its renowned research division to look for ways to transfer technology from its other divisions to make new products.[41] One outcome of this cross-divisional combination: a new tartar-fighting ingredient from toothpaste that's included in all of its dry adult pet foods.

As this example shows, innovation strategies aren't necessarily focused on just the radical, breakthrough products. They can include applying existing technology to new uses. And organizations have successfully used both approaches. What types of innovation strategies do organizations need in today's environment? Those strategies should reflect their innovation philosophy, which is shaped by two strategic decisions: innovation emphasis and innovation timing.

Managers must first decide where the emphasis of their innovation efforts will be. Is the organization going to focus on basic scientific research, product development, or process improvement? Basic scientific research requires the most resource commitment because it involves the nuts-and-bolts work of scientific research. In numerous industries (for instance, genetics engineering, pharmaceuticals, information technology, or cosmetics), an organization's expertise in basic research is the key to a sustainable competitive advantage. However, not every organization requires this extensive commitment to scientific research to achieve high performance levels. Instead, many depend on product development strategies. Although this strategy also requires a significant resource investment, it's not in areas associated with scientific research. Instead, the organization takes existing technology and improves on it or applies it in new ways, just as Procter & Gamble did when it applied tartar-fighting knowledge to pet food products. Both of these first two strategic approaches to innovation (basic scientific research and product development) can help an organization achieve high levels of differentiation, which can be a significant source of competitive advantage.

Finally, the last strategic approach to innovation emphasis is a focus on process development. Using this strategy, an organization looks for ways to improve and enhance its work processes. The organization innovates new and improved ways for employees to do their work in all organizational areas. This innovation strategy can lead to lower costs, which, as we know, also can be a significant source of competitive advantage.

Once managers have determined the focus of their innovation efforts, they must decide their innovation timing strategy. Some organizations want to be the first with innovations whereas others are content to follow or mimic the innovations. An organization that's first to bring a product innovation to the market or to use a new process innovation is called a **first mover**. Being a first mover has certain strategic advantages and disadvantages as shown in Exhibit 9-6. Some organizations pursue this route, hoping to develop a sustainable competitive advantage. Others have successfully developed a sustainable competitive advantage by being the followers in the industry. They let the first movers pioneer the innovations and then mimic their products or processes. Which approach managers choose depends on their organization's innovation philosophy and specific resources and capabilities.

first mover
An organization that's first to bring a product innovation to the market or to use a new process innovation

Advantages	Disadvantages
• Reputation for being innovative and industry leader	• Uncertainty over exact direction technology and market will go
• Cost and learning benefits	• Risk of competitors imitating innovations
• Control over scarce resources and keeping competitors from having access to them	• Financial and strategic risks
• Opportunity to begin building customer relationships and customer loyalty	• High development costs

Exhibit 9-6
First-Mover Advantages and Disadvantages

CHAPTER

PREPARING FOR: Exams/Quizzes
CHAPTER SUMMARY by Learning Outcomes

9.1 [LEARNING OUTCOME]

Define strategic management and explain why it's important.

Strategic management is what managers do to develop the organization's strategies. Strategies are the plans for how the organization will do whatever it's in business to do, how it will compete successfully, and how it will attract and satisfy its customers in order to achieve its goals. A business model is how a company is going to make money. Strategic management is important for three reasons. First, it makes a difference in how well organizations perform. Second, it's important for helping managers cope with continually changing situations. Finally, strategic management helps coordinate and focus employee efforts on what's important.

9.2 [LEARNING OUTCOME]

Explain what managers do during the six steps of the strategic management process.

The six steps in the strategic management process encompass strategy planning, implementation, and evaluation. These steps include the following: (1) identify the current mission, goals, and strategies; (2) do an external analysis; (3) do an internal analysis (steps 2 and 3 collectively are known as SWOT analysis); (4) formulate strategies; (5) implement strategies; and (6) evaluate strategies. Strengths are any activities the organization does well or its unique resources. Weaknesses are activities the organization doesn't do well or resources it needs. Opportunities are positive trends in the external environment. Threats are negative trends.

9.3 [LEARNING OUTCOME]

Describe the three types of corporate strategies.

A growth strategy is when an organization expands the number of markets served or products offered, either through current or new businesses. The types of growth strategies include concentration, vertical integration (backward and forward), horizontal integration, and diversification (related and unrelated). A stability strategy is when an organization makes no significant changes in what it's doing. Both renewal strategies—retrenchment and turnaround—address organizational weaknesses leading to performance declines. The BCG matrix is a way to analyze a company's portfolio of businesses by looking at a business's market share and its industry's anticipated growth rate. The four categories of the BCG matrix are cash cows, stars, question marks, and dogs.

9.4 [LEARNING OUTCOME]

Describe competitive advantage and the competitive strategies organizations use to get it.

An organization's competitive advantage is what sets it apart, its distinctive edge. A company's competitive advantage becomes the basis for choosing an appropriate competitive strategy. Porter's five forces model assesses the five competitive forces that dictate the rules of competition in an industry: threat of new entrants, threat of substitutes, bargaining power of buyers, bargaining power of suppliers, and current rivalry. Porter's three competitive strategies are as follows: cost leadership (competing on the basis of having the lowest costs in the industry), differentiation (competing on the basis of having unique products that are widely valued by customers), and focus (competing in a narrow segment with either a cost advantage or a differentiation advantage).

9.5 | LEARNING OUTCOME

Discuss current strategic management issues.

Managers face three current strategic management issues: strategic leadership, strategic flexibility, and important types of strategies for today's environment. Strategic leadership is the ability to anticipate, envision, maintain flexibility, think strategically, and work with others in the organization to initiate changes that will create a viable and valuable future for the organization and includes eight key dimensions. Strategic flexibility—that is, the ability to recognize major external environmental changes, to quickly commit resources, and to recognize when a strategic decision isn't working—is important because managers often face highly uncertain environments. Managers can use e-business strategies to reduce costs, to differentiate their firm's products and services, to target (focus on) specific customer groups, or to lower costs by standardizing certain office functions. Another important e-business strategy is the clicks-and-bricks strategy, which combines online and traditional, stand-alone locations. Strategies managers can use to become more customer oriented include giving customers what they want, communicating effectively with them, and having a culture that emphasizes customer service. Strategies managers can use to become more innovative include deciding their organization's innovation emphasis (basic scientific research, product development, or process development) and its innovation timing (first mover or follower).

REVIEW AND DISCUSSION QUESTIONS ✪

1. Describe the six steps in the strategic management process.

2. How could the Internet be helpful to managers as they follow the steps in the strategic management process?

3. How might the process of strategy formulation, implementation, and evaluation differ for (a) large businesses, (b) small businesses, (c) not-for-profit organizations, and (d) global businesses?

4. Should ethical considerations be included in analyses of an organization's internal and external environments? Why or why not?

5. Describe the three major types of corporate strategies and how the BCG matrix is used to manage those corporate strategies.

6. Describe the role of competitive advantage and how Porter's competitive strategies help an organization develop competitive advantage.

7. "The concept of competitive advantage is as important for not-for-profit organizations as it is for for-profit organizations." Do you agree or disagree with this statement? Explain, using examples to make your case.

8. Describe e-business, customer service, and innovation strategies.

PREPARING FOR: My Career
ETHICS DILEMMA ✪

Many "social technology companies are presenting an antisocial attitude to callers."[42] If you try to call someone at or get a phone number for LinkedIn, Facebook, Twitter, or Quora (and probably others), well, you're out of luck! Google is one of a few companies that actually publishes phone numbers on its Web site. Yet, its phone system sends callers back to the Web 11 times. At Facebook, a caller who goes through a long phone tree trying to reach a real person is told that "Facebook is, in fact, an Internet-based company" and suggests trying e-mail.

Twitter's phone system hangs up after providing Web or e-mail addresses three times. Although voice calls aren't necessarily important to teenagers or twenty-somethings, has this strategy become a matter of policy for technology companies? Yes, phones cost money as do people to answer those phones. What do you think? What ethical dilemmas are involved with this strategic decision? What factors would influence the decision? (Think in terms of the various stakeholders who might be affected by this decision.)

SKILLS EXERCISE Developing Your Business Planning Skill

About the Skill

An important step in starting a business or in determining a new strategic direction is preparing a business plan.[43] Not only does the business plan aid in thinking about what to do and how to do it, but it can be a sound basis from which to obtain funding and resources.

Steps in Practicing the Skill

1. *Describe your company's background and purpose.* Provide the history of the company. Briefly describe the company's history and what this company does that's unique. Describe what your product or service will be, how you intend to market it, and what you need to bring your product or service to the market.

2. *Identify your short- and long-term goals.* What is your intended goal for this organization? Clearly, for a new company three broad objectives are relevant: creation, survival, and profitability. Specific objectives can include such things as sales, market share, product quality, employee morale, and social responsibility. Identify how you plan to achieve each objective, how you intend to determine whether you met the objective, and when you intend the objective to be met (e.g., short or long term).

3. *Do a thorough market analysis.* You need to convince readers that you understand what you are doing, what your market is, and what competitive pressures you'll face. In this analysis, you'll need to describe the overall market trends, the specific market you intend to compete in, and who the competitors are. In essence, in this section you'll perform your SWOT analysis.

4. *Describe your development and production emphasis.* Explain how you're going to produce your product or service. Include time frames from start to finish. Describe the difficulties you may encounter in this stage as well as how much you believe activities in this stage will cost. Provide an explanation of what decisions (e.g., make or buy?) you will face and what you intend to do.

5. *Describe how you'll market your product or service.* What is your selling strategy? How do you intend to reach your customers? In this section, describe your product or service in terms of your competitive advantage and demonstrate how you'll exploit your competitors' weaknesses. In addition to the market analysis, provide sales forecasts in terms of the size of the market, how much of the market you can realistically capture, and how you'll price your productor service.

6. *Put together your financial statements.* What's your bottom line? Investors want to know this information. In the financial section, provide projected profit-and-loss statements (income statements) for approximately three to five years, a cash flow analysis, and the company's projected balance sheets. In the financial section, give thought to how much start-up costs will be as well as develop a financial strategy—how you intend to use funds received from a financial institution and how you'll control and monitor the financial well-being of the company.

7. *Provide an overview of the organization and its management.* Identify the key executives, summarizing their education, experience, and any relevant qualifications. Identify their positions in the organization and their job roles. Explain how much salary they intend to earn initially. Identify others who may assist the organization's management (e.g., company lawyer, accountant, board of directors). This section should also include, if relevant, a subsection on how you intend to deal with employees. For example, how will employees be paid, what benefits will be offered, and how will employee performance be assessed?

8. *Describe the legal form of the business.* Identify the legal form of the business. For example, is it a sole proprietor, a partnership, a corporation? Depending on the legal form, you may need to provide information regarding equity positions, shares of stock issued, and the like.

9. *Identify the critical risks and contingencies facing the organization.* In this section, identify what you'll do if problems arise. For instance, if you don't meet sales forecasts, what then? Similar responses to such questions as problems with suppliers, inability to hire qualified employees, poor-quality products, and so on should be addressed. Readers want to see if you've anticipated potential problems and if you have contingency plans. This is the "what if" section.

10. *Put the business plan together.* Using the information you've gathered from the previous nine steps, it's now time to put the business plan together into a well-organized document. A business plan should contain a cover page that shows the company name, address, contact person, and numbers at which the individual can be reached. The cover page should also contain the date the business was established and, if one exists, the company logo. The next page of the business plan should be a table of contents. Here you'll want to list and identify the location of each major section and subsection in the business plan. Remember to use proper outlining techniques. Next comes the executive summary, the first section the readers will actually read. Thus, it's one of the more critical elements of the business plan, because if the executive summary is poorly done, readers may not read any further. In a two- to three-page summary, highlight information about the company, its management, its

market and competition, the funds requested, how the funds will be used, financial history (if available), financial projections, and when investors can expect to get their money back (called the exit). Next come the main sections of your business plan; that is, the material you've researched and written about in steps 1 through 9. Close out the business plan with a section that summarizes the highlights of what you've just presented. Finally, if you have charts, exhibits, photographs, tables, and the like, you might want to include an appendix in the back of the business plan. If you do, remember to cross-reference this material to the relevant section of the report.

Practicing the Skill

You have a great idea for a business and need to create a business plan to present to a bank. Choose one of the following products or services and draft the part of your plan that describes how you will price and market it (see step 5).

1. Haircuts at home (you make house calls)
2. Olympic snowboarding computer game
3. Online apartment rental listing
4. Voice-activated house alarm

Now choose a different product or service from the list and identify critical risks and contingencies (see step 9).

WORKING TOGETHER Team Exercise

Organizational mission statements. Are they a promise, a commitment, or just a bunch of hot air? Form small groups of three to four individuals and find examples of three different organizational mission statements. Your first task is to evaluate the mission statements. How do they compare to the items listed in Exhibit 9-2? Would you describe each

as an effective mission statement? Why or why not? How might you rewrite each mission statement to make it better? Your second task is to use the mission statements to describe the types of corporate and competitive strategies each organization might use to fulfill that mission statement. Explain your rationale for choosing each strategy.

MY TURN TO BE A MANAGER

- Do a personal SWOT analysis. Assess your personal strengths and weaknesses (skills, talents, abilities). What are you good at? What are you not so good at? What do you enjoy doing? What don't you enjoy doing? Then, identify career opportunities and threats by researching job prospects in the industry you're interested in. Look at trends and projections. You might want to check out the Bureau of Labor Statistics information on job prospects. Once you have all this information, write a specific career action plan. Outline five-year career goals and what you need to do to achieve those goals.

- Using current business periodicals, find two examples of each of the corporate and competitive strategies. Write a description of what these businesses are doing and how it represents that particular strategy.

- Pick five companies from the latest version of *Fortune*'s "Most Admired Companies" list. Research these companies and identify their (a) mission statement, (b) strategic goals, and (c) strategies used.

- Steve's and Mary's suggested readings: Adrian Slywotzky and Richard Wise, *How to Grow When Markets Don't* (Warner Business Books, 2003); Jim Collins, *Good to Great: Why Some Companies Make the Leap…and Others Don't* (Harper Business, 2001); Michael E. Porter, *On Competition* (Harvard Business School Press, 1998);

James C. Collins and Jerry I. Porras, *Built to Last: Successful Habits of Visionary Companies* (Harper Business, 1994); and Gary Hamel and C. K. Prahalad, *Competing for the Future* (Harvard Business School Press, 1994).

- Customer service, e-business, and innovation strategies are particularly important to managers today. We described specific ways companies can pursue these strategies. Your task is to pick customer service, e-business, or innovation and find one example for each of the specific approaches in that category. For instance, if you choose customer service, find an example of (a) giving customers what they want, (b) communicating effectively with them, and (c) providing employees with customer service training. Write a report describing your examples.

- In your own words, write down three things you learned in this chapter about being a good manager.

- Self-knowledge can be a powerful learning tool. Go to mymanagementlab.com and complete these self-assessment exercises: How Well Do I Handle Ambiguity? How Creative Am I? How Well Do I Respond to Turbulent Change? Using the results of your assessments, identify personal strengths and weaknesses. What will you do to reinforce your strengths and improve your weaknesses?

MyManagementLab

Go to **mymanagementlab.com** for Auto-graded writing questions as well as the following Assisted-graded writing questions:

9-1. Explain why strategic management is important.

9-2. Explain why strategic leadership and strategic flexibility are important.

9-3. Mymanagementlab Only – comprehensive writing assignment for this chapter.

CASE APPLICATION 1 Fast Fashion

When Amancio Ortega, a former Spanish bath-robe maker, opened his first Zara clothing store, his business model was simple: sell high-fashion look-alikes to price-conscious Europeans.[44] After succeeding in this, he decided to tackle the outdated clothing industry in which it took six months from a garment's design to consumers being able to purchase it in a store. What Ortega envisioned was "fast fashion"—getting designs to customers quickly. And that's exactly what Zara has done!

The company has been described as having more style than Gap, faster growth than Target, and logistical expertise rivaling Walmart's. Zara, owned by the Spanish fashion retail group Inditex SA, recognizes that success in the fashion world is based on a simple rule—get products to market quickly. Accomplishing this, however, isn't so simple. It involves a clear and focused understanding of fashion, technology, and their market, *and* the ability to adapt quickly to trends.

The success of Spanish fashion retail group Inditex SA is based on its competitive strategy of getting clothing designs to customers at its Zara stores quickly. Company reps from Spain, northern Europe, and Japan shown here sorting clothing samples at the Inditex plant are part of the fast and flexible process that takes about two weeks from drawing board to store floor.
Source: © Larry Mangino/The Image Works

Inditex, the world's largest fashion retailer by sales worldwide, has seven chains: Zara (including Zara Kids and Zara Home), Pull and Bear, Massimo Dutti, Stradivarius, Bershka, Oysho, and Uterqüe. The company has more than 5,618 stores in 84 countries, although Zara pulls in more than 60 percent of the company's revenues. Despite its global presence, Zara is not yet a household name in the United States, with just over 50 stores open, including a flagship store in New York City.

What is Zara's secret to excelling at fast fashion? It takes approximately two weeks to get a new design from drawing board to store floor. And stores are stocked with new designs twice a week as clothes are shipped directly to the stores from the factory. Thus, each aspect of Zara's business contributes to the fast turnaround. Sales managers at "the Cube"—what employees call their futuristic-looking headquarters—sit at a long row of computers and scrutinize sales at every store. They see the hits and the misses almost instantaneously. They ask the in-house designers, who work in teams, sketching out new styles and deciding which fabrics will provide the best combination of style and price, for new designs. Once a design is drawn, it's sent electronically to Zara's factory across the street, where a clothing sample is made. To minimize waste, computer programs arrange and rearrange clothing patterns on the massive fabric rolls before a laser-guided machine does the cutting. Zara produces most of its designs close to home—in Morocco, Portugal, Spain, and Turkey. Finished garments are returned to the factory within a week. Finishing touches (buttons, trim, detailing, etc.) are added, and each garment goes through a quality check. Garments that don't pass are discarded while those that do pass are individually pressed. Then, garment labels (indicating to which country garments will be shipped) and security tags are added. The bundled garments proceed along a moving carousel of hanging rails via a maze of tunnels to the warehouse, a four-story, 5-million-square-foot building (about the size of 90 football fields). As the merchandise bundles move along the rails, electronic bar code tags are read by equipment that send them to the right "staging area," where specific merchandise is first sorted by country and then by individual store, ensuring that each store gets exactly the shipment it's supposed to. From there, merchandise for European stores is sent to a loading dock and packed on a truck with other shipments in order of delivery. Deliveries to other locations go by plane. Some 60,000 items each hour—more than 2.6 million items a week—move through this ultrasophisticated distribution center. And this takes place with only a handful of workers who monitor the entire process. The company's just-in-time production (an idea borrowed from the auto industry) gives it a competitive edge in terms of speed and flexibility.

Despite Zara's success at fast fashion, its competitors are working to be faster. But CEO Pablo Isla isn't standing still. To maintain Zara's leading advantage, he's introducing new methods that enable store managers to order and display merchandise faster and is adding new cargo routes for shipping goods. And the company has finally made the jump into online retailing. One analyst forecasts that the company could quadruple sales in the United States by 2014, with a majority of that coming from online sales.

DISCUSSION QUESTIONS ✪

1. How is strategic management illustrated by this case story?
2. How might SWOT analysis be helpful to Inditex executives? To Zara store managers?
3. What competitive advantage do you think Zara is pursuing? How does it exploit that competitive advantage?
4. Do you think Zara's success is due to external or internal factors or both? Explain.
5. What strategic implications does Zara's move into online retailing have? (Hint: Think in terms of resources and capabilities.)

CASE APPLICATION 2 Rewind and Replay

Following the success of his online DVD movie subscription service, Netflix founder and CEO Reed Hastings is countering the intense competition in the in-home film entertainment industry by focusing the company's competitive strengths on a streaming media service. In this photo Hastings speaks during the launch of streaming internet subscription service for movies and TV shows in Canada, marking the first availability of the Netflix service outside of the United States.
Source: Reuters/Mike Cassese

There's no doubt that people like to watch movies, but *how* they watch those movies has changed.[45] Although many people still prefer going to an actual movie theater, more and more are settling back in their easy chairs in front of home entertainment systems, especially now that technology has improved to the point where those systems are affordable and offer many of the same features as those found in movie theaters. Along with the changes in *where* people watch movies, *how* people get those movies has changed. For many, the weekend used to start with a trip to the video rental store to search the racks for something good to watch, an approach Blockbuster built its business on. Today's consumers can choose a movie by going to their computer and visiting an online DVD subscription and delivery site where the movies come to the customers—a model invented by Netflix.

Launched in 1999, Netflix's subscriber base grew rapidly. It now has more than 23.4 million subscribers and more than 100,000 movie titles from which to choose. "The company's appeal and success are built on providing the most expansive selection of DVDs, an easy way to choose movies, and fast, free delivery." A company milestone was reached in late February 2007, when Netflix delivered its one billionth DVD, a goal that took about seven-and-a-half years to accomplish— "about seven months less than it took McDonald's Corporation to sell one billion hamburgers after opening its first restaurant."

Netflix founder and CEO Reed Hastings believed in the approach he pioneered and set some ambitious goals for his company: build the world's best Internet movie service and grow earnings per share (EPS) and subscribers every year. In 2011, though, Hastings made a decision that had customers complaining loudly. Netflix's troubles began when it announced it would charge separate prices for its DVDs-by-mail and streaming video plans. Then, it decided to rebrand its DVD service as Qwikster. Customers raged so much that Netflix reversed that decision and pulled the plug on the entire Qwikster plan. As Netflix regained its focus with customers, it was once again ready to refocus on its competitors.

Success ultimately attracts competition. Other businesses want a piece of the market. Trying to gain an edge in how customers get the movies they want, when and where they want them, has led to an all-out competitive war. Now, what Netflix did to Blockbuster, Blockbuster and other competitors are doing to Netflix. Hastings said he has learned never to underestimate the competition. He says, "We erroneously concluded that Blockbuster probably wasn't going to launch a competitive effort when they hadn't by 2003. Then, in 2004, they did. We thought...well they won't put much money behind it. Over the past four years, they've invested more than $500 million against us." Not wanting to suffer the same fate as Blockbuster (it filed for bankruptcy protection in 2010 and was sold to Satellite TV service provider DISH Network in 2011), Netflix is bracing for other onslaughts. In fact, CEO Hastings defending his misguided decisions in 2011 said, "We did so many difficult things this year that we got overconfident. Our big obsession for the year was streaming, the idea that 'let's not die with DVDs.'"

The in-home filmed entertainment industry is intensely competitive and continually changing. Many customers have multiple providers (e.g., HBO, renting a DVD from Red Box, buying a DVD, streaming a movie from providers such as Hulu, Apple, and Amazon) and may use any or all of those services in the same month. Video-on-demand and streaming are becoming extremely competitive.

To counter such competitive challenges, Hastings is focusing the company's competitive strengths on a select number of initiatives. He says, "Streaming is the future; we're focused on it. DVD is going to do whatever it's going to do. We don't want to hurt it, but we're not putting much time or energy into it." Others include continually developing profitable partnerships with content providers, controlling the cost of streaming content, and even licensing it on original series. In fact, it just licensed its first original series called "House of Cards" and starring Kevin Spacey. With other companies hoping to get established in the market, the competition is intense. Does Netflix have the script it needs to be a dominant player? CEO Hastings says, "If it's true that you should be judged by the quality of your competitors, we must be doing pretty well."

DISCUSSION QUESTIONS ✪

1. Using Porter's framework, describe Netflix's competitive strategy. Explain your choice.

2. What competitive advantage(s) do you think Netflix has? Have its resources, capabilities, or core competencies contributed to its competitive advantage(s)? Explain.

3. How will Netflix's functional strategies have to support its competitive strategy? Explain.

4. What do you think Netflix is going to have to do to maintain its competitive position, especially as its industry changes?

CHAPTER 10 — Managerial Controls

SPOTLIGHT: *Manager at Work*

"Prisons are easier to enter than Visa's top-secret Operations Center East (OCE), its biggest, newest and most advanced U.S. data center."[1] And Rick Knight, Visa's head of global operations and engineering, is responsible for its security and functioning. Why all the precautions? Because Visa acknowledges that (1) hackers are increasingly savvy, (2) data is an increasingly desirable black-market commodity, and (3) the best way to keep itself safe is with an information network in a fortress that instantly responds to threats.

Every day, Visa processes some 150 million retail electronic payments from around the globe. (Its current record for processing transactions? 300.7 million on December 23, 2011.) And every day, Visa's system connects up to 2 billion debit and credit cards, millions of acceptance locations, 1.9 million ATMs, and 15,000 financial institutions. So what seems to us a simple swipe of a card or keying in our card numbers on an online transaction actually triggers a robust set of activities, including the basic sales transaction processing, risk management, and information-based services. That's why OCE's 130 workers have two jobs: "Keep hackers out and keep the network up, no matter what." And that's why Visa doesn't reveal the location of OCE—on the eastern seaboard is as specific as the description gets.

Beneath the road leading to the OCE, hydraulic posts can rise up fast enough to stop a car going 50 miles per hour. And a car won't be able to go that fast or it will miss a "vicious hairpin turn" and drive off into a drainage pond. Back in medieval days, that would have been known as the castle moat, which was also designed as protection. There are also hundreds of security cameras and a superb security team of former military personnel. If you're lucky enough to be invited as a guest to OCE

Source: © Realimage/Alamy

Source: Reuters/Chip East

(which few people are), you'll have your photo taken and right index fingerprint encoded on a badge. Then you're locked into a "mantrap portal" where you put your badge on a reader that makes sure you are you, and then put it on another reader with

"Prisons are easier to enter than Visa's top-secret Operations Center East (OCE), its biggest, newest and most advanced U.S. data center."

your finger on a fingerprint detector. If you make it through, you're clear to enter the network operations center. With a wall of screens in front of them, each employee sits at a desk with four monitors. In a room behind the main center, three security üexperts keep an eye on things. "Knight says about 60 incidents a day warrant attention."

Although hackers are a primary concern, Knight also worries about network capacity. Right now, maximum capacity is currently at 24,000 transactions per second. "At some point, over that 24,000-message limit, 'the network doesn't stop processing one message. It stops processing all of them,'" Knight says. So far, on its busiest day, OCE hit 11,613

MyManagementLab®
⭐ Improve Your Grade!
Over 10 million students improved their results using the Pearson MyLabs.
Visit **mymanagementlab.com** for simulations, tutorials, and end-of-chapter problems.

LEARNING OUTCOMES

10.1 | *Explain* the nature and importance of control.

10.2 | *Describe* the three steps in the control process.

10.3 | *Explain* how organizational and employee performance are measured.

10.4 | *Describe* tools used to measure organizational performance.

10.5 | *Discuss* contemporary issues in control.

messages processed. OCE is described as a "Tier-4" center, which is a certification from a data center organization. To achieve that certification, every (and yes, we mean every) mainframe, air conditioner, and battery has a back-up. **Why is this level of managerial controls necessary? What other managerial controls might be useful to Rick Knight?**

Although the controlled environment at Visa's OCE might seem extreme, it does illustrate how important controls are to managers. Company executives have created a system that works for them. And that's what all managers are looking for. Appropriate controls that can help pinpoint specific or critical performance gaps and areas for improvement.

10.1 | **Explain** *the nature and importance of control.*

WHAT Is Controlling and Why Is It Important?

A press operator at the Denver Mint noticed a flaw—an extra up leaf or an extra down leaf—on Wisconsin state quarters being pressed at one of his five press machines. He stopped the machine and left for a meal break. When he returned, he saw the machine running and assumed that someone had changed the die in the machine. However, after a routine inspection, the machine operator realized the die had not been changed. The faulty press had likely been running for over an hour and thousands of the flawed coins were now commingled with unblemished quarters. As many as 50,000 of the faulty coins entered circulation, setting off a coin collector buying frenzy.[2] Can you see why controlling is such an important managerial function?

controlling
The process of monitoring, comparing, and correcting work performance

What is **controlling**? It's the process of monitoring, comparing, and correcting work performance. All managers should control even if their units are performing as planned because they can't really know that unless they've evaluated what activities have been done and compared actual performance against the desired standard.[3] Effective controls ensure that activities are completed in ways that lead to the attainment of goals. Whether controls are effective, then, is determined by how well they help employees and managers achieve their goals.[4]

In David Lee Roth's autobiography (yes, *that* David Lee Roth, the former front man for Van Halen), he tells the story of how he had a clause (article 126) in his touring contract asking for a bowl of M&Ms backstage, but no brown ones.[5] Now, you might think that it is just typical demanding rock star behavior, but instead it was a well-planned effort by Roth to see whether the venue management had paid attention. With the technical complexity of his show, he figured if they couldn't get the M&Ms right, he needed to demand a line check of the entire production to ensure that no technical errors would occur during a performance. Now that's what control should do!

Why is control so important? Planning can be done, an organizational structure created to facilitate efficient achievement of goals, and employees motivated through effective leadership. But there's no assurance that activities are going as planned and that the goals employees and managers are working toward are, in fact, being attained. Control is important, therefore, because it's the only way that managers know whether organizational goals are being met and if not, the reasons why. The value of the control function can be seen in three specific areas: planning, empowering employees, and protecting the workplace.

In Chapter 8, we described goals, which provide specific direction to employees and managers, as the foundation of planning. However, just stating goals or having employees accept goals doesn't guarantee that the necessary actions to accomplish those goals have been taken. As the old saying goes, "The best-laid plans often go awry." The effective manager follows up to ensure that what employees are supposed

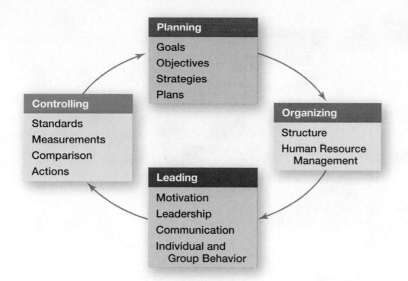

Exhibit 10-1
Planning-Controlling Link

to do is, in fact, being done and goals are being achieved. Controlling provides a critical link back to planning. (See Exhibit 10-1.) If managers didn't control, they'd have no way of knowing whether their goals and plans were being achieved and what future actions to take.

The second reason controlling is important is because of employee empowerment. Many managers are reluctant to empower their employees because they fear something will go wrong for which they would be held responsible. But an effective control system can provide information and feedback on employee performance and minimize the chance of potential problems.

The final reason why managers control is to protect the organization and its assets.[6] Today's environment brings heightened threats from natural disasters, financial scandals, workplace violence, global supply chain disruptions, security breaches, and even possible terrorist attacks. Managers must protect organizational assets in the event that any of these things should happen. Comprehensive controls and back-up plans will help assure minimal work disruptions.

THE CONTROL Process

Describe the three **10.2**
steps in the control
process.

- Security lapses, including unlocked doors and faulty airflow, have been found at the Centers for Disease Control bioterror lab in Atlanta.
- During December 2011, Best Buy had a massive breakdown in fulfilling many online orders in time for Christmas.
- An Apple employee lost a prototype for a new but unreleased iPhone at a northern California bar.
- A rogue trader at London's UBS Bank lost $2 billion in fraudulent trading.
- At Dropbox, a cloud storage site used by some 25 million customers, all of its customers' data (including sensitive documents) were left unprotected and exposed.[7]

In all these situations, company managers relied on the control process to address the issues leading to and resolving the problems.

The **control process** is a three-step process of measuring actual performance, comparing actual performance against a standard, and taking managerial action to correct deviations or to address inadequate standards. (See Exhibit 10-2.) The control process assumes that performance standards already exist, and they do. They're the specific goals created during the planning process.

control process
A three-step process of measuring actual performance, comparing actual performance against a standard, and taking managerial action to correct deviations or inadequate standards

Exhibit 10-2
The Control Process

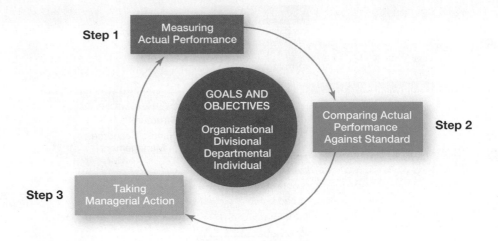

Step 1: Measuring Actual Performance

To determine what actual performance is, a manager must first get information about it. Thus, the first step in control is measuring.

HOW WE MEASURE Four approaches used by managers to measure and report actual performance are personal observations, statistical reports, oral reports, and written reports. Exhibit 10-3 summarizes the advantages and drawbacks of each approach. Most managers use a combination of these approaches.

WHAT WE MEASURE At Office Depot, customer service was measured by metrics—such as the cleanliness of bathrooms—that didn't drive sales. The company's president is trying to address this by identifying what measures are most important and then retraining the staff on achieving those measures.[8] Yes, what is measured is probably more critical to the control process than how it's measured. Why? Because selecting the wrong criteria can create serious problems. Besides, *what* is measured often determines what employees will do.[9] What control criteria might managers use?

Exhibit 10-3
Sources of Information for Measuring Performance

	Benefits	Drawbacks
Personal Observations	• Get firsthand knowledge • Information isn't filtered • Intensive coverage of work activities	• Subject to personal biases • Time-consuming • Obtrusive
Statistical Reports	• Easy to visualize • Effective for showing relationships	• Provide limited information • Ignore subjective factors
Oral Reports	• Fast way to get information • Allow for verbal and nonverbal feedback	• Information is filtered • Information can't be documented
Written Reports	• Comprehensive • Formal • Easy to file and retrieve	• Take more time to prepare

Some control criteria can be used for any management situation. For instance, all managers deal with people, so criteria such as employee satisfaction or turnover and absenteeism rates can be measured. Keeping costs within budget is also a fairly common control measure. Other control criteria should recognize the different activities that managers supervise. For instance, a manager at a pizza delivery location might use measures such as number of pizzas delivered per day, average delivery time, or number of coupons redeemed. A manager in a governmental agency might use applications typed per day, client requests completed per hour, or average time to process paperwork.

Most work activities can be expressed in quantifiable terms. However, managers should use subjective measures when they can't. Although such measures may have limitations, they're better than having no standards at all and doing no controlling.

Step 2: Comparing Actual Performance Against the Standard

The comparing step determines the variation between actual performance and the standard. Although some variation in performance can be expected in all activities, it's critical to determine an acceptable **range of variation** (see Exhibit 10-4). Deviations outside this range need attention. Let's work through an example.

Chris Tanner is a sales manager for Green Earth Gardening Supply, a distributor of specialty plants and seeds in the Pacific Northwest. Chris prepares a report during the first week of each month that describes sales for the previous month, classified by product line. Exhibit 10-5 displays both the sales goals (standard) and actual sales figures for the month of June. After looking at the numbers, should Chris be concerned? Sales were a bit higher than originally targeted, but does that mean there were no significant deviations? That depends on what Chris thinks is *significant*; that is, outside the acceptable range of variation. Even though overall performance was generally quite favorable, some product lines need closer scrutiny. For instance, if sales of heirloom seeds, flowering bulbs, and annual flowers continue to be over what was expected, Chris might need to order more product from nurseries to meet customer demand. Because sales of vegetable plants were 15 percent below goal, Chris may need to run a special on them. As this example shows, both overvariance and undervariance may require managerial attention, which is the third step in the control process.

range of variation
The acceptable parameters of variance between actual performance and the standard

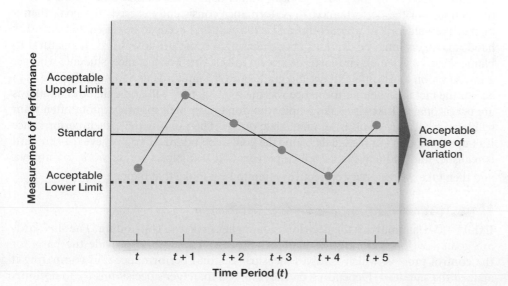

Exhibit 10-4
Acceptable Range of Variation

Exhibit 10-5

Green Earth Gardening Supply—
June Sales

Product	Standard	Actual	Over (Under)
Vegetable plants	1,075	913	(162)
Perennial flowers	630	634	4
Annual flowers	800	912	112
Herbs	160	140	(20)
Flowering bulbs	170	286	116
Flowering bushes	225	220	(5)
Heirloom seeds	540	672	132
Total	3,600	3,777	177

Step 3: Taking Managerial Action

Managers can choose among three possible courses of action: do nothing, correct the actual performance, or revise the standards. Because "do nothing" is self-explanatory, let's look at the other two.

CORRECT ACTUAL PERFORMANCE Sports coaches understand the importance of correcting actual performance. During a game, they'll often correct a player's actions. But if the problem is recurring or encompasses more than one player, they'll devote time during practice before the next game to correcting the actions.[10] That's what managers need to do as well.

Depending on what the problem is, a manager could take different corrective actions. For instance, if unsatisfactory work is the reason for performance variations, the manager could correct it by things such as training programs, disciplinary action, changes in compensation practices, and so forth. One decision a manager must make is whether to take **immediate corrective action**, which corrects problems at once to get performance back on track, or to use **basic corrective action**, which looks at how and why performance deviated before correcting the source of deviation. It's not unusual for managers to rationalize that they don't have time to find the source of a problem (basic corrective action) and continue to perpetually "put out fires" with immediate corrective action. Effective managers analyze deviations and, if the benefits justify it, take the time to pinpoint and correct the causes of variance.

immediate corrective action
Corrective action that corrects problems at once to get performance back on track

basic corrective action
Corrective action that looks at how and why performance deviated before correcting the source of deviation

REVISE THE STANDARD It's possible that the variance was a result of an unrealistic standard—too low or too high a goal. In that situation, the standard needs the corrective action, not the performance. If performance consistently exceeds the goal, then a manager should look at whether the goal is too easy and needs to be raised. On the other hand, managers must be cautious about revising a standard downward. It's natural to blame the goal when an employee or a team falls short. For instance, students who get a low score on a test often attack the grade cut-off standards as too high. Rather than accept the fact that their performance was inadequate, they will argue that the standards are unreasonable. Likewise, salespeople who don't meet their monthly quota often want to blame what they think is an unrealistic quota. The point is that when performance isn't up to par, don't immediately blame the goal or standard. If you believe the standard is realistic, fair, and achievable, tell employees that you expect future work to improve, and then take the necessary corrective action to help make that happen.

Managerial Decisions in Controlling

Exhibit 10-6 summarizes the decisions a manager makes in controlling. The standards are goals developed during the planning process. These goals provide the basis for the control process, which involves measuring actual performance and comparing it against the standard. Depending on the results, a manager's decision is to do nothing, correct the performance, or revise the standard.

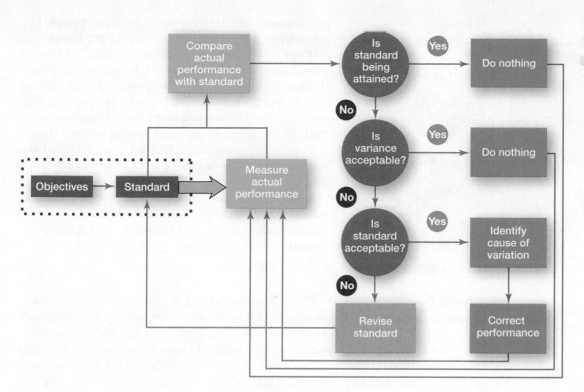

Exhibit 10-6
Managerial Decisions in the Control Process

CONTROLLING for Organizational and Employee Performance

Cost efficiency. The length of time customers are kept on hold. Customer satisfaction with service provided. These are just a few of the important performance indicators that executives in the intensely competitive call-center service industry measure. To make good decisions, managers in this industry want and need this type of information so they can manage organizational and employee performance. Managers in all types of businesses are responsible for managing organizational and employee performance.

Explain how 10.3 *organizational performance is measured.*

What Is Organizational Performance?

When you hear the word *performance,* what do you think of? A summer evening concert by a local community orchestra? An Olympic athlete striving for the finish line in a close race? A Southwest Airlines ramp agent in Ft. Myers, Florida, loading passengers as efficiently as possible in order to meet the company's 20-minute gate turnaround goal? **Performance** is all of these things. It's the end result of an activity. And whether that activity is hours of intense practice before a concert or race or whether it's carrying out job responsibilities as efficiently and effectively as possible, performance is what results from that activity.

Managers are concerned with **organizational performance**—the accumulated results of all the organization's work activities. It's a multifaceted concept, but managers need to understand the factors that contribute to organizational performance. After all, it's unlikely that they want (or intend) to manage their way to mediocre performance. They *want* their organizations, work units, or work groups to achieve high levels of performance.

performance
The end result of an activity

organizational performance
The accumulated results of all the organization's work activities

Measures of Organizational Performance

Theo Epstein, executive vice president and general manager of the Boston Red Sox, uses some unusual statistics to evaluate his players' performance instead of the old standards like batting average, home runs, and runs batted in. These "new"

Industry and company rankings determined by specific performance measures are one way managers can assess their company's performance. With sales topping $11 billion, Ebay is the world's largest marketplace that connects buyers and sellers. The company appears on the Forbes Global 2000, a list of the world's largest companies based on a composite ranking of sales, profits, assets, and market value. Ebay is also included on the Forbes Global High Performers list, an industry-specific ranking of fast-growing and well-managed global companies in 26 industries based on measures such as growth in sales, income, and earnings per share. Ebay is ranked as one of the five best companies in the retailing industry.
Source: DDAA/ZOB WENN Photos/Newscom

productivity
The amount of goods or services produced divided by the inputs needed to generate that output

organizational effectiveness
A measure of how appropriate organizational goals are and how well those goals are being met

performance measures include on-base percentage, pitches per plate appearance, at-bats per home run, and on-base plus slugging percentage.[11] Also, by using these statistics to predict future performance, Epstein has identified some potential star players and signed them for a fraction of the cost of a big-name player. His management team is defining new statistics to measure the impact of a player's defensive skills. As a manager, Epstein has identified the performance measures that are most important to his decisions.

Like Epstein, all managers must know which measures will give them the information they need about organizational performance. Commonly used ones include organizational productivity, organizational effectiveness, and industry rankings.

ORGANIZATIONAL PRODUCTIVITY **Productivity** is the amount of goods or services produced divided by the inputs needed to generate that output. Organizations and individual work units want to be productive. They want to produce the most goods and services using the least amount of inputs. Output is measured by the sales revenue an organization receives when goods are sold (selling price × number sold). Input is measured by the costs of acquiring and transforming resources into outputs.

It's management's job to increase this ratio. Of course, the easiest way to do this is to raise prices of the outputs. But in today's competitive environment, that may not be an option. The only other option, then, is to decrease the inputs side. How? By being more efficient in performing work and thus decreasing the organization's expenses.

ORGANIZATIONAL EFFECTIVENESS **Organizational effectiveness** is a measure of how appropriate organizational goals are and how well those goals are met. That's the bottom line for managers, and it's what guides managerial decisions in designing strategies and work activities and in coordinating the work of employees.

INDUSTRY AND COMPANY RANKINGS Rankings are a popular way for managers to measure their organization's performance. And there's not a shortage of these rankings as Exhibit 10-7 shows. Rankings are determined by specific performance measures, which are different for each list. For instance, *Fortune's* Best Companies to

Exhibit 10-7
Popular Industry and Company Rankings

Fortune (www.fortune.com)	*IndustryWeek* (www.industryweek.com)
Fortune 500	*IndustryWeek* 1000
Global 500	*IndustryWeek* U.S. 500
World's Most Admired Companies	50 Best Manufacturers
100 Best Companies to Work For	*IndustryWeek* Best Plants
25 Top Companies for Leaders	
100 Fastest-Growing Companies	
Forbes (www.forbes.com)	**Customer Satisfaction Indexes**
25 Fastest-Growing Tech Companies	American Customer Satisfaction Index— University of Michigan Business School
Best Places for Business and Careers	Customer Satisfaction Measurement Association

Work For are chosen by answers given by thousands of randomly selected employees on a questionnaire called "The Great Place to Work® Trust Index®" and on materials filled out by thousands of company managers, including a corporate culture audit created by the Great Place to Work Institute. These rankings give managers (and others) an indicator of how well their company performs in comparison to others.

Controlling for Employee Performance

Since managers manage employees, they also have to be concerned about controlling for employee performance; that is, making sure employees' work efforts are of the quantity and quality needed to accomplish organizational goals. How do managers do that? By following the control process: measure actual performance; compare that performance to standard (or expectations); and take action, if needed. It's particularly important for managers to deliver effective performance feedback and to be prepared, if needed, to use **disciplinary actions**—actions taken by a manager to enforce the organization's work standards and regulations.[12] Let's look first at effective performance feedback.

disciplinary actions
Actions taken by a manager to enforce the organization's work standards and regulations

DELIVERING EFFECTIVE PERFORMANCE FEEDBACK Throughout the semester, do you keep track of all your scores on homework, exams, and papers? If you do, why do you like to know that information? For most of us, it's because we like to know where we stand in terms of where we'd like to be and what we'd like to accomplish in our work. We like to know how we're doing. Managers need to provide their employees with feedback so that the employees know where they stand in terms of their work. When giving performance feedback, both parties need to feel heard, understood, and respected. And if done that way, positive outcomes can result. "In a productive performance discussion, organizations have the opportunity to reinforce company values, strengthen workplace culture, and achieve strategic goals."[13] Sometimes, however, performance feedback doesn't work. An employee's performance may continue to be an issue. Under those circumstances, disciplinary actions may be necessary to address the problems.

USING DISCIPLINARY ACTIONS Fortunately, most employees do their jobs well and never need formal correction. Yet, sometimes it is needed. Exhibit 10-8 lists some common types of work discipline problems and examples of each. In those circumstances, it's important for a manager to know what the organization's policies are on discipline. Is there a process for dealing with unsatisfactory job performance? Do warnings need to be given when performance is inadequate? What happens if after the warnings, performance or the troublesome behavior doesn't improve? Disciplinary actions are never easy or pleasant; however, discipline can be used to both control and correct employee performance, and managers must know how to discipline.

Attendance	Absenteeism, tardiness, abuse of sick leave
On-the-Job Behaviors	Insubordination, failure to use safety devices, alcohol or drug abuse
Dishonesty	Theft, lying to supervisors, falsifying information on employment application or on other organizational forms
Outside Activities	Criminal activities, unauthorized strike activities, working for a competing organization (if no-compete clause is part of employment)

Exhibit 10-8
Types of Discipline Problems and Examples of Each

let's get REAL

The Scenario:

Maddy Long supervises a team of data specialists. One of her team members doesn't like to be told what to do even though that's part of her responsibility as the manager—to outline the work that has to be done each week. Some of the other team members are starting to complain among themselves. Maddy knows she needs to address this problem before it reaches a crisis stage.

What should Maddy do now?

Maddy should immediately confront her employee via a private meeting and present the concrete examples in which she felt her employee behaved inappropriately, along with the negative effect it is having on team morale and work efficacy. Maddy should remain calm, impartial, and keep defensiveness at bay while presenting her point of view. It is of utmost importance in the meeting that she also asks her employee powerful leading questions to better understand her employee's view of the situation, source of frustration, and any recommendations her employee may have to solve the issue at hand. A final solution, as well as a plan to monitor improvement, should be agreed upon in the meeting. Depending on the severity of the offense and if it continues to occur, Maddy may also need to get additional guidance from Human Resources on the situation.

Shanise King
Associate Director, Marketing

Source: Shanise King

10.4 | ***Describe*** *tools used to measure organizational performance.*

TOOLS for Measuring Organizational Performance

- Missoni-loving fashionistas scrambling to buy the high-end Italian designer's clothes at Target crashed the company's Web site. Target executives admitted being unprepared for online shoppers' demand for the items.
- When someone typed the word "bailout" into a Domino's promo code window and found it was good for a free medium pizza, the news spread like wildfire across the Web. Domino's ended up having to give away thousands of free pizzas.
- A simple mistyped Web address by a Google employee caused all search results worldwide during a 55-minute period to warn, "This site may be harmful to your computer"—even though it wasn't.[14]

What kinds of tools could managers at these companies have used for monitoring and measuring performance?

All managers need appropriate tools for monitoring and measuring organizational performance. Before describing some specific types of control tools, let's look at the concept of feedforward, concurrent, and feedback control.

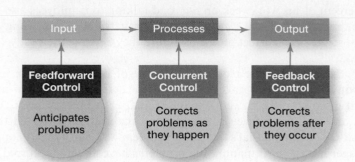

Exhibit 10-9
Types of Control

Feedforward/Concurrent/Feedback Controls

Managers can implement controls *before* an activity begins, *during* the time the activity is going on, and *after* the activity has been completed. The first type is called feedforward control; the second, concurrent control; and the last, feedback control (see Exhibit 10-9).

FEEDFORWARD CONTROL   The most desirable type of control—**feedforward control**—prevents problems because it takes place before the actual activity.[15] For instance, hospital emergency rooms are looking to prevent mistakes such as an 18-year-old with fever and chills being sent home from the emergency room with Tylenol and later dying of sepsis, a blood infection. Or a 42-year-old woman with chest pains being discharged, only to suffer a heart attack two hours later. Medical experts know that a serious ailment can look a lot like something else in the hubbub and chaos of the ER. So that's why many are setting protocols and oversights in place to prevent these kinds of mistakes.[16] When McDonald's opened its first restaurant in Moscow, it sent company quality control experts to help Russian farmers learn techniques for growing high-quality potatoes and to help bakers learn processes for baking high-quality breads. Why? McDonald's demands consistent product quality no matter the geographical location. They want a cheeseburger in Moscow to taste like one in Omaha. Still another example of feedforward control is the scheduled preventive maintenance programs on aircraft done by the major airlines. These programs are designed to detect and hopefully to prevent structural damage that might lead to an accident.

The key to feedforward controls is taking managerial action *before* a problem occurs. That way, problems can be prevented rather than having to correct them after any damage (poor-quality products, lost customers, lost revenue, etc.) has already been done. However, these controls require timely and accurate information that isn't always easy to get. Thus, managers frequently end up using the other two types of control.

CONCURRENT CONTROL   **Concurrent control**, as its name implies, takes place while a work activity is in progress. For instance, Nicholas Fox is director of business product management at Google. He and his team keep a watchful eye on one of Google's most profitable businesses—online ads. They watch "the number of searches and clicks, the rate at which users click on ads, the revenue this generates—everything is tracked hour by hour, compared with the data from a week earlier and charted."[17] If they see something that's not working particularly well, they fine-tune it.

The best-known form of concurrent control is direct supervision. Another term for it is **management by walking around**, which is when a manager is in the work area interacting directly with employees. For example, Nvidia's CEO Jen-Hsun Huang tore down his cubicle and replaced it with a conference table so he's available to employees at all times to discuss what's going on.[18] Even GE's CEO Jeff Immelt

feedforward control
Control that takes place before a work activity is done

concurrent control
Control that takes place while a work activity is in progress

management by walking around
A term used to describe when a manager is out in the work area interacting directly with employees

spends 60 percent of his workweek on the road talking to employees and visiting the company's numerous locations.[19] All managers can benefit from using concurrent control because they can correct problems before they become too costly.

feedback control
Control that takes place after a work activity is done

FEEDBACK CONTROL   The most popular type of control relies on feedback. In **feedback control**, the control takes place *after* the activity is done. For instance, the Denver Mint discovered the flawed Wisconsin quarters using feedback control. The damage had already occurred even though the organization corrected the problem once it was discovered. And that's the major problem with this type of control. By the time a manager has the information, the problems have already occurred, leading to waste or damage. However, in many work areas (for example, financial), feedback is the only viable type of control.

Feedback controls have two advantages.[20] First, feedback gives managers meaningful information on how effective their planning efforts were. Feedback that shows little variance between standard and actual performance indicates that the planning was generally on target. If the deviation is significant, a manager can use that information to formulate new plans. Second, feedback can enhance motivation. People want to know how well they're doing and feedback provides that information. Now, let's look at some specific control tools that managers can use.

Financial Controls

Every business wants to earn a profit. To achieve this goal, managers need financial controls. For instance, they might analyze quarterly income statements for excessive expenses. They might also calculate financial ratios to ensure that sufficient cash is available to pay ongoing expenses, that debt levels haven't become too high, or that assets are used productively.

Managers might use traditional financial measures such as ratio analysis and budget analysis. Exhibit 10-10 summarizes some of the most popular financial ratios. Liquidity ratios measure an organization's ability to meet its current debt obligations. Leverage ratios examine the organization's use of debt to finance its assets and

let's get REAL

The Scenario:

Lily Wong manages a product testing lab. Although her team works normal hours (8 to 5), there are times when the product testers need to work after hours or even on the weekend. She doesn't have a supervisor there when these associates are working but is wondering whether she needs to.

What would you suggest to Lily?

I would recommend that Lily appoint an after hours team leader to provide an update on productivity outside of normal business hours. She should compare the cost of adding a supervisor against the potential increased revenue for the lab. Furthermore, she must consistently ask her team for feedback and spot check for results.

Shawn Linett
Sales Manager

Source: Shawn Linett

Objective	Ratio	Calculation	Meaning
Liquidity	Current ratio	$$\frac{\text{Current assets}}{\text{Current liabilities}}$$	Tests the organization's ability to meet short-term obligations
	Acid test	$$\frac{\text{Current assets less inventories}}{\text{Current liabilities}}$$	Tests liquidity more accurately when inventories turn over slowly or are difficult to sell
Leverage	Debt to assets	$$\frac{\text{Total debt}}{\text{Total assets}}$$	The higher the ratio, the more leveraged the organization
	Times interest earned	$$\frac{\text{Profits before interest and taxes}}{\text{Total interest charges}}$$	Measures how many times the organization is able to meet its interest expenses
Activity	Inventory turnover	$$\frac{\text{Sales}}{\text{Inventory}}$$	The higher the ratio, the more efficiently inventory assets are used
	Total asset turnover	$$\frac{\text{Sales}}{\text{Total assets}}$$	The fewer assets used to achieve a given level of sales, the more efficiently management uses the organization's total assets
Profitability	Profit margin on sales	$$\frac{\text{Net profit after taxes}}{\text{Total sales}}$$	Identifies the profits that are generated
	Return on investment	$$\frac{\text{Net profit after taxes}}{\text{Total assets}}$$	Measures the efficiency of assets to generate profits

Exhibit 10-10
Popular Financial Ratios

whether it's able to meet the interest payments on the debt. Activity ratios assess how efficiently a company uses its assets. Finally, profitability ratios measure how efficiently and effectively the company uses its assets to generate profits. These ratios are calculated using selected information from the organization's two primary financial statements (the balance sheet and the income statement), which are then expressed as a percentage or ratio. Because you've probably studied these ratios in other accounting or finance courses, or will in the near future, we aren't going to elaborate on how they're calculated. We mention them here to remind you that managers use such ratios as internal control tools.

Budgets are planning and control tools. (See the Planning and Control Techniques module for more information on budgeting.) When a budget is formulated, it's a planning tool because it indicates which work activities are important and what and how much resources should be allocated to those activities. But budgets are also used for controlling because they provide managers with quantitative standards against which to measure and compare resource consumption. If deviations are significant enough to require action, the manager examines what has happened and tries to uncover why. With this information, necessary action can be taken. For example, if you use a personal budget for monitoring and controlling your monthly expenses, you might find that one month your miscellaneous expenses were higher than you had budgeted for. At that point, you might cut back spending in another area or work extra hours to get more income.

Information Controls

Cyber-attackers from China targeted Google and 34 other companies in an attempt to steal information. The largest ever criminal stealing of credit card data—account information belonging to millions of people—happened to Heartland Payment Systems, a payments processor. An ex-worker at Goldman Sachs stole "black box" computer programs that Goldman uses to make lucrative, rapid-fire trades in the financial markets. Even the U.S. government is getting serious about controlling information. Financial-market sensitive data (think Consumer Price Index, housing starts, inflation numbers, gas prices, corn yields, etc.) will be guarded as a precaution against anyone who might want to take advantage of an accidental or covert leak to get an insider's edge in the financial markets.[21] Talk about the need for information controls! Managers deal with information controls in two ways: (1) as a tool to help them control other organizational activities and (2) as an organizational area they need to control.

HOW IS INFORMATION USED IN CONTROLLING? Managers need the right information at the right time and in the right amount to monitor and measure organizational activities and performance.

In measuring actual performance, managers need information about what is happening within their area of responsibility and about the standards in order to be able to compare actual performance with the standard. They also rely on information to help them determine if deviations are acceptable. Finally, they rely on information to help them develop appropriate courses of action. Information *is* important! Most of the information tools managers use come from the organization's management information system.

management information system (MIS)

A system used to provide management with needed information on a regular basis

A **management information system (MIS)** is a system used to provide managers with needed information on a regular basis. In theory, this system can be manual or computer-based, although most organizations have moved to computer-supported applications. The term *system* in MIS implies order, arrangement, and purpose. Further, an MIS focuses specifically on providing managers with *information* (processed and analyzed data), not merely *data* (raw, unanalyzed facts). A library provides a good analogy. Although it can contain millions of volumes, a library doesn't do you any good if you can't find what you want quickly. That's why librarians spend a great deal of time cataloging a library's collections and ensuring that materials are returned to their proper locations. Organizations today are like well-stocked libraries. The issue is not a lack of data; instead, the issue is whether an organization has the ability to process that data so that the right information is available to the right person when he or she needs it. An MIS collects data and turns them into relevant information for managers to use.

CONTROLLING INFORMATION It seems that every week, there's another news story about information security breaches. A survey shows that 85 percent of privacy and security professionals acknowledge a reportable data breach occurred within their organizations within the last year alone.[22] Because information is critically important to everything an organization does, managers must have comprehensive and secure controls in place to protect that information. Such controls can range from data encryption to system firewalls to data back-ups, and other techniques as well.[23] Problems can lurk in places that an organization might not even have considered, like blogs, search engines, and Twitter accounts. Sensitive, defamatory, confidential, or embarrassing organizational information has found its way into search engine results. For instance, detailed monthly expenses and employee salaries on the National Speleological Society's Web site turned up in a Google search.[24] Equipment such as tablet and laptop computers, smart phones, and even RFID (radio-frequency identification) tags are vulnerable to viruses and hacking. Needless to say, information controls should be monitored regularly to ensure that all possible precautions are in place to protect important information.

Balanced Scorecard

The **balanced scorecard** approach is a way to evaluate organizational performance from more than just the financial perspective.[25] A balanced scorecard typically looks at four areas that contribute to a company's performance: financial, customer, internal processes, and people/innovation/growth assets. According to this approach, managers should develop goals in each of the four areas and then measure whether the goals are being met.

Although a balanced scorecard makes sense, managers will tend to focus on areas that drive their organization's success and use scorecards that reflect those strategies.[26] For example, if strategies are customer-centered, then the customer area is likely to get more attention than the other three areas. Yet, you can't focus on measuring only one performance area because others are affected as well. For instance, at IBM Global Services in Houston, managers developed a scorecard around an overriding strategy of customer satisfaction. However, the other areas (financial, internal processes, and people/innovation/growth) support that central strategy. The division manager described it as follows, "The internal processes part of our business is directly related to responding to our customers in a timely manner, and the learning and innovation aspect is critical for us since what we're selling our customers above all is our expertise. Of course, how successful we are with those things will affect our financial component."[27]

Benchmarking of Best Practices

The Cleveland Clinic is world renowned for delivering high-quality health care, with a top-ranked heart program that attracts patients from around the world. But what you may not realize is that it's also a model of cost-effective health care.[28] It could serve as a model for other health care organizations looking to be more effective and efficient.

Managers in such diverse industries as health care, education, and financial services are discovering what manufacturers have long recognized—the benefits of **benchmarking**, which is the search for the best practices among competitors or noncompetitors that lead to their superior performance. Benchmarking should identify various **benchmarks**, the standards of excellence against which to measure and compare. For instance, the American Medical Association developed more than 100 standard measures of performance to improve medical care. Carlos Ghosn, CEO of Nissan, benchmarked Walmart operations in purchasing, transportation, and logistics.[29] At its most basic, benchmarking means learning from others. As a tool for monitoring and measuring organizational performance, benchmarking can be used to identify specific performance gaps and potential areas of improvement. But best practices aren't just found externally.

Sometimes those best practices can be found inside the organization and just need to be shared. One fertile area for finding good performance improvement ideas is an employee suggestion box, which we'll discuss in Chapter 16. Research shows that best practices frequently already exist within an organization but usually go unidentified and unnoticed.[31] In today's environment, organizations seeking high performance levels can't afford to ignore such potentially valuable information. For example, Ameren Corporation's power plant managers used internal benchmarking to help identify performance gaps and opportunities.[32] Exhibit 10-11 provides some suggestions for internal benchmarking.

balanced scorecard
A performance measurement tool that looks at more than just the financial perspective

benchmarking
The search for the best practices among competitors or noncompetitors that lead to their superior performance

benchmark
The standard of excellence against which to measure and compare

Source: Rex Features via AP Images

LEADER who made a DIFFERENCE

Walt Disney Company is one of the world's largest entertainment and media companies and has had a long record of success.[30] When Bob Iger was named CEO in 2005, analysts believed that the Disney brand had become outdated. The perception was too many Disney products in the marketplace lacking the quality people expected. Iger decided to address that perception with what he called the Disney Difference. What is the Disney Difference? It's "high-quality creative content, backed up by a clear strategy for maximizing that content's value across platforms and markets." Now the company's obsessive focus on product quality led it to a number one ranking in Fortune's Most Admired list for product quality. What can you learn from this leader who made a difference?

Exhibit 10-11

Suggestions for Internal Benchmarking

1. *Connect best practices to strategies and goals.* The organization's strategies and goals should dictate what types of best practices might be most valuable to others in the organization.

2. *Identify best practices throughout the organization.* Organizations must have a way to find out what practices have been successful in different work areas and units.

3. *Develop best practices reward and recognition systems.* Individuals must be given an incentive to share their knowledge. The reward system should be built into the organization's culture.

4. *Communicate best practices throughout the organization.* Once best practices have been identified, that information needs to be shared with others in the organization.

5. *Create a best practices knowledge-sharing system.* There needs to be a formal mechanism for organizational members to continue sharing their ideas and best practices.

6. *Nurture best practices on an ongoing basis.* Create an organizational culture that reinforces a "we can learn from everyone" attitude and emphasizes sharing information.

Source: Based on "Extracting Diamonds in the Rough" by Tad Leahy, from *Business Finance*, August 2000.

10.5 *Discuss* contemporary issues in control.

CONTEMPORARY Issues in Control

The employees of Integrated Information Systems Inc. didn't think twice about exchanging digital music over a dedicated office server they had set up. Like office betting on college and pro sports, it was technically illegal, but harmless, or so they thought. But after the company had to pay a $1 million settlement to the Recording Industry Association of America, managers wished they had controlled the situation better.[33] Control is an important managerial function. We're going to look at four control issues that managers face today: cross-cultural differences, workplace concerns, customer interactions, and corporate governance.

Adjusting Controls for Cross-Cultural Differences and Global Turmoil

The concepts of control that we've been discussing are appropriate for an organization whose work units are not geographically separated or culturally distinct. But control techniques can be quite different for different countries. The differences are primarily in the measurement and corrective action steps of the control process. In a global corporation, managers of foreign operations tend to be less controlled by the home office, if for no other reason than distance keeps managers from being able to observe work directly. Because distance creates a tendency to formalize controls, such organizations often rely on extensive formal reports for control, most of which are communicated electronically.

Technology's impact on control is also seen when comparing technologically advanced nations with less technologically advanced countries. Managers in countries where technology is more advanced often use indirect control devices such as computer-generated reports and analyses in addition to standardized rules and direct supervision to ensure that work activities are going as planned. In less technologically advanced countries, however, managers tend to use more direct supervision and highly centralized decision making for control.

Managers in foreign countries also need to be aware of constraints on corrective actions they can take. Some countries' laws prohibit closing facilities, laying off employees, taking money out of the country, or bringing in a new management team from outside the country.

Another challenge for global managers in collecting data for measurement and comparison is comparability. For instance, a company that manufactures apparel in Cambodia might produce the same products at a facility in Scotland. However, the Cambodian facility might be more labor intensive than its Scottish counterpart to take advantage of lower labor costs in Cambodia. This difference makes it hard to compare, for instance, labor costs per unit.

Finally, global organizations need to have controls in place for protecting their workers and other assets during times of global turmoil and disasters. For instance, when the earthquake/tsunami hit Japan in March 2011, companies scrambled to activate their disaster management plans. In the volatile Middle East, many companies have had to evacuate workers during times of crisis. The best time to be prepared is before an emergency occurs, and many organizations are doing just that so that if a crisis occurs, employees and other organizational assets are protected as best as possible.

Workplace Concerns

The month-long World Cup games are a big drain on global productivity. A survey by the Chartered Management Institute says that in the United Kingdom, productivity losses could total just under 1 billion pounds ($1.45 billion). In the United States, March Madness also leads to a drop in productivity—estimated at $1.8 billion during the first week of the tournament—as employees fill out their brackets and survey the message boards and blogs.[34]

Today's workplaces present considerable control challenges for managers. From monitoring employees' computer usage at work to protecting the workplace against disgruntled employees intent on doing harm, managers need controls to ensure that work can be done efficiently and effectively as planned.

WORKPLACE PRIVACY If you work, do you think you have a right to privacy at your job? What can your employer find out about you and your work? You might be surprised at the answers! Employers can (and do), among other things, read your e-mail (even those marked "personal or confidential"), tap your telephone, monitor your work by computer, store and review computer files, monitor you in an employee bathroom or dressing room, and track your whereabouts in a company vehicle. And these actions aren't that uncommon. In fact, some 26 percent of companies have fired an employee for e-mail misuse; 26 percent have fired workers for misusing the Internet; 6 percent have fired employees for inappropriate cell phone use; 4 percent have fired someone for instant messaging misuse; and 3 percent have fired someone for inappropriate text messaging.[35]

Why do managers feel they need to monitor what employees are doing? A big reason is that employees are hired to work, not to surf the Web checking stock prices, watching online videos, playing fantasy baseball, or shopping for presents for family or friends. Recreational on-the-job Web surfing is thought to cost billions of dollars in lost work productivity annually. In fact, a survey of U.S. employers said that 87 percent of employees look at non-work-related Web sites while at work and more than half engage in personal Web site surfing every day.[36] Watching online video has become an increasingly serious problem not only because of the time being wasted by employees but because it clogs already-strained corporate computer networks.[37] All this nonwork adds up to significant costs to businesses.

Another reason why managers monitor employee e-mail and computer usage is that they don't want to risk being sued for creating a hostile workplace environment because of offensive messages or an inappropriate image displayed on a coworker's computer screen. Concerns about racial or sexual harassment are one reason

Most cases of organizational theft and fraud are committed by employees such as Hanjuan Jin, who worked as a software engineer for Motorola, Inc. for nine years. Stopped during a random security check at Chicago's O'Hare International Airport before boarding a flight to China, Jin was carrying $31,000 and more than 1,000 confidential Motorola documents that were stored on a laptop, four external hard drives, thumb drives, and other devices. Jin is shown here entering a federal courthouse before being sentenced to four years in prison for stealing trade secrets from Motorola. With the ready availability of information technology, employee theft is increasing and presenting considerable control challenges for managers.
Source: AP Photo/M. Spencer Green

datapoints[41]

27 percent of employees say the most common cause of on-the-job distraction is people stopping by their office.

52 percent of workers say they have witnessed or heard about workplace violence.

47 percent of employees say they play online games at work throughout the day.

16 percent more productivity resulted when students spent 10 minutes surfing the Web after completing a tedious task.

69 percent of U.S. adults are concerned about security when using popular social network sites.

45 percent of employees say they can't go more than 15 minutes, on average, without an interruption at work.

employee theft
Any unauthorized taking of company property by employees for their personal use

companies might want to monitor or keep back-up copies of all e-mail. Electronic records can help establish what actually happened so managers can react quickly.[38]

Finally, managers want to ensure that company secrets aren't being leaked.[39] In addition to typical e-mail and computer usage, companies are monitoring instant messaging and banning camera phones in the office. Managers need to be certain that employees are not, even inadvertently, passing information on to others who could use that information to harm the company.

Because of the potentially serious costs and given the fact that many jobs now entail computers, many companies have workplace monitoring policies. Such policies should control employee behavior in a nondemeaning way and employees should be informed about those policies.[40]

EMPLOYEE THEFT At the Saks flagship store in Manhattan, a 23-year-old sales clerk was caught ringing up $130,000 in false merchandise returns and putting the money onto a gift card.[42] And such practices have occurred at other retailers as well.

Would you be surprised to find that up to 85 percent of all organizational theft and fraud is committed by employees, not outsiders?[43] And it's a costly problem—estimated to be around $4,500 per worker per year.[44]

Employee theft is defined as any unauthorized taking of company property by employees for their personal use.[45] It can range from embezzlement to fraudulent filing of expense reports to removing equipment, parts, software, or office supplies from company premises. Although retail businesses have long faced serious potential losses from employee theft, loose financial controls at start-ups and small companies and the ready availability of information technology have made employee stealing an escalating problem in all kinds and sizes of organizations. Managers need to educate themselves about this control issue and be prepared to deal with it.[46]

Why do employees steal? The answer depends on whom you ask.[47] Experts in various fields—industrial security, criminology, clinical psychology—have different perspectives. The industrial security people propose that people steal because the opportunity presents itself through lax controls and favorable circumstances. Criminologists say it's because people have financial-based pressures (such as personal financial problems) or vice-based pressures (such as gambling debts). And the clinical psychologists suggest that people steal because they can rationalize whatever they're doing as being correct and appropriate behavior ("everyone does it," "they had it coming," "this company makes enough money and they'll never miss anything this small," "I deserve this for all that I put up with," and so forth).[48] Although each approach provides compelling insights into employee theft and has been instrumental in attempts to deter it, unfortunately, employees continue to steal. What can managers do?

The concept of feedforward, concurrent, and feedback control is useful for identifying measures to deter or reduce employee theft.[49] Exhibit 10-12 summarizes several possible managerial actions.

Workplace Violence

In August 2010, a driver about to lose his job at Hartford Distributors in Hartford, Connecticut, opened fire killing eight other employees and himself. In July 2010, a former employee at a solar products manufacturer in Albuquerque, New Mexico, walked into the business and opened fire killing two people and wounding four others. On November 6, 2009, in Orlando, Florida, an engineer who had been dismissed from his job for poor performance returned and shot and killed one person while wounding five others. This incident happened only one day after an Army psychiatrist went on a shooting rampage at Fort Hood Army post killing 13 and wounding 27. On June 25, 2008, in Henderson, Kentucky, an employee at a plastics plant returned hours after arguing with his supervisor over his not wearing safety goggles and for using his cell phone while working on the assembly line. He shot and killed the supervisor, four coworkers, and himself. On January 30, 2006, a former employee

Feedforward	Concurrent	Feedback
Use careful prehiring screening.	Treat employees with respect and dignity.	Make sure employees know when theft or fraud has occurred—not naming names but letting people know this is not acceptable.
Establish specific policies defining theft and fraud and discipline procedures.	Openly communicate the costs of stealing.	Use the services of professional investigators.
Involve employees in writing policies.	Let employees know on a regular basis about their successes in preventing theft and fraud.	Redesign control measures.
Educate and train employees about the policies.	Use video surveillance equipment if conditions warrant.	Evaluate your organization's culture and the relationships of managers and employees.
Have a professional review of your internal security controls.	Install "lock-out" options on computers, telephones, and e-mail.	
	Use corporate hotlines for reporting incidences.	
	Set a good example.	

Exhibit 10-12

Controlling Employee Theft

Sources: Based on A. H. Bell and D. M. Smith, "Protecting the Company Against Theft and Fraud," *Workforce Management Online,* December 3, 2000; J. D. Hanson, "To Catch a Thief," *Journal of Accountancy,* March 2000, pp. 43–46; and J. Greenberg, "The Cognitive Geometry of Employee Theft," in S. B. Bacharach, A. O'Leary-Kelly, J. M. Collins, and R. W. Griffin (eds.), *Dysfunctional Behavior in Organizations: Nonviolent and Deviant Behavior* (Stamford, CT: JAI Press, 1998), pp. 147–193.

who was once removed from a Santa Barbara, California, postal facility because of "strange behavior" came back and shot five workers to death, critically wounded another, and killed herself. On January 26, 2005, an autoworker at a Jeep plant in Toledo, Ohio, who had met the day before with plant managers about a problem with his work, came in and killed a supervisor and wounded two other employees before killing himself. In April 2003, a manager of a Boston Market restaurant in Indianapolis was killed by a fellow employee after the restaurant closed because the manager had refused the employee's sexual advances. In July 2003, an employee at an aircraft assembly plant in Meridian, Mississippi, walked out of a mandatory class on ethics and respect in the workplace, returned with firearms and ammunition, shot 14 of his coworkers, killing five and himself.[50] Is workplace violence really an issue for managers? Yes. Despite these examples, thankfully the number of workplace shootings has decreased.[51] However, the U.S. National Institute of Occupational Safety and Health still says that each year, some 2 million American workers are victims of some form of workplace violence. In an average week, one employee is killed and at least 25 are seriously injured in violent assaults by current or former coworkers. And according to a Department of Labor survey, 58 percent of firms reported that managers received verbal threats from workers.[52] Anger, rage, and violence in the workplace are intimidating to coworkers and adversely affect their productivity. The annual cost to U.S. businesses is estimated to be between $20 billion and $35 billion.[53] And office rage isn't a uniquely American problem. A survey of aggressive behavior in Britain's workplaces found that 18 percent of managers say they have personally experienced harassment or verbal bullying, and 9 percent claim to have experienced physical attacks.[54]

What factors are believed to be contributing to workplace violence? Undoubtedly, employee stress caused by an uncertain economic environment, job uncertainties, declining value of retirement accounts, long hours, information overload, other daily interruptions, unrealistic deadlines, and uncaring managers play a role. Even office layout designs with small cubicles where employees work amid the noise and commotion from those around them have been cited as contributing to the problem.[55] Other experts have described dangerously dysfunctional work environments characterized by the following as primary contributors to the problem:[56]

- Employee work driven by TNC (time, numbers, and crises).
- Rapid and unpredictable change where instability and uncertainty plague employees.
- Destructive communication style where managers communicate in an excessively aggressive, condescending, explosive, or passive-aggressive styles; excessive workplace teasing or scapegoating.
- Authoritarian leadership with a rigid, militaristic mindset of managers versus employees; employees aren't allowed to challenge ideas, participate in decision making, or engage in team-building efforts.
- Defensive attitude where little or no performance feedback is given; only numbers count; and yelling, intimidation, or avoidance is the preferred way of handling conflict.
- Double standards in terms of policies, procedures, and training opportunities for managers and employees.

Exhibit 10-13

Controlling Workplace Violence

Sources: Based on M. Gorkin, "Five Strategies and Structures for Reducing Workplace Violence," *Workforce Management Online*, December 3, 2000; "Investigating Workplace Violence: Where Do You Start? *Workforce Management Online*, December 3, 2000; "Ten Tips on Recognizing and Minimizing Violence," *Workforce Management Online*, December 3, 2000; and "Points to Cover in a Workplace Violence Policy," *Workforce Management Online*, December 3, 2000.

Feedforward	Concurrent	Feedback
Use MBWA (managing by walking around) to identify potential problems; observe how employees treat and interact with each other.	Ensure management commitment to functional, not dysfunctional, work environments.	Communicate openly about incidences and what's being done.
Provide employee assistance programs (EAPs) to help employees with behavioral problems.	Allow employees or work groups to "grieve" during periods of major organizational change.	Investigate incidences and take appropriate action.
Enforce organizational policy that any workplace rage, aggression, or violence will not be tolerated.	Be a good role model in how you treat others.	Review company policies and change, if necessary.
Use careful prehiring screening.	Use corporate hotlines or some other mechanism for reporting and investigating incidences.	
Never ignore threats.	Use quick and decisive intervention.	
Train employees about how to avoid danger if situation arises.	Get expert professional assistance if violence erupts.	
Clearly communicate policies to employees.	Provide necessary equipment or procedures for dealing with violent situations (cell phones, alarm system, code names or phrases, and so forth).	

- Unresolved grievances because the organization provides no mechanisms or only adversarial ones for resolving them; dysfunctional individuals may be protected or ignored because of long-standing rules, union contract provisions, or reluctance to take care of problems.
- Emotionally troubled employees and no attempt by managers to get help for these people.
- Repetitive, boring work with no chance for doing something else or for new people coming in.
- Faulty or unsafe equipment or deficient training, which keeps employees from being able to work efficiently or effectively.
- Hazardous work environment in terms of temperature, air quality, repetitive motions, overcrowded spaces, noise levels, excessive overtime, and so forth. To minimize costs, no additional employees are hired when workload becomes excessive, leading to potentially dangerous work expectations and conditions.
- Culture of violence that has a history of individual violence or abuse; violent or explosive role models; or tolerance of on-the-job alcohol or drug abuse.

Reading through this list, you surely hope that workplaces where you'll spend your professional life won't be like this. However, the competitive demands of succeeding in a 24/7 global economy put pressure on organizations and employees in many ways.

What can managers do to deter or reduce possible workplace violence? Once again, the concept of feedforward, concurrent, and feedback control can help identify actions that managers can take.[57] Exhibit 10-13 summarizes several suggestions.

Controlling Customer Interactions

Every month, every local branch of Enterprise Rent-a-Car conducts telephone surveys with customers.[58] Each branch earns a ranking based on the percentage of its customers who say they were "completely satisfied" with their last Enterprise experience—a level of satisfaction referred to as "top box." Top box performance is important to Enterprise because completely satisfied customers are far more likely to be repeat customers. By using this service quality index measure, employees' careers and financial aspirations are linked with the organizational goal of providing consistently superior service to each and every customer. Managers at Enterprise Rent-a-Car understand the connection between employees and customers and the importance of controlling these customer interactions.

Shown here at the Canadian International Auto Show is the new Jaguar C-X16. From its beginning as a manufacturer of motorcycle sidecars in 1922, Jaguar has grown to become one of the world's premier manufacturers of luxury sedans and sports cars. The company's strategy of producing beautiful fast cars that are desired throughout the world includes controlling customer interactions that create and build long-term relationships among the company, employees, and customers. The high quality of Jaguar's customer service staff and service policies results in customer satisfaction and loyalty that improves the company's growth and profitability.
Source: AP Photo/The Canadian Press, Nathan Denette

There's probably no better area to see the link between planning and controlling than in customer service. If a company proclaims customer service as one of its goals, it quickly and clearly becomes apparent whether that goal is being achieved by seeing how satisfied customers are with their service! How can managers control the interactions between the goal and the outcome when it comes to customers? The concept of a service profit chain can help.[59]

A **service profit chain** is the service sequence from employees to customers to profit. According to this concept, the company's strategy and service delivery system influence how employees deal with customers; that is, how productive they are in providing service and the quality of that service. The level of employee service productivity and service quality influences customer perceptions of service value. When service value is high, it has a positive impact on customer satisfaction, which leads to customer loyalty. And customer loyalty improves organizational revenue growth and profitability.

What does this concept mean for managers? Managers who want to control customer interactions should work to create long-term and mutually beneficial relationships among the company, employees, and customers. How? By creating a work

service profit chain
The service sequence from employees to customers to profit

environment that enables employees to deliver high levels of quality service and which makes them feel they're capable of delivering top-quality service. In such a service climate, employees are motivated to deliver superior service. Employee efforts to satisfy customers, coupled with the service value provided by the organization, improve customer satisfaction. And when customers receive high service value, they're loyal and return, which ultimately improves the company's growth and profitability.

There's no better example of this concept in action than Southwest Airlines, which is the most consistently profitable U.S. airline (the year 2011 marked 39 straight profitable years). Its customers are fiercely loyal because the company's operating strategy (hiring, training, rewards and recognition, teamwork, and so forth) is built around customer service. Employees consistently deliver outstanding service value to customers. And Southwest's customers reward the company by coming back. It's through efficiently and effectively controlling these customer interactions that companies like Southwest and Enterprise have succeeded.

Corporate Governance

Although Andrew Fastow—Enron's former chief financial officer who pled guilty to wire and securities fraud—had an engaging and persuasive personality, that still didn't explain why Enron's board of directors failed to raise even minimal concerns about management's questionable accounting practices. The board even allowed Fastow to set up off-balance-sheet partnerships for his own profit at the expense of Enron's shareholders.

corporate governance
The system used to govern a corporation so that the interests of corporate owners are protected

Corporate governance, the system used to govern a corporation so that the interests of corporate owners are protected, failed abysmally at Enron, as it has at many companies caught in financial scandals. In the aftermath of these scandals, corporate governance has been reformed. Two areas where reform has taken place are the role of boards of directors and financial reporting. Such reforms aren't limited to U.S. corporations; corporate governance problems are global.[60] Some 75 percent of senior executives at U.S. and Western European corporations expect their boards of directors to take a more active role.[61]

THE ROLE OF BOARDS OF DIRECTORS The original purpose of a board of directors was to have a group, independent from management, looking out for the interests of shareholders who were not involved in the day-to-day management of the organization. However, it didn't always work that way. Board members often enjoyed a cozy relationship with managers in which each took care of the other.

This type of "quid pro quo" arrangement has changed. The Sarbanes-Oxley Act puts greater demands on board members of publicly traded companies in the United States to do what they were empowered and expected to do.[62] To help boards do this better, researchers at the Corporate Governance Center at Kennesaw State University developed governance principles for U.S. public companies. (See [http://coles.kennesaw.edu/centers/corporate-governance/corporate-governance-documents/21stcentury_2002.pdf] for a list and discussion of these principles.)

FINANCIAL REPORTING AND THE AUDIT COMMITTEE In addition to expanding the role of boards of directors, the Sarbanes-Oxley Act also called for more disclosure and transparency of corporate financial information. In fact, senior managers in the United States are now required to certify their companies' financial results. Such changes have led to better information—that is, information that is more accurate and reflective of a company's financial condition. In fulfilling their financial reporting responsibilities, managers might want to follow the principles also developed by the researchers at the Corporate Governance Center at Kennesaw State University. These principles also can be found at [coles.kennesaw.edu/centers/corporate-governance/white-papers.htm].

CHAPTER **10**

PREPARING FOR: Exams/Quizzes

CHAPTER SUMMARY by Learning Outcomes

10.1 LEARNING OUTCOME

Explain the nature and importance of control.

Controlling is the process of monitoring, comparing, and correcting work performance. As the final step in the management process, controlling provides the link back to planning. If managers didn't control, they'd have no way of knowing whether goals were being met.

Control is important because (1) it's the only way to know if goals are being met, and if not, why; (2) it provides information and feedback so managers feel comfortable empowering employees; and (3) it helps protect an organization and its assets.

10.2 LEARNING OUTCOME

Describe the three steps in the control process.

The three steps in the control process are measuring, comparing, and taking action. Measuring involves deciding how to measure actual performance and what to measure. Comparing involves looking at the variation between actual performance and the standard (goal). Deviations outside an acceptable range of variation need attention.

Taking action can involve doing nothing, correcting the actual performance, or revising the standards. Doing nothing is self-explanatory. Correcting the actual performance can involve different corrective actions, which can either be immediate or basic. Standards can be revised by either raising or lowering them.

10.3 LEARNING OUTCOME

Explain how organizational and employee performance are measured.

Organizational performance is the accumulated results of all the organization's work activities. Three frequently used organizational performance measures include (1) productivity, the output of goods or services produced divided by the inputs needed to generate that output; (2) effectiveness, a measure of how appropriate organizational goals are and how well those goals are being met; and (3) industry and company rankings compiled by various business publications.

Employee performance is controlled through effective performance feedback and through disciplinary actions, when needed.

10.4 LEARNING OUTCOME

Describe tools used to measure organizational performance.

Feedforward controls take place before a work activity is done. Concurrent controls take place while a work activity is being done. Feedback controls take place after a work activity is done.

Financial controls that managers can use include financial ratios (liquidity, leverage, activity, and profitability) and budgets. One information control managers can use is an MIS, which provides managers with needed information on a regular basis. Others include comprehensive and secure controls such as data encryption, system firewalls, data back-ups, and so forth that protect the organization's information.

Balanced scorecards provide a way to evaluate an organization's performance in four different areas rather than just from the financial perspective.

Benchmarking provides control by finding the best practices among competitors or noncompetitors and from inside the organization itself.

10.5 [LEARNING OUTCOME] **Discuss** contemporary issues in control.
Adjusting controls for cross-cultural differences may be needed primarily in the areas of measuring and taking corrective actions.

Workplace concerns include workplace privacy, employee theft, and workplace violence. For each of these issues, managers need to have policies in place to control inappropriate actions and ensure that work is getting done efficiently and effectively.

Control is important to customer interactions because employee service productivity and service quality influences customer perceptions of service value. Organizations want long-term and mutually beneficial relationships among their employees and customers.

Corporate governance is the system used to govern a corporation so that the interests of corporate owners are protected.

REVIEW AND DISCUSSION QUESTIONS ✪

1. What are the three steps in the control process? Describe in detail.
2. What is organizational performance?
3. Contrast feedforward, concurrent, and feedback controls.
4. Discuss the various types of tools used to monitor and measure organizational performance.
5. What workplace concerns do managers have to deal with? How might those concerns be controlled?
6. Why is control important to customer interactions?

7. In Chapter 7 we discussed the white-water rapids view of change, which refers to situations in which unpredictable change is normal and expected, and managing it is a continual process. Do you think it's possible to establish and maintain effective standards and controls in this type of environment? Discuss.
8. "Every individual employee in an organization plays a role in controlling work activities." Do you agree with this statement, or do you think control is something that only managers are responsible for? Explain.

PREPARING FOR: My Career
ETHICS DILEMMA ✪

"The restaurant industry faces a sobering image mess: how to convince consumers it will stop accidentally serving alcohol drinks to toddlers."[63] In separate incidents, a 10-year-old boy was accidently served a drink with rum in it. In another incident, a toddler was served alcoholic sangria instead of orange juice. And in another incident, a toddler was served a margarita. Other than the obvious, what problems do you see here, especially as it relates to control? How would you handle this? How could organizations make sure they're addressing work controls ethically?

SKILLS EXERCISE Developing Your Performance Feedback Skill

About the Skill
One of the more critical feedback sessions will occur when you, as a manager, are using feedback control to address performance issues.

Steps in Practicing the Skill
1. *Schedule the feedback session in advance and be prepared.* One of the biggest mistakes you can make is to treat feedback control lightly. Simply calling in an employee

and giving feedback that's not well organized serves little purpose for you and your employee. For feedback to be effective, you must plan ahead. Identify the issues you wish to address and cite specific examples to reinforce what you are saying. Furthermore, set aside the time for the meeting with the employee. Make sure what you do is done in private and can be completed without interruptions. That may mean closing your office door (if you have one), not taking phone calls, and the like.

2. *Put the employee at ease.* Regardless of how you feel about the feedback, you must create a supportive climate for the employee. Recognize that giving and getting this feedback can be an emotional event even when the feedback is positive. By putting your employee at ease, you begin to establish a supportive environment in which understanding can take place.

3. *Make sure the employee knows the purpose of this feedback session.* What is the purpose of the meeting? That's something any employee will be wondering. Clarifying what you are going to do sets the appropriate stage for what is to come.

4. *Focus on specific rather than general work behaviors.* Feedback should be specific rather than general. General statements are vague and provide little useful information—especially if you are attempting to correct a problem.

5. *Keep comments impersonal and job-related.* Feedback should be descriptive rather than judgmental or evaluative, especially when you are giving negative feedback. No matter how upset you are, keep the feedback job-related and never criticize someone personally because of an inappropriate action. You're correcting job-related behavior, not the person.

6. *Support feedback with hard data.* Tell your employee how you came to your conclusion on his or her performance. Hard data help your employees to identify with specific behaviors. Identify the "things" that were done correctly and provide a detailed critique. And if you need to criticize, state the basis of your conclusion that a good job was not completed.

7. *Direct the negative feedback toward work-related behavior that the employee controls.* Negative feedback should be directed toward work-related behavior that the employee can do something about. Indicate what he or she can do to improve the situation. This practice

helps take the sting out of the criticism and offers guidance to an individual who understands the problem but doesn't know how to resolve it.

8. *Let the employee speak.* Get the employee's perceptions of what you are saying, especially if you are addressing a problem. Of course, you're not looking for excuses, but you need to be empathetic to the employee. Get his or her side. Maybe something has contributed to the issue. Letting the employee speak involves your employee and just might provide information you were unaware of.

9. *Ensure that the employee has a clear and full understanding of the feedback.* Feedback must be concise and complete enough so that your employee clearly and fully understands what you have said. Consistent with active listening techniques, have your employee rephrase the content of your feedback to check whether it fully captures your meaning.

10. *Detail a future plan of action.* Performing doesn't stop simply because feedback occurred. Good performance must be reinforced and new performance goals set. However, when performance deficiencies are the issue, time must be devoted to helping your employee develop a detailed, step-by-step plan to correct the situation. This plan includes what has to be done and when and how you will monitor the activities. Offer whatever assistance you can to help the employee, but make it clear that it is the employee, not you, who has to make the corrections.

Practicing the Skill

Think of a skill you would like to acquire or improve, or a habit you would like to break. Perhaps you would like to learn a foreign language, start exercising, quit smoking, ski better, or spend less. For the purpose of this exercise, assume you have three months to make a start on your project and all the necessary funds. Draft a plan of action that outlines what you need to do, when you need to do it, and how you will know that you have successfully completed each step of your plan. Be realistic, but don't set your sights too low either.

Review your plan. What outside help or resources will you require? How will you get them? Add these to your plan. Could someone else follow the steps you've outlined to achieve the goal you set? What modifications would you have to make, if any?

WORKING TOGETHER Team Exercise

Research says that up to 80 percent of U.S. teens have worked for pay at some time during high school.[64] As the number of employed teens has risen, so has the likelihood of their getting hurt on the job. How can organizations keep teen workers safe?

Form small groups of three to four students. Come up with some ideas about things an organization could do to keep its teen workers safe. Put your ideas in a bulleted list format and be prepared to share those ideas with the class.

MY TURN TO BE A MANAGER

- You have a major class project due in a month. Identify some performance measures you could use to help determine whether the project is going as planned and will be completed efficiently (on time) and effectively (high quality).

- How could you use the concept of control in your personal life? Be specific. (Think in terms of feedforward, concurrent, and feedback controls as well as specific controls for the different aspects of your life—school, work, family relationships, friends, hobbies, etc.)

- Survey 30 people as to whether they have experienced office rage. Ask them specifically whether they have experienced any of the following: yelling or other verbal abuse, yelled at coworkers themselves, cried over work-related issues, seen someone purposely damaged machines or furniture, seen physical violence in the workplace, or struck a coworker. Compile your findings in a table. Are you surprised at the results? Be prepared to present these in class.

- Pretend you're the manager of a customer call center for timeshare vacations. What types of control measures would you use to see how efficient and effective an employee is? How about measures for evaluating the entire call center?

- Disciplining employees is one of the least favorite tasks of managers, but is something that all managers have to do. Survey three managers about their experiences with employee discipline. What types of employee actions have caused the need for disciplinary action? What disciplinary actions have they used? What do they think is the most difficult thing to do when disciplining employees? What suggestions do they have for disciplining employees?

- Steve's and Mary's recommended readings: Marcus Buckingham, *Go Put Your Strengths to Work* (Free Press, 2007); W. Steven Brown, *13 Fatal Errors Managers Make and How You Can Avoid Them* (Berkley Business, 1987); and Peter F. Drucker, *Management: Tasks, Responsibilities, Practices* (Harper Business, 1974).

- Research "The Great Package Race." Write a paper describing what it is and how it's a good example of organizational control.

- In your own words, write down three things you learned in this chapter about being a good manager.

- Self-knowledge can be a powerful learning tool. Go to mymanagementlab.com and complete these self-assessment exercises: How Good Am I at Disciplining Others? How Willing Am I to Delegate? What Time of Day Am I Most Productive? How Good Am I at Giving Performance Feedback? Using the results of your assessments, identify personal strengths and weaknesses. What will you do to reinforce your strengths and improve your weaknesses?

MyManagementLab

Go to **mymanagementlab.com** for Auto-graded writing questions as well as the following Assisted-graded writing questions:

10-1. Why is control important to customer interactions?

10-2. What are some work activities in which the acceptable range of variation might be higher than average? What about lower than average? (Hint: Think in terms of the output from the work activities, who it might affect, and how it might affect them.)

10-3. Mymanagementlab Only – comprehensive writing assignment for this chapter.

CASE APPLICATION 1 Deepwater in Deep Trouble

When all is said and done, which may not be for many years, it's likely to be one of the worst environmental disasters, if not the worst, in U.S. history.[65] When British Petroleum's (BP) Deepwater Horizon off-shore rig in the Gulf of Mexico exploded in a ball of flames on April 20, 2010, killing 11 employees, it set in motion frantic efforts to stop the flow of oil and to initiate the long and arduous clean-up process. Although the impacts of the explosion and oil spill were felt most intensely by businesses and residents along the coast and by coastal wildlife, those of us inland who watched the disaster unfold were also stunned and dismayed by what we saw happening. What led to this disaster, and what can BP do to ensure that the likelihood of it ever happening again is minimized?

Strong warning signs indicated serious problems with well equipment and other safety aspects of the Deepwater Horizon oil rig, but a lack of effective controls needed to protect the rig as the employees' workplace resulted in a tragic explosion and oil spill.
Source: ZUMA Press/Newscom

One thing that has come to light in the disaster investigation is that it's no surprise that something like this happened. After Hurricane Dennis blew through in July 2005, a passing ship was shocked to see BP's new massive $1 billion Thunder Horse oil platform "listing precariously to one side, looking for all the world as if it were about to sink." Thunder Horse "was meant to be the company's crowning glory, the embodiment of its bold gamble to outpace its competitors in finding and exploiting the vast reserves of oil beneath the waters of the gulf." But the problems with this rig soon became evident. A valve installed backwards caused it to flood during the hurricane even before any oil had been pumped. Other problems included a welding job so shoddy that it left underwater pipelines brittle and full of cracks. "The problems at Thunder Horse were not an anomaly, but a warning that BP was taking too many risks and cutting corners in pursuit of growth and profits."

Then came the tragic explosion on the Deepwater Horizon. Before the rig exploded, strong warning signs indicated that something was terribly wrong with the oil well. Among the red flags were several equipment readings suggesting that gas was bubbling into the well, a potential sign of an impending blowout. Those red flags were ignored. Other decisions made in the 24 hours before the explosion included a critical decision to replace heavy mud in the pipe rising from the seabed with seawater, again possibly increasing the risk of an explosion. Internal BP documents also show serious problems and safety concerns with Deepwater. Those problems involved the well casing and blowout preventer. One BP senior drilling engineer warned, "This would certainly be a worst-case scenario."

The federal panel charged with investigating the spill has been examining 20 "anomalies in the well's behavior and the crew's response." The panel is also investigating in particular why "rig workers missed telltale signs that the well was close to an uncontrolled blowout." The U.S. Coast Guard's report found that "poor maintenance, inadequate training, and a lax safety culture contributed to the lethal explosion and sinking of the company's Deepwater Horizon drilling rig." And finally, the U.S. Justice Department was getting closer to civil and criminal settlements with BP and with Transocean over the Deepwater Horizon disaster—deals that would likely include billions of dollars in fines and penalties.

DISCUSSION QUESTIONS ✪

1. What type(s) of control—feedforward, concurrent, or feedback—do you think would have been most useful in this situation? Explain your choice(s).

2. Using Exhibit 10-2, explain what BP could have done better.

3. Why do you think company employees ignored the red flags? How could such behavior be changed in the future?

4. What could other organizations learn from BP's mistakes?

CASE APPLICATION 2 — Baggage Blunders and Wonders

Inappropriate controls contributed to the baggage handling problems that developed on the opening day of British Airways Terminal 5 and resulted in flight delays and cancellations for the passengers shown here, but the airline worked quickly to resolve the problems and since then has received high marks in customer satisfaction surveys.
Source: © Daily Mail/Rex/Alamy

Terminal 5 (T5), built by British Airways for $8.6 billion, is London Heathrow Airport's newest state-of-the-art facility.[66] Made of glass, concrete, and steel, it's the largest free-standing building in the United Kingdom and has more than 10 miles of belts for moving luggage. At the terminal's unveiling in March 2008, Queen Elizabeth II called it a "twenty-first-century gateway to Britain." Alas, the accolades didn't last long! After two decades in planning and 100 million hours in manpower, opening day didn't work out as planned. Endless lines and major baggage handling delays led to numerous flight cancellations, stranding many irate passengers. Airport operators said the problems were triggered by glitches in the terminal's high-tech baggage-handling system.

With its massive automation features, T5 was planned to ease congestion at Heathrow and improve the flying experience for the 30 million passengers expected to pass through it annually. With 96 self-service check-in kiosks, more than 90 fast check-in bag drops, 54 standard check-in desks, and miles of suitcase-moving belts estimated to be able to process 12,000 bags per hour, the facility's design seemed to support those goals.

However, within the first few hours of the terminal's operation, problems developed. Presumably understaffed, baggage workers were unable to clear incoming luggage fast enough. Arriving passengers waited more than an hour for their bags. Departing passengers tried in vain to check in for flights. Flights left with empty cargo holds. Sometime on day one, the airline checked in only those passengers with no luggage. And it didn't help that the moving belt system jammed at one point. Lesser problems also became apparent: a few broken escalators, some hand dryers that didn't work, a gate that wouldn't function at the new underground station, and inexperienced ticket sellers who didn't know the fares between Heathrow and various stations on the Piccadilly line. By the end of the first full day of operation, Britain's Department of Transportation released a statement calling for British Airways and the airport operator BAA to "work hard to resolve these issues and limit disruptions to passengers."

You might be tempted to think that all of this could have been prevented if British Airways had only tested the system. But thorough runs of all systems "from toilets to check in and seating" took place six months before opening, including four full-scale test runs using 16,000 volunteers.

Although T5's debut was far from perfect, things have certainly changed. A recent customer satisfaction survey showed that 80 percent of passengers waited less than five minutes to check in. And those passengers are extremely satisfied with the terminal's lounges, catering, facilities, and ambience.

With the Summer Olympics in London, London's Heathrow (and T5) grappled with a record passenger surge as competitors, spectators, and media arrived. To cope with the deluge, some 1,000 volunteers greeted arrivals, and special teams were assigned to deal with athletes' oversize items like javelins, bikes, and other sports equipment. Despite the chaotic "birth" of T5, it's become a valued component of Heathrow and British Airways.

DISCUSSION QUESTIONS ✪

1. What type of control—feedforward, concurrent, or feedback—do you think would be most important in this situation? Explain your choice.

2. How might immediate corrective action have been used in this situation? How about basic corrective action?

3. Could British Airways' controls have been more effective? How?

4. What role would information controls play in this situation? Customer interaction controls? Benchmarking?

5. What could companies learn from the smooth handling of the throngs of arrivals and departures for the Summer 2012 Olympics?

Planning and Control Techniques Module

Managers in baseball team front offices have discovered certain factors dictate whether they can charge more for tickets—namely, weather reports, winning streaks, and a big factor: pitching matchups.[1] The San Francisco Giants are the first Major League Baseball team to try and ride these shifts in demand by repricing tickets daily, a technique known as dynamic pricing. How well does it work? In 2009, the Giants were able to earn an extra $500,000 in revenue from dynamic pricing. In 2010, revenues increased about 6 percent.

As this example shows, managers use planning tools and techniques to help their organizations be more efficient and effective. In this module, we discuss three categories of basic planning tools and techniques: techniques for assessing the environment, techniques for allocating resources, and contemporary planning techniques.

TECHNIQUES for Assessing the Environment

Leigh Knopf, former senior manager for strategic planning at the AICPA, says that many larger accounting firms have set up external analysis departments to "study the wider environment in which they, and their clients, operate." These organizations have recognized that, "What happens in India in today's environment may have an impact on an American accounting firm in North Dakota."[2] In our description of the strategic management process in Chapter 9, we discussed the importance of assessing the organization's environment. Three techniques help managers do that: environmental scanning, forecasting, and benchmarking.

Environmental Scanning

How important is environmental scanning? While looking around on competitor Google's company Web site, Bill Gates found a help-wanted page with descriptions of all the open jobs. What piqued his interest, however, was that many of these posted job qualifications were identical to Microsoft's job requirements. He began to wonder why Google—a Web search company—would be posting job openings for software engineers with backgrounds that "had nothing to do with web searches and everything to do with Microsoft's core business of operating-system design, compiler optimization, and distributed-systems architecture." Gates e-mailed an urgent message to some of his top executives saying that Microsoft had better be on its toes because it sure looked like Google was preparing to move into being more of a software company.[3]

How can managers become aware of significant environmental changes such as a new law in Germany permitting shopping for "tourist items" on Sunday; the increased trend of counterfeit consumer products in South Africa; the precipitous decline in the working-age populations in Japan, Germany, Italy, and Russia; or the decrease in family size in Mexico? Managers in both small and large organizations use **environmental scanning**, the screening of large amounts of information to anticipate and interpret changes in the environment. Extensive environmental scanning is likely to reveal issues and concerns that could affect an organization's current or planned activities. Research has shown that companies that use environmental scanning have higher performance.[4] Organizations that don't keep on top of environmental changes are likely to experience the opposite!

COMPETITOR INTELLIGENCE   A fast-growing area of environmental scanning is **competitor intelligence**.[5] It's a process by which organizations gather information about their competitors and get answers to questions such as Who are they? What are they doing? How will what they're doing affect us? Let's look at an example of how one organization used competitor intelligence in its planning. Dun & Bradstreet (D&B), a leading provider of business information, has an active business intelligence division. The division manager received a call from an assistant vice president for sales in one of the company's geographic territories. This person had been on a sales call with a major customer and the customer happened to mention in passing that another company had visited and made a major presentation about its services. It was interesting because, although D&B had plenty of competitors, this particular company wasn't one of them. The manager gathered together a team that sifted through dozens of sources (research services, Internet, personal contacts, and other external sources) and quickly became convinced that there was something to this; that this company was "aiming its guns right at us." Managers at D&B jumped into action to develop plans to counteract this competitive attack.[6]

Competitor intelligence experts suggest that 80 percent of what managers need to know about competitors can be found out from their own employees, suppliers, and customers.[7] Competitor intelligence doesn't have to involve spying. Advertisements, promotional materials, press releases, reports filed with government agencies, annual reports, want ads, newspaper reports, and industry studies are examples of readily accessible sources of information. Attending trade shows and debriefing the company's salesforce can be other good sources of competitor information. Many firms regularly buy competitors' products and have their own engineers study them (through a process called *reverse engineering*) to learn about new technical innovations. In addition, the Internet has opened up vast sources of competitor intelligence as many corporate Web pages include new product information and other press releases.

Managers need to be careful about the way competitor information is gathered to prevent any concerns about whether it's legal or ethical. For instance, at Procter & Gamble, executives hired competitive intelligence firms to spy on its competitors in the hair-care business. At least one of these firms misrepresented themselves to competitor Unilever's employees, trespassed at Unilever's hair-care headquarters in Chicago, and went through trash dumpsters to gain information. When P&G's CEO found out, he immediately fired the individuals responsible and apologized to Unilever.[8] Competitor intelligence becomes illegal corporate spying when it involves the theft of proprietary materials or trade secrets by any means. The Economic Espionage Act makes it a crime in the United States to engage in economic espionage or to steal a trade secret.[9] The difficult decisions about competitive intelligence arise because often there's a fine line between what's considered *legal and ethical* and what's considered *legal but unethical*. Although the top manager at one competitive intelligence firm contends that 99.9 percent of intelligence gathering is legal, there's no question that some people or companies will go to any lengths—some unethical—to get information about competitors.[10]

GLOBAL SCANNING   One type of environmental scanning that's particularly important is global scanning. Because world markets are complex and dynamic, managers have expanded the scope of their scanning efforts to gain vital information on global forces that might affect their organizations.[11] The value of global scanning to managers,

environmental scanning
The screening of large amounts of information to anticipate and interpret changes in the environment

competitor intelligence
Environmental scanning activity by which organizations gather information about competitors

of course, largely depends on the extent of the organization's global activities. For a company with significant global interests, global scanning can be quite valuable. For instance, Sealed Air Corporation of Elmwood Park, New Jersey—you've probably seen and used its most popular product, Bubble Wrap—tracks global demographic changes. Company managers found that as countries move from agriculture-based societies to industrial ones, the population tends to eat out more and favor prepackaged foods, which translates to more sales of its food packaging products.[12]

Because the sources that managers use for scanning the domestic environment are too limited for global scanning, managers must globalize their perspectives. For instance, they can subscribe to information-clipping services that review world newspapers and business periodicals and provide summaries of desired information. Also, numerous electronic services will provide topic searches and automatic updates in global areas of special interest to managers.

Forecasting

forecasts
Predictions of outcome

The second technique managers can use to assess the environment is forecasting. Forecasting is an important part of planning, and managers need forecasts that will allow them to predict future events effectively and in a timely manner. Environmental scanning establishes the basis for **forecasts**, which are predictions of outcomes. Virtually any component in an organization's environment can be forecasted. Let's look at how managers forecast and the effectiveness of those forecasts.

quantitative forecasting
Forecasting that applies a set of mathematical rules to a series of past data to predict outcome

qualitative forecasting
Forecasting that uses the judgment and opinions of knowledgeable individuals to predict outcomes

FORECASTING TECHNIQUES Forecasting techniques fall into two categories: quantitative and qualitative. **Quantitative forecasting** applies a set of mathematical rules to a series of past data to predict outcomes. These techniques are preferred when managers have sufficient hard data that can be used. **Qualitative forecasting**, in contrast, uses the judgment and opinions of knowledgeable individuals to predict outcomes. Qualitative techniques typically are used when precise data are limited or hard to obtain. Exhibit PCM-1 describes some popular forecasting techniques.

Today, many organizations collaborate on forecasts using an approach known as CPFR, which stands for collaborative planning, forecasting, and replenishment.[13] CPFR provides a framework for the flow of information, goods, and services between retailers and manufacturers. Each organization relies on its own data to calculate a demand forecast for a particular product. If their respective forecasts differ by a certain amount (say 10 percent), the retailer and manufacturer exchange data and written comments until they arrive at a more accurate forecast. Such collaborative forecasting helps both organizations do a better job of planning.

FORECASTING EFFECTIVENESS The goal of forecasting is to provide managers with information that will facilitate decision making. Despite its importance to planning, managers have had mixed success with it.[14] For instance, prior to a holiday weekend at the Procter & Gamble factory in Lima, Ohio, managers were preparing to shut down the facility early so as not to have to pay employees for just sitting around and to give them some extra time off. The move seemed to make sense since an analysis of purchase orders and historical sales trends indicated that the factory had already produced enough cases of Liquid Tide detergent to meet laundry demand over the holiday. However, managers got a real surprise. One of the company's largest retail customers placed a sizable—and unforeseen—order. They had to reopen the plant, pay the workers overtime, and schedule emergency shipments to meet the retailer's request.[15] As this example shows, managers' forecasts aren't always accurate. In a survey of financial managers in the United States, United Kingdom, France, and Germany, 84 percent of the respondents said their financial forecasts were inaccurate by 5 percent or more; 54 percent of the respondents reported inaccuracy of 10 percent or more.[16] Results of another survey showed that 39 percent of financial executives said they could reliably forecast revenues only one quarter out. Even more disturbing

Technique	Description	Application
Quantitative		
Time series analysis	Fits a trend line to a mathematical equation and projects into the future by means of this equation	Predicting next quarter's sales on the basis of 4 years of previous sales data
Regression models	Predicts one variable on the basis of known or assumed other variables	Seeking factors that will predict a certain level of sales (e.g., price, advertising expenditures)
Econometric models	Uses a set of regression equations to simulate segments of the economy	Predicting change in car sales as a result of changes in tax laws
Economic indicators	Uses one or more economic indicators to predict a future state of the economy	Using change in GNP to predict discretionary income
Substitution effect	Uses a mathematical formula to predict how, when, and under what circumstances a new product or technology will replace an existing one	Predicting the effect of DVD players on the sale of VHS players
Qualitative		
Jury of opinion	Combines and averages the opinions of experts	Polling the company's human resource managers to predict next year's college recruitment needs
Salesforce composition	Combines estimates from field sales personnel of customers' expected purchases	Predicting next year's sales of industrial lasers
Customer evaluation	Combines estimates from established customers' purchases	Surveying major car dealers by a car manufacturer to determine types and quantities of products desired

Exhibit PCM-1
Forecasting Techniques

is that 16 percent of those executives said they were "in the dark" about revenue forecasts.[17] But it is important to try to make forecasting as effective as possible because research shows that a company's forecasting ability can be a distinctive competence.[18] Here are some suggestions for making forecasting more effective.[19]

First, it's important to understand that forecasting techniques are most accurate when the environment is not rapidly changing. The more dynamic the environment, the more likely managers are to forecast ineffectively. Also, forecasting is relatively ineffective in predicting nonseasonal events such as recessions, unusual occurrences, discontinued operations, and the actions or reactions of competitors. Next, use simple forecasting methods. They tend to do as well as, and often better than, complex methods that may mistakenly confuse random data for meaningful information. For instance, at St. Louis–based Emerson Electric, chairman emeritus Chuck Knight found that forecasts developed as part of the company's planning process indicated that the competition wasn't just domestic anymore, but global. He didn't use any complex mathematical techniques to come to this conclusion but instead relied on the information already collected as part of his company's planning process. Next, look at involving more people in the process. At *Fortune* 100 companies, it's not unusual to have 1,000 to 5,000 managers providing forecasting input. These businesses are finding that as more people are involved in the process, the more the reliability of the outcomes improves.[20] Next, compare every forecast with "no change." A no change forecast is accurate approximately half the time. Next, use *rolling* forecasts that look 12 to 18 months ahead, instead of using a single, static forecast. These types of forecasts can help managers spot trends better and help their organizations be more adaptive in changing environments.[21] It's also important to not rely on a single forecasting method. Make forecasts with several models and average them, especially when making longer-range forecasts. Next, don't assume you can accurately identify turning points in a trend. What is typically perceived as a significant turning point often turns out to be simply a random event. And, finally, remember that forecasting *is* a managerial skill and as such can be practiced and improved. Forecasting software has made the task somewhat less mathematically challenging, although the "number crunching" is only a small part of the activity. Interpreting the forecast and incorporating that information into planning decisions is the challenge facing managers.

Benchmarking

benchmarking
The search for the best practices among competitors or noncompetitors that lead to their superior performance

Suppose you're a talented pianist or gymnast. To make yourself better, you want to learn from the best so you watch outstanding musicians or athletes for motions and techniques they use as they perform. That same approach is involved in the final technique for assessing the environment we're going to discuss—**benchmarking**, the search for the best practices among competitors or noncompetitors that lead to their superior performance.[22] Does benchmarking work? Studies show that users have achieved 69 percent faster growth and 45 percent greater productivity.[23]

The basic idea behind benchmarking is that managers can improve performance by analyzing and then copying the methods of the leaders in various fields. Organizations such as Nissan, Payless Shoe Source, the U.S. military, General Mills, United Airlines, and Volvo Construction Equipment have used benchmarking as a tool in improving performance. In fact, some companies have chosen some pretty unusual benchmarking partners! IBM studied Las Vegas casinos for ways to discourage employee theft. Many hospitals have benchmarked their admissions processes against Marriott Hotels. And Giordano Holdings Ltd., a Hong Kong–based manufacturer and retailer of mass-market casual wear, borrowed its "good quality, good value" concept from Marks & Spencer, used Limited Brands to benchmark its point-of-sales computerized information system, and modeled its simplified product offerings on McDonald's menu.[24]

What does benchmarking involve? Exhibit PCM-2 illustrates the four steps typically used in benchmarking.

Exhibit PCM-2
Steps in Benchmarking

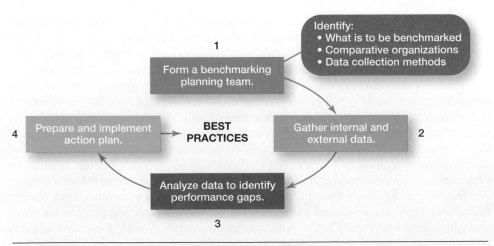

Source: Based on "Aiming High: Competitive Benchmarking for Superior Performance" by Y. K. Shetty, from *Long Range Planning*, February 1993 Volume 26(1).

TECHNIQUES for Allocating Resources

Once an organization's goals have been established, it's important to determine how those goals are going to be accomplished. Before managers can organize and lead as goals are implemented, they must have **resources**, the assets of the organization (financial, physical, human, and intangible). How can managers allocate these resources effectively and efficiently so that organizational goals are met? Although managers can choose from a number of techniques for allocating resources (many of which are covered in courses on accounting, finance, and operations management), we'll discuss four techniques here: budgeting, scheduling, breakeven analysis, and linear programming.

resources
The assets of the organization including financial, physical, human, intangible, and structural/cultural

Budgeting

Most of us have had some experience, as limited as it might be, with budgets. We probably learned at an early age that unless we allocated our "revenues" carefully, our weekly allowance was spent on "expenses" before the week was half over.

A **budget** is a numerical plan for allocating resources to specific activities. Managers typically prepare budgets for revenues, expenses, and large capital expenditures such as equipment. It's not unusual, though, for budgets to be used for improving time, space, and use of material resources. These types of budgets substitute nondollar numbers for dollar amounts. Such items as person-hours, capacity utilization, or units of production can be budgeted for daily, weekly, or monthly activities. Exhibit PCM-3 describes the different types of budgets that managers might use.

budget
A numerical plan for allocating resources to specific activities

Why are budgets so popular? Probably because they're applicable to a wide variety of organizations and work activities within organizations. We live in a world in which almost everything is expressed in monetary units. Dollars, rupees, pesos, euros, yuan, yen, and the like are used as a common measuring unit within a country. That's why monetary budgets are a useful tool for allocating resources and guiding work in such diverse departments as manufacturing and information systems or at various levels in an organization. Budgets are one planning technique that most managers use—regardless of organizational level. It's an important managerial activity because it forces financial discipline and structure throughout the organization. However, many managers don't like preparing budgets because they feel the process is time consuming, inflexible, inefficient, and ineffective.[25] How can the budgeting process be improved? Exhibit PCM-4 provides some suggestions. Organizations such as Texas Instruments, IKEA, Volvo, and Svenska Handelsbanken have incorporated several of these suggestions as they revamped their budgeting processes.

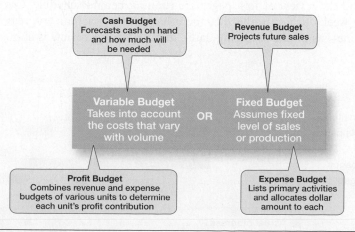

Cash Budget
Forecasts cash on hand and how much will be needed

Revenue Budget
Projects future sales

Variable Budget
Takes into account the costs that vary with volume

OR

Fixed Budget
Assumes fixed level of sales or production

Profit Budget
Combines revenue and expense budgets of various units to determine each unit's profit contribution

Expense Budget
Lists primary activities and allocates dollar amount to each

Exhibit PCM-3
Types of Budgets

Source: Based on *Production and Operations Management,* by R. S. Russell and B. W. Taylor III.

Exhibit PCM-4
How to Improve Budgeting

- Collaborate and communicate.
- Be flexible.
- Goals should drive budgets—budgets should not determine goals.
- Coordinate budgeting throughout the organization.
- Use budgeting/planning software when appropriate.
- Remember that budgets are tools.
- Remember that profits result from smart management, not because you budgeted for them.

Scheduling

Jackie is a manager at a Chico's store in San Francisco. Every week, she determines employees' work hours and the store area where each employee will be working. If you observed any group of supervisors or department managers for a few days, you would see them doing much the same—allocating resources by detailing what activities have to be done, the order in which they are to be completed, who is to do each, and when they are to be completed. These managers are **scheduling**. In this section, we'll review some useful scheduling devices, including Gantt charts, load charts, and PERT network analysis.

GANTT CHARTS The **Gantt chart** was developed during the early 1900s by Henry Gantt, an associate of Frederick Taylor, the scientific management expert. The idea behind a Gantt chart is simple. It's essentially a bar graph with time on the horizontal axis and the activities to be scheduled on the vertical axis. The bars show output, both planned and actual, over a period of time. The Gantt chart visually shows when tasks are supposed to be done and compares those projections with the actual progress on each task. It's a simple but important device that lets managers detail easily what has yet to be done to complete a job or project and to assess whether an activity is ahead of, behind, or on schedule.

Exhibit PCM-5 depicts a simplified Gantt chart for book production developed by a manager in a publishing company. Time is expressed in months across the top of the chart. The major work activities are listed down the left side. Planning involves deciding what activities need to be done to get the book finished, the order in which those activities need to be completed, and the time that should be allocated to each activity. Where a box sits within a time frame reflects its planned sequence. The shading represents actual progress. The chart also serves as a control tool because the manager can see deviations from the plan. In this example, both the design of the cover and the review of first pages are running behind schedule. Cover design is about three weeks behind (note that there has been no actual progress—shown by blue color line—as of the reporting date), and first pages review is about two weeks

scheduling
Detailing what activities have to be done, the order in which they are to be completed, who is to do each, and when they are to be completed

Gantt chart
A scheduling chart developed by Henry Gantt that shows actual and planned output over a period of time

Exhibit PCM-5
A Gantt Chart

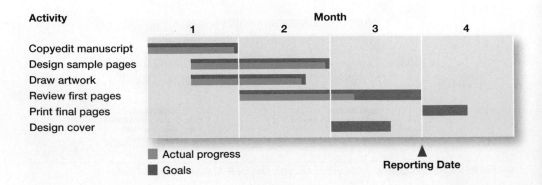

behind schedule (note that as of the report date, actual progress—shown by blue color line—is about six weeks, out of a goal of completing in two months). Given this information, the manager might need to take some action to either make up for the two lost weeks or to ensure that no further delays will occur. At this point, the manager can expect that the book will be published at least two weeks later than planned if no action is taken.

LOAD CHARTS A **load chart** is a modified Gantt chart. Instead of listing activities on the vertical axis, load charts list either entire departments or specific resources. This arrangement allows managers to plan and control capacity utilization. In other words, load charts schedule capacity by work areas.

For example, Exhibit PCM-6 shows a load chart for six production editors at the same publishing company. Each editor supervises the production and design of several books. By reviewing a load chart, the executive editor, who supervises the six production editors, can see who is free to take on a new book. If everyone is fully scheduled, the executive editor might decide not to accept any new projects, to accept new projects and delay others, to make the editors work overtime, or to employ more production editors. As this exhibit shows, only Antonio and Maurice are completely scheduled for the next six months. The other editors have some unassigned time and might be able to accept new projects or be available to help other editors who get behind.

PERT NETWORK ANALYSIS Gantt and load charts are useful as long as the activities scheduled are few in number and independent of each other. But what if a manager had to plan a large project such as a departmental reorganization, the implementation of a cost-reduction program, or the development of a new product that required coordinating inputs from marketing, manufacturing, and product design? Such projects require coordinating hundreds and even thousands of activities, some of which must be done simultaneously and some of which can't begin until preceding activities have been completed. If you're constructing a building, you obviously can't start putting up the walls until the foundation is laid. How can managers schedule such a complex project? The program evaluation and review technique (PERT) is highly appropriate for such projects.

A **PERT network** is a flowchart diagram that depicts the sequence of activities needed to complete a project and the time or costs associated with each activity. With a PERT network, a manager must think through what has to be done, determine which events depend on one another, and identify potential trouble spots. PERT also makes it easy to compare the effects alternative actions might have on scheduling and costs. Thus, PERT allows managers to monitor a project's progress, identify possible bottlenecks, and shift resources as necessary to keep the project on schedule.

To understand how to construct a PERT network, you need to know four terms. **Events** are end points that represent the completion of major activities. **Activities** represent the time or resources required to progress from one event to another. **Slack time** is the amount of time an individual activity can be delayed without delaying the whole project. The **critical path** is the longest or most time-consuming sequence of

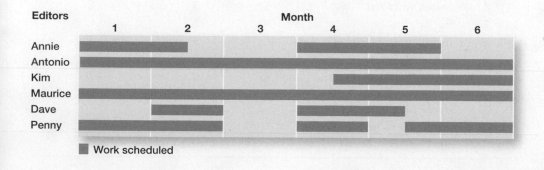

Exhibit PCM-6
A Load Chart

Work scheduled

Exhibit PCM-7

Steps in Developing a PERT
Network

1. *Identify every significant activity that must be achieved for a project to be completed.* The accomplishment of each activity results in a set of events or outcomes.

2. *Determine the order in which these events must be completed.*

3. *Diagram the flow of activities from start to finish, identifying each activity and its relationship to all other activities.* Use circles to indicate events and arrows to represent activities. This results in a flowchart diagram called a PERT network.

4. *Compute a time estimate for completing each activity.* This is done with a weighted average that uses an *optimistic* time estimate (t_o) of how long the activity would take under ideal conditions, a *most likely* estimate (t_m) of the time the activity normally should take, and a *pessimistic* estimate (t_p) that represents the time that an activity should take under the worst possible conditions. The formula for calculating the expected time (t_e) is then

$$t_e = \frac{t_o + 4t_m + t_p}{6}$$

5. *Using the network diagram that contains time estimates for each activity, determine a schedule for the start and finish dates of each activity and for the entire project.* Any delays that occur along the critical path require the most attention because they can delay the whole project.

events and activities in a PERT network. Any delay in completing events on this path would delay completion of the entire project. In other words, activities on the critical path have zero slack time.

Developing a PERT network requires that a manager identify all key activities needed to complete a project, rank them in order of occurrence, and estimate each activity's completion time. Exhibit PCM-7 explains the steps in this process.

Most PERT projects are complicated and include numerous activities. Such complicated computations can be done with specialized PERT software. However, let's work through a simple example. Assume you're the superintendent at a construction company and have been assigned to oversee the construction of an office building. Because time really is money in your business, you must determine how long it will take to get the building completed. You've determined the specific activities and events. Exhibit PCM-8 outlines the major events in the construction project and your estimate of the expected time to complete each. Exhibit PCM-9 shows the actual

Exhibit PCM-8

Events and Activities in
Constructing an Office Building

Event	Description	Expected Time (in weeks)	Preceding Event
A	Approve design and get permits	10	None
B	Dig subterranean garage	6	A
C	Erect frame and siding	14	B
D	Construct floor	6	C
E	Install windows	3	C
F	Put on roof	3	C
G	Install internal wiring	5	D, E, F
H	Install elevator	5	G
I	Put in floor covering and paneling	4	D
J	Put in doors and interior decorative trim	3	I, H
K	Turn over to building management group	1	J

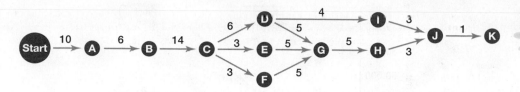

Exhibit PCM-9
PERT Network for Constructing an
Office Building

PERT network based on the data in Exhibit PCM-8. You've also calculated the length of time that each path of activities will take:

A-B-C-D-I-J-K (44 weeks)

A-B-C-D-G-H-J-K (50 weeks)

A-B-C-E-G-H-J-K (47 weeks)

A-B-C-F-G-H-J-K (47 weeks)

Your PERT network shows that if everything goes as planned, the total project completion time will be 50 weeks. This is calculated by tracing the project's critical path (the longest sequence of activities): A-B-C-D-G-H-J-K and adding up the times. You know that any delay in completing the events on this path would delay the completion of the entire project. Taking six weeks instead of four to put in the floor covering and paneling (Event I) would have no effect on the final completion date. Why? Because that event isn't on the critical path. However, taking seven weeks instead of six to dig the subterranean garage (Event B) would likely delay the total project. A manager who needed to get back on schedule or to cut the 50-week completion time would want to concentrate on those activities along the critical path that could be completed faster. How might the manager do this? He or she could look to see if any of the other activities *not* on the critical path had slack time in which resources could be transferred to activities that *were* on the critical path.

Breakeven Analysis

Managers at Glory Foods want to know how many units of their new sensibly seasoned canned vegetables must be sold in order to break even—that is, the point at which total revenue is just sufficient to cover total costs. **Breakeven analysis** is a widely used resource allocation technique to help managers determine breakeven point.[26]

Breakeven analysis is a simple calculation, yet it's valuable to managers because it points out the relationship between revenues, costs, and profits. To compute breakeven point *(BE)*, a manager needs to know the unit price of the product being sold *(P)*, the variable cost per unit *(VC)*, and total fixed costs *(TFC)*. An organization breaks even when its total revenue is just enough to equal its total costs. But total cost has two parts: fixed and variable. *Fixed costs* are expenses that do not change regardless of volume. Examples include insurance premiums, rent, and property taxes. *Variable costs* change in proportion to output and include raw materials, labor costs, and energy costs.

Breakeven point can be computed graphically or by using the following formula:

breakeven analysis
A technique for identifying the point at which total revenue is just sufficient to cover total costs

$$BE = \frac{TFC}{P - VC}$$

This formula tells us that (1) total revenue will equal total cost when we sell enough units at a price that covers all variable unit costs, and (2) the difference between price and variable costs, when multiplied by the number of units sold, equals the fixed costs. Let's work through an example.

Assume that Randy's Photocopying Service charges $0.10 per photocopy. If fixed costs are $27,000 a year and variable costs are $0.04 per copy, Randy can compute his breakeven point as follows: $27,000 ÷ ($0.10 – $0.04) = 450,000 copies, or when annual revenues are $45,000 (450,000 copies × $0.10). This same relationship is shown graphically in Exhibit PCM-10.

Exhibit PCM-10
Breakeven Analysis

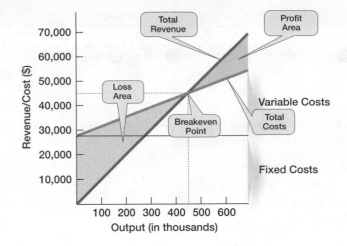

As a planning tool, breakeven analysis could help Randy set his sales goal. For example, he could determine his profit goal and then calculate what sales level is needed to reach that goal. Breakeven analysis could also tell Randy how much volume has to increase to break even if he's currently operating at a loss or how much volume he can afford to lose and still break even.

Linear Programming

Maria Sanchez manages a manufacturing plant that produces two kinds of cinnamon-scented home fragrance products: wax candles and a woodchip potpourri sold in bags. Business is good, and she can sell all of the products she can produce. Her dilemma: Given that the bags of potpourri and the wax candles are manufactured in the same facility, how many of each product should she produce to maximize profits? Maria can use **linear programming** to solve her resource allocation problem.

Although linear programming can be used here, it can't be applied to all resource allocation problems because it requires that resources be limited, that the goal be outcome optimization, that resources can be combined in alternative ways to produce a number of output mixes, and that a linear relationship exist between variables (a change in one variable must be accompanied by an exactly proportional change in the other).[27] For Maria's business, that last condition would be met if it took exactly twice the amount of raw materials and hours of labor to produce two of a given home fragrance product as it took to produce one.

What kinds of problems can be solved with linear programming? Some applications include selecting transportation routes that minimize shipping costs, allocating a limited advertising budget among various product brands, making the optimal assignment of people among projects, and determining how much of each product to make with a limited number of resources. Let's return to Maria's problem and see how linear programming could help her solve it. Fortunately, her problem is relatively simple, so we can solve it rather quickly. For complex linear programming problems, managers can use computer software programs designed specifically to help develop optimizing solutions.

First, we need to establish some facts about Maria's business. She has computed the profit margins on her home fragrance products at $10 for a bag of potpourri and $18 for a scented candle. These numbers establish the basis for Maria to be able to express her *objective function* as maximum profit = $10P + \$18S$, where P is the number of bags of potpourri produced and S is the number of scented candles produced. The objective function is simply a mathematical equation that can predict the outcome of all proposed alternatives. In addition, Maria knows how much time each fragrance product must spend in production and the monthly production capacity (1,200 hours in manufacturing and 900 hours in assembly) for manufacturing and

linear programming
A mathematical technique that solves resource allocation problems

| | Number of Hours Required (per unit) | | Monthly Production |
Department	Potpourri Bags	Scented Candles	Capacity (in hours)
Manufacturing	2	4	1,200
Assembly	2	2	900
Profit per unit	$10	$18	

Exhibit PCM-11

Production Data for Cinnamon-Scented Products

assembly. (See Exhibit PCM-11.) The production capacity numbers act as *constraints* on her overall capacity. Now Maria can establish her constraint equations:

$$2P + 4S \leq 1,200$$

$$2P + 2S \leq 900$$

Of course, Maria can also state that $P \geq 0$ and $S \geq 0$ because neither fragrance product can be produced in a volume less than zero.

Maria has graphed her solution in Exhibit PCM-12. The shaded area represents the options that don't exceed the capacity of either department. What does this mean? Well, let's look first at the manufacturing constraint line BE. We know that total manufacturing capacity is 1,200 hours, so if Maria decides to produce all potpourri bags, the maximum she can produce is 600 (1,200 hours ÷ 2 hours required to produce a bag of potpourri). If she decides to produce all scented candles, the maximum she can produce is 300 (1,200 hours ÷ 4 hours required to produce a scented candle). The other constraint Maria faces is that of assembly, shown by line DF. If Maria decides to produce all potpourri bags, the maximum she can assemble is 450 (900 hours production capacity ÷ 2 hours required to assemble). Likewise, if Maria decides to produce all scented candles, the maximum she can assemble is also 450 because the scented candles also take 2 hours to assemble. The constraints imposed by these capacity limits establish Maria's *feasibility region*. Her optimal resource allocation will be defined at one of the corners within this feasibility region. Point C provides the maximum profits within the constraints stated. How do we know? At point A, profits would be 0 (no production of either potpourri bags or scented candles). At point B, profits would be $5,400 (300 scented candles × $18 profit and 0 potpourri bags produced = $5,400]). At point D, profits would be $4,500 (450 potpourri bags produced × $10 profit and 0 scented candles produced = $4,500). At point C, however, profits would be $5,700 (150 scented candles produced × $18 profit and 300 potpourri bags produced × $10 profit = $5,700).

Exhibit PCM-12

Graphical Solution to Linear Programming Problem

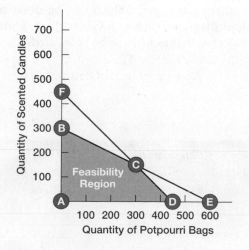

CONTEMPORARY Planning and Control Techniques

Lowest home mortgage rates since 1950s. H1N1 flu pandemic. Chemical/biological attacks. Recession/inflation worries. Category 4 or 5 hurricanes. Changing competition. Today's managers face the challenges of planning in an environment that's both dynamic and complex. Two planning techniques appropriate for this type of environment are project management and scenarios. Both techniques emphasize *flexibility*, something that's important to making planning more effective and efficient in this type of organizational environment.

Project Management

project
A one-time-only set of activities that has a definite beginning and ending point in time

project management
The task of getting a project's activities done on time, within budget, and according to specifications

Different types of organizations, from manufacturers such as Coleman and Boeing to software design firms such as SAS and Microsoft, use projects. A **project** is a one-time-only set of activities that has a definite beginning and ending point in time.[28] Projects vary in size and scope—from Boston's "big dig" downtown traffic tunnel to a sorority's holiday formal. **Project management** is the task of getting a project's activities done on time, within budget, and according to specifications.[29]

More and more organizations are using project management because the approach fits well with the need for flexibility and rapid response to perceived market opportunities. When organizations undertake projects that are unique, have specific deadlines, contain complex interrelated tasks requiring specialized skills, and are temporary in nature, these projects often do not fit into the standardized planning procedures that guide an organization's other routine work activities. Instead, managers use project management techniques to effectively and efficiently accomplish the project's goals. What does the project management process involve?

PROJECT MANAGEMENT PROCESS In the typical project, work is done by a project team whose members are assigned from their respective work areas to the project and who report to a project manager. The project manager coordinates the project's activities with other departments. When the project team accomplishes its goals, it disbands and members move on to other projects or back to their permanent work area.

The essential features of the project planning process are shown in Exhibit PCM-13. The process begins by clearly defining the project's goals. This step is necessary because the manager and the team members need to know what's expected. All activities in the project and the resources needed to do them must then be identified. What materials and labor are needed to complete the project? This step may be time-consuming and complex, particularly if the project is unique and the managers have no history or experience with similar projects. Once the activities have been identified, the sequence of completion needs to be determined. What activities must be completed before others can begin? Which can be done simultaneously? This step often uses flowchart diagrams such as a Gantt chart, a load chart, or a PERT network. Next, the project activities need to be scheduled. Time estimates for each

Exhibit PCM-13
Project Planning Process

Source: Based on *Production and Operations Management*, by R. S. Russell and B. W. Taylor III.

activity are done, and these estimates are used to develop an overall project schedule and completion date. Then the project schedule is compared to the goals, and any necessary adjustments are made. If the project completion time is too long, the manager might assign more resources to critical activities so they can be completed faster.

Today, the project management process can take place online as a number of Web-based software packages are available. These packages cover aspects from project accounting and estimating to project scheduling and bug and defect tracking.[30]

THE ROLE OF THE PROJECT MANAGER The temporary nature of projects makes managing them different from, say, overseeing a production line or preparing a weekly tally of costs on an ongoing basis. The one-shot nature of the work makes project managers the organizational equivalent of a hired gunman. There's a job to be done. It has to be defined—in detail. And the project manager is responsible for how it's done. At J.B. Hunt Transport Services, the head of project management trains project managers on both technical and interpersonal skills so that they know how to "...run a project effectively."[31]

Even with the availability of sophisticated computerized and online scheduling programs and other project management tools, the role of project manager remains difficult because he or she is managing people who typically are still assigned to their permanent work areas. The only real influence project managers have is their communication skills and their power of persuasion. To make matters worse, team members seldom work on just one project. They're usually assigned to two or three at any given time. So project managers end up competing with each other to focus a worker's attention on his or her particular project.

Scenario Planning

During the 1990s, business was so good at Colgate-Palmolive that then-chairman Reuben Mark worried about what "might go wrong." He installed an "early-warning system to flag problems before they blew up into company-wrecking crises." For instance, a red-flag report alerted Mark "that officials in Baddi, India, had questions about how a plant treated wastewater." Mark's response was to quickly assign an engineering team to check it out and prevent potential problems.[32]

We already know how important it is that today's managers do what Reuben Mark was doing—monitor and assess the external environment for trends and changes. As they assess the environment, issues and concerns that could affect their organization's current or planned operations are likely to be revealed. All of these issues won't be equally important, so it's usually necessary to focus on a limited set that are most important and to develop scenarios based on each.

A **scenario** is a consistent view of what the future is likely to be. Developing scenarios also can be described as *contingency planning*; that is, if this event happens, then we need to take these actions. If, for instance, environmental scanning reveals increasing interest by U.S. Congress for raising the national minimum wage, managers at Subway could create multiple scenarios to assess the possible consequences of such an action. What would be the implications for its labor costs if the minimum wage was raised to $10 an hour? How about $12 an hour? What effect would these changes have on the chain's bottom line? How might competitors respond? Different assumptions lead to different outcomes. The intent of scenario planning is not to try to predict the future but to reduce uncertainty by playing out potential situations under different specified conditions.[33] Subway could, for example, develop a set of scenarios ranging from optimistic to pessimistic in terms of the minimum wage issue. It would then be prepared to implement new strategies to get and keep a competitive advantage. An expert in scenario planning said, "Just the process of doing scenarios causes executives to rethink and clarify the essence of the business environment in ways they almost certainly have never done before."[34]

scenario
A consistent view of what the future is likely to be

Although scenario planning is useful in anticipating events that *can be* anticipated, it's difficult to forecast random events—the major surprises and aberrations that can't be foreseen. For instance, an outbreak of deadly and devastating tornadoes in southwest Missouri in May 2011 was a scenario that could be anticipated. The disaster recovery planning that took place after the storms was effective because this type of scenario had been experienced before. A response had already been planned and people knew what to do. But the planning challenge comes from those totally random and unexpected events. For instance, the 9/11 terrorist attacks in New York and Washington, D.C., were random, unexpected, and a total shock to many organizations. Scenario planning was of little use because no one could have envisioned this scenario. As difficult as it may be for managers to anticipate and deal with these random events, they're not totally vulnerable to the consequences. One suggestion identified by risk experts as particularly important is to have an early warning system in place. (A similar idea is the tsunami warning systems in the Pacific and in Alaska, which alert officials to potentially dangerous tsunamis and give them time to take action.) Early warning indicators for organizations can give managers advance notice of potential problems and changes—such as it did Reuben Mark at Colgate-Palmolive—so they, too, can take action. Then, managers need to have appropriate responses (plans) in place if these unexpected events occur.

Planning tools and techniques can help managers prepare confidently for the future. But they should remember that all the tools we've described in this module are just that—tools. They will never replace the manager's skills and capabilities in using the information gained to develop effective and efficient plans.

REVIEW AND DISCUSSION QUESTIONS

1. Describe the different approaches to assessing the environment.

2. Describe the four techniques for allocating resources.

3. How does PERT network analysis work?

4. Why is flexibility so important to today's planning techniques?

5. What is project management, and what are the steps managers use in planning projects?

6. "It's a waste of time and other resources to develop a set of sophisticated scenarios for situations that may never occur." Do you agree or disagree? Support your position.

7. Do intuition and creativity have any relevance in quantitative planning tools and techniques? Explain.

8. The *Wall Street Journal* and other business periodicals often carry reports of companies that have not met their sales or profit forecasts. What are some reasons a company might not meet its forecast? What suggestions could you make for improving the effectiveness of forecasting?

9. In what ways is managing a project different from managing a department or other structured work area? In what ways are they the same?

10. What might be some early warning signs of (a) a new competitor coming into your market, (b) an employee work stoppage, or (c) a new technology that could change demand for your product?

Managing Operations Module

Using millions of parts as small as rivets and as large as five-story buildings, employees at Hyundai Heavy Industries Inc. build as many as 30 ships at one time.[1] And the "factory" stretches for miles over land and sea. "It's an environment that is too large and complex to be able to keep track of the movement in parts and inventory in real time." Hwang See-young, chief information officer at Hyundai Heavy, knew that production efficiency was limited without real-time data. The solution? High-speed wireless networks that employees can access at anytime and anywhere with notebook computers.

With the new technology, data fly around the shipyard complex at 4 megabits per second. Radio sensors track the movements of parts from fabrication shops to the dry dock and onto a ship being constructed. Also, workers on a ship can access plans using notebook computers or handheld phones. They're also able to hold two-way video conversations with ship designers in the office over a mile away. Eventually, they hope to establish communication capabilities with workers inside a ship that is below ground or at sea level. Now, however, Hyundai Heavy wants to implement the technology in its other construction divisions. Suppose you were in charge of doing this. What would you do?

As the world's largest maker of ships, Hyundai hopes its new technology helps it reduce expenses and streamline production, an important consideration in today's environment. You've probably never given much thought to how organizations "produce" the goods and services that you buy or use. But it's an important process. Without it, you wouldn't have a car to drive or McDonald's fries to snack on, or even a hiking trail in a local park to enjoy. Organizations need to have well-thought-out and well-designed operating systems, organizational control systems, and quality programs to survive in today's increasingly competitive global environment. And it's the manager's job to manage those systems and programs.

THE Role of Operations Management

operations management
The transformation process that converts resources into finished goods and services

What is **operations management**? The term refers to the transformation process that converts resources into finished goods and services. Exhibit MOM-1 portrays this process in a simplified fashion. The system takes in inputs—people, technology, capital, equipment, materials, and information—and transforms them through various processes, procedures, work activities, and so forth into finished goods and services. Because every unit in an organization produces something, managers need to be familiar with operations management concepts in order to achieve goals efficiently and effectively.

Operations management is important to organizations and managers for three reasons: (1) it encompasses both services and manufacturing; (2) it's important in effectively and efficiently managing productivity; and (3) it plays a strategic role in an organization's competitive success.

Services and Manufacturing

With a menu that offers more than 200 items, The Cheesecake Factory restaurants rely on a finely tuned production system. One food-service consultant says, "They've evolved with this highly complex menu combined with a highly efficient kitchen."[2]

manufacturing organizations
Organizations that produce physical goods

service organizations
Organizations that produce nonphysical products in the form of services

Every organization produces something. Unfortunately, this fact is often overlooked except in obvious cases such as in the manufacturing of cars, cell phones, or lawnmowers. After all, **manufacturing organizations** produce physical goods. It's easy to see the operations management (transformation) process at work in these types of organizations because raw materials are turned into recognizable physical products. But the transformation process isn't as readily evident in **service organizations** that produce nonphysical outputs in the form of services. For instance, hospitals provide medical and health care services that help people manage their personal health, airlines provide transportation services that move people from one location to another, a cruise line provides a vacation and entertainment service, military forces provide defense capabilities, and the list goes on. These service organizations also transform inputs into outputs, although the transformation process isn't as easily recognizable as that in manufacturing organizations. Take a university, for example. University administrators bring together inputs—professors, books, academic journals, technology materials, computers, classrooms, and similar resources—to transform "unenlightened" students into educated and skilled individuals who are capable of making contributions to society.

The reason we're making this point is that the U.S. economy, and to a large extent the global economy, is dominated by the creation and sale of services. Most of the world's developed countries are predominantly service economies. In the United States, for instance, almost 80 percent of all economic activity is services and in the European Union, it's over 73 percent. In lesser-developed countries, the services sector is less important. For instance, in Nigeria, it accounts for only 31 percent of economic activity; in Laos, only 37 percent; and in Vietnam, about 38 percent.[3]

Exhibit MOM-1
The Operations System

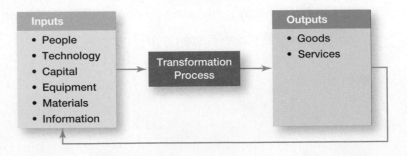

Managing Productivity

One jetliner has roughly 4 million parts. Efficiently assembling such a finely engineered product requires intense focus. Boeing and Airbus, the two major global manufacturers, have copied techniques from Toyota. However, not every technique can be copied because airlines demand more customization than do car buyers and significantly more rigid safety regulations apply to jetliners than to cars.[4] At the Evans Findings Company in East Providence, Rhode Island, which makes the tiny cutting devices on dental-floss containers, one production shift each day is run without people.[5] The company's goal is to do as much as possible with no labor. And it's not because they don't care about their employees. Instead, like many U.S. manufacturers, Evans needed to raise productivity in order to survive, especially against low-cost competitors. So they turned to "lights-out" manufacturing where machines are designed to be so reliable that they make flawless parts on their own, without people operating them.

Although most organizations don't make products that have 4 million parts and most organizations can't function without people, improving productivity has become a major goal in virtually every organization. For countries, high productivity can lead to economic growth and development. Employees can receive higher wages and company profits can increase without causing inflation. For individual organizations, increased productivity gives them a more competitive cost structure and the ability to offer more competitive prices.

Over the past decade, U.S. businesses have made dramatic improvements to increase their efficiency. For example, at Latex Foam International's state-of-the-art digital facility in Shelton, Connecticut, engineers monitor all of the factory's operations. The facility boosted capacity by 50 percent in a smaller space but with a 30 percent efficiency gain.[6] And it's not just in manufacturing that companies are pursuing productivity gains. Pella Corporation's purchasing office improved productivity by reducing purchase order entry times anywhere from 50 percent to 86 percent, decreasing voucher processing by 27 percent, and eliminating 14 financial systems. Its information technology department slashed e-mail traffic in half and implemented work design improvements for heavy PC users such as call center users. The human resources department cut the time to process benefit enrollment by 156.5 days. And the finance department now takes 2 days instead of 6 to do its end-of-month closeout.[7]

Organizations that hope to succeed globally are looking for ways to improve productivity. For example, McDonald's Corporation drastically reduced the time it takes to cook its french fries—65 seconds as compared to the 210 seconds it once took, saving time and other resources.[8] The Canadian Imperial Bank of Commerce, based in Toronto, automated its purchasing function, saving several million dollars annually.[9] And Skoda, the Czech car company that's a subsidiary of Germany's Volkswagen AG, improved its productivity through an intensive restructuring of its manufacturing process.[10]

Productivity is a composite of people and operations variables. To improve productivity, managers must focus on both. The late W. Edwards Deming, a renowned quality expert, believed that managers, not workers, were the primary source of increased productivity. Some of his suggestions for managers included planning for the long-term future, never being complacent about product quality, understanding whether problems were confined to particular parts of the production process or stemmed from the overall process itself, training workers for the job they're being asked to perform, raising the quality of line supervisors, requiring workers to do quality work, and so forth.[11] As you can see, Deming understood the interplay between people and operations. High productivity can't come solely from good "people management." The truly effective organization will maximize productivity by successfully integrating people into the overall operations system. For instance, at Simplex Nails Manufacturing in Americus, Georgia, employees were an integral part of the company's much-needed turnaround effort.[12] Some production workers were redeployed on a plant-wide cleanup and organization effort, which freed up floor space. The company's sales force was retrained and refocused to sell what customers wanted rather than what was in inventory. The results were dramatic. Inventory was reduced by more than 50 percent, the plant had 20 percent more floor space, orders were more consistent, and employee morale improved. Here's a company that recognized the important interplay between people and the operations system.

Strategic Role of Operations Management

Modern manufacturing originated over 100 years ago in the United States, primarily in Detroit's automobile factories. The success that U.S. manufacturers experienced during World War II led manufacturing executives to believe that troublesome production problems had been conquered. These executives focused, instead, on improving other functional areas such as finance and marketing and paid little attention to manufacturing.

However, as U.S. executives neglected production, managers in Japan, Germany, and other countries took the opportunity to develop modern, computer-based, and technologically advanced facilities that fully integrated manufacturing operations into strategic planning decisions. The competition's success realigned world manufacturing leadership. U.S. manufacturers soon discovered that foreign goods were made not only less expensively but also with better quality. Finally, by the late 1970s, U.S. executives recognized they were facing a true crisis and responded. They invested heavily in improving manufacturing technology, increased the corporate authority and visibility of manufacturing executives, and began incorporating existing and future production requirements into the organization's overall strategic plan. Today, successful organizations recognize the crucial role that operations management plays as part of the overall organizational strategy to establish and maintain global leadership.[13]

The strategic role that operations management plays in successful organizational performance can be seen clearly as more organizations move toward managing their operations from a value chain perspective, which we're going to discuss next.

WHAT Is Value Chain Management and Why Is It Important?

It's 11 p.m., and you're reading a text message from your parents saying they want to buy you a laptop for your birthday this year and to order it. You log on to Dell's Web site and configure your dream machine. You hit the order button and not long after, your dream computer is delivered to your front door, built to your exact specifications, ready to set up and use immediately to type that management assignment due tomorrow. Or consider Siemens AG's Computed Tomography manufacturing plant in Forchheim, Germany, which has established partnerships with about 30 suppliers. These suppliers are partners in the truest sense as they share responsibility with the plant for overall process performance. This arrangement has allowed Siemens to eliminate all inventory warehousing and has streamlined the number of times paper changes hands to order parts from 18 to one. At the Timken's plant in Canton, Ohio, electronic purchase orders are sent across the street to an adjacent "Supplier City" where many of its key suppliers have set up shop. The process takes milliseconds and costs less than 50 cents per purchase order. And when Black & Decker extended its line of handheld tools to include a glue gun, it totally outsourced the entire design and production to the leading glue gun manufacturer. Why? Because they understood that glue guns don't require motors, which was what Black & Decker did best.[14]

As these examples show, closely integrated work activities among many different players are possible. How? The answer lies in value chain management. The concepts of value chain management have transformed operations management strategies and turned organizations around the world into finely tuned models of efficiency and effectiveness strategically positioned to exploit competitive opportunities.

WHAT Is Value Chain Management?

Every organization needs customers if it's going to survive and prosper. Even a not-for-profit organization must have "customers" who use its services or purchase its products. Customers want some type of value from the goods and services they purchase or use, and these customers decide what has value. Organizations must provide that value to attract and keep customers. **Value** is defined as the performance characteristics, features, and attributes and any other aspects of goods and services for which customers are willing to give up resources (usually money). For example, when you purchase Rihanna's new CD at Best Buy, a new pair of Australian sheepskin Ugg boots online at Zappos, a Wendy's bacon cheeseburger at the drive-through location on campus, or a haircut from your local hair salon, you're exchanging (giving up) money in return for the value you need or desire from these products—providing music during your evening study time, keeping your feet warm *and* fashionable during winter's cold weather, alleviating the lunchtime hunger pangs quickly since your next class starts in 15 minutes, or looking professionally groomed for the job interview you've got next week.

How *is* value provided to customers? Through transforming raw materials and other resources into some product or service that end users need or desire when, where, and how they want it. However, that seemingly simple act of turning varied resources into something that customers value and are willing to pay for involves a vast array of interrelated work activities performed by different participants (suppliers, manufacturers, and even customers)—that is, it involves the value chain. The **value chain** is the entire series of organizational work activities that add value at each step from raw materials to finished product. In its entirety, the value chain can encompass the supplier's suppliers to the customer's customer.[15]

Value chain management is the process of managing the sequence of activities and information along the entire value chain. In contrast to supply chain management, which is *internally* oriented and focuses on efficient flow of incoming materials (resources) to the organization, value chain management is *externally* oriented and focuses on both incoming materials and outgoing products and services. Although supply chain management is efficiency oriented (its goal is to reduce costs and make the organization more productive), value chain management is effectiveness oriented and aims to create the highest value for customers.[16]

value
The performance characteristics, features, and attributes, and any other aspects of goods and services for which customers are willing to give up resources

value chain
The entire series of organizational work activities that add value at each step from raw materials to finished product

value chain management
The process of managing the sequence of activities and information along the entire value chain

Goal of Value Chain Management

Who has the power in the value chain? Is it the suppliers providing needed resources and materials? After all, they have the ability to dictate prices and quality. Is it the manufacturer who assembles those resources into a valuable product or service? Their contribution in creating a product or service is quite obvious. Is it the distributor that makes sure the product or service is available where and when the customer needs it? Actually, it's none of these! In value chain management, ultimately customers are the ones with power.[17] They're the ones who define what value is and how it's created and provided. Using value chain management, managers hope to find that unique combination that offers customers solutions to truly meet their unique needs incredibly fast and at a price that can't be matched by competitors.

With these factors in mind then, the goal of value chain management is to create a value chain strategy that meets and exceeds customers' needs and desires and allows for full and seamless integration among all members of the chain. A good value chain involves a sequence of participants working together as a team, each adding some component of value—such as faster assembly, more accurate information, better customer response and service, and so forth—to the overall process.[18] The better the collaboration among the various chain participants, the better the customer solutions. When value is created for customers and their needs and desires are satisfied, everyone along the chain benefits. For example, at Johnson Controls Inc., managing the value chain started first with improved relationships with internal suppliers, then expanded out to external suppliers and customers. As the company's experience with value chain management improved, so did its connection with its customers, which ultimately paid off for all its value chain partners.[19]

Benefits of Value Chain Management

Collaborating with external and internal partners in creating and managing a successful value chain strategy requires significant investments in time, energy, and other resources, and a serious commitment by all chain partners. Given these demands, why would managers ever choose to implement value chain management? A survey of manufacturers noted four primary benefits of value chain management: improved procurement, improved logistics, improved product development, and enhanced customer order management.[20]

MANAGING Operations Using Value Chain Management

Even though it's the world's largest retailer, Walmart still looks for ways to more effectively and efficiently manage its value chain. Its current efforts involve taking over U.S. transportation services from suppliers in an effort to reduce the cost of transporting goods. The goal: "to handle suppliers' deliveries in instances where Walmart can do the same job for less, then use those savings to reduce prices in stores." Walmart believes it has the size and scale to allow it to ship most products more efficiently than the companies that produce the goods.[21]

Even if you're Walmart, managing an organization from a value chain perspective isn't easy. Approaches to giving customers what they want that may have worked in the past are likely no longer efficient or effective. Today's dynamic competitive environment demands new solutions from global organizations. Understanding how and why value is determined by the marketplace has led some organizations to experiment with a new business model, a concept we introduced in Chapter 9. For example, IKEA transformed itself from a small Swedish mail-order furniture operation into one of the world's largest furniture retailers by reinventing the value chain in that industry. The company offers customers well-designed products at substantially lower prices in return for their willingness to take on certain key tasks traditionally done by manufacturers and retailers—assembling furniture and getting it home.[22] The company's creation of a new business model and willingness to abandon old methods and processes has worked well.

Value Chain Strategy

Exhibit MOM-2 shows the six main requirements of a successful value chain strategy: coordination and collaboration, technology investment, organizational processes, leadership, employees, and organizational culture and attitudes.

COORDINATION AND COLLABORATION For the value chain to achieve its goal of meeting and exceeding customers' needs and desires, collaborative relationships among all chain participants must exist.[23] Each partner must identify things he or she may not value but that customers do. Sharing information and being flexible as far as who in the value chain does what are important steps in building coordination and collaboration. This sharing of information and analysis requires more open

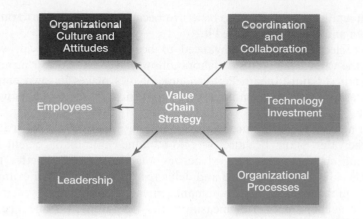

communication among the various value chain partners. For example, Kraft Foods believes that better communication with customers and with suppliers has facilitated timely delivery of goods and services.[24]

TECHNOLOGY INVESTMENT   Successful value chain management isn't possible without a significant investment in information technology. The payoff from this investment, however, is that information technology can be used to restructure the value chain to better serve end users. For example, each year the Houston-based food distributor Sysco ships 21.5 million tons of produce, meats, prepared meals, and other food-related products to restaurants, cafeterias, and sports stadiums. To get all that food safely to the right place at the right time, Sysco relies on a complex web of software, databases, scanning systems, and robotics.[25]

ORGANIZATIONAL PROCESSES   At Pactiv Corporation, which manufactures consumer and food-service packaging, the company relied on a planning process that included three-year breakthrough goals, which were then translated into one-year goals, annual improvement priorities, and measurable targets. This disciplined approach to planning has helped the company grow and achieve its goals.[26]

Value chain management radically changes **organizational processes**—that is, the ways that organizational work is done. When managers decide to manage operations using value chain management, old processes are no longer appropriate. All organizational processes must be critically evaluated from beginning to end to see where value is being added. Non-value-adding activities should be eliminated. Questions such as "Where can internal knowledge be leveraged to improve the flow of material and information?" "How can we better configure our product to satisfy both customers and suppliers?" "How can the flow of material and information be improved?" and "How can we improve customer service?" should be asked for each and every process. For example, when managers at Deere and Company implemented value chain management, a thorough process evaluation revealed that work activities needed to be better synchronized and interrelationships between multiple links in the value chain better managed. They changed numerous work processes division-wide in order to realize greater value.[27]

Three important conclusions can be made about organizational processes. First, better demand forecasting is necessary *and* possible because of closer ties with customers and suppliers. For example, in an effort to make sure that Listerine was on the store shelves when customers wanted it (known in the retail industry as *product replenishment rates*), Walmart and Pfizer's Consumer Healthcare Group collaborated on improving product demand forecast information. Through their mutual efforts, the partners boosted Walmart's sales of Listerine, an excellent outcome for both

organizational processes
The ways that organizational work is done

supplier and retailer. Customers also benefited because they were able to purchase the product when and where they wanted it.

Second, selected functions may need to be done collaboratively with other partners in the value chain. This collaboration may even extend to sharing employees. For instance, Saint-Gobain Performance Plastics places its own employees in customer sites and brings in employees of suppliers and customers to work on its premises.[28]

Finally, new measures are needed for evaluating performance of various activities along the value chain. Because the goal in value chain management is meeting and exceeding customers' needs and desires, managers need a better picture of how well this value is being created and delivered to customers. For example, when Nestlé USA implemented value chain management, it redesigned its metrics system to focus on one consistent set of measurements—including, for instance, accuracy of demand forecasts and production plans, on-time delivery, and customer-service levels—that allowed them to more quickly identify problem areas and take actions to resolve them.[29]

LEADERSHIP Successful value chain management isn't possible without strong and committed leadership. From top organizational levels to lower levels, managers must support, facilitate, and promote the implementation and ongoing practice of value chain management. Managers must seriously commit to identifying what value is, how that value can best be provided, and how successful those efforts have been. A culture where all efforts are focused on delivering superb customer value isn't possible without a serious commitment on the part of the organization's leaders.

Also, it's important that managers outline expectations for what's involved in the organization's pursuit of value chain management. Ideally, managers start with a vision or mission statement that expresses the organization's commitment to identifying, capturing, and providing the highest possible value to customers. For instance, when American Standard began using value chain management, the CEO held dozens of meetings across the United States to explain the new competitive environment and why the company needed to create better working relationships with its value chain partners in order to better serve the needs of its customers.[30]

Then, managers should clarify expectations regarding each employee's role in the value chain. But clear expectations aren't just important for internal partners. Being clear about expectations also extends to external partners. For example, managers at American Standard identified clear requirements for suppliers and were prepared to drop any that couldn't meet them, and did so. The upside, though, was that those suppliers who met the expectations benefited from more business and American Standard had partners willing to work with them in delivering better value to customers.

EMPLOYEES/HUMAN RESOURCES When new employees at the Thermo Fisher Scientific plant in Marietta, Ohio, have work-related questions, they can consult with a member of the facility's "Tree of Knowledge." The "tree" is actually a bulletin board with pictures of employees who have worked at the plant for decades.[31]

We know from our discussions of management theories throughout this text that employees are an organization's most important resource. Without employees, no products are produced and no services are delivered—in fact, no organized efforts in the pursuit of common goals would be possible. So not surprisingly, employees play an important role in value chain management. The three main human resource requirements for value chain management are flexible approaches to job design, effective hiring process, and ongoing training.

Flexibility is the key to job design in value chain management. Traditional functional job roles—such as marketing, sales, accounts payable, customer service, and so forth—won't work. Instead, jobs must be designed around work processes that create and provide value to customers. It takes flexible jobs and flexible employees. For instance, at Nordson Corporation's facility in Swainsboro, Georgia, workers are trained to do several different tasks, which isn't all that uncommon in many manufacturing plants. What's unique about this facility is that even salaried employees are expected to spend four hours every month building products on the shop floor.[32]

In a value chain organization, employees may be assigned to work teams that tackle a given process and may be asked to do different things on different days depending on need. In such an environment where customer value is best delivered through collaborative relationships that may change as customer needs change and where processes or job descriptions are not standardized, an employee's ability to be flexible is critical. Therefore, the organization's hiring process must be designed to identify those employees who have the ability to learn and adapt.

Finally, the need for flexibility also requires a significant investment in continual and ongoing employee training. Whether that training involves learning how to use information technology software, how to improve the flow of materials throughout the chain, how to identify activities that add value, how to make better decisions faster, or how to improve any other number of potential work activities, managers must see to it that employees have the knowledge and tools they need to do their jobs efficiently and effectively.

ORGANIZATIONAL CULTURE AND ATTITUDES   The last requirement for value chain management is having a supportive organizational culture and attitudes. From our extensive description of value chain management, you could probably guess the type of organizational culture that's going to support its successful implementation! Those cultural attitudes include sharing, collaborating, openness, flexibility, mutual respect, and trust. These attitudes encompass not only the internal partners in the value chain, but extend to external partners as well.

Obstacles to Value Chain Management

As desirable as these benefits may be, managers must tackle several obstacles in managing the value chain including organizational barriers, cultural attitudes, required capabilities, and people (see Exhibit MOM-3).

ORGANIZATIONAL BARRIERS   At General Cable's manufacturing facility in Manchester, New Hampshire, one of the most interesting challenges faced by managers and employees in maintaining its world-class competitiveness is the 23 different nationalities that speak 12 languages besides English. Multiple languages make getting new messages out about anything that comes up especially tricky. But they've made it work using visual cues throughout the plant.[33]

Organizational barriers are among the most difficult obstacles to handle. These barriers include refusal or reluctance to share information, reluctance to shake up the status quo, and security issues. Without shared information, close coordination

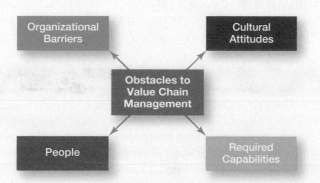

Exhibit MOM-3
Obstacles to Value Chain Management

and collaboration is impossible. And the reluctance or refusal of employees to shake up the status quo can impede efforts toward value chain management and prevent its successful implementation. Finally, because value chain management relies heavily on a substantial information technology infrastructure, system security and Internet security breaches are issues that need to be addressed.

CULTURAL ATTITUDES Unsupportive cultural attitudes—especially trust and control—also can be obstacles to value chain management. The trust issue is a critical one, both lack of trust and too much trust. To be effective, partners in a value chain must trust each other. A mutual respect for, and honesty about, each partner's activities all along the chain is essential. When that trust doesn't exist, the partners will be reluctant to share information, capabilities, and processes. But too much trust also can be a problem. Just about any organization is vulnerable to theft of **intellectual property**—that is, proprietary information that's critical to an organization's efficient and effective functioning and competitiveness. You need to be able to trust your value chain partners so your organization's valuable assets aren't compromised.[34] Another cultural attitude that can be an obstacle is the belief that when an organization collaborates with external and internal partners, it no longer controls its own destiny. However, this lack of control just isn't the case. Even with the intense collaboration that's important to value chain management, organizations still control critical decisions such as what customers value, how much value they desire, and what distribution channels are important.[35]

REQUIRED CAPABILITIES We know from our earlier discussion of requirements for the successful implementation of value chain management that value chain partners need numerous capabilities. Several of these capabilities—coordination and collaboration, the ability to configure products to satisfy customers and suppliers, and the ability to educate internal and external partners—aren't easy, but they're essential to capturing and exploiting the value chain. Many of the companies we've described throughout this section endured critical, and oftentimes difficult, self-evaluations of their capabilities and processes in order to become more effective and efficient at managing their value chains.

PEOPLE The final obstacles to successful value chain management can be an organization's people. Without their unwavering commitment to do whatever it takes, value chain management won't be successful. If employees refuse to be flexible in their work—how and with whom they work—collaboration and cooperation throughout the value chain will be hard to achieve.

In addition, value chain management takes an incredible amount of time and energy on the part of an organization's employees. Managers must motivate those high levels of effort from employees, which is not an easy thing to do.

Finally, a major human resource problem is the lack of experienced managers who can lead value chain management initiatives. It's not that widespread, so there aren't a lot of managers who've done it successfully. However, progressive organizations see the benefits to be gained from value chain management and pursue it despite obstacles.

CURRENT Issues in Managing Operations

Rowe Furniture had an audacious goal: make a sofa in 10 days. It wanted to "become as efficient at making furniture as Toyota is at making cars." Reaching that goal, however, required revamping its operations management process to exploit technology *and* maintaining quality.[36] Rowe's actions illustrate three of today's most important operations management issues: technology, quality, and mass customization and lean organizations.

---

intellectual property
Proprietary information that's critical to an organization's efficient and effective functioning and competitiveness

Technology's Role in Operations Management

Global positioning systems (GPS) are changing a number of enterprises from shipping to shopping, from health care to law enforcement, and even farming.[37] Like many other technologies, GPS was invented for military use to track weapons and personnel as they moved. Now GPS is being used to track shipping fleets, revitalize consumer products such as watches or photos, and monitor parolees or sex offenders.

As we know from our previous discussion of value chain management, today's competitive marketplace has put tremendous pressure on organizations to deliver products and services that customers value in a timely manner. Smart companies are looking at ways to harness technology to improve operations management. Many fast-food companies are competing to see who can provide faster and better service to drive-through customers. With drive-through now representing a huge portion of sales, faster and better delivery can be a significant competitive edge. For instance, Wendy's has added awnings to some of its menu boards and replaced some of the text with pictures. Others use confirmation screens, a technology that helped McDonald's boost accuracy by more than 11 percent. Technology used by two national chains tells managers how much food they need to prepare by counting vehicles in the drive-through line and factoring in demand for current promotional and popular staple items. Even Domino's is using a new point-of-sale system to attract customers and streamline online orders.[38]

Although an organization's production activities are driven by the recognition that the customer is king, managers still need to be more responsive. For instance, operations managers need systems that can reveal available capacity, status of orders, and product quality while products are in the process of being manufactured, not just after the fact. To connect more closely with customers, production must be synchronized across the enterprise. To avoid bottlenecks and slowdowns, the production function must be a full partner in the entire business system.

What's making such extensive collaboration possible is technology. Technology is also allowing organizations to control costs particularly in the areas of predictive maintenance, remote diagnostics, and utility cost savings. For instance, new Internet-compatible equipment contains embedded Web servers that can communicate proactively—that is, if a piece of equipment breaks or reaches certain preset parameters indicating that it's about to break, it asks for help. But technology can do more than sound an alarm or light up an indicator button. For instance, some devices have the ability to initiate e-mail or signal a pager at a supplier, the maintenance department, or contractor describing the specific problem and requesting parts and service. How much is such e-enabled maintenance control worth? It can be worth quite a lot if it prevents equipment breakdowns and subsequent production downtime.

Managers who understand the power of technology to contribute to more effective and efficient performance know that managing operations is more than the traditional view of simply producing the product. Instead, the emphasis is on working together with all the organization's business functions to find solutions to customers' business problems. Even service providers understand the power of technology for these tasks. For example, Southwest Airlines upgraded its cockpit software, enabling its pilots (who have been extensively trained) to fly precise satellite-based navigation approaches to airports, thus saving fuel, reducing delays, and cutting noise.[39]

Quality Initiatives

Quality problems are expensive. For example, even though Apple has had phenomenal success with its iPod, the batteries in the first three versions died after 4 hours instead of lasting the up-to-12 hours that buyers expected. Apple's settlement with consumers cost close to $100 million. At Schering-Plough, problems with inhalers and other pharmaceuticals were traced to chronic quality control shortcomings, for which the company eventually paid a $500 million fine. And the auto industry paid $14.5 billion to cover the cost of warranty and repair work in one year.[40]

Many experts believe that organizations unable to produce high-quality products won't be able to compete successfully in the global marketplace. What is quality? When you consider a product or service to have quality, what does that mean? Does it mean that the product doesn't break or quit working—that is, that it's reliable? Does it mean that the service is delivered in a way that you intended? Does it mean that the product does what it's supposed to do? Or does quality mean something else? We're going to define **quality** as the ability of a product or service to reliably do what it's supposed to do and to satisfy customer expectations.

How is quality achieved? That's an issue managers must address. A good way to look at quality initiatives is with the management functions—planning, organizing, leading, and controlling—that need to take place.

quality
The ability of a product or service to reliably do what it's supposed to do and to satisfy customer expectations

PLANNING FOR QUALITY Managers must have quality improvement goals and strategies and plans to achieve those goals. Goals can help focus everyone's attention toward some objective quality standard. For instance, Caterpillar's goal is to apply quality improvement techniques to help cut costs.[41] Although this goal is specific and challenging, managers and employees are partnering together to pursue well-designed strategies to achieve the goals, and are confident they can do so.

ORGANIZING AND LEADING FOR QUALITY Because quality improvement initiatives are carried out by organizational employees, it's important for managers to look at how they can best organize and lead them. For instance, at the Moosejaw, Saskatchewan, plant of General Cable Corporation, every employee participates in continual quality assurance training. In addition, the plant manager believes wholeheartedly in giving employees the information they need to do their jobs better. He says, "Giving people who are running the machines the information is just paramount. You can set up your cellular structure, you can cross-train your people, you can use lean tools, but if you don't give people information to drive improvement, there's no enthusiasm." Needless to say, this company shares production data and financial performance measures with all employees.[42]

Organizations with extensive and successful quality improvement programs tend to rely on two important people approaches: cross-functional work teams, and self-directed or empowered work teams. Because achieving product quality is something that all employees from upper to lower levels must participate in, it's not surprising that quality-driven organizations rely on well-trained, flexible, and empowered employees.

CONTROLLING FOR QUALITY Quality improvement initiatives aren't possible without having some way to monitor and evaluate their progress. Whether it involves standards for inventory control, defect rate, raw materials procurement, or other operations management areas, controlling for quality is important. For instance, at the Northrup Grumman Corporation plant in Rolling Meadows, Illinois, several quality controls have been implemented, such as automated testing and IT that integrates product design and manufacturing and tracks process quality improvements. Also, employees are empowered to make accept/reject decisions about products throughout the manufacturing process. The plant manager explains, "This approach helps build quality into the product rather than trying to inspect quality into the product." But one of the most important things they do is "go to war" with their customers—soldiers preparing for war or in live combat situations. Again, the plant manager says, "What discriminates us is that we believe if we can understand our customer's mission as well as they do, we can help them be more effective. We don't wait for our customer to ask us to do something. We find out what our customer is trying to do and then we develop solutions."[43]

These types of quality improvement success stories aren't just limited to U.S. operations. For example, at a Delphi assembly plant in Matamoros, Mexico, employees worked hard to improve quality and made significant strides. Their customer rejection rate on shipped products is now 10 ppm (parts per million), down from 3,000 ppm—an improvement of almost 300 percent.[44] Quality initiatives at several Australian companies including Alcoa of Australia, Wormald Security, and Carlton and United Breweries have led to significant quality improvements.[45] And at Valeo Klimasystemme GmbH of Bad Rodach, Germany, assembly teams build different climate-control systems for high-end German cars including Mercedes and BMW. Quality initiatives by Valeo's employee teams have led to significant improvements in various quality standards.[46]

Quality Goals

To publicly demonstrate their quality commitment, many organizations worldwide have pursued challenging quality goals—the two best-known being ISO 9000 and Six Sigma.

ISO 9000 **ISO 9000** is a series of international quality management standards established by the International Organization for Standardization (www.iso.org), which set uniform guidelines for processes to ensure that products conform to customer requirements. These standards cover everything from contract review to product design to product delivery. The ISO 9000 standards have become the internationally recognized standard for evaluating and comparing companies in the global marketplace. In fact, this type of certification can be a prerequisite for doing business globally. Achieving ISO 9000 certification provides proof that a quality operations system is in place.

As of 2012, more than 1 million certifications had been awarded to organizations in 175 countries. Almost 40,000 U.S. businesses are ISO 9000 certified. Over 200,000 Chinese firms have received certification.[47]

ISO 9000
A series of international quality management standards that set uniform guidelines for processes to ensure products conform to customer requirements

SIX SIGMA Motorola popularized the use of stringent quality standards more than 30 years ago, through a trademarked quality improvement program called Six Sigma.[48] Very simply, **Six Sigma** is a quality program designed to reduce defects to help lower costs, save time, and improve customer satisfaction. It's based on the statistical standard that establishes a goal of no more than 3.4 defects per million units or procedures. What does the name mean? Sigma is the Greek letter that statisticians use to define a standard deviation from a bell curve. The higher the sigma, the fewer the deviations from the norm—that is, the fewer the defects. At One Sigma, two-thirds of whatever is being measured falls within the curve. Two Sigma covers about 95 percent. At Six Sigma, you're about as close to defect-free as you can get.[49] It's an ambitious quality goal! Although it is an extremely high standard to achieve, many quality-driven businesses are using it and benefiting from it. For instance, General Electric estimates that it has saved billions in costs since 1995, according to company executives.[50] Other well-known companies pursuing Six Sigma include ITT Industries, Dow Chemical, 3M Company, American Express, Sony Corporation, Nokia Corporation, and Johnson & Johnson. Although manufacturers seem to make up the bulk of Six Sigma users, service companies such as financial institutions, retailers, and health care organizations are beginning to apply it. What impact can Six Sigma have? Let's look at an example.

Six Sigma
A quality program designed to reduce defects and help lower costs, save time, and improve customer satisfaction

It used to take Wellmark Blue Cross & Blue Shield, a managed-care health care company, 65 days or more to add a new doctor to its medical plans. Now, thanks to Six Sigma, the company discovered that half the processes they used were redundant. With those unnecessary steps gone, the job now gets done in 30 days or less and with reduced staff. The company also has been able to reduce its administrative expenses by $3 million per year, an amount passed on to consumers through lower health care premiums.[51]

Although it's important for managers to recognize that many positive benefits come from reaching Six Sigma or obtaining ISO 9000 certification, the key benefit comes from the quality improvement journey itself. In other words, the goal of quality certification should be having work processes and an operations system in place that enable organizations to meet customers' needs and employees to perform their jobs in a consistently high-quality way.

Mass Customization and Lean Organization

The term *mass customization* seems an oxymoron. However, the design-to-order concept is becoming an important operations management issue for today's managers. **Mass customization** provides consumers with a product when, where, and how they want it.[52] Companies as diverse as BMW, Ford, Levi Strauss, Wells Fargo, Mattel, and Dell are adopting mass customization to maintain or attain a competitive advantage. Mass customization requires flexible manufacturing techniques and continual customer dialogue.[53] Technology plays an important role in both.

With flexible manufacturing, companies have the ability to quickly readjust assembly lines to make products to order. Using technology such as computer-controlled factory equipment, intranets, industrial robots, barcode scanners, digital printers, and logistics software, companies can manufacture, assemble, and ship customized products with customized packaging to customers in incredibly short timeframes. Dell is a good example of a company that uses flexible manufacturing techniques and technology to custom-build computers to customers' specifications.

Technology also is important in the continual dialogue with customers. Using extensive databases, companies can keep track of customers' likes and dislikes. And the Internet has made it possible for companies to have ongoing dialogues with customers to learn about and respond to their exact preferences. For instance, on Amazon's Web site, customers are greeted by name and can get personalized recommendations of books and other products. The ability to customize products to a customer's desires and specifications starts an important relationship between the organization and the customer. If the customer likes the product and it provides value, he or she is more likely to be a repeat customer.

An intense focus on customers is also important to be a **lean organization**, which is an organization that understands what customers want, identifies customer value by analyzing all activities required to produce products, and then optimizes the entire process from the customer's perspective.[54] Lean organizations drive out all activities that do not add value in customers' eyes. For instance, companies like United Parcel Service, LVMH Moet Hennessy Louis Vuitton, and Harley-Davidson have pursued lean operations. "Lean operations adopt a philosophy of minimizing waste by striving for perfection through continuous learning, creativity, and teamwork."[55] As more manufacturers and service organizations adopt lean principles, they must realize that it's a never-ending journey toward being efficient and effective.

mass customization
Providing customers with a product when, where, and how they want it

lean organization
An organization that understands what customers want, identifies customer value by analyzing all activities required to produce products, and then optimizes the entire process from the customer's perspective

REVIEW AND DISCUSSION QUESTIONS

1. What is operations management?

2. Do you think that manufacturing or service organizations have the greater need for operations management? Explain.

3. What is a value chain and what is value chain management? What is the goal of value chain management? What are the benefits of value chain management?

4. What is required for successful value chain management? What obstacles exist to successful value chain management?

5. How could you use value chain management in your everyday life?

6. How does technology play a role in manufacturing?

7. What are ISO 9000 and Six Sigma?

8. Describe lean management and explain why it's important.

9. How might operations management apply to other managerial functions besides control?

10. Which is more critical to success in organizations: continuous improvement or quality control? Support your position.

PART 4 Management Practice

A Manager's Dilemma

Habitat for Humanity is a nonprofit, ecumenical Christian housing ministry dedicated to building affordable housing for individuals dealing with poverty or homelessness. Habitat's approach is simple. Families in need of decent housing apply to a local Habitat affiliate. Homeowners are chosen based on their level of need, their willingness to become partners in the program, and their ability to repay the loan. And that's the unique thing about Habitat's approach. It's not a giveaway program. Families chosen to become homeowners have to make a down payment and monthly mortgage payments, and invest hundreds of hours of their own labor into building their Habitat home. And they have to commit to helping build other Habitat houses. Habitat volunteers (maybe you've been involved on a Habitat build) provide labor and donations of money and materials as well.

Social service organizations often struggle financially to provide services that are never enough to meet the overwhelming need. Habitat for Humanity, however, was given an enormous financial commitment—$100 million—from an individual who had worked with Habitat and seen the gift it offers to families in poverty. That amount of money means that Habitat can have a huge impact now and in the future. But the management team wants to use the gift wisely—a definite planning, strategy, and control challenge.

Pretend you're part of that management team. Using what you've learned in the chapters on planning, strategic management, and managerial controls in Part 4, what five things would you suggest the team focus on? Think carefully about your suggestions to the team.

Global Sense

Manufacturers have spent years building low-cost global supply chains. However, when those businesses are dependent on a global supply chain, any unplanned disruptions (political, economic, weather, natural disaster, etc.) can wreak havoc on plans, schedules, and budgets. The Icelandic Eyjafjallajokull volcano in 2010 and the Japanese earthquake/tsunami and Thailand flooding in 2011 are still fresh in the minds of logistics, transportation, and operations managers around the globe. Although unexpected problems in the supply chain have always existed, now the far-reaching impact of something happening not in your own facility but thousands of miles away has created additional volatility and risk for managers and organizations. For instance, when the Icelandic volcano erupted, large portions of European airspace

were shut down for more than a week, which affected air traffic worldwide. At BMW's plant in Spartanburg, South Carolina, air shipments of car components were delayed and workers' hours had to be scaled back and plans made for a possible shutdown of the entire facility. During the Thailand floods in late 2011, industrial parks that manufactured semiconductors for companies like Apple and Samsung were underwater and crawling with crocodiles. After the Japanese earthquake and tsunami in early 2011 shut down dozens of contractors and subcontractors that supply many parts to the auto and technology industries, companies like Toyota, Honda, and Hewlett-Packard had to adjust to critical parts shortages.

Discuss the following questions in light of what you learned in Part 4:

- *You see the challenges associated with a global supply chain; what are some of the benefits of it?*
- *What types of plans would be best in these unplanned events?*
- *As Chapter 9 asks, how can managers plan effectively in dynamic environments?*
- *Could SWOT analysis be useful in these instances? Explain.*
- *How might managers use scenario planning in preparing for such disasters? (Scenario planning is discussed in the Planning and Control Techniques module.)*
- *What types of managerial controls might be useful to managers during these events?*
- *How is the operations system, especially of manufacturing companies, affected by such global disruptions? What can managers do to minimize the impact of those disruptions?*

Sources: R. Teijken, "Local Issues in Global Supply Chains," Logistics & Transport Focus, April 2012, pp. 41–43; J. Beer, "Sighted: The Ends of the Earth," Canadian Business, Winter 2011/2012, pp. 19–22; B. Powell, "When Supply Chains Break," Fortune, December 26, 2011, pp. 29–32; A. H. Merrill, R. E. Scale, and M. D. Sullivan, "Post-Natural Disaster Appraisal and Valuation: Lessons from the Japan Experience," The Secured Lender, November/December 2011, pp. 30–33; J. Rice, "Alternate Supply," Industrial Engineer, May 2011, p. 10; and "Risk Management: An Increasingly Small World," Reactions, April 2011, p. 252.

Continuing Case
Starbucks—Planning and Control

All managers plan. The planning they do may be extensive or it may be limited. It might be for the next week or month or it might be for the next couple of years. It might cover a work group or it might cover an entire division or the entire organization. No matter what type or extent of planning

Scott McMartin, Starbuck's director of global coffee advocacy, poses in the cupping room at company headquarters where quality control tastings take place daily. Starbucks coffee buyers, tasters, and quality control team members taste an average 1,000 cups per day as part of Starbucks stringent control activities to meet its goal of providing customers with a unique product of the highest quality.
Source: Reuters/Marcus Donner

a manager does, the important thing is that planning takes place. Without planning, there would be nothing for managers to organize, lead, or control.

Starbucks—Planning

Based on Starbucks' numerous achievements, there's no doubt that managers have done their planning. Let's take a look.

Company Goals

As of July 2012, Starbucks had over 17,200 stores in more than 58 countries. The company's goal for 2013 is 1,200 net new stores (new stores opened minus existing stores closed). Starbucks financial goals for 2013 include revenue growth of 10 percent to 13 percent and earnings per share growth of 15 percent to 20 percent. In addition to the quantitative/fiscal goals, Starbucks focuses on continuing to develop new coffee products in multiple forms and staying true to its global social responsibilities.

Company Strategies

Starbucks has been called the most dynamic retail brand over the last two decades. It has been able to rise above the commodity nature of its product and become a global

brand leader by reinventing the coffee experience. Over 60 million times a week, a customer receives a product (hot drink, chilled drink, food, etc.) from a Starbucks partner. It's a reflection of the success that Howard Schultz has had in creating something that never really existed in the United States—café life. And in so doing, he created a cultural phenomenon. Starbucks is changing what we eat and drink. It's shaping how we spend our time and money.

Starbucks has found a way to appeal to practically every customer demographic as its customers cover a broad base. It's not just the affluent or the urban professionals and it's not just the intellectuals or the creative types who frequent Starbucks. You'll find soccer moms, construction workers, bank tellers, and office assistants at Starbucks. And despite the high price of its products, customers pay it because they think it's worth it. What they get for that price is some of the finest coffee available commercially, custom preparation, and, of course, that Starbucks ambiance—the comfy chairs, the music, the aromas, the hissing steam from the espresso machine—all invoking that warm feeling of community and connection that Schultz experienced on his first business trip to Italy and knew instinctively could work elsewhere.

As the world's number one specialty coffee retailer, Starbucks sells coffee drinks, food items, coffee beans, Tazo

Teas, Starbucks VIA® Ready brew and other VIA-branded products, coffee-related accessories and equipment, chilled drinks, and many other products. Recent product introductions include a new line of "natural" energy drinks, single-serve K-Cup® packs for use in the single-cup machines, and a light roast coffee called Starbucks Blonde Roast. Starbucks' loyalty program continues to distinguish it from competitors. Its My Starbucks Rewards™ has more than 3.6 million active members. And the company has made a huge investment in mobile payments. Its Starbucks Card apps for Android phones and iPhones were hugely popular. The company also announced a partnership with Square, the mobile payments start-up. Square processes all credit and debit card transactions at Starbucks stores in the United States. Eventually, customers will be able to charge their order to their credit card simply by saying their names.

Starbucks' primary competition comes from quick-service restaurants and specialty coffee shops. McDonalds, for one, has invested heavily in its McCafé concept, which offers coffee, real fruit smoothies, shakes, and frappés. And there are numerous specialty coffee shops, but most of these tend to be in local markets only.

Starbucks—Controlling

Once managers have established goals and plans and organized and structured to pursue those goals, the manager's job isn't done. Quite the opposite! Managers must now monitor work activities to make sure they're being done as planned and correct any significant deviations. At Starbucks, managers control various functions, activities, processes, and procedures to ensure that desired performance standards are achieved at all organizational levels.

Controlling the Coffee Experience

Why has Starbucks been so successful? Although many factors have contributed to its success, one significant factor is its ability to provide customers with a unique product of the highest quality delivered with exceptional service. Everything that each Starbucks' partner does, from top level to bottom level, contributes to the company's ability to do that efficiently and effectively. And managers need controls in place to help monitor and evaluate what's being done and how it's being done. Starbuck's managers use different types of controls to ensure that the company meets its goals. These controls include transactions controls, security controls, employee controls, and organizational performance controls.

A legal recruiter stops by Starbucks on her way to her office in downtown Chicago and orders her daily Caffè Mocha tall. A construction site supervisor pulls into the drive-through line at the Starbucks store in Rancho Cucamonga, California, for a cinnamon chip scone and Tazo tea. It's 11 P.M. and, needing a break from studying for her next-day's management exam, a student heads to the local Starbucks for a tasty treat—a Raspberry Pomegranate Starbucks Refresher. Now she's ready again to tackle that chapter material on managerial controls.

Every week, an average 60 million transactions take place at a Starbucks store. The average dollar sale per transaction is $7.01. These transactions between partners (employees) and customers—the exchange of products for money—are the major source of sales revenue for Starbucks. Measuring and evaluating the efficiency and effectiveness of these transactions for both walk-in customers and customers at drive-through windows is important. As Starbucks has been doing walk-in transactions for a number of years, numerous procedures and processes are in place to make those transactions go smoothly. However, as Starbucks adds more drive-through windows, the focus of the transaction is on being fast as well as on quality—a different metric than for walk-in transactions. When a customer walks into a store and orders, he can step aside while the order is being prepared; that's not possible in a drive-through line. Recognizing these limitations, the company is taking steps to improve its drive-through service. For instance, digital timers are placed where employees can easily see them to measure service times; order confirmation screens are used to help keep accuracy rates high; and additional pastry racks have been conveniently located by the drive-through windows.

Security is also an important issue for Starbucks. Keeping company assets (such as people, equipment, products, financial information, and so forth) safe and secure requires security controls. The company is committed to providing all partners with a clean, safe, and healthy work environment. All partners share the responsibility to follow all safety rules and practices; to cooperate with officials who enforce those rules and practices; to take necessary steps to protect ourselves and other partners; to attend required safety training; and to report immediately all accidents, injuries, and unsafe practices or conditions. When hired, each partner is provided with a manual that covers safety, security, and health standards and is trained on the requirements outlined in the manual. In addition, managers receive ongoing training about these issues and are expected to keep employees trained and up-to-date on any changes. And at any time, any partner can contact the Partner & Asset Protection Department for information and advice.

One security area that has been particularly important to Starbucks has been with its gift cards, in which it does an enormous volume of business. With gift cards, there are lots of opportunities for an unethical employee to "steal" from the company. The company's director of compliance has said that detecting such fraud can be difficult because it's often not apparent from an operations standpoint. However, Starbucks uses transactional data analysis technology to detect multiple card redemptions in a single day and has identified other "telltale" activities that pinpoint possible fraud. When the company's technology detects transaction activity outside the norm, Starbucks' corporate staff is alerted and a panel of company experts reviews the data. Investigators have found individuals at stores who confess to stealing as much as $42,000. When smaller exceptions are noted, the individuals are sent letters asking them to explain what's going on. Employees who have been so "notified" often quit.

Starbucks' part-time and full-time hourly partners are the primary—and most important—source of contact between the company and the customer, and exemplary customer service is a top priority at Starbucks. Partners are encouraged to strive to make every customer's experience pleasant and fulfilling and to treat customers with respect and dignity. What kinds of employee controls does Starbucks use to ensure that this happens? Partners are trained in and are required to follow all proper procedures relating to the storage, handling, preparation, and service of Starbucks' products. In addition, partners are told to notify their managers immediately if they see anything that suggests a product may pose a danger to the health or safety of themselves or of customers. Partners also are taught the warning signs associated with possible workplace violence and how to reduce their vulnerability if faced with a potentially violent situation. In either circumstance where product or partner safety and security are threatened, store managers have been trained as far as the appropriate steps to take if such a situation occurs.

The final types of control that are important to Starbucks' managers are the organizational performance and financial controls. Starbucks uses the typical financial control measures, but also looks at growth in sales at stores open at least one year as a performance standard. One continual challenge is trying to control store operating costs. There's a fine balance the company has to achieve between keeping costs low and keeping quality high. However, there are steps the company has taken to control costs. For instance, new thinner garbage bags will save the company half a million dollars a year.

In addition to the typical financial measures, corporate governance procedures and guidelines are an important part of Starbucks' financial controls as they are at any public corporation that's covered by Sarbanes-Oxley legislation. The company has identified guidelines for its board of directors with respect to responsibilities, processes, procedures, and expectations.

Starbucks' Value Chain: From Bean to Cup

The steaming cup of coffee placed in a customer's hand at any Starbucks' store location starts as coffee beans (berries) plucked from fields of coffee plants. From harvest to storage to roasting to retail to cup, Starbucks understands the important role each participant in its value chain plays.

Starbucks offers a selection of coffees from around the world, and its coffee buyers personally travel to the coffee-growing regions of Latin America, Africa/Arabia, and Asia/Pacific in order to select and purchase the highest-quality *arabica* beans. Once the beans arrive at any one of the five roasting facilities in the United States and three global facilities, Starbucks' master professional roasters take over. These individuals know coffee and do their "magic" in creating the company's rich signature roast coffee in a process that brings balance to all of its flavor attributes. There are many potential challenges to "transforming" the raw material into the quality product and experience that customers have come to expect at Starbucks. Weather, shipping and logistics, technology, political instability, and so forth all could potentially impact what Starbucks is in business to do.

One issue of great importance to Starbucks is environmental protection. Starbucks has taken actions throughout its entire supply chain to minimize its "environmental footprint." For instance, suppliers are asked to sign a code of conduct that deals with certain expectations in business standards and practices. Even company stores are focused on the environmental impact of their store operations. For instance, partners at stores around the world have found innovative ways to reuse coffee grounds. In Japan, for example, a team of Starbucks partners realized that coffee grounds could be used as an ingredient to make paper. A local printing company uses this paper to print the official Starbucks Japan newsletter. In Bahrain, partners dry coffee grounds in the sun, package them, and give them to customers as fertilizer for house plants.

Discussion Questions

1. Make a list of Starbucks' goals. Describe what type of goal each is. Then, describe how that stated goal might affect how the following employees do their job: (a) a part-time store employee—a barista—in Omaha; (b) a quality assurance technician at the company's roasting plant in Amsterdam; (c) a regional sales manager; (d) the executive vice president of global supply chain operations; and (e) the CEO.

2. Discuss the types of growth strategies that Starbucks has used. Be specific.

3. What competitive advantages do you think Starbucks has? What will it have to do to maintain that (those) advantage (s)?

4. Do you think the Starbucks brand can become too saturated—that is, extended to too many different products? Why or why not?

5. What companies might be good benchmarks for Starbucks? Why? What companies might want to benchmark Starbucks? Why?

6. Describe how the following Starbucks managers might use forecasting, budgeting, and scheduling (be specific): (a) a retail store manager; (b) a regional marketing manager; (c) the manager for global development; and (d) the CEO

7. Describe Howard Schultz as a strategic leader.

8. Is Starbucks "living" its mission? (You can find the company mission on its Web site at www.starbucks.com) Discuss.

9. What control criteria might be useful to a retail store manager? To a barista at one of Starbucks's walk-in-only retail stores? How about for a store that has a drive-through?

10. What types of feedforward, concurrent, and feedback controls does Starbucks use? Are there others that might be important to use? If so, describe.

11. What "red flags" might indicate significant deviations from standard for (a) an hourly partner; (b) a store manager; (c) a district manager; (d) the executive vice president of finance; and (e) the CEO? Are there any similarities? Why or why not?

12. Evaluate the control measures Starbucks is using with its gift cards from the standpoint of the three steps in the control process.

13. Using the company's most current financial statements, calculate the following financial ratios: current, debt to assets, inventory turnover, total asset turnover, profit margin on sales, and return on investment. What do these ratios tell managers?

14. Would you describe Starbucks production/operations technology in its retail stores as unit, mass, or process? How about in its roasting plants? (Hint: you might need to review material in Chapter 11, as well, in order to answer this question.)

15. Can Starbucks manage the uncertainties in its value chain? If so, how? If not, why not?

16. Go to the company's Web site [www.starbucks.com]. Find the information on the company's environmental activities from bean to cup. Select one of the steps in the chain (or your professor may assign you one). Describe and evaluate what environmental actions it's taking. How might these affect the planning, organizing, and controlling taking place in these areas?

17. Look at the company's mission and guiding principles on its Web site. How might these affect the way Starbucks controls? How do the ways Starbucks controls contribute to the attainment or pursuit of these?

Notes for the Part 4 Continuing Case

C. Cain Miller, "Starbucks and Square to Team Up," *New York Times Online,* August 8, 2012; Starbucks Corporation 2011 Annual Report, www.investor.starbucks.com, August 6, 2012; Starbucks News Release, "Starbucks Reports Record Third Quarter Results," www.investor.starbucks.com, July 26, 2012; R. Ahmed, "Tata Setting Up Starbucks Coffee Roasting Facility," www.online.wsj.com, July 26, 2012; B. Horovitz, "Starbucks Rolling Out Pop with Pep," *USA Today,* March 22, 2012, p. 1B; Starbucks News Release, "Starbucks Spotlights Connection Between Record Performance, Shareholder Value, and Company Values at Annual Meeting of Shareholders," news.starbucks.com, March 21, 2012; D. A. Kaplan, "Strong Coffee," *Fortune,* December 12, 2011, pp. 100–116; J. A. Cooke, Editor, "From Bean to Cup: How Starbucks Transformed Its Supply Chain," www.supplychainquarterly.com, Quarter 4, 2010; R. Ruggless, "Starbucks Exec: Security from Employee Theft Important When Implementing Gift Card Strategies," *Nation's Restaurant News,* December 12, 2005, p. 24; and R. Ruggless, "Transaction Monitoring Boosts Safety, Perks Up Coffee Chain Profits," *Nation's Restaurant News,* November 28, 2005, p. 35.

11 Basic Organizational Design

SPOTLIGHT: *Manager at Work*

$10 billion. *That's how much Eli Lilly & Co. stands to lose in annual revenues between now and 2016 as three of its major drug patents expire.[1] Replacing that revenue is high on the list of "must-do's" for CEO John Lechleiter (see photo). The solution is speeding up the pace of drug development, but his challenge is: How?*

Unlike its global competitors that have addressed similar product development challenges by using large-scale mergers and acquisitions, Lechleiter's focus has been on acquiring smaller drug companies. He said large-scale combinations "provide short-term relief but don't fundamentally address the issue of innovation and how to make [product development] pipelines more productive." Developing new products and moving them forward as quickly as possible on the thorough and mandatory approval process, which can be agonizingly slow, is critical to the company's present and future success.

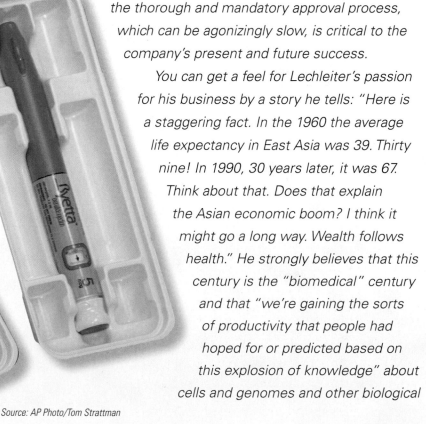

You can get a feel for Lechleiter's passion for his business by a story he tells: "Here is a staggering fact. In the 1960 the average life expectancy in East Asia was 39. Thirty nine! In 1990, 30 years later, it was 67. Think about that. Does that explain the Asian economic boom? I think it might go a long way. Wealth follows health." He strongly believes that this century is the "biomedical" century and that "we're gaining the sorts of productivity that people had hoped for or predicted based on this explosion of knowledge" about cells and genomes and other biological

Source: AP Photo/Tom Strattman

Source: Bloomberg via Getty Images

functioning. His optimism is tempered by what has happened in his company (and other pharmaceutical companies)—what he calls the "patent cliff—the intellectual-property expirations" that threaten research and development.

$10 billion. That's how much Eli Lilly & Co. stands to lose in annual revenues.

One action Lechleiter took was revamping the company's operational structure into five global business units: oncology, diabetes, established markets, emerging markets, and animal health. Part of the restructuring also involved creating an improved product research and development center. Another was encouraging the company's R&D unit to look at ways in which modern technology—improved communications, always-available

Internet, and high-bandwidth systems—could be harnessed as alternatives to how R&D had always been done. And despite the challenges, Lilly's operational performance has been steady. More than 60 percent of the company's project milestones were met or accelerated. **What other organizational design elements might Lechleiter use to ensure that Lilly achieves its goal of speeding up its product development process?**

MyManagementLab®
⭐ **Improve Your Grade!**
Over 10 million students improved their results using the Pearson MyLabs.
Visit **mymanagementlab.com** for simulations, tutorials, and end-of-chapter problems.

LEARNING OUTCOMES

11.1 | *Describe* six key elements in organizational design.

11.2 | *Contrast* mechanistic and organic structures.

11.3 | *Discuss* the contingency factors that favor either the mechanistic model or the organic model of organizational design.

11.4 | *Describe* traditional organizational designs.

Replacing $10 billion in revenue can't and won't be easy. However, Lechleiter understands the importance of organizational structure and design, especially when it comes to the difficult product development challenges facing his company. His initial restructuring actions are ones that many companies undergo when faced with radical environmental challenges in an attempt to become a stronger, more successful organization. His actions also illustrate the importance of designing or redesigning a structure that helps an organization accomplish its goals efficiently and effectively. In this chapter, we'll look at what's involved with that.

11.1 *Describe* six *key elements in organizational design.*

DESIGNING Organizational Structure

A short distance south of McAlester, Oklahoma, employees in a vast factory complex make products that must be perfect. These people "are so good at what they do and have been doing it for so long that they have a 100 percent market share."[2] They make bombs for the U.S. military and doing so requires a work environment that's an interesting mix of the mundane, structured, and disciplined, coupled with high levels of risk and emotion. The work gets done efficiently and effectively here. Work also gets done efficiently and effectively at Cisco Systems although not in such a structured and formal way. At Cisco, some 70 percent of the employees work from home at least 20 percent of the time.[3] Both of these organizations get needed work done although each does so using a different structure.

Few topics in management have undergone as much change in the past few years as that of organizing and organizational structure. Managers are reevaluating traditional approaches to find new structural designs that best support and facilitate employees' doing the organization's work—designs that can achieve efficiency but are also flexible.[4]

The basic concepts of organization design formulated by early management writers, such as Henri Fayol and Max Weber, offered structural principles for managers to follow. (Those principles are described on pp. 29–31.) Over 90 years have passed since many of those principles were originally proposed. Given that length of time and all the changes that have taken place, you'd think that those principles would be pretty worthless today. Surprisingly, they're not. For the most part, they still provide valuable insights into designing effective and efficient organizations. Of course, we've also gained a great deal of knowledge over the years as to their limitations.

In Chapter 1, we defined **organizing** as arranging and structuring work to accomplish organizational goals. It's an important process during which managers design an organization's structure. **Organizational structure** is the formal arrangement of jobs within an organization. This structure, which can be shown visually in an **organizational chart**, also serves many purposes. (See Exhibit 11-1.) When managers create or change the structure, they're engaged in **organizational design**, a process that involves decisions about six key elements: work specialization, departmentalization, chain of command, span of control, centralization and decentralization, and formalization.[5]

organizing
Arranging and structuring work to accomplish the organization's goals

organizational structure
The formal arrangement of jobs within an organization

organizational chart
The visual representation of an organization's structure

organizational design
Creating or changing an organization's structure

Exhibit 11-1
Purposes of Organizing

- Divides work to be done into specific jobs and departments.
- Assigns tasks and responsibilities associated with individual jobs.
- Coordinates diverse organizational tasks.
- Clusters jobs into units.
- Establishes relationships among individuals, groups, and departments.
- Establishes formal lines of authority.
- Allocates and deploys organizational resources.

Work Specialization

At the Wilson Sporting Goods factory in Ada, Ohio, 150 workers (with an average work tenure exceeding 20 years) make every football used in the National Football League and most of those used in college and high school football games. To meet daily output goals, the workers specialize in job tasks such as molding, stitching and sewing, lacing, and so forth.[6] This is an example of **work specialization**, which is dividing work activities into separate job tasks. Individual employees "specialize" in doing part of an activity rather than the entire activity in order to increase work output. It's also known as division of labor, a concept we introduced in the management history module.

Work specialization makes efficient use of the diversity of skills that workers have. In most organizations, some tasks require highly developed skills; others can be performed by employees with lower skill levels. If all workers were engaged in all the steps of, say, a manufacturing process, all would need the skills necessary to perform both the most demanding and the least demanding jobs. Thus, except when performing the most highly skilled or highly sophisticated tasks, employees would be working below their skill levels. In addition, skilled workers are paid more than unskilled workers, and, because wages tend to reflect the highest level of skill, all workers would be paid at highly skilled rates to do easy tasks—an inefficient use of resources. This concept explains why you rarely find a cardiac surgeon closing up a patient after surgery. Instead, doctors doing their residencies in open-heart surgery and learning the skill usually stitch and staple the patient after the surgeon has finished the surgery.

Early proponents of work specialization believed it could lead to great increases in productivity. At the beginning of the twentieth century, that generalization was reasonable. Because specialization was not widely practiced, its introduction almost always generated higher productivity. But, as Exhibit 11-2 illustrates, a good thing can be carried too far. At some point, the human diseconomies from division of labor—boredom, fatigue, stress, low productivity, poor quality, increased absenteeism, and high turnover—exceed the economic advantages.[7]

TODAY'S VIEW Most managers today continue to see work specialization as important because it helps employees be more efficient. For example, McDonald's uses

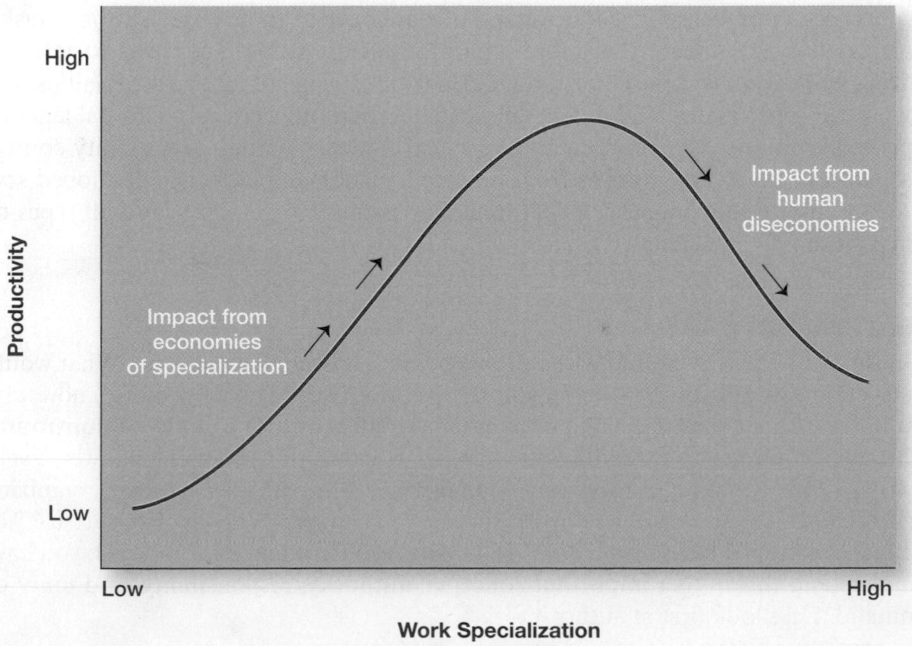

work specialization
Dividing work activities into separate job tasks

Exhibit 11-2
Economies and Diseconomies of Work Specialization

high work specialization to get its products made and delivered to customers efficiently and quickly—that's why it's called "fast" food. One person takes orders at the drive-through window, others cook and assemble the hamburgers, another works the fryer, another gets the drinks, another bags orders, and so forth. Such single-minded focus on maximizing efficiency has contributed to increasing productivity. In fact, at many McDonald's, you'll see a clock that times how long it takes employees to fill the order; look closer and you'll probably see posted somewhere an order fulfillment time goal. At some point, however, work specialization no longer leads to productivity. That's why companies such as Avery-Dennison, Ford Australia, Hallmark, and American Express use minimal work specialization and instead give employees a broad range of tasks to do.

Departmentalization

Does your college have a department of student services or financial aid department? Are you taking this course through a management department? After deciding what job tasks will be done by whom, common work activities need to be grouped back together so work gets done in a coordinated and integrated way. How jobs are grouped together is called **departmentalization**. Five common forms of departmentalization are used, although an organization may develop its own unique classification. (For instance, a hotel might have departments such as front desk operations, sales and catering, housekeeping and laundry, and maintenance.) Exhibit 11-3 illustrates each type of departmentalization as well as the advantages and disadvantages of each.

departmentalization
The basis by which jobs are grouped together

TODAY'S VIEW Most large organizations continue to use combinations of most or all of these types of departmentalization. For example, a major Japanese electronics firm organizes its divisions along functional lines, its manufacturing units around processes, its sales units around seven geographic regions, and its sales regions into four customer groupings. Black & Decker organizes its divisions along functional lines, its manufacturing units around processes, its sales around geographic regions, and its sales regions around customer groupings.

One popular departmentalization trend is the increasing use of customer departmentalization. Because getting and keeping customers is essential for success, this approach works well because it emphasizes monitoring and responding to changes in customers' needs. Another popular trend is the use of teams, especially as work tasks have become more complex and diverse skills are needed to accomplish those tasks. One specific type of team that more organizations are using is a **cross-functional team**, a work team composed of individuals from various functional specialties. For instance, at Ford's material planning and logistics division, a cross-functional team of employees from the company's finance, purchasing, engineering, and quality control areas, along with representatives from outside logistics suppliers, has developed several work improvement ideas.[8] We'll discuss cross-functional teams (and all types of teams) more fully in Chapter 14.

cross-functional team
A work team composed of individuals from various functional specialties

Chain of Command

Suppose you were at work and had a problem with an issue that came up. What would you do? Who would you go to help you resolve that issue? People need to know who their boss is. That's what the chain of command is all about. The **chain of command** is the line of authority extending from upper organizational levels to lower levels, which clarifies who reports to whom. Managers need to consider it when organizing work because it helps employees with questions such as "Who do I report to?" or "Who do I go to if I have a problem?" To understand the chain of command, you have to understand three other important concepts: authority, responsibility, and unity of command. Let's look first at authority.

chain of command
The line of authority extending from upper organizational levels to the lowest levels, which clarifies who reports to whom

FUNCTIONAL DEPARTMENTALIZATION—Groups Jobs According to Function

Exhibit 11-3
The Five Common
Forms of
Departmentalization

Plant Manager

- Manager, Engineering
- Manager, Accounting
- Manager, Manufacturing
- Manager, Human Resources
- Manager, Purchasing

+ Efficiencies from putting together similar specialties and people with common skills, knowledge, and orientations
+ Coordination within functional area
+ In-depth specialization
− Poor communication across functional areas
− Limited view of organizational goals

GEOGRAPHICAL DEPARTMENTALIZATION—Groups Jobs According to Geographic Region

Vice President for Sales

- Sales Director, Western Region
- Sales Director, Southern Region
- Sales Director, Midwestern Region
- Sales Director, Eastern Region

+ More effective and efficient handling of specific regional issues that arise
+ Serve needs of unique geographic markets better
− Duplication of functions
− Can feel isolated from other organizational areas

PRODUCT DEPARTMENTALIZATION—Groups Jobs by Product Line

Source: Bombardier Annual Report.

Bombardier, Ltd.

- Mass Transit Sector
  - Mass Transit Division
  - Bombardier–Rotax (Vienna)
- Recreational and Utility Vehicles Sector
  - Recreational Products Division
  - Logistic Equipment Division
  - Industrial Equipment Division
  - Bombardier–Rotax (Gunskirchen)
- Rail Products Sector
  - Rail and Diesel Products Division

+ Allows specialization in particular products and services
+ Managers can become experts in their industry
+ Closer to customers
− Duplication of functions
− Limited view of organizational goals

PROCESS DEPARTMENTALIZATION—Groups Jobs on the Basis of Product or Customer Flow

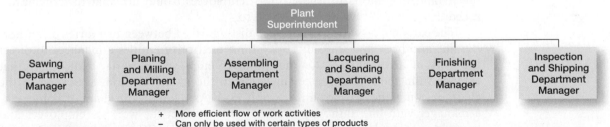

Plant Superintendent

- Sawing Department Manager
- Planing and Milling Department Manager
- Assembling Department Manager
- Lacquering and Sanding Department Manager
- Finishing Department Manager
- Inspection and Shipping Department Manager

+ More efficient flow of work activities
− Can only be used with certain types of products

CUSTOMER DEPARTMENTALIZATION—Groups Jobs on the Basis of Specific and Unique Customers Who Have Common Needs

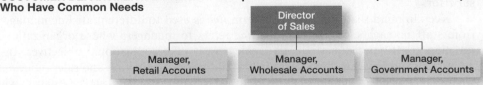

Director of Sales

- Manager, Retail Accounts
- Manager, Wholesale Accounts
- Manager, Government Accounts

+ Customers' needs and problems can be met by specialists
− Duplication of functions
− Limited view of organizational goals

These waiters and waitresses stand in line while attending a meeting held by their managers before they start their work day at a restaurant at the Beijing Airport. The managers have the authority to give employees instructions for their work day as it is an inherent right in their position as managers to tell people what to do and to expect them to do it. The concept of authority is part of the chain of command that extends from higher organizational levels to lower levels and clarifies who reports to whom. The concept of authority also includes the perspective that subordinates are willing to accept it when they understand what they are told to do and are able to perform the task.
Source: © Lou Linwei/Alamy

authority
The rights inherent in a managerial position to tell people what to do and to expect them to do it

acceptance theory of authority
The view that authority comes from the willingness of subordinates to accept it

line authority
Authority that entitles a manager to direct the work of an employee

AUTHORITY Authority was a major concept discussed by the early management writers; they viewed it as the glue that held an organization together. **Authority** refers to the rights inherent in a managerial position to tell people what to do and to expect them to do it.[9] Managers in the chain of command had authority to do their job of coordinating and overseeing the work of others. Authority could be delegated downward to lower-level managers, giving them certain rights while also prescribing certain limits within which to operate. These writers emphasized that authority was related to one's position within an organization and had nothing to do with the personal characteristics of an individual manager. They assumed that the rights and power inherent in one's formal organizational position were the sole source of influence and that if an order was given, it would be obeyed.

Another early management writer, Chester Barnard, proposed another perspective on authority. This view, the **acceptance theory of authority**, says that authority comes from the willingness of subordinates to accept it.[10] If an employee didn't accept a manager's order, there was no authority. Barnard contended that subordinates *will* accept orders only if the following conditions are satisfied:

1. They understand the order.
2. They feel the order is consistent with the organization's purpose.
3. The order does not conflict with their personal beliefs.
4. They are able to perform the task as directed.

Barnard's view of authority seems to make sense, especially when it comes to an employee's ability to do what he or she is told to do. For instance, if my manager (my department chair) came into my classroom and told me to do open-heart surgery on one of my students, the traditional view of authority said that I would have to follow that order. Barnard's view would say, instead, that I would talk to my manager about my lack of education and experience to do what he's asked me to do and that it's probably not in the best interests of the student (or our department) for me to follow that order. Yes, this is an extreme—and highly unrealistic—example. However, it does point out that simply viewing a manager's authority as total control over what an employee does or doesn't do is unrealistic also, except in certain circumstances like the military where soldiers are expected to follow their commander's orders. However, understand that Barnard believed most employees would do what their managers asked them to do if they were able to do so.

The early management writers also distinguished between two forms of authority: line authority and staff authority. **Line authority** entitles a manager to direct the work of an employee. It is the employer–employee authority relationship that extends from the top of the organization to the lowest echelon, according to the chain of command, as shown in Exhibit 11-4. As a link in the chain of command, a manager with line authority has the right to direct the work of employees and to make certain decisions without consulting anyone. Of course, in the chain of command, every manager is also subject to the authority or direction of his or her superior.

Keep in mind that sometimes the term *line* is used to differentiate line managers from staff managers. In this context, *line* refers to managers whose organizational function contributes directly to the achievement of organizational objectives. In a manufacturing firm, line managers are typically in the production and sales functions, whereas managers in human resources and payroll are considered staff managers with staff authority. Whether a manager's function is classified as line or staff depends on the organization's objectives. For example, at Staff Builders, a supplier of temporary employees, interviewers have a line function. Similarly, at the payroll firm of ADP, payroll is a line function.

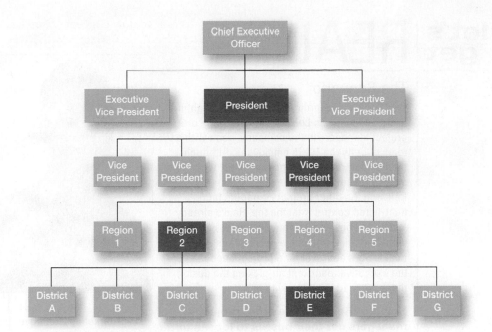

Exhibit 11-4
Chain of Command and Line Authority

As organizations get larger and more complex, line managers find that they do not have the time, expertise, or resources to get their jobs done effectively. In response, they create **staff authority** functions to support, assist, advise, and generally reduce some of their informational burdens. For instance, a hospital administrator who cannot effectively handle the purchasing of all the supplies the hospital needs creates a purchasing department, which is a staff function. Of course, the head of the purchasing department has line authority over the purchasing agents who work for him. The hospital administrator might also find that she is overburdened and needs an assistant, a position that would be classified as a staff position. Exhibit 11-5 illustrates line and staff authority.

staff authority
Positions with some authority that have been created to support, assist, and advise those holding line authority

RESPONSIBILITY   When managers use their authority to assign work to employees, those employees take on an obligation to perform those assigned duties. This obligation or expectation to perform is known as **responsibility**. And employees should be held accountable for their performance! Assigning work authority without

responsibility
The obligation or expectation to perform any assigned duties

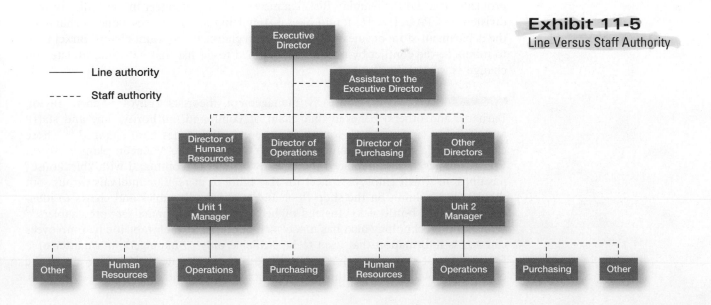

Exhibit 11-5
Line Versus Staff Authority

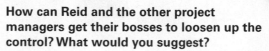

Source: Paul Baranda

The Scenario:

Reid Lawson is a project manager for a lighting design company in Los Angeles. He's one of 30 project managers in the company, each with a team of between 10–15 employees. Although the company's top managers say they want employees to be "innovative" in their work, Reid and the other project managers face tight-fisted control from the top. Reid's already lost two of his most talented designers (who went to work for a competitor) because he couldn't get approval for a project because the executive team kept nit-picking the design these two had been working on.

Paul Baranda
Marketing Executive
Director

How can Reid and the other project managers get their bosses to loosen up the control? What would you suggest?

Innovation is the driving force to a successful business and is usually hindered by red tape in the workplace. It is important to examine internal processes to ensure company procedures are not creating road blocks. The project manager should work with the executive team to ensure their ability to empower their employees as well as keep them engaged and inspired. With the proper support and understanding of expectations from the executive team, the project managers can assure their teams that their ingenious ideas would be approved or implemented.

responsibility and accountability can create opportunities for abuse. Likewise, no one should be held responsible or accountable for work tasks over which he or she has no authority to complete those tasks.

unity of command
The management principle that each person should report to only one manager

UNITY OF COMMAND   Finally, the **unity of command** principle (one of Fayol's 14 management principles) states that a person should report to only one manager. Without unity of command, conflicting demands from multiple bosses may create problems as it did for Damian Birkel, a merchandising manager in the Fuller Brands division of CPAC, Inc. He found himself reporting to two bosses—one in charge of the department-store business and the other in charge of discount chains. Birkel tried to minimize the conflict by making a combined to-do list that he would update and change as work tasks changed.[11]

TODAY'S VIEW   Although early management theorists (Fayol, Weber, Taylor, Barnard, and others) believed that chain of command, authority (line and staff), responsibility, and unity of command were essential, times have changed.[12] Those elements are far less important today. For example, at the Michelin plant in Tours, France, managers have replaced the top-down chain of command with "birdhouse" meetings, in which employees meet for five minutes at regular intervals throughout the day at a column on the shop floor and study simple tables and charts to identify production bottlenecks. Instead of being bosses, shop managers are enablers.[13] Information technology also has made such concepts less relevant today. Employees can access information that used to be available only to managers in a matter of a few seconds. It also means that employees can communicate with anyone else in the organization without going through the chain of command. Also, many employees, especially in organizations where work revolves around projects, find themselves reporting to more than one boss, thus violating the unity of command principle. However, such arrangements can and do work if communication, conflict, and other issues are managed well by all involved parties.

Span of Control

How many employees can a manager efficiently and effectively manage? That's what **span of control** is all about. The traditional view was that managers could not—and should not—directly supervise more than five or six subordinates. Determining the span of control is important because to a large degree, it determines the number of levels and managers in an organization—an important consideration in how efficient an organization will be. All other things being equal, the wider or larger the span, the more efficient the organization. Here's why.

span of control
The number of employees a manager can efficiently and effectively manage

Assume two organizations both have approximately 4,100 employees. As Exhibit 11-6 shows, if one organization has a span of four and the other a span of eight, the organization with the wider span will have two fewer levels and approximately 800 fewer managers. At an average manager's salary of $42,000 a year, the organization with the wider span would save over $33 million a year! Obviously, wider spans are more efficient in terms of cost. However, at some point, wider spans may reduce effectiveness if employee performance worsens because managers no longer have the time to lead effectively.

TODAY'S VIEW The contemporary view of span of control recognizes there is no magic number. Many factors influence the number of employees a manager can efficiently and effectively manage. These factors include the skills and abilities of the manager and the employees and the characteristics of the work being done. For instance, managers with well-trained and experienced employees can function well with a wider span. Other contingency variables that determine the appropriate span include similarity and complexity of employee tasks, the physical proximity of subordinates, the degree to which standardized procedures are in place, the sophistication of the organization's information system, the strength of the organization's culture, and the preferred style of the manager.[14]

The trend in recent years has been toward larger spans of control, which is consistent with managers' efforts to speed up decision making, increase flexibility, get closer to customers, empower employees, and reduce costs. Managers are beginning to recognize that they can handle a wider span when employees know their jobs well and when those employees understand organizational processes. For instance, at PepsiCo's Gamesa cookie plant in Mexico, 56 employees now report to each manager. However, to ensure that performance doesn't suffer because of these wider spans, employees were thoroughly briefed on company goals and processes. Also, new pay systems reward quality, service, productivity, and teamwork.[15]

Members at Each Level

Exhibit 11-6
Contrasting Spans of Control

Organizational Level	(Highest) Assuming Span of 4	Assuming Span of 8
1	1	1
2	4	8
3	16	64
4	64	512
5	256	4,096
6	1,024	
7	4,096	

(Lowest)

Span of 4:
Employees: = 4,096
Managers (level 1–6) = 1,365

Span of 8:
Employees: = 4,096
Managers (level 1–4) =   585

centralization
The degree to which decision making is concentrated at upper levels of the organization

decentralization
The degree to which lower-level employees provide input or actually make decisions

Centralization and Decentralization

One of the questions that needs to be answered when organizing is "At what organizational level are decisions made?" **Centralization** is the degree to which decision making takes place at upper levels of the organization. If top managers make key decisions with little input from below, then the organization is more centralized. On the other hand, the more that lower-level employees provide input or actually make decisions, the more **decentralization** there is. Keep in mind that centralization-decentralization is not an either-or concept. The decision is relative, not absolute—that is, an organization is never completely centralized or decentralized.

Early management writers proposed that the degree of centralization in an organization depended on the situation.[16] Their goal was the optimum and efficient use of employees. Traditional organizations were structured in a pyramid, with power and authority concentrated near the top of the organization. Given this structure, historically centralized decisions were the most prominent, but organizations today have become more complex and responsive to dynamic changes in their environments. As such, many managers believe decisions need to be made by those individuals closest to the problems, regardless of their organizational level. In fact, the trend over the past several decades—at least in U.S. and Canadian organizations—has been a movement toward more decentralization in organizations.[17] Exhibit 11-7 lists some of the factors that affect an organization's use of centralization or decentralization.[18]

TODAY'S VIEW   Today, managers often choose the amount of centralization or decentralization that will allow them to best implement their decisions and achieve organizational goals.[19] What works in one organization, however, won't necessarily work in another, so managers must determine the appropriate amount of decentralization for each organization and work units within it.

employee empowerment
Giving employees more authority (power) to make decisions

As organizations have become more flexible and responsive to environmental trends, there's been a distinct shift toward decentralized decision making.[20] This trend, also known as **employee empowerment**, gives employees more authority (power) to make decisions. (We'll address this concept more thoroughly in our discussion of leadership in Chapter 18.) In large companies especially, lower-level managers are "closer to the action" and typically have more detailed knowledge about problems and how best to solve them than top managers. For instance, at Terex Corporation, CEO Ron Defeo, a big proponent of decentralized management, tells his managers that, "You gotta' run the company you're given." And they have! The company generated revenues of more than $4 billion in 2009 with about 16,000 employees

Exhibit 11-7
Centralization or Decentralization

More Centralization	More Decentralization
• Environment is stable.	• Environment is complex, uncertain.
• Lower-level managers are not as capable or experienced at making decisions as upper-level managers.	• Lower-level managers are capable and experienced at making decisions.
• Lower-level managers do not want a say in decisions.	• Lower-level managers want a voice in decisions.
• Decisions are relatively minor.	• Decisions are significant.
• Organization is facing a crisis or the risk of company failure.	• Corporate culture is open to allowing managers a say in what happens.
• Company is large.	• Company is geographically dispersed.
• Effective implementation of company strategies depends on managers retaining say over what happens.	• Effective implementation of company strategies depends on managers having involvement and flexibility to make decisions.

let's get REAL

Source: Julie Colon

The Scenario:

An old saying goes like this: "If you want something done right, do it yourself." But Alicia Nunez, customer service manager at a party imports company in Guadalajara, Mexico, wants to do just the opposite! She wants to delegate tasks to her team of 25 customer service representatives. But she also wants to do it in a way that her team is still productive and functional.

Julie Colon
Creative Project Manager

What can Alicia do to make sure her employee delegation is successful?

It is most important in any business to delegate tasks to employees so they feel empowered to make decisions. This is essential for building teams that support their leader and feel like they have an important role to play within the organization. Delegating tasks gives the team ownership of the work and drives them to be more passionate about the work. Delegation must be done in a way that takes into account the skills of the team as well as consideration of what tasks will give them a challenge. When we are challenged, we tend to work smarter in order to solve issues that arise, and that can be a very rewarding result of delegation.

worldwide and a small corporate headquarters staff.[21] Another example can be seen at the General Cable plant in Piedras Negras, Coahuila, Mexico, where employees are responsible for managing nearly 6,000 active raw material SKUs (stock-keeping units) in inventory and on the plant floor. And company managers continue to look for ways to place more responsibility in the hands of workers.[22]

Formalization

Formalization refers to how standardized an organization's jobs are and the extent to which employee behavior is guided by rules and procedures. In highly formalized organizations, there are explicit job descriptions, numerous organizational rules, and clearly defined procedures covering work processes. Employees have little discretion over what's done, when it's done, and how it's done. However, where formalization is low, employees have more discretion in how they do their work.

formalization
How standardized an organization's jobs are and the extent to which employee behavior is guided by rules and procedures

TODAY'S VIEW Although some formalization is necessary for consistency and control, many organizations today rely less on strict rules and standardization to guide and regulate employee behavior. For instance, consider the following situation:

> A customer comes into a branch of a large national drug store and drops off a roll of film for same-day developing 37 minutes after the store policy cut-off time. Although the sales clerk knows he's supposed to follow rules, he also knows he could get the film developed with no problem and wants to accommodate the customer. So he accepts the film, violating policy, hoping that his manager won't find out.[23]

Has this employee done something wrong? He did "break" the rule. But by "breaking" the rule, he actually brought in revenue and provided good customer service.

Considering there are numerous situations where rules may be too restrictive, many organizations have allowed employees some latitude, giving them sufficient

mechanistic organization
An organizational design that's rigid and tightly controlled

organic organization
An organizational design that's highly adaptive and flexible

11.2 *Contrast* mechanistic and organic structures.

*data*points[29]

24 percent of job seekers said they preferred to work at a company with more than 1,000 employees; 27 percent they preferred a company with fewer than 200 employees.

80 percent of a company's total workforce is what typical frontline managers directly supervise.

34 percent of HR executives said they had retrained employees for new positions over the last six months.

68 percent of organizations said they've increased centralization in the last five years.

51 percent of white-collar workers say teleworking is a good idea.

42 percent of U.S. companies offer some form of telework arrangement.

55 percent of workers believe their work quality is perceived the same when working remotely as when working in the office.

autonomy to make those decisions that they feel are best under the circumstances. It doesn't mean throwing out all organizational rules because there *will* be rules that are important for employees to follow—and these rules should be explained so employees understand why it's important to adhere to them. But for other rules, employees may be given some leeway.[24]

MECHANISTIC and Organic Structures

Stocking extra swimsuits in retail stores near water parks seems to make sense, right? And if size 11 women's shoes have been big sellers in Chicago, then stocking more size 11s seems to be a no-brainer. After suffering through 16 months of declining same-store sales, Macy's CEO Terry Lundgren decided it was time to restructure the organization to make sure these types of smart retail decisions are made.[25] He's making the company both more centralized and more locally focused. Although that may seem a contradiction, the redesign seems to be working. Lundgren centralized Macy's purchasing, planning, and marketing operations from seven regional offices to one office at headquarters in New York. He also replaced regional merchandise managers with more local managers—each responsible for a dozen stores—who spend more time figuring out what's selling. Designing (or redesigning) an organizational structure that works is important. Basic organizational design revolves around two organizational forms, described in Exhibit 11-8.[26]

The **mechanistic organization** (or bureaucracy) was the natural result of combining the six elements of structure. Adhering to the chain-of-command principle ensured the existence of a formal hierarchy of authority, with each person controlled and supervised by one superior. Keeping the span of control small at increasingly higher levels in the organization created tall, impersonal structures. As the distance between the top and the bottom of the organization expanded, top management would increasingly impose rules and regulations. Because top managers couldn't control lower-level activities through direct observation and ensure the use of standard practices, they substituted rules and regulations. The early management writers' belief in a high degree of work specialization created jobs that were simple, routine, and standardized. Further specialization through the use of departmentalization increased impersonality and the need for multiple layers of management to coordinate the specialized departments.[27]

The **organic organization** is a highly adaptive form that is as loose and flexible as the mechanistic organization is rigid and stable. Rather than having standardized jobs and regulations, the organic organization's loose structure allows it to change rapidly as required.[28] It has division of labor, but the jobs people do are not standardized. Employees tend to be professionals who are technically proficient and trained to handle diverse problems. They need few formal rules and little direct supervision because their training has instilled in them standards of professional conduct. For instance, a petroleum engineer doesn't need to follow specific procedures on how to locate oil sources miles offshore. The engineer can solve most problems alone or after conferring with colleagues. Professional standards guide his or her behavior. The organic organization is low in centralization so that the professional can respond quickly to problems and because top-level managers cannot be expected to possess the expertise to make necessary decisions.

Exhibit 11-8
Mechanistic Versus Organic Organizations

Mechanistic	Organic
• High specialization	• Cross-functional teams
• Rigid departmentalization	• Cross-hierarchical teams
• Clear chain of command	• Free flow of information
• Narrow spans of control	• Wide spans of control
• Centralization	• Decentralization
• High formalization	• Low formalization

CONTINGENCY Factors Affecting Structural Choice

Discuss the contingency factors that favor either the mechanistic model or the organic model of organizational design.   **11.3**

When Carol Bartz took over the CEO position at Yahoo! from cofounder Jerry Yang, she found a company "hobbled by slow decision making and ineffective execution on those decisions."[30] Bartz said, "There's plenty that has bogged this company down." For a company that was once the darling of Web search, Yahoo! seemed to have lost its way, a serious misstep in an industry where change is continual and rapid. Bartz (who is no longer the CEO) implemented a new streamlined structure intended to "make the company a lot faster on its feet." Top managers typically put a lot of thought into designing an appropriate organizational structure. What that appropriate structure is depends on four contingency variables: the organization's strategy, size, technology, and degree of environmental uncertainty.

Strategy and Structure

An organization's structure should facilitate goal achievement. Because goals are an important part of the organization's strategies, it's only logical that strategy and structure are closely linked. Alfred Chandler initially researched this relationship.[31] He studied several large U.S. companies and concluded that changes in corporate strategy led to changes in an organization's structure that support the strategy.

Research has shown that certain structural designs work best with different organizational strategies.[32] For instance, the flexibility and free-flowing information of the organic structure works well when an organization is pursuing meaningful and unique innovations. The mechanistic organization with its efficiency, stability, and tight controls works best for companies wanting to tightly control costs.

Size and Structure

There's considerable evidence that an organization's size affects its structure.[33] Large organizations—typically considered to be those with more than 2,000 employees—tend to have more specialization, departmentalization, centralization, and rules and regulations than do small organizations. However, once an organization grows past a certain size, size has less influence on structure. Why? Essentially, once there are around 2,000 employees, it's already fairly mechanistic. Adding another 500 employees won't impact the structure much. On the other hand, adding 500 employees to an organization with only 300 employees is likely to make it more mechanistic.

Technology and Structure

Every organization uses some form of technology to convert its inputs into outputs. For instance, workers at Whirlpool's Manaus, Brazil, facility build microwave ovens and air conditioners on a standardized assembly line. Employees at FedEx Kinko's Office and Print Services produce custom design and print jobs for individual customers. And employees at Bayer's facility in Karachi, Pakistan, are involved in producing pharmaceuticals on a continuous-flow production line.

LEADER who made a DIFFERENCE

Source: Wang Jun/EyePress EPN/Newscom

As chairman and CEO of Haier Group, Zhang Ruimin runs a successful enterprise with annual revenues of more than $20 billion by turning it into one of China's first global brands.[34] Zhang is considered by many to be China's leading corporate executive. When he took over a floundering refrigerator plant in Qingdao, he quickly found out it produced terrible refrigerators. The story goes that he gave the workers sledgehammers and ordered them to destroy every one. His message: Poor quality would no longer be tolerated. Using his business training, Zhang successfully organized Haier for efficient mass production. But here in the twenty-first century, Zhang believes success requires a different competency. So he reorganized the company into self-managed groups, each devoted to a customer or group of similar customers. Zhang gets it! He understands clearly how an organization's design can help it be successful. What can you learn from this leader who made a difference?

Exhibit 11-9
Woodward's Findings on
Technology and Structure

	Unit Production	Mass Production	Process Production
Structural characteristics:	Low vertical differentiation	Moderate vertical differentiation	High vertical differentiation
	Low horizontal differentiation	High horizontal differentiation	Low horizontal differentiation
	Low formalization	High formalization	Low formalization
Most effective structure:	Organic	Mechanistic	Organic

unit production
The production of items in units or small batches

mass production
The production of items in large batches

process production
The production of items in continuous processes

The initial research on technology's effect on structure can be traced to Joan Woodward, who studied small manufacturing firms in southern England to determine the extent to which structural design elements were related to organizational success.[35] She couldn't find any consistent pattern until she divided the firms into three distinct technologies that had increasing levels of complexity and sophistication. The first category, **unit production**, described the production of items in units or small batches. The second category, **mass production**, described large-batch manufacturing. Finally, the third and most technically complex group, **process production**, included continuous-process production. A summary of her findings is shown in Exhibit 11-9.

Other studies also have shown that organizations adapt their structures to their technology depending on how routine their technology is for transforming inputs into outputs.[36] In general, the more routine the technology, the more mechanistic the structure can be, and organizations with more nonroutine technology are more likely to have organic structures.[37]

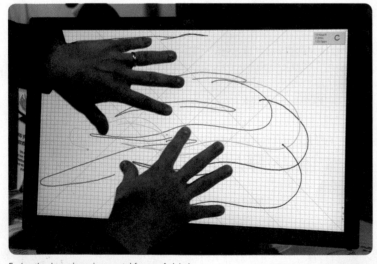

Facing the dynamic environmental forces of global competition and accelerated product innovation by competitors, 3M Company has a flexible and decentralized organic structure that enables it to respond quickly to customer demands for high quality products and fast service. Describing itself as "a global innovation company that never stops inventing," 3M has 35 business units that operate as small companies to keep the company agile and entrepreneurial. The 10-finger multi-touch screen shown in this photo is an innovation of 3M's Touch System business unit designed for customers in the medical and engineering industries. With its organic structure, 3M is poised to adapt quickly to the fast-growing demand for touch-screen products.
Source: Ethan Miller/Getty Images

Environmental Uncertainty and Structure

Some organizations face stable and simple environments with little uncertainty; others face dynamic and complex environments with a lot of uncertainty. Managers try to minimize environmental uncertainty by adjusting the organization's structure.[38] In stable and simple environments, mechanistic designs can be more effective. On the other hand, the greater the uncertainty, the more an organization needs the flexibility of an organic design. For example, the uncertain nature of the oil industry means that oil companies need to be flexible. Soon after he was named CEO of Royal Dutch Shell PLC, Jeroen van der Veer (now the former CEO) streamlined the corporate structure to counteract some of the industry volatility. One thing he did was eliminate the company's cumbersome, overly analytical process of making deals with OPEC countries and other major oil producers.[39]

TODAY'S VIEW   The evidence on the environment-structure relationship helps explain why so many managers today are restructuring their organizations to be lean, fast, and flexible. Worldwide economic downturns, global competition, accelerated product innovation by competitors, and increased demands from customers for high quality and faster deliveries are examples of dynamic environmental forces. Mechanistic organizations are not equipped to respond to rapid environmental change and environmental uncertainty. As a result, we're seeing organizations become more organic.

TRADITIONAL **Organizational Designs**

Describe *traditional* **11. 4**
organizational designs.

They're a big hit with the elementary-school crowd, and millions of them were sold every month. Ever heard of Silly Bandz?[40] If you're over the age of 10, you probably haven't! These colorful rubber bands retain the shapes they're twisted in and kids love them. The small business that created Silly Bandz—BCP Imports of Toledo, Ohio—increased its employee count from 20 to 200 and added 22 phone lines to keep up with inquiries. The person behind those organizing decisions is company president Robert Croak. In making structural decisions, managers have some common designs from which to choose. In this chapter, we're going to describe the traditional organizational designs. In the next chapter, we'll be looking at more contemporary types of organizational designs.

When designing a structure, managers may choose one of the traditional organizational designs. These structures tend to be more mechanistic in nature. A summary of the strengths and weaknesses of each can be found in Exhibit 11-10.

Simple Structure

Most companies start as entrepreneurial ventures using a **simple structure**, an organizational design with low departmentalization, wide spans of control, authority centralized in a single person, and little formalization.[41] As employees are added, however, most don't remain as simple structures. The structure tends to become more specialized and formalized. Rules and regulations are introduced, work becomes specialized, departments are created, levels of management are added, and the organization becomes increasingly bureaucratic. At this point, managers might choose a functional structure or a divisional structure.

simple structure
An organizational design with low departmentalization, wide spans of control, centralized authority, and little formalization

Functional Structure

A **functional structure** is an organizational design that groups similar or related occupational specialties together. You can think of this structure as functional departmentalization applied to the entire organization.

functional structure
An organizational design that groups together similar or related occupational specialties

Divisional Structure

The **divisional structure** is an organizational structure made up of separate business units or divisions.[42] In this structure, each division has limited autonomy, with a division manager who has authority over his or her unit and is responsible for

divisional structure
An organizational structure made up of separate, semiautonomous units or divisions

Simple Structure

- Strengths: Fast; flexible; inexpensive to maintain; clear accountability.
- Weaknesses: Not appropriate as organization grows; reliance on one person is risky.

Functional Structure

- Strengths: Cost-saving advantages from specialization (economies of scale, minimal duplication of people and equipment); employees are grouped with others who have similar tasks.
- Weaknesses: Pursuit of functional goals can cause managers to lose sight of what's best for the overall organization; functional specialists become insulated and have little understanding of what other units are doing.

Divisional Structure

- Strengths: Focuses on results—division managers are responsible for what happens to their products and services.
- Weaknesses: Duplication of activities and resources increases costs and reduces efficiency.

Exhibit 11-10
Traditional Organizational Designs

performance. In divisional structures, however, the parent corporation typically acts as an external overseer to coordinate and control the various divisions, and often provides support services such as financial and legal. Walmart, for example, has two divisions: retail (Walmart Stores, International, Sam's Clubs, and others) and support (distribution centers).

Hopefully, you've seen in this chapter that organizational structure and design (or redesign) are important managerial tasks. Also, we hope that you recognize that organizing decisions aren't only important for upper-level managers. Managers at all levels may have to deal with work specialization or authority or span of control decisions. In the next chapter, we'll continue our discussion of the organizing function by looking at contemporary organizational designs.

CHAPTER

PREPARING FOR: Exams/Quizzes

CHAPTER SUMMARY by Learning Outcomes

11.1 ⌈ LEARNING OUTCOME

Describe six key elements in organizational design.

The key elements in organizational design are work specialization, chain of command, span of control, departmentalization, centralization-decentralization, and formalization. Traditionally, work specialization was viewed as a way to divide work activities into separate job tasks. Today's view is that it is an important organizing mechanism but it can lead to problems. The chain of command and its companion concepts—authority, responsibility, and unity of command—were viewed as important ways of maintaining control in organizations. The contemporary view is that they are less relevant in today's organizations. The traditional view of span of control was that managers should directly supervise no more than five to six individuals. The contemporary view is that the span of control depends on the skills and abilities of the manager and the employees and on the characteristics of the situation.

The various forms of departmentalization are as follows: *Functional* groups jobs by functions performed; *product* groups jobs by product lines; *geographical* groups jobs by geographical region; *process* groups jobs on product or customer flow; and *customer* groups jobs on specific and unique customer groups.

Authority refers to the rights inherent in a managerial position to tell people what to do and to expect them to do it. The acceptance view of authority says that authority comes from the willingness of subordinates to accept it. Line authority entitles a manager to direct the work of an employee. Staff authority refers to functions that support, assist, advise, and generally reduce some of managers' informational burdens. Responsibility is the obligation or expectation to perform assigned duties. Unity of command states that a person should report to only one manager. Centralization-decentralization is a structural decision about who makes decisions—upper-level managers or lower-level employees. Formalization concerns the organization's use of standardization and strict rules to provide consistency and control.

11.2 ⌈ LEARNING OUTCOME

Contrast mechanistic and organic structures.

A mechanistic organization is a rigid and tightly controlled structure. An organic organization is highly adaptive and flexible.

11.3 ⌈ LEARNING OUTCOME

Discuss the contingency factors that favor either the mechanistic model or the organic model of organizational design.

An organization's structure should support the strategy. If the strategy changes, the structure also should change. An organization's size can affect its structure up to a certain point. Once an organization reaches a certain size (usually around 2,000 employees), it's fairly mechanistic. An organization's technology can affect its structure. An organic structure is most effective with unit production and process production technology. A mechanistic structure is most effective with mass production technology. The more uncertain an organization's environment, the more it needs the flexibility of an organic design.

11.4 ⎡ **LEARNING OUTCOME**

Describe traditional organizational designs.
A simple structure is one with low departmentalization, wide spans of control, authority centralized in a single person, and little formalization. A functional structure groups similar or related occupational specialties together. A divisional structure is made up of separate business units or divisions.

REVIEW AND DISCUSSION QUESTIONS ✪

1. Discuss the traditional and contemporary views of each of the six key elements of organizational design.

2. Contrast mechanistic and organic organizations.

3. Would you rather work in a mechanistic or an organic organization? Why?

4. Contrast the three traditional organizational designs.

5. With the availability of advanced information technology that allows an organization's work to be done anywhere at any time, is organizing still an important managerial function? Why or why not?

6. Researchers are now saying that efforts to simplify work tasks actually have negative results for both companies and their employees. Do you agree? Why or why not?

PREPARING FOR: My Career
ETHICS DILEMMA ✪

Thomas Lopez, a lifeguard in the Miami area, was fired for leaving his assigned area to save a drowning man.[43] His employer, Jeff Ellis and Associates, which has a contract with the Florida city of Hallandale, said Lopez "left his patrol area unmonitored and exposed the company to legal liability." Lopez said he had no choice but to do what he did. "I'm not going to put my job over helping someone. I'm going to do what I felt was right, and I did." After this story hit the media, the company offered Lopez his job back, but he declined. What do you think? What ethical concerns do you see? What lessons can be applied to organizational design from this story?

SKILLS EXERCISE Developing Your Empowering People (Delegating) Skill

About the Skill
Managers get things done through other people. Because there are limits to any manager's time and knowledge, effective managers need to understand how to delegate.[44] Delegation is the assignment of authority to another person to carry out specific duties. It allows an employee to make decisions. Delegation should not be confused with participation. In participative decision making, authority is shared. In delegation, employees make decisions on their own.

Steps in Practicing the Skill
A number of actions differentiate the effective delegator from the ineffective delegator. The following five behaviors are used by effective delegators.

1. *Clarify the assignment.* Determine *what* is to be delegated and *to whom.* You need to identify the person who's most capable of doing the task and then determine whether he or she has the time and motivation to do the task. If you have a willing and able employee, it's your responsibility to provide clear information on what is delegated, the results you expect, and any time or performance expectations you may have. Unless there's an overriding need to adhere to specific methods, you should delegate only the results expected. Get agreement on what is to be done and the results expected, but let the employee decide the best way to complete the task.

2. *Specify the employee's range of discretion.* Every situation of delegation comes with constraints. Although you're delegating to an employee the authority to perform some task or tasks, you're not delegating unlimited authority. You are delegating authority to act on certain issues within certain parameters. You need to specify what those parameters are so that employees know, without any doubt, the range of their discretion.

3. *Allow the employee to participate.* One of the best ways to decide how much authority will be necessary to accomplish a task is to allow the employee who will be held accountable for that task to participate in that decision. Be aware, however, that allowing employees to participate can present its own set of potential problems as a result of employees' self-interests and biases in evaluating their own abilities.

4. *Inform others that delegation has occurred.* Delegation shouldn't take place behind the scenes. Not only do the manager and employee need to know specifically what has been delegated and how much authority has been given, but so does anyone else who's likely to be affected by the employee's decisions and actions. This includes people inside and outside the organization. Essentially, you need to communicate what has been delegated (the task and amount of authority) and to whom.

5. *Establish feedback channels.* To delegate without establishing feedback controls is inviting problems. The establishment of controls to monitor the employee's performance increases the likelihood that important problems will be identified and that the task will be completed on time and to the desired specifications. Ideally, these controls should be determined at the time of the initial assignment. Agree on a specific time for the completion of the task and then set progress dates when the employee will report back on how well he or she is doing and any major problems that may have arisen. These controls can be supplemented with periodic checks to ensure that authority guidelines aren't being abused, organizational policies are being followed, proper procedures are being met, and the like.

Practicing the Skill
Read through the following scenario. Write a paper describing how you would handle the situation described. Be sure to refer to the five behaviors described for delegating.

Scenario
Ricky Lee is the manager of the contracts group of a large regional office supply distributor. His boss, Anne Zumwalt, has asked him to prepare by the end of the month the department's new procedures manual that will outline the steps followed in negotiating contracts with office products manufacturers who supply the organization's products. Because Ricky has another major project he's working on, he went to Anne and asked her if it would be possible to assign the rewriting of the procedures manual to Bill Harmon, one of his employees who's worked in the contracts group for about three years. Anne said she had no problems with Ricky reassigning the project as long as Bill knew the parameters and the expectations for the completion of the project. Ricky is preparing for his meeting in the morning with Bill regarding this assignment.

WORKING TOGETHER Team Exercise

An organizational chart can be a useful tool for understanding certain aspects of an organization's structure. Form small groups of three to four individuals. Among yourselves, choose an organization with which one of you is familiar (where you work, a student organization to which you belong, your college or university, etc.). Draw an organizational chart of this organization. Be careful to show departments (or groups) and especially be careful to get the chain of command correct. Be prepared to share your chart with the class.

MY TURN TO BE A MANAGER

- Find three different examples of an organizational chart. (Company's annual reports are a good place to look.) In a report, describe each of these. Try to decipher the organization's use of organizational design elements, especially departmentalization, chain of command, centralization-decentralization, and formalization.

- Survey at least 10 different managers as to how many employees they supervise. Also ask them whether they feel they could supervise more employees or whether they feel the number they supervise is too many. Graph your survey results and write a report describing what you found. Draw some conclusions about span of control.

- Using the organizational chart you created in the team exercise, redesign the structure. What structural changes might make this organization more efficient and effective? Write a report describing what you would do and why. Be sure to include an example of the original organizational chart as well as a chart of your proposed revision of the organizational structure.

- Steve's and Mary's suggested readings: Gary Hamel, *The Future of Management* (Harvard Business School Press, 2007); Thomas Friedman, *The World Is Flat 3.0* (Picador, 2007); Harold J. Leavitt, *Top Down: Why Hierarchies Are Here to Stay and How to Manage Them More Effectively*

(Harvard Business School Press, 2005); and Thomas W. Malone, *The Future of Work* (Harvard Business School Press, 2004).

• In your own words, write down three things you learned in this chapter about being a good manager.

• Self-knowledge can be a powerful learning tool. Go to mymanagementlab.com and complete these self-assessment exercises: How Well Do I Handle Ambiguity? What Type of Organizational Structure Do I Prefer? Do I Like Bureaucracy? How Good Am I at Playing Politics? How Willing Am I to Delegate? Using the results of your assessments, identify personal strengths and weaknesses. What will you do to reinforce your strengths and improve your weaknesses?

MyManagementLab

Go to **mymanagementlab.com** for Auto-graded writing questions as well as the following Assisted-graded writing questions:

11-1. Can an organization's structure be changed quickly? Why or why not? Should it be changed quickly? Explain.

11-2. Explain the contingency factors that affect organizational design.

11-3. Mymanagementlab Only – comprehensive writing assignment for this chapter.

CASE APPLICATION 1   Ask Chuck

The Charles Schwab Corporation (Charles Schwab) is a San Francisco-based financial services company.[45] Like many companies in that industry, Charles Schwab struggled during the economic recession.

Founded in 1971 by its namesake as a discount brokerage, the company has now "grown up" into a full-service traditional brokerage firm, with more than 300 offices in some 45 states and in London and Hong Kong. It still offers discount brokerage services, but also financial research, advice, and planning; retirement plans; investment management; and proprietary financial products including mutual funds, mortgages, CDs, and other banking products through its Charles Schwab Bank unit. However, its primary business is still making stock trades for investors who make their own financial decisions. The company has a reputation for being conservative, which helped it avoid the financial meltdown suffered by other investment firms. Founder Charles R. Schwab has a black bowling ball perched on his desk. "It's a memento of the long-forgotten bubble of 1961, when shares of bowling-pin companies, shoemakers, chalk manufacturers, and lane operators were thought to be can't-miss plays on the limitless potential of suburbia—and turned out to be duds." He keeps the ball as a reminder not to "buy into hype or take excessive risks."

Effective communication with customers that helps them become "better investors" plays an important role in Charles Schwab's customer service strategy as the company strives to succeed in a challenging economic environment. Each day managers of the company's offices receive customer feedback reports and empower employees to respond quickly to customer concerns.
Source: AP Photo/Eric Risberg

Like many companies, Charles Schwab is fanatical about customer service. By empowering front-line employees to respond fast to customer issues and concerns, Cheryl Pasquale, a manager at one of Schwab's branches, is on the front line of Schwab's efforts to prosper in a "resource-challenged economy." Every workday morning, she pulls up a customer feedback report for her branch generated by a brief survey the investment firm e-mails out daily. The report allows her to review how well her six financial consultants handled the previous day's transactions. She's able to see comments of customers who gave both high and low marks and whether a particular transaction garnered praise or complaint. On one particular day, she notices that several customers commented on how difficult it was to use the branch's in-house information kiosks. "She decides she'll ask her team for insights about this in their weekly meeting." One thing that she pays particular attention to is a "manager alert—a special notice triggered by a client who has given Schwab a poor rating for a delay in posting a transaction to his account." And she's not alone. Every day, Pasquale and the managers at all the company's branches receive this type of customer feedback. It's been particularly important to have this information in the challenging economic climate of the last few years.

DISCUSSION QUESTIONS ✪

1. Describe and evaluate what Charles Schwab is doing.

2. How might the company's culture of not buying into hype and not taking excessive risks affect its organizational structural design?

3. What structural implications—good and bad—might Schwab's intense focus on customer feedback have?

4. Do you think this arrangement would work for other types of organizations? Why or why not?

CASE APPLICATION 2 A New Kind of Structure

After finding that employees were spending too much time on menial and time-consuming tasks, Pfizer created an arrangement called PfizerWorks for its global employees that helps them work more efficiently and effectively by allowing them to use the services of several Indian outsourcing firms for support work such as creating documents and manipulating data.
Source: Bloomberg via Getty Images

Admit it. Sometimes the projects you're working on (school, work, or both) can get pretty boring and monotonous. Wouldn't it be great to have a magic button you could push to get someone else to do that boring, time-consuming stuff? At Pfizer, that "magic button" is a reality for a large number of employees.[46]

As a global pharmaceutical company, Pfizer is continually looking for ways to help employees be more efficient and effective. The company's senior director of organizational effectiveness found that the "Harvard MBA staff we hired to develop strategies and innovate were instead Googling and making PowerPoints." Indeed, internal studies conducted to find out just how much time its valuable talent was spending on menial tasks was startling. The average Pfizer employee was spending 20 percent to 40 percent of his or her time on support work (creating documents, typing notes, doing research, manipulating data, scheduling meetings) and only 60 percent to 80 percent on knowledge work (strategy, innovation, networking, collaborating, critical thinking). And the problem wasn't just at lower levels. Even the highest-level employees were affected. Take, for instance, David Cain, an executive director for global engineering. He enjoys his job—assessing environmental real estate risks, managing facilities, and controlling a multimillion-dollar budget. But he didn't so much enjoy having to go through spreadsheets and put together PowerPoints. Now, however, with Pfizer's "magic button," those tasks are passed off to individuals outside the organization.

Just what is this "magic button?" Originally called the Office of the Future (OOF), the renamed PfizerWorks allows employees to shift tedious and time-consuming tasks with the click of a single button on their computer desktop. They describe what they need on an online form, which is then sent to one of two Indian service-outsourcing firms. When a request is received, a team member in India calls the Pfizer employee to clarify what's needed and by when. The team member then e-mails back a cost specification for the requested work. If the Pfizer employee decides to proceed, the costs involved are charged to the employee's department. About this unique arrangement, Cain said that he relishes working with what he prefers to call his "personal consulting organization."

The number 66,500 illustrates just how beneficial PfizerWorks has been for the company. That's the number of work hours estimated to have been saved by employees who've used PfizerWorks. What about Joe Cain's experiences? When he gave the Indian team a complex project researching strategic actions that worked when consolidating company facilities, the team put the report together in a month, something that would have taken him six months to do alone. He says, "Pfizer pays me not to work tactically, but to work strategically."

DISCUSSION QUESTIONS ✪

1. Describe and evaluate what Pfizer is doing with its PfizerWorks.

2. What structural implications—good and bad—does this approach have? (Think in terms of the six organizational design elements.)

3. Do you think this arrangement would work for other types of organizations? Why or why not? What types of organizations might it also work for?

4. What role do you think organizational structure plays in an organization's efficiency and effectiveness? Explain.

12 Adaptive Organizational Design

SPOTLIGHT: *Manager at Work*

Self-governance. *Sounds like a term you'd read in a political science textbook, but not a management textbook. However, a self-governing organization is what Dov Seidman (see photo) has created in his own company, LRN (a consulting firm), and it's what he advocates for other organizations that want to prosper in the new realities of today's environment of interdependence.[1] Here's his story.*

LRN consults with companies on legal and regulatory compliance, reputation and principled performance, environmental sustainability, business ethics, governance, leadership, and culture change. Seidman has long argued that the most moral businesses were also the most successful. Through research and experience, he began to realize that the old system of top-down command and control in organizations wasn't working. A large-scale study (a survey of almost 5,000 managers and executives in the United States) gave Seidman interesting insights into values by asking questions such as: "When people go around their boss because they believe it's the right thing to do, are they punished or rewarded? Are people trusted to make decisions?" and so forth. The results showed three general categories of organizations: (1) "blind obedience," which rely on coercion, formal authority, policing, and command-and-control leadership; (2) "informed acquiescence," which have clear-cut rules and policies, well-established procedures,

Source: Andrey_Popov/Shutterstock.com

and performance-based rewards and punishments; and (3) "self-governance," where there's a shared purpose and common values guiding people at all levels of the company and who are trusted to act on their own initiative and to collaboratively innovate. Siedman calls this a "theory

Source: Bloomberg via Getty Images

Seidman has long argued that the most moral businesses were also the most successful.

of organizational evolution: from blind obedience to informed acquiescence to self-governance. So, he decided to make his organization self-governing.

Seidman's company had an organizational chart that showed the formal arrangement of jobs and who reported to whom. One day, in front of his 300 colleagues at LRN, Seidman ripped up

the organizational chart and announced that "none of us would report to a boss anymore. From that point on, we would all 'report' to our company mission." Thus began LRN's journey to become a self-governing company. Seidman would be the first to admit that it's not been an easy process. Self-governance doesn't just mean making the organization flatter

LEARNING OUTCOMES

12.1	**Describe** contemporary organizational designs.
12.2	**Discuss** how organizations organize for collaboration.
12.3	**Explain** flexible work arrangements used by organizations.
12.4	**Discuss** organizing issues associated with a contingent workforce.
12.5	**Describe** today's organizational design challenges.

(that is, eliminating reporting levels) nor is it about empowering, since the concept of empowerment reinforces the idea of "bestowing" power from someone at a higher level. It does mean power and authority are used in a "highly collaborative way. Information is shared openly and immediately. Employees make decisions and behave not in reaction to rules or a supervisor's directive, but in accordance with a company mission built on shared values." Elected employee councils at LRN handle things like recruiting, performance management, and conflict resolution. Seidman says, "Our effort to become self-governing has been enlightening, frustrating, nerve-racking, authentic and urgent. It remains a work in progress." **What's your reaction to this concept of self-governing organizations? Could you see yourself working in such an organization?**

Welcome to the fascinating world of organizational structure and design in the twenty-first century! Did you ever consider that a business might actually be structured so that employees wouldn't report to a boss and instead would all work together collaboratively? Dov Seidman and LRN were open to trying new ways to do what they're in business to do, and the unusual structural

experiment seems to be working well. Although organizational self-governance is still fairly rare—a survey done by LRN shows that only 3 percent of employees observed high levels of self-governing behavior within their organization—the trust, shared values, and deep understanding and commitment to a purpose-inspired mission can help self-governed organizations gain competitive advantage and achieve superior business performance.

In the last chapter, we introduced the basic concepts of traditional organizational design, including the six building blocks of an organization's structure: work specialization, departmentalization, chain of command, span of control, centralization and decentralization, and formalization. In this chapter, we're going to explore contemporary aspects of organizational design as organizations adapt to the demands of today's environment. We're going to first look at some contemporary organizational designs and then move on to discussing how organizations are coping with those demands through collaborative work efforts, flexible work arrangements, and a contingent workforce. We'll wrap up the chapter by describing some organizational design challenges facing today's managers.

12.1 | ***Describe*** *contemporary organizational designs.*

CONTEMPORARY Organizational Designs

Microsoft's Windows 7 was the outcome of a three-year project marked by close collaboration among the thousands of people working on various aspects of the product.[2] This approach contrasted sharply with the development of Windows Vista, where the development team had evolved into "a rigid set of silos—each responsible for specific technical features—that didn't share their plans widely." With Vista, programming code created by each group might have worked fine on its own, but it caused technical problems when integrated with code created by other groups. Those design issues, as well as internal communications breakdowns, contributed to numerous product delays and defects. CEO Steve Ballmer was adamant about not repeating that mistake. Thus, to "rebuild Windows, Microsoft razed walls"—that is, organizational structure walls that acted as barriers and impediments to efficient and effective work.

Like Steve Ballmer, many managers are finding that the traditional designs (discussed on pp. 345–346) often aren't appropriate for today's increasingly dynamic and complex environment. Instead, organizations need to be lean, flexible, and innovative;

Exhibit 12-1
Contemporary Organizational
Designs

Team Structure

- What it is: A structure in which the entire organization is made up of work groups or teams.
- Advantages: Employees are more involved and empowered.
  Reduced barriers among functional areas.
- Disadvantages: No clear chain of command.
  Pressure on teams to perform.

Matrix-Project Structure

- What it is: Matrix is a structure that assigns specialists from different functional areas to work on projects who then return to their areas when the project is completed. Project is a structure in which employees continuously work on projects. As one project is completed, employees move on to the next project.
- Advantages: Fluid and flexible design that can respond to environmental changes. Faster decision making.
- Disadvantages: Complexity of assigning people to projects.
  Task and personality conflicts.

Boundaryless Structure

- What it is: A structure not defined by or limited to artificial horizontal, vertical, or external boundaries; includes *virtual* and *network* types of organizations.
- Advantages: Highly flexible and responsive.
  Utilizes talent wherever it's found.
- Disadvantages: Lack of control.
  Communication difficulties.

Learning Structure

- What it is: A structure in which employees continually acquire and share new knowledge and apply that knowledge.
- Advantages: Sharing of knowledge throughout organization. Sustainable source of competitive advantage.
- Disadvantages: Reluctance on part of employees to share knowledge for fear of losing their power.
  Large numbers of experienced employees on the verge of retiring.

that is, they need to be more organic. So managers are finding creative ways to structure and organize work. These contemporary designs include team structures, matrix and project structures, boundaryless organizations, and learning organizations. (See Exhibit 12-1 for a summary of these designs.)

Team Structures

Larry Page and Sergey Brin, cofounders of Google, created a corporate structure that "tackles most big projects in small, tightly focused teams."[3] A **team structure** is one in which the entire organization is made up of work teams that do the organization's work.[4] In this structure, employee empowerment is crucial because no line of managerial authority flows from top to bottom. Rather, employee teams design and do work in the way they think is best, but the teams are also held responsible for all work performance results in their respective areas.

In large organizations, the team structure complements what is typically a functional or divisional structure and allows the organization to have the efficiency of a bureaucracy *and* the flexibility that teams provide. Companies such as Amazon, Boeing,

team structure
An organizational structure in which the entire organization is made up of work teams

Exhibit 12-2
Example of a Matrix Organization

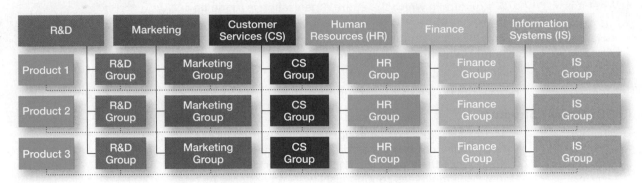

Hewlett-Packard, Louis Vuitton, Motorola, and Xerox, for instance, extensively use employee teams to improve productivity.

Matrix and Project Structures

matrix structure
An organizational structure that assigns specialists from different functional departments to work on one or more projects

Other popular contemporary designs are the matrix and project structures. The **matrix structure** assigns specialists from different functional departments to work on projects being led by a project manager. (See Exhibit 12-2.) One unique aspect of this design is that it creates a *dual chain of command* because employees in a matrix organization have two managers: their functional area manager and their product or project manager, who share authority. The project manager has authority over the functional members who are part of his or her project team in areas related to the project's goals. However, any decisions about promotions, salary recommendations, and annual reviews typically remain the functional manager's responsibility. The matrix design "violates" the unity of command principle, which says that each person should report to only one boss; however, it can—and does—work effectively if both managers communicate regularly, coordinate work demands on employees, and resolve conflicts together.[5]

project structure
An organizational structure in which employees continuously work on projects

Many organizations use a **project structure**, in which employees continuously work on projects. Unlike the matrix structure, a project structure has no formal departments where employees return at the completion of a project. Instead, employees take their specific skills, abilities, and experiences to other projects. Also, all work in project structures is performed by teams of employees. For instance, at design firm IDEO, project teams form, disband, and form again as the work requires. Employees "join" project teams because they bring needed skills and abilities to that project. Once a project is completed, however, they move on to the next one.[6]

Project structures tend to be more flexible organizational designs, without the departmentalization or rigid organizational hierarchy that can slow down making decisions or taking action. In this structure, managers serve as facilitators, mentors, and coaches. They eliminate or minimize organizational obstacles and ensure that teams have the resources they need to effectively and efficiently complete their work.

The Boundaryless Organization

The Large Hadron Collider is a $6 billion particle accelerator lying in a tunnel that's 27 kilometers (17 miles) in circumference and 175 meters (574 feet) below ground near Geneva, Switzerland. "The atom smasher is so large that a brief status report lists 2,900 authors, so complex that scientists in 34 countries have readied 100,000 computers to process its data, and so fragile that a bird dropping a bread crust can short-circuit its power supply."[7] But exploiting the collider's potential to expand the frontiers of knowledge has required that scientists around the world cut across "boundaries of place, organization, and technical specialty to conduct ever more ambitious experiments."

The structural arrangement for getting work done that has developed around the massive collider is an example of another contemporary organizational design called the **boundaryless organization**, an organization whose design is not defined by, or limited to, the horizontal, vertical, or external boundaries imposed by a predefined structure.[8] Former GE chairman Jack Welch coined the term because he wanted to eliminate vertical and horizontal boundaries within GE and break down external barriers between the company and its customers and suppliers. Although the idea of eliminating boundaries may seem odd, many of today's most successful organizations find that they can operate most effectively by remaining flexible and *un*structured: that the ideal structure for them is *not* having a rigid, bounded, and predefined structure.[9]

What do we mean by *boundaries*? There are two types: (1) *internal*—the horizontal ones imposed by work specialization and departmentalization and the vertical ones that separate employees into organizational levels and hierarchies; and (2) *external*—the boundaries that separate the organization from its customers, suppliers, and other stakeholders. To minimize or eliminate these boundaries, managers might use virtual or network structural designs.

VIRTUAL ORGANIZATIONS Is an internship something you've ever thought about doing (or maybe have done)? How about an internship that you could do, not in a workplace cubicle, but from your couch using your computer?[10] Such virtual internships are becoming quite popular, especially with smaller and midsize companies and, of course, with online businesses. The type of work virtual interns do typically involves "researching, sales, marketing, and social media development"—tasks that can be done anywhere with a computer and online access. Some organizations are structured in a way that allows most employees to be virtual employees.

A **virtual organization** typically consists of a small core of full-time employees and outside specialists temporarily hired as needed to work on projects.[11] An example is when Second Life, a company creating a virtual world of colorful online avatars, was building its software. Founder Philip Rosedale hired programmers from around the world and divided up the work into about 1,600 individual tasks, "from setting up databases to fixing bugs." The process worked so well, the company used it for all sorts of work.[12] Another example is Nashville-based Emma Inc., an e-mail marketing firm with 100 employees who work from home or offices in Austin, Denver, New York, and Portland.[13] The biggest challenge they've faced is creating a "virtual" culture, a task made more challenging by the fact that the organization is virtual.

NETWORK ORGANIZATIONS Food marketer Smart Balance Inc. helps people stay trim and lean with its heart-healthy products.[14] The company's organizational structure is also trim and lean. With only 67 employees, the company outsources almost every other organizational function, including manufacturing, product distribution, and sales. Smart Balance's structural approach is one that also eliminates organizational boundaries and can be described as a **network organization**, which uses its own employees to do some work activities and networks of outside suppliers to provide other needed product components or work processes.[15] This organizational form is sometimes called a modular organization by manufacturing firms.[16] Such an approach allows organizations to concentrate on what they do best by contracting out other activities to companies that do those activities best. For instance, the strategy of British company ARM, a microchip designer, is to find a lot of partners. It contracts with those partners for manufacturing and sales. Because ARM doesn't manufacture, it can encourage its customers (ARM's chip designs serve as the brains of 98 percent of the world's cell phones)

boundaryless organization
An organization whose design is not defined by, or limited to, the horizontal, vertical, or external boundaries imposed by a predefined structure

Rekha Menon, executive vice president of India geographic services and human capital and diversity at Accenture India, works from her home. Accenture, an international consulting, technology, and outsourcing firm, is a virtual organization that operates in 120 countries. Like Menon, most of Accenture's quarter of a million employees do not work in company offices but from home or at their clients' offices. Accenture achieves high productivity and collaboration by using an innovative videoconferencing system that connects with clients and enables employees of its worldwide virtual workplace to operate as a unified team.
Source: India Today Group/Getty Images

virtual organization
An organization that consists of a small core of full-time employees and outside specialists temporarily hired as needed to work on projects

network organization
An organization that uses its own employees to do some work activities and networks of outside suppliers to provide other needed product components or work processes

FUTURE VISION | Flexible Organizations

By 2025, a considerably smaller proportion of the labor force will hold full-time jobs. Organizations will increasingly rely on contract employees and part-timers to get the work done, giving the organization greater flexibility. Many workers will be doing pieces of what is today a single job. From the employee's standpoint, it will mean greater individual control of the employee's future rather than being dependent on a single employer.

Future workers will be more like outside consultants than full-time employees. Assignments will be temporary. They might last a few weeks or a few years, but the presumption is—on the part of both workers and employers—that the relationship will not become permanent. As such, you will find yourself consistently working on new projects with a different group of coworkers.

Additionally, expect to see fewer large corporate headquarter buildings and centralized corporate centers. Work demands will not require organizations to house large numbers of workers in one place. "Headquarter" cities such as New York, Toronto, or London will find themselves with lots of empty office space. Conversely, job opportunities will be geographically dispersed, and in many cases, not dependent at all on where employees reside. An increasing proportion of the labor force will work from home. And many organizations will create regional satellite centers where employees meet or work. These centers will be less costly to operate than centralized offices and will cut down on commuting distances for workers.

to request whatever they like. Such flexibility is particularly valuable in the cell phone market where having custom chips and software can provide an edge.[17] At Boeing, the company's head of development for the 787 Dreamliner manages thousands of employees and some 100 suppliers at more than 100 sites in different countries.[18] Sweden's Ericsson contracts its manufacturing and even some of its research and development to more cost-effective contractors in New Delhi, Singapore, California, and other global locations.[19] And at Penske Truck Leasing, dozens of business processes, such as securing permits and titles, entering data from drivers' logs, and processing data for tax filings and accounting, have been outsourced to Mexico and India.[20]

Learning Organizations

learning organization
An organization that has developed the capacity to continuously learn, adapt, and change

Doing business in an intensely competitive global environment, British retailer Tesco realizes how important it is for its stores to run well behind the scenes.[21] And it does so using a proven "tool" called Tesco in a Box, a self-contained complete IT system and matching set of business processes that provides the model for all of Tesco's international business operations. This approach promotes consistency in operations and is a way to share innovations.[22] Tesco is an example of a **learning organization**, an organization that has developed the capacity to continuously learn, adapt, and change. "Today's managerial challenge is to inspire and enable knowledge workers to solve, day in and day out, problems that cannot be anticipated."[23] In a learning organization, employees continually acquire and share new knowledge and apply that knowledge in making decisions or doing their work. Some organizational theorists even go so far as to say that an organization's ability to do this—that is, to learn and to apply that learning—may be the only sustainable source of competitive advantage.[24] What structural characteristics does a learning organization need?

Employees throughout the entire organization—across different functional specialties and even at different organizational levels—must share information and collaborate on work activities. Such an environment requires minimal structural and physical barriers, which allows employees to work together in doing the organization's work the best way they can and, in the process, learn from each other. Finally, empowered work teams tend to be an important feature of a learning organization's structural design. These teams make decisions about doing whatever work needs to be done or resolving issues. With empowered employees and teams, there's little need for "bosses" to direct and control. Instead, managers serve as facilitators, supporters, and advocates.

ORGANIZING for Collaboration

In 3M's dental products division, Sumita Mitra, a research scientist, helped develop coatings that prevent tooth plaque and innovative cement bonding materials that could be set by light.[25] However, as cosmetic dentistry's popularity increased, she sensed an opportunity for developing a product that had both the strength and the natural appearance that dentists wanted. Finding that product meant venturing outside the realm of traditional dental materials. Mitra first turned to 3M's database of technical reports written by the company's approximately 7,000 scientists. Although this database is invaluable for spreading knowledge throughout the company, "the real work of collaboration happens face-to-face, often at events sponsored by TechForum, an employee-run organization designed to foster communications between scientists in different labs or division." There, Mitra found valuable information and guidance from other scientists in different divisions of the company. 3M also has an R&D Workcenter networking Web site, which Mitra describes as "a LinkedIn for 3M scientists." It also proved to be a valuable collaborative tool. Both the TechForum and the R&D Workcenter proved beneficial for Mitra's research efforts. Three years after starting her research, 3M introduced Filtek Supreme Plus, a strong, polishable dental material and the first to include nanoparticles. At 3M, employees are expected to collaborate and are evaluated on their success. Such collaborations among the company's scientists have led to several breakthroughs in product technology.

It's fair to say that the world of work has changed. Organizations need to be more flexible in how work gets done, although it still needs to get done efficiently and effectively. Throw in the fact that innovation and the ability to bring innovations to market quickly is critical, and you can begin to appreciate how traditional top-down decision making that strictly follows the chain of command and narrowly defined functional arrangements might not be the best structural mechanisms to do this. Many organizations, like 3M, are encouraging collaborative work among employees. Exhibit 12-3 lists some of the benefits and drawbacks of working collaboratively. An organization's collaboration efforts can be internal—that is, among employees within the organization. Or those efforts can be external collaborations with any stakeholders. In both types, it's important that managers recognize how such collaborative efforts "fit" with the organization's structure and the challenges of making all the pieces work together successfully. Let's take a look at each of these types of collaboration.

Internal Collaboration

When managers believe collaboration among employees is needed for more coordinated and integrated work efforts, they can use several different structural options. Some of the more popular include cross-functional teams, task forces, and communities of practice.

Discuss how organizations organize for collaboration. **12.2**

Benefits	Drawbacks
• Increased communication and coordination	• Potential interpersonal conflict
• Greater innovative output	• Different views and competing goals
• Enhanced ability to address complex problems	• Logistics of coordinating
• Sharing of information and best practices	

Exhibit 12-3
Benefits and Drawbacks of Collaborative Work

Sources: Based on R. Wagner and G. Muller, "The Pinnacle of Partnership: Unselfishness," *Gallup Management Journal Online* [http://gmj.gallup.com], February 18, 2010; M.T. Hansen, "When Internal Collaboration Is Bad for Your Company," *Harvard Business Review*, April 2009, pp. 83–88; G. Ahuja, "Collaboration Networks, Structural Holes and Innovation: A Longitudinal Study," *Academy of Management Proceedings Online*, 1998; and M. Pincher, "Collaboration: Find a New Strength in Unity," *Computer Weekly*, November 27, 2007, p. 18.

Cross-functional teamwork is a vital component of Procter & Gamble's internal collaboration strategy. Teams that include employees from research and development, marketing, engineering, logistics, supply management, and other functional areas enable the company to organize and utilize their resources effectively and efficiently on a global basis. P&G uses teams to create corporate plans and strategy, reduce operating costs, speed up product development, drive new products and services to market, and provide solutions for complicated business problems. Shown here are team members during a launch meeting of eStore, an online shopping service developed by PFSweb for P&G consumer brands.
Source: AP Photo/Al Behrman

cross-functional team
A work team composed of individuals from various functional specialties

CROSS-FUNCTIONAL TEAMS You'd probably agree that hospitals would be challenging organizations to manage. When Wright L. Lassiter took on the job as CEO of the Alameda County Medical Center in Oakland, California, he had a massive challenge on his hands. Nurses followed doctors' orders only when they felt like it, a doctor was beaten and strangled to death by a patient and his body left on the floor for 30 minutes until a janitor found it, the organization lost millions of dollars every year, and so on. However, Lassiter turned a "shockingly mismanaged urban safety-net hospital system in one of America's most violent cities into a model for other public hospitals." And one of the approaches he took was what he called "odd-couple arrangements"—what we would call cross-functional teams—of doctors, nurses, technicians, and other managers and made them responsible for finding ways to be more efficient and effective.[26]

Organizations use team-based structures because they've found that teams are more flexible and responsive to changing events than traditional departments or other permanent work groups. Teams have the ability to quickly assemble, deploy, refocus, and disband. In Chapter 11, we introduced the concept of a **cross-functional team** in our discussion of the various forms of departmentalization. Remember that it's a work team composed of individuals from various functional specialties. When a cross-functional team is formed, team members are brought together to collaborate on resolving mutual problems that affect the respective functional areas. Ideally, the artificial boundaries that separate functions disappear, and the team focuses on working together to achieve organizational goals. For instance, at ArcelorMittal, the world's biggest steel company, cross-functional teams of scientists, plant managers, and salespeople review and monitor product innovations.[27] The concept of cross-functional teams is being applied in health care, as we noted in the example at the beginning of this section. And, at Suburban Hospital in Bethesda, Maryland, intensive care unit (ICU) teams composed of a doctor trained in intensive care medicine, a pharmacist, a social worker, a nutritionist, the chief ICU nurse, a respiratory therapist, and a chaplain meet daily with every patient's bedside nurse to discuss and debate the best course of treatment. The hospital credits this team care approach with reducing errors, shortening the amount of time patients spent in ICU, and improving communication between families and the medical staff.[28] We'll discuss teams in more detail in Chapter 14.

task force (or ad hoc committee)
A temporary committee or team formed to tackle a specific short-term problem affecting several departments

TASK FORCES Another structural option organizations might use is a **task force** (also called an **ad hoc committee**), a temporary committee or team formed to tackle a specific short-term problem affecting several departments. The temporary nature of a task force is what differentiates it from a cross-functional team. Task force members usually perform many of their normal work tasks while serving on the task force; however, the members of a task force must collaborate to resolve the issue that's been assigned to them. When the issue or problem is solved, the task force is no longer needed and members return to their regular assignments. Many organizations, from government agencies to universities to businesses, use task forces. For instance, at San Francisco–based accounting firm Eichstaedt & Devereaux, employee task forces have helped develop formal recruiting, mentoring, and training programs. And at Frito-Lay, a subsidiary of PepsiCo, Inc., a task force that included members of the company's Hispanic employees' resource group helped in the development of two new products: Lay's Cool Guacamole potato chips and Doritos Guacamole tortilla chips.[29]

COMMUNITIES OF PRACTICE Early in 2008, American soldiers training Afghan and Iraqi armies were having problems using a rocket-propelled grenade launcher.

let's get REAL

The Scenario:

Leann Breur is the human resources (HR) manager at a large grocery supply company that has locations in four Midwestern states and more than 800 employees. Leann's team, which includes all four locations, has 18 people. At the home office, she sees her staff being quite innovative in getting their work done, and she's certain the HR offices at the other offices have great ideas, too. How can Leann get her employees to share their knowledge with each other?

What advice would you give to Leann?

Leann should schedule a set of conference calls where the team can get to know each other first, and then be comfortable with sharing ideas and best practices. If budget permits, a one-day gathering would be ideal.

Kelly Osorio
Human Resources Manager

Source: Kelly Osorio

The frustrated unit commander posted a question to one of the U.S. Army's online forums where soldiers ask questions and share ideas with peers around the world. Within a few days, someone who had a similar experience with the launcher posted a simple solution on the Web site on how to safely prevent misfiring. Problem solved![30] Such types of internal collaborations are called **communities of practice**, which are "groups of people who share a concern, a set of problems, or a passion about a topic, and who deepen their knowledge and expertise in that area by interacting on an ongoing basis."[31] For example, repair technicians at Xerox share "war stories" to communicate their experiences and to help others solve difficult problems with repairing machines.[32] At pharmaceutical firm Pfizer, communities of practice are integrated into the company's formal structure. Called employee councils and networks, these communities share knowledge and help product development teams on difficult issues such as safety.[33] Pfizer's more structured approach to recognizing the value of such collaboration is becoming more common. But how effective are these communities of practice? Research studies have found that communities of practice can "create value by contributing to increased effectiveness in employees' job performance through greater access that they provide to the ideas, knowledge, and best practices shared among community members."[34] Exhibit 12-4 lists some suggestions for making such communities work.

communities of practice
Groups of people who share a concern, a set of problems, or a passion about a topic and who deepen their knowledge and expertise in that area by interacting on an ongoing basis

- Have top management support and set clear expectations.
- Create an environment that will attract people and make them want to return for advice, conversation, and knowledge sharing.
- Encourage regular meetings of the community, whether in person or online.
- Establish regular communication among community members.
- Focus on real problems and issues important to the organization.
- Have clear accountability and managerial oversight.

Exhibit 12-4
Making Communities of Practice Work

Sources: Based on R. McDermott and D. Archibald, "Harnessing Your Staff's Informal Networks," *Harvard Business Review,* March 2010, pp. 82–89; S. F. Gale, "The Power of Community, *Workforce Management Online,* March 2009; and E. Wenger, R. McDermott, and W. Snyder, *Cultivating Communities of Practice: A Guide to Managing Knowledge* (Boston: Harvard Business School Press, 2002).

External Collaboration

Intuit has figured out a way to get its customers involved. Devoted users of QuickBooks can access a site—QuickBooks Live Community—and exchange helpful information with others. For customers, that often means faster answers to problems. And for the company, this "volunteer army" means less investment in paid technicians.[35] External collaboration efforts have become quite popular for organizations, especially in the area of product innovation. We're going to look at two forms of external collaboration: open innovation and strategic partnerships. Each of these can provide organizations with needed information, support, and contributions to getting work done and achieving organizational goals. But it's important that managers understand the challenges of how each might fit into the organization's structural design.

OPEN INNOVATION Frito Lay offered a cool $1 million to the winner of the company's contest for a new potato chip flavor. The winner was selected by a Facebook vote. Pharmaceutical giant GlaxoSmithKline PLC opened to the public the designs behind 13,500 chemical compounds associated with the parasite that causes malaria. Glaxo "hopes that sharing information and working together will lead scientists to come up with a drug for treating the mosquito-borne disease faster than the company could do on its own."[36]

The days may be numbered when businesses generate their own product development ideas and develop, manufacture, market, and deliver those products to customers. Today, many companies are trying **open innovation**, opening up the search for new ideas beyond the organization's boundaries and allowing innovations to easily transfer inward and outward. For instance, Procter & Gamble, Starbucks, Dell, Best Buy, and Nike have all created digital platforms that allow customers to help them create new products and messages.[37] As you can see, many of today's successful companies are collaborating directly with customers in the product development process. Others are partnering with suppliers, other outsiders, and even competitors. Exhibit 12-5 describes some of the benefits and drawbacks of open innovation.

STRATEGIC PARTNERSHIPS Companies worldwide are finding ways to connect to each other. Once bitter rivals, Nokia and Qualcomm formed a cooperative agreement to develop next-generation cell phones for North America. Nokia also collaborated with Microsoft in a partnership where Microsoft's software powers e-mail and chat services on most Nokia phones.[38]

open innovation
Opening up the search for new ideas beyond the organization's boundaries and allowing innovations to easily transfer inward and outward

Exhibit 12-5
Benefits and Drawbacks of Open Innovation

Benefits	Drawbacks
• Gives customers what they want—a voice	• High demands of managing the process
• Allows organizations to respond to complex problems	• Extensive support needed
• Nurtures internal and external relationships	• Cultural challenges
• Brings focus back to marketplace	• Greater need for flexibility
• Provides way to cope with rising costs and uncertainties of product development	• Crucial changes required in how knowledge is controlled and shared

Sources: Based on S. Lindegaard, "The Side Effects of Open Innovation," *Bloomberg BusinessWeek Online,* June 7, 2010; H. W. Chesbrough and A. R. Garman, "How Open Innovation Can Help You Cope in Lean Times," *Harvard Business Review,* December 2009, pp. 68–76; A. Gabor, "The Promise [and Perils] of Open Collaboration," *Strategy & Business Online,* Autumn 2009; and J. Winsor, "Crowdsourcing: What It Means for Innovation," *BusinessWeek Online,* June 15, 2009.

In today's environment, organizations are looking for advantages wherever they can get them. One way they can do this is with **strategic partnerships**, collaborative relationships between two or more organizations in which they combine their resources and capabilities for some business purpose. Here are some reasons why such partnerships make sense: flexibility and informality of arrangements promote efficiencies, provide access to new markets and technologies, and entail less paperwork when creating and disbanding projects; risks and expenses are shared by multiple parties; independent brand identification is kept and can be exploited; working with partners possessing multiple skills can create major synergies; rivals can often work together harmoniously; partnerships can take on varied forms from simple to complex; dozens of participants can be accommodated in partnership arrangements; and antitrust laws can protect R&D activities.[39] Strategic partnerships are growing in popularity. However, as with all the collaborative arrangements we've described— external and internal—the challenge for managers is finding ways to exploit the benefits of such collaboration while incorporating the collaborative efforts seamlessly into the organization's structural design.

strategic partnerships
Collaborative relationships between two or more organizations in which they combine their resources and capabilities for some business purpose

FLEXIBLE Work Arrangements

Explain flexible work arrangements used by organizations. **12.3**

Accenture consultant Keyur Patel's job arrangement is becoming the norm, rather than the exception.[40] During his recent consulting assignment, he had three clocks on his desk: one set to Manila time (where his software programmers were), one to Bangalore (where another programming support team worked), and the third for San Francisco, where he was spending four days a week helping a major retailer implement IT systems to track and improve sales. And his cell phone kept track of the time in Atlanta, his home, where he headed on Thursday evenings.

For this new breed of professionals, life is a blend of home and office, work and leisure. Thanks to technology, work can now be done anywhere, anytime. As organizations adapt their structural designs to these new realities, we see more of them adopting flexible working arrangements. Such arrangements not only exploit the power of technology, but give organizations the flexibility to deploy employees when and where needed. In this section, we're going to take a look at some different types of flexible work arrangements, including telecommuting and compressed workweeks, flextime, and job sharing. As with the other structural options we've looked at, managers must evaluate these types in light of the implications for decision making, communication, authority relationships, work task accomplishment, and so forth.

Telecommuting

Eve Gelb used to endure hour-and-a-half commutes morning and evening on the 405 freeway in Los Angeles to her job as a project manager at SCAN Health Plan.[41] Now, she's turned her garage into an office and works from home as a telecommuter. On the days when she does have to go in to the corporate office, she shares a space with her three subordinates who also work flexibly. Information technology has made telecommuting possible, and external environmental changes have made it necessary for many organizations. **Telecommuting** is a work arrangement in which employees work at home and are linked to the workplace by computer. Needless to say, not every job is a candidate for telecommuting, but many are.

Working from home used to be considered a "cushy perk" for a few lucky employees, and such an arrangement wasn't allowed very often. Now, many businesses view telecommuting as a business necessity. For instance, at SCAN Health Plan, the company's chief financial officer said that getting more employees to telecommute provided the company a way to grow without having to incur any additional fixed costs such as office buildings, equipment, or parking lots. In addition, some

telecommuting
A work arrangement in which employees work at home and are linked to the workplace by computer

data*points* [42]

84 percent of employees who work remotely did so at least once a week.

62 percent of workers want the option to telecommute.

67 percent of respondents to a survey said they want greater flexibility at work.

32 percent of organizations have ad hoc alternative workplace programs such as mobile work, hoteling, and telecommuting.

69 percent of human resource consultants say that the use of a flexible workforce is a permanent change and not a temporary response to economic conditions.

48 percent of respondents to a survey say that compared with now, the office of 2021 will have disappeared and employees will work from wherever they are.

32 percent of workers say the biggest advantage of working from home is no commute.

50 percent of adults surveyed said they preferred a traditional 9 to 5 shift for their workdays; 50 percent said they'd like some other option.

33 percent of employees say they often receive e-mails from their bosses during the weekend.

companies view the arrangement as a way to combat high gas prices and to attract talented employees who want more freedom and control over their work.

Despite its apparent appeal, many managers are reluctant to have their employees become "laptop hobos."[43] They argue that employees will waste time surfing the Internet or playing online games instead of working, that they'll ignore clients, and that they'll desperately miss the camaraderie and social exchanges of the workplace. In addition, managers wonder how they'll "manage" these employees. How do you interact with an employee and gain his or her trust when they're not physically present? And what if their work performance isn't up to par? How do you make suggestions for improvement? Another significant challenge is making sure that company information is kept safe and secure when employees are working from home, as we discussed in Chapter 10.

Employees often express the same concerns about working remotely, especially when it comes to the isolation of not being "at work." At Accenture, where employees are scattered around the world, the chief human resources officer says it isn't easy to maintain that esprit de corps.[44] However, the company has put in place a number of programs and processes to create that sense of belonging for its workforce, including Web-conferencing tools, assigning each employee to a career counselor, and holding quarterly community events at its offices. In addition, the telecommuter employee may find that the line between work and home becomes even more blurred, which can be stressful.[45] Managers and organizations must address these important organizing issues as they move toward having employees telecommute.

So, once an organization decides that it wants to establish telecommuting opportunities for employees, what needs to happen next? One of the first issues to address is encouraging employees to make that decision to become remote workers. For instance, at SCAN Health Plan, the company offered free high-speed Internet access

let's get REAL

The Scenario:

Isabella Castillo, vice president of professional services at a consulting company that helps IT organizations deliver better service to their customers, needs help with her professional staff of 16 consultants, who all work from home. Her problem: dealing with the realities of telecommuting—lack of direct interaction, lack of camaraderie, feeling isolated and out-of-the-loop, etc. For their type of business, remote work makes good business sense, but how can she connect and engage her employees?

What advice would you give Isabella?

Isabella's predicament is quite common among teams that don't interact in person. She will first need to form a direct relationship with each employee. Isabella will then be charged with uniting the employees as a team through a common ground. She can set a numerical goal for the team, or another metric in order to judge them as a whole. That should help them work together, rather than individually. Finally, she will need to ensure that her language and direction to the team are all aimed at identifying them as a unit.

Mina Nematalla
Business Owner & Manager

and free office furniture, along with help in setting it up to encourage more of its workforce to work from home. Other companies have encouraged employees to work anywhere but at the office by pointing to the pay "increase" employees would receive from money saved on gas, dry cleaning, and eating out at lunch. Other companies have used the "green" angle…emphasizing the carbon-free aspect of not driving long distances to and from the workplace. Managing the telecommuters then becomes a matter of keeping employees feeling like they're connected and engaged—a topic we delve into at the end of the chapter as we look at today's organizational design challenges.

Compressed Workweeks, Flextime, and Job Sharing

During the global economic crisis in the United Kingdom, accounting firm KPMG needed to reduce costs.[46] It decided to use flexible work options as a way of doing so. The company's program, called Flexible Futures, offered employees four options to choose from: a four-day workweek with a 20 percent salary reduction; a two- to twelve-week sabbatical at 30 percent of pay; both options; or continue with their regular schedule. Some 85 percent of the U.K. employees agreed to the reduced-workweek plan. "Since so many people agreed to the flexible work plans, KPMG was able to cap the salary cut at about 10 percent for the year in most cases." The best thing, though, was that as a result of the plan, KPMG didn't have to do large-scale employee layoffs.

As this example shows, organizations may sometimes find they need to restructure work using forms of flexible work arrangements. One approach is a **compressed workweek**, a workweek where employees work longer hours per day but fewer days per week. The most common arrangement is four 10-hour days (a 4–40 program). For example, in Utah, state employees have a mandated (by law) four-day workweek, with offices closed on Fridays in an effort to reduce energy costs. After a year's time, the state found that its compressed workweek resulted in a 13 percent reduction in energy use and estimated that state employees saved as much as $6 million in gasoline costs.[47] Another alternative is **flextime** (also known as **flexible work hours**), a scheduling system in which employees are required to work a specific number of hours a week but are free to vary those hours within certain limits. A flextime schedule typically designates certain common core hours when all employees are required to be on the job, but allows starting, ending, and lunch-hour times to be flexible. According to a survey of companies by the Families and Work Institute, 81 percent of the respondents now offer flextime benefits. Another survey by Watson Wyatt of mid- and large-sized companies found that a flexible work schedule was the most commonly offered benefit.[48]

In Great Britain, McDonald's experimented with an unusual program—dubbed the Family Contract—to reduce absenteeism and turnover at some of its restaurants. Under this Family Contract, employees from the same immediate family can fill in for one another for any work shift without having to clear it first with their manager.[49] This type of job scheduling is called **job sharing**—the practice of having two or more people split a full-time job. Although something like McDonald's Family Contract may be appropriate for a low-skilled job, other organizations might offer job sharing to professionals who want to work but don't want the demands and hassles of a full-time position. For instance, at Ernst & Young, employees in many of the company's locations can choose from a variety of flexible work arrangements, including job sharing. Also, many companies have used job sharing during the economic downturn to avoid employee layoffs.[50]

compressed workweek
A workweek where employees work longer hours per day but fewer days per week

flextime (or flexible work hours)
A scheduling system in which employees are required to work a specific number of hours a week but are free to vary those hours within certain limits

job sharing
The practice of having two or more people split a full-time job

As an employee of Ernst & Young's advanced security operations, this young man can choose from a variety of flexible working arrangements including day-to-day work-hour flexibility, reduced work-hour schedules, telecommuting, compressed workweeks, and job sharing. Designed to allow employees to schedule their jobs around life events, the company's flexible work initiatives are part of its "People First" culture. Ernst & Young's management believes that by helping its employees balance their work-life commitments, the clients of the national accounting firm will also be served well by its employees.
Source: AP Photo/The Honolulu Advertiser, Bruce Asato

12.4 *Discuss* organizing
issues associated with
a contingent workforce.

contingent workers
Temporary, freelance, or contract
workers whose employment is
contingent on demand for their services

CONTINGENT Workforce

At Conrad & Co., a small private accounting firm in Spartanburg, South Carolina, Diana Galvin started as a temporary, part-time employee before moving into a full-time staff accountant position. She got her full-time job by learning how to do and then doing her assignments well and offering suggestions on how the company could improve.[51] But not every temporary worker gets offered a full-time job (or wants to be offered one). Prior to her full-time employment, Diana was part of what has been called the contingent workforce. **Contingent workers** are temporary, freelance, or contract workers whose employment is *contingent* on demand for their services. Some are now referring to these workers as the *independent* work force, since there's no dependent relationship between worker and organization.[52]

"Stung by massive and disruptive layoffs that accompanied the latest recession, companies are starting to rethink the way they get work done."[53] As organizations eliminate full-time jobs through downsizing and other organizational restructurings, they often rely on a contingent workforce to fill in as needed. Also, one of the top-ranking forecasts in a survey that asked HR experts to look ahead to 2018 was that "Firms will become adept at sourcing and engaging transient talent around short-term needs, and will focus considerable energy on the long-term retention of smaller core talent groups."[54] The model for the contingent worker structural approach can be seen in the film industry. There, people are essentially "free agents" who move from project to project applying their skills—directing, talent casting, costuming, makeup, set design, and so forth—as needed. They assemble for a movie, then disband once it's finished and move on to the next project. This type of contingent worker is common in project organizations. But contingent workers can also be temporary employees brought in to help with special needs such as seasonal work. Let's look at some of the organizational issues associated with contingent workers.

One of the main issues businesses face with their contingent workers, especially those who are independent contractors or freelancers, is classifying who actually qualifies as one.[55] The decision on who is and who isn't an independent contractor isn't as easy or as unimportant as it may seem. Companies don't have to pay Social Security, Medicare, or unemployment insurance taxes on workers classified as independent contractors. And those individuals also aren't covered by most workplace laws. So it's an important decision. For instance, FedEx treats some 12,000 of its package deliverers in its FedEx Ground Division as contractors. Their classification of these workers as independent contractors has caused battles with the Internal Revenue Service and state governments and riled competitor UPS, whose drivers are unionized employees and argues that FedEx's policy is "unfair to taxpayers, competitors, and the workers themselves."[56] The federal government is also looking at increased power to penalize employers that misclassify workers. So, there is an incentive to be totally above board in classifying who is and who is not an independent contractor. The legal definition of a contract worker depends on how much control a company has over the person; that is, does the company control what the worker does and how the worker does his or her job? The more control the company has, "the more likely the individual will be considered an employee rather than an independent contractor."[57] And it isn't just the legal/tax issues that are important in how workers are classified. The structural implications, especially in terms of getting work done and how performance problems are resolved, are important, as well.

Another issue with contingent workers is the process for recruiting, screening, and placing these contingent workers where their work skills and efforts are needed.[58] As we'll discuss in the next chapter on human resource management, these important steps help ensure that the right people are in the right places at the right times in order to get work done efficiently and effectively. Any organization that wants to minimize potential problems with its contingent workers needs to pay attention to hiring.

The final issue we want to look at is the importance of a contingent employee's performance. Just like a regular employee, a contingent employee is brought on board to do some specific work task(s). It's important that managers have a method of establishing goals, schedules, and deadlines with the contingent employees.[59] And it's also important that mechanisms be in place to monitor work performance and goal achievement, especially if the contingent employee is working off-site.

TODAY'S Organizational Design Challenges

As managers look for organizational designs that will best support and facilitate employees doing their work efficiently and effectively, they must contend with certain challenges. These challenges include keeping employees connected and managing global structural issues.

Describe today's **12.5**
organizational design
challenges.

Keeping Employees Connected

Many organizational design concepts were developed during the twentieth century when work was done at an employer's place of business under a manager's supervision, work tasks were fairly predictable and constant, and most jobs were full-time and continued indefinitely.[60] But that's not the way it is today at many companies. For instance, thousands of Cisco Systems employees sit at unassigned desks in team rooms interspersed with communal break areas. At some IBM divisions, only a small percentage of employees—mostly top managers and their assistants—have fixed desks or offices. All others are either mobile employees or they share desks when they need to be at work. At Sabre Holdings, teams are assigned to neighborhoods of workspaces and employees find places for themselves when they arrive.[61]

As these examples show, a major structural design challenge for managers is finding a way to offer flexibility but also keeping widely dispersed and mobile employees connected to the organization. Mobile computing and communication technology have given organizations and employees ways to stay connected and to be more productive. For instance, handheld devices have e-mail, calendars, and contacts that can be used anywhere there's a wireless network. And these devices can be used to log into corporate databases and company intranets. Employees can videoconference using broadband networks and Webcams. Many companies are giving employees key fobs with constantly changing encryption codes that allow them to log onto the corporate network to access e-mail and company data from any computer hooked up to the Internet. Cell phones switch seamlessly between cellular networks and corporate Wi-Fi connections. The biggest issue in doing work anywhere, anytime, however, is security. Companies must protect their important and sensitive information. Fortunately, software and other disabling devices have minimized security issues considerably. Even insurance providers are more comfortable giving their mobile employees access to information. For instance, Health Net Inc. gave BlackBerry phones to many of its managers so they can tap into customer records from anywhere. As one tech company CEO

LEADER who made a DIFFERENCE

Source: Daniel Barry/EPA/Newscom

One senior vice president at Cisco Systems belongs to more internal company teams than "he can count on both hands." While that may sound like a nightmare to some, that's part of the organizational structure "web" created by CEO John T. Chambers.[62] The structure is so complex that it takes about 15 minutes and a whiteboard to explain it. However, Chambers uses three words to describe its benefits: "speed, skill, and flexibility." His idea for the company's structure originated at the end of the 2001 downturn after Cisco wrote off some $2.2 billion in losses. Chambers realized that the "company's hierarchical structure precluded it from moving quickly into new markets." So he began grouping executives into cross-functional teams figuring that this would help break down traditional silos and lead to faster decision making. At first, the executives didn't like it. Some couldn't handle working with unfamiliar colleagues; others were upset with the new team-based compensation structure. However, the company's decision making has accelerated—it took executives only eight days to figure out that it made sense to acquire Web-conferencing company WebEx. And as the chaotic tech industry continues to evolve, it's important for Chamber's organization to stay on top of things, and its structural arrangement contributes to being able to do that. *What can you learn from this leader who made a difference?*

said, "Companies now can start thinking about innovative apps [applications] they can create and deliver to their workers anywhere."[63]

Managing Global Structural Issues

Are there global differences in organizational structures? Are Australian organizations structured like those in the United States? Are German organizations structured like those in France or Mexico? Given the global nature of today's business environment, managers need to be familiar with this issue. Researchers have concluded that the structures and strategies of organizations worldwide are similar, "while the behavior within them is maintaining its cultural uniqueness."[64] What does this distinction between strategy and culture mean for designing effective and efficient structures? When designing or changing structure, managers may need to think about the cultural implications of certain design elements. For instance, one study showed that formalization—rules and bureaucratic mechanisms—may be more important in less economically developed countries and less important in more economically developed countries where employees may have higher levels of professional education and skills.[65] Another study found that organizations with people from high power-distance countries (such as Greece, France, and most of Latin America) find that their employees are much more accepting of mechanistic structures than are employees from low power-distance countries. Other structural design elements may be affected by cultural differences as well.

No matter what structural design managers choose for their organizations, the design should help employees do their work in the best—most efficient and effective—way they can. The structure should support and facilitate organizational members as they carry out the organization's work. After all, an organization's structure is simply a means to an end.

MyManagementLab
Go to **mymanagementlab.com** to complete the problems marked with this icon .

CHAPTER

PREPARING FOR: Exams/Quizzes
CHAPTER SUMMARY by Learning Outcomes

12.1 LEARNING OUTCOME

Describe contemporary organizational designs.
In a team structure, the entire organization is made up of work teams. The matrix structure assigns specialists from different functional departments to work on one or more projects being led by project managers. A project structure is one in which employees continuously work on projects. A virtual organization consists of a small core of full-time employees and outside specialists temporarily hired as needed to work on projects. A network organization is an organization that uses its own employees to do some work activities and networks of outside suppliers to provide other needed product components or work processes. A learning organization is one that has developed the capacity to continuously learn, adapt, and change. It has certain structural characteristics including an emphasis on sharing information and collaborating on work activities, minimal structural and physical barriers, and empowered work team.

12.2 LEARNING OUTCOME

Discuss how organizations organize for collaboration.
An organization's collaboration efforts can be internal or external. Internal collaborative structural options include cross-functional teams, task forces, and communities of practice. A cross-functional team is a work team composed of individuals from various functional specialties. A task force is a temporary committee or team formed to tackle a specific short-term problem affecting several departments. Communities of practice are groups of people who share a concern, a set of problems, or a passion about a topic and who deepen their knowledge and expertise in that area by interacting on an ongoing basis. External collaborative options include open innovation and strategic partnerships. Open innovation expands the search for new ideas beyond the organization's boundaries and allows innovations to easily transfer inward and outward. Strategic partnerships are collaborative relationships between two or more organizations in which they combine resources and capabilities for some business purpose.

12.3 LEARNING OUTCOME

Explain flexible work arrangements used by organizations.
Flexible work arrangements give organizations the flexibility to deploy employees when and where they're needed. Structural options include telecommuting, compressed workweeks, flextime, and job sharing. Telecommuting is a work arrangement in which employees work at home and are linked to the workplace by computer. A compressed workweek is one in which employees work longer hours per day but fewer days per week. Flextime is a scheduling system in which employees are required to work a specific number of hours a week but are free to vary those hours within certain limits. Job sharing is when two or more people split a full-time job.

12.4 LEARNING OUTCOME

Discuss organizing issues associated with a contingent workforce.
Contingent workers are temporary, freelance, or contract workers whose employment is contingent on demand for their services. Organizing issues include classifying who actually qualifies as an independent contractor; setting up a

process for recruiting, screening, and placing contingent workers; and having a method in place for establishing goals, schedules, and deadlines and for monitoring work performance.

12.5 (LEARNING OUTCOME)   **Describe** today's organizational design challenges.
The two main organizational design challenges for today include keeping employees connected and managing global structural issues.

REVIEW AND DISCUSSION QUESTIONS ✪

1. Describe the four contemporary organizational designs. How are they similar? Different?

2. Differentiate between matrix and project structures.

3. How can an organization operate without boundaries?

4. What types of skills would a manager need to effectively work in a project structure? In a boundaryless organization? In a learning organization?

5. How does each of the different types of collaboration (both internal and external) contribute to more coordinated and integrated work efforts?

6. What structural issues might arise in managing employees' flexible work arrangements? Think about what you've learned about organizational design. How might that information help a manager address those issues?

7. Does the idea of a flexible work arrangement appeal to you? Why or why not?

8. Why is it a challenge to "keep employees connected" in today's organizations?

PREPARING FOR: My Career
ETHICS DILEMMA ✪

"Ethical hacking." It's probably an understatement to say that people were excited about the introduction of Apple's iPad.[66] Then the news broke that a small group of computer experts calling themselves Goatse Security had hacked into AT&T's Web site and found numbers that identified iPads connected to AT&T's mobile network. Those numbers allowed the group to uncover 114,000 e-mail addresses of thousands of first-adopter iPad customers, including prominent officials in companies, politics, and the military. AT&T called it an act of malice, condemned the hackers, and apologized to its affected customers. The group that exposed the flaw said that it did a "public service."

One analyst for CNET also said that the group did a good thing. "Security researchers often disclose holes to keep vendors honest. Many sources complain that they notify companies of security vulnerabilities and that the companies take months, or even years, to provide a fix to customers. In the meantime, malicious hackers may have discovered the same hole and may be using it to steal data, infect computers, or attack systems without the computer owner knowing there is even a risk."[67] What do you think? Is there such a thing as "ethical hacking?" What ethical issues do you see here? What are the implications for various stakeholders in this situation?

SKILLS EXERCISE   Developing Your Acquiring Power Skill

About the Skill
Power is a natural process in any group or organization, and to perform their jobs effectively, managers need to know how to acquire and use power.[68] Why is having power important? Because power makes you less dependent on others. When a manager has power, he or

she is not as dependent on others for critical resources. And if the resources a manager controls are important, scarce, and nonsubstitutable, her power will increase because others will be more dependent on her for those resources. (See Chapter 18 for more information on leader power.)

Steps in Practicing the Skill
You can be more effective at acquiring and using power if you use the following eight behaviors.

1. *Frame arguments in terms of organizational goals.* To be effective at acquiring power means camouflaging your self-interests. Discussions over who controls what resources should be framed in terms of the benefits that will accrue to the organization; do not point out how you personally will benefit.

2. *Develop the right image.* If you know your organization's culture, you already understand what the organization wants and values from its employees in terms of dress, associates to cultivate and those to avoid, whether to appear risk taking or risk aversive, the preferred leadership style, the importance placed on getting along well with others, and so forth. With this knowledge, you're equipped to project the appropriate image. Because the assessment of your performance isn't always a fully objective process, you need to pay attention to style as well as substance.

3. *Gain control of organizational resources.* Controlling organizational resources that are scarce *and* important is a source of power. Knowledge and expertise are particularly effective resources to control. They make you more valuable to the organization and therefore more likely to have job security, chances for advancement, and a receptive audience for your ideas.

4. *Make yourself appear indispensable.* Because we're dealing with appearances rather than objective facts, you can enhance your power by appearing to be indispensable. You don't really have *to be* indispensable, as long as key people in the organization believe that you are.

5. *Be visible.* If you have a job that brings your accomplishments to the attention of others, that's great. However, if you don't have such a job, you'll want to find ways to let others in the organization know what you're doing by highlighting successes in routine reports, having satisfied customers relay their appreciation to senior executives, being seen at social functions, being active in your professional associations, and developing powerful allies who speak positively about your accomplishments. Of course, you'll want to be on the lookout for those projects that will increase your visibility.

6. *Develop powerful allies.* To get power, it helps to have powerful people on your side. Cultivate contacts with potentially influential people above you, at your own level, and at lower organizational levels. These allies often can provide you with information that's otherwise not readily available. In addition, having allies can provide you with a coalition of support—if and when you need it.

7. *Avoid "tainted" members.* In almost every organization, there are fringe members whose status is questionable. Their performance and/or loyalty may be suspect. Keep your distance from such individuals.

8. *Support your boss.* Your immediate future is in the hands of your current boss. Because he or she evaluates your performance, you'll typically want to do whatever is necessary to have your boss on your side. You should make every effort to help your boss succeed, make her look good, support her if she is under siege, and spend the time to find out the criteria she will use to assess your effectiveness. Don't undermine your boss. And don't speak negatively of her to others.

Practicing the Skill
The following suggestions are activities you can do to practice the behaviors associated with acquiring power.

1. Keep a one-week journal of your behavior describing incidences when you tried to influence others around you. Assess each incident by asking: Were you successful at these attempts to influence them? Why or why not? What could you have done differently?

2. Review recent issues of a business periodical (such as *Bloomberg BusinessWeek, Fortune, Forbes, Fast Company, Industry Week,* or the *Wall Street Journal*). Look for articles on reorganizations, promotions, or departures from management positions. Find at least two articles where you believe power issues are involved. Relate the content of the articles to the concepts introduced in this skill module.

WORKING TOGETHER Team Exercise

A company's future may well depend on how well it's able to learn.

Form small groups of three to four individuals. Your team's "job" is to find some current information on learning organizations. You'll probably be able to find numerous articles about the topic, but limit your report to five of what you consider to be the best sources of information on the topic. Using this information, write a one-page bulleted list discussing your reactions to the statement set in bold at the beginning of this exercise. Be sure to include bibliographic information for your five chosen articles at the end of your one-page bulleted list.

MY TURN TO BE A MANAGER

- Since you may be a telecommuter some time during your career (or may manage employees who are telecommuters), do some research on tips for making telecommuting work.

- Find the most current list of *Fortune*'s Best Companies to Work For (usually published in early February). Look through the list, and tally how many of the top 50 provide some type of flexible work arrangements for their employees and the type of flexible work arrangements they use.

- Using current business periodicals, do some research on open innovation efforts by companies. Choose three examples of businesses using this and describe and evaluate what each is doing.

- Create a chart describing each adaptive organizational design discussed in this chapter along with what you perceive as potential advantages and disadvantages of each.

- Steve's and Mary's suggested readings: Richard Donkin, *The Future of Work* (Palgrave Macmillan, 2010); Philip Kotler and John A. Caslione, *Chaotics: The Business of Managing and Marketing in the Age of Turbulence* (Amacom, 2009); Paul Osterman, *The Truth About Middle Managers* (Harvard Business School Press, 2008); and Gary Hamel, *The Future of Management* (Harvard Business School Press, 2007).

- In your own words, write down three things you learned in this chapter about being a good manager.

- Self-knowledge can be a powerful learning tool. Go to mymanagementlab.com and complete these self-assessment exercises: How Well Do I Handle Ambiguity? Do I Trust Others? Do Others See Me as Trustworthy? How Well Do I Respond to Turbulent Change? Using the results of your assessments, identify personal strengths and weaknesses. What will you do to reinforce your strengths and improve your weaknesses?

MyManagementLab

Go to **mymanagementlab.com** for Auto-graded writing questions as well as the following Assisted-graded writing questions:

12-1. The boundaryless organization has the potential to create a major shift in the way we work. Do you agree or disagree? Explain.

12-2. What structural issues might arise in managing employees' flexible work arrangements? Think about what you've learned about organizational design. How might that information help a manager address those issues?

12-3. Mymanagementlab Only – comprehensive writing assignment for this chapter.

CASE APPLICATION 1 Organizational Volunteers

They're individuals you might never have thought of as being part of an organization's structure, but for many organizations, volunteers provide a much-needed source of labor.[69] Maybe you've volunteered at a Habitat for Humanity build, a homeless shelter, or some nonprofit organization. However, what if the volunteer assignment was at a for-profit business and the job description read like this: "Spend a few hours a day at your computer, supplying answers online to customer questions about technical matters like how to set up an Internet home network or how to program a new high-definition television," all for no pay. Many large corporations, start-up companies, and venture capitalists are betting that this "emerging corps of Web-savvy helpers will transform the field of customer service."

Setting up an experimental structure with a rating system for Web-savvy volunteers who answer customer-service calls may help Verizon boost its productivity by eliminating many calls usually handled at a Verizon call center. The payoff for volunteers who work without pay include respect from their peers and development of their skills.
Source: © Pixellover RM 6/Alamy

Self check-outs. Self check-ins. Pumping your own gas (although most of you are probably too young to remember having an attendant that pumped your gas, checked your oil, and washed your windshield). Filling out online forms. Businesses have become very good at getting customers to do free work. Now, they're taking the concept even further, especially in customer service settings, by getting "volunteers" to perform specialized work tasks.

The role that these volunteer "enthusiasts" have played, especially in contributing innovations to research and development efforts, has been closely researched in recent years. For example, case studies highlight the product tweaks made by early skateboarders and mountain bikers to their gear. Researchers have also studied the programmers behind open-source software like the Linux operating system. It seems that individuals who do this type of "volunteering" are motivated mainly by a payoff in enjoyment and respect among their peers and to some extent the skills they're able to develop. Now, as the concept of individuals volunteering for work tasks moves to the realm of customer service, can it work and what does it mean for managers?

For instance, at Verizon's high-speed fiber optic Internet, television, and telephone service, "volunteers" are answering customer questions about technical matters on a company-sponsored customer-service Web site for no pay. Mark Studness, director of Verizon's e-commerce unit was familiar with sites where users offered tips and answered questions. His challenge? Find a way to use that potential resource for customer service. His solution? "Super" or lead users—that is, users who provided the best answers and dialogue in Web forums.

The experiment at Verizon "suggests that company-sponsored online communities for customer service, if handled adeptly, hold considerable promise." Studness says that "you have to make an environment that attracts these super users of the world because that's where the magic happens." A company that worked with Verizon to set up its structure said that "the mentality of super-users in online customer-service communities is similar to that of devout gamers." So they set up the structure with an elaborate rating system for contributors with ranks, badges, and "kudos counts." So far, Studness is happy with how it's gone. He says the company-sponsored customer-service site is "a very productive tool, partly because it absorbs many thousands of questions that would otherwise be expensive calls to a Verizon call center."

DISCUSSION QUESTIONS ✪

1. What do you think about using "volunteers" to do work that other people get paid to do?

2. If you were in Mark Studness's position, what would you be most concerned about in this arrangement? How would you "manage" that concern?

3. How do these "volunteers" fit into an organization's structure? Take each of the six elements of organizational design (see Chapter 11, pp. 333–342) and discuss how each would affect this structural approach.

4. Do you think this approach could work for other types of work being done or in other types of organizations? Explain.

CASE APPLICATION 2 The Anti-Hierarchy

Top-down decision making at Apple produced phenomenal results, with Steve Jobs initiating the creative process by providing the vision and direction for innovations and then relying on talented leaders like Jonathan Ive, shown here, to complete the process. As Apple's senior vice president of industrial design reporting directly to Jobs, Ive has brought to life such innovations as the iMac, iPod, and iPhone.
Source: Paul Harris, Pacific Coast News/Newscom

A major function of an organization's hierarchy is to increase standardization and control for managers. Using the chain of command, managers can direct the activities of subordinates toward a common purpose. If the right person with a creative vision is in charge of a hierarchy, the results can be phenomenal. For instance, the late Steve Jobs would be an example. At Apple, where he was CEO, there was a strongly top-down creative process in which most major decisions and innovations flowed directly through Jobs and then were delegated to sub-teams as specific assignments to complete. This approach worked—and worked well for Apple.

On the other hand, there's "creative deviance," in which individuals create extremely successful products despite being told by senior management to stop working on them.[70] For instance, the electrostatic displays used in more than half of Hewlett-Packard's instruments, the tape slitter that was one of 3M's most important process innovations, and Nichia's development of multi-billion-dollar LED bright lighting technology were all officially rejected by the organizational management hierarchy. In all these examples, an approach like Apple's would have turned away some of the most successful products these companies ever produced. Doing "business as usual" can be so entrenched in a hierarchical organization that new ideas—creative deviance—are seen as threats rather than opportunities for development.

We don't know why top-down decision making works so well for one highly creative company like Apple, and why hierarchy nearly ruined innovations at other organizations. It might be that Apple's structure is actually quite simple, with relatively few layers, and a great deal of responsibility placed on each individual for his or her outcomes. Or it might be that Apple simply had a very unique leader who was able to rise above the conventional boundaries of a CEO to create a culture of constant innovation.

DISCUSSION QUESTIONS ✪

1. Do you think it's possible for an organization to deliberately create an "anti-hierarchy" to encourage employees to engage in acts of creative deviance? What steps might a company take to encourage creative deviance?

2. What are the drawbacks of an approach that encourages creative deviance?

3. Why do you think a company like Apple is able to be creative with a strongly hierarchical structure, while other companies find hierarchy limiting?

4. Do you think Apple's success has been entirely dependent on Steve Jobs in his role as head of the hierarchy? What are the potential drawbacks when a company is so strongly connected to the decision making of a single individual?

13 Managing Human Resources

SPOTLIGHT: *Manager at Work*

Would you lie on your résumé to get a job you want? In a survey of college students, 70 percent said they would. Human resource (HR) managers say that 53 percent of résumés and job applications contain falsification, and 21 percent of falsified résumés state a fraudulent degree. In this age of digital and social media, it's hard to imagine anyone falsifying their records, much less someone who's in a company's top position as CEO.[1]

After a thorough search, Scott Thompson (see photo) was named as Yahoo's CEO in early 2012. Prior to his appointment at Yahoo, Thompson was president of PayPal and prior to that was PayPal's chief technology officer. Thompson replaced Carol Bartz, a well-known computer industry executive, who after two years on the job had been unable to resolve Yahoo's troubles. In his first months on the job, Thompson formulated a strategic plan for turning around the company, including a massive layoff of employees. Then, the whole situation started to unravel. In early May 2012, an activist investor sent a letter to Yahoo's board of directors expressing concern about an SEC regulatory filing signed by Thompson "that stated to the best of his knowledge its contents were accurate." That document said that Thompson had earned a college degree in accounting and computer science in 1979 from a small university south of Boston. The activist investor said he had reason to believe that the degree was in accounting only. And, the university didn't have a computer science program until the early 1980s, and school officials confirmed that Mr. Thompson received a bachelor's of science degree in business administration. The activist investor questioned if Thompson

Source: © MTP/Alamy

had embellished his academic credentials and if the board had failed to exercise due "diligence and oversight in one of its most important tasks—identifying and hiring the Chief Executive Officer."

After all this came down, a person close to the company said that, "In the absence of

Source: Terrence McCarthy/Paypal/Handout/EPA/Newscom

Would you lie on your résumé to get a job you want?

evidence that Mr. Thompson actively misled Yahoo about his résumé, Yahoo's directors likely won't force him out. Maintaining him as CEO of Yahoo at this time is more important than whether he had a computer science degree or not." And at first, that was the stance Yahoo's board took. However, the controversy continued to grow. In a meeting with senior Yahoo officials, Thompson said he "regretted not finding an error in his

public biography." He then suggested that maybe an executive search firm might have inserted this information more than seven years earlier. Yet, this blame game backfired. Some of his comments ended up on tech blogs, angering the search firm and leading it to produce documents from Mr. Thompson showing his inaccurate biography. As one person close to the situation said, "The cover-up became worse

---

MyManagementLab®

⭐ **Improve Your Grade!**

Over 10 million students improved their results using the Pearson MyLabs.
Visit **mymanagementlab.com** for simulations, tutorials, and end-of-chapter problems.

LEARNING OUTCOMES

13.1 | **_Explain_** the importance of the human resource management process and the external influences that might affect that process.

13.2 | **_Discuss_** the tasks associated with identifying and selecting competent employees.

13.3 | **_Explain_** the different types of orientation and training.

13.4 | **_Describe_** strategies for retaining competent, high-performing employees.

13.5 | **_Discuss_** contemporary issues in managing human resources.

than the crime." Not long after, Thompson ended up resigning his position. Although the board did not give him severance pay, he did get to keep $7 million of the cash and stock he received when appointed to the position. Not a bad haul for only four months' work. **What does this story tell you about the importance of checking a job applicant's background?**

Maybe you were surprised that a person with the most powerful organization position as CEO would lie on a résumé. Well, the surprising thing is that this Yahoo story isn't the first one where a CEO or another senior executive claimed false credentials. RadioShack, Bausch & Lomb, MGM Mirage, CSX, and FEMA are a few of the others where this scenario has played out in recent years. As we embark on this chapter on managing a company's human resources, it's a powerful message that emphasizes the importance of the process. With the organization's structure in place, managers have to find people to fill the jobs that have been created or to remove people from jobs

(even the CEO) if business circumstances require. That's where human resource management (HRM) comes in. It's an important task that involves having the right number of the right people in the right place at the right time. In this chapter, we'll look at the process managers use to do just that. In addition, we'll look at some contemporary HRM issues facing managers.

A major HRM challenge for managers is ensuring that their company has a high-quality workforce. Getting and keeping competent and talented employees is critical to the success of every organization, whether an organization is just starting or has been in business for years. If an organization doesn't take its HRM responsibilities seriously, performance may suffer. Therefore, part of every manager's job when organizing is human resource management. All managers engage in some HRM activities such as interviewing job candidates, orienting new employees, and evaluating their employees' work performance, even if there is a separate HRM department.

13.1 | *Explain* the importance of the human resource management process and the external influences that might affect that process.

THE HUMAN Resource Management Process

"At L'Oreal, success starts with people. Our people are our most precious asset. Respect for people, their ideas and differences, is the only path to our sustainable long-term growth."[2] Many organizations profess that their people are their most important asset and acknowledge the important role that employees play in organizational success. However, why is HRM important, and what external factors influence the HRM process?

Why Is HRM Important?

HRM is important for three reasons. First, as various studies have concluded, it can be a significant source of competitive advantage.[3] And that's true for organizations around the world, not just U.S. firms. The Human Capital Index, a comprehensive study of more than 2,000 global firms, concluded that people-oriented HR gives an organization an edge by creating superior shareholder value.[4]

Second, HRM is an important part of organizational strategies. Achieving competitive success through people means managers must change how they think about their employees and how they view the work relationship. They must work with people and treat them as partners, not just as costs to be minimized or avoided. That's what people-oriented organizations such as Southwest Airlines and W. L. Gore do.

Finally, the way organizations treat their people has been found to significantly impact organizational performance.[5] For instance, one study reported that improving work practices could increase market value by as much as 30 percent.[6] Another study

- Self-managed teams
- Decentralized decision making
- Training programs to develop knowledge, skills, and abilities
- Flexible job assignments
- Open communication
- Performance-based compensation
- Staffing based on person–job and person–organization fit
- Extensive employee involvement
- Giving employees more control over decision making
- Increasing employee access to information

Exhibit 13-1
High-Performance Work Practices

Sources: C. H. Chuang and H. Liao, "Strategic Human Resource Management in Service Context: Taking Care of Business by Taking Care of Employees and Customers," *Personnel Psychology,* Spring 2010, pp. 153–196; M. Subramony, "A Meta-Analytic Investigation of the Relationship Between HRM Bundles and Firm Performance," *Human Resource Management,* September–October 2009, pp. 745–768; M. M. Butts et al., "Individual Reactions to High Involvement Work Practices: Investigating the Role of Empowerment and Perceived Organizational Support," *Journal of Occupational Health Psychology,* April 2009, pp. 122–136; and W. R. Evans and W. D. Davis, "High-Performance Work Systems and Organizational Performance: The Mediating Role of Internal Social Structure," *Journal of Management,* October 2005, p. 760.

that tracked average annual shareholder returns of companies on *Fortune's* list of 100 Best Companies to Work For found that these companies significantly beat the S&P 500 over 10-year, 5-year, 3-year, and 1-year periods.[7] Work practices that lead to both high individual and high organizational performance are known as **high-performance work practices**. (See some examples in Exhibit 13-1.) The common thread among these practices seems to be a commitment to involving employees; improving the knowledge, skills, and abilities of an organization's employees; increasing their motivation; reducing loafing on the job; and enhancing the retention of quality employees while encouraging low performers to leave.

Even if an organization doesn't use high-performance work practices, other specific HRM activities must be completed in order to ensure that the organization has qualified people to perform the work that needs to be done—activities that comprise the HRM process. Exhibit 13-2 shows the eight activities in this process. The first

high-performance work practices
Work practices that lead to both high individual and high organizational performance

Exhibit 13-2
HRM Process

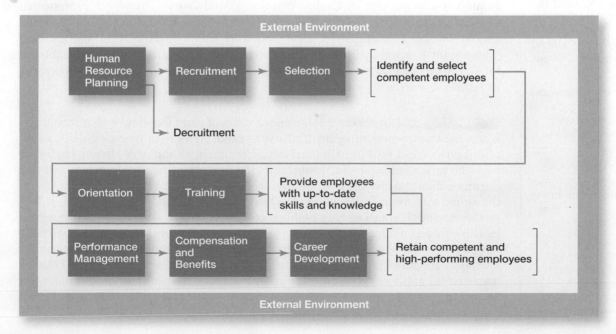

*data*points [8]

83 percent of companies cite a shortage of talent as their number one hiring challenge.

91 percent of recent college graduates say that if they started a job and didn't like it, they would stay in that job for up to a year.

52 percent of HR professionals say they don't use social networking sites to research job candidates.

85 percent of survey respondents said the top reason for why an employee should be terminated is sexually harassing a co-worker.

6.25 seconds is the time recruiters spend looking at a resume before deciding whether the candidate is a good fit for a job.

61 percent of workers surveyed say they're never late for work.

15 percent of employers say they have fired a worker for calling in sick without a legitimate excuse.

36 percent of respondents say the top reason why someone hired would not work out in a position (other than poor performance) is a mismatched skill set.

39 percent of HR managers say that annual performance reviews are not an accurate appraisal of employees' work.

38 percent of senior managers say the most common mistake candidates make during job interviews is having little or no knowledge of the company.

82 percent of employees say they'd give up more than 5 percent of their salary to get a guaranteed retirement income.

three activities ensure that competent employees are identified and selected; the next two involve providing employees with up-to-date knowledge and skills; and the final three ensure that the organization retains competent and high-performing employees. Before we discuss those specific activities, we need to look at external factors that affect the HRM process.

External Factors That Affect the HRM Process

The administrative assistant job opening paying $13 an hour at a Burns Harbor, Indiana, truck driver training school for C. R. England, a nationwide trucking company, was posted on a Friday afternoon.[9] By the time the company's head of corporate recruiting arrived at work on Monday morning, there were about 300 applications in the company's e-mail inbox. And an inch-and-a-half stack of résumés was piled up by the now out-of-paper fax machine. Out of those 500 plus applicants, one person, who had lost her job four months earlier, impressed the hiring manager so much that the job was hers, leaving the remaining 499 plus people—including a former IBM analyst with 18 years of experience, a former director of human resources, and someone with a master's degree and 12 years of experience at accounting firm Deloitte & Touche—still searching for a job. This is not a unique example. The economic slowdown has made filling a job opening an almost mind-boggling exercise.

Such is the new reality facing HRM. The entire HRM process is influenced by the external environment. Those factors most directly influencing it include the economy, employee labor unions, governmental laws and regulations, and demographic trends.

THE ECONOMY'S EFFECT ON HRM The global economic downturn has left what many experts believe to be an enduring mark on HRM practices worldwide. For instance, in Japan, workers used to count on two things: a job for life and a decent pension. Now, lifetime employment is long gone and corporate pension plans are crumbling.[10] In the European Union, the 2011 jobless rate was 9.5 percent, with Spain being hit hardest with an unemployment rate of 21.7 percent.[11] And in Thailand, employees in the automotive industry dealt with reduced work hours, which affected their pay and their skill upgrades.[12] In the United States, labor economists say that although jobs may be coming back slowly, they aren't the same ones that employees were used to. Many of these jobs are temporary or contract positions, rather than full-time jobs with benefits. And many of the more than 8.4 million jobs lost during the recession aren't coming back at all, but may be replaced by other types of work in growing industries.[13] All of these changes have affected employers and workers. A Global Workforce Study survey by global professional services company Towers Watson confirmed that the recession has "fundamentally altered the way U.S. employees view their work and leaders. ...U.S. workers have dramatically lowered their career and retirement expectations for the foreseeable future."[14] Such findings have profound implications for how an organization manages its human resources.

EMPLOYEE LABOR UNIONS A planned series of three five-day work stoppages by Unite, the union representing British Airways cabin crews, had the potential for a serious negative effect on Europe's third-largest airline in an industry already struggling from the prolonged economic downturn.[15] If negotiations between management and the union didn't resolve the disputes over work practices, then employees vowed to hit the airline with more strikes during the busy summer period. Then, in China, strikes at Honda and Toyota factories highlighted that country's struggle with income inequality, rising inflation, and soaring property prices. Factory workers, who had been "pushed to work 12-hour days, six days a week on monotonous low-wage assembly line tasks, are pushing back."[16] Work stops, labor disputes, and negotiations between management and labor are just a few of the challenges organizations and managers face when their workforce is unionized.

A **labor union** is an organization that represents workers and seeks to protect their interests through collective bargaining. In unionized organizations, many HRM decisions are dictated by collective bargaining agreements, which usually define things such as recruitment sources; criteria for hiring, promotions, and layoffs; training eligibility; and disciplinary practices. Due to information availability, it's difficult to pin down how unionized global workforces are. Current estimates are that about 11.8 percent of the U.S. workforce is unionized.[17] But the percentage of unionized workers tends to be higher in other countries except in France, where some 9.6 percent of workers are unionized. For instance, in Japan, some 19.6 percent of the labor force belongs to a union; in Germany, 27 percent; in Denmark, 75 percent; in Australia, 27.4 percent; in Canada, 30.4 percent; and in Mexico, 19 percent.[18] One union membership trend we're seeing, especially in the more industrialized countries, is that the rate in private enterprise is declining while that in the public sector (which includes teachers, police officers, firefighters, and government workers) is climbing. Although labor unions can affect an organization's HRM practices, the most significant environmental constraint is governmental laws, especially in North America.

LEGAL ENVIRONMENT OF HRM $250 million. That's the amount a New York City jury awarded in punitive damages to plaintiffs who claim drug company Novartis AG discriminated against women.[19] As this example shows, an organization's HRM practices are governed by a country's laws. (See Exhibit 13-3 for some of the important U.S. laws that affect the HRM process.) For example, decisions regarding who will be hired or which employees will be chosen for a training program or what an employee's compensation will be must be made without regard to race, sex, religion, age, color, national origin, or disability. Exceptions can occur only in special circumstances. For instance, a community fire department can deny employment to a firefighter applicant who is confined to a wheelchair; but if that same individual is applying for a desk job, such as a dispatcher, the disability cannot be used as a reason to deny employment. The issues, however, are rarely that clear-cut. For example, employment laws protect most employees whose religious beliefs require a specific style of dress—robes, long shirts, long hair, and the like. However, if the specific style of dress may be hazardous or unsafe in the work setting (such as when operating machinery), a company could refuse to hire a person who won't adopt a safer dress code.

As you can see, a number of important laws and regulations affect what you can and cannot do legally as a manager. Because workplace lawsuits are increasingly targeting supervisors, as well as their organizations, managers must know what they can and cannot do by law.[20] Trying to balance the "shoulds and should nots" of many laws often falls within the realm of **affirmative action**. Many U.S. organizations have affirmative action programs to ensure that decisions and practices enhance the employment, upgrading, and retention of members from protected groups such as minorities and females. That is, an organization refrains from discrimination and actively seeks to enhance the status of members from protected groups. However, U.S. managers are not completely free to choose whom they hire, promote, or fire, or free to treat employees any way they want. Although laws have helped reduce employment discrimination and unfair work practices, they have, at the same time, reduced managers' discretion over HRM decisions.

We do want to mention two current U.S. laws that each have the potential to affect future HRM practices. The first of these, the Patient Protection and Affordable Care Act (PPACA and commonly called the Health Care Reform Act), was signed into law in March 2010 and upheld by the Supreme Court of the United States in 2012.[21] Employers are beginning to sort through the requirements of the law and the deadlines for compliance. The other proposed law—the Social Networking Online Protection Act (SNOPA) has been introduced and would prohibit employers from requiring a username, password, or other access to online content.[22]

labor union
An organization that represents workers and seeks to protect their interests through collective bargaining

affirmative action
Organizational programs that enhance the status of members of protected groups

Exhibit 13-3
Major HRM Laws

Laws

Law or Ruling	Year	Description
Equal Employment Opportunity and Discrimination		
Equal Pay Act	1963	Prohibits pay differences for equal work based on gender
Civil Rights Act, Title VII	1964 (amended in 1972)	Prohibits discrimination based on race, color, religion, national origin, or gender
Age Discrimination in Employment Act	1967 (amended in 1978)	Prohibits discrimination against employees 40 years and older
Vocational Rehabilitation Act	1973	Prohibits discrimination on the basis of physical or mental disabilities
Americans with Disabilities Act	1990	Prohibits discrimination against individuals who have disabilities or chronic illnesses; also requires reasonable accommodations for these individuals
Compensation/Benefits		
Worker Adjustment and Retraining Notification Act	1990	Requires employers with more than 100 employees to provide 60 days' notice before a mass layoff or facility closing
Family and Medical Leave Act	1993	Gives employees in organizations with 50 or more employees up to 12 weeks of unpaid leave each year for family or medical reasons
Health Insurance Portability and Accountability Act	1996	Permits portability of employees' insurance from one employer to another
Lilly Ledbetter Fair Pay Act	2009	Changes the statute of limitations on pay discrimination to 180 days from each paycheck
Patient Protection and Affordable Care Act	2010	Health care legislation that puts in place comprehensive health insurance reforms
Health/Safety		
Occupational Safety and Health Act (OSHA)	1970	Establishes mandatory and health standards in organizations
Privacy Act	1974	Gives employees the legal right to examine personnel files and letters of reference
Consolidated Omnibus Reconciliation Act (COBRA)	1985	Requires continued health coverage following termination (paid by employee)

What about HRM laws globally? It's important that managers in other countries be familiar with the specific laws that apply there. Let's take a look at some of the federal legislation in countries such as Canada, Mexico, Australia, and Germany.

Canadian laws pertaining to HRM practices closely parallel those in the United States. The Canadian Human Rights Act prohibits discrimination on the basis of race, religion, age, marital status, sex, physical or mental disability, or national origin. This act governs practices throughout the country. Canada's HRM environment, however, is somewhat different from that in the United States in that it involves more decentralization of lawmaking to the provincial level. For example, discrimination on the basis of language is not prohibited anywhere in Canada except in Quebec.

In Mexico, employees are more likely to be unionized than they are in the United States. Labor matters in Mexico are governed by the Mexican Federal Labor Law. One hiring law states that an employer has 28 days to evaluate a new employee's work performance. After that period, the employee is granted job security and termination is quite difficult and expensive. Those who violate the Mexican Federal Labor Law are subject to severe penalties, including criminal action that can result in steep fines and even jail sentences for employers who fail to pay, for example, the minimum wage.

Australia's discrimination laws were not enacted until the 1980s and generally apply to discrimination and affirmative action for women. Yet, gender opportunities for women in Australia appear to lag behind those in the United States. In Australia, however, a significant proportion of the workforce is unionized. The higher percentage of unionized workers has placed increased importance on industrial relations specialists in Australia and reduced the control of line managers over workplace labor issues. In 1997, Australia overhauled its labor and industrial relations laws with the objective of increasing productivity and reducing union power. The Workplace Relations Bill gives employers greater flexibility to negotiate directly with employees on pay, hours, and benefits. It also simplifies federal regulation of labor–management relations.

Our final example, Germany, is similar to most Western European countries when it comes to HRM practices. Legislation requires companies to practice representative participation, in which the goal is to redistribute power within the organization, putting labor on a more equal footing with the interests of management and stockholders. The two most common forms of representative participation are work councils and board representatives. **Work councils** link employees with management. They are groups of nominated or elected employees who must be consulted when management makes decisions involving personnel. **Board representatives** are employees who sit on a company's board of directors and represent the interests of the firm's employees.

LEADER who made a DIFFERENCE

Source: PRNewsFotc/AutoTrader.com/APImages.com

Chances are when a hurricane threatens, a snow storm looms, or any other type of weather emergency is on the horizon, you, along with millions of other viewers, turn to the Weather Channel at some point.[23] *The Weather Channel has a reputation for live, on-the-spot reporting during severe weather events. What is a warning for some becomes entertainment for the rest of us. On camera and behind the scenes, though, are all the employees who make it happen. And the individual responsible for managing the HR function and ensuring that the right people, processes, and structures are in place is Sylvia Taylor, executive vice president of human resources. The company's CEO says, "Sylvia makes sure we are growing the team to meet our growth potential on multiple fronts—television, digital, mobile and business-to-business." One of her accomplishments at the Weather Channel has been developing performance scorecards for senior executives. She says, "Executive scorecards demonstrate that everyone is accountable for achieving business goals and that senior-level management supports and lives by the same corporate values system." What can you learn from this leader who made a difference?*

work councils
Groups of nominated or elected employees who must be consulted when management makes decisions involving personnel

board representatives
Employees who sit on a company's board of directors and represent the interests of the firm's employees

DEMOGRAPHIC TRENDS Back in 2007, the head of BMW's 2,500-employee power train plant in Dingolfing, Lower Bavaria, was worried about the potential inevitable future decline in productivity due to an aging workforce.[24] That's when company executives decided to redesign its factory for older workers. With input from employees, they implemented physical changes to the workplace—for instance, new wooden floors to reduce joint strain and special chairs for sitting down or relaxing for short periods—that would reduce wear and tear on workers' bodies. Other organizations worldwide are preparing for a shift as baby boomers retire. Many older workers delayed their retirement during the recession, reducing the threat of mass turnover for a few years. "But now it's sneaking up on companies." Companies are responding by creating succession plans, bringing retirees on as consultants, and increasing cross-training efforts to prepare younger workers to fill the void. Almost half of HR

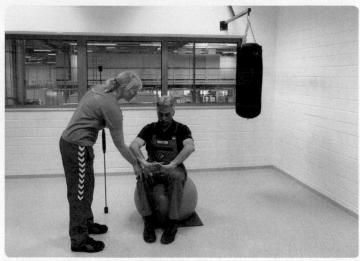

BMW is managing the challenges of an aging workforce by redesigning factories to accommodate older workers. At its plant in Dingolfing, BMW adapted a production line to meet the needs of aging employees that include ergonomic back supports for monkey-wrench turners, enhanced lighting to ease the strain on older eyes, mobile tool trolleys so workers don't have to strain themselves to reach for equipment, and new work benches that can be adjusted to an individual's height. Shown in this photo is a physiotherapist helping a BMW employee perform stretching exercises in the plant's new relaxation room.
Source: Christof Stache/AFP/Getty Images/ Newscome

professionals surveyed said this potential loss of talent over the next decade is a problem for their organizations.[25] As these examples show, demographic trends are impacting HRM practices, worldwide and in the United States.

Much of the change in the U.S. workforce over the last 50 years can be attributed to federal legislation enacted in the 1960s that prohibited employment discrimination. With these laws, avenues opened up for minority and female job applicants. These two groups dramatically changed the workplace in the latter half of the twentieth century. Women, in particular, have changed the composition of the workforce as they now hold some 49.1 percent of jobs. And that percentage may increase as some 82 percent of jobs lost during the economic crisis were ones held by men. Why the disproportion? Because women tend to be employed in education and health care industries, which are less sensitive to economic ups and downs.[26] If this trend continues, women are set to become the majority group in the workforce.

Workforce trends in the first half of the twenty-first century will be notable for three reasons: (1) changes in racial and ethnic composition, (2) an aging baby boom generation, and (3) an expanding cohort of Gen Y workers. By 2050, Hispanics will grow from today's 13 percent of the workforce to 24 percent, blacks will increase from 12 percent to 14 percent, and Asians will increase from 5 percent to 11 percent. Meanwhile, the labor force is aging. The 55-and-older age group, which currently makes up 13 percent of the workforce, will increase to 20 percent by 2014. Another group that's having a significant impact on today's workforce is Gen Y, a population group that includes individuals born from about 1978 to 1994. Gen Y has been the fastest-growing segment of the workforce—increasing from 14 percent to more than 24 percent. With Gen Y now in the workforce, analysts point to the four generations that are working side-by-side in the workplace[27]:

- The oldest, most experienced workers (those born before 1946) make up 6 percent of the workforce.
- The baby boomers (those born between 1946 and 1964) make up 41.5 percent of the workforce.
- Gen Xers (those born 1965 to 1977) make up almost 29 percent of the workforce.
- Gen Yers (those born 1978 to 1994) make up almost 24 percent of the workforce.

These and other demographic trends are important because of the impact they're having on current and future HRM practices.

13.2 | *Discuss* the tasks associated with identifying and selecting competent employees.

IDENTIFYING and Selecting Competent Employees

Executives at Texas-based global engineering giant Fluor are "required to identify and mentor high-performing employees, and at any given time 10 percent of the 42,000 global employees are being tracked through Fluor's leadership development program." The company's senior vice president of human resources and administration says such efforts are necessary because "you can't create a senior mechanical engineer overnight. It takes years." Here's a company that understands the importance of tracking talent on a global scale.[28] Is a job in the insurance industry on your list of jobs you'll apply for after graduation? Unfortunately for the insurance industry, it's not for many college graduates. Like many other nonglamorous industries, including transportation, utilities, and manufacturing, the insurance industry is not "particularly attractive to the so-called 'millennials'—people who turned 21 in 2000 or later."

In all these industries, the number of skilled jobs is already starting to overtake the number of qualified people available to fill them.[29]

Every organization needs people to do whatever work is necessary for doing what the organization is in business to do. How do they get those people? And more importantly, what can they do to ensure they get competent, talented people? This first phase of the HRM process involves three tasks: human resource planning, recruitment and decruitment, and selection.

Human Resource Planning

Human resource planning is the process by which managers ensure that they have the right number and kinds of capable people in the right places and at the right times. Through planning, organizations avoid sudden people shortages and surpluses.[30] HR planning entails two steps: (1) assessing current human resources and (2) meeting future HR needs.

human resource planning
Ensuring that the organization has the right number and kinds of capable people in the right places and at the right times

CURRENT ASSESSMENT Managers begin HR planning by inventorying current employees. This inventory usually includes information on employees such as name, education, training, prior employment, languages spoken, special capabilities, and specialized skills. Sophisticated databases make getting and keeping this information quite easy. For example, Stephanie Cox, Schlumberger's director of personnel for North and South America, uses a company planning program called PeopleMatch to help pinpoint managerial talent. Suppose she needs a manager for Brazil. She types in the qualifications: someone who can relocate, speak Portuguese, and is a "high potential" employee. Within a minute, 31 names of possible candidates pop up.[31] At Hoover's Inc., a Dun & Bradstreet subsidiary, getting a clear picture of employees' skills and finding the right people for projects is done through a sophisticated software program and an internally developed employee appraisal system that charts employees' progress along their career paths.[32] That's what good HR planning should do—help managers identify the people they need.

An important part of a current assessment is **job analysis**, an assessment that defines a job and the behaviors necessary to perform it. For instance, what are the duties of a level 3 accountant who works for General Motors? What minimal knowledge, skills, and abilities are necessary to adequately perform this job? How do these requirements compare with those for a level 2 accountant or for an accounting manager? Information for a job analysis is gathered by directly observing individuals on the job, interviewing employees individually or in a group, having employees complete a questionnaire or record daily activities in a diary, or having job "experts" (usually managers) identify a job's specific characteristics.

job analysis
An assessment that defines jobs and the behaviors necessary to perform them

Using this information from the job analysis, managers develop or revise job descriptions and job specifications. A **job description** (sometimes called a position description) is a written statement describing a job—typically job content, environment, and conditions of employment. A **job specification** states the minimum qualifications that a person must possess to successfully perform a given job. It identifies the knowledge, skills, and attitudes needed to do the job effectively. Both the job description and job specification are important documents when managers begin recruiting and selecting.

job description
A written statement that describes a job

job specification
A written statement of the minimum qualifications a person must possess to perform a given job successfully

MEETING FUTURE HR NEEDS Future HR needs are determined by the organization's mission, goals, and strategies. Demand for employees results from demand for the organization's products or services. For instance, Corning's expansion into developing countries was slowed by the lack of qualified employees. To continue its growth strategy, it had to plan how to find those qualified employees.[33]

After assessing both current capabilities and future needs, managers can estimate areas in which the organization will be understaffed or overstaffed. Then they're ready to proceed to the next step in the HRM process.

Recruitment and Decruitment

Competition for talent by India's two largest technology outsourcing companies has led to an all-out recruiting war. In the United States, the tech sector is also in a hiring push, pitting start-up companies against giants such as Google and Intel in the hunt for employees.[34]

recruitment
Locating, identifying, and attracting capable applicants

decruitment
Reducing an organization's workforce

If employee vacancies exist, managers should use the information gathered through job analysis to guide them in **recruitment**—that is, locating, identifying, and attracting capable applicants.[35] On the other hand, if HR planning shows a surplus of employees, managers may want to reduce the organization's workforce through **decruitment**.[36]

RECRUITMENT   Some organizations have interesting approaches to finding employees. For instance, on one day in April 2011, McDonald's, the world's largest hamburger chain, held its first National Hiring Day hoping to hire 50,000 people. The chain and its franchisees actually hired 62,000 workers.[37] Microsoft launched a new Web site that integrated 103 country sites into one career-related site. There, potential applicants find employee blogs on everything from interview tips to whether a failed start-up on a résumé hurts in applying for a job at the company.[38] Even Google, which receives 3,000 applications a day and can afford to be picky about whom it hires, still needs qualified computer science and engineering candidates. One fun thing the company does is Google Games, a day devoted to student team competitions on the company's campus.[39] Accounting firm Deloitte & Touche created its Deloitte Film Festival to get employee team-produced films about "life" at Deloitte to use in college recruiting.[40] Even the U.S. Army is getting social by seeking recruits using social media.[41] Exhibit 13-4 explains different recruitment sources managers can use to find potential job candidates.[42]

Although online recruiting is popular and allows organizations to identify applicants cheaply and quickly, applicant quality may not be as good as other sources. Research has found that employee referrals generally produce the best candidates.[43] Why? Because current employees know both the job and the person being recommended, they tend to refer applicants who are well qualified. Also, current employees often feel their reputation is at stake and refer others only when they're confident that the person will not make them look bad.

DECRUITMENT   The other approach to controlling labor supply is decruitment, which is not a pleasant task for any manager. Decruitment options are shown in

Exhibit 13-4
Recruiting Sources

Source	Advantages	Disadvantages
Internet	Reaches large numbers of people; can get immediate feedback	Generates many unqualified candidates
Employee referrals	Knowledge about the organization provided by current employee; can generate strong candidates because a good referral reflects on the recommender	May not increase the diversity and mix of employees
Company Web site	Wide distribution; can be targeted to specific groups	Generates many unqualified candidates
College recruiting	Large centralized body of candidates	Limited to entry-level positions
Professional recruiting organizations	Good knowledge of industry challenges and requirements	Little commitment to specific organization

Option	Description
Firing	Permanent involuntary termination
Layoffs	Temporary involuntary termination; may last only a few days or extend to years
Attrition	Not filling openings created by voluntary resignations or normal retirements
Transfers	Moving employees either laterally or downward; usually does not reduce costs but can reduce intraorganizational supply–demand imbalances
Reduced workweeks	Having employees work fewer hours per week, share jobs, or perform their jobs on a part-time basis
Early retirements	Providing incentives to older and more senior employees for retiring before their normal retirement date
Job sharing	Having employees share one full-time position

Exhibit 13-5
Decruitment Options

Exhibit 13-5. Although employees can be fired, other choices may be better. However, no matter how you do it, it's never easy to reduce an organization's workforce.

Selection

Once you have a pool of candidates, the next step in the HRM process is **selection**, screening job applicants to determine who is best qualified for the job. Managers need to "select" carefully since hiring errors can have significant implications. For instance, a driver at Fresh Direct, an online grocer that delivers food to masses of apartment-dwelling New Yorkers, was charged with, and later pled guilty to, stalking and harassing female customers.[44] At T-Mobile, lousy customer service led to its last-place ranking in the J.D. Power's customer-satisfaction survey. The first step in a total overhaul of the customer service area was revamping the company's hiring practices to increase the odds of hiring employees who would be good at customer service.[45]

selection
Screening job applicants to ensure that the most appropriate candidates are hired

WHAT IS SELECTION?   In the all-important Game 6 of the 2011 World Series, officials made the decision to call off the game based on a fairly strong forecast of rain. If it did rain, it was a good decision. However, if it didn't, then maybe it wasn't such a good decision. (As it turned out, it was a good decision with the postponed game ending up being a nail-biter won by the St. Louis Cardinals in the 11th inning on a walk-off home run and sending the Series into the deciding Game 7.) Although most hiring decisions aren't nail-biters, that's a lot like the hiring process. Selection involves predicting which applicants will be successful if hired. For example, in hiring for a sales position, the selection process should predict which applicants will generate a high volume of sales. As shown in Exhibit 13-6, any selection decision can result in four possible outcomes—two correct and two errors.

Exhibit 13-6
Selection Decision Outcomes

A decision is correct when the applicant was predicted to be successful and proved to be successful on the job, or when the applicant was predicted to be unsuccessful and was not hired. In the first instance, we have successfully accepted; in the second, we have successfully rejected.

Problems arise when errors are made in rejecting candidates who would have performed successfully on the job (reject errors) or accepting those who ultimately perform poorly (accept errors). These problems can be significant. Given today's HR laws and regulations, reject errors can cost more than the additional screening needed to find acceptable candidates. Why? Because they can expose the organization to discrimination charges, especially if applicants from protected groups are disproportionately rejected. For instance, two written firefighter exams used by the New York City Fire Department were found to have had a disparate impact on black and Hispanic candidates.[46] On the other hand, the costs of accept errors include the cost of training the employee, the profits lost because of the employee's incompetence, the cost of severance, and the subsequent costs of further recruiting and screening. The major emphasis of any selection activity should be reducing the probability of reject errors or accept errors while increasing the probability of making correct decisions. Managers do this by using selection procedures that are both valid and reliable.

VALIDITY AND RELIABILITY A valid selection device is characterized by a proven relationship between the selection device and some relevant criterion. Federal employment laws prohibit managers from using a test score to select employees unless clear evidence shows that, once on the job, individuals with high scores on this test outperform individuals with low test scores. The burden is on managers to support that any selection device they use to differentiate applicants is validly related to job performance.

A reliable selection device indicates that it measures the same thing consistently. On a test that's reliable, any single individual's score should remain fairly consistent over time, assuming that the characteristics being measured are also stable. No selection device can be effective if it's not reliable. Using such a device would be like weighing yourself every day on an erratic scale. If the scale is unreliable—randomly fluctuating, say 5 to 10 pounds every time you step on it—the results don't mean much.

A growing number of companies are adopting a new measure of recruitment effectiveness called "quality of fill."[47] This measure looks at the contributions of good hires versus those of hires who have failed to live up to their potential. Five key factors are considered in defining this quality measure: employee retention, performance evaluations, number of first-year hires who make it into high-potential training programs, number of employees who are promoted, and what surveys of new hires indicate. Such measures help an organization assess whether its selection process is working well.

TYPES OF SELECTION TOOLS The best-known selection tools include application forms, written and performance-simulation tests, interviews, background investigations, and in some cases, physical exams. Exhibit 13-7 lists the strengths and weaknesses of each.[48] Because many selection tools have limited value for making selection decisions, managers should use ones that effectively predict performance for a given job.

REALISTIC JOB PREVIEWS One thing managers need to carefully watch is how they portray the organization and the work an applicant will be doing. If they tell applicants only the good aspects, they're likely to have a workforce that's dissatisfied

Exhibit 13-7
Selection Tools

Application Forms
- Almost universally used
- Most useful for gathering information
- Can predict job performance but not easy to create one that does

Written Tests
- Must be job related
- Include intelligence, aptitude, ability, personality, and interest tests
- Are popular (e.g., personality tests; aptitude tests)
- Relatively good predictor for supervisory positions

Performance-Simulation Tests
- Use actual job behaviors
- Work sampling—test applicants on tasks associated with that job; appropriate for routine or standardized work
- Assessment center—simulate jobs; appropriate for evaluating managerial potential

Interviews
- Almost universally used
- Must know what can and cannot be asked
- Can be useful for managerial positions

Background Investigations
- Used for verifying application data—valuable source of information
- Used for verifying reference checks—not a valuable source of information

Physical Examinations
- Are for jobs that have certain physical requirements
- Mostly used for insurance purposes

and prone to high turnover.[49] Negative things can happen when the information an applicant receives is excessively inflated. First, mismatched applicants probably won't withdraw from the selection process. Second, inflated information builds unrealistic expectations, so new employees may quickly become dissatisfied and leave the organization. Third, new hires become disillusioned and less committed to the organization when they face the unexpected harsh realities of the job. In addition, these individuals may feel they were misled during the hiring process and then become problem employees.

To increase employee job satisfaction and reduce turnover, managers should consider a **realistic job preview (RJP),** one that includes both positive and negative information about the job and the company. For instance, in addition to the positive comments typically expressed during an interview, the job applicant might be told there are limited opportunities to talk to coworkers during work hours, that promotional advancement is unlikely, or that work hours are erratic and they may have to work weekends. Research indicates that applicants who receive an RJP have more realistic expectations about the jobs they'll be performing and are better able to cope with the frustrating elements than applicants who receive only inflated information.

realistic job preview (RJP)
A preview of a job that provides both positive and negative information about the job and the company

let's get REAL

The Scenario:

José Salinas is the HR director at a large food processor. Within the last couple of years, he has seen more frequent parental involvement in their adult child's job hunt. In fact, one candidate's parents actually contacted the company after their child got a job offer wanting to discuss their daughter's salary, relocation package, and educational reimbursement opportunities. He's not sure how to handle these occurrences.

Sarah Saracino
Human Resources Manager

What advice would you give José?

This new challenge that employers face is typically known as "helicopter parenting." In recent history, we have seen adult employees' parents hovering and these overprotective parents are attempting to get involved in their children's terms and conditions of employment, most often compensation. When a manager receives a call from a parent, the manager is faced with two options. First, she may inform the parent that they cannot discuss the terms and conditions of employment with anyone other then the employee. Or, a new approach that some employers have adopted would be to recruit the parents' guidance, encouraging them to promote loyalty, healthcare choices, and retirement plans, in exchange for their involvement in their adult children's employment.

13.3 *Explain* the different types of orientation and training.

PROVIDING Employees with Needed Skills and Knowledge

As one of the nation's busiest airports, Miami International Airport served more than 38 million passengers in 2011. But Miami International is doing something that no other airport has done. It's "trying to persuade disparate groups of employees to think and act as ambassadors for regional tourism. Airport workers in all jobs are learning the importance of finding solutions to the myriad issues that beset travelers on their way to and from Miami." Accomplishing that means that all employees who work on airport grounds are required to master customer service through a series of tourism training efforts. The required training is tied to renewal of airport ID badges, providing a critical incentive for employees to participate.[50]

If we've done our recruiting and selecting properly, we should have hired competent individuals who can perform successfully on the job. But successful performance requires more than possessing certain skills. New hires must be acclimated to the organization's culture and be trained and given the knowledge to do the job in a manner consistent with the organization's goals. Current employees, like those at Miami International Airport, may have to complete training programs to improve or update their skills. For these acclimation and skill improvement tasks, HRM uses orientation and training.

Orientation

Did you participate in some type of organized "introduction to college life" when you started school? If so, you may have been told about your school's rules and the procedures for activities such as applying for financial aid, cashing a check, or registering for classes, and you were probably introduced to some of the college administrators.

A person starting a new job needs the same type of introduction to his or her job and the organization. This introduction is called **orientation**.

There are two types of orientation. *Work unit orientation* familiarizes the employee with the goals of the work unit, clarifies how his or her job contributes to the unit's goals, and includes an introduction to his or her new coworkers. *Organization orientation* informs the new employee about the company's goals, history, philosophy, procedures and rules. It should also include relevant HR policies and maybe even a tour of the facilities.

Many organizations have formal orientation programs, while others use a more informal approach in which the manager assigns the new employee to a senior member of the work group who introduces the new hire to immediate coworkers and shows him or her where important things are located. And then there are intense orientation programs like that at Randstad USA, a staffing company based in Atlanta. The company's 16-week program covers everything from the company's culture to on-the-job training. The executive in charge of curriculum development says, "It's a very defined process. It's not just about what new hires have to learn and do, but also about what managers have to do."[51] And managers do have an obligation to effectively and efficiently integrate any new employee into the organization. They should openly discuss mutual obligations of the organization and the employee.[52] It's in the best interests of both the organization and the new employee to get the person up and running in the job as soon as possible. Successful orientation results in an outsider-insider transition that makes the new employee feel comfortable and fairly well adjusted, lowers the likelihood of poor work performance, and reduces the probability of a surprise resignation only a week or two into the job.

orientation
Introducing a new employee to his or her job and the organization

Employee Training

On the whole, planes don't cause airline accidents, people do. Most collisions, crashes, and other airline mishaps—nearly three-quarters of them—result from errors by the pilot or air traffic controller, or from inadequate maintenance. Weather and structural failures typically account for the remaining accidents.[53] We cite these statistics to illustrate the importance of training in the airline industry. Such maintenance and human errors could be prevented or significantly reduced by better employee training, as shown by the amazing "landing" of US Airways Flight 1549 in the Hudson River in January 2009 with no loss of life. Pilot Captain Chesley Sullenberger attributed the positive outcome to the extensive and intensive training that all pilots and flight crews undergo.[54] At management and technology consulting firm BearingPoint, the ethics and compliance training program became a series of fictional films modeled after *The Office*, even with a "Michael Scott-esque leader."[55] The film episodes were an immediate sensation in the company with comments like, "This is the best training I've ever had" or "I think that episode was based on my team." The new episodes became so popular that employees started tracking them down on the company's staging server, which is pretty amazing considering these training videos covered issues that most employees find boring even though it's critical information. Everything that employees at Ruth's Chris Steak House restaurants need to know can be found on sets of 4 × 8½-inch cards. Whether it's a recipe for caramelized banana cream pie or how to acknowledge customers, it's on the cards. And since the cards for all jobs are readily available, employees know the behaviors and skills it takes to get promoted. It's a unique approach to employee training, but it seems to work. Since the card system was implemented, employee turnover has decreased, something that's not easy to accomplish in the restaurant industry.[56] Training is just as important at other restaurants with servers trained to "read" diners and make the service more personal.[57]

Employee training is an important HRM activity. As job demands change, employee skills have to change. In 2011, U.S. business firms spent more than $59 billion

These pilots and cabin crew members of Hainan Airlines in China learn how to use an escape slide in evacuating an airplane quickly during emergency situations. Training for emergencies and evacuations such as the operation of escape slides, slide rafts, and life rafts and the mechanical workings of aircraft doors is a top priority of airlines' extensive and intensive safety training programs. To ensure the safety of passengers and employees during a flight where medical attention may not be available, cabin crew members receive first aid training that focuses on illnesses and injuries that can occur mid-air such as airsickness and oxygen deprivation.
Source: Wang Jianhua/Xinhua/Photoshot/Newscom

Exhibit 13-8
Types of Training

Type	Includes
General	Communication skills, computer systems application and programming, customer service, executive development, management skills and development, personal growth, sales, supervisory skills, and technological skills and knowledge
Specific	Basic life–work skills, creativity, customer education, diversity/cultural awareness, remedial writing, managing change, leadership, product knowledge, public speaking/presentation skills, safety, ethics, sexual harassment, team building, wellness, and others

Source: Based on "2005 Industry Report—Types of Training." *Training*, December 2005, p. 22.

on formal employee training.[58] Managers, of course, are responsible for deciding what type of training employees need, when they need it, and what form that training should take.

TYPES OF TRAINING Exhibit 13-8 describes the major types of training that organizations provide. Some of the most popular types include profession/industry-specific training, management/supervisory skills, mandatory/compliance information (such as sexual harassment, safety, etc.), and customer service training. For many organizations, employee interpersonal skills training—communication, conflict resolution, team building, customer service, and so forth—is a high priority. For example, the director of training and development for Vancouver-based Boston Pizza International said, "Our people know the Boston Pizza concept; they have all the hard skills. It's the soft skills they lack."[59] So the company launched Boston Pizza College, a training program that uses hands-on, scenario-based learning about many interpersonal skills topics. For Canon, Inc., it's the repair personnel's technical skills that are important.[60] As part of their training, repair people play a video game based on the familiar kids' board game Operation in which "lights flashed and buzzers sounded if copier parts were dragged and dropped poorly." The company found that comprehension levels were 5 to 8 percent higher than when traditional training manuals were used.

TRAINING METHODS Although employee training can be done in traditional ways, many organizations are relying more on technology-based training methods because of their accessibility, cost, and ability to deliver information. Exhibit 13-9 provides

Exhibit 13-9
Traditional Training Methods

On-the-job—Employees learn how to do tasks simply by performing them, usually after an initial introduction to the task.

Job rotation—Employees work at different jobs in a particular area, getting exposure to a variety of tasks.

Mentoring and coaching—Employees work with an experienced worker who provides information, support, and encouragement; also called apprenticeships in certain industries.

Experiential exercises—Employees participate in role playing, simulations, or other face-to-face types of training.

Workbooks/manuals—Employees refer to training workbooks and manuals for information.

Classroom lectures—Employees attend lectures designed to convey specific information.

(continued)

Technology-Based Training Methods

CD-ROM/DVD/videotapes/audiotapes/podcasts—Employees listen to or watch selected media that convey information or demonstrate certain techniques.

Videoconferencing/teleconferencing/satellite TV—Employees listen to or participate as information is conveyed or techniques demonstrated.

E-learning—Internet-based learning where employees participate in multimedia simulations or other interactive modules.

Mobile learning—Learning delivered via mobile devices.

---

a description of the various traditional and technology-based training methods that managers might use. Of all these training methods, experts believe that organizations will increasingly rely on e-learning and mobile applications to deliver important information and to develop employees' skills.

RETAINING Competent, High-Performing Employees

At Procter & Gamble, mid-year employee evaluations were used to adjust work goals to reflect more accurately what could be achieved in such a challenging economic environment. The company has directed managers to focus on employees' achievements rather than just to point out areas that need improvement. P&G's director of human resources said, "Particularly in this economy, people are living in the survival zone. Setting attainable targets was important to keeping up morale."[61]

> **Describe** strategies for **13.4**
> retaining competent,
> high-performing
> employees.

Once an organization has invested significant dollars in recruiting, selecting, orienting, and training employees, it wants to keep them, especially the competent, high-performing ones! Two HRM activities that play a role in this area are managing employee performance and developing an appropriate compensation and benefits program.

Employee Performance Management

A recent survey found that two-thirds of surveyed organizations have inefficient performance management processes in place.[62] That's scary because managers need to know whether their employees are performing their jobs efficiently and effectively. That's what a **performance management system** does—establishes performance standards used to evaluate employee performance. How do managers evaluate employees' performance? That's where the different performance appraisal methods come in.

performance management system
Establishes performance standards used to evaluate employee performance

PERFORMANCE APPRAISAL METHODS More than 70 percent of managers admit they have trouble giving a critical performance review to an underachieving employee.[63] It's particularly challenging when managers and employees alike sense they're not beneficial.[64] And some companies—about 1 percent—are eliminating the formal performance review entirely.[65] Although appraising someone's performance is never easy, especially with employees who aren't doing their jobs well, managers can be better at it by using any of the seven different performance appraisal methods. A description of each of these methods, including advantages and disadvantages, is shown in Exhibit 13-10.

Compensation and Benefits

Executives at Discovery Communications Inc. had an employee morale problem on their hands. Many of the company's top performers were making the same salaries as the poorer performers, and the company's compensation program didn't allow for

Exhibit 13-10
Performance Appraisal Methods

Written Essay

Evaluator writes a description of employee's strengths and weaknesses, past performance, and potential; provides suggestions for improvement.

+ Simple to use
− May be better measure of evaluator's writing ability than of employee's actual performance

Critical Incident

Evaluator focuses on critical behaviors that separate effective and ineffective performance.

+ Rich examples, behaviorally based
− Time-consuming, lacks quantification

Graphic Rating Scale

Popular method that lists a set of performance factors and an incremental scale; evaluator goes down the list and rates employee on each factor.

+ Provides quantitative data; not time-consuming
− Doesn't provide in-depth information on job behavior

BARS (Behaviorally Anchored Rating Scale)

Popular approach that combines elements from critical incident and graphic rating scale; evaluator uses a rating scale, but items are examples of actual job behaviors.

+ Focuses on specific and measurable job behaviors
− Time-consuming; difficult to develop

Multiperson Comparison

Employees are rated in comparison to others in work group.

+ Compares employees with one another
− Difficult with large number of employees; legal concerns

MBO

Employees are evaluated on how well they accomplish specific goals.

+ Focuses on goals; results oriented
− Time-consuming

360-Degree Appraisal

Utilizes feedback from supervisors, employees, and coworkers.

+ Thorough
− Time-consuming

giving raises to people who stayed in the same position. The only way for managers to reward the top performers was to give them a bonus or promote them to another position. Executives were discovering that not only was that unfair, it was counterproductive. So they overhauled the program.[66]

Just in case you think that compensation and benefits decisions aren't important, a recent survey showed that 71 percent of workers surveyed said their benefits package would influence their decision to leave their job.[67] Most of us expect to receive appropriate compensation from our employer. Developing an effective and appropriate compensation system is an important part of the HRM process.[68] It can help attract and retain competent and talented individuals who help the organization accomplish its mission and goals. In addition, an organization's compensation system has been shown to have an impact on its strategic performance.[69]

Managers must develop a compensation system that reflects the changing nature of work and the workplace in order to keep people motivated. Organizational compensation can include many different types of rewards and benefits such as base wages and salaries, wage and salary add-ons, incentive payments, and other benefits and services. Some organizations offer employees some unusual, but popular, benefits. For instance, at Qualcomm, employees can receive surfing lessons, kayaking tours, and baseball game tickets. Employees at CHG Healthcare Services enjoy an on-site fitness center, fresh fruit baskets every morning, and an annual wellness fair. And at J. M. Smucker, new hires get a gift basket sent to their homes and all employees enjoy softball games and bowling nights.[70]

How do managers determine who gets paid what? Several factors influence the compensation and benefit packages that different employees receive. Exhibit 13-11 summarizes these factors, which are job-based and business- or industry-based. Many organizations, however, are using alternative approaches to determining compensation: skill-based pay and variable pay.

Skill-based pay systems reward employees for the job skills and competencies they can demonstrate. Under this type of pay system, an employee's job title doesn't define his or her pay category, skills do.[71] Research shows these types of pay systems tend to be more successful in manufacturing organizations than in service organizations and organizations pursuing technical innovations.[72] On the other hand, many organizations use **variable pay** systems, in which an individual's compensation is contingent on performance—90 percent of U.S. organizations use some type of variable pay plans, and 81 percent of Canadian and Taiwanese organizations do.[73] In Chapter 17, we'll discuss variable pay systems further as they relate to employee motivation.

Although many factors influence the design of an organization's compensation system, flexibility is a key consideration. The traditional approach to paying people reflected a more stable time when an employee's pay was largely determined by seniority and job level. Given the dynamic environments that many organizations face, the trend is to make pay systems more flexible and to reduce the number of pay levels. However, whatever approach managers use, they must establish a fair, equitable, and motivating compensation system that allows the organization to recruit and keep a talented and productive workforce.

skill-based pay
A pay system that rewards employees for the job skills they can demonstrate

variable pay
A pay system in which an individual's compensation is contingent on performance

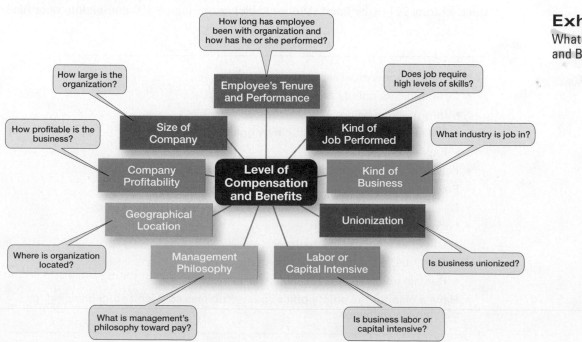

Exhibit 13-11
What Determines Pay and Benefits

Discuss contemporary
issues in managing
human resources.

13.5

CONTEMPORARY Issues in Managing Human Resources

We'll conclude this chapter by looking at some contemporary HR issues facing today's managers. These concerns include managing downsizing, sexual harassment, work–life balance, and controlling HR costs.

Managing Downsizing

downsizing
The planned elimination of jobs in an organization

"Before 1981, the word 'layoff' in the sense of permanent separation from a job with no prospects for recall, was so uncommon that the U.S. Bureau of Labor Statistics didn't even keep track of such cuts."[74] How things have changed!

Downsizing (or layoffs) is the planned elimination of jobs in an organization. When an organization has too many employees—which can happen when it's faced with an economic recession, declining market share, too aggressive growth, or poorly managed operations—one option for improving profits is to eliminate some of those excess workers. During the most current economic recession, many well-known companies downsized—including, among others, Boeing, Nokia, Procter & Gamble, Hewlett-Packard, Volkswagen, Dell, General Motors, Unisys, Siemens, Merck, Honeywell, and eBay. Now, some HR experts are suggesting that a "cost" associated with mass layoffs is the damage they can cause to long-term growth prospects.[75]

How can managers best manage a downsized workplace? Disruptions in the workplace and in employees' personal lives should be expected. Stress, frustration, anxiety, and anger are typical reactions of both individuals being laid off and the job survivors. Exhibit 13-12 lists some ways that managers can lessen the trauma both for the employees being laid off and for the survivors.[76]

Managing Sexual Harassment

A Kentucky appeals court said that McDonald's Corporation is liable in the sexual assault case of an employee detained by supervisors who were following the instructions of a prank caller pretending to be a police officer. The ruling said that McDonald's knew of 30 hoax telephone calls made to its restaurants from 1994 to 2004, including several calls to Kentucky restaurants in which the caller persuaded managers and employees to conduct strip searches and sexual assaults.[77]

Sexual harassment is a serious issue in both public and private sector organizations. During 2011 (the latest data available), more than 8,300 complaints were filed

Exhibit 13-12

Tips for Managing Downsizing

- Treat everyone with respect.
- Communicate openly and honestly:
  - Inform those being let go as soon as possible.
  - Tell surviving employees the new goals and expectations.
  - Explain impact of layoffs.
- Follow any laws regulating severance pay or benefits.
- Provide support/counseling for surviving (remaining) employees.
- Reassign roles according to individuals' talents and backgrounds.
- Focus on boosting morale:
  - Offer individualized reassurance.
  - Continue to communicate, especially one-on-one.
  - Remain involved and available.
- Have a plan for the empty office spaces/cubicles so it isn't so depressing for surviving employees.

with the Equal Employment Opportunity Commission (EEOC), a substantial drop from 13,867 in 2008, 12,696 in 2009, and 11,717 in 2010.[78] Although most complaints are filed by women, the percentage of charges filed by males reached an all-time high of almost 24 percent.[79] The costs of sexual harassment are high. Almost all *Fortune* 500 companies in the United States have had complaints lodged by employees, and at least a third have been sued.[80] Settlements typically average over $15 million.[81] In addition, it's estimated that sexual harassment costs a "typical *Fortune* 500 company $6.7 million per year in absenteeism, low productivity, and turnover."[82]

Sexual harassment isn't a problem just in the United States. It's a global issue. For instance, data collected by the European Commission found that 30 to 50 percent of female employees in European Union countries had experienced some form of sexual harassment.[83] And sexual harassment charges have been filed against employers in other countries such as Japan, Australia, New Zealand, and Mexico.[84]

Even though discussions of sexual harassment cases often focus on the large awards granted by a court, there are other concerns for employers. It creates an unpleasant, oftentimes hostile, work environment and undermines workers' ability to perform their job.

So what is **sexual harassment**? It's defined as any unwanted action or activity of a sexual nature that explicitly or implicitly affects an individual's employment, performance, or work environment. And as we indicated earlier, it can occur between members of the opposite sex or of the same sex.

Many problems associated with sexual harassment involve determining exactly what constitutes this illegal behavior. The EEOC defines sexual harassment this way: "Unwelcome sexual advances, requests for sexual favors, and other verbal or physical conduct of a sexual nature constitute sexual harassment when this conduct explicitly or implicitly affects an individual's employment, unreasonably interferes with an individual's work performance, or creates an intimidating, hostile or offensive work environment."[85] For many organizations, it's the offensive or hostile environment issue that is problematic. Managers must be aware of what constitutes such an environment. Another thing that managers must understand is that the victim doesn't necessarily have to be the person harassed but could be anyone affected

sexual harassment
Any unwanted action or activity of a sexual nature that explicitly or implicitly affects an individual's employment, performance, or work environment

---

let's get REAL

The Scenario:

Lisa Brown is the HR director at a health care facility. She says, "I have a great employee who has a troubling habit of being 'touchy' in the workplace. Whenever, this person is standing next to someone, she likes to touch the person's arm, hand, or shoulder. Just last week, I saw her talking to a male employee and she had her hand on his chest. Other than this habit, she's an outstanding worker."

What advice would you give Lisa?

Lisa should start the conversation by telling the employee about all the great things she does and how valued she is to the company. Then mention that she has noticed the employee's tendency to be a little too touchy at times with coworkers and give specific examples. Lisa should say that she appreciates her friendliness, but she needs to curb her touching because that puts her and potentially the company at risk for misconduct.

Braeden Rogers
Emerging Solutions
Manager

by the offensive conduct.[86] The key is being attuned to what makes fellow employees uncomfortable—and if we don't know, we should ask![87]

What can an organization do to protect itself against sexual harassment claims?[88] The courts want to know two things: First, did the organization know about, or should it have known about, the alleged behavior? And secondly, what did managers do to stop it? With the number and dollar amounts of the awards against organizations increasing, it's vital that all employees be educated on sexual harassment matters. In addition, organizations need to ensure that no retaliatory actions—such as cutting back hours, assigning back-to-back work shifts without a rest break, etc.—are taken against a person who has filed harassment charges, especially in light of a U.S. Supreme Court ruling that broadened the definition of retaliation.[89] One final area of interest we want to discuss in terms of sexual harassment is workplace romances.

WORKPLACE ROMANCES   If you're employed, have you ever dated someone at work? If not, have you ever been attracted to someone in your workplace and thought about pursuing a relationship? Such situations are more common than you might think—40 percent of employees surveyed by the *Wall Street Journal* said they have had an office romance.[90] And another survey found that 43 percent of single men and 28 percent of single women said they would be open to dating a coworker.[91] The environment in today's organizations with mixed-gender work teams and long work hours has likely contributed to this situation. "People realize they're going to be at work such long hours, it's almost inevitable that this takes place," said one survey director.[92] And some 67 percent of employees feel there's no need to hide their office relationships.[93]

But workplace romances can potentially become big problems for organizations.[94] In addition to the potential conflicts and retaliation between coworkers who decide to stop dating or to end a romantic relationship, more serious problems stem from the potential for sexual harassment accusations, especially when it's between supervisor and subordinate. The standard used by judicial courts has been that workplace sexual conduct is prohibited sexual harassment *if* it is unwelcome. If it's welcome, it still may be inappropriate, but usually is not unlawful. However, a ruling by the California Supreme Court concerning specifically a supervisor–subordinate relationship that got out of hand is worth noting. That ruling said "completely consensual workplace romances can create a hostile work environment for others in the workplace."[95]

What should managers do about workplace romances? Over the last decade, companies have become more flexible about workplace romances. People spend so much time at the office that coworker romances are almost inevitable.[96] However, it's important to educate employees about the potential for sexual harassment. And because the potential liability is more serious when it comes to supervisor–subordinate relationships, a more proactive approach is needed in terms of discouraging such relationships and perhaps even requiring supervisors to report any such relationships to the HR department. At some point, the organization may even want to consider banning such relationships, although an outright ban may be difficult to put into practice.

Managing Work–Life Balance

In 2009, Verizon employees contacted VZ-LIFE, the company's employee assistance program, more than 1,100 times a month by phone and logged more than 35,000 visits a month to the Web site. This program provides resources on parenting and childcare, adult care, health and wellness, moving and relocation, and much more.[97]

Smart managers recognize that employees don't leave their families and personal lives behind when they come to work. Although managers can't be sympathetic with every detail of an employee's family life, organizations are becoming more attuned to the fact that employees have sick children, elderly parents who need special care, and other family issues that may require special arrangements. In response, many organizations are offering **family-friendly benefits**, which accommodate employees' needs

family-friendly benefits
Benefits that accommodate employees' needs for work–life balance

for work–family life balance. They've introduced programs such as on-site child care, summer day camps, flextime, job sharing, time off for school functions, telecommuting, and part-time employment. Work–family life conflicts are as relevant to male workers with children and women without children as they are for female employees with children. Heavy workloads and increased travel demands have made it hard for many employees to satisfactorily juggle both work and personal responsibilities. A *Fortune* survey found that 84 percent of male executives surveyed said that "they'd like job options that let them realize their professional aspirations while having more time for things outside work." [98] Also, 87 percent of these executives believed that any company that restructured top-level management jobs in ways that would both increase productivity and make more time available for life outside the office would have a competitive advantage in attracting talented employees. Younger employees, particularly, put a higher priority on family and a lower priority on jobs and are looking for organizations that give them more work flexibility. [99]

Today's progressive workplaces must accommodate the varied needs of a diverse workforce. How? By providing a wide range of scheduling options and benefits that allow employees more flexibility at work and to better balance or integrate their work and personal lives. Despite these organizational efforts, work–family life programs certainly have room for improvement. One survey showed that more than 31 percent of college-educated male workers spend 50 or more hours a week at work (up from 22 percent in 1980) and that about 40 percent of American adults get less than seven hours of sleep on weekdays (up from 34 percent in 2001). [100] What about women? Another survey showed that the percentage of American women working 40 hours or more per week had increased. By the way, this same survey showed that the percentage of European women working 40 hours or more had actually declined. [101] Other workplace surveys still show high levels of employee stress stemming from work–family life conflicts. And large groups of women and minority workers remain unemployed or underemployed because of family responsibilities and bias in the workplace. [102] So what can managers do?

Research on work–family life balance has shown positive outcomes when individuals are able to combine work and family roles. [103] As one study participant noted, "I think being a mother and having patience and watching someone else grow has made me a better manager. I am better able to be patient with other people and let them grow and develop in a way that is good for them." [104] In addition, individuals who have family-friendly workplace support appear to be more satisfied on the job. [105] This finding seems to strengthen the notion that organizations benefit by creating a workplace in which employee work–family life balance is possible. And the benefits are financial as well. Research has shown a significant, positive relationship

Discovery Communications provides flexible work arrangements, work-life initiatives, and wellness programs to accommodate employees' different life styles, life stages, and life events. To help employees balance work and personal responsibilities, the media company offers telework, compressed workweeks, job sharing, and a summer-hours program. Discovery's wellness initiatives include on-site wellness centers at several U.S. locations, physical fitness reimbursement, annual flu shots, wellness fairs, and wellness classes such as early morning yoga shown here. A showpiece of Discovery's family support program is an on-site child care center at company headquarters for employees' children from 6 weeks to 5 years old.
Source: Reuters/Reuters Staff

FUTURE VISION | **24/7 Work Life**

Technology and globalization have played major roles in blurring the lines between work and leisure time. It's increasingly expected that today's professional worker be available 24/7. So employees regularly check their e-mail before going to bed, take calls from the boss during dinner, participate in global conference calls at 6 A.M., and read tweets from colleagues on weekends.

The 24/7 work life eventually undermines real social relationships. Face-to-face interactions with family and friends suffer and people are likely to feel stressed out and emotionally empty. In response, employees are likely to demand real and virtual barriers that can separate their work and personal lives. For instance, you'll set up separate accounts, Web sites, and networks for work and friends. Employers will find that employees balk at work demands outside defined work hours. In order to get and keep good employees, organizations will need to restructure work communications so as to confine them to more traditional hours.

between work–family life initiatives and an organization's stock price.[106] However, managers need to understand that people do differ in their preferences for work–family life scheduling options and benefits.[107] Some prefer organizational initiatives that better *segment* work from their personal lives. Others prefer programs that facilitate *integration*. For instance, flextime schedules segment because they allow employees to schedule work hours that are less likely to conflict with personal responsibilities. On the other hand, on-site child care integrates the boundaries between work and family responsibilities. People who prefer segmentation are more likely to be satisfied and committed to their jobs when offered options such as flextime, job sharing, and part-time hours. People who prefer integration are more likely to respond positively to options such as on-site child care, gym facilities, and company-sponsored family picnics.

Controlling HR Costs

It's estimated that worker obesity costs U.S. companies as much as $153 billion annually.[108] HR costs are skyrocketing, especially employee health care and employee pensions. Organizations are looking for ways to control these costs.

EMPLOYEE HEALTH CARE COSTS At AOL, almost 1,000 employees enrolled in an 11-week activity challenge to take as many steps as possible. By the end of the challenge, those employees had taken more than 530 million total steps—equivalent to walking around the globe more than 10 times. Employees at Paychex who undergo a confidential health screening and risk assessment, and for those who smoke who agree to enroll in a smoking cessation program, can get free annual physicals, colonoscopies, and 100 percent coverage of preventive care as well as lower deductibles and costs. At Black and Decker Corporation, employees and dependents who certify in an honor system that they have been tobacco-free for at least six months pay $75 less per month for their medical and dental coverage. At Amerigas Propane, employees were given an ultimatum: get their medical check-ups or lose their health insurance.[109]

All these examples illustrate how companies are trying to control skyrocketing employee health care costs. Since 2002, health care costs have risen an average of 15 percent a year and are expected to double by the year 2016 from the $2.2 trillion spent in 2007.[110] And smokers cost companies even more—about 25 percent more for health care than nonsmokers.[111] However, the biggest health care cost for companies—estimated at $153 billion a year—is obesity and its related costs arising from medical expenditures and absenteeism.[112] A study of manufacturing organizations found that presenteeism, defined as employees not performing at full capacity, was 1.8 percent higher for workers with moderate to severe obesity than for all other employees.[113] The reason for the lost productivity is likely the result of reduced mobility because of body size or pain problems such as arthritis. Is it any wonder that organizations are looking for ways to control their health care costs? How? First, many organizations are providing opportunities for employees to lead healthy lifestyles. From financial incentives to company-sponsored health and wellness programs, the goal is to limit rising health care costs. About 41 percent of companies use some type of positive incentives aimed at encouraging healthy behavior, up from 34 percent in 1996.[114] Another study indicated that nearly 90 percent of companies surveyed planned to aggressively promote healthy lifestyles to their employees during the next three to five years.[115] Many are starting sooner: Google, Yamaha Corporation of America, Caterpillar, and others are putting health food in company break rooms, cafeterias, and vending machines; providing deliveries of fresh organic fruit; and putting "calorie taxes" on fatty foods.[116] In the case of smokers, however, some companies have taken a more aggressive stance by increasing the amount smokers pay for health insurance or by firing them if they refuse to stop smoking.

EMPLOYEE PENSION PLAN COSTS The other area where organizations are looking to control costs is employee pension plans. Corporate pensions have been around since the nineteenth century.[117] But the days when companies could afford to give employees a broad-based pension that provided them a guaranteed retirement income have changed. Pension commitments have become such an enormous burden that companies can no longer afford them. In fact, the corporate pension system has been described as "fundamentally broken."[118] Many companies no longer provide pensions. Even IBM, which closed its pension plan to new hires in December 2004, told employees that their pension benefits would be frozen.[119] In a 2011 survey, a consulting firm found that only 57 percent of employers surveyed offered both a traditional pension plan and a defined contribution plan (down from 64 percent in 2009). Of those with traditional pension plans, only 44 percent remained open to new hires.[120] Obviously, the pension issue is one that directly affects HR decisions. On the one hand, organizations want to attract talented, capable employees by offering them desirable benefits such as pensions. But on the other hand, organizations have to balance offering benefits with the costs of providing such benefits.

CHAPTER  PREPARING FOR: Exams/Quizzes

CHAPTER SUMMARY by Learning Outcome

13.1 ⌈ LEARNING OUTCOME ⌉

Explain the importance of the human resource management process and the external influences that might affect that process.
HRM is important for three reasons. First, it can be a significant source of competitive advantage. Second, it's an important part of organizational strategies. Finally, the way organizations treat their people has been found to significantly impact organizational performance.

The external factors that most directly affect the HRM process are the economy, labor unions, legal environment, and demographic trends.

13.2 ⌈ LEARNING OUTCOME ⌉

Discuss the tasks associated with identifying and selecting competent employees.
A job analysis is an assessment that defines a job and the behaviors necessary to perform it. A job description is a written statement describing a job, and typically includes job content, environment, and conditions of employment. A job specification is a written statement that specifies the minimum qualifications a person must possess to successfully perform a given job.

The major sources of potential job candidates include the Internet, employee referrals, company Web site, college recruiting, and professional recruiting organizations.

The different selection devices include application forms (best used for gathering employee information), written tests (must be job-related), work sampling (appropriate for complex nonmanagerial and routine work), assessment centers (most appropriate for top-level managers), interviews (widely used, but most appropriate for managerial positions, especially top-level managers), background investigations (useful for verifying application data, but reference checks are essentially worthless), and physical exams (useful for work that involves certain physical requirements and for insurance purposes).

A realistic job preview is important because it gives an applicant more realistic expectations about the job, which in turn should increase employee job satisfaction and reduce turnover.

13.3 ⌈ LEARNING OUTCOME ⌉

Explain the different types of orientation and training.
Orientation is important because it results in an outsider-insider transition that makes the new employee feel comfortable and fairly well-adjusted, lowers the likelihood of poor work performance, and reduces the probability of an early surprise resignation.

The two types of training are general (includes communication skills, computer skills, customer service, personal growth, etc.) and specific (includes basic life/work skills, customer education, diversity/cultural awareness, managing change, etc.). This training can be provided using traditional training methods (on-the-job, job rotation, mentoring and coaching, experiential exercises, workbooks/manuals, and classroom lectures) or by technology-based methods (CD/DVD/videotapes/audiotapes, videoconferencing or teleconferencing, or e-learning).

13.4 [LEARNING OUTCOME]
Describe strategies for retaining competent, high-performing employees.
The different performance appraisal methods are written essays, critical incidents, graphic rating scales, BARS, multiperson comparisons, MBO, and 360-degree appraisals.

The factors that influence employee compensation and benefits include the employee's tenure and performance, kind of job performed, kind of business/industry, unionization, labor or capital intensive, management philosophy, geographical location, company profitability, and size of company.

Skill-based pay systems reward employees for the job skills and competencies they can demonstrate. In a variable pay system, an employee's compensation is contingent on performance.

13.5 [LEARNING OUTCOME]
Discuss contemporary issues in managing human resources.
Managers can manage downsizing by communicating openly and honestly, following appropriate laws regarding severance pay or benefits, providing support/counseling for surviving employees, reassigning roles according to individuals' talents and backgrounds, focusing on boosting morale, and having a plan for empty office spaces.

Sexual harassment is any unwanted action or activity of a sexual nature that explicitly or implicitly affects an individual's employment, performance, or work environment. Managers need to be aware of what constitutes an offensive or hostile work environment, educate employees on sexual harassment, and ensure that no retaliatory actions are taken against any person who files harassment charges. Also, they may need to have a policy in place for workplace romances.

Organizations are dealing with work–family life balance issues by offering family-friendly benefits such as on-site child care, flextime, telecommuting, and so on. Managers need to understand that people may prefer programs that segment work and personal lives, while others prefer programs that integrate their work and personal lives.

Organizations are controlling HR costs by controlling employee health care costs through employee health initiatives (encouraging healthy behavior and penalizing unhealthy behaviors) and controlling employee pension plans by eliminating or severely limiting them.

REVIEW AND DISCUSSION QUESTIONS ✪

1. Discuss the external environmental factors that most directly affect the HRM process.

2. Some critics claim that corporate HR departments have outlived their usefulness and are not there to help employees, but to keep the organization from legal problems. What do you think? What benefits are there to having a formal HRM process? What drawbacks?

3. Describe the different selection devices and which work best for different jobs.

4. What are the benefits and drawbacks of realistic job previews? (Consider this question from the perspective of both the organization and the employee.)

5. Describe the different types of orientation and training and how each of the types of training might be provided.

6. List the factors that influence employee compensation and benefits.

7. Describe the different performance appraisal methods.

8. What, in your view, constitutes sexual harassment? Describe how companies can minimize sexual harassment in the workplace.

PREPARING FOR: My Career
ETHICS DILEMMA ✪

It's likely to be a challenging issue for HR managers.[121] "It" is the use of medical marijuana by employees. Seventeen states and the District of Columbia have laws or constitutional amendments that allow patients with certain medical conditions such as cancer, glaucoma, or chronic pain to use marijuana without fear of being prosecuted. Federal prosecutors have been directed by the Obama administration not to bring criminal charges against marijuana users who follow their states' laws. However, that puts employers in a difficult position as they try to accommodate state laws on medical marijuana use while having to enforce federal rules or company drug-use policies based on federal law. Although courts have generally ruled that companies do not have to accommodate medical marijuana users, legal guidance is still not all that clear. Legal experts have warned employers to "not run afoul of disability and privacy laws." In addition to the legal questions, employers are concerned about the challenge of maintaining a safe workplace. What ethical issues do you see here? How might this issue affect HR processes such as recruitment, selection, performance management, compensation and benefits, and safety and health? What other stakeholders might be impacted by this? In what ways might they be impacted?

SKILLS EXERCISE Developing Your Interviewing Skills

About the Skill
Every manager needs to develop his or her interviewing skills. The following discussion highlights the key behaviors associated with this skill.

Steps in Practicing the Skill
1. *Review the job description and job specification.* Reviewing pertinent information about the job provides valuable information about how to assess the candidate. Furthermore, relevant job requirements help to eliminate interview bias.

2. *Prepare a structured set of questions to ask all applicants for the job.* By having a set of prepared questions, you ensure that the information you wish to elicit is attainable. Furthermore, if you ask all applicants similar questions, you're better able to compare their answers against a common base.

3. *Before meeting an applicant, review his or her application form and résumé.* Doing so helps you to create a complete picture of the applicant in terms of what is represented on the résumé or application and what the job requires. You will also begin to identify areas to explore in the interview. That is, areas not clearly defined on the résumé or application but essential for the job will become a focal point of your discussion with the applicant.

4. *Open the interview by putting the applicant at ease and by providing a brief preview of the topics to be discussed.* Interviews are stressful for job applicants. By opening with small talk (e.g., the weather), you give the person time to adjust to the interview setting. By providing a preview of topics to come, you're giving the applicant an agenda that helps the individual begin framing what he or she will say in response to your questions.

5. *Ask your questions and listen carefully to the applicant's answers.* Select follow-up questions that naturally flow from the answers given. Focus on the responses as they relate to information you need to ensure that the applicant meets your job requirements. Any uncertainty you may still have requires a follow-up question to probe further for the information.

6. *Close the interview by telling the applicant what's going to happen next.* Applicants are anxious about the status of your hiring decision. Be honest with the applicant regarding others who will be interviewed and the remaining steps in the hiring process. If you plan to make a decision in two weeks or so, let the individual know what you intend to do. In addition, tell the applicant how you will let him or her know about your decision.

7. *Write your evaluation of the applicant while the interview is still fresh in your mind.* Don't wait until the end of your day, after interviewing several applicants, to write your analysis of each one. Memory can fail you. The sooner you complete your write-up after an interview, the better chance you have of accurately recording what occurred in the interview.

Practicing the Skill
Review and update your résumé. Then have several friends critique it who are employed in management-level positions or in management training programs. Ask them to explain their comments and make any changes to your résumé they think will improve it.

Now inventory your interpersonal and technical skills and any practical experiences that do not show up in your résumé. Draft a set of leading questions you would like to be asked in an interview that would give you a chance to discuss the unique qualities and attributes you could bring to the job.

WORKING TOGETHER Team Exercise

The increasing popularity of body art is posing challenges for employers and HR departments in every profession and industry.[122] A Pew Research Center survey reported that 36 percent of 18- to 25-year-olds and 40 percent of 26- to 40-year-olds have at least one tattoo. In those same age groups, 30 percent and 22 percent, respectively, have a piercing somewhere other than their ears. The same survey found that even in the 40- to 60-year-old age group, more than 10 percent had tattoos or piercings outside of their ears.

Form small groups of three to four individuals. Your team's task is to come up with a dress code and grooming policy that clearly spells out guidelines as far as body art and what is permitted. You can do this in the form of a bulleted list. Be prepared to share your proposed policy with the class.

MY TURN TO BE A MANAGER

- Studies show that women's salaries still lag behind men's and even with equal opportunity laws and regulations, women are paid about 82 percent of what men are paid.[123] Do some research on designing a compensation system that would address this issue. Write up your findings in a bulleted list format.

- Go the Society for Human Resource Management Web site [www.shrm.org] and find the HR News section. Pick one of the News Stories to read. (Note: Some of these will be available only to SHRM members, but others will be generally available.) Write a summary of the information. At the end of your summary, discuss the implications of the topic for managers.

- Use the Internet to research five different companies that interest you and check out what they say about careers or their people. Put this information in a bulleted-format report. Be prepared to make a presentation to the class on your findings.

- Work on your résumé. If you don't have one already, research what a good résumé should include. If you have one already, make sure it provides specific information that explicitly describes your work skills and experience rather than meaningless phrases such as "results-oriented."

- If you're working, note what types of HRM activities your managers do (such as interview, appraise performance, etc.). Ask them what they've found to be effective in getting and keeping good employees. What hasn't been effective? What can you learn from this? If you're not working, interview three different managers as to what HRM activities they do and which they've found to be effective or not effective.

- Research your chosen career by finding out what it's going to take to be successful in that career in terms of education, skills, experience, and so forth. Write a Personal Career Guide detailing this information.

- Steve's and Mary's suggested readings: D. Shilling, *2010 Complete Guide to Human Resources and the Law* (Wolters Kluwer, 2010); Brian E. Becker, Mark A. Huselid, and Richard W. Beatty, *The Differentiated Workforce* (Harvard Business School Press, 2009); Thomas W. Malone, *The Future of Work* (Harvard Business School Press, 2004); Charles A. O'Reilly III and Jeffrey Pfeffer, *Hidden Value* (Harvard Business School Press, 2000); Jeffrey Pfeffer, *The Human Equation* (Harvard Business School Press, 1998); Richard W. Judy and Carol D'Amico, *Workforce 2020* (Hudson Institute, 1997); and Robert Johansen and Rob Swigart, *Upsizing the Individual in the Downsized Organization* (Addison-Wesley, 1996).

- Pick one of the four topics in the section on contemporary issues in managing human resources. Research this topic and write a paper about it. Focus on finding current information and current examples of companies dealing with these issues.

- In your own words, write down three things you learned in this chapter about being a good manager.

- Self-knowledge can be a powerful learning tool. Go to mymanagementlab.com and complete these self-assessment exercises: How Good Am I at Giving Performance Feedback? How Satisfied Am I with My Job? Am I Experiencing Work–Family Conflict? What Are My Attitudes Toward Workplace Diversity? How Much Do I Know About HRM? Using the results of your assessments, identify personal strengths and weaknesses. What will you do to reinforce your strengths and improve your weaknesses?

MyManagementLab

Go to **mymanagementlab.com** for Auto-graded writing questions as well as the following Assisted-graded writing questions:

13-1. How does HRM affect all managers?

13-2. Should an employer have the right to choose employees without governmental interference? Support your conclusion.

13-3. Mymanagementlab Only – comprehensive writing assignment for this chapter.

CASE APPLICATION 1 Thinking Outside the Box

Replacing its traditional classroom training for drivers based on books and lectures, UPS now prepares applicants for the rigorous task of delivering packages and documents efficiently by using high-tech methods that include videogames, a "slip and fall" simulator, and an obstacle course around a mock village.

Source: Bloomberg/Getty Images

It's the world's largest package delivery company with the instantly recognizable brown trucks.[124] Every day United Parcel Service (UPS) transports more than 15 million packages and documents throughout the United States to more than 220 countries and territories. Delivering those packages efficiently is what it gets paid to do, and that massive effort wouldn't be possible without its 102,000-plus drivers. UPS recognizes that it has an HR challenge: hiring and training some 25,000 drivers over the next five years to replace retiring baby boomers. But the company has a plan in place that combines its tested business model of uniformity and efficiency (for instance, drivers are trained to hold their keys on a pinky finger so they don't waste time fumbling in their pockets for the keys) with a new approach to driver training.

UPS's traditional classroom driver training obviously wasn't working as some 30 percent of its driver candidates didn't make it. The company was convinced that the twenty-somethings—the bulk of its driver recruits—responded best to high-tech instruction instead of books and lectures. Now, trainees use videogames, a "slip and fall simulator which combines a greased floor with slippery shoes," and an obstacle course around a mock village.

At a UPS training center outside of Washington, D.C., applicants for a driver's job, which pays an average of $74,000 annually, spend one week practicing and training to be a driver. They move from one station to the next practicing the company's "340 Methods," techniques developed by industrial engineers "to save seconds and improve safety in every task from lifting and loading boxes to selecting a package from a shelf in the truck." Applicants play a videogame where they're in the driver's seat and must identify obstacles. From computer simulations, they move to "Clarksville," a mock village with miniature houses and faux businesses. There, they drive a real truck and "must successfully execute five deliveries in 19 minutes." And, in the interest of safety and efficiency, trainees learn to carefully walk on ice with the slip and fall simulator.

How are the new training methods working? So far, so good. Of the 1,629 trainees who have completed it, "only 10 percent have failed the training program, which takes a total of six weeks overall, including 30 days of driving a truck in the real world."

DISCUSSION QUESTIONS ✪

1. What external factors were affecting UPS's HR practices? How did UPS respond to these trends?

2. Why is efficiency and safety so important to UPS? What role do the company's industrial engineers play in how employees do their work?

3. What changes did the company make to its driver training program? What do you think of these changes?

4. What advantages and drawbacks do you see to this training approach for (a) the trainee and (b) the company?

CASE APPLICATION 2 Spotting Talent

Attracting and selecting the right talent is critical to a company's success. For tech companies, the process is even more critical since it's the knowledge, skills, and abilities of their employees that determines these companies' efficiency, innovation, and ultimately, financial achievements.[125] So, how *do* companies like Google and Facebook and even IBM and Microsoft attract the talent they need? As you'll see, these companies use some unique approaches.

Modis, a global provider of IT staffing and recruiting, has an interesting philosophy about searching for talented tech types. As pressure has mounted on businesses to find qualified employees, the search for the "perfect" candidate has become increasingly competitive. This company calls this "search for perfection the quest for the 'purple squirrel.'" Sometimes you just have to realize that, like the purple squirrel, the "perfect" candidate isn't available or doesn't exist. But that doesn't mean you don't try to find the best available talent. How do some of the big tech names spot talent?

In trying to attract qualified candidates with technical skills and knowledge to consider a career at IBM, the mature tech company brought its Watson computer that beat two former *Jeopardy* champions in a televised match to Carnegie Mellon's campus where students got a chance to challenge the computer during a symposium on Watson.
Source: Associated Press

For "mature" tech companies like IBM, Microsoft, and Hewlett-Packard (H-P), the challenge can be especially difficult since they don't have the allure of start-ups or the younger, "sexier" tech companies. So these businesses have to "pour on the charm." Take IBM, for instance. After its Watson computer beat two former *Jeopardy* champions in a televised match, the company hauled the machine to Carnegie Mellon, a top school, where students got a chance to challenge the computer. IBM's goal: lure some of those students to consider a career at IBM. H-P is using the pizza party/tech talk approach at various schools trying to lure younger students before they get "snatched away by other tech companies and start-ups." Microsoft, which was once one of those start-ups, has sent alumni back to schools to promote why Microsoft is a great place to take their talents. And it also hosts game nights, final-exam study parties, and app-building sessions and other events to try to lure students.

For companies like Facebook and Google, the search for talent is still challenging because of the increasing demand for and limited supply of potential employees. So even these companies have to be creative in spotting talent. Google, for instance, found they had been looking at resumes too narrowly by focusing (as expected) on education, GPA, and even SAT scores trying to find those candidates with the highest IQs. But they found that some of those so-called geniuses weren't as effective on the job as expected. So, they began to "take a wider view." Rather than looking at resumes the "traditional way, from top to bottom," it began to look "upside down" at resumes, trying to find some "rare, special attribute that could point the way to greatness." Facebook found that old-fashioned hiring channels weren't getting the talent it needed fast enough. So it tried online puzzles and programming challenges to attract and spot talent. It was an easy, fast, and cheap approach to get submissions from potential candidates. Despite these unique approaches, it's also true that younger tech companies, like these and many others, have a built-in appeal for candidates primarily because they're what's "in" and what's "hot" right now. Also, in many of the younger tech companies, there's no entrenched bureaucracy or cultural restrictions. If an employee wants to come to work in cargo shorts, t-shirts, and flip-flops, they do. In fact, what attracts many talented employees to companies like these is the fact that they can set their own hours, bring their pets to work, have access to free food and drinks, and a variety of other perks.

DISCUSSION QUESTIONS ✪

1. What does this case imply about the supply of and demand for employees and the implications for businesses?

2. What's the meaning behind the "search for the purple squirrel" in relation to spotting talent? Is this relevant to non-tech companies, as well? Discuss.

3. Do you think "mature" tech companies are always going to have a more difficult time attracting tech talent? Discuss.

4. What do you think of the approaches that Google and Facebook have tried? Explain.

5. Put on your "creative" hat. You're in charge of HR at a tech start-up. What suggestions can you come up with for "spotting talent?"

Managing Your Career Module

Jeffrey Hollender is chief inspired protagonist, cofounder, and executive chairperson of Seventh Generation Inc., the country's largest distributor of nontoxic, all-natural cleaning, paper, and personal products. He would undoubtedly be considered a successful businessperson. However, every time Hollender visits Canada, he is detained for extra security screening "because of an incident where authorities arrested and deported the then 23-year-old American for operating an adult education school in Toronto without a work permit."[1] Other prominent businesspeople also had setbacks early in their career but went on to be successful.

If you want to be successful in your career, maybe you'll face setbacks, but maybe you won't. The main thing to keep in mind is that you are responsible for your career.[2] No one else is going to do it for you, including your employer. That's why we've included this—to help you better manage your career. The information in this module is set up by topic area so you can pick and choose what you're most interested in. Have fun reading it, and good luck in your future career!

CAREER OPPORTUNITIES in Management

If you've paid any attention to news reports over the last few years, you know about the widespread layoffs both in the United States and worldwide: Merck cut about 11 percent of its workforce. Unisys reduced its workforce by 10 percent. Pfizer Japan Inc. cut its workforce by 5 percent. Kodak eliminated up to 25,000 jobs. So, are management jobs disappearing? You might think so based on these reports. The truth is: The future looks bright! Business administration and management continues to be one of the top 10 most popular college majors, and jobs are likely to be waiting for those graduates!

It's hard to get an exact number of individuals in the United States that are employed as managers because the numbers are aggregated with business and financial operations occupations. According to the U.S. Bureau of Labor Statistics (BLS), almost 30 million individuals are employed in those categories.[3] The BLS estimates a 5 to 28 percent growth in executive, administrative, and managerial jobs through the year 2018.[4] The point is that there will be managerial jobs, but these jobs may not be in the organizations or fields that you'd expect. The demand for managers in traditional *Fortune* 500 organizations, and particularly in the area of traditional manufacturing, is not going to be as strong as the demand for managers in small and medium-sized organizations in the services field, particularly information and health care services. Keep in mind that a good place to land a management position can be a smaller organization.

Finding a Culture That Fits

Richard D'Ambrosio thought he had found the perfect job at an accounting firm. It had all the outward appearances of a good workplace—employee recognition awards and managers with "politically correct" answers to work–life questions. Yet, as soon as he signed on, he found himself in a culture that prized working long hours just for the sake of working long hours and where junior accountants were expected to be at the beck and call of the partners. If it was your wedding anniversary, too bad. If it was a holiday, too bad. It only took a few months before he quit. How can you avoid the same problem? How can you find a culture that fits?[5] Here are some suggestions.

First, *figure out what suits you.* For instance, do you like working in teams or on your own? Do you like to go out after work with colleagues or go straight home? Are you comfortable in a more formal or a more casual environment? Then, narrow your job search to those kinds of employers.

Once you've gotten through the initial job-screening process and begin interviewing, the real detective work begins, which involves more than investigating the "official" information provided by the employer. *Try to uncover the values that drive the organization.* Ask questions such as the proudest accomplishments or how it responded to past emergencies and crises. Ask, "If I have an idea, how do I make it happen?" Ask if you can talk to someone who's on the "fast track" to promotions and find out what they're doing and why they're being rewarded. Ask how you'll be evaluated—after all, if you're going to be in the game, shouldn't you know how the score is kept? Also, look for nonverbal clues. What do people have at their desks—family pictures or only work stuff? Are office doors closed or open? Are there doors? How does the physical climate feel? Is it relaxed and casual or more formal? Do people seem to be helping each other as they work? Are the bathrooms dirty, which might indicate a low value placed on anything to do with employees? Look at the material symbols and who seems to have access to them. And finally, during your investigation, *pay particular attention to the specific department or unit where you'd work.* After all, it is the place where you'd spend the majority of your working hours. Can you see yourself being happy there?

Taking Risks

"IYAD-WYAD-YAG-WYAG: If you always do what you've always done, you'll always get what you've always got! So if your life is ever going to improve, you'll have to take chances."—Anonymous[6]

How will you approach your various career moves over the course of your lifetime? Will you want to do what you've always done? Or will you want to take chances, and how comfortable will you be taking chances? Taking career risks doesn't have to be a gamble. Responsible risk taking can make outcomes more predictable. Here are some suggestions for being a responsible, effective risk taker in career decisions. It's important to thoroughly evaluate the risk. Before committing to a career risk, consider what you could lose or who might be hurt. How important are those things or those people to you? Explore whether you can reach your goal in another way, thus making the risk unnecessary. Find out everything you can about what's involved with taking this career risk—the timing; the people involved; the changes it will entail; and the potential gains and losses, both in the short run and the long run. Examine closely your feelings about taking this risk: Are you afraid? Are you ready to act now? Will you know if you have risked more than you can afford to lose? Finally, ensure your employability. The most important thing you can do is ensuring that you have choices by keeping your skills current and continually learning new skills.

As with any decision involving risk, the more information you have available, the better able you are to assess the risk. Then, armed with this information, you can make a more informed decision. Even though you won't be able to eliminate all the negatives associated with taking the risk, you can, at least, know about them.

Reinventing Yourself

Face it. The only constant thing about change is that it is constant. These days, you don't have the luxury of dealing with change only once in a while. No, the workplace seems to change almost continuously. How can you reinvent yourself to deal with the demands of a constantly changing workplace?[7]

Being prepared isn't a credo just for the Boy Scouts; it should be your motto for dealing with a workplace that is constantly changing. Being prepared means taking the initiative and being responsible for your own personal career development. Rather than depending on your organization to provide you with career development and training opportunities, do it yourself. Take advantage of continuing education or graduate courses at local colleges. Sign up for workshops and seminars that can help enhance your skills. Upgrading your skills to keep them current is one of the most important things you can do to reinvent yourself.

It's also important for you to be a positive force when faced with workplace changes. We don't mean you should routinely accept any change that's being implemented. If you think that a proposed change won't work, speak up. Voice your concerns in a constructive manner. Being constructive may mean suggesting an alternative. However, if you feel that the change is beneficial, support it wholeheartedly and enthusiastically.

The changes that organizations make in response to a dynamic environment can be overwhelming and stressful. However, you can take advantage of these changes by reinventing yourself.

Learning to Get Along with Difficult People

We've all been around people who, to put it nicely, are difficult to get along with. These people might be chronic complainers, they might be meddlers who think they know everything about everyone else's job and don't hesitate to tell you so, or they might exhibit any number of other unpleasant interpersonal characteristics. They can make your job as a manager extremely hard and your work day very stressful if you don't know how to deal with them. Being around difficult people tends to bring out the worst in all of us. What can you do? How do you learn to get along with these difficult people?[8]

Getting along with difficult people takes a little bit of patience, planning, and preparation. What you need is an approach that helps you diffuse a lot of the negative aspects of dealing with these individuals. For instance, it helps to write down a detailed description of the person's behavior. Describe what this person does that bothers you. Then, try to understand that behavior. Put yourself in that person's shoes and attempt to see things from his or her perspective. Doing these things initially might help you better understand, predict, and influence behavior.

Unfortunately, trying to understand the person usually isn't enough for getting along. You'll also need some specific strategies for coping with different types of difficult personalities. Here are some of the most common types of difficult people you'll meet and some strategies for dealing with them.

THE HOSTILE, AGGRESSIVE TYPES. With this type, you need to stand up for yourself; give them time to run down; don't worry about being polite, just jump in if you need to; get their attention carefully; get them to sit down; speak from your own point of view; avoid a head-on fight; and be ready to be friendly.

THE COMPLAINERS. With the complainers you need to listen attentively; acknowledge their concerns; be prepared to interrupt their litany of complaints; don't agree, but do acknowledge what they're saying; state facts without comment or apology; and switch them to problem solving.

THE SILENT OR NONRESPONSIVE TYPES With this type, you need to ask open-ended questions; use the friendly, silent stare; don't fill the silent pauses for them in conversations; comment on what's happening; and help break the tension by making them feel more at ease.

THE KNOW-IT-ALL EXPERTS The keys to dealing with this type are to be on top of things; listen and acknowledge their comments; question firmly, but don't confront; avoid being a counterexpert; and work with them to channel their energy in positive directions.

What Do I Want from My Job?

If you're reading this textbook, you're likely enrolled in a class that's helping you earn credit toward a college degree. You're also likely taking the courses you need to earn a college degree because you hope to get a good job (or a better job, if you're already working) upon graduating. With all this effort you're putting forth, have you ever stopped to think about what you really want from your job?[9] A high salary? Work that challenges you? Autonomy and flexibility? Perhaps the results of surveys of workers will give you some insights into what you might want from your job. The top reasons that employees took their jobs and stay with their jobs are as follows:

Work–life balance and flexibility	29%
The work itself	27
Compensation offered	26
Coworkers	25
Work culture	13
Training opportunities	5
Advancement opportunities	5

(Total adds up to more than 100% because individuals indicated more than one factor.)

Do any of these characteristics describe what you want from your job? Whether they do or don't, you should spend some time reflecting on what you want your job to provide you. Then, when it's time to do that all-important job search, look for situations that will provide you what you're looking for.

How Can I Have a Successful Career?

Leaving college after graduation to enter the workforce is always a scary step. However, you can make that transition much easier through one "undeniable element: personal accountability."[10] And because you're likely to be the youngest team member, it's especially important that you take responsibility for your actions and behaviors. By taking an active role in managing your career, your work life can be more exciting, enjoyable, satisfying, and rewarding. So, here are some suggestions that will help you on the path to a successful career:

- Understand yourself—your abilities and disabilities; your strengths and weaknesses.
- Protect your personal brand—watch what you share online and in interactions with others, and watch your e-mails.[11]
- Be a team player—focus on knowing your peer group and your organization and on the best ways to work within them.
- Dress appropriately—first impressions count, but so do other impressions that you make every day.

- Network—develop and keep your links to other professionals open and active by participating in professional organizations, staying in touch with classmates and friends, using online networking sites, and so forth.[12]
- Ask for help—if you find yourself facing an issue you're not sure how to handle, ask someone for advice or guidance; seek out a mentor.
- Keep your skills updated—although you might think you know it all, you don't; keep learning about your profession and your industry.
- Set goals and then work hard to achieve them—showing your boss that you're able to set goals and reach them is always impressive.
- Do good work—above all, having a successful career means doing your job well, whatever that job might be.

14 Managing Teams

SPOTLIGHT: *Manager at Work*

As the world's largest semiconductor manufacturer, Intel's technological capabilities are known the world over. One of Intel's most important locations is in Haifa, Israel, on the Mediterranean coast where its Israel Development Center (IDC) was established in 1974 as the company's first development center outside the United States.[1] The Israeli team of engineers (two IDC employees are shown here) has been instrumental in developing many of the company's most successful innovations. The group has been described as having a "strong culture of debate and confrontation. Sometimes too much." The technology behind the highly successful Centrino chips for laptops came out of this lab, as has the technology for other processors. The group atmosphere at IDC actually helped Centrino get off the ground and become a marketplace and financial success for Intel. Getting there, however, wasn't easy.

During the initial design stages of Centrino, the focus, as always, was on processor chip speed. But the reality is that fast chips consume more power and shorten battery life. And when designing a product for use in wireless computers, that's not a good thing. An engineer at IDC came to the team leader and suggested that by giving up half the chip speed, power consumption could be cut by half as well. Such a suggestion probably wouldn't have survived long at the home office because it involved challenging everything the company stood for. However, here in a location where the group wasn't bound by such

Source: Bloomberg via Getty Images

organizational culture constraints, it led to the development of a winning product.

Another benefit of having design groups thousands of miles from headquarters in Santa Clara, California (almost 30 percent

Source: Reuters/Steve Marcus

Intel's managers have found ways to keep the teams connected and the innovations flowing.

of the company's R&D employees are located in more than 20 countries outside the United States), is that these off-site locations don't suffer from bureaucratic inertia associated with constant meetings and committees. Team members can instead focus on the tasks to be done.

However, a major challenge for Intel's geographically dispersed teams is that when team members live and work in different countries, the time zones,

diverse cultures, and dissimilar languages "add complexities to the difficult tasks associated with successful teamwork." One thing that has worked for Intel is the virtual retrospective.

A retrospective is "a formal method for evaluating project performance, extracting lessons learned, and making recommendations for the future." Intel's

LEARNING OUTCOMES

14.1 | ***Define*** *groups and the stages of group development.*

14.2 | ***Describe*** *the major components that determine group performance and satisfaction.*

14.3 | ***Define*** *teams and best practices influencing team performance.*

14.4 | ***Discuss*** *contemporary issues in managing teams.*

design teams collaborate virtually over an audio or video connection. Such retrospectives allow Intel's teams to connect and share ideas and information and to deal with problems. The biggest challenges have been finding acceptable common meeting times, dealing with cultural differences (speaking styles, family commitments), and promoting an atmosphere of safety and fairness in which all participants feel their input is valued. **What could other organizations learn from Intel's teams?**

You've probably had a lot of experience working in groups—class project teams, maybe an athletic team, a fundraising committee, or even a sales team at work. Work teams are one of the realities—and challenges—of managing in today's dynamic global environment. Many organizations have made the move to restructure work around teams rather than individuals. Why? What do these teams look like? And, like the challenges facing Intel's R&D teams, how can managers build effective teams? We will look at answers to these questions throughout this chapter. Before we can understand teams, however, we first need to understand some basics about groups and group behavior.

14.1 | **Define** groups and the stages of group development.

GROUPS and Group Development

Each person in the group had his or her assigned role: The Spotter, The Back Spotter, The Gorilla, and the Big Player. For over 10 years, this group—former MIT students who were members of a secret Black Jack Club—used their extraordinary mathematical abilities, expert training, teamwork, and interpersonal skills to take millions of dollars from some of the major casinos in the United States.[2] Although most groups aren't formed for such dishonest purposes, the success of this group at its task was impressive. Managers would like their groups to be successful at their tasks also. The first step is understanding what a group is and how groups develop.

What Is a Group?

group
Two or more interacting and interdependent individuals who come together to achieve specific goals

A **group** is defined as two or more interacting and interdependent individuals who come together to achieve specific goals. *Formal groups* are work groups defined by the organization's structure and have designated work assignments and specific tasks directed at accomplishing organizational goals. Exhibit 14-1 provides some examples. *Informal groups* are social groups. These groups occur naturally in the workplace and tend to form around friendships and common interests. For example, five employees from different departments who regularly eat lunch together are an informal group.

Stages of Group Development

Research shows that groups develop through five stages.[3] As shown in Exhibit 14-2, these five stages are *forming*, *storming*, *norming*, *performing*, and *adjourning*.

Exhibit 14-1
Examples of Formal Work Groups

- *Command groups*—Groups determined by the organizational chart and composed of individuals who report directly to a given manager.
- *Task groups*—Groups composed of individuals brought together to complete a specific job task; their existence is often temporary because when the task is completed, the group disbands.
- *Cross-functional teams*—Groups that bring together the knowledge and skills of individuals from various work areas or groups whose members have been trained to do each others' jobs.
- *Self-managed teams*—Groups that are essentially independent and that, in addition to their own tasks, take on traditional managerial responsibilities such as hiring, planning and scheduling, and evaluating performance.

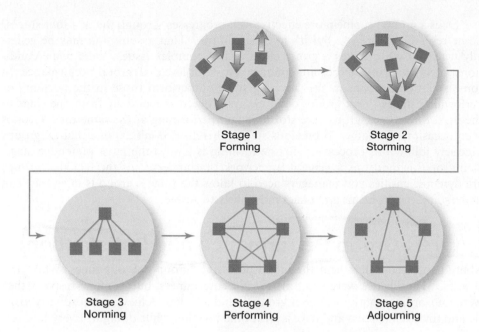

Stage 1
Forming

Stage 2
Storming

Stage 3
Norming

Stage 4
Performing

Stage 5
Adjourning

Exhibit 14-2
Stages of Group Development

The **forming stage** has two phases. The first occurs as people join the group. In a formal group, people join because of some work assignment. Once they've joined, the second phase begins: defining the group's purpose, structure, and leadership. This phase involves a great deal of uncertainty as members "test the waters" to determine what types of behavior are acceptable. This stage is complete when members begin to think of themselves as part of a group.

The **storming stage** is appropriately named because of the intragroup conflict. There's conflict over who will control the group and what the group needs to be doing. During this stage, a relatively clear hierarchy of leadership and agreement on the group's direction emerge.

The **norming stage** is one in which close relationships develop and the group becomes cohesive. There's now a strong sense of group identity and camaraderie. This stage is complete when the group structure solidifies and the group has assimilated a common set of expectations (or norms) regarding member behavior.

The fourth stage is the **performing stage**. The group structure is in place and accepted by group members. Their energies have moved from getting to know and understand each other to working on the group's task. This is the last stage of development for permanent work groups. However, for temporary groups—project teams, task forces, or similar groups that have a limited task to do—the final stage is **adjourning**. In this stage, the group prepares to disband. The group focuses its attention on wrapping up activities instead of task performance. Group members react in different ways. Some are upbeat and thrilled about the group's accomplishments. Others may be sad over the loss of camaraderie and friendships.

Many of you have probably experienced these stages as you've worked on a group project for a class. Group members are selected or assigned and then meet for the first time. There's a "feeling out" period to assess what the group is going to do and how it's going to be done. What usually follows is a battle for control: Who's going to be in charge? Once this issue is resolved and a "hierarchy" agreed on, the group identifies specific work that needs to be done, who's going to do each part, and dates by which the assigned work needs to be completed. General expectations are established. These decisions form the foundation for what you hope will be a coordinated group effort culminating in a project that's been done well. Once the project is complete and turned in, the group breaks up. Of course, some groups don't get much beyond the forming or storming stages. These groups may have serious interpersonal conflicts, turn in disappointing work, and get lower grades.

forming stage
The first stage of group development in which people join the group and then define the group's purpose, structure, and leadership

storming stage
The second stage of group development, characterized by intragroup conflict

norming stage
The third stage of group development, characterized by close relationships and cohesiveness

performing stage
The fourth stage of group development when the group is fully functional and works on group task

adjourning
The final stage of group development for temporary groups during which group members are concerned with wrapping up activities rather than task performance

Does a group become more effective as it progresses through the first four stages? Some researchers say yes, but it's not that simple.[4] That assumption may be generally true, but what makes a group effective is a complex issue. Under some conditions, high levels of conflict are conducive to high levels of group performance. In some situations, groups in the storming stage outperform those in the norming or performing stages. Also, groups don't always proceed sequentially from one stage to the next. Sometimes, groups are storming and performing at the same time. Groups even occasionally regress to previous stages; therefore, don't assume that all groups precisely follow this process or that performing is always the most preferable stage. Think of this model as a general framework that underscores the fact that groups are dynamic entities and managers need to know the stage a group is in so they can understand the problems and issues most likely to surface.

14.2 **Describe** *the major components that determine group performance and satisfaction.*

WORK **Group Performance and Satisfaction**

Many people consider them the most successful "group" of our times. Who? The Beatles. "The Beatles were great artists and entertainers, but in many respects they were four ordinary guys who, as a group, found a way to achieve extraordinary artistic and financial success and have a great time together while doing it. Every business team can learn from their story."[5]

Why *are* some groups more successful than others? Why do some groups achieve high levels of performance and high levels of member satisfaction and others do not? The answers are complex, but include variables such as the abilities of the group's members, the size of the group, the level of conflict, and the internal pressures on members to conform to the group's norms. Exhibit 14-3 presents the major factors that determine group performance and satisfaction.[6] Let's look at each.

External Conditions Imposed on the Group

Work groups are affected by the external conditions imposed on it such as the organization's strategy, authority relationships, formal rules and regulations, availability of resources, employee selection criteria, the performance management system and culture, and the general physical layout of the group's work space. For instance, some groups have modern, high-quality tools and equipment to do their jobs while other groups don't. Or the organization might be pursuing a strategy of lowering costs or improving quality, which will affect what a group does and how it does it.

Group Member Resources

A group's performance potential depends to a large extent on the resources each individual brings to the group. These resources include knowledge, abilities, skills, and personality traits, and they determine what members can do and how effectively they will perform in a group. Interpersonal skills—especially conflict management and resolution, collaborative problem solving, and communication—consistently emerge as important for high performance by work groups.[7]

Personality traits also affect group performance because they strongly influence how the individual will interact with other group members. Research has shown that

role
Behavior patterns expected of someone occupying a given position in a social unit

norms
Standards or expectations that are accepted and shared by a group's members

Exhibit 14-3
Group Performance/Satisfaction Model

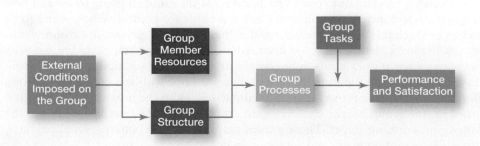

traits viewed as positive in our culture (such as sociability, self-reliance, and independence) tend to be positively related to group productivity and morale. In contrast, negative personality characteristics, such as authoritarianism, dominance, and unconventionality, tend to be negatively related to group productivity and morale.[8]

Group Structure

Work groups aren't unorganized crowds. They have an internal structure that shapes members' behavior and influences group performance. The structure defines roles, norms, conformity, status systems, group size, group cohesiveness, and leadership. Let's look at the first six of these aspects of structure. Leadership is discussed in Chapter 18.

ROLES We introduced the concept of roles in Chapter 1 when we discussed what managers do. (Remember Mintzberg's managerial roles?) Of course, managers aren't the only individuals in an organization who play various roles. The concept of roles applies to all employees and to their life outside an organization as well. (Think of the various roles you play: student, sibling, employee, spouse or significant other, etc.)

A **role** refers to behavior patterns expected of someone occupying a given position in a social unit. In a group, individuals are expected to do certain things because of their position (role) in the group. These roles are generally oriented toward either getting work done or keeping group members happy.[10] Think about groups you've been in and the roles you played in those groups. Were you continually trying to keep the group focused on getting its work done? If so, you were performing a task accomplishment role. Or were you more concerned that group members had the opportunity to offer ideas and that they were satisfied with the experience? If so, you were performing a group member satisfaction role. Both roles are important to the group's ability to function effectively and efficiently.

A problem arises when individuals play multiple roles and adjust their roles to the group to which they belong at the time. However, the differing expectations of these roles often mean that employees face *role conflicts*.

NORMS All groups have **norms**—standards or expectations that are accepted and shared by a group's members. Norms dictate things such as work output levels, absenteeism, promptness, and the amount of socializing on the job.

For example, norms dictate the "arrival ritual" among office assistants at Coleman Trust Inc. where the workday begins at 8 a.m. Most employees typically arrive a few minutes before and hang up their coats and put their purses and other personal items on their desk so everyone knows they're "at work." They then go to the break room to get coffee and chat. Anyone who violates this norm by starting work at 8 a.m. is pressured to behave in a way that conforms to the group's standard.

Although a group has its own unique set of norms, common organizational norms focus on effort and performance, dress, and loyalty. The most widespread norms are those related to work effort and performance. Work groups typically provide their members with explicit cues on how hard to work, level of output, when to look busy, when it's acceptable to goof off, and the like. These norms are powerful influences on an individual employee's performance. They're so powerful that you can't predict someone's performance based solely on his or her ability and personal motivation. Dress norms frequently dictate what's acceptable to wear to work. If the norm is more formal dress, anyone who dresses casually may face subtle pressure to conform. Finally, loyalty norms will influence whether individuals work late, work on weekends, or move to locations they might not prefer to live.

One negative thing about group norms is that being part of a group can increase an individual's antisocial actions. If the norms of the group include tolerating deviant behavior, someone who normally wouldn't engage in such behavior might be more likely to do so. For instance, one study found that those working in a group were

---

*data*points[9]

58 percent of adults say they would not report a colleague who's seriously underperforming but would instead help the friend with work; 27 percent said they would report a colleague if the team's success was on the line.

65 percent to 95 percent of workers across a wide range of industries and occupations are members of more than one project team at a time.

25 percent of managers say the most challenging thing is dealing with issues between coworkers on their team; 22 percent say it's motivating team members.

70 percent of employees say the biggest benefit of workplace friendships is that it creates a more supportive workplace.

85 percent of Fortune 1000 companies use team- or group-based pay.

69 percent of workers say their teams are not given enough resources.

83 percent of respondents to a survey identify teams as a key ingredient to organizational success.

33 percent of females want more face-to-face group meetings; 27 percent of males do.

40 percent of senior executives say meeting deadlines is the most important characteristic of a good team player.

Liam Maimon, CEO and co-founder of Stagee.com, makes a shot at a mini basketball hoop as he takes a break from work to have fun with his co-workers. Casual dress and an informal work environment are norms at Stagee, a new social networking platform where actors, singers, songwriters, musicians, models, comedians, and dancers can promote their careers and expand their reach to new audiences. High worker output is a performance norm accepted and shared by Stagee's employees as they invested many months of hard work and long hours to build and launch their new venture and continue to work hard to grow their community of talent and expand their business by connecting entertainers with casting agents, directors, and producers.
Source: © *PhotoStock-Israel/Alamy*

groupthink
When a group exerts extensive pressure on an individual to align his or her opinion with others' opinions

status
A prestige grading, position, or rank within a group

more likely to lie, cheat, and steal than individuals working alone.[11] Why? Because groups provide anonymity, thus giving individuals—who might otherwise be afraid of getting caught—a false sense of security.

CONFORMITY Because individuals want to be accepted by groups to which they belong, they're susceptible to pressures to conform. Early experiments done by Solomon Asch demonstrated the impact conformity has on an individual's judgment and attitudes.[12] In these experiments, groups of seven or eight people were asked to compare two cards held up by the experimenter. One card had three lines of different lengths and the other had one line that was equal in length to one of the three lines on the other card (see Exhibit 14-4). Each group member was to announce aloud which of the three lines matched the single line. Asch wanted to see what would happen if members began to give incorrect answers. Would pressures to conform cause individuals to give wrong answers just to be consistent with the others? The experiment was "fixed" so that all but one of the members (the unsuspecting subject) were told ahead of time to start giving obviously incorrect answers after one or two rounds. Over many experiments and trials, the unsuspecting subject conformed over a third of the time.

Are these conclusions still valid? Research suggests that conformity levels have declined since Asch's studies. However, managers can't ignore conformity because it can still be a powerful force in groups.[13] Group members often want to be seen as one of the group and avoid being visibly different. We find it more pleasant to agree than to be disruptive, even if being disruptive may improve the group's effectiveness. So we conform. But conformity can go too far, especially when an individual's opinion differs significantly from that of others in the group. In such a case, the group often exerts intense pressure on the individual to align his or her opinion to conform to others' opinions, a phenomenon known as **groupthink**. Groupthink seems to occur when group members hold a positive group image they want to protect and when the group perceives a collective threat to this positive image.[14]

STATUS SYSTEMS Status systems are an important factor in understanding groups. **Status** is a prestige grading, position, or rank within a group. As far back as researchers have been able to trace groups, they have found status hierarchies. Status can be a significant motivator with behavioral consequences especially when individuals see a disparity between what they perceive their status to be and what others perceive it to be.

Status may be informally conferred by characteristics such as education, age, skill, or experience. Anything can have status value if others in the group evaluate it that way. Of course, just because status is informal doesn't mean it's unimportant or hard to determine who has it or who does not. Group members have no problem placing people into status categories and usually agree about who has high or low status.

Exhibit 14-4
Examples of Asch's Cards

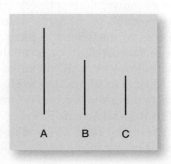

Status is also formally conferred, and it's important for employees to believe the organization's formal status system is congruent—that is, the system shows consistency between the perceived ranking of an individual and the status symbols he or she is given by the organization. For instance, status incongruence would occur when a supervisor earns less than his or her subordinates, a desirable office is occupied by a person in a low-ranking position, or paid country club memberships are provided to division managers but not to vice presidents. Employees expect the "things" an individual receives to be congruent with his or her status. When they're not, employees may question the authority of their managers and may not be motivated by job promotion opportunities.

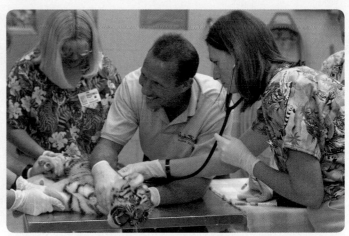

Group cohesiveness is high for the veterinarians at The Detroit Zoo. Shown here is Dr. Ann Duncan (right, with stethoscope), chief veterinarian at the zoo, and staff members as they perform a physical examination and vaccinate a nine-week-old Amur tiger cub, an endangered species native to Siberia with only several hundred left in the wild. The veterinary staff is passionate about sharing the zoo's mission of "saving and celebrating wildlife," and they contribute to the zoo's recognition as a leader in animal conservation and welfare. Committed to their work, they cooperate with each other in overseeing the care of wild and exotic animals to achieve the goals of maintaining animal health, preventing disease, and developing treatment approaches.
Source: © Jim West/PhotoEdit

GROUP SIZE   What's an appropriate size for a group? At Amazon, work teams have considerable autonomy to innovate and to investigate their ideas. And Jeff Bezos, founder and CEO, uses a "two-pizza" philosophy; that is, a team should be small enough that it can be fed with two pizzas. This "two-pizza" philosophy usually limits groups to five to seven people depending, of course, on team member appetites.[15]

Group size affects performance and satisfaction, but the effect depends on what the group is supposed to accomplish.[16] Research indicates, for instance, that small groups are faster than larger ones at completing tasks. However, for groups engaged in problem solving, large groups consistently get better results than smaller ones. What do these findings mean in terms of specific numbers? Large groups—those with a dozen or more members—are good for getting diverse input. Thus, if the goal of the group is to find facts, a larger group should be more effective. On the other hand, smaller groups—from five to seven members—are better at doing something productive with those facts.

One important research finding related to group size concerns **social loafing**, which is the tendency for an individual to expend less effort when working collectively than when working individually.[17] Social loafing may occur because people believe others in the group aren't doing their fair share. Thus, they reduce their work efforts in an attempt to make the workload more equivalent. Also, the relationship between an individual's input and the group's output is often unclear. Thus, individuals may become "free riders" and coast on the group's efforts because individuals believe their contribution can't be measured.

The implications of social loafing are significant. When managers use groups, they must find a way to identify individual efforts. If not, group productivity and individual satisfaction may decline.[18]

GROUP COHESIVENESS   Cohesiveness is important because it has been found to be related to a group's productivity. Groups in which there's a lot of internal disagreement and lack of cooperation are less effective in completing their tasks than groups in which members generally agree, cooperate, and like each other. Research in this area has focused on **group cohesiveness**, or the degree to which members are attracted to a group and share the group's goals.[19]

Research has generally shown that highly cohesive groups are more effective than less cohesive ones.[20] However, the relationship between cohesiveness and effectiveness is complex. A key moderating variable is the degree to which the group's attitude aligns with its goals or with the goals of the organization.[21] (See Exhibit 14-5.) The more cohesive the group, the more its members will follow its goals. If the goals are desirable (for instance, high output, quality work, cooperation with individuals outside the group), a cohesive group is more productive than a less cohesive group. But if cohesiveness is high and attitudes are unfavorable, productivity decreases. If cohesiveness is low but goals are supported, productivity increases but not as much as

social loafing
The tendency for individuals to expend less effort when working collectively than when working individually

group cohesiveness
The degree to which group members are attracted to one another and share the group's goals

Exhibit 14-5

Group Cohesiveness and Productivity

		Cohesiveness	
		High	Low
Alignment of Group and Organizational Goals	High	Strong Increase in Productivity	Moderate Increase in Productivity
	Low	Decrease in Productivity	No Significant Effect on Productivity

when both cohesiveness and support are high. When cohesiveness is low and goals are not supported, productivity is not significantly affected.

GROUP PROCESSES The next factor that determines group performance and satisfaction concerns the processes that go on within a work group such as communication, decision making, conflict management, and the like. These processes are important to understanding work groups because they influence group performance and satisfaction positively or negatively. An example of a positive process factor is the synergy of four people on a marketing research team who are able to generate far more ideas as a group than the members could produce individually. However, the group also may have negative process factors such as social loafing, high levels of conflict, or poor communication, which may hinder group effectiveness. We'll look at two important group processes: group decision making and conflict management.

GROUP DECISION MAKING It's a rare organization that doesn't use committees, task forces, review panels, study teams, or other similar groups to make decisions. Studies show that managers may spend up to 30 hours a week in group meetings.[22] Undoubtedly, a large portion of that time is spent formulating problems, developing solutions, and determining how to implement the solutions. It's possible, in fact, for groups to be assigned any of the eight steps in the decision-making process. (Refer to Chapter 6 to review these steps.)

What advantages do group decisions have over individual decisions? One is that groups generate more complete information and knowledge. They bring a diversity of experience and perspectives to the decision process that an individual cannot. In addition, groups generate more diverse alternatives because they have a greater amount and diversity of information. Next, groups increase acceptance of a solution. Group members are reluctant to fight or undermine a decision they helped develop. Finally, groups increase legitimacy. Decisions made by groups may be perceived as more legitimate than decisions made by one person.

Group decisions also have disadvantages. One is that groups almost always take more time to reach a solution than it would take an individual. Another is that a dominant and vocal minority can heavily influence the final decision. In addition, groupthink can undermine critical thinking in the group and harm the quality of the final decision.[23] Finally, in a group, members share responsibility, but the responsibility of any single member is ambiguous.

Determining whether groups are effective at making decisions depends on the criteria used to assess effectiveness.[24] If accuracy, creativity, and degree of acceptance are important, then a group decision may work best. However, if speed and efficiency are important, then an individual decision may be the best. In addition, decision effectiveness is influenced by group size. Although a larger group provides more diverse representation, it also requires more coordination and time for members to contribute their ideas. Evidence indicates that groups of five, and to a lesser extent seven, are the most

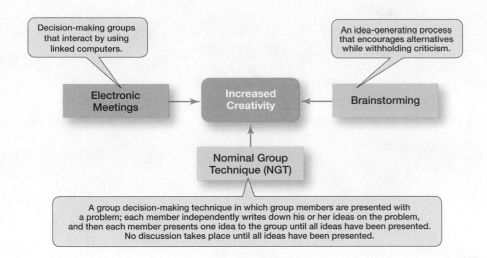

Exhibit 14-6
Creative Group Decision Making

effective for making decisions.[25] Having an odd number in the group helps avoid decision deadlocks. Also, these groups are large enough for members to shift roles and withdraw from unfavorable positions but still small enough for quieter members to participate actively in discussions.

What techniques can managers use to help groups make more creative decisions? Exhibit 14-6 describes three possibilities.

CONFLICT MANAGEMENT Another important group process is how a group manages conflict. As a group performs its assigned tasks, disagreements inevitably arise. **Conflict** is *perceived* incompatible differences resulting in some form of interference or opposition. Whether the differences are real is irrelevant. If people in a group perceive that differences exist, then there is conflict.

Three different views have evolved regarding conflict.[26] The **traditional view of conflict** argues that conflict must be avoided—that it indicates a problem within the group. Another view, the **human relations view of conflict**, argues that conflict is a natural and inevitable outcome in any group and need not be negative but has

conflict
Perceived incompatible differences that result in interference or opposition

traditional view of conflict
The view that all conflict is bad and must be avoided

human relations view of conflict
The view that conflict is a natural and inevitable outcome in any group

let's get REAL

The Scenario:

Fran Waller is the manager of a retail store that's part of a large national chain. Many of her employees are going to school and working. But she also has some full-time employees. A conflict over vacation and holiday work schedules has been building for some time now and it's creating a very tense atmosphere, which isn't good for customer service. She's got to resolve it NOW.

What suggestions would you give Fran for managing this conflict?

I would advise Fran to create a vacation/ holiday schedule at the beginning of the year. Start with the tenured employees, and ask each employee to select the days they would like to take vacation/holiday. In the event that several employees choose the same date, I would suggest they work it out as a team to promote synergy.

Source: Patricia Ficco

Patricia Ficco
Retail General Manager

Exhibit 14-7
Conflict and Group
Performance

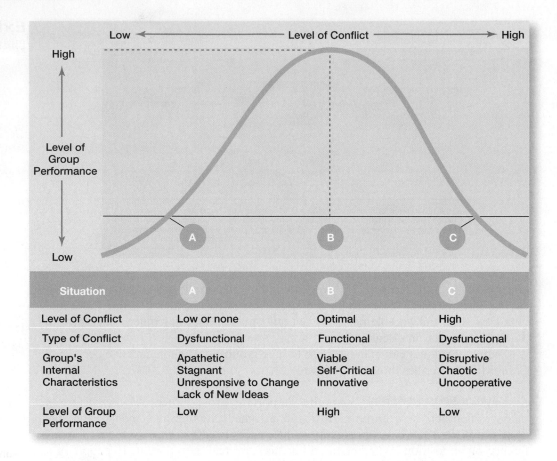

Situation	A	B	C
Level of Conflict	Low or none	Optimal	High
Type of Conflict	Dysfunctional	Functional	Dysfunctional
Group's Internal Characteristics	Apathetic Stagnant Unresponsive to Change Lack of New Ideas	Viable Self-Critical Innovative	Disruptive Chaotic Uncooperative
Level of Group Performance	Low	High	Low

interactionist view of conflict
The view that some conflict is necessary for a group to perform effectively

functional conflicts
Conflicts that support a group's goals and improve its performance

dysfunctional conflicts
Conflicts that prevent a group from achieving its goals

task conflict
Conflicts over content and goals of the work

relationship conflict
Conflict based on interpersonal relationships

process conflict
Conflict over how work gets done

potential to be a positive force in contributing to a group's performance. The third and most recent view, the **interactionist view of conflict**, proposes that not only can conflict be a positive force in a group but that some conflict is *absolutely necessary* for a group to perform effectively.

The interactionist view doesn't suggest that all conflicts are good. Some conflicts—**functional conflicts**—are constructive and support the goals of the work group and improve its performance. Other conflicts—**dysfunctional conflicts**—are destructive and prevent a group from achieving its goals. Exhibit 14-7 illustrates the challenge facing managers.

When is conflict functional and when is it dysfunctional? Research indicates that you need to look at the *type* of conflict.[27] **Task conflict** relates to the content and goals of the work. **Relationship conflict** focuses on interpersonal relationships. **Process conflict** refers to how the work gets done. Research shows that *relationship* conflicts are almost always dysfunctional because the interpersonal hostilities increase personality clashes and decrease mutual understanding and the tasks don't get done. On the other hand, low levels of process conflict and low-to-moderate levels of task conflict are functional. For *process* conflict to be productive, it must be minimal. Otherwise, intense arguments over who should do what may become dysfunctional and can lead to uncertainty about task assignments, increase the time to complete tasks, and result in members working at cross-purposes. However, a low-to-moderate level of *task* conflict consistently has a positive effect on group performance because it stimulates discussion of ideas that help groups be more innovative.[28] Because we don't yet have a sophisticated measuring instrument for assessing whether conflict levels are optimal, too high, or too low, the manager must try to judge that intelligently.

When group conflict levels are too high, managers can select from five conflict management options: avoidance, accommodation, forcing, compromise, and collaboration.[29] (See Exhibit 14-8 for a description of these techniques.) Keep in mind that no one option is ideal for every situation. Which approach to use depends on the circumstances.

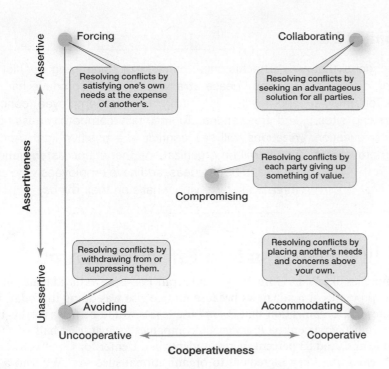

Exhibit 14-8
Conflict-Management Techniques

Source: K. Thomas, "Conflict and Negotiation Process in Organizations," in M. D. Dunnette and L. J. Hough (eds.), *Handbook of Industrial and Organizational Psychology*, 2 ed. vol. 3 (Palo Alto, CA: Consulting Psychologists Press, 1992), p. 668. Used with permission by Leaetta Hough-Dunnette.

Have you ever been part of a class group in which all teammates received the same grade, even though some team members didn't fulfill their responsibilities? How did that make you feel? Did it create conflict within the group, and did you feel that the process and outcome were unfair? Recent research also has shown that organizational justice or fairness is an important aspect of managing group conflict.[30] How group members feel about how they're being treated both by each other within the group and by outsiders can affect their work attitudes and behaviors. To promote the sense of fairness, it's important that group leaders build a strong sense of community based on fair and just treatment.

Group Tasks

At Hackensack University Medical Center in New Jersey, daily reviews of each patient in each nursing unit are conducted in MDRs (multidisciplinary rounds) by teams of nurses, case managers, social workers, and an in-hospital doctor. These teams perform tasks such as prescribing drugs or even recommending a patient be discharged. Employee teams at Lockheed Martin's New York facility custom build complex products such as ground-based radar systems using continuous quality improvement techniques. The six people in the Skinny Improv group in Springfield, Missouri, perform their unique brand of comedy every weekend in a downtown venue.[31] Each of these groups has a different type of task to accomplish.

As the group performance/satisfaction model shows, the impact that group processes have on group performance and member satisfaction is modified by the task the group is doing. More specifically, it's the *complexity* and *interdependence* of tasks that influence a group's effectiveness.[32]

Tasks are either simple or complex. Simple tasks are routine and standardized. Complex tasks tend to be novel or nonroutine. It appears that the more complex the task, the more a group benefits from group discussion about alternative work methods. Group members don't need to discuss such alternatives for a simple task, but can rely on standard operating procedures. Similarly, a high degree of interdependence among the tasks that group members must perform means they'll need to interact more. Thus, effective communication and controlled conflict are most relevant to group performance when tasks are complex and interdependent.

FUTURE VISION | Conflict 2.0

Successful organizations will come to recognize that functional conflict—in the form of tolerating dissent—makes an organization stronger, not weaker. Tomorrow's organizations will use blogs, social networking sites, and other vehicles to allow employees to question practices, criticize decisions, and offer improvement suggestions.

The historical practice of minimizing conflict and seeking "peace at any price" didn't produce harmony and loyalty. It merely masked employee concerns and frustrations. To maintain competitiveness, organizations will see conflict in a positive light. And the result will be organizations that adapt faster, generate more and better ideas, and have employees who aren't threatened by saying what's on their minds.

14.3 *Define teams and best practices influencing team performance.*

TURNING Groups into Effective Teams

When companies like W. L. Gore, Volvo, and Kraft Foods introduced teams into their production processes, it made news because no one else was doing it. Today, it's just the opposite—the organization that *doesn't* use teams would be newsworthy. It's estimated that some 80 percent of *Fortune* 500 companies have at least half of their employees on teams. And 83 percent of respondents in a Center for Creative Leadership study said teams are a key ingredient to organizational success.[33] Without a doubt, team-based work is a core feature of today's organizations. And teams are likely to continue to be popular. Why? Research suggests that teams typically outperform individuals when the tasks being done require multiple skills, judgment, and experience.[34] Organizations are using team-based structures because they've found that teams are more flexible and responsive to changing events than traditional departments or other permanent work groups. Teams have the ability to quickly assemble, deploy, refocus, and disband. In this section, we'll discuss what a work team is, the different types of teams organizations might use, and how to develop and manage work teams.

What Is a Work Team?

Most of you are probably familiar with teams, especially if you've watched or participated in organized sports events. Work *teams* differ from work *groups* and have their own unique traits (see Exhibit 14-9). Work groups interact primarily to share information and to make decisions to help each member do his or her job more efficiently and effectively.

Exhibit 14-9
Groups Versus Teams

Work Teams	Work Groups
• Leadership role is shared	• One leader clearly in charge
• Accountable to self and team	• Accountable only to self
• Team creates specific purpose	• Purpose is same as broader organizational purpose
• Work is done collectively	• Work is done individually
• Meetings characterized by open-ended discussion and collaborative problem-solving	• Meetings characterized by efficiency; no collaboration or open-ended discussion
• Performance is measured directly by evaluating collective work output	• Performance is measured indirectly according to its influence on others
• Work is decided upon and done together	• Work is decided upon by group leader and delegated to individual group members
• Can be quickly assembled, deployed, refocused, and disbanded	

Sources: J. R. Katzenbach and D. K. Smith, "The Wisdom of Teams," *Harvard Business Review*, July–August 2005, p. 161; A. J. Fazzari and J. B. Mosca, "Partners in Perfection: Human Resources Facilitating Creation and Ongoing Implementation of Self-Managed Manufacturing Teams in a Small Medium Enterprise," *Human Resource Development Quarterly*, Fall 2009, pp. 353–376.

There's no need or opportunity for work groups to engage in collective work that requires joint effort. On the other hand, **work teams** are groups whose members work intensely on a specific, common goal using their positive synergy, individual and mutual accountability, and complementary skills. For instance, at the Sparta, Tennessee, facility of Philips Professional Luminaires, a work team came up with a startling innovation. One team member was commenting on the efficient way that Subway restaurants make their sandwiches with workers lining up all their ingredients in an easy-to-reach, highly adaptable format. The team decided to apply that same flexible principle to their work of producing lighting fixtures and together figured out a way to make that happen.[35]

Types of Work Teams

Teams can do a variety of things. They can design products, provide services, negotiate deals, coordinate projects, offer advice, and make decisions.[36] For instance, at Rockwell Automation's facility in North Carolina, teams are used in work process optimization projects. At Sylvania, the New Ventures Group creates cool LED-based products. At Arkansas-based Acxiom Corporation, a team of human resource professionals planned and implemented a cultural change. And every summer weekend at any NASCAR race, you can see work teams in action during drivers' pit stops.[37] The four most common types of work teams are problem-solving teams, self-managed work teams, cross-functional teams, and virtual teams.

When work teams first became popular, most were **problem-solving teams**, teams from the same department or functional area involved in efforts to improve work activities or to solve specific problems. Members share ideas or offer suggestions on how work processes and methods can be improved. However, these teams are rarely given the authority to implement any of their suggested actions.

Although problem-solving teams were helpful, they didn't go far enough in getting employees involved in work-related decisions and processes. This shortcoming led to another type of team, a **self-managed work team**, a formal group of employees who operate without a manager and are responsible for a complete work process or segment. A self-managed team is responsible for getting the work done *and* for managing themselves, which usually includes planning and scheduling of work, assigning tasks to members, collective control over the pace of work, making operating decisions, and taking action on problems. For instance, teams at Corning have no shift supervisors and work closely with other manufacturing divisions to solve production-line problems and coordinate deadlines and deliveries. The teams have the authority to make and implement decisions, finish projects, and address problems.[38] Other organizations such as Xerox, Boeing, PepsiCo, and Hewlett-Packard also use self-managed teams. An estimated 30 percent of U.S. employers now use this form of team; among large firms, the number is probably closer to 50 percent.[39] Most organizations that use self-managed teams find them to be effective.[40]

The third type of team is the **cross-functional team**, which we introduced in Chapters 11 and 12 and defined as a work team composed of individuals from various functional specialties. Many organizations use cross-functional teams. For example, ArcelorMittal, the world's biggest steel company, uses cross-functional teams of scientists, plant managers, and salespeople to review and monitor product innovations.[41] The concept of cross-functional teams is even applied in health care. For instance, at Suburban Hospital in Bethesda, Maryland, intensive care unit (ICU) teams composed of a doctor trained in intensive care medicine, a pharmacist, a social worker, a nutritionist, the chief ICU nurse, a respiratory therapist, and a chaplain meet daily with every patient's bedside nurse to discuss and debate the best course of treatment. The hospital credits this team care approach with reducing errors, shortening the amount of time patients spent in ICU, and improving communication between families and the medical staff.[42]

To improve its organizational performance, Florida Power & Light Company has restructured its work processes around teams. Throughout the company, high-performing problem-solving teams from the same department or functional area focus on improving work activities or solving specific problems. Shown in this photo are members of a materials management team participating in a companywide emergency response and restoration drill. This team, along with many other emergency teams that respond to accidents and storms, enable FPL to achieve its goals of quickly and safely deploying equipment and crews to prepare for power outages, activating emergency response plans, and restoring power to customers.
Source: Bruce R. Bennett/ZUMA Press/Newscom

work teams
Groups whose members work intensely on a specific, common goal using their positive synergy, individual and mutual accountability, and complementary skills

problem-solving team
A team from the same department or functional area that's involved in efforts to improve work activities or to solve specific problems

self-managed work team
A type of work team that operates without a manager and is responsible for a complete work process or segment

cross-functional team
A work team composed of individuals from various functional specialties

virtual team
A type of work team that uses technology to link physically dispersed members in order to achieve a common goal

The final type of team is the **virtual team**, a team that uses technology to link physically dispersed members to achieve a common goal. For instance, a virtual team at Boeing-Rocketdyne played a pivotal role in developing a radically new product.[43] Another company, Decision Lens, uses a virtual team environment to generate and evaluate creative ideas.[44] In a virtual team, members collaborate online with tools such as wide-area networks, videoconferencing, fax, e-mail, or Web sites where the team can hold online conferences.[45] Virtual teams can do all the things that other teams can—share information, make decisions, and complete tasks; however, they lack the normal give-and-take of face-to-face discussions. That's why virtual teams tend to be more task-oriented, especially if the team members have never met in person.

Creating Effective Work Teams

As our chapter opener illustrated, teams are not always effective. They don't always achieve high levels of performance. However, research on teams provides insights into the characteristics typically associated with effective teams.[46] These characteristics are listed in Exhibit 14-10. One element you might notice is missing but think is important to being an effective team is that a team be harmonious and friendly.[47] In fact, friendliness is not a necessary ingredient. Even a grumpy team can be effective if these other team characteristics are present. When a team is productive, has done something good together, and is recognized for its efforts, team members can feel good about their effectiveness.

CLEAR GOALS High-performance teams have a clear understanding of the goal to be achieved. Members are committed to the team's goals, know what they're expected to accomplish, and understand how they will work together to achieve these goals.

RELEVANT SKILLS Effective teams are composed of competent individuals who have the necessary technical and interpersonal skills to achieve the desired goals while working well together. This last point is important because not everyone who is technically competent has the interpersonal skills to work well as a team member.

MUTUAL TRUST Effective teams are characterized by high mutual trust among members. That is, members believe in each other's ability, character, and integrity. But as you probably know from personal relationships, trust is fragile. Maintaining this trust requires careful attention by managers.[48]

Exhibit 14-10
Characteristics of Effective Teams

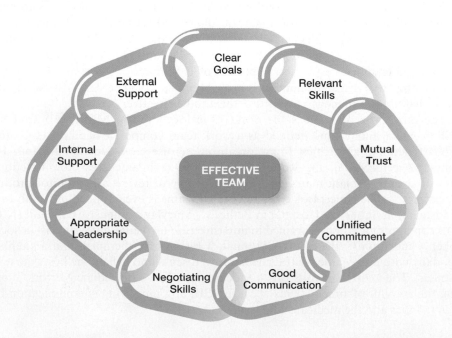

UNIFIED COMMITMENT   Unified commitment is characterized by dedication to the team's goals and a willingness to expend extraordinary amounts of energy to achieve them. Members of an effective team exhibit intense loyalty and dedication to the team and are willing to do whatever it takes to help their team succeed.

GOOD COMMUNICATION   Not surprisingly, effective teams are characterized by good communication.[49] Members convey messages, verbally and nonverbally, between each other in ways that are readily and clearly understood. Also, feedback helps guide team members and correct misunderstandings. Like a couple who has been together for many years, members of high-performing teams are able to quickly and efficiently share ideas and feelings.

NEGOTIATING SKILLS   Effective teams are continually making adjustments to whom does what. This flexibility requires team members to possess negotiating skills. Because problems and relationships regularly change within teams, members need to be able to confront and reconcile differences.

APPROPRIATE LEADERSHIP   Effective leaders are important. They can motivate a team to follow them through the most difficult situations. How? By clarifying goals, demonstrating that change is possible by overcoming inertia, increasing the self-confidence of team members, and helping members to more fully realize their potential. Increasingly, effective team leaders act as coaches and facilitators. They help guide and support the team, but don't control it. Studies have shown that when a team leader's emotional displays—positive *and* negative—are used at appropriate times, the team's functioning and performance can be enhanced.[50]

INTERNAL AND EXTERNAL SUPPORT.   The final condition necessary for an effective team is a supportive climate. Internally, the team should have a sound

let's get REAL

Source: Joe Binef

Joe Binef
Director of Global Process Development

The Scenario:

Barry Murphy is the HR manager at a large agricultural services company. He says, "We've always had an internal recognition program that focused on individual efforts. This recognition provides highly public praise for employees who have exceeded expectations or shown extraordinary effort, plus they get a small monetary incentive. Now, however, since our company is moving to an approach that recognizes team goals rather than individual, how can I make this work?"

What advice would you give Barry?

I would advise Barry to look at this as a team building opportunity, highlighting individuals' strengths and pointing out how they are all an essential part of the company's success. In order to make everyone feel accountable, managers can assign individual tasks within their teams and then personally recognize those outstanding achievements that have an impact on the team. Lastly, since employees are no longer eligible for individual monetary incentives, Barry should allocate that money in a way that collectively recognizes outstanding group performance, such as a departmental breakfast, so that everyone can equally enjoy the team's success.

infrastructure, which means proper training, a clear and reasonable measurement system that team members can use to evaluate their overall performance, an incentive program that recognizes and rewards team activities, and a supportive human resource system. The right infrastructure should support members and reinforce behaviors that lead to high levels of performance. Externally, managers should provide the team with the resources needed to get the job done.

14.4 *Discuss* contemporary issues in managing teams.

CURRENT Challenges in Managing Teams

Few trends have influenced how work gets done in organizations as much as the use of work teams. The shift from working alone to working on teams requires employees to cooperate with others, share information, confront differences, and sublimate personal interests for the greater good of the team. Managers can build effective teams by understanding what influences performance and satisfaction. However, managers also face some current challenges in managing teams, primarily those associated with managing global teams, building team skills, and understanding organizational social networks.

Managing Global Teams

Two characteristics of today's organizations are obvious: They're global and work is increasingly done by teams. These two aspects mean that any manager is likely to have to manage a global team. What do we know about managing global teams? We know there are both drawbacks and benefits in using global teams (see Exhibit 14-11). Using our group model as a framework, we can see some of the issues associated with managing global teams.

GROUP MEMBER RESOURCES IN GLOBAL TEAMS In global organizations, understanding the relationship between group performance and group member resources is more challenging because of the unique cultural characteristics represented by members of a global team. In addition to recognizing team members' abilities, skills, knowledge, and personality, managers need to be familiar with and clearly understand the cultural characteristics of the groups and the group members they manage.[51] For instance, is the global team from a culture in which uncertainty avoidance is high? If so, members will not be comfortable dealing with unpredictable and ambiguous tasks. Also, as managers work with global teams, they need to be aware of the potential for stereotyping, which can lead to problems.

GROUP STRUCTURE Some of the structural areas where we see differences in managing global teams include conformity, status, social loafing, and cohesiveness.

Are conformity findings generalizable across cultures? Research suggests that Asch's findings are culture-bound.[52] For instance, as might be expected, conformity to social norms tends to be higher in collectivistic cultures than in individualistic cultures. Despite this tendency, however, groupthink tends to be less of a problem in global teams because members are less likely to feel pressured to conform to the ideas, conclusions, and decisions of the group.[53]

Exhibit 14-11
Global Teams

Drawbacks	Benefits
• Dislike of team members • Mistrust of team members • Stereotyping • Communication problems • Stress and tension	• Greater diversity of ideas • Limited groupthink • Increased attention on understanding others' ideas, perspectives, etc.

Source: Based on N. Adler, *International Dimensions in Organizational Behavior*, 4th ed. (Cincinnati, OH: South-Western Publishing, 2002), pp. 141–147.

Also, the importance of status varies between cultures. The French, for example, are extremely status conscious. Also, countries differ on the criteria that confer status. For instance, in Latin America and Asia, status tends to come from family position and formal roles held in organizations. In contrast, while status is important in countries like the United States and Australia, it tends to be less "in your face." And it tends to be given based on accomplishments rather than on titles and family history. Managers must understand who and what holds status when interacting with people from a culture different from their own. An American manager who doesn't understand that office size isn't a measure of a Japanese executive's position or who fails to grasp the importance the British place on family genealogy and social class is likely to unintentionally offend others and lessen his or her interpersonal effectiveness.

Social loafing has a Western bias. It's consistent with individualistic cultures, like the United States and Canada, which are dominated by self-interest. It's not consistent with collectivistic societies, in which individuals are motivated by group goals. For instance, in studies comparing employees from the United States with employees from the People's Republic of China and Israel (both collectivistic societies), the Chinese and Israelis showed no propensity to engage in social loafing. In fact, they actually performed better in a group than when working alone.[55]

Cohesiveness is another group structural element where managers may face special challenges. In a cohesive group, members are unified and "act as one." These groups exhibit a great deal of camaraderie, and group identity is high. In global teams, however, cohesiveness is often more difficult to achieve because of higher levels of "mistrust, miscommunication, and stress."[56]

GROUP PROCESSES   The processes global teams use to do their work can be particularly challenging for managers. For one thing, communication issues often arise because not all team members may be fluent in the team's working language. This can lead to inaccuracies, misunderstandings, and inefficiencies.[57] However, research also has shown that a multicultural global team is better able to capitalize on the diversity of ideas represented if a wide range of information is used.[58]

Managing conflict in global teams isn't easy, especially when those teams are virtual teams. Conflict can interfere with how information is used by the team. However, research shows that in collectivistic cultures, a collaborative conflict management style can be most effective.[59]

MANAGER'S ROLE   Despite the challenges associated with managing global teams, managers can provide the group with an environment in which efficiency and effectiveness are enhanced.[60] First, because communication skills are vital, managers should focus on developing those skills. Also, as we've said earlier, managers must consider cultural differences when deciding what type of global team to use. For instance, evidence suggests that self-managed teams have not fared well in Mexico largely due to that culture's low tolerance of ambiguity and uncertainty and employees' strong respect for hierarchical authority.[61] Finally, it's vital that managers be sensitive to the unique

Source: Reuters/Michaela Rehle

LEADER *who made a* DIFFERENCE

Answering the world's toughest questions is what the some 360,000 employees of Siemens, one of the largest electronics and industrial engineering companies in the world, do.[54] CEO Peter Löscher plays an important role in helping those employees do that. Löscher was brought in as CEO after a traumatic time in the company's history when it was disgraced internationally and paid a $1.6 billion fine for bribery charges. Under his strong leadership, Löscher has turned around the company and returned it to its role of being a leader in the global marketplace. But Löscher didn't do that single-handedly. Employee teams made up of highly dedicated and skilled individuals have been a critical component. For instance, Zhang Wei Ping leads a sales team at Siemens Energy in Shanghai and says the open culture at Siemens is what helps make the company great. "It's like one big family." Löscher also says that trust within a team where "you're no longer just playing individually at your best, but you're also trying to understand what you can do to make the team better" is what he strives for. And that type of culture and atmosphere can be pretty powerful tools in helping make a company strong and competitive in today's world. What can you learn from this leader who made a difference?

Because a team-focused mindset is so critical to the success of U.S. Navy SEAL operations, candidates train together so they can work together and accomplish their goals together. The extremely rigorous team-building training for the SEALs includes physical-endurance exercises with a 600-pound log that helps trainees bond, support, cooperate with, and rely on each other. Team-building training for the SEALs emphasizes that each person is a valuable asset to the team and then prepares individuals to be ready and willing to implement a unified approach of working together to achieve the team's mission.
Source: U.S. Navy/AFLO/Newscom

social network structure
The patterns of informal connections among individuals within a group

differences of each member of the global team, but it's also important that team members be sensitive to each other.

Building Team Skills

Have you ever participated in a team-building exercise? Such exercises are commonly used to illustrate and develop specific aspects or skills of being on a team. For instance, maybe you've completed *Lost on the Moon* or *Stranded at Sea* or some other written exercise in which you rank-order what items are most important to your survival. Then, you do the same thing with a group—rank-order the most important items. The rank-ordered items are compared against some expert ranking to see how many you got "right." The intent of the exercise is to illustrate how much more effective decisions can be when made as a team. Or maybe you've been part of a trust-building exercise in which you fall back and team members catch you or an exercise in which your team had to figure out how to get all members across an imaginary river or up a rock wall. Such exercises help teams bond or connect and learn to rely on one another. One of the important tasks managers have is building effective teams.[62] These types of team-building exercises can be an important part of that process. And team-building efforts can work. For example, a research project that looked at star performers with poor team skills who went through two cycles of team-building exercises found that those individuals learned how to collaborate better.[63]

With the emphasis on teams in today's organizations, managers need to recognize that people don't automatically know how to be part of a team or to be an effective team member. Like any behavior, sometimes you have to learn about the skill and then keep practicing and reinforcing it. In building team skills, managers must view their role as more of being a coach and developing team members in order to create more committed, collaborative, and inclusive teams.[64] It's important to recognize that not everyone is a team player or can learn to be a team player. If attempts at team building aren't working, then maybe it's better to put those people in positions where their work is done individually.

Understanding Social Networks

We can't leave this chapter on managing teams without looking at the patterns of informal connections among individuals within groups—that is, at the **social network structure**.[65] What actually happens *within* groups? How *do* group members relate to each other and how does work get done?

Managers need to understand the social networks and social relationships of work groups. Why? Because a group's informal social relationships can help or hinder its effectiveness. For instance, research on social networks has shown that when people need help getting a job done, they'll choose a friendly colleague over someone who may be more capable.[66] Another recent review of team studies showed that teams with high levels of interpersonal interconnectedness actually attained their goals better and were more committed to staying together.[67] Organizations are recognizing the practical benefits of knowing the social networks within teams. For instance, when Ken Loughridge, an IT manager with MWH Global, was transferred from Cheshire, England, to New Zealand, he had a "map" of the informal relationships and connections among company IT employees. This map had been created a few months before using the results of a survey that asked employees who they "consulted most frequently, who they turned to for expertise, and who either boosted or drained their energy levels." Not only did this map help him identify well-connected technical experts, it helped him minimize potential problems when a key manager in the Asia region left the company because Loughridge knew who this person's closest contacts were. Loughridge said, "It's as if you took the top off an ant hill and could see where there's a hive of activity. It really helped me understand who the players were."[68]

CHAPTER

PREPARING FOR: Exams/Quizzes

CHAPTER SUMMARY by Learning Outcomes

14.1 [LEARNING OUTCOME]

Define groups and the stages of group development.

A group is two or more interacting and interdependent individuals who come together to achieve specific goals. Formal groups are work groups defined by the organization's structure and have designated work assignments and specific tasks directed at accomplishing organizational goals. Informal groups are social groups.

The forming stage consists of two phases: joining the group and defining the group's purpose, structure, and leadership. The storming stage is one of intragroup conflict over who will control the group and what the group will be doing. The norming stage is when close relationships and cohesiveness develop as norms are determined. The performing stage is when group members began to work on the group's task. The adjourning stage is when the group prepares to disband.

14.2 [LEARNING OUTCOME]

Describe the major components that determine group performance and satisfaction.

The major components that determine group performance and satisfaction include external conditions, group member resources, group structure, group processes, and group tasks.

External conditions, such as availability of resources, organizational goals, and other factors, affect work groups. Group member resources (knowledge, skills, abilities, personality traits) can influence what members can do and how effectively they will perform in a group.

Group roles generally involve getting the work done or keeping group members happy. Group norms are powerful influences on a person's performance and dictate things such as work output levels, absenteeism, and promptness. Pressures to conform can heavily influence a person's judgment and attitudes. If carried to extremes, groupthink can be a problem. Status systems can be a significant motivator with individual behavioral consequences, especially if incongruence is a factor. What size group is most effective and efficient depends on the task the group is supposed to accomplish. Cohesiveness is related to a group's productivity.

Group decision making and conflict management are important group processes that play a role in performance and satisfaction. If accuracy, creativity, and degree of acceptance are important, a group decision may work best. Relationship conflicts are almost always dysfunctional. Low levels of process conflicts and low-to-moderate levels of task conflicts are functional. Effective communication and controlled conflict are most relevant to group performance when tasks are complex and interdependent.

14.3 [LEARNING OUTCOME]

Define teams and best practices influencing team performance.

Characteristics of work groups include a strong, clearly focused leader; individual accountability; purpose that's the same as the broader organizational mission; individual work product; efficient meetings; effectiveness measured by influence on others; and discusses, decides, and delegates together. Characteristics of teams include shared leadership roles; individual and mutual accountability;

specific team purpose; collective work products; meetings with open-ended discussion and active problem solving; performance measured directly on collective work products; and discusses, decides, and does real work.

A problem-solving team is one that's focused on improving work activities or solving specific problems. A self-managed work team is responsible for a complete work process or segment and manages itself. A cross-functional team is composed of individuals from various specialties. A virtual team uses technology to link physically dispersed members in order to achieve a common goal.

The characteristics of an effective team include clear goals, relevant skills, mutual trust, unified commitment, good communication, negotiating skills, appropriate leadership, and internal and external support.

14.4 [LEARNING OUTCOME]

Discuss contemporary issues in managing teams.

The challenges of managing global teams can be seen in the group member resources, especially the diverse cultural characteristics; group structure, especially conformity, status, social loafing, and cohesiveness; group processes, especially with communication and managing conflict; and the manager's role in making it all work.

With the emphasis on teams in today's organizations, managers need to recognize that people don't automatically know how to be part of a team or to be an effective team member. Like any behavior, team members have to learn about the skill and then keep practicing and reinforcing it. In building team skills, managers must view their role as more of being a coach and developing others to create more committed, collaborative, and inclusive teams.

Managers need to understand the patterns of informal connections among individuals within groups because those informal social relationships can help or hinder the group's effectiveness.

REVIEW AND DISCUSSION QUESTIONS ✪

1. Describe the different types of groups and the five stages of group development.

2. Explain how external conditions and group member resources affect group performance and satisfaction.

3. Discuss how group structure, group processes, and group tasks influence group performance and satisfaction.

4. Compare groups and teams.

5. Describe the four most common types of teams.

6. List the characteristics of effective teams.

7. Explain the role of informal (social) networks in managing teams.

8. How do you think scientific management theorists would react to the increased reliance on teams in organizations? How would behavioral science theorists react?

PREPARING FOR: My Career

ETHICS DILEMMA ✪

When coworkers work closely on a team project, is there such a thing as TMI (too much information)?[69] At one company, a team that had just finished a major project went out to lunch to celebrate. During lunch, one colleague mentioned that he was training for a 20-mile bike race. In addition to a discussion of his new helmet and Lycra shorts, the person also described shaving his whole body to reduce aerodynamic drag. Later, another team member said, "Why, why, why do we need to go there? This is information about a coworker, not someone I really consider a friend, and now it's forever burned in my brain." What do you think? Why are work colleagues sharing increasingly personal information? How have social media and technology contributed to this type of information disclosure? What are the ethical implications of sharing such personal information in the workplace?

SKILLS EXERCISE Developing Your Coaching Skills

About the Skill

Effective managers are increasingly being described as coaches rather than bosses. Just like coaches, they're expected to provide instruction, guidance, advice, and encouragement to help team members improve their job performance.

Steps in Practicing the Skill

1. *Analyze ways to improve the team's performance and capabilities.* A coach looks for opportunities for team members to expand their capabilities and improve performance. How? You can use the following behaviors. Observe your team members' behaviors on a day-to-day basis. Ask questions of them: Why do you do a task this way? Can it be improved? What other approaches might be used? Show genuine interest in team members as individuals, not merely as employees. Respect them individually. Listen to each employee.

2. *Create a supportive climate.* It's the coach's responsibility to reduce barriers to development and to facilitate a climate that encourages personal performance improvement. How? You can use the following behaviors. Create a climate that contributes to a free and open exchange of ideas. Offer help and assistance. Give guidance and advice when asked. Encourage your team. Be positive and upbeat. Don't use threats. Ask, "What did we learn from this that can help us in the future?" Reduce obstacles. Assure team members that you value their contribution to the team's goals. Take personal responsibility for the outcome, but don't rob team members of their full responsibility. Validate team members' efforts when they succeed.

Point to what was missing when they fail. Never blame team members for poor results.

3. *Influence team members to change their behavior.* The ultimate test of coaching effectiveness is whether an employee's performance improves. You must encourage ongoing growth and development. How can you do this? Try the following behaviors. Recognize and reward small improvements and treat coaching as a way of helping employees to continually work toward improvement. Use a collaborative style by allowing team members to participate in identifying and choosing among improvement ideas. Break difficult tasks down into simpler ones. Model the qualities you expect from your team. If you want openness, dedication, commitment, and responsibility from your team members, demonstrate these qualities yourself.

Practicing the Skill

Collaborative efforts are more successful when every member of the group or team contributes a specific role or task toward the completion of the goal. To improve your skill at nurturing team effort, choose two of the following activities and break each one into at least six to eight separate tasks or steps. Be sure to indicate which steps are sequential, and which can be done simultaneously with others. What do you think is the ideal team size for each activity you choose?

a. Making an omelet
b. Washing the car
c. Creating a computerized mailing list
d. Designing an advertising poster
e. Planning a ski trip
f. Restocking a supermarket's produce department

WORKING TOGETHER Team Exercise

Derek Yach, senior vice president for global health policy at PepsiCo, is assembling a team of "idealistic scientists to find alternatives to Doritos."[70] These physicians and researchers with doctorate degrees, many of whom have built their reputations at places like the Mayo Clinic, the World Health Organization, and like-minded organizations, are tasked with creating healthier options by "making the bad stuff less bad." Suppose you were put in charge of this elite team. How would you lead it?

Form small groups of three to four individuals. Your team's task is to come up with some suggestions for leading this team. (Hint: Look at Exhibit 14-10.) Come up with a bulleted list of your ideas. Be prepared to share your ideas with the class.

MY TURN TO BE A MANAGER

• Think of a group to which you belong (or have belonged). Trace its development through the stages of group development as shown in Exhibit 14-2. How closely did its development parallel the group development model? How

might the group development model be used to improve this group's effectiveness?

• Using this same group, write a report describing the following things about this group: types of roles played by whom, group norms, group conformity issues, status system, size of group and how effective/efficient it is, and group cohesiveness.

- Using the same group, describe how decisions are made. Is the process effective? Efficient? Describe what types of conflicts seem to arise most often (relationship, process, or task) and how those conflicts are handled. Add this information to your report on the group's development and structure.

- What traits do you think good team players have? Do some research to answer this question and write up a report detailing your findings using a bulleted list format.

- Select two of the characteristics of effective teams listed in Exhibit 14-10 and develop a team-building exercise for each characteristic that will help a group improve that characteristic. Be creative. Write a report describing your exercises, and be sure to explain how your exercise will help a group improve or develop that characteristic.

- When working in a group (any group to which you're assigned or to which you belong), pay careful attention to what happens in the group as tasks are completed. How does the group's structure or its processes affect how successful the group is at completing its task?

- Steve's and Mary's suggested readings: Tom Rath, *Vital Friends* (Gallup Press, 2006); Jon R. Katzenbach and Douglas K. Smith, *The Wisdom of Teams: Creating the High Performance Organization* (McGraw-Hill, 2005); Patrick Lencioni, *Overcoming the 5 Dysfunctions of a Team* (Jossey-Bass, 2005); Ben Mezrich, *Bringing Down the House: The Inside Story of Six MIT Students Who Took Vegas for Millions* (Free Press, 2002); Jon R. Katzenbach and Douglas K. Smith, *The Discipline of Teams* (Wiley, 2001); and Jean Lipman-Blumen and Harold J. Leavitt, *Hot Groups* (Oxford, 1999).

- Research brainstorming and write a report to your professor explaining what it is and listing suggestions for making it an effective group decision-making tool.

- In your own words, write down three things you learned in this chapter about being a good manager.

- Self-knowledge can be a powerful learning tool. Go to mymanagementlab.com and complete these self-assessment exercises: What's My Attitude Toward Working in Groups? Do I Trust Others? Do Others See Me As Trusting? How Good Am I at Building and Leading a Team? What's My Preferred Conflict-Handing Style? Using the results of your assessments, identify personal strengths and weaknesses. What will you do to reinforce your strengths and improve your weaknesses?

MyManagementLab

Go to **mymanagementlab.com** for Auto-graded writing questions as well as the following Assisted-graded writing questions:

14-1. What challenges do managers face in managing global teams? How should those challenges be handled?

14-2. Why might a manager want to stimulate conflict in a group or team? How could conflict be stimulated?

14-3. Mymanagementlab Only – comprehensive writing assignment for this chapter.

A lot of people around the world love to travel. How about you? Have you visited other countries, or do you hope to visit other countries some day? For those who do travel outside their home country, travel advice guides can be quite valuable. Lonely Planet, an Australian company, has set the benchmark for providing accurate, up-to-date travel guides that have accompanied millions of travelers on their journeys worldwide.[71]

Lonely Planet was started by husband-and-wife team Tony and Maureen Wheeler who in 1971, after Tony finished graduate school in London, decided to embark on an adventurous trip before settling into "real" jobs. They drove through Europe armed with a few maps and sold their car in Afghanistan. From there, they continued their journey using local buses, trains, and boats or by hitchhiking whenever they needed to keep within their daily budget of $6 AUD. Their nine-month journey took them

By developing an effective team of professional writers, cartographers, designers, image researchers, and other independent contractors, Tony and Maureen Wheeler, founders of Lonely Planet Publications, grew their company from a simple, self-published guidebook to the world's largest publisher of travel guidebooks.
Source: AP Photo/Chiang Ying-ying

through Pakistan, Kashmir, India, Nepal, Thailand, Malaysia, and Indonesia on their way to their ultimate destination, Australia. The story is they arrived in Sydney on Boxing Day 1971 and had 27 cents left between them. Their plan was to find jobs in Sydney until they had earned enough for plane tickets back to London. However, they found that a lot of people were interested in hearing about their travel experiences. Urged on by friends, they started working on a travel guide title *Across Asia on the Cheap*. Within a week of the 96-page book's completion and placement in a Sydney bookstore, they had sold 1,500 copies, and the publishing company Lonely Planet was born. They financed their second trip through Asia with profits from the first book and published their second guidebook, *South-East Asia on a Shoestring*. A succession of basic travel guides written by Tony and Maureen produced enough income to cover their own traveling and publishing expenses, but just enough to break even. Their decision to produce a 700-page guidebook to India almost overwhelmed them, but that guidebook was an immediate success, giving Lonely Planet financial stability for the future. Finally, they could afford to hire editors, cartographers, and writers, all of whom worked on a contract basis on individual team projects.

So, how does Lonely Planet produce a product like a guidebook? It's all about teamwork. Commissioning editors (CEs) have a specific geographic area for which they're responsible for commissioning authors of regional content for Lonely Planet's digital and print travel products. CEs research a destination thoroughly to see what travelers are looking for—what's hot and what's not. CEs also get input from specialists and regional experts. Based on this information, the CEs write an author brief. Then, they commission freelance authors who do a lot of pre-trip research before packing their bags. Armed with author briefs, an empty notebook, and a laptop, an author goes on the road doing all the diligent groundwork on location. After concluding their research, the writing of the manuscript begins, which must be completed by a deadline. Once a manuscript is done, it's worked on by CEs and editors at Lonely Planet headquarters to ensure it meets the company's standards of style and quality. Cartographers create new maps from the author's material. The layout designers work with the editors to bring the text, maps, and images together. The design team and image researchers create the cover and photo sections. A proofreader makes sure there are no typographical or layout errors. The book is then sent to a printer, where it's printed, bound, and shipped to bookstores for sale.

From its first simple self-published guidebook, Lonely Planet Publications has grown to become the world's largest independent guidebook publisher. Tony and Maureen realized the business needed a partner that had the necessary resources for future growth, especially in the digital side of the business. BBC Worldwide acquired a 75 percent share in October 2007. In 2011, BBC acquired the remaining 25 percent share of Lonely Planet Publishing.

DISCUSSION QUESTIONS ✪

1. What challenges would there be to creating an effective team in an organization staffed by independent contractors? How could managers deal with these challenges?

2. Why do you think teamwork is crucial to Lonely Planet's business model?

3. Using Exhibit 14-10, what characteristics of effective teams would be most important to Lonely Planet's guidebook teams? Explain your choices.

CASE APPLICATION 2 · 737 Teaming Up for Take Off

Management team members of Boeing's 737 jet airplanes applauded the company's employee innovation teams during a celebration honoring them for devising ways to improve their work processes. These improvements resulted in increased production to meet customers' demands for new planes needed to replace their aging jet fleets.
Source: AP Photo/Stephen Brashear

The Boeing 737, a short- to medium-range twin-engine, narrow-body jet, first rolled off the assembly line in 1967.[72] Here, almost half a century later, it's the best-selling jet airliner in the history of aviation. The 737 is Boeing's only narrow-body airliner in production, with the -600, -700, -800, and -900ER series currently being built. The re-engined and redesigned 737MAX is set for debut in 2017. As airlines replace their aging jet fleets, the burden is on Boeing to ramp up production to meet demand and to do so efficiently. As Boeing managers state, "How do you produce more aircraft without expanding the building?" Managing production of the multimillion dollar product—a 737-800 is sold for $84.4 million—means "walking an increasingly fine line between generating cash and stoking an airplane glut." And Boeing is relying on its employee innovation teams to meet the challenge.

Boeing has been using employee-generated ideas since the 1990s when its manufacturing facility in Renton, Washington, began adopting "lean" manufacturing techniques. Today, employee teams are leaving "few stones unturned." For instance, a member of one team thought of a solution to a problem of stray metal fasteners sometimes puncturing the tires as the airplane advanced down the assembly line. The solution? A canvas wheel cover that hugs the four main landing-gear tires. Another team figured out how to rearrange its work space to make four engines at a time instead of three. Another team of workers in the paint process revamped their work routines and cut 10 minutes to 15 minutes per worker off each job. It took five years for another employee team to perfect a process for installing the plane's landing gear hydraulic tubes, but it eventually paid off.

These employee teams are made up of seven to ten workers with "varying backgrounds"—from mechanics to assembly workers to engineers—and tend to focus on a specific part of a jet, such as the landing gear or the passenger seats or the galleys. These teams may meet as often as once a week. What's the track record of these teams? Today, it takes about 11 days for the final assembly of a 737 jet. That's down from 22 days about a decade ago. The near-term goal is to "whittle that number down to nine days."

DISCUSSION QUESTIONS ✪

1. What type of team(s) do these employee teams appear to be? Explain.

2. As this story illustrated, sometimes it may take a long time for a team to reach its goal. As a manager, how would you motivate a team to keep on trying?

3. What role do you think a team leader needs to play in this type of setting? Explain.

4. Using Exhibit 14-10, what characteristics of effective teams would these teams need? Explain.

PART 5 Management Practice

A Manager's Dilemma

Management theory suggests that compared to an individual, a diverse group of people will be more creative because team members will bring a variety of ideas, perspectives, and approaches to the group. For an organization like Google, innovation is critical to its success, and teams are a way of life. If management theory about teams is on target, then Google's research and development center in India should excel at innovation. Why? Because there you'll find broad diversity, even though all employees are from India. These Googlers include Indians, Sikhs, Hindus, Muslims, Buddhists, Christians, and Jains. And they speak English, Hindi, Tamil, Bengali, and more of India's 22 officially recognized languages. One skill Google looks for in potential hires is the ability to work as a team member. As Google continues to grow at a rapid pace, new Googlers are continually added to teams.

> Suppose you're a manager at Google's Hyderabad facility. How would you gauge a potential hire's ability to work as a team member, and how would you maintain your team's innovation when new engineers and designers join the group?

Global Sense

Workforce productivity. It's a performance measure that's important to managers and policy makers around the globe. Governments want their labor forces to be productive. Managers want their employees to be productive. Being productive encompasses both efficiency and effectiveness. Think back to our discussion of efficiency and effectiveness in Chapter 1. Efficiency was getting the most output from the least amount of inputs or resources. Or said another way, doing things the right way. Effectiveness was doing those work activities that would result in achieving goals, or doing the right things that would lead to goal achievement. So how does workforce productivity stack up around the world? Here are some of the most recent data on productivity growth rates from the Organization for Economic Cooperation and Development (OECD): Australia, 0.7 percent; Belgium, –1.2 percent; Canada, 0.7 percent; Estonia, –1.7 percent; Greece, –0.9 percent; Ireland, 2.4 percent; Korea, 1.8 percent; Poland, 3.4 percent; Turkey, 2.4 percent; United Kingdom, 1.9 percent; and United States, 0.2 percent. One factor that has had a significant effect on workforce productivity rates is the ongoing global economic recession. Productivity seems to have spiked through the early part of the downturn, but as the slowdown dragged on, productivity rates, for many countries, including the United States, fell. Labor economists suggest that perhaps companies are approaching the limits of how much they can squeeze from the workforce.

Discuss the following questions in light of what you learned in Part 5:

- *How might workforce productivity be affected by organizational design? Look at the six key elements of organizational design.*
- *What types of adaptive organizational design might be conducive to increasing worker productivity? Which might be detrimental to worker productivity?*
- *How might an organization's human resource management approach affect worker productivity? How could managers use their HR processes to improve worker productivity?*
- *This question is designed to make you think! Are teams more productive than individuals? Discuss and explain.*
- *What's your reaction to the statement by experts that perhaps companies are approaching the limits of how much they can squeeze from the workforce? What are the implications for managers as they make organizing decisions?*

Sources: C. Dougherty, "Workforce Productivity Falls," Wall Street Journal, *May 4, 2012, p. A5; "Labour Productivity Growth in the Total Economy," Organization for Economic Cooperation and Development, http://stats.oecd.org/Index.aspx?DatasetCode=PDYGTH, February 2012; and "International Comparisons of Manufacturing Productivity and Unit Labor Cost Trends, 2010," Bureau of Labor Statistics, U.S. Department of Labor, [www.bls.gov], December 1, 2011.*

Continuing Case

Starbucks—Organizing

Organizing is an important task of managers. Once the organization's goals and plans are in place, the organizing function sets in motion the process of seeing that those goals and plans are pursued. When managers organize, they're defining what work needs to get done and creating a structure that enables work activities to be completed efficiently and effectively by organizational members hired to do that work. As Starbucks continues its global expansion and pursues innovative strategic initiatives, managers must deal with the realities of continually organizing and reorganizing its work efforts.

Structuring Starbucks

Like many start-up businesses, Starbucks' original founders organized their company around a simple structure based on each person's unique strengths: Zev Siegl became the retail expert; Jerry Baldwin took over the administrative

Michelle Gass, president of Starbucks Europe, Middle East, and Africa, is a senior corporate officer who, as a former Procter & Gamble employee, had experience working at a $10 billion company. Reporting directly to Schultz, Gass provides leadership to Starbucks company-operated markets in the United Kingdom, France, and Germany and is responsible for developing joint ventures and licensed operations in Europe, Russia, and the Middle East. *Source: REUTERS/Robert Sorbo*

functions; and Gordon Bowker was the dreamer who called himself "the magic, mystery, and romance man" and recognized from the start that a visit to Starbucks could "evoke a brief escape to a distant world." As Starbucks grew to the point where Jerry recognized that he needed to hire professional and experienced managers, Howard Schultz (now Starbucks' chairman, CEO, and president) joined the company, bringing his skills in sales, marketing, and merchandising. When the original owners eventually sold the company to Schultz, he was able to take the company on the path to becoming what it is today and what it hopes to be in the future.

As Starbucks has expanded, its organizational structure has changed to accommodate that growth. However, the company prides itself on its "lean" corporate structure. Howard Schultz is at the top of the structure and has focused on hiring a team of executives from companies like Nestlé, Procter & Gamble, Corbis, Microsoft, and PepsiCo. He says, "I wanted to bring in people who had experience working at $10 billion companies." These senior corporate officers include the following: four presidents (Starbucks Americas, Starbucks Coffee China and Asia Pacific, Starbucks Europe, Middle East and Africa, and Channel Development and Emerging Brands); four chief officers (chief financial officer/chief administrative officer, chief creative officer, chief digital officer, and chief information officer); four executive vice presidents (general counsel and secretary, global supply chain operations, partner resources, and public affairs); and two senior vice presidents (global coffee and global strategy). A full description of the team of Starbucks executives and what each is responsible for can be found on the company's Web site.

Although the executive team provides the all-important strategic direction, the "real" work of Starbucks gets done at the company's support center, zone offices, retail stores, and roasting plants. The support center provides support to and assists all other aspects of corporate operations in the areas of accounting, finance, information technology, and sales and supply chain management.

The zone offices oversee the regional operations of the retail stores and provide support in human resource management, facilities management, account management, financial management, and sales management. The essential link between the zone offices and each retail store is the district manager, each of whom oversees 8 to 10 stores, down from the dozen or so stores they used to oversee. Since district managers need to be out working with the stores, most use mobile technology that allows them to spend more time in the stores and still remain connected to their own office. These district managers have been called "the most important in the company" because it's out in the stores that the Starbucks vision and goals are being carried out. Thus, keeping those district managers connected is vital.

In the retail stores, hourly employees (baristas) service customers under the direction of shift supervisors, assistant store managers, and store managers. These managers are responsible for the day-to-day operations of each Starbucks location. One of the organizational challenges for many store managers has been the company's decision to add more drive-through windows to retail stores, which appears to be a smart strategic move since the average annual volume at a store with a drive-through window is about 30 percent higher than a store without one. However, a drive-through window often takes up to 4 people to operate: one to take orders, one to operate the cash register, one to work the espresso machine, and a "floater" who can fill in where needed. And these people have to work rapidly and carefully to get the cars in and out in a timely manner, since the drive-through lane can get congested quickly. Other organizing challenges arise any time the company introduces new products and new, more efficient work approaches.

Finally, without coffee and other beverages to sell, there would be no Starbucks. The coffee beans are processed at the company's domestic roasting plants in Washington, Pennsylvania, Nevada, South Carolina, Georgia, and internationally in Amsterdam. There's also a manufacturing plant for Tazo Tea in Oregon, and the company recently reached an agreement with Tata Global Beverages to set up a coffee roasting facility in India. At each manufacturing facility, the production team produces the coffee and other products and the distribution team manages the inventory and distribution of products and equipment to company stores. Because product quality is so essential to Starbucks' success, each person in the manufacturing facilities must be focused on maintaining quality control at every step in the process. The roasting plant in Sandy Run, South Carolina, is a state-of-the art facility that's also an example of the company's commitment to green design. The plant has been awarded LEED® Silver certification for new construction. And the newest plant in Augusta, Georgia, will also be built to LEED® standards.

People Management at Starbucks

Starbucks recognizes that what it's been able to accomplish is due to the people it hires. When you have talented and committed people offering their ideas and expertise, success will follow.

Since the beginning, Starbucks has strived to be an employer that nurtured employees and gave them opportunities to grow and be challenged. The company says it is "pro-partner" and has always been committed to providing a flexible and progressive work environment and treating one another with respect and dignity.

As Starbucks continues its expansion both in the United States and internationally, it needs to make sure it has the right number of the right people in the right place at the right time. What kinds of people are "right" for Starbucks? They state they want "people who are adaptable, self-motivated, passionate, creative team players." Starbucks uses a variety of methods to attract potential partners. The company has an interactive and easy-to-use online career center. Job seekers—who must be at least 16—can search and apply online for jobs in the home office (Seattle) support center and in the zone offices, roasting plants, store management, and store hourly (barista) positions in any geographic location. Starbucks also has recruiting events in various locations in the United States throughout the year, which allow job seekers to talk to recruiters and partners face-to-face about working at Starbucks. In addition, job seekers for part-time and full-time hourly positions can also submit an application at any Starbucks store location. The company also has a limited number of internship opportunities for students during the summer.

Starbucks' workplace policies provide for equal employment opportunities and strictly prohibit discrimination. Diversity and inclusion are very important to Starbucks as the following statistics from its U.S. workforce illustrate: 65 percent of its total workforce are women and 32 percent of its total workforce are people of color. That commitment to diversity starts at the top. At one point, senior executives participated in a 360-degree diversity assessment to identify their strengths and needed areas of improvement. Also, an executive diversity learning series, including a full-day diversity immersion exercise, was developed for individuals at the vice-president level and above to build their diversity competencies.

Although diversity training is important to Starbucks, it isn't the only training provided. The company continually invests in training programs and career development initiatives: baristas, who get a "green apron book" that exhorts them to be genuine and considerate, receive 23 hours of initial training; an additional 29 hours of training as shift supervisor; 112 hours as assistant store manager; and 320 hours as store manager. District manager trainees receive 200 hours of training. And every partner takes a class on coffee education, which focuses on Starbucks' passion for coffee and understanding the core product. In addition, the Starbucks corporate support center offers a variety of classes ranging from basic computer skills to conflict resolution to management training. Starbucks' partners aren't "stuck" in their jobs. The company's rapid growth creates tremendous opportunities for promotion and advancement for all store partners. If they desire, they can utilize career counseling, executive coaching, job rotation, mentoring, and leadership development to help them create a career path that meets their needs. One example of the company's training efforts: When oxygen levels in coffee bags were too high in one of the company's roasting plants (which affected product freshness), partners were retrained on procedures and given additional coaching. After the training, the number of bags of coffee placed on "quality hold" declined by 99 percent. Then, on one day in February 2008, Starbucks did something quite unusual—it closed all its U.S. stores for three-and-a-half hours to train and retrain baristas on espresso. A company spokesperson said, "We felt this training was an investment in our baristas and in the Starbucks' experience." The training, dubbed Perfecting the Art of Espresso, was about focusing on the core product, espresso, as well as on the customer experience. Feedback was quite positive. Customers said they appreciated the company taking the time to do the training and felt it had resulted in a better customer experience. The company also embarked on a series of training for partners to find ways to do work more efficiently. A 10-person "lean team" went from region to region encouraging managers and partners to find ways to be more efficient.

One human resource issue that has haunted Starbucks is its position on labor unions. The company takes the position that the fair and respectful "direct employment relationship" it has with its partners— not a third party that acts on behalf of the partners—is the best way to help ensure a great work environment. Starbucks prides itself on how it treats its employees. However, the company did settle a complaint issued by the National Labor Relations Board that contained more than two dozen unfair labor practice allegations brought against the company by the union, Industrial Workers of the World. This settlement arose from disputes at three stores in New York City. Then, in 2011, a strike by partners in Chile—which is the only country where the company has a sizable union presence—over low wages led baristas in other countries to call for a "global week of solidarity" in support of the strikers. The Chilean workers eventually abandoned that strike without reaching an agreement with the company. As Starbucks continues to expand globally, it will face challenges in new markets where local labor groups and government requirements honor collective bargaining. And Starbucks realizes it needs to be cautious so that its "we care" image isn't diminished by labor woes.

Discussion Questions

1. What types of departmentalization are being used? Explain your choices. (Hint: In addition to information in the case, you might want to look at the

complete list and description of corporate executives on the company's Web site.)

2. Do you think it's a good idea to have a president for the U.S. division and for the other international divisions? What are the advantages of such an arrangement? Disadvantages?

3. What examples of the six organizational structural elements do you see discussed in the case? Describe.

4. Considering the expense associated with having more managers, what are some reasons why you think Starbucks decided to decrease the number of stores each district manager was responsible for, thus increasing the number of managers needed? Other than the expense, can you think of any disadvantages to this decision?

5. Why do you think it was important for Starbucks to keep its mobile workforce "connected?" In addition to the technology used to do this, what other things might the company do to make its adaptive organizational design efficient and effective?

6. Starbucks has said its goal is to open 1,200 new stores globally. In addition, the company has set a financial goal of attaining total net revenue growth of 10 to 13 percent and earnings per share growth between 15 to 20 percent. How will the organizing function contribute to the accomplishment of these goals?

7. Starbucks has said that it wants people who are "adaptable, self-motivated, passionate, and creative team players." How does the company ensure that its hiring and selection process identifies those kinds of people?

8. Select one of the job openings posted on the company's Web site. Do you think the job description and job specification for this job are adequate? Why or why not? What changes might you suggest?

9. Evaluate Starbucks' training efforts. What types of training are available? What other type(s) of training might be necessary? Explain your choices.

10. Pretend that you're a local Starbucks' store manager. You have three new hourly partners (baristas) joining your team. Describe the orientation you would provide these new hires.

11. Which of the company's principles affect the organizing function of management? Explain how

the one(s) you chose would affect how Starbucks' managers deal with (a) structural issues; (b) HRM issues; and (c) issues in managing teams. (Hint: The principles can be found on the company's Web site.)

Notes for the Part 5 Continuing Case

Reuters, "Chile Fines, Blacklists Starbucks, Wal-Mart Over Labor Practices," www.reuters.com, August 9, 2012; R. Ahmed, "Tata Setting Up Starbucks Coffee Roasting Facility," online.wsj.com, July 26, 2012; News Release, "Starbucks Spotlights Connection Between Record Performance, Shareholder Value and Company Values at Annual Meeting of Shareholders," news.starbucks.com, March 21, 2012; M. Moskowitz and R. E. Levering, "The 100 Best Companies To Work For," *Fortune,* February 6, 2012, pp. 117+; J. Jargon, "Baristas Put Pressure on Starbucks," *Wall Street Journal,* July 26, 2011, p. B3; "Starbucks Finds Ways to Speed Up," *Training Online,* August 11, 2009; M. Herbst, "Starbucks' Karma Problem," *BusinessWeek,* January 12, 2009, p. 26; "Fresh Cup of Training," *Training Online,* May 1, 2008; "Training 135,000 Employees In One Day—Starbucks Closes Store To Do It," www.thecareerrevolution.com, February 27, 2008; K. Maher and J. Adamy," Do Hot Coffee and 'Wobblies' Go Together?" *Wall Street Journal,* March 21, 2006, pp. B1+; A. Serwer, Interview with Howard Schultz," *Fortune (Europe),* March 20, 2006, pp. 35–36; S. Gray, "Fill 'er Up—With Latte," *Wall Street Journal,* January 6, 2006, pp. A9+; W. Meyers, "Conscience in a Cup of Coffee," *US News & World Report,* October 31, 2005, pp. 48–50; . Sellers, "J. M. Cohn, R. Khurana, and L. Reeves, "Growing Talent as if Your Business Depended It," *Harvard Business Review,* October 2005, pp. 62–70; P. B. Nussbaum, R. Berner, and D. Brady, "Get Creative," *BusinessWeek,* August 1, 2005, pp. 60–68; S. Holmes, "A Bitter Aroma at Starbucks," *BusinessWeek,* June 6, 2005, p. 13; J. Cummings, "Legislative Grind," *Wall Street Journal,* April 12, 2005, pp. A1+; Starbucks: The Next Generation," *Fortune,* April 4, 2005, p. 20; P. Kafka, "Bean Counter," *Forbes,* February 28, 2005, pp. 78–80; A. Lustgarten, "A Hot, Steaming Cup of Customer Awareness," *Fortune,* November 15, 2004, p. 192; and A. Serwer and K. Bonamici, "Hot Starbucks to Go," *Fortune,* January 26, 2004, pp. 60–74.

15 Understanding Individual Behavior

SPOTLIGHT: *Manager at Work*

HCL Technologies is headquartered in the world's largest democracy, so it's quite fitting that the New Delhi-based company is attempting a radical experiment in workplace democracy. As one of the largest companies in India, HCL sells various information technology product services, such as laptop, custom software development, and technology consulting. Luring and keeping top talent is one of the challenges HCL faces. And at its size, it doesn't have the atmosphere of a fun and quirky start-up. CEO Vineet Nayar (see photo next page) is committed to creating a company where the job of company leaders is to enable people to find their own destiny by gravitating to their strengths. One thing Nayar has done is to pioneer a culture in which employees are first. That's the most important and crucial cultural value that he believes will take his company into the future.[1] What has Nayar done to put employees first? Part of the cultural initiative dealt with the organization's structure. HCL inverted its organizational structure and placed more power in the hands of front-line employees, especially those in direct contact with customers and clients. It increased its investment in employee development and improved communication through greater transparency. Employees were encouraged to communicate directly with Nayar. Through a forum called U&I (You and I), Nayar fielded more than a hundred questions from employees every week. "I threw open the door and invited criticism," he said. However, the signature

Source: AP Photo/M. Lakshman

Source: AP Photo/Michel Euler

piece of the company's cultural mission is probably what HCL called "trust pay." In contrast to the industry standard in which the average employee's pay is 30 percent variable, HCL decided to pay higher fixed salaries and reduce the variable component.

One thing Vineet Nayar has done is to pioneer a culture in which employees are first.

And Nayar recently implemented an experiment designed to help pinpoint talent from the workers' perspective in which he gave a group of 100 employees virtual currency units in an online exchange and told them to spend the imaginary currency on the group members they thought brought the most value to the company.

Does the unique "employees first" culture at HCL Technologies attract unique employees? Rajeev Sawhney, HCL's European president would say it does. He says entrepreneurialism is a key value of the HCL culture. "You can still tell an HCL person from a mile off." They exhibit a very high need for achievement and are very persuasive.

MyManagementLab®
★ Improve Your Grade!
Over 10 million students improved their results using the Pearson MyLabs.
Visit **mymanagementlab.com** for simulations, tutorials, and end-of-chapter problems.

LEARNING OUTCOMES

15.1	**Identify** the focus and goals of individual behavior within organizations.
15.2	**Explain** the role that attitudes play in job performance.
15.3	**Describe** different personality theories.
15.4	**Describe** perception and factors that influence it.
15.5	**Discuss** learning theories and their relevance in shaping behavior.
15.6	**Discuss** contemporary issues in organizational behavior.

They're also very energetic and willing to try new and different work approaches.

*Part of that "employee first" philosophy is a no layoff policy, which has been difficult to uphold during the pressures of the economic downturn. Like its competitors, HCL had excess employees and had suspended raises. But HCL kept its promise and didn't lay off any HCLites (Nayar's name for HCL employees). As business has picked up, however, employees began looking at competitors' job offers. Maybe it's time to monitor and track employee satisfaction. **What should Vineet Nayar do now?***

Although most managers will not go as far as Vineet Nayar to promote employee satisfaction, many organizations are concerned with the attitudes of their employees. Like him, most managers want to attract and retain employees with the right attitudes and personality. They want people who show up and work hard, get along with coworkers and customers, have good attitudes, and exhibit good work behaviors in other ways. But as you're probably already aware, people don't always behave like that "ideal" employee. They job hop at the first opportunity or they may post critical comments in blogs. People differ in their behaviors and even the same person can behave one way one day and a completely different way another day. For instance, haven't you seen family members, friends, or coworkers behave in ways that prompted you to wonder: Why did they do that?

15.1 *Identify the focus and goals of individual behavior within organizations.*

behavior
The actions of people

organizational behavior
The study of the actions of people at work

FOCUS and Goals of Organizational Behavior

Managers need good people skills. The material in this and the next three chapters draws heavily on the field of study that's known as *organizational behavior (OB)*. Although it's concerned with the subject of **behavior**—that is, the actions of people—**organizational behavior** is the study of the actions of people at work.

One of the challenges in understanding organizational behavior is that it addresses issues that aren't obvious. Like an iceberg, OB has a small visible dimension and a much larger hidden portion. (See Exhibit 15-1.) What we see when we look at an organization is its visible aspects: strategies, goals, policies and procedures, structure, technology, formal authority relationships, and chain of command. But under the surface are other elements that managers need to understand—elements that also influence how employees behave at work. As we'll show, OB provides managers with

Exhibit 15-1
Organization as Iceberg

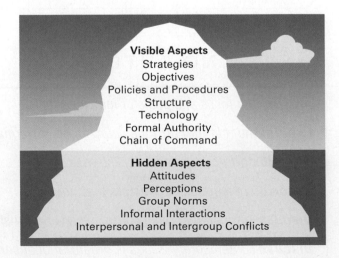

considerable insights into these important, but hidden, aspects of the organization. For instance, Tony Levitan, founder and former CEO of EGreetings (now a part of AG Interactive), found out the hard way about the power of behavioral elements. When he tried to "clean up" the company's online greeting-card site for a potential partnership with a large greeting card company, his employees rebelled. He soon realized that he shouldn't have unilaterally made such a major decision without getting input from his staff, and he reversed the move.[2]

Focus of Organizational Behavior

Organizational behavior focuses on three major areas. First, OB looks at *individual behavior*. Based predominantly on contributions from psychologists, this area includes such topics as attitudes, personality, perception, learning, and motivation. Second, OB is concerned with *group behavior*, which includes norms, roles, team building, leadership, and conflict. Our knowledge about groups comes basically from the work of sociologists and social psychologists. Finally, OB also looks at *organizational* aspects including structure, culture, and human resource policies and practices. We've addressed group and organizational aspects in previous chapters. In this chapter, we'll look at individual behavior.

Goals of Organizational Behavior

The goals of OB are to *explain, predict,* and *influence* behavior. Managers need to be able to *explain* why employees engage in some behaviors rather than others, *predict* how employees will respond to various actions and decisions, and *influence* how employees behave.

What employee behaviors are we specifically concerned with explaining, predicting, and influencing? Six important ones have been identified: employee productivity, absenteeism, turnover, organizational citizenship behavior (OCB), job satisfaction, and workplace misbehavior. **Employee productivity** is a performance measure of both efficiency and effectiveness. Managers want to know what factors will influence the efficiency and effectiveness of employees. **Absenteeism** is the failure to show up for work. It's difficult for work to get done if employees don't show up. Studies have shown that unscheduled absences cost companies around $660 per employee per year and result in the highest net loss of productivity per day.[3] Although absenteeism can't be totally eliminated, excessive levels have a direct and immediate impact on the organization's functioning. **Turnover** is the voluntary and involuntary permanent withdrawal from an organization. It can be a problem because of increased recruiting, selection, and training costs and work disruptions. Just like absenteeism, managers can never eliminate turnover, but it is something they want to minimize, especially among high-performing employees. **Organizational citizenship behavior (OCB)** is discretionary behavior that's not part of an employee's formal job requirements but promotes the effective functioning of the organization.[4] Examples of good OCBs include helping others on one's work team, volunteering for extended job activities, avoiding unnecessary conflicts, and making constructive statements about one's work group and the organization. Organizations need individuals who will do more than their usual job duties, and the evidence indicates that organizations that have such employees outperform those that don't.[5] However, drawbacks of OCB occur when employees experience work overload, stress, and work–family life conflicts.[6] **Job satisfaction** refers to an employee's general attitude toward his or her job. Although job satisfaction is an attitude rather than a behavior, it's an outcome that concerns many managers because satisfied employees are more likely to show up for work, have higher levels of performance, and stay with an organization. **Workplace misbehavior** is any intentional employee behavior that is potentially harmful to the organization or individuals within the organization. Workplace misbehavior shows up in organizations in four ways: deviance, aggression, antisocial behavior, and violence.[7] Such behaviors can range from playing loud music just to

employee productivity
A performance measure of both efficiency and effectiveness

absenteeism
The failure to show up for work

turnover
The voluntary and involuntary permanent withdrawal from an organization

organizational citizenship behavior (OCB)
Discretionary behavior that is not part of an employee's formal job requirements, but which promotes the effective functioning of the organization

job satisfaction
An employee's general attitude toward his or her job

workplace misbehavior
Any intentional employee behavior that is potentially damaging to the organization or to individuals within the organization

irritate coworkers to verbal aggression to sabotaging work, all of which can create havoc in any organization. In the following sections, we'll address how an understanding of four psychological factors—employee attitudes, personality, perception, and learning—can help us predict and explain these employee behaviors.

ATTITUDES and Job Performance

15.2 **Explain** the role that attitudes play in job performance.

Attitudes are evaluative statements—favorable or unfavorable—concerning objects, people, or events. They reflect how an individual feels about something. When a person says, "I like my job," he or she is expressing an attitude about work.

An attitude is made up of three components: cognition, affect, and behavior.[8] The **cognitive component** of an attitude refers to the beliefs, opinions, knowledge, or information held by a person (for instance, the belief that "discrimination is wrong"). The **affective component** of an attitude is the emotional or feeling part of an attitude. Using our example, this component would be reflected by the statement, "I don't like Pat because he discriminates against minorities." Finally, affect can lead to behavioral outcomes. The **behavioral component** of an attitude refers to an intention to behave in a certain way toward someone or something. To continue our example, I might choose to avoid Pat because of my feelings about him. Understanding that attitudes are made up of three components helps show their complexity. But keep in mind that the term *attitude* usually refers only to the affective component.

Naturally, managers aren't interested in every attitude an employee has. They're especially interested in job-related attitudes. The three most widely known are job satisfaction, job involvement, and organizational commitment. Another concept that's generating widespread interest is employee engagement.[9]

attitudes
Evaluative statements, either favorable or unfavorable, concerning objects, people, or events

cognitive component
That part of an attitude that's made up of the beliefs, opinions, knowledge, or information held by a person

affective component
That part of an attitude that's the emotional or feeling part

behavioral component
That part of an attitude that refers to an intention to behave in a certain way toward someone or something

Job Satisfaction

As we know from our earlier definition, job satisfaction refers to a person's general attitude toward his or her job. A person with a high level of job satisfaction has a positive attitude toward his or her job. A person who is dissatisfied has a negative attitude. When people speak of employee attitudes, they usually are referring to job satisfaction.

HOW SATISFIED ARE EMPLOYEES? Studies of U.S. workers over the past 30 years generally indicated that the majority of workers were satisfied with their jobs. A Conference Board study in 1995 found that some 60 percent of Americans were satisfied with their jobs.[10] However, since then the number has been declining. By 2010, that percentage was down to its lowest level, 42.6 percent, but rose slightly in 2011 to 47.2 percent.[11] Although job satisfaction tends to increase as income increases, only 58 percent of individuals earning more than $50,000 are satisfied with their jobs. For individuals earning less than $15,000, about 45 percent of workers say they are satisfied with their jobs.[12] Even though it's possible that higher pay translates into higher job satisfaction, an alternative explanation for the difference in satisfaction levels is that higher pay reflects different types of jobs. Higher-paying jobs generally require more advanced skills, give jobholders greater responsibilities, are more stimulating and provide more challenges, and allow workers more control. It's more likely that the reports of higher satisfaction among higher-income levels reflect those factors rather than the pay itself.

What about job satisfaction levels in other countries? Surveys of European workers show regional variations. For instance, only 68 percent of Scandinavian workers, 67 percent of Italian workers, and 53 percent of Swiss workers report being satisfied with their jobs. Other numbers from Europe are somewhat higher: 80 percent of workers in France, 73 percent of German workers, and 72 percent of workers in Great Britain say they're satisfied with their jobs.[13] On the other hand, 60 percent of Canadian workers report being satisfied with their jobs, while 61 percent of Asia-Pacific employees are.[14]

The global recession has likely had an impact on global job satisfaction rates. For instance, a study by a British consulting group found that 67 percent of workers surveyed were putting in unpaid overtime. Also, 63 percent said their employers did not appreciate their extra effort, and 57 percent felt that employees were treated like dispensable commodities.[15]

SATISFACTION AND PRODUCTIVITY After the Hawthorne Studies (discussed in the Management History Module), managers believed that happy workers were productive workers. Because it's not been easy to determine whether job satisfaction caused job productivity or vice versa, some management researchers felt that belief was generally wrong. However, we can say with some certainty that the correlation between satisfaction and productivity is fairly strong.[16] Also, organizations with more satisfied employees tend to be more effective than organizations with fewer satisfied employees.[17]

SATISFACTION AND ABSENTEEISM Although research shows that satisfied employees have lower levels of absenteeism than dissatisfied employees, the correlation isn't strong.[18] It certainly makes sense that dissatisfied employees are more likely to miss work, but other factors affect the relationship. For instance, organizations that provide liberal sick leave benefits are encouraging all their employees—including those who are highly satisfied—to take "sick" days. Assuming your job has some variety in it, you can find work satisfying and yet still take a "sick" day to enjoy a three-day weekend or to golf on a warm spring day if taking such days results in no penalties.

SATISFACTION AND TURNOVER Research on the relationship between satisfaction and turnover is much stronger. Satisfied employees have lower levels of turnover while dissatisfied employees have higher levels of turnover.[19] Yet, things such as labor-market conditions, expectations about alternative job opportunities, and length of employment with the organization also affect an employee's decision to leave.[20] Research suggests that the level of satisfaction is less important in predicting turnover for superior performers because the organization typically does everything it can to keep them—pay raises, praise, increased promotion opportunities, and so forth.[21]

Southwest Airlines understands the connection between satisfied employees and customer satisfaction. The airline's marketing staff employees shown here handing out free tickets during a promotion embody the friendly, fun-loving, upbeat, and helpful behavior that customers appreciate and value. Southwest helps shape a positive on-the-job attitude by giving employees extensive customer-service training and by empowering them to make on-the-spot decisions to meet customer needs and help fellow workers. By treating employees well and giving them a supportive work environment, Southwest encourages all of its employees to deliver the high levels of quality service that satisfy customers.
Source: AP Photo/David Zalubowski

JOB SATISFACTION AND CUSTOMER SATISFACTION Is job satisfaction related to positive customer outcomes? For frontline employees who have regular contact with customers, the answer is "yes." Satisfied employees increase customer satisfaction and loyalty.[22] Why? In service organizations, customer retention and defection are highly dependent on how frontline employees deal with customers. Satisfied employees are more likely to be friendly, upbeat, and responsive, which customers appreciate. And because satisfied employees are less likely to leave their jobs, customers are more likely to encounter familiar faces and receive experienced service. These qualities help build customer satisfaction and loyalty. However, the relationship also seems to work in reverse. Dissatisfied customers can increase an employee's job dissatisfaction. Employees who have regular contact with customers report that rude, thoughtless, or unreasonably demanding customers adversely affect their job satisfaction.[23]

A number of companies appear to understand this connection. Service-oriented businesses, such as L.L. Bean, Southwest Airlines, and Starbucks, obsess about pleasing their customers. They also focus on building employee satisfaction—recognizing that satisfied employees will go a long way toward contributing to their goal of having happy customers. These firms seek to hire upbeat and friendly employees, they train employees in customer service, they reward customer service, they provide positive work climates, and they regularly track employee satisfaction through attitude surveys. For instance, at shoe retailer Zappos (now part of Amazon.com), employees are encouraged to "create fun and a little weirdness" and have been given high levels of discretion to make customers satisfied. Zappos even offers a $2,000 bribe to employees to quit the company after training if they're not happy working there.[24]

JOB SATISFACTION AND OCB   It seems logical to assume that job satisfaction should be a major determinant of an employee's OCB.[25] Satisfied employees would seem more likely to talk positively about the organization, help others, and go above and beyond normal job expectations. Research suggests a modest overall relationship between job satisfaction and OCB.[26] But that relationship is tempered by perceptions of fairness.[27] Basically, if you don't feel as though your supervisor, organizational procedures, or pay policies are fair, your job satisfaction is likely to suffer significantly. However, when you perceive that these things are fair, you have more trust in your employer and are more willing to voluntarily engage in behaviors that go beyond your formal job requirements. Another factor that influences individual OCB is the type of citizenship behavior a person's work group exhibits. In a work group with low group-level OCB, any individual in that group who engaged in OCB had higher job performance ratings. One possible explanation may be that the person was trying to find some way to "stand out" from the crowd.[28] No matter why it happens, the point is that OCB can have positive benefits for organizations.

JOB SATISFACTION AND WORKPLACE MISBEHAVIOR   When employees are dissatisfied with their jobs, they'll respond somehow. The problem comes from the difficulty in predicting *how* they'll respond. One person might quit. Another might respond by using work time to play computer games. And another might verbally abuse a coworker. If managers want to control the undesirable consequences of job dissatisfaction, they'd be better off to attack the problem—job dissatisfaction—than trying to control the different employee responses. Three other job-related attitudes we need to look at include job involvement, organizational commitment, and employee engagement.

Job Involvement and Organizational Commitment

job involvement
The degree to which an employee identifies with his or her job, actively participates in it, and considers his or her job performance to be important to self-worth

Job involvement is the degree to which an employee identifies with his or her job, actively participates in it, and considers his or her job performance to be important to his or her self-worth.[29] Employees with a high level of job involvement strongly identify with and really care about the kind of work they do. Their positive attitude leads them to contribute in positive ways to their work. High levels of job involvement have been found to be related to fewer absences, lower resignation rates, and higher employee engagement with their work.[30]

organizational commitment
The degree to which an employee identifies with a particular organization and its goals and wishes to maintain membership in that organization

Organizational commitment is the degree to which an employee identifies with a particular organization and its goals and wishes to maintain membership in that organization.[31] Whereas job involvement is identifying with your job, organizational commitment is identifying with your employing organization. Research suggests that organizational commitment also leads to lower levels of both absenteeism and turnover and, in fact, is a better indicator of turnover than job satisfaction.[32] Why? Probably because it's a more global and enduring response to the organization than satisfaction with a particular job.[33] However, organizational commitment is less important as a work-related attitude than it once was. Employees don't generally stay with a single organization for most of their career and the relationship they have with their employer has changed considerably.[34] Although the commitment of *an employee to an organization* may not be as important as it once was, research about **perceived organizational support**—employees' general belief that their organization values their contribution and cares about their well-being—shows that the commitment of *the organization to the employee* can be beneficial. High levels of perceived organizational support lead to increased job satisfaction and lower turnover.[35]

perceived organizational support
Employees' general belief that their organization values their contribution and cares about their well-being

Employee Engagement

A low-level trader employed by Société Générale, a giant French bank, loses billions of dollars through dishonest trades and no one reports suspicious behavior. An internal investigation uncovered evidence that many back office employees failed to alert their supervisors about the suspicious trades.[36] Employee indifference can have serious consequences.

Managers want their employees to be connected to, satisfied with, and enthusiastic about their jobs. This concept is known as **employee engagement**.[37] Highly engaged employees are passionate about and deeply connected to their work. Disengaged employees have essentially "checked out" and don't care. They show up for work, but have no energy or passion for it. A global study of more than 12,000 employees found the following factors as contributing to employee engagement: respect, type of work, work-life balance, providing good service to customers, base pay, people you work with, benefits, long-term career potential, learning and development opportunities, flexible work, promotion opportunities, and variable pay/bonuses.[38]

A number of benefits come from having highly engaged employees. First, highly engaged employees are two-and-a-half times more likely to be top performers than their less-engaged coworkers. In addition, companies with highly engaged employees have higher retention rates, which help keep recruiting and training costs low. And both of these outcomes—higher performance and lower costs—contribute to superior financial performance.[39]

Employee engagement is high at St. Jude Children's Research Hospital where employees share a deep commitment to patients and are passionate about their work in the research and treatment of children with cancer and other catastrophic diseases. Embracing the hospital's powerful mission of "finding cures, saving children" and its culture of compassion and collaboration, employees feel their contributions at work are important and meaningful and make a difference in the lives of their young patients. Shown here are costumed employees bringing treats to a patient who couldn't leave his bed during the hospital's Halloween celebration.
Source: PRNewsFoto/St. Jude Children's Research Hospital/AP Photo

employee engagement
When employees are connected to, satisfied with, and enthusiastic about their jobs

Attitudes and Consistency

Have you ever noticed that people change what they say so it doesn't contradict what they do? Perhaps a friend of yours has repeatedly said that she thinks joining a sorority is an important part of college life. But then she goes through rush and doesn't get accepted. All of a sudden, she's saying that sorority life isn't all that great.

Research has generally concluded that people seek consistency among their attitudes *and* between their attitudes and behavior.[40] This tendency means that individuals try to reconcile differing attitudes and align their attitudes and behavior so they appear rational and consistent. When they encounter an inconsistency, individuals will do something to make it consistent by altering the attitudes, altering the behavior, or rationalizing the inconsistency.

For example, a campus recruiter for R&S Information Services who visits college campuses and sells students on the advantages of R&S as a good place to work would experience inconsistency if he personally believed that R&S had poor working conditions and few opportunities for promotion. This recruiter could, over time, find his attitudes toward R&S becoming more positive. He might actually convince himself by continually articulating the merits of working for the company. Another alternative is that the recruiter could become openly negative about R&S and the opportunities within the company for prospective applicants. The original enthusiasm the recruiter might have had would dwindle and might be replaced by outright cynicism toward the company. Finally, the recruiter might acknowledge that R&S is an undesirable place to work, but as a professional, realize that his obligation is to present the positive aspects of working for the company. He might further rationalize that no workplace is perfect and that his job is to present a favorable picture of the company, not to present both sides.

Cognitive Dissonance Theory

Can we assume from this consistency principle that an individual's behavior can always be predicted if we know his or her attitude on a subject? The answer isn't a simple "yes" or "no." Why? Cognitive dissonance theory.

cognitive dissonance
Any incompatibility or inconsistency between attitudes or between behavior and attitudes

Cognitive dissonance theory sought to explain the relationship between attitudes and behavior.[41] **Cognitive dissonance** is any incompatibility or inconsistency between attitudes or between behavior and attitudes. The theory argued that inconsistency is uncomfortable and that individuals will try to reduce the discomfort and thus, the dissonance.

Of course, no one can avoid dissonance. You know you should floss your teeth every day but don't do it. There's an inconsistency between attitude and behavior. How do people cope with cognitive dissonance? The theory proposed that how hard we'll try to reduce dissonance is determined by three things: (1) the *importance* of the factors creating the dissonance, (2) the degree of *influence* the individual believes he or she has over those factors, and (3) the *rewards* that may be involved in dissonance.

If the factors creating the dissonance are relatively unimportant, the pressure to correct the inconsistency will be low. However, if those factors are important, individuals may change their behavior, conclude that the dissonant behavior isn't so important, change their attitude, or identify compatible factors that outweigh the dissonant ones.

How much influence individuals believe they have over the factors also affects their reaction to the dissonance. If they perceive the dissonance is something about which they have no choice, they're won't be receptive to attitude change or feel a need to do so. If, for example, the dissonance-producing behavior was required as a result of a manager's order, the pressure to reduce dissonance would be less than if the behavior had been performed voluntarily. Although dissonance exists, it can be rationalized and justified by the need to follow the manager's orders—that is, the person had no choice or control.

Finally, rewards also influence the degree to which individuals are motivated to reduce dissonance. Coupling high dissonance with high rewards tends to reduce the discomfort by motivating the individual to believe that consistency exists.

Attitude Surveys

attitude surveys
Surveys that elicit responses from employees through questions about how they feel about their jobs, work groups, supervisors, or the organization

Many organizations regularly survey their employees about their attitudes.[42] Exhibit 15-2 shows an example of an actual attitude survey. Typically, **attitude surveys** present the employee with a set of statements or questions eliciting how they feel about their jobs, work groups, supervisors, or the organization. Ideally, the items will be designed to obtain the specific information that managers desire. An attitude score is achieved by summing up responses to individual questionnaire items. These scores can then be averaged for work groups, departments, divisions, or the organization as a whole. For instance, the Tennessee Valley Authority, the largest U.S. government-run energy company, came up with a "Cultural Health Index" to measure employee attitudes. The organization found business units that scored high on the attitude surveys also were the ones whose performance was high. For poorly performing business units, early signs of potential trouble had shown up in the attitude surveys.[43]

Regularly surveying employee attitudes provides managers with valuable feedback on how employees perceive their working conditions. Policies and practices that

Exhibit 15-2

Sample Employee Attitude Survey

Here are some sample statements from an employee attitude survey:

- I have ample opportunities to use my skills/abilities in my job.
- My manager has a good relationship with my work group.
- My organization provides me professional development opportunities.
- I am told if I'm doing good work or not.
- I feel safe in my work environment.
- My organization is a great place to work.

---

managers view as objective and fair may not be seen that way by employees. The use of regular attitude surveys can alert managers to potential problems and employees' intentions early so that action can be taken to prevent repercussions.[44]

Implications for Managers

Managers should be interested in their employees' attitudes because they influence behavior. Satisfied and committed employees, for instance, have lower rates of turnover and absenteeism. If managers want to keep resignations and absences down—especially among their more productive employees—they'll want to do things that generate positive job attitudes.

Satisfied employees also perform better on the job. So managers should focus on those factors that have been shown to be conducive to high levels of employee job satisfaction: making work challenging and interesting, providing equitable rewards, creating supportive working conditions, and encouraging supportive colleagues.[46] These factors are likely to help employees be more productive.

Managers should also survey employees about their attitudes. As one study put it, "A sound measurement of overall job attitude is one of the most useful pieces of information an organization can have about its employees."[47]

Finally, managers should know that employees will try to reduce dissonance. If employees are required to do things that appear inconsistent to them or that are at odds with their attitudes, managers should remember that pressure to reduce the dissonance is not as strong when the employee perceives that the dissonance is externally imposed and uncontrollable. It's also decreased if rewards are significant enough to offset the dissonance. So the manager might point to external forces such as competitors, customers, or other factors when explaining the need to perform some work that the individual may have some dissonance about. Or the manager can provide rewards that an individual desires.

LEADER who made a DIFFERENCE

As one of the top-ranked airlines for customer service, Singapore Airlines (SIA) has a stellar reputation in the fiercely competitive commercial aviation business.[45] Goh Choon Phong was promoted to the company's top leader role in 2011 and continues to emphasize its legendary culture in which employees excel at what they do and enjoy what they do. SIA was ranked number twenty-three on Fortune's The World's Most Admired Companies List in 2012. Passengers appreciate the outstanding customer service provided by the airline's satisfied frontline employees who have earned a reputation as friendly, upbeat, and responsive. In recruiting flight attendants, the company carefully selects people who are warm, hospitable, and happy to serve others. All employees—from bottom to top—are proud to be part of the SIA family. What can you learn from this leader who made a difference?

Source: Bloomberg via Getty Images

PERSONALITY

"Let's face it, dating is a drag. There was a time when we thought the computer was going to make it all better.... But most of us learned the hard way that finding someone who shares our love of film noir and obscure garage bands does not a perfect match make."[48] Using in-depth personality assessment and profiling, Chemistry.com has tried to do something about making the whole dating process better.

Personality. We all have one. Some of us are quiet and passive; others are loud and aggressive. When we describe people using terms such as *quiet, passive, loud, aggressive, ambitious, extroverted, loyal, tense,* or *sociable,* we're describing their personalities. An individual's **personality** is a unique combination of emotional, thought, and behavioral patterns that affect how a person reacts to situations and interacts with others. It's our natural way of doing things and relating to others. Personality is most often described in terms of measurable traits a person exhibits. We're interested in looking at personality because just like attitudes, it too, affects how and why people behave the way they do.

Over the years, researchers have attempted to identify those traits that best describe personality. The two most well-known approaches are: the Myers Briggs Type Indicator® (MBTI) and the Big Five model.

Describe different personality theories. **15.3**

personality
The unique combination of emotional, thought, and behavioral patterns that affect how a person reacts to situations and interacts with others

MBTI®

One popular approach to classifying personality traits is the personality-assessment instrument known as the MBTI®. This 100-question assessment asks people how they usually act or feel in different situations.[49] On the basis of their answers, individuals are classified as exhibiting a preference in four categories: extraversion or introversion (E or I), sensing or intuition (S or N), thinking or feeling (T or F), and judging or perceiving (J or P). These terms are defined as follows:

- *Extraversion (E) versus Introversion (I).* Individuals showing a preference for extraversion are outgoing, social, and assertive. They need a work environment that's varied and action oriented, that lets them be with others, and that gives them a variety of experiences. Individuals showing a preference for introversion are quiet and shy. They focus on understanding and prefer a work environment that is quiet and concentrated, that lets them be alone, and that gives them a chance to explore in depth a limited set of experiences.
- *Sensing (S) versus Intuition (N).* Sensing types are practical and prefer routine and order. They dislike new problems unless there are standard ways to solve them, have a high need for closure, show patience with routine details, and tend to be good at precise work. On the other hand, intuition types rely on unconscious processes and look at the "big picture." They're individuals who like solving new problems, dislike doing the same thing over and over again, jump to conclusions, are impatient with routine details, and dislike taking time for precision.
- *Thinking (T) versus Feeling (F).* Thinking types use reason and logic to handle problems. They're unemotional and uninterested in people's feelings, like analysis and putting things into logical order, are able to reprimand people and fire them when necessary, may seem hard-hearted, and tend to relate well only to other thinking types. Feeling types rely on their personal values and emotions. They're aware of other people and their feelings, like harmony, need occasional praise, dislike telling people unpleasant things, tend to be sympathetic, and relate well to most people.
- *Judging (J) versus Perceiving (P).* Judging types want control and prefer their world to be ordered and structured. They're good planners, decisive, purposeful, and exacting. They focus on completing a task, make decisions quickly, and want only the information necessary to get a task done. Perceiving types are flexible and spontaneous. They're curious, adaptable, and tolerant. They focus on starting a task, postpone decisions, and want to find out all about the task before starting it.

Combining these preferences provides descriptions of 16 personality types, with every person identified with one of the items in each of the four pairs. Exhibit 15-3 summarizes two of them. As you can see from these descriptions, each personality type would approach work and relationships differently—neither one better than the other, just different.

Exhibit 15-3
Examples of MBTI®
Personality Types

Type	Description
I–S–F–P (introversion, sensing, feeling, perceiving)	Sensitive, kind, modest, shy, and quietly friendly. Such people strongly dislike disagreements and will avoid them. They are loyal followers and quite often are relaxed about getting things done.
E–N–T–J (extraversion, intuition, thinking, judging)	Warm, friendly, candid, and decisive; also skilled in anything that requires reasoning and intelligent talk, but may sometimes overestimate what they are capable of doing.

Source: Based on I. Briggs-Myers, *Introduction to Type* (Palo Alto, CA: Consulting Psychologists Press, 1980), pp. 7–8.

More than 2 million people a year take the MBTI® in the United States alone. Some organizations that have used the MBTI® include Apple, AT&T, GE, 3M, hospitals, educational institutions, and even the U.S. Armed Forces. No hard evidence shows that the MBTI® is a valid measure of personality, but that doesn't seem to deter its widespread use.

How could the MBTI® help managers? Proponents believe it's important to know these personality types because they influence the way people interact and solve problems. For instance, if your boss is an intuition type and you're a sensing type, you'll gather information in different ways. An intuitive type prefers gut reactions, whereas a sensor prefers facts. To work well with your boss, you would have to present more than just facts about a situation and bring out how you feel about it. Also, the MBTI® has been used to help managers better match employees to certain types of jobs.

The Big Five Model

In recent years, research has shown that five basic personality dimensions underlie all others and encompass most of the significant variation in human personality.[50] The five personality traits in the **Big Five Model** are:

1. *Extraversion:* The degree to which someone is sociable, talkative, assertive, and comfortable in relationships with others.
2. *Agreeableness:* The degree to which someone is good-natured, cooperative, and trusting.
3. *Conscientiousness:* The degree to which someone is reliable, responsible, dependable, persistent, and achievement oriented.
4. *Emotional stability:* The degree to which someone is calm, enthusiastic, and secure (positive) or tense, nervous, depressed, and insecure (negative).
5. *Openness to experience:* The degree to which someone has a wide range of interests and is imaginative, fascinated with novelty, artistically sensitive, and intellectual.

Big Five Model
Personality trait model that includes extraversion, agreeableness, conscientiousness, emotional stability, and openness to experience

The Big Five Model provides more than just a personality framework. Research has shown that important relationships exist between these personality dimensions and job performance. For example, one study examined five categories of occupations: *professionals* (such as engineers, architects, and attorneys), *police, managers, salespeople,* and *semiskilled and skilled employees.*[51] The results showed that conscientiousness predicted job performance for all five occupational groups. Predictions for the other personality dimensions depended on the situation and on the occupational group. For example, extraversion predicted performance in managerial and sales positions— occupations in which high social interaction is necessary. Openness to experience was found to be important in predicting training competency. Ironically, emotional security wasn't positively related to job performance in any of the occupations. Another study that looked at whether the five-factor model could predict managerial performance found it could if 360-degree performance ratings (that is, performance ratings from supervisors, peers, and subordinates) were used.[52] Other studies have shown that employees who score higher in conscientiousness develop higher levels of job knowledge, probably because highly conscientious people learn more. In fact, a review of 138 studies revealed that conscientiousness was rather strongly related to GPA.[53]

Additional Personality Insights

Although the traits in the Big Five are highly relevant to understanding behavior, they aren't the only personality traits that can describe someone's personality. Five other personality traits are powerful predictors of behavior in organizations.

1. *Locus of Control.* Some people believe they control their own fate. Others see themselves as pawns, believing that what happens to them in their lives is due to luck or chance. The **locus of control** in the first case is *internal*; these people believe they control their own destiny. The locus of control in the second case

locus of control
The degree to which people believe they are masters of their own fate

is *external*; these people believe their lives are controlled by outside forces.[54] Research indicates that employees who are externals are less satisfied with their jobs, more alienated from the work setting, and less involved in their jobs than those who rate high on internality.[55] A manager might also expect externals to blame a poor performance evaluation on their boss's prejudice, their coworkers, or other events outside their control; internals would explain the same evaluation in terms of their own actions.

Machiavellianism
A measure of the degree to which people are pragmatic, maintain emotional distance, and believe that ends justify means

2. *Machiavellianism.* The second characteristic is called **Machiavellianism** (Mach), named after Niccolo Machiavelli, who wrote in the sixteenth century on how to gain and manipulate power. An individual high in Machiavellianism is pragmatic, maintains emotional distance, and believes that ends can justify means.[56] "If it works, use it" is consistent with a high Mach perspective. Do high Machs make good employees? That depends on the type of job and whether you consider ethical factors in evaluating performance. In jobs that require bargaining skills (such as a purchasing manager) or that have substantial rewards for excelling (such as a salesperson working on commission), high Machs are productive.

self-esteem
An individual's degree of like or dislike for himself or herself

3. *Self-Esteem.* People differ in the degree to which they like or dislike themselves, a trait called **self-esteem**.[57] Research on self-esteem (SE) offers some interesting behavioral insights. For example, self-esteem is directly related to expectations for success. High SEs believe they possess the ability they need to succeed at work. Individuals with high SEs will take more risks in job selection and are more likely to choose unconventional jobs than people with low SEs.

The most common finding on self-esteem is that low SEs are more susceptible to external influence than high SEs. Low SEs are dependent on receiving positive evaluations from others. As a result, they're more likely to seek approval from others and are more prone to conform to the beliefs and behaviors of those they respect than high SEs. In managerial positions, low SEs will tend to be concerned with pleasing others and, therefore, will be less likely to take unpopular stands than high SEs. Finally, self-esteem has also been found to be related to job satisfaction. A number of studies confirm that high SEs are more satisfied with their jobs than low SEs.

self-monitoring
A personality trait that measures the ability to adjust behavior to external situational factors

4. *Self-Monitoring.* Have you ever had the experience of meeting someone new and feeling a natural connection and hitting it off right away? At some time or another, we've all had that experience. That natural ability to "click" with other people may play a significant role in determining career success[58] and is another personality trait called **self-monitoring**, which refers to the ability to adjust behavior to external, situational factors.[59] Individuals high in self-monitoring show considerable adaptability in adjusting their behavior. They're highly sensitive to external cues and can behave differently in different situations. High self-monitors are capable of presenting striking contradictions between their public persona and their private selves. Low self-monitors can't adjust their behavior. They tend to display their true dispositions and attitudes in every situation, and there's high behavioral consistency between who they are and what they do.

Research on self-monitoring suggests that high self-monitors pay closer attention to the behavior of others and are more flexible than low self-monitors.[60] In addition, high self-monitoring managers tend to be more mobile in their careers, receive more promotions (both internal and cross-organizational), and are more likely to occupy central positions in an organization.[61] The high self-monitor is capable of putting on different "faces" for different audiences, an important trait for managers who must play multiple, or even contradicting roles.

proactive personality
People who identify opportunities, show initiative, take action, and persevere until meaningful change occurs.

resilience
An individual's ability to overcome challenges and turn them into opportunities

5. *Risk-Taking.* People differ in their willingness to take chances. Differences in the propensity to assume or to avoid risk have been shown to affect how long it takes managers to make a decision and how much information they require before making their choice. For instance, in one study where managers worked on simulated exercises that required them to make hiring decisions, high

risk-taking managers took less time to make decisions and used less information in making their choices than low-risk taking managers.[62] Interestingly, the decision accuracy was the same for the two groups. To maximize organizational effectiveness, managers should try to align employee risk-taking propensity with specific job demands.

OTHER PERSONALITY TRAITS A couple of other personality traits deserve mention. In Chapter 7, we introduced the Type A personality, which describes someone who is continually and aggressively struggling to achieve more and more in less and less time.[64] In the North American culture, the Type A personality is highly valued. Type A individuals subject themselves to continual time pressure and deadlines and have moderate to high levels of stress. They emphasize quantity over quality. On the other hand, a Type B person isn't harried by the desire to achieve more and more. Type Bs don't suffer from a sense of time urgency and are able to relax without guilt.

Another interesting trait that's been studied extensively is the **proactive personality**, which describes people who identify opportunities, show initiative, take action, and persevere until meaningful change occurs. Not surprisingly, research has shown that proactives have many desirable behaviors that organizations want.[65] For instance, they are more likely to be seen as leaders and more likely to act as change agents in organizations; they're more likely to challenge the status quo; they have entrepreneurial abilities; and they're more likely to achieve career success.

Finally, the economic recession has prompted a reexamination of **resilience**, an individual's ability to overcome challenges and turn them into opportunities.[66] A recent study by a global consulting firm showed that it is a key factor in keeping a job: A resilient person is likely to be more adaptable, flexible, and goal-focused. OB researchers also have looked at resilience and other individual characteristics including efficacy, hope, and optimism in a concept called positive psychological capital.[67] These characteristics have been found to be related to higher feelings of well-being and less work stress, which ultimately affect how and why people behave the way they do at work.

Personality Types in Different Cultures

Do personality frameworks, like the Big Five model, transfer across cultures? Are dimensions like locus of control relevant in all cultures? Let's try to answer these questions.

The five personality factors studied in the Big Five model appear in almost all cross-cultural studies.[68] These studies include a wide variety of diverse cultures such as China, Israel, Germany, Japan, Spain, Nigeria, Norway, Pakistan, and the United States. Differences are found in the emphasis on dimensions. Chinese, for example, use the category of conscientiousness more often and use the category of agreeableness less often than do Americans. But a surprisingly high amount of agreement is found, especially among individuals from developed countries. As a case in point, a comprehensive review of studies covering people from the European Community found that conscientiousness was a valid predictor of performance across jobs and occupational groups.[69] Studies in the United States found the same thing.

We know that no personality type is common for a given country. You can, for instance, find high risk takers and low risk takers in almost any culture. Yet a country's culture influences the *dominant* personality characteristics of its people. We can see this effect of national culture by looking at one of the personality traits we just discussed: locus of control.

National cultures differ in terms of the degree to which people believe they control their environment. For instance, North Americans believe they can dominate their environment; other societies, such as those in Middle Eastern countries, believe life is essentially predetermined. Notice how closely this distinction parallels the concept of internal and external locus of control. On the basis of this particular cultural characteristic, we should expect a larger proportion of internals in the U.S. and Canadian workforces than in the workforces of Saudi Arabia or Iran.

The Scenario:

"Why can't we all just get along?" wondered Bonnie, as she sat in her office. Today, she had already dealt with an employee who came in nearly every day with a complaint about something another coworker had said or done. Then, on top of that, Bonnie had to soothe over the hurt feelings of another employee who had overheard a conversation in the break room. She thought to herself, "I love being a manager, but there are days when the emotional tension in this place is too much."

What would you tell Bonnie about emotions in the workplace and how to deal with them?

Emotional stability and rationalization can be extremely difficult in the work environment. This is why it is important to have a solid foundation of rules and regulations in place as well as open lines of communications with everyone on your team. In the case of the two employees, I always believe it is important to sit two employees down together and discuss the efficiencies and inefficiencies each individual is complaining about. If there is a consistent behavioral pattern, it is the manager's responsibility to then do something about it. Whether it's a write-up or some form of disciplinary action, the negative behavior must come to an end as it will eventually begin to affect the rest of the team.

Aniece Meinhold
Restaurant Owner

Source: Aniece Meinhold

As we have seen throughout this section, personality traits influence employees' behavior. For global managers, understanding how personality traits differ takes on added significance when looking at it from the perspective of national culture.

Emotions and Emotional Intelligence

"Trying to sell wedding gowns to anxious brides-to-be" can be quite a stressful experience for the salesperson, needless to say. To help its employees stay "cheery," David's Bridal, a chain of more than 270 stores, relied on research into joyful emotions. Now, when "faced with an indecisive bride," salespeople have been taught emotional coping techniques and know how to focus on "things that bring them joy."[70]

We can't leave the topic of personality without looking at the important behavioral aspect of emotions. Employees rarely check their feelings at the door to the workplace nor are they unaffected by things that happen throughout the workday.[71] How we respond emotionally and how we deal with our emotions are typically functions of our personality. **Emotions** are intense feelings directed at someone or something. They're object-specific; that is, emotions are reactions to an object.[72] For instance, when a work colleague criticizes you for the way you spoke to a client, you might become angry at him. That is, you show emotion (anger) toward a specific object (your colleague). Because employees bring an emotional component with them to work every day, managers need to understand the role that emotions play in employee behavior.[73]

How many emotions are there? Although you could probably name several dozen, research has identified six universal emotions: anger, fear, sadness, happiness, disgust, and surprise.[74] Do these emotions surface in the workplace? Absolutely! I get *angry*

emotions
Intense feelings that are directed at someone or something

FUTURE VISION | Increased Reliance on Emotional Intelligence

Whether it goes by the name of emotional intelligence, social intelligence, or something else, the ability to understand yourself and others will be a skill that organizations will seek when hiring employees. In fact, in a survey of critical skills for the workforce in 2020, social intelligence ranked second on a list of the most critical skills.[75] (FYI: the number one skill was sense-making, that is, being able to determine the deeper meaning or significance of what's being expressed.) The ability to get along with others—coworkers, colleagues, team members, bosses, and customers—will be critical to success in most jobs. While more employees are likely to work off-site, there will still be ongoing contact with others. Those employees who have strong technical skills but are weak on emotional intelligence will find it increasingly difficult to find and hold a job.

after receiving a poor performance appraisal. I *fear* that I could be laid off as a result of a company cutback. I'm *sad* about one of my coworkers leaving to take a new job in another city. I'm *happy* after being selected as employee-of-the-month. I'm *disgusted* with the way my supervisor treats women on our team. And I'm *surprised* to find out that management plans a complete restructuring of the company's retirement program.

People respond differently to identical emotion-provoking stimuli. In some cases, differences can be attributed to a person's personality and because people vary in their ability to express emotions. For instance, you undoubtedly know people who almost never show their feelings. They rarely get angry or show rage. In contrast, you probably also know people who seem to be on an emotional roller coaster. When they're happy, they're ecstatic. When they're sad, they're deeply depressed. And two people can be in the exact same situation—one showing excitement and joy, the other remaining calm.

However, at other times how people respond emotionally is a result of job requirements. Jobs make different demands in terms of what types and how much emotion needs to be displayed. For instance, air traffic controllers, ER nurses, and trial judges are expected to be calm and controlled, even in stressful situations. On the other hand, public-address announcers at sporting events and lawyers in a courtroom must be able to alter their emotional intensity as the need arises.

One area of emotions research with interesting insights into personality is **emotional intelligence (EI)**, the ability to notice and to manage emotional cues and information.[76] It's composed of five dimensions:

Self-awareness: The ability to be aware of what you're feeling.

Self-management: The ability to manage one's own emotions and impulses.

Self-motivation: The ability to persist in the face of setbacks and failures.

Empathy: The ability to sense how others are feeling.

Social skills: The ability to handle the emotions of others.

EI has been shown to be positively related to job performance at all levels. For instance, one study looked at the characteristics of Lucent Technologies' engineers who were rated as stars by their peers. The researchers concluded that stars were better at relating to others. That is, it was EI, not academic intelligence, that characterized high performers. A study of Air Force recruiters generated similar findings. Top-performing recruiters exhibited high levels of EI. Despite these findings, EI has been a controversial topic in OB.[77] Supporters say EI has intuitive appeal and predicts important behavior.[78] Critics say that EI is vague, can't be measured, and has questionable validity.[79] One thing we can conclude is that EI appears to be relevant to success in jobs that demand a high degree of social interaction.

emotional intelligence (EI)
The ability to notice and to manage emotional cues and information

Implications for Managers

More than 62 percent of companies are using personality tests when recruiting and hiring.[80] Perhaps the major value in understanding personality differences lies in this area. Managers are likely to have higher-performing and more satisfied employees if consideration is given to matching personalities with jobs. The best-documented personality-job fit theory was developed by psychologist John Holland who identified six basic personality types.[81] His theory states that an employee's satisfaction with his or her job, as well as his or her likelihood of leaving that job, depends on the degree to which the individual's personality matches the job environment. Exhibit 15-4 describes the six types, their personality characteristics, and examples of suitable occupations for each.

Holland's theory proposes that satisfaction is highest and turnover lowest when personality and occupation are compatible. Social individuals should be in "people" type jobs, and so forth. The key points of this theory are that (1) intrinsic differences in personality are apparent among individuals; (2) the types of jobs vary; and (3) people in job environments compatible with their personality types should be more satisfied and less likely to resign voluntarily than people in incongruent jobs.

In addition, other benefits arise from understanding personality. By recognizing that people approach problem solving, decision making, and job interactions differently, a manager can better understand why an employee is uncomfortable with making quick decisions or why another employee insists on gathering as much information as possible before addressing a problem. Or, for instance, managers can

Exhibit 15-4

Holland's Personality–Job Fit

Type	Personality Characteristics	Sample Occupations
Realistic. Prefers physical activities that require skill, strength, and coordination	Shy, genuine, persistent, stable, conforming, practical	Mechanic, drill press operator, assembly-line worker, farmer
Investigative. Prefers activities involving thinking, organizing, and understanding	Analytical, original, curious, independent	Biologist, economist, mathematician, news reporter
Social. Prefers activities that involve helping and developing others	Sociable, friendly, cooperative, understanding	Social worker, teacher, counselor, clinical psychologist
Conventional. Prefers rule-regulated, orderly, and unambiguous activities	Conforming, efficient, practical, unimaginative, inflexible	Accountant, corporate manager, bank teller, file clerk
Enterprising. Prefers verbal activities that offer opportunities to influence others and attain power	Self-confident, ambitious, energetic, domineering	Lawyer, real estate agent, public relations specialist, small business manager
Artistic. Prefers ambiguous and unsystematic activities that allow creative expression	Imaginative, disorderly, idealistic, emotional, impractical	Painter, musician, writer, interior decorator

Source: Based on J. L. Holland, *Making Vocational Choices: A Theory of Vocational Personalities and Work Environments* (Odessa, FL: Psychological Assessment Resources, 1997).

expect that individuals with an external locus of control may be less satisfied with their jobs than internals and that they may be less willing to accept responsibility for their actions.

Finally, being a successful manager and accomplishing goals means working well together with others both inside and outside the organization. In order to work effectively together, you need to understand each other. This understanding comes, at least in part, from an appreciation of personality traits and emotions. Also, one of the skills you have to develop as a manager is learning to fine-tune your emotional reactions according to the situation. In other words, you have to learn to recognize when "you have to smile and when you have to bark."[82]

PERCEPTION

Describe *perception* **15.4** *and factors that influence it.*

Maybe you've seen this come in a Facebook post or on some other online source: AOCRNDICG TO RSCHEEARCH AT CMABRIGDE UINERVTISY, IT DSENO'T MTAETR WAHT OERDR THE LTTERES IN A WROD ARE, THE OLNY IPROAMTNT TIHNG IS TAHT   THE FRSIT AND LSAT LTTEER BE IN THE RGHIT PCLAE. TIHS IS BCUSEAE THE HUAMN MNID DEOS NOT RAED ERVEY LTETER BY ISTLEF, BUT THE WROD AS A WLOHE. IF YOU CAN RAED...TIHS, PSOT IT TO YUOR WLAL. OLNY 55% OF PLEPOE CAN.[83] How'd you do in trying to read this? If you were able to make sense out of this jumbled message, that's the perceptual process at work. **Perception** is a process by which we give meaning to our environment by organizing and interpreting sensory impressions. Research on perception consistently demonstrates that individuals may look at the same thing yet perceive it differently. One manager, for instance, can interpret the fact that her assistant regularly takes several days to make important decisions as evidence that the assistant is slow, disorganized, and afraid to make decisions. Another manager with the same assistant might interpret the same tendency as evidence that the assistant is thoughtful, thorough, and deliberate. The first manager would probably evaluate her assistant negatively; the second manager would probably evaluate the person positively. The point is that none of us sees reality. We interpret what we see and call it reality. And, of course, as the example shows, we behave according to our perceptions.

perception
A process by which we give meaning to our environment by organizing and interpreting sensory impressions

Factors That Influence Perception

How do we explain the fact that people can perceive the same thing differently? A number of factors act to shape and sometimes distort perception. These factors are in the *perceiver*, in the *target* being perceived, or in the *situation* in which the perception occurs.

When a person looks at a target and attempts to interpret what he or she sees, the individual's personal characteristics will heavily influence the interpretation. These personal characteristics include attitudes, personality, motives, interests, experiences, or expectations.

The characteristics of the target being observed can also affect what's perceived. Loud people are more likely than quiet people to be noticed in a group as are extremely attractive or unattractive individuals. The relationship of a target to its background also influences perception, as does our tendency to group close things and similar things together. You can experience these tendencies by looking at the visual perception examples shown in Exhibit 15-5. Notice how what you see changes as you look differently at each one.

Finally, the context in which we see objects or events is also important. The time at which an object or event is seen can influence perception, as can location, light, heat, color, and any number of other situational factors.

Exhibit 15-5
What Do You See?

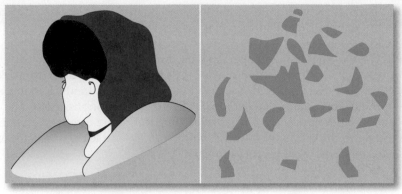

Old woman or young woman?   A knight on a horse?

Attribution Theory

Much of the research on perception is directed at inanimate objects. Managers, however, are concerned with people. Our perceptions of people differ from our perception of inanimate objects because we make inferences about the behaviors of people that we don't make about objects. Objects don't have beliefs, motives, or intentions; people do. The result is that when we observe an individual's behavior, we try to develop explanations of why they behave in certain ways. Our perception and judgment of a person's actions are significantly influenced by the assumptions we make about the person.

Attribution theory was developed to explain how we judge people differently depending on what meaning we attribute to a given behavior.[84] Basically, the theory suggests that when we observe an individual's behavior, we attempt to determine whether it was internally or externally caused. Internally caused behaviors are those believed to be under the personal control of the individual. Externally caused behavior results from outside factors; that is, the person is forced into the behavior by the situation. That determination, however, depends on three factors: distinctiveness, consensus, and consistency.

Distinctiveness refers to whether an individual displays different behaviors in different situations. Is the employee who arrived late today the same person who some employees complain of as being a "goof-off"? What we want to know is whether this behavior is unusual. If it's unusual, the observer is likely to attribute the behavior to external forces, something beyond the control of the person. However, if the behavior isn't unusual, it will probably be judged as internal.

If everyone who's faced with a similar situation responds in the same way, we can say the behavior shows *consensus*. A tardy employee's behavior would meet this criterion if all employees who took the same route to work were also late. From an attribution perspective, if consensus is high, you're likely to give an external attribution to the employee's tardiness; that is, some outside factor—maybe road construction or a traffic accident—caused the behavior. However, if other employees who come the same way to work made it on time, you would conclude that the cause of the late behavior was internal.

Finally, an observer looks for *consistency* in a person's actions. Does the person engage in the behaviors regularly and consistently? Does the person respond the same way over time? Coming in 10 minutes late for work isn't perceived in the same way if, for one employee, it represents an unusual case (she hasn't been late in months), while for another employee, it's part of a routine pattern (she's late two or three times every week). The more consistent the behavior, the more the observer is inclined to attribute it to internal causes. Exhibit 15-6 summarizes the key elements of attribution theory.

One interesting finding from attribution theory is that errors or biases distort our attributions. For instance, substantial evidence supports the fact that when we make judgments about the behavior of other people, we have a tendency to *under*estimate the influence of external factors and to *over*estimate the influence of internal or personal factors.[85] This tendency is called the **fundamental attribution error** and can explain

attribution theory
A theory used to explain how we judge people differently depending on what meaning we attribute to a given behavior

fundamental attribution error
The tendency to underestimate the influence of external factors and overestimate the influence of internal factors when making judgments about the behavior of others

Observation	Interpretation	Attribution of Cause
Does person behave this way in other situations?	Yes: Low distinctiveness No: High distinctiveness	Internal attribution External attribution
Do other people behave the same way in similar situations?	Yes: High consensus No: Low consensus	External attribution Internal attribution
Does person behave this way consistently?	Yes: High consistency No: Low consistency	Internal attribution External attribution

Exhibit 15-6
Attribution Theory

self-serving bias
The tendency for individuals to attribute their own successes to internal factors while putting the blame for failures on external factors

assumed similarity
The assumption that others are like oneself

stereotyping
Judging a person on the basis of one's perception of a group to which he or she belongs

halo effect
A general impression of an individual based on a single characteristic

why a sales manager may attribute the poor performance of her sales representative to laziness rather than to the innovative product line introduced by a competitor. Another tendency is to attribute our own successes to internal factors, such as ability or effort, while putting the blame for personal failure on external factors, such as luck. This tendency is called the **self-serving bias** and suggests that feedback provided to employees in performance reviews will be distorted by them depending on whether it's positive or negative.

Are these errors or biases that distort attributions universal across different cultures? We can't say for sure, but preliminary evidence indicates cultural differences.[86] For instance, a study of Korean managers found that, contrary to the self-serving bias, they tended to accept responsibility for group failure "because I was not a capable leader" instead of attributing it to group members.[87] Attribution theory was developed largely based on experiments with Americans and Western Europeans. But the Korean study suggests caution in making attribution theory predictions in non-Western societies, especially in countries with strong collectivist traditions.

Shortcuts Used in Judging Others

Perceiving and interpreting people's behavior is a lot of work, so we use shortcuts to make the task more manageable. These techniques can be valuable when they let us make accurate interpretations quickly and provide valid data for making predictions. However, they aren't perfect. They can and do get us into trouble.

It's easy to judge others if we assume they're similar to us. In **assumed similarity**, or the "like me" effect, the observer's perception of others is influenced more by the observer's own characteristics than by those of the person observed. For example, if you want challenges and responsibility in your job, you'll assume that others want the same. People who assume that others are like them can, of course, be right, but not always.

When we judge someone on the basis of our perception of a group he or she is part of, we're using the shortcut called **stereotyping**. For instance, "Married people are more stable employees than single persons" is an example of stereotyping. To the degree that a stereotype is based on fact, it may produce accurate judgments. However, many stereotypes aren't factual and distort our judgment.[88]

When we form a general impression about a person on the basis of a single characteristic, such as intelligence, sociability, or appearance, we're influenced by the **halo effect**. This effect frequently occurs when students evaluate their classroom instructor. Students may isolate a single trait such as enthusiasm and allow their entire evaluation to be slanted by the perception of this one trait. An instructor may be quiet, assured, knowledgeable, and highly qualified, but if his classroom teaching style lacks enthusiasm, he might be rated lower on a number of other characteristics.

Marissa Mayer, shown here arriving at the opening night gala of The San Francisco Opera, is a computer scientist who held a top management position at Google where she worked for 13 years before being named president and CEO of Yahoo. As a computer expert and enthusiast who is passionate about computer science, Mayer challenges the stereotypical view of computer scientists that inaccurately generalizes them as white males who wear thick glasses and pocket protectors, are poorly dressed and disorganized, and have no social skills and no social life. Mayer is concerned that negative stereotyping may be hindering women from pursuing careers in computer science.
Source: © Laura Morton/Corbis

Implications for Managers

Managers need to recognize that their employees react to perceptions, not to reality. So whether a manager's appraisal of an employee's performance is actually objective and unbiased or whether the organization's wage levels are among the highest in the community is less relevant than what employees perceive them to be. If individuals perceive appraisals to be biased or wage levels as low, they'll behave as if those conditions actually exist. Employees organize and interpret what they see, so the potential for perceptual distortion is always present. The message is clear: Pay close attention to how employees perceive both their jobs and management actions.

LEARNING

15.5 | *Discuss* learning theories and their relevance in shaping behavior.

When 20-year-old Elvis Andrus was signed by the Texas Rangers, he was excited to find out that the Rangers had signed another shortstop—11-time Gold Glove winner and fellow Venezuelan Omar Vizquel. Vizquel's role was clear: to be a mentor to the talented young player. Managers of major league baseball teams "regularly mix savvy veterans with talented young players, hoping tricks of the trade and advice on everything from how to turn a double play to how to avoid trouble in night spots on the road will rub off."[89]

Mentoring is a good example of the last individual behavior concept we're going to look at—learning. Learning is included in our discussion of individual behavior for the obvious reason that almost all behavior is learned. If we want to explain, predict, and influence behavior, we need to understand how people learn.

The psychologists' definition of learning is considerably broader than the average person's view that "it's what we do in school." Learning occurs all the time as we continuously learn from our experiences. A workable definition of **learning** is any relatively permanent change in behavior that occurs as a result of experience. Two learning theories help us understand how and why individual behavior occurs.

learning
Any relatively permanent change in behavior that occurs as a result of experience

Operant Conditioning

operant conditioning
A theory of learning that says behavior is a function of its consequences

Operant conditioning argues that behavior is a function of its consequences. People learn to behave to get something they want or to avoid something they don't want. Operant behavior is voluntary or learned behavior, not reflexive or unlearned behavior. The tendency to repeat learned behavior is influenced by reinforcement or lack of reinforcement that happens as a result of the behavior. Reinforcement strengthens a behavior and increases the likelihood that it will be repeated. Lack of reinforcement weakens a behavior and lessens the likelihood that it will be repeated.

B. F. Skinner's research widely expanded our knowledge of operant conditioning.[90] Behavior is assumed to be determined from without—that is, *learned*—rather than from within—reflexive or unlearned. Skinner argued that people will most likely engage in desired behaviors if they are positively reinforced for doing so, and rewards are most effective if they immediately follow the desired response. In addition, behavior that isn't rewarded or is punished is less likely to be repeated.

You see examples of operant conditioning everywhere. Any situation in which it's either explicitly stated or implicitly suggested that reinforcement (rewards) are contingent on some action on your part is an example of operant conditioning. Your instructor says that if you want a high grade in this course, you must perform well on tests by giving correct answers. A salesperson working on commission knows that earning a sizeable income is contingent on generating high sales in his or her territory. Of course, the linkage between behavior and reinforcement can also work to teach the individual to behave in ways that work against the best interests of the organization. Assume your boss tells you that if you'll work overtime during the next three-week busy season, you'll be compensated for it at the next performance appraisal. Then, when performance appraisal time comes, you are given no positive reinforcements (such as being praised for pitching in and helping out when needed). What will you do the next time your boss asks you to work overtime? You'll probably refuse. Your behavior can be explained by operant conditioning: If a behavior isn't positively reinforced, the probability that the behavior will be repeated declines.

Social Learning

Some 60 percent of the Radio City Rockettes have danced in prior seasons. The veterans help newcomers with "Rockette style"—where to place their hands, how to hold their hands, how to keep up stamina, and so forth.[91]

As the Rockettes are well aware, individuals can also learn by observing what happens to other people and just by being told about something as well as by direct experiences. Much of what we have learned comes from watching others (models)— parents, teachers, peers, television and movie actors, managers, and so forth. This view that we can learn both through observation and direct experience is called **social learning theory**.

The influence of others is central to the social learning viewpoint. The amount of influence these models have on an individual is determined by four processes:

1. *Attentional processes.* People learn from a model when they recognize and pay attention to its critical features. We're most influenced by models who are attractive, repeatedly available, thought to be important, or seen as similar to us.
2. *Retention processes.* A model's influence will depend on how well the individual remembers the model's action, even after the model is no longer readily available.

social learning theory
A theory of learning that says people can learn through observation and direct experience

let's get REAL

The Scenario:

Paul Taylor manages an advertising agency in Sydney. Although he runs his business quite loosely, he has one employee who is chronically late to everything: meetings, appointments, even getting to work. It's gotten to the point where the other employees are "rumbling" about it. It's time to do something.

What advice would you give Paul in "shaping" this employee's behavior?

Paul needs to provide his employee with immediate feedback. He should structure his feedback according to the SBIA Feedback Tool, ensuring it is SPECIFIC, in reference to the actual BEHAVIOR Paul has observed (not what was "rumbled" from the team); he should clearly state the IMPACT it is having on the team/business; and finally, he should propose a more effective, positive ALTERNATIVE behavior he'd like to see from his employee. After providing feedback, Paul should ask his employee to repeat what he/she has heard to ensure the message was effectively communicated and received. Finally, he and his employee should discuss the appropriate next steps and action plan to ensure the inappropriate behavior is no longer exhibited.

Shanise King
Associate Director, Marketing

Source: Shanise King

3. *Motor reproduction processes.* After a person has seen a new behavior by observing the model, the watching must become doing. This process then demonstrates that the individual can actually do the modeled activities.
4. *Reinforcement processes.* Individuals will be motivated to exhibit the modeled behavior if positive incentives or rewards are provided. Behaviors that are reinforced will be given more attention, learned better, and performed more often.

Shaping: A Managerial Tool

shaping behavior
The process of guiding learning in graduated steps using reinforcement or lack of reinforcement

Because learning takes place on the job as well as prior to it, managers are concerned with how they can teach employees to behave in ways that most benefit the organization. Thus, managers will often attempt to "mold" individuals by guiding their learning in graduated steps, through a method called **shaping behavior**.

Consider the situation in which an employee's behavior is significantly different from that sought by a manager. If the manager reinforced the individual only when he or she showed desirable responses, the opportunity for reinforcement might occur too infrequently. Shaping offers a logical approach toward achieving the desired behavior. We shape behavior by systematically reinforcing each successive step that moves the individual closer to the desired behavior. If an employee who has chronically been a half-hour late for work comes in only 20 minutes late, we can reinforce the improvement. Reinforcement would increase as an employee gets closer to the desired behavior.

Four ways to shape behavior include positive reinforcement, negative reinforcement, punishment, and extinction. When a behavior is followed by something pleasant, such as praising an employee for a job well done, it's called *positive reinforcement.* Positive reinforcement increases the likelihood that the desired behavior will be repeated. Rewarding a response by eliminating or withdrawing something unpleasant is *negative reinforcement.* A manager who says, "I won't dock your pay if you start getting to work on time" is using negative reinforcement. The desired behavior (getting to work on time) is being encouraged by the withdrawal of something unpleasant (the employee's pay being docked). On the other hand, *punishment* penalizes undesirable behavior and will eliminate it. Suspending an employee for two days without pay for habitually coming to work late is an example of punishment. Finally, eliminating any reinforcement that's maintaining a behavior is called *extinction.* When a behavior isn't reinforced, it gradually disappears. In meetings, managers who wish to discourage employees from continually asking irrelevant or distracting questions can eliminate this behavior by ignoring those employees when they raise their hands to speak. Soon this behavior should disappear.

Both positive and negative reinforcement result in learning. They strengthen a desired behavior and increase the probability that the desired behavior will be repeated. Both punishment and extinction also result in learning but do so by weakening an undesired behavior and decreasing its frequency.

Implications for Managers

Employees are going to learn on the job. The only issue is whether managers are going to manage their learning through the rewards they allocate and the examples they set, or allow it to occur haphazardly. If marginal employees are rewarded with pay raises and promotions, they will have little reason to change their behavior. In fact, productive employees, who see marginal performance rewarded, might change their behavior. If managers want behavior A, but reward behavior B, they shouldn't be surprised to find employees' learning to engage in behavior B. Similarly, managers should expect that employees will look to them as models. Managers who are consistently late to work, or take two hours for lunch, or help themselves to company office supplies for personal use should expect employees to read the message they are sending and model their behavior accordingly.

CONTEMPORARY Issues in Organizational Behavior

Discuss contemporary issues in organizational behavior. 15.6

By this point, you're probably well aware of the reasons managers need to understand how and why employees behave the way they do. We conclude this chapter by looking at two OB issues with a major influence on managers' jobs today.

Managing Generational Differences

Since 1998, Beloit College in Wisconsin has assembled a Mindset List© that helps identify the experiences that have shaped the lives of incoming freshmen.[92] The authors of the list state that it is an effort to better understand the "experiences that have shaped the lives and formed the mindset of students." Here are some of the observations from the 2016 list (generated in 2012):

- They have always lived in cyberspace.
- They're a "tribal" generation and despise being separated from contact with their similar-aged friends.
- They have little knowledge of Bill Clinton's presidency, knowing him only as a senior statesman.
- For most of their lives, there has been a woman as head of the U.S. Department of State.
- Exposed bra straps have been a fashion statement, not a wardrobe malfunction.
- Women have always piloted war planes and space shuttles.
- There have always been blue M&Ms, but no tan ones.

What will *this* group of young employees be like when they enter the workforce after graduation? Will they share the characteristics of the earlier members of Gen Y? Let's take a look at how Gen Y is changing the workplace since by 2014, they'll make up about 50 percent of the workforce, and by 2025 more than 75 percent.[93]

They're bright, curious, and eager to learn. But they can also be brash. They wear flip-flops to the office and listen to iPods at their desk. They want to work, but don't want work to be their life. Communicating with them means being concise and being mobile. They get excited about the opportunity to work on exciting or innovative projects, but not so much about job titles. Keeping them engaged in the workplace requires continual feedback and recognition. This is Generation Y, some 70 million of them, many of whom are embarking on their careers, taking their place in an increasingly multigenerational workplace.[94]

JUST WHO IS GEN Y?   There's no consensus about the exact timespan that Gen Y comprises, but most definitions include those individuals born from about 1982 to 1997. One thing is for sure—they're bringing new attitudes with them to the workplace. Gen Ys have grown up with an amazing array of experiences and opportunities. And they want their work life to provide that as well. For instance, Stella Kenyi, who is passionately interested in international development, was sent by her employer, the National Rural Electric Cooperative Association, to Yai, Sudan, to survey energy use.[95] At Best Buy's corporate offices, Beth Trippie, a senior scheduling specialist, feels that as long as the results are there, why should it matter how it gets done. She says, "I'm constantly playing video games, on a call, doing work, and the thing is, all of it gets done, and it gets done well."[96] And Katie Patterson, an assistant account executive in Atlanta, says, "We are willing and not afraid to challenge the status quo. An environment where creativity and independent thinking are looked upon as a positive is appealing to people my age. We're very independent and tech savvy."[97]

DEALING WITH THE MANAGERIAL CHALLENGES   Managing Gen Y workers presents some unique challenges. Conflicts and resentment can arise over issues such as appearance, technology, and management style.

Richard Pollack of Berkowitz Dick Pollack & Brant values the enthusiasm, eagerness to learn, and hard work that his Gen Y employee Rachel Merritt brings to the multigenerational CPA firm. After only a year with the firm, Merritt contributed key analyses for a major litigation case in her department that required frequently working late at night to research data. Merritt appreciates that her supervisors gave her job responsibilities quickly, a stimulating assignment, recognition for her achievements, and the opportunity to learn from employees at levels above her. As her supervisor, Pollack enjoys his role as mentor in teaching her how to develop as a professional.
Source: MCT via Getty Images

How flexible must an organization be in terms of "appropriate" office attire? It may depend on the type of work being done and the size of the organization. In many organizations, jeans, t-shirts, and flip-flops are acceptable. However, in other settings, employees are expected to dress more conventionally. But even in those more conservative organizations, one possible solution to accommodate the more casual attire preferred by Gen Y is to be more flexible in what's acceptable. For instance, the guideline might be that when the person is not interacting with someone outside the organizations, more casual wear (with some restrictions) can be worn.

What about technology? This generation has lived much of their lives with ATMs, DVDs, cell phones, e-mail, texting, laptops, and the Internet. When they don't have information they need, they just simply enter a few keystrokes to get it. Having grown up with technology, Gen Ys tend to be totally comfortable with it. They're quite content to meet virtually to solve problems, while bewildered baby boomers expect important problems to be solved with an in-person meeting. Baby boomers complain about Gen Y's inability to focus on one task, while Gen Ys see nothing wrong with multitasking. Again, flexibility from both is the key.

Finally, what about managing Gen Ys? Like the old car advertisement that used to say, "This isn't your father's car," we can say, "This isn't your father's or mother's way of managing." Gen Y employees want bosses who are open minded; experts in their field, even if they aren't tech-savvy; organized; teachers, trainers, and mentors; not authoritarian or paternalistic; respectful of their generation; understanding of their need for work–life balance; providing constant feedback; communicating in vivid and compelling ways; and providing stimulating and novel learning experiences.[98]

Gen Y employees have a lot to offer organizations in terms of their knowledge, passion, and abilities. Mangers, however, have to recognize and understand the behaviors of this group in order to create an environment in which work can be accomplished efficiently, effectively, and without disruptive conflict.

Managing Negative Behavior in the Workplace

Jerry notices the oil is low in his forklift but continues to drive it until it overheats and can't be used. After enduring 11 months of repeated insults and mistreatment from her supervisor, Maria quits her job. An office clerk slams her keyboard and then shouts profanity whenever her computer freezes up. Rudeness, hostility, aggression, and other forms of workplace negativity and incivility have become all too common in today's organizations. In a survey of U.S. employees, 10 percent said they witnessed rudeness daily within their workplaces and 20 percent said they were direct targets of incivility at work at least once a week. In a survey of Canadian workers, 25 percent reported seeing incivility daily, and 50 percent said they were the direct targets at least once per week.[99] Some estimates put the costs of negativity to the U.S. economy at $300 billion a year.[100] Most managers dread having to deal with difficult employees. However, they can't just ignore the problems. So, what can managers do to manage negative behavior in the workplace?

The main thing is to recognize that it's there. Pretending that negative behavior doesn't exist or ignoring such misbehaviors will only confuse employees about what is expected and acceptable behavior. Although some debate among researchers questions whether preventive or responsive actions to negative behaviors are more effective, in reality, both are needed.[101] Preventing negative behaviors by carefully screening potential employees for certain personality traits and responding immediately and decisively to unacceptable negative behaviors can go a long way toward managing negative workplace behaviors. But it's also important to pay attention to employee attitudes, because negativity will show up there as well. As we said earlier, when employees are dissatisfied with their jobs, they *will* respond somehow.

CHAPTER

PREPARING FOR: Exams/Quizzes

CHAPTER SUMMARY by Learning Outcomes

15.1 [LEARNING OUTCOME]

Identify the focus and goals of individual behavior within organizations.

Just like an iceberg, it's the hidden organizational elements (attitudes, perceptions, norms, etc.) that make understanding individual behavior so challenging.

Organization behavior (OB) focuses on three areas: individual behavior, group behavior, and organizational aspects. The goals of OB are to explain, predict, and influence behavior.

Employee productivity is a performance measure of both efficiency and effectiveness. Absenteeism is the failure to report to work. Turnover is the voluntary and involuntary permanent withdrawal from an organization. Organizational citizenship behavior (OCB) is discretionary behavior that's not part of an employee's formal job requirements but it promotes the effective functioning of an organization. Job satisfaction is an individual's general attitude toward his or her job. Workplace misbehavior is any intentional employee behavior that is potentially harmful to the organization or individuals within the organization.

15.2 [LEARNING OUTCOME]

Explain the role that attitudes play in job performance.

The cognitive component refers to the beliefs, opinions, knowledge, or information held by a person. The affective component is the emotional or feeling part of an attitude. The behavioral component refers to an intention to behave in a certain way toward someone or something.

Job satisfaction refers to a person's general attitude toward his or her job. Job involvement is the degree to which an employee identifies with his or her job, actively participates in it, and considers his or her job performance to be important to his or her self-worth. Organizational commitment is the degree to which an employee identifies with a particular organization and its goals and wishes to maintain membership in that organization. Employee engagement is when employees are connected to, satisfied with, and enthusiastic about their jobs.

Job satisfaction positively influences productivity, lowers absenteeism levels, lowers turnover rates, promotes positive customer satisfaction, moderately promotes OCB, and helps minimize workplace misbehavior.

Individuals try to reconcile attitude and behavior inconsistencies by altering their attitudes, altering their behavior, or rationalizing the inconsistency.

15.3 [LEARNING OUTCOME]

Describe different personality theories.

The MBTI measures four dimensions: social interaction, preference for gathering data, preference for decision making, and style of making decisions. The Big Five Model consists of five personality traits: extraversion, agreeableness, conscientiousness, emotional stability, and openness to experience.

The five personality traits that help explain individual behavior in organizations are locus of control, Machiavellianism, self-esteem, self-monitoring, and risk-taking. Other personality traits include Type A/Type B personalities, proactive personality, and resilience.

How a person responds emotionally and how they deal with their emotions is a function of personality. A person who is emotionally intelligent has the ability to notice and to manage emotional cues and information.

15.4 LEARNING OUTCOME

Describe perception and factors that influence it.

Perception is how we give meaning to our environment by organizing and interpreting sensory impressions. Because people behave according to their perceptions, managers need to understand it.

Attribution theory depends on three factors. Distinctiveness is whether an individual displays different behaviors in different situations (that is, is the behavior unusual). Consensus is whether others facing a similar situation respond in the same way. Consistency is when a person engages in behaviors regularly and consistently. Whether these three factors are high or low helps managers determine whether employee behavior is attributed to external or internal causes.

The fundamental attribution error is the tendency to underestimate the influence of external factors and overestimate the influence of internal factors. The self-serving bias is the tendency to attribute our own successes to internal factors and to put the blame for personal failure on external factors.

Three shortcuts used in judging others are assumed similarity, stereotyping, and the halo effect.

15.5 LEARNING OUTCOME

Discuss learning theories and their relevance in shaping behavior.

Operant conditioning argues that behavior is a function of its consequences. Managers can use it to explain, predict, and influence behavior.

Social learning theory says that individuals learn by observing what happens to other people and by directly experiencing something.

Managers can shape behavior by using positive reinforcement (reinforcing a desired behavior by giving something pleasant), negative reinforcement (reinforcing a desired response by withdrawing something unpleasant), punishment (eliminating undesirable behavior by applying penalties), or extinction (not reinforcing a behavior to eliminate it).

15.6 LEARNING OUTCOME

Discuss contemporary issues in organizational behavior.

The challenge of managing Gen Y workers is that they bring new attitudes to the workplace. The main challenges are over issues such as appearance, technology, and management style.

Workplace misbehavior can be dealt with by recognizing that it's there; carefully screening potential employees for possible negative tendencies; and most importantly, by paying attention to employee attitudes through surveys about job satisfaction and dissatisfaction.

REVIEW AND DISCUSSION QUESTIONS ✪

1. Does the importance of knowledge of OB differ based on a manager's levels in the organization? If so, how? If not, why not? Be specific.

2. Explain why the concept of an organization as an iceberg is important.

3. Define the six important employee behaviors.

4. Describe the three components of an attitude and explain the four job-related attitudes.

5. Contrast the MBTI and the Big Five model. Describe five other personality traits that help explain individual behavior in organizations.

6. Explain how an understanding of perception can help managers better understand individual behavior. Name three shortcuts used in judging others.

7. Describe the key elements of attribution theory. Discuss the fundamental attribution error and self-serving bias.

8. Describe operant conditioning and how managers can shape behavior.

ETHICS DILEMMA ✪

It's been called the "desperation hustle."[102] Employees who are "anxious about layoffs want to look irreplaceable." So they clean up their act. Those who might not have paid much attention to their manner of dress now do. Those who were mouthy and argumentative are now quiet and

compliant. Those who used to "watch the clock" are now the last to leave. The fear is there, and it's noticeable. "Managing that fear can be challenging." What ethical issues might arise for both employees and for managers? How could managers approach these circumstances ethically?

SKILLS EXERCISE Developing Your Shaping Behavior Skill

About the Skill
In today's dynamic work environments, learning is continual. But this learning shouldn't be done in isolation or without any guidance. Most employees need to be shown what's expected of them on the job. As a manager, you must teach your employees the behaviors most critical to their, and the organization's, success.

Steps in Practicing the Skill

1. *Identify the critical behaviors that have a significant impact on an employee's performance.* Not everything employees do on the job is equally important in terms of performance outcomes. A few critical behaviors may, in fact, account for the majority of one's results. These high impact behaviors need to be identified.

2. *Establish a baseline of performance.* A baseline is obtained by determining the number of times the identified behaviors occur under the employee's present job conditions.

3. *Analyze the contributing factors to performance and their consequences.* A number of factors, such as the norms of a group, may be contributing to the baseline performance. Identify these factors and their effect on performance.

4. *Develop a shaping strategy.* The change that may occur will entail changing some element of performance—structure, processes, technology, groups, or the task. The purpose of the strategy is to strengthen the desirable behaviors and weaken the undesirable ones.

5. *Apply the appropriate strategy.* Once the strategy has been developed, it needs to be implemented. In this step, an intervention occurs.

6. *Measure the change that has occurred.* An intervention should produce the desired results in performance behaviors. Evaluate the number of times the identified behaviors now occur. Compare these with the baseline evaluation in step 2.

7. *Reinforce desired behaviors.* If an intervention has been successful and the new behaviors are producing the desired results, maintain these behaviors through reinforcement mechanisms.

Practicing the Skill

a. Imagine that your assistant is ideal in all respects but one—he or she is hopeless at taking phone messages for you when you're not in the office. You're often in training sessions and the calls are sales leads you want to follow up, so you have identified taking accurate messages as a high impact behavior for your assistant.

b. Focus on steps 3 and 4, and devise a way to shape your assistant's behavior. Identify some factors that might contribute to his or her failure to take messages—these could range from a heavy workload to a poor understanding of the task's importance (you can rule out insubordination). Then develop a shaping strategy by determining what you can change—the available technology, the task itself, the structure of the job, or some other element of performance.

c. Now plan your intervention and take a brief meeting with your assistant in which you explain the change you expect. Recruit a friend to help you role-play your intervention. Do you think you would succeed in a real situation?

WORKING TOGETHER Team Exercise

You may not like it or want to believe it, but unprofessional dress can be a career-killer.[103] Pretend you're a manager in a large, multinational company. Your company has a dress code policy, but men and women alike "cross the line." One of your female subordinates is the worst offender. Several times, she has come to work dressed in sheer, low-cut, sleeveless blouses with a

micro-mini skirt and strappy sandals. How would you change her behavior?

Form small groups of three to four individuals. Your team's task is to come up with a specific plan for changing (shaping) the behavior of any employee who violates the dress code policy. Write this up and be prepared to share your ideas with the class.

MY TURN TO BE A MANAGER

- For one week, pay close attention to how people around you behave, especially those who are close to you (roommates, siblings, significant others, coworkers, etc.). Use what you've learned about attitudes, personality, perception, and learning to understand and explain how and why they're behaving the way they do. Write your observations and your explanations in a journal.

- Write down three attitudes you have. Identify the cognitive, affective, and behavioral components of those attitudes.

- Survey 15 employees (at your place of work or at some campus office). Be sure to obtain permission before doing this anonymous survey. Ask them what rude or negative behaviors they've seen at work. Compile your findings in a report and be prepared to discuss this in class. If you were the manager in this workplace, how would you handle this behavior?

- If you've never taken a personality or career compatibility test, contact your school's testing center to see if you can take one. Once you get your results, evaluate what they mean for your career choice. Have you chosen a career that "fits" your personality? What are the implications?

- Have you ever heard of the "waiter rule"? A lot of business people think that how you treat service workers says a lot about your character and attitudes. What do you think this means? Do you agree with this idea? Why or why not? How would you be evaluated on the "waiter rule"?

- Like it or not, each of us is continually shaping the behavior of those around us. For one week, keep track of how many times you use positive reinforcement, negative reinforcement, punishment, or extinction to shape behaviors. At the end of the week, which one did you tend to use most? What were you trying to do; that is, what behaviors were you trying to shape? Were your attempts successful? Evaluate. What could you have done differently if you were trying to change someone's behavior?

- Create a job satisfaction survey for a business you're familiar with.

- Now, do a Web search for sample job satisfaction surveys. Find one or two samples. Write a report describing, comparing, and evaluating the examples you found and the survey you created.

- Steve's and Mary's recommended readings: Jonathan Littman and Mark Herson, *I Hate People!* (Little-Brown, 2009); Yoav Vardi and Ely Weitz, *Misbehavior in Organizations* (Lawrence Erlbaum Associates, 2004); Murray R. Barrick and A. M. Ryan, eds., *Personality and Work* (Jossey-Bass, 2003); Daniel Goleman, *Destructive Emotions: How Can We Overcome Them?* (Bantam, 2003); L. Thomson, *Personality Type: An Owner's Manual* (Shambhala, 1998); and Daniel Goleman, *Working with Emotional Intelligence* (Bantam, 1998).

- Survey 10 Gen Yers. Ask them three questions: (1) What do you think is appropriate office attire? (2) How comfortable are you with using technology, and what types of technology do you rely on most? (3) What do you think the "ideal" boss would be like? Compile your results into a paper that reports your data and summarizes your findings in a bulleted list format.

- In your own words, write down three things you learned in this chapter about being a good manager.

- Self-knowledge can be a powerful learning tool. Go to mymanagementlab.com and complete these self-assessment exercises: What's My Basic Personality? What's My Jungian 16-Type Personality? (Note that this is a miniature version of the MBTI.) Am I a Type A? What Do I Value? How Involved Am I in My Job? How Satisfied Am I With My Job? Am I Engaged? How Are You Feeling Right Now? What's My Affect Intensity? What's My Emotional Intelligence Score? How Committed Am I to My Organization? Using the results of your assessments, identify personal strengths and weaknesses. What will you do to reinforce your strengths and improve your weaknesses?

MyManagementLab

Go to **mymanagementlab.com** for Auto-graded writing questions as well as the following Assisted-graded writing questions:

15-1. Describe the focus and goals of OB.

15-2. Explain the challenges facing managers in managing generational differences and negative behavior in the workplace.

15-3. Mymanagementlab Only – comprehensive writing assignment for this chapter.

CASE APPLICATION 1 Great Place to Work

Have you heard of SAS Institute, Inc.?[104] Maybe, just maybe, you've used a school-based version of their analytical software in a research class. SAS (originally called Statistical Analysis System) is based in Cary, North Carolina, and its analytics and business intelligence software is used by corporations and other customers to analyze operations and forecast trends. For 15 years, SAS has been named to *Fortune's* Best Companies to Work For list. In 2010 and 2011, it was ranked number one, and it was ranked number three in 2012. One thing that distinguishes SAS is its highly employee-friendly culture.

The beautifully landscaped grounds with walking paths for employees at its campus in Cary, North Carolina, onsite massages, free onsite healthcare, a fitness and recreation center, free M&Ms every Wednesday, and a no-layoff policy all attest to SAS Institute's fundamental belief that keeping employees happy and healthy enhances their job satisfaction and productivity.
Source: AP Photo/Karen Tam

The good life for employees began some 26 years ago with free M&Ms every Wednesday. Now the sweets have become even sweeter. Today, SAS's almost 13,000 employees enjoy perks such as free onsite health care, subsidized Montessori child care, unlimited sick time, onsite massage, summer camp for employees' children, an enormous fitness and recreation center, car cleaning, soda fountains and snacks in every break room, and others. The SAS dress code is...well, there is no dress code. "Laidback is the unofficial posture here and convenience the motto." To be sure, these benefits help make SAS a desirable place to work. But, the company's commitment to employees goes beyond nice perks. Even in the economic downturn, SAS has refused to lay off employees and has, in fact, even extended its benefits. As SAS's VP of Human Resources says, "SAS's continued success proves our core belief: Happy, healthy employees are more productive."

The masses of programmers who churn out the company's products are paid a competitive wage, but are not offered stock options. SAS is a privately held company so there is no stock. Yet, the extraordinary perks helps SAS keep turnover low. The 2012 Best Companies to Work For list cited SAS as the company with the lowest turnover of the 100 companies on the list, with a turnover rate of just 2.2 percent in 2011. On the survey instrument used to determine those Best Companies, one SAS employee wrote that in his or her opinion, employees continue to work at SAS because the company respects them and cares for them. The company's CEO and co-founder Jim Goodnight would say there's nothing wrong with treating your people well. And it's worked for his company. In 2011, SAS sold almost $2.75 billion of its sophisticated software, and it has never had a losing year.

DISCUSSION QUESTIONS ✪

1. What is your impression of this employee-friendly culture? Would this work in other organizations? Why or why not? What would it take to make it work?

2. How might an understanding of organizational behavior help CEO Jim Goodnight lead his company? Be specific. How about first-line company supervisors? Again, be specific.

3. What do you think has contributed to SAS's low turnover? Why is low turnover good for a company?

4. Look back at the statement made by the SAS employee on the Best Companies survey. What does that tell you about the importance of understanding individual behavior?

CASE APPLICATION 2 Odd Couples

With the goal of boosting productivity, the founders of Randstad established a work arrangement of partnering two employees to share a job and alternate work tasks. To ensure that young employees work well with older and more experienced partners, the company seeks to hire individuals who have the ability to work in a team environment and who are willing to both teach and learn from their job partner.
Source: © *Caro/Alamy*

A 29-year-old and a 68-year-old. How much could they possibly have in common? And what could they learn from each other? At Randstad USA's Manhattan office, such employee pairings are common.[105] One such pair of colleagues sits inches apart facing each other. As they work closely together, they share communications, including telephone calls and e-mails, and they sometimes even finish each other's sentences

Randstad Holding NV, a Dutch company, has been using this pairing idea since its founding more than 40 years ago. The founder's motto was "Nobody should be alone." The original intent was to boost productivity by having sales agents share one job and trade off job responsibilities. Today, these partners in the home office have an arrangement where one is in the office one week while the other one is out making sales calls, then the next week, they switch. The company brought its partner arrangement to the United States in the late 1990s. But when it began recruiting new employees, the vast majority of whom were in their twenties, it realized the challenges and the potential of pairing different generations together. Randstad's managers had done their homework and knew that members of Gen Y enjoy collaborating with others and feeling nurtured. So the managers figured that both of those needs could be satisfied if a Gen Y employee could share a job with another employee, with both depending on each other for mutual success.

Randstad doesn't simply pair up people and hope it works. There's more to it than that! The company looks for people who will work well with others by conducting extensive interviews and requiring job applicants to shadow a sales agent for half a day. During the interview process, managers will ask potential employees to share their "most memorable moment" as part of a team. If the recruit mentions anything that indicates an individual achievement, that's a deal breaker. This organization is about being part of a team. When a new hire is paired with an experienced agent, both individuals have some adjusting. One of the most interesting elements of Randstad's program is that neither person is "the boss." And both are expected to teach each other.

DISCUSSION QUESTIONS ✪

1. What topics of individual behavior do you see in this story? Explain.

2. What do you think about this pairing-up idea? Would you be comfortable with such an arrangement? Why or why not?

3. What personality traits would be most needed for this type of work arrangement? Why?

4. What types of issues might a Gen Y employee and an older, more experienced employee face? How could two people in such a close-knit work arrangement deal with those issues? That is, how could both make the adjustment easier?

5. Design an employee attitude survey for Randstad's employees.

16 Managers and Communication

SPOTLIGHT: *Manager at Work*

Tweets. Twittering. Prior to 2006, the only definition we would have known for these words would have involved birds and the sounds they make. Now, practically everyone knows that Twitter is also an online service—as of early 2012 with 500 million registered users, 340 million tweets daily, and 1.6 billion daily search queries—used to trade short messages of 140 characters or less via the Web, cell phones, and other devices.[1] According to its founders (Evan Williams, Biz Stone, and Jack Dorsey; see photo next page), Twitter is many things: a messaging service, a customer-service tool to reach customers, real-time search, and microblogging. And as the numbers show, it's become quite popular!

One place where Twitter has caught on is the sports world, especially in college sports. For instance, Les Miles, head football coach at Louisiana State University calls himself "a Twittering kind of guy." He understands the power of instant communication. Miles wants to stay ahead of the competition, especially when it comes to recruiting and keeping fans informed. He said, "It (Twittering) allows us to communicate blasts of information to those people that subscribe. And it's also an opportunity for those recruiting prospects that subscribe to communicate to us." On game days, he Twitters (via a staff assistant) before games, at halftime, and after games. If it's okay for coaches to tweet, what about student athletes? That's often a different story.

Many universities and college coaches are monitoring and, in some cases, banning athletes' use of social media. "They're nervous because an ill-considered tweet can embarrass the program, draw the ire of administrators and boosters, and possibly violate NCAA recruitment rules." Here are a couple

Source: Cal Sport Media via AP Images

of tweeting slip-ups: a Western Kentucky running back was suspended after he tweeted critical comments about the team's fans; the NCAA pulled 15 football scholarships after an investigation based on a player's tweet; and a Lehigh

Source: Kevin Mazur/Getty Images

One place where Twitter has caught on is the sports world, especially in college sports.

University wide receiver was suspended for re-tweeting a racial slur. We even saw how tweeting backfired at the London Olympics. The first "casualty"—a Greek triple jumper—was banned from the Games over some racially charged tweets. That seems to be good reason for the managers (i.e., coaches and administrators) of these programs to attempt to control the information flow. But is banning the answer? Some analysts say no. They argue that those setting up rules and regulations don't understand what social media is all about and the value it provides as a marketing and recruiting tool, and they argue that it's necessary to understand First Amendment rights (part of which includes freedom of speech). Rather than

---

MyManagementLab®

⭐ **Improve Your Grade!**

Over 10 million students improved their results using the Pearson MyLabs.
Visit **mymanagementlab.com** for simulations, tutorials, and end-of-chapter problems.

LEARNING OUTCOMES

16.1	***Define*** the nature and function of communication.
16.2	***Compare*** and contrast methods of interpersonal communication.
16.3	***Identify*** barriers to effective interpersonal communication and how to overcome them.
16.4	***Explain*** how communication can flow most effectively in organizations.
16.5	***Describe*** how technology affects managerial communication and organizations.
16.6	***Discuss*** contemporary issues in communication.

banning the use of social media, many universities are hiring companies to monitor athletes' posts. This, however, requires athletes to give access to their accounts, which some call an invasion of privacy. **What do you think? How is this relevant to managers in business organizations?**

Ahhhh…welcome to the new world of communication! In this "world," managers are going to have to understand both the importance and the drawbacks of communication—all forms of communication. Communication between managers and employees is important because it provides the information necessary to get work done in organizations. Thus, there's no doubt that communication is fundamentally linked to managerial performance.[2]

16.1 **Define** the nature and function of communication.

THE NATURE and Function of Communication

Southwest Airlines suspended a pilot who accidentally broadcast a vulgar criticism that was picked up on an air traffic control frequency and heard by air traffic controllers and other pilots.[3] In the middle of the pilot's profanity-laced rant about the flight attendants on his plane, a Houston air-traffic controller interrupted and said, "Whoever's transmitting, better watch what you're saying." The Federal Aviation Administration sent the audio recording to Southwest, calling it "inappropriate." Southwest suspended the 12-year veteran pilot without pay for an undisclosed amount of time for making comments that were contrary to employee policy and sent him to sensitivity training. This example shows why it's important for managers to understand the impact of communication.

The ability to communicate effectively is a skill that must be mastered by any manager who wants to be an effective manager. The importance of effective communication for managers can't be overemphasized for one specific reason: Everything a manager does involves communicating. Not *some* things, but everything! A manager can't make a decision without information. That information has to be communicated. Once a decision is made, communication must again take place. Otherwise, no one would know that a decision was made. The best idea, the most creative suggestion, the best plan, or the most effective job redesign can't take shape without communication.

What Is Communication?

communication
The transfer and understanding of meaning

Communication is the transfer and understanding of meaning. Note the emphasis on the *transfer* of meaning: If information or ideas have not been conveyed, communication hasn't taken place. The speaker who isn't heard or the writer whose materials aren't read hasn't communicated. More importantly, however, communication involves the *understanding* of meaning. For communication to be successful, the meaning must be imparted and understood. A letter written in Spanish addressed to a person who doesn't read Spanish can't be considered communication until it's translated into a language the person does read and understand. Perfect communication, if such a thing existed, would be when a transmitted thought or idea was received and understood by the receiver exactly as it was envisioned by the sender.

Another point to keep in mind is that *good* communication is often erroneously defined by the communicator as *agreement* with the message instead of clear understanding of the message.[4] If someone disagrees with us, we assume that the person just didn't fully understand our position. In other words, many of us define good communication as having someone accept our views. But I can clearly understand what you mean and just *not* agree with what you say.

interpersonal communication
Communication between two or more people

organizational communication
All the patterns, networks, and systems of communication within an organization

The final point we want to make about communication is that it encompasses both **interpersonal communication**—communication between two or more people—and **organizational communication**, which is all the patterns, networks, and systems of communication within an organization. Both types are important to managers.

Functions of Communication

Irene Lews, CEO of SAIT Polytechnic, a Calgary, Alberta, Canada-based technical institute, was awarded the 2012 Excellence in Communication Leadership (EXCEL) Award by the International Association of Business Communicators. This award recognizes leaders who foster excellence in communication and contribute to the development and support of organizational communication. The selection committee noted Lewis' leadership and commitment to communication and her impact on SAIT's reputation and growth. "She is involved in a wide variety of issues and uses communications wisely to engage relevant stakeholders."[5]

Throughout SAIT Polytechnic and many other organizations, communication serves four major functions: control, motivation, emotional expression, and information.[6] Each function is equally important.

Communication acts to *control* employee behavior in several ways. As we know from Chapter 11, organizations have authority hierarchies and formal guidelines that employees are expected to follow. For instance, when employees are required to communicate any job-related grievance to their immediate manager, to follow their job description, or to comply with company policies, communication is being used to control. Informal communication also controls behavior. When a work group teases a member who's ignoring the norms by working too hard, they're informally controlling the member's behavior.

Next, communication acts to *motivate* by clarifying to employees what is to be done, how well they're doing, and what can be done to improve performance if it's not up to par. As employees set specific goals, work toward those goals, and receive feedback on progress toward goals, communication is required.

For many employees, their work group is a primary source of social interaction. The communication that takes place within the group is a fundamental mechanism by which members share frustrations and feelings of satisfaction. Communication, therefore, provides a release for *emotional expression* of feelings and for fulfillment of social needs.

Finally, individuals and groups need information to get things done in organizations. Communication provides that *information.*

Communication with new employees at Columbus Company, Ltd., a shoe care products company in Tokyo, serves the functions of information, motivation, and socialization. During their initiation, college graduates first attend a lecture to learn about the company's polishing creams and other shoe supplies. Then they are paired with a senior master polisher who teaches them how to shine shoes with the spirit of "polishing shoes is like polishing the heart." The new recruits also polish their mentors' shoes and receive feedback about their performance. Communication also provides a release for emotional expressions and feelings as new recruits interact socially with each other and senior staff members.
Source: Everett Kennedy Brown/EPA/Newscom

METHODS of Interpersonal Communication

Before communication can take place, a purpose, expressed as a **message** to be conveyed, must exist. It passes between a source (the sender) and a receiver. The message is converted to symbolic form (called **encoding**) and passed by way of some medium (**channel**) to the receiver, who retranslates the sender's message (called **decoding**). The result is the transfer of meaning from one person to another.[7]

Exhibit 16-1 illustrates the elements of the **communication process**. Note that the entire process is susceptible to **noise**—disturbances that interfere with the transmission, receipt, or feedback of a message. Typical examples of noise include illegible print, phone static, inattention by the receiver, or background sounds of machinery or coworkers. However, anything that interferes with understanding can be noise, and noise can create distortion at any point in the communication process.

A personal written letter from a U.S. Army commander in Afghanistan to his troops assured them that they are "contributing to the overall success of the mission" here. Colonel David Haight, of the 10th Mountain Division's 3rd Brigade Combat team, sent the letter to each of the 3,500 men and women after two of their fellow soldiers were killed in combat and his chaplains reported that many were disillusioned about the war. In that letter, Haight said it's important for a leader to explain why certain tasks are important to the accomplishment of the overall mission. Communicating in that way ensures that the mission is not only accomplished, but is accomplished in

Compare and contrast 16.2
methods of interpersonal communication.

message
A purpose to be conveyed

encoding
Converting a message into symbols

channel
The medium a message travels along

decoding
Retranslating a sender's message

communication process
The seven elements involved in transferring meaning from one person to another

noise
Any disturbances that interfere with the transmission, receipt, or feedback of a message

Exhibit 16-1
The Interpersonal Communication Process

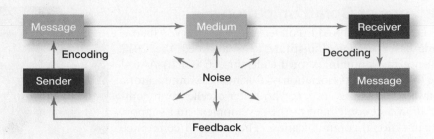

an exemplary way.[8] Here's a manager who understands the role of communication and how best to communicate to his subordinates.

You need to communicate to your employees the organization's new policy on sexual harassment; you want to compliment one of your workers on the extra hours she's put in to help your team complete a customer's order; you must tell one of your employees about changes to his job; or you would like to get employees' feedback on your proposed budget for next year. In each of these instances, how would you communicate? Managers have a wide variety of communication methods from which to choose and can use 12 questions to help them evaluate these methods.[9]

1. *Feedback:* How quickly can the receiver respond to the message?
2. *Complexity capacity:* Can the method effectively process complex messages?
3. *Breadth potential:* How many different messages can be transmitted using this method?
4. *Confidentiality:* Can communicators be reasonably sure their messages are received only by those intended?
5. *Encoding ease:* Can sender easily and quickly use this channel?
6. *Decoding ease:* Can receiver easily and quickly decode messages?
7. *Time-space constraint:* Do senders and receivers need to communicate at the same time and in the same space?
8. *Cost:* How much does it cost to use this method?
9. *Interpersonal warmth:* How well does this method convey interpersonal warmth?
10. *Formality:* Does this method have the needed amount of formality?
11. *Scanability:* Does this method allow the message to be easily browsed or scanned for relevant information?
12. *Time of consumption:* Does the sender or receiver exercise the most control over when the message is dealt with?

Exhibit 16-2 provides a comparison of various communication methods. Which method a manager ultimately chooses should reflect the needs of the sender, the attributes of the message, the attributes of the channel, and the needs of the receiver. For instance, if you need to communicate to an employee about the changes being made in her job, face-to-face communication would be a better choice than a memo because you want to be able to address immediately any questions and concerns she might have.

An important part of interpersonal communication is **nonverbal communication**—that is, communication transmitted without words. Some of the most meaningful communications are neither spoken nor written. When a college instructor is teaching a class, she doesn't need words to tell her that students are tuned out when they begin to read a newspaper in the middle of class. Similarly, when students start putting their book, papers, and notebooks away, the message is clear: Class time is about over. The size of a person's office or the clothes he or she wears also convey messages to others. Among these various forms of nonverbal communication, the best-known types are body language and verbal intonation.

Body language refers to gestures, facial expressions, and other body movements that convey meaning. A person frowning "says" something different from one who's smiling. Hand motions, facial expressions, and other gestures can communicate

nonverbal communication
Communication transmitted without words

body language
Gestures, facial configurations, and other body movements that convey meaning

Exhibit 16-2
Comparison of Communication Methods

High Feedback Potential
- Face-to-face
- Telephone
- Computer conference

Low Feedback Potential
- Publications

High Complexity Capacity
- Face-to-face

Low Complexity Capacity
- Bulletin boards

High Breadth Potential
- Face-to-face
- Bulletin boards
- E-mail

Low Breadth Potential
- Postal mail
- Audio-videotapes

High Confidentiality
- Face-to-face
- Voice mail

Low Confidentiality
- Publications
- Bulletin boards
- Audio-videotapes
- Teleconference

High Encoding Ease
- Face-to-face
- Telephone

Low Encoding Ease
- Publications

High Time-Decoding Ease
- Face-to-face
- Telephone
- Hotlines
- Voice mail

Low Time-Decoding Ease
- Memos
- Postal mail
- Fax
- Publications

High Space Constraint
- Face-to-face
- Group meetings
- Formal presentations

Low Space Constraint
- Memos
- Postal mail
- Fax
- Publications
- Voice mail

High Cost
- Group meetings
- Formal presentations
- Videoconference

Low Cost
- Bulletin boards

High Personal Warmth
- Face-to-face

Low Personal Warmth
- Memos
- Bulletin boards

High Formality
- Postal mail
- Publications

Low Formality
- Face-to-face
- Telephone
- Voice mail

High Scanability
- Memos
- Postal mail
- Fax
- Publications
- Bulletin boards

Low Scanability
- Formal presentations
- Face-to-face
- Telephone
- Group meetings
- Audio-videotapes
- Hotlines
- E-mail
- Computer conference
- Voice mail
- Teleconference
- Videoconference

Source: Based on P. G. Clampitt, *Communicating for Managerial Effectiveness* (Newbury Park, CA: Sage Publications, 1991), p. 136.

LEADER *who made a* DIFFERENCE

Zappos, the quirky Las Vegas-based online shoe retailer (now a part of Amazon.com, which purchased the company for $1.2 billion), has a reputation for being a fun place to work.[11] Much of that is due to its CEO Tony Hsieh, who also understands the power of communication. And one thing that's communicated well and frequently is the company's values. He says that maintaining that corporate culture is "the number one priority." At the company's headquarters, employees use only one entrance and exit to encourage them to "literally run into" each other in the lobby. Hsieh believes that's a way to encourage opportune interactions to share ideas. His next project? Revitalizing downtown Las Vegas by using his own money to buy property, subsidize schools, and fund new business ventures. What can you learn from this leader who made a difference?

verbal intonation
An emphasis given to words or phrases that conveys meaning

emotions or temperaments such as aggression, fear, shyness, arrogance, joy, and anger. Knowing the meaning behind someone's body moves and learning how to put forth your best body language can help you personally and professionally.[10]

Verbal intonation refers to the emphasis someone gives to words or phrases in order to convey meaning. To illustrate how intonations can change the meaning of a message, consider the student who asks the instructor a question. The instructor replies, "What do you mean by that?" The student's reaction will vary, depending on the tone of the instructor's response. A soft, smooth vocal tone conveys interest and creates a different meaning from one that is abrasive and puts a strong emphasis on saying the last word. Most of us would view the first intonation as coming from someone sincerely interested in clarifying the student's concern, whereas the second suggests that the person resents the question.

Managers need to remember that as they communicate, the nonverbal component usually carries the greatest impact. It's not *what* you say, but *how* you say it.

16.3 *Identify barriers to effective interpersonal communication and how to overcome them.*

EFFECTIVE Interpersonal Communication

A company with 100 employees can expect to lose approximately $450,000 a year, or more, because of e-mail blunders, inefficiencies, and misunderstandings.[12] The chief executive of a marketing firm in New York was in a meeting with a potential client. For the entire hour-and-a-half meeting, the client was fiddling with his iPhone. Doing what? Playing a racing game, although he did glance up occasionally and ask questions.[13] Research done by an HR consulting firm found that U.S. and U.K. employees cost their businesses $37 billion every year because they don't really understand their jobs.[14]

Somewhere, somehow communication isn't being as effective as it needs to be. One reason is that managers face barriers that can distort the interpersonal communication process. Let's look at these barriers to effective communication.

Barriers to Communication

filtering
The deliberate manipulation of information to make it appear more favorable to the receiver

FILTERING **Filtering** is the deliberate manipulation of information to make it appear more favorable to the receiver. For example, when a person tells his or her manager what the manager wants to hear, information is being filtered. Or if information being communicated up through organizational levels is condensed by senders, that's filtering.

How much filtering takes place tends to be a function of the number of vertical levels in the organization and the organizational culture. The more vertical levels in an organization, the more opportunities there are for filtering. As organizations use more collaborative, cooperative work arrangements, information filtering may become less of a problem. In addition, e-mail reduces filtering because communication is more direct. Finally, the organizational culture encourages or discourages filtering by the type of behavior it rewards. The more that organizational rewards emphasize style and appearance, the more managers may be motivated to filter communications in their favor.

EMOTIONS How a receiver feels when a message is received influences how he or she interprets it. Extreme emotions are most likely to hinder effective communication.

In such instances, we often disregard our rational and objective thinking processes and substitute emotional judgments.

INFORMATION OVERLOAD   A marketing manager goes on a week-long sales trip to Spain where he doesn't have access to his e-mail, and he faces 1,000 messages on his return. It's not possible to fully read and respond to each message without facing **information overload**, which is when information exceeds our processing capacity. Today's employees frequently complain of information overload. Statistics show that 87 percent of employees use e-mail and that the average business e-mail user devotes 107 minutes a day to e-mail—about 25 percent of the workday. Other statistics show that employees send and receive an average of 112 e-mail messages every day. And the number of worldwide e-mail messages (not just workplace e-mails) sent daily is a staggering 294 billion.[15] The demands of keeping up with e-mail, text messages, phone calls, faxes, meetings, and professional reading create an onslaught of data. What happens when individuals have more information than they can process? They tend to ignore, pass over, forget, or selectively choose information. Or they may stop communicating. Regardless, the result is lost information and ineffective communication.

> **information overload**
> When information exceeds our processing capacity

DEFENSIVENESS   When people feel they're being threatened, they tend to react in ways that hinder effective communication and reduce their ability to achieve mutual understanding. They become defensive—verbally attacking others, making sarcastic remarks, being overly judgmental, or questioning others' motives.[16]

LANGUAGE   Conservative author/journalist Ann Coulter and rapper Nelly both speak English, but the language each uses is vastly different. Words mean different things to different people. Age, education, and cultural background are three of the more obvious variables that influence the language a person uses and the definitions he or she gives to words.

In an organization, employees come from diverse backgrounds and have different patterns of speech. Even employees who work for the same organization but in different departments often have different **jargon**—specialized terminology or technical language that members of a group use to communicate among themselves.

> **jargon**
> Specialized terminology or technical language that members of a group use to communicate among themselves

NATIONAL CULTURE   For technological and cultural reasons, the Chinese people dislike voice mail.[17] This general tendency illustrates how communication differences can arise from national culture as well as different languages. For example, let's compare countries that value individualism (such as the United States) with countries that emphasize collectivism (such as Japan).[18]

In an individualistic country like the United States, communication is more formal and is clearly spelled out. Managers rely heavily on reports, memos, and other formal forms of communication. In a collectivist country like Japan, more interpersonal contact takes place, and face-to-face communication is encouraged. A Japanese manager extensively consults with subordinates over an issue first and draws up a formal document later to outline the agreement that was made.

Overcoming the Barriers

On average, an individual must hear new information seven times before he or she truly understands.[19] In light of this fact and the communication barriers just described, what can managers do to be more effective communicators?

USE FEEDBACK   Many communication problems are directly attributed to misunderstanding and inaccuracies. These problems are less likely to occur if the manager gets feedback, both verbal and nonverbal.

A manager can ask questions about a message to determine whether it was received and understood as intended. Or the manager can ask the receiver to restate the message in his or her own words. If the manager hears what was intended, understanding and accuracy should improve. Feedback can also be more subtle, and general comments can give a manager a sense of the receiver's reaction to a message.

Feedback also doesn't have to be verbal. If a sales manager e-mails information about a new monthly sales report that all sales representatives will need to complete and some of them don't turn it in, the sales manager has received feedback. This feedback suggests that the sales manager needs to clarify the initial communication. Similarly, managers can look for nonverbal cues to tell whether someone's getting the message.

SIMPLIFY LANGUAGE Because language can be a barrier, managers should consider the audience to whom the message is directed and tailor the language to them.[20] Remember, effective communication is achieved when a message is both received and *understood*. For example, a hospital administrator should always try to communicate in clear, easily understood terms and to use language tailored to different employee groups. Messages to the surgical staff should be purposefully different from those used with office employees. Jargon can facilitate understanding if it's used within a group that knows what it means, but can cause problems when used outside that group.

LISTEN ACTIVELY When someone talks, we hear, but too often we don't listen. Listening is an active search for meaning, whereas hearing is passive. In listening, the receiver is also putting effort into the communication.

Many of us are poor listeners. Why? Because it's difficult, and most of us would rather do the talking. Listening, in fact, is often more tiring than talking. Unlike hearing, **active listening**, which is listening for full meaning without making premature judgments or interpretations, demands total concentration. The average person normally speaks at a rate of about 125 to 200 words per minute. However, the average listener can comprehend up to 400 words per minute.[21] The difference leaves lots of idle brain time and opportunities for the mind to wander.

Active listening is enhanced by developing empathy with the sender—that is, by putting yourself in the sender's position. Because senders differ in attitudes, interests, needs, and expectations, empathy makes it easier to understand the actual content of a message. An empathetic listener reserves judgment on the message's content and carefully listens to what is being said. The goal is to improve one's ability to get the full meaning of a communication without distorting it by premature judgments or interpretations. Other specific behaviors that active listeners demonstrate are listed in Exhibit 16-3. As you can see, active listening takes effort, but it can help make communication much more effective.

active listening
Listening for full meaning without making premature judgments or interpretations

Exhibit 16-3
Active Listening Behaviors

Sources: Based on J. V. Thill and C. L. Bovee, *Excellence in Business Communication*, 9th ed. (Upper Saddle River, NJ: Prentice Hall, 2011), pp. 48–49; and S. P. Robbins and P. L. Hunsaker, *Training in Interpersonal Skills*, 5th ed. (Upper Saddle River, NJ: Prentice Hall, 2009), pp. 90–92.

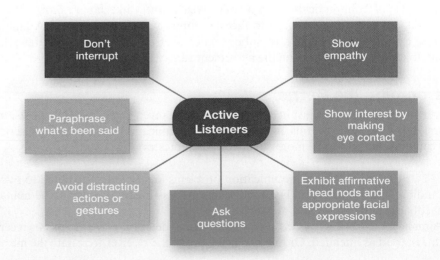

let's get REAL

The Scenario:

Jason Broughton manages a diverse team of corporate security system installers. On his most recent evaluation, his boss told him that his employees have complained that he never listens to what they're telling him. Because Jason hopes to eventually move into positions with more responsibility, he knows he needs to work on this.

What advice would you give Jason?

I would advise Jason to start working on creating a better forum between him and his employees for listening to their feedback. It could be that he listens but does not follow up; and to an employee, this can feel like they were not heard. He may want to implement a monthly meeting to update his team on the business, any structural changes in the company and also as a check in to hear any issues that may have come up. An open door policy can help his team to get more time with Jason and feel comfortable approaching him with issues.

Julie Colon
Creative Project Manager

Source: Julie Colon

CONSTRAIN EMOTIONS It would be naïve to assume that managers always communicate in a rational manner. We know that emotions can cloud and distort communication. A manager who's upset over an issue is more likely to misconstrue incoming messages and fail to communicate his or her outgoing messages clearly and accurately. What to do? The simplest answer is to calm down and get emotions under control before communicating.

WATCH NONVERBAL CUES If actions speak louder than words, then it's important to make sure your actions align with and reinforce the words that go along with them. An effective communicator watches his or her nonverbal cues to ensure that they convey the desired message.

ORGANIZATIONAL Communication

Explain how **16.4**
communication can flow most effectively in organizations.

The European economic crisis has employees everywhere on edge. So when all 1,300 workers at Aviva Investors, the asset management division of a United Kingdom insurance company, opened their e-mail one morning, they found out they'd been fired. Except—it was a mistake. Only one unfortunate employee was supposed to get the message. Can you imagine the stunned silence in that office? A spokesman for the company said an apology was quickly issued for the mistaken e-mail message, but had damage already been done?[22]

Maybe you've had the experience of sitting in an employee meeting with managers when they ask if anyone has any questions—only to be met with deafening silence.[23] Communication can be an interesting thing, especially in organizations. As we've seen, managerial communication is important, but it is a two-way street. An understanding of managerial communication isn't possible without looking at organizational communication. In this section, we look at several important aspects of organizational communication, including formal versus informal communication, the flow patterns of communication, formal and informal communication networks, and workplace design.

Formal Versus Informal Communication

Communication within an organization is described as formal or informal. **Formal communication** refers to communication that takes place within prescribed organizational work arrangements. For example, when a manager asks an employee to complete a task, that's formal communication. Another example of formal communication occurs when an employee communicates a problem to his or her manager.

Informal communication is organizational communication not defined by the organization's structural hierarchy. When employees talk with each other in the lunch room, as they pass in hallways, or as they're working out at the company wellness facility, they engage in informal communication. Employees form friendships and communicate with each other. The informal communication system fulfills two purposes in organizations: (1) it permits employees to satisfy their need for social interaction, and (2) it can improve an organization's performance by creating alternative, and frequently faster and more efficient, channels of communication.

Direction of Communication Flow

Let's look at the ways that organizational communication can flow: downward, upward, laterally, or diagonally.

DOWNWARD   Every morning and often several times a day, managers at UPS package delivery facilities gather workers for mandatory meetings that last precisely three minutes. During those 180 seconds, managers relay company announcements and go over local information like traffic conditions or customer complaints. Then, each meeting ends with a safety tip. The three-minute meetings have proved so successful that many of the company's office workers are using the idea.[24] CEOs at companies such as Starbucks and Apple use **town hall meetings** to communicate with employees. These town hall meetings are informal public meetings where top executives relay information, discuss issues, or bring employees together to celebrate accomplishments. These are examples of **downward communication** which is communication that flows from a manager to employees. It's used to inform, direct, coordinate, and evaluate employees. When managers assign goals to their employees, they're using downward communication. They're also using downward communication when providing employees with job descriptions, informing them of organizational policies and procedures, pointing out problems that need attention, or evaluating their performance. Downward communication can take place through any of the communication methods we described earlier.

UPWARD COMMUNICATION   Managers rely on their employees for information. For instance, reports are given to managers to inform them of progress toward goals or to report any problems. **Upward communication** is communication that flows from employees to managers. It keeps managers aware of how employees feel about their jobs, their coworkers, and the organization in general. Managers also rely on upward communication for ideas on how things can be improved. Some examples of upward communication include performance reports prepared by employees, suggestion boxes, employee attitude surveys, grievance procedures, manager-employee discussions, and informal group sessions in which employees have the opportunity to discuss problems with their manager or representatives of top-level management.

How much upward communication is used depends on the organizational culture. If managers have created a climate of trust and respect and use participative decision making or empowerment, considerable upward communication will occur as employees provide input to decisions. In a more highly structured and authoritarian environment, upward communication still takes place, but is limited.

LATERAL COMMUNICATION   Communication that takes place among employees on the same organizational level is called **lateral communication**. In today's dynamic environment, horizontal communications are frequently needed to save

---

formal communication
Communication that takes place within prescribed organizational work arrangements

informal communication
Communication that is not defined by the organization's structural hierarchy

town hall meeting
Informal public meetings where information can be relayed, issues can be discussed, or just as a way to bring employees together to celebrate accomplishments

downward communication
Communication that flows downward from a manager to employees

upward communication
Communication that flows upward from employees to managers

lateral communication
Communication that takes place among any employees on the same organizational level

time and facilitate coordination. Cross-functional teams, for instance, rely heavily on this form of communication interaction. However, conflicts can arise if employees don't keep their managers informed about decisions they've made or actions they've taken.

DIAGONAL COMMUNICATION   **Diagonal communication** is communication that crosses both work areas *and* organizational levels. A credit analyst who communicates directly with a regional marketing manager about a customer's problem—note the different department and different organizational level—uses diagonal communication. Because of its efficiency and speed, diagonal communication can be beneficial. Increased e-mail use facilitates diagonal communication. In many organizations, any employee can communicate by e-mail with any other employee, regardless of organizational work area or level, even with upper-level managers. In many organizations, CEOs have adopted an "open inbox" e-mail policy. For example, William H. Swanson, head of defense contractor Raytheon Company, figures he has received and answered more than 150,000 employee e-mails. And Henry McKinnell Jr., former CEO of Pfizer, says the approximately 75 internal e-mails he received every day were "an avenue of communication I didn't otherwise have."[25] However, diagonal communication also has the potential to create problems if employees don't keep their managers informed.

diagonal communication
Communication that cuts across work areas and organizational levels

Organizational Communication Networks

The vertical and horizontal flows of organizational communication can be combined into a variety of patterns called **communication networks**. Exhibit 16-4 illustrates three common communication networks.

communication networks
The variety of patterns of vertical and horizontal flows of organizational communication

TYPES OF COMMUNICATION NETWORKS   In the *chain* network, communication flows according to the formal chain of command, both downward and upward. The *wheel* network represents communication flowing between a clearly identifiable and strong leader and others in a work group or team. The leader serves as the hub through whom all communication passes. Finally, in the *all-channel* network, communication flows freely among all members of a work team.

Which form of network you should use depends on your goal. Exhibit 16-4 also summarizes each network's effectiveness according to four criteria: speed, accuracy, the probability that a leader will emerge, and the importance of member satisfaction. One observation is immediately apparent: No single network is best for all situations.

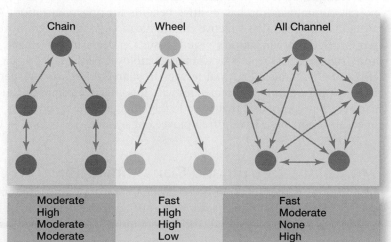

Exhibit 16-4
Organizational Communication Networks

CRITERIA	Chain	Wheel	All Channel
Speed	Moderate	Fast	Fast
Accuracy	High	High	Moderate
Emergence of leader	Moderate	High	None
Member satisfaction	Moderate	Low	High

let's get REAL

The Scenario:

Alexandra Pavlou has a delicate, potentially touchy issue she needs to discuss with her team of real estate appraisers. How can she approach this discussion with care and yet address the issue frankly?

What advice would you give Alexandra?

The discussion should be held in a private setting with all the facts at hand. Alexandra should be prepared to address any concerns as to how this will directly affect each of her team members. Depending on the severity, she should consider individual conversations, instead of a group meeting.

Kelly Osorio
Human Resources Manager

---

grapevine
The informal organizational communication network

THE GRAPEVINE We can't leave our discussion of communication networks without discussing the **grapevine**—the informal organizational communication network. The grapevine is active in almost every organization. Is it an important source of information? You bet! One survey reported that 63 percent of employees say they hear about important matters first through rumors or gossip on the grapevine.[26]

Certainly, the grapevine is an important part of any communication network and well worth understanding.[27] Acting as both a filter and a feedback mechanism, it pinpoints those bewildering issues that employees consider important. More importantly, from a managerial point of view, it *is* possible to analyze what is happening on the grapevine—what information is being passed, how information seems to flow, and what individuals seem to be key information conduits. By staying aware of the grapevine's flow and patterns, managers can identify issues that concern employees and in turn use the grapevine to disseminate important information. Because the grapevine can't be eliminated, managers should "manage" it as an important information network.

Rumors that flow along the grapevine also can never be eliminated entirely. However, managers can minimize the negative consequences of rumors. How? By communicating openly, fully, and honestly with employees, particularly in situations where employees may not like proposed or actual managerial decisions. Open and honest communication has positive benefits for an organization. A study by Towers Watson concluded that effective communication "connects employees to the business, reinforces the organization's vision, fosters process improvement, facilitates change, and drives business results by changing employee behavior." For those companies with effective communication, total returns to shareholders were 91 percent higher over a five-year period than for companies with less effective communication. This study also showed that companies that were highly effective communicators were four times as likely to report high levels of employee engagement as firms that communicated less effectively.[28]

Workplace Design and Communication

In addition to the direction of communication flow and organizational communication networks, another factor that influences organizational communication is workplace design. Despite all the information technology and associated employee mobility (which we'll discuss in the next section), much of an organization's communication still occurs in the workplace. In fact, some 74 percent of an employee's average workweek is spent in an office.[29] How that office workspace is designed and configured can affect the communication that occurs as well as influence an organization's overall performance. In fact, in a survey of American workers, 90 percent believed that better workplace design and layout result in better overall employee performance.[30]

Research shows that a workplace design should successfully support four types of employee work: focused work, collaboration, learning, and socialization.[31] Focused work is when an employee needs to concentrate on completing a task. In collaboration, employees need to work together to complete a task.

Learning is when employees are engaged in training or doing something new and could involve both focused work and collaboration. And socialization happens when employees informally gather to chat or to exchange ideas. A survey found that when workers had these types of "oases" or informal meeting places nearby, they had 102 percent more face-to-face communication than people who had only minimal access to such spots.[32] Because communication can and does take place in each of these settings, the workplace design needs to accommodate these organizational and interpersonal communications—all directions and all types—in order to be most effective.

As managers design the physical work environment, two common design elements have the greatest impact on communication.[33] First, the enclosures and barriers used in the workspace. Many organizational workplaces today—some 68 percent—are **open workplaces**; that is, they include few physical barriers and enclosures.[34] Research has shown both the merits and the drawbacks of an open workplace.[35] One of the things we know for sure about this type of arrangement and its effect on communication is *visibility*. People in open cubicles placed along main routes of circulation or adjacent to atria reported almost 60 percent more face-to-face communication with team members than did those in lower-visibility locations. Another thing is *density*. More people populating an immediate work area meant that more face-to-face interactions took place. Workspaces with a high density yielded 84 percent more team-member communication than did workspace arrangements with a low density. If it's important that employees communicate and collaborate, managers need to consider visibility and density in workplace design. Another consideration in any open workplace is making sure to have some area where sensitive discussions can take place when needed. For instance, when private personnel matters need to be addressed, those shouldn't take place where interruptions or "eavesdropping" can occur.

Another workplace design element is the availability of adjustable work arrangements, equipment, and furnishings. As organizations have moved toward nontraditional work arrangements, the adjustability and customizability of employee workspace have become essential and influence organizational communication. For instance, one study found that adjustable partitions were associated with both greater perceived privacy and better communication.

As companies shrink workspaces to save money, managers need to ensure that the smaller and generally more open workspaces are useful and contribute to efficient and effective work.[36] By providing workspaces where employees can have some privacy and still have opportunities for collaborative efforts, both interpersonal and organizational communication can flourish and contribute to the organization's overall performance.

Skype's business goal is to break down the barriers to communication by developing technology that is inventive, dependable, easy to use, and affordable. In support of this goal, open workplace designs at Skype's offices throughout the world provide a comfortable and relaxed environment that encourages concentration, productivity, and creativity and in which employees can easily communicate and collaborate with each other. Skype's core development team of engineers and designers work from offices in Tallinn, Estonia, shown here, where informal spaces support focused work, collaboration, learning, and socialization.
Source: Amruth/Caro Fotos/SIPA/Newscom

open workplaces
Workplaces with few physical barriers and enclosures

16.5 | *Describe* how technology affects managerial communication and organizations.

INFORMATION Technology and Communication

Technology is changing the way we live and work. Take the following four examples: Chefs are using digital approaches to solve a kitchen crisis—recipe clutter. Japanese employees, managers, housewives, and teens use wireless interactive Web phones to send e-mail, surf the Web, swap photos, and play computer games. At DreamWorks Animation, a sophisticated videoconferencing system allows animators in three different locations to collaboratively edit films. Several thousand employees at Ford use cell phones exclusively at work. A recent survey of employees showed that 93 percent of those polled use the Internet at work. Employees at Lockheed Martin Corporation can access an internal social media site called Unity, which includes tools such as blogs, wikis, file-sharing, discussion forums, and social bookmarking.[37]

The world of communication isn't what it used to be! Although changing technology has been a significant source of the environmental uncertainty facing organizations, these same technological changes have enabled managers to coordinate employees' work efforts in more efficient and effective ways. Information technology (IT) now touches every aspect of almost every company's business. The implications for the ways managers communicate are profound.

How Technology Affects Managerial Communication

IT has radically changed the way organizational members communicate. For example, it has significantly improved a manager's ability to monitor individual and team performance, has allowed employees to have more complete information to make faster decisions, and has provided employees more opportunities to collaborate and share information. In addition, IT has made it possible for people in organizations to be fully accessible, any time, regardless of where they are. Employees don't have to be at their desk with their computer running to communicate with others in the

FUTURE VISION | Office of Tomorrow

The office of tomorrow is still likely to resemble the office of today. There probably won't be mail delivery by robots on hovercraft nor any teleportation devices. Most of the changes, however, will likely be in the way we communicate.[38] Employees will rely on multiple channels of communication with heavy reliance on social networks, text messaging, and instant messaging. Smartphones will be as powerful as today's mainframes, meaning employees will be able to do heavy computing on the go. Software will be able to track where employees are and blend that data with information about current projects and suggest potential collaborators. E-mail is likely to decline in popularity, largely because other channels are faster, more fluid, and more immediate.

Accurately forecasting tomorrow's technology is impossible. But several patterns seem to be evolving. For instance, the combining of functions in a single device is likely to result in employees having a single product that will combine phone, text messaging, Internet access, video camera, teleconferencing, and language translator. It will allow people to read proposals, legal papers, news, or almost any document digitally. It won't need a keyboard and will operate via voice commands. It's also likely not to be handheld but rather something akin to combining reading glasses and an earpiece. You'll read documents through the lenses of what look like normal reading glasses and the earpiece/microphone will make it hands-free.

Another outcome made possible by technology will be a significant decrease in business travel. Improvements in computer-mediated groupware will allow individuals to conduct meetings in environments that closely simulate face-to-face interactions. In settings where employees use different languages, real-time translations will be transcribed and displayed on screen and teleconferencers will be able to hear and see the words.

organization. Two IT developments that are most significant for managerial communication are networked systems and wireless capabilities.

NETWORKED SYSTEMS In a networked system, an organization's computers are linked. Organizational members can communicate with each other and tap into information whether they're down the hall, across town, or halfway across the world. We're not looking at the mechanics of how a network system works, but some of its communication applications include e-mail; instant messaging; social media such as blogs, wikis, and Twitter; webinars; voice-mail; fax; teleconferencing and videoconferencing; and intranets.

WIRELESS CAPABILITIES At Seattle-based Starbucks Corporation, district managers use mobile technology, giving them more time to spend in the company's stores. A company executive says, "These are the most important people in the company. Each has between 8 to 10 stores that he or she services. And while their primary job is outside of the office—and in those stores—they still need to be connected."[39] As this example shows, wireless communication technology has the ability to improve work for managers and employees. Even Internet access is available through Wi-Fi and WiMax hot spots, which are locations where users gain wireless access. The number of these hot spot locations continues to grow. With more than 50 million "mobile" workers in the United States, smartphones, notebook computers, computing devices such as iPad, and other pocket communication devices have generated whole new ways for managers to "keep in touch." And the number of mobile communication users keeps increasing.[40] Employees don't have to be at their desks to communicate with others in the organization. As wireless technology continues to improve, we'll see more organizational members using it as a way to collaborate and share information.

How Information Technology Affects Organizations

Monsanto Company wanted to raise the visibility of some projects and to make a stronger argument for bioengineered crops. Using a YouTube approach, the company sent camera crews to the Philippines, Australia, and other countries to film testimonials from farmers using Monsanto products to grow these crops. The clips were posted on a company Web site, which now attracts more than 15,000 visitors a month. The PR manager in charge of the project said, "When the people involved relate how their life has changed and you actually see it, it's more compelling."[41] That's the power of IT at work. Employees—working in teams or as individuals—need information to make decisions and to do their work. It's clear that technology *can* significantly affect the way that organizational members communicate, share information, and do their work.

Communication and the exchange of information among organizational members are no longer constrained by geography or time. Collaborative work efforts among widely dispersed individuals and teams, sharing of information, and integration of decisions and work throughout an entire organization have the potential to increase organizational efficiency and effectiveness. And while the economic benefits of IT are obvious, managers must not forget the psychological drawbacks.[42] For instance, what is the psychological cost of an employee always being accessible? Will it lead to increased pressure for employees to "check in" even during their off hours? How important is it for employees to separate their work and personal lives? These questions don't come with easy answers, and managers will have to face these and similar issues.

IT technology has affected the communication and exchange of information among doctors, medical staff, and patients by removing the constraints of geography and time. Shown here is Doctor Nir Cohen working on his Apple iPad before visiting a patient at the Mayanei Hayeshua Medical Center in Bnei Brak, Israel. Using iPads enables Dr. Cohen and his medical staff to check patients' records, test results, and other medical information; to study high-resolution X-rays and CT scans from both within and outside the hospital; and to diagnose and prescribe treatment immediately at any time.
Source: Reuters/Nir Elias

16.6 ⌈ **Discuss**
*contemporary issues in
communication.*

COMMUNICATION Issues in Today's Organizations

"Pulse lunches." That's what managers at Citibank's offices throughout Malaysia used to address pressing problems of declining customer loyalty and staff morale and increased employee turnover. By connecting with employees and listening to their concerns—that is, taking their "pulse"—during informal lunch settings, managers were able to make changes that boosted both customer loyalty and employee morale by more than 50 percent and reduced employee turnover to nearly zero.[43]

Being an effective communicator in today's organizations means being connected—not only to employees and customers, but to any of the organization's stakeholders. In this section, we examine five communication issues of particular significance to today's managers: managing communication in an Internet world, managing the organization's knowledge resources, communicating with customers, getting employee input, and communicating ethically.

Managing Communication in an Internet World

Lars Dalgaard, founder and chief executive of SuccessFactors, a human resource management software company, recently sent an e-mail to his employees banning in-house e-mail for a week. His goal? Getting employees to "authentically address issues amongst each other."[44] And he's not alone. Other companies have tried the same thing. (See Case Application 1 at the end of the chapter.) As we discussed earlier, e-mail can consume employees, but it's not always easy for them to let go of it, even when they know it can be "intexticating." But e-mail is only one communication challenge in this Internet world. A recent survey found that 20 percent of employees at large companies say they contribute regularly to blogs, social networks, wikis, and other Web services.[45] Managers are learning, the hard way sometimes, that all this new technology has created special communication challenges. The two main ones are (1) legal and security issues, and (2) lack of personal interaction.

LEGAL AND SECURITY ISSUES Chevron paid $2.2 million to settle a sexual-harassment lawsuit stemming from inappropriate jokes being sent by employees over company e-mail. U.K. firm Norwich Union had to pay £450,000 in an out-of-court settlement after an employee sent an e-mail stating that their competitor Western Provident Association was experiencing financial difficulties. Whole Foods Market was investigated by federal regulators and its board after CEO John P. Mackey used a pseudonym to post comments on a blog attacking the company's rival Wild Oats Markets.[46]

Although e-mail, blogs, tweets, and other forms of online communication are quick and easy ways to communicate, managers need to be aware of potential legal problems from inappropriate usage. Electronic information is potentially admissible in court. For instance, during the Enron trial, prosecutors entered into evidence e-mails and other documents they say showed that the defendants defrauded investors. Says one expert, "Today, e-mail and instant messaging are the electronic equivalent of DNA evidence."[47] But legal problems aren't the only issue—security concerns are as well.

A survey addressing outbound e-mail and content security found that 26 percent of the companies surveyed saw their businesses affected by the exposure of sensitive or embarrassing information.[48] Managers need to ensure that confidential information is kept confidential. Employee e-mails and blogs should not communicate—inadvertently or purposely—proprietary information. Corporate computer and e-mail systems should be protected against hackers (people who try to gain unauthorized access) and spam (electronic junk mail). These serious issues must be addressed if the benefits of communication technology are to be realized.

PERSONAL INTERACTION It may be called social media, but another communication challenge posed by the Internet age we live and work in is the lack of personal interaction.[49] Even when two people are communicating face-to-face, understanding is not always achieved. However, it can be especially challenging to achieve understanding and collaborate on getting work done when communication takes place in a virtual environment. In response, some companies have banned e-mail on certain days, as we saw earlier. Others have simply encouraged employees to collaborate more in-person. Yet, in some situations and at certain times, personal interaction isn't physically possible—your colleagues work across the continent or even across the globe. In those instances, real-time collaboration software (such as private workplace wikis, blogs, instant messengers, and other types of groupware) may be a better communication choice than sending an e-mail and waiting for a response.[50] Instead of fighting it, other companies are encouraging employees to utilize the power of social networks to collaborate on work and to build strong connections. This form of interaction is especially appealing to younger workers who are comfortable with this communication medium. Some companies have gone as far as creating their own in-house social networks. For instance, employees at Starcom MediaVest Group tap into SMG Connected to find colleague profiles that outline their jobs, list the brands they admire, and describe their values. A company vice president says, "Giving our employees a way to connect over the Internet around the world made sense because they were doing it anyway."[51]

Managing the Organization's Knowledge Resources

Kara Johnson is a materials expert at product design firm IDEO. To make finding the right materials easier, she's building a master library of samples linked to a database that explains their properties and manufacturing processes.[52] What Johnson is doing is managing knowledge and making it easier for others at IDEO to learn and benefit from her knowledge. That's what today's managers need to do with the organization's knowledge resources—make it easy for employees to communicate and share their knowledge so they can learn from each other ways to do their jobs more effectively and efficiently. One way organizations can do this is to build online information databases that employees can access. For example, William Wrigley Jr. Co. launched an interactive Web site that allows sales agents to access marketing data and other product information. The sales agents can question company experts about products or search an online knowledge bank. In its first year, Wrigley estimates that the site cut research time of the sales force by 15,000 hours, making them more efficient and effective.[53]

In addition to online information databases for sharing knowledge, companies could create communities of practice, a concept that we introduced in Chapter 12, as a type of internal collaboration. To make these communities of practice work, however, it's important to maintain strong human interactions through communication using such essential tools as interactive Web sites, e-mail, and videoconferencing. In addition, these groups face the same communication problems that individuals face—filtering, emotions, defensiveness, overdocumentation, and so forth. However, groups can resolve these issues by focusing on the same suggestions we discussed earlier.

The Role of Communication in Customer Service

You've been a customer many times; in fact, you probably find yourself in a customer service encounter several times a day. So what does this have to do with communication? As it turns out, a lot! *What* communication takes place and *how* it takes place can have a significant impact on a customer's satisfaction with the service and the likelihood of being a repeat customer. Managers in service organizations need to make sure that employees who interact with customers are communicating appropriately and effectively with those customers. How? By first recognizing the three components in any service delivery process: the customer, the service organization, and the individual service provider.[54] Each plays a role in whether communication is

*data*points[55]

53 percent of companies have a policy for managing employees' use of social media.

176 square feet is now the average office space per workers. In 2010, it was 225 square feet; in 2017, it's forecasted to be 151 square feet.

70 percent of executives ranked in-person meetings as most valuable for an initial interaction with a new team member.

83 percent of employers use e-mail to engage employees and foster productivity; 75 percent use their organization's intranet to do so.

45 percent of North American workers use their mobile devices during lunch; 44 percent use it before going to work.

38 percent of employees have a negative view of workers with a messy desk.

15 percent of employees say that if there were no consequences, they'd say to their boss that they need a chance to express their ideas.

28 percent of survey respondents said that phone calls were the most common workplace distraction; 23 percent cited e-mails.

1 of every 7 communications by managers is redundant with a previous communication using a different technology.

No. 1 form of evidence in any employment law dispute is … e-mail.

44 percent of the time, e-mails are misinterpreted.

working. Obviously, managers don't have a lot of control over what or how the customer communicates, but they can influence the other two.

An organization with a strong service culture already values taking care of customers—finding out what their needs are, meeting those needs, and following up to make sure that their needs were met satisfactorily. Each of these activities involves communication, whether face-to-face, by phone or e-mail, or through other channels. In addition, communication is part of the specific customer service strategies the organization pursues. One strategy that many service organizations use is personalization. For instance, at Ritz-Carlton Hotels, customers are provided with more than a clean bed and room. Customers who have stayed at a location previously and indicated that certain items are important to them—such as extra pillows, hot chocolate, or a certain brand of shampoo—will find those items waiting in their room at arrival. The hotel's database allows service to be personalized to customers' expectations. In addition, all employees are asked to communicate information related to service provision. For instance, if a room attendant overhears guests talking about celebrating an anniversary, he or she is supposed to relay the information so something special can be done.[56] Communication plays an important role in the hotel's customer personalization strategy.

The opinions and ideas of employees are valued by sisters Jenny Briones (left) and Lisa De Bono (right), who, along with their mother, are owner-operators of nine McDonald's restaurants. Communication plays a big part in the growth and success of the family business. Jenny and Lisa engender trust and respect among their managers, employees, and customers by frequently visiting restaurants and encouraging everyone to voice their opinions and share information that will improve their business. In this photo, they seek out feedback from one of their managers about a new incentive plan for their restaurant crew members.
Source: ZUMA Press/Newscom

Communication also is important to the individual service provider or contact employee. The quality of the interpersonal interaction between the customer and that contact employee does influence customer satisfaction, especially when the service encounter isn't up to expectations.[57] People on the front line involved with those "critical service encounters" are often the first to hear about or notice service failures or breakdowns. They must decide *how* and *what* to communicate during these instances. Their ability to listen actively and communicate appropriately with the customer goes a long way in whether the situation is resolved to the customer's satisfaction or spirals out of control. Another important communication concern for the individual service provider is making sure that he or she has the information needed to deal with customers efficiently and effectively. If the service provider doesn't personally have the information, some way needs to be devised to get the information easily and promptly.[58]

Getting Employee Input

Nokia recently set up an intranet soapbox known as Blog-Hub, opening it up to employee bloggers around the world. There, employees have griped about their employer, but rather than shutting it down, Nokia managers want them to "fire away." They feel that Nokia's growth and success can be attributed to a "history of encouraging employees to say whatever's on their minds, with faith that smarter ideas will result."[59]

In today's challenging environment, companies need to get input from their employees. Have you ever worked somewhere that had an employee suggestion box? When an employee had an idea about a new way of doing something—such as reducing costs, improving delivery time, and so forth—it went into the suggestion box where it usually sat until someone decided to empty the box. Businesspeople frequently joked about the suggestion box, and cartoonists lambasted the futility of putting ideas in the employee suggestion box. And unfortunately, this attitude about suggestion boxes still persists in many organizations, and it shouldn't. Managers do business in a world today where you can't afford to ignore such potentially valuable information. Exhibit 16-5 lists some suggestions for letting employees know that their opinions matter.

- *Hold town-hall meetings* where information is shared and input solicited.
- *Provide information* about what's going on, good and bad.
- *Invest in training* so that employees see how they impact the customer experience.
- *Analyze problems together*—managers and employees.
- *Make it easy* for employees to give input by setting up different ways for them to do so (online, suggestion box, preprinted cards, and so forth).

Exhibit 16-5
How to Let Employees Know Their Input Matters

Communicating Ethically

It's particularly important today that a company's communication efforts be ethical. **Ethical communication** "includes all relevant information, is true in every sense, and is not deceptive in any way."[60] On the other hand, unethical communication often distorts the truth or manipulates audiences. What are some ways that companies communicate unethically? It could be by omitting essential information. For instance, not telling employees that an impending merger is going to mean some of them will lose their jobs is unethical. It's unethical to plagiarize, which is "presenting someone else's words or other creative product as your own."[61] It would also be unethical communication to selectively misquote, misrepresent numbers, distort visuals, and fail to respect privacy or information security needs. For instance, although British Petroleum attempted to communicate openly and truthfully about the Gulf Coast oil spill in the summer of 2010, the public still felt that much of the company's communication contained some unethical elements.

ethical communication
Communication that includes all relevant information, is true in every sense, and is not deceptive in any way

So how can managers encourage ethical communications? One thing is to "establish clear guidelines for ethical behavior, including ethical business communication.[62] In a global survey by the International Association of Business Communicators, 70 percent of communication professionals said their companies clearly define what is considered ethical and unethical behavior."[63] If no clear guidelines exist, it's important to answer the following questions:

- Has the situation been defined fairly and accurately?
- Why is the message being communicated?
- How will the people who may be affected by the message or who receive the message be impacted?
- Does the message help achieve the greatest possible good while minimizing possible harm?
- Will this decision that appears to be ethical now seem so in the future?
- How comfortable are you with your communication effort? What would a person you admire think of it?[64]

Remember that as a manager, you have a responsibility to think through your communication choices and the consequences of those choices. If you always operate with these two things in mind, you're likely to have ethical communication.

CHAPTER

PREPARING FOR: Exams/Quizzes
CHAPTER SUMMARY by Learning Outcomes

16.1 [LEARNING OUTCOME]

Define the nature and function of communication.

Communication is the transfer and understanding of meaning. Interpersonal communication is communication between two or more people. Organizational communication includes all the patterns, networks, and systems of communication within an organization.

    The functions of communication include controlling employee behavior, motivating employees, providing a release for emotional expression of feelings and fulfillment of social needs, and providing information.

16.2 [LEARNING OUTCOME]

Compare and contrast methods of interpersonal communication.

The communication process contains seven elements. First, a *sender* has a message. A *message* is a purpose to be conveyed. *Encoding* converts a message into symbols. A *channel* is the medium a message travels along. *Decoding* happens when the *receiver* retranslates a sender's message. Finally, *feedback* occurs.

    Managers can evaluate the various communication methods according to their feedback, complexity capacity, breadth potential, confidentiality, encoding ease, decoding ease, time-space constraint, cost, interpersonal warmth, formality, scanability, and time of consumption.

    The communication methods include face-to-face, telephone, group meetings, formal presentations, memos, traditional mail, fax, employee publications, bulletin boards, other company publications, audio- and videotapes, hotlines, e-mail, computer conferencing, voice mail, teleconferences, and videoconferences.

16.3 [LEARNING OUTCOME]

Identify barriers to effective interpersonal communication and how to overcome them.

The barriers to effective communication include filtering, emotions, information overload, defensiveness, language, and national culture.

    Managers can overcome these barriers by using feedback, simplifying language, listening actively, constraining emotions, and watching for nonverbal clues.

16.4 [LEARNING OUTCOME]

Explain how communication can flow most effectively in organizations.

Formal communication is communication that takes place within prescribed organizational work arrangements. Informal communication is not defined by the organization's structural hierarchy.

    Communication in an organization can flow downward, upward, laterally, and diagonally.

    The three communication networks include the chain, in which communication flows according to the formal chain of command; the wheel, in which communication flows between a clearly identifiable and strong leader and others in a work team; and the all-channel, in which communication flows freely among all members of a work team.

    Managers should manage the grapevine as an important information network. The negative consequences of rumors can be minimized by communicating openly, fully, and honestly with employees.

Workplace design also influences organizational communication. That design should support four types of employee work: focused work, collaboration, learning, and socialization. In each of these circumstances, communication must be considered.

16.5 [LEARNING OUTCOME]

Describe how technology affects managerial communication and organizations.

Technology has radically changed the way organizational members communicate. It improves a manager's ability to monitor performance; it gives employees more complete information to make faster decisions; it has provided employees more opportunities to collaborate and share information; and it has made it possible for people to be fully accessible, anytime anywhere.

IT affects organizations by influencing the way that organizational members communicate, share information, and do their work.

16.6 [LEARNING OUTCOME]

Discuss contemporary issues in communication.

The two main challenges of managing communication in an Internet world are the legal and security issues and the lack of personal interaction.

Organizations can manage knowledge by making it easy for employees to communicate and share their knowledge, which can help them learn from each other ways to do their jobs more effectively and efficiently. One way is through online information databases and another way is through creating communities of practice.

Communicating with customers is an important managerial issue since *what* communication takes place and *how* it takes place can significantly affect a customer's satisfaction with the service and the likelihood of being a repeat customer.

It's important for organizations to get input from their employees. Such potentially valuable information should not be ignored.

Finally, a company's communication efforts need to be ethical. Ethical communication can be encouraged through clear guidelines and through answering questions that force a communicator to think through the communication choices made and the consequences of those choices.

REVIEW AND DISCUSSION QUESTIONS ⭐

1. Define communication, interpersonal communication, and organizational communication. Why isn't effective communication synonymous with *agreement?*

2. What are the functions of communication?

3. Explain the components in the communication process.

4. What are the various communication methods managers can use? What criteria can managers use to evaluate those communication methods?

5. Contrast formal and informal communication.

6. Explain communication flow, the three common communication networks, and how managers should handle the grapevine.

7. Discuss the five contemporary communication issues facing managers.

8. Which do you think is more important for a manager: speaking accurately or listening actively? Why?

PREPARING FOR: My Career
ETHICS DILEMMA ⭐

Social networking Web sites can be fun. Staying in touch with old friends or even family is one of the pleasures of joining. However, what happens when colleagues or even your boss want to "friend" you? Experts say that you should proceed with caution.[65] What do you think? Is it okay to provide people you know in a professional sense a "window into your personal life?" What ethical issues might arise in such a situation?

SKILLS EXERCISE Developing Your Active Listening Skill

About the Skill

Active listening requires you to concentrate on what is being said. It's more than just hearing the words. It involves a concerted effort to understand and interpret the speaker's message.

Steps in Practicing the Skill

1. *Make eye contact.* How do you feel when somebody doesn't look at you when you're speaking? If you're like most people, you're likely to interpret this behavior as aloofness or disinterest. Making eye contact with the speaker focuses your attention, reduces the likelihood that you will become distracted, and encourages the speaker.

2. *Exhibit affirmative nods and appropriate facial expressions.* The effective listener shows interest in what is being said through nonverbal signals. Affirmative nods and appropriate facial expressions, when added to good eye contact, convey to the speaker that you're listening.

3. *Avoid distracting actions or gestures that suggest boredom.* In addition to showing interest, you must avoid actions that suggest that your mind is somewhere else. When listening, don't look at your watch, shuffle papers, play with your pencil, or engage in similar distractions. They make the speaker feel that you're bored or disinterested or indicate that you aren't fully attentive.

4. *Ask questions.* The critical listener analyzes what he or she hears and asks questions. This behavior provides clarification, ensures understanding, and assures the speaker that you're listening.

5. *Paraphrase what's been said.* The effective listener uses phrases such as "What I hear you saying is..." or "Do you mean...?" Paraphrasing is an excellent control device to check on whether you're listening carefully and to verify that what you heard is accurate.

6. *Avoid interrupting the speaker.* Let the speaker complete his or her thought before you try to respond. Don't try to second-guess where the speaker's thoughts are going. When the speaker is finished, you'll know it.

7. *Stay motivated to listen.* Most of us would rather express our own ideas than listen to what someone else says. Talking might be more fun and silence might be uncomfortable, but you can't talk and listen at the same time. The good listener recognizes this fact and doesn't overtalk.

8. *Make smooth transitions between the roles of speaker and listener.* The effective listener makes transitions smoothly from speaker to listener and back to speaker. From a listening perspective, this means concentrating on what a speaker has to say and practicing not thinking about what you're going to say as soon as you get your chance.

Practicing the Skill

Ask a friend to tell you about his or her day and listen without interrupting. When your friend has finished speaking, ask two or three questions if needed to obtain more clarity and detail. Listen carefully to the answers. Now summarize your friend's day in no more than five sentences.

How well did you do? Let your friend rate the accuracy of your paraphrase (and try not to interrupt).

WORKING TOGETHER Team Exercise

We've all watched and laughed at the oddball videos on YouTube and other online video sites. But what about using online video for work purposes?[66] What uses do you see for online video at work? What would be the advantages and drawbacks of using online video?

Form small groups of three to four individuals. Your team's task is to look at these issues. Answer the questions and be prepared to share your answers with the class.

MY TURN TO BE A MANAGER

• Research the characteristics of a good communicator. Keeping these characteristics in mind, practice being a good communicator—both as a sender and a listener.

• For one day, keep track of the types of communication you use (see Exhibit 16-2 for a list of various types). Which do you use most? Least? Were your choices of communication methods effective? Why or why not? Could they have been improved? How?

• For one day, track nonverbal communication that you notice in others. What types did you observe? Was the nonverbal communication always consistent with the verbal communication taking place? Describe.

• Research new types of IT devices. Write a report describing these devices (at least three) and their applicability to employees and organizations. Be sure to look at both the positive and negative aspects.

- Survey five different managers for their advice on being a good communicator. Put this information in a bulleted list format and be prepared to present it in class.
- Steve's and Mary's recommended readings: Phillip G. Clampitt, *Communicating for Managerial Effectiveness,* 4th ed. (Sage Publications, 2009); John Baldoni, *Great Communication Secrets of Great Leaders* (McGraw-Hill, 2003); Robert Mai and Alan Akerson, *The Leader as Communicator* (AMACOM, 2003); Boyd Clarke, *The Leader's Voice: How Communication Can Inspire Action and Get Results!* (Select Books, 2002); Jo-Ellan Dimitrius and Mark Mazzarella, *Reading People* (Random House, 1998).
- Survey 10 office workers. Ask them: (1) the number of e-mail messages they receive daily, on average; (2) how many times in one day they check their e-mail; and (3) if they think a ban on e-mail messages one day a week would be a good idea and why or why not. Compile this information into a report.
- Pick one of the five topics addressed in the section on Communication Issues in Today's Organizations and do some additional research. Put your findings in a bulleted list and be prepared to discuss in class. Be sure to cite your sources!
- In your own words, write down three things you learned in this chapter about being a good manager.
- Self-knowledge can be a powerful learning tool. Go to mymanagementlab.com and complete these self-assessment exercises: What's My Face-to-Face Communication Style? How Good Are My Listening Skills? How Good Am I at Giving Performance Feedback? Am I a Gossip? Using the results of your assessments, identify personal strengths and weaknesses. What will you do to reinforce your strengths and improve your weaknesses?

MyManagementLab

Go to **mymanagementlab.com** for Auto-graded writing questions as well as the following Assisted-graded writing questions:

16-1. What are the barriers to effective communication? How can those barriers be overcome?

16-2. How does technology affect managerial communication? How does it affect organizations?

16-3. Mymanagementlab Only – comprehensive writing assignment for this chapter.

CASE APPLICATION 1 E-Mail Ban

Believing that most internal e-mail messages are a waste of employees' time and wanting to work with the tools that the young generation is using, Atos CEO Thierry Breton has banned internal e-mails and is replacing them with communication tools that include social networks like Facebook, instant messaging, and microblogging.
Source: Sipa via AP Images

It's estimated that the average corporate user sends and received some 112 e-mails daily.[67] That's about 14 e-mails per hour and even if half of those don't require a lot of time and concentration, that level of e-mail volume can be stressful and lead to unproductive time. Once imagined to be a time-saver, has the inbox become a burden? Back in 2007, U.S. Cellular's executive vice president, Jay Ellison (who has since retired) implemented a ban on e-mail every Friday. In his memo announcing the change to employees, he told them to get out and meet the people they work with rather than sending an e-mail. That directive went over with a thud. One employee confronted him saying that Ellison didn't understand how much work had to get done and how much easier it was when using e-mail. Eventually, however, employees were won over. Forced to use the phone, one employee learned that a co-worker he thought was across the country, was instead, across the hall. Now, in 2012, other executives are discovering the benefits of banning e-mail.

Jessica Rovello, co-founder and president of Arkadium, which develops games, has described e-mail as "a form of business attention-deficit disorder." She found herself—and her employees—putting e-mail in the inbox ahead of everything else being worked on. What she decided to do was only check her e-mail four times a day and to turn off her e-mail notification. Another executive, Tim Fry of Weber Shandwick, a global public relations firm, spent a year preparing to "wean" his employees off their e-mail system. His goal: dramatically reduce how much e-mail employees send and receive. His approach started with the firm's interoffice communication system, which became an internal social network, with elements of Facebook, work group collaboration software, and an employee bulletin board. And then there's Thierry Breton, head of Europe's largest IT firm, Atos. He announced a "zero e-mail policy" to be replaced with a service more like Facebook and Twitter combined.

DISCUSSION QUESTIONS ✪

1. What do you think of this? Do you agree that e-mail can be unproductive in the workplace?

2. Were you surprised at the volume of e-mail an average employee receives daily? What are the challenges of dealing with this volume of e-mail? How much e-mail would you say you receive daily? Has your volume of e-mail increased? Have your had to change your e-mail habits?

3. What do you think of the e-mail "replacement" some businesses are using—more of a social media tool? In what ways might it be better? Worse?

4. What implications can you see for managers and communication from this story?

CASE APPLICATION 2 Delivery Disaster

When two Domino's Pizza employees filmed a gross prank in the kitchen of the restaurant in Conover, North Carolina, the company suddenly had a major public relations crisis on its hands.[68] The video ended up posted on YouTube and other sites and showed a Domino's employee performing unsanitary and vulgar actions while preparing food, with another employee providing narration. By the next day, over a million disgusted people had viewed the video and discussion about Domino's had spread throughout Twitter and Google.

As Domino's quickly realized, social media has the power to take tiny incidents and turn them into marketing crises. A company spokesperson said Domino's had no idea the video had been shot and posted online. When the company first learned about the video, executives decided not to respond aggressively, hoping the controversy would quiet down. What they missed, though, was how these videos can go viral so quickly. The chief marketing officer of a social media marketing firm said companies make a mistake when they assume a negative video will not spread because all too often it does—as Domino's discovered in this case. In just a matter of days, Domino's reputation was damaged. Customers' perception of its quality went from positive to negative. One brand expert said videos showing what this one did, even if the employees never intended to sell the tainted food, can create a situation where customers will think twice about purchasing that product.

So what happened to the two employees? Although they told Domino's executives they never actually delivered the tainted food, they were fired and charged with a felony. And Domino's posted its own video featuring its top manager addressing the incident on YouTube not long after it occurred.

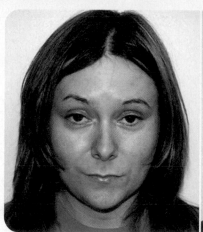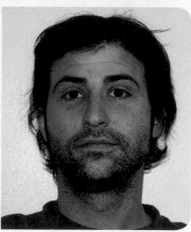

A slow response by Domino's Pizza management to the fast-spreading video posted on YouTube and other sites by these two former employees contaminating the food they were preparing tarnished the company's reputation and changed customers' perception of its product and service quality.
Source: Splash News/Conover P.D./Newscom

DISCUSSION QUESTIONS ✪

1. Beyond its being vulgar and disgusting, what do you think of this situation from the perspective of managing communications?

2. Why do you think Domino's executives took a wait-and-see attitude? Why was this response a problem?

3. How could this type of communication problem be prevented at other Domino's Pizza restaurants?

4. Do incidents like this one and the possibility of them happening anywhere, anytime, mean that all forms of social media should be banned from workplaces? What are the implications for policies regarding communication technology? Discuss.

17 Motivating Employees

SPOTLIGHT: *Manager at Work*

Google gets more than 3,000 applications a day.[1]

And in one week alone, after it had announced a recruitment push, it received 75,000 job applications. Why all the love for Google? It's not surprising since it has set the gold standard for workplace conditions and employee perks. The director of benefits at Google says some of the company's perks include on-site gyms, cafés with healthy food, free all-you-can-eat gourmet meals, swimming pool and spa, onsite laundry, and other over-the-top surprises like a wave pool brought in one day during the summer so employees who wanted to surf could do so. At the Googleplex, the company's "campus" in Mountain View, California, you'd find an indoor treehouse, apiaries, volleyball court, and yes—a yellow brick road. At its New York City office, employees can chow down at a food truck—inside the facility. What more could an employee want? Sounds like an ideal job, doesn't it? However, many employees are demonstrating by their decision to leave the company that all those perks (and there are more) aren't enough to keep them there.

Google is number one on the list of "ideal" employers, and has been in the top five of Fortune's list of "best companies to work for" for six years running and was number one on that list for three of those years, including 2012. But make no mistake. Google's executives offer these fabulous perks for several reasons: to attract the best knowledge workers it can in an intensely competitive, cutthroat market; to help employees work long hours and not have to deal with time-consuming personal chores; to show employees they're valued; and to have employees remain Googlers (the name used for employees) for many years. However, as one employee

Source: Peter DaSilva/Polaris/Newscom

said, "When you get to a place like this, it can tear you apart if you don't find a way to handle the hard-driving culture." And employees continue to jump ship. One analyst wondered why with Google's success and abounding with smart people,

Source: Seth Wenig/AP Photo

Google has set the gold standard for workplace conditions and employee perks.

so many are giving up what appears to be a dream job and going out on their own.

For instance, Sean Knapp and two colleagues, brothers Bismarck and Belsasar Lepe, came up with an idea on how to handle Web video. Google really wanted them—and their project—to stay and offered them a "blank check." But the trio realized they would do all the hard work and Google would own the product. So off they went! If this were an isolated occurrence, it would be easy to write off. But it's not. Other talented Google employees have done the same thing. In fact, there are so many of them who have left that they've formed an informal alumni club.

Google's CEO (and co-founder) Larry Page (see photo above) understands that people are crucial to the company's long-term success. His goal is to hire the very best AND keep them. Page also realizes that while work environment is an important aspect, challenging work is, too.

MyManagementLab®

⭐ **Improve Your Grade!**

Over 10 million students improved their results using the Pearson MyLabs.
Visit **mymanagementlab.com** for simulations, tutorials, and end-of-chapter problems.

LEARNING OUTCOMES

17.1	***Define*** motivation.
17.2	***Compare*** and contrast early theories of motivation.
17.3	***Compare*** and contrast contemporary theories of motivation.
17.4	***Discuss*** current issues in motivation.

He cites projects, such as Google Translate, which has turned mobile phones into pocket translators, and says, "When you work on projects of this magnitude, it's impossible not to wake up excited about work; the chance to make a difference is the greatest motivation anyone can have." **What do you think? Is this motivation "the greatest"?**

Successful managers, like Larry Page, need to understand that what motivates them personally may have little or no effect on others. Just because *you're* motivated by being part of a cohesive work team, don't assume everyone is. Or just because *you're* motivated by your job doesn't mean that everyone is. Effective managers who get employees to put forth maximum effort know how and why those employees are motivated and tailor motivational practices to satisfy their needs and wants.

17.1 *Define* motivation.

WHAT Is Motivation?

According to LinkedIn Corporation, a Web site that provides networking for more than 175 million professionals, "ninja" has far outpaced the growth of other trendy job titles.[2] Although most individuals using that title are computer programmers—who attack writing code like a ninja, with tons of tools available to do battle—the term also has been used to describe expertise in everything from customer service to furniture movers. For instance, in Salt Lake City, one business owner sells the services of "ninja workers" who will do everything from hauling junk to personal security to house-sitting. And at Bonobos, Inc., a New York City start-up that makes and sells men's apparel online, customer-service employees are also called ninjas. Why would a job title matter to employees? Many people, especially the young and young-at-heart, like vivid and unusual titles that celebrate their hard work. And ninja, like other popular job titles before it (guru, evangelist, barista, or even sandwich artist) shows employees that their efforts aren't plain and ordinary, but appreciated.

Would you ever have thought that a job title might be motivating? Have you ever thought about how to motivate someone? It's an important topic in management, and researchers have long been interested in it.[3] All managers need to be able to motivate their employees, which first requires understanding what motivation is. Let's begin by pointing out what motivation is not. Why? Because many people incorrectly view motivation as a personal trait; that is, they think some people are motivated and others aren't. Our knowledge of motivation tells us that we can't label people that way because individuals differ in motivational drive and their overall motivation varies from situation to situation. For instance, you're probably more motivated in some classes than in others.

Motivation refers to the process by which a person's efforts are energized, directed, and sustained toward attaining a goal.[4] This definition has three key elements: energy, direction, and persistence.[5]

The *energy* element is a measure of intensity, drive, and vigor. A motivated person puts forth effort and works hard. However, the quality of the effort must be considered as well as its intensity. High levels of effort don't necessarily lead to favorable job performance unless the effort is channeled in a *direction* that benefits the organization. Effort directed toward and consistent with organizational goals is the kind of effort we want from employees. Finally, motivation includes a *persistence* dimension. We want employees to persist in putting forth effort to achieve those goals.

Motivating high levels of employee performance is an important organizational concern, and managers keep looking for answers. For instance, a Gallup poll found that a large majority of U.S. employees—some 73 percent—are not excited about their work. As the researchers stated, "These employees have essentially 'checked out.' They're sleepwalking through their workday, putting time, but not energy or passion, into their work."[6] It's no wonder then that both managers and academics want to understand and explain employee motivation.

motivation
The process by which a person's efforts are energized, directed, and sustained toward attaining a goal

EARLY Theures of Motivation

We begin by looking at four early motivation theories: *Maslow's hierarchy of needs*, *McGregor's theories X and Y*, *Herzberg's two-factor theory*, and *McClelland's three-needs theory*. Although more valid explanations of motivation have been developed, these early theories are important because they represent the foundation from which contemporary motivation theories were developed and because many practicing managers still use them.

Compare *and contrast* **17.2**
*early theories of
motivation.*

Maslow's Hierarchy of Needs Theory

Having a car to get to work is a necessity for many workers. When two crucial employees of Vurv Technology in Jacksonville, Florida, had trouble getting to work, owner Derek Mercer decided to buy two inexpensive used cars for the employees. He said, "I felt that they were good employees and a valuable asset to the company." One of the employees who got one of the cars said it wasn't the nicest or prettiest car, but it gave him such a sense of relief to know that he had a reliable way to get to work. So when the company needed him to work hard, he was willing to do so.[7] Derek Mercer understands employee needs and their impact on motivation. The first motivation theory we're going to look at addresses employee needs.

The best-known theory of motivation is probably Abraham Maslow's **hierarchy of needs theory**.[8] Maslow was a psychologist who proposed that within every person is a hierarchy of five needs:

1. **Physiological needs**: A person's needs for food, drink, shelter, sex, and other physical requirements.
2. **Safety needs**: A person's needs for security and protection from physical and emotional harm as well as assurance that physical needs will continue to be met.
3. **Social needs**: A person's needs for affection, belongingness, acceptance, and friendship.
4. **Esteem needs**: A person's needs for internal esteem factors such as self-respect, autonomy, and achievement and external esteem factors such as status, recognition, and attention.
5. **Self-actualization needs**: A person's needs for growth, achieving one's potential, and self-fulfillment; the drive to become what one is capable of becoming.

Maslow argued that each level in the needs hierarchy must be substantially satisfied before the next need becomes dominant. An individual moves up the needs hierarchy from one level to the next. (See Exhibit 17-1.) In addition, Maslow separated the five needs into higher and lower levels. Physiological and safety needs were considered *lower-order needs*; social, esteem, and self-actualization needs were considered *higher-order needs*. Lower-order needs are predominantly satisfied externally while higher-order needs are satisfied internally.

How does Maslow's theory explain motivation? Managers using Maslow's hierarchy to motivate employees do things to satisfy employees' needs. But the

hierarchy of needs theory
Maslow's theory that human needs—physiological, safety, social, esteem, and self-actualization—form a sort of hierarchy

physiological needs
A person's needs for food, drink, shelter, sexual satisfaction, and other physical needs

safety needs
A person's needs for security and protection from physical and emotional harm

social needs
A person's needs for affection, belongingness, acceptance, and friendship

esteem needs
A person's needs for internal factors such as self-respect, autonomy, and achievement, and external factors such as status, recognition, and attention

self-actualization needs
A person's need to become what he or she is capable of becoming

Exhibit 17-1
Maslow's Hierarchy of Needs

Source: Abraham H. Maslow, Robert D. Frager, Robert D., and James Fadiman, *Motivation and Personality*, 3rd Edition, © 1987. Adapted by permission of Pearson Education, Inc., Upper Saddle River, NJ.

Satisfying physiological, safety, and social needs may be the most important motivators for these men and women hired to work at a new Procter & Gamble factory in Urlati, Romania. According to Maslow's hierarchy of needs theory, after these employees are assured that their lower-order needs of a salary, a safe job, benefits, and job security are satisfied, they will move up to the next level of social needs. Managers can motivate employees to satisfy their needs for belongingness, acceptance, and friendship by creating an environment that fosters good relationships with co-workers and supervisors, by forming work groups or teams, and by providing leisure and recreational activities that give employees opportunities to socialize.
Source: Bloomberg via Getty Images

Theory X
The assumption that employees dislike work, are lazy, avoid responsibility, and must be coerced to perform

Theory Y
The assumption that employees are creative, enjoy work, seek responsibility, and can exercise self-direction

two-factor theory (motivation-hygiene theory)
The motivation theory that intrinsic factors are related to job satisfaction and motivation, whereas extrinsic factors are associated with job dissatisfaction

theory also says that once a need is substantially satisfied, an individual is no longer motivated to satisfy that need. Therefore, to motivate someone, you need to understand what need level that person is on in the hierarchy and focus on satisfying needs at or above that level.

Maslow's need theory was widely recognized during the 1960s and 1970s, especially among practicing managers, probably because it was intuitively logical and easy to understand. But Maslow provided no empirical support for his theory, and several studies that sought to validate it could not.[9]

McGregor's Theory X and Theory Y

Andy Grove, cofounder of Intel Corporation and now a senior advisor to the company, was known for being open with his employees. However, he was also known for his tendency to yell. Intel's current CEO, Paul Otellini said, "When Andy was yelling at you, it wasn't because he didn't care about you. He was yelling at you because he wanted you to do better."[10] Although managers like Andy Grove want their employees to do better, that approach might not have been the best way to motivate employees as McGregor's Theory X and Theory Y suggest.

Douglas McGregor is best known for proposing two assumptions about human nature: Theory X and Theory Y.[11] Very simply, **Theory X** is a negative view of people that assumes workers have little ambition, dislike work, want to avoid responsibility, and need to be closely controlled to work effectively. **Theory Y** is a positive view that assumes employees enjoy work, seek out and accept responsibility, and exercise self-direction. McGregor believed that Theory Y assumptions should guide management practice and proposed that participation in decision making, responsible and challenging jobs, and good group relations would maximize employee motivation.

Unfortunately, no evidence confirms that either set of assumptions is valid or that being a Theory Y manager is the only way to motivate employees. For instance, Jen-Hsun Huang, founder of Nvidia Corporation, an innovative and successful microchip manufacturer, has been known to use both reassuring hugs and tough love in motivating employees. He also has little tolerance for screw-ups. In one meeting, he supposedly screamed at a project team for its tendency to repeat mistakes. "Do you suck?" he asked the stunned employees. "Because if you suck, just get up and say you suck."[12] His message, delivered in classic Theory X style, was that if you need help, ask for it. It's a harsh approach, but in this case, it worked.

Herzberg's Two-Factor Theory

Frederick Herzberg's **two-factor theory** (also called **motivation-hygiene theory**) proposes that intrinsic factors are related to job satisfaction, while extrinsic factors are associated with job dissatisfaction.[13] Herzberg wanted to know when people felt exceptionally good (satisfied) or bad (dissatisfied) about their jobs. (These findings are shown in Exhibit 17-2.) He concluded that the replies people gave when they felt good about their jobs were significantly different from the replies they gave when they felt badly. Certain characteristics were consistently related to job satisfaction (factors on the left side of the exhibit), and others to job dissatisfaction (factors on the right side). When people felt good about their work, they tended to cite intrinsic factors arising from the job itself such as achievement, recognition, and responsibility. On the other hand, when they were dissatisfied, they tended to cite extrinsic factors arising from the job context such as company policy and administration, supervision, interpersonal relationships, and working conditions.

Motivators	Hygiene Factors
• Achievement	• Supervision
• Recognition	• Company Policy
• Work Itself	• Relationship with
• Responsibility	Supervisor
• Advancement	• Working Conditions
• Growth	• Salary
	• Relationship with Peers
	• Personal Life
	• Relationship with
	Subordinates
	• Status
	• Security
Extremely Satisfied	Neutral	Extremely Dissatisfied

Exhibit 17-2
Herzberg's Two Factor Theory

Source: Based on F. Herzberg, B. Mausner, and B. B. Snyderman, *The Motivation to Work* (New York: John Wiley, 1959).

In addition, Herzberg believed the data suggested that the opposite of satisfaction was not dissatisfaction, as traditionally had been believed. Removing dissatisfying characteristics from a job would not necessarily make that job more satisfying (or motivating). As shown in Exhibit 17-3, Herzberg proposed that a dual continuum existed: The opposite of "satisfaction" is "no satisfaction," and the opposite of "dissatisfaction" is "no dissatisfaction."

Again, Herzberg believed the factors that led to job satisfaction were separate and distinct from those that led to job dissatisfaction. Therefore, managers who sought to eliminate factors that created job dissatisfaction could keep people from being dissatisfied but not necessarily motivate them. The extrinsic factors that create job dissatisfaction were called **hygiene factors**. When these factors are adequate, people won't be dissatisfied, but they won't be satisfied (or motivated) either. To motivate people, Herzberg suggested emphasizing **motivators**, the intrinsic factors having to do with the job itself.

Herzberg's theory enjoyed wide popularity from the mid-1960s to the early 1980s, despite criticisms of his procedures and methodology. Although some critics said his theory was too simplistic, it has influenced how we currently design jobs, especially when it comes to job enrichment, which we'll discuss at a later point in this chapter.

Three-Needs Theory

David McClelland and his associates proposed the **three-needs theory**, which says three acquired (not innate) needs are major motives in work.[14] These three needs include the **need for achievement (nAch)**, the drive to succeed and excel in relation to a set of standards; the **need for power (nPow)**, the need to make others behave in a way they would not have behaved otherwise; and the **need for affiliation (nAff)**, the desire for friendly and close interpersonal relationships. Of these three needs, the need for achievement has been researched the most.

People with a high need for achievement are striving for personal achievement rather than for the trappings and rewards of success. They have a desire to do something better or more efficiently than it's been done before.[15] They prefer jobs that offer personal responsibility for finding solutions to problems, in which they

hygiene factors
Factors that eliminate job dissatisfaction, but don't motivate

motivators
Factors that increase job satisfaction and motivation

three-needs theory
The motivation theory that says three acquired (not innate) needs— achievement, power, and affiliation—are major motives in work

need for achievement (nAch)
The drive to succeed and excel in relation to a set of standards

need for power (nPow)
The need to make others behave in a way that they would not have behaved otherwise

need for affiliation (nAff)
The desire for friendly and close interpersonal relationships

Traditional View	
Satisfied	Dissatisfied

Herzberg's View			
Motivators		Hygiene Factors	
Satisfaction	No Satisfaction	No Dissatisfaction	Dissatisfaction

Exhibit 17-3
Contrasting Views of Satisfaction– Dissatisfaction

Exhibit 17-4
TAT Pictures

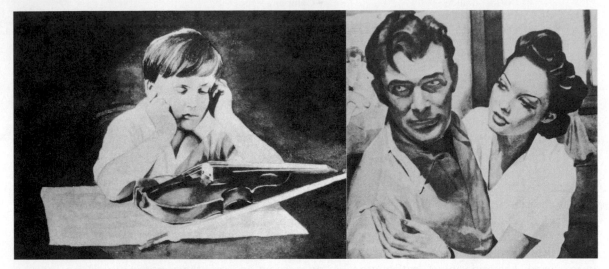

nAch: Indicated by someone in the story wanting to perform or do something better.
nAff: Indicated by someone in the story wanting to be with someone else and enjoy mutual friendship.
nPow: Indicated by someone in the story desiring to have an impact or make an impression on others in the story.

Source for photos: Bill Aron/PhotoEdit, Inc.

can receive rapid and unambiguous feedback on their performance in order to tell whether they're improving, and in which they can set moderately challenging goals. High achievers avoid what they perceive to be very easy or very difficult tasks. Also, a high need to achieve doesn't necessarily lead to being a good manager, especially in large organizations. That's because high achievers focus on their *own* accomplishments, while good managers emphasize helping *others* accomplish their goals.[16] McClelland showed that employees can be trained to stimulate their achievement need by being in situations where they have personal responsibility, feedback, and moderate risks.[17]

The other two needs in this theory haven't been researched as extensively as the need for achievement. However, we do know that the best managers tend to be high in the need for power and low in the need for affiliation.[18]

All three of these needs can be measured by using a projective test (known as the Thematic Apperception Test or TAT) in which respondents react to a set of pictures. Each picture is briefly shown to a person who writes a story based on the picture. (See Exhibit 17-4 for some examples.) Trained interpreters then determine the individual's levels of nAch, nPow, and nAff from the stories written.

17.3 *Compare* and contrast contemporary theories of motivation.

CONTEMPORARY **Theories of Motivation**

The theories we look at in this section represent current explanations of employee motivation. Although these theories may not be as well known as those we just discussed, they are supported by research.[19] These contemporary motivation approaches include goal-setting theory, reinforcement theory, job design theory, equity theory, expectancy theory, and high-involvement work practices.

Goal-Setting Theory

At Wyeth's research division, scientists were given challenging new product quotas in an attempt to bring more efficiency to the innovation process, and their bonuses were contingent on meeting those goals.[20] Before a big assignment or major class project presentation, has a teacher ever encouraged you to "Just do your best"? What does that vague statement mean? Would your performance on a class project have been higher had that teacher said you needed to score a 93 percent to keep your A in the class? Research on goal-setting theory addresses these issues, and the findings, as you'll see, are impressive in terms of the effect that goal specificity, challenge, and feedback have on performance.[21]

Research provides substantial support for **goal-setting theory**, which says that specific goals increase performance and that difficult goals, when accepted, result in higher performance than do easy goals. What does goal-setting theory tell us?

First, working toward a goal is a major source of job motivation. Studies on goal setting have demonstrated that specific and challenging goals are superior motivating forces.[22] Such goals produce a higher output than the generalized goal of "do your best." The specificity of the goal itself acts as an internal stimulus. For instance, when a sales rep commits to making eight sales calls daily, this intention gives him a specific goal to try to attain.

It's not a contradiction that goal-setting theory says that motivation is maximized by *difficult* goals, whereas achievement motivation (from three-needs theory) is stimulated by *moderately challenging* goals.[23] First, goal-setting theory deals with people in general, whereas the conclusions on achievement motivation are based on people who have a high nAch. Given that no more than 10 to 20 percent of North Americans are high achievers (a proportion that's likely lower in underdeveloped countries), difficult goals are still recommended for the majority of employees. Second, the conclusions of goal-setting theory apply to those who accept and are committed to the goals. Difficult goals will lead to higher performance *only* if they are accepted.

Next, will employees try harder if they have the opportunity to participate in the setting of goals? Not always. In some cases, participatively set goals elicit superior performance; in other cases, individuals performed best when their manager assigned goals. However, participation is probably preferable to assigning goals when employees might resist accepting difficult challenges.[25]

LEADER who made a DIFFERENCE

Source: Karl Deblaker/AP Photo

His privately held software company (the world's largest) has made Fortune magazine's list of "Best Companies to Work For" for all 15 years that it's been published.[24] "He" is Jim Goodnight, CEO and co-founder of Cary, North Carolina–based SAS. (See the Case Application about SAS on p. 475.) Goodnight has always believed in taking care of his employees. His company's approach to giving employees flexibility and perks is "so legendary that even Google uses SAS as a model." Goodnight fashioned SAS's culture around the idea of "trust between our employees and the company." And employees love it! Annual turnover is a low 2 percent, and the company is highly profitable. There's something to be said for recognizing that your employees are your most important asset! What can you learn from this leader who made a difference?

Finally, we know people will do better if they get feedback on how well they're progressing toward their goals because feedback helps identify discrepancies between what they have done and what they want to do. But all feedback isn't equally effective. Self-generated feedback—where an employee monitors his or her own progress—has been shown to be a more powerful motivator than feedback coming from someone else.[26]

Three other contingencies besides feedback influence the goal-performance relationship: goal commitment, adequate self-efficacy, and national culture.

First, goal-setting theory assumes an individual is committed to the goal. Commitment is most likely when goals are made public, when the individual has an internal locus of control, and when the goals are self-set rather than assigned.[27]

Next, **self-efficacy** refers to an individual's belief that he or she is capable of performing a task.[28] The higher your self-efficacy, the more confidence you have in your ability to succeed in a task. So, in difficult situations, we find that people with low self-efficacy are likely to reduce their effort or give up altogether, whereas those with high self-efficacy will try harder to master the challenge.[29] In addition, individuals

Exhibit 17-5
Goal-Setting Theory

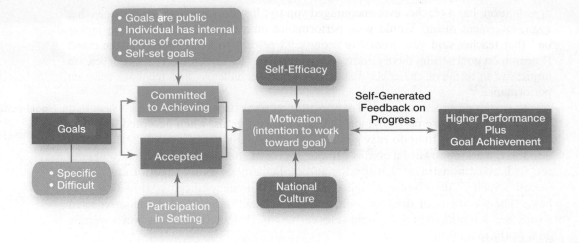

with high self-efficacy seem to respond to negative feedback with increased effort and motivation, whereas those with low self-efficacy are likely to reduce their effort when given negative feedback.[30]

Finally, the value of goal-setting theory depends on the national culture. It's well adapted to North American countries because its main ideas align reasonably well with those cultures. It assumes that subordinates will be reasonably independent (not a high score on power distance), that people will seek challenging goals (low in uncertainty avoidance), and that performance is considered important by both managers and subordinates (high in assertiveness). Don't expect goal setting to lead to higher employee performance in countries where the cultural characteristics aren't like this.

Exhibit 17-5 summarizes the relationships among goals, motivation, and performance. Our overall conclusion is that the intention to work toward hard and specific goals is a powerful motivating force. Under the proper conditions, it can lead to higher performance. However, no evidence indicates that such goals are associated with increased job satisfaction.[31]

Reinforcement Theory

reinforcement theory
The theory that behavior is a function of its consequences

reinforcers
Consequences immediately following a behavior, which increase the probability that the behavior will be repeated

Reinforcement theory says that behavior is a function of its consequences. Those consequences that immediately follow a behavior and increase the probability that the behavior will be repeated are called **reinforcers**.

Reinforcement theory ignores factors such as goals, expectations, and needs. Instead, it focuses solely on what happens to a person when he or she does something. For instance, Walmart improved its bonus program for hourly employees. Employees who provide outstanding customer service get a cash bonus. And all Walmart hourly full- and part-time store employees are eligible for annual "My$hare" bonuses, which are allocated on store performance and distributed quarterly so that workers are rewarded more frequently.[32] The company's intent: keep the workforce motivated to meet goals by rewarding them when they did, thus reinforcing the behaviors.

In Chapter 15 we showed how managers use reinforcers to shape behavior, but the concept is also widely believed to explain motivation. According to B. F. Skinner, people will most likely engage in desired behaviors if they are rewarded for doing so. These rewards are most effective if they immediately follow a desired behavior; and behavior that isn't rewarded, or is punished, is less likely to be repeated.[33]

Using reinforcement theory, managers can influence employees' behavior by using positive reinforcers for actions that help the organization achieve its goals. And managers should ignore, not punish, undesirable behavior. Although punishment eliminates undesired behavior faster than nonreinforcement, its effect is often temporary and may have unpleasant side effects, including dysfunctional behavior such as workplace conflicts, absenteeism, and turnover. Although reinforcement is an important influence on work behavior, it isn't the only explanation for differences in employee motivation.[34]

Designing Motivating Jobs

It's not unusual to find shop-floor workers at Cordis LLC's San German, Puerto Rico, facility interacting directly with customers, especially if that employee has special skills or knowledge that could help come up with a solution to a customer's problem.[35] One company executive said, "Our sales guys often encourage this in specific situations because they don't always have all the answers. If by doing this, we can better serve the customers, then we do it." As this example shows, the tasks an employee performs in his or her job are often determined by different factors, such as providing customers what they need—when they need it.

Because managers want to motivate individuals on the job, we need to look at ways to design motivating jobs. If you look closely at what an organization is and how it works, you'll find that it's composed of thousands of tasks. These tasks are, in turn, aggregated into jobs. We use the term **job design** to refer to the way tasks are combined to form complete jobs. The jobs people perform in an organization should not evolve by chance. Managers should design jobs deliberately and thoughtfully to reflect the demands of the changing environment; the organization's technology; and employees' skills, abilities, and preferences.[36] When jobs are designed like that, employees are motivated to work hard. Let's look at some ways that managers can design motivating jobs.[37]

JOB ENLARGEMENT As we saw in the Management History Module and Chapter 11, job design historically has been to make jobs smaller and more specialized. It's difficult to motivate employees when jobs are like this. An early effort at overcoming the drawbacks of job specialization involved horizontally expanding a job through increasing **job scope**—the number of different tasks required in a job and the frequency with which these tasks are repeated. For instance, a dental hygienist's job could be enlarged so that in addition to cleaning teeth, he or she is pulling patients' files, refiling them when finished, and sanitizing and storing instruments. This type of job design option is called **job enlargement**.

Most job enlargement efforts that focused solely on increasing the number of tasks don't seem to work. As one employee who experienced such a job redesign said, "Before, I had one lousy job. Now, thanks to job enlargement, I have three lousy jobs!" However, research has shown that *knowledge* enlargement activities (expanding the scope of knowledge used in a job) lead to more job satisfaction, enhanced customer service, and fewer errors.[38]

JOB ENRICHMENT Another approach to job design is the vertical expansion of a job by adding planning and evaluating responsibilities—**job enrichment**. Job enrichment increases **job depth**, which is the degree of control employees have over their work. In other words, employees are empowered to assume some of the tasks typically done by their managers. Thus, an enriched job allows workers to do an entire activity with increased freedom, independence, and responsibility. In addition, workers get feedback so they can assess and correct their own performance. For instance, if our dental hygienist had an enriched job, he or she could, in addition to cleaning teeth, schedule appointments (planning) and follow up with clients (evaluating). Although job enrichment may improve the quality of work, employee motivation, and satisfaction, research evidence has been inconclusive as to its usefulness.[39]

JOB CHARACTERISTICS MODEL Even though many organizations implemented job enlargement and job enrichment programs and experienced mixed results, neither approach provided an effective framework for managers to design motivating jobs.

job design
The way tasks are combined to form complete jobs

job scope
The number of different tasks required in a job and the frequency with which those tasks are repeated

job enlargement
The horizontal expansion of a job by increasing job scope

job enrichment
The vertical expansion of a job by adding planning and evaluating responsibilities

job depth
The degree of control employees have over their work

Dr. Sigrid Heuer, a senior scientist at the International Rice Research Institute, is the leader of an international multidisciplinary team of research scientists whose work scores high on the core dimensions of skill variety, task identity, and task significance. Heuer and her team discovered a gene that increases grain production substantially by enabling rice plants to grow stronger root systems that take in more phosphorus, an important plant nutrient. Their discovery will help poor rice farmers grow more rice for sale to poor countries. Believing their work is meaningful because it has a significant impact on the lives of others gives the scientists great motivation and job satisfaction.
Source: Reuters/Cheryl Ravelo

job characteristics model (JCM)
A framework for analyzing and designing jobs that identifies five primary core job dimensions, their interrelationships, and their impact on outcomes

skill variety
The degree to which a job requires a variety of activities so that an employee can use a number of different skills and talents

task identity
The degree to which a job requires completion of a whole and identifiable piece of work

task significance
The degree to which a job has a substantial impact on the lives or work of other people

autonomy
The degree to which a job provides substantial freedom, independence, and discretion to the individual in scheduling work and determining the procedures to be used in carrying it out

feedback
The degree to which carrying out work activities required by a job results in the individual's obtaining direct and clear information about his or her performance effectiveness

But the **job characteristics model (JCM)** does.[40] It identifies five core job dimensions, their interrelationships, and their impact on employee productivity, motivation, and satisfaction. These five core job dimensions are:

1. **Skill variety**, the degree to which a job requires a variety of activities so that an employee can use a number of different skills and talents.
2. **Task identity**, the degree to which a job requires completion of a whole and identifiable piece of work.
3. **Task significance**, the degree to which a job has a substantial impact on the lives or work of other people.
4. **Autonomy**, the degree to which a job provides substantial freedom, independence, and discretion to the individual in scheduling the work and determining the procedures to be used in carrying it out.
5. **Feedback**, the degree to which doing work activities required by a job results in an individual obtaining direct and clear information about the effectiveness of his or her performance.

The JCM is shown in Exhibit 17-6. Notice how the first three dimensions—skill variety, task identity, and task significance—combine to create meaningful work. In other words, if these three characteristics exist in a job, we can predict that the person will view his or her job as being important, valuable, and worthwhile. Notice, too, that jobs that possess autonomy give the jobholder a feeling of personal responsibility for the results and that if a job provides feedback, the employee will know how effectively he or she is performing.

The JCM suggests that employees are likely to be motivated when they *learn* (knowledge of results through feedback) that they *personally* (experienced responsibility through autonomy of work) performed well on tasks that they *care about* (experienced meaningfulness through skill variety, task identity, or task significance).[41] The more a job is designed around these three elements, the greater the employee's motivation, performance, and satisfaction and the lower his or her absenteeism and likelihood of resigning. As the model shows, the links between the job dimensions and the outcomes are moderated by the strength of the individual's growth need (the person's desire for self-esteem and self-actualization). Individuals with a high growth need are more likely than low-growth need individuals to experience the critical psychological states and respond positively when their jobs include the core dimensions. This distinction may explain the mixed results with job enrichment: Individuals with low growth need aren't likely to achieve high performance or satisfaction by having their jobs enriched.

The JCM provides specific guidance to managers for job design. These suggestions specify the types of changes most likely to lead to improvement in the five core

Exhibit 17-6
Job Characteristics Model

Source: "Job Characteristics Model" from *Work Redesign*, by J. R. Hackman & G. R. Oldham. Copyright © 1980 by Addison-Wesley (a division of Pearson). Reprinted with permission.

job dimensions. You'll notice that two suggestions incorporate job enlargement and job enrichment, although the other suggestions involve more than vertical and horizontal expansion of jobs.

1. *Combine tasks.* Put fragmented tasks back together to form a new, larger work module (job enlargement) to increase skill variety and task identity.
2. *Create natural work units.* Design tasks that form an identifiable and meaningful whole to increase employee "ownership" of the work. Encourage employees to view their work as meaningful and important rather than as irrelevant and boring.
3. *Establish client (external or internal) relationships.* Whenever possible, establish direct relationships between workers and their clients to increase skill variety, autonomy, and feedback.
4. *Expand jobs vertically.* Vertical expansion gives employees responsibilities and controls that were formerly reserved for managers, which can increase employee autonomy.
5. *Open feedback channels.* Direct feedback lets employees know how well they're performing their jobs and whether their performance is improving or not.

Research into the JCM continues. For instance, one recent study looked at using job redesign efforts to change job characteristics and improve employee well-being.[42] Another study examined psychological ownership—that is, a personal feeling of "mine-ness" or "our-ness"—and its role in the JCM.[43]

REDESIGNING JOB DESIGN APPROACHES[44] Although the JCM has proven to be useful, it may not be totally appropriate for today's jobs that are more service and knowledge-oriented. The nature of these jobs has also changed the tasks that employees do in those jobs. Two emerging viewpoints on job design are causing a rethink of the JCM and other standard approaches. Let's take a look at each perspective.

The first perspective, the **relational perspective of work design**, focuses on how people's tasks and jobs are increasingly based on social relationships. In jobs today, employees have more interactions and interdependence with coworkers and others both inside and outside the organization. In doing their job, employees rely more and more on those around them for information, advice, and assistance. So what does this mean for designing motivating jobs? It means that managers need to look at important components of those employee relationships such as access to and level of social support in an organization, types of interactions outside an organization, amount of task interdependence, and interpersonal feedback.

The second perspective, the **proactive perspective of work design**, says that employees are taking the initiative to change how their work is performed. They're much more involved in decisions and actions that affect their work. Important job design factors according to this perspective include autonomy (which *is* part of the JCM), amount of ambiguity and accountability, job complexity, level of stressors, and social or relationship context. Each of these has been shown to influence employee proactive behavior.

One stream of research that's relevant to proactive work design is **high-involvement work practices**, which are designed to elicit greater input or involvement from workers.[45] The level of employee proactivity is believed to increase as employees become more involved in decisions that affect their work. Another term for this approach, which we discussed in an earlier chapter, is employee empowerment.

relational perspective of work design
An approach to job design that focuses on how people's tasks and jobs are increasingly based on social relationships

proactive perspective of work design
An approach to job design in which employees take the initiative to change how their work is performed

high-involvement work practices
Work practices designed to elicit greater input or involvement from workers

Equity Theory

Do you ever wonder what kind of grade the person sitting next to you in class makes on a test or on a major class assignment? Most of us do! Being human, we tend to compare ourselves with others. If someone offered you $50,000 a year on your first job after graduating from college, you'd probably jump at the offer and report to work enthusiastic, ready to tackle whatever needed to be done, and certainly satisfied with your pay. How would you react, though, if you found out a month into the job that a coworker—another recent graduate, your age, with comparable grades from a comparable school, and with comparable work experience—was getting $55,000 a year? You'd probably be upset! Even though in absolute terms, $50,000 is a lot of money for a new graduate to make (and you know it!), that suddenly isn't the issue. Now you see the issue as what you believe is *fair*—what is *equitable*. The term *equity* is related to the concept of fairness and equitable treatment compared with others who behave in similar ways. Evidence indicates that employees compare themselves to others and that inequities influence how much effort employees exert.[46]

Equity theory, developed by J. Stacey Adams, proposes that employees compare what they get from a job (outcomes) in relation to what they put into it (inputs), and then they compare their inputs–outcomes ratio with the inputs–outcomes ratios of relevant others (Exhibit 17-7). If an employee perceives her ratio to be equitable in comparison to those of relevant others, there's no problem. However, if the ratio is inequitable, she views herself as underrewarded or overrewarded. When inequities occur, employees attempt to do something about it.[47] The result might be lower or higher productivity, improved or reduced quality of output, increased absenteeism, or voluntary resignation.

The **referent**—the other persons, systems, or selves individuals compare themselves against in order to assess equity—is an important variable in equity theory.[48] Each of the three referent categories is important. The "persons" category includes other individuals with similar jobs in the same organization but also includes friends, neighbors, or professional associates. Based on what they hear at work or read about in newspapers or trade journals, employees compare their pay with that of others. The "system" category includes organizational pay policies, procedures, and allocation. The "self" category refers to inputs–outcomes ratios that are unique to the individual. It reflects past personal experiences and contacts and is influenced by criteria such as past jobs or family commitments.

Originally, equity theory focused on **distributive justice**, the perceived fairness of the amount and allocation of rewards among individuals. More recent research has focused on looking at issues of **procedural justice**, the perceived fairness of the process used to determine the distribution of rewards. This research shows that distributive justice has a greater influence on employee satisfaction than procedural justice, while procedural justice tends to affect an employee's organizational commitment, trust in his or her boss, and intention to quit.[49] What are the implications for managers? They should consider openly sharing information on how allocation decisions are made, follow consistent and unbiased procedures, and engage in similar practices to increase the perception of procedural justice. By increasing the perception of procedural justice, employees are likely to view their bosses and the organization as positive even if they're dissatisfied with pay, promotions, and other personal outcomes.

equity theory
The theory that an employee compares his or her job's input–outcomes ratio with that of relevant others and then corrects any inequity

referents
The persons, systems, or selves against which individuals compare themselves to assess equity

distributive justice
Perceived fairness of the amount and allocation of rewards among individuals

procedural justice
Perceived fairness of the process used to determine the distribution of rewards

Exhibit 17-7
Equity Theory

Perceived Ratio Comparison[a]		Employee's Assessment
$\dfrac{\text{Outcomes A}}{\text{Inputs A}} < \dfrac{\text{Outcomes B}}{\text{Inputs B}}$		Inequity (underrewarded)
$\dfrac{\text{Outcomes A}}{\text{Inputs A}} = \dfrac{\text{Outcomes B}}{\text{Inputs B}}$		Equity
$\dfrac{\text{Outcomes A}}{\text{Inputs A}} > \dfrac{\text{Outcomes B}}{\text{Inputs B}}$		Inequity (overrewarded)

[a]Person A is the employee, and person B is a relevant other or referent.

Expectancy Theory

The most comprehensive explanation of how employees are motivated is Victor Vroom's **expectancy theory**.[50] Although the theory has its critics,[51] most research evidence supports it.[52]

Expectancy theory states that an individual tends to act in a certain way based on the expectation that the act will be followed by a given outcome and on the attractiveness of that outcome to the individual. It includes three variables or relationships (see Exhibit 17-8):

1. *Expectancy* or *effort–performance linkage* is the probability perceived by the individual that exerting a given amount of effort will lead to a certain level of performance.
2. *Instrumentality* or *performance–reward linkage* is the degree to which the individual believes that performing at a particular level is instrumental in attaining the desired outcome.
3. *Valence* or *attractiveness of reward* is the importance an individual places on the potential outcome or reward that can be achieved on the job. Valence considers both the goals and needs of the individual.

This explanation of motivation might sound complicated, but it really isn't. It can be summed up in the questions: How hard do I have to work to achieve a certain level of performance, and can I actually achieve that level? What reward will performing at that level of performance get me? How attractive is the reward to me, and does it help me achieve my own personal goals? Whether you are motivated to put forth effort (that is, to work hard) at any given time depends on your goals and your perception of whether a certain level of performance is necessary to attain those goals. Let's look at an example. Your second author had a student many years ago who went to work for IBM as a sales rep. Her favorite work "reward" was having an IBM corporate jet fly into Springfield, Missouri, to pick up her best customers and her and take them for a weekend of golfing at some fun location. But to get that particular "reward," she had to achieve at a certain level of performance, which involved exceeding her sales goals by a specified percentage. How hard she was willing to work (that is, how motivated she was to put forth effort) was dependent on the level of performance that had to be met and the likelihood that if she achieved at that level of performance she would receive that reward. Because she "valued" that reward, she always worked hard to exceed her sales goals. And the performance–reward linkage was clear because her hard work and performance achievements were always rewarded by the company with the reward she valued (access to the corporate jet).

The key to expectancy theory is understanding an individual's goal and the linkage between effort and performance, between performance and rewards, and finally, between rewards and individual goal satisfaction. It emphasizes payoffs, or rewards. As a result, we have to believe that the rewards an organization is offering align with what the individual wants. Expectancy theory recognizes that no

Just Born candy company—makers of Peeps, Mike and Ike's, Hot Tamales, and Teenie Beanie brands—uses expectancy theory in motivating employees to achieve annual corporate sales goals. Members of Just Born's sales team shown here expected that their efforts to reach their goal of increasing sales by 4 percent over the previous year would earn them an all-expense paid trip to Hawaii if they met their target. The 24-employee sales team had a good year of boosting sales by 2 percent but, in failing to meet their goal, they were given fleece jackets and bomber hats and a trip to Fargo, North Dakota.
Source: Ann Arbor Miller/AP Photo

expectancy theory
The theory that an individual tends to act in a certain way based on the expectation that the act will be followed by a given outcome and on the attractiveness of that outcome to the individual

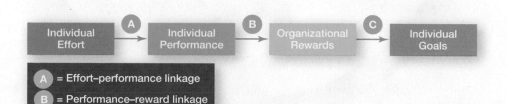

Exhibit 17-8
Expectancy Model

universal principle explains what motivates individuals and thus stresses that managers understand why employees view certain outcomes as attractive or unattractive. After all, we want to reward individuals with those things they value positively. Also, expectancy theory emphasizes expected behaviors. Do employees know what is expected of them and how they'll be evaluated? Finally, the theory is concerned with perceptions. Reality is irrelevant. An individual's own perceptions of performance, reward, and goal outcomes—not the outcomes themselves—will determine his or her motivation (level of effort).

Integrating Contemporary Theories of Motivation

Many of the ideas underlying the contemporary motivation theories are complementary, and you'll understand better how to motivate people if you see how the theories fit together.[53] Exhibit 17-9 presents a model that integrates much of what we know about motivation. Its basic foundation is the expectancy model. Let's work through the model, starting on the left.

The individual effort box has an arrow leading into it. This arrow flows from the individual's goals. Consistent with goal-setting theory, this goals–effort link is meant to illustrate that goals direct behavior. Expectancy theory predicts that an employee will exert a high level of effort if he or she perceives a strong relationship between effort and performance, performance and rewards, and rewards and satisfaction of personal goals. Each of these relationships is in turn influenced by certain factors. You can see from the model that the level of individual performance

Exhibit 17-9

Integrating Contemporary Theories of Motivation

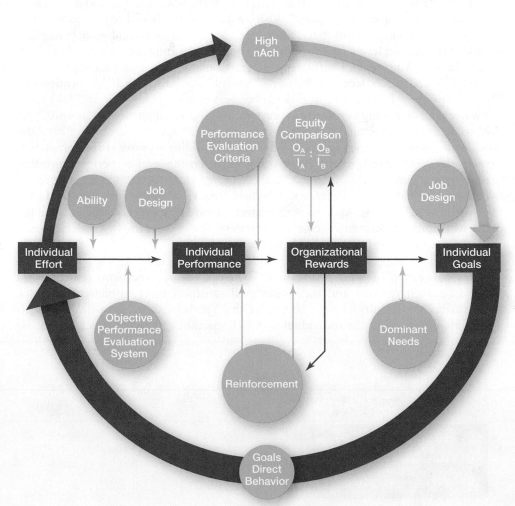

is determined not only by the level of individual effort but also by the individual's ability to perform and by whether the organization has a fair and objective performance evaluation system. The performance–reward relationship will be strong if the individual perceives that performance (rather than seniority, personal favorites, or some other criterion) is what is rewarded. The final link in expectancy theory is the rewards–goal relationship. The traditional need theories come into play at this point. Motivation would be high to the degree that the rewards an individual received for his or her high performance satisfied the dominant needs consistent with his or her individual goals.

A closer look at the model also shows that it considers the achievement–need, reinforcement, equity, and JCM theories. The high achiever isn't motivated by the organization's assessment of his or her performance or organizational rewards; hence the jump from effort to individual goals for those with a high nAch. Remember that high achievers are internally driven as long as the jobs they're doing provide them with personal responsibility, feedback, and moderate risks. They're not concerned with the effort–performance, performance–reward, or rewards–goals linkages.

Reinforcement theory is seen in the model by recognizing that the organization's rewards reinforce the individual's performance. If managers have designed a reward system that is seen by employees as "paying off" for good performance, the rewards will reinforce and encourage continued good performance. Rewards also play a key part in equity theory. Individuals will compare the rewards (outcomes) they have received from the inputs or efforts they made with the inputs–outcomes ratio of relevant others. If inequities exist, the effort expended may be influenced.

Finally, the JCM is seen in this integrative model. Task characteristics (job design) influence job motivation at two places. First, jobs designed around the five job dimensions are likely to lead to higher actual job performance because the individual's motivation will be stimulated by the job itself—that is, they will increase the linkage between effort and performance. Second, jobs designed around the five job dimensions also increase an employee's control over key elements in his or her work. Therefore, jobs that offer autonomy, feedback, and similar task characteristics help to satisfy the individual goals of employees who desire greater control over their work.

let's get REAL

The Scenario:

Sam Grisham is the plant manager at a bathroom vanity manufacturer. When business is brisk, employees have to work overtime to meet customers' demands. Aside from a few people, he has a horrible time getting employees to work overtime. "I practically have to beg for volunteers."

Source: Patricia Ficco

Patricia Ficco
Retail General Manager

What suggestions do you have for Sam?

Employees will work overtime without hesitation if the manager makes them feel valued. In order to make them feel appreciated, I would recommend Sam think of ways to reward them for going above and beyond. He could try to provide his team with dinner on extra-long work days; buy them coffee on Mondays to start off the week; or maybe award gift cards to top performers. If Sam makes his team feel appreciated, they will work longer and harder to achieve the goals.

17.4 *Discuss* current issues in motivation.

CURRENT Issues in Motivation

After Vincent Stevens's church ran an experiment in which 10 members were each given $100 to help their communities, some used it as seed capital to raise thousands more. As a partner in a Bellevue, Washington, accounting firm, he wondered what would happen if he tried the same thing with his employees. To find out, his company launched Caring, Serving, and Giving—a program that lets employees apply for grants of up to $500 to fund community service projects. By empowering employees to use the seed money as they saw fit, they were motivated to make the best use of it. Another benefit was a boost in employee morale.[54]

Understanding and predicting employee motivation is one of the most popular areas in management research. We've introduced you to several motivation theories. However, even the contemporary theories of employee motivation are influenced by some significant workplace issues—motivating in tough economic circumstances, managing cross-cultural challenges, motivating unique groups of workers, and designing appropriate rewards programs.

Motivating in Tough Economic Circumstances

Zappos, the quirky Las Vegas–based online shoe retailer (now a part of Amazon.com), has always had a reputation for being a fun place to work.[55] However, during the economic recession, it, like many companies, had to cut staff—124 employees in total. CEO Tony Hsieh wanted to get out the news fast to lessen the stress for his employees. So he announced the layoff in an e-mail, on his blog, and on his Twitter account. Although some might think these are terrible ways to communicate that kind of news, most employees thanked him for being so open and so honest. The company also took good care of those who were laid off. Laid-off employees with less than two years of service were paid through the end of the year. Longer-tenured employees got four weeks for every year of service. All got six months of continued paid health coverage and, at the request of the employees, got to keep their 40 percent merchandise discount through the Christmas season. Zappos had always been a model of how to nurture employees in good times; now it showed how to treat employees in bad times.

The economic recession of the last few years was difficult for many organizations, especially when it came to their employees. Layoffs, tight budgets, minimal or no pay raises, benefit cuts, no bonuses, long hours doing the work of those who had been laid off—this was the reality that many employees faced. As conditions deteriorated, employee confidence, optimism, and job engagement plummeted as well. As you can imagine, it wasn't an easy thing for managers to keep employees motivated under such challenging circumstances.

Managers came to realize that in an uncertain economy, they had to be creative in keeping their employees' efforts energized, directed, and sustained toward achieving goals. They were forced to look at ways to motivate employees that didn't involve money or that were relatively inexpensive.[56] So they relied on actions such as holding meetings with employees to keep the lines of communication open and to get their input on issues; establishing a common goal, such as maintaining excellent customer service, to keep everyone focused; creating a community feel so employees could see that managers cared about them and their work; and giving employees opportunities to continue to learn and grow. And, of course, an encouraging word always went a long way.

Managing Cross-Cultural Motivational Challenges

Scores of employees at Denmark's largest brewer, Carlsberg A/S, walked off their jobs in protest after the company tightened rules on workplace drinking and removed beer coolers from work sites.[57] Now that's a motivational challenge you don't often see in U.S. workplaces!

In today's global business environment, managers can't automatically assume motivational programs that work in one geographic location are going to work in others.

Most current motivation theories were developed in the United States by Americans and about Americans.[59] Maybe the most blatant pro-American characteristic in these theories is the strong emphasis on individualism and achievement. For instance, both goal-setting and expectancy theories emphasize goal accomplishment as well as rational and individual thought. Let's look at the motivation theories to see their level of cross-cultural transferability.

Maslow's need hierarchy argues that people start at the physiological level and then move progressively up the hierarchy in order. This hierarchy, if it has any application at all, aligns with American culture. In countries like Japan, Greece, and Mexico, where uncertainty avoidance characteristics are strong, security needs would be the foundational layer of the need hierarchy. Countries that score high on nurturing characteristics—Denmark, Sweden, Norway, the Netherlands, and Finland—would have social needs as their foundational level.[60] We would predict, for instance, that group work will be more motivating when the country's culture scores high on the nurturing criterion.

Another motivation concept that clearly has an American bias is the achievement need. The view that a high achievement need acts as an internal motivator presupposes two cultural characteristics—a willingness to accept a moderate degree of risk (which excludes countries with strong uncertainty avoidance characteristics) and a concern with performance (which applies almost singularly to countries with strong achievement characteristics). This combination is found in Anglo-American countries such as the United States, Canada, and Great Britain.[61] On the other hand, these characteristics are relatively absent in countries such as Chile and Portugal.

Equity theory has a relatively strong following in the United States, which is not surprising given that U.S.-style reward systems are based on the assumption that workers are highly sensitive to equity in reward allocations. In the United States, equity is meant to closely link pay to performance. However, recent evidence suggests that in collectivist cultures, especially in the former socialist countries of Central and Eastern Europe, employees expect rewards to reflect their individual needs as well as their performance.[62] Moreover, consistent with a legacy of communism and centrally planned economies, employees exhibited a greater "entitlement" attitude—that is, they expected outcomes to be greater than their inputs.[63] These findings suggest that U.S.-style pay practices may need to be modified in some countries in order to be perceived as fair by employees.

Another research study of more than 50,000 employees around the world examined two cultural characteristics from the GLOBE framework—individualism and masculinity—(see Chapter 3 for a discussion of these characteristics) in relation to motivation.[64] The researchers found that in individualistic cultures such as the United States and Canada, individual initiative, individual freedom, and individual achievement are highly valued. In more collective cultures such as Iran, Peru, and China, however, employees may be less interested in receiving individual praise but place a greater emphasis on harmony, belonging, and consensus. They also found that in masculine (achievement/assertive) cultures such as Japan and Slovakia, the focus is on material success. Those work environments are designed to push employees hard and then reward top performers with high earnings. However, in more feminine (nurturing) cultures such as Sweden and the Netherlands, smaller wage gaps among employees are common, and employees are likely to have extensive quality-of-life benefits.

Despite these cross-cultural differences in motivation, some cross-cultural consistencies are evident. In a recent study of employees in thirteen countries, the top motivators included (ranked from number one on down): being treated with respect, work-life balance, the type of work done, the quality of people worked with and the quality of the organization's leadership (tied), base pay, working in an environment where good service can be provided to others, long-term career potential, flexible working arrangements, learning and development opportunities and benefits (tied), promotion opportunities, and incentive pay or bonus.[65] And other studies have shown that the desire for interesting work seems important to almost all workers, regardless

*data*points[58]

92 percent of executives have the perception that favoritism occurs in large organizations.

29 percent of HR professionals and employees were satisfied with their organization's recognition efforts.

50 percent of HR professionals said they believe managers and supervisors acknowledge and appreciate employees effectively.

100 percent of senior executives indicated that satisfied and engaged employees positively affect an organization's bottom line.

65 percent of American adults polled said rewards in the workplace are distributed less fairly today than five years ago.

92 percent of employers have variable pay plans or performance-based award programs.

12 percent of employees believe their company listens to and cares about them.

56 percent of HR professionals believe rewards are based on job performance.

67 percent of employees said their manager acknowledges and appreciates them at work.

21 percent of adults surveyed said job security was the most important thing to them about their job.

of their national culture. For instance, employees in Belgium, Britain, Israel, and the United States ranked "interesting work" number one among 11 work goals. It was ranked either second or third in Japan, the Netherlands, and Germany.[66] Similarly, in a study comparing job-preference outcomes among graduate students in the United States, Canada, Australia, and Singapore, growth, achievement, and responsibility were rated the top three and had identical rankings.[67] Both studies suggest some universality to the importance of intrinsic factors identified by Herzberg in his two-factor theory. Another recent study examining workplace motivation trends in Japan also seems to indicate that Herzberg's model is applicable to Japanese employees.[68]

Motivating Unique Groups of Workers

At Deloitte, employees are allowed to "dial up" or "dial down" their job responsibilities to fit their personal and professional goals.[69] The company's program called Mass Career Customization has been a huge hit with its employees! In the first 12 months after it was rolled out, employee satisfaction with "overall career/life fit" rose by 25 percent. Also, the number of high-performing employees staying with Deloitte increased.

Motivating employees has never been easy! Employees come into organizations with different needs, personalities, skills, abilities, interests, and aptitudes. They have different expectations of their employers and different views of what they think their employer has a right to expect of them. And they vary widely in what they want from their jobs. For instance, some employees get more satisfaction out of their personal interests and pursuits and only want a weekly paycheck—nothing more. They're not interested in making their work more challenging or interesting or in "winning" performance contests. Others derive a great deal of satisfaction in their jobs and are motivated to exert high levels of effort. Given these differences, how can managers do an effective job of motivating the unique groups of employees found in today's workforce? One thing is to understand the motivational requirements of these groups including diverse employees, professionals, contingent workers, and low-skilled minimum-wage employees.

MOTIVATING A DIVERSE WORKFORCE   To maximize motivation among today's workforce, managers need to think in terms of *flexibility*. For instance, studies tell us that men place more importance on having autonomy in their jobs than women. In contrast, the opportunity to learn, convenient and flexible work hours, and good interpersonal relations are more important to women.[70] Having the opportunity to be independent and to be exposed to different experiences is important to Gen Y employees whereas older workers may be more interested in highly structured work opportunities.[71] Managers need to recognize that what motivates a single mother with

FUTURE VISION | Individualized Rewards

Organizations have historically assumed that "one size fits all" when it comes to allocating rewards. Managers typically assumed that everyone wants more money and more vacation time. But as organizations become less bureaucratic and more capable of differentiating rewards, managers will be encouraged to differentiate rewards among employees as well as for individual employees over time.

Organizations control a vast number of potential rewards that employees might find appealing. A partial list would include increased base pay, bonuses, shortened workweeks, extended vacations, paid sabbaticals, flexible work hours, part-time employment, guaranteed job security, increased pension contributions, college tuition reimbursement, personal days off, help in purchasing a home, recognition awards, paid club memberships, and work-from-home options. In the future, most organizations will structure individual reward packages in ways that will maximize employee motivation.

two dependent children who's working full time to support her family may be very different from the needs of a single part-time employee or an older employee who is working only to supplement his or her retirement income. A diverse array of rewards is needed to motivate employees with such diverse needs. Many of the work–life balance programs (see Chapter 13) that organizations have implemented are a response to the varied needs of a diverse workforce. In addition, many organizations have developed flexible work arrangements—such as compressed workweeks, flextime, and job sharing, which we discussed in Chapter 12—that recognize different needs. Another job alternative we also discussed earlier is telecommuting. However, keep in mind that not all employees embrace the idea of telecommuting. Some workers relish the informal interactions at work that satisfy their social needs as well as being a source of new ideas.

Do flexible work arrangements motivate employees? Although such arrangements might seem highly motivational, both positive and negative relationships have been found. For instance, a recent study that looked at the impact of telecommuting on job satisfaction found that job satisfaction initially increased as the extent of telecommuting increased, but as the number of hours spent telecommuting increased, job satisfaction started to level off, decreased slightly, and then stabilized.[72]

MOTIVATING PROFESSIONALS In contrast to a generation ago, the typical employee today is more likely to be a professional with a college degree than a blue-collar factory worker. What special concerns should managers be aware of when trying to motivate a team of engineers at Intel's India Development Center, software designers at SAS Institute in North Carolina, or a group of consultants at Accenture in Singapore?

Professionals are different from nonprofessionals.[73] They have a strong and long-term commitment to their field of expertise. To keep current in their field, they need to regularly update their knowledge, and because of their commitment to their profession, they rarely define their workweek as 8 a.m. to 5 p.m. five days a week.

What motivates professionals? Money and promotions typically are low on their priority list. Why? They tend to be well paid and enjoy what they do. In contrast, job challenge tends to be ranked high. They like to tackle problems and find solutions. Their chief reward is the work itself. Professionals also value support. They want others to think that what they are working on is important. That may be true for all employees, but professionals tend to be focused on their work as their central life interest, whereas nonprofessionals typically have other interests outside of work that can compensate for needs not met on the job.

MOTIVATING CONTINGENT WORKERS We discussed in Chapter 12 the increased number of contingent workers employed by organizations. There's no simple solution for motivating these employees. For that small set of individuals who prefer the freedom of their temporary status, the lack of stability may not be an issue. In addition, temporariness might be preferred by highly compensated physicians, engineers, accountants, or financial planners who don't want the demands of a full-time job. But these individuals are the exceptions. For the most part, temporary employees are not temporary by choice.

What will motivate involuntarily temporary employees? An obvious answer is the opportunity to become a permanent employee. In cases in which permanent employees are selected from a pool of temps, the temps will often work hard in hopes of becoming permanent. A less obvious answer is the opportunity for training. The ability of a temporary employee to find a new job is largely dependent on his or her skills. If an employee sees that the job he or she is doing can help develop marketable skills, then motivation is increased. From an equity standpoint, when temps work alongside permanent

Chrislyn Hamilton, a crew member at a McDonald's restaurant in Brisbane, Australia, won first place in the Voice of McDonald's, a global singing competition to discover, recognize, and reward the most talented singers among the company's 1.8 million restaurant employees throughout the world. As top winner in the contest, Hamilton received $25,000, will lend her voice to a DreamWorks Animation movie, and will appear in a McDonald's TV commercial in her market. In addition to this recognition program, McDonald's motivates its crew members by providing them with a relaxed work environment, a low-stress job, social interaction with co-workers, a flexible work schedule, and an opportunity to advance to a higher position.
Source: Reinhold Matay/AP Photo

employees who earn more and get benefits too for doing the same job, the performance of temps is likely to suffer. Separating such employees or perhaps minimizing interdependence between them might help managers counteract potential problems.[74]

MOTIVATING LOW-SKILLED, MINIMUM-WAGE EMPLOYEES Suppose in your first managerial position after graduating, you're responsible for managing a work group of low-skilled, minimum-wage employees. Offering more pay to these employees for high levels of performance is out of the question: your company just can't afford it. In addition, these employees have limited education and skills. What are your motivational options at this point?

One trap we often fall into is thinking that people are motivated only by money. Although money is important as a motivator, it's not the only reward that people seek and that managers can use. In motivating minimum-wage employees, managers might look at employee recognition programs. Many managers also recognize the power of praise although these "pats on the back" must be sincere and given for the right reasons.

Designing Appropriate Rewards Programs

Blue Cross of California, one of the nation's largest health insurers, pays bonuses to doctors serving its health maintenance organization members based on patient satisfaction and other quality standards. FedEx's drivers are motivated by a pay system that rewards them for timeliness and how much they deliver.[75] Employee rewards programs play a powerful role in motivating appropriate employee behavior.

open-book management
A motivational approach in which an organization's financial statements (the "books") are shared with all employees

OPEN-BOOK MANAGEMENT Within 24 hours after managers of the Heavy Duty Division of Springfield Remanufacturing Company (SRC) gather to discuss a multi-page financial document, every plant employee will have seen the same information. If the employees can meet shipment goals, they'll all share in a large year-end bonus.[76] Many organizations of various sizes involve their employees in workplace decisions by opening up the financial statements (the "books"). They share that information so employees will be motivated to make better decisions about their work and better able to understand the implications of what they do, how they do it, and the ultimate impact on the bottom line. This approach is called **open-book management** and many organizations are using it.[77] For instance, at Parrish Medical Center in Titusville, Florida, CEO George Mikitarian was struggling with the prospect of massive layoffs, facilities closing, and profits declining. So he turned to "town hall meetings" in which employees received updates on the financial condition of the hospital. He also told his employees it would require their commitment to help find ways to reduce expenses and cut costs.[78] At giant insurance broker Marsh, its 25,000 employees are being taught the ABCs of finance and accounting.[79]

The goal of open-book management is to get employees to think like an owner by seeing the impact their decisions have on financial results. Since many employees don't have the knowledge or background to understand the financials, they have to be taught how to read and understand the organization's financial statements. Once employees have this knowledge, however, managers need to regularly share the numbers with them. By sharing this information, employees begin to see the link between their efforts, level of performance, and operational results.

employee recognition programs
Personal attention and expressing interest, approval, and appreciation for a job well done

EMPLOYEE RECOGNITION PROGRAMS **Employee recognition programs** consist of personal attention and expressing interest, approval, and appreciation for a job well done.[80] They can take numerous forms. For instance, Kelly Services introduced a new version of its points-based incentive system to better promote productivity and retention among its employees. The program, called Kelly Kudos, gives employees more choices of awards and allows them to accumulate points over a longer time period. It's working. Participants generate three times more revenue and hours than employees not receiving points.[81] Nichols Foods, a British manufacturer, has a comprehensive recognition program. The main hallway in the production department is hung with "bragging boards" on which the accomplishments of employee teams are noted. Monthly awards are presented to people who have been nominated by peers for extraordinary effort on the job. And monthly award winners are eligible for further recognition at an off-site meeting for all employees.[82] At Wayfair.com, a seller of home furnishings, a recognition wall provides space where anyone in the company can write about anyone else in the company and give them rewards dollars. It's used to recognize someone for something they did for a customer or some other accomplishment.[83] Most managers, however, use a far more informal approach. For example, when Julia Stewart was president of Applebee's restaurants (she's currently the president and CEO of DineEquity, which includes IHOP International and Applebee's Restaurants), she would frequently leave sealed notes on the chairs of employees after everyone had gone home.[84] These notes explained how important Stewart thought the person's work was or how much she appreciated the completion of a project. Stewart also relied heavily on voice mail messages left after office hours to tell employees how appreciative she was for a job well done. And recognition doesn't have to come only from managers. Some 35 percent of companies encourage coworkers to recognize peers for outstanding work efforts.[85] For instance, managers at Yum Brands Inc. (the Kentucky-based parent of food chains Taco Bell, KFC, and Pizza Hut) were looking for ways to reduce employee turnover. They found a successful customer-service program involving peer recognition at KFC restaurants in Australia. Workers there spontaneously rewarded fellow workers with "Champs cards, an acronym for attributes such as cleanliness, hospitality, and accuracy." Yum implemented the program in other restaurants around the world, and credits the peer recognition with reducing hourly employee turnover from 181 percent to 109 percent.[86]

A recent survey of organizations found that 84 percent had some type of program to recognize worker achievements.[87] And do employees think these programs are important? You bet! In a survey conducted a few years ago, a wide range of employees was asked what they considered the most powerful workplace motivator. Their response? Recognition, recognition, and more recognition![88]

Consistent with reinforcement theory, rewarding a behavior with recognition immediately following that behavior is likely to encourage its repetition. And recognition can take many forms. You can personally congratulate an employee in private for a good job. You can send a handwritten note or e-mail message acknowledging something positive that the employee has done. For employees with a strong need for social acceptance, you can publicly recognize accomplishments. To enhance group cohesiveness and motivation, you can celebrate team successes. For instance, you can do something as simple as throw a pizza party to celebrate a team's accomplishments. During the economic recession, managers got quite creative in how they showed employees they were appreciated.[89] For instance, employees at one company got to take home fresh vegetables from the company vegetable garden. In others, managers treated employees who really put forth efforts on a project to a special meal or movie tickets. Also, managers can show employees that no matter his or her role, their contributions matter. Some of these things may seem simple, but they can go a long way in showing employees they're valued.

PAY-FOR-PERFORMANCE Here's a survey statistic that may surprise you: 40 percent of employees see no clear link between performance and pay.[90] So what are the companies where these employees work paying for? They're obviously not clearly communicating performance expectations.[91] **Pay-for-performance programs** are variable compensation plans that pay employees on the basis of some performance measure.[92] Piece-rate pay plans, wage incentive plans, profit-sharing, and lump-sum bonuses are examples. What differentiates these forms of pay from more traditional compensation plans is that instead of paying a person for time on the job, pay is adjusted to reflect some performance measure. These performance measures might include such things as

pay-for-performance programs
Variable compensation plans that pay employees on the basis of some performance measure

let's get REAL

The Scenario:

Penny Collins manages an audio supply store in Atlanta. The work hours can be long and work conditions difficult for her three teams of 10 installers. She'd like to implement a recognition program to reward and motivate her employees.

What advice would you give Penny?

Penny is in a situation that, if executed correctly, will highly improve her employees' morale, satisfaction, and productivity! I would suggest she implement two methods jointly to start and evolve the recognition program in her company. First, a reward based on team performance where she recognizes the team that achieves the best results in comparison to the others. As a second approach, Penny should reward a single employee per cycle (monthly or quarterly), like an employee of the month/quarter with her own creative spin. Combining both methods will ensure that a foundation for a recognition program is in place. Now, all Penny has to do is monitor and tweak the system to her employees' reception and to the needs of the business.

Mina Nematalla
Business Owner & Manager

Source: Mina Nematalla

individual productivity, team or work group productivity, departmental productivity, or the overall organization's profit performance.

Pay-for-performance is probably most compatible with expectancy theory. Individuals should perceive a strong relationship between their performance and the rewards they receive for motivation to be maximized. If rewards are allocated only on nonperformance factors—such as seniority, job title, or across-the-board pay raises—then employees are likely to reduce their efforts. From a motivation perspective, making some or all an employee's pay conditional on some performance measure focuses his or her attention and effort toward that measure, then reinforces the continuation of the effort with a reward. If the employee's team's or organization's performance declines, so does the reward. Thus, there's an incentive to keep efforts and motivation strong.

Pay-for-performance programs are popular. Some 92 percent of large U.S. companies have some form of variable pay plan.[93] These types of pay plans have also been tried in other countries such as Canada and Japan. About 30 percent of Canadian companies and 22 percent of Japanese companies have company-wide pay-for-performance plans.[94]

Do pay-for-performance programs work? The jury is still out. For the most part, studies seem to indicate that they do. For instance, one study found companies that used pay-for-performance programs performed better financially than those that did not.[95] Another study showed pay-for-performance programs with outcome-based incentives had a positive impact on sales, customer satisfaction, and profits.[96] In organizations that use work teams, managers should consider group-based performance incentives that will reinforce team effort and commitment. However, others say that linking pay to performance doesn't work.[97] So if a business decides it wants to use pay-for-performance programs, managers need to ensure they're specific about the relationship between an individual's pay and his or her expected level of appropriate performance. Employees must clearly understand exactly how performance—theirs and the organization's—translates into dollars on their paychecks.[98]

CHAPTER

PREPARING FOR: Exams/Quizzes

CHAPTER SUMMARY by Learning Outcomes

17.1 LEARNING OUTCOME

Define motivation.

Motivation is the process by which a person's efforts are energized, directed, and sustained toward attaining a goal.

The *energy* element is a measure of intensity, drive, or vigor. The high level of effort needs to be *directed* in ways that help the organization achieve its goals. Employees must *persist* in putting forth effort to achieve those goals.

17.2 LEARNING OUTCOME

Compare and contrast early theories of motivation.

In Maslow's hierarchy, individuals move up the hierarchy of five needs (physiological, safety, social, esteem, and self-actualization) as needs are substantially satisfied. A need that's substantially satisfied no longer motivates.

A Theory X manager believes people don't like to work or won't seek out responsibility so they have to be threatened and coerced to work. A Theory Y manager assumes people like to work and seek out responsibility, so they will exercise self-motivation and self-direction.

Herzberg's theory proposed that intrinsic factors associated with job satisfaction were what motivated people. Extrinsic factors associated with job dissatisfaction simply kept people from being dissatisfied.

Three-needs theory proposed three acquired needs that are major motives in work: need for achievement, need for affiliation, and need for power.

17.3 LEARNING OUTCOME

Compare and contrast contemporary theories of motivation.

Goal-setting theory says that specific goals increase performance, and difficult goals, when accepted, result in higher performance than easy goals. Important points in goal-setting theory include intention to work toward a goal as a major source of job motivation; specific hard goals that produce higher levels of output than generalized goals; participation in setting goals as preferable to assigning goals, but not always; feedback that guides and motivates behavior, especially self-generated feedback; and contingencies that affect goal setting—goal commitment, self-efficacy, and national culture. Reinforcement theory says that behavior is a function of its consequences. To motivate, use positive reinforcers to reinforce desirable behaviors. Ignore undesirable behavior rather than punishing it.

Job enlargement involves horizontally expanding job scope by adding more tasks or increasing how many times the tasks are done. Job enrichment vertically expands job depth by giving employees more control over their work. The job characteristics model says five core job dimensions (skill variety, task identity, task significance, autonomy, and feedback) are used to design motivating jobs. Another job design approach proposed looking at relational aspects and proactive aspects of jobs.

Equity theory focuses on how employees compare their inputs–outcomes ratios to relevant others' ratios. A perception of inequity will cause an employee to do something about it. Procedural justice has a greater influence on employee satisfaction than distributive justice.

Expectancy theory says an individual tends to act in a certain way based on the expectation that the act will be followed by a desired outcome. Expectancy is the effort–performance linkage (how much effort do I need to exert to achieve a certain level of performance?); instrumentality is the performance–reward linkage (achieving at a certain level of performance will get me a specific reward); and valence is the attractiveness of the reward (is it the reward that I want?).

17.4 LEARNING OUTCOME

Discuss current issues in motivation.

Managers must cope with four current motivation issues: motivating in tough economic circumstances, managing cross-cultural challenges, motivating unique groups of workers, and designing appropriate rewards programs.

During tough economic conditions, managers must look for creative ways to keep employees' efforts energized, directed, and sustained toward achieving goals.

Most motivational theories were developed in the United States and have a North American bias. Some theories (Maslow's need hierarchy, achievement need, and equity theory) don't work well for other cultures. However, the desire for interesting work seems important to all workers and Herzberg's motivator (intrinsic) factors may be universal.

Managers face challenges in motivating unique groups of workers. A diverse workforce is looking for flexibility. Professionals want job challenge and support and are motivated by the work itself. Contingent workers want the opportunity to become permanent or to receive skills training. Recognition programs and sincere appreciation for work done can be used to motivate low-skilled, minimum-wage workers.

Open-book management is when financial statements (the books) are shared with employees who have been taught what they mean. Employee recognition programs consist of personal attention, approval, and appreciation for a job well done. Pay-for-performance programs are variable compensation plans that pay employees on the basis of some performance measure.

REVIEW AND DISCUSSION QUESTIONS ✪

1. What is motivation? Explain the three key elements of motivation.

2. Describe each of the four early theories of motivation.

3. How do goal-setting, reinforcement, and equity theories explain employee motivation?

4. What are the different job design approaches to motivation?

5. Explain the three key linkages in expectancy theory and their role in motivation.

6. What challenges do managers face in motivating today's workforce?

7. Describe open-book management, employee recognition, and pay-for-performance programs.

8. Can an individual be too motivated? Discuss.

PREPARING FOR: My Career

ETHICS DILEMMA ✪

Kodak, once the premier maker of photographic film, has struggled to make it in a world of digital photography and camera phones.[99] It filed for bankruptcy in early 2012. In July 2012, the company's CEO went back to bankruptcy court asking permission to pay 15 top executives and managers (including himself) up to $8.82 million in cash and deferred stock if they successfully restructured the company and brought it back out of bankruptcy. Although incentive plans in bankruptcy have been controversial, Kodak said a committee of the company's unsecured creditors supported the pay plan. What do you think? What potential ethical issues do you see here? What stakeholders might be impacted and how?

SKILLS EXERCISE Developing Your Motivating Employees Skill

About the Skill

Because a simple, all-encompassing set of motivational guidelines is not available, the following suggestions draw on the essence of what we know about motivating employees.

Steps in Practicing the Skill

1. *Recognize individual differences.* Almost every contemporary motivation theory recognizes that employees are not homogeneous. They have different needs. They also differ in terms of attitudes, personality, and other important individual variables.

2. *Match people to jobs.* A great deal of evidence shows the motivational benefits of carefully matching people to jobs. People who lack the necessary skills to perform successfully will be at a disadvantage.

3. *Use goals.* You should ensure that employees have hard, specific goals and feedback on how well they're doing in pursuit of those goals. In many cases, these goals should be participatively set.

4. *Ensure goals are perceived as attainable.* Regardless of whether goals are actually attainable, employees who see goals as unattainable will reduce their effort. Be sure, therefore, that employees feel confident that increased efforts can lead to achieving performance goals.

5. *Individualize rewards.* Because employees have different needs, what acts as a reinforcer for one may not do

so for another. Use your knowledge of employee differences to individualize the rewards over which you have control. Some of the more obvious rewards that you can allocate include pay, promotions, autonomy, and the opportunity to participate in goal setting and decision making.

6. *Link rewards to performance.* You need to make rewards contingent on performance. Rewarding factors other than performance will only reinforce the importance of those other factors. Key rewards such as pay increases and promotions should be given for the attainment of employees' specific goals.

7. *Check the system for equity.* Employees should perceive that rewards or outcomes are equal to the inputs given. On a simplistic level, experience, ability, effort, and other obvious inputs should explain differences in pay, responsibility, and other obvious outcomes.

8. *Don't ignore money.* It's easy to get so caught up in setting goals, creating interesting jobs, and providing opportunities for participation that you forget that money is a major reason why most people work. Thus, the allocation of performance-based wage increases, piece-work bonuses, employee stock ownership plans, and other pay incentives are important in determining employee motivation.

WORKING TOGETHER Team Exercise

List five criteria (for example, pay, recognition, challenging work, friendships, status, the opportunity to do new things, the opportunity to travel, and so forth) that would be most important to you in a job. Rank them by order of importance.

Break into small groups of three or four and compare your responses. What patterns, if any, did you find?

MY TURN TO BE A MANAGER

- A good habit to get into if you don't already do it is goal-setting. Set goals for yourself using the suggestions from goal-setting theory. Write these down and keep them in a notebook. Track your progress toward achieving these goals.

- Describe a task you've done recently for which you exerted a high level of effort. Explain your behavior, using any three of the motivation approaches described in this chapter.

- Pay attention to times when you're highly motivated and times when you're not as motivated. Write down a description of these. What accounts for the difference in your level of motivation?

- Interview three managers about how they motivate their employees. What have they found that works the best? Write up your findings in a report and be prepared to present it in class.

- Using the job characteristics model, redesign the following jobs to be more motivating: retail store sales associate, utility company meter reader, and checkout cashier at a discount store. In a written report, describe for each job at least two specific actions you would take for each of the five core job dimensions.

- Do some serious thinking about what you want from your job after graduation. Make a list of what's important to you. Are you looking for a pleasant work environment, challenging work, flexible work hours, fun coworkers, or what? Discuss how you will discover whether a particular job will help you get those things.

- Steve's and Mary's recommended readings: Teresa Amabile and Steven Kramer, *The Progress Principle: Using Small Wins to Ignite Joy, Engagement, and Creativity at Work* (Harvard Business Review Press, 2011); Daniel H. Pink, *Drive: The Surprising Truth About What Motivates Us* (Riverhead Books: The Penguin Group, 2009); C. Ressler and J. Thompson, *Why Work Sucks and How To Fix It* (Portfolio: The Penguin Group, 2008); Terry R. Bacon, *What People Want* (Davies-Black Publishing, 2006); Dennis W. Bakke, *Joy at Work* (PVG, 2005); Leon Martel, *High Performers* (Jossey-Bass, 2002); Jon R. Katzenbach, *Peak Performance* (Harvard Business School Press, 2000); and Steven Kerr (ed.), *Ultimate Rewards: What Really Motivates People to Achieve* (Harvard Business School Press, 1997).

- Find five different examples of employee recognition programs from organizations with which you're familiar or from articles that you find. Write a report describing your examples and evaluating what you think about the various approaches.

- Find the Web site of Great Place to Work Institute [www.greatplacetowork.com]. What does the Institute say about what makes an organization a great place to work? Next, locate the lists of the Best Companies to Work For. Choose one company from each of the international lists. Now research that company and describe what it does that makes it a great place to work.

- In your own words, write down three things you learned in this chapter about being a good manager.

- Self-knowledge can be a powerful learning tool. Go to mymanagementlab.com and complete these self-assessment exercises: What Motivates Me? What Are My Dominant Needs? What Rewards Do I Value Most? What's My View on the Nature of People? What's My Job's Motivating Potential? Do I Want an Enriched Job? How Confident Am I in My Ability to Succeed? What's My Attitude Toward Achievement? Using the results of your assessments, identify personal strengths and weaknesses. What will you do to reinforce your strengths and improve your weaknesses?

MyManagementLab

Go to **mymanagementlab.com** for Auto-graded writing questions as well as the following Assisted-graded writing questions:

17-1. What economic and cross-cultural challenges do managers face when motivating employees?

17-2. Most of us have to work for a living, and a job is a central part of our lives. So why do managers have to worry so much about employee motivation issues?

17-3. Mymanagementlab Only – comprehensive writing assignment for this chapter.

CASE APPLICATION **1** Passion for the Outdoors and for People

At its headquarters in Ventura, California, Patagonia's office space feels more like a national park lodge than the main office of a $400 million retailer.[100] It has a Douglas fir staircase and a portrait of Yosemite's El Capitan. The company's café serves organic food and drinks. There's an infant and toddler child-care room for employees' children. An easy one-block walk from the Pacific Ocean, employees' surfboards are lined up by the cafeteria, ready at a moment's notice to catch some waves. (Current wave reports are noted on a whiteboard in the lobby.) After surfing or jogging or biking, employees can freshen up in the showers in the restrooms. And no one has a private office. If an employee doesn't want to be disturbed, he or she wears headphones. Visitors are evident by the business attire they wear. The company encourages celebrations to boost employee morale. For instance, at the Reno store, the "Fun Patrol" organizes parties throughout the year.

Attracting people who share its strong passion for the outdoors and the environment, Patagonia motivates its loyal employees by giving them responsibility for the outcomes of their work and a high level of task significance that their work is meaningful because it contributes to the purpose of protecting and preserving the environment.
Source: Rich Reid/Glow Images

Patagonia has long been recognized as a great workplace for mothers. And it's also earned a reputation for loyal employees, something that many retailers struggle with. Its combined voluntary and involuntary turnover in its retail stores was around 25 percent, while it was only 7 percent at headquarters. (The industry average for retail is around 44 percent.) Patagonia's CEO Casey Sheahan says the company's culture, camaraderie, and way of doing business is very meaningful to employees and they know that "what they do each day is contributing toward a higher purpose—protecting and preserving the areas that most of them love spending time in." Managers are coached to define expectations, communicate deadlines, and then let employees figure out the best way to meet those.

Founded by Yvon Chouinard (his profile as a Leader Who Made a Difference can be found on p. 134), Patagonia's first and strongest passion is for the outdoors and the environment. And that attracts employees who are also passionate about those things. But Patagonia's executives do realize that they are first and foremost a business and, even though they're committed to doing the right thing, the company needs to remain profitable to be able to continue to do the things it's passionate about. But that hasn't seemed to be an issue since the recession in the early 1990s when the company had to make its only large-scale layoffs in its history.

DISCUSSION QUESTIONS ✪

1. What would it be like to work at Patagonia? (Hint: Go to Patagonia's Web site and find the section on jobs.) What's your assessment of the company's work environment?

2. Using what you've learned from studying the various motivation theories, what does Patagonia's situation tell you about employee motivation?

3. What do you think might be Patagonia's biggest challenge in keeping employees motivated?

4. If you were managing a team of Patagonia employees in the retail stores, how would you keep them motivated?

CASE APPLICATION 2 Best Practices at Best Buy

Best Buy's Results-Only Work Environment program that changed the company's culture of evaluating and rewarding employees on the results of their work rather than on the number of hours they work increased worker productivity and job satisfaction and decreased voluntary turnover.

Source: Richard Sennott/ZUMA Press/Newscom

Do traditional workplaces reward long hours instead of efficient hours? Wouldn't it make more sense to have a workplace in which "people can do whatever they want, whenever they want, as long as the work gets done?" Well, that's the approach Best Buy is taking.[101] And this radical workplace experiment, which obviously has many implications for employee motivation, has been an interesting and enlightening journey for the company.

In 2002, then CEO Brad Anderson introduced a carefully crafted program called ROWE—Results-Only Work Environment. ROWE was the inspiration of two HRM managers at Best Buy, Cali Ressler and Jody Thompson, who had been given the task of taking a flexible work program in effect at corporate headquarters in Minnesota and developing it for everyone in the company. Ressler and Thompson said, "We realized that the flexible work program was successful as employee engagement was up, productivity was higher, but the problem was the participants were being viewed as 'not working.'" And that was a common reaction from managers who didn't really view flexible work employees as "really working because they aren't in the office working traditional hours." The two women set about to change that by creating a program in which "everyone would be evaluated solely on their results, not on how long they worked."

The first thing to understand about ROWE is that it's not about schedules. Instead, it's about changing the work culture of an organization, which is infinitely more difficult than changing schedules. With Anderson's blessing and support, they embarked on this journey to overhaul the company's corporate workplace.

The first step in implementing ROWE was a culture audit at company headquarters, which helped them establish a baseline for how employees perceived their work environment. After four months, the audit was repeated. During this time, Best Buy executives were being educated about ROWE and what it was all about. Obviously, it was important to have their commitment to the program. The second phase involved explaining the ROWE philosophy to all the corporate employees and training managers on how to maintain control in a ROWE workplace. In the third phase, work unit teams were free to figure out how to implement the changes. Each team found a different way to keep the flexibility from spiraling into chaos. For instance, the public relations team got pagers to make sure someone was always available in an emergency. Some employees in the finance department used software that turns voice mail into e-mail files accessible from anywhere, making it easier for them to work at home. Four months after ROWE was implemented, Ressler and Thompson followed up with another culture check to see how everyone was doing.

So what's the bottom line for Best Buy? Productivity jumped 41 percent, and voluntary turnover fell to 8 percent from 12 percent. They also discovered that when employees' engagement with their jobs increased, average annual sales increased 2 percent. And employees said the freedom changed their lives. "They don't know if they work fewer hours—they've stopped counting—but they are more productive." ROWE reduced work-family conflict and increased employees' control over their schedules. As Ressler and Thompson stated, "Work isn't a place you go—it's something you do."

DISCUSSION QUESTIONS ⭐

1. Describe the elements of ROWE. What do you think might be the advantages and drawbacks of this program?

2. Using one or more motivation theories from the chapter, explain why you think ROWE works.

3. What might be the challenges for managers in motivating employees in a program like this?

4. Does this sound like something you would be comfortable with? Why or why not?

5. What's your interpretation of the statement that "Work isn't a place you go—it's something you do"? Do you agree? Why or why not?

SPOTLIGHT: *Manager at Work*

A lot has been written about the late Steve Jobs.[1]
How he took Apple, a niche business, and turned it into the most valuable company in the world as measured by market capitalization. How he was extremely charismatic and extremely compelling in getting people to join with him and believe in his vision. But also how he was despotic, tyrannical, abrasive, uncompromising, and a perfectionist. So what is his leadership legacy?

Everything Jobs did and how he did it was motivated by his desire to have Apple make innovative products—products that were "insanely great"— "insanely" being one of his favorite descriptors. That singular focus shaped his leadership style which has been described as autocratic and yet persuasive. As one reporter said, Jobs "violated every rule of management. He was not a consensus builder but a dictator who listened mainly to his own intuition. He was a maniacal micromanager...He could be absolutely brutal in meetings." His verbal assaults on staff could be terrifying. The story is told that when Apple launched its first version of the iPhone that worked on 3G mobile networks, it included MobileMe, an email system that was supposed to provide seamless synchronization features similar to that used by the fanatical corporate users of Blackberrys. The problem: It didn't work well at all, and product reviews were quite critical. Since "Steve Jobs doesn't tolerate duds," it wasn't long after the launch that he gathered the MobileMe team in an auditorium on Apple's campus. According to a participant in that meeting, Jobs walked in—in his trademark black mock turtleneck and jeans—and "asked a simple question: 'Can you tell me what MobileMe is supposed to do?' Having received a satisfactory answer, he responded, 'So why the @#$% doesn't it do that?'" Then, for the next 30 minutes, Jobs blasted criticisms at the team. "You've tarnished Apple's reputation. You should hate each

Source: Paul Sakuma/AP Photo

What is Steve Jobs' leadership legacy?

other for having let each other down." Ouch. And this wasn't the only example of his taking employees to task. He was tough on the people around him. When asked about his tendency to be rough on people, Jobs responded, "Look at the results. These are all smart people I work with, and any of them could get a top job at another place if they were truly feeling brutalized. But they don't."

On the other hand, Steve Jobs could be thoughtful, passionate, and "insanely" charismatic. He could "push people to do the impossible." And there's no argument with the fact that the results from the company he co-founded have been market-changing. From the Macs and iPods to the iPhones and iPads, Apple's products have revolutionized industries and created a fan base of consumers who

LEARNING OUTCOMES

18.1	*Define* leader and leadership.
18.2	*Compare* and contrast early theories of leadership.
18.3	*Describe* the three major contingency theories of leadership.
18.4	*Describe* contemporary views of leadership.
18.5	*Discuss* contemporary issues affecting leadership.

are very loyal to the Apple brand and employees who are very loyal to the company. **Would Steve Jobs' leadership approach work for others? What do you think?**

Steve Jobs of Apple provides a fascinating example of the what's and how's of leadership. His leadership approach and style is totally not what you'd read about in most books on leadership. Yet, how he led Apple probably wouldn't work in all situations, if any others. But leadership *is* needed in all organizations. Why? Because it's the leaders in organizations who make things happen.

18.1 ⎰ *Define* leader and leadership.

leader
Someone who can influence others and who has managerial authority

leadership
A process of influencing a group to achieve goals

WHO **Are Leaders and What Is Leadership?**

Let's begin by clarifying who leaders are and what leadership is. Our definition of a **leader** is someone who can influence others and who has managerial authority. **Leadership** is a process of leading a group and influencing that group to achieve its goals. It's what leaders do.

Are all managers leaders? Because leading is one of the four management functions, yes, ideally, all managers *should* be leaders. Thus, we're going to study leaders and leadership from a managerial perspective.[2] However, even though we're looking at these from a managerial perspective, we're aware that groups often have informal leaders who emerge. Although these informal leaders may be able to influence others, they have not been the focus of most leadership research and are not the types of leaders we're studying in this chapter.

Leaders and leadership, like motivation, are organizational behavior topics that have been researched a lot. Most of that research has been aimed at answering the question: *What is an effective leader?* We'll begin our study of leadership by looking at some early leadership theories that attempted to answer that question.

18.2 ⎰ *Compare* and contrast early theories of leadership.

EARLY **Leadership Theories**

People have been interested in leadership since they started coming together in groups to accomplish goals. However, it wasn't until the early part of the twentieth century that researchers actually began to study leadership. These early leadership theories focused on the *leader* (leadership trait theories) and how the *leader interacted* with his or her group members (leadership behavior theories).

Leadership Trait Theories

Researchers at the University of Cambridge in England recently reported that men with longer ring fingers, compared to their index fingers, tended to be more successful in the frantic high-frequency trading in the London financial district.[3] What does a study of the finger lengths of financial traders have to do with trait theories of leadership? Well, that's also what leadership trait theories have attempted to do—identify certain traits that all leaders have.

Leadership research in the 1920s and 1930s focused on isolating leader traits—that is, characteristics—that would differentiate leaders from nonleaders. Some of the traits studied included physical stature, appearance, social class, emotional stability, fluency of speech, and sociability. Despite the best efforts of researchers, it proved impossible to identify a set of traits that would *always* differentiate a leader (the person) from a nonleader. Maybe it was a bit optimistic to think that a set of consistent and unique traits would apply universally to all effective leaders, no matter whether they were in charge of Mondelez International (formerly Kraft Foods), the Moscow Ballet, the country of France, a local collegiate chapter of Alpha Chi Omega, Ted's Malibu Surf Shop, or Oxford University. However, later attempts to identify traits consistently associated with

1. *Drive*. Leaders exhibit a high effort level. They have a relatively high desire for achievement, they are ambitious, they have a lot of energy, they are tirelessly persistent in their activities, and they show initiative.

2. *Desire to lead*. Leaders have a strong desire to influence and lead others. They demonstrate the willingness to take responsibility.

3. *Honesty and integrity*. Leaders build trusting relationships with followers by being truthful or nondeceitful and by showing high consistency between word and deed.

4. *Self-confidence*. Followers look to leaders for an absence of self-doubt. Leaders, therefore, need to show self-confidence in order to convince followers of the rightness of their goals and decisions.

5. *Intelligence*. Leaders need to be intelligent enough to gather, synthesize, and interpret large amounts of information, and they need to be able to create visions, solve problems, and make correct decisions.

6. *Job-relevant knowledge*. Effective leaders have a high degree of knowledge about the company, industry, and technical matters. In-depth knowledge allows leaders to make well-informed decisions and to understand the implications of those decisions.

7. *Extraversion*. Leaders are energetic, lively people. They are sociable, assertive, and rarely silent or withdrawn.

8. *Proneness to guilt*. Guilt proneness is positively related to leadership effectiveness because it produces a strong sense of responsibility for others.

Exhibit 18-1
Eight Traits Associated with Leadership

Sources: Based on S. A. Kirkpatrick and E. A. Locke, "Leadership: Do Traits Really Matter?" *Academy of Management Executive,* May 1991, pp. 48–60; T. A. Judge, J. E. Bono, R. Ilies, and M. W. Gerhardt, "Personality and Leadership: A Qualitative and Quantitative Review," *Journal of Applied Psychology,* August 2002, pp. 765–780; and R. L. Schaumberg and F. J. Flynn, "Uneasy Lies the Head That Wears the Crown: The Link Between Guilt Proneness and Leadership," *Journal of Personality and Social Psychology,* August 2012, pp. 327–342.

---

leadership (the process of leading, not the person) were more successful. The eight traits shown to be associated with effective leadership are described briefly in Exhibit 18-1.[4]

Researchers eventually recognized that traits alone were not sufficient for identifying effective leaders since explanations based solely on traits ignored the interactions of leaders and their group members as well as situational factors. Possessing the appropriate traits only made it more likely that an individual would be an effective leader. Therefore, leadership research from the late 1940s to the mid-1960s concentrated on the preferred behavioral styles that leaders demonstrated. Researchers wondered whether something unique in what effective leaders *did*—in other words, in their *behavior*—was the key.

Leadership Behavior Theories

Bill Watkins, former CEO of disk drive manufacturer Seagate Technology, once responded when asked how he handled his board of directors, "You never ask board members what they think. You tell them what you're going to do." In contrast, Joe Lee, CEO of Darden Restaurants during the aftermath of 9/11, was focused on only two things that morning: his Darden people who were traveling and his company's Muslim colleagues.[5] These two leaders of successful companies, as you can see, behaved in two very different ways. What do we know about leader behavior and how can it help us in our understanding of what an effective leader is?

Researchers hoped that the **behavioral theories** approach would provide more definitive answers about the nature of leadership than did the trait theories.[6] The four main leader behavior studies are summarized in Exhibit 18-2.

UNIVERSITY OF IOWA STUDIES The University of Iowa studies explored three leadership styles to find which was the most effective.[7] The **autocratic style** described

behavioral theories
Leadership theories that identify behaviors that differentiated effective leaders from ineffective leaders

autocratic style
A leader who dictates work methods, makes unilateral decisions, and limits employee participation

Exhibit 18-2
Behavioral Theories of Leadership

	Behavioral Dimension	Conclusion
University of Iowa	*Democratic style:* involving subordinates, delegating authority, and encouraging participation *Autocratic style:* dictating work methods, centralizing decision making, and limiting participation *Laissez-faire style:* giving group freedom to make decisions and complete work	Democratic style of leadership was most effective, although later studies showed mixed results.
Ohio State	*Consideration:* being considerate of followers' ideas and feelings *Initiating structure:* structuring work and work relationships to meet job goals	High–high leader (high in consideration and high in initiating structure) achieved high subordinate performance and satisfaction, but not in all situations
University of Michigan	*Employee oriented:* emphasized interpersonal relationships and taking care of employees' needs *Production oriented:* emphasized technical or task aspects of job	Employee-oriented leaders were associated with high group productivity and higher job satisfaction.
Managerial Grid	*Concern for people:* measured leader's concern for subordinates on a scale of 1 to 9 (low to high) *Concern for production:* measured leader's concern for getting job done on a scale 1 to 9 (low to high)	Leaders performed best with a 9,9 style (high concern for production and high concern for people).

democratic style
A leader who involves employees in decision making, delegates authority, and uses feedback as an opportunity for coaching employees

laissez-faire style
A leader who lets the group make decisions and complete the work in whatever way it sees fit

a leader who dictated work methods, made unilateral decisions, and limited employee participation. The **democratic style** described a leader who involved employees in decision making, delegated authority, and used feedback as an opportunity for coaching employees. Finally, the **laissez-faire style** leader let the group make decisions and complete the work in whatever way it saw fit. The researchers' results seemed to indicate that the democratic style contributed to both good quantity and quality of work. Had the answer to the question of the most effective leadership style been found? Unfortunately, it wasn't that simple. Later studies of the autocratic and democratic styles showed mixed results. For instance, the democratic style sometimes produced higher performance levels than the autocratic style, but at other times, it didn't. However, more consistent results were found when a measure of employee satisfaction was used. Group members were more satisfied under a democratic leader than under an autocratic one.[8]

Now leaders had a dilemma! Should they focus on achieving higher performance or on achieving higher member satisfaction? This recognition of the dual nature of a leader's behavior—that is, focus on the task and focus on the people—was also a key characteristic of the other behavioral studies.

THE OHIO STATE STUDIES The Ohio State studies identified two important dimensions of leader behavior.[9] Beginning with a list of more than 1,000 behavioral dimensions, the researchers eventually narrowed it down to just two that accounted for most of the leadership behavior described by group members. The first was called **initiating structure**, which referred to the extent to which a leader defined his or her role and the roles of group members in attaining goals. It included behaviors that involved attempts to organize work, work relationships, and goals. The second was called **consideration**, which was defined as the extent to which a leader had work relationships characterized by mutual trust and respect for group members' ideas and feelings. A leader who was high in consideration helped group members with personal problems, was friendly and approachable, and treated all group members as equals. He or she showed concern for (was considerate of) his or her followers' comfort, well-being, status, and satisfaction. Research found that a leader who was high in both initiating structure and consideration (a **high–high leader**) sometimes achieved high group task performance and high group member satisfaction, but not always.

initiating structure
The extent to which a leader defines his or her role and the roles of group members in attaining goals

consideration
The extent to which a leader has work relationships characterized by mutual trust and respect for group members' ideas and feelings

high–high leader
A leader high in both initiating structure and consideration behaviors

UNIVERSITY OF MICHIGAN STUDIES Leadership studies conducted at the University of Michigan at about the same time as those done at Ohio State also hoped to identify behavioral characteristics of leaders that were related to performance effectiveness. The Michigan group also came up with two dimensions of leadership behavior, which they labeled employee oriented and production oriented.[10] Leaders who were *employee oriented* were described as emphasizing interpersonal relationships. The *production-oriented* leaders, in contrast, tended to emphasize the task aspects of the job. Unlike the other studies, the Michigan researchers concluded that leaders who were employee oriented were able to get high group productivity and high group member satisfaction.

managerial grid
A two-dimensional grid for appraising leadership styles

THE MANAGERIAL GRID The behavioral dimensions from these early leadership studies provided the basis for the development of a two-dimensional grid for appraising leadership styles. This **managerial grid** used the behavioral dimensions "concern for people" (the vertical part of the grid) and "concern for production" (the horizontal part of the grid) and evaluated a leader's use of these behaviors, ranking them on a scale from 1 (low) to 9 (high).[11] Although the grid had 81 potential categories into which a leader's behavioral style might fall, only five styles were named: impoverished management (1,1 or low concern for production, low concern for people), task management (9,1 or high concern for production, low concern for people), middle-of-the-road management (5,5 or medium concern for production, medium concern for people), country club management (1,9 or low concern for production, high concern for people), and team management (9,9 or high concern for production, high concern for people). Of these five styles, the researchers concluded that managers performed best when using a 9,9 style. Unfortunately, the grid offered no answers to the question of what made a manager an effective leader; it only provided a framework for conceptualizing leadership style. In fact, little substantive evidence supports the conclusion that a 9,9 style is most effective in all situations.[12]

Chanda Kochhar is the managing director and chief executive officer of ICICI Bank in India. She is an employee-oriented leader whose behavior towards subordinates is compassionate, nurturing, and understanding. Kochhar sets high performance goals, encourages employees to work hard, motivates them to perform to the best of their abilities, and helps them realize their full potential. Her leadership behavior of emphasizing interpersonal relationships and being sensitive to employees has resulted in high group member satisfaction and high group productivity. Under her leadership, ICICI Bank has grown to become the largest private retail bank in India.
Source: Reuters/Vivek Prakash

Leadership researchers were discovering that predicting leadership success involved something more complex than isolating a few leader traits or preferable behaviors. They began looking at situational influences. Specifically, which leadership styles might be suitable in different situations and what were these different situations?

18.3 *Describe* the three major contingency theories of leadership.

CONTINGENCY Theories of Leadership

"The corporate world is filled with stories of leaders who failed to achieve greatness because they failed to understand the context they were working in."[13] In this section, we examine three contingency theories—Fiedler, Hersey-Blanchard, and path-goal. Each looks at defining leadership style and the situation, and attempts to answer the *if-then* contingencies (that is, *if* this is the context or situation, *then* this is the best leadership style to use).

The Fiedler Model

The first comprehensive contingency model for leadership was developed by Fred Fiedler.[14] The **Fiedler contingency model** proposed that effective group performance depended on properly matching the leader's style and the amount of control and influence in the situation. The model was based on the premise that a certain leadership style would be most effective in different types of situations. The keys were to (1) define those leadership styles and the different types of situations, and then (2) identify the appropriate combinations of style and situation.

Fiedler proposed that a key factor in leadership success was an individual's basic leadership style, either task oriented or relationship oriented. To measure a leader's style, Fiedler developed the **least-preferred coworker (LPC) questionnaire**. This questionnaire contained 18 pairs of contrasting adjectives—for example, pleasant–unpleasant, cold–warm, boring–interesting, or friendly–unfriendly. Respondents were asked to think of all the coworkers they had ever had and to describe that one person they *least enjoyed* working with by rating him or her on a scale of 1 to 8 for each of the 18 sets of adjectives (the 8 always described the positive adjective out of the pair and the 1 always described the negative adjective out of the pair).

If the leader described the least preferred coworker in relatively positive terms (in other words, a "high" LPC score—a score of 64 or above), then the respondent was primarily interested in good personal relations with coworkers, and the style would be described as *relationship oriented*. In contrast, if you saw the least preferred coworker in relatively unfavorable terms (a low LPC score—a score of 57 or below), you were primarily interested in productivity and getting the job done; thus, your style would be labeled as *task oriented*. Fiedler did acknowledge that a small number of people might fall in between these two extremes and not have a cut-and-dried leadership style. One other important point is that Fiedler assumed a person's leadership style was fixed regardless of the situation. In other words, if you were a relationship-oriented leader, you'd always be one, and the same for task-oriented.

After an individual's leadership style had been assessed through the LPC, it was time to evaluate the situation in order to be able to match the leader with the situation. Fiedler's research uncovered three contingency dimensions that defined the key situational factors in leader effectiveness.

- **Leader–member relations**: the degree of confidence, trust, and respect employees had for their leader; rated as either good or poor.
- **Task structure**: the degree to which job assignments were formalized and structured; rated as either high or low.
- **Position power**: the degree of influence a leader had over activities such as hiring, firing, discipline, promotions, and salary increases; rated as either strong or weak.

Each leadership situation was evaluated in terms of these three contingency variables, which when combined produced eight possible situations that were either favorable or unfavorable for the leader. (See the bottom of the chart in Exhibit 18-3.) Situations I, II, and III were classified as highly favorable for the leader. Situations IV, V, and VI were moderately favorable for the leader. And situations VII and VIII were described as highly unfavorable for the leader.

Fiedler contingency model
A leadership theory proposing that effective group performance depends on the proper match between a leader's style and the degree to which the situation allows the leader to control and influence

least-preferred coworker (LPC) questionnaire
A questionnaire that measures whether a leader is task or relationship oriented

leader–member relations
One of Fiedler's situational contingencies that describes the degree of confidence, trust, and respect employees had for their leader

task structure
One of Fiedler's situational contingencies that describes the degree to which job assignments are formalized and structured

position power
One of Fiedler's situational contingencies that describes the degree of influence a leader has over activities such as hiring, firing, discipline, promotions, and salary increases

Exhibit 18-3
The Fiedler Model

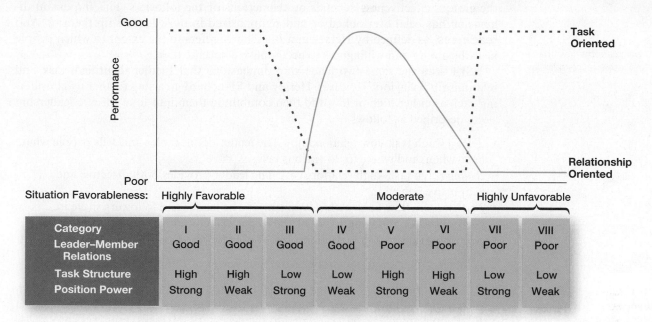

Category	I	II	III	IV	V	VI	VII	VIII
Leader–Member Relations	Good	Good	Good	Good	Poor	Poor	Poor	Poor
Task Structure	High	High	Low	Low	High	High	Low	Low
Position Power	Strong	Weak	Strong	Weak	Strong	Weak	Strong	Weak

Situation Favorableness: Highly Favorable — Moderate — Highly Unfavorable

Once Fiedler had described the leader variables and the situational variables, he had everything he needed to define the specific contingencies for leadership effectiveness. To do so, he studied 1,200 groups where he compared relationship-oriented versus task-oriented leadership styles in each of the eight situational categories. He concluded that task-oriented leaders performed better in very favorable situations and in very unfavorable situations. (See the top of Exhibit 18-3 where performance is shown on the vertical axis and situation favorableness is shown on the horizontal axis.) On the other hand, relationship-oriented leaders performed better in moderately favorable situations.

Because Fiedler treated an individual's leadership style as fixed, only two ways could improve leader effectiveness. First, you could bring in a new leader whose style better fit the situation. For instance, if the group situation was highly unfavorable but was led by a relationship-oriented leader, the group's performance could be improved by replacing that person with a task-oriented leader. The second alternative was to change the situation to fit the leader. This could be done by restructuring tasks; by increasing or decreasing the power that the leader had over factors such as salary increases, promotions, and disciplinary actions; or by improving the leader–member relations.

Research testing the overall validity of Fiedler's model has shown considerable evidence to support the model.[15] However, his theory wasn't without criticisms. The major one is that it's probably unrealistic to assume that a person can't change his or her leadership style to fit the situation. Effective leaders can, and do, change their styles. Another is that the LPC wasn't very practical. Finally, the situation variables were difficult to assess.[16] Despite its shortcomings, the Fiedler model showed that effective leadership style needed to reflect situational factors.

Hersey and Blanchard's Situational Leadership Theory

Paul Hersey and Ken Blanchard developed a leadership theory that has gained a strong following among management development specialists.[17] This model, called **situational leadership theory (SLT)**, is a contingency theory that focuses on followers' readiness. Before we proceed, two points need clarification: Why a leadership theory focuses on the followers and what is meant by the term *readiness*.

situational leadership theory (SLT)
A leadership contingency theory that focuses on followers' readiness

readiness
The extent to which people have the ability and willingness to accomplish a specific task

The emphasis on the followers in leadership effectiveness reflects the reality that it *is* the followers who accept or reject the leader. Regardless of what the leader does, the group's effectiveness depends on the actions of the followers. This important dimension has been overlooked or underemphasized in most leadership theories. And **readiness**, as defined by Hersey and Blanchard, refers to the extent to which people have the ability and willingness to accomplish a specific task.

SLT uses the same two leadership dimensions that Fiedler identified: task and relationship behaviors. However, Hersey and Blanchard go a step further by considering each as either high or low and then combining them into four specific leadership styles described as follows:

- *Telling* (high task–low relationship): The leader defines roles and tells people what, how, when, and where to do various tasks.
- *Selling* (high task–high relationship): The leader provides both directive and supportive behavior.
- *Participating* (low task–high relationship): The leader and followers share in decision making; the main role of the leader is facilitating and communicating.
- *Delegating* (low task–low relationship): The leader provides little direction or support.

The final component in the model is the four stages of follower readiness:

- *R1:* People are both *unable and unwilling* to take responsibility for doing something. Followers aren't competent or confident.
- *R2:* People are *unable but willing* to do the necessary job tasks. Followers are motivated but lack the appropriate skills.
- *R3:* People are *able but unwilling* to do what the leader wants. Followers are competent, but don't want to do something.
- *R4:* People are both *able and willing* to do what is asked of them.

path-goal theory
A leadership theory that says the leader's job is to assist followers in attaining their goals and to provide direction or support needed to ensure that their goals are compatible with the goals of the group or organization

SLT essentially views the leader–follower relationship as like that of a parent and a child. Just as a parent needs to relinquish control when a child becomes more mature and responsible, so too should leaders. As followers reach higher levels of readiness, the leader responds not only by decreasing control over their activities but also decreasing relationship behaviors. The SLT says if followers are at R1 (*unable* and *unwilling* to do a task), the leader needs to use the telling style and give clear and specific directions; if followers are at R2 (*unable* and *willing*), the leader needs to use the selling style and display high task orientation to compensate for the followers' lack of ability and high relationship orientation to get followers to "buy into" the leader's desires; if followers are at R3 (*able* and *unwilling*), the leader needs to use the participating style to gain their support; and if employees are at R4 (both *able* and *willing*), the leader doesn't need to do much and should use the delegating style.

SLT has intuitive appeal. It acknowledges the importance of followers and builds on the logic that leaders can compensate for ability and motivational limitations in their followers. However, research efforts to test and support the theory generally have been disappointing.[18] Possible explanations include internal inconsistencies in the model as well as problems with research methodology. Despite its appeal and wide popularity, we have to be cautious about any enthusiastic endorsement of SLT.

Meg Whitman, CEO and president of Hewlett-Packard and formerly president and CEO of eBay, can be described as a supportive leader who is friendly and shows concern for the needs of followers. Believing that people are basically good, she trusts her subordinates, emotionally supports them, and treats them with care and respect. During her ten years at eBay, she led the company to incredible success, expanding it from 30 employees and $4 million in sales to 15,000 employees and $8 billion in sales. Her supportive leadership at eBay resulted in high employee performance and satisfaction.
Source: LiPo Ching/MCT/Newscom

Path-Goal Model

Another approach to understanding leadership is **path-goal theory**, which states that the leader's job is to assist followers in attaining their goals and to provide direction or support needed to ensure that their goals are compatible with the goals of the group or organization. Developed by Robert House, path-goal theory takes key elements from the expectancy theory of motivation.[19] The term *path-goal* is derived from the belief that effective leaders remove the roadblocks and pitfalls so that followers have a clearer path to help them get from where they are to the achievement of their work goals.

House identified four leadership behaviors:

- *Directive leader:* Lets subordinates know what's expected of them, schedules work to be done, and gives specific guidance on how to accomplish tasks.
- *Supportive leader:* Shows concern for the needs of followers and is friendly.
- *Participative leader:* Consults with group members and uses their suggestions before making a decision.
- *Achievement oriented leader:* Sets challenging goals and expects followers to perform at their highest level.

In contrast to Fiedler's view that a leader couldn't change his or her behavior, House assumed that leaders are flexible and can display any or all of these leadership styles depending on the situation.

As Exhibit 18-4 illustrates, path-goal theory proposes two situational or contingency variables that moderate the leadership behavior–outcome relationship: those in the *environment* that are outside the control of the follower (factors including task structure, formal authority system, and the work group) and those that are part of the personal characteristics of the *follower* (including locus of control, experience, and perceived ability). Environmental factors determine the type of leader behavior required if subordinate outcomes are to be maximized; personal characteristics of the follower determine how the environment and leader behavior are interpreted. The theory proposes that a leader's behavior won't be effective if it's redundant with what the environmental structure is providing or is incongruent with follower characteristics. For example, some predictions from path-goal theory are:

- Directive leadership leads to greater satisfaction when tasks are ambiguous or stressful than when they are highly structured and well laid out. The followers aren't sure what to do, so the leader needs to give them some direction.
- Supportive leadership results in high employee performance and satisfaction when subordinates are performing structured tasks. In this situation, the leader only needs to support followers, not tell them what to do.
- Directive leadership is likely to be perceived as redundant among subordinates with high perceived ability or with considerable experience. These followers are quite capable, so they don't need a leader to tell them what to do.

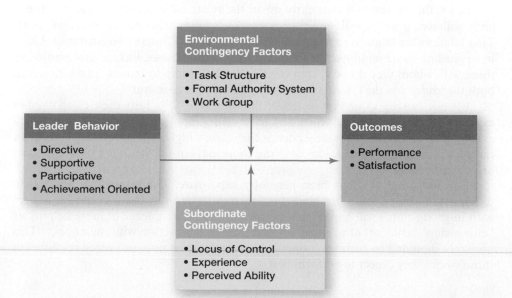

Exhibit 18-4

Path-Goal Model

- The clearer and more bureaucratic the formal authority relationships, the more leaders should exhibit supportive behavior and deemphasize directive behavior. The organizational situation has provided the structure as far as what is expected of followers, so the leader's role is simply to support.
- Directive leadership will lead to higher employee satisfaction when there is substantive conflict within a work group. In this situation, the followers need a leader who will take charge.
- Subordinates with an internal locus of control will be more satisfied with a participative style. Because these followers believe they control what happens to them, they prefer to participate in decisions.
- Subordinates with an external locus of control will be more satisfied with a directive style. These followers believe that what happens to them is a result of the external environment, so they would prefer a leader who tells them what to do.
- Achievement-oriented leadership will increase subordinates' expectancies that effort will lead to high performance when tasks are ambiguously structured. By setting challenging goals, followers know what the expectations are.

Testing path-goal theory has not been easy. A review of the research suggests mixed support.[20] To summarize the model, however, an employee's performance and satisfaction are likely to be positively influenced when the leader chooses a leadership style that compensates for shortcomings in either the employee or the work setting. However, if the leader spends time explaining tasks that are already clear or when the employee has the ability and experience to handle them without interference, the employee is likely to see such directive behavior as redundant or even insulting.

18.4 *Describe* contemporary views of leadership.

CONTEMPORARY Views of Leadership

What are the latest views of leadership? We want to look at four of these views: leader–member exchange theory, transformational-transactional leadership, charismatic-visionary leadership, and team leadership.

Leader–Member Exchange (LMX) Theory

leader–member exchange theory (LMX)
The leadership theory that says leaders create in-groups and out-groups and those in the in-group will have higher performance ratings, less turnover, and greater job satisfaction

Have you ever been in a group in which the leader had "favorites" who made up his or her in-group? If so, that's the premise behind leader–member exchange (LMX) theory.[21] **Leader–member exchange theory (LMX)** says leaders create in-groups and out-groups and those in the in-group will have higher performance ratings, less turnover, and greater job satisfaction.

LMX theory suggests that early on in the relationship between a leader and a given follower, a leader will implicitly categorize a follower as an "in" or as an "out." That relationship tends to remain fairly stable over time. Leaders also encourage LMX by rewarding those employees with whom they want a closer linkage and punishing those with whom they do not.[22] For the LMX relationship to remain intact, however, both the leader and the follower must "invest" in the relationship.

It's not exactly clear how a leader chooses who falls into each category, but evidence shows that in-group members have demographic, attitude, personality, and even gender similarities with the leader or they have a higher level of competence than out-group members.[23] The leader does the choosing, but the follower's characteristics drive the decision.

Research on LMX has been generally supportive. It appears that leaders do differentiate among followers; that these disparities are not random; and followers with in-group status will have higher performance ratings, engage in more helping or "citizenship" behaviors at work, and report greater satisfaction with their boss.[24] This probably shouldn't be surprising since leaders invest their time and other resources in those whom they expect to perform best.

Transformational-Transactional Leadership

Many early leadership theories viewed leaders as **transactional leaders**; that is, leaders who lead primarily by using social exchanges (or transactions). Transactional leaders guide or motivate followers to work toward established goals by exchanging rewards for their productivity.[26] But another type of leader—a **transformational leader**—stimulates and inspires (transforms) followers to achieve extraordinary outcomes. Examples include Jim Goodnight of SAS Institute and Andrea Jung of Avon. They pay attention to the concerns and developmental needs of individual followers; they change followers' awareness of issues by helping those followers look at old problems in new ways; and they are able to excite, arouse, and inspire followers to exert extra effort to achieve group goals.

LEADER who made a DIFFERENCE

Ajay Banga, CEO of MasterCard, has had well-rounded leadership experiences.[25] Born in India, Banga honed his leadership skills at Nestlé and PepsiCo before moving to Citigroup to head up its Asia-Pacific division. Citigroup was a challenging situation as he found a vast banking group that "worked fluidly in its product clusters but lacked coordination, synergy, or vision." Banga undertook the painful process of breaking down those "silos and stitching them together again under a single umbrella structure." When he was offered a position at MasterCard as president and chief operating officer, Banga jumped at the chance. Now as CEO, Banga is the company's cheerleader, shaking up the company's low-key corporate culture with hugs and fist bumps in the hallways. One analyst describes him as "energetic, open, and engaging." What can you learn from this leader who made a difference?

Source: Reuters/Keith Bedford

Transactional and transformational leadership shouldn't be viewed as opposing approaches to getting things done.[27] Transformational leadership develops from transactional leadership. Transformational leadership produces levels of employee effort and performance that go beyond what would occur with a transactional approach alone. Moreover, transformational leadership is more than charisma because the transformational leader attempts to instill in followers the ability to question not only established views but those views held by the leader.[28]

The evidence supporting the superiority of transformational leadership over transactional leadership is overwhelmingly impressive. For instance, studies that looked at managers in different settings, including the military and business, found that transformational leaders were evaluated as more effective, higher performers, more promotable than their transactional counterparts, and more interpersonally sensitive.[29] In addition, evidence indicates that transformational leadership is strongly correlated with lower turnover rates and higher levels of productivity, employee satisfaction, creativity, goal attainment, follower well-being, and corporate entrepreneurship, especially in start-up firms.[30]

transactional leaders
Leaders who lead primarily by using social exchanges (or transactions)

transformational leaders
Leaders who stimulate and inspire (transform) followers to achieve extraordinary outcomes

Charismatic-Visionary Leadership

Jeff Bezos, founder and CEO of Amazon.com, is a person who exudes energy, enthusiasm, and drive.[31] He's fun-loving (his legendary laugh has been described as a flock of Canadian geese on nitrous oxide), but has pursued his vision for Amazon with serious intensity and has demonstrated an ability to inspire his employees through the ups and downs of a rapidly growing company. Bezos is what we call a **charismatic leader**—that is, an enthusiastic, self-confident leader whose personality and actions influence people to behave in certain ways.

Several authors have attempted to identify personal characteristics of the charismatic leader.[32] The most comprehensive analysis identified five such characteristics: they have a vision, the ability to articulate that vision, a willingness to take risks to achieve that vision, a sensitivity to both environmental constraints and follower needs, and behaviors that are out of the ordinary.[33]

An increasing body of evidence shows impressive correlations between charismatic leadership and high performance and satisfaction among followers.[34] Although one study found that charismatic CEOs had no impact on subsequent organizational performance, charisma is still believed to be a desirable leadership quality.[35]

charismatic leader
An enthusiastic, self-confident leader whose personality and actions influence people to behave in certain ways

If charisma is desirable, can people learn to be charismatic leaders? Or are charismatic leaders born with their qualities? Although a small number of experts still think that charisma can't be learned, most believe that individuals can be trained to exhibit charismatic behaviors.[36] For example, researchers have succeeded in teaching undergraduate students to "be" charismatic. How? They were taught to articulate a far-reaching goal, communicate high performance expectations, exhibit confidence in the ability of subordinates to meet those expectations, and empathize with the needs of their subordinates; they learned to project a powerful, confident, and dynamic presence; and they practiced using a captivating and engaging voice tone. The researchers also trained the student leaders to use charismatic nonverbal behaviors, including leaning toward the follower when communicating, maintaining direct eye contact, and having a relaxed posture and animated facial expressions. In groups with these "trained" charismatic leaders, members had higher task performance, higher task adjustment, and better adjustment to the leader and to the group than did group members who worked in groups led by noncharismatic leaders.

One last thing we should say about charismatic leadership is that it may not always be necessary to achieve high levels of employee performance. It may be most appropriate when the follower's task has an ideological purpose or when the environment involves a high degree of stress and uncertainty.[37] This distinction may explain why, when charismatic leaders surface, it's more likely to be in politics, religion, or wartime or when a business firm is starting up or facing a survival crisis. For example, Martin Luther King Jr. used his charisma to bring about social equality through nonviolent means, and Steve Jobs achieved unwavering loyalty and commitment from Apple's technical staff in the early 1980s by articulating a vision of personal computers that would dramatically change the way people lived.

Although the term *vision* is often linked with charismatic leadership, **visionary leadership** is different; it's the ability to create and articulate a realistic, credible, and attractive vision of the future that improves on the present situation.[38] This vision, if properly selected and implemented, is so energizing that it "in effect jump-starts the future by calling forth the skills, talents, and resources to make it happen."[39]

An organization's vision should offer clear and compelling imagery that taps into people's emotions and inspires enthusiasm to pursue the organization's goals. It should be able to generate possibilities that are inspirational and unique and offer new ways of doing things that are clearly better for the organization and its members. Visions that are clearly articulated and have powerful imagery are easily grasped and accepted. For instance, Michael Dell (Dell Computer) created a vision of a business that sells and delivers customized PCs directly to customers in less than a week. The late Mary Kay Ash's vision of women as entrepreneurs selling products that improved their self-image gave impetus to her cosmetics company, Mary Kay Cosmetics.

visionary leadership
The ability to create and articulate a realistic, credible, and attractive vision of the future that improves upon the present situation

This young man is a team leader who manages the bakery department at a Whole Foods Market store. As leader of a 13-member team, he needs to possess good communication skills, work well with others, and convey enthusiasm. He serves as a coach in training and motivating team members to excellence in all aspects of the department, from maintaining good relationships with each other and with vendors to achieving team goals for sales, growth, and productivity. Whole Foods is completely organized around employee teams, with team leaders for each store department. Team leaders in each store also function as a team, store leaders in each region are a team, and regional presidents work as a team.
Source: © *Daily Mail/Rex/Alamy*

Team Leadership

Because leadership is increasingly taking place within a team context and more organizations are using work teams, the role of the leader in guiding team members has become increasingly important. The role of team leader *is* different from the traditional leadership role, as J. D. Bryant, a supervisor at Texas Instruments' Forest Lane plant in Dallas, discovered.[40] One day he was contentedly overseeing a staff of 15 circuit board assemblers. The next day, he was told that the company was going to use employee teams and he was to become a "facilitator." He said, "I'm supposed to teach the teams everything I know and then let them make their own decisions." Confused about his new role, he admitted, "There was no clear plan on what I was supposed to do." What *is* involved in being a team leader?

Many leaders are not equipped to handle the change to employee teams. As one consultant noted, "Even the most capable managers have trouble making the transition because all the command-and-control type things they were encouraged to do before are no longer appropriate. There's no reason to have any skill or sense of this."[42] This same consultant estimated that "probably 15 percent of managers are natural team leaders; another 15 percent could never lead a team because it runs counter to their personality—that is, they're unable to sublimate their dominating style for the good of the team. Then there's that huge group in the middle: Team leadership doesn't come naturally to them, but they can learn it."[43]

The challenge for many managers is learning how to become an effective team leader. They have to learn skills such as patiently sharing information, being able to trust others and to give up authority, and understanding when to intervene. And effective team leaders have mastered the difficult balancing act of knowing when to leave their teams alone and when to get involved. New team leaders may try to retain too much control at a time when team members need more autonomy, or they may abandon their teams at times when the teams need support and help.[44]

One study looking at organizations that reorganized themselves around employee teams found certain common responsibilities of all leaders. These leader responsibilities included coaching, facilitating, handling disciplinary problems, reviewing team and individual performance, training, and communication.[45] However, a more meaningful way to describe the team leader's job is to focus on two priorities: (1) managing the team's external boundary and (2) facilitating the team process.[46] These priorities entail four specific leadership roles, which are identified in Exhibit 18-5.

let's get REAL

The Scenario:

Linda Bustamante owns a thriving company that manufactures scented potpourris and other products. She's getting ready to expand her sales team again and wants to promote one of the current sales reps to team leader. This is a big step, and Linda desperately wants that person to succeed because it would take a load off her shoulders.

What advice could Linda give her newly appointed team leader?

Linda should advise her newly promoted team leader to meet with her team members one-on-one and let each know she is there to support them to achieve individual and department goals. Linda should devote time during her first few weeks in her new position to observe and listen to her team and their clients before implementing any major changes. She should take advantage of all of the training available within the company and look for a mentor she will feel comfortable working with.

Shawn Linett
Sales Manager

Source: Shawn Linett

Exhibit 18-5
Team Leadership Roles

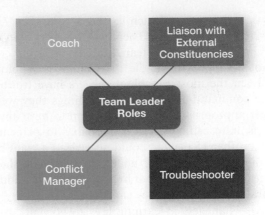

18.5 | *Discuss* contemporary issues affecting leadership.

LEADERSHIP Issues in the Twenty-First Century

It's not easy being a chief information officer (CIO) today. The person responsible for managing a company's information technology activities will find that the task comes with a lot of external and internal pressures. Technology continues to change rapidly—almost daily, it sometimes seems. Business costs continue to rise. Rob Carter, CIO of FedEx, is on the hot seat facing such challenges.[47] He's responsible for all the computer and communication systems that provide around-the-clock and around-the-globe support for FedEx's products and services. If anything goes wrong, you know who takes the heat. However, Carter has been an effective leader in this seemingly chaotic environment.

Leading effectively in today's environment is likely to involve such challenging circumstances for many leaders. In addition, twenty-first-century leaders do face some important leadership issues. In this section, we look at these issues that include managing power, developing trust, empowering employees, leading across cultures, and becoming an effective leader.

Managing Power

Where do leaders get their power—that is, their right and capacity to influence work actions or decisions? Five sources of leader power have been identified: legitimate, coercive, reward, expert, and referent.[48]

Legitimate power and authority are the same. Legitimate power represents the power a leader has as a result of his or her position in the organization. Although people in positions of authority are also likely to have reward and coercive power, legitimate power is broader than the power to coerce and reward.

Coercive power is the power a leader has to punish or control. Followers react to this power out of fear of the negative results that might occur if they don't comply. Managers typically have some coercive power, such as being able to suspend or demote employees or to assign them work they find unpleasant or undesirable.

Reward power is the power to give positive rewards. A reward can be anything a person values such as money, favorable performance appraisals, promotions, interesting work assignments, friendly colleagues, and preferred work shifts or sales territories.

Expert power is power based on expertise, special skills, or knowledge. If an employee has skills, knowledge, or expertise that's critical to a work group, that person's expert power is enhanced.

Finally, **referent power** is the power that arises because of a person's desirable resources or personal traits. If I admire you and want to be associated with you, you can exercise power over me because I want to please you. Referent power develops out of admiration of another and a desire to be like that person.

legitimate power
The power a leader has as a result of his or her position in the organization

coercive power
The power a leader has to punish or control

reward power
The power a leader has to give positive rewards

expert power
Power that's based on expertise, special skills, or knowledge

referent power
Power that arises because of a person's desirable resources or personal traits

Most effective leaders rely on several different forms of power to affect the behavior and performance of their followers. For example, the commanding officer of one of Australia's state-of-the-art submarines, the HMAS *Sheean,* employs different types of power in managing his crew and equipment. He gives orders to the crew (legitimate), praises them (reward), and disciplines those who commit infractions (coercive). As an effective leader, he also strives to have expert power (based on his expertise and knowledge) and referent power (based on his being admired) to influence his crew.

Developing Trust

Christine Day joined Lululemon Athletica as CEO in 2008 (after 20 years at Starbucks) and helped the company grow by trusting her employees to make decisions.[49] In today's uncertain environment, an important consideration for leaders is building trust and credibility, both of which can be extremely fragile. Before we can discuss ways leaders can build trust and credibility, we have to know what trust and credibility are and why they're so important.

The main component of credibility is honesty. Surveys show that honesty is consistently singled out as the number one characteristic of admired leaders. "Honesty is absolutely essential to leadership. If people are going to follow someone willingly, whether it be into battle or into the boardroom, they first want to assure themselves that the person is worthy of their trust."[50] In addition to being honest, credible leaders are competent and inspiring. They are personally able to effectively communicate their confidence and enthusiasm. Thus, followers judge a leader's **credibility** in terms of his or her honesty, competence, and ability to inspire.

Trust is closely entwined with the concept of credibility, and, in fact, the terms are often used interchangeably. **Trust** is defined as the belief in the integrity, character, and ability of a leader. Followers who trust a leader are willing to be vulnerable to the leader's actions because they are confident that their rights and interests will not be abused.[51] Research has identified five dimensions that make up the concept of trust:[52]

- *Integrity:* honesty and truthfulness
- *Competence:* technical and interpersonal knowledge and skills
- *Consistency:* reliability, predictability, and good judgment in handling situations
- *Loyalty:* willingness to protect a person, physically and emotionally
- *Openness:* willingness to share ideas and information freely

Of these five dimensions, integrity seems to be the most critical when someone assesses another's trustworthiness.[53] Both integrity and competence were seen in our earlier discussion of leadership traits found to be consistently associated with leadership. Workplace changes have reinforced why such leadership qualities are important. For instance, the trends toward empowerment and self-managed work teams have reduced many of the traditional control mechanisms used to monitor employees. If a work team is free to schedule its own work, evaluate its own performance, and even make its own hiring decisions, trust becomes critical. Employees have to trust managers to treat them fairly, and managers have to trust employees to conscientiously fulfill their responsibilities.

Also, leaders have to increasingly lead others who may not be in their immediate work group or may even be physically separated—members of cross-functional or virtual teams, individuals who work for suppliers or customers, and perhaps even people who represent other organizations through strategic alliances. These situations don't allow leaders the luxury of falling back on their formal positions for influence. Many of these relationships, in fact, are fluid and fleeting. So the ability to quickly develop trust and sustain that trust is crucial to the success of the relationship.

Why is it important that followers trust their leaders? Research has shown that trust in leadership is significantly related to positive job outcomes including job

credibility

The degree to which followers perceive someone as honest, competent, and able to inspire

trust

The belief in the integrity, character, and ability of a leader

Exhibit 18-6
Building Trust

> *Practice openness.*
> *Be fair.*
> *Speak your feelings.*
> *Tell the truth.*
> *Show consistency.*
> *Fulfill your promises.*
> *Maintain confidences.*
> *Demonstrate competence.*

performance, organizational citizenship behavior, job satisfaction, and organizational commitment.[54] Given the importance of trust to effective leadership, how can leaders build trust? Exhibit 18-6 lists some suggestions. (Also, see the Building Your Skill exercise in Chapter 5.)[55]

Now, more than ever, managerial and leadership effectiveness depends on the ability to gain the trust of followers.[56] Downsizing, financial challenges, and the increased use of temporary employees have undermined employees' trust in their leaders and shaken the confidence of investors, suppliers, and customers. A survey found that only 39 percent of U.S. employees and 51 percent of Canadian employees trusted their executive leaders.[57] Today's leaders are faced with the challenge of rebuilding and restoring trust with employees and with other important organizational stakeholders.

Empowering Employees

Employees at DuPont's facility in Uberaba, Brazil, planted trees to commemorate the site's 10th anniversary. Although they had several things to celebrate, one of the most important was the fact that since production began, the facility has had zero environmental incidents and no recordable safety violations. The primary reason for

let's get | REAL

The Scenario:

Adhita Chopra is stumped. Three months ago, he was assigned to lead a team of phone app designers, and although no one has come out and said anything directly, he feels like his team doesn't trust him. They have been withholding information and communicating only selectively when asked questions. And they have persistently questioned the team's goals and strategies and even Adhita's actions and decisions. How can he build trust with his team?

What advice would you give Adhita?

To inspire and build trust, trust needs to be extended through communication and clarification of the team's goals and expectations. Adhita's actions and decisions need to be transparent and consistent and should demonstrate a commitment to achieving the team's objectives.

Susan Mathew
Program Manager

Source: Susan Mathew

this achievement was the company's STOP (Safety Training Observation Program) program—a program in which empowered employees were responsible for observing one another, correcting improper procedures, and encouraging safe procedures.[58]

As we've described in different places throughout the text, managers are increasingly leading by empowering their employees. As we've said before, empowerment involves increasing the decision-making discretion of workers. Millions of individual employees and employee teams are making the key operating decisions that directly affect their work. They're developing budgets, scheduling workloads, controlling inventories, solving quality problems, and engaging in similar activities that until very recently were viewed exclusively as part of the manager's job.[59] For instance, at The Container Store, any employee who gets a customer request has permission to take care of it. Garret Boone, chairman emeritus, says, "Everybody we hire, we hire as a leader. Anybody in our store can take an action that you might think of typically being a manager's action."[60]

One reason more companies are empowering employees is the need for quick decisions by those people who are most knowledgeable about the issues—often those at lower organizational levels. If organizations want to successfully compete in a dynamic global economy, employees have to be able to make decisions and implement changes quickly. Another reason is that organizational downsizings left many managers with larger spans of control. In order to cope with the increased work demands, managers had to empower their people. Although empowerment is not a universal answer, it can be beneficial when employees have the knowledge, skills, and experience to do their jobs competently.

Leading Across Cultures

"In the United States, leaders are expected to look great, sound great, and be inspiring. In other countries—not so much."[61] In this global economy, how can managers account for cross-cultural differences as they lead?

One general conclusion that surfaces from leadership research is that effective leaders do not use a single style. They adjust their style to the situation. Although not mentioned explicitly, national culture is certainly an important situational variable in determining which leadership style will be most effective. What works in China isn't likely to be effective in France or Canada. For instance, one study of Asian leadership styles revealed that Asian managers preferred leaders who were competent decision makers, effective communicators, and supportive of employees.[62]

National culture affects leadership style because it influences how followers will respond. Leaders can't (and shouldn't) just choose their styles randomly. They're constrained by the cultural conditions their followers have come to expect. Exhibit 18-7 provides some findings from selected examples of cross-cultural leadership studies. Because most leadership theories were developed in the United States, they have an American bias. They emphasize follower responsibilities rather than rights; assume self-gratification rather than commitment to duty or altruistic motivation; assume centrality of work and democratic value orientation; and stress rationality rather than spirituality, religion, or superstition.[63] However, the GLOBE research program, which we first introduced in Chapter 3, is the most extensive and comprehensive cross-cultural study of leadership ever undertaken. The GLOBE study found that leadership has some universal aspects. Specifically, a number of elements of transformational leadership appear to be associated with effective leadership regardless of what country the leader is in.[64] These elements include vision, foresight, providing encouragement, trustworthiness, dynamism, positiveness, and proactiveness. The results led two members of the GLOBE team to conclude that "effective business leaders in any country are expected by their subordinates to provide a powerful and proactive vision to guide the company into the future, strong motivational skills to stimulate all employees to fulfill the vision, and excellent planning skills to assist in implementing the vision."[65] Some people suggest that the universal appeal of these transformational

Exhibit 18-7
Cross-Cultural Leadership

- Korean leaders are expected to be paternalistic toward employees.
- Arab leaders who show kindness or generosity without being asked to do so are seen by other Arabs as weak.
- Japanese leaders are expected to be humble and speak frequently.
- Scandinavian and Dutch leaders who single out individuals with public praise are likely to embarrass, not energize, those individuals.
- Effective leaders in Malaysia are expected to show compassion while using more of an autocratic than a participative style.
- Effective German leaders are characterized by high performance orientation, low compassion, low self-protection, low team orientation, high autonomy, and high participation.

Sources: Based on J. C. Kennedy, "Leadership in Malaysia: Traditional Values, International Outlook," *Academy of Management Executive,* August 2002, pp. 15–17; F. C. Brodbeck, M. Frese, and M. Javidan, "Leadership Made in Germany: Low on Compassion, High on Performance," *Academy of Management Executive,* February 2002, pp. 16–29; M. F. Peterson and J. G. Hunt, "International Perspectives on International Leadership," *Leadership Quarterly,* Fall 1997, pp. 203–231; R. J. House and R. N. Aditya, "The Social Scientific Study of Leadership: Quo Vadis?" *Journal of Management,* vol. 23, no. 3, 1997, p. 463; and R. J. House, "Leadership in the Twenty-First Century," in A. Howard (ed.), *The Changing Nature of Work* (San Francisco: Jossey-Bass, 1995), p. 442.

As part of their leadership training, some 300 executives of Samsung Heavy Industries Ship Construction attended a one-week military training camp at an airbase in South Korea. Developing effective leaders who will act as agents of change is a top priority for Samsung in executing its plan of reaching $400 billion in revenue and becoming one of the world's top five brands by 2020. Through military-style training, participants learn how to develop mentally, physically, and emotionally; how to become a source of influence to inspire others through vision, courage, and commitment; and how to motivate others to attain higher levels of performance.
Source: Reuters/Handout

leader characteristics is due to the pressures toward common technologies and management practices, as a result of global competitiveness and multinational influences.

Becoming an Effective Leader

Organizations need effective leaders. Two issues pertinent to becoming an effective leader are leader training and recognizing that sometimes being an effective leader means *not* leading. Let's take a look at these issues.

LEADER TRAINING Organizations around the globe spend billions of dollars, yen, and euros on leadership training and development.[66] These efforts take many forms—from $50,000 leadership programs offered by universities such as Harvard to sailing experiences at the Outward Bound School. Although much of the money spent on leader training may provide doubtful benefits, our review suggests that managers can do some things to get the maximum effect from such training.[67]

First, let's recognize the obvious. Some people don't have what it takes to be a leader. Period. For instance, evidence indicates that leadership training is more likely to be successful with individuals who are high self-monitors than with low self-monitors. Such individuals have the flexibility to change their behavior as different situations may require. In addition, organizations may find that individuals with higher levels of a trait called motivation to lead are more receptive to leadership development opportunities.[68]

What kinds of things can individuals learn that might be related to being a more effective leader? It may be a bit optimistic to think that "vision-creation" can be taught, but implementation skills can be taught. People can be trained to develop "an understanding about content themes critical to effective visions."[69] We can also teach skills such as trust-building and mentoring. And leaders can be taught situational analysis skills. They can learn how to evaluate situations, how to modify situations to make them fit better with their style, and how to assess which leader behaviors might be most effective in given situations.

SUBSTITUTES FOR LEADERSHIP Despite the belief that some leadership style will always be effective regardless of the situation, leadership may not always be important! Research indicates that, in some situations, any behaviors a leader exhibits are irrelevant. In other words, certain individual, job, and organizational variables can act as "substitutes for leadership," negating the influence of the leader.[70]

For instance, follower characteristics such as experience, training, professional orientation, or need for independence can neutralize the effect of leadership. These characteristics can replace the employee's need for a leader's support or ability to create structure and reduce task ambiguity. Similarly, jobs that are inherently unambiguous and routine or intrinsically satisfying may place fewer demands on leaders. Finally, such organizational characteristics as explicit formalized goals, rigid rules and procedures, or cohesive work groups can substitute for formal leadership.

MyManagementLab
Go to **mymanagementlab.com** to complete the problems marked with this icon ⭐.

CHAPTER

PREPARING FOR: Exams/Quizzes
CHAPTER SUMMARY by Learning Outcomes

18.1 [LEARNING OUTCOME]

Define leader and leadership.
A leader is someone who can influence others and who has managerial authority. Leadership is a process of leading a group and influencing that group to achieve its goals. Managers should be leaders because leading is one of the four management functions.

18.2 [LEARNING OUTCOME]

Compare and contrast early theories of leadership.
Early attempts to define leader traits were unsuccessful although later attempts found eight traits associated with leadership.

    The University of Iowa studies explored three leadership styles. The only conclusion was that group members were more satisfied under a democratic leader than under an autocratic one. The Ohio State studies identified two dimensions of leader behavior—initiating structure and consideration. A leader high in both those dimensions at times achieved high group task performance and high group member satisfaction, but not always. The University of Michigan studies looked at employee-oriented leaders and production-oriented leaders. They concluded that leaders who were employee oriented could get high group productivity and high group member satisfaction. The Managerial Grid looked at leaders' concern for production and concern for people and identified five leader styles. Although it suggested that a leader who was high in concern for production and high in concern for people was the best, there was no substantive evidence for that conclusion.

    As the behavioral studies showed, a leader's behavior has a dual nature: a focus on the task and a focus on the people.

18.3 [LEARNING OUTCOME]

Describe the three major contingency theories of leadership.
Fiedler's model attempted to define the best style to use in particular situations. He measured leader style—relationship oriented or task oriented—using the least-preferred coworker questionnaire. Fiedler also assumed a leader's style was fixed. He measured three contingency dimensions: leader–member relations, task structure, and position power. The model suggests that task-oriented leaders performed best in very favorable and very unfavorable situations, and relationship-oriented leaders performed best in moderately favorable situations.

    Hersey and Blanchard's situational leadership theory focused on followers' readiness. They identified four leadership styles: telling (high task–low relationship), selling (high task–high relationship), participating (low task–high relationship), and delegating (low task–low relationship). They also identified four stages of readiness: unable and unwilling (use telling style), unable but willing (use selling style), able but unwilling (use participative style), and able and willing (use delegating style).

    The path-goal model developed by Robert House identified four leadership behaviors: directive, supportive, participative, and achievement-oriented. He assumed that a leader can and should be able to use any of these styles. The two situational contingency variables were found in the environment and in the follower. Essentially the path-goal model says that a leader should provide direction and support as needed; that is, structure the path so the followers can achieve goals.

18.4 ⌈ LEARNING OUTCOME ⌉

Describe contemporary views of leadership.
Leader–member exchange theory (LMX) says that leaders create in-groups and out-groups and those in the in-group will have higher performance ratings, less turnover, and greater job satisfaction.

A transactional leader exchanges rewards for productivity where a transformational leader stimulates and inspires followers to achieve goals.

A charismatic leader is an enthusiastic and self-confident leader whose personality and actions influence people to behave in certain ways. People can learn to be charismatic. A visionary leader is able to create and articulate a realistic, credible, and attractive vision of the future.

A team leader has two priorities: manage the team's external boundary and facilitate the team process. Four leader roles are involved: liaison with external constituencies, troubleshooter, conflict manager, and coach.

18.5 ⌈ LEARNING OUTCOME ⌉

Discuss contemporary issues affecting leadership.
The five sources of a leader's power are legitimate (authority or position), coercive (punish or control), reward (give positive rewards), expert (special expertise, skills, or knowledge), and referent (desirable resources or traits).

Today's leaders face the issues of managing power, developing trust, empowering employees, leading across cultures, and becoming an effective leader.

REVIEW AND DISCUSSION QUESTIONS ✪

1. What does each of the four behavioral leadership theories say about leadership?
2. Explain Fiedler's contingency model of leadership.
3. How do situational leadership theory and path-goal theory each explain leadership?
4. What is leader–member exchange theory, and what does it say about leadership?
5. Differentiate between transactional and transformational leaders and between charismatic and visionary leaders.
6. What are the five sources of a leader's power?
7. Do you think most managers in real life use a contingency approach to increase their leadership effectiveness? Explain.
8. Do the followers make a difference in whether a leader is effective? Discuss.

PREPARING FOR: My Career
ETHICS DILEMMA ✪

Have you ever watched the show *Undercover Boss?* It features a company's "boss" working undercover in his or her own company to find out how the organization really works. Typically, the executive works undercover for a week, and then the employees the leader has worked with are summoned to company headquarters and either rewarded or punished for their actions. Bosses from organizations ranging from Waste Management and White Castle to NASCAR and Yankee Candle have participated. What do you think? Is it ethical for a leader to go undercover in his or her organization? Why or why not? What ethical issues could arise?

SKILLS EXERCISE   Developing Your Choosing an Effective Leadership Style Skill

About the Skill
Effective leaders are skillful at helping the groups they lead be successful as the group goes through various stages of development. No leadership style is consistently effective. Situational factors, including follower characteristics, must be taken into consideration in the selection of an effective leadership style. The key situational factors that determine leadership effectiveness include stage of group development,

task structure, position power, leader–member relations, the work group, employee characteristics, organizational culture, and national culture.

Steps in Practicing the Skill

You can choose an effective leadership style if you use the following six suggestions.

1. *Determine the stage in which your group or team is operating: forming, storming, norming, or performing.* Because each team stage involves specific and different issues and behaviors, it's important to know in which stage your team is. *Forming* is the first stage of group development during which people join a group and then help define the group's purpose, structure, and leadership. *Storming* is the second stage characterized by intragroup conflict. *Norming* is the third stage characterized by close relationships and cohesiveness. *Performing* is the fourth stage when the group is fully functional.

2. *If your team is in the forming stage, you want to exhibit certain leader behaviors.* These include making certain that all team members are introduced to one another, answering member questions, working to establish a foundation of trust and openness, modeling the behaviors you expect from the team members, and clarifying the team's goals, procedures, and expectations.

3. *If your team is in the storming stage, you want to exhibit certain leader behaviors.* These behaviors include identifying sources of conflict and adopting a mediator role, encouraging a win-win philosophy, restating the team's vision and its core values and goals, encouraging open discussion, encouraging an analysis of team processes in order to identify ways to improve, enhancing team cohesion and commitment, and providing recognition to individual team members as well as the team.

4. *If your team is in the norming stage, you want to exhibit certain leader behaviors.* These behaviors include clarifying the team's goals and expectations, providing performance feedback to individual team members and

the team, encouraging the team to articulate a vision for the future, and finding ways to publicly and openly communicate the team's vision.

5. *If your team is in the performing stage, you want to exhibit certain leader behaviors.* These behaviors include providing regular and ongoing performance feedback, fostering innovation and innovative behavior, encouraging the team to capitalize on its strengths, celebrating achievements (large and small), and providing the team whatever support it needs to continue doing its work.

6. *Monitor the group for changes in behavior and adjust your leadership style accordingly.* Because a group is not a static entity, it will go through up periods and down periods. You should adjust your leadership style to the needs of the situation. If the group appears to need more direction from you, provide it. If it appears to be functioning at a high level on its own, provide whatever support is necessary to keep it functioning at that level.

Practicing the Skill

The following suggestions are activities you can do to practice the behaviors in choosing an effective leadership style.

1. Think of a group or team to which you currently belong or of which you have been a part. What type of leadership style did the leader of this group appear to exhibit? Give some specific examples of the types of leadership behaviors he or she used. Evaluate the leadership style. Was it appropriate for the group? Why or why not? What would you have done differently? Why?

2. Observe a sports team (either college or professional) that you consider extremely successful and one that you would consider not successful. What leadership styles appear to be used in these team situations? Give some specific examples of the types of leadership behaviors you observe. How would you evaluate the leadership style? Was it appropriate for the team? Why or why not? To what degree do you think leadership style influenced the team's outcomes?

WORKING TOGETHER Team Exercise

Everybody's probably had at least one experience with a *bad boss.* But what *is* a bad boss? And more importantly, what can you do in such a situation?

Break into small groups of three to four other class members. Come up with a bulleted list of characteristics and

behaviors you believe a bad boss would have or exhibit. Then, come up with another bulleted list of what you can do if you find yourself in a situation with a bad boss. Be realistic about your suggestions; that is, don't suggest tampering with the person's coffee or slashing the person's tires!

MY TURN TO BE A MANAGER

- Think of the different organizations to which you belong. Note the different styles of leadership used by the leaders in these organizations. Write a paper describing these individual's style of leading (no names, please) and evaluate the styles being used.

- Write down three people you consider effective leaders. Make a bulleted list of the characteristics these individuals exhibit that you think make them effective leaders.

- Think about the times you have had to lead. Describe your own personal leadership style. What could you do to improve your leadership style? Come up with an action plan of steps you can take. Put all this information into a brief paper.

- Managers say that increasingly they must use influence to get things done. Do some research on the art of persuasion. Make a bulleted list of suggestions you find on how to improve your skills at influencing others.

- Here's a list of leadership skills. Choose two and develop a training exercise that will help develop or improve that skill: building employee communities; building teams; coaching and motivating others; communicating with impact, confidence, and energy; leading by example; leading change; making decisions; providing direction and focus; and valuing diversity.

- Steve's and Mary's recommended readings: Stephen M. R. Covey with Rebecca Merrell, *The Speed of Trust: The One Thing That Changes Everything* (Free Press, 2006); Nancy S. Ahlrichs, *Manager of Choice* (Davies-Black Publishing, 2003); John H. Zenger and Joseph Folkman, *The Extraordinary Leader: Turning Good Managers into Great Leaders* (McGraw-Hill, 2002); Robert H. Rosen, *Leading People* (Viking Penguin Publishing, 1996); Margaret J. Wheatley, *Leadership and the New Science* (Berrett-Koehler Publishers, 1994); Max DePree, *Leadership Jazz* (Dell Publishing, 1992); and Max DePree, *Leadership Is an Art* (Dell Publishing, 1989).

- Select one of the topics in the section on leadership issues in the twenty-first century. Do some additional research on the topic, and put your findings in a bulleted list that you are prepared to share in class. Be sure to cite your sources.

- Interview three managers about what they think it takes to be a good leader. Write up your findings in a report and be prepared to present it in class.

- In your own words, write down three things you learned in this chapter about being a good manager.

- Self-knowledge can be a powerful learning tool. Go to mymanagementlab.com and complete these self-assessment exercises: What's My Leadership Style? What Is My LPC Score? How Charismatic Am I? Do I Trust Others? Do Others See Me as Trustworthy? How Good Am I at Building and Leading a Team? Am I an Ethical Leader? Using the results of your assessments, identify personal strengths and weaknesses. What will you do to reinforce your strengths and improve your weaknesses?

MyManagementLab

Go to **mymanagementlab.com** for Auto-graded writing questions as well as the following Assisted-graded writing questions:

18-1. Define leader and leadership and explain why managers should be leaders.

18-2. What issues do today's leaders face?

18-3. Mymanagementlab Only – comprehensive writing assignment for this chapter.

CASE APPLICATION 1 Growing Leaders

3M's new CEO Inge Thulin (left) and former CEO George Buckley reinforce the company's pursuit of leadership excellence based on six leadership attributes: the ability to "chart the course; energize and inspire others; demonstrate ethics, integrity, and compliance; deliver results; raise the bar; and innovate resourcefully."
Source: © ZUMA Press, Inc./Alamy

How important are excellent leaders to organizations? If you were to ask the recently-retired 3M CEO George Buckley, he'd say extremely important.[71] But he'd also say that excellent leaders don't just pop up out of nowhere. A company has to cultivate leaders who have the skills and abilities to help it survive and thrive. And like a successful baseball team with strong performance statistics that has a player development plan in place, 3M has its own farm system. Except its farm system is designed to develop company leaders.

3M's leadership development program is so effective that it has been one of the "Top 20 Companies for Leadership" in three of the last four years and ranks as one of the top 25 companies for grooming leadership talent according to Hay Consulting Group and *Fortune* magazine. What is 3M's leadership program all about? About 10 years ago, the company's former CEO (Jim McNerney, who is now Boeing's CEO) and his top team spent 18 months developing a new leadership model for the company. After numerous brainstorming sessions and much heated debate, the group finally agreed on six "leadership attributes" they believed were essential for the company to become skilled at executing strategy and being accountable. Those six attributes included the ability to "chart the course; energize and inspire others; demonstrate ethics, integrity, and compliance; deliver results; raise the bar; and innovate resourcefully." And under Buckley's guidance and continued under the leadership of newly appointed CEO Inge Thulin, the company is continuing and reinforcing its pursuit of leadership excellence with these six attributes.

When asked about his views on leadership, Buckley said he believes leaders differ from managers. "A leader is as much about inspiration as anything else. A manager is more about process." He believes the key to developing leaders is to focus on those things that can be developed—like strategic thinking. Buckley also believes leaders should not be promoted up and through the organization too quickly. They need time to experience failures and what it takes to rebuild.

Finally, when asked about his own leadership style. Buckley responded, "The absolutely best way for me to be successful is to have people working for me who are better. Having that kind of emotional self-confidence is vital to leaders. You build respect in those people because you admire what they do. Having built respect, you build trust. However hokey it sounds, it works." And it must be working as the company was ranked number 18 on *Fortune's* most admired global companies list for 2012.

DISCUSSION QUESTIONS ✪

1. What do you think about Buckley's statement that leaders and managers differ? Do you agree? Why or why not?

2. What leadership models/theories/issues do you see in this case? List and describe.

3. Take each of the six leadership attributes that the company feels is important. Explain what you think each one involves. Then discuss how those attributes might be developed and measured.

4. What did this case teach you about leadership?

CASE APPLICATION 2 Radical Leadership

Ricardo Semler, CEO of Semco Group of São Paulo, Brazil, is considered by many to be a radical.[72] He's never been the type of leader that most people might expect to be in charge of a multimillion-dollar business. Why? Semler breaks all the traditional "rules" of leading. He's the ultimate hands-off leader who doesn't even have an office at the company's headquarters. As the "leading proponent and most tireless evangelist" of participative management, Semler says his philosophy is simple: Treat people like adults and they'll respond like adults.

Underlying his participative management approach is the belief that "organizations thrive best by entrusting employees to apply their creativity and ingenuity in service of the whole enterprise, and to make important decisions close to the flow of work, conceivably including the selection and election of their bosses." And according to Semler, his approach works...and works well. But how does it work in reality?

The radical leadership of Ricardo Semler that entrusts employees to make important decisions about their work hours, pay levels, supervisors, corporate leadership, and strategic initiatives is based on his belief that self-governance is necessary to create a flexible organization that will survive and thrive in a chaotic political and economic environment.
Source: Kali9/Getty Images

At Semler, you won't find most of the trappings of organizations and management. There are no organizational charts, no long-term plans, no corporate values statements, no dress codes, and no written rules or policy manuals. The company's employees decide their work hours and their pay levels. Subordinates decide who their bosses will be and they also review their boss's performance. The employees also elect the corporate leadership and decide most of the company's new strategic initiatives. Each person has one vote—including Ricardo Semler.

Why did Semler decide that his form of radical leadership was necessary, and does it work? Semler didn't pursue such radical self-governance out of some altruistic ulterior motive. Instead, he felt it was the only way to build an organization that was flexible and resilient enough to flourish in chaotic and turbulent times. He maintains that this approach has enabled Semco to survive the roller-coaster nature of Brazilian politics and economy. Although the country's political leadership and economy have gone from one extreme to another and countless Brazilian banks and companies have failed, Semco has survived. And not just survived—prospered. And Semler attributes that fact to flexibility—of his company and most importantly, of his employees.

DISCUSSION QUESTIONS ✪

1. Describe Ricardo Semler's leadership style. What do you think the advantages and drawbacks of his style might be?

2. What challenges might a radically "hands-off" leader face? How could those challenges be addressed?

3. How could future leaders be identified in this organization? Would leadership training be important to this organization? Discuss.

4. What could other businesses learn from Ricardo Semler's approach to leadership?

PART 6 Management Practice

A Manager's Dilemma

How would you feel as a new employee if your boss asked you to do something and you had to admit that you didn't know how to do it? Most of us would probably feel pretty inadequate and incompetent. Now imagine how strange and uncomfortable it would be if, after experiencing such an incident, you went home with the boss because you were roommates and have been friends since fourth grade. That's the situation faced by John, Glen, and Kurt. John and Kurt are employees at a software company that their friend Glen and four others started. The business now has 39 employees, and the "friends" are finding out that mixing work and friendships can be tricky! At home, they're equals. They share a three-bedroom condo and divide up housework and other chores. However, at work, equality is out the door. Glen is John's boss and Kurt's boss is another company manager. Recently, the company moved into a new workspace. As part of the four-person management team, Glen has a corner office with windows. However, John was assigned a cubicle and is annoyed at Glen for not standing up for him when offices were assigned. But John didn't complain because he didn't want to get an office only because of his friendship with Glen. Another problem brewing is that the roommates compete to outlast one another working late. Kurt's boss is afraid that he's going to burn out. Other awkward moments arise whenever the company's performance is discussed. When Glen wants to get something off his chest about work matters, he has to stop himself. And then there's the "elephant in the room." If the software company is ever bought out by a larger company, Glen (and his three partners) stand to profit dramatically, thereby creating some interesting emotional issues for the roommates. Although it might seem easy to say the solution is to move, real estate is too expensive and besides that, these guys are good friends.

Put yourself in Glen's shoes. Using what you've learned in Part 6 about individual behavior, communication, employee motivation, and leadership, how would you handle this situation?

Global Sense

As you discovered in this part of the text, employee engagement is an important focus for managers. Managers want their employees to be connected to, satisfied with, and enthusiastic about their jobs; that is, to be engaged. Why is employee engagement so important? The level of employee engagement serves as an indicator of organizational health and ultimately business results—success or failure. The latest available data (2011) on global employee engagement

levels showed a slight increase, up to 58 percent from 56 percent in 2010. That is, 58 percent of employees worldwide say they're engaged—passionate about and deeply connected to their work. The largest upward movement was seen in the Asia Pacific region; a slight increase was seen in Europe; a small downward movement was noted in Latin America; and in North America, the level of employee engagement stayed the same. Think about the other side of this, though. With 58 percent of employees saying they're engaged with their jobs and organizations, that means four employees out of ten worldwide are somewhat or completely disengaged.

So what can managers do to keep employees engaged? Some important efforts include providing opportunities for career advancement, offering recognition, and having a good organization reputation.

Discuss the following questions in light of what you learned in Part 6.

- *What role do you think external factors such as the global economic downturn or a country's culture play in levels of employee engagement? Discuss.*
- *What role does an organization's motivational programs play in whether an employee is engaged or not? Discuss.*
- *How might a manager's leadership style affect an employee's level of engagement? Discuss.*
- *Look at what we discussed about managerial communication in this part. What could a manager do in the way he or she communicates to affect an employee's level of engagement?*
- *You're a manager of a workplace that has different "generations." How will you approach engaging your employees? Do you think Gen Y employees are going to be more difficult to "engage"? Discuss.*

Sources: M. Wilson, "Study: Employee Engagement Ticking Up, But It's Not All Good News," [www.hrcommunication.com], June 18, 2012; "2012 Trends in Global Employee Engagement," www.aon.com, June 17, 2012; K. Gurchiek, "Engagement Erosion Plagues Employers Worldwide," HR Magazine, June 2012, p. 17; and T. Maylett and J. Nielsen, "There Is No Cookie-Cutter Approach to Engagement," T&D, April 2012, pp. 54–59.

Continuing Case
Starbucks—Leading

Once people are hired or brought into organizations, managers must oversee and coordinate their work so that organizational goals can be pursued and achieved. This is the leading function of management. And it's an important one! However, it also can be quite challenging. Managing people successfully means understanding their attitudes,

Knowing that its people are the heart and soul of its success, Starbucks values its employees and has created an environment that motivates them to work efficiently and effectively, rewards their accomplishments, and gives them training opportunities and generous benefits. The baristas shown here handing out gift bags to shareholders at an annual meeting represent Starbucks' "ideal" employee who is adaptable, self-motivated, passionate, and a creative team player.
Source: Elaine Thompson/AP Photo

behaviors, personalities, individual and team work efforts, motivation, conflicts, and so forth. That's not an easy thing to do. In fact, understanding how people behave and why they do the things they do is downright difficult at times. Starbucks has worked hard to create a workplace environment in which employees (partners) are *encouraged to* and *want to* put forth their best efforts. Howard Schultz says, "We all want the same thing as people—to be respected and valued as employees and appreciated as customers."

Starbucks—Focus on Individuals

Even with some 149,000 full- and part-time partners around the world, one thing that's been important to Howard Schultz from day one is the relationship he has with employees. He says, "We know that our people are the heart and soul of our success. They are invaluable and we treat them that way." And one way Starbucks demonstrates the concern it has for the relationship with its partners is through an attitude survey that gives partners an opportunity to voice their opinions about their experiences. It also measures overall satisfaction and engagement—the degree to which partners are connected to the company. It's been an effective way for Starbucks to show that it cares about what its employees think.

For example, a partner view survey was conducted in early 2010 with partners in the United States and Canada and in the international regional support centers in Europe/Middle East/Africa, Asia Pacific and Latin America, at Starbucks Coffee Trading Company in Switzerland, at Starbucks Coffee Agronomy Company in Costa Rica, and at the coffee roasting facility in Amsterdam. At the end of the survey, Howard Schultz thanked partners for taking the survey. He also acknowledged that the previous year and a half had been difficult (it was the time of Schultz

transitioning back into the CEO position) and that partners had been asked to do a lot during that time. The tough and emotional decisions to be made and the company's financial crisis weren't easy for any of them—from top to bottom of the organization. But, Schultz also reiterated that his number one commitment was to the company's partners and reinventing the partner experience at Starbucks. Although results aren't publicly available, it's likely that managers heard the good and the bad stuff that partners experienced and were feeling. It was a good barometer for gauging employee attitudes after a difficult time of transition and transformation for the company. Earlier partner surveys have provided relevant and important clues to employee attitudes. For instance, in a survey from 2005, well over half (64 percent) of partners responded to the survey—much higher than the number of respondents to the previous survey in 2003 in which the partner response rate was only 46 percent. Responses to questions about partner satisfaction and partner engagement were extremely positive: 87 percent of partners said they were satisfied or very satisfied, and 73 percent said they were engaged with the company. (The numbers in 2003 were 82 percent satisfied and 73 percent engaged.) In addition, partners specifically said they "Know what is expected of them at work; believe someone at work cares about them; and work for managers who promote work/life balance." But partners identified some areas where they felt improvements were needed. These included "Celebrate successes more; provide more effective coaching and feedback; and improve communication with partners." And Starbucks' managers try to address any concerns raised in these surveys or concerns expressed in other ways.

Every organization needs employees who will be able to do their jobs efficiently and effectively. Starbucks states that it wants employees who are "adaptable, self-motivated, passionate, creative team players." As you can see, this "ideal" Starbucks' partner should have individual strengths and should be able to work as part of a team. In the retail store setting, especially, individuals must work together as a team to provide the experience that customers expect when they walk into a Starbucks. If that doesn't happen, the company's ability to pursue its mission and goals are likely to be affected.

Communication at Starbucks

Keeping organizational communication flowing in all directions is important to Starbucks. And that commitment starts at the top. Howard Schultz tries to visit at least 30 to 40 stores a week. Not only does this give him an upfront view of what's happening out in the field, it gives partners a chance to talk with the top guy in the company. The CEO also likes to "get out in the field" by visiting the stores and roasting facilities. Schultz recently spent time in Beijing with more than 1,200 Starbucks partners and their parents and family members. The event recognized the special role Chinese families play and highlighted Starbucks commitment to its partners. Despite these efforts by the top executives, partners have indicated on past employee surveys that communication needed improvement. Managers listened and made some changes.

An initial endeavor was the creation of an internal video newsletter that conveyed information to partners about company news and announcements. Another change was the implementation of an internal communication audit that asks randomly selected partners for feedback on how to make company communication more effective. In addition, partners can voice concerns about actions or decisions where they believe the company is not operating in a manner consistent with the guiding principles to the Mission Review team, a group formed in 1991 and consisting of company managers and partners. The concept worked so well in North America that many of Starbucks' international units have provided similar communication forums to their partners.

Starbucks—Motivating Employees

A story from Howard Schultz's childhood provides some clues into what has shaped his philosophy about how to treat people. Schultz's father worked hard at various blue-collar jobs. However, when he didn't work, he didn't get paid. When his father broke his ankle when Howard was 7 years old, the family "had no income, no health insurance, no worker's compensation, nothing to fall back on." The image of his father with his leg in a cast unable to work left a lasting impression on the young Schultz. Many years later, when his father died of lung cancer, "he had no savings, no pension, and more important, he had never attained fulfillment and dignity from work he found meaningful." The sad realities of the types of work environments his father endured had a powerful effect on Howard, and he vowed that if he were "ever in a position where I could make a difference, I wouldn't leave people behind." And those personal experiences have shaped the way that Starbucks cares for its partners—the relationships and commitments the company has with each and every employee. In fact, during the recent economic recession, Schultz was contacted by an institutional shareholder about trimming the health insurance for part-time employees. Schultz's reply? There's no way that benefit at Starbucks is being cut.

One of the best reflections of how Starbucks treats its eligible part- and full-time partners is its Total Pay package, which includes competitive base pay, bonuses, a comprehensive health plan, paid time-off plans, stock options, a savings program, and partner perks (which includes a pound of coffee each week). Although specific benefits differ between regions and countries, all Starbucks international partners share the "Total Pay" philosophy. For instance, in Malaysia and Thailand, partners are provided extensive training opportunities to further their careers in addition to health insurance, paid vacation, sick leave, and other benefits. In Turkey, the "Total Pay" package for Starbucks' partners includes transportation subsidies and access to a company doctor who provides free treatment.

Partner (employee) recognition is important to Starbucks. The company has several formal recognition programs in place that partners can use as tools to encourage, reward, and inspire one another. These programs range from formal company awards to informal special acknowledgments given by coworkers. One tool—developed in response to suggestions on the partner survey—is an on-the-spot recognition card that celebrates partner and team successes.

To assist partners who are facing particularly difficult circumstances (such as natural disaster, fire, illness), the company has a CUP (Caring Unites Partners) fund that provides financial support. After Hurricanes Katrina and Rita in 2005, more than 300 partners from the Gulf Coast region received more than $225,000 in assistance from the CUP fund. In China, Starbucks has set aside RMB1 million (about $158,000 in today's currency exchange) for the Starbucks China CUP fund to be used to provide financial assistance to partners in times of significant or immediate needs. This is the type of caring and compassion that Howard Schultz vowed to provide after seeing his father not able to work and have an income because of a broken ankle.

In 2012, Starbucks again was named one of *Fortune* magazine's 100 Best Companies to Work For—the fourteenth time since 1998 that Starbucks has received this recognition. Although being recognized as a great company to work for is commendable, Starbucks has seen its ranking drop. In 2008, it was ranked #7; in 2009, #24; in 2010, #93; in 2011 #98. However, in 2012, its ranking rose to #73. Like many companies, Starbucks had to make some tough strategic decisions during one of the toughest economic periods faced recently. Yet, despite the challenges, it's a testament to Starbucks' treatment of its partners that it still makes the top 100 list.

Starbucks—Fostering Leadership

Not surprisingly, Howard Schultz has some definite views about leading and leadership. He says being a great leader involves finding a balance between celebrating what's made a company successful in the past and knowing when to not continue following the status quo. He also said being a great leader means identifying a path your organization needs to follow and then creating enough confidence in your people so they follow that path and don't "veer off course because it's an easier route to go." He also said leaders, particularly of growing companies, need to stay true to those values and principles that have guided how their business is done and not let those values be compromised by ambitions of growth.

Since 1982, Howard Schultz has led Starbucks in a way that has allowed the company to successfully grow and meet and exceed its goals *and* to do so ethically and responsibly. From the creation of the company's Guiding Principles to the various innovative strategic initiatives, Schultz has never veered from his belief about what Starbucks, the company, could be and should be. In 2011, *Fortune* named Howard Schultz the Businessperson of the Year.

Unlike many companies, Starbucks and Howard Schultz have taken their leadership succession responsibilities seriously. In 2000 when Schultz was still CEO, he decided to move into the chairman's position. His replacement, Orin Smith (president and chief operating officer of Starbucks Coffee U.S.), had been "groomed" to take over the CEO position. Smith made it a top priority to plan his own succession. First, he established an exit date—in 2005 at age 62. Then he monitored the leadership skills development of his top executives. Two years into the job, Smith recognized that the internal candidates most likely to replace him would still be too "unseasoned" to assume the CEO position by his stated exit date. At that point, the decision was made to look externally for a promising successor. That's when Jim Donald was hired from Pathmark, a regional grocery chain, where he was chairman, president, and CEO. For 3 years, Donald was immersed in Starbucks' business as president of the largest division, the North American unit, before assuming the CEO position in 2005, as planned. As described in earlier parts, in early 2008, Jim Donald stepped down from the CEO position, and Howard Schultz once again assumed the position. At that time, Schultz realized his job was to step up as a leader to transform and revitalize Starbucks.

Starbucks also recognizes the importance of having individuals with excellent leadership skills throughout the company. In addition to the leadership development training for upper-level managers, Starbucks offers a program called Learning to Lead for hourly employees (baristas) to develop leadership skills. This training program also covers store operations and effective management practices. In addition, Starbucks offers to managers at all organizational levels additional training courses on coaching and providing feedback to help managers improve their people skills.

Discussion Questions

1. Do the overwhelmingly positive results from the 2005 partner survey surprise you? Why or why not? Do you think giving employees an opportunity to express their opinions in something like an attitude survey is beneficial? Why or why not?
2. How might the results of the partner survey affect the way a local store manager does his or her job? How about a district manager? How about the president of global development? Do you think there are differences in the impact of employee surveys on how managers at different organizational levels lead? Why or why not?
3. As Starbucks continues to expand globally, what factors might affect partner responses on a partner view survey? What are the implications for managers?
4. Look at the description of the types of people Starbucks seeks. What individual behavior issues might arise in managing these types of people? (Think

in terms of attitudes, personality, etc.) What work team issues might arise? (Think in terms of what makes teams successful. Hint: Can a person be self-motivated and passionate *and* be a good team player?)
5. Discuss the "ideal" Starbucks employee in terms of the various personality trait theories.
6. Describe in your own words the workplace environment Starbucks has tried to create. What impact might such an environment have on motivating employees?
7. Using the Job Characteristics Model in Exhibit 17–6, re-design a part-time hourly worker's job to be more motivating. Do the same with a store manager's job.
8. Does Starbucks "care" too much for its partners? Can a company ever treat its employees too well? Why or why not?
9. Howard Schultz says, "We all want the same thing as people—to be respected and valued as employees and appreciated as customers." Does the company respect and value its partners (employees)? Explain. What do you think this implies for its employee relationships?
10. Former CEO Jim Donald once said, "Spending money to put people first is smart money." Do you agree or disagree? Why?
11. If you were an executive, would you be concerned about the drastic drop in ranking on the list of best companies to work for? Why or why not? What actions might you take?
12. Give some examples of the types of communication taking place at Starbucks.
13. Suppose you're a Starbucks store manager in Birmingham, Alabama. How do you find out what's going on in the company? How might you communicate your concerns or issues?
14. Describe Howard Schultz's leadership style. Would his approach be appropriate in other types of organizations? Why or why not?
15. Do you agree that leadership succession planning is important? Why or why not?
16. What is Starbucks doing "right" with respect to the leading function? Are they doing anything "wrong?" Explain.
17. Which of the company's principles (see Web site) influence the leading function of management? Explain how the one(s) you chose would affect how Starbucks' managers deal with (a) individual behavior issues; (b) communication issues; (c) motivational techniques; and (d) leadership styles or approaches.

Notes for the Part 6 Continuing Case

News Release, "Starbucks Strengthens Commitment to Being the Employer of Choice in China," news.starbucks.com, April 18, 2012; J. Certner, "Starbucks: For Infusing a Steady Stream of New Ideas to Revive Its Business," *Fast Company,* March 2012, pp. 112+; D. A. Kaplan, "Strong

Coffee," *Fortune,* December 12, 2011, pp. 100+; "Howard Schultz, On Getting A Second Shot," *Inc.,* April 2011, pp. 52–54; C. Cain Miller, "A Changed Starbucks. A Changed CEO," *New York Times Online,* March 12, 2011; "Howard Schultz Promises Partners a Better Starbucks Experience in the Future," *StarbucksMelody.com,* www.starbucksmelody.com/2010/03/06/howard-schultz-promises-partners-a-better-starbucks-experience-in-the-future/, March 6, 2010; M. Moskowitz, R. Levering, and C. Tkaczyk, "The List: 100 Best Companies to Work For," *Fortune,* February 8, 2010, pp. 75+; Starbucks Ad, *USA Today,* May 19, 2009, p. 9A; Interview with Jim Donald, *Smart Money,* May 2006, pp. 31–32; A. Serwer, "Interview with Howard Schultz," *Fortune (Europe),* March 20, 2006, pp. 35–36; W. Meyers, "Conscience in a Cup of Coffee," *US News & World Report,* October 31, 2005, pp. 48–50; J. M. Cohn, R. Khurana, and L. Reeves, "Growing Talent As If Your Business Depended It," *Harvard Business Review,* October 2005, pp. 62–70; Interview with Jim Donald, *Fortune,* April 4, 2005, p. 30; P. Kafka, "Bean Counter," *Forbes,* February 28, 2005, pp. 78–80; S. Gray, "Starbucks's CEO Announces Plan to Retire in March," *Wall Street Journal,* October 13, 2004, p. A6; and A. Serwer and K. Bonamici, "Hot Starbucks to Go," *Fortune,* January 26, 2004, pp. 60–74.

Appendix

Managing Entrepreneurial Ventures

THE CONTEXT of Entrepreneurship

Russell Simmons is an entrepreneur.[1] He cofounded Def Jam Records because the emerging group of New York hip-hop artists needed a record company, and the big record companies refused to take a chance on unknown artists. Def Jam was just one piece of Simmons's corporation, Rush Communications, which also included a management company, a clothing company called Phat Farm, a movie production house, television shows, a magazine, and an advertising agency. In 1999, Simmons sold his stake in Def Jam to Universal Music Group, and in 2004, he sold Phat Farm. Today, Simmons is involved in UniRush, a Cincinnati company that sells a prepaid Visa debit card, and Russell Simmons Argyle Culture, a clothing line aimed at older men. *USA Today* named Simmons one of the top 25 Influential People, while *Inc.* magazine named him one of America's 25 Most Fascinating Entrepreneurs.

In this appendix, we're going to look at the activities that entrepreneurs like Russell Simmons engage in. We'll start by looking at the context of entrepreneurship and then examining entrepreneurship from the perspective of the four managerial functions: planning, organizing, leading, and controlling.

What Is Entrepreneurship?

Entrepreneurship is the process of starting new businesses, generally in response to opportunities. Entrepreneurs are pursuing opportunities by changing, revolutionizing, transforming, or introducing new products or services. For example, Hong Liang Lu of UTStarcom knew that less than 10 percent of the Chinese population was served by a land-line phone system and service was very poor.[2] He decided that wireless technology might be the answer. Now, his company's inexpensive cell phone service is a hit in China with more than 66 million subscribers and growing. Looking to continue his success, Lu's company is moving into other markets including Africa, Southeast Asia, India, and Panama.

Many people think that entrepreneurial ventures and small businesses are one and the same, but they're not. Some key differences distinguish the two. Entrepreneurs create **entrepreneurial ventures**—organizations that pursue opportunities, are characterized by innovative practices, and have growth and profitability as their main goals. On the other hand, a **small business** is one that is independently owned, operated, and financed; has fewer than 100 employees; doesn't necessarily engage in any new or innovative practices; and has relatively little impact on its industry.[3] A small business isn't necessarily entrepreneurial because it's small. To be entrepreneurial means that the business must be innovative, seeking out new opportunities. Even though entrepreneurial ventures may start small, they pursue growth. Some new small firms may grow, but many remain small businesses, by choice or by default.

Why Is Entrepreneurship Important?

Entrepreneurship is, and continues to be, important to every industry sector in the United States and in most advanced countries.[4] Its importance in the United States can be shown in three areas: innovation, number of new start-ups, and job creation.

INNOVATION Innovating is a process of changing, experimenting, transforming, revolutionizing, and a key aspect of entrepreneurial activity. The "creative destruction"

entrepreneurship
The process of starting new businesses, generally in response to opportunities

entrepreneurial ventures
Organizations that pursue opportunities, are characterized by innovative practices, and have growth and profitability as their main goals

small business
An organization that is independently owned, operated, and financed; has fewer than 100 employees; doesn't necessarily engage in any new or innovative practices; and has relatively little impact on its industry

565

process that characterizes innovation leads to technological changes and employment growth. Entrepreneurial firms act as "agents of change" by providing an essential source of new and unique ideas that may otherwise go untapped.[5] Statistics back this up. New small organizations generate 24 times more innovations per research and development dollar spent than do *Fortune* 500 organizations, and they account for more than 95 percent of new and "radical" product developments.[6] In addition, the U.S. Small Business Administration's Office of Advocacy reports that small entrepreneurial firms produce 13 to 14 times more patents per employee than large patenting firms.[7] These statistics are further proof of how important small business is to innovation in America.

NUMBER OF NEW START-UPS   Because all businesses—whether they fit the definition of entrepreneurial ventures or not—were new start-ups at one point in time, the most suitable measure we have of the important role of entrepreneurship is to look at the number of new firms over a period of time. Data collected by the U.S. Small Business Administration shows that the number of new start-ups has increased every year since 2002. Estimates for 2008, the latest available data, showed that some 627,200 new businesses were created.[8]

JOB CREATION   We know that job creation is important to the overall long-term economic health of communities, regions, and nations. The latest figures show that small businesses accounted for most of the net new jobs. In fact, over the last 15 years, small businesses have created some 65 percent of the net new jobs.[9] Small organizations have been creating jobs at a fast pace even as many of the world's largest and well-known global corporations continued to downsize. These numbers reflect the importance of entrepreneurial firms as job creators.

GLOBAL ENTREPRENEURSHIP   What about entrepreneurial activity outside the United States? What kind of impact has it had? An annual assessment of global entrepreneurship called the Global Entrepreneurship Monitor (GEM) studies the impact of entrepreneurial activity on economic growth in various countries. The GEM 2009 report covered 54 countries that were divided into three clusters identified by phase of economic development: Factor-Driven economies, Efficiency-Driven economies, and Innovation-Driven economies. What did the researchers find? One of the principal aspects that GEM examines is "total early-stage entrepreneurial activity (TEA)," or the proportion of people who are involved in setting up a business. Generally, as economic development increases, the overall levels of TEA declines. With large variations found in the three different categories, however, it's obvious that countries have "unique sets of economic and social conditions that affect entrepreneurial activity." The GEM report concludes, "There is wide agreement on the importance of entrepreneurship for economic development."[10]

The Entrepreneurial Process

Entrepreneurs must address four key steps as they start and manage their entrepreneurial ventures.

The first is *exploring the entrepreneurial context*. The context includes the realities of today's economic, political/legal, social, and work environment. It's important to look at each of these aspects of the entrepreneurial context because they determine the "rules" of the game and which decisions and actions are likely to meet with success. Also, it's through exploring the context that entrepreneurs confront the next critically important step in the entrepreneurial process—*identifying opportunities and possible competitive advantages*. We know from our definition of entrepreneurship that the pursuit of opportunities is an important aspect.

Once entrepreneurs have explored the entrepreneurial context and identified opportunities and possible competitive advantages, they must look at the issues involved with actually bringing their entrepreneurial venture to life. Therefore, the next step in the entrepreneurial process is *starting the venture.* Included in this phase are researching the feasibility of the venture, planning the venture, organizing the venture, and launching the venture.

Finally, once the entrepreneurial venture is up and running, the last step in the entrepreneurial process is *managing the venture*, which an entrepreneur does by managing processes, managing people, and managing growth. We can explain these important steps in the entrepreneurial process by looking at what it is that entrepreneurs do.

What Do Entrepreneurs Do?

Describing what entrepreneurs do isn't an easy or simple task! No two entrepreneurs' work activities are exactly alike. In a general sense, entrepreneurs create something new, something different. They search for change, respond to it, and exploit it.

Initially, an entrepreneur is engaged in assessing the potential for the entrepreneurial venture and then dealing with start-up issues. In exploring the entrepreneurial context, entrepreneurs gather information, identify potential opportunities, and pinpoint possible competitive advantage(s). Then, armed with this information, the entrepreneur researches the venture's feasibility—uncovering business ideas, looking at competitors, and exploring financing options.

After looking at the potential of the proposed venture and assessing the likelihood of pursuing it successfully, the entrepreneur proceeds to plan the venture. Planning includes such activities as developing a viable organizational mission, exploring organizational culture issues, and creating a well-thought-out business plan. Once these planning issues have been resolved, the entrepreneur must look at organizing the venture, which involves choosing a legal form of business organization, addressing other legal issues such as patent or copyright searches, and coming up with an appropriate organizational design for structuring how work is going to be done.

Only after these start-up activities have been completed is the entrepreneur ready to actually launch the venture. Such a launch involves setting goals and strategies, and establishing the technology-operations methods, marketing plans, information systems, financial-accounting systems, and cash flow management systems.

Once the entrepreneurial venture is up and running, the entrepreneur's attention switches to managing it. What's involved with actually managing the entrepreneurial venture? An important activity is managing the various processes that are part of every business: making decisions, establishing action plans, analyzing external and internal environments, measuring and evaluating performance, and making needed changes. Also, the entrepreneur must perform activities associated with managing people including selecting and hiring, appraising and training, motivating, managing conflict, delegating tasks, and being an effective leader. Finally, the entrepreneur must manage the venture's growth including such activities as developing and designing growth strategies, dealing with crises, exploring various avenues for financing growth, placing a value on the venture, and perhaps even eventually exiting the venture.

Social Responsibility and Ethics Issues Facing Entrepreneurs

As they launch and manage their ventures, entrepreneurs are faced with the often-difficult issues of social responsibility and ethics. Just how important are these issues to entrepreneurs? An overwhelming majority of respondents (95%) in a study of small companies believed that developing a positive reputation and relationship in communities where they do business is important for achieving business goals.[11] However, despite the importance these individuals placed on corporate citizenship, more than half lacked formal programs for connecting with their communities. In fact, some 70 percent of the respondents admitted that they failed to consider community goals in their business plans.

Yet, some entrepreneurs take their social responsibilities seriously. For example, Alicia Polak used to work on Wall Street, helping companies go public. In 2004, she founded the Khayelitsha Cookie Company in Khayelitsha, South Africa, 30 minutes from Cape Town. She now employs 11 women from the impoverished community to bake cookies and brownies that are sold to high-end hotels, restaurants, and coffee houses throughout South Africa. Polak says, "My driving force in this company is that I want them [the hundreds of thousands of people living in poverty in South Africa] out of those shacks. I want to help change their lives using this company as a vehicle."[12]

Other entrepreneurs have pursued opportunities with products and services that protect the global environment. For example, Univenture Inc. of Columbus, Ohio, makes recyclable sleeves and packaging for disc media. Its products are better for the environment as compared with the traditional jewel boxes most compact disks are packaged in. Ross Youngs, founder and president/CEO, says, "Our products won't break. If someone throws it away, it's because they don't want it. Hopefully they will end up in the recycle bin because our products are recyclable."[13]

Ethical considerations also play a role in decisions and actions of entrepreneurs. Entrepreneurs do need to be aware of the ethical consequences of what they do. The example they set—particularly for other employees—can be profoundly significant in influencing behavior.

If ethics are important, how do entrepreneurs stack up? Unfortunately, not well! In a survey of employees from different sizes of businesses who were asked if they thought their organization was highly ethical, 20 percent of employees at companies with 99 or fewer employees disagreed.[14]

START-UP and Planning Issues

Although pouring a bowl of cereal may seem like a simple task, even the most awake and alert morning person has probably ended up with cereal on the floor. Philippe Meert, a product designer based in Erpe-Mere, Belgium, has come up with a better way. Meert sensed an opportunity to correct the innate design flaw of cereal boxes and developed the Cerealtop, a plastic cover that snaps onto a cereal box and channels the cereal into a bowl.[15]

The first thing that entrepreneurs like Philippe Meert must do is to identify opportunities and possible competitive advantages. Once they've identified the opportunities, they're ready to start the venture by researching its feasibility and then planning for its launch. These start-up and planning issues are what we're going to look at in this section.

Identifying Environmental Opportunities and Competitive Advantage

How important is the ability to identify environmental opportunities? Consider the following: More than 4 million baby boomers turn 50 every year. Almost 8,000 turned 60 each day in starting in 2006. More than 57.5 million baby boomers are projected to be alive in 2030, which would put them between the ages of 66 and 84. J. Raymond Elliott, CEO of Zimmer Holdings, is well aware of that demographic trend. Why? His company, which makes orthopedic products, including reconstructive implants for hips, knees, shoulders, and elbows, sees definite marketing opportunities.[16]

In 1994, when Jeff Bezos first saw that Internet usage was increasing by 2,300 percent a month, he knew that something dramatic was happening. "I hadn't seen growth that fast outside of a Petri dish," he said. Bezos was determined to be a part of it. He quit his successful career as a stock market researcher and hedge fund manager on Wall Street and pursued his vision for online retailing, now the Amazon.com Web site.[17]

What would you have done had you seen that type of number somewhere? Ignored it? Written it off as a fluke? The skyrocketing Internet usage that Bezos observed and the recognition of the baby boomer demographic by Elliott's Zimmer Holdings are prime examples of identifying environmental opportunities. Remember the discussion in Chapter 9 that opportunities are positive trends in external environmental factors. These trends provide unique and distinct possibilities for innovating and creating value. Entrepreneurs need to be able to pinpoint these pockets of opportunities that a changing context provides. After all, "organizations do not see opportunities, individuals do."[18] And they need to do so quickly, especially in dynamic environments, before those opportunities disappear or are exploited by others.[19]

The late Peter Drucker, a well-known management author, identified seven potential sources of opportunity that entrepreneurs might look for in the external context.[20] These include the unexpected, the incongruous, the process need, industry and market structures, demographics, changes in perception, and new knowledge.

1. *The unexpected.* When situations and events are unanticipated, opportunities can be found. The event may be an unexpected success (positive news) or an unexpected failure (bad news). Either way, it may present opportunities for entrepreneurs to pursue. For instance, the dramatic increase in fuel prices has proved to be a bonanza for companies that offer solutions. For instance, Jeff Pink, CEO of EV Rental Cars, uses only hybrid vehicles. The company's utilization rate—the percentage of days a vehicle is out generating revenue—is about 90 percent.[21] The unexpected increase in fuel prices proved to be an opportunity for this entrepreneur. And for RSA Security, the unexpected opportunity came in the form of identity theft. Art Coviello's company develops software that helps make online transactions more secure. He stated, "A lot of factors are about to turn in RSA's favor, namely the need for more secure, traceable financial transactions in a world beset by online fraud and identity theft."[22]

2. *The incongruous.* When something is incongruous, it exhibits inconsistencies and incompatibilities in the way it appears. Things "ought to be" a certain way, but aren't. When conventional wisdom about the way things should be no longer holds true, for whatever reason, opportunities are present. Entrepreneurs who are willing to "think outside the box"—that is, to think beyond the traditional and conventional approaches—may find pockets of potential profitability. Sigi Rabinowicz, founder and president of Tefron, an Israeli firm, recognized incongruities in the way that women's lingerie was made. He knew that a better way was possible. His company spent more than a decade adapting a circular hosiery knitting machine to make intimate apparel that is nearly seamless.[23] Another example of how the incongruous can be a potential source of entrepreneurial opportunity is Fred Smith, founder of FedEx, who recognized in the early 1970s the inefficiencies in the delivery of packages and documents. His approach was: Why not? Who says that overnight delivery isn't possible? Smith's recognition of the incongruous led to the creation of FedEx, now a multibillion-dollar corporation.

3. *The process need.* What happens when technology doesn't immediately come up with the "big discovery" that's going to fundamentally change the nature of some product or service? What happens is the emergence of pockets of entrepreneurial opportunity in the various stages of the process as researchers and technicians continue to work for the monumental breakthrough. Because the full leap hasn't been possible, opportunities abound in the tiny steps. Take the medical products industry, for example. Although researchers haven't yet discovered a cure for cancer, many successful entrepreneurial biotechnology ventures have been created as knowledge about a possible cure continues to grow.

4. *Industry and market structures.* When changes in technology change the structure of an industry and market, existing firms can become obsolete if they're not attuned to the changes or are unwilling to change. Even changes in social values and consumer tastes can shift the structures of industries and markets. These markets and industries become open targets for nimble and smart entrepreneurs. For instance, while working part-time at an auto body shop while finishing his

engineering graduate degree, Joe Born wondered if the industrial paint buffer used to smooth out a car's paint job could be used to smooth out scratches on CDs. He tried it out on his favorite Clint Black CD that had been ruined and the newly polished CD played flawlessly. After this experience, Born spent almost four years perfecting his disk repair kit invention, the SkipDr.[24] The arena of the Internet provides several good examples of existing industries and markets being challenged by upstart entrepreneurial ventures. For instance, eBay has prospered as an online intermediary between buyers and sellers. eBay's CEO says that the company's job is connecting people, not selling them things. And connect them, they do! The online auction firm has more than 275 million registered users.[25]

5. *Demographics.* The characteristics of the world population are changing. These changes influence industries and markets by altering the types and quantities of products and services desired and customers' buying power. Although many of these changes are fairly predictable if you stay alert to demographic trends, others aren't as obvious. Either way, significant entrepreneurial opportunities can be realized by anticipating and meeting the changing needs of the population. For example, Thay Thida was one of three partners in Khmer Internet Development Services (KIDS) in Phnom Penh, Cambodia. She and her cofounders saw the opportunities in bringing Internet service to Cambodians and profited from their entrepreneurial venture.[26]

6. *Changes in perception.* Perception is one's view of reality. When changes in perception take place, the facts do not vary, but their meanings do. Changes in perception get at the heart of people's psychographic profiles—what they value, what they believe in, and what they care about. Changes in these attitudes and values create potential market opportunities for alert entrepreneurs. For example, think about your perception of healthy foods. Changes in our perception of whether certain food groups are good has brought about product and service opportunities for entrepreneurs to recognize and capture. For example, John Mackey started Whole Foods Market in Austin, Texas, as a place for customers to purchase food and other items free of pesticides, preservatives, sweeteners, and cruelty. Now, as the world's number one natural foods chain, Mackey's entrepreneurial venture consists of about 275 stores in the United States, Canada, and the United Kingdom.[27] Michael and Ellen Diamant changed the perception that baby necessities—diaper bags, bottle warmers, and bottle racks—couldn't be fashionable. Their baby gear company, Skip Hop, offers pricey products that design-conscious new parents have embraced.[28]

7. *New knowledge.* New knowledge is a significant source of entrepreneurial opportunity. Although not all knowledge-based innovations are significant, new knowledge ranks pretty high on the list of sources of entrepreneurial opportunity! It takes more than just having new knowledge, though. Entrepreneurs must be able to do something with that knowledge and to protect important proprietary information from competitors. For example, French scientists are using new knowledge about textiles to develop a wide array of innovative products to keep wearers healthy and smelling good. Neyret, the Parisian lingerie maker, created lingerie products woven with tiny perfume microcapsules that stay in the fabric through about 10 washings. Another French company, Francital, developed a fabric treated with chemicals to absorb perspiration and odors.[29]

Being alert to entrepreneurial opportunities is only part of an entrepreneur's initial efforts. He or she must also understand competitive advantage. As we discussed in Chapter 9, when an organization has a competitive advantage, it has something that other competitors don't; does something better than other organizations; or does something that others can't. Competitive advantage is a necessary ingredient for an entrepreneurial venture's long-term success and survival. Getting and keeping a competitive advantage is tough. However, it is something that entrepreneurs must consider as they begin researching the venture's feasibility.

Researching the Venture's Feasibility—Generating and Evaluating Ideas

On a trip to New York, Miho Inagi got her first taste of the city's delicious bagels. After her palate-expanding experience, she had the idea of bringing bagels to Japan. Five years after her first trip to New York and a subsequent apprenticeship at a New York bagel business, Miho opened Maruichi Bagel in Tokyo. After a struggle to get the store up and running, it now has a loyal following of customers.[30]

It's important for entrepreneurs to research the venture's feasibility by generating and evaluating business ideas. Entrepreneurial ventures thrive on ideas. Generating ideas is an innovative, creative process. It's also one that will take time, not only in the beginning stages of the entrepreneurial venture, but throughout the life of the business. Where do ideas come from?

GENERATING IDEAS Studies of entrepreneurs have shown that the sources of their ideas are unique and varied. One survey found that "working in the same industry" was the major source of ideas for an entrepreneurial venture (60% of respondents).[31] Other sources included personal interests or hobbies, looking at familiar and unfamiliar products and services, and opportunities in external environmental sectors (technological, sociocultural, demographics, economic, or legal-political).

What should entrepreneurs look for as they explore these idea sources? They should look for limitations of what's currently available, new and different approaches, advances and breakthroughs, unfilled niches, or trends and changes. For example, John C. Diebel, founder of Meade Instruments Corporation, the Irvine, California, telescope maker, came up with the idea of putting computerized attachments on the company's inexpensive consumer models so that amateur astronomers could enter on a keypad the coordinates of planets or stars they wanted to see. The telescope would then automatically locate and focus on the desired planetary bodies. It took the company's engineers two years to figure out how to do it, but Meade now controls more than half the amateur astronomy market.[32]

EVALUATING IDEAS Evaluating entrepreneurial ideas revolves around personal and marketplace considerations. Each of these assessments will provide an entrepreneur with key information about the idea's potential. Exhibit A-1 describes some questions that entrepreneurs might ask as they evaluate potential ideas.

Exhibit A-1
Evaluating Potential Ideas

Personal Considerations	Marketplace Considerations
• Do you have the capabilities to do what you've selected?	• Who are the potential customers for your idea: who, where, how many?
• Are you ready to be an entrepreneur?	• What similar or unique product features does your proposed idea have compared to what's currently on the market?
• Are you prepared emotionally to deal with the stresses and challenges of being an entrepreneur?	
• Are you prepared to deal with rejection and failure?	• How and where will potential customers purchase your product?
• Are you ready to work hard?	• Have you considered pricing issues and whether the price you'll be able to charge will allow your venture to survive and prosper?
• Do you have a realistic picture of the venture's potential?	
• Have you educated yourself about financing issues?	• Have you considered how you will need to promote and advertise your proposed entrepreneurial venture?
• Are you willing and prepared to do continual financial and other types of analyses?	

feasibility study
An analysis of the various aspects of a proposed entrepreneurial venture designed to determine its feasibility

A more structured evaluation approach that an entrepreneur might want to use is a **feasibility study**—an analysis of the various aspects of a proposed entrepreneurial venture designed to determine its feasibility. Not only is a well-prepared feasibility study an effective evaluation tool to determine whether an entrepreneurial idea is a potentially successful one, it can serve as a basis for the all-important business plan.

A feasibility study should give descriptions of the most important elements of the entrepreneurial venture and the entrepreneur's analysis of the viability of these elements. Exhibit A-2 provides an outline of a possible approach to a feasibility study.

Exhibit A-2
Feasibility Study

A. Introduction, historical background, description of product or service
 1. Brief description of proposed entrepreneurial venture
 2. Brief history of the industry
 3. Information about the economy and important trends
 4. Current status of the product or service
 5. How you intend to produce the product or service
 6. Complete list of goods or services to be provided
 7. Strengths and weaknesses of the business
 8. Ease of entry into the industry, including competitor analysis

B. Accounting considerations
 1. Pro forma balance sheet
 2. Pro forma profit and loss statement
 3. Projected cash flow analysis

C. Management considerations
 1. Personal expertise—strengths and weaknesses
 2. Proposed organizational design
 3. Potential staffing requirements
 4. Inventory management methods
 5. Production and operations management issues
 6. Equipment needs

D. Marketing considerations
 1. Detailed product description
 2. Identify target market (who, where, how many)
 3. Describe place product will be distributed (location, traffic, size, channels, etc.)
 4. Price determination (competition, price lists, etc.)
 5. Promotion plans (role of personal selling, advertising, sales promotion, etc.)

E. Financial considerations
 1. Start-up costs
 2. Working capital requirements
 3. Equity requirements
 4. Loans—amounts, type, conditions
 5. Breakeven analysis
 6. Collateral
 7. Credit references
 8. Equipment and building financing—costs and methods

F. Legal considerations
 1. Proposed business structure (type; conditions, terms, liability, responsibility; insurance needs; buyout and succession issues)
 2. Contracts, licenses, and other legal documents

G. Tax considerations: sales/property/employee; federal, state, and local

H. Appendix: charts/graphs, diagrams, layouts, résumés, etc.

Yes, it covers a lot of territory and takes a significant amount of time, energy, and effort to prepare it. However, an entrepreneur's potential future success is worth that investment.

Researching the Venture's Feasibility—Competitors

Part of researching the venture's feasibility is looking at the competitors. What would entrepreneurs like to know about their potential competitors? Here are some possible questions:

What types of products or services are competitors offering?

What are the major characteristics of these products or services?

What are their products' strengths and weaknesses?

How do they handle marketing, pricing, and distributing?

What do they attempt to do differently from other competitors?

Do they appear to be successful at it? Why or why not?

What are they good at?

What competitive advantage(s) do they appear to have?

What are they not so good at?

What competitive disadvantage(s) do they appear to have?

How large and profitable are these competitors?

For instance, the CEO of The Children's Place carefully examined the competition as he took his chain of children's clothing stores nationwide. Although he faces stiff competition from the likes of GapKids, J.C. Penney, and Gymboree, he feels that his company's approach to manufacturing and marketing will give it a competitive edge.[33]

Once an entrepreneur has this information, he or she should assess how the proposed entrepreneurial venture is going to "fit" into this competitive arena. Will the entrepreneurial venture be able to compete successfully? This type of competitor analysis becomes an important part of the feasibility study and the business plan. If, after all this analysis, the situation looks promising, the final part of researching the venture's feasibility is to look at the various financing options. This step isn't the final determination of how much funding the venture will need or where this funding will come from but is simply gathering information about various financing alternatives.

Researching the Venture's Feasibility—Financing

Getting financing isn't always easy. For instance, when William Carey first proposed building a liquor distributor business in Poland, more than 20 investment banking houses in New York passed on funding his idea. Carey recalls, "They didn't know Poland, and the business was small. We were ready to give up." Then, a New York investment banking boutique agreed to fund the venture. Today, Carey's company, CEDC (Central European Distribution), has more than 3,000 employees and sales revenues that top $1.1 billion.[34]

Because funds likely will be needed to start the venture, an entrepreneur must research the various financing options. Possible financing options available to entrepreneurs are shown in Exhibit A-3.

Planning the Venture—Developing a Business Plan

Planning is also important to entrepreneurial ventures. Once the venture's feasibility has been thoroughly researched, the entrepreneur then must look at planning the venture. The most important thing that an entrepreneur does in planning the venture is developing a **business plan**—a written document that summarizes a business opportunity and defines and articulates how the identified opportunity is to be seized and exploited.

business plan
A written document that summarizes a business opportunity and defines and articulates how the identified opportunity is to be seized and exploited

Exhibit A-3
Possible Financing Options

- Entrepreneur's personal resources (personal savings, home equity, personal loans, credit cards, etc.)
- Financial institutions (banks, savings and loan institutions, government-guaranteed loan, credit unions, etc.)
- **Venture capitalists**—external equity financing provided by professionally managed pools of investor money
- **Angel investors**—a private investor (or group of private investors) who offers financial backing to an entrepreneurial venture in return for equity in the venture
- **Initial public offering (IPO)**—the first public registration and sale of a company's stock
- National, state, and local governmental business development programs
- Unusual sources (television shows, judged competitions, etc.)

venture capitalists
External equity financing provided by professionally managed pools of investor money

angel investors
A private investor (or group of private investors) who offers financial backing to an entrepreneurial venture in return for equity in the venture

initial public offering (IPO)
The first public registration and sale of a company's stock

For many would-be entrepreneurs, developing and writing a business plan seems like a daunting task. However, a good business plan is valuable. It pulls together all of the elements of the entrepreneur's vision into a single coherent document. The business plan requires careful planning and creative thinking. But if done well, it can be a convincing document that serves many functions. It serves as a blueprint and road map for operating the business. And the business plan is a "living" document, guiding organizational decisions and actions throughout the life of the business, not just in the start-up stage.

If an entrepreneur has completed a feasibility study, much of the information included in it becomes the basis for the business plan. A good business plan covers six major areas: executive summary, analysis of opportunity, analysis of the context, description of the business, financial data and projections, and supporting documentation.

EXECUTIVE SUMMARY The executive summary summarizes the key points that the entrepreneur wants to make about the proposed entrepreneurial venture. These points might include a brief mission statement; primary goals; brief history of the entrepreneurial venture, maybe in the form of a timeline; key people involved in the venture; nature of the business; concise product or service descriptions; brief explanations of market niche, competitors, and competitive advantage; proposed strategies; and selected key financial information.

ANALYSIS OF OPPORTUNITY In this section of the business plan, an entrepreneur presents the details of the perceived opportunity. Essentially, details include (1) sizing up the market by describing the demographics of the target market, (2) describing and evaluating industry trends, and (3) identifying and evaluating competitors.

ANALYSIS OF THE CONTEXT Whereas the opportunity analysis focuses on the opportunity in a specific industry and market, the context analysis takes a much broader perspective. Here, the entrepreneur describes the broad external changes and trends taking place in the economic, political-legal, technological, and global environments.

DESCRIPTION OF THE BUSINESS In this section, an entrepreneur describes how the entrepreneurial venture is going to be organized, launched, and managed. It includes a thorough description of the mission statement; a description of the desired organizational culture; marketing plans including overall marketing strategy, pricing, sales tactics, service-warranty policies, and advertising and promotion tactics; product development plans such as an explanation of development status, tasks, difficulties and risks, and anticipated costs; operational plans including a description of proposed geographic location, facilities and needed improvements, equipment, and work flow; human resource plans including a description of key management persons, composition of board of directors including their background experience and skills, current and future staffing needs, compensation and benefits, and training needs; and an overall schedule and timetable of events.

FINANCIAL DATA AND PROJECTIONS Every effective business plan contains financial data and projections. Although the calculations and interpretation may be difficult, they are absolutely critical. No business plan is complete without financial information. Financial plans should cover at least three years and contain projected income statements, pro forma cash flow analysis (monthly for the first year and quarterly for the next two), pro forma balance sheets, breakeven analysis, and cost controls. If major equipment or other capital purchases are expected, the items, costs, and available collateral should be listed. All financial projections and analyses should include explanatory notes, especially where the data seem contradictory or questionable.

SUPPORTING DOCUMENTATION For this important component of an effective business plan, the entrepreneur should back up his or her descriptions with charts, graphs, tables, photographs, or other visual tools. In addition, it might be important to include information (personal and work-related) about the key participants in the entrepreneurial venture.

Just as the idea for an entrepreneurial venture takes time to germinate, so does the writing of a good business plan. It's important for the entrepreneur to put serious thought and consideration into the plan. It's not an easy thing to do. However, the resulting document should be valuable to the entrepreneur in current and future planning efforts.

ORGANIZING Issues

Donald Hannon, president of Graphic Laminating Inc. in Solon, Ohio, redesigned his organization's structure by transforming it into an employee-empowered company. He wanted to drive authority down through the organization so employees were responsible for their own efforts. One way he did this was by creating employee teams to handle specific projects. Employees with less experience were teamed with veteran employees. He says, "I want to build a good team and give people the ability to succeed. Sometimes that means giving them the ability to make mistakes, and I have to keep that in perspective. The more we allow people to become better at what they do, the better they will become—and the better we all will do."[35]

Once the start-up and planning issues for the entrepreneurial venture have been addressed, the entrepreneur is ready to begin organizing the entrepreneurial venture. Then, the entrepreneur must address five organizing issues: the legal forms of organization, organizational design and structure, human resource management, stimulating and making changes, and the continuing importance of innovation.

Legal Forms of Organization

The first organizing decision that an entrepreneur must make is a critical one. It's the form of legal ownership for the venture. The two primary factors affecting this decision are taxes and legal liability. An entrepreneur wants to minimize the impact of both of these factors. The right choice can protect the entrepreneur from legal liability as well as save tax dollars, in both the short run and the long run.

What alternatives are available? The three basic ways to organize an entrepreneurial venture are sole proprietorship, partnership, and corporation. However, when you include the variations of these basic organizational alternatives, you end up with six possible choices, each with its own tax consequences, liability issues, and pros and cons.

These six choices are sole proprietorship, general partnership, limited liability partnership (LLP), C corporation, S corporation, and limited liability company (LLC). Let's briefly look at each one with their advantages and drawbacks. (Exhibit A-4 summarizes the basic information about each organizational alternative.)

SOLE PROPRIETORSHIP A **sole proprietorship** is a form of legal organization in which the owner maintains sole and complete control over the business and is personally liable for business debts. The legal requirements for establishing a sole proprietorship consist of obtaining the necessary local business licenses and permits. In a sole proprietorship, income and losses "pass through" to the owner and are taxed at the owner's personal income tax rate. The biggest drawback, however, is the unlimited personal liability for any and all debts of the business.

GENERAL PARTNERSHIP A **general partnership** is a form of legal organization in which two or more business owners share the management and risk of the business. Even though a partnership is possible without a written agreement, the potential and inevitable problems that arise in any partnership make a written partnership agreement drafted by legal counsel a highly recommended thing to do.

LIMITED LIABILITY PARTNERSHIP (LLP) The **limited liability partnership (LLP)** is a legal organization formed by general partner(s) and limited partner(s). The general partners actually operate and manage the business. They are the ones who have unlimited liability. At least one general partner is necessary in an LLP, but any number of limited partners are allowed. These partners are usually passive investors, although they can make management suggestions to the general partners. They also have the right to inspect the business and make copies of business records. The limited partners are entitled to a share of the business's profits as agreed to in the partnership agreement, and their risk is limited to the amount of their investment in the LLP.

C CORPORATION Of the three basic types of ownership, the corporation (also known as a C corporation) is the most complex to form and operate. A **corporation** is a legal business entity that is separate from its owners and managers. Many entrepreneurial ventures are organized as a **closely held corporation** which, very simply, is a corporation owned by a limited number of people who do not trade the stock publicly. Whereas the sole proprietorship and partnership forms of organization do not exist separately from the entrepreneur, the corporation does. The corporation functions as a distinct legal entity and, as such, can make contracts, engage in business activities, own property, sue and be sued, and of course, pay taxes. A corporation must operate in accordance with its charter and the laws of the state in which it operates.

S CORPORATION The **S corporation** (also called a subchapter S corporation) is a specialized type of corporation that has the regular characteristics of a corporation but is unique in that the owners are taxed as a partnership as long as certain criteria are met. The S corporation has been the classic organizing approach for getting the limited liability of a corporate structure without incurring corporate tax. However, this form of legal organization must meet strict criteria. If any of these criteria are violated, a venture's S status is automatically terminated.

LIMITED LIABILITY COMPANY (LLC) The **limited liability company (LLC)** is a relatively new form of business organization that's a hybrid between a partnership and a corporation. The LLC offers the liability protection of a corporation, the tax benefits of a partnership, and fewer restrictions than an S corporation. However, the main drawback of this approach is that it's quite complex and expensive to set up. Legal and financial advice is an absolute necessity in forming the LLC's **operating agreement**, the document that outlines the provisions governing the way the LLC will conduct business.

---

sole proprietorship
A form of legal organization in which the owner maintains sole and complete control over the business and is personally liable for business debts

general partnership
A form of legal organization in which two or more business owners share the management and risk of the business

limited liability partnership (LLP)
A form of legal organization consisting of general partner(s) and limited liability partner(s)

corporation
A legal business entity that is separate from its owners and managers

closely held corporation
A corporation owned by a limited number of people who do not trade the stock publicly

S corporation
A specialized type of corporation that has the regular characteristics of a C corporation but is unique in that the owners are taxed as a partnership as long as certain criteria are met

limited liability company (LLC)
A form of legal organization that's a hybrid between a partnership and a corporation

operating agreement
The document that outlines the provisions governing the way an LLC will conduct business

Exhibit A-4
Legal Forms of Business Organization

Structure	Ownership Requirements	Tax Treatment	Liability	Advantages	Drawbacks
Sole proprietorship	One owner	Income and losses "pass through" to owner and are taxed at personal rate	Unlimited personal liability	*Low start-up costs* Freedom from most regulations *Owner has direct control* All profits go to owner *Easy to exit business*	Unlimited personal liability *Personal finances at risk* Miss out on many business tax deductions *Total responsibility* May be more difficult to raise financing
General partnership	Two or more owners	Income and losses "pass through" to partners and are taxed at personal rate; *flexibility in profit-loss allocations to partners*	Unlimited personal liability	*Ease of formation* Pooled talent *Pooled resources* Somewhat easier access to financing *Some tax benefits*	Unlimited personal liability *Divided authority and decisions* Potential for conflict *Continuity of transfer of ownership*
Limited liability partnership (LLP)	Two or more owners	Income and losses "pass through" to partner and are taxed at personal rate; *flexibility in profit-loss allocations to partners*	Limited, although one partner must retain unlimited liability	*Good way to acquire capital from limited partners*	Cost and complexity of forming can be high *Limited partners cannot participate in management of business without losing liability protection*
C corporation	Unlimited number of shareholders; *no limits on types of stock or voting arrangements*	Dividend income is taxed at corporate and personal shareholder levels; *losses and deductions are corporate*	Limited	*Limited liability* Transferable ownership *Continuous existence* Easier access to resources	Expensive to set up *Closely regulated* Double taxation *Extensive record keeping* Charter restrictions
S corporation	Up to 75 shareholders; *no limits on types of stock or voting arrangements*	Income and losses "pass through" to partners and are taxed at personal rate; *flexibility in profit-loss allocation to partners*	Limited	*Easy to set up* Enjoy limited liability protection and tax benefits of partnership *Can have a tax-exempt entity as a shareholder*	Must meet certain requirements *May limit future financing options*
Limited liability company (LLC)	Unlimited number of "members"; *flexible membership arrangements for voting rights and income*	Income and losses "pass through" to partners and are taxed at personal rate; *flexibility in profit-loss allocations to partners*	Limited	*Greater flexibility* Not constrained by regulations on C and S corporations *Taxed as partnership, not as corporation*	Cost of switching from one form to this can be high *Need legal and financial advice in forming operating agreement*

SUMMARY OF LEGAL FORMS OF ORGANIZATION The organizing decision regarding the legal form of organization is an important one because it can have significant tax and liability consequences. Although the legal form of organization can be changed, it's not an easy thing to do. An entrepreneur needs to think carefully about what's important, especially in the areas of flexibility, taxes, and amount of personal liability in choosing the best form of organization.

Organizational Design and Structure

The choice of an appropriate organizational structure is also an important decision when organizing an entrepreneurial venture. At some point, successful entrepreneurs find that they can't do everything alone. More people are needed. The entrepreneur must then decide on the most appropriate structural arrangement for effectively and efficiently carrying out the organization's activities. Without some suitable type of organizational structure, the entrepreneurial venture may soon find itself in a chaotic situation.

In many small firms, the organizational structure tends to evolve with little intentional or deliberate planning by the entrepreneur. For the most part, the structure may be simple—one person does whatever is needed. As the entrepreneurial venture grows and the entrepreneur finds it increasingly difficult to go it alone, employees are brought on board to perform certain functions or duties that the entrepreneur can't handle. These individuals tend to perform those same functions as the company grows. Then, as the entrepreneurial venture continues to grow, each of these functional areas may require managers and employees.

With the evolution to a more deliberate structure, the entrepreneur faces a whole new set of challenges. All of a sudden, he or she must share decision making and operating responsibilities. This transition is typically one of the most difficult things for an entrepreneur to do—letting go and allowing someone else to make decisions. *After all*, he or she reasons, *how can anyone know this business as well as I do*? Also, what might have been a fairly informal, loose, and flexible atmosphere that worked well when the organization was small may no longer be effective. Many entrepreneurs are greatly concerned about keeping that "small company" atmosphere alive even as the venture grows and evolves into a more structured arrangement. But having a structured organization doesn't necessarily mean giving up flexibility, adaptability, and freedom. In fact, the structural design may be as fluid as the entrepreneur feels comfortable with and yet still have the rigidity it needs to operate efficiently.

Organizational design decisions in entrepreneurial ventures revolve around the six key elements of organizational structure discussed in Chapter 10: work specialization, departmentalization, chain of command, span of control, amount of centralization-decentralization, and amount of formalization. Decisions about these six elements will determine whether an entrepreneur designs a more mechanistic or organic organizational structure (concepts also discussed in Chapter 10). When would each be preferable? A mechanistic structure would be preferable when cost efficiencies are critical to the venture's competitive advantage, when more control over employees' work activities is important, if the venture produces standardized products in a routine fashion, and when the external environment is relatively stable and certain. An organic structure would be most appropriate when innovation is critical to the organization's competitive advantage; for smaller organizations where rigid approaches to dividing and coordinating work aren't necessary; if the organization produces customized products in a flexible setting; and where the external environment is dynamic, complex, and uncertain.

Human Resource Management Issues in Entrepreneurial Ventures

As an entrepreneurial venture grows, additional employees will need to be hired to perform the increased workload. As employees are brought on board, the entrepreneur faces certain human resource management (HRM) issues. Two HRM issues of particular importance to entrepreneurs are employee recruitment and employee retention.

EMPLOYEE RECRUITMENT An entrepreneur wants to ensure that the venture has the people to do the required work. Recruiting new employees is one of the biggest challenges that entrepreneurs face. In fact, the ability of small firms to successfully recruit appropriate employees is consistently rated as one of the most important factors influencing organizational success.

Entrepreneurs, particularly, are looking for high-potential people who can perform multiple roles during various stages of venture growth. They look for individuals who "buy into" the venture's entrepreneurial culture—individuals who have a passion for the business. Unlike their corporate counterparts who often focus on filling a job by matching a person to the job requirements, entrepreneurs look to fill in critical skills gaps. They're looking for people who are exceptionally capable and self-motivated, flexible, multi-skilled, and who can help grow the entrepreneurial venture. While corporate managers tend to focus on using traditional HRM practices and techniques, entrepreneurs are more concerned with matching characteristics of the person to the values and culture of the organization; that is, they focus on matching the person to the organization.

EMPLOYEE RETENTION Getting competent and qualified people into the venture is just the first step in effectively managing the human resources. An entrepreneur wants to keep the people he or she has hired and trained. Sabrina Horn, president of The Horn Group based in San Francisco, understands the importance of having good people on board and keeping them. In the rough-and-tumble, intensely competitive public relations industry, Sabrina knows that the loss of talented employees could harm client services. To contend with this issue, she offers employees a wide array of desirable benefits such as raises each year, profit sharing, trust funds for employees' children, paid sabbaticals, personal development funds, and so forth. But more importantly, Sabrina recognizes that employees have a life outside the office and treats them accordingly. This type of HRM approach has kept her employees loyal and productive.[36]

A unique and important employee retention issue entrepreneurs must deal with is compensation. Whereas traditional organizations are more likely to view compensation from the perspective of monetary rewards (base pay, benefits, and incentives), smaller entrepreneurial firms are more likely to view compensation from a total rewards perspective. For these firms, compensation encompasses psychological rewards, learning opportunities, and recognition in addition to monetary rewards (base pay and incentives).[37]

Stimulating and Making Changes

We know that the context facing entrepreneurs is one of dynamic change. Both external and internal forces (see Chapter 7) may bring about the need for making changes in the entrepreneurial venture. Entrepreneurs need to be alert to problems and opportunities that may create the need to change. In fact, of the many hats an entrepreneur wears, that of change agent may be one of the most important.[38] If changes are needed in the entrepreneurial venture, often it is the entrepreneur who first recognizes the need for change and acts as the catalyst, coach, cheerleader, and chief change consultant. Change isn't easy in any organization, but it can be particularly challenging for entrepreneurial ventures. Even if a person is comfortable with taking risks—as entrepreneurs usually are—change can be hard. That's why it's important for an entrepreneur to recognize the critical role he or she plays in stimulating and implementing change. For instance, Jeff Fluhr, CEO of StubHub, Inc., is well aware of the important role he plays in stimulating and implementing changes. As the leading Internet player in the ticket reselling market, Fluhr had to continually look for ways to keep his company competitive. One change was the creation of an exclusive advertising agreement with the National Hockey League to promote StubHub.com on NHL.com.[39] StubHub is now a division of eBay.

During any type of organizational change, an entrepreneur also may have to act as chief coach and cheerleader. Because organizational change of any type can be disruptive and scary, the entrepreneur must explain the change to employees and encourage change efforts by supporting employees, getting them excited about the change, building them up, and motivating them to put forth their best efforts.

Finally, the entrepreneur may have to guide the actual change process as changes in strategy, technology, products, structure, or people are implemented. In this role, the entrepreneur answers questions, makes suggestions, gets needed resources, facilitates conflict, and does whatever else is necessary to get the change(s) implemented.

The Importance of Continuing Innovation

In today's dynamically chaotic world of global competition, organizations must continually innovate new products and services if they want to compete successfully. Innovation is a key characteristic of entrepreneurial ventures and, in fact, it's what makes the entrepreneurial venture "entrepreneurial."

What must an entrepreneur do to encourage innovation in the venture? Having an innovation-supportive culture is crucial. What does such a culture look like?[40] It's one in which employees perceive that supervisory support and organizational reward systems are consistent with a commitment to innovation. It's also important in this type of culture that employees not perceive their workload pressures to be excessive or unreasonable. And research has shown that firms with cultures supportive of innovation tend to be smaller, have fewer formalized human resource practices, and less abundant resources.[41]

LEADING Issues

The employees at designer Liz Lange's company have to be flexible. Many don't have job descriptions, and everyone is expected to contribute ideas and pitch in with tasks in all departments. Lange says, "The phrase 'That's not my job' doesn't belong here." In return, Lange is a supportive leader who gives her employees considerable latitude.[42]

Leading is an important function of entrepreneurs. As an entrepreneurial venture grows and people are brought on board, an entrepreneur takes on a new role—that of a leader. In this section, we want to look at what's involved with the leading function. First, we're going to look at the unique personality characteristics of entrepreneurs. Then we're going to discuss the important role entrepreneurs play in motivating employees through empowerment and leading the venture and employee teams.

Personality Characteristics of Entrepreneurs

Think of someone you know who is an entrepreneur. Maybe it's someone you personally know or maybe it's someone like Bill Gates of Microsoft. How would you describe this person's personality? One of the most researched areas of entrepreneurship has been the search to determine what—if any—psychological characteristics entrepreneurs have in common, what types of personality traits entrepreneurs have that might distinguish them from non-entrepreneurs, and what traits entrepreneurs have that might predict who will be a successful entrepreneur.

Is there a classic "entrepreneurial personality"? Trying to pinpoint specific personality characteristics that all entrepreneurs share has the same problem as identifying the trait theories of leadership—that is, being able to identify specific personality traits that *all* entrepreneurs share. This challenge hasn't stopped entrepreneurship researchers from listing common traits, however. For instance, one list of personality characteristics included the following: high level of motivation, abundance of self-confidence, ability to be involved for the long term, high energy level, persistent problem solver, high degree of initiative, ability to set goals, and moderate risk-taker. Another list of characteristics of "successful" entrepreneurs included high energy level, great persistence, resourcefulness, the desire and ability to be self-directed, and relatively high need for autonomy.

Another development in defining entrepreneurial personality characteristics was the proactive personality scale to predict an individual's likelihood of pursuing entrepreneurial ventures. We introduced the **proactive personality** trait in Chapter 14. Recall that it's a personality trait of individuals who are more prone to take actions to influence their environment—that is, they're more proactive. Obviously, an entrepreneur is likely to exhibit proactivity as he or she searches for opportunities and acts to take advantage of those opportunities. Various items on the proactive personality scale were found to be good indicators of a person's likelihood of becoming an entrepreneur, including gender, education, having an entrepreneurial parent, and possessing a proactive personality. In addition, studies have shown that entrepreneurs have greater risk propensity than do managers. However, this propensity is moderated by the entrepreneur's primary goal. Risk propensity is greater for entrepreneurs whose primary goal is growth versus those whose focus is on producing family income.

proactive personality
A personality trait that describes individuals who are more prone to take actions to influence their environments

Motivating Employees Through Empowerment

At Sapient Corporation (creators of Internet and software systems for e-commerce and automating back-office tasks such as billing and inventory), cofounders Jerry Greenberg and J. Stuart Moore recognized that employee motivation was vitally important to their company's ultimate success.[43] They designed their organization so individual employees are part of an industry-specific team that works on an entire project rather than on one small piece of it. Their rationale was that people often feel frustrated when they're doing a small part of a job and never get to see the whole job from start to finish. They figured people would be more productive if they got the opportunity to participate in all phases of a project.

When you're motivated to do something, don't you find yourself energized and willing to work hard at doing whatever it is you're excited about? Wouldn't it be great if all of a venture's employees were energized, excited, and willing to work hard at their jobs? Having motivated employees is an important goal for any entrepreneur, and employee empowerment is an important motivational tool entrepreneurs can use.

Although it's not easy for entrepreneurs to do, employee empowerment—giving employees the power to make decisions and take actions on their own—is an important motivational approach. Why? Because successful entrepreneurial ventures must be quick and nimble, ready to pursue opportunities and go off in new directions. Empowered employees can provide that flexibility and speed. When employees are empowered, they often display stronger work motivation, better work quality, higher job satisfaction, and lower turnover.

For example, employees at Butler International, Inc., a technology consulting services firm based in Montvale, New Jersey, work at client locations. President and CEO Ed Kopko recognized that employees had to be empowered to do their jobs if they were going to be successful.[44] Another entrepreneurial venture that found employee empowerment to be a strong motivational approach is Stryker Instruments in Kalamazoo, Michigan, a division of Stryker Corporation. Each of the company's production units is responsible for its operating budget, cost reduction goals, customer-service levels, inventory management, training, production planning and forecasting, purchasing, human resource management, safety, and problem solving. In addition, unit members work closely with marketing, sales, and R&D during new product introductions and continuous improvement projects. Says one team supervisor, "Stryker lets me do what I do best and rewards me for that privilege."[45]

Empowerment is a philosophical concept that entrepreneurs have to "buy into." This doesn't come easily. In fact, it's hard for many entrepreneurs to do. Their life is tied up in the business. They've built it from the ground up. But continuing to grow the entrepreneurial venture is eventually going to require handing over more responsibilities to employees. How can entrepreneurs empower employees? For many entrepreneurs, it's a gradual process.

Entrepreneurs can begin by using participative decision making in which employees provide input into decisions. Although getting employees to participate in decisions isn't quite taking the full plunge into employee empowerment, at least it's a way to begin tapping into the collective array of employees' talents, skills, knowledge, and abilities.

Another way to empower employees is through delegation—the process of assigning certain decisions or specific job duties to employees. By delegating decisions and duties, the entrepreneur is turning over the responsibility for carrying them out.

When an entrepreneur is finally comfortable with the idea of employee empowerment, fully empowering employees means redesigning their jobs so they have discretion over the way they do their work. It's allowing employees to do their work effectively and efficiently by using their creativity, imagination, knowledge, and skills.

If an entrepreneur implements employee empowerment properly—that is, with complete and total commitment to the program and with appropriate employee training—results can be impressive for the entrepreneurial venture and for the empowered employees. The business can enjoy significant productivity gains, quality improvements, more satisfied customers, increased employee motivation, and improved morale. Employees can enjoy the opportunities to do a greater variety of work that is more interesting and challenging.

In addition, employees are encouraged to take the initiative in identifying and solving problems and doing their work. For example, at Mine Safety Appliances Company in Pittsburgh, Pennsylvania, employees are empowered to change their work processes in order to meet the organization's challenging quality improvement goals. Getting to this point took an initial 40 hours of classroom instruction per employee in areas such as engineering drawing, statistical process control, quality certifications, and specific work instruction. However, the company's commitment to an empowered workforce has resulted in profitability increasing 57 percent over the last four years and 95 percent of the company's employees achieving multi-skill certifications.[46]

The Entrepreneur as Leader

The last topic we want to discuss in this section is the role of the entrepreneur as a leader. In this role, the entrepreneur has certain leadership responsibilities in leading the venture and in leading employee work teams.

LEADING THE VENTURE   Today's successful entrepreneur must be like the leader of a jazz ensemble known for its improvisation, innovation, and creativity. Max DePree, former head of Herman Miller, Inc., a leading office furniture manufacturer known for its innovative leadership approaches, said it best in his book, *Leadership Jazz*, "Jazz band leaders must choose the music, find the right musicians, and perform—in public. But the effect of the performance depends on so many things—the environment, the volunteers playing the band, the need for everybody to perform as individuals and as a group, the absolute dependence of the leader on the members of the band, the need for the followers to play well....The leader of the jazz band has the beautiful opportunity to draw the best out of the other musicians. We have much to learn from jazz band leaders, for jazz, like leadership, combines the unpredictability of the future with the gifts of individuals."[47]

The way an entrepreneur leads the venture should be much like the jazz leader—drawing the best out of other individuals, even given the unpredictability of the situation. One way an entrepreneur leads is through the vision he or she creates for the organization. In fact, the driving force through the early stages of the entrepreneurial venture is often the visionary leadership of the entrepreneur. The entrepreneur's ability to articulate a coherent, inspiring, and attractive vision of the future is a key test of his or her leadership. But if an entrepreneur can articulate such a vision, the results can be worthwhile. A study contrasting visionary and nonvisionary companies showed that visionary companies outperformed the nonvisionary ones by six times on standard financial criteria, and their stocks outperformed the general market by 15 times.[48]

LEADING EMPLOYEE WORK TEAMS As we know from Chapter 13, many organizations—entrepreneurial and otherwise—are using employee work teams to perform organizational tasks, create new ideas, and resolve problems.

Employee work teams tend to be popular in entrepreneurial ventures. An *Industry Week* Census of Manufacturers showed that nearly 68 percent of survey respondents used teams to varying degrees.[49] The three most common ones respondents said they used included empowered teams (teams that have the authority to plan and implement process improvements), self-directed teams (teams that are nearly autonomous and responsible for many managerial activities), and cross-functional teams (work teams composed of individuals from various specialties who work together on various tasks).

These entrepreneurs also said that developing and using teams is necessary because technology and market demands are forcing them to make their products faster, cheaper, and better. Tapping into the collective wisdom of the venture's employees and empowering them to make decisions just may be one of the best ways to adapt to change. In addition, a team culture can improve the overall workplace environment and morale.

For team efforts to work, however, entrepreneurs must shift from the traditional command-and-control style to a coach-and-collaboration style (refer to the discussion of team leadership in Chapter 17). They must recognize that individual employees can understand the business and can innovate just as effectively as they can. For example, at Marque, Inc., of Goshen, Indiana, CEO Scott Jessup recognized that he wasn't the smartest guy in the company as far as production problems, but he was smart enough to realize that, if he wanted his company to expand its market share in manufacturing medical-emergency-squad vehicles, new levels of productivity needed to be reached. He formed a cross-functional team—bringing together people from production, quality assurance, and fabrication—that could spot production bottlenecks and other problems and then gave the team the authority to resolve the constraints.[50]

CONTROLLING Issues

Philip McCaleb still gets a kick out of riding the scooters his Chicago-based company, Genuine Scooter Co., makes. However, in building his business, McCaleb has had to acknowledge his own limitations. As a self-described "idea" guy, he knew that he would need someone else to come in and ensure that the end product was *what* it was supposed to be, *where* it was supposed to be, and *when* it was supposed to be there.[51]

Entrepreneurs must look at controlling their venture's operations in order to survive and prosper in both the short run and long run. Those unique control issues that face entrepreneurs include managing growth, managing downturns, exiting the venture, and managing personal life choices and challenges.

Managing Growth

Growth is a natural and desirable outcome for entrepreneurial ventures. Growth is what distinguishes an entrepreneurial venture. Entrepreneurial ventures pursue growth. Growing slowly can be successful, but so can rapid growth.

Growing successfully doesn't occur randomly or by luck. Successfully pursuing growth typically requires an entrepreneur to manage all the challenges associated with growing—in other words, planning, organizing, and controlling for growth.

PLANNING FOR GROWTH Although it may seem we've reverted back to discussing planning issues instead of controlling issues, actually controlling is closely tied to planning, as we know from our discussion in Chapter 18 (see Exhibit 18-1). And the best growth strategy is a well-planned one.[52] Ideally, the decision to grow doesn't come about spontaneously, but instead is part of the venture's overall business goals and plan. Rapid growth without planning can be disastrous. Entrepreneurs need to address growth strategies as part of their business planning but shouldn't be overly rigid in that planning. The plans should be flexible enough to exploit unexpected opportunities that arise. With plans in place, the successful entrepreneur must then organize for growth.

ORGANIZING FOR GROWTH   The key challenges for an entrepreneur in organizing for growth include finding capital, finding people, and strengthening the organizational culture. Norbert Otto is the founder of Sport Otto, an online business based in Germany that sold almost $2 million worth of skates, skis, snowboards, and other sporting goods on eBay. As the company grows, Otto is finding that he has to be more organized.[53]

Having enough capital is a major challenge facing growing entrepreneurial ventures. The money issue never seems to go away, does it? It takes capital to expand. The processes of finding capital to fund growth are much like going through the initial financing of the venture. Hopefully, at this time the venture has a successful track record to back up the request. If it doesn't, it may be extremely difficult to acquire the necessary capital. That's why we said earlier that the best growth strategy is a planned one.

Part of that planning should be how growth will be financed. For example, The Boston Beer Company, America's largest microbrewer and producer of Samuel Adams beer, grew rapidly by focusing almost exclusively on increasing its top-selling product line. However, the company was so focused on increasing market share that it had few financial controls and an inadequate financial infrastructure. During periods of growth, cash flow difficulties would force company chairman and brewmaster Jim Koch to tap into a pool of unused venture capital funding. However, when a chief financial officer joined the company, he developed a financial structure that enabled the company to manage its growth more efficiently and effectively by setting up a plan for funding growth.[54]

Another important issue that a growing entrepreneurial venture needs to address is finding people. If the venture is growing quickly, this challenge may be intensified because of time constraints. It's important to plan the numbers and types of employees needed as much as possible in order to support the increasing workload of the growing venture. It may also be necessary to provide additional training and support to employees to help them handle the increased pressures associated with the growing organization.

Finally, when a venture is growing, it's important to create a positive, growth-oriented culture that enhances the opportunities to achieve success, both organizationally and individually. Encouraging the culture can sometimes be difficult to do, particularly when changes are rapidly happening. However, the values, attitudes, and beliefs that are established and reinforced during these times are critical to the entrepreneurial venture's continued and future success. Exhibit A-5 lists some suggestions that entrepreneurs might use to ensure that their venture's culture is one that embraces and supports a climate in which organizational growth is viewed as desirable and important. Keeping employees focused and committed to what the venture is doing is critical to the ultimate success of its growth strategies. If employees don't "buy into" the direction the entrepreneurial venture is headed, it's unlikely the growth strategies will be successful.

CONTROLLING FOR GROWTH   Another challenge that growing entrepreneurial ventures face is reinforcing already established organizational controls. Maintaining good financial records and financial controls over cash flow, inventory, customer data, sales orders, receivables, payables, and costs should be a priority of every entrepreneur—whether pursuing growth or not. However, it's particularly important

Exhibit A-5
Achieving a Supportive,
Growth-Oriented Culture

- Keep the lines of communication open—inform employees about major issues.
- Establish trust by being honest, open, and forthright about the challenges and rewards of being a growing organization.
- Be a good listener—find out what employees are thinking and facing.
- Be willing to delegate duties.
- Be flexible—be willing to change your plans if necessary.
- Provide consistent and regular feedback by letting employees know the outcomes—good and bad.
- Reinforce the contributions of each person by recognizing employees' efforts.
- Continually train employees to enhance their capabilities and skills.
- Maintain the focus on the venture's mission even as it grows.
- Establish and reinforce a "we" spirit that supports the coordinated efforts of all the employees and helps the growing venture be successful.

to reinforce these controls when the entrepreneurial venture is expanding. It's all too easy to let things "get away" or to put them off when there's an unrelenting urgency to get things done. Rapid growth—or even slow growth—does not excuse the need to have effective controls in place. In fact, it's particularly important to have established procedures, protocols, and processes and to use them. Even though mistakes and inefficiencies can never be eliminated entirely, an entrepreneur should at least ensure that every effort is being made to achieve high levels of productivity and organizational effectiveness. For example, at Green Gear Cycling, cofounder Alan Scholz recognized the importance of controlling for growth. How? By following a "Customers for Life" strategy, which meant continually monitoring customer relationships and orienting organizational work decisions around their possible impacts on customers. Through this type of strategy, Green Gear hopes to keep customers for life. That's significant because they figured that, if they could keep a customer for life, the value would range from $10,000 to $25,000 per lifetime customer.[55]

Managing Downturns

Although organizational growth is a desirable and important goal for entrepreneurial ventures, what happens when things don't go as planned—when the growth strategies don't result in the intended outcomes and, in fact, result in a decline in performance? Significant challenges can come in managing the downturns.

Nobody likes to fail, especially entrepreneurs. However, when an entrepreneurial venture faces times of trouble, what can be done? How can downturns be managed successfully? The first step is recognizing that a crisis is brewing.

RECOGNIZING CRISIS SITUATIONS An entrepreneur should be alert to the warning signs of a business in trouble. Some signals of potential performance decline include inadequate or negative cash flow, excess number of employees, unnecessary and cumbersome administrative procedures, fear of conflict and taking risks, tolerance of work incompetence, lack of a clear mission or goals, and ineffective or poor communication within the organization.[56]

Another perspective on recognizing performance declines revolves around what is known as the **"boiled frog" phenomenon** in which subtly declining situations are difficult to recognize.[57] The "boiled frog" is a classic psychological response experiment. In one case, a live frog that's dropped into a boiling pan of water reacts instantaneously and jumps out of the pan. But in the second case, a live frog that's dropped into a pan of mild water that is gradually heated to the boiling point fails to react and dies. A small firm may be particularly vulnerable to the boiled frog phenomenon because the entrepreneur may not recognize the "water heating up"—that

"boiled frog" phenomenon
A perspective on recognizing performance declines that suggests watching out for subtly declining situations

is, the subtle decline of the situation. When changes in performance are gradual, a serious response may never be triggered or may be initiated too late to intervene effectively in the situation.

So what does the boiled frog phenomenon teach us? It teaches us that entrepreneurs need to be alert to signals that the venture's performance may be worsening. Don't wait until the water has reached the boiling point before you react.

DEALING WITH DOWNTURNS, DECLINES, AND CRISES   Although an entrepreneur hopes to never have to deal with organizational downturns, declines, or crises, a time may come when he or she must do just that. After all, nobody likes to think about things going bad or taking a turn for the worse. But that's exactly what the entrepreneur should do—think about it *before* it happens (remember feedforward control from Chapter 18).[58] It's important to have an up-to-date plan for covering crises. It's like mapping exit routes from your home in case of a fire. An entrepreneur wants to be prepared before an emergency hits. This plan should focus on providing specific details for controlling the most fundamental and critical aspects of running the venture—cash flow, accounts receivable, costs, and debt. Beyond having a plan for controlling the venture's critical inflows and outflows, other actions would involve identifying specific strategies for cutting costs and restructuring the venture.

Exiting the Venture

Getting out of an entrepreneurial venture may seem to be a strange thing for entrepreneurs to do. However, the entrepreneur may decide at some point that it's time to move on. That decision may be based on the fact that the entrepreneur hopes to capitalize financially on the investment in the venture—called **harvesting**—or that the entrepreneur is facing serious organizational performance problems and wants to get out, or even on the entrepreneur's desire to focus on other pursuits (personal or business). The issues involved with exiting the venture include choosing a proper business valuation method and knowing what's involved in the process of selling a business.

harvesting
Exiting a venture when an entrepreneur hopes to capitalize financially on the investment in the venture

BUSINESS VALUATION METHODS   Valuation techniques generally fall into three categories: (1) asset valuations, (2) earnings valuations, and (3) cash flow valuations.[59] Setting a value on a business can be a little tricky. In many cases, the entrepreneur has sacrificed much for the business and sees it as his or her "baby." Calculating the value of the baby based on objective standards such as cash flow or some multiple of net profits can sometimes be a shock. That's why it's important for an entrepreneur who wishes to exit the venture to get a comprehensive business valuation prepared by professionals.

OTHER IMPORTANT CONSIDERATIONS IN EXITING THE VENTURE   Although the hardest part of preparing to exit a venture is valuing it, other factors also should be considered.[60] These factors include being prepared, deciding who will sell the business, considering the tax implications, screening potential buyers, and deciding whether to tell employees before or after the sale. The process of exiting the entrepreneurial venture should be approached as carefully as the process of launching it. If the entrepreneur is selling the venture on a positive note, he or she wants to realize the value built up in the business. If the venture is being exited because of declining performance, the entrepreneur wants to maximize the potential return.

Managing Personal Life Choices and Challenges

Being an entrepreneur is extremely exciting and fulfilling, yet extremely demanding, often with long hours and high stress. Yet, being an entrepreneur can offer a variety of rewards, as well. In this section, we want to look at how entrepreneurs can make it work—that is, how can they be successful and effectively balance the demands of their work and personal lives?[61]

Entrepreneurs are a special group. They are focused, persistent, hardworking, and intelligent. Because they put so much of themselves into launching and growing their entrepreneurial ventures, many may neglect their personal lives. Entrepreneurs often have to make sacrifices to pursue their entrepreneurial dreams. However, they can make it work. They can balance their work and personal lives. But how?

One of the most important things an entrepreneur can do is *become a good time manager.* Prioritize what needs to be done. Use a planner (daily, weekly, monthly) to help schedule priorities. Some entrepreneurs don't like taking the time to plan or prioritize, or they think it's a ridiculous waste of time. Yet identifying the important duties and distinguishing them from those that aren't so important actually makes an entrepreneur more efficient and effective. In addition, part of being a good time manager is delegating those decisions and actions the entrepreneur doesn't have to be personally involved in to trusted employees. Although it may be hard to let go of some of the things they've always done, entrepreneurs who delegate effectively will see their personal productivity levels rise.

Another suggestion for finding that balance is to *seek professional advice* in those areas of business where it's needed. Although entrepreneurs may be reluctant to spend scarce cash, the time, energy, and potential problems saved in the long run are well worth the investment. Competent professional advisers can provide entrepreneurs with information to make more intelligent decisions. Also, it's important to *deal with conflicts* as they arise—both workplace and family conflicts. If an entrepreneur doesn't deal with conflicts, negative feelings are likely to crop up and lead to communication breakdowns. When communication falls apart, vital information may get lost, and people (employees *and* family members) may start to assume the worst. It can turn into a nightmare situation that feeds upon itself. The best strategy is to deal with conflicts as they come up. Talk, discuss, argue (if you must), but an entrepreneur shouldn't avoid the conflict or pretend it doesn't exist.

Another suggestion for achieving that balance between work and personal life is to *develop a network of trusted friends and peers.* Having a group of people to talk with is a good way for an entrepreneur to think through problems and issues. The support and encouragement offered by these people can be an invaluable source of strength for an entrepreneur.

Finally, *recognize when your stress levels are too high.* Entrepreneurs *are* achievers. They like to make things happen. They thrive on working hard. Yet, too much stress can lead to significant physical and emotional problems (as we discussed in Chapter 12). Entrepreneurs have to learn when stress is overwhelming them and to do something about it. After all, what's the point of growing and building a thriving entrepreneurial venture if you're not around to enjoy it?

REVIEW AND DISCUSSION QUESTIONS

1. What do you think would be the hardest thing about being an entrepreneur? What do you think would be the most fun thing?

2. How does the concept of social entrepreneurship (see Chapter 5) relate to entrepreneurs and entrepreneurial ventures?

3. Would a good manager be a good entrepreneur? Discuss.

4. Why do you think many entrepreneurs find it hard to step aside and let others manage their business?

5. Do you think a person can be taught to be an entrepreneur? Why or why not?

6. What do you think it means to be a successful entrepreneurial venture? How about a successful entrepreneur?

Endnotes

CHAPTER 1

1. J. Graham, "Zynga's Office Shows Off Its Wild Side," *USA Today,* March 29, 2012, p. 2B; C. Rose, "Charlie Rose Talks to Zynga CEO Mark Pincus," *Bloomberg BusinessWeek,* March 12–18, 2012, p. 44; "Can Zynga Justify the Hype? Looking Beyond 'Farmville;'" *Wall Street Journal,* January 17, 2012, pp. B1+; M. Helft, "Check Out Zynga's Zany New Offices," *Fortune,* November 7, 2011, pp. 59–60; A. Shahani, "Farmville Makers Putting Stock in Virtual Goods," [www.npr.org], November 6, 2011; S. Raice, "Zynga Devises a New Plan to Break Its Facebook Habit, *Wall Street Journal,* October 12, 2011, p. B1; J. Swartz, "Zynga Goes on a Big Game Blitz," *USA Today,* October 12, 2011, p. 1B; D. Streitfield, "Zynga Releases New Games and a New Platform," *New York Times Online,* October 11, 2011; F. Manjdoo, "The Zynga Conundrum," *Fast Company,* October 2011, p. 54; C. Nuttall, "Zynga IPO Odds Lengthen As Profits Fall," *Financial Times Blog,* September 22, 2011; N. Wingfield, "Virtual Products, Real Profits," *Wall Street Journal,* September 9, 2011, pp. A1+; N. Wingfield, "Zynga Secures $1 Billion Cushion," *Wall Street Journal,* August 12, 2011, p. B4; D. MacMillan and B. Stone, "Zynga's Little-Known Addiction: 'Whales,'" *Bloomberg BusinessWeek,* July 11–July 17, 2011, pp. 37–38; and N. Wingfield and L. Cowan, "Virtual Farms, Rich Harvest," *Wall Street Journal,* July 2–3, 2011, pp. B1+.

2. J. Welch and S. Welch, "An Employee Bill of Rights," *Bloomberg BusinessWeek,* March 16, 2009, p. 72.

3. A. Taylor III, "Survival on Dealers' Row," *CNNMoney.com,* March 26, 2008.

4. E. Frauenheim, "Managers Don't Matter," *Workforce Management Online,* April 2010; and K. A. Tucker and V. Allman, "Don't Be a Cat-and-Mouse Manager," The Gallup Organization [www.brain.gallup.com], September 9, 2004.

5. "Work USA 2008/2009 Report: Driving Business Results through Continuous Engagement," Watson Wyatt Worldwide, Washington, DC.

6. "The New Employment Deal: How Far, How Fast and How Enduring? Insights from the 2010 Global Workforce Study," Towers Watson, Washington, DC.

7. R. R. Hastings, "Study: Supervisors Drive Employee Engagement," *HR Magazine,* August 2011, p. 22.

8. T. R. Holcomb, R. M. Holmes, Jr., and B. L. Connelly, "Making the Most of What You Have: Managerial Ability as a Source of Resource Value Creation," *Strategic Management Journal,* May 2009, pp. 457–485.

9. data points box based on J. Yang and V. Bravo, "Would You Like to Have Your Manager's Job?" *USA Today Snapshots,* November 15, 2011, p. 1B; J. Yang and S. Ward, "Do You Think You Could Do a Better Job Than Your Boss?" *USA Today Snapshots,* November 7, 2011, p. 1B; J. Yang and S. Ward, "Is Working Part Time in a Management Position Possible?" *USA Today Snapshots,* October 11, 2011, p. 1B; R. J. Alsop, "The Last Word: Misery in Your Company," *Workforce Management Online,* August 9, 2011; J. Yang and

K. Geiles, "The 'Horrible Boss' I Had Was..." *USA Today Snapshots,* August 4, 2011, p. 1B; and R. R. Hastings, "Study: Employees' Trust in Leaders Has Declined," *HR Magazine,* September 2011, p. 15.

10. http://www.catalyst.org/publication/271/women-ceos-of-the-fortune-1000, March 2012.

11. D. J. Campbell, "The Proactive Employee: Managing Workplace Initiative," *Academy of Management Executive,* August 2000, pp. 52–66.

12. J. S. McClenahen, "Prairie Home Champion," *Industry Week,* October 2005, pp. 45–47.

13. "Interaction: First, Let's Fire All the Managers," *Harvard Business Review,* March 2012, pp. 20–21; and G. Hamel, "First, Let's Fire All the Managers," *Harvard Business Review,* December 2011, pp. 48–60.

14. Future Vision box based on: Quote attributed to Charles F. Kettering, WikipediaQuote; M. Gladwell, *The Tipping Point* (Little, Brown and Company, 2000); and H. Yen, The Associated Press, "Minorities Making Up Almost Half of Births," *Springfield, Missouri News-Leader,* March 10, 2010, p. 3B.

15. L. I. Alpert, "Majority of Babies Born in America Are Minorities, Census Shows," *NewYorkDailyNews.com,* June 23, 2011.

16. Q. Hardy, "Google Thinks Small," *Forbes,* November 14, 2005, pp. 198–202.

17. P. Panchak, "Sustaining Lean," *Industry Week,* October 2005, pp. 48–50.

18. H. Fayol, *Industrial and General Administration* (Paris: Dunod, 1916).

19. For a comprehensive review of this question, see C. P. Hales, "What Do Managers Do? A Critical Review of the Evidence," *Journal of Management,* January 1986, pp. 88–115.

20. J. T. Straub, "Put on Your Manager's Hat," *USA Today Online* [www.usatoday.com], October 29, 2002; and H. Mintzberg, *The Nature of Managerial Work* (New York: Harper & Row, 1973).

21. E. C. Dierdorff, R. S. Rubin, and F. P. Morgeson, "The Milieu of Managerial Work: An Integrative Framework Linking Work Context to Role Requirements," *Journal of Applied Psychology,* June 2009, pp. 972–988.

22. H. Mintzberg and J. Gosling, "Educating Managers Beyond Borders," *Academy of Management Learning and Education,* September 2002, pp. 64–76.

23. See, for example, M. J. Martinko and W. L. Gardner, "Structured Observation of Managerial Work: A Replication and Synthesis," *Journal of Management Studies,* May 1990, pp. 330–357; A. I. Kraut, P. R. Pedigo, D. D. McKenna, and M. D. Dunnette, "The Role of the Manager: What's Really Important in Different Management Jobs," *Academy of Management Executive,* November 1989, pp. 286–293; and C. M. Pavett and A. W. Lau, "Managerial Work: The Influence of Hierarchical Level and Functional Specialty," *Academy of Management Journal,* March 1983, pp. 170–77.

24. Pavett and Lau, "Managerial Work."
25. "What Managers Really Do," *Wall Street Journal,* August 17, 2009, p. R2; and H. Mintzberg, *Managing* (San Francisco: Berrett Koehler), 2009.
26. S. J. Carroll and D. J. Gillen, "Are the Classical Management Functions Useful in Describing Managerial Work?" *Academy of Management Review,* January 1987, p. 48.
27. "What Do CEOs Admire?" *Fortune,* March 19, 2012, p. 143; N. Kolakowski, "Ursula Burns: Focused on the Core," *eWeek,* February 13, 2012, pp. 10–13; E. McGert, "Fresh Copy," *Fast Company,* December 2011/January 2012, pp. 132–138; and D. Mattioli, "Xerox Chief Looks Beyond Photocopiers Toward Services," *Wall Street Journal,* June 13, 2011, p. B9.
28. E. White, "Firms Step Up Training for Front-Line Managers," *Wall Street Journal,* August 27, 2007, p. B3.
29. See, for example, J. G. Harris, D. W. DeLong, and A. Donnellon, "Do You Have What It Takes to Be an E-Manager?" *Strategy and Leadership,* August 2001, pp. 10–14; C. Fletcher and C. Baldry, "A Study of Individual Differences and Self-Awareness in the Context of Multi-Source Feedback," *Journal of Occupational and Organizational Psychology,* September 2000, pp. 303–319; and R. L. Katz, "Skills of an Effective Administrator," *Harvard Business Review,* September/October 1974, pp. 90–102.
30. K. Fivecoat-Campbell, "Up the Corporate Ladder," *Springfield, Missouri, Business Journal,* March 12–18, 2012, pp. 9+.
31. S. Miller, "Study: Flexible Schedules Reduce Conflict, Lower Turnover," www.shrm.org, April 13, 2011; K. M. Butler, "We Can ROWE Our Way to a Better Work Environment," *EBN.BenefitNews.com,* April 1, 2011, p. 8; P. Moen, E. L. Kelly, and R. Hill, "Does Enhancing Work -Time Control and Flexibility Reduce Turnover? A Naturally Occurring Experiment," *Social Problems,* February 2011, pp. 69-98; and T. J. Erickson, "Task, Not Time: Profile of a Gen Y Job," *Harvard Business Review,* February 2008, p. 19.
32. C. Ansberry, "Firms Map Routes to Recovery," *Wall Street Journal,* March 2, 2010, pp. B1+.
33. F. F. Reichheld, "Lead for Loyalty," *Harvard Business Review,* July/August 2001, Vol. 79(7) p. 76.
34. Cited in E. Naumann and D. W. Jackson, Jr., "One More Time: How Do You Satisfy Customers?" *Business Horizons,* May/June 1999, p. 73.
35. Data from *The World Factbook 2012,* [https://www.cia.gov/library/publications/the-world-factbook/], April 7, 2012.
36. C. B. Blocker, D. J. Flint, M. B. Myers, and S. F. Slater, "Proactive Customer Orientation and Its Role for Creating Customer Value in Global Markets," *Journal of the Academy of Marketing Science,* April 2011, pp. 216–233; D. Dougherty and A. Murthy, "What Service Customers Really Want," *Harvard Business Review,* September 2009, p. 22; and K. A. Eddleston, D. L. Kidder, and B. E. Litzky, "Who's the Boss? Contending With Competing Expectations From Customers and Management," *Academy of Management Executive,* November 2002, pp. 85–95.
37. See, for instance, D. Meinert, "Aim to Serve," *HR Magazine,* December 2011, p. 18; D. M. Mayer, M. G. Ehrhart, and B. Schneider, "Service Attribute Boundary Conditions of the Service Climate-Customer Satisfaction Link," *Academy of Management Journal,* October 2009, pp. 1034–1050; M. Groth, T. Hennig-Thurau, and G. Walsh, "Customer Reactions to Emotional Labor: The Roles of Employee Acting Strategies and Customer Detection Accuracy," *Academy of Management Journal,* October 2009, pp. 958–974; J. W. Grizzle, A. R. Zablah, T. J. Brown, J. C. Mowen, and J. M. Lee, "Employee Customer Orientation in Context: How the Environment Moderates the Influence of Customer Orientation on Performance Outcomes," *Journal of Applied Psychology,* September 2009, pp. 1227–1242; B. A. Gutek, M. Groth, and B. Cherry, "Achieving Service Success Through Relationships and Enhanced Encounters," *Academy of Management Executive,* November 2002, pp. 132–144; Eddleston, Kidder, and Litzky, "Who's the Boss? Contending With Competing Expectations From Customers and Management"; S. D. Pugh, J. Dietz, J. W. Wiley, and S. M. Brooks, "Driving Service Effectiveness Through Employee-Customer Linkages," *Academy of Management Executive,* November 2002, pp. 73–84; S. D. Pugh, "Service With a Smile: Emotional Contagion in the Service Encounter," *Academy of Management Journal,* October 2001, pp. 1018–1027; W. C. Tsai, "Determinants and Consequences of Employee Displayed Positive Emotions," *Journal of Management,* vol. 27, no. 4, 2001, pp. 497–512; Naumann and Jackson, Jr., "One More Time: How Do You Satisfy Customers?"; and M. D. Hartline and O. C. Ferrell, "The Management of Customer-Contact Service Employees: An Empirical Investigation," *Journal of Marketing,* October 1996, pp. 52–70.
38. J. Swartz, "Twitter Helps Customer Service," *USA Today,* November 18, 2009, p. 3B; and J. Swartz, "Businesses Get Cheap Help from a Little Birdie," *USA Today,* June 26, 2009, p. 1B.
39. M. J. Piskorski, "Social Strategies That Work," *Harvard Business Review,* November 2011, pp. 116–122.
40. D. Ferris, "Social Studies: How to Use Social Media to Build a Better Organization," *Workforce Online,* February 12, 2012.
41. R. A. Hattori and J. Wycoff, "Innovation DNA," *Training and Development,* January 2002, p. 24.
42. R. Wagner, "One Store, One Team at Best Buy," *Gallup Brain,* August 12, 2004 [http://brain.gallup.com/content/], November 28, 2005.
43. M. Kripalani, "Tata Taps A Vast R&D Shop—Its Own," *Bloomberg BusinessWeek Magazine,* April 8, 2009, p. 50.
44. S. Rosenbloom, "Wal-Mart Unveils Plan to Make Supply Chain Greener," *New York Times Online,* February 25, 2010.
45. S. Clifford, "Unexpected Ally Helps Wal-Mart Cut Waste," *New York Times Online,* April 13, 2012.
46. KPMG Global Sustainability Services, *Sustainability Insights,* October 2007.
47. *Symposium on Sustainability—Profiles in Leadership,* New York, October 2001.
48. R. E. Silverman, "Where's the Boss? Trapped in a Meeting," *Wall Street Journal,* February 14, 2012, pp. B1+; and J. Sandberg, "Down over Moving Up: Some New Bosses Find They Hate Their Jobs," *Wall Street Journal,* July 27, 2005, p. B1.
49. Silverman, "Where's the Boss? Trapped in a Meeting."
50. M. S. Plakhotnik and T. S. Rocco, "A Succession Plan for First-Time Managers," *T&D,* December 2011, pp. 42-45; P. Brotherton, "New Managers Feeling Lost at Sea," *T&D,* June 2011, p. 25; and "How Do We Help a New Manager Manage?" *Workforce Management Online,* June 16, 2011.

51. S. Y. Todd, K. J. Harris, R. B. Harris, and A. R. Wheeler, "Career Success Implications of Political Skill," *Journal of Social Psychology,* June 2009, pp. 179–204; G. R. Ferris, D. C. Treadway, P. L. Perrewé, R. L. Brouer, C. Douglas, and S. Lux, "Political Skill in Organizations," *Journal of Management,* June 2007, pp. 290–329; K. J. Harris, K. M. Kacmar, S. Zivnuska, and J. D. Shaw, "The Impact of Political Skill on Impression Management Effectiveness," *Journal of Applied Psychology,* January 2007, pp. 278–285; and G. R. Ferris, D. C. Treadway, R. W. Kolodinsky, W. A. Hochwarter, C. J. Kacmar, C. Douglas, and D. D. Frink, "Development and Validation of the Political Skill Inventory," *Journal of Management,* February 2005, pp. 126–152.

52. R. D'Aprix, "A Simple Effective Formula for Leadership," *Strategic Communication Management,* May 2011, p. 14; R. Jaish, "Pieces of Eight," *e-learning age,* May 2011, p. 6; M. L. Stallard, "Google's Project Oxygen: A Case-Study in Connection Culture," [www.humanresourcesiq.com], March 25, 2011; J. Aquino, "8 Traits of Stellar Managers, Defined by Googlers," *Business Insider,* March 15, 2011. Copyright © 2011 by Business Insider, Inc. Reprinted with permission; and A. Bryant, "Google's Quest to Build a Better Boss," *New York Times Online,* March 12, 2011.

53. C. Drew and V. G. Kopytoff, "Deploying New Tools to Stop the Hackers," *New York Times Online,* June 17, 2011; A. Vance, "Have You Seen This Android?" *Bloomberg BusinessWeek,* March 12–March 18, 2012, pp. 37–38; "Are We Winning the Cybersecurity War?" www.networkworld.com, February 13, 2012, pp. 19–20; "Symantec Corporation: Company Profile," *Datamonitor,* February 10, 2012; A. Greenberg, "As Hackers Leak Symantec's Source Code, Firm Says Cops Set Up Extortion Sting Operation," *Forbes.com,* February 7, 2012, p. 8; "Under Siege," *Best's Review,* January 2012, p. 77; E. Savits and A. K. Ghosh, "Cyber Spies Are Winning: Time to Reinvent Online Security," *Forbes.com,* November 18, 2011, p. 3; and "The Virus Hunters," *Management Today,* December 2010, p. 98; S. Kirsner, "Sweating In the Hot Zone" *Fast Company,* October 1, 2005.

MANAGEMENT HISTORY MODULE

1. C. S. George, Jr., *The History of Management Thought,* 2d ed. (Upper Saddle River, NJ: Prentice Hall, 1972), p. 4.

2. Ibid., pp. 35–41.

3. F. W. Taylor, *Principles of Scientific Management* (New York: Harper, 1911), p. 44. For other information on Taylor, see S. Wagner-Tsukamoto, "An Institutional Economic Reconstruction of Scientific Management: On the Lost Theoretical Logic of Taylorism," *Academy of Management Review,* January 2007, pp. 105–117; R. Kanigel, *The One Best Way: Frederick Winslow Taylor and the Enigma of Efficiency* (New York: Viking, 1997); and M. Banta, *Taylored Lives: Narrative Productions in the Age of Taylor, Veblen, and Ford* (Chicago: University of Chicago Press, 1993).

4. See for example, F. B. Gilbreth, *Motion Study* (New York: Van Nostrand, 1911); and F. B. Gilbreth and L. M. Gilbreth, *Fatigue Study* (New York: Sturgis and Walton, 1916).

5. H. Fayol, *Industrial and General Administration* (Paris: Dunod, 1916).

6. M. Weber, *The Theory of Social and Economic Organizations,* ed. T. Parsons, trans. A. M. Henderson and T. Parsons (New York: Free Press, 1947); and M. Lounsbury and E. J.

Carberry, "From King to Court Jester? Weber's Fall from Grace in Organizational Theory," *Organization Studies,* vol. 26, no. 4, 2005, pp. 501–525.

7. E. Mayo, *The Human Problems of an Industrial Civilization* (New York: Macmillan, 1933); and F. J. Roethlisberger and W. J. Dickson, *Management and the Worker* (Cambridge, MA: Harvard University Press, 1939).

8. See, for example, G. W. Yunker, "An Explanation of Positive and Negative Hawthorne Effects: Evidence from the Relay Assembly Test Room and Bank Wiring Observation Room Studies," paper presented, Academy of Management Annual Meeting, August 1993, Atlanta, Georgia; S. R. Jones, "Was There a Hawthorne Effect?" *American Sociological Review,* November 1992, pp. 451–468; and S. R. G. Jones, "Worker Interdependence and Output: The Hawthorne Studies Reevaluated," *American Sociological Review,* April 1990, pp. 176–190; J. A. Sonnenfeld, "Shedding Light on the Hawthorne Studies," *Journal of Occupational Behavior,* April 1985, pp. 111–130; B. Rice, "The Hawthorne Defect: Persistence of a Flawed Theory," *Psychology Today,* February 1982, pp. 70–74; R. H. Franke and J. Kaul, "The Hawthorne Experiments: First Statistical Interpretations," *American Sociological Review,* October 1978, pp. 623–643; and A. Carey, "The Hawthorne Studies: A Radical Criticism," *American Sociological Review,* June 1967, pp. 403–416.

9. N. Zamiska, "Plane Geometry: Scientists Help Speed Boarding of Aircraft," *Wall Street Journal,* November 2, 2005, p. A1+.

10. See, for example, J. Jusko, "Tried and True," *IW,* December 6, 1999, pp. 78–84; T. A. Stewart, "A Conversation with Joseph Juran," *Fortune,* January 11, 1999, pp. 168–170; J. R. Hackman and R. Wageman, "Total Quality Management: Empirical, Conceptual, and Practical Issues," *Administrative Science Quarterly,* June 1995, pp. 309–42; T. C. Powell, "Total Quality Management as Competitive Advantage: A Review and Empirical Study," *Strategic Management Journal,* January 1995, pp. 15–37; R. K. Reger, L. T. Gustafson, S. M. Demarie, and J. V. Mullane, "Reframing the Organization: Why Implementing Total Quality Is Easier Said Than Done," *Academy of Management Review,* July 1994, pp. 565–584; C. A. Reeves and D. A. Bednar, "Defining Quality: Alternatives and Implications," *Academy of Management Review,* July 1994, pp. 419–445; J. W. Dean Jr. and D. E. Bowen, "Management Theory and Total Quality: Improving Research and Practice through Theory Development," *Academy of Management Review,* July 1994, pp. 392–418; B. Krone, "Total Quality Management: An American Odyssey," *The Bureaucrat,* Fall 1990, pp. 35–38; and A. Gabor, *The Man Who Discovered Quality* (New York: Random House, 1990).

11. M. Barbaro, "A Long Line for a Shorter Wait at the Supermarket," *New York Times Online,* June 23, 2007.

12. S. Haines, "Become a Strategic Thinker," *Training,* October/November 2009, p. 64; and K. B. DeGreene, *Sociotechnical Systems: Factors in Analysis, Design, and Management* (Upper Saddle River, NJ: Prentice Hall, 1973), p. 13.

CHAPTER 2

1. The Indian Hotels Company Limited, Hoovers Online [www.hoovers.com], April 27, 2012; "*Interaction,*" *Harvard Business Review,* March 2012, p. 22; R. Deshpandé and A. Raina,

"The Ordinary Heroes of the Taj," *Harvard Business Review*, December 2011, pp. 119–123; M. S. Balakrishnan, "Protecting from Brand Burn During Times of Crisis," *Management Research Review*, vol. 34, no. 12, 2011, pp. 1309–1333; and G. Anand and E. Bellman, "Terror-Shattered Hotels Reopen as Mumbai Returns to Business," *Wall Street Journal*, December 22, 2008, pp. A1+.

2. "Industry & People," *Food Engineering*, November 2011, p. 16; and M. Esterl, "PepsiCo Shakes Up Management," *Wall Street Journal*, September 15, 2011, p. B3.

3. A. Oreskovic and E. Chan, "Yahoo CEO Bartz Fired Over the Phone, Rocky Run Ends," Reuters.com, September 7, 2011; and J. McGregor, "Yahoo CEO Carol Bartz Gets Fired by Phone, Gets Real by Email," WashingtonPost.com, September 7, 2011.

4. P. Rozenzweig, "The Halo Effect and Other Managerial Delusions," *The McKinsey Quarterly Online Journal*, no. 1, March 9, 2007.

5. For insights into the symbolic view, see "Why CEO Churn Is Healthy," *BusinessWeek*, November 13, 2000, p. 230; S. M. Puffer and J. B. Weintrop, "Corporate Performance and CEO Turnover: The Role of Performance Expectations," *Administrative Science Quarterly*, March 1991, pp. 1–19; C. R. Schwenk, "Illusions of Management Control? Effects of Self-Serving Attributions on Resource Commitments and Confidence in Management," *Human Relations*, April 1990, pp. 333–347; J. R. Meindl and S. B. Ehrlich, "The Romance of Leadership and the Evaluation of Organizational Performance," *Academy of Management Journal*, March 1987, pp. 91–109; J. A. Byrne, "The Limits of Power," *BusinessWeek*, October 23, 1987, pp. 33–35; D. C. Hambrick and S. Finkelstein, "Managerial Discretion: A Bridge between Polar Views of Organizational Outcomes," in L. L. Cummings and B. M. Staw (eds.), *Research in Organizational Behavior*, vol. 9 (Greenwich, CT: JAI Press, 1987), pp. 369–406; and J. Pfeffer, "Management as Symbolic Action: The Creation and Maintenance of Organizational Paradigms," in L. L. Cummings and B. M. Staw (eds.), *Research in Organizational Behavior*, vol. 3 (Greenwich, CT: JAI Press, 1981), pp. 1–52.

6. T. M. Hout, "Are Managers Obsolete?" *Harvard Business Review*, March–April 1999, pp. 161–168; and Pfeffer, "Management as Symbolic Action."

7. P. Svensson, "Microsoft Backs B&N In Battle of the e-Books," The Associated Press, *USA Today*, May 1, 2012, p. 3B; J. A. Trachtenberg and M. Peers, "Barnes & Noble Seeks Next Chapter," *Wall Street Journal*, January 6, 2012, pp. A1+; J. Bosman and M. J. De La Merced, "Barnes & Noble Considers Spinning Off Its Nook Unit," IPO Offerings.com, January 5, 2012; M. Maxwell, "Barnes & Noble's Digital Strategy Gaining Traction," *Wall Street Journal*, August 31, 2011, p. B3; J. A. Trachtenberg, S. Schechner, and G. Chon, "B&N Vulnerable to Rivals: Amazon, Apple Loom as Bookseller's Takeover Offer Dies," *Wall Street Journal Online*, August 20, 2011; A. Flood, "Hardback Sales Plummeting in Age of the ebook," *The Guardian*, [www.guardian.co.uk], August 12, 2011; and J. Bosman, "Publishing Gives Hints of Revival, Data Show," *New York Times Online*, August 9, 2011.

8. R. Roberson, "Are High Commodity Prices Here to Stay?" *Southeast Farm Press*, October 5, 2011, pp. 18–20; A. Hanacek, "Deli Processing: Cost Crunch," *National Provisioner*, October 2011, pp. 111–114; and T. Mulier, "Nestlé's Recipe for Juggling Volatile Commodity Costs," *Bloomberg BusinessWeek*, March 21–March 27, 2011, pp. 29–30.

9. D. Das, Gaea News Network, "Men Lost More Jobs than Women Worldwide: Accenture," *Reuters*, March 9, 2010; P. Izzo, "Economists Expect Shifting Work Force," *Wall Street Journal Online*, February 11, 2010; and BBC News, "Recession May See 25m Jobs Lost," *BBC News Online*, September 16, 2009.

10. S. Reddy, M. Walker, and A. Batson, "Factories Revive Economy," *Wall Street Journal*, April 2, 2010, pp. A1+; and S. Shinn, "Banking on Customers," *BizEd*, March/April 2010, pp. 16–21.

11. E. Pfanner, "Economic Troubles Cited as the Top Risks in 2012," *New York Times Online*, January 11, 2012; and E. Pfanner, "Divining the Business and Political Risks of 2012," *New York Times Online*, January 11, 2012.

12. C. Hausman, "Americans See Inequality as a Major Problem," Ethics Newsline [www.globalethics.org/newsline], April 9, 2012.

13. E. Porter, "Inequality Undermines Democracy," *New York Times Online*, March 20, 2012.

14. J. Cox, "Occupy Wall Street: They're Back, But Does Anyone Care?" CNBC.com, April 30, 2012; L. Visconti, "Ask the White Guy: Why Are Disparities in Income Distribution Increasing?" DiversityInc.com, April 10, 2012; P. Meyer, "Income Inequality *Does* Matter," *USA Today*, March 28, 2012, p. 9A; E. Porter, "Inequality Undermines Democracy," *New York Times Online*, March 20, 2012; T. Cowen, "Whatever Happened to Discipline and Hard Work?" *New York Times Online*, November 12, 2011; and A. Davidson, "It's Not Just About the Millionaires," *New York Times Online*, November 9, 2011.

15. A. Zolli, "Demographics: The Population Hourglass," Fast Company, March 2006, pp. 56–63.

16. S. Jayson, "iGeneration Has No Off Switch," *USA Today*, February 10, 2010, pp. 1D+; and L. Rosen, *Rewired: Understanding the iGeneration and the Way They Learn* (Palgrave-McMillan), 2010.

17. B. Horovitz, "Generation Whatchamacallit," *USA Today*, May 4, 2012, p. 1B+.

18. S. Cardwell, "Where Do Babies Come From?" *Newsweek*, October 19, 2009, p. 56.

19. Y. Hori, J-P. Lehmann, T. Ma Kam Wah, and V. Wang, "Facing Up to the Demographic Dilemma," *Strategy & Business Online*, Spring 2010; and E. E. Gordon, "Job Meltdown or Talent Crunch?" *Training*, January 2010, p. 10.

20. P. Izzo, "Economists Expect Shifting Work Force," *Wall Street Journal Online*, February 11, 2010; and J. Lanhart, "Even In a Recovery, Some Jobs Won't Return," *Wall Street Journal*, January 12, 2010, p. A15.

21. S. Jayson, "Recession Has Broad Effects for Ages 18–34," *USA Today*, February 9, 2012, p. 4D; and M. Rich, "For Jobless, Little Hope of Restoring Better Days," *New York Times Online*, December 1, 2011.

22. S. G. Hauser, "Independent Contractors Helping to Shape the New World of Work," Workforce.com, February 3, 2012; H. G. Jackson, "Flexible Workplaces: A Business Imperative," *HRMagazine*, October 2011, p. 10; I. Speitzer, "Contingent Staffing," Workforce.com, October 4, 2011; M. Steen, "More Employers Take on Temps, but Planning Is Paramount," Workforce.com, May 2011; P. Davidson, "More Temp Workers Are Getting Hired," *USA Today*, March 8, 2010, p. 1B; S. Reddy, "Wary Companies Rely on Temporary Workers," *Wall Street Journal*, March 6/7, 2010, p. A4; P. Davidson, "Cuts in

Hours Versus Cuts in Jobs," *USA Today,* February 25, 2010, p. 1B; and S. A. Hewlett, L. Sherbin, and K. Sumberg, "How Gen Y and Boomers Will Reshape Your Agenda," *Harvard Business Review,* July–August, 2009, pp. 71–76.

23. A. Taylor III, "Akio Toyda: Toyota's Comeback Kid," *Fortune,* February 27, 2012, pp. 72–79; J. E. Vascellaro and others, "Twelve Global Executives to Watch in 2012," *Wall Street Journal,* December 29, 2011, pp. B1+; "Steeled by 3 Years of Crises, Toyoda Steers Toward Growth," *Automotive News,* November 14, 2011, p. 18; W. Boccard, M. Francis, B. Powell, and R. Arora, "The Changing Face of Asian Business," *Fortune,* May 2, 2011, pp. 81+; "A New-Model Toyoda Is at Ease in Media Spotlight," *Automotive News,* March 14, 2011, p. 22; and K. Mitra, "Still Apologizing," *Business Today,* January 23, 2011, p. 125.

24. J. P. Walsh, "Book Review Essay: Taking Stock of Stakeholder Management," *Academy of Management Review,* April 2005, pp. 426–438; R. E. Freeman, A. C. Wicks, and B. Parmar, "Stakeholder Theory and 'The Corporate Objective Revisited,'" *Organization Science,* 15, 2004, pp. 364–369; T. Donaldson and L. E. Preston, "The Stakeholder Theory of the Corporation: Concepts, Evidence, and Implications," *Academy of Management Review,* January 1995, pp. 65–91; and R. E. Freeman, *Strategic Management: A Stakeholder Approach* (Boston: Pitman/Ballinger), 1984.

25. J. S. Harrison and C. H. St. John, "Managing and Partnering With External Stakeholders," *Academy of Management Executive,* May 1996, pp. 46–60.

26. S. L. Berman, R. A. Phillips, and A. C. Wicks, "Resource Dependence, Managerial Discretion, and Stakeholder Performance," *Academy of Management Proceedings* Best Conference Paper, August 2005; A. J. Hillman and G. D. Keim, "Shareholder Value, Stakeholder Management, and Social Issues: What's the Bottom Line?" *Strategic Management Journal,* March 2001, pp. 125–139; J. S. Harrison and R. E. Freeman, "Stakeholders, Social Responsibility, and Performance: Empirical Evidence and Theoretical Perspectives," *Academy of Management Journal,* July 1999, pp. 479–487; and J. Kotter and J. Heskett, *Corporate Culture and Performance* (New York: The Free Press, 1992).

27. M. Moskowitz, R. Levering, C. Tkaczyk, C. Keating, A. Konrad, A. Vandermey, and C. Kapelke, "The 100 Best Companies to Work For," *Fortune,* February 6, 2012, pp. 117+; M. Moskowitz, R. Levering, and C. Tkaczyk, "The List," *Fortune,* February 8, 2010, pp. 75–88; E. Ruth, "Gore-Tex Maker Decides It's Time to Demand Some Attention," The Wilmington, DE *News Journal, USA Today,* October 24, 2007, p. 5B; and A. Deutschman, "The Fabric of Creativity," *Fast Company,* December 2004, pp. 54–62.

28. K. Shadur and M. A. Kienzle, "The Relationship Between Organizational Climate and Employee Perceptions of Involvement," *Group & Organization Management,* December 1999, pp. 479–503; M. J. Hatch, "The Dynamics of Organizational Culture," *Academy of Management Review,* October 1993, pp. 657–693; D. R. Denison, "What Is the Difference between Organizational Culture and Organizational Climate? A Native's Point of View on a Decade of Paradigm Wars," paper presented at Academy of Management Annual Meeting, 1993, Atlanta, GA; and L. Smircich, "Concepts of Culture and Organizational Analysis," *Administrative Science Quarterly,* September 1983, p. 339.

29. J. A. Chatman and K. A. Jehn, "Assessing the Relationship between Industry Characteristics and Organizational Culture: How Different Can You Be?" *Academy of Management Journal,* June 1994, pp. 522–553; and C. A. O'Reilly III, J. Chatman, and D. F. Caldwell, "People and Organizational Culture: A Profile Comparison Approach to Assessing Person-Organization Fit," *Academy of Management Journal,* September 1991, pp. 487–516.

30. Y. Berson, S. Oreg, and T. Dvir, "CEO Values, Organizational Culture, and Firm Outcomes," *Journal of Organizational Behavior,* July 2008, pp. 615–633; and E. H. Schien, *Organizational Culture and Leadership* (San Francisco: Jossey-Bass, 1985), pp. 314–315.

31. A. E. M. Va Vianen, "Person-Organization Fit: The Match Between Newcomers' and Recruiters' Preferences for Organizational Cultures," *Personnel Psychology,* Spring 2000, pp. 113–149; K. Shadur and M. A. Kienzle, *Group & Organization Management;* P. Lok and J. Crawford, "The Relationship Between Commitment and Organizational Culture, Subculture, and Leadership Style," *Leadership & Organization Development Journal,* vol. 20, no. 6/7, 1999, pp. 365–374; C. Vandenberghe, "Organizational Culture, Person-Culture Fit, and Turnover: A Replication in the Health Care Industry," *Journal of Organizational Behavior,* March 1999, pp. 175–184; and C. Orphen, "The Effect of Organizational Cultural Norms on the Relationships between Personnel Practices and Employee Commitment," *Journal of Psychology,* September 1993, pp. 577–579.

32. See, for example, J. B. Sorensen, "The Strength of Corporate Culture and the Reliability of Firm Performance," *Administrative Science Quarterly,* 2002, vol. 47, no. 1, pp. 70–91; R. Goffee and G. Jones, "What Holds the Modern Company Together?" *Harvard Business Review,* November–December 1996, pp. 133–148; Collins and Porras, "Building Your Company's Vision," *Harvard Business Review,* September–October 1996, pp. 65–77; J. C. Collins and J. I. Porras, *Built to Last* (New York: HarperBusiness, 1994); G. G. Gordon and N. DiTomaso, "Predicting Corporate Performance from Organizational Culture," *Journal of Management Studies,* November 1992, pp. 793–798; J. P. Kotter and J. L. Heskett, *Corporate Culture and Performance* (New York: Free Press, 1992), pp. 15–27; and D. R. Denison, *Corporate Culture and Organizational Effectiveness* (New York: Wiley, 1990).

33. Sorensen, pp. 70–91; and L. B. Rosenfeld, J. M. Richman, and S. K. May, "Information Adequacy, Job Satisfaction, and Organizational Culture in a Dispersed-Network Organization," *Journal of Applied Communication Research,* vol. 32, 2004, pp. 28–54.

34. C. Edwards, "Why Tech Bows to Best Buy," *BusinessWeek Online,* December 10, 2009.

35. S. E. Ante, "The New Blue," *BusinessWeek,* March 17, 2003, p. 82.

36. C. C. Miller, "Now at Starbucks: A Rebound," *New York Times Online,* January 21, 2010; J. Jargon, "Latest Starbucks Buzzword: 'Lean' Japanese Techniques," *Wall Street Journal,* August 4, 2009, pp. A1+; P. Kafka, "Bean Counter," *Forbes,* February 28, 2005, pp. 78–80; A. Overholt, "Listening to Starbucks," *Fast Company,* July 2004, pp. 50–56; and B. Filipczak, "Trained by Starbucks," *Training,* June 1995, pp. 73–79.

37. P. Guber, "The Four Truths of the Storyteller," *Harvard Business Review,* December 2007, pp. 53–59; S. Denning,

"Telling Tales," *Harvard Business Review*, May 2004, pp. 122–129; T. Terez, "The Business of Storytelling," *Workforce*, May 2002, pp. 22–24; J. Forman, "When Stories Create an Organization's Future," *Strategy & Business*, Second Quarter 1999, pp. 6–9; C. H. Deutsch, "The Parables of Corporate Culture," *New York Times*, October 13, 1991, p. F25; and D. M. Boje, "The Storytelling Organization: A Study of Story Performance in an Office-Supply Firm," *Administrative Science Quarterly*, March 1991, pp. 106–126.

38. G. Colvin, "Value Driven," *Fortune*, November 23, 2009, p. 24.

39. J. Useem, "Jim McNerney Thinks He Can Turn 3M From a Good Company Into a Great One—With a Little Help From His Former Employer, General Electric," *Fortune*, August 12, 2002, pp. 127–132.

40. Denning, 2004; and A. M. Pettigrew, "On Studying Organizational Cultures," *Administrative Science Quarterly*, December 1979, p. 576.

41. J. E. Vascellaro, "Facebook CEO in No Rush to 'Friend' Wall Street," *Wall Street Journal*, March 4, 2010, p. A1+.

42. E. H. Schein, "Organizational Culture," *American Psychologist*, February 1990, pp. 109–119.

43. M. Zagorski, "Here's the Drill," *Fast Company*, February 2001, p. 58.

44. "Slogans That Work," Forbes.com Special, January 7, 2008, p. 99.

45. P. Keegan, "Best Companies to Work For: Maxine Clark and Kip Tindell Exchange Jobs," *Fortune*, February 8, 2010, pp. 68–72.

46. data points box based on R. J. Alsop, "The Last Word: Tapping Social Workers," *Workforce Management*, May 2011, p. 50; R. E. Silverman, "Latest Game Theory Mixes Work and Play," *Wall Street Journal*, October 10, 2011, p. B11; K. E. Ayers, "A Culture of Proactive Employees Will Let the Boss Know if His Fly Is Unzipped," *Workforce Management Online*, August 23, 2011; R. Wartzman, "Executives Are Wrong to Devalue Values," *Bloomberg BusinessWeek Online*, October 30, 2009; J. MacIntyre, "Hurdles to Re-Entry," *Springfield, Missouri Business Journal*, August 16–22, 2010, p. 16; G. Kranz, "Fit to be Tied? Recession May Inspire More Formal Work Attire," *Workforce Management Online*, October 18, 2008; and *Global Firms in 2020* (Economist Intelligence Unit, 2010), [www.shrm.org], July 2, 2011.

47. C. Palmeri, "The Fastest Drill in the West," *BusinessWeek*, October 24, 2005, pp. 86–88.

48. J. Levine, "Dare to Be Boring," *Time*, February 1, 2010, pp. Global Business 1–2.

49. J. Guthrie, "David Kelley of IDEO Raises Level of Design," SFGate.com, October 23, 2011; C. T. Greer, "Innovation 101," WSJ.com, October 17, 2011; "The World's 50 Most Innovative Companies," *Fast Company*, March 2010, p. 90; L. Tischler, "A Designer Takes On His Biggest Challenge," *Fast Company*, February 2009, pp. 78+; T. Kelley and J. Littman, *The Ten Faces of Innovation: IDEO's Strategies for Defeating the Devil's Advocate and Driving Creativity Throughout Your Organization* (New York: Currency, 2005); C. Fredman, "The IDEO Difference," *Hemispheres*, August 2002, pp. 52–57; and T. Kelley and J. Littman, *The Art of Innovation* (New York: Currency, 2001).

50. D. Lyons, "Think Really Different," *Newsweek*, April 5, 2010, pp. 46–51; and R. Brands, "Innovation Made Incarnate," *Bloomberg BusinessWeek Online*, January 11, 2010.

51. J. Yang and R. W. Ahrens, "Culture Spurs Innovation," *USA Today*, February 25, 2008, p. 1B.

52. J. Cable, "Building an Innovative Culture," *Industry Week*, March 2010, pp. 32–37; M. Hawkins, "Create a Climate of Creativity," *Training*, January 2010, p. 12; and L. Simpson, "Fostering Creativity," *Training*, December 2001, p. 56.

53. M. Millstein, "Customer Relationships Make Playing the Odds Easy," *Chain Store Age*, December 2007, p. 22A; and L. Gary, "Simplify and Execute: Words to Live By in Times of Turbulence," *Harvard Management Update*, January 2003, p. 12.

54. Based on J. McGregor, "Customer Service Champs," *BusinessWeek*, March 3, 2008, pp. 37–57; B. Schneider, M. G. Ehrhart, D. M. Mayer, J. L. Saltz, and K. Niles-Jolly, "Understanding Organization-Customer Links in Service Settings," *Academy of Management Journal*, December 2006, pp. 1017–1032; B. A. Gutek, M. Groth, and B. Cherry, "Achieving Service Success Through Relationships and Enhanced Encounters," *Academy of Management Executive*, November 2002, pp. 132–144; K. A. Eddleston, D. L. Kidder, and B. E. Litzky, "Who's the Boss? Contending With Competing Expectations From Customers and Management," *Academy of Management Executive*, November 2002, pp. 85–95; S. D. Pugh, J. Dietz, J. W. Wiley, and S. M. Brooks, "Driving Service Effectiveness Through Employee-Customer Linkages," *Academy of Management Executive*, November 2002, pp. 73–84; L. A. Bettencourt, K. P. Gwinner, and M. L. Mueter, "A Comparison of Attitude, Personality, and Knowledge Predictors of Service-Oriented Organizational Citizenship Behaviors," *Journal of Applied Psychology*, February 2001, pp. 29–41; M. D. Hartline, J. G. Maxham III, and D. O. McKee, "Corridors of Influence in the Dissemination of Customer-Oriented Strategy to Customer Contact Service Employees," *Journal of Marketing*, April 2000, pp. 35–50; L. Lengnick-Hall and C. A. Lengnick-Hall, "Expanding Customer Orientation in the HR Function," *Human Resource Management*, Fall 1999, pp. 201–214; M. D. Hartline and O. C. Ferrell, "The Management of Customer-Contact Service Employees: An Empirical Investigation," *Journal of Marketing*, October 1996, pp. 52–70; and M. J. Bitner, B. H. Booms, and L. A. Mohr, "Critical Service Encounters: The Employee's Viewpoint," *Journal of Marketing*, October 1994, pp. 95–106.

55. R. A. Giacalone and C. L. Jurkiewicz (eds.), *Handbook of Workplace Spirituality and Organizational Performance* (New York: M. E. Sharp, 2003).

56. M. B. Marklein, "Study: College Students Seeking Meaning of Life," USA Today, *Springfield News-Leader*, December 22, 2007, p. 6C.

57. This section is based on L. Lambert III, "God Goes to the Office," *USA Today*, February 8, 2010, p. 7A; B. S. Pawar, "Workplace Spirituality Facilitation: A Comprehensive Model," *Journal of Business Ethics*, December 2009, pp. 375–386; "Faith and Spirituality in the Workplace," *Walton Business Perspective*, Fall 2009, p. 22; B. S. Pawar, "Some of the Recent Organizational Behavior Concepts as Precursors to Workplace Spirituality," *Journal of Business Ethics*, August 2009, pp. 245–261; L. Lambert III, *Spirituality Inc: Religion in the American Workplace*, (New York University Press), 2009; A. Gross-Schaefer, "Reaching for the Stars: Effective Tools for the Creation of a More Spiritual Workplace," *Employee Relations Law Journal*, Summer 2009, pp. 25–42; D. Grant, "What Should a Science of Workplace Spirituality Study? The Case for a Relational Approach," *Academy of Management Proceedings* Best

Paper, August 2005; C. D. Pielstick, "Teaching Spirituality Synchronicity in a Business Leadership Class," *Journal of Management Education*, February 2005, pp. 153–168; H. Ashar and M. Lane-Maher, "Success and Spirituality in the New Business Paradigm," *Journal of Management Inquiry*, June 2004, pp. 249–260; G. A. Gull and J. Doh, "The 'Transmutation' of the Organization: Toward a More Spiritual Workplace," *Journal of Management Inquiry*, June 2004, pp. 128–139; K. C. Cash and G. R. Gray, "A Framework for Accommodating Religion and Spirituality in the Workplace," *Academy of Management Executive*, August 2000, pp. 124–133; F. Wagner-Marsh and J. Conley, "The Fourth Wave: The Spiritually-Based Firm," *Journal of Organizational Change Management*, vol. 12, no. 3, 1999, pp. 292–302; E. H. Burack, "Spirituality in the Workplace," *Journal of Organizational Change Management*, vol. 12, no. 3, 1999, pp. 280–291; J. Milliman, J. Ferguson, D. Trickett, and B. Condemi, "Spirit and Community at Southwest Airlines: An Investigation of a Spiritual Values-Based Model," *Journal of Organizational Change Management*, vol. 12, no. 3, 1999, pp. 221–233; and I. A. Mitroff and E. A. Denton, *A Spiritual Audit of Corporate America: A Hard Look at Spirituality, Religion, and Values in the Workplace* (San Francisco: Jossey-Bass, 1999).

58. J. Reingold, "Walking the Walk," *Fast Company*, November 2005, p. 82.

59. C. H. Liu and P. J. Robertson, "Spirituality in the Workplace: Theory and Measurement," *Journal of Management Inquiry*, March 2011, pp. 35–50.

60. M. Lips-Wiersma, K. L. Dean, and C. J. Fornaciari, "Theorizing the Dark Side of the Workplace Spirituality Movement," *Journal of Management Inquiry*, December 2009, pp. 288–300; P. Paul, "A Holier Holiday Season," *American Demographics*, December 2001, pp. 41–45; and M. Conlin, "Religion in the Workplace: The Growing Presence of Spirituality in Corporate America," *Business Week*, November 1, 1999, pp. 151–158.

61. Cited in M. Conlin, "Religion in the Workplace," p. 153.

62. C. P. Neck and J. F. Milliman, "Thought Self-Leadership: Finding Spiritual Fulfillment in Organizational Life," *Journal of Managerial Psychology*, vol. 9, no. 8, 1994, p. 9.

63. J. Marques, "Toward Greater Consciousness in the 21st Century Workplace: How Buddhist Practices Fit In," *Journal of Business Ethics*, March 2010, pp. 211–225; L. Kim, "Improving the Workplace with Spirituality," *Journal for Quality and Participation*, October 2009, pp. 32–35; M. Stevenson, "Toward a Greater Understanding of Spirit at Work: A Model of Spirit at Work and Outcomes," *Academy of Management Proceedings Online*, August 2009; P. D. Corner, "Workplace Spirituality and Business Ethics: Insights from an Eastern Spiritual Tradition," *Journal of Business Ethics*, March 2009, pp. 377–389; M. L. Lynn, M. J. Naughton, and S. VanderVeen, "Faith at Work Scale (FWS): Justification, Development, and Validation of a Measure of Judaeo-Christian Religion in the Workplace," *Journal of Business Ethics*, March 2009, pp. 227–243; R. W. Kolodinsky, R. A. Giacalone, and C. L. Jurkiewicz, "Workplace Values and Outcomes: Exploring Personal, Organizational, and Interactive Workplace Spirituality," *Journal of Business Ethics*, August 2008, pp. 465–480; and J. Millman, A. Czaplewski, and J. Ferguson, "An Exploratory Empirical Assessment of the Relationship Between Spirituality and Employee Work

Attitudes," paper presented at Academy of Management, Washington, DC, August 2001.

64. M. V. Copeland, "Can the Ski Suit Make the Man (and Woman)?" *Fortune Online*, February 16, 2010; C. Hausman, "New and Old Technologies Keep Officials, Ethicists, Debating Questions of Fairness," *Global Ethics Newsline Online*, February 8, 2010; and S. Sataline, "Some Aging Competitors Call High-Tech Swimsuits Dirty Pool," *Wall Street Journal*, November 3, 2009, pp. A1.

65. Based on C. K. Prahalad, "Best Practices Get You Only So Far," *Harvard Business Review*, April 2010, p. 32; J. R. Oreja-Rodriguez and V. Yanes-Estévez, "Environmental Scanning: Dynamism with Rack and Stack Rasch Model," *Management Decision*, vol. 48, no. 2, 2010, pp. 260–276; C. Heavey, Z. Simsek, F. Roche, and A. Kelly, "Decision Comprehensiveness and Corporate Entrepreneurship: The Moderating Role of Managerial Uncertainty Preferences and Environmental Dynamism," *Journal of Management Studies*, December 2009, pp. 1289–1314; R. Subramanian, N. Fernandes, and E. Harper, "Environmental Scanning in U.S. Companies: Their Nature and Their Relationship to Performance," *Management International Review*, July 1993, pp. 271–286; E. H. Burack and N. J. Mathys, "Environmental Scanning Improves Strategic Planning," *Personnel Administrator*, 1989, pp. 82–87; and L. M. Fuld, *Monitoring the Competition* (New York: Wiley, 1988).

66. M. Moskowitz, R. Levering, C. Tkaczyk, C. Keating, A. Konrad, A. Vandermey, and C. Kapelke, "The 100 Best Companies to Work For," *Fortune*, February 6, 2012, pp. 117+; K. Gurchiek, "Delivering HR at Zappos," *HRMagazine*, June 2011, pp. 44-45; "V. Nayar, "Employee Happiness: Zappos vs. HCL," Businessweek.com, January 5, 2011; D. Richards, "At Zappos, Culture Pays," *Strategy+Business Online*, August 2010; T. Hseih, "Zappos's CEO on Going to Extremes for Customers," *Harvard Business Review*, July–August 2010, pp. 41–45; A. Perschel, "Work-Life Flow: How Individuals, Zappos, and Other Innovative Companies Achieve High Engagement," *Global Business & Organizational Excellence*, July 2010, pp. 17–30; T. Hseih, "Why I Sold Zappos," *Inc.*, June 2010, pp. 100–104; T. Hseih, "Happy Feet," *Newsweek*, June 21, 2010, p. 10; M. Betts, "Zappos Earns No. 1 Ranking for E-retailing," *Computerworld*, June 7, 2010, p. 4; S. Elliott, "Tireless Employees Get Their Tribute, Even if It's in Felt and Polyester," *New York Times Online*, March 4, 2010; C. Palmeri, "Now for Sale, Zappos Culture," *Bloomberg Businessweek*, January 11, 2010, p. 57; E. Frauenheim, "Can Zappos Culture Survive the Amazon Jungle?"; and Zappos, *Culture Book. Workforce Management Online*, September 14, 2009.

67. "U.S. Movie Market Summary 1995 to 2012," www.the-numbers.com/market, January 15, 2012; D. Germain, "Hollywood's 2011: Lower Attendance and Revenue," NorthJersey.com, December 29, 2011; M. Rosenbaum, "Box Office Bust: Movie Attendance Hits 16-Year Low," ABCNews.com, December 28, 2011; M. Cieply, "Charging a Premium for Movies, At a Cost," *New York Times Online*, July 31, 2011; M. Healy and K. Gelles, "Number of Movie Screens in the USA," *USA Today*, May 26, 2011, p. 1D; B. Barnes and M. Cieply, "Graying Audience Returns to Movies," *New York Times Online*, February 25, 2011; L. A. E. Schuker, "Double Feature: Dinner and a Movie," *Wall Street Journal*, January 5, 2011, p. D1+; J. O'Donnell, "Going to the Movies - At Home," *USA Today*, January 5,

2011, p. 3B; M. DeCuir, "Some Food and Alcohol with Your Flick? Cinemas Hope So," *USA Today,* March 27, 2008, p. 3A; B. Barnes, "At Cineplexes, Sports, Opera, Maybe a Movie," *New York Times Online,* March 23, 2008; D. Stuckey and K. Gelles, "Entertainment Sold Online," *USA Today,* February 26, 2008; and J. Carroll, "Americans Dislike the Cost of Going to the Movies," *Gallup News Service,* December 22, 2006.

CHAPTER 3

1. S. Terlep and M. Ramsey, "Ford Bets $5 Billion on Made in China," *Wall Street Journal,* April 20, 2012, pp. B1+; K. Bradsher, "Ford to Build New Plant in China to Bolster Global Sales," *New York Times Online,* April 19, 2012; Ford Motor Company [www.ford.com], March 5, 2012; A. Censky, "Our Love-Hate Relationship with China," CNN. com, February 13, 2012; M. Ramsey, "Ford SUV Marks New World Car Strategy," *Wall Street Journal,* November 16, 2011, pp. B1+; A. Mulally, address at annual shareholders meeting; and "Charlie Rose Talks to Alan Mulally," *Bloomberg BusinessWeek,* August 1–August 7, 2011, p. 27.

2. G. Koretz, "Things Go Better with Multinationals—Except Jobs," *BusinessWeek,* May 2, 1994, p. 20.

3. The idea for this quiz was adapted from R. M. Hodgetts and F. Luthans, *International Management,* 2d ed. (New York: McGraw-Hill, 1994).

4. Reuters Limited, *USA Today Online* [www.usatoday.com], February 21, 2006; D. Graddol, "Indian English Challenge Hurts Bahrain," *The Telegraph* (Calcutta, India), February 22, 2006; and "Learning the Lingo," *USA Today,* January 26, 2006, p. 1A.

5. Ibid.

6. N. Adler, *International Dimensions of Organizational Behavior,* 5th ed. (Cincinnati: South-Western, 2008).

7. M. R. F. Kets De Vries and E. Florent-Treacy, "Global Leadership From A to Z: Creating High Commitment Organizations," *Organizational Dynamics,* Spring 2002, pp. 295–309; P. R. Harris and R. T. Moran, *Managing Cultural Differences,* 4th ed. (Houston: Gulf Publishing Co., 1996); R. T. Moran, P. R. Harris, and W. G. Stripp, *Developing the Global Organization: Strategies for Human Resource Professionals,* (Houston: Gulf Publishing Co., 1993); Y. Wind, S. P. Douglas, and H. V. Perlmutter, "Guidelines for Developing International Marketing Strategies," *Journal of Marketing,* April 1973, pp. 14–23; and H. V. Perlmutter, "The Tortuous Evolution of the Multinational Corporation," *Columbia Journal of World Business,* January–February 1969, pp. 9–18.

8. Leader Who Made a Difference box based on B. Kowitt and R. Arora, "50 Most Powerful Women," *Fortune,* October 17, 2011, pp. 125–130; P. Sellers, "The Queen of Pop," *Fortune,* September 28, 2009, p. 108; M. Egan and others, "The Top 100," *Forbes,* September 7, 2009, pp. 72–76; I. K. Nooyi, "Leading to the Future," *Vital Speeches of the Day,* September 2009, pp. 404–410; B. Einhorn, "Pepsi Chief on Trip to China," *BusinessWeek Online,* July 3, 2009; G. Fairclough and V. Bauerlein, "Pepsi CEO Tours China to Get a Feel for Market," *Wall Street Journal,* July 1, 2009, p. B5; H. Jackson, "America's Best CEOs," *Institutional Investor,* April 2009, pp. 66–70; "Women to Watch: The 50 Women to Watch," *Wall Street Journal,* November 10, 2008, p. R3; B. McKay, "Boss Talk: PepsiCo CEO Adapts to Tough Climate,"

Wall Street Journal, September 11, 2008, p. B1; and H. Schultz, "Indra Nooyi," *Time,* May 12, 2008, pp. 116–117.

9. T. K. Grose, "When in Rome, Do as Roman CEOs Do," *U.S. News & World Report,* November 2009, pp. 38–41.

10. S. Kotkin, "The World as an Imperfect Globe," *New York Times Online,* December 2, 2007.

11. "Panorama of the European Union," http://www.ec.europa. eu/publications/booklets/eu_glance/79/en.pdf, May 30, 2012; and "EU Enlargement: The Next Eight," *BBC News Europe* [www.bbc.co.uk], December 9, 2011.

12. Europa [www.europa.eu/index_en.htm], May 30, 2012.

13. Ibid.

14. Ibid.

15. S. Erlanger and S. Castle, "Growing Economic Crisis Threatens the Idea of One Europe," *New York Times Online,* March 2, 2009.

16. M. Walker and A. Galloni, "Europe's Choice: Growth or Safety Net," *Wall Street Journal,* March 25, 2010, p. A1.

17. J. Kanter and P. Geitner, "E.U. Cautions France and Warns of Challenges in Spain," *New York Times Online,* May 30, 2012.

18. F. Norris, "In Economic Deluge, a World That Can't Bail Together," *New York Times Online,* June 2, 2012; S. Castle, "Future in Mind, E.U. Plans for Less Unanimity," *New York Times Online,* January 1, 2012; M. Walker, C. Forelle, and S. Meichtry, "Deepening Crisis Over Euro Pits Leader Against Leader," *Wall Street Journal,* December 30, 2011, pp. A1+; J. Bhatti and N. Apostolou, "In Europe, Economic Meltdown Tears at Unity," *USA Today,* October 12, 2011, pp. 1A+; D. Melvin, "Will the European Union Survive?" *Springfield, Missouri, News-Leader,* September 29, 2011, p. 4B; D. Macshane, "Europe Agrees to Disagree on Foreign Policy," *Newsweek,* April 12, 2010, p. 6; and C. Forelle and M. Walker, "Europeans Agree on Bailout for Greece," *Wall Street Journal,* March 26, 2010, p. A1.

19. N. Popper, "Europe's Fade Becomes Drag on Sales for U.S. Companies," *New York Times Online,* June 4, 2012; V. Fuhrmans and D. Cimiluca, "Business Braces for Europe's Worst," *Wall Street Journal,* June 1, 2012, pp. B1+; and J. Revill, "Food Makers Rethink Europe," *Wall Street Journal,* May 29, 2012, p. B8.

20. *CIA World Factbook* [www.cia.gov/library/publications/the-world-factbook/], 2012.

21. "Results: North Americans Are Better Off After 15 Years of NAFTA," www.naftanow.org/results/default_en.asp, April 3, 2012.

22. D. Cave, "Better Lives for Mexicans Cut Allure of Going North," *New York Times Online,* July 6, 2011.

23. J. Lyons, "Costa Rica CAFTA Vote Bolsters U.S. Policy," *Wall Street Journal,* October 9, 2007, p. A2.

24. J. Forero, "U.S. and Colombia Reach Trade Deal After 2 Years of Talks," *New York Times Online* [www.nytimes.com], February 28, 2006.

25. "Free Trade Area of the Americas" www.[en.wikipedia.org], April 6, 2010; "Ministerial Declaration," Web site of the Free Trade Area of the Americas [www.ftaa-alca.org], January 23, 2006; and M. Moffett and J. D. McKinnon, "Failed Summit Casts Shadow on Global Trade Talks," *Wall Street Journal,* November 7, 2005, pp. A1+.

26. "ASEAN Stats" [www.aseansec.org], March 15, 2010.

27. J. Hookway, "Asian Nations Push Ideas for Trade," *Wall Street Journal,* October 26, 2009, p. A12; and Bloomberg

News, "Southeast Asian Nations Talk of Economic Union," *New York Times Online,* March 2, 2009.

28. "Asia's Never-Closer Union," *Economist,* February 6, 2010, p. 48; "East Asia Summit: Regional Unity Decades Away," *Business Monitor International* [www.asia-monitor.com], 2009/2010; and "Southeast Asian Nations Talk of Economic Union."

29. "China-ASEAN FTA: Winners and Losers," *China & North East Asia,* February 2010, p. 2.

30. "2009–2012 Strategic Plan," *Commission of the African Union* [www.africa-union.org]; and D. Kraft, "Leaders Question, Praise African Union," *Springfield News-Leader,* July 10, 2002, p. 8A.

31. J. Guo, "Africa Is Booming Like Never Before," *Newsweek,* March 1, 2010, p. 6.

32. "It Really May Happen," *Economist,* January 2, 2010, p. 36; and "Five Into One?" *Business Africa,* December 1, 2009, p. 1.

33. SAARC Official Web site [www.saarc-sec.org]; and N. George, "South Asia Trade Zone in Works," *Springfield News-Leader,* January 4, 2004, p. 1E+.

34. This section is based on materials from the World Trade Organization Web site [www.wto.org]; "What's Up at the WTO?" *Industry Week,* February 2010, p. 20; and D. A. Irwin, "GATT Turns 60," *Wall Street Journal,* April 9, 2007, p. A13.

35. data points box based on M. J. Slaughter and L. D. Tyson, "A Warning Sign from Global Companies," *Harvard Business Review,* March 2012, p. 74; J. Schramm, "Think Globally," *HRMagazine,* June 2011, p. 156; A. R. Carey and V. Salazar, "Speaking a Foreign Language," *USA Today,* October 4, 2010, p. 1A; J. Jargon and J.S. Lublin, "Uprooted Again?" *Wall Street Journal,* September 2, 2011, p. B1; P. Brotherton, "Top Global Leadership Programs Tied to Business Results," *T&D,* August 2011, p. 20; A. R. Carey and S. Ward, "What Are the Most Common Foreign Languages Taught in U.S. Schools?" *USA Today,* February 16, 2010, p. 1A; J. Yang and V. Salazar, "Foreign Relations," *USA Today,* December 5, 2007, p. 1B; D. Stuckey and S. Parker, "Young Americans Staying Home," *USA Today,* August 4, 2006, p. 1A; and J. Yang and K. Simmons, "Global Travel and Career," *USA Today,* November 26, 2008, p. 1B.

36. J. W. Miller and M. Dalton, "WTO Finds EU Aid to Airbus Is Illegal," *Wall Street Journal,* March 24, 2010, p. A10; and C. Drew and N. Clark, "WTO Affirms Ruling of Improper Airbus Aid," *New York Times Online,* March 23, 2010.

37. "Internet Censorship: Showdown at the WTO?" *Bloomberg BusinessWeek,* March 15, 2010, p. 12.

38. 2010 Press Release, "Trade to Expand by 9.5 Percent in 2010 After a Dismal 2009, WTO Reports" [www.wto.org], March 26, 2010.

39. International Monetary Fund Web site [www.imf.org], March 15, 2010.

40. S. Johnson, "Can the I.M.F. Save the World?" *New York Times Online,* September 22, 2011; and Associated Press, "IMF Warns Global Instability Demands Strong Policies," *USA Today,* September 21, 2011, p. 3B.

41. World Bank Group Web site [www.worldbank.org], March 15, 2010.

42. News Release, "World Bank Group: Record US $100 Billion Response Lays Foundation for Recovery from Global Economic Crisis" [www.worldbank.org], April 7, 2010.

43. Organization for Economic Cooperation and Development Web site [www.oecd.org], March 15, 2010.

44. D. Searcey, "Small-Scale Bribes Targeted by OECD," *Wall Street Journal,* December 10, 2009, p. A4.

45. S. Schonhardt, "7-Eleven Finds a Niche by Adapting to Indonesian Ways," *New York Times Online,* May 28, 2012; E. Glazer, "P&G Unit Bids Goodbye to Cincinnati, Hello to Asia," *Wall Street Journal,* May 11, 2012, p. B1; D. Jolly, "Daimler, Nissan, and Renault Unveil Partnership," *New York Times Online,* April 7, 2010; B. Becht, "Building a Company Without Borders," *Harvard Business Review,* April 2010, pp. 103–106; and "Statistical Information" [www.mosers.org], March 15, 2010.

46. C. A. Bartlett and S. Ghoshal, *Managing Across Borders: The Transnational Solution,* 2d ed. (Boston: Harvard Business School Press), 2002; and N. J. Adler, *International Dimensions of Organizational Behavior,* 4th ed. (Cincinnati, OH: South-Western, 2002), pp. 9–11.

47. M. Bustillo, "After Early Errors, Wal-Mart Thinks Locally to Act Globally," *Wall Street Journal,* August 14, 2009, pp. A1+.

48. P. F. Drucker, "The Global Economy and the Nation-State," *Foreign Affairs,* September–October, 1997, pp. 159–171.

49. P. Dvorak, "Why Multiple Headquarters Multiply," *Wall Street Journal,* November 19, 2007, pp. B1+.

50. B. Becht, "Building a Company Without Borders"; D. A. Aaker, *Developing Business Strategies,* 5th ed. (New York: John Wiley & Sons, 1998); and J.A. Byrne et al., "Borderless Management," *BusinessWeek,* May 23, 1994, pp. 24–26.

51. B. Davis, "Migration of Skilled Jobs Abroad Unsettles Global-Economy Fans," *Wall Street Journal,* January 26, 2004, p. A1.

52. J. Teresko, "United Plastics Picks China's Silicon Valley," *Industry Week,* January 2003, p. 58.

53. M. Celarier, "Global Positioning," *CFO,* January/February 2012, pp. 51–55.

54. F. Mutsaka and P. Wonacott, "Mugabe Presses Law Requiring Foreign Entities to Cede Control," *Wall Street Journal,* February 19, 2010, p. A9.

55. D. Roberts, "Closing for Business," *Bloomberg BusinessWeek,* April 5, 2010, pp. 32–37; and A. Browne and J. Dean, "Business Sours on China," *Wall Street Journal,* March 17, 2010, pp. A1+.

56. J. Bush, "Ikea in Russia: Enough Is Enough," *Bloomberg BusinessWeek,* July 13, 2009, p. 33.

57. W. Mauldin, "Russians Search BP Office Second Day," *Wall Street Journal,* September 2, 2011, p. B6; and A. E. Kramer, "Memo to Exxon: Business With Russia Might Involve Guns and Balaclavas," *New York Times Online,* August 31, 2011.

58. Aon Political 2012 Political Risk Map," [www.aon.com], June 12, 2012.

59. Roberts, "Closing for Business"; and Browne and Dean, "Business Sours on China."

60. "Leading Indicator," *Newsweek,* September 14, 2009, p. 14.

61. M. Landler, "Germany's Export-Led Economy Finds Global Niche," *New York Times Online,* April 13, 2007.

62. "Country Comparison: Inflation Rate," *CIA World Factbook* [www.cia.gov/library/publications/the-world-factbook/rankorder/2092rank], 2012.

63. D. M. Airoldi, "Starwood Studies Abroad," *CFO,* September 2011, pp. 29–30; A. Sheivachman, "Starwood Puts Priority on Chinese Development," *Hotel Management,* August 1, 2011, p. 15; and A. Berzon, "Frits Van Paasschen: Starwood CEO Moves to China to Grow Brand," *Wall Street Journal,* June 6, 2011, p. B6.

64. J. McGregor and S. Hamm, "Managing the Global Workforce," *Bloomberg BusinessWeek,* January 28, 2008, pp. 34–51.

65. These examples taken from L. Khosla, "You Say Tomato," *Forbes,* May 21, 2001, p. 36; and T. Raphael, "Savvy Companies Build Bonds with Hispanic Employees," *Workforce,* September 2001, p. 19.

66. See G. Hofstede, *Culture's Consequences: International Differences in Work-Related Values,* 2d ed. (Thousand Oaks, CA: Sage Publications, 2001), pp. 9–15.

67. S. Bhaskaran and N. Sukumaran, "National Culture, Business Culture and Management Practices: Consequential Relationships?" *Cross Cultural Management: An International Journal,* vol. 14, no. 7, 2007, pp. 54–67; G. Hofstede, *Culture's Consequences;* and G. Hofstede, "The Cultural Relativity of Organizational Practices and Theories," *Journal of International Business Studies,* Fall 1983, pp. 75–89.

68. M. Minkov and G. Hofstede, "The Evolution of Hofstede's Doctrine," *Cross Cultural Management,* February 2011, pp. 10–20.

69. R. R. McCrae, A. Terracciano, A. Realo, and J. Allik, "Interpreting GLOBE Societal Practices Scale," *Journal of Cross-Cultural Psychology,* November 2008, pp. 805–810; J. S. Chhokar, F. C. Brodbeck, and R. J. House, *Culture and Leadership Across the World: The GLOBE Book of In-Depth Studies of 25 Societies,* (Philadelphia: Lawrence Erlbaum Associates), 2007; and R. J. House, P. J. Hanges, M. Javidan, P. W. Dorfman, and V. Gupta, *Culture, Leadership, and Organizations: The GLOBE Study of 62 Societies* (Thousand Oaks, CA: Sage Publications), 2004.

70. For instance, see D. A. Waldman, M. S. de Luque, and D. Wang, "What Can We Really Learn About Management Practices Across Firms and Countries?" *Academy of Management Perspectives,* February 2012, pp. 34–40; A. E. Munley, "Culture Differences in Leadership," *IUP Journal of Soft Skills,* March 2011, pp. 16–30; and R. J. House, N. R. Quigley, and M. S. deLuque, "Insights from Project GLOBE: Extending Advertising Research Through a Contemporary Framework," *International Journal of Advertising,* 29, no. 1 (2010), pp. 111–139.

71. D. Yergin, "Globalization Opens Door to New Dangers," *USA Today,* May 28, 2003, p. 11A; K. Lowrey Miller, "Is It Globaloney?" *Newsweek,* December 16, 2002, pp. E4–E8; L. Gomes, "Globalization Is Now a Two-Way Street—Good News for the U.S.," *Wall Street Journal,* December 9, 2002, p. B1; J. Kurlantzick and J. T. Allen, "The Trouble With Globalism," *U.S. News and World Report,* February 11, 2002, pp. 38–41; and J. Guyon, "The American Way," *Fortune,* November 26, 2001, pp. 114–120.

72. Guyon, "The American Way," p. 114.

73. H. Seligson, "For American Workers in China, a Culture Clash," *New York Times Online,* December 23, 2009.

74. G. N. Powell, A. M. Francesco, and Y. Ling, "Toward Culture-Sensitive Theories of the Work-Family Interface," *Journal of Organizational Behavior,* July 2009, pp. 597–616.

75. J. S. Lublin, "Cultural Flexibility in Demand," *Wall Street Journal,* April 11, 2011, pp. B1+; S. Russwurm, L. Hernández, S. Chambers, and K. Chung, "Developing Your Global Know-How," *Harvard Business Review,* March 2011, pp. 70–75; "Are You Cued in to Cultural Intelligence?" *Industry Week,* November 2009, p. 24; M. Blasco, "Cultural Pragmatists? Student Perspectives on Learning Culture at a Business School," *Academy of Management Learning & Education,* June 2009, pp. 174–187; and D. C. Thomas and K. Inkson, "Cultural Intelligence: People Skills for a Global Workplace," *Consulting to Management,* vol. 16, no. 1, pp. 5–9.

76. M. Javidan, M. Teagarden, and D. Bowen, "Making It Overseas," *Harvard Business Review,* April 2010, pp. 109–113.

77. S. Deffree, "Foxconn Explosion Ignites Conversation on Corporate Responsibility," *EDN,* June 23, 2011, p. 8; J. Bussey, "Measuring the Human Cost of an iPad Made in China," *Wall Street Journal,* June 3, 2011, pp. B1+; A. Satariano, "Apple Risks iPad Production Loss of 500,000 After Blast," *Bloomberg BusinessWeek,* May 26, 2011; and E. Savitz, "Apple: Analysts See Limited Risks From Hon Hai Plant Explosion," *Forbes.com,* May 23, 2011, p. 4.

78. S. Clifford, "Bribery Case at Wal-Mart May Widen," *New York Times Online,* May 17, 2012; S. Clifford, "Pension Plan Sues Wal-Mart Officials Over Failures," *New York Times Online,* May 3, 2012; E. Lichtblau, "Wal-Mart's Good-Citizen Efforts Face a Test," *New York Times Online,* April 30, 2012; S. Clifford and S. Greenhouse, "Wal-Mart's U.S. Expansion Plans Complicated by Bribery Scandal," *New York Times Online,* April 29, 2012; "Walmart's Mexican Morass," The Economist.com, April 28, 2012; A. Hartung, "WalMart's Mexican Bribery Scandal Will Sink It Like an Iceberg Sank the Titanic," Forbes.com, April 26, 2012; D. Brady, "Wal-Mart, Avon Execs Should Stop Hiding Behind Boards," *Bloomberg BusinessWeek Online,* April 25, 2012; C. Savage, "With Wal-Mart Claims, Greater Attention on a Law," *New York Times Online,* April 25, 2012; D. Barstow, "Wal-Mart Hushed Up a Vast Mexican Bribery Case," *New York Times Online,* April 21, 2012; L. Wayne, "Hits, and Misses, in a War on Bribery," *New York Times Online,* March 10, 2012; A. Strom, "Web Sites Shine Light on Petty Bribery Worldwide," *New York Times Online,"* March 6, 2012; M. Bustillo and J. Palazzolo, "Wal-Mart Discloses A Corruption Probe," *Wall Street Journal,* December 9, 2011, p. B2; J. Katz, "Schooled by Scandals," *Industry Week,* April 2011, pp. 34–36; and "FCPA: History," PBS.org, February 2009.

79. "Nomura Falls Out of Love with Lehman Dream Team," *Euroweek,* January 13, 2012, p. 108; A. House and K. Johnson, "Delivering Integrated Global Training," *Chief Learning Officer,* December 2011, pp. 68–72; A. Tudor, "Bhattal's Goal; Keep Lehman Talent," *Wall Street Journal,* April 19, 2010, p. C5; A. Tudor, "Lehman Defections Continue at Nomura," *Wall Street Journal,* March 23, 2010, p. C5; A. Tudor, "Nomura Turns to a Foreigner from Lehman," *Wall Street Journal,* March 18, 2010, p. C1; A. Or, "More Quit Nomura as Bonuses Lapse," *Wall Street Journal,* March 12, 2010, p. C2; A. Rozens, "The Return of Nomura," *Investment Dealers' Digest,* February 12, 2010, p. 1+; "Nomura Set for Fight on All Fronts," *Euroweek,* December 4, 2009, p. 49; L. Peacock, untitled, *Personnel Today,* November 10, 2009, p. 25; and A. Tudor, "Nomura Stumbles in New Global Push," *Wall Street Journal,* July 29, 2009, pp. A1+.

CHAPTER 4

1. "Global Diversity: Our Strategy Framework," Coca-Cola Web site, May 25, 2012; "The 2012 DiversityInc Top 10 Companies for Blacks," *DiversityInc.com,* April 24, 2012; J. J. Sapolek, "Coca-Cola Division Refreshes Its Talent With Diversity Push on Campus," *Workforce Management Online,* March 24, 2011; J. Lewis Jr., "The Ground Up," *Inside Counsel,* August 2010, p. 10; R. Hastings, "Diversity Speakers Encourage Innovation, Global Mindset," *HR Magazine,* January 2009, p. 85; J. Wiscombe, "Corporate America's Scariest Opponent," *Workforce,* April 2003, pp. 34–39; D. Maharaj, "Coca-Cola to

Settle Racial Bias Lawsuit" *Los Angeles Times,* November 17, 2000; "Coca-Cola's 2010 U.S. Diversity Stewardship Report," May 2011; and B. McKay, "Coca-Cola Concedes Its Diversity Efforts Have Been Slow, Says It Will Do Better," *Wall Street Journal,* February 10, 2000, p. A11.

2. J. S. Lublin and K. Eggers, "More Women Are Primed to Land CEO Roles," *Wall Street Journal,* April 30, 2012, pp. B1+; http://www.catalyst.org/publication/271/women-ceos-of-the-fortune-1000, March 2012; N. M. Carter and C. Silva, "Pipeline's Broken Promise," *Catalyst* [www.catalyst.org], 2010, p. 1; and "Women in Management in the United States, 1950–Present," *Catalyst* [www.catalyst.org], April, 2010.

3. S. Caminiti, "The Diversity Factor," *Fortune,* October 19, 2007, pp. 95–105; and B. Velez, "People and Places," *DiversityInc Online* [www.diversityinc.com], October 2006.

4. R. Anand and M. Frances Winters, "A Retrospective View of Corporate Diversity Training from 1964 to the Present," *Academy of Management Learning & Education,* September 2008, pp. 356–372.

5. State Farm [www.statefarm.com/aboutus/diversity/workplace/definition.asp], June 5, 2012.

6. Society for Human Resource Management [www.shrm.org], April 14, 2010.

7. M. L. Wheeler, "Diversity: Business Rationale and Strategies," The Conference Board, Report No. 1130-95-RR, 1995, p. 14.

8. S. P. Robbins and P. L. Hunsaker, *Training in Interpersonal Skills: TIPS for Managing People at Work* (Upper Saddle River, NJ: Pearson Prentice Hall, 2009), p. 285.

9. This section is based on S. P. Robbins and T. A. Judge, *Organizational Behavior,* 15th ed. (Upper Saddle River, NJ: Pearson Prentice Hall, 2013), p. 42.

10. "The 2012 DiversityInc Top 50 Companies for Diversity," *DiversityInc.com,* April 24, 2012; and "Top 50 Companies for Diversity," *Diversity Inc.,* May/June 2009, p. 42.

11. J. Rosenthal, "Strength in Diversity—Large Corporations Find Working with Minority-Owned Firms Is Good Business," *Workforce Management Online,* February 2010.

12. A. Joshi and H. Roh, "The Role of Context in Work Team Diversity Research: A Meta-Analytic Review," *Academy of Management Journal,* June 2009, pp. 599–627.

13. M. Bello, USA Today, "Controversy Shrouds Scarves," *Springfield, Missouri News-Leader,* April 17, 2010, p. 8A.

14. "All Statutes: FY 1997–FY2011," U. S. Equal Employment Opportunity Commission, [www.1.eeoc.gov/eeoc/statistics/enforcement/all], March 6, 2012; and "Charges Filed with EEOC Hit Record High in Fiscal 2011," [www.shrm.org], November 17, 2011.

15. D. Gilgoff, "Investing in Diversity," *U.S. News & World Report,* November 2009, pp. 72–74.

16. E. B. King, J. F. Dawson, M. A. West, V. I. Gilrane, C. I. Peddie, and L. Bastin, "Why Organizational and Community Diversity Matter: Representativeness and the Emergence of Incivility and Organizational Performance," *Academy of Management Journal,* December 2011, pp. 1103–1118.

17. Ernst & Young, "The New Global Mindset: Driving Innovation Through Diversity," EYGM Limited, 2010, p. 1.

18. Ibid.

19. C. Dougherty and M. Jordan, "Minority Births Are New Majority," *Wall Street Journal,* May 17, 2012, p. A4; and S. Tavernise, "Whites Account for Under Half of Births in U.S.," *New York Times Online,* May 17, 2012.

20. H. El Nasser and P. Overberg, "1990–2010: How America Changed," *USA Today,* August 10, 2011, pp. 1A+; and D. Meinert, "Census Data Reflect Older, More Diverse U.S. Workforce," *HR Magazine,* July 2011, pp. 18–19.

21. Information in this section from: H. El Nasser, "U.S. Hispanic Population to Triple by 2050," *USA Today Online* [www.usatoday.com], February 12, 2008; "U.S. Population Projections: 2005–2050," Pew Research Center [www.pewhispanic.org/reports/)], February 11, 2008; U.S. Department of Labor, The Bureau of Labor Statistics, "Report of the Taskforce on the Aging of the American Workforce" [www.bls.gov], 2008; and L. B. Shrestha, "The Changing Demographic Profile of the United States," *Congressional Research Service/The Library of Congress,* May 5, 2006.

22. CIA *World Factbook* [www.cia.gov/library/publications/the-world-factbook/], 2012.

23. "The Changing Demographic Profile of the United States," p. CRS-16.

24. L. Visconti, "The Business Case for Diversity," *DiversityInc Online* [www.diversityinc.com], July/August 2009.

25. "Report of the Taskforce on the Aging of the American Workforce."

26. S. Roberts, "Census Finds Rise in Foreign Workers," *New York Times Online,* December 8, 2009.

27. J. Preston, "Immigrants in Work Force: Study Belies Image," *New York Times Online,* April 15, 2010.

28. Ernst & Young, "The New Global Mindset: Driving Innovation Through Diversity."

29. Y. Hori, J.-P. Lehmann, T. Ma Kam Wah, and V. Wang, "Facing Up to the Demographic Dilemma," *Strategy + Business Online,* Issue 58 [www.strategy-business.com/article], Spring 2010.

30. Information in this section from "Facing Up to the Demographic Dilemma," International Data Base Information Gateway, U.S. Census Bureau [www.census.gov/ipc/www/idb/worldpopgraph.php], December 2009; K. Kinsella and W. He, "An Aging World: 2008," U.S. Census Bureau/International Population Reports, June 2009; and J. Hookway, "Affirmative Action Spurs Asian Debate," *Wall Street Journal,* July 8, 2009, pp. A1+.

31. "World POPClock Projection," U.S. Census Bureau [www.census.gov/population/popclockworld.html], July 1, 2012. (The number on this page is automatically updated daily.)

32. Hori, Lehmann, and Wah, "Facing Up to the Demographic Dilemma."

33. Kinsella and He, "An Aging World: 2008."

34. K. Gurchiek, "Options for Older Workers," *HR Magazine,* June 2012, p. 18.

35. Material in this section adapted from Robbins and Judge, *Organizational Behavior,* 15th ed., p. 44.

36. L. Wolgemuth, "How to Stand Out from the Crowd and Kick-Start Your Own Recovery," *U.S. News & World Report,* May 2010, pp. 14–16.

37. F. Norris, "The Number of Those Working Past 65 Is at a Record High," *New York Times Online,* May 18, 2012.

38. P. Kujawa, "Older Workers Exercising Plans to Delay Retirement," *Workforce Management Online,* July 5, 2011.

39. R. B. Williams, "Generation Y Poised to Dominate the Workplace" [network.nationalpost.com/np/blogs], June 13, 2009.

40. "Most Common Gen Y Job Titles Today," *T&D,* April 2012, p. 23; and P. Ketter, "Value Proposition? Oh, Yes!" *T&D,* November 2011, p. 10.

41. S. G. Hauser, "The Women's Movement in the '70s, Today: 'You've Come A Long Way,' But..." *Workforce Management Online,* June 4, 2012; and N. Gibbs, "What Women Want Now," *Time,* October 26, 2009, pp. 24–33.

42. H. Hartmann, A. Hegewisch, H. Liepmann, and C. Williams, "Fact Sheet: The Gender Wage Gap: 2009," *Institute for Women's Policy Research* [www.iwpr.org], March 2010.

43. C. Rampell, "Young Women are More Career-Driven than Men," New York Times Online, April 19, 2012.

44. P. Korkki, "For Women, Parity Is Still a Subtly Steep Climb," New York Times Online, October 8, 2011; and The Associated Press, "Women with Degrees Equal Men," *Springfield, Missouri News-Leader,* April 21, 2010, p. 4B.

45. N. M. Carter and C. Silva, "Women in Management: Delusions of Progress," *Harvard Business Review,* March 2010, pp. 19–21.

46. Material in this section adapted from Robbins and Judge, *Organizational Behavior,* 14th ed., pp. 45–46.

47. G. N. Powell, D. A. Butterfield, and J. D. Parent, "Gender and Managerial Stereotypes: Have the Times Changed?" *Journal of Management,* vol. 28 (2), 2002, pp. 177–193.

48. "Women Leaders: The Hard Truth About Soft Skills," *Bloomberg BusinessWeek Online,* February 16, 2010; and A. Bryant, "No Doubts: Women Are Better Managers," New York Times Online, July 26, 2009.

49. "Women Leaders: The Hard Truth About Soft Skills."

50. Lublin and Eggers, "More Women Are Primed to Land CEO Roles."

51. A. M. Carton and A. S. Rosette, "Explaining Bias Against Black Leaders: Integrating Theory on Information Processing and Goal-Based Stereotyping," *Academy of Management Journal,* December 2011, pp. 1141–1156; and "I Didn't Get the Job Because I'm Black," *DiversityInc.,* [diversityinc.com/legal-issues/didnt-get-job/], June 2011.

52. H. El Nasser, "Multiracial No Longer Boxed In By the Census," *USA Today,* March 3, 2010, pp. 1A+.

53. Ibid.

54. Material in this section adapted from Robbins and Judge, *Organizational Behavior,* 14th ed., p. 47.

55. J. L. S. Wittmer, "Take a Walk in Our Shoes," *T&D,* November 2011, pp. 57–59.

56. D. Meinert, "Opening Doors," *HR Magazine,* June 2012, pp. 55–57.

57. U.S. Department of Labor/Office of Disability Employment Policy, "Survey of Employer Perspectives on the Employment of People with Disabilities" [www.dol.gov/odep/documents/survey_report_jan_09.doc], November 2008.

58. A. Merrick, "Erasing 'Un' From 'Unemployable'; Walgreen Program Trains the Disabled to Take on Regular Wage-Paying Jobs," *Wall Street Journal,* August 2, 2007, pp. B1+.

59. M. Bello, "Controversy Shrouds Muslim Women's Head Coverings" *USA Today,* April 15, 2010.

60. Daily Mail Reporter, "Muslim Woman Wins $5 Million in Discrimination Lawsuit Against AT&T For 'Harassment From Her Co-Workers Because of Her Religion,'" Daily Mail Online, May 5, 2012.

61. Material in this section adapted from Robbins and Judge, *Organizational Behavior,* 15th ed., pp. 50–51; S. Greenhouse, "Muslims Report Rising Discrimination at Work," New York Times Online, September 23, 2010; and S. Ghumman and L. Jackson, "The Downside of Religious Attire: The Muslim Headscarf and Expectations of Obtaining Employment," *Journal of Organizational Behavior,* January 2010, pp. 4–23.

62. "Facts & Figures: Number of Religious Discrimination Complaints Received," *Diversity Inc.* November/December 2009, p. 52.

63. "Religion-Based Charges," *U.S. Equal Opportunity Employment Commission,* [www.eeoc.gov/eeoc/statistics/enforcement/religion.cfm], June 10, 2012.

64. P. Wang and J. L. Schwartz, "Stock Price Reactions to GLBT Nondiscrimination Policies," *Human Resource Management,* March–April 2010, pp. 195–216.

65. S. A. Hewlett and K. Sumberg, "For LGBT Workers, Being 'Out' Brings Advantages," *Harvard Business Review,* July-August 2011, p. 28.

66. L. Sullivan, "Sexual Orientation—The Last 'Acceptable' Bias," *Canadian HR Reporter,* December 20, 2004, pp. 9–11.

67. S. A. Hewlett and K. Sumberg, "For LGBT Workers, Being 'Out' Brings Advantages."

68. F. Colgan, T. Wright, C. Creegan, and A. McKearney, "Equality and Diversity in the Public Services: Moving Forward on Lesbian, Gay and Bisexual Equality?" *Human Resource Management Journal,* vol. 19, no. 3, 2009, pp. 280–301.

69. J. Hempel, "Coming Out in Corporate America," *BusinessWeek,* December 15, 2003, pp. 64–72.

70. S. A. Hewlett and K. Sumberg, "For LGBT Workers, Being 'Out' Brings Advantages."

71. Material in this section adapted from Robbins and Judge, *Organizational Behavior,* 15th ed., pp. 51–52.

72. "Domestic-Partner Perks Most Likely to Come from Large Companies," *HRFocus,* June 2009, p. 12.

73. data points box based on K. Piombino, "Infographic: Gen Y Women Have the Most Positive Attitude at Work," *Ragan Communications,* [www.ragan.com], March 12, 2012; "Are You Ready to Commit?" *Wall Street Journal,* May 7, 2012, p. B9; "Facts & Figures," *DiversityInc.,* Summer 2011, p. 30; A. Tugend, "Bridging the Workplace Generation Gap: It Starts with a Text," New York Times Online, November 7, 2009; J. MacIntyre, "Minority Viewpoints at Work," *Springfield Business Journal,* August 10–16, 2009, p. 15; and J. Yang and K. Simmons, "Diversity and Reality," *USA Today,* August 25, 2008, p. 1B.

74. B. Leonard, "Transgender Issues Test Diversity Limits," *HRMagazine,* June 2007, pp. 32–34.

75. S. A. Hewlett and K. Sumberg, "For LGBT Workers, Being 'Out' Brings Advantages."

76. Wang and Schwartz, "Stock Price Reactions to GLBT Nondiscrimination Policies."

77. L. Eaton, "Black Workers' Complaints Advance," *Wall Street Journal,* April 16, 2010, p. B4.

78. Robbins and Judge, *Organizational Behavior,* 15th ed., p. 42.

79. N. Rigoglioso, "Steering the No. 1 Company for Diversity: 5 Minutes with Rohini Anand," Diversitywoman.com, February 6, 2012; "Sodexo," *DiversityInc,* Summer 2011, p. 34; "Case Study No. 1: Sodexo," *DiversityInc,* Early Fall 2011, pp. 48-50; DiversityInc Staff, "Sodexo's Rohini Anand: Breaking Gender Barriers and Creating Change," *DiversityInc,* June 7, 2010; and "Rohini Anand: Leading Sodexho's Commitment to a Globally Diverse Workforce," *Nation's Restaurant News,* February 10, 2003, p. 24.

80. Catalyst, "Workforce Metrics: Level of First Position," Workforce Management Online [www.workforce.com], April 8, 2010.

81. J. M. Hoobler, S. J. Wayne, and G. Lemmon, "Bosses' Perceptions of Family-Work Conflict and Women's Promotability: Glass Ceiling Effects," *Academy of Management Journal,* October 2009, pp. 939–957.

82. C. Hymowitz and T. D. Schellhardt, "The Glass Ceiling," *Wall Street Journal: A Special Report—The Corporate Woman,* March 24, 1986, pp. D1+.

83. Hoobler, Wayne, and Lemmon, "Bosses' Perceptions of Family-Work Conflict and Women's Promotability: Glass Ceiling Effects."

84. "Top 50 Companies for Diversity: Marriott International," *DiversityInc,* April 24, 2012.

85. K. A. Cañas and H. Sondak, *Opportunities and Challenges of Workplace Diversity,* 2nd ed. (Upper Saddle River, NJ: Pearson Prentice Hall, 2011), p. 26.

86. "Leaders Create Sustainable Approaches to Diversity," *DiversityInc.,* February 2010, p. 20.

87. K. E. O'Brien, A. Biga, S. R. Kessler, and T. D. Allen, "A Meta-Analytic Investigation of Gender Differences in Mentoring," *Journal of Management,* March 2010, pp. 537–554.

88. D. Jones, "Often, Men See Women to the Top," *USA Today,* August 5, 2009, pp. 1B+.

89. J. Prime and C. A. Moss-Racusin, "Engaging Men in Gender Initiatives: What Change Agents Need to Know," *Catalyst* [www.catalyst.org], 2009.

90. L. Visconti, "Diversity Is Not in Your DNA, Says White Guy," *DiversityInc Online* [www.diversityinc.com], March 3, 2010.

91. K. L. Allers, "Won't It Be Grand When We Don't Need Diversity Lists?" *Fortune,* August 22, 2005, p. 101.

92. Press release, "Sodexho Named 2010 Straight for Equality in Business Award Winner," *DiversityInc Online* [www.diversityinc.com], April 9, 2010.

93. Kellogg Company, "Our Commitment to Diversity" [www.kelloggcompany.com], April 22, 2010.

94. P. Brotherton, "Employee Resource Groups Still Going Strong," *T&D,* August 2011, p. 25; B. Frankel, "Are Employee-Resource Groups Still Relevant?" *DiversityInc,* Spring 2011, p. 12; and B. Frankel, Editor's Letter, "The *Most* Critical Diversity Initiative," *DiversityInc.,* September/ October 2009, p. 12.

95. Based on P. L. Hunsaker, *Training in Management Skills* (Upper Saddle River, NJ: Prentice Hall, 2009); C. Harvey and J. Allard, *Understanding and Managing Diversity: Readings, Cases, and Exercises,* 3rd ed. (Upper Saddle River, NJ: Prentice Hall, 2005); and J. Greenberg, *Managing Behavior in Organizations: Science in Service to Practice,* 2nd ed. (Upper Saddle River, NJ: Prentice Hall, 1999).

96. "No. 1: PricewaterhouseCoopers," *DiversityInc Online,* April 24, 2012; L. Kwor, "Firms Hail Chiefs (of Diversity)," *Wall Street Journal,* January 5, 2012, p. B10; S. Ali, "PWC Chairman Bob Moritz Makes Diversity Personal," *DiversityInc,* Fall 2011, pp. 42–43; "PwC Tops Global Ranking of Firms," *Accountancy,* November 2011, p. 10.

97. K. Gurchiek, "The Global Battle for Female Talent," *HRMagazine,* June 2012, pp. 48–52; T. Sattleberger, "HR Report 2010/2011: Facts and Figures," Deutsche Telekom [www.e-paper.telekom.com/hr-report-2010-2011/epaper/ HR2010_11_eng.pdf], June 2012; N. Clark, "Deutsche Telekom Struggles With Gender Goal," *New York Times Online,* October 2, 2011;

98. K. Bennhold, "Women Nudged Out of German Workforce," *New York Times Online,* June 28, 2011; L. Stevens and J. Espinoza, "Deutsche Telekom Sets Women-Manager Quota," Wall Street Journal Online, March 22, 2010; J. Blaue, "Deutsche Telekom Launches Quota for Top Women Managers" [www.german-info.com/business_shownews]; N. Clark, "Goal at Deutsche Telekom: More Women as Managers," New York Times Online, March 15, 2010; R. Foroohar and S. H. Greenberg, "Working Women Are Poised to Become the Biggest Economic Engine the World Has Ever Known," *Newsweek,* November 2, 2009, pp. B2–B5; News Release, "Women Still Hold Less Than a Quarter of Senior Management Positions in Privately Held Businesses," *Grant Thornton International* [www.gti.org], March 5, 2009; and Catalyst Research Report, "Different Cultures, Similar Perceptions: Stereotyping of Western European Business Leaders" *Catalyst* [www.catalyst.org], 2006.

CHAPTER 5

1. A. Fredin, "The Unexpected Cost of Staying Silent," *Strategic Finance,* April 2012, pp. 53–59; D. Meinert, "Whistle-Blowers: Threat or Asset?" *HR Magazine,* April 2011, pp. 27–32; S. Moffett, "Renault's No. 2 Executive Quits: Pelata to Take Lesser Post at Nissan Alliance as He, Others Absorb Blame for Bogus Espionage Debacle," *WallStreet Journal,* April 12, 2011, p. B1; J. Reed and J. Thompson, "Renault's Pélata to Go Over Spy Scandal," *Financial Times Online,* April 11, 2011; B. Crumley, "An Apology and a New Suspect in the Renault Spying Debacle," *Time.com,* March 16, 2011; S. Moffett, "France Criticizes Renault," *Wall Street Journal,* March 16, 2011, p. B3; D. Gauthier-Villars, "Police Probe if Renault Was Victim of Fraud in Spy Case," *Wall Street Journal,* March 14, 2011, p. B1; A. Jones and J. S. Lublin," Firms Revisit Whistleblowing," *Wall Street Journal,* March 14, 2011, p. B5; "Renault Security Held inSpy Case," *Wall Street Journal Online,* March 11, 2011; M. Saltmarsh, "Doubt Cast on Renault Spying Charges," *New York Times Online,* March 4, 2011; S. Moffett, "Ghosn: Spy Risks Were Too Big to Ignore," *Wall Street Journal,* February 11, 2011, p. B8; S. Moffett, "Renault Manager Sues Firm," *Wall Street Journal,* January 19, 2011, p. B3; D. Jolly, "Renault Espionage Gained No Key Secrets, Official Says," *New York Times Online,* January 8, 2011; and D. Pearson, "Renault Probes Ethics Complaint," *Wall Street Journal,* January 6, 2011, p. B3.

2. M. L. Barnett, "Stakeholder Influence Capacity and the Variability of Financial Returns to Corporate Social Responsibility," *Academy of Management Review,* July 2007, pp. 794–816; A. Mackey, T. B. Mackey, and J. B. Barney, "Corporate Social Responsibility and Firm Performance: Investor Preferences and Corporate Strategies," *Academy of Management Review,* July 2007, pp. 817–835; and A. B. Carroll, "A Three-Dimensional Conceptual Model of Corporate Performance," *Academy of Management Review,* October 1979, p. 499.

3. See K. Basu and G. Palazzo, "Corporate Social Performance: A Process Model of Sensemaking," *Academy of Management Review,* January 2008, pp. 122–136; and S. P. Sethi, "A Conceptual Framework for Environmental Analysis of Social Issues and Evaluation of Business Response Patterns," *Academy of Management Review,* January 1979, pp. 68–74.

4. M. Friedman, *Capitalism and Freedom* (Chicago: University of Chicago Press, 1962); and Friedman, "The Social Responsibility of Business Is to Increase Profits," *New York Times Magazine,* September 13, 1970, p. 33.

5. V. Vermaelen, "An Innovative Approach to Funding CSR Projects," *Harvard Business Review,* June 2011, p. 28; S. Strom, "To Be Good Citizens, Report Says companies Should Just Focus on Bottom Line," *New York Times Online,* June 14, 2011; and A. Karnani, "The Case Against Social Responsibility," *Wall Street Journal,* August 23, 2010, pp. R1+.

6. S. Lohr, "First, Make Money. Also, Do Good," *New York Times Online,* August 13, 2011; and S. Liebs, "Do Companies Do Good Well?" *CFO,* July 2007, p. 16.

7. See, for example, D. J. Wood, "Corporate Social Performance Revisited," *Academy of Management Review*, October 1991, pp. 703–708; and S. L. Wartick and P. L. Cochran, "The Evolution of the Corporate Social Performance Model, *Academy of Management Review,* October 1985, p. 763.

8. N. Bunkley, "Ford Backs Ban on Text Messaging by Drivers," *New York Times Online,* September 11, 2009.

9. B. X. Chen, "Tech Companies Respond to Japan Quake With Resources, Support," *wired.com,* March 15, 2011; and J. O'Donnell, "UPS Workers Head to Haiti to Provide Help," *USA Today,* January 25, 2010, p. 4B.

10. See, for example, R. A. Buchholz, *Essentials of Public Policy for Management,* 2d ed. (Upper Saddle River, NJ: Prentice Hall, 1990).

11. I. Brat, "The Extra Step," *Wall Street Journal,* March 24, 2008, p. R12.

12. Wal-Mart [www.walmartstores.com], March 16, 2006; and an advertisement from *USA Today,* March 6, 2006, p. 5A.

13. This section is based on J. D. Margolis and J. P. Walsh, "Misery Loves Companies: Rethinking Social Initiatives by Business," *Administrative Science Quarterly,* vol. 48, no. 2, 2003, pp. 268–305; K. Davis and W. C. Frederick, *Business and Society: Management, Public Policy, Ethics,* 5th ed. (New York: McGraw-Hill, 1984), pp. 28–41; and R. J. Monsen Jr., "The Social Attitudes of Management," in J. M. McGuire (ed.), *Contemporary Management: Issues and Views* (Upper Saddle River, NJ: Prentice Hall, 1974), p. 616.

14. See, for instance, J. Surroca, J. A. Tribo, and S. Waddock, "Corporate Responsibility and Financial Performance: The Role of Intangible Resources," *Strategic Management Journal,* May 2010, pp. 463–490; R. Garcia-Castro, M. A. Ariño, and M. A. Canela, "Does Social Performance Really Lead to Financial Performance? Accounting for Endogeneity," *Journal of Business Ethics,* March 2010, pp. 107–126; J. Peloza, "The Challenge of Measuring Financial Impacts from Investments in Corporate Social Performance," *Journal of Management,* December 2009, pp. 1518–1541; J. D. Margolis and H. Anger Elfenbein, "Do Well by Doing Good? Don't Count on It," *Harvard Business Review,* January 2008, pp. 19–20; M. L. Barnett, "Stakeholder Influence Capacity and the Variability of Financial Returns to Corporate Social Responsibility," 2007; D. O. Neubaum and S. A. Zahra, "Institutional Ownership and Corporate Social Performance: The Moderating Effects of Investment Horizon, Activism, and Coordination," *Journal of Management,* February 2006, pp. 108–131; B. A. Waddock and S. B. Graves, "The Corporate Social Performance–Financial Performance Link," *Strategic Management Journal,* April 1997, pp. 303–319; J. B. McGuire, A. Sundgren, and T. Schneeweis, "Corporate Social Responsibility and Firm Financial Performance," *Academy of Management Journal,* December 1988, pp. 854–872; K. Aupperle, A. B. Carroll, and J. D. Hatfield, "An Empirical Examination of the Relationship Between Corporate Social Responsibility and Profitability," *Academy of Management Journal,* June 1985, pp. 446–463; and P. Cochran and R. A. Wood, "Corporate Social Responsibility and Financial Performance," *Academy of Management Journal,* March 1984, pp. 42–56.

15. Peloza, "The Challenge of Measuring Financial Impacts from Investments in Corporate Social Performance."

16. B. Seifert, S. A. Morris, and B. R. Bartkus, "Having, Giving, and Getting: Slack Resources, Corporate Philanthropy, and Firm Financial Performance," *Business & Society,* June 2004, pp. 135–161; and McGuire, Sundgren, and Schneeweis, "Corporate Social Responsibility and Firm Financial Performance."

17. A. McWilliams and D. Siegel, "Corporate Social Responsibility and Financial Performance: Correlation or Misspecification?" *Strategic Management Journal,* June 2000, pp. 603–609.

18. A. J. Hillman and G. D. Keim, "Shareholder Value, Stakeholder Management, and Social Issues: What's the Bottom Line?" *Strategic Management Journal,* vol. 22, 2001, pp. 125–139.

19. M. Orlitzky, F. L. Schmidt, and S. L. Rynes, "Corporate Social and Financial Performance," *Organization Studies,* vol. 24, no. 3, 2003, pp. 403–441.

20. R. Kapadia, "Blind Faith," *SmartMoney,* February 2011, pp. 72-76; and A. Hughey and P. Villareal, "Socially Responsible Investing," *National Center for Policy Analysis* [www.ncpa.org/pdfs/ba657.pdf], May 11, 2009.

21. Social Investment Forum, "Socially Responsible Mutual Fund Charts: Financial Performance" [www.socialinvest.org/resources/performance.cfm], April 28, 2010.

22. A. Salkever, "Why Are Coke Drinkers Smiling? Vending Machines to Be More Eco-Friendly," *Daily Finance Online* [www.dailyfinance.com], December 3, 2009.

23. "Hive Mentality," *Body + Soul,* December 2009, p. 26.

24. "The Total Package," *Bloomberg BusinessWeek,* March 19 - March 25, 2012, p. 6.

25. D. A. Lubin and D. C. Esty, "The Sustainability Imperative," *Harvard Business Review,* May 2010, pp. 42–50; J. Pfeffer, "Building Sustainable Organizations: The Human Factor," *Academy of Management Perspectives,* February 2010, pp.34–45; R. Nidumolu, C. K. Prahalad, and M. R. Rangaswami, "Why Sustainability Is Now the Key Driver of Innovation," *Harvard Business Review,* September 2009, pp. 56–64; A. A. Marcus and A. R. Fremeth, "Green Management Matters Regardless," *Academy of Management Perspectives,* August 2009, pp. 17–27; D. S. Siegel, "Green Management Matters Only If It Yields More Green: An Economic/Strategic Perspective," *Academy of Management Perspectives,* August 2009, pp. 5–16; and A. White, "The Greening of the Balance Sheet," *Harvard Business Review,* March 2006, pp. 27–28.

26. The concept of shades of green can be found in R. E. Freeman, J. Pierce, and R. Dodd, *Shades of Green: Business Ethics and the Environment* (New York: Oxford University Press, 1995).

27. Leader Who Made a Difference box based on One Percent for the Planet, http://www.onepercentfortheplanet.org/en/, June 12, 2012; S. Stevenson, "Patagonia's Founder Is America's Most Unlikely Business Guru," *Wall Street Journal Magazine,* May 2012; "Responsible Company," *Wall Street Journal Online,* April 25, 2012; T. Henneman, "Patagonia Fills Payroll With People Who Are Passionate,"

Workforce Management Online, November 4, 2011; M. J. Ybarra, "Book Review: The Fun Hog Expedition Revisited," *Wall Street Journal,* February 19, 2010, p. W8; K. Garber, "Not in the Business of Hurting the Planet," *US News & World Report,* November 2009, p. 63; and T. Foster, "No Such Thing As Sustainability," *Fast Company,* July/August 2009, pp. 46–48.

28. The Global 100 list is a collaborative effort of Corporate Knights Inc. and Innovest Strategic Value Advisors. Information from Global 100 Web site [www.global100.org], January 25, 2012.

29. C. Hausman, "Financial News Focuses on Questions of Ethics," *Ethics Newsline* [www.globalethics.org/newsline], April 20, 2010; C. Hausman, "Privacy Issues Prominent in Week's Tech News," *Ethics Newsline* [www.globalethics.org/newsline], March 9, 2010; and H. Maurer and C. Lindblad, "Madoff Gets the Max," *Bloomberg BusinessWeek,* July 13 & 20, 2009, p. 6.

30. This last example is based on J. F. Viega, T. D. Golden, and K. Dechant, "Why Managers Bend Company Rules," *Academy of Management Executive,* May 2004, pp. 84–90.

31. K. Davis and W. C. Frederick, *Business and Society,* p. 76.

32. F. D. Sturdivant, *Business and Society: A Managerial Approach,* 3rd ed. (Homewood, IL: Richard D. Irwin, 1985), p. 128.

33. L. K. Treviño, G. R. Weaver, and S. J. Reynolds, "Behavioral Ethics in Organizations: A Review," *Journal of Management,* December 2006, pp. 951–990; T. Kelley, "To Do Right or Just to Be Legal," *New York Times,* February 8, 1998, p. BU12; J. W. Graham, "Leadership, Moral Development, and Citizenship Behavior," *Business Ethics Quarterly,* January 1995, pp. 43–54; L. Kohlberg, *Essays in Moral Development: The Psychology of Moral Development,* vol. 2 (New York: Harper & Row, 1984); and L. Kohlberg, *Essays in Moral Development: The Philosophy of Moral Development,* vol. 1 (New York: Harper & Row, 1981).

34. See, for example, J. Weber, "Managers' Moral Reasoning: Assessing Their Responses to Three Moral Dilemmas," *Human Relations,* July 1990, pp. 687–702.

35. W. C. Frederick and J. Weber, "The Value of Corporate Managers and Their Critics: An Empirical Description and Normative Implications," in W. C. Frederick and L. E. Preston (eds.) *Business Ethics: Research Issues and Empirical Studies* (Greenwich, CT: JAI Press, 1990), pp. 123–144; and J. H. Barnett and M. J. Karson, "Personal Values and Business Decisions: An Exploratory Investigation," *Journal of Business Ethics,* July 1987, pp. 371–382.

36. M. E. Baehr, J. W. Jones, and A. J. Nerad, "Psychological Correlates of Business Ethics Orientation in Executives," *Journal of Business and Psychology,* Spring 1993, pp. 291–308; and L. K. Treviño and S. A. Youngblood, "Bad Apples in Bad Barrels: A Causal Analysis of Ethical Decision-Making Behavior," *Journal of Applied Psychology,* August 1990, pp. 378–385.

37. M. E. Schweitzer, L. Ordonez, and B. Douma, "Goal Setting as a Motivator of Unethical Behavior," *Academy of Management Journal,* June 2004, pp. 422–432.

38. M. C. Jensen, "Corporate Budgeting is Broken—Let's Fix It," *Harvard Business Review,* June 2001, pp. 94–101.

39. R. L. Cardy and T. T. Selvarajan, "Assessing Ethical Behavior Revisited: The Impact of Outcomes on Judgment Bias," paper presented at the Annual Meeting of the Academy of Management, Toronto, 2000.

40. M. H. Bazerman and A. E. Tenbrunsel, "Ethical Breakdowns," *Harvard Business Review,* April 2011, pp. 58–65.

41. M. C. Gentile, "Keeping Your Colleagues Honest," *Harvard Business Review,* March 2010, pp. 114–117; J. R. Edwards and D. M. Cable, "The Value of Value Congruence," *Journal of Applied Psychology,* May 2009, pp. 654–677; G. Weaver, "Ethics and Employees: Making the Connection," *Academy of Management Executive,* May 2004, pp. 121–125; V. Anand, B. E. Ashforth, and M. Joshi, "Business as Usual: The Acceptance and Perpetuation of Corruption in Organizations," *Academy of Management Executive,* May 2004, pp. 39–53; J. Weber, L. B. Kurke, and D. W. Pentico, "Why Do Employees Steal?" *Business & Society,* September 2003, pp. 359–380; V. Arnold and J. C. Lampe, "Understanding the Factors Underlying Ethical Organizations: Enabling Continuous Ethical Improvement," *Journal of Applied Business Research,* Summer 1999, pp. 1–19.

42. data points box based on J. Yang and A. Gonzalez, "Do You Feel Guilty Calling In Sick When You Aren't?" *USA Today,* June 14, 2012, p. 1B; M. Heller, "Ethics Group Warns of 'Steep Declines' in Workforce Trust," *Workforce Management Online,* March 20, 2012; S. Bates, "Surge Predicted in Workplace Ethical Lapses," *HR Magazine,* March 2012, p. 11; J. Yang and P. Trap, "If Granted Access to Confidential Document Accidently, I'd…" *USA Today,* September 13, 2010, p. 1B; and R. R. Hastings," Study: Employees' Trust in Leaders Has Decline," *HR Magazine,* September 2011, p. 15.

43. P. Van Lee, L. Fabish, and N. McCaw, "The Value of Corporate Values," *Strategy & Business,* Summer 2005, pp. 52–65.

44. F. O. Walumba and J. Schaubroeck, "Leader Personality Traits and Employee Voice Behavior: Mediating Roles of Ethical Leadership and Work Group Psychological Safety," *Journal of Applied Psychology,* September 2009, pp. 1275–1286; G. Weaver, "Ethics and Employees: Making the Connection," May 2004; G. Weaver, L. K. Treviño, and P. L. Cochran, "Integrated and Decoupled Corporate Social Performance: Management Commitments, External Pressures, and Corporate Ethics Practices," *Academy of Management Journal,* October 1999, pp. 539–552; G. R. Weaver, L. K. Treviño, and P. L. Cochran, "Corporate Ethics Programs as Control Systems: Influences of Executive Commitment and Environmental Factors," *Academy of Management Journal,* February 1999, pp. 41–57; R. B. Morgan, "Self- and Co-Worker Perceptions of Ethics and Their Relationships to Leadership and Salary," *Academy of Management Journal,* February 1993, pp. 200–214; and B. Z. Posner and W. H. Schmidt, "Values and the American Manager: An Update," *California Management Review,* Spring 1984, pp. 202–216.

45. IBM Corporate Responsibility Report, 2007 [www.ibm.com]; and A. Schultz, "Integrating IBM," *CRO,* March/April 2007, pp. 16–21.

46. T. Barnett, "Dimensions of Moral Intensity and Ethical Decision Making: An Empirical Study," *Journal of Applied Social Psychology,* May 2001, pp. 1038–1057; and T. M. Jones, "Ethical Decision Making by Individuals in Organizations: An Issue-Contingent Model," *Academy of Management Review,* April 1991, pp. 366–395.

47. W. Bailey and A. Spicer, "When Does National Identity Matter? Convergence and Divergence in International Business Ethics," *Academy of Management Journal,* December 2007, pp. 1462–1480; and R. L. Sims, "Comparing Ethical Attitudes Across Cultures," *Cross Cultural Management: An International Journal,* vol. 13, no. 2, 2006, pp. 101–113.

48. BBC News Online, "Legal Review of Overseas Bribery," November 29, 2007.

49. C. Hausman, "British Defense Giant BAE Must Hire Ethics Monitor and Pay Huge Penalties Under Corruption Settlement," *Ethics Newsline* [www.globalethics.org], February 15, 2010.

50. M. Koehler, "2011 DOF Enforcement of the FCPA—Year in Review," www.corporatecomplianceinsights.com, January 12, 2012.

51. L. Paine, R. Deshpande, J. D. Margolis, and K. E. Bettcher, "Up to Code: Does Your Company's Conduct Meet World-Class Standards?" *Harvard Business Review,* December 2005, pp. 122–133; G. R. Simpson, "Global Heavyweights Vow 'Zero Tolerance' for Bribes," *Wall Street Journal,* January 27, 2005, pp. A2+; A. Spicer, T. W. Dunfee, and W. J. Bailey, "Does National Context Matter in Ethical Decision Making? An Empirical Test of Integrative Social Contracts Theory," *Academy of Management Journal,* August 2004, pp. 610–620; J. White and S. Taft, "Frameworks for Teaching and Learning Business Ethics Within the Global Context: Background of Ethical Theories," *Journal of Management Education,* August 2004, pp. 463–477; J. Guyon, "CEOs on Managing Globally," *Fortune,* July 26, 2004, p. 169; A. B. Carroll, "Managing Ethically with Global Stakeholders: A Present and Future Challenge," *Academy of Management Executive,* May 2004, pp. 114–120; and C. J. Robertson and W. F. Crittenden, "Mapping Moral Philosophies: Strategic Implications for Multinational Firms," *Strategic Management Journal,* April 2003, pp. 385–392.

52. United Nations Global Compact [www.unglobalcompact.org/AboutTheGC/index.html], June 10, 2012.

53. Organization for Economic Cooperation and Development, "About Bribery in International Business" [www.oecd.org], April 30, 2010.

54. R. M. Kidder, "Can Disobedience Save Wall Street?" *Ethics Newsline* [www.globalethics.org], May 3, 2010.

55. Enron example taken from P. M. Lencioni, "Make Your Values Mean Something," *Harvard Business Review,* July 2002, p. 113; and Sears example taken from series of posters called "Sears Ethics and Business Practices: A Century of Tradition," in *Business Ethics,* May/June 1999, pp. 12–13; and B. J. Feder, "The Harder Side of Sears," *New York Times,* July 20, 1997, pp. BU1+.

56. B. Roberts, "Your Cheating Heart," *HR Magazine,* June 2011, pp. 55–60.

57. J. R. Edwards and D. M. Cable, "The Value of Value Congruence," *Journal of Applied Psychology,* May 2009, pp. 654–677; and Treviño and Youngblood, "Bad Apples in Bad Barrels," p. 384.

58. K. Bart, "UBS Lays Out Employee Ethics Code," *Wall Street Journal Online* [online.wsj.com], January 12, 2010; J. L. Lunsford, "Transformer in Transition," *Wall Street Journal,* May 17, 2007, pp. B1+; and J. S. McClenahen, "UTC's Master of Principle," *Industry Week,* January 2003, pp. 30–36.

59. M. Weinstein, "Survey Says: Ethics Training Works," *Training,* November 2005, p. 15.

60. J. E. Fleming, "Codes of Ethics for Global Corporations," *Academy of Management News,* June 2005, p. 4.

61. "Corporate Codes of Ethics Spread," *Ethics Newsline* [www.globalethics.org], October 12, 2009; "Global Ethics Codes Gain Importance As a Tool to Avoid Litigation and Fines," *Wall Street Journal,* August 19, 1999, p. A1; and J. Alexander, "On the Right Side," *World Business,* January/February 1997, pp. 38–41.

62. F. R. David, "An Empirical Study of Codes of Business Ethics: A Strategic Perspective," paper presented at the 48th Annual Academy of Management Conference; Anaheim, California, August 1988.

63. National Business Ethics Survey 2011, *Ethics Resource Center* [www.ethics.org], March, 2012.

64. J. B. Singh, "Determinants of the Effectiveness of Corporate Codes of Ethics: An Empirical Study," *Journal of Business Ethics,* July 2011, pp. 385–395; P. M. Erwin, "Corporate Codes of Conduct: The Effects of Code Content and Quality on Ethical Performance," *Journal of Business Ethics,* April 2011, pp. 535–548; "Codes of Conduct," Center for Ethical Business Cultures [www.cebcglobal.org], February 15, 2006; L. Paine, R. Deshpande, J. D. Margolis, and K. E. Bettcher, "Up to Code: Does Your Company's Conduct Meet World-Class Standards"; and A. K. Reichert and M. S. Webb, "Corporate Support for Ethical and Environmental Policies: A Financial Management Perspective," *Journal of Business Ethics,* May 2000.

65. D. Jones, "CEO's Moral Compass Steers Siemens," *USA Today,* February 15, 2010, p. 3B.

66. V. Wessler, "Integrity and Clogged Plumbing," *Straight to the Point,* newsletter of VisionPoint Corporation, Fall 2002, pp. 1–2.

67. T. A. Gavin, "Ethics Education," *Internal Auditor*, April 1989, pp. 54–57.

68. L. Myyry and K. Helkama, "The Role of Value Priorities and Professional Ethics Training in Moral Sensitivity," *Journal of Moral Education,* 2002, vol. 31, no. 1, pp. 35–50; W. Penn and B. D. Collier, "Current Research in Moral Development as a Decision Support System," *Journal of Business Ethics,* January 1985, pp. 131–136.

69. J. A. Byrne, "After Enron: The Ideal Corporation," *Business Week,* August 19, 2002, pp. 68–71; D. Rice and C. Dreilinger, "Rights and Wrongs of Ethics Training," *Training & Development Journal,* May 1990, pp. 103–109; and J. Weber, "Measuring the Impact of Teaching Ethics to Future Managers: A Review, Assessment, and Recommendations," *Journal of Business Ethics*, April 1990, pp. 182–190.

70. E. White, "What Would You Do? Ethics Courses Get Context," *Wall Street Journal,* June 12, 2006, p. B3; and D. Zielinski, "The Right Direction: Can Ethics Training Save Your Company," *Training,* June 2005, pp. 27–32.

71. G. Farrell and J. O'Donnell, "Ethics Training As Taught by Ex-Cons: Crime Doesn't Pay," *USA Today,* November 16, 2005, p. 1B+.

72. J. Weber, "The New Ethics Enforcers," *Business Week,* February 13, 2006, pp. 76–77.

73. The Ethics and Compliance Officer Association [www.theecoa.org], April 30, 2010; and K. Maher, "Global Companies Face Reality of Instituting Ethics Programs," *Wall Street Journal,* November 9, 2004, p. B8.

74. "Survey Reveals How Many Workers Commit Office Taboos," *Ethics Newsline* [www.globalethics.org], September 18, 2007.

75. C. Hausman, "Men Are Less Ethical than Women, Claims Researcher," *Ethics Newsline,* www.globaletehics.org/newsline, June 25, 2012; and C. May, "When Men Are Less Moral Than Women," *Scientific American.com,* June 19, 2012.

76. H. Oh, "Biz Majors Get an F for Honesty," *Business Week,* February 6, 2006, p. 14.

77. "Students Aren't Squealers," *USA Today,* March 27, 2003, p. 1D; and J. Merritt, "You Mean Cheating Is Wrong?" *Business Week,* December 9, 2002, p. 8.

78. J. Hyatt, "Unethical Behavior: Largely Unreported in Offices and Justified by Teens," *The CRO Online,* February 13, 2008.

79. D. Lidsky, "Transparency: It's Not Just for Shrink Wrap Anymore," *Fast Company,* January 2005, p. 87.

80. D. M. Mayer, K. Aquino, R. L. Greenbaum, and M. Kuenze, "Who Displays Ethical Leadership, and Why Does It Matter? An Examination of Antecedents and Consequences of Ethical Leadership," *Academy of Management Journal,* February 2012, pp. 151-171; and F. O. Walumbwa, D. M. Mayer, P. Wang, H. Wang, K. Workman, and A. L. Christensen, "Linking Ethical Leadership to Employee Performance: The Roles of Leader-Member Exchange, Self-Efficacy, and Organizational Identification," *Organizational Behavior & Human Decision Processes,* July 2011, pp. 204–213.

81. W. Zellner, "A Hero—and a Smoking-Gun Letter," *Business Week,* January 28, 2002, pp. 34–35.

82. National Business Ethics Survey, Ethics Resource Center (Arlington, VA), 2007.

83. S. Armour, "More Companies Urge Workers to Blow the Whistle," *USA Today,* December 16, 2002, p. 1B.

84. J. Wiscombe, "Don't Fear Whistleblowers," *Workforce,* July 2002, pp. 26–27.

85. T. Reason, "Whistle Blowers: The Untouchables," *CFO,* March 2003, p. 18; and C. Lachnit, "Muting the Whistle-Blower?" *Workforce,* September 2002, p. 18.

86. J. Hyatt, "Corporate Whistleblowers Might Need a Monetary Nudge, Researchers Suggest," *CRO Newsletter Online,* April 11, 2007; J. O'Donnell, "Blowing the Whistle Can Lead to Harsh Aftermath, Despite Law"; *USA Today,* August 1, 2005, p. 2B; and D. Solomon, "For Financial Whistle-Blowers, New Shield Is An Imperfect One," *Wall Street Journal,* October 4, 2004, pp. A1+.

87. A. Smith, "Bottled Up," *Time,* August 14, 2009, p. Global 6.

88. This definition based on P. Tracey and N. Phillips, "The Distinctive Challenge of Educating Social Entrepreneurs: A Postscript and Rejoinder to the Special Issue on Entrepreneurship Education," *Academy of Management Learning & Education,* June 2007, pp. 264–271; Schwab Foundation for Social Entrepreneurship [www.schwabfound.org], February 20, 2006; and J. G. Dees, J. Emerson, and P. Economy, *Strategic Tools for Social Entrepreneurs* (New York: John Wiley & Sons, Inc.), 2002.

89. P. Margulies, "Linda Rottenberg's High-Impact Endeavor," *Strategy + Business Online,* Spring 2012; S. Moran, "Some Ways to Get Started as a Social Entrepreneur," *New York Times Online,* June 22, 2011; P. A. Dacin, M. T. Dacin, and M. Matear, "Social Entrepreneurship: Why We Don't Need a New Theory and How We Move Forward From Here," *Academy of Management Perspective,* August 2010, pp. 37–57; and D. Bornstein, *How to Change the World: Social Entrepreneurs and the Power of New Ideas* (New York: Oxford University Press), 2004, inside cover jacket.

90. A. Kamenetz, "Five Social Capitalists Who Will Change the World in 2010," *Fast Company Online* [www.fastcompany.com], February 1, 2010.

91. K. H. Hammonds, "Now the Good News," *Fast Company,* December 2007/January 2008, pp. 110–121; C. Dahle, "Filling the Void," *Fast Company,* January/February 2006, pp. 54–57; and PATH [www.path.org].

92. R. J. Bies, J. M. Bartunek, T. L. Fort, and M. N. Zald, "Corporations as Social Change Agents: Individual, Interpersonal, Institutional, and Environmental Dynamics," *Academy of Management Review,* July 2007, pp. 788–793.

93. "The State of Corporate Philanthropy: A McKinsey Global Survey," *The McKinsey Quarterly Online,* February 2008.

94. R. Nixon, The Associated Press, "Bottom Line for (Red)," *New York Times Online,* February 6, 2008; and G. Mulvihill, "Despite Cause, Not Everyone Tickled Pink by Campaign," *Springfield News-Leader,* October 15, 2007, p. 2E.

95. Giving in Numbers: 2011 Edition, http://www.corporatephilanthropy.org/measurement/benchmarking-reports/giving-in-numbers/2011-edition.

96. K. J. Delaney, "Google: From 'Don't be Evil' to How to Do Good," *Wall Street Journal,* January 18, 2008, pp. B1+; H. Rubin, "Google Offers a Map for Its Philanthropy," *New York Times Online,* January 18, 2008; and K. Hafner, "Philanthropy Google's Way: Not the Usual," *New York Times Online,* September 14, 2006.

97. A. Tergesen, "Doing Good to Do Well," *Wall Street Journal,* January 9, 2012,p. B7.

98. Committee to Encourage Corporate Philanthropy [www.corporatephilanthropy.org], April 7, 2008; "Investing in Society," *Leaders,* July–September 2007, pp. 12+; M. C. White, "Doing Good on Company Time," *New York Times Online,* May 8, 2007; and M. Lowery, "How Volunteerism is Changing the Face of Philanthropy," *DiversityInc,* December 2006, pp. 45–47.

99. S. Deffree, "Foxconn Explosion Ignites Conversation on Corporate Responsibility," *EDN,* June 23, 2011, p. 8; J. Bussey, "Measuring the Human Cost of an iPad Made in China," *Wall Street Journal,* June 3, 2011, pp. B1+; A. Satariano, "Apple Risks iPad Production Loss of 500,000 After Blast," *Bloomberg BusinessWeek*, May 26, 2011; and E. Savitz, "Apple: Analysts See Limited Risks From Hon Hai Plant Explosion," *Forbes.com,* May 23, 2011, p. 4.

100. Skills Exercise based on F. Bartolome, "Nobody Trusts the Boss Completely—Now What?" *Harvard Business Review*, March–April 1989, pp. 135–142; and J. K. Butler Jr., "Toward Understanding and Measuring Conditions of Trust: Evolution of a Condition of Trust Inventory," *Journal of Management*, September 1991, pp. 643–663.

101. "20 Odd Questions: Sole Man Blake Mycoskie," *Wall Street Journal,* January 2012, p. D8; "Your Childhood Saw It Coming," *Fast Company,* December 2011/January 2012, p. 25; C. Garton, "Consumers Are Drawn to Products With a Charitable Connection," *USA Today Online,* July 18, 2011; "Ten Companies With Social Responsibility at the Core," *Advertising Age,* April 19, 2010, p. 88; C. Binkley, "Charity Gives Shoe Brand Extra Shine," *Wall Street Journal,* April 1, 2010, p. D7; J. Shambora, "How I Got Started: Blake Mycoskie, Founder of TOMS Shoes," *Fortune,* March 22, 2010, p. 72; and "Making A Do-Gooder's Business Model Work," *BusinessWeek Online,* January 26, 2009.

102. J. Sterngold, "Who Cares About Another $200 Million?" *Bloomberg BusinessWeek,* May 3–9, 2010, pp. 56–59; L. Story and E. Dash, "Lehman Channeled Risks Through Alter Ego Firm," *New York Time Online,* April 12, 2010; P. M. Barrett, "Cold Case: Lessons From the Lehman Autopsy," *Bloomberg BusinessWeek,* April 5, 2010, pp. 20–22; A. Smith, "What's Left of Lehman: A Plan," *CNNMoney* [www.money.cnn.com], March 16, 2010; and G. Wong and A. Smith, "What Killed Lehman," *CNNMoney* [www.money.cnn.com], March 15, 2010.

CHAPTER 6

1. C. Ravneberg, "MenuMasters 2012: Sonic, America's Drive-In," *Nation's Restaurant News,* April 20, 2012, p. 58; R. Ruggless, "Sonic's New Hot Dog Spices Up Popular Menu Line," *Nation's Restaurant News Online,* July 6, 2011; and

S. E. Lockyer, "Hot Dogs, New Ads Help Sonic," *Nation's Restaurant News Online,* April 29, 2011.

2. M. Trottman, "Choices in Stormy Weather," *Wall Street Journal,* February 14, 2006, p. B1+.

3. S. Minter, "The Season of Snap Judgments," *Industry Week,* May 2010, p. 6; and D. A. Garvin and M. A. Roberto, "What You Don't Know About Making Decisions," *Harvard Business Review,* September 2001, pp. 108–116.

4. "A Bold Alternative to the Worst 'Best' Practices," *BusinessWeek Online* [www.businessweek.com], September 15, 2009.

5. W. Pounds, "The Process of Problem Finding," *Industrial Management Review,* Fall 1969, pp. 1–19.

6. R. J. Volkema, "Problem Formulation: Its Portrayal in the Texts," *Organizational Behavior Teaching Review,* 11, No. 3 (1986–1987), pp. 113–26.

7. T. A. Stewart, "Did You Ever Have to Make Up Your Mind?" *Harvard Business Review,* January 2006, p. 12; and E. Pooley, "Editor's Desk," *Fortune,* June 27, 2005, p. 16.

8. J. Pfeffer and R. I. Sutton, "Why Managing by Facts Works," *Strategy & Business,* Spring 2006, pp. 9–12.

9. See A. Langley, "In Search of Rationality: The Purposes Behind the Use of Formal Analysis in Organizations," *Administrative Science Quarterly,* December 1989, pp. 598–631; and H. A. Simon, "Rationality in Psychology and Economics," *Journal of Business,* October 1986, pp. 209–224.

10. J. G. March, "Decision-Making Perspective: Decisions in Organizations and Theories of Choice," in A. H. Van de Ven and W.F. Joyce (eds.), *Perspectives on Organization Design and Behavior* (New York: Wiley-Interscience, 1981), pp. 232–233.

11. See P. Hemp, "Death by Information Overload," *Harvard Business Review,* September 2009, pp. 82–89; D. Heath and C. Heath, "The Gripping Statistic," *Fast Company,* September 2009, pp. 59–60; D. R. A. Skidd, "Revisiting Bounded Rationality," *Journal of Management Inquiry,* December 1992, pp. 343–347; B. E. Kaufman, "A New Theory of Satisficing," *Journal of Behavioral Economics,* Spring 1990, pp. 35–51; and N. M. Agnew and J. L. Brown, "Bounded Rationality: Fallible Decisions in Unbounded Decision Space," *Behavioral Science,* July 1986, pp. 148–161.

12. See, for example, G. McNamara, H. Moon, and P. Bromiley, "Banking on Commitment: Intended and Unintended Consequences of an Organization's Attempt to Attenuate Escalation of Commitment," *Academy of Management Journal,* April 2002, pp. 443–452; V. S. Rao and A. Monk, "The Effects of Individual Differences and Anonymity on Commitment to Decisions," *Journal of Social Psychology,* August 1999, pp. 496–515; C. F. Camerer and R. A. Weber, "The Econometrics and Behavioral Economics of Escalation of Commitment: A Re-examination of Staw's Theory," *Journal of Economic Behavior and Organization,* May 1999, pp. 59–82; D. R. Bobocel and J. P. Meyer, "Escalating Commitment to a Failing Course of Action: Separating the Roles of Choice and Justification," *Journal of Applied Psychology,* June 1994, pp. 360–363; and B. M. Staw, "The Escalation of Commitment to a Course of Action," *Academy of Management Review,* October 1981, pp. 577–587.

13. W. Cole, "The Stapler Wars," *Time Inside Business,* April 2005, p. A5.

14. See E. Dane and M. G. Pratt, "Exploring Intuition and Its Role in Managerial Decision Making," *Academy of Management Review,* January 2007, pp. 33–54; M. H. Bazerman and D. Chugh, "Decisions Without Blinders," *Harvard Business Review,* January 2006, pp. 88–97; C. C. Miller and R. D. Ireland, "Intuition in Strategic Decision Making: Friend or Foe in the Fast-Paced 21st Century," *Academy of Management Executive,* February 2005, pp. 19–30; E. Sadler-Smith and E. Shefy, "The Intuitive Executive: Understanding and Applying 'Gut Feel' in Decision Making," *Academy of Management Executive,* November 2004, pp. 76–91; and L. A. Burke and M. K. Miller, "Taking the Mystery Out of Intuitive Decision Making," *Academy of Management Executive,* October 1999, pp. 91–99.

15. C. C. Miller and R. D. Ireland, "Intuition in Strategic Decision Making: Friend or Foe," p. 20.

16. E. Sadler-Smith and E. Shefy, "Developing Intuitive Awareness in Management Education," *Academy of Management Learning & Education,* June 2007, pp. 186–205.

17. M. G. Seo and L. Feldman Barrett, "Being Emotional During Decision Making—Good or Bad? An Empirical Investigation," *Academy of Management Journal,* August 2007, pp. 923–940.

18. B. Roberts, "Hire Intelligence," *HR Magazine,* May 2011, p. 63.

19. R. B. Briner, D. Denyer, and D. M. Rousseau, "Evidence-Based Management: Concept Cleanup Time?" *Academy of Management Perspective,* November 2009, p. 22.

20. J. Pfeffer and R. Sutton, "Trust the Evidence, Not Your Instincts," *New York Times Online,* September 3, 2011; and T. Reay, W. Berta, and M. K. Kohn, "What's the Evidence on Evidence-Based Management?" *Academy of Management Perspectives,* November 2009, p. 5.

21. K. R. Brousseau, M. J. Driver, G. Hourihan, and R. Larsson, "The Seasoned Executive's Decision-Making Style," *Harvard Business Review,* February 2006, pp. 111–121.

22. Future Vision box based on A. Alter, "Your E-Book Is Reading You," *Wall Street Journal,* June 29, 2012, pp. D1+; R. Kurzweil, "Man or Machine?" *Wall Street Journal,* June 29, 2012, p. C12; D. Jones and A. Shaw, "Slowing Momentum: Why BPM Isn't Keeping Pace with Its Potential," *BPM Magazine,* February 2006, pp. 4–12; B. Violino, "IT Directions," *CFO,* January 2006, pp. 68–72; D. Weinberger, "Sorting Data to Suit Yourself," *Harvard Business Review,* March 2005, pp. 16–18; and C. Winkler, "Getting a Grip on Performance," *CFO-IT,* Winter 2004, pp. 38–48.

23. Leader Who Made a Difference box based on M. Mazzeo, "Deron Williams to Meet with Nets," *espn.go.com,* May 11, 2012; T. Bontemps, "Nets Owner Mentions 'Kickboxing' Mavericks Over Deron," *NYPost.com,* April 11, 2012; R. Sandomir, "Nets' Likely Owner Faces a Nation," *New York Times Online,* March 28, 2010; Y. Humber, "Your Handy Guide to Russia's Oligarchs," *BusinessWeek,* March 8, 2010, pp. 62–63; and M. Futterman, "Russia Billionaire to Buy NBA's Nets in Deal to Help Save Brooklyn Arena," *Wall Street Journal,* September 24, 2009, p. B1.

24. S. Holmes, "Inside the Coup at Nike," *BusinessWeek,* February 6, 2006, pp. 34–37; and M. Barbaro, "Slightly Testy Nike Divorce Came Down to Data vs. Feel," *New York Times Online* [www.nytimes.com], January 28, 2006.

25. C. M. Vance, K. S. Groves, Y. Paik, and H. Kindler, "Understanding and Measuring Linear–NonLinear Thinking Style for Enhanced Management Education and Professional Practice," *Academy of Management Learning & Education,* June 2007, pp. 167–185.

26. E. Teach, "Avoiding Decision Traps," *CFO,* June 2004, pp. 97–99; and D. Kahneman and A. Tversky, "Judgment Under Uncertainty: Heuristics and Biases," *Science* 185 (1974), pp. 1124–1131.

27. Information for this section taken from D. Kahneman, D. Lovallo, and O. Sibony, "Before You Make That Decision…" *Harvard Business Review,* June 2011, pp. 50–60; and S. P. Robbins, *Decide & Conquer* (Upper Saddle River, NJ: Financial Times/Prentice Hall), 2004.

28. data points box based on D. Kahneman, D. Lovallo, and O. Siboney, "Before You Make That Big Decision," *Harvard Business Review,* June 2011, pp.50–60; N. Tasler, "Prime Your Mind for Action," *BusinessWeek Online,* November 3, 2009; B. Dumaine, "The Trouble with Teams," *Fortune,* September 5, 1994, pp. 86–92; A. S. Wellner, "A Perfect Brainstorm," *Inc.,* October 2003, pp. 31–35; "Hurry Up and Decide," *BusinessWeek,* May 14, 2001, p. 16; J. MacIntyre, "Bosses and Bureaucracy," *Springfield, Missouri Business Journal,* August 1–7, 2005, p. 29; J. Crick, "Hand Jive," *Fortune,* June 13, 2005, pp. 40–41; and "On the Road to Invention," *Fast Company,* February 2005, p. 16.

29. L. Margonelli, "How IKEA Designs Its Sexy Price Tags," *Business 2.0,* October 2002, p. 108.

30. P. C. Chu, E. E. Spires, and T. Sueyoshi, "Cross-Cultural Differences in Choice Behavior and Use of Decision Aids: A Comparison of Japan and the United States," *Organizational Behavior & Human Decision Processes,* vol. 77, no. 2 (1999), pp. 147–170.

31. D. Ariely, "Good Decisions. Bad Outcomes," *Harvard Business Review,* December 2010, p. 40.

32. S. Thurm, "Seldom-Used Executive Power: Reconsidering," *Wall Street Journal,* February 6, 2006, p. B3.

33. J. S. Hammond, R. L. Keeney, and H. Raiffa, *Smart Choices: A Practical Guide to Making Better Decisions* (Boston, MA: Harvard Business School Press, 1999), p. 4.

34. This discussion is based on E. W. Ford, W. J. Duncan, A. G. Bedeian, P. M. Ginter, M. D. Rousculp, and A. M. Adams, "Mitigating Risks, Visible Hands, Inevitable Disasters, and Soft Variables: Management Research That Matters," *Academy of Management Executive,* November 2005, pp. 24–38; K. H. Hammonds, "5 Habits of Highly Reliable Organizations: An Interview with Karl Weick," *Fast Company,* May 2002, pp. 124–128; and K. E. Weick, "Drop Your Tools: An Allegory for Organizational Studies," *Administrative Science Quarterly,* vol. 41, no. 2 (1996), pp. 301–313.

35. D. Dunne and R. Martin, "Design Thinking and How It Will Change Management Education: An Interview and Discussion," *Academy of Management Learning & Education,* December 2006, p. 512.

36. M. Korn and R. E. Silverman, "Forget B-School, D-School Is Hot," *Wall Street Journal,* June 7, 2012, pp. B1+; R. Martin and J. Euchner, "Design Thinking," *Research Technology Management,* May/June 2012, pp. 10-14; T. Larsen and T. Fisher, "Design Thinking: A Solution to Fracture-Critical Systems," *DMI News & Views,* May 2012, p. 31; T. Berno, "Design Thinking versus Creative Intelligence," *DMI News & Views,* May 2012, p. 28; J. Liedtka and Tim Ogilvie, "Helping Business Managers Discover Their Appetite for Design Thinking," *Design Management Review,* Issue 1, 2012, pp. 6-13; and T. Brown, "Strategy By Design," *Fast Company,* June 2005, pp. 52–54.

37. C. Guglielmo, "Apple Loop: The Week in Review," *Forbes.com,* May 25, 2012, p. 2.

38. D. Dunne and R. Martin, "Design Thinking and How It Will Change Management Education: An Interview and Discussion," p. 514.

39. M. Morrison and E. J. Schultz, "Beer-at-Burger-Chain Fad May Leave Hangover," *Advertising Age,* May 21, 2012, p. 2-16; C. Ravneberg, "Sonic, America's Drive-In;" S. Clifford, "Alcohol Isn't Worth the Trouble for Some Chain Restaurants," *New York Times Online,* September 26, 2011; and J. Scarpa, "A Thirst for Sales," *Nation's Restaurant News,* August 22, 2011, pp. 1–22.

40. Developing Your Creative Skill exercise based on S. P. Robbins, *Essentials of Organizational Behavior,* 8th ed. (Upper Saddle River, NJ: Prentice Hall, 2004); C. W. Wang and R. Y. Horng, "The Effects of Creative Problem Solving Training on Creativity, Cognitive Type, and R & D Performance," *R&D Management* (January 2002), pp. 35–46; S. Caudron, "Creativity 101," *Workforce* (March 2002), pp. 20, 24; and T. M. Amabile, "Motivating Creativity in Organizations," *California Management Review* (Fall 1997), pp. 42–52.

41. T. Caporale and T.C. Collier, "Scouts versus Stats: The Impact of Moneyball on the Major League Baseball Draft," *Applied Economics,* vol. 45, issue 15, 2013, pp. 1983-1990; B. Cohen, "College Baseball Showing Signs of a Revolution," *Wall Street Journal,* June 22, 2012, p. D10; T. Van Riper and C. Semmimi, "The New Moneyball," *Forbes,* April 9, 2012, pp. 70-76; D. K. Berman, "So, What's Your Algorithm?" *Wall Street Journal,* January 4, 2012, pp. B1+; P. White, "The Suits Behind the Uniforms," *USA Today,* December 7, 2011, pp. 1C+; K. L. Papps, A. Bryson, and R. Gomez, "Heterogeneous Worker Ability and Team-Based Production: Evidence from Major League Baseball, 1920–2009," *Labour Economics,* June 2011, pp. 310–319; Michael Lewis, *Moneyball,* (W. W. Norton & Co., 2011); and B. Curtis, "Debating America's Pastime(s)," *New York Times Online,* January 2, 2009.

42. "Eurotunnel Boosts Capacity," *Rail Business Intelligence,* May 31, 2012, p. 2; "Eurostar Trains Disrupted by French Power Cable Fault," *BBCNews Online,* March 6, 2012; N. Clark, "Eurostar Criticized for Winter Breakdowns," *New York Times Online,* February 13, 2010; B. Mellor and S. Rothwell, "Eurostar Cuts Service Amid Cold Snap," *BusinessWeek,* January 11, 2010, p. 10; D. Jolly, "Eurostar Service Disrupted as Train Stalls in Channel Tunnel," *New York Times Online,* January 8, 2010; and G. Corkindale, "Does Your Company's Reputation Matter?" *BusinessWeek Online,* December 29, 2009.

CHAPTER 7

1. I. Klotz, "NASA Unveils Mars Rover Curiosity's Travel Plans," www.washingtonpost.com, August 18, 2012; A. Pasztor, "NASA Finds Overseas Ventures More Elusive," *Wall Street Journal,* July 9, 2012, p. B4; "This Week at NASA," [www.nasa.gov], May 18, 2012; K. Chang, "NASA Hitches a Ride on a Russian Craft, and Begins a New Dependent Era," *New York Times Online,* November 12, 2011; A. Campo-Flores and R. L. Hotz," Touchdown Brings Shuttle Era to a Close," *Wall Street Journal,* July 22, 2011, p. A6; "Lost in Space: Jobs," *Time,* July 18, 2011, p. 16; T. Dokoupil, "The Next Space Race," *Newsweek,* July 18, 2011, pp. 58–60; A. Pasztor, "Senators Push NASA to Set Rocket Plans," *Wall Street Journal,* July 15, 2011, p. A6; A. Campos-Flores, and R. L. Hotz, "One More Spin Around the Planet," *Wall Street Journal,* July 9–10, 2011, p. A5; M. W. Walsh, "Shuttle's End Leaves NASA a Pension Bill," *New York Times Online,* June 14, 2011; J. J. Salopek, "NASA's Mission: Launching More Young Careers," *Workforce Management Online,* May 24, 2011; A. Pasztor and A. Campo-Flores, "Blastoff

Obscures NASA's Troubles," *Wall Street Journal,* April 29, 2011, p. A3; A. Pasztor, "NASA Stresses New Mission," *Wall Street Journal,* May 18, 2012, p. A3; O. Kharf, "Reentry," *Bloomberg BusinessWeek,* April 9–April 15, 2012, pp. 45–46; and G. Easterbrook, "Give NASA A Real Mission," *Harvard Business Review,* January–February 2012, pp. 56–57.

2. A. Weintraub and M. Tirrell, "Eli Lilly's Drug Assembly Line," *Bloomberg BusinessWeek,* March 8, 2010, pp. 56–57.

3. "Clear Direction in a Complex World: How Top Companies Create Clarity, Confidence and Community to Build Sustainable Performance," Towers Watson [www.towerswatson.com], 2011–2012; R. Soparnot, "The Concept of Organizational Change Capacity," *Journal of Organizational Change,* vol. 24, no. 1, 2011, pp. 640–661; A. H. Van de Ven and K. Sun, "Breakdowns in Implementing Models of Organization Change," *Academy of Management Perspectives,* August 2011, pp. 58–74; L. Dragoni, P. E. Tesluk, J. E. A. Russell, and I. S. Oh, "Understanding Managerial Development: Integrating Developmental Assignments, Learning Orientation, and Access to Developmental Opportunities in Predicting Managerial Competencies," *Academy of Management Journal,* August 2009, pp. 731–743; G. Nadler and W. J. Chandon, "Making Changes: The FIST Approach," *Journal of Management Inquiry,* September 2004, pp. 239–246; and C. R. Leana and B. Barry, "Stability and Change as Simultaneous Experiences in Organizational Life," *Academy of Management Review,* October 2000, pp. 753–759.

4. The idea for these metaphors came from J. E. Dutton, S. J. Ashford, R. M. O'Neill, and K. A. Lawrence, "Moves That Matter: Issue Selling and Organizational Change," *Academy of Management Journal,* August 2001, pp. 716–736; B. H. Kemelgor, S. D. Johnson, and S. Srinivasan, "Forces Driving Organizational Change: A Business School Perspective," *Journal of Education for Business,* January/February 2000, pp. 133–137; G. Colvin, "When It Comes to Turbulence, CEOs Could Learn a Lot from Sailors," *Fortune,* March 29, 1999, pp. 194–196; and P. B. Vaill, *Managing as a Performing Art: New Ideas for a World of Chaotic Change* (San Francisco: Jossey-Bass, 1989).

5. K. Lewin, *Field Theory in Social Science* (New York: Harper & Row, 1951).

6. R. Safian, "Generation Flux," *FastCompany.com,* February 2012, p. 62.

7. "Who's Next," *FastCompany.com,* December 2010/January 2011, p. 39.

8. D. Lieberman, "Nielsen Media Has Cool Head at the Top," *USA Today,* March 27, 2006, p. 3B.

9. S. A. Mohrman and E. E. Lawler III, "Generating Knowledge That Drives Change," *Academy of Management Perspectives,* February 2012, pp. 41–51; S. Ante, "Change Is Good—So Get Used to It," *BusinessWeek,* June 22, 2009, pp. 69–70; L. S. Lüscher and M. W. Lewis, "Organizational Change and Managerial Sensemaking: Working Through Paradox," *Academy of Management Journal,* April 2008, pp. 221–240; F. Buckley and K. Monks, "Responding to Managers' Learning Needs in an Edge-of-Chaos Environment: Insights from Ireland," *Journal of Management,* April 2008, pp. 146–163; and G. Hamel, "Take It Higher," *Fortune,* February 5, 2001, pp. 169–170.

10. "Electrolux Cops Top Design Honors," *This Week in Consumer Electronics,* June 4, 2012, p. 48; A. Wolf, "Electrolux Q1 Profits Up 23%," *This Week in Consumer Electronics,* May 7, 2012, p. 30; M. Boyle, "Persuading Brits to Give Up Their Dishrags," *Bloomberg BusinessWeek,* March 26, 2012, pp.

20–21; "Electrolux Earnings Down in 2011, Hopeful for 2012," *Appliance Design.com,* March 2012, pp. 7–8; "Electrolux Breaks Ground on Memphis Factory," *Kitchen & Bath Design News,* December 2011, p. 15; J. R. Hagerty and B. Tita, "Appliance Sales Tumble," *Wall Street Journal,* October 29, 2011, p. B1; and A. Sains and S. Reed, "Electrolux Cleans Up," *BusinessWeek,* February 27, 2006, pp. 42–43.

11. J. Cohen, "Business As Usual," *Training,* February 2010, pp. 46–50.

12. R. Lawrence, "Many Fish In A Global Development Pond," *Chief Learning Officer,* November 2011, pp. 26–31; K. Roose, "Outsiders' Ideas Help Bank of America Cut Jobs and Costs," *New York Times Online,* September 12, 2011; and "How HR Made A Difference," *PeopleManagement.co.uk,* February 2011, p. 31.

13. J. Zhiguo, "How I Did It: Tsingtao's Chairman on Jump-Starting a Sluggish Company," *Harvard Business Review,* April 2012, pp. 41–44.

14. M. De Giovanni, "Tallahassee CEO Lisa Brown Says 'Sleep Is for Sissies," *Credit Union Times,* December 4, 2011, p. 24; and C. B. Class, "Teaching New Technologies and Life-Long Learning Skills: A Sample Approach and Its Evaluation," *International Journal of Advanced Corporate Learning,* November 2011, pp. 10–19.

15. J. Jesitus, "Change Management: Energy to the People," *Industry Week,* September 1, 1997, pp. 37, 40.

16. D. Lavin, "European Business Rushes to Automate," *Wall Street Journal,* July 23, 1997, p. A14.

17. See, for example, B. B. Bunker, B. T. Alban, and R. J. Lewicki, "Ideas in Currency and OD Practice," *The Journal of Applied Behavioral Science,* December 2004, pp. 403–422; L. E. Greiner and T. G. Cummings, "Wanted: OD More Alive Than Dead!" *Journal of Applied Behavioral Science,* December 2004, pp. 374–391; S. Hicks, "What Is Organization Development?" *Training & Development,* August 2000, p. 65; W. Nicolay, "Response to Farias and Johnson's Commentary," *Journal of Applied Behavioral Science,* September 2000, pp. 380–381; and G. Farias, "Organizational Development and Change Management," *Journal of Applied Behavioral Science,* September 2000, pp. 376–379.

18. T. White, "Supporting Change: How Communicators at Scotiabank Turned Ideas into Action," *Communication World,* April 2002, pp. 22–24.

19. M. Javidan, P. W. Dorfman, M. S. deLuque, and R. J. House, "In the Eye of the Beholder: Cross-Cultural Lessons in Leadership from Project GLOBE," *Academy of Management Perspective,* February 2006, pp. 67–90; and E. Fagenson-Eland, E. A. Ensher, and W. W. Burke, "Organization Development and Change Interventions: A Seven-Nation Comparison," *The Journal of Applied Behavioral Science,* December 2004, pp. 432–464.

20. E. Fagenson-Eland, Ensher, and Burke, "Organization Development and Change Interventions: A Seven-Nation Comparison," p. 461.

21. S. Shinn, "Stairway to Reinvention," *BizEd,* January/February 2010, p. 6; M. Scott, "A Stairway to Marketing Heaven," *BusinessWeek,* November 2, 2009, p. 17; and The Fun Theory [http://thefuntheory.com], November 10, 2009.

22. See, for example, J. D. Ford, L. W. Ford, and A. D'Amelio, "Resistance to Change: The Rest of the Story," *Academy of Management Review,* April 2008, pp. 362–377; A. Deutschman, "Making Change: Why Is It So Hard to Change Our Ways?" *Fast Company,* May 2005, pp. 52–62; S. B. Silverman, C. E. Pogson, and A. B. Cober, "When Employees at Work Don't

Get It: A Model for Enhancing Individual Employee Change in Response to Performance Feedback," *Academy of Management Executive,* May 2005, pp. 135–147; C. E. Cunningham, C. A. Woodward, H. S. Shannon, J. MacIntosh, B. Lendrum, D. Rosenbloom, and J. Brown, "Readiness for Organizational Change: A Longitudinal Study of Workplace, Psychological and Behavioral Correlates," *Journal of Occupational and Organizational Psychology,* December 2002, pp. 377–392; M. A. Korsgaard, H. J. Sapienza, and D. M. Schweiger, "Beaten Before Begun: The Role of Procedural Justice in Planning Change," *Journal of Management,* 2002, vol. 28, no. 4, pp. 497–516; R. Kegan and L. L. Lahey, "The Real Reason People Won't Change," *Harvard Business Review,* November 2001, pp. 85–92; S. K. Piderit, "Rethinking Resistance and Recognizing Ambivalence: A Multidimensional View of Attitudes Toward an Organizational Change," *Academy of Management Review,* October 2000, pp. 783–794; C. R. Wanberg and J. T. Banas, "Predictors and Outcomes of Openness to Changes in a Reorganizing Workplace," *Journal of Applied Psychology,* February 2000, pp. 132–142; A. A. Armenakis and A. G. Bedeian, "Organizational Change: A Review of Theory and Research in the 1990s," *Journal of Management,* vol. 25, no. 3, 1999, pp. 293–315; and B. M. Staw, "Counterforces to Change," in P. S. Goodman and Associates (eds.), *Change in Organizations* (San Francisco: Jossey-Bass, 1982), pp. 87–121.

23. A. Reichers, J. P. Wanous, and J. T. Austin, "Understanding and Managing Cynicism about Organizational Change," *Academy of Management Executive,* February 1997, pp. 48–57; P. Strebel, "Why Do Employees Resist Change?" *Harvard Business Review,* May–June 1996, pp. 86–92; and J. P. Kotter and L. A. Schlesinger, "Choosing Strategies for Change," *Harvard Business Review,* March–April 1979, pp. 107–109.

24. A. Foege, "Wii at Work," *CNNMoney* [cnnmoney.com], June 5, 2009.

25. R. Yu, "Korean Air Upgrades Service, Image," *USA Today,* August 24, 2009, pp. 1B+.

26. See P. Anthony, *Managing Culture* (Philadelphia: Open University Press, 1994); P. Bate, *Strategies for Cultural Change* (Boston: Butterworth-Heinemann, 1994); C. G. Smith and R. P. Vecchio, "Organizational Culture and Strategic Management: Issues in the Strategic Management of Change," *Journal of Managerial Issues,* Spring 1993, pp. 53–70; P. F. Drucker, "Don't Change Corporate Culture—Use It!" *Wall Street Journal,* March 28, 1991, p. A14; and T. H. Fitzgerald, "Can Change in Organizational Culture Really Be Managed?" *Organizational Dynamics,* Autumn 1988, pp. 5–15.

27. K. Maney, "Famously Gruff Gerstner Leaves IBM a Changed Man," *USA Today,* November 11, 2002, pp. 1B+; and Louis V. Gerstner, *Who Says Elephants Can't Dance: Inside IBM's Historic Turnaround* (New York: Harper Business, 2002).

28. See, for example, D. C. Hambrick and S. Finkelstein, "Managerial Discretion: A Bridge between Polar Views of Organizational Outcomes," in L. L. Cummings and B. M. Staw (eds.), *Research in Organizational Behavior,* vol. 9 (Greenwich, CT: JAI Press, 1987), p. 384; and R. H. Kilmann, M. J. Saxton, and R. Serpa (eds.), *Gaining Control of the Corporate Culture* (San Francisco: Jossey-Bass, 1985).

29. P. Davidson, "Moonlighting Becomes a Way of Life for Many," *USA Today,* June 24, 2009, p. 3B.

30. P. Korkki, "Driven to Worry, and to Procrastinate," *New York Times Online,* February 25, 2012; E. Frauenheim, "To the Limit," *Workforce Management Online,* December 16,

2011; A. Kadet, "Surviving the Superjob," *SmartMoney,* June 2011, pp. 75–79; L. J. Dugan, "Working Two Jobs and Still Underemployed," *Wall Street Journal,* December 1, 2009, p. A15; N. Parmar, "The New Balancing Act," *Smart Money,* October 2009, p. 59; and Davidson "Moonlighting Becomes a Way of Life for Many."

31. S. Ilgenfritz, "Are We Too Stressed to Reduce Our Stress?" *Wall Street Journal,* November 10, 2009, p. D2; C. Daniels, "The Last Taboo," *Fortune,* October 28, 2002, pp. 137–144; J. Laabs, "Time-Starved Workers Rebel," *Workforce,* October 2000, pp. 26–28; M. A. Verespej, "Stressed Out," *Industry Week,* February 21, 2000, pp. 30–34; and M. A. Cavanaugh, W. R. Boswell, M. V. Roehling, and J. W. Boudreau, "An Empirical Examination of Self-Reported Work Stress Among U.S. Managers," *Journal of Applied Psychology,* February 2000, pp. 65–74.

32. A report on job stress compiled by the American Institute of Stress [www.stress.org/job], 2002–2003.

33. M. Conlin, "Go-Go-Going to Pieces in China," *Business Week,* April 23, 2007, p. 88; V. P. Sudhashree, K. Rohith, and K. Shrinivas, "Issues and Concerns of Health Among Call Center Employees," *Indian Journal of Occupational Environmental Medicine,"* vol. 9, no. 3, 2005, pp. 129–132; E. Muehlchen, "An Ounce of Prevention Goes A Long Way," Wilson Banwell [www.wilsonbanwell.com], January 2004; UnionSafe, "Stressed Employees Worked to Death" [unionsafe.labor.net.au/news], August 23, 2003; O. Siu, "Occupational Stressors and Well-Being Among Chinese Employees: The Role of Organizational Commitment," *Applied Psychology: An International Review,* October 2002, pp. 527–544; O. Siu, P. E. Spector, C. L. Cooper, L. Lu, and S. Yu, "Managerial Stress in Greater China: The Direct and Moderator Effects of Coping Strategies and Work Locus of Control," *Applied Psychology: An International Review,* October 2002, pp. 608–632; A. Oswald, "New Research Reveals Dramatic Rise in Stress Levels in Europe's Workplaces," University of Warwick [www.warwick.ac.uk/news/pr], 1999; and Y. Shimizu, S. Makino, and T. Takata, "Employee Stress Status During the Past Decade [1982–1992] Based on a Nation-Wide Survey Conducted by the Ministry of Labour in Japan," Japan Industrial Safety and Health Association, July 1997, pp. 441–450.

34. G. Kranz, "Job Stress Viewed Differently by Workers, Employers," *Workforce Management* [www.workforce.com], January 15, 2008.

35. Adapted from the UK National Work-Stress Network [www.workstress.net].

36. R. S. Schuler, "Definition and Conceptualization of Stress in Organizations," *Organizational Behavior and Human Performance,* April 1980, p. 191.

37. data points box based on T. Rath and J. Harter, "Unhealthy, Stressed Employees Are Hurting Your Business," *Gallup Business Journal Online,* May 22, 2012; C. Allen, "Burned Out and Fed Up? Maybe All You Need Is a Break," *T&D,* December 2011, p. 72; R. Higgins and K. Gelles, "How Americans Feel About Their Workload Today vs. At Start of Recession," *USA Today,* October 26, 2011, p. 1A; "Stress: By the Numbers," *AARP The Magazine,* September/October 2011, p. 30; J. Yang and S. Ward, "Which Is the More Stress-Inducing Aspect of Your Job?" *USA Today,* September 11, 2011, p. 1B; K. Foster, "Prod the Turtle," *HR Magazine,* September 2011, p. 122; D. Meinert, "Full Speed Ahead," *HR Magazine,* March 2011, p. 18; L. Kwoh, "You Call That Innovation?" *Wall Street Journal,* May 23, 2012, pp. B1+; and E. Pofeldt, "Build the Right Skills," *Money,* May 2011, p. 24.

38. J. B. Rodell and T. A. Judge, "Can 'Good' Stressors Spark 'Bad' Behaviors? The Mediating Role of Emotions in Links of Challenge and Hindrance Stressors with Citizenship and Counterproductive Behaviors," *Journal of Applied Psychology*, November 2009, pp. 1438–1451; and see, for example, "Stressed Out: Extreme Job Stress: Survivors' Tales," *Wall Street Journal* (January 17, 2001), p. B1.

39. See, for instance, S. Bates, "Expert: Don't Overlook Employee Burnout," *HR Magazine* (August 2003), p. 14.

40. "The Japanese Are Dying to Get to Work," www.tofugu.com, January 26, 2012; A. Kanai, "Karoshi (Work to Death) in Japan, *Journal of Business Ethics*, January 2009 Supplement 2, pp. 209–216; "Jobs for Life," *The Economist* [www.economist.com], December 19, 2007; and B. L. de Mente, "Karoshi: Death from Overwork," Asia Pacific Management Forum [www.apmforum.com], May 2002.

41. H. Benson, "Are You Working Too Hard?" *Harvard Business Review*, November 2005, pp. 53–58; B. Cryer, R. McCraty, and D. Childre, "Pull the Plug on Stress," *Harvard Business Review*, July 2003, pp. 102–107; C. Daniels, "The Last Taboo;" C. L. Cooper and S. Cartwright, "Healthy Mind, Healthy Organization—A Proactive Approach to Occupational Stress," *Human Relations*, April 1994, pp. 455–471; C. A. Heaney et al., "Industrial Relations, Worksite Stress Reduction and Employee Well-Being: A Participatory Action Research Investigation," *Journal of Organizational Behavior*, September 1993, pp. 495–510; C. D. Fisher, "Boredom at Work: A Neglected Concept," *Human Relations*, March 1993, pp. 395–417; and S. E. Jackson, "Participation in Decision Making as a Strategy for Reducing Job-Related Strain," *Journal of Applied Psychology*, February 1983, pp. 3–19.

42. C. Mamberto, "Companies Aim to Combat Job-Related Stress," *Wall Street Journal*, August 13, 2007, p. B6.

43. J. Goudreau, "Dispatches from the War on Stress," *BusinessWeek*, August 6, 2007, pp. 74–75.

44. Well Workplace 2008 Award Executive Summaries, Wellmark BlueCross BlueShield and Zimmer Holdings, Inc., available on Wellness Councils of America Web site [www.welcoa.org].

45. P. A. McLagan, "Change Leadership Today," *T&D*, November 2002, pp. 27–31.

46. Ibid, p. 29.

47. K. Kingsbury, "Road to Recovery," *Time*, March 18, 2010, pp. Global 14–16; and C. Haddad, "UPS: Can It Keep Delivering?" *BusinessWeek Online Extra* [www.businessweek.com], Spring 2003.

48. W. Pietersen, "The Mark Twain Dilemma: The Theory and Practice for Change Leadership," *Journal of Business Strategy*, September/October 2002, p. 35.

49. P. A. McLagan, "The Change-Capable Organization," *T&D*, January 2003, pp. 50–58.

50. A. Saha-Bubna and M. Jarzemsky, "MasterCard President Is Named CEO," *Wall Street Journal*, April 13, 2010, p. C3; and S. Vandebook, "Quotable," *Industry Week*, April 2010, p. 18.

51. R. M. Kanter, "Think Outside the Building," *Harvard Business Review*, March 2010, p. 34; T. Brown, "Change By Design," *BusinessWeek*, October 5, 2009, pp. 54–56; J. E. Perry-Smith and C. E. Shalley, "The Social Side of Creativity: A Static and Dynamic Social Network Perspective," *Academy of Management Review*, January 2003, pp. 89–106; and P. K. Jagersma, "Innovate or Die: It's Not Easy, But It Is Possible to Enhance Your Organization's Ability to Innovate," *Journal of Business Strategy*, January–February 2003, pp. 25–28.

52. E. Brynjolfsson and M. Schrage, "The New Faster Face of Innovation," *Wall Street Journal*, August 17, 2009, p. R3.

53. Ibid.

54. L. Kwoh, "You Call That Innovation?" *Wall Street Journal*, May 23, 2012, pp. B1+.

55. These definitions are based on E. Miron-Spektor, M. Erez, and E. Naveh, "The Effect of Conformist and Attentive-to-Detail Members on Team Innovation: Reconciling the Innovation Paradox," *Academy of Management Journal*, August 2011, pp. 740–760; and T. M. Amabile, *Creativity in Context* (Boulder, CO: Westview Press, 1996)

56. U. R. Hülsheger, N. Anderson, and J. F. Salgado, "Team-Level Predictors of Innovation at Work: A Comprehensive Meta-Analysis Spanning Three Decades of Research," *Journal of Applied Psychology*, September 2009, pp. 1128–1145; R. W. Woodman, J. E. Sawyer, and R. W. Griffin, "Toward a Theory of Organizational Creativity," *Academy of Management Review*, April 1993, pp. 293–321.

57. G. Hirst, D. Van Knippenberg, C. H. Chen, and C. A. Sacramento, "How Does Bureaucracy Impact Individual Creativity? A Cross-Level Investigation of Team Contextual Influences on Goal Orientation-Creativity Relationships," *Academy of Management Journal*, June 2011, pp. 624–641; L. Sagiv, S. Arieli, J. Goldenberg, and A. Goldschmidt, "Structure and Freedom in Creativity: The Interplay Between Externally Imposed Structure and Personal Cognitive Style," *Journal of Organizational Behavior*, November 2010, pp. 1086–1100; J. van denEnde and G. Kijkuit, "Nurturing Good Ideas," *Harvard Business Review*, April 2009, p. 24; T. M. Egan, "Factors Influencing Individual Creativity in the Workplace: An Examination of Quantitative Empirical Research," *Advances in Developing Human Resources*, May 2005, pp. 160–181; N. Madjar, G. R. Oldham, and M. G. Pratt, "There's No Place Like Home? The Contributions of Work and Nonwork Creativity Support to Employees' Creative Performance," *Academy of Management Journal*, August 2002, pp. 757–767; T. M. Amabile, C. N. Hadley, and S. J. Kramer, "Creativity Under the Gun," *Harvard Business Review*, August 2002, pp. 52–61; J. B. Sorensen and T. E. Stuart, "Aging, Obsolescence, and Organizational Innovation," *Administrative Science Quarterly*, March 2000, pp. 81–112; G. R. Oldham and A. Cummings, "Employee Creativity: Personal and Contextual Factors at Work," *Academy of Management Journal*, June 1996, pp. 607–634; and F. Damanpour, "Organizational Innovation: A Meta-Analysis of Effects of Determinants and Moderators," *Academy of Management Journal*, September 1991, pp. 555–590.

58. J. S. Lublin, "Smart Balance Keeps Tight Focus on Creativity," *Wall Street Journal*, June 8, 2009, p. B4.

59. P. R. Monge, M. D. Cozzens, and N. S. Contractor, "Communication and Motivational Predictors of the Dynamics of Organizational Innovations," *Organization Science*, May 1992, pp. 250–274.

60. D. Dobson, "Integrated Innovation at Pitney Bowes," *Strategy+Business* [www.strategy-business.com], October 26, 2009.

61. T. M. Amabile, C. N. Hadley, and S. J. Kramer, "Creativity Under the Gun."

62. T. Jana, "Dusting Off A Big Idea in Hard Times," *BusinessWeek*, June 22, 2009, pp. 44–46.

63. N. Madjar, G. R. Oldham, and M. G. Pratt, "There's No Place Like Home? The Contributions of Work and Nonwork Creativity Support to Employees' Creative Performance."

64. Leader Who Made a Difference Box based on N. Karmali, "Bill Gates, Azim Premji, Ratan Tata to Host Bangalore Philanthropy Meet," *Forbes.com,* May 12, 2012; A. Chaze, "Mistry To Take Helm At Tata Sons," *Global Finance,* January 2012, p. 6; C. Chynoweth, "Dare to Try, the Indian Way," *The Sunday Times Online,* April 17, 2011; C. K. Prahalad, "Best Practices Get You Only So Far," *Harvard Business Review,* April 2010, p. 32; A. Graham, "Too Good to Fail," *Strategy+Business Online* [www.strategy-business.com], February 23, 2010; J. Scanlon, "How to Build a Culture of Innovation," *BusinessWeek Online* [www.businessweek.com], August 19, 2009; and J. Scanlon, "Tata Group's Innovation Competition," *BusinessWeek Online* [www.businessweek.com], June 17, 2009.

65. C. Salter, "Mattel Learns to 'Throw the Bunny,'" *Fast Company,* November 2002, p. 22.

66. See, for instance, K. E. M. De Stobbeleir, S. J. Ashford, and D. Buyens, "Self-Regulation of Creativity At Work: The Role of Feedback-Seeking Behavior in Creative Performance," *Academy of Management Journal,* August 2011, pp. 811–831; J. Cable, "Building an Innovation Culture," *Industry Week,* March 2010, pp. 32–37; M. Hawkins, "Create a Climate of Creativity," *Training,* January 2010, p. 12; D. C. Wyld, "Keys to Innovation: The Right Measures and the Right Culture?" *Academy of Management Perspective,* May 2009, pp. 96–98; J. E. Perry-Smith, "Social Yet Creative: The Role of Social Relationships in Facilitating Individual Creativity," *Academy of Management Journal,* February 2006, pp. 85–101; C. E. Shalley, J. Zhou, and G. R. Oldham, "The Effects of Personal and Contextual Characteristics on Creativity: Where Should We Go from Here?" *Journal of Management,* vol. 30, no. 6, 2004, pp. 933–958; J. E. Perry-Smith and C. E. Shalley, "The Social Side of Creativity: A Static and Dynamic Social Network Perspective;" J. M. George and J. Zhou, "When Openness to Experience and Conscientiousness are Related to Creative Behavior: An Interactional Approach," *Journal of Applied Psychology,* June 2001, pp. 513–524; J. Zhou, "Feedback Valence, Feedback Style, Task Autonomy, and Achievement Orientation: Interactive Effects on Creative Behavior," *Journal of Applied Psychology,* 1998, vol. 83, pp. 261–276; T. M. Amabile, R. Conti, H. Coon, J. Lazenby, and M. Herron, "Assessing the Work Environment for Creativity," *Academy of Management Journal,* October 1996, pp. 1154–1184; S. G. Scott and R. A. Bruce, "Determinants of Innovative People: A Path Model of Individual Innovation in the Workplace," *Academy of Management Journal,* June 1994, pp. 580–607; R. Moss Kanter, "When a Thousand Flowers Bloom: Structural, Collective, and Social Conditions for Innovation in Organization," in B. M. Staw and L. L. Cummings (eds.), *Research in Organizational Behavior,* vol. 10 (Greenwich, CT: JAI Press, 1988), pp. 169–211; and Amabile, *Creativity in Context.*

67. L. A. Schlesinger, C. F. Kiefer, and P. B. Brown, "New Project? Don't Analyze—Act," *Harvard Business Review,* March 2012, pp. 154–158.

68. T. L. Stanley, "Creating a No-Blame Culture," *Supervision,* October 2011, pp. 3-6; S. Shellenbarger, "Better Ideas Through Failure," *Wall Street Journal,* October 27, 2011, pp. D1+; and R. W. Goldfarb, "When Fear Stifles Initiative," *New York Times Online,* May 14, 2011.

69. S. Shellenbarger, "Better Ideas Through Failure."

70. F. Yuan and R. W. Woodman, "Innovative Behavior in the Workplace: The Role of Performance and Image Outcome Expectations," *Academy of Management Journal,* April 2010, pp. 323–342.

71. K. E. M. De Stobbeleir, S. J. Ashford, and D. Buyens, "Self-Regulation of Creativity At Work: The Role of Feedback-Seeking Behavior in Creative Performance."

72. J. McGregor, "The World's Most Innovative Companies," *BusinessWeek,* April 24, 2006, p. 70.

73. X. Zhang and K. M. Bartol, "Linking Empowering Leadership and Employee Creativity: The Influence of Psychological Empowerment, Intrinsic Motivation, and Creative Process Engagement," *Academy of Management Journal,* February 2010, pp. 107–128.

74. J. H. Dyer, H. B. Gregersen, and C. M. Christensen, "The Innovator's DNA," *Harvard Business Review,* December 2009, pp. 60–67; J. Gong, J-C Huang, and J-L. Farh, "Employee Learning Orientation, Transformational Leadership, and Employee Creativity: The Mediating Role of Employee Creative Self-Efficacy," *Academy of Management Journal,* August 2009, pp. 765–778; B. Buxton, "Innovation Calls for I-Shaped People," *BusinessWeek Online* [www.businessweek.com], July 13, 2009; J. Ramos, "Producing Change That Lasts," *Across the Board,* March 1994, pp. 29–33; T. Stjernberg and A. Philips, "Organizational Innovations in a Long-Term Perspective: Legitimacy and Souls-of-Fire as Critical Factors of Change and Viability," *Human Relations,* October 1993, pp. 1193–2023; and J. M. Howell and C. A. Higgins, "Champions of Change," *Business Quarterly,* Spring 1990, pp. 31–32.

75. J. Liedtka and T. Ogilvie, *Designing for Growth: A Design Thinking Tool Kit for Managers,* (New York: Columbia Business School Press), 2011.

76. R. E. Silverman, "Companies Change Their Way of Thinking," *Wall Street Journal,* June 7, 2012, p. B8; and R. L. Martin, "The Innovation Catalysts," *Harvard Business Review,* June 2011, pp. 82–87.

77. Ethics Dilemma based on T. Roth and J. Harter, "Unhealthy, Stressed Employees Are Hurting Your Business," *Gallup Business Journal Online,* May 22, 2012; R. Vesely, "EAPs Modernize, But Employees Are Slow to Catch On," *Workforce Management Online,* February 20, 2012; A. Kadet, "Surviving the Superjob;" P. F. Weisberg, "Wellness Programs: Legal Requirements and Risks," *Workforce Management Online* [www.workforce.com], March 2010; S. S. Wang, "Workplace Mental-Health Services Expand," *Wall Street Journal,* December 15, 2009, p. D8; and D. Cole, "The Big Chill," *US News & World Report,* December 6, 2004, pp. EE2–EE5.

78. Developing Your Skill box based on J. P. Kotter and L. A. Schlesinger, "Choosing Strategies for Change," *Harvard Business Review,* March–April 1979, pp. 106–114; and T. A. Stewart, "Rate Your Readiness to Change," *Fortune,* February 7, 1994, pp. 106–110.

79. Team Exercise based on M. Fuchs, "Getting Your Organization Ready for Converting to International Financial Reporting Standards," *Workforce Management Online* [www.workforce.com], September 2009.

80. B. Horovitz, "In Search of Next Big Thing," *USA Today,* July 9, 2012, pp. 1B+; Press Release, "Under Armour Reports Fourth Quarter Net Revenues Growth of 34% and Fourth Quarter EPS Growth of 40%," [investor.underarmour.com], January 26, 2012; D. Roberts, "Under Armour Gets Serious," *Fortune,* November

7, 2011, pp. 153–162; E. Olson, "Under Armour Applies Its Muscle to Shoes," *New York Times Online,* August 8, 2011, M. Townsend, "Under Armour's Daring Half-Court Shot," *Bloomberg BusinessWeek,* November 1–November 7, 2010, pp. 24–25; and E. Olson, "Under Armour Wants to Dress Athletic Young Women," *New York Times Online,* August 31, 2010.

81. J. Clare, "Foxconn Says Another Worker Committed Suicide," Reuters, [www.businessinsider.com], June 14, 2012; M. Moore, "Mass Suicide Protest at Apple Manufacturer Foxconn Factory," [www.telegraph.co.uk], January 11, 2012; C. Campbell, "Foxconn's Robot Empire," *Macleans,* November 21, 2011, p. 41; T. Culpan, Z. Lifei, B. Einhorn, "How to Beat the High Cost of Happy Workers," *Bloomberg BusinessWeek,* May 9, 2011, pp. 39–40; A. Chrisafis, "France Télécom Worker Kills Himself in Office Car Park," [www.guardian.co.uk], April 26, 2011; M. Saltmarsh, "France Télécom Suicides Prompt an Investigation," *New York Times Online,* April 9, 2010; C. Stievenard, "France's Approach to Workplace Bullying," *Workforce Management Online* [www.workforce.com], March 2010; R. Bender and M. Colchester, "Morale Is Priority for France Télécom," *Wall Street Journal,* February 4, 2010, p. B2; The Associated Press, "Executive Quits After Suicides at France Télécom," *New York Times Online,* October 6, 2009; and D. Jolly and M. Saltmarsh, "Suicides in France Put Focus on Workplace," *New York Times Online,* September 30, 2009.

CHAPTER 8

1. K. O'Brien, "How McDonald's Came Back Bigger Than Ever," *New York Times Online,* May 4, 2012; C. Choi, "McDonald's Aims to Stay Fresh With New Seasonal Menu Items," Associated Press, *Springfield, Missouri News-Leader,* May 4, 2012, p. 7B; L. Patton, "McDonald's Pursuit of the Perfect French Fry," *Bloomberg BusinessWeek Online,* April 19, 2012; McDonald's [www.mcdonalds.com],February 29, 2012; L. Burkitt, "McDonald's Pushes for More Gains in China," *Wall Street Journal,* February 29, 2012, p. B7; "Food CPI and Expenditures," *USDA Economic Research Service,* [www.ers.usda.gov], February 29, 2012; "Fish McBites, Mcdonald's Newest Snack, Makes It to Select Stores in Time for Lent," *Huffington Post,* [www.huffingtonpost.com], February 23, 2012; S. Strom, "McDonald's Set to Phase Out Suppliers' Use of Sow Crates," *New York Times Online,* February 13, 2012; N. Kruse, "Tailoring the Menu to Meet Customers' Needs," *Nation's Restaurant News,* February 6, 2012, p. 8; J. Jargon, "Late-Night Sales on a Roll For U.S. Fast-Food Outlets," *Wall Street Journal,* January 25, 2012, pp. B1+; "Fast Food Industry Profile: Global," Datamonitor Plc, January 2012, pp. 12+; A. Gasparro and M. Warner, "McDonald's Sells, 24/7," *Wall Street Journal,* December 9, 2011, p. B2; B. Kowitt, "Why McDonald's Wins in Any Economy," *Fortune,* September 5, 2011, pp. 70-78; J. Jargon, "Under Pressure, McDonald's Adds Apples to Kids Meals," *Wall Street Journal,* July 27, 2011, pp. B1+; S. Strom, "McDonald's Trims Its Happy Meal," *New York Times Online,* July 26, 2011; A. Schachtel, "McDonald's New Menu to Focus on Healthy Options," [http://wallstcheatsheet.com], July 26, 2011; Press Release, "Effie Worldwide and Warc Reveal First Global Effectiveness Rankings: The Most Effective Agencies, Advertisers and Brands," *Effie Worldwide,* [www.effie.org], June 23, 2011.

2. D. Gates and M. Allison, "Boeing, ANA Celebrate First 787 Delivery," *Seattle Times Online,* September 26, 2011; P.

Sanders, "Boeing Says Flaw Slows 787 Assembly," *Wall Street Journal,* May 18, 2010, p. B1; Boeing News Release, "ANA Pilots First Customer Crew to Fly Boeing 787 Dreamliner" [boeingmediaroom.com], May 13, 2010; *Seattle Times* Business Staff, "25 More Orders Canceled for Boeing's New 787," *Seattle Times Online,* July 5, 2009; J. L. Lunsford, "Boeing Delays Dreamliner Delivery Again," *Wall Street Journal,* April 10, 2008, p. B3; and J. Teresko, "The Boeing 787: A Matter of Materials," *Industry Week,* December 2007, pp. 34–38.

3. See, for example, A. Ghobadian, N. O'Regan, H. Thomas, and J. Liu, "Formal Strategic Planning, Operating Environment, Size, Sector, and Performance," *Journal of General Management,* Winter 2008, pp. 1–19; F. Delmar and S. Shane, "Does Business Planning Facilitate the Development of New Ventures?" *Strategic Management Journal,* December 2003, pp. 1165–1185; R. M. Grant, "Strategic Planning in a Turbulent Environment: Evidence from the Oil Majors," *Strategic Management Journal,* June 2003, pp. 491–517; P. J. Brews and M. R. Hunt, "Learning to Plan and Planning to Learn: Resolving the Planning School/Learning School Debate," *Strategic Management Journal,* December 1999, pp. 889–913; C. C. Miller and L. B. Cardinal, "Strategic Planning and Firm Performance: A Synthesis of More Than Two Decades of Research," *Academy of Management Journal,* March 1994, pp. 1649–1685; N. Capon, J. U. Farley, and J. M. Hulbert, "Strategic Planning and Financial Performance: More Evidence," *Journal of Management Studies,* January 1994, pp. 22–38; D. K. Sinha, "The Contribution of Formal Planning to Decisions," *Strategic Management Journal,* October 1990, pp. 479–492; J. A. Pearce II, E. B. Freeman, and R. B. Robinson Jr., "The Tenuous Link between Formal Strategic Planning and Financial Performance," *Academy of Management Review,* October 1987, pp. 658–675; L. C. Rhyne, "Contrasting Planning Systems in High, Medium, and Low Performance Companies," *Journal of Management Studies,* July 1987, pp. 363–385; and J. A. Pearce II, K. K. Robbins, and R. B. Robinson, Jr., "The Impact of Grand Strategy and Planning Formality on Financial Performance," *Strategic Management Journal,* March–April 1987, pp. 125–134.

4. R. Molz, "How Leaders Use Goals," *Long Range Planning,* October 1987, p. 91.

5. C. Hymowitz, "When Meeting Targets Becomes the Strategy, CEO Is on Wrong Path," *Wall Street Journal,* March 8, 2005, p. B1.

6. McDonald's 2010 Proxy Statement [www.mcdonalds.com], May 24, 2010; and McDonald's Annual Report 2007 [www.mcdonalds.com], April 21, 2008.

7. S. Clifford and J. Creswell, "At Bloomberg, Modest Strategy to Rule the World," *New York Times Online,* November 15, 2009.

8. Nike [www.nikebiz.com/crreport/] Deutsche Bank [www.db.com/en/content/company/mission_and_brand.htm] and EnCana Corporate Constitution (2010) [www.encana.com].

9. See, for instance, J. Pfeffer, *Organizational Design* (Arlington Heights, IL: AHM Publishing, 1978), pp. 5–12; and C. K. Warriner, "The Problem of Organizational Purpose," *Sociological Quarterly,* Spring 1965, pp. 139–146.

10. J. D. Hunger and T. L. Wheelen, *Strategic Management and Business Policy,* 10th ed. (Upper Saddle River, NJ: Prentice Hall, 2006).

11. Leader Who Made a Difference box based on R. L. Brandt, "Birth of a Salesman," *Wall Street Journal,* October 15–16,

2012, pp. C1+; D. Lyons, "Jeff Bezos," *Newsweek,* December 28, 2009/January 4, 2010, pp. 85–86; B. Stone, "Can Amazon Be Wal-Mart of the Web?" *New York Times Online,* September 20, 2009; and K. Kelleher, "Why Amazon Is Bucking the Trend," *CNNMoney.com,* March 2, 2009.

12. J. L. Roberts, "Signed. Sealed. Delivered?" *Newsweek,* June 20, 2005, pp. 44–46.

13. J. Jusko, "Unwavering Focus," *Industry Week,* January 2010, p. 26.

14. P. N. Romani, "MBO By Any Other Name is Still MBO," *Supervision,* December 1997, pp. 6–8; and A. W. Schrader and G. T. Seward, "MBO Makes Dollar Sense," *Personnel Journal,* July 1989, pp. 32–37.

15. R. Rodgers and J. E. Hunter, "Impact of Management by Objectives on Organizational Productivity," *Journal of Applied Psychology*, April 1991, pp. 322–336.

16. E. A. Locke and G. P. Latham, "Has Goal Setting Gone Wild, or Have Its Attackers Abandoned Good Scholarship?" *Academy of Management Perspectives,* February 2009, pp. 17–23; and G. P. Latham, "The Motivational Benefits of Goal-Setting," *Academy of Management Executive,* November 2004, pp. 126–129.

17. L. Wayne, "P&G Sees the World as Its Client," *New York Times Online,* December 12, 2009.

18. For additional information on goals, see, for instance, P. Drucker, *The Executive in Action* (New York: HarperCollins Books, 1996), pp. 207–214; and E. A. Locke and G. P. Latham, *A Theory of Goal Setting and Task Performance* (Upper Saddle River, NJ: Prentice Hall, 1990).

19. data points box based on American Management Association, "Mercer Study Shows Workforce Priorities for 2010" [www. amanet.org], October 21, 2009; M. Weinstein, "Coming Up Short? Join the Club," *Training,* April 2006, p. 14; G. Kranz, "Workers Unprepared," *Workforce Management Online,* March 13, 2008; J. Yang, "Disaster Recovery Plan," *USA Today,* November 13, 2005, p. 1B; and American Management Association, "2003 Survey on Leadership Challenges" [www. amanet.org], April 24, 2004.

20. Several of these factors were suggested by R. K. Bresser and R. C. Bishop, "Dysfunctional Effects of Formal Planning: Two Theoretical Explanations," Academy of Management Review, October 1983, pp. 588–599; and J. S. Armstrong, "The Value of Formal Planning for Strategic Decisions: Review of Empirical Research," Strategic Management Journal, July–September 1982, pp. 197–211.

21. Brews and Hunt, "Learning to Plan and Planning to Learn: Resolving the Planning School/Learning School Debate."

22. D. Rowinski, "As Apple Dominates U.S. Sales, Smartphone Focus Shifts Overseas," [http://www.readwriteweb.com/mobile/2012/04/as-apple-dominates-us-sales-smartphone-focus-shifts-overseas.php], April 26, 2012.

23. R. Farzad, "AT&T's iMess," *Bloomberg BusinessWeek,* February 15, 2010, pp. 34–40.

24. A. Campbell, "Tailored, Not Benchmarked: A Fresh Look at Corporate Planning," *Harvard Business Review*, March–April 1999, pp. 41–50.

25. J. H. Sheridan, "Focused on Flow," *IW,* October 18, 1999, pp. 46–51.

26. A. Taylor III, "Hyundai Smokes the Competition," *Fortune,* January 18, 2010, pp. 62–71.

27. J. Vance, "Ten Cloud Computing Leaders," *IT Management Online,* May 26, 2010; A. Rocadela, "Amazon Looks to Widen Lead in Cloud Computing," *Bloomberg BusinessWeek Online,* April 28, 2010; and S. Lawson, "Cloud Computing Could Be a Boon for Flash Storage," *Bloomberg Business Week Online,* August 24, 2009.

28. Brews and Hunt, "Learning to Plan and Planning to Learn: Resolving the Planning School/Learning School Debate."

29. J. Ribeiro, "Wipro Sees Drop in Outsourcing Revenue," *Bloomberg BusinessWeek Online,* July 22, 2009; S. N. Mehta, "Schooled by China and India," *CNNMoney Online,* May 5, 2009; R. J. Newman, "Coming and Going," *US News and World Report,* January 23, 2006, pp. 50–52; T. Atlas, "Bangalore's Big Dreams," *US News and World Report,* May 2, 2005, pp. 50–52; and K. H. Hammonds, "Smart, Determined, Ambitious, Cheap: The New Face of Global Competition," *Fast Company,* February 2003, pp. 90–97.

30. G. Fairclough and V. Bauerlein, "Pepsi CEO Tours China to Get a Feel for Market," *Wall Street Journal,* July 1, 2009, p. B5.

31. See, for example, P. Tarraf and R. Molz, "Competitive Intelligence," *SAM Advanced Management Journal,* Autumn 2006, pp. 24–34; W. M. Fitzpatrick, "Uncovering Trade Secrets: The Legal and Ethical Conundrum of Creative Competitive Intelligence," *S.A.M Advanced Management Journal,* Summer 2003, pp. 4–12; L. Lavelle, "The Case of the Corporate Spy," *BusinessWeek*, November 26, 2001, pp. 56–58; C. Britton, "Deconstructing Advertising: What Your Competitor's Advertising Can Tell You About Their Strategy," *Competitive Intelligence,* January/February 2002, pp. 15–19; and L. Smith, "Business Intelligence Progress in Jeopardy," *Information Week,* March 4, 2002, p. 74.

32. S. Greenbard, "New Heights in Business Intelligence," *Business Finance,* March 2002, pp. 41–46; K. A. Zimmermann, "The Democratization of Business Intelligence," *KN World,* May 2002, pp. 20–21; and C. Britton, "Deconstructing Advertising: What Your Competitor's Advertising Can Tell You About Their Strategy," *Competitive Intelligence,* January/February 2002, pp. 15–19.

33. L. Weathersby, "Take This Job and ***** It," *Fortune,* January 7, 2002, p. 122.

34. D. Leonard, "The Corporate Side of Snooping," *New York Times Online,* March 5, 2010; B. Acohido, "Corporate Espionage Surges in Tough Times," *USA Today,* July 29, 2009, pp. 1B+; and B. Rosner, "HR Should Get a Clue: Corporate Spying is Real," *Workforce,* April 2001, pp. 72–75.

35. P. Lattman, "Hotel Feud Prompts Probe by Grand Jury," *Wall Street Journal,* October 7, 2009, p. A1+; "Starwood vs. Hilton," *Hotels' Investment Outlook,* June 2009, p. 14; R. Kidder, "Hotel Industry Roiled by Corporate Espionage Claim," *Ethics Newsline* [www.globalethicslorg/newsline] Reuters, "Hilton Hotels Is Subpoenaed in Espionage Case," *New York Times Online,* April 22, 2009; T. Audi, "U.S. Probes Hilton Over Theft Claims," *Wall Street Journal,* April 22, 2009, p. B1; and T. Audi, "Hilton Is Sued Over Luxury Chain," *Wall Street Journal,* April 17, 2009, p. B1.

36. S. Bergsman, "Corporate Spying Goes Mainstream," *CFO,* December 1997, p. 24; and K. Western, "Ethical Spying," *Business Ethics,* September–October 1995, pp. 22–23.

37. "Wayward At Safeway," *Workforce.com,* November 8, 2011; S. Halzack, "Safeway Sandwich Theft Allegation: Charges Dropped; What Do You Think?" *Washingtonpost.com,* November 2, 2011; and "Couple Jailed, Lose Custody of Daughter, Over Stolen Sandwiches," *Reuters.com,* October 30, 2011.

38. C. Herring, "Schools' New Math: The Four-Day Week," *Wall Street Journal,* March 8, 2010, pp. A1+.

39. The Associated Press, "Habitat for Humanity Gets $100 Million from Developer," *Wall Street Journal,* May 15, 2009, p. A5; G. Bluestein, The Associated Press, "Record Gift for Habitat for Humanity," *Springfield, Missouri, News-Leader,* May 15, 2009, p. 3B; The Associated Press, "Habitat for Humanity Gets $100 Million Gift," *MSNBC. com* [www.msnbc.msn.com], May 14, 2009; and "$100 Million Commitment Made to Habitat for Humanity by J. Ronald Terwilliger" [www.habitat.org], May 14, 2009.

40. "Garmin Finds Route Higher," *Forbes.com,* May 2, 2012; "Come on Baby, Drive My Car," *Tech Talk,* April 2012, pp. 24–28; E. Rhey, "A GPS Maker Shifts Gears," *Fortune,* March 19, 2012, p. 62; "Garmin® Arrives at a Milestone: 100 Million Products Sold," *Garmin.com,* May 2, 2012; and B. Charny, "Garmin's Positioning Comes Under Scrutiny," *Wall Street Journal,* April 2, 2008, p. A5.

CHAPTER 9

1. A. Troianovski and S. Grundberg, "Nokia's Bad Call on Smartphones," *Wall Street Journal,* July 19, 2012, pp. A1+; J. D. Stoll, "Nokia Late to the Silicon Valley Party," *Wall Street Journal,* June 21, 2012, pp. B1+; K. J. O'Brien, "One Year Later, Nokia and Microsoft Deliver," *New York Times Online,* February 27, 2012; C. Huston, "Nokia Corporation," *Hoover's Online,* February 26, 2012; C. Lawton, "Nokia Takes Aim at High-End U.S. Market," *Wall Street Journal,* January 10, 2012, p. B5; C. Lawton, "It's Crunch Time for Nokia," *Wall Street Journal,* October 25, 2011, p. B6; K. J. O'Brien, "Nokia to Cut 3,500 More Jobs," *New York Times Online,* September 29, 2011; C. Lawton, "Nokia's Troubles Hit Suppliers," *Wall Street Journal,* September 27, 2011, p. B8; C. Lawton, "Nokia Aims Software At Low-End Phones," *Wall Street Journal,* September 29, 2011, p. B11; B. Dummett, "Nokia Sells 2,000 Patents," *Wall Street Journal,* September 2, 2011, p. B2; C. Lawton and C. H. Wong, "Nokia Shows Off New Phones," *Wall Street Journal,* June 22, 2011, p. B6; C. Lawton, "Missed Call: Nokia Reversal of Fortune Is Also Finland's," *Wall Street Journal,* June 3, 2011, p. A12; C. Lawton, "Investors Hang Up on Nokia," *Wall Street Journal,* June 1, 2011, pp. B1+; S. Lohr, "Playing Catch-Up, Nokia and H.P. Try to Innovate," *New York Times Online,* February 9, 2011; J. S. Lublin and C. Lawton, "New CEO of Nokia Readies Shake-Up," *Wall Street Journal,* February 7, 2011, pp. B1+; G. Sandstrom and C. Lawton, "Nokia CEO Makes His Mark," *Wall Street Journal,* October 22, 2010, p. B3; and J. Ewing and C. Kharif, "Nokia Takes Aim at Apple," *Bloomberg BusinessWeek Online,* August 27, 2009.

2. S. Martin, "Tablet Wars Heat Up With Mini iPad," *USA Today,* July 6-8, 2012, p. 1A; D. Michaels, J. Ostrower, and D. Pearson, "Airbus's New Push: Made In the U.S.A." *Wall Street Journal,* July 3, 2012, p. A1+; "Applebee's Gets Fresh," *USA Today,* July 2, 2012, pp. 1B+; and A. Sharma and J. Hansegard, "IKEA Says It Is Ready To Give India A Try," *Wall Street Journal,* June 25, 2012, p. B1.

3. J. W. Dean, Jr. and M. P. Sharfman, "Does Decision Process Matter? A Study of Strategic Decision-Making Effectiveness," *Academy of Management Journal,* April 1996, pp. 368–396.

4. Based on A. A. Thompson Jr., A. J. Strickland III, and J. E. Gamble, *Crafting and Executing Strategy,* 14th ed. (New York: McGraw-Hill Irwin, 2005).

5. J. Magretta, "Why Business Models Matter," *Harvard Business Review,* May 2002, pp. 86–92.

6. B. Carter, "'American Idol' and Its Owner to Undergo a Retooling," *New York Times Online,* May 30, 2012; B. Keveney, "'Idol' May be Down, But It's Not Out," *USA Today,* May 22, 2012, p. 1D; G. Levin and B. Keveney, "NBC Upstart 'The Voice' Calls Out 'American Idol'," *USA Today,* February 16, 2012, pp. 1B+; S. Schechner, "Fewer Viewers Tune in for Cowell's 'Idol' Finale," *Wall Street Journal,* May 28, 2010, p. B7; B. Keveny, "Idol Ratings Take A Tumble," *USA Today,* May 4, 2010, p. 1D; R. Bianco, "Time for Producers to Fix 'Idol' Franchise," *USA Today,* May 4, 2010, p. 7D; and D. J. Lang, Associated Press *Springfield, Missouri News-Leader,* May 3, 2008, p. 4C.

7. M. Song, S. Im, H. van der Bij, and L. Z. Song, "Does Strategic Planning Enhance or Impede Innovation and Firm Performance?" *Journal of Product Innovation Management,* July 2011, pp. 503–520; M. Reimann, O. Schilke, and J. S. Thomas, "Customer Relationship Management and Firm Performance: The Mediating Role of Business Strategy," *Journal of the Academy of Marketing Science,* Summer 2010, pp. 326–346; J. Aspara, J. Hietanen, and H. Tikkanen, "Business Model Innovation vs. Replication: Financial Performance Implications of Strategic Emphases," *Journal of Strategic Marketing,* February 2010, pp. 39–56; J. C. Short, D. J. Ketchen Jr., T. B. Palmer, and G. T. M. Hult, "Firm, Strategic Group, and Industry Influences on Performance," *Strategic Management Journal,* February 2007, pp. 147–167; H. J. Cho and V. Pucik, "Relationship Between Innovativeness, Quality, Growth, Profitability, and Market Value," *Strategic Management Journal,* June 2005, pp. 555–575; A. Carmeli and A. Tischler, "The Relationships Between Intangible Organizational Elements and Organizational Performance," *Strategic Management Journal,* December 2004, pp. 1257–1278; D. J. Ketchen, C. C. Snow, and V. L. Street, "Improving Firm Performance by Matching Strategic Decision-Making Processes to Competitive Dynamics," *Academy of Management Executive,* November 2004, pp. 29–43; E. H. Bowman and C. E. Helfat, "Does Corporate Strategy Matter?" *Strategic Management Journal,* 22 (2001), pp. 1–23; P. J. Brews and M. R. Hunt, "Learning to Plan and Planning to Learn: Resolving the Planning School-Learning School Debate," *Strategic Management Journal,* 20 (1999), pp. 889–913; D. J. Ketchen Jr., J. B. Thomas, and R. R. McDaniel Jr., "Process, Content and Context; Synergistic Effects on Performance," *Journal of Management,* 22, no. 2 (1996), pp. 231–257; C. C. Miller and L. B. Cardinal, "Strategic Planning and Firm Performance: A Synthesis of More Than Two Decades of Research," *Academy of Management Journal,* December 1994, pp. 1649–1665; and N. Capon, J. U. Farley, and J. M. Hulbert, "Strategic Planning and Financial Performance: More Evidence," *Journal of Management Studies,* January 1994, pp. 105–110.

8. J. S. Lublin and D. Mattioli, "Strategic Plans Lose Favor," *Wall Street Journal,* January 25, 2010, p. B7.

9. J. Liberto, "Postal Plants to Shrink, 28,000 Jobs At Stake," *CNNMoney.com,* May 17, 2012; C. Boles, "Postal Rescue Passes Senate," *Wall Street Journal,* April 26, 2012, p. A2; J. Liberto, "Congress Ready to Tackle Postal Reform," *CNNMoney.com,* April 16, 2012; D. Leinwand, "Postal Service Seeks 5-Day Delivery," *USA Today,* March 2, 2010, p. 3A; and Wire Reports, "Postal Chief Calls for 5-Day Delivery to Save $3.5 Billion Yearly," *USA Today,* March 26, 2009, p. 4A.

10. You can see this document at the United States Postal Service Web site at [www.usps.com/strategicplanning/].

11. B. Stone, "The Education of Larry Page," *Bloomberg BusinessWeek,* April 9–April 15, 2012, pp. 12–14.

12. C. Armario, "More Young Adults Earn College Degrees," Associated Press, *Springfield, Missouri, News-Leader,* July 13, 2012, p. 3A; A. R. Sorkin, "Angry Birds Maker Posted Revenue of $106.3 Million in 2011," *New York Times Online,* May 7, 2012; J. Wortham, "Cellphones Now Used More for Data Than for Calls," *New York Times Online,* May 13, 2010; and S. Rosenbloom, "Calorie Data to Be Posted at Most Chains," *New York Times Online,* March 23, 2010.

13. C. K. Prahalad and G. Hamel, "The Core Competence of the Corporation," *Harvard Business Review*, May–June 1990, pp. 79–91.

14. Leader Who Made a Difference box based on M. Quinn and A. Stuart, "Not Just Bean Counters," *Wall Street Journal,* July 31, 2012, pp. B1+; J. Lahart, "Lowe's Still Needs Repair to Compete With Home Depot," *Wall Street Journal,* June 6, 2012, p. C16; N. Janowitz, "Rolling in the Depot," *Fast Company,* May 2012, p. 38; M. Bustillo and D. Mattioli, "From Home Depot to Saks, Some Retailers Gain Edge," *Wall Street Journal,* February 22, 2012, p. B1; C. Burritt, "Home Depot's Fix-It Lady," *Bloomberg BusinessWeek,* January 17–January 23, 2011, pp. 64–67; P. Wahlstrom, "Home Depot: Shifting From the Art of Retail to the Science of Retail," *Morningstar Stock Investor,* August 15, 2010, pp. 12–13; and G. Colvin, "Renovating Home Depot," *Fortune,* August 31, 2009, pp. 45–50.

15. H. Quarls, T. Pernsteiner, and K. Rangan, "Love Your Dogs," *Strategy & Business,* Spring 2006, pp. 58–65; and P. Haspeslagh, "Portfolio Planning: Uses and Limits," *Harvard Business Review*, January–February 1982, pp. 58–73.

16. *Perspective on Experience* (Boston: Boston Consulting Group, 1970).

17. "100 Best Global Brands," *BusinessWeek,* September 28, 2009, pp. 50–56.

18. J. B. Barney, "Looking Inside for Competitive Advantage," *Academy of Management Executive*, November 1995, pp. 49–61; M. A. Peteraf, "The Cornerstones of Competitive Advantage: A Resource-Based View," *Strategic Management Journal*, March 1993, pp. 179–191; J. Barney, "Firm Resources and Sustained Competitive Advantage," *Journal of Management* 17, No. 1 (1991), pp. 99–120; M. E. Porter, *Competitive Advantage: Creating and Sustaining Superior Performance* (New York: Free Press, 1985); and R. Rumelt, "Towards a Strategic Theory of the Firm," in R. Lamb (ed.), *Competitive Strategic Management* (Upper Saddle River, NJ: Prentice Hall, 1984), pp. 556–570.

19. R. D. Spitzer, "TQM: The Only Source of Sustainable Competitive Advantage," *Quality Progress,* June 1993, pp. 59–64; T. C. Powell, "Total Quality Management as Competitive Advantage: A Review and Empirical Study," *Strategic Management Journal,* January 1995, pp. 15–37; and N. A. Shepherd, "Competitive Advantage: Mapping Change and the Role of the Quality Manager of the Future," *Annual Quality Congress,* May 1998, pp. 53–60.

20. See special issue of *Academy of Management Review* devoted to TQM, July 1994, pp. 390–584; B. Voss, "Quality's Second Coming," *Journal of Business Strategy*, March–April 1994, pp. 42–46; R. Krishnan, A. B. Shani, R. M. Grant, and R. Baer, "In Search of Quality Improvement Problems of

Design and Implementation," *Academy of Management Executive,* November 1993, pp. 7–20; C. A. Barclay, "Quality Strategy and TQM Policies: Empirical Evidence," *Management International Review*, Special Issue 1993, pp. 87–98; and R. Jacob, "TQM: More Than a Dying Fad?" *Fortune,* October 18, 1993, pp. 66–72; and R. J. Schonenberger, "Is Strategy Strategic? Impact of Total Quality Management on Strategy," *Academy of Management Executive,* August 1992, pp. 80–87.

21. "Executive Insight: An Interview with Peter Blair, Senior Director of Marketing, Kiva Systems," *Apparel Magazine,* June 2012, p. 24; A. Noto, "Amazon's Robotics Play Underscores Industry Trend," *Mergers & Acquisitions: The Dealmaker's Journal,* May 2012, p. 14; "Amazon to Acquire Kiva Systems for $775 Million," *Material Handling & Logistics,*" April 2012, p. 7; and C. Chaey, "The World's 50 Most Innovative Companies: Kiva Systems," *FastCompany.com,* March 2012, p. 110.

22. D. Dunne and R. Martin, "Design Thinking and How It Will Change Management Education: An Interview and Discussion," *Academy of Management Learning & Education,* December 2006, pp. 512–523.

23. See, for example, A. Brandenburger, "Porter's Added Value: High Indeed!" *Academy of Management Executive,* May 2002, pp. 58–60; N. Argyres and A. M. McGahan, "An Interview with Michael Porter," *Academy of Management Executive,* May 2002, pp. 43–52; D. F. Jennings and J. R. Lumpkin, "Insights between Environmental Scanning Activities and Porter's Generic Strategies: An Empirical Analysis," *Strategic Management Journal*, 18, No. 4 (1992), pp. 791–803; I. Bamberger, "Developing Competitive Advantage in Small and Medium-Sized Firms," *Long Range Planning*, October 1989, pp. 80–88; C. W. L. Hill, "Differentiation versus Low Cost or Differentiation and Low Cost: A Contingency Framework," *Academy of Management Review*, July 1988, pp. 401–412; A. I. Murray, "A Contingency View of Porter's 'Generic Strategies,'" *Academy of Management Review*, July 1988, pp. 390–400; M. E. Porter, "From Competitive Advantage to Corporate Strategy," *Harvard Business Review*, May–June 1987, pp. 43–59; G. G. Dess and P. S. Davis, "Porter's (1980) Generic Strategies and Performance: An Empirical Examination with American Data—Part II: Performance Implications," *Organization Studies*, No. 3 (1986), pp. 255–261; G. G. Dess and P. S. Davis, "Porter's (1980) Generic Strategies and Performance: An Empirical Examination with American Data—Part I: Testing Porter," *Organization Studies*, no. 1 (1986), pp. 37–55; G. G. Dess and P. S. Davis, "Porter's (1980) Generic Strategies as Determinants of Strategic Group Membership and Organizational Performance," *Academy of Management Journal*, September 1984, pp. 467–488; Porter, *Competitive Advantage: Creating and Sustaining Superior Performance*; and M. E. Porter, *Competitive Strategy: Techniques for Analyzing Industries and Competitors* (New York: Free Press, 1980).

24. J. W. Bachmann, "Competitive Strategy: It's O.K. to Be Different," *Academy of Management Executive,* May 2002, pp. 61–65; S. Cappel, P. Wright, M. Kroll, and D. Wyld, "Competitive Strategies and Business Performance: An Empirical Study of Select Service Businesses," *International Journal of Management*, March 1992, pp. 1–11; D. Miller, "The Generic Strategy Trap," *Journal of Business Strategy*, January–February 1991, pp. 37–41; R. E. White, "Organizing to Make Business Unit Strategies Work," in H. E. Glass

(ed.), *Handbook of Business Strategy*, 2d ed. (Boston: Warren Gorham and Lamont, 1991), pp. 1–24; and Hill, "Differentiation versus Low Cost or Differentiation and Low Cost: A Contingency Framework."

25. data points box based on M. E. Mangelsdorf, "Interview with Dr. Peter Weill: Getting an Edge from IT," *Wall Street Journal*, November 30, 2009, p. R2; M. E. Raynor, M. Ahmed, and A. D. Henderson, "Are 'Great' Companies Just Lucky?" *Harvard Business Review*, April 2009, pp. 18–19; J. Yang and M. E. Mullins, "Employee's Concerns in Mergers and Acquisitions," *USA Today*, June 6, 2007, p. 1B; and J. Choi, D. Lovallo, and A. Tarasova, "Better Strategy for Business Units: A McKinsey Global Survey," *The McKinsey Quarterly Online* [www.mckinseyquarterly.com], July 2007.

26. B. Sisario, "Out to Shake Up Music, Often With Sharp Words," *New York Times Online*, May 6, 2012; and J. Plambeck, "As CD Sales Wane, Music Retailers Diversify," *New York Times Online*, May 30, 2010.

27. S. Clifford, "Amazon Leaps Into High End of the Fashion Pool," *New York Times Online*, May 7, 2012 and "Can Amazon Be A Fashion Player?" *Women's Wear Daily*, May 4, 2012, p. 1.

28. S. Ghoshal and C. A. Bartlett, "Changing the Role of Top Management: Beyond Structure to Process," *Harvard Business Review*, January–February 1995, pp. 86–96.

29. R. Calori, G. Johnson, and P. Sarnin, "CEO's Cognitive Maps and the Scope of the Organization," *Strategic Management Journal*, July 1994, pp. 437–457.

30. R. D. Ireland and M. A. Hitt, "Achieving and Maintaining Strategic Competitiveness in the 21st Century: The Role of Strategic Leadership," *Academy of Management Executive*, February 1999, pp. 43–57.

31. J. P. Wallman, "Strategic Transactions and Managing the Future: A Druckerian Perspective," *Management Decision*, vol. 48, no. 4, 2010, pp. 485–499; D. E. Zand, "Drucker's Strategic Thinking Process: Three Key Techniques," *Strategy & Leadership*, vol. 38, no. 3, 2010, pp. 23–28; and R. D. Ireland and M. A. Hitt, "Achieving and Maintaining Strategic Competitiveness in the 21st Century: The Role of Strategic Leadership."

32. Lublin and Mattioli, "Strategic Plans Lose Favor."

33. Ibid.

34. K. Shimizu and M. A. Hitt, "Strategic Flexibility: Organizational Preparedness to Reverse Ineffective Decisions," *Academy of Management Executive*, November 2004, p. 44.

35. B. Barnes, "Across U.S., ESPN Aims to Be the Home Team," *New York Times Online*, July 20, 2009; P. Sanders and M. Futterman, "Competition Pushes Up Content Costs for ESPN," *Wall Street Journal*, February 23, 2009, pp. B1+; T. Lowry, "ESPN's Cell-Phone Fumble," *Business Week Online*, October 30, 2006; and T. Lowry, "In the Zone," *Business Week*, October 17, 2005, pp. 66–77.

36. E. Kim, D. Nam, and J. L. Stimpert, "The Applicability of Porter's Generic Strategies in the Digital Age: Assumptions, Conjectures, and Suggestions," *Journal of Management*, vol. 30, no. 5 (2004), pp. 569–589; and G. T. Lumpkin, S. B. Droege, and G. G. Dess, "E-Commerce Strategies: Achieving Sustainable Competitive Advantage and Avoiding Pitfalls," *Organizational Dynamics*, Spring 2002, pp. 325–340.

37. Kim, Nam, and Stimpert, "The Applicability of Porter's Generic Strategies in the Digital Age: Assumptions, Conjectures, and Suggestions."

38. S. Clifford, "Luring Online Shoppers Offline," *New York Times Online*, July 4, 2012.

39. J. Gaffney, "Shoe Fetish," *Business 2.0*, March 2002, pp. 98–99.

40. D. Fickling, "The Singapore Girls Aren't Smiling Anymore," *Bloomberg BusinessWeek*, May 21–May 27, 2012, pp. 25–26; L. Heracleous and J. Wirtz, "Singapore Airlines' Balancing Act," *Harvard Business Review*, July-August 2010, pp. 145–149; and J. Doebele, "The Engineer," *Forbes*, January 9, 2006, pp. 122–124.

41. S. Ellison, "P&G to Unleash Dental Adult-Pet Food," *Wall Street Journal*, December 12, 2002, p. B4.

42. A. O'Leary, "Tech Companies Leave Phone Calls Behind," *New York Times Online*, July 6, 2012.

43. Materials for developing a business plan can be found at Small Business Administration, *The Business Plan Workbook* (Washington, DC, May 17, 2001); and on the Small Business Administration Web site [www.sba.gov]. In addition, readers may find software such as Business Plan Pro Software, available at [www.businessplanpro.com], useful.

44. D. Roman and W. Kemble-Diaz, "Owner of Fast-Fashion Retailer Zara Keeps Up Emerging-Markets Push," *Wall Street Journal*, June 14, 2012, p. B3; Press Releases, "Inditex Achieves Net Sales of 9,709 Million Euros, An Increase of 10 percent," [www.inditex.com], February 22, 2012; C. Bjork, "'Cheap Chic' Apparel Sellers Heat Up U.S. Rivalry on Web," *Wall Street Journal*, September 6, 2011, pp. B1+; A. Kenna, "Zara Plays Catch-up With Online Shoppers," *Bloomberg BusinessWeek*, August 29–September 4, 2011, pp. 24–25; K. Girotra and S. Netessine, "How to Build Risk Into Your Business Model," *Harvard Business Review*, May 2011, pp. 100–105; M. Dart and R. Lewis, "Break the Rules the Way Zappos and Amazon Do," *Bloomberg BusinessWeek Online*, April 29, 2011; K. Cappell, "Zara Thrives by Breaking All the Rules," *BusinessWeek*, October 20, 2008, p. 66; and C. Rohwedder and K. Johnson, "Pace-Setting Zara Seeks More Speed to Fight Its Rising Cheap-Chic Rivals," *Wall Street Journal*, February 20, 2008, pp. B1+.

45. D. Reisinger, "Dark Days Ahead for Netflix?" *Fortune.com*, July 12, 2012; S. Woo and I. Sherr, "Netflix's Growth Disappoints," *Wall Street Journal*, April 24, 2012, pp. B1+; S. Woo and I. Sherr, "Netflix Recovers Subscribers," *Wall Street Journal*, January 26, 2012, pp. B1+; J. Pepitone, "Netflix CEO: We Got Overconfident," *CNNMoney.com*, December 6, 2011; D. McDonald, "Netflix: Down, But Not Out," *CNN.com*, November 23, 2011; H. W. Jenkins, Jr., "Netflix Isn't Doomed," *Wall Street Journal*, October 26, 2011, p. A13; C. Edwards, "Netflix Drops Most Since 2004 After Losing 800,000 Customers," *BusinessWeek.com*, October 25, 2011; N. Wingfield and B. Stelter, "How Netflix Lost 800,000 Members and Good Will," *New York Times Online*, October 24, 2011; C. Edwards and R. Grover, "Can Netflix Regain Lost Ground," *BusinessWeek.com*, October 19, 2011; and R. Grover, C. Edwards, and A. Fixmer, "Can Netflix Find Its Future By Abandoning the Past?" *Bloomberg BusinessWeek*, September 26–October 2, 2011, pp. 29–30.

CHAPTER 10

1. J. Swartz, "Visa Stores Data Like Gold: In Its Own Fort Knox," *USA Today*, March 26, 2012, p. 4B; M. Fitzgerald, "How Visa Protects Your Data" *Fast Company*, October 19, 2011; M. Fitzgerald, "Visa Is Ready for Anything," *FastCompany.com*, November 2011, pp. 54–58; and "Visa Launches New Operating System, Data Center," *CardLine*, November 20, 2009, p. 37.

2. B. Hagenbaugh, "State Quarters Extra Leaf Grew Out of Lunch Break," *USA Today*, January 20, 2006, p. 1B.

3. K. A. Merchant, "The Control Function of Management," *Sloan Management Review,* Summer 1982, pp. 43–55.

4. E. Flamholtz, "Organizational Control Systems Managerial Tool," *California Management Review,* Winter 1979, p. 55.

5. D. Heath and C. Heath, "The Telltale Brown M&M," *Fast Company,* March 2010, pp. 36–38.

6. T. Vinas and J. Jusko, "5 Threats That Could Sink Your Company," *Industry Week,* September 2004, pp. 52–61; "Workplace Security: How Vulnerable Are You?" Special section in *Wall Street Journal,* September 29, 2003, pp. R1–R8; P. Magnusson, "Your Jitters Are Their Lifeblood," *BusinessWeek,* April 14, 2003, p. 41; and T. Purdum, "Preparing for the Worst," *Industry Week,* January 2003, pp. 53–55.

7. A. Young, "Security Lapses Found at CDC Bioterror Lab in Atlanta," *USA Today,* June 28, 2012, p. 5A; J. O'Donnell, "Best Buy Blames Processes for Holiday Mixups," *USA Today,* January 13, 2012, p. 3B; M. Wohlsen, "Lost iPhone Just One Headache for Apple," The Associated Press, *Springfield, Missouri News-Leader,* September 20, 2011, p. 6A; M. Saltmarsh, "UBS Reports $2 Billion Loss by Rogue Trader," *New York Times Online,* September 15, 2011; and J. Pepitone, "Dropbox's Password Nightmare Highlights Cloud Risks," *CNNMoney.com,* June 22, 2011.

8. K. Peters, "Office Depot's President on How 'Mystery Shopping' Helped Spark a Turnaround," *Harvard Business Review,* November 2011, pp. 47–50.

9. S. Kerr, "On the Folly of Rewarding A, While Hoping for B," *Academy of Management Journal,* December 1975, pp. 769–783.

10. D. Heath and C. Heath, "Watch the Game Film," *Fast Company,* June 2010, pp. 52–54.

11. M. Starr, "State-of-the-Art Stats," *Newsweek,* March 24, 2003, pp. 47–49.

12. A. H. Jordan and P. G. Audia, "Self-Enhancement and Learning from Performance Feedback," *Academy of Management Review,* April 2012, pp. 211–231; D. Busser, "Delivering Effective Performance Feedback," *T&D,* April 2012, pp. 32–34; and "U.S. Employees Desire More Sources of Feedback for Performance Reviews," *T&D,* February 2012, p. 18.

13. D. Busser, "Delivering Effective Performance Feedback."

14. S. Clifford, "Demand at Target for Fashion Line Crashes Web Site," *New York Times Online,* September 13, 2011; "Domino's Delivered Free Pizzas," *Springfield, Missouri, News-Leader,* April 3, 2009, p. 3B; and L. Robbins, "Goggle Error Sends Warning Worldwide," *New York Times Online,* February 1, 2009.

15. H. Koontz and R. W. Bradspies, "Managing Through Feedforward Control," *Business Horizons,* June 1972, pp. 25–36.

16. L. Landro, "Hospitals Overhaul ERs to Reduce Mistakes," *Wall Street Journal,* May 10, 2011, p. D3.

17. M. Helft, "The Human Hands Behind the Google Money Machine," *New York Times Online,* June 2, 2008.

18. B. Caulfield, "Shoot to Kill," *Forbes,* January 7, 2008, pp. 92–96.

19. T. Laseter and L. Laseter, "See for Yourself," *Strategy+Business* [www.strategy-business.com], November 29, 2007.

20. W. H. Newman, *Constructive Control: Design and Use of Control Systems* (Upper Saddle River, NJ: Prentice Hall, 1975), p. 33.

21. J. H. Cushman, Jr., "U.S. Tightens Security for Economic Data," *New York Times Online,* July 16, 2012; B. Worthen, "Private Sector Keeps Mum on Cyber Attacks," *Wall Street Journal,* January 19, 2010, p. B4; G. Bowley, "Ex-Worker Said to Steal Goldman Code," *New York Times Online,* July 7, 2009; and R. King, "Lessons from the Data Breach at Heartland," *BusinessWeek Online,* July 6, 2009.

22. Deloitte & Touche and the Ponemon Institute, "Research Report: Reportable and Multiple Privacy Breaches Rising at Alarming Rate," *Ethics Newsline* [www.ethicsnewsline. wordpress.com], January 1, 2008.

23. B. Grow, K. Epstein, and C-C. Tschang, "The New E-Spionage Threat," *BusinessWeek,* April 21, 2008, pp. 32–41; S. Leibs, "Firewall of Silence," *CFO,* April 2008, pp. 31–35; J. Pereira, "How Credit-Card Data Went Out Wireless Door," *Wall Street Journal,* May 4, 2007, pp. A1+; and B. Stone, "Firms Fret as Office E-Mail Jumps Security Walls," *New York Times Online,* January 11, 2007.

24. D. Whelan, "Google Me Not," *Forbes,* August 16, 2004, pp. 102–104.

25. K. Hendricks, M. Hora, L. Menor, and C. Wiedman, "Adoption of the Balance Scorecard: A Contingency Variables Analysis," *Canadian Journal of Administrative Sciences,* June 2012, pp. 124–138; E. R. Iselin, J. Sands, and L. Mia, "Multi-Perspective Performance Reporting Systems, Continuous Improvement Systems, and Organizational Performance," *Journal of General Management,* Spring 2011, pp. 19–36; T. L. Albright, C. M. Burgess, A. R. Hibbets, and M. L. Roberts, "Four Steps to Simplify Multimeasure Performance Evaluations Using the Balanced Scorecard," *Journal of Corporate Accounting & Finance,* July–August 2010, pp. 63–68; H. Sundin, M. Granlund, and D. A. Brown, "Balancing Multiple Competing Objectives with a Balanced Scorecard," *European Accounting Review,* vol. 19, no. 2, 2010, pp. 203–246; R. S. Kaplan and D. P. Norton, "How to Implement a New Strategy Without Disrupting Your Organization," *Harvard Business Review,* March 2006, pp. 100–109; L. Bassi and D. McMurrer, "Developing Measurement Systems for Managers in the Knowledge Era," *Organizational Dynamics,* May 2005, pp. 185–196; G. M. J. DeKoning, "Making the Balanced Scorecard Work (Part 2)," *Gallup Brain* [brain.gallup.com], August 12, 2004; G. J. J. DeKoning, "Making the Balanced Scorecard Work (Part 1)," *Gallup Brain* [brain.gallup.com], July 8, 2004; K. Graham, "Balanced Scorecard," *New Zealand Management,* March 2003, pp. 32–34; K. Ellis, "A Ticket to Ride: Balanced Scorecard," *Training,* April 2001, p. 50; and T. Leahy, "Tailoring the Balanced Scorecard," *Business Finance,* August 2000, pp. 53–56.

26. T. Leahy, "Tailoring the Balanced Scorecard."

27. Ibid.

28. V. Fuhrmans, "Replicating Cleveland Clinic's Success Poses Major Challenges," *Wall Street Journal,* July 23, 2009, p. A4.

29. R. Pear, "A.M.A. to Develop Measure of Quality of Medical Care," *New York Times Online,* February 21, 2006; and A. Taylor III, "Double Duty," *Fortune,* March 7, 2005, pp. 104–110.

30. Leader Who Made a Difference box based on J. Reingold and M. Adamo, "The Fun King," *Fortune,* May 21, 2012, pp. 166-174; "The World's Most Admired Companies," *Fortune,* March 19, 2012, pp. 139+; P. Sanders, "Disney Angles for Cash, Loyalty," *Wall Street Journal,* March 11, 2009, p. B4; and R. Siklos, "Bob Iger Rocks Disney," *CNN Online* [www. cnnmoney.com], January 5, 2009.

31. S. Minter, "How Good Is Your Benchmarking?" *Industry Week,* October 2009, pp. 24–26; and T. Leahy, "Extracting Diamonds in the Rough," *Business Finance,* August 2000, pp. 33–37.

32. B. Bruzina, B. Jessop, R. Plourde, B. Whitlock, and L. Rubin, "Ameren Embraces Benchmarking As a Core Business Strategy," *Power Engineering,* November 2002, pp. 121–124.

33. J. Yaukey and C. L. Romero, "Arizona Firm Pays Big for Workers' Digital Downloads," Associated Press, *Springfield, Missouri, News-Leader,* May 6, 2002, p. 6B.

34. L.Petrecca, "Office Madness," *USA Today,* March 15, 2012, pp. 1A+; D. Mattioli and J. Espinoza, "World Cup Poses Challenge to Bosses," *Wall Street Journal,* June 14, 2010, p. B9; "March Madness Leads to Drop in Productivity," *Delaware County Daily Times Online,* March 16, 2010; and "March Madness at Work Raises Questions of Priorities, Productivity," *FoxSports Online,* March 15, 2010.

35. L. Petrecca, "Feel Like Someone's Watching? You're Right," *USA Today,* March 17, 2010, pp. 1B+.

36. S. Armour, "Companies Keep an Eye on Workers' Internet Use," *USA Today,* February 21, 2006, p. 2B.

37. B. White, "The New Workplace Rules: No Video-Watching," *Wall Street Journal,* March 4, 2008, pp. B1+.

38. P-W. Tam, E. White, N. Wingfield, and K. Maher, "Snooping E-Mail by Software Is Now a Workplace Norm," *Wall Street Journal,* March 9, 2005, pp. B1+; D. Hawkins, "Lawsuits Spur Rise in Employee Monitoring," *U.S. News & World Report,* August 13, 2001, p. 53; and L. Guernsey, "You've Got Inappropriate Mail," *New York Times,* April 5, 2000, pp. C1+.

39. S. Armour, "More Companies Keep Track of Workers' E-Mail," *USA Today,* June 13, 2005, p. 4B; and E. Bott, "Are You Safe? Privacy Special Report," *PC Computing,* March 2000, pp. 87–88.

40. B. Acohido, "An Invitation to Crime," *USA Today,* March 4, 2010, pp. A1+; W. P. Smith and F. Tabak, "Monitoring Employee E-mails: Is There Any Room for Privacy?" *Academy of Management Perspectives,* November 2009, pp. 33–38; and S. Boehle, "They're Watching You," *Training,* September 2008, pp. 23–29.

41. data points box based on J. Yang and B. Bravo, "What Is the Most Common Cause of On-the-Job Distraction?" *USA Today,* July 11, 2012, p. 1B; J. Yang and S. Ward, "Safe Workplace?" *USA Today,* March 5, 2012, p. 1B; A. R. Carey and V. Salazar, "When Are People Playing Online Games at Work?" *USA Today,* July 13, 2011, p. 1A; "There's No Shame in Cyberloafing," *Harvard Business Review,* December 2011, p. 30; M. Saltzman, "Poll: 69% Worry About Security," *USA Today,* June 24, 2011, p. 3B; and T. Mullaney, "Distractions for Workers Add Up," *USA Today,* May 18, 2011, p. 1B.

42. S. Greenhouse, "Shoplifters? Studies Say Keep an Eye on Workers," *New York Times Online,* December 30, 2009.

43. A. M. Bell and D. M. Smith, "Theft and Fraud May Be an Inside Job," *Workforce Online* [www.workforce.com], December 3, 2000.

44. C. C. Verschoor, "New Evidence of Benefits from Effective Ethics Systems," *Strategic Finance,* May 2003, pp. 20–21; and E. Krell, "Will Forensic Accounting Go Mainstream?" *Business Finance,* October 2002, pp. 30–34.

45. J. Greenberg, "The STEAL Motive: Managing the Social Determinants of Employee Theft," in R. Giacalone and J. Greenberg (eds.), *Antisocial Behavior in Organizations* (Newbury Park, CA: Sage, 1997), pp. 85–108.

46. B. E. Litzky, K. A. Eddleston, and D. L. Kidder, "The Good, the Bad, and the Misguided: How Managers Inadvertently Encourage Deviant Behaviors," *Academy of Management Perspective,* February 2006, pp. 91–103; "Crime Spree,"

BusinessWeek, September 9, 2002, p. 8; B. P. Niehoff and R. J. Paul, "Causes of Employee Theft and Strategies That HR Managers Can Use for Prevention," *Human Resource Management,* Spring 2000, pp. 51–64; and G. Winter, "Taking at the Office Reaches New Heights: Employee Larceny Is Bigger and Bolder," *New York Times,* July 12, 2000, pp. C1+.

47. This section is based on J. Greenberg, *Behavior in Organizations: Understanding and Managing the Human Side of Work,* 8th ed. (Upper Saddle River, NJ: Prentice Hall, 2003), pp. 329–330.

48. A. H. Bell and D. M. Smith, "Why Some Employees Bite the Hand That Feeds Them," *Workforce Management Online,* December 3, 2000.

49. B. E. Litzky et al., "The Good, the Bad, and the Misguided"; A. H. Bell and D. M. Smith, "Protecting the Company Against Theft and Fraud," *Workforce Management Online,* December 3, 2000; J. D. Hansen, "To Catch a Thief," *Journal of Accountancy,* March 2000, pp. 43–46; and J. Greenberg, "The Cognitive Geometry of Employee Theft," in *Dysfunctional Behavior In Organizations: Nonviolent and Deviant Behavior* (Stamford, CT: JAI Press, 1998), pp. 147–193.

50. R. Rivera and L. Robbins, "Troubles Preceded Connecticut Workplace Killing," *New York Times Online,* August 3, 2010; J. Griffin, "Workplace Violence News" [www.workplaceviolencenews.com], July 16, 2010; J. Smerd, "Workplace Shootings in Florida, Texas Again Put Focus on Violence on the Job," *Workforce Management Online,* November 6, 2009; R. Lenz, Associated Press, "Gunman Kills Five, Himself At Plant," *Springfield, Missouri, News-Leader,* June 26, 2008, p. 6A; CBS News, "Former Postal Worker Kills 5, Herself" [www.cbsnews.com/stories], January 31, 2006; CBS News, "Autoworker's Grudge Turns Deadly" [www.cbsnews.com/stories], January 27, 2005; D. Sharp, "Gunman Just Hated a Lot of People," *USA Today,* July 10, 2003, p. 3A; and M. Prince, "Violence in the Workplace on the Rise; Training, Zero Tolerance Can Prevent Aggression," *Business Insurance,* May 12, 2003, p. 1.

51. "Workplace Shootings: Fact Sheet," U.S. Bureau of Labor Statistics [www.bls.gov/data/], July 2010; Occupational Health and Safety, "BLS: Workplace Homicides Drop to Lowest Number on Record" [www.ohsonline.com], August 17, 2007.

52. J. McCafferty, "Verbal Chills," *CFO,* June 2005, p. 17; S. Armour, "Managers Not Prepared for Workplace Violence," July 15, 2004, pp. 1B+; and "Workplace Violence," OSHA Fact Sheet, U.S. Department of Labor, Occupational Safety and Health Administration, 2002.

53. "Ten Tips on Recognizing and Minimizing Violence," *Workforce Management Online,* December 3, 2000.

54. "Bullying Bosses Cause Work Rage Rise," *Management Issues News* [www.management-issues.com], January 28, 2003.

55. R. McNatt, "Desk Rage," *BusinessWeek,* November 27, 2000, p. 12.

56. M. Gorkin, "Key Components of a Dangerously Dysfunctional Work Environment," *Workforce Management Online,* December 3, 2000.

57. "Ten Tips on Recognizing and Minimizing Violence"; M. Gorkin, "Five Strategies and Structures for Reducing Workplace Violence"; "Investigating Workplace Violence: Where Do You Start?"; and "Points to Cover in a Workplace Violence Policy," all articles from *Workforce Management Online,* December 3, 2000.

58. A. Taylor, "Enterprise Asks What Customer's Thinking and Acts," *USA Today,* May 22, 2006, p. 6B; and A. Taylor, "Driving Customer Satisfaction," *Harvard Business Review,* July 2002, pp. 24–25.

59. S. D. Pugh, J. Dietz, J. W. Wiley, and S. M. Brooks, "Driving Service Effectiveness Through Employee–Customer Linkages," *Academy of Management Executive,* November 2002, pp. 73–84; J. L. Heskett, W. E. Sasser, and L. A. Schlesinger, *The Service Profit Chain* (New York: Free Press, 1997); and J. L. Heskett, T. O. Jones, G. W. Loveman, W. E. Sasser, Jr., and L. A. Schlesinger, "Putting the Service Profit Chain to Work," *Harvard Business Review,* March–April 1994, pp. 164–170.

60. T. Buck and A. Shahrim, "The Translation of Corporate Governance Changes Across National Cultures: The Case of Germany," *Journal of International Business Studies,* January 2005, pp. 42–61; and "A Revolution Where Everyone Wins: Worldwide Movement to Improve Corporate-Governance Standards," *BusinessWeek,* May 19, 2003, p. 72.

61. J. S. McClenahen, "Executives Expect More Board Input," *Industry Week,* October 2002, p. 12.

62. D. Salierno, "Boards Face Increased Responsibility," *Internal Auditor,* June 2003, pp. 14–15.

63. "Restaurant Serves Rum Drink to Boy, 10," www.wishtv. com, April 20, 2012; B. Horovitz, "Restaurants Reel After Babies Get Booze," *USA Today,* April 15, 2011, p. 1B; "Toddler Given Sangria at Restaurant," www.wishtv.com, April 14, 2011; and A. Hillaker, "Applebee's Serves Alcohol to 15-month-old Child Instead of Apple Juice," *MiNBCnews. com,* April 11, 2011.

64. A. Andors, "Keeping Teen Workers Safe," *HR Magazine,* June 2010, pp. 76–80.

65. T. Fowler, "U.S. Nears BP Settlement," *Wall Street Journal,* June 29, 2012, p. A3; T. Tracy, "BP, Contractors Cited," *Wall Street Journal,* October 13, 2011, p. B3; J. M. Broder, "Companies, Crews and Regulators Share Blame in Coast Guard Report on Oil Spill," *New York Times Online,* April 22, 2011; R. Brown, "Oil Rig's Siren Was Kept Silent, Technician Says," *New York Times Online,* July 23, 2010; I. Urbina, "Workers on Doomed Rig Voiced Concern About Safety," *New York Times Online,* July 21, 2010; R. Gold, "Rig's Final Hours Probed," *Wall Street Journal,* July 19, 2010, pp. A1+; S. Lyall, "In BP's Record, a History of Boldness and Costly Blunders," *New York Times Online,* July 12, 2010; B. Casselman and R. Gold, "Unusual Decisions Set Stage for BP Disaster," *Wall Street Journal,* May 27, 2010, pp. A1+; H. Fountain and T. Zeller, Jr., "Panel Suggests Signs of Trouble Before Rig Explosion," *New York Times Online,* May 25, 2010; and R. Gold and N. King Jr., "The Gulf Oil Spill: Red Flags Were Ignored Aboard Doomed Rig," *Wall Street Journal,* May 13, 2010, p. A6.

66. D. Kirka, "Heathrow Handles Record Numbers for Olympics," www.aviationpros.com, July 17, 2012; E. Lawrie, "London Heathrow Olympic Surge Spurs Record Traffic Plan," www. bloomberg.com, July 16, 2012; K. Kühn, "How Has T5 Taken Off?" *Caterer & Hotelkeeper,* March 12, 2010, pp. 22–25; C. Dosh, "Debunking T5 Terror," *Successful Meetings,* April 2009, p. 99; M. Frary, "A Tale of Two Terminals," *Business Travel World,* August 2008, pp. 16–19; K. Capell, "British Airways Hit by Heathrow Fiasco," *BusinessWeek,* April 3, 2008, p. 6; The Associated Press, "Problems Continue at Heathrow's Terminal 5," *International Herald Tribune* [www. iht.com], March 31, 2008; M. Scott, "New Heathrow Hub: Slick, but No Savior," *BusinessWeek,* March 28, 2008, p. 11; and G. Katz, "Flights Are Canceled, Baggage Stranded, as London's New Heathrow Terminal Opens," *The Seattle Times Online* [www.seattletimes.nwsource.com], March 27, 2008.

PLANNING AND CONTROLS TECHNIQUE MODULE

1. J. Brustein, "Star Pitchers in a Duel? Tickets Will Cost More," *New York Times Online,* June 27, 2010; and A. Satariano, "Innovator: Barry Kahn," *Bloomberg BusinessWeek,* May 24–May 30, 2010, p. 39.

2. J. Trotsky, "The Futurists," *US News & World Report,* April 19, 2004, pp. EE4–EE6.

3. F. Vogelstein, "Search and Destroy," *Fortune,* May 2, 2005, pp. 73–82.

4. S. C. Jain, "Environmental Scanning in U.S. Corporations," *Long Range Planning,* April 1984, pp. 117–128; see also L. M. Fuld, *Monitoring the Competition* (New York: John Wiley & Sons, 1988); E. H. Burack and N. J. Mathys, "Environmental Scanning Improves Strategic Planning," *Personnel Administrator,* April 1989, pp. 82–87; R. Subramanian, N. Fernandes, and E. Harper, "Environmental Scanning in U.S. Companies: Their Nature and Their Relationship to Performance," *Management International Review,* July 1993, pp. 271–286; B. K. Boyd and J. Fulk, "Executive Scanning and Perceived Uncertainty: A Multidimensional Model," *Journal of Management,* vol. 22, no. 1, 1996, pp. 1–21; D. S. Elkenov, "Strategic Uncertainty and Environmental Scanning: The Case for Institutional Influences on Scanning Behavior," *Strategic Management Journal,* vol. 18, 1997, pp. 287–302; K. Kumar, R. Subramanian, and K. Strandholm, "Competitive Strategy, Environmental Scanning and Performance: A Context Specific Analysis of Their Relationship," *International Journal of Commerce and Management,* Spring 2001, pp. 1–18; C. G. Wagner, "Top 10 Reasons to Watch Trends," *The Futurist,* March–April 2002, pp. 68–69; and V. K. Garg, B. A. Walters, and R. L. Priem, "Chief Executive Scanning Emphases, Environmental Dynamism, and Manufacturing Firm Performance," *Strategic Management Journal,* August 2003, pp. 725–744.

5. B. Gilad, "The Role of Organized Competitive Intelligence in Corporate Strategy," *Columbia Journal of World Business,* Winter 1989, pp. 29–35; L. Fuld, "A Recipe for Business Intelligence," *Journal of Business Strategy,* January–February 1991, pp. 12–17; J. P. Herring, "The Role of Intelligence in Formulating Strategy," *Journal of Business Strategy,* September–October 1992, pp. 54–60; K. Western, "Ethical Spying," *Business Ethics,* September–October 1995, pp. 22–23; D. Kinard, "Raising Your Competitive IQ: The Payoff of Paying Attention to Potential Competitors," *Association Management,* February 2003, pp. 40–44; K. Girard, "Snooping on a Shoestring," *Business 2.0,* May 2003, pp. 64–66; and "Know Your Enemy," *Business 2.0,* June 2004, p. 89.

6. C. Davis, "Get Smart," *Executive Edge,* October–November 1999, pp. 46–50.

7. B. Ettore, "Managing Competitive Intelligence," *Management Review,* October 1995, pp. 15–19.

8. A. Serwer, "P&G's Covert Operation," *Fortune,* September 17, 2001, pp. 42–44.

9. B. Rosner, "HR Should Get a Clue: Corporate Spying Is Real," *Workforce,* April 2001, pp. 72–75.

10. Western, "Ethical Spying."

11. W. H. Davidson, "The Role of Global Scanning in Business Planning," *Organizational Dynamics,* Winter 1991, pp. 5–16.

12. T. Smart, "Air Supply," *US News & World Report,* February 28, 2005, p. EE10.
13. "Is Supply Chain Collaboration Really Happening?" *ERI Journal* [www.eri.com], January–February 2006; L. Denend and H. Lee, "West Marine: Driving Growth Through Shipshape Supply Chain Management, A Case Study," *Stanford Graduate School of Business* [www.vics.org], April 7, 2005; N. Nix, A. G. Zacharia, R. F. Lusch, W. R. Bridges, and A. Thomas, "Keys to Effective Supply Chain Collaboration: A Special Report from the Collaborative Practices Research Program," *Neeley School of Business, Texas Christian University* [www.vics.org], November 15, 2004; Collaborative, Planning, Forecasting, and Replenishment Committee Web site [www.cpfr.org], May 20, 2003; and J. W. Verity, "Clearing the Cobwebs From the Stockroom," *BusinessWeek*, October 21, 1996, p. 140.
14. See A. B. Fisher, "Is Long-Range Planning Worth It?" *Fortune*, April 23, 1990, pp. 281–284; J. A. Fraser, "On Target," *Inc.*, April 1991, pp. 113–114; P. Schwartz, *The Art of the Long View* (New York: Doubleday/Currency, 1991); G. Hamel and C. K. Prahalad, "Competing for the Future," *Harvard Business Review*, July–August 1994, pp. 122–128; F. Elikai and W. Hall, Jr., "Managing and Improving the Forecasting Process," *Journal of Business Forecasting Methods & Systems*, Spring 1999, pp. 15–19; L. Lapide, "New Developments in Business Forecasting," *Journal of Business Forecasting Methods & Systems*, Summer 1999, pp. 13–14; and T. Leahy, "Building Better Forecasts," *Business Finance*, December 1999, pp. 10–12.
15. J. Goff, "Start with Demand," *CFO*, January 2005, pp. 53–57.
16. L. Brannen, "Upfront: Global Planning Perspectives," *Business Finance,* March 2006, pp. 12+.
17. V. Ryan, "Future Tense," *CFO*, December 2008, pp. 37–42.
18. R. Durand, "Predicting a Firm's Forecasting Ability: The Roles of Organizational Illusion of Control and Organizational Attention," *Strategic Management Journal,* September 2003, pp. 821–838.
19. J. Katz, "Forecasts Demand Change," *Industry Week,* May 2010, pp. 26–29; A. Stuart, "Imperfect Futures," *CFO,* July–August 2009, pp. 48–53; C. L. Jain and M. Covas, "Thinking About Tomorrow," *Wall Street Journal,* July 7, 2008, p. R10+; T. Leahy, "Turning Managers into Forecasters," *Business Finance,* August 2002, pp. 37–40; M. A. Giullian, M. D. Odom, and M. W. Totaro, "Developing Essential Skills for Success in the Business World: A Look at Forecasting," *Journal of Applied Business Research*, Summer 2000, pp. 51–65; F. Elikai and W. Hall, Jr., "Managing and Improving the Forecasting Process;" and N. Pant and W. H. Starbuck, "Innocents in the Forest: Forecasting and Research Methods," *Journal of Management*, June 1990, pp. 433–460.
20. T. Leahy, "Turning Managers into Forecasters."
21. J. Hope, "Use a Rolling Forecast to Spot Trends," *Harvard Business School Working Knowledge* [hbswk.hbs.edu], March 13, 2006.
22. This section is based on Y. K. Shetty, "Benchmarking for Superior Performance," *Long Range Planning* vol. 1, April 1993, pp. 39–44; G. H. Watson, "How Process Benchmarking Supports Corporate Strategy," *Planning Review*, January–February 1993, pp. 12–15; S. Greengard, "Discover Best Practices," *Personnel Journal*, November 1995, pp. 62–73; J. Martin, "Are You as Good as You Think You Are?" *Fortune*, September 30, 1996, pp. 142–152; R. L. Ackoff, "The Trouble with Benchmarking," *Across the Board*, January 2000, p. 13; V. Prabhu, D. Yarrow, and G. Gordon-Hart, "Best Practice and Performance Within Northeast Manufacturing," *Total Quality Management*, January 2000, pp. 113–121; "E-Benchmarking: The Latest E-Trend," *CFO*, March 2000, p. 7; E. Krell, "Now Read This," *Business Finance*, May 2000, pp. 97–103; and H. Johnson, "All in Favor Say Benchmark!" *Training*, August 2004, pp. 30–34.
23. "Newswatch," *CFO,* July 2002, p. 26.
24. Benchmarking examples from the following: S. Carey, "Racing to Improve," *Wall Street Journal,* March 24, 2006, pp. B1+; D. Waller, "NASCAR: The Army's Unlikely Adviser," *Time,* July 4, 2005, p. 19; A. Taylor, III, "Double Duty," *Fortune,* March 7, 2005, p. 108; P. Gogoi, "Thinking Outside the Cereal Box," *BusinessWeek,* July 28, 2003, pp. 74–75; "Benchmarkers Make Strange Bedfellows," *Industry Week,* November 15, 1993, p. 8; G. Fuchsberg, "Here's Help in Finding Corporate Role Models," *Wall Street Journal,* June 1, 1993, p. B1; and A. Tanzer, "Studying at the Feet of the Masters," *Forbes,* May 10, 1993, pp. 43–44.
25. E. Krell, "The Case Against Budgeting," *Business Finance,* July 2003, pp. 20–25; J. Hope and R. Fraser, "Who Needs Budgets?" *Harvard Business Review,* February 2003, pp. 108–115; T. Leahy, "The Top 10 Traps of Budgeting," *Business Finance,* November 2001, pp. 20–26; T. Leahy, "Necessary Evil," *Business Finance,* November 1999, pp. 41–45; J. Fanning, "Businesses Languishing in a Budget Comfort Zone?" *Management Accounting,* July/August 1999, p. 8; "Budgeting Processes: Inefficiency or Inadequate?" *Management Accounting,* February 1999, p. 5; A. Kennedy and D. Dugdale, "Getting the Most From Budgeting," *Management Accounting,* February 1999, pp. 22–24; G. J. Nolan, "The End of Traditional Budgeting," *Bank Accounting & Finance,* Summer 1998, pp. 29–36; and J. Mariotti, "Surviving the Dreaded Budget Process," *IW,* August 17, 1998, p. 150.
26. See, for example, S. Stiansen, "Breaking Even," *Success,* November 1988, p. 16.
27. S. E. Barndt and D. W. Carvey, *Essentials of Operations Management* (Upper Saddle River, NJ: Prentice Hall, 1982), p. 134.
28. E. E. Adam Jr. and R. J. Ebert, *Production and Operations Management*, 5th ed. (Upper Saddle River, NJ: Prentice Hall, 1992), p. 333.
29. See, for instance, C. Benko and F. W. McFarlan, *Connecting the Dots: Aligning Projects with Objectives in Unpredictable Times* (Boston, MA: Harvard Business School Press, 2003); M. W. Lewis, M. A. Welsh, G. E. Dehler, and S. G. Green, "Product Development Tensions: Exploring Contrasting Styles of Project Management," *Academy of Management Journal,* June 2002, pp. 546–564; C. E. Gray and E. W. Larsen, *Project Management: The Managerial Process* (Columbus, OH: McGraw-Hill Higher Education, 2000); J. Davidson Frame, *Project Management Competence: Building Key Skills for Individuals, Teams, and Organizations* (San Francisco, CA: Jossey-Bass, 1999).
30. For more information, see Project Management Software Directory [www.infogoal.com/pmc/pmcswr.htm].
31. D. Zielinski, "Soft Skills, Hard Truth," *Training,* July 2005, pp. 19–23.
32. H. Collingwood, "Best Kept Secrets of the World's Best Companies: Secret 05, Bad News Folders," *Business 2.0,* April 2006, p. 84.
33. G. Colvin, "An Executive Risk Handbook," *Fortune,* October 3, 2005, pp. 69–70; A. Long and A. Weiss, "Using Scenario Planning to Manage Short-Term Uncertainty,"

Outward Insights [www.outwardinsights.com], 2005;
B. Fiora, "Use Early Warning to Strengthen Scenario
Planning," *Outward Insights* [www.outwardinsights.com],
2003; L. Fahey, "Scenario Learning," *Management Review,*
March 2000, pp. 29–34; S. Caudron, "Frontview Mirror,"
Business Finance, December 1999, pp. 24–30; and J. R.
Garber, "What if...?," *Forbes,* November 2, 1998, pp. 76–79.
34. S. Caudron, "Frontview Mirror," p. 30.

MANAGING OPERATIONS MODULE

1. K. Baxter, "Seoul Showcases Its Talent," *MEED: Middle
East Economic Digest,* May 14, 2010, pp. 13–24; E. Ramstad,
"High-Speed Wireless Transforms a Shipyard," *Wall Street
Journal,* March 16, 2010, p. B6; and Datamonitor, "Company
Profile: Hyundai Heavy Industries Co., Ltd." [www.
datamonitor.com], November 27, 2009.
2. D. McGinn, "Faster Food," *Newsweek,* April 19, 2004, pp.
E20–E22.
3. *World Factbook 2012,* available online at https://www.cia.gov/
library/publications/the-world-factbook/.
4. D. Michaels and J. L. Lunsford, "Streamlined Plane Making,"
Wall Street Journal, April 1, 2005, pp. B1+.
5. T. Aeppel, "Workers Not Included," *Wall Street Journal,*
November 19, 2002, pp. B1+.
6. A. Aston and M. Arndt, "The Flexible Factory,"
BusinessWeek, May 5, 2003, pp. 90–91.
7. P. Panchak, "Pella Drives Lean Throughout the Enterprise,"
Industry Week, June 2003, pp. 74–77.
8. J. Ordonez, "McDonald's to Cut the Cooking Time of Its
French Fries," *Wall Street Journal,* May 19, 2000, p. B2.
9. C. Fredman, "The Devil in the Details," *Executive Edge,*
April–May, 1999, pp. 36–39.
10. Information from [http://new.skoda-auto.com/Documents/
AnnualReports/skoda_auto_annual_report_2007_%20EN_
FINAL.pdf], July 8, 2008; and T. Mudd, "The Last Laugh,"
Industry Week, September 18, 2000, pp. 38–44.
11. W. E. Deming, "Improvement of Quality and Productivity
Through Action by Management," *National Productivity
Review,* Winter 1981–1982, pp. 12–22.
12. T. Vinas, "Little Things Mean a Lot," *Industry Week,*
November 2002, p. 55.
13. "The Future of Manufacturing 2009," *Industry
Week,* November 2009, pp. 25–31; T. D. Kuczmarski,
"Remanufacturing America's Factory Sector," *BusinessWeek
Online,* September 9, 2009; P. Panchak, "Shaping the Future
of Manufacturing," *Industry Week,* January 2005, pp. 38–44;
M. Hammer, "Deep Change: How Operational Innovation
Can Transform Your Company," *Harvard Business Review,*
April 2004, pp. 84–94; S. Levy, "The Connected Company,"
Newsweek, April 28, 2003, pp. 40–48; and J. Teresko, "Plant
Floor Strategy," *Industry Week,* July 2002, pp. 26–32.
14. T. Laseter, K. Ramdas, and D. Swerdlow, "The Supply Side of
Design and Development," *Strategy+Business,* Summer 2003,
p. 23; J. Jusko, "Not All Dollars and Cents," *Industry Week,*
April 2002, p. 58; and D. Drickhamer, "Medical Marvel,"
Industry Week, March 2002, pp. 47–49.
15. J. H. Sheridan, "Managing the Value Chain," *Industry Week*
[www.industryweek.com], September 6, 1999, pp. 1–4.
16. Ibid, p. 3.
17. J. Teresko, "Forward, March!" *Industry Week,* July 2004,
pp. 43–48; D. Sharma, C. Lucier, and R. Molloy, "From
Solutions to Symbiosis: Blending with Your Customers,"

Strategy+Business, Second Quarter 2002, pp. 38–48; and S.
Leibs, "Getting Ready: Your Suppliers," *Industry Week* [www.
industryweek.com], September 6, 1999.
18. D. Bartholomew, "The Infrastructure," *Industry Week* [www.
industryweek.com], September 6, 1999, p. 1.
19. T. Stevens, "Integrated Product Development," *Industry
Week,* June 2002, pp. 21–28.
20. T. Vinas, "A Map of the World: IW Value-Chain Survey,"
Industry Week, September 2005, pp. 27–34.
21. C. Burritt, C. Wolf, and M. Boyle, "Why Wal-Mart Wants to
Take the Driver's Seat," *Bloomberg BusinessWeek,* May 31–
June 6, 2010, pp. 17–18.
22. R. Normann and R. Ramirez, "From Value Chain to Value
Constellation," *Harvard Business Review on Managing the
Value Chain* (Boston, MA: Harvard Business School Press,
2000), pp. 185–219.
23. "Collaboration Is the Key to Reducing Costs," *Industry Week,*
October 2009, p. 35; J. Teresko, "The Tough Get Going,"
Industry Week, March 2005, pp. 25–32; D. M. Lambert and
A. M. Knemeyer, "We're in This Together," *Harvard Business
Review,* December 2004, pp. 114–122; and V. G. Narayanan
and A. Raman, "Aligning Incentives in Supply Chains,"
Harvard Business Review, November 2004, pp. 94–102.
24. D. Drickhamer, "Looking for Value," *Industry Week,*
December 2002, pp. 41–43.
25. J. L. Yang, "Veggie Tales," *Fortune,* June 8, 2009, pp. 25–30.
26. J. Jusko, "Focus. Discipline. Results," *Industry Week,* June
2010, pp. 16–17.
27. J. H. Sheridan, "Managing the Value Chain," p. 3.
28. S. Leibs, "Getting Ready: Your Customers," *Industry Week*
[www.industryweek.com], September 6, 1999, p. 1.
29. G. Taninecz, "Forging the Chain," *Industry Week,* May 15,
2000, pp. 40–46.
30. S. Leibs, "Getting Ready: Your Customers."
31. J. Katz, "Empowering the Workforce," *Industry Week,*
January 2009, p. 43.
32. D. Blanchard, "In the Rotation," *Industry Week,* January
2009, p. 42.
33. N. Zubko, "Mindful of the Surroundings," *Industry Week,*
January 2009, p. 38.
34. "Top Security Threats and Management Issues Facing
Corporate America: 2003 Survey of *Fortune* 1000
Companies," ASIS International and Pinkerton [www.
asisonline.org].
35. J. H. Sheridan, "Managing the Value Chain," p. 4.
36. R. Russell and B. W. Taylor, *Operations Management,* 5th ed.
(New York: Wiley, 2005); C. Liu-Lien Tan, "U.S. Response:
Speedier Delivery," *Wall Street Journal,* November 18, 2004,
pp. D1+; and C. Salter, "When Couches Fly," *Fast Company,*
July 2004, pp. 80–81.
37. D. Joseph, "The GPS Revolution: Location, Location,
Location," *BusinessWeek Online,* May 27, 2009.
38. J. Jargon, "Domino's IT Staff Delivers Slick Site, Ordering
System," *Wall Street Journal,* November 24, 2009, p. B5; and
S. Anderson, The Associated Press, "Restaurants Gear Up for
Window Wars," *Springfield, Missouri, News-Leader,* January
27, 2006, p. 5B.
39. S. McCartney, "A Radical Cockpit Upgrade Southwest Fliers
Will Feel," *Wall Street Journal,* April 1, 2010, p. D1.
40. D. Bartholomew, "Quality Takes a Beating," *Industry Week,*
March 2006, pp. 46–54; J. Carey and M. Arndt, "Making Pills
the Smart Way," *BusinessWeek,* May 3, 2004, pp. 102–103;

and A. Barrett, "Schering's Dr. Feelbetter?" *BusinessWeek,* June 23, 2003, pp. 55–56.

41. T. Vinas, "Six Sigma Rescue," *Industry Week,* March 2004, p. 12.

42. J. S. McClenahen, "Prairie Home Companion," *Industry Week,* October 2005, pp. 45–46.

43. T. Vinas, "Zeroing In on the Customer," *Industry Week,* October 2004, pp. 61–62.

44. W. Royal, "Spotlight Shines on Maquiladora," *Industry Week,* October 16, 2000, pp. 91–92.

45. See B. Whitford and R. Andrew (eds.), *The Pursuit of Quality* (Perth: Beaumont Publishing, 1994).

46. D. Drickhamer, "Road to Excellence," *Industry Week,* October 16, 2000, pp. 117–118.

47. J. Heizer and B. Render, *Operations Management,* 10th ed. (Upper Saddle River, NJ: Prentice Hall, 2011), p. 193.

48. G. Hasek, "Merger Marries Quality Efforts," *Industry Week,* August 21, 2000, pp. 89–92.

49. M. Arndt, "Quality Isn't Just for Widgets," *BusinessWeek,* July 22, 2002, pp. 72–73.

50. E. White, "Rethinking the Quality Improvement Program," *Wall Street Journal,* September 19, 2005, p. B3.

51. M. Arndt, "Quality Isn't Just for Widgets."

52. S. McMurray, "Ford's F-150: Have It Your Way," *Business 2.0,* March 2004, pp. 53–55; "Made-to-Fit Clothes Are on the Way," *USA Today,* July 2002, pp. 8–9; and L. Elliott, "Mass Customization Comes a Step Closer," *Design News,* February 18, 2002, p. 21.

53. E. Schonfeld, "The Customized, Digitized, Have-it-Your-Way Economy," *Fortune,* October 28, 1998, pp. 114–120.

54. Heizer and Render, *Operations Management,* p. 636; and S. Minter, "Measuring the Success of Lean," *Industry Week,* February 2010, pp. 32–35.

55. Heizer and Render, *Operations Management,* p. 636.

CHAPTER 11

1. A. Bingham "Building on Open Business Models," *Research-Technology Management,* July–August 2012, p. 64; J. Brown, "Harnessing the Power of the Crowd," *Public CIO,* Spring 2012, pp. 16–21; J. Rago, "The Weekend Interview with John Lechleiter: The Biomedical Century," *Wall Street Journal,* November 19, 2011, p. A13; J. C. Lechleiter, "The Return on Innovation," *Vital Speeches of the Day,* January 2011, pp. 13–18; P. Loftus, "Eli Lilly Will Take New Path," *Wall Street Journal,* June 8, 2010, p. B6; J. Miller, "The Lilly Way," *Pharmaceutical Technology,* May 2010, pp. 82–84; L. Lallos, "Retired—But in the Game," *Bloomberg BusinessWeek,* April 25, 2010, p. 62; A. Weintraub and M. Tirrell, "Eli Lilly's Drug Assembly Line," *Bloomberg BusinessWeek,* March 8, 2010, pp. 56–57; J. D. Rockoff, "Lilly Taps Contractors to Revive Pipeline," *Wall Street Journal,* January 5, 2010, pp. B1+; J. Pepitone, "Eli Lilly to Cut 5,500 Jobs," *CNNMoney.com,* September 14, 2009; and P. Loftus, "Lilly to Revamp, Cut Jobs as Patents Expire," *Wall Street Journal,* May 15, 2009, p. B1.

2. B. Fenwick, "Oklahoma Factory Turns Out US Bombs Used in Iraq," *Planet Ark* [www.planetark.com], November 4, 2003; A. Meyer, "Peeking Inside the Nation's Bomb Factory," *KFOR TV* [www.kfor.com], February 27, 2003; G. Tuchman, "Inside America's Bomb Factory," *CNN* [articles.cnn.com], December 5, 2002; and C. Fishman, "Boomtown, U.S.A.," *Fast Company,* June 2002, pp. 106–114.

3. D. Hudepohl, "Finesse a Flexible Work Schedule," *Wall Street Journal,* February 19, 2008, p. B8.

4. J. Nickerson, C. J. Yen, and J. T. Mahoney, "Exploring the Problems-Finding and Problem-Solving Approach for Designing Organizations," *Academy of Management Perspectives,* February 2012, pp. 52–72; R. Greenwood and D. Miller, "Tackling Design Anew: Getting Back to the Heart of Organizational Theory," *Academy of Management Perspectives,* November 2010, pp. 78–89.

5. See, for example, R. L. Daft, *Organization Theory and Design,* 10th ed. (Mason, OH: South-Western College Publishing), 2009.

6. S. Peterson, Associated Press, "Wilson Sporting Goods Football Factory" [www.chron.com], February 3, 2010; T. Arbel, Associated Press, "Factory Activity Fuels Economic Recovery," *OnlineAthens Banner-Herald* [www.onlineathens. com], February 2, 2010; and M. Hiestand, "Making a Stamp on Football," *USA Today,* January 25, 2005, pp. 1C+.

7. C. Dougherty, "Workforce Productivity Falls," *Wall Street Journal,* May 4, 2012, p. A5; and S. E. Humphrey, J. D. Nahrgang, and F. P. Morgeson, "Integrating Motivational, Social, and Contextual Work Design Features: A Meta-Analytic Summary and Theoretical Expansion of the Work Design Literature," *Journal of Applied Psychology,* September 2007, pp. 1332–1356.

8. D. Drickhamer, "Moving Man," *IW,* December 2002, pp. 44–46.

9. For a discussion of authority, see W. A. Kahn and K. E. Kram, "Authority at Work: Internal Models and Their Organizational Consequences," *Academy of Management Review,* January 1994, pp. 17–50.

10. C. I. Barnard, *The Functions of the Executive,* 30th Anniversary Edition (Cambridge, MA: Harvard University Press, 1968), pp. 165–166.

11. E. P. Gunn, "Who's the Boss?" *Smart Money,* April 2003, p. 121.

12. R. Ashkenas, "Simplicity-Minded Management," *Harvard Business Review,* December 2007, pp. 101–109; and P. Glader, "It's Not Easy Being Lean," *Wall Street Journal,* June 19, 2006, pp. B1+.

13. R. C. Morais, "The Old Lady Is Burning Rubber," *Forbes,* November 26, 2007, pp. 146–150.

14. G. L. Neilson and J. Wulf, "How Many Direct Reports?" *Harvard Business Review,* April 2012, pp. 112–119; and D. Van Fleet, "Span of Management Research and Issues," *Academy of Management Journal,* September 1983, pp. 546–552.

15. G. Anders, "Overseeing More Employees—With Fewer Managers," *Wall Street Journal,* March 24, 2008, p. B6.

16. H. Fayol, *General and Industrial Management,* trans. C. Storrs (London: Pitman Publishing, 1949), pp. 19–42.

17. J. Zabojnik, "Centralized and Decentralized Decision Making in Organizations," *Journal of Labor Economics,* January 2002, pp. 1–22.

18. See, for example, H. Mintzberg, *Power In and Around Organizations* (Upper Saddle River, NJ: Prentice Hall, 1983); and J. Child, *Organization: A Guide to Problems and Practices* (London: Kaiser & Row, 1984).

19. See P. Kenis and D. Knoke, "How Organizational Field Networks Shape InterOrganizational Tie-Formation Rates," *Academy of Management Review* (April 2002), pp. 275–293.

20. A. D. Amar, C. Hentrich, and V. Hlupic, "To Be a Better Leader, Give Up Authority," *Harvard Business Review,* December 2009, pp. 22–24.

21. P. Siekman, "Dig It!" *Fortune,* May 3, 2004, pp. 128[B]–128[L].

22. J. Cable, "Operators Lead the Way," *Industry Week,* January 2010, p. 31.

23. "Doing the Job Well: An Investigation of Pro-Social Rule Breaking" by Elizabeth W. Morrison, from *Journal of Management*, February 2006, Volume 32(1).

24. Ibid.

25. M. Boyle, "A Leaner Macy's Tries Catering to Local Tastes," *Bloomberg BusinessWeek,* September 14, 2009, p. 13.

26. D. A. Morand, "The Role of Behavioral Formality and Informality in the Enactment of Bureaucratic versus Organic Organizations," *Academy of Management Review*, October 1995, pp. 831–872; and T. Burns and G. M. Stalker, *The Management of Innovation* (London: Tavistock, 1961).

27. C. Feser, "Long Live Bureaucracy!," *Leader to Leader,* Summer 2012, pp. 57–62.

28. "How to Bust Corporate Barriers," *Gallup Management Journal Online,* August 18, 2011; and D. Dougherty, "Re-imagining the Differentiation and Integration of Work for Sustained Product Innovation," *Organization Science* (September–October 2001), pp. 612–631.

29. data points box based on J. Yang and P. Trap, "What Size Company Do You Prefer?" *USA Today,* March 19, 2012, p. 1 B; F. Hassan, "The Frontline Advantage," *Harvard Business Review,* May 2011, p. 109; P. Dvorak, "Firms Shift Underused Workers," *Wall Street Journal,* June 22, 2009, p. B2; M. Weinstein, "It's A Balancing Act," *Training,* May 2009, p. 10; J. Yang and A. Lewis, "Is Teleworking a Good Idea?" *USA Today*, October 28, 2008, p. 1 B; Drive Time: More Employees Get to Work Remotely," *Workforce Management Online* [www.workforce.com], September 23, 2008; J. Yang and K. Gelles, "Working Remotely vs. In the Office," *USA Today,* April 24, 2008, p. 1 B; A. R. Carey and S. Parker, "Workers Take Home Their Offices," *USA Today,* October 7, 2008, p. 1 A.

30. R. D. Hof, "Yahoo's Bartz Shows Who's Boss," *Business Week Online,* February 27, 2009; and J. E. Vascellaro, "Yahoo CEO Set to Install Top-Down Management," *Wall Street Journal,* February 23, 2009, p. B1.

31. A. D. Chandler, Jr., *Strategy and Structure: Chapters in the History of the Industrial Enterprise* (Cambridge, MA: MIT Press, 1962).

32. See, for instance, W. Chan Kim and R. Mauborgne, "How Strategy Shapes Structure," *Harvard Business Review,* September 2009, pp. 73–80; L. L. Bryan and C. I. Joyce, "Better Strategy Through Organizational Design," *The McKinsey Quarterly,* 2007, Number 2, pp. 21–29; D. Jennings and S. Seaman, "High and Low Levels of Organizational Adaptation: An Empirical Analysis of Strategy, Structure, and Performance," *Strategic Management Journal*, July 1994, pp. 459–475; D. C. Galunic and K. M. Eisenhardt, "Renewing the Strategy-Structure-Performance Paradigm," in B. M. Staw and L. L. Cummings (eds.), *Research in Organizational Behavior*, vol. 16 (Greenwich, CT: JAI Press, 1994), pp. 215–255; R. Parthasarthy and S. P. Sethi, "Relating Strategy and Structure to Flexible Automation: A Test of Fit and Performance Implications," *Strategic Management Journal*, 14, no. 6 (1993), pp. 529–549; H. A. Simon, "Strategy and Organizational Evolution," *Strategic Management Journal*, January 1993, pp. 131–142; H. L. Boschken, "Strategy and Structure: Re-conceiving the Relationship," *Journal of Management*, March 1990, pp. 135–150; D. Miller, "The Structural and Environmental Correlates of Business Strategy," *Strategic Management Journal*, January–February 1987, pp. 55–76; and R. E. Miles and C. C. Snow, *Organizational Strategy, Structure, and Process* (New York: McGraw-Hill, 1978).

33. See, for instance, R. Z. Gooding and J. A. Wagner III, "A Meta-Analytic Review of the Relationship between Size and Performance: The Productivity and Efficiency of Organizations and Their Subunits," *Administrative Science Quarterly*, December 1985, pp. 462–481; D. S. Pugh, "The Aston Program of Research: Retrospect and Prospect," in A. H. Van de Ven and W. F. Joyce (eds.), *Perspectives on Organization Design and Behavior* (New York: John Wiley, 1981), pp. 135–166; and P. M. Blau and R. A. Schoenherr, *The Structure of Organizations* (New York: Basic Books, 1971).

34. Leader Who Made a Difference box based on R. Gluckman, "Every Customer Is Always Right," *Forbes,* May 21, 2012, pp. 38–40; G. Colvin, "The Next Management Icon: Would You Believe He's From China?" *Fortune,* July 25, 2011, p. 77; and D. J. Lynch, CEO Pushes China's Haier as Global Brand," *USA Today,* January 3, 2003, pp. 1B+.

35. J. Woodward, *Industrial Organization: Theory and Practice* (London: Oxford University Press, 1965).

36. See, for instance, J. Zhang and C. Baden-Fuller, "The Influence of Technological Knowledge Base and Organizational Structure on Technology Collaboration," *Journal of Management Studies,* June 2010, pp. 679–704; C. C. Miller, W. H. Glick, Y. D. Wang, and G. Huber, "Understanding Technology-Structure Relationships: Theory Development and Meta-Analytic Theory Testing," *Academy of Management Journal,* June 1991, pp. 370–399; J. Hage and M. Aiken, "Routine Technology, Social Structure, and Organizational Goals," *Administrative Science Quarterly*, September 1969, pp. 366–377; J. D. Thompson, *Organizations in Action* (New York: McGraw-Hill, 1967); and C. Perrow, "A Framework for the Comparative Analysis of Organizations," *American Sociological Review*, April 1967, pp. 194–208.

37. D. M. Rousseau and R. A. Cooke, "Technology and Structure: The Concrete, Abstract, and Activity Systems of Organizations," *Journal of Management*, Fall–Winter 1984, pp. 345–361; and D. Gerwin, "Relationships between Structure and Technology," in P. C. Nystrom and W. H. Starbuck (eds.), *Handbook of Organizational Design*, vol. 2 (New York: Oxford University Press, 1981), pp. 3–38.

38. S. Rausch and J. Birkinshaw, "Organizational Ambidexterity: Antecedents, Outcomes, and Moderators," *Journal of Management,* June 2008, pp. 375–409; M. Yasai-Ardekani, "Structural Adaptations to Environments," *Academy of Management Review*, January 1986, pp. 9–21; P. Lawrence and J. W. Lorsch, *Organization and Environment: Managing Differentiation and Integration* (Boston: Harvard Business School, Division of Research, 1967); and F. E. Emery and E. Trist, "The Causal Texture of Organizational Environments," *Human Relations*, February 1965, pp. 21–32.

39. S. Reed, "He's Brave Enough to Shake Up Shell," *BusinessWeek,* July 18, 2005, p. 53.

40. B. Rochman, "Banning the Bandz," *Time,* June 14, 2010, p. 99; and S. Berfield, "The Man Behind the Bandz," *Bloomberg BusinessWeek Online,* June 10, 2010.

41. H. Mintzberg, *Structure in Fives: Designing Effective Organizations* (Upper Saddle River, NJ: Prentice Hall, 1983), p. 157.

42. R. J. Williams, J. J. Hoffman, and B. T. Lamont, "The Influence of Top Management Team Characteristics on M-Form Implementation Time," *Journal of Managerial Issues*, Winter 1995, pp. 466–480.

43. C. Hausman, "Lifeguard Fired for Leaving Patrol Zone to Save Drowning Man," *Ethics Newsline Online,* July 9, 2012; S. Grossman, "Lifeguard Who Got Fired for Saving Drowning Swimmer Declines Offer to Return," *newsfeed.time.com,* July 6, 2012; E. Illades and C. Teproff, "Fired Lifeguard Says 'No Thanks' When He's Re-offered Job," *MiamiHerald.com,* July 5, 2012; and W. Lee, "Florida Lifeguard Helps Save Life, Gets Fired," *USA Today Online,* July 4, 2012.

44. Based on S. P. Robbins and P. L. Hunsaker, *Training in Interpersonal Skills* (Upper Saddle River, New Jersey: Pearson Prentice Hall), 2009, pp. 173–188; S. Caudron, "Delegate for Results," *Industry Week,* February 6, 1995, pp. 27–30; and R. T. Noel, "What You Say to Your Employees When You Delegate," *Supervisory Management*, December 1993, p. 13.

45. B. Philbin, "Schwab's Net Drops 20%," *Wall Street Journal,* April 17, 2012, p. C9; M. Tian, "Charles Schwab—An Unnoticed Transformation," *Morningstar OpportunisticInvestor,* March 2012, pp. 6–9; B. Morris, "Chuck Schwab Is Worried About the Small Investor," *Bloomberg BusinessWeek,* May 31–June 6, 2010, pp. 58–64; L. Gibbs, "Chuck Would Like a Word With You," *Money,* January/February 2010, pp. 98–103; R. Markey, F. Reichheld, and A. Dullweber, "Closing the Customer Feedback Loop," *Harvard Business Review,* December 2009, pp. 43–47; and R. Farzad and C. Palmeri, "Can Schwab Seize the Day?" *Bloomberg BusinessWeek,* July 27, 2009, pp. 36–39.

46. S. Silbermann, "How Culture and Regulation Demand New Ways to Sell," *Harvard Business Review,* July/August 2012, pp. 104–105; P. Miller and T. Wedell-Wedellsborg, "How to Make an Offer That Managers Can't Refuse?" *IESE Insight,* 2011 (second quarter), issue 9, pp. 66–67; S. Hernández, "Prove Its Worth," *IESE Insight,* 2011 (second quarter), issue 9, p. 68; T. Koulopoulos, "Know Thyself," *IESE Insight,* 2011 (second quarter), issue 9, p. 69; M. Weinstein, "Retrain and Restructure Your Organization," *Training,* May 2009, p. 36; J. McGregor, "The Chore Goes Offshore," *BusinessWeek,* March 23 & 30, 2009, pp. 50–51; "Pfizer: Making It 'Leaner, Meaner, More Efficient,'" *BusinessWeek Online,* March 2, 2009; and A. Cohen, "Scuttling Scut Work," *Fast Company,* February 2008, pp. 42–43.

CHAPTER 12

1. A. Kleiner, "The Thought Leader Interview: Dov Seidman," *Strategy+Business,* Summer 2012, pp. 1–8; D. Seidman, "Letting the Mission Govern a Company," *New York Times Online,* June 23, 2012; D. Seidman, "To Inspire Others, It's How You Do It That Counts," *CNN.com,* May 3, 2012; "The How Report: New Metrics for a New Reality," LRN [www.lrn.com], 2012; E. De Vita, "How," *Third Sector,* January 17, 2012, p. 21; S. Pastoor, "The New Competitive Advantage: Values," *Official Board Markets,* December 10, 2011, p. 6; and E. Frauenheim and D. Seidman, "Inspiration as Worker Incentive," *Workforce Management,* May 2010, p. 8.

2. N. Wingfield, "To Rebuild Windows, Microsoft Razed Walls," *Wall Street Journal,* October 20, 2009, p. B9.

3. Q. Hardy, "Google Thinks Small," *Forbes,* November 14, 2005, pp. 198–202.

4. See, for example, A. C. Edmondson, "Teamwork On the Fly," *Harvard Business Review,* April 2012, pp. 72–80; D. R. Denison, S. L. Hart, and J. A. Kahn, "From Chimneys to Cross-Functional Teams: Developing and Validating a Diagnostic Model," *Academy of Management Journal,* December 1996, pp. 1005–1023; D. Ray and H. Bronstein, *Teaming Up: Making the Transition to a Self-Directed Team-Based Organization* (New York: McGraw Hill, 1995); J. R. Katzenbach and D. K. Smith, *The Wisdom of Teams* (Boston: Harvard Business School Press, 1993); J. A. Byrne, "The Horizontal Corporation," *BusinessWeek,* December 20, 1993, pp. 76–81; B. Dumaine, "Payoff from the New Management," *Fortune,* December 13, 1993, pp. 103–110; and H. Rothman, "The Power of Empowerment," *Nation's Business,* June 1993, pp. 49–52.

5. E. Krell, "Managing the Matrix," *HR Magazine,* April 2011, pp. 69–71.

6. J. Hyatt, "Engineering Inspiration," *Newsweek,* June 14, 2010, p. 44; T. McKeough, "Blowing Hot and Cold," *Fast Company,* December 2009–January 2010, p. 66; H. Walters, "Inside the Design Thinking Process," *BusinessWeek Online,* December 15, 2009; P. Kaihla, "Best-Kept Secrets of the World's Best Companies," *Business 2.0,* April 2006, p. 83; C. Taylor, "School of Bright Ideas," *Time Inside Business,* April 2005, pp. A8–A12; and B. Nussbaum, "The Power of Design," *BusinessWeek,* May 17, 2004, pp. 86–94.

7. R. L. Hotz, "More Scientists Treat Experiments as a Team Sport," *Wall Street Journal,* November 20, 2009, p. A23.

8. See, for example, G. G. Dess, A. M. A. Rasheed, K. J. McLaughlin, and R. L. Priem, "The New Corporate Architecture," *Academy of Management Executive*, August 1995, pp. 7–20.

9. For additional readings on boundaryless organizations, see Rausch and Birkinshaw, June 2008; M. F. R. Kets de Vries, "Leadership Group Coaching in Action: The Zen of Creating High-Performance Teams," *Academy of Management Executive,* February 2005, pp. 61–76; J. Child and R. G. McGrath, "Organizations Unfettered: Organizational Form in an Information-Intensive Economy," *Academy of Management Journal,* December 2001, pp. 1135–1148; M. Hammer and S. Stanton, "How Process Enterprises Really Work," *Harvard Business Review*, November–December 1999, pp. 108–118; T. Zenger and W. Hesterly, "The Disaggregation of Corporations: Selective Intervention, High-Powered Incentives, and Modular Units," *Organization Science,* 1997, vol. 8, pp. 209–222; R. Ashkenas, D. Ulrich, T. Jick, and S. Kerr, *The Boundaryless Organization: Breaking the Chains of Organizational Structure* (San Francisco: Jossey-Bass, 1997); R. M. Hodgetts, "A Conversation with Steve Kerr," *Organizational Dynamics,* Spring 1996, pp. 68–79; and J. Gebhardt, "The Boundaryless Organization," *Sloan Management Review*, Winter 1996, pp. 117–119. For another view of boundaryless organizations, see B. Victor, "The Dark Side of the New Organizational Forms: An Editorial Essay," *Organization Science*, November 1994, pp. 479–482.

10. J. Marte, "An Internship from Your Couch," *Wall Street Journal,* September 9, 2009, pp. D1+.

11. See, for instance, R. J. King, "It's a Virtual World," *Strategy+Business* [www.strategy-business.com], April 21, 2009; Y. Shin, "A Person-Environment Fit Model for Virtual Organizations," *Journal of Management,* December 2004, pp. 725–743; D. Lyons, "Smart and Smarter," *Forbes,* March 18, 2002, pp. 40–41; W. F. Cascio, "Managing a Virtual Workplace," *Academy of Management Executive,* August 2000, pp. 81–90; G. G. Dess, A. M. A. Rasheed, K. J. McLaughlin, and R. L. Priem, "The New Corporate Architecture"; H. Chesbrough and D. Teece, "When Is Virtual Virtuous: Organizing for Innovation," *Harvard Business Review,* January–February 1996, pp. 65–73; and W. H.

Davidow and M. S. Malone, *The Virtual Corporation* (New York: Harper Collins, 1992).

12. Q. Hardy, "Bit by Bit, Work Exchange Site Aims to Get Jobs Done," *New York Times Online,* November 6, 2011.

13. M. V. Rafter, "Cultivating A Virtual Culture," *Workforce Management Online,* April 5, 2012.

14. R. Reisner, "A Smart Balance of Staff and Contractors," *BusinessWeek Online,* June 16, 2009; and J. S. Lublin, "Smart Balance Keeps Tight Focus on Creativity," *Wall Street Journal,* June 8, 2009, p. B4.

15. R. Merrifield, J. Calhoun, and D. Stevens, "The Next Revolution in Productivity," *Harvard Business Review,* June 2008, pp. 73–80; R. E. Miles et al., "Organizing in the Knowledge Age: Anticipating the Cellular Form," *Academy of Management Executive,* November 1997, pp. 7–24; C. Jones, W. Hesterly, and S. Borgatti, "A General Theory of Network Governance: Exchange Conditions and Social Mechanisms," *Academy of Management Review,* October 1997, pp. 911–945; R. E. Miles and C. C. Snow, "The New Network Firm: A Spherical Structure Built on Human Investment Philosophy," *Organizational Dynamics,* Spring 1995, pp. 5–18; and R. E. Miles and C. C. Snow, "Causes of Failures in Network Organizations," *California Management Review,* 1992, vol. 34, no. 4, pp. 53–72.

16. G. Hoetker, "Do Modular Products Lead to Modular Organizations?" *Strategic Management Journal,* June 2006, pp. 501–518; C. H. Fine, "Are You Modular or Integral?" *Strategy & Business,* Summer 2005, pp. 44–51; D. A. Ketchen, Jr. and G. T. M. Hult, "To Be Modular or Not to Be? Some Answers to the Question," *Academy of Management Executive,* May 2002, pp. 166–167; M. A. Schilling, "The Use of Modular Organizational Forms: An Industry-Level Analysis," *Academy of Management Journal,* December 2001, pp. 1149–1168; D. Lei, M. A. Hitt, and J. D. Goldhar, "Advanced Manufacturing Technology: Organizational Design and Strategic Flexibility," *Organization Studies,* 1996, vol. 17, pp. 501–523; R. Sanchez and J. Mahoney, "Modularity Flexibility and Knowledge Management in Product and Organization Design," *Strategic Management Journal,* 1996, vol. 17, pp. 63–76; and R. Sanchez, "Strategic Flexibility in Product Competition," *Strategic Management Journal,* 1995, vol. 16, pp. 135–159.

17. J. Fortt, "The Chip Company That Dares to Battle Intel," *Fortune,* July 20, 2009, pp. 51–56.

18. C. Hymowitz, "Have Advice, Will Travel," *Wall Street Journal,* June 5, 2006, pp. B1+.

19. S. Reed, A. Reinhardt, and A. Sains, "Saving Ericsson," *BusinessWeek,* November 11, 2002, pp. 64–68.

20. P. Engardio, "The Future of Outsourcing," *BusinessWeek,* January 30, 2006, pp. 50–58.

21. P. Sonne, "Tesco's CEO-to-Be Unfolds Map for Global Expansion," *Wall Street Journal,* June 9, 2010, p. B1; T. Shifrin, "Grocery Giant Tesco Is Creating a Storm in the US Market with Its Tesco in a Box Set of Systems" [www.computerworlduk.com], January 14, 2008; P. Olson, "Tesco's Landing," *Forbes,* June 4, 2007, pp. 116–118; and P. M. Senge, *The Fifth Discipline: The Art and Practice of Learning Organizations* (New York: Doubleday, 1990).

22. J. J. Salopek, "Keeping Learning Well-Oiled," *T&D,* October 2011, pp. 32-35.

23. A. C. Edmondson, "The Competitive Imperative of Learning," *Harvard Business Review,* July–August 2008, pp. 60–67.

24. S. A. Sackmann, P. M. Eggenhofer-Rehart, and M. Friesl, "Long-Term Efforts Toward Developing a Learning Organization," *Journal of Applied Behavioral Science,* December 2009, pp. 521–549; D. A. Garvin, A. C. Edmondson, and F. Gino, "Is Yours a Learning Organization?" *Harvard Business Review,* March 2008, pp. 109–116; A. N. K. Chen and T. M. Edgington, "Assessing Value in Organizational Knowledge Creation: Considerations for Knowledge Workers," *MIS Quarterly,* June 2005, pp. 279–309; K. G. Smith, C. J. Collins, and K. D. Clark, "Existing Knowledge, Knowledge Creation Capability, and The Rate of New Product Introduction in High-Technology Firms," *Academy of Management Journal,* April 2005, pp. 346–357; R. Cross, A. Parker, L. Prusak, and S. P. Borgati, "Supporting Knowledge Creation and Sharing in Social Networks," *Organizational Dynamics,* Fall, 2001, pp. 100–120; M. Schulz, "The Uncertain Relevance of Newness: Organizational Learning and Knowledge Flows," *Academy of Management Journal,* August 2001, pp. 661–681; G. Szulanski, "Exploring Internal Stickiness: Impediments to the Transfer of Best Practice within the Firm," *Strategic Management Journal,* Winter Special Issue, 1996, pp. 27–43; and J. M. Liedtka, "Collaborating across Lines of Business for Competitive Advantage," *Academy of Management Executive,* April 1996, pp. 20–37.

25. J. Scanlon, "How 3M Encourages Collaboration," *BusinessWeek Online,* September 2, 2009.

26. R. Mitchell, "The Cure," *Fast Company.com,* May 2011, pp. 108+.

27. "Meet the New Steel," *Fortune,* October 1, 2007, pp. 68–71.

28. J. Appleby and R. Davis, "Teamwork Used to Save Money; Now It Saves Lives," *USA Today* [www.usatoday.com], March 1, 2001.

29. C. Kauffman, "Employee Involvement: A New Blueprint for Success," *Journal of Accountancy,* May 2010, pp. 46–49; and R. L. Daft, *Management,* 9th ed. (Mason, OH: South-Western Cengage Learning, 2010), p. 262.

30. S. F. Gale, "The Power of Community," *Workforce Management Online,* March 2009.

31. C. G. Cataldo, "Book Review," *Academy of Management Learning & Education,* June 2009, pp. 301–303; E. Wenger, R. McDermott, and W. Snyder, *Cultivating Communities of Practice: A Guide to Managing Knowledge* (Boston: Harvard Business School Press, 2002), p. 4.

32. E. Wenger, R. McDermott, and W. Snyder, *Cultivating Communities of Practice: A Guide to Managing Knowledge* (Boston: Harvard Business School Press, 2002), p. 39.

33. R. McDermott and D. Archibald, "Harnessing Your Staff's Informal Networks," *Harvard Business Review,* March 2010, pp. 82–89.

34. T. L. Griffith and J. E. Sawyer, "Multilevel Knowledge and Team Performance," *Journal of Organizational Behavior,* October 2010, pp. 1003-1031; and M. Hemmasi and C. M. Csanda, "The Effectiveness of Communities of Practice: An Empirical Study," *Journal of Managerial Issues,* Summer 2009, pp. 262–279.

35. R. Jana, "How Intuit Makes a Social Network Pay," *BusinessWeek Online,* July 2, 2009.

36. B. Horovitz, "Tasty Potato Chip Offer: $1 Million Prize," *USA Today,* July 19, 2012, p. 1A; and R. A. Guth, "Glaxo Tries a Linux Approach," *Wall Street Journal,* May 26, 2010, p. B4.

37. J. Winsor, "Crowdsourcing: What It Means for Innovation," *BusinessWeek Online,* June 15, 2009.

38. K. J. O'Brien, "One Year Later, Nokia and Microsoft Deliver," *New York Times Online,* February 27, 2012.

39. D. Lavie, U. Stettner, and M. L. Tushman, "Exploration and Exploitation Within and Across Organizations," *Academy of Management Annals,* June 2010, pp. 109–155; H. Mitsuhashi and H. R. Greve, "A Matching Theory of Alliance Formation and Organizational Success: Complementarity and Compatibility," *Academy of Management Journal,* October 2009, pp. 975–995; D. Durfee, "Try Before You Buy," *CFO,* May 2006, pp. 48–54; B. McEvily and A. Marcus, "Embedded Ties and the Acquisition of Competitive Capabilities," *Strategic Management Journal,* November 2005, pp. 1033–1055; R. D. Ireland, M. A. Hitt, and D. Vaidyanath, "Alliance Management as a Source of Competitive Advantage," *Journal of Management,* 2002, vol. 28, no. 3, pp. 413–446; E. Krell, "The Alliance Advantage," *Business Finance,* July 2002, pp. 16–23; D. Sparks, "Partners," *BusinessWeek,* October 25, 1999, pp. 106–112; and D. Brady, "When Is Cozy Too Cozy?," *BusinessWeek,* October 25, 1999, pp. 127–130.

40. J. Marquez, "Connecting a Virtual Workforce," *Workforce Management Online,* February 3, 2009.

41. M. Conlin, "Home Offices: The New Math," *BusinessWeek,* March 9, 2009, pp. 66–68.

42. data points box based on S. Shellenbarger, "More Workers Keep the Office at a Distance," *Wall Street Journal,* June 20, 2012, p. B8; SHRM Online Staff, "People Really Love Telecommuting," *HR Magazine,* April 2012, p. 20; A. Quick, "The Business Case for Flex," *HR Magazine,* April 2012, pp. 44–46; P. Brotherton, "Alternative Workplace Programs Are on the Rise," *T&D,* March 2012, p. 28; "Staffing Industry Analysts Report," *Workforce Management Online,* January 18, 2012; J. Yang and S. Ward, "Compared With Now, the Office of 2021 Will…" *USA Today,* November 1, 2011, p. 1B; R. Huggins and S. Ward, "Which is the Biggest Advantage of Working From Home?" *USA Today,* October 7–9, 2011, p. 1A; J. Yang and P. Trap, "For My Workdays, I Prefer," *USA Today,* October 6, 2011, p. 1B; and "Weekend Work," *HR Magazine,* October 2011, p. 32.

43. Ibid.

44. J. Marquez, "Connecting a Virtual Workforce."

45. S. Jayson, "Working At Home: Family-Friendly," *USA Today,* April 15, 2010, pp. 1A+; T. D. Hecht and N. J. Allen, "A Longitudinal Examination of the Work-Nonwork Boundary Strength Construct," *Journal of Organizational Behavior,* October 2009, pp. 839–862; and G. E. Kreiner, E. C. Hollensbe, and M. L. Sheep, "Balancing Borders and Bridges: Negotiating the Work-Home Interface via Boundary Work Tactics," *Academy of Management Journal,* August 2009, pp. 704–730.

46. J. T. Marquez, "The Future of Flex," *Workforce Management Online,* January 2010.

47. B. Walsh, "Thank God It's Thursday," *Time,* September 7, 2009, p. 58.

48. J. Sahadi, "Flex-time, Time Off—Who's Getting These Perks?" *CNNMoney.com,* June 25, 2007.

49. M. Arndt, "The Family That Flips Together…" *BusinessWeek,* April 17, 2006, p. 14.

50. S. Greenhouse, "Work-Sharing May Help Companies Avoid Layoffs," *New York Times Online,* June 16, 2009.

51. M. Korn, "Making a Temporary Stint Stick," *Wall Street Journal,* February 9, 2010, p. D6.

52. A. Levit, "The Rise of the Independent Work Force," *New York Times Online,* April 14, 2012.

53. I. Speizer, "Special Report on Contingency Staffing—The Future of Contingent Staffing Could Be Like Something Out of a Movie," *Workforce Management Online,* October 19, 2009.

54. E. Frauenheim, "Special Report on HR Technology: Tracking the Contingents," *Workforce Management Online,* April 2010.

55. S. G. Hauser, "Independent Contractors Helping to Shape the New World of Work," *Workforce Management Online,* February 3, 2012; S. Greenhouse, "U.S. Cracks Down on 'Contractors' As a Tax Dodge," *New York Times Online,* February 18, 2010; and M. Orey, "They're Employees. No, They're Not," *BusinessWeek,* November 16, 2009, pp. 73–74.

56. M. Orey, "They're Employees. No, They're Not."

57. Ibid.

58. V. Smith and E. B. Neuwirth, "Temporary Help Agencies and the Making of a New Employment Practice," *Academy of Management Perspectives,* February 2009, pp. 56–72.

59. E. Frauenheim, "Special Report on HR Technology: Tracking the Contingents."

60. C. E. Connelly and D. G. Gallagher, "Emerging Trends in Contingent Work Research," *Journal of Management,* November, 2004, pp. 959–983.

61. K. Holland, "The Anywhere, Anytime Office," *New York Times Online,* September 28, 2008.

62. Leader Who Made a Difference box based on C. Rose, "Charlie Rose Talks to Cisco's John Chambers," *Bloomberg BusinessWeek,* April 23, 2012, p. 41; M. T. Hansen et al., "The Best-Performing CEOs in the World," *Harvard Business Review,* January–February 2010, pp. 104–113; P. Burrows, "Cisco's Extreme Ambitions," *BusinessWeek,* November 30, 2009, pp. 26–27; P. Burrows and A. Ricadela, "Cisco Seizes the Moment," *BusinessWeek,* May 25, 2009, pp. 46–48; and "Cisco Systems Layers It On," *Fortune,* December 8, 2008, p. 24.

63. E. Frauenheim, "Special Report on HR Technology: Tracking the Contingents"; A. P. McAfee, "How a Connected Workforce Innovates," *Harvard Business Review,* December 2009, p. 80; R. Yu, "Work Away from Work Gets Easier with Technology," *USA Today,* November 28, 2006, p. 8B; M. Weinstein, "GOing Mobile," *Training,* September 2006, pp. 24–29; C. Cobbs, "Technology Helps Boost Multitasking," *Springfield, Missouri News-Leader,* June 15, 2006, p. 5B; C. Edwards, "Wherever You Go, You're on the Job," *BusinessWeek,* June 20, 2005, pp. 87–90; and S. E. Ante, "The World Wide Work Space," *BusinessWeek,* June 6, 2005, pp. 106–108.

64. N. M. Adler, *International Dimensions of Organizational Behavior,* 5th ed. (Cincinnati, OH: South-Western), 2008, p. 62.

65. P. B. Smith and M. F. Peterson, "Demographic Effects on the Use of Vertical Sources of Guidance by Managers in Widely Differing Cultural Contexts," *International Journal of Cross Cultural Management,* April 2005, pp. 5–26.

66. C. Hausman, "Was AT&T's iPad Security Breach 'Ethical' Hacking?" *Ethics Newsline* [www.globalethics.org], June 21, 2010; S. E. Ante and B. Worthen, "FBI to Probe iPad Breach—Group That Exposed AT&T Flaw to See Addresses Says It Did a Public Service," *Wall Street Journal,* June 11, 2010, p. B1; and S. E. Ante, "AT&T Discloses Breach of iPad Owner Data," *Wall Street Journal Online,* June 9, 2010.

67. "Hackers Were Right to Disclose AT&T-iPad Site Hole" by Elinor Mills from CNET, June 14, 2010.

68. Based on H. Mintzberg, *Power In and Around Organizations* (Upper Saddle River, NJ: Prentice Hall, 1983), p. 24; P. L. Hunsaker, *Training in Management Skills* (Upper Saddle River, NJ: Prentice Hall, 2001), pp. 339–364; G. Ferris, S.

Davidson, and P. Perrewé, "Developing Political Skill at Work," *Training,* November 2005, pp. 40 45; B. Uzzi and S. Dunlap, "How to Build Your Network," *Harvard Business Review,* December 2005, pp. 53–60; and B. Brim, "The Best Way to Influence Others," *Gallup Management Journal,* February 9, 2006 [http://gmj.gallup.com].

69. J. Graham, "Product Fans Can Become Customer Service Reps," *USA Today,* May 31, 2012, p. 3B; A. Fox, "Pave the Way for Volunteers," *HR Magazine,* June 2010, pp. 70–74; G. Morse, "The Power of Unwitting Workers," *Harvard Business Review,* October 2009, p. 27; S. Lohr, "Customer Service? Ask A Volunteer," *New York Times Online,* April 26, 2009; and B. Xu, D. R. Jones, and B. Shao, "Volunteers' Involvement in Online Community Based Software Development," *Information & Management,* April 2009, pp. 151–158.

70. A. Hill, "How to Conform to Creative Deviance," *Financial Times Online,* April 30, 2012; A. Lashinsky, "Inside Apple," May 23, 2011, pp. 125–134; and C. Mainemelis, "Stealing Fire: Creative Deviance in the Evolution of New Ideas," *Academy of Management Review,* December 2010, pp. 558–578.

CHAPTER 13

1. A. Ford, "Liar, Liar. How Faux Credentials Felled Yahoo!'s CEO, Among Others," *Time,* May 28, 2012, p. 18; G. Strauss and L. Petrecca, "CEOs Stumble Over Ethics Violations, Mismanagement," *USA Today Online,* May 22, 2012; C. Hausman, "CEOs' Ethics in Spotlight," *Ethics Newsline,* May 21, 2012; A. Efrati and J. S. Lublin, "Yahoo CEO's Downfall," *Wall Street Journal,* May 15, 2012, p. B5; J. Pepitone, "Ousted Yahoo CEO Will Get No Severance," *CNNMoney.com,* May 15, 2012; S. Martin and J. Swartz, "Yahoo Ousts CEO In New Shake-Up," *USA Today,* May 14, 2012, p. 1B; A. Efrati and J. S. Lublin, "Thompson Resigns As CEO of Yahoo," *Wall Street Journal,* May 14, 2012, pp. A1+; and A. Efrati and J. S. Lublin, "Résumé Trips Up Yahoo's Chief," *Wall Street Journal,* May 5-6, 2012, pp. A1+.

2. L'Oreal advertisement, *Diversity Inc.,* November 2006, p. 9.

3. A. Carmeli and J. Shaubroeck, "How Leveraging Human Resource Capital With Its Competitive Distinctiveness Enhances the Performance of Commercial and Public Organizations," *Human Resource Management,* Winter 2005, pp. 391–412; L. Bassi and D. McMurrer, "How's Your Return on People?" *Harvard Business Review,* March 2004, p. 18; C. J. Collins and K. D. Clark, "Strategic Human Resource Practices, Top Management Team Social Networks, and Firm Performance: The Role of Human Resource Practices in Creating Organizational Competitive Advantage," *Academy of Management Journal,* December 2003, pp. 740–751; J. Pfeffer, *The Human Equation* (Boston: Harvard Business School Press, 1998); J. Pfeffer, *Competitive Advantage Through People* (Boston: Harvard Business School Press, 1994); A. A. Lado and M. C. Wilson, "Human Resource Systems and Sustained Competitive Advantage," *Academy of Management Review*, October 1994, pp. 699–727; and P. M. Wright and G. C. McMahan, "Theoretical Perspectives for Strategic Human Resource Management," *Journal of Management* 18, no. 1 (1992), pp. 295–320.

4. "Maximizing the Return on Your Human Capital Investment: The 2005 Watson Wyatt Human Capital Index® Report," "WorkAsia 2004/2005: A Study of Employee Attitudes in Asia," and "European Human Capital Index 2002," Watson Wyatt Worldwide (Washington, DC).

5. See, for example, C. H. Chuang and H. Liao, "Strategic Human Resource Management in Service Context: Taking Care of Business by Taking Care of Employees and Customers," *Personnel Psychology,* Spring 2010, pp. 153–196; M. Subramony, "A Meta-Analytic Investigation of the Relationship Between HRM Bundles and Firm Performance," *Human Resource Management,* September–October 2009, pp. 745–768; M. M. Butts et al., "Individual Reactions to High Involvement Work Practices: Investigating the Role of Empowerment and Perceived Organizational Support," *Journal of Occupational Health Psychology,* April 2009, pp. 122–136; L. Sun, S. Aryee, and K. S. Law, "High-Performance Human Resource Practices, Citizenship Behavior, and Organizational Performance: A Relational Perspective," *Academy of Management Journal,* June 2007, pp. 558–577; A. Carmeli and J. Shaubroeck, "How Leveraging Human Resource Capital with Its Competitive Distinctiveness Enhances the Performance of Commercial and Public Organizations," 2005; Y. Y. Kor and H. Leblebici, "How Do Interdependencies Among Human-Capital Deployment, Development, and Diversification Strategies Affect Firms' Financial Performance?" *Strategic Management Journal,* October 2005, pp. 967–985; D. E. Bowen and C. Ostroff, "Understanding HRM–Firm Performance Linkages: The Role of the 'Strength' of the HRM System," *Academy of Management Review,* April 2004, pp. 203–221; A. S. Tsui, J. L. Pearce, L. W. Porter, and A. M. Tripoli, "Alternative Approaches to the Employee-Organization Relationship: Does Investment in Employees Pay Off?" *Academy of Management Journal,* October 1997, pp. 1089–1121; M. A. Huselid, S. E. Jackson, and R. S. Schuler, "Technical and Strategic Human Resource Management Effectiveness as Determinants of Firm Performance," *Academy of Management Journal*, January 1997, pp. 171–188; J. T. Delaney and M. A. Huselid, "The Impact of Human Resource Management Practices on Perceptions of Organizational Performance," *Academy of Management Journal,* August 1996, pp. 949–969; B. Becker and B. Gerhart, "The Impact of Human Resource Management on Organizational Performance: Progress and Prospects," *Academy of Management Journal,* August 1996, pp. 779–801; M. J. Koch and R. G. McGrath, "Improving Labor Productivity: Human Resource Management Policies Do Matter," *Strategic Management Journal,* May 1996, pp. 335–354; and M. A. Huselid, "The Impact of Human Resource Management Practices on Turnover, Productivity, and Corporate Financial Performance," *Academy of Management Journal,* June 1995, pp. 635–672.

6. "Human Capital a Key to Higher Market Value," *Business Finance,* December 1999, p. 15.

7. M. Boyle, "Happy People, Happy Returns," *Fortune,* January 11, 2006, p. 100.

8. data points box based on "Find the Sharpest Needle in the Stack," *HR Magazine,* June 2012, p. 16; J. Yang and P. Trap, "If You Started a Job and You Didn't Like It, How Long Would You Stay?" *USA Today,* June 11, 2012, p. 1B; J. Yang and P. Trap, "Do You Use Social Networking Sites to Research Candidates?" *USA Today,* June 5, 2012, p. 1B; J. Yang and A. Gonzalez, "Top Actions Workers Feel Are Grounds for Termination," *USA Today,* May 7, 2012, p. 1B; L. Weber," Little Time for Resumes," *Wall Street Journal,* March 21, 2012, p. B8; J. Yang and V. Bravo, "How Often Are You Late for Work?" *USA Today,* February 8, 2012, p. 1B; K. Madden, "Playing Hooky From the Office," Careerbuilder, *Springfield, Missouri News-Leader,* November 6, 2011, p. 1G; J. Yang and P. Trap, "Top Reasons Why Someone

Hired Would Not Work Out in the Position," *USA Today,* October 26, 2011, p. 1B; J. Yang and V. Salazar, "Are Annual Performance Reviews An Accurate Appraisal for Employees' Work?" *USA Today,* September 27, 2011, p. 1B; J. Yang and S. Ward, "What Are the Most Common Mistakes Candidates Make During Job Interviews?" *USA Today,* August 15, 2011, p. 1B; and P. Kujawa, "For Some Workers, the Piggy Bank Is Fat for Retirement," *Workforce Management Online,* July 16, 2012.

9. M. Luo, "$13 an Hour? 500 Sign Up, 1 Wins a Job," *New York Times Online,* October 22, 2009.

10. J. Clenfield, "A Tear in Japan's Safety Net," *Bloomberg BusinessWeek,* April 12, 2010, pp. 60–61.

11. CIA World Factbook, https://www.cia.gov/library/publications/the-world-factbook/geos/ee.html, 2012; and "EU: Not Working," *Business Europe,* March 1, 2010, p. 1.

12. A. Kohpaiboon et al., "Global Recession: Labour Market Adjustment and International Production Networks," *ASEAN Economic Bulletin,* April 2010, pp. 98–120.

13. J. Schramm, "Tomorrow's Workforce," *HR Magazine,* March 2012, p. 112; C. Isidore, "Say Goodbye to Full-Time Jobs with Benefits," *CNNMoney.com,* June 1, 2010; C. Rampell, "In a Job Market Realignment, Some Left Behind," *New York Times Online,* May 12, 2010; and P. Izzo, "Economists Expect Shifting Work Force," *Wall Street Journal Online,* February 11, 2010.

14. F. Hansen, "Jobless Recovery Is Leaving a Trail of Recession-Weary Employees in Its Wake," *Compensation & Benefits Review,* May/June 2010, pp. 135–136; J. Hollon, "Worker 'Deal' Is Off," *Workforce Management,* April 2010, p. 42; and "The New Employment Deal: How Far, How Fast, and How Enduring? The 2010 Global Workforce Study," *Towers Watson* [www.towerswatson.com], April 2010.

15. K. Niththyananthan, "BA, Union Set to Restart Talks," *Wall Street Journal Online,* June 1, 2010; The Associated Press, "No Deal in Talks on British Airway," *MSNBC.com,* May 27, 2010; D. Cameron and D. Michaels, "BA Crews Begin Walkout," *Wall Street Journal,* May 25, 2010, p. B2; and J. Brustein, "British Airways Cabin Crew Walks Out," *New York Times Online,* May 24, 2010.

16. K. Bradsher and D. Barboza, "Strike in China Highlights Gap in Workers' Pay," *New York Times Online,* May 28, 2010.

17. A. Smith, "Union Membership Inches Up," www.shrm.org, January 27, 2012.

18. "Union Membership in Canada—2008," *Labour Program, Human Resources and Skills Development Canada* [www.labour.gc.ca], June 29, 2010; C. Barratt, "Trade Union Membership 2008," *Department for Business Enterprise and Regulatory Reform* [www.stats.berr.gov.au], April 2009; and J. Visser, "Union Membership Statistics in 24 Countries," *Monthly Labor Review,* January 2006, pp. 38–49.

19. C. Hausman, "Novartis Hit With Punitive Damages in Sex Discrimination Case," *Ethics Newsline* [www.globalethics.org/newsline], May 24, 2010.

20. S. Armour, "Lawsuits Pin Target on Managers," *USA Today* [www.usatoday.com], October 1, 2002.

21. G. B. Kushner, "Special Report: What HR Professionals Should Do Now," www.shrm.org, June 28, 2012; and S. G. Stolberg and R. Pear, "Obama Signs Health Care Overhaul Bill, With a Flourish," *New York Times Online,* March 23, 2010.

22. A. Smith, "Social Networking Online Protection Act Introduced," www.shrm.org, May 1, 2012.

23. B. Leonard, "The Right Career Forecast," *HR Magazine,* June 2012, pp. 46–47; S. Vranica and S. Schechner, "Weather Channel Taps Digital Expert as CEO," *Wall Street Journal,* January 25, 2012, p. B5; and B. Stelter, "A Warning for Some, Entertainment for Others," *New York Times Online,* August 28, 2011.

24. C. H. Loch, F. J. Sting, N. Bauer, and J. Mauermann, "How BMW Is Defusing the Demographic Time Bomb," *Harvard Business Review,* March 2010, pp. 99–102.

25. M. Korn, "As Baby Boomers Retire, Firms Prepare for Shift," *Wall Street Journal,* April 18, 2012, p. B8; and T. Minton-Eversole, "Concerns Grow Over Workforce Retirements and Skills Gaps," [www.shrm.org], April 9, 2012.

26. C. Rampell, "As Layoffs Surge, Women May Pass Men in Job Force," *New York Times Online,* February 6, 2009.

27. B. Tulgan, "Generation Y Defined: The New Young Workforce," *HR Tools Online* [www.hrtools.com/insights/bruce_tulgan], February 25, 2009.

28. S. F. Gale, "From Texas to Timbuktu—How Fluor Tracks Talent on a Global Scale," *Workforce Management Online,* March 7, 2012.

29. M. A. Costonis and R. Salkowitz, "The Tough Match of Young Workers and Insurance," *New York Times Online,* June 11, 2010.

30. E. Seubert, "What Are Your Organization's Critical Positions," *Workforce Management Online,* December 2009; F. Hansen, "Strategic Workforce Planning in an Uncertain World," *Workforce Management Online,* July 2009; and J. Sullivan, "Workforce Planning: Why to Start Now," *Workforce,* September 2002, pp. 46–50.

31. N. Byrnes, "Star Search," *BusinessWeek,* October 10, 2005, pp. 68–78.

32. D. Robb, "Sizing Up Talent," *HR Magazine,* April 2011, p. 77.

33. J. W. Boudreau and P. M. Ramstad, "Where's Your Pivotal Talent?" *Harvard Business Review,* April 2005, pp. 23–24.

34. J. Swartz, "Tech Firms Go On A Hiring Binge Again," *USA Today,* April 21, 2011, pp. 1B+; B. Einhorn and K. Gokhale, "Bangalore's Paying Again to Keep the Talent," *Bloomberg BusinessWeek,* May 24–May 30, 2010, pp. 14–16; D. A. Thoppil, "Pay War Breaks Out as India's Tech Firms Vie for Talent," *Wall Street Journal,* April 27, 2010, p. B8; and C. Tuna, J. E. Vascellaro, and P-W. Tam, "Tech Sector in Hiring Drive," *Wall Street Journal,* April 16, 2010, pp. A1+.

35. A. S. Bargerstock and G. Swanson, "Four Ways to Build Cooperative Recruitment Alliances," *HRMagazine,* March 1991, p. 49; and T. J. Bergmann and M. S. Taylor, "College Recruitment: What Attracts Students to Organizations?" *Personnel,* May–June 1984, pp. 34–46.

36. J. R. Gordon, *Human Resource Management: A Practical Approach* (Boston: Allyn and Bacon, 1986), p. 170.

37. C. Reynolds, "McDonald's Hiring Day Draws Crowds, High Hopes," AP Business Writer, *Springfield, Missouri News-Leader,* April 20, 2011, p. 6A; and A. Gasparro, "Fast-Food Chain Aims to Alter 'McJob' Image," *Wall Street Journal,* April 5, 2011, p. B9.

38. J. Walker, "Firms Invest Big in Career Sites," *Wall Street Journal Online,* June 8, 2010.

39. L. Petrecca, "With 3,000 Applications a Day, Google Can Be Picky," *USA Today,* May 19, 2010, p. 2B; and M. Helft, "In Fierce Competition, Google Finds Novel Ways to Feed Hiring Machine," *New York Times Online,* May 28, 2007.

40. K. Plourd, "Lights, Camera, Audits!" *CFO,* November 2007, p. 18.

41. S. Elliott, "Army Seeks Recruits in Social Media," *New York Times Online,* May 24, 2011.

42. S. Burton and D. Warner, "The Future of Hiring—Top 5 Sources for Recruitment Today," *Workforce Vendor Directory 2002,* p. 75.

43. See, for example, L. G. Klaff, "New Internal Hiring Systems Reduce Cost and Boost Morale," *Workforce Management,* March 2004, pp. 76–79; M. N. Martinez, "The Headhunter Within," *HR Magazine,* August 2001, pp. 48–55; R. W. Griffeth, P. W. Hom, L. S. Fink, and D. J. Cohen, "Comparative Tests of Multivariate Models of Recruiting Sources Effects," *Journal of Management,* vol. 23, no. 1, 1997, pp. 19–36; and J. P. Kirnan, J. E. Farley, and K. F. Geisinger, "The Relationship between Recruiting Source, Applicant Quality, and Hire Performance: An Analysis by Sex, Ethnicity, and Age," *Personnel Psychology*, Summer 1989, pp. 293–308.

44. J. McGregor, "Background Checks That Never End," *BusinessWeek,* March 20, 2006, p. 40.

45. A. Fisher, "For Happier Customers, Call HR," *Fortune,* November 28, 2005, p. 272.

46. J. Greenwald, "Judge Rules New York City Fire Department Exams Showed Racial Bias," *Workforce Management Online,* July 28, 2009.

47. A. Douzet, "Quality of Fill an Emerging Recruitment Metric," *Workforce Management Online,* June 24, 2010; and "Quality of Hire Metrics Help Staffing Unit Show Its Contribution to Bottom Line," *Society for Human Resource Management Online,* January 25, 2009.

48. A. Shadday, "Assessments 101: An Introduction to Candidate Testing," *Workforce Management Online,* January 2010; A. M. Ryan and R. E. Ployhart, "Applicants' Perceptions of Selection Procedures and Decisions: A Critical Review and Agenda for the Future," *Journal of Management,* vol. 26, no. 3 (2000), pp. 565–606; C. Fernandez-Araoz, "Hiring Without Firing," *Harvard Business Review,* July–August, 1999, pp. 108–120; A. K. Korman, "The Prediction of Managerial Performance: A Review," *Personnel Psychology,* Summer 1986, pp. 295–322; G. C. Thornton, *Assessment Centers in Human Resource Management* (Reading, MA: Addison-Wesley, 1992); I. T. Robertson and R. S. Kandola, "Work Sample Tests: Validity, Adverse Impact, and Applicant Reaction," *Journal of Occupational Psychology,* vol. 55, no. 3 (1982), pp. 171–183; E. E. Ghiselli, "The Validity of Aptitude Tests in Personnel Selection," *Personnel Psychology,* Winter 1973, p. 475; G. Grimsley and H. F. Jarrett, "The Relation of Managerial Achievement to Test Measures Obtained in the Employment Situation: Methodology and Results," *Personnel Psychology,* Spring 1973, pp. 31–48; J. J. Asher, "The Biographical Item: Can It Be Improved?" *Personnel Psychology,* Summer 1972, p. 266; and G. W. England, *Development and Use of Weighted Application Blanks*, rev. ed. (Minneapolis: Industrial Relations Center, University of Minnesota, 1971).

49. See, for example, M. A. Tucker, "Show and Tell," *HR Magazine,* January 2012, p. 51; Y. Ganzach, A. Pazy, Y. Ohayun, and E. Brainin, "Social Exchange and Organizational Commitment: Decision-Making Training for Job Choice as an Alternative to the Realistic Job Preview," *Personnel Psychology,* Autumn 2002, pp. 613–637; B. M. Meglino, E. C. Ravlin, A. S. DeNisi, "A Meta-Analytic Examination of Realistic Job Preview Effectiveness: A Test of Three Counterintuitive Propositions," *Human Resource Management Review,* vol. 10, no. 4 (2000), pp. 407–434; J. A. Breaugh and M. Starke, "Research on Employee Recruitment: So Many Studies, So Many Remaining Questions," *Journal of Management,* vol. 26,

no. 3 (2000), pp. 405–434; and S. L. Premack and J. P. Wanous, "A Meta-Analysis of Realistic Job Preview Experiments," *Journal of Applied Psychology,* November 1985, pp. 706–720.

50. G. Kranz, "Tourism Training Takes Flight in Miami," *Workforce Management Online,* May 2010.

51. K. Gustafson, "A Better Welcome Mat," *Training,* June 2005, pp. 34–41.

52. M. Jokisaari and J-E. Nurmi, "Change in Newcomers' Supervisor Support and Socialization Outcomes After Organizational Entry," *Academy of Management Journal,* June 2009, pp. 527–544; D. G. Allen, "Do Organizational Socialization Tactics Influence Newcomer Embeddedness and Turnover?" *Journal of Management,* April 2006, pp. 237–256; C. L. Cooper, "The Changing Psychological Contract at Work: Revisiting the Job Demands-Control Model," *Occupational and Environmental Medicine,* June 2002, p. 355; D. M. Rousseau and S. A. Tijoriwala, "Assessing Psychological Contracts: Issues, Alternatives and Measures," *Journal of Organizational Behavior,* vol. 19 (1998), pp. 679–695; S. L. Robinson, M. S. Kraatz, and D. M. Rousseau, "Changing Obligations and the Psychological Contract: A Longitudinal Study," *Academy of Management Journal,* February 1994, pp. 137–152.

53. See, for instance, E. G. Tripp, "Aging Aircraft and Coming Regulations: Political and Media Pressures Have Encouraged the FAA to Expand Its Pursuit of Real and Perceived Problems of Older Aircraft and Their Systems. Operators Will Pay," *Business and Commercial Aviation,* March 2001, pp. 68–75.

54. "A&S Interview: Sully's Tale," *Air & Space Magazine* [www.airspacemag.com], February 18, 2009; A. Altman, "Chesley B. Sullenberger III," *Time* [www.time.com], January 16, 2009; and K. Burke, Pete Donohue, and C. Siemaszko, "US Airways Airplane Crashes in Hudson River—Hero Pilot Chesley Sullenberger III Saves All Aboard," *New York Daily News* [www.nydailynews.com], January 16, 2009.

55. D. Heath and C. Heath, "The Power of Razzle-Dazzle," *Fast Company,* December 2009–January 2010, pp. 69–70.

56. T. Raphael, "It's All in the Cards," *Workforce,* September 2002, p. 18.

57. S. Nassauer, "How Waiters Read Your Table," *Wall Street Journal,* February 22, 2012, pp. D1+.

58. "2011 Training Industry Report," [www.trainingmag.com], November 23, 2011.

59. B. Hall, "The Top Training Priorities for 2003," *Training,* February 2003, p. 40.

60. D. Heath and C. Heath, "The Power of Razzle-Dazzle."

61. J. McGregor, "The Midyear Review's Sudden Impact," *BusinessWeek,* July 6, 2009, pp. 50–52.

62. A. Pace, "The Performance Management Dilemma," *T&D,* July 2011, p. 22.

63. K. Sulkowicz, "Straight Talk at Review Time," *BusinessWeek,* September 10, 2007, p. 16.

64. J. Pfeffer, "Low Grades for Performance Appraisals," *BusinessWeek,* August 3, 2009, p. 68.

65. R. E. Silverman, "Work Reviews Losing Steam," *Wall Street Journal,* December 19, 2011, p. B7.

66. J. D. Glater, "Seasoning Compensation Stew," *New York Times,* March 7, 2001, pp. C1+.

67. M. Korn, "Benefits Matter," *Wall Street Journal,* April 4, 2012, p. B8.

68. This section based on R. I. Henderson, *Compensation Management in a Knowledge-Based World*, 10th ed. (Upper Saddle River, NJ: Prentice Hall, 2006).

69. M. P. Brown, M. C. Sturman, and M. J. Simmering, "Compensation Policy and Organizational Performance: The Efficiency, Operational and Financial Implications of Pay Levels and Pay Structure," *Academy of Management Journal,* December 2003, pp. 752–762; J. D. Shaw, N. P. Gupta, and J. E. Delery, "Pay Dispersion and Workforce Performance: Moderating Effects of Incentives and Interdependence," *Strategic Management Journal,* June 2002, pp. 491–512; E. Montemayor, "Congruence between Pay Policy and Competitive Strategy in High-Performing Firms," *Journal of Management,* vol. 22, no. 6 (1996), pp. 889–908; and L. R. Gomez-Mejia, "Structure and Process of Diversification, Compensation Strategy, and Firm Performance," *Strategic Management Journal,* 13 (1992), pp. 381–397.

70. M. Moskowitz, R. Levering, and C. Tkaczyk, "100 Best Companies to Work For," *Fortune,* February 8, 2010, pp. 75–88.

71. J. D. Shaw, N. Gupta, A. Mitra, and G. E. Ledford, Jr., "Success and Survival of Skill-Based Pay Plans," *Journal of Management,* February 2005, pp. 28–49; C. Lee, K. S. Law, and P. Bobko, "The Importance of Justice Perceptions on Pay Effectiveness: A Two-Year Study of a Skill-Based Pay Plan," *Journal of Management,* vol. 26, no. 6 (1999), pp. 851–873; G. E. Ledford, "Paying for the Skills, Knowledge and Competencies of Knowledge Workers," *Compensation and Benefits Review,* July–August 1995, pp. 55–62; and E. E. Lawler III, G. E. Ledford Jr., and L. Chang, "Who Uses Skill-Based Pay and Why," *Compensation and Benefits Review,* March–April 1993, p. 22.

72. J. D. Shaw, N. Gupta, A. Mitra, and G. E. Ledford Jr., "Success and Survival of Skill-Based Pay Plans."

73. Information from Hewitt Associates Studies: "Aftermath of the Recession on 2009–2010 Compensation Spending," February 2010; "As Fixed Costs Increase, Employers Turn to Variable Pay Programs as Preferred Way to Reward Employees," August 21, 2007; "Hewitt Study Shows Pay-for-Performance Plans Replacing Holiday Bonuses," December 6, 2005; "Salaries Continue to Rise in Asia Pacific, Hewitt Annual Study Reports," November 23, 2005; and "Hewitt Study Shows Base Pay Increases Flat for 2006 With Variable Pay Plans Picking Up the Slack," Hewitt Associates, LLC [www.hewittassociates.com], August 31, 2005.

74. T. J. Erickson, "The Leaders We Need Now," *Harvard Business Review,* May 2010, pp. 63–66.

75. S. Thurm, "Recalculating the Cost of Big Layoffs," *Wall Street Journal,* May 5, 2010, pp. B1+; and J. Pfeffer, "Lay Off the Layoffs," *Newsweek,* February 15, 2010, pp. 32–37.

76. W. F. Cascio, "Use and Management of Downsizing as a Corporate Strategy," *HR Magazine,* June 2010, special insert; D. K. Datta, J. P. Guthrie, D. Basuil, and A. Pandey, "Causes and Effects of Employee Downsizing: A Review and Synthesis," *Journal of Management,* January 2010, pp. 281–348; B. Conaty, "Cutbacks: Don't Neglect the Survivors," *Bloomberg BusinessWeek,* January 11, 2010, p. 68; and P. Korkki, "Accentuating the Positive After a Layoff," *New York Times Online,* August 16, 2009;

77. R. Ceniceros, "Court Finds McDonald's Liable in Employee's Sexual Assault Case," *Workforce Management Online,* November 25, 2009.

78. H. Stout, "Less 'He Said, She Said' in Sex Harassment Cases," *New York Times Online,* November 5, 2011.

79. R. Huggins and P. Trap, "Number of Sexual Harassment Claims Filed By Men," *USA Today,* January 23, 2012, p. 1A.

80. A. B. Fisher, "Sexual Harassment, What to Do," *Fortune,* August 23, 1993, pp. 84–88.

81. M. Velasquez, "Sexual Harassment Today: An Update—Looking Back and Looking Forward," *Diversity Training Group* [www.diversitydtg.com], 2004.

82. "Quick Takes: Sex Discrimination and Sexual Harassment," *Catalyst* [www.catalyst.org], November 9, 2007; P. M. Buhler, "The Manager's Role in Preventing Sexual Harassment," *Supervision,* April 1999, p. 18; and "Cost of Sexual Harassment in the U.S.," *The Webb Report: A Newsletter on Sexual Harassment* (Seattle, WA: Premier Publishing, Ltd.), January 1994, pp. 4–7, and April 1994, pp. 2–5.

83. "Effects of Sexual Harassment," *Stop Violence Against Women* [www.catalyst.org], May 9, 2007; and V. Di Martino, H. Hoel, and C. L. Cooper, "Preventing Violence and Harassment in the Workplace," *European Foundation for the Improvement of Living and Working Conditions,* 2003, p. 39.

84. The Associated Press, "Corruption, Sexual Harassment Charges Cloud Oxford Debating Club Presidential Election," *International Herald Tribune* [www.iht.com], February 6, 2008; G. L. Maatman, Jr., "A Global View of Sexual Harassment: Global Human Resource Strategies," *HR Magazine,* July 2000, pp. 151–156; and W. Hardman and J. Heidelberg, "When Sexual Harassment Is a Foreign Affair," *Personnel Journal,* April 1996, pp. 91–97.

85. "Sexual Harassment," *The U.S. Equal Employment Opportunity Commission* [www.eeoc.gov].

86. Ibid.

87. A. R. Karr, "Companies Crack Down on the Increasing Sexual Harassment by E-Mail," *Wall Street Journal,* September 21, 1999, p. A1; and A. Fisher, "After All This Time, Why Don't People Know What Sexual Harassment Means?" *Fortune,* January 12, 1998, p. 68.

88. See T. S. Bland and S. S. Stalcup, "Managing Harassment," *Human Resource Management,* Spring 2001, pp. 51–61; K. A. Hess and D. R. M. Ehrens, "Sexual Harassment—Affirmative Defense to Employer Liability," *Benefits Quarterly,* Second Quarter 1999, p. 57; J. A. Segal, "The Catch-22s of Remedying Sexual Harassment Complaints," *HR Magazine,* October 1997, pp. 111–117; S. C. Bahls and J. E. Bahls, "Hand-Off Policy," *Entrepreneur,* July 1997, pp. 74–76; J. A. Segal, "Where Are We Now?" *HR Magazine,* October 1996, pp. 69–73; B. McAfee and D. L. Deadrick, "Teach Employees to Just Say No," *HR Magazine,* February 1996, pp. 86–89; G. D. Block, "Avoiding Liability for Sexual Harassment," *HR Magazine,* April 1995, pp. 91–97; and J. A. Segal, "Stop Making Plaintiffs' Lawyers Rich," *HR Magazine,* April 1995, pp. 31–35. Also, it should be noted here that under the Title VII and the Civil Rights Act of 1991, the maximum award that can be given, under the Federal Act, is $300,000. However, many cases are tried under state laws that permit unlimited punitive damages, such as the $7.1 million that Rena Weeks received in her trial based on California statutes.

89. S. Shellenbarger, "Supreme Court Takes on How Employers Handle Worker Harassment Complaints," *Wall Street Journal,* April 13, 2006, p. D1.

90. S. Jayson, "Workplace Romance No Longer Gets the Kiss-Off," *USA Today,* February 9, 2006, p. 9D.

91. J. Yang and V. Salazar, "Would You Date a Co-Worker?" *USA Today,* February 14, 2008, p. 1B.

92. Jayson, "Workplace Romance No Longer Gets the Kiss-off."

93. S. Shellenbarger, "For Office Romance, The Secret's Out," *Wall Street Journal,* February 10, 2010, pp. D1+.

94. C. Boyd, "The Debate Over the Prohibition of Romance in the Workplace," *Journal of Business Ethics,* December 2010, pp. 325–338; R. Mano and Y. Gabriel, "Workplace Romances in Cold and Hot Organizational Climates: The Experience of Israel and Taiwan," *Human Relations,* January 2006, pp. 7–35; J. A. Segal, "Dangerous Liaisons," *HR Magazine,* December 2005, pp. 104–108; "Workplace Romance Can Create Unforeseen Issues for Employers," *HR Focus,* October 2005, p. 2; C. A. Pierce and H. Aguinis, "Legal Standards, Ethical Standards, and Responses to Social-Sexual Conduct At Work," *Journal of Organizational Behavior,* September 2005, pp. 727–732; and C. A. Pierce, B. J. Broberg, J. R. McClure, and H. Aguinis, "Responding to Sexual Harassment Complaints: Effects of a Dissolved Workplace Romance on Decision-Making Standards," *Organizational Behavior and Human Decision Processes,* September 2004, pp. 66–82.

95. J. A. Segal, "Dangerous Liaisons."

96. E. Zimmerman, "When Cupid Strikes at the Cubicle," *New York Times Online,* April 9, 2010.

97. S. Ali and B. Frankel, "The Work/Life Balancing Act: How 4 Companies Do It," *DiversityInc,* May 18, 2010, pp. 62–68.

98. J. Miller and M. Miller, "Get a Life!" *Fortune,* November 28, 2005, pp. 108–124.

99. L. Vanderkam, "Graduates, You Can Have It All," *USA Today,* May 27, 2010, p. 11A; and M. Elias, "The Family-First Generation," *USA Today,* December 13, 2004, p. 5D.

100. M. Mandel, "The Real Reasons You're Working So Hard…and What You Can Do About It," *BusinessWeek,* October 3, 2005, pp. 60–67.

101. C. Farrell, "The Overworked, Networked Family," *BusinessWeek,* October 3, 2005, p. 68.

102. F. Hansen, "Truths and Myths about Work/Life Balance," *Workforce,* December 2002, pp. 34–39.

103. P. Brough and T. Kalliath, "Work-Family Balance: Theoretical and Empirical Advancements," *Journal of Organizational Behavior,* July 2009, pp. 581–585; E. F. Van Steenbergen and N. Ellemers, "Is Managing the Work-Family Interface Worthwhile? Benefits for Employee Health and Performance," *Journal of Organizational Behavior,* July 2009, pp. 617–642; K. Palmer, "The New Mommy Track," *US News and World Report,* September 3, 2007, pp. 40–45; and J. H. Greenhaus and G. N. Powell, "When Work and Family Are Allies: A Theory of Work-Family Enrichment," *Academy of Management Review,* January 2006, pp. 72–92.

104. Ibid., p. 73.

105. S. Shellenbarger, "What Makes A Company A Great Place to Work Today," *Wall Street Journal,* October 4, 2007, p. D1; and L. B. Hammer, M. B. Neal, J. T. Newsom, K. J. Brockwood, and C. L. Colton, "A Longitudinal Study of the Effects of Dual-Earner Couples' Utilization of Family-Friendly Workplace Supports on Work and Family Outcomes," *Journal of Applied Psychology,* July 2005, pp. 799–810.

106. M. M. Arthur, "Share Price Reactions to Work-Family Initiatives: An Institutional Perspective," *Academy of Management Journal,* August 2003, pp. 497–505.

107. L. B. Hammer et al., "Development and Validation of a Multidimensional Measure of Family Supportive Supervisor Behaviors," *Journal of Management,* August 2009, pp. 837–856; and N. P. Rothbard, T. L. Dumas, and K. W. Phillips, "The Long Arm of the Organization: Work-Family Policies and Employee Preferences for Segmentation," paper presented at the 61st Annual Academy of Management meeting, Washington, DC, August 2001.

108. R. Ceniceros, "Workforce Obesity," *Workforce Management Online,* October 19, 2011; and J. Walsh, "Special Report: Creating a Culture of Wellness Helps Companies Tighten Their Belt," *Workforce Management Online,* April 2011.

109. A. W. Matthews, "Pitting Employees Against Each Other…for Health," *Wall Street Journal,* May 1, 2012, pp. D1+; R. King, "Slimming Down Employees to Cut Costs"; C. Tkaczyk, "Lowering Health-Care Costs," *Fortune,* November 23, 2009, p. 16; and A. W. Matthews, "When All Else Fails: Forcing Workers into Healthy Habits," *Wall Street Journal,* July 8, 2009, pp. D1+.

110. L. Cornwell, "More Companies Penalize Workers with Health Risks," The Associated Press, *Springfield, Missouri News-Leader,* September 10, 2007, p. 10A.

111. B. Pyenson and K. Fitch, "Smoking May Be Hazardous to Your Bottom Line," *Workforce Management Online* [www.workforce.com], December 2007; and L. Cornwell, The Associated Press, "Companies Tack on Fees on Insurance for Smokers," *Springfield, Missouri News-Leader,* February 17, 2006, p. 5B.

112. R. Ceniceros, "Workforce Obesity," J. Walsh, "Special Report: Creating a Culture of Wellness Helps Companies Tighten Their Belt," and M. Scott, "Obesity More Costly to U.S. Companies Than Smoking, Alcoholism," *Workforce Management Online* [www.workforce.com], April 9, 2008.

113. "Obesity Weighs Down Production," *Industry Week,* March 2008, pp. 22–23.

114. J. Appleby, "Companies Step Up Wellness Efforts," *USA Today,* August 1, 2005, pp. 1A+.

115. G. Kranz, "Prognosis Positive: Companies Aim to Get Workers Healthy," *Workforce Management Online* [www.workforce.com], April 15, 2008.

116. M. Conlin, "Hide the Doritos! Here Comes HR," *BusinessWeek,* April 28, 2008, pp. 94–96.

117. J. Fox, "Good Riddance to Pensions," *CNN Money,* January 12, 2006.

118. M. Adams, "Broken Pension System in Crying Need of a Fix," *USA Today,* November 15, 2005, p. 1B+.

119. J. Appleby, "Traditional Pensions Are Almost Gone. Is Employer-Provided Health Insurance Next?" *USA Today,* November 13, 2007, pp. 1A+; S. Kelly, "FedEx, Goodyear Make Big Pension Plan Changes," *Workforce Management Online* [www.workforce.com], March 1, 2007; G. Colvin, "The End of a Dream," *Fortune* [www.cnnmoney.com], June 22, 2006; E. Porter and M. Williams Nash, "Benefits Go the Way of Pensions," *NY Times Online,* February 9, 2006; and J. Fox, "Good Riddance to Pensions."

120. L. Beyer, "The Rise and Fall of Employer-Sponsored Pension Plans," *Workforce Management Online,* February 6, 2012.

121. Based on R. Pyrillis, "Workers Using Medical Marijuana Hold Their Breath, but Employers Worry They'll Take a Hit," *Workforce Management Online,* April 2011; "Puffing Up Over Pot in Workplace," *Workforce Management,* March 2011, p. 41; D. Cadrain, "The Marijuana Exception," *HR Magazine,* November 2010, pp. 40–42; D. Cadrain, "Do Medical Marijuana Laws Protect Usage by Employees?" *HR Magazine,* November 2010, p. 12; A. K. Wiwi and N. P. Crifo, "The Unintended Impact of New Jersey's New Medical Marijuana Law on the Workplace," *Employee Relations Law Journal,* Summer 2010, pp. 33–37; S. Simon, "At Work, A Drug Dilemma," *Wall Street Journal,* August 3, 2010, p. D1;

and J. Greenwald, "Medical Marijuana Laws Create Dilemma for Firms," *Business Insurance,* February 15, 2010, pp. 1–20.

122. D. S. Urban, "What to Do About 'Body Art' at Work?" *Workforce Management Online,* March 2010.

123. P. Coy and E. Dwoskin, "Shortchanged: Why Women Get Paid Less Than Men," *Bloomberg BusinessWeek Online,* June 21, 2012.

124. T. Bingham and P. Galagan, "Delivering 'On-Time, Every Time' Knowledge and Skills to a World of Employees," *T&D,* July 2012, pp. 32–37; J. Levitz, "UPS Thinks Outside the Box on Driver Training," *Wall Street Journal,* April 6, 2010, pp. B1+; and K. Kingsbury, "Road to Recovery," *Time,* March 8, 2010, pp. Global 14–Global 16.

125. "Digital Report: Tug-of-War for Digital Talent," *Campaign Asia-Pacific,* June 2012, p. 12; N. Blacksmith and Y. Yang, "Executives: Your Company Isn't Attracting the Best Talent," *Gallup Management Journal Online,* May 29, 2012, p. 1; J. Cullen, "Stop Searching for the Elusive Purple Squirrel," *Computerworld,* April 9, 2012, p. 25; G. Anders, "The Rare Find," *Bloomberg BusinessWeek,* October 17–October 23, 2011, pp. 106–112; and J. Light, "At Mature Techs, A Young Vibe," *Wall Street Journal,* June 13, 2011, p. B7.

MANAGING YOUR CAREER MODULE

1. J. S. Lublin, "Three Who Thrived After Early Gaffes," *Wall Street Journal,* May 4, 2010, p. D4.

2. S. E. Sullivan and Y. Baruch, "Advances in Career Theory and Research: A Critical Review and Agenda for Future Exploration," *Journal of Management,* December 2009, pp. 1542–1571.

3. "The Employment Situation—July 2012," http://www.bls.gov/news.release/pdf/empsit.pdf, August 3, 2012.

4. "Management and Business and Financial Occupations," *Occupational Outlook Handbook, 2010–11 Edition* [http://www.bls.gov/oco/oco1001.htm#management].

5. J. Sandberg, "Sometimes an Office Visit Can Feel Like a Visit to a Very Foreign Land," *Wall Street Journal,* October 20, 2005, p. B1; D. Sacks, "Scout's Honor," *Fast Company,* April 2005, p. 94; D. W. Brown, "Searching for Clues," *Black Enterprise,* November 2002, pp. 114–120; L. Bower, "Weigh Values to Decide If Working for 'Beasts' Worthwhile," *Springfield Business Journal,* November 4, 2002, p. 73; S. Shellenbarger, "How to Find Out If You're Going to Hate a New Job Before You Agree to Take It," *Wall Street Journal,* June 13, 2002, p. D1; and M. Boyle, "Just Right," *Fortune,* June 10, 2002, pp. 207–208.

6. S. Caudron, "Some New Rules for the New World of Work," *Business Finance,* October 2001, p. 24; C. Kanchier, *Dare to Change Your Job and Your Life,* 2d ed. (Indianapolis, IN: Jist Publishing, 2000); and S. Hagevik, "Responsible Risk Taking," *Journal of Environmental Health,* November 1999, pp. 29+.

7. A. Feldman, "The Road to Reinvention," *Bloomberg BusinessWeek,* March 8, 2010, pp. 68–70; E. Zimmerman, "Making Yourself Indispensable," *New York Times Online,* February 14, 2010; S. E. Needleman, "Revving a Career While It's in Neutral," *Wall Street Journal,* January 19, 2010, p. D5; and D. Schawbel, "Upping Your Value at Work," *BusinessWeek Online,* December 18, 2009.

8. D. Nishi, "What To Do If Your Boss Is the Problem," *Wall Street Journal,* April 20, 2010, p. D4; M. Weinstein, "Mind Your Manners," *Training,* July–August 2009, pp. 24–29; M. Solomon, *Working With Difficult People* (Upper Saddle River, NJ: Prentice Hall, 2002); M. Gaskill, "Bigger Bullies," *American Way,* August 2001, pp. 92–96; R. Cooper, "Dealing Effectively with Difficult People," *Nursing,* September 1993, pp. 97–100; and R. M. Bramson, *Coping with Difficult People* (Garden City, NY: Anchor Press/Doubleday, 1981).

9. A. Ebron, "All Work and No Play," *Woman's Day,* October 6, 2009, p. 50; and J. Yang and K. Simmons, "Work–Life Balance Tops Pay," *USA Today,* March 13, 2008, p. 1B.

10. D. Hannah, "Just Out of School? Six Ways You Can Get Ahead at Work," *Diversity Inc.,* May 2008, pp. 46–47.

11. S. Lohr, "How Privacy Vanishes Online," *New York Times Online,* March 16, 2010; and A. Bruzzese, "Online Postings Can Sabotage One's Career," Gannett News Service, *Springfield, Missouri, News-Leader,* August 11, 2009, p. 9B; and D. Hannah, "Just Out of School? Six Ways You Can Get Ahead at Work."

12. J. Hempel, "How LinkedIn Will Fire Up Your Career," *Fortune,* April 12, 2010, pp. 74–82; and J. S. Lublin, "A Networking Pro Learns Some New Tricks," *Wall Street Journal,* March 2, 2010, p. D4.

CHAPTER 14

1. "Jobs at Haifa," Intel Corporation, www.intel.com, July 24, 2012; M. Fleisher, "Intel and Israeli Universities Team Up to Create 'Human Brain' Applications," *TheJewishPress.com,* May 24, 2012; J. Terzakis, "Virtual Retrospectives for Geographically Dispersed Software Teams," *IEEE Computer Society,* May–June 2011, pp. 12–15; "Virtual Teams Must Function Correctly," *Strategic Direction,* April 2011, pp. 22–24; C. Scovotti and L. D. Spiller, "Cross-Border Student Collaborations: Opportunities for Videoconferencing," *Marketing Education Review,* Spring 2011, pp. 57–61; E. Markowitz, "Are the Best Leaders Revolutionaries?" *Inc. Online,* March 28, 2011; L. J. Grcssgård, "Virtual Team Collaboration and Innovation in Organizations," *Team Performance Management,* March 2011, pp. 102–119; L. Tischler, "Intel's Virtual Footwear Wall for Adidas Turns Boutiques into Shoe-Topias," *Fast Company Online,* January 11, 2011; O. Coren, "Israel Offers $110 Million for commitment to Stay in the Country," *Haaretz.com,* August 26, 2010; and R. R. Nelson, "Project Retrospectives: Evaluating Project Success, Failure, and Everything In Between," *MIS Quarterly Executive,* September 2005, pp. 361–372.

2. B. Mezrich, *Bringing Down the House: The Inside Story of Six MIT Students Who Took Vegas for Millions* (New York: Free Press, 2002). The 2008 film *21* was a fictional work based loosely on the story.

3. M. F. Maples, "Group Development: Extending Tuckman's Theory," *Journal for Specialists in Group Work,* Fall 1988, pp. 17–23; and B. W. Tuckman and M. C. Jensen, "Stages of Small-Group Development Revisited," *Group and Organizational Studies,* December 1977, pp. 419–427.

4. D. Coutou, interview with J. R. Hackman, "Why Teams Don't Work," *Harvard Business Review,* May 2009, pp. 99–105; M. Kactcr, "Repotting Mature Work Teams," *Training,* April 1994, pp. 54–56; and L. N. Jewell and H. J. Reitz, *Group Effectiveness in Organizations* (Glenview, IL: Scott, Foresman, 1981).

5. A. Sobel, "The Beatles Principles," *Strategy & Business,* Spring 2006, p. 42.

6. This model is based on the work of P. S. Goodman, E. Ravlin, and M. Schminke, "Understanding Groups in Organizations," in L. L. Cummings and B. M. Staw (eds.), *Research in Organizational Behavior*, vol. 9 (Greenwich, CT: JAI Press, 1987), pp. 124–128; J. R. Hackman, "The Design of Work Teams," in J. W. Lorsch (ed.), *Handbook of Organizational Behavior* (Upper Saddle River, NJ: Prentice Hall, 1987),

pp. 315–342; G. R. Bushe and A. L. Johnson, "Contextual and Internal Variables Affecting Task Group Outcomes in Organizations," *Group and Organization Studies,* December 1989, pp. 462–482; M. A. Campion, C. J. Medsker, and A. C. Higgs, "Relations Between Work Group Characteristics and Effectiveness: Implications for Designing Effective Work Groups," *Personnel Psychology,* Winter 1993, pp. 823–850; D. E. Hyatt and T. M. Ruddy, "An Examination of the Relationship Between Work Group Characteristics, and Performance: Once More into the Breach," *Personnel Psychology,* Autumn 1997, pp. 553–585; and P. E. Tesluk and J. E. Mathieu, "Overcoming Roadblocks to Effectiveness: Incorporating Management of Performance Barriers into Models of Work Group Effectiveness," *Journal of Applied Psychology,* April 1999, pp. 200–217.

7. G. L. Stewart, "A Meta-Analytic Review of Relationships Between Team Design Features and Team Performance," *Journal of Management,* February 2006, pp. 29–54; T. Butler and J. Waldroop, "Understanding 'People' People," *Harvard Business Review,* June 2004, pp. 78–86; J. S. Bunderson, "Team Member Functional Background and Involvement in Management Teams: Direct Effects and the Moderating Role of Power Centralization," *Academy of Management Journal,* August 2003, pp. 458–474; and M. J. Stevens and M. A. Campion, "The Knowledge, Skill, and Ability Requirements for Teamwork: Implications for Human Resource Management," *Journal of Management,* Summer 1994, pp. 503–530.

8. V. U. Druskat and S. B. Wolff, "The Link between Emotions and Team Effectiveness: How Teams Engage Members and Build Effective Task Processes," *Academy of Management Proceedings,* August 1999; D. C. Kinlaw, *Developing Superior Work Teams: Building Quality and the Competitive Edge* (San Diego, CA: Lexington, 1991); and M. E. Shaw, *Contemporary Topics in Social Psychology* (Morristown, NJ: General Learning Press, 1976), pp. 350–351.

9. data points box based on J. Yang and S. Ward, "Would You Report a Colleague Who's Seriously Underperforming?" *USA Today,* September 21, 2011, p. 1B; M. B. O'Leary, M. Mortensen, and A. W. Woolley, "Multiple Team Membership: A Theoretical Model of Its Effects on Productivity and Learning for Individuals and Teams," *Academy of Management Review,* July 2011, p. 461; J. Yang and P. Trap, "As a Manager, It's Most Challenging To…," *USA Today,* April 19, 2011, p. 1B; J. Yang and K. Gelles, "Workplace Friendships," *USA Today,* April 13, 2010, p. 1B; K. Merriman, "Low-Trust Teams Prefer Individualized Pay," *Harvard Business Review,* November 2008, p. 32; M. Weinstein, "Coming Up Short? Join the Club," *Training,* April 2006, p. 14; B. J. West, J. L. Patera, and M. K. Carsten, "Team Level Positivity: Investigating Positive Psychological Capacities and Team Level Outcomes"; L. G. Boiney, "Gender Impacts Virtual Work Teams," *The Graziadio Business Report,* Fall 2001, Pepperdine University; and J. Yang and K. Simmons, "Traits of Good Team Players," *USA Today,* November 21, 2007, p. 1B.

10. McMurry, Inc., "The Roles Your People Play," *Managing People at Work,* October 2005, p. 4; G. Prince, "Recognizing Genuine Teamwork," *Supervisory Management*, April 1989, pp. 25–36; R. F. Bales, *SYMOLOG Case Study Kit* (New York: Free Press, 1980); and K. D. Benne and P. Sheats, "Functional Roles of Group Members," *Journal of Social Issues*, vol. 4 (1948), pp. 41–49.

11. A. Erez, H. Elms, and E. Fong, "Lying, Cheating, Stealing: Groups and the Ring of Gyges," paper presented at the Academy of Management Annual meeting, Honolulu: HI: August 8, 2005.

12. S. E. Asch, "Effects of Group Pressure upon the Modification and Distortion of Judgments," in H. Guetzkow (ed.), *Groups, Leadership and Men* (Pittsburgh: Carnegie Press, 1951), pp. 177–190; and S. E. Asch, "Studies of Independence and Conformity: A Minority of One Against a Unanimous Majority," *Psychological Monographs: General and Applied,* vol. 70, no. 9 (1956), pp. 1–70.

13. R. Bond and P. B. Smith, "Culture and Conformity: A Meta-Analysis of Studies Using Asch's [1952, 1956] Line Judgment Task," *Psychological Bulletin,* January 1996, pp. 111–137.

14. M. E. Turner and A. R. Pratkanis, "Mitigating Groupthink by Stimulating Constructive Conflict," in C. DeDreu and E. Van deVliert (eds.), *Using Conflict in Organizations* (London: Sage, 1997), pp. 53–71.

15. A. Deutschman, "Inside the Mind of Jeff Bezos," *Fast Company,* August 2004, pp. 50–58.

16. See, for instance, E. J. Thomas and C. F. Fink, "Effects of Group Size," *Psychological Bulletin*, July 1963, pp. 371–384; and M. E. Shaw, *Group Dynamics: The Psychology of Small Group Behavior*, 3rd ed. (New York: McGraw-Hill, 1981).

17. A. Jassawalla, H. Sashittal, and A. Malshe, "Students' Perceptions of Social Loafing: Its Antecedents and Consequences in Undergraduate Business Classroom Teams," *Academy of Management Learning & Education,* March 2009, pp. 42–54; R. C. Liden, S. J. Wayne, R. A. Jaworski, and N. Bennett, "Social Loafing: A Field Investigation," *Journal of Management,* April 2004, pp. 285–304; and D. R. Comer, "A Model of Social Loafing in Real Work Groups," *Human Relations,* June 1995, pp. 647–667.

18. S. G. Harkins and K. Szymanski, "Social Loafing and Group Evaluation," *Journal of Personality and Social Psychology,* December 1989, pp. 934–941.

19. C. R. Evans and K. L. Dion, "Group Cohesion and Performance: A Meta-Analysis," *Small Group Research,* May 1991, pp. 175–186; B. Mullen and C. Copper, "The Relation between Group Cohesiveness and Performance: An Integration," *Psychological Bulletin*, March 1994, pp. 210–227; and P. M. Podsakoff, S. B. MacKenzie, and M. Ahearne, "Moderating Effects of Goal Acceptance on the Relationship between Group Cohesiveness and Productivity," *Journal of Applied Psychology,* December 1997, pp. 974–983.

20. See, for example, L. Berkowitz, "Group Standards, Cohesiveness, and Productivity," *Human Relations*, November 1954, pp. 509–519; and B. Mullen and C. Copper, "The Relation between Group Cohesiveness and Performance: An Integration."

21. S. E. Seashore, *Group Cohesiveness in the Industrial Work Group* (Ann Arbor: University of Michigan, Survey Research Center, 1954).

22. C. Shaffran, "Mind Your Meeting: How to Become the Catalyst for Culture Change," *Communication World,* February–March 2003, pp. 26–29.

23. I. L. Janis, *Victims of Groupthink* (Boston: Houghton Mifflin, 1972); R. J. Aldag and S. Riggs Fuller, "Beyond Fiasco: A Reappraisal of the Groupthink Phenomenon and a New Model of Group Decision Processes," *Psychological Bulletin*, May 1993, pp. 533–552; and T. Kameda and S. Sugimori, "Psychological Entrapment in Group Decision Making: An Assigned Decision

Rule and a Groupthink Phenomenon," *Journal of Personality and Social Psychology,* August 1993, pp. 282–292.

24. See, for example, L. K. Michaelson, W. E. Watson, and R. H. Black, "A Realistic Test of Individual vs. Group Consensus Decision Making," *Journal of Applied Psychology,* vol. 74, no. 5 (1989), pp. 834–839; R. A. Henry, "Group Judgment Accuracy: Reliability and Validity of Postdiscussion Confidence Judgments," *Organizational Behavior and Human Decision Processes,* October 1993, pp. 11–27; P. W. Paese, M. Bieser, and M. E. Tubbs, "Framing Effects and Choice Shifts in Group Decision Making," *Organizational Behavior and Human Decision Processes,* October 1993, pp. 149–165; N. J. Castellan Jr. (ed.), *Individual and Group Decision Making* (Hillsdale, NJ: Lawrence Erlbaum Associates, 1993); and S. G. Straus and J. E. McGrath, "Does the Medium Matter? The Interaction of Task Type and Technology on Group Performance and Member Reactions," *Journal of Applied Psychology,* February 1994, pp. 87–97.

25. E. J. Thomas and C. F. Fink, "Effects of Group Size," *Psychological Bulletin,* July 1963, pp. 371–384; F. A. Shull, A. L. Delbecq, and L.L. Cummings, *Organizational Decision Making* (New York: McGraw-Hill, 1970), p. 151; A. P. Hare, *Handbook of Small Group Research* (New York: Free Press, 1976); M. E. Shaw, *Group Dynamics: The Psychology of Small Group Behavior,* 3rd ed. (New York: McGraw-Hill, 1981); and P. Yetton and P. Bottger, "The Relationships Among Group Size, Member Ability, Social Decision Schemes, and Performance," *Organizational Behavior and Human Performance,* October 1983, pp. 145–159.

26. This section is adapted from S. P. Robbins, *Managing Organizational Conflict: A Nontraditional Approach* (Upper Saddle River, NJ: Prentice Hall, 1974), pp. 11–14. Also, see D. Wagner-Johnson, "Managing Work Team Conflict: Assessment and Preventative Strategies," Center for the Study of Work Teams, University of North Texas [www.workteams. unt.edu/reports], November 3, 2000; and M. Kennedy, "Managing Conflict in Work Teams," Center for the Study of Work Teams, University of North Texas [www.workteams. unt.edu/reports], November 3, 2000.

27. See K. J. Behfar, E. A. Mannix, R. S. Peterson, and W. M. Trochim, "Conflict in Small Groups: The Meaning and Consequences of Process Conflict," *Small Group Research,* April 2011, pp. 127–176; M. A. Korsgaard et al., "A Multilevel View of Intragroup Conflict," *Journal of Management,* December 2008, pp. 1222–1252; C. K. W. DeDreu, "The Virtue and Vice of Workplace Conflict: Food for (Pessimistic) Thought," *Journal of Organizational Behavior,* January 2008, pp. 5–18; K. A. Jehn, "A Multimethod Examination of the Benefits and Detriments of Intragroup Conflict," *Administrative Science Quarterly,* June 1995, pp. 256–282; K. A. Jehn, "A Qualitative Analysis of Conflict Type and Dimensions in Organizational Groups," *Administrative Science Quarterly,* September 1997, pp. 530–557; K. A. Jehn, "Affective and Cognitive Conflict in Work Groups: Increasing Performance Through Value-Based Intragroup Conflict," in C. DeDreu and E. Van deVliert (eds.), *Using Conflict in Organizations* (London: Sage Publications, 1997), pp. 87–100; K. A. Jehn and E. A. Mannix, "The Dynamic Nature of Conflict: A Longitudinal Study of Intragroup Conflict and Group Performance," *Academy of Management Journal,* April 2001, pp. 238–251; C. K. W. DeDreu and A. E. M. Van Vianen, "Managing Relationship Conflict and the Effectiveness of Organizational Teams," *Journal of Organizational Behavior,* May 2001, pp. 309–328; and J. Weiss and J. Hughes, "Want

Collaboration? Accept—and Actively Manage—Conflict," *Harvard Business Review,* March 2005, pp. 92–101.

28. C. K. W. DeDreu, "When Too Little or Too Much Hurts: Evidence for a Curvilinear Relationship Between Task Conflict and Innovation in Teams," *Journal of Management,* February 2006, pp. 83–107.

29. A. Somech, H. S. Desivilya, and H. Lidogoster, "Team Conflict Management and Team Effectiveness: The Effects of Task Interdependence and Team Identification," *Journal of Organizational Behavior,* April 2009, pp. 359–378; K. W. Thomas, "Conflict and Negotiation Processes in Organizations," in M. D. Dunnette and L. M. Hough (eds.), *Handbook of Industrial and Organizational Psychology,* 2 ed., vol. 3 (Palo Alto, CA: Consulting Psychologists Press, 1992), pp. 651–717.

30. A. Li and R. Cropanzano, "Fairness at the Group Level: Justice Climate and Intraunit Justice Climate," *Journal of Management,* June 2009, pp. 564–599.

31. K. E. Culp, "Improv Teaches Work Team Building," *Springfield, Missouri News-Leader,* December 9, 2005, p. 5B; T. J. Mullaney and A. Weintraub, "The Tech Guru: Dr. Gerard Burns," *BusinessWeek,* March 28, 2005, p. 84; and J. S. McClenahen, "Lean and Teams: More Than Blips," *Industry Week,* October 2003, p. 63.

32. See, for example, J. R. Hackman and C. G. Morris, "Group Tasks, Group Interaction Process, and Group Performance Effectiveness: A Review and Proposed Integration," in L. Berkowitz (ed.), *Advances in Experimental Social Psychology* (New York: Academic Press, 1975), pp. 45–99; R. Saavedra, P. C. Earley, and L. Van Dyne, "Complex Interdependence in Task-Performing Groups," *Journal of Applied Psychology,* February 1993, pp. 61–72; M. J. Waller, "Multiple-Task Performance in Groups," *Academy of Management Proceedings on Disk,* 1996; and K. A. Jehn, G. B. Northcraft, and M. A. Neale, "Why Differences Make A Difference: A Field Study of Diversity, Conflict, and Performance in Workgroups," *Administrative Science Quarterly,* December 1999, pp. 741–763.

33. B. J. West, J. L. Patera, and M. K. Carsten, "Team Level Positivity: Investigating Positive Psychological Capacities and Team Level Outcomes," *Journal of Organizational Behavior,* February 2009, pp. 249–267; T. Purdum, "Teaming, Take 2," *Industry Week,* May 2005, p. 43; and C. Joinson, "Teams at Work," *HRMagazine,* May 1999, p. 30.

34. See, for example, S. A. Mohrman, S. G. Cohen, and A. M. Mohrman, Jr., *Designing Team-Based Organizations* (San Francisco: Jossey-Bass, 1995); P. MacMillan, *The Performance Factor: Unlocking the Secrets of Teamwork* (Nashville, TN: Broadman & Holman, 2001); and E. Salas, C. A. Bowers, and E. Eden (eds.), *Improving Teamwork in Organizations: Applications of Resource Management Training* (Mahwah, NJ: Lawrence Erlbaum, 2002).

35. P. Alpern, "Spreading the Light," *Industry Week,* January 2010, p. 35.

36. See, for instance, J. R. Hollenbeck, B. Beersma, and M. E. Schouten, "Beyond Team Types and Taxonomies: A Dimensional Scaling Conceptualization for Team Description," *Academy of Management Review,* January 2012, p. 85; and E. Sundstrom, K. P. DeMeuse, and D. Futrell, "Work Teams: Applications and Effectiveness," *American Psychologist,* February 1990, pp. 120–133.

37. M. Fitzgerald, "Shine a Light," *Fast Company,* April 2009, pp. 46–48; J. S. McClenahen, "Bearing Necessities," *Industry Week,* October 2004, pp. 63–65; P. J. Kiger, "Acxiom Rebuilds

from Scratch," *Workforce,* December 2002, pp. 52–55; and T. Boles, "Viewpoint—Leadership Lessons from NASCAR," *Industry Week* [www.industryweek.com], May 21, 2002.

38. M. Cianni and D. Wanuck, "Individual Growth and Team Enhancement: Moving Toward a New Model of Career Development," *Academy of Management Executive,* February 1997, pp. 105–115.

39. "Teams," *Training,* October 1996, p. 69; and C. Joinson, "Teams at Work," p. 30.

40. G. M. Spreitzer, S. G. Cohen, and G. E. Ledford, Jr., "Developing Effective Self-Managing Work Teams in Service Organizations," *Group & Organization Management,* September 1999, pp. 340–366.

41. "Meet the New Steel," *Fortune,* October 1, 2007, pp. 68–71.

42. J. Appleby and R. Davis, "Teamwork Used to Save Money; Now It Saves Lives," *USA Today* [www.usatoday.com], March 1, 2001.

43. A. Malhotra, A. Majchrzak, R. Carman, and V. Lott, "Radical Innovation without Collocation: A Case Study at Boeing-Rocketdyne," *MIS Quarterly,* June 2001, pp. 229–249.

44. A. Stuart, "Virtual Agreement," *CFO,* November 2007, p. 24.

45. F. Siebdrat, M. Hoegl, and H. Ernst, "How to Manage a Virtual Team," *MIT Sloan Management Review,* Summer 2009, pp. 63–68; A. Malhotra, A. Majchrzak, and B. Rosen, "Leading Virtual Teams," *Academy of Management Perspectives,* February 2007, pp. 60–70; B. L. Kirkman and J. E. Mathieu, "The Dimensions and Antecedents of Team Virtuality," *Journal of Management,* October 2005, pp. 700–718; J. Gordon, "Do Your Virtual Teams Deliver Only Virtual Performance?" *Training,* June 2005, pp. 20–25; L. L. Martins, L. L. Gilson, and M. T. Maynard, "Virtual Teams: What Do We Know and Where Do We Go From Here?" *Journal of Management,* December 2004, pp. 805–835; S. A. Furst, M. Reeves, B. Rosen, and R. S. Blackburn, "Managing the Life Cycle of Virtual Teams," *Academy of Management Executive,* May 2004, pp. 6–20; B. L. Kirkman, B. Rosen, P. E. Tesluk, and C. B. Gibson, "The Impact of Team Empowerment on Virtual Team Performance: The Moderating Role of Face-to-Face Interaction," *Academy of Management Journal,* April 2004, pp. 175–192; F. Keenan and S. E. Ante, "The New Teamwork," *Business Week e.biz,* February 18, 2002, pp. EB12–EB16; and G. Imperato, "Real Tools for Virtual Teams?" *Fast Company,* July 2000, pp. 378–387.

46. B. L. Kirkman, C. B. Gibson, and D. L. Shapiro, "Exporting Teams: Enhancing the Implementation and Effectiveness of Work Teams in Global Affiliates," *Organizational Dynamics,* Summer 2001, pp. 12–29; J. W. Bing and C. M. Bing, "Helping Global Teams Compete," *Training & Development,* March 2001, pp. 70–71; C. G. Andrews, "Factors That Impact Multi-Cultural Team Performance," Center for the Study of Work Teams, University of North Texas [www.workteams.unt.edu/reports/], November 3, 2000; P. Christopher Earley and E. Mosakowski, "Creating Hybrid Team Cultures: An Empirical Test of Transnational Team Functioning," *Academy of Management Journal,* February 2000, pp. 26–49; J. Tata, "The Cultural Context of Teams: An Integrative Model of National Culture, Work Team Characteristics, and Team Effectiveness," *Academy of Management Proceedings,* 1999; D. I. Jung, K. B. Baik, and J. J. Sosik, "A Longitudinal Investigation of Group Characteristics and Work Group Performance: A Cross-Cultural Comparison," *Academy of Management Proceedings,* 1999; and C. B. Gibson, "They Do What They Believe They Can? Group-Efficacy Beliefs and Group Performance across Tasks and Cultures," *Academy of Management Proceedings,* 1996.

47. D. Coutou, interview with J. R. Hackman, "Why Teams Don't Work."

48. A. C. Costa and N. Anderson, "Measuring Trust in Teams: Development and Validation of a Multifaceted Measure of Formative and Reflective Indicators of Team Trust," *European Journal of Work and Organizational Psychology,* vol. 20, no. 1 (2011), pp. 119–154.

49. A. Pentland, "The New Science of Building Great Teams," *Harvard Business Review,* April 2012, pp. 60–70.

50. J. C. Santora and M. Esposito, "Do Happy Leaders Make for Better Team Performance," *Academy of Management Perspective,* November 2011, pp. 88–90; G. A. Van Kleef et al., "Searing Sentiment or Cold Calculation? The Effects of Leader Emotional Displays on Team Performance Depend on Followers Epistemic Motivation," *Academy of Management Journal,* June 2009, pp. 562–580.

51. R. Bond and P. B. Smith, "Culture and Conformity: A Meta-Analysis of Studies Using Asch's [1952, 1956] Line Judgment Task," *Psychological Bulletin,* January 1996, pp. 111–137.

52. I. L. Janis, *Groupthink,* 2nd ed. (New York: Houghton Mifflin Company, 1982), p. 175.

53. See P. C. Earley, "Social Loafing and Collectivism: A Comparison of the United States and the People's Republic of China," *Administrative Science Quarterly,* December 1989, pp. 565–581; and P. C. Earley, "East Meets West Meets Mideast: Further Explorations of Collectivistic and Individualistic Work Groups," *Academy of Management Journal,* April 1993, pp. 319–348.

54. Siemens Web site, www.siemens.com/jobs, July 25, 2012; G. Barlett, "Customer Centricity: Siemens' Cultural Centerpiece," *Velocity,* vol. 13, Issue 3, 2011, pp. 17–18; A. Bryant, "The Trust That Makes a Team Click," *New York Times Online,* July 30, 2011; H. Struck, D. Fisher, N. Karmali, and G. Epstein, "Urban Outfitter," *Forbes,* May 9, 2011, pp. 80–98; "Siemens Hunts for New Hires As Nation Watches Unemployment Rate," *Forbes. com,* May 5, 2011, p. 62; R. Weiss and B. Kammel, " How Seimens Got Its Geist Back," *Bloomberg BusinessWeek,* January 31, 2011, pp. 18–209; and D. Roberts, "Never Miss A Good Crisis," *Bloomberg BusinessWeek,* October 4, 2010, pp. 79–80.

55. N. J. Adler, *International Dimensions of Organizational Behavior,* 4th ed. (Cincinnati, OH: Southwestern, 2002), p. 142.

56. Ibid., p. 144.

57. K. B. Dahlin, L. R. Weingart, and P. J. Hinds, "Team Diversity and Information Use," *Academy of Management Journal,* December 2005, pp. 1107–1123.

58. Adler, *International Dimensions of Organizational Behavior,* p. 142.

59. P. S. Hempel, Z-X. Zhang, and D. Tjosvold, "Conflict Management Between and Within Teams for Trusting Relationships and Performance in China," *Journal of Organizational Behavior,* January 2009, pp. 41–65; and S. Paul, I. M. Samarah, P. Seetharaman, and P. P. Mykytyn, "An Empirical Investigation of Collaborative Conflict Management Style in Group Support System-Based Global Virtual Teams," *Journal of Management Information Systems,* Winter 2005, pp. 185–222.

60. S. Chang and P. Tharenou, "Competencies Needed for Managing a Multicultural Workgroup," *Asia Pacific Journal of Human Resources* vol. 42, no. 1 (2004), pp. 57–74; and Adler, *International Dimensions of Organizational Behavior,* p. 153.

61. C. E. Nicholls, H. W. Lane, and M. Brehm Brechu, "Taking Self-Managed Teams to Mexico," *Academy of Management Executive,* August 1999, pp. 15–27.

62. M. O'Neil, "Leading the Team," *Supervision,* April 2011, pp. 8-10; and A. Gilley, J. W. Gilley, C. W. McConnell, and A. Veliquette, "The Competencies Used by Effective Managers to Build Teams: An Empirical Study," *Advances in Developing Human Resources,* February 2010, pp. 29–45.

63. B. V. Krishnamurthy, "Use Downtime to Enhance Skills," *Harvard Business Review,* December 2008, pp. 29–30.

64. "Women Leaders: The Hard Truth About Soft Skills," *BusinessWeek Online,* February 17, 2010, p. 8.

65. J. Reingold and J. L. Yang, "The Hidden Workplace: What's Your OQ?" *Fortune,* July 23, 2007, pp. 98–106; and P. Balkundi and D. A. Harrison, "Ties, Leaders, and Time in Teams: Strong Inference About Network Structures' Effects on Team Viability and Performance," *Academy of Management Journal,* February 2006, pp. 49–68.

66. T. Casciaro and M. S. Lobo, "Competent Jerks, Lovable Fools, and the Formation of Social Networks," *Harvard Business Review,* June 2005, pp. 92–99.

67. Balkundi and Harrison, "Ties, Leaders, and Time in Teams: Strong Inference About Network Structures' Effects on Team Viability and Performance."

68. P. Dvorak, "Engineering Firm Charts Ties," *Wall Street Journal,* January 26, 2009, p. B7; and J. McGregor, "The Office Chart That Really Counts," *Business Week,* February 27, 2006, pp. 48–49.

69. P. Klaus, "Thank You for Sharing. But Why at the Office? *New York Times Online,* August 18, 2012; and E. Bernstein, "You Did *What?* Spare the Office the Details," *Wall Street Journal,* April 6, 2010, pp. D1+.

70. N. Byrnes, "Pepsi Brings in the Health Police," *Bloomberg BusinessWeek,* January 25, 2010, pp. 50–51.

71. A. Schein, "Lonely Planet Publications," *Hoovers.com,* July 25, 2012; J. Koppisch, "2012 Australian Philanthropists," *Forbes.com,* June 20, 2012, p. 1; N. Denny, "Digital and the Bookshop," *Bookseller,* June 8, 2012, p. 3; M. Costa, "Travel Guru Explores New Routes," *Marketing Week,* April 12, 2012, p. 20; and K. Cuthbertson and R. Haynes, "Duo Came With 27 cents and left with $100 million," *The Herald Sun,* October 2, 2007, p. 11.

72. D. Michaels and J. Ostrower, "Airbus, Boeing Walk a Fine Line on Jetliner Production," *Wall Street Journal,* July 16, 2012, p. B3; D. Kesmodel, "Boeing Teams Speed Up 737 Output," *Wall Street Journal,* February 7, 2012, p. B10; and A. Cohen, "Boeing Sees Demand for Existing, Re-engined 737s," blog on *Seattle Post-Intelligencer Online,* October 26, 2011.

CHAPTER 15

1. R. E. Silverman, "My Colleague, My Paymaster," *Wall Street Journal,* April 4, 2012, pp. B1+; "Indian IT Firm Says It Will Create 10,000 Jobs in West," *Mechanical Engineering,* March 2012, p. 14; A. Bhattacharya and J. Anand, "Business Buddhas, " *Business Today,* January 22, 2012, pp. 2–5; D. Woodward, "Long and Winding Road," *Director.co.uk,* March 2011, pp. 5053; V. Nayar, "A Maverick CEO Explains How He Persuaded His Team to Leap into the Future," *Harvard Business Review,* June 2010, pp. 110–113; B. Einhorn and K. Gokhale, "Bangalore's Paying Again to Keep the Talent," *Bloomberg BusinessWeek,* May 24, 2010, pp. 14–16; M. Srivastava and S. Hamm, "Using the Slump to Get Bigger in Bangalore," *BusinessWeek,* September 3, 2009, pp. 50–51; and S. Lauchlan, "HCL Embraces *Slumdog* Effect," *Computer Weekly,* June 23, 2009, p. 8.

2. K. O'Toole, "Cold-Calling Van Horne," *Stanford Business Magazine* [www.gsb.stanford.edu], May 2005; and S. Orenstein, "Feeling Your Way to the Top," *Business 2.0,* June 2004, p. 146.

3. "Unplanned Absence Costs Organizations 8.7 Percent of Payroll, Mercer/Kronos Study" [www.mercer.com], June 28, 2010; and K. M. Kroll, "Absence-Minded," *CFO Human Capital,* 2006, pp. 12–14.

4. D. W. Organ, *Organizational Citizenship Behavior: The Good Soldier Syndrome* (Lexington, MA: Lexington Books, 1988), p. 4. See also J. L. Lavell, D. E. Rupp, and J. Brockner, "Taking a Multifoci Approach to the Study of Justice, Social Exchange, and Citizenship Behavior: The Target Similarity Model," *Journal of Management,* December 2007, pp. 841–866; and J. A. LePine, A. Erez, and D. E. Johnson, "The Nature and Dimensionality of Organizational Citizenship Behavior: A Critical Review and Meta-Analysis," *Journal of Applied Psychology,* February 2002, pp. 52–65.

5. R. Ilies, B. A. Scott, and T. A. Judge, "The Interactive Effects of Personal Traits and Experienced States on Intraindividual Patterns of Citizenship Behavior," *Academy of Management Journal,* June 2006, pp. 561–575; P. Cardona, B. S. Lawrence, and P. M. Bentler, "The Influence of Social and Work Exchange Relationships on Organizational Citizenship Behavior," *Group & Organization Management,* April 2004, pp. 219–247; M. C. Bolino and W. H. Turnley, "Going the Extra Mile: Cultivating and Managing Employee Citizenship Behavior," *Academy of Management Executive,* August 2003, pp. 60–73; M. C. Bolino, W. H. Turnley, and J. J. Bloodgood, "Citizenship Behavior and the Creation of Social Capital in Organizations," *Academy of Management Review,* October 2002, pp. 505–522; and P. M. Podsakoff, S. B. MacKenzie, J. B. Paine, and D. G. Bachrach, "Organizational Citizenship Behaviors: A Critical Review of the Theoretical and Empirical Literature and Suggestions for Future Research," *Journal of Management,* vol. 26, no. 3, 2000, pp. 543–548.

6. M. C. Bolino and W. H. Turnley, "The Personal Costs of Citizenship Behavior: The Relationship Between Individual Initiative and Role Overload, Job Stress, and Work-Family Conflict," *Journal of Applied Psychology,* July 2005, pp. 740–748.

7. This definition adapted from R. W. Griffin and Y. P. Lopez, "Bad Behavior in Organizations: A Review and Typology for Future Research," *Journal of Management,* December 2005, pp. 988–1005.

8. S. J. Breckler, "Empirical Validation of Affect, Behavior, and Cognition as Distinct Components of Attitude," *Journal of Personality and Social Psychology,* May 1984, pp. 1191–1205; and S. L. Crites, Jr., L. R. Fabrigar, and R. E. Petty, "Measuring the Affective and Cognitive Properties of Attitudes: Conceptual and Methodological Issues," *Personality and Social Psychology Bulletin,* December 1994, pp. 619–634.

9. D. R. May, R. L. Gilson, and L. M. Harter, "The Psychological Conditions of Meaningfulness, Safety and Availability and the Engagement of the Human Spirit at Work," *Journal of Occupational and Organizational Psychology,* March 2004, pp. 11–37; R. T. Keller, "Job Involvement and Organizational Commitment as Longitudinal Predictors of Job Performance: A Study of Scientists and Engineers," *Journal of Applied Psychology,* August 1997, pp. 539–545; W. Kahn, "Psychological Conditions of Personal Engagement and Disengagement at Work," *Academy of Management Journal,* December 1990, pp. 692–794; and P. P. Brooke, Jr., D. W. Russell, and J. L. Price,

"Discriminant Validation of Measures of Job Satisfaction, Job Involvement, and Organizational Commitment," *Journal of Applied Psychology,* May 1988, pp. 139–145.

10. P. Korkki, "With Jobs Few, Most Workers Aren't Satisfied," *New York Times Online,* January 10, 2010.

11. The Conference Board, "Workers Less Miserable, But Hardly Happy," [www.conference-board.org], June 27, 2012.

12. Ibid.

13. "Six Nation Survey Finds Satisfaction with Current Job," *Harris Interactive* [www.harrisinteractive.com], October 9, 2007; and SwissInfo, "Swiss Like Work, But Not Their Salaries" [www.swissinfo.org], June 7, 2005.

14. Watson Wyatt Worldwide, "A Comparison of Attitudes Around the Globe" [www.watsonwyatt.com/research], 2006.

15. "Overstretched," *The Economist* [www.economist.com], May 20, 2010.

16. T. A. Judge, C. J. Thoresen, J. E. Bono, and G. K. Patton, "The Job Satisfaction-Job Performance Relationship: A Qualitative and Quantitative Review," *Psychological Bulletin,* May 2001, pp. 376–407.

17. J. K. Harter, F. L. Schmidt, and T. L. Hayes, "Business-Unit Level Relationship Between Employee Satisfaction, Employee Engagement, and Business Outcomes: A Meta-Analysis," *Journal of Applied Psychology,* April 2002, pp. 268–279; A. M. Ryan, M. J. Schmit, and R. Johnson, "Attitudes and Effectiveness: Examining Relations at an Organizational Level," *Personnel Psychology,* Winter 1996, pp. 853–882; and C. Ostroff, "The Relationship Between Satisfaction, Attitudes, and Performance: An Organizational Level Analysis," *Journal of Applied Psychology,* December 1992, pp. 963–974.

18. E. A. Locke, "The Nature and Causes of Job Satisfaction," in M. D. Dunnette (ed.), *Handbook of Industrial and Organizational Psychology* (Chicago: Rand McNally, 1976), p. 1331; S. L. McShane, "Job Satisfaction and Absenteeism: A Meta-Analytic Re-Examination," *Canadian Journal of Administrative Science,* June 1984, pp. 61–77; R. D. Hackett and R. M. Guion, "A Reevaluation of the Absenteeism-Job Satisfaction Relationship," *Organizational Behavior and Human Decision Processes,* June 1985, pp. 340–381; K. D. Scott and G. S. Taylor, "An Examination of Conflicting Findings on the Relationship Between Job Satisfaction and Absenteeism: A Meta-Analysis," *Academy of Management Journal,* September 1985, pp. 599–612; R. D. Hackett, "Work Attitudes and Employee Absenteeism: A Synthesis of the Literature," paper presented at the 1988 National Academy of Management Meeting, Anaheim, CA, August 1988; and R. Steel and J. R. Rentsch, "Influence of Cumulation Strategies on the Long-Range Prediction of Absenteeism," *Academy of Management Journal,* December 1995, pp. 1616–1634.

19. P. W. Hom and R. W. Griffeth, *Employee Turnover* (Cincinnati, OH: Southwestern, 1995); R. W. Griffith, P. W. Hom, and S. Gaertner, "A Meta-Analysis of Antecedents and Correlates of Employee Turnover: Update, Moderator Tests, and Research Implications for the Next Millennium," *Journal of Management,* vol. 26, no. 3, 2000, p. 479; and P. W. Hom and A. J. Kinicki, "Toward a Greater Understanding of How Dissatisfaction Drives Employee Turnover," *Academy of Management Journal,* October 2001, pp. 975–987.

20. See, for example, J. M. Carsten and P. E. Spector, "Unemployment, Job Satisfaction, and Employee Turnover: A Meta-Analytic Test of the Muchinsky Model," *Journal*

of Applied Psychology, August 1987, pp. 374–381; and C. L. Hulin, M. Roznowski, and D. Hachiya, "Alternative Opportunities and Withdrawal Decisions: Empirical and Theoretical Discrepancies and an Integration," *Psychological Bulletin,* July 1985, pp. 233–250.

21. T. A. Wright and D. G. Bonett, "Job Satisfaction and Psychological Well-Being as Nonadditive Predictors of Workplace Turnover," *Journal of Management,* April 2007, pp. 141–160; and D. G. Spencer and R. M. Steers, "Performance as a Moderator of the Job Satisfaction-Turnover Relationship," *Journal of Applied Psychology,* August 1981, pp. 511–514.

22. See, for instance, M. Schulte, C. Ostroff, S. Shmulyian, and A. Kinicki, "Organizational Climate Configurations: Relationships to Collective Attitudes, Customer Satisfaction, and Financial Performance," *Journal of Applied Psychology,* May 2009, pp. 618–634; S. P. Brown and S. K. Lam, "A Meta-analysis of Relationships Linking Employee Satisfaction to Customer Responses," *Journal of Retailing,* vol. 84, 2008, pp. 243–255; X. Luo and C. Homburg, "Neglected Outcomes of Customer Satisfaction," *Journal of Marketing,* April 2007, pp. 133–149; P. B. Barger and A. A. Grandey, "Service With a Smile and Encounter Satisfaction: Emotional Contagion and Appraisal Mechanisms," *Academy of Management Journal,* December 2006, pp. 1229–1238; C. Homburg and R. M. Stock, "The Link Between Salespeople's Job Satisfaction and Customer Satisfaction in a Business-to-Business Context: A Dyadic Analysis," *Journal of the Academy of Marketing Science,* Spring 2004, pp. 144–158; J. K. Harter, F. L. Schmidt, and T. L. Hayes, "Business-Unit-Level Relationship Between Employee Satisfaction, Employee Engagement, and Business Outcomes: A Meta-Analysis," *Journal of Applied Psychology,* April 2002, pp. 268–279; J. Griffith, "Do Satisfied Employees Satisfy Customers? Support-Services Staff Morale and Satisfaction Among Public School Administrators, Students, and Parents," *Journal of Applied Social Psychology,* August 2001, pp. 1627–1658; D. J. Koys, "The Effects of Employee Satisfaction, Organizational Citizenship Behavior, and Turnover on Organizational Effectiveness: A Unit-Level, Longitudinal Study," *Personnel Psychology,* Spring 2001, pp. 101–114; E. Naumann and D. W. Jackson, Jr., "One More Time: How Do You Satisfy Customers?" *Business Horizons,* May–June 1999, pp. 71–76; W. W. Tornow and J. W. Wiley, "Service Quality and Management Practices: A Look at Employee Attitudes, Customer Satisfaction, and Bottom-Line Consequences," *Human Resource Planning,* vol. 4, no. 2, 1991, pp. 105–116; and B. Schneider and D. E. Bowen, "Employee and Customer Perceptions of Service in Banks: Replication and Extension," *Journal of Applied Psychology,* August 1985, pp. 423–433.

23. M. J. Bitner, B. H. Blooms, and L. A. Mohr, "Critical Service Encounters: The Employees' Viewpoint," *Journal of Marketing,* October 1994, pp. 95–106.

24. J. M. O'Brien, "Zappos Knows How to Kick It," *Fortune,* February 2, 2009, pp. 55–60.

25. See T. M. Glomb, D. P. Bhave, A. G. Miner, and M. Wall, "Doing Good, Feeling Good: Examining the Role of Organizational Citizenship Behaviors in Changing Mood," *Personnel Psychology,* Spring 2011, pp. 191-223; L. M. Little, D. L. Nelson, J. C. Wallace, and P. D. Johnson, "Integrating Attachment Style, Vigor at Work, and Extra-Role Performance," *Journal of Organizational Behavior,* April 2011, pp. 464–484; N. P. Podsakoff, P. J. Podsakoff, S. W. Whiting, and P. Hisra,

"Effects of Organizational Citizenship Behavior on Selection Decisions in Employment Interviews," *Journal of Applied Psychology,* March 2011, pp. 310–326; J. A. LePine, A. Erez, and D. E. Johnson, "The Nature and Dimensionality of Organizational Citizenship Behavior: A Critical Review and Meta-Analysis," 2002; P. Podsakoff, S. B. Mackenzie, J. B. Paine, and D. G. Bachrach, "Organizational Citizenship Behaviors: A Critical Review of the Theoretical and Empirical Literature and Suggestions for Future Research," *Journal of Management,* May 2000, pp. 513–563; T. S. Bateman and D. W. Organ, "Job Satisfaction and the Good Soldier: The Relationship between Affect and Employee 'Citizenship,'" *Academy of Management Journal,* December 1983, pp. 587–595.

26. B. J. Hoffman, C. A. Blair, J. P. Maeriac, and D. J. Woehr, "Expanding the Criterion Domain? A Quantitative Review of the OCB Literature," *Journal of Applied Psychology,* vol. 92, no. 2, 2007, pp. 555–566; J. A. LePine, A. Erez, and D. E. Johnson, "The Nature and Dimensionality of Organizational Citizenship Behavior: A Critical Review and Meta-Analysis," 2002; and D. W. Organ and K. Ryan, "A Meta-Analytic Review of Attitudinal and Dispositional Predictors of Organizational Citizenship Behavior," *Personnel Psychology,* Winter 1995, pp. 775–802.

27. N. A. Fassina, D. A. Jones, and K. L. Uggerslev, "Relationship Clean-Up Time: Using Meta-Analysis and Path Analysis to Clarify Relationships Among Job Satisfaction, Perceived Fairness, and Citizenship Behaviors," *Journal of Management,* April 2008, pp. 161–188; M. A. Konovsky and D. W. Organ, "Dispositional and Contextual Determinants of Organizational Citizenship Behavior," *Journal of Organizational Behavior,* May 1996, pp. 253–266; R. H. Moorman, "Relationship Between Organization Justice and Organizational Citizenship Behaviors: Do Fairness Perceptions Influence Employee Citizenship?" *Journal of Applied Psychology,* December 1991, pp. 845–855; and J. Fahr, P. M. Podsakoff, and D. W. Organ, "Accounting for Organizational Citizenship Behavior: Leader Fairness and Task Scope versus Satisfaction," *Journal of Management,* December 1990, pp. 705–722.

28. W. H. Bommer, E. C. Dierdorff, and R. S. Rubin, "Does Prevalence Mitigate Relevance? The Moderating Effect of Group-Level OCB on Employee Performance," *Academy of Management Journal,* December 2007, pp. 1481–1494.

29. See, for example, S. Rabinowitz and D. T. Hall, "Organizational Research in Job Involvement," *Psychological Bulletin,* March 1977, pp. 265–288; G. J. Blau, "A Multiple Study Investigation of the Dimensionality of Job Involvement," *Journal of Vocational Behavior,* August 1985, pp. 19–36; and N. A. Jans, "Organizational Factors and Work Involvement," *Organizational Behavior and Human Decision Processes,* June 1985, pp. 382–396.

30. D. A. Harrison, D. A. Newman, and P. L. Roth, "How Important Are Job Attitudes?: Meta-Analytic Comparisons of Integrative Behavioral Outcomes and Time Sequences," *Academy of Management Journal,* April 2006, pp. 305–325; G. J. Blau, "Job Involvement and Organizational Commitment as Interactive Predictors of Tardiness and Absenteeism," *Journal of Management,* Winter 1986, pp. 577–584; and K. Boal and R. Cidambi, "Attitudinal Correlates of Turnover and Absenteeism: A Meta-Analysis," paper presented at the meeting of the American Psychological Association, Toronto, Canada, 1984.

31. G. J. Blau and K. Boal, "Conceptualizing How Job Involvement and Organizational Commitment Affect Turnover and Absenteeism," *Academy of Management Review,* April 1987, p. 290.

32. See, for instance, P. W. Hom, R. Katerberg, and C. L. Hulin, "Comparative Examination of Three Approaches to the Prediction of Turnover," *Journal of Applied Psychology,* June 1979, pp. 280–290; R. T. Mowday, L. W. Porter, and R. M. Steers, *Employee Organization Linkages: The Psychology of Commitment, Absenteeism, and Turnover* (New York: Academic Press, 1982); H. Angle and J. Perry, "Organizational Commitment: Individual and Organizational Influence," *Work and Occupations,* May 1983, pp. 123–145; and J. L. Pierce and R. B. Dunham, "Organizational Commitment: Pre-Employment Propensity and Initial Work Experiences," *Journal of Management,* Spring 1987, pp. 163–178.

33. L. W. Porter, R. M. Steers, R. T. Mowday, and V. Boulian, "Organizational Commitment, Job Satisfaction, and Turnover among Psychiatric Technicians," *Journal of Applied Psychology,* October 1974, pp. 603–609.

34. D. M. Rousseau, "Organizational Behavior in the New Organizational Era," in J. T. Spence, J. M. Darley, and D. J. Foss (eds.), *Annual Review of Psychology,* vol. 48 (Palo Alto, CA: Annual Reviews, 1997), p. 523.

35. P. Eder and R. Eisenberger, "Perceived Organizational Support: Reducing the Negative Influence of Coworker Withdrawal Behavior," *Journal of Management,* February 2008, pp. 55–68; R. Eisenberger, F. Stinglhamber, C. Vandenberghe, I. L. Sucharski, and L. Rhoades, "Perceived Supervisor Support: Contributions to Perceived Organizational Support and Employee Retention," *Journal of Applied Psychology,* June 2002, pp. 565–573; L. Rhoades and R. Eisenberger, "Perceived Organizational Support: A Review of the Literature," *Journal of Applied Psychology,* August 2002, pp. 698–714; J. L. Kraimer and S. J. Wayne, "An Examination of Perceived Organizational Support as a Multidimensional Construct in the Context of an Expatriate Assignment," *Journal of Management,* vol. 30, no. 2, 2004, pp. 209–237; J. W. Bishop, K. D. Scott, J. G. Goldsby, and R. Cropanzano, "A Construct Validity Study of Commitment and Perceived Support Variables," *Group & Organization Management,* April 2005, pp. 153–180; and J. A-M. Coyle-Shapiro and N. Conway, "Exchange Relationships: Examining Psychological Contracts and Perceived Organizational Support," *Journal of Applied Psychology,* July 2005, pp. 774–781.

36. J. Marquez, "Disengaged Employees Can Spell Trouble at Any company," *Workforce Management* [www.workforce.com], May 13, 2008.

37. J. Smythe, "Engaging Employees to Drive Performance," *Communication World,* May–June 2008, pp. 20–22; A. B. Bakker and W. B. Schaufeli, "Positive Organizational Behavior: Engaged Employees in Flourishing Organizations," *Journal of Organizational Behavior,* February 2008, pp. 147–154; U. Aggarwal, S. Datta, and S. Bhargava, "The Relationship between Human Resource Practices, Psychological Contract, and Employee Engagement—Implications for Managing Talent," *IIMB Management Review,* September 2007, pp. 313–325; M. C. Christian and J. E. Slaughter, "Work Engagement: A Meta-Analytic Review and Directions for Research in an Emerging Area," *AOM Proceedings,* August 2007, pp. 1–6; C. H. Thomas, "A New Measurement Scale for Employee Engagement: Scale Development, Pilot Test, and Replication," *AOM Proceedings,* August 2007, pp. 1–6; A. M. Saks,

"Antecedents and Consequences of Employee Engagement," *Journal of Managerial Psychology,* vol. 21, no. 7, 2006, pp. 600–619; and A. Parsley, "Road Map for Employee Engagement," *Management Services,* Spring 2006, pp. 10–11.

38. J. Katz, "The Engagement Dance," *Industry Week,* April 2008, p. 24.

39. "Driving Employee Engagement in a Global Workforce," *Watson Wyatt Worldwide,* 2007–2008, p. 2.

40. A. J. Elliott and P. G. Devine, "On the Motivational Nature of Cognitive Dissonance: Dissonance as Psychological Discomfort," *Journal of Personality and Social Psychology,* September 1994, pp. 382–394.

41. L. Festinger, *A Theory of Cognitive Dissonance* (Stanford, CA: Stanford University Press, 1957; and C. Crossen, "Cognitive Dissonance Became a Milestone in 1950s Psychology," *Wall Street Journal,* December 4, 2006, p. B1.

42. See, for example, S. V. Falletta, "Organizational Intelligence Surveys," *T&D,* June 2008, pp. 52–58; R. Fralicx, P. Foley, H. Friedman, P. Gilberg, D. P. McCauley, and L. F. Parra, "Point of View: Using Employee Surveys to Drive Business Decisions," Mercer Human Resource Consulting, July 1, 2004; L. Simpson, "What's Going on in Your Company? If You Don't Ask, You'll Never Know," *Training,* June 2002, pp. 30–34; and B. Fishel, "A New Perspective: How to Get the Real Story from Attitude Surveys," *Training,* February 1998, pp. 91–94.

43. A. Kover, "And the Survey Says…," *Industry Week,* September 2005, pp. 49–52.

44. See J. Welch and S. Welch, "Employee Polls: A Vote in Favor," *BusinessWeek,* January 28, 2008, p. 90; E. White, "How Surveying Workers Can Pay Off," *Wall Street Journal,* June 18, 2007, p. B3; A. Kover, "And the Survey Says…," R. Fralicx, P. Foley, H. Friedman, P. Gilberg, D. P. McCauley, and L. F. Parra, "Point of View: Using Employee Surveys to Drive Business Decisions"; and S. Shellenbarger, "Companies Are Finding It Really Pays to be Nice to Employees," *Wall Street Journal,* July 22, 1998, p. B1.

45. Leader Who Made a Difference Box based on "The World's Most Admired Companies," *Fortune,* March 19, 2012, pp. 139+; "Goh Choon Phong Is Next SIA CEO," [www.asiaone.com.sg], September 3, 2010; L. Heracleous and J. Wirtz, "Singapore Airlines' Balancing Act," *Harvard Business Review,* July–August 2010, pp. 145–149; S. Cendrowski, "Singapore Airlines," *Fortune,* June 14, 2010, p. 22; and S. Govindasamy, "A State of Mind," *Airline Business,* February 2010, pp. 18–21.

46. L. Saari and T. A. Judge, "Employee Attitudes and Job Satisfaction," *Human Resource Management,* Winter 2004, pp. 395–407; and T. A. Judge and A. H. Church, "Job Satisfaction: Research and Practice," in C. L. Cooper and E. A. Locke (eds.), *Industrial and Organizational Psychology: Linking Theory with Practice* (Oxford, UK: Blackwell, 2000).

47. Harrison, Newman, and Roth, "How Important Are Job Attitudes?" pp. 320–321.

48. A. Tugend, "Blinded by Science in the Online Dating Game," *New York Times Online,* July 18, 2009; and "Better Loving Through Chemistry?" by Catherine Arnst, from *Bloomberg Business Week,* October 23, 2010.

49. I. Briggs-Myers, *Introduction to Type* (Palo Alto, CA: Consulting Psychologists Press, 1980); W. L. Gardner and M. J. Martinko, "Using the Myers-Briggs Type Indicator to Study Managers: A Literature Review and Research Agenda," *Journal of Management,* vol. 22, no. 1, 1996, pp. 45–83; and

N. L. Quenk, *Essentials of Myers-Briggs Type Indicator Assessment* (New York: Wiley, 2000).

50. R. D. Meyer, R. S. Dalal, and S. Bonaccio, "A Meta-Analytic Investigation into the Moderating Effects of Situational Strength on the Conscientiousness–Performance Relationship," *Journal of Organizational Behavior,* November 2009, pp. 1077–1102; C. G. DeYoung, L. C. Quilty, and J. B. Peterson, "Between Facets and Domains: 10 Aspects of the Big Five," *Journal of Personality and Social Psychology,* November 2007, pp. 880–896; T. A. Judge, D. Heller, and M. K. Mount, "Five-Factor Model of Personality and Job Satisfaction: A Meta-Analysis," *Journal of Applied Psychology,* June 2002, pp. 530–541; G. M. Hurtz and J. J. Donovan, "Personality and Job Performance: The Big Five Revisited," *Journal of Applied Psychology,* December 2000, pp. 869–879; M. K. Mount, M. R. Barrick, and J. P. Strauss, "Validity of Observer Ratings of the Big Five Personality Factors," *Journal of Applied Psychology,* April 1996, pp. 272–280; O. P. John, "The Big Five Factor Taxonomy: Dimensions of Personality in the Natural Language and in Questionnaires," in L. A. Pervin (ed.), *Handbook of Personality Theory and Research* (New York: Guilford Press, 1990), pp. 66–100; and J. M. Digman, "Personality Structure: Emergence of the Five-Factor Model," in M. R. Rosenweig and L. W. Porter (eds.), *Annual Review of Psychology,* vol. 41 (Palo Alto, CA: Annual Review, 1990), pp. 417–440.

51. M. R. Barrick and M. K. Mount, "The Big Five Personality Dimensions and Job Performance: A Meta-Analysis," *Personnel Psychology,* vol. 44, 1991, pp. 1–26; A. J. Vinchur, J. S. Schippmann, F. S. Switzer III, and P. L. Roth, "A Meta-Analytic Review of Predictors of Job Performance for Salespeople," *Journal of Applied Psychology,* August 1998, pp. 586–597; G. M. Hurtz and J. J. Donovan, "Personality and Job Performance Revisited," *Journal of Applied Psychology,* December 2000, pp. 869–879; T. A. Judge and J. E. Bono, "Relationship of Core Self-Evaluations Traits—Self Esteem, Generalized Self-Efficacy, Locus of Control, and Emotional Stability—With Job Satisfaction and Job Performance: A Meta-Analysis," *Journal of Applied Psychology,* February 2001, pp. 80–92; T. A. Judge, D. Heller, and M. K. Mount, "Five-Factor Model of Personality and Job Satisfaction: A Meta-Analysis"; and D. M. Higgins, J. B. Peterson, R. O. Pihl, and A. G. M. Lee, "Prefrontal Cognitive Ability, Intelligence, Big Five Personality, and the Prediction of Advanced Academic and Workplace Performance," *Journal of Personality and Social Psychology,* August 2007, pp. 298–319.

52. I-S. Oh and C. M. Berry, "The Five-Factor Model of Personality and Managerial Performance: Validity Gains Through the Use of 360 Degree Performance Ratings," *Journal of Applied Psychology,* November 2009, pp. 1498–1513.

53. A. E. Poropat, "A Meta-Analysis of the Five-Factor Model of Personality and Academic Performance," *Psychological Bulletin,* vol. 135, no. 2, 2009, pp. 322–338.

54. J. B. Rotter, "Generalized Expectancies for Internal versus External Control of Reinforcement," *Psychological Monographs* 80, no. 609, 1966.

55. See, for instance, D. W. Organ and C. N. Greene, "Role Ambiguity, Locus of Control, and Work Satisfaction," *Journal of Applied Psychology,* February 1974, pp. 101–102; and T. R. Mitchell, C. M. Smyser, and S. E. Weed, "Locus of Control: Supervision and Work Satisfaction," *Academy of Management Journal,* September 1975, pp. 623–631.

56. S. Weinberg, "Poor, Misunderstood Little Machiavelli," *USA Today*, June 13, 2011, p. 2B; S. R. Kessler, P. E. Spector, W. C. Borman, C. E. Nelson, A. C. Bandelli, and L. J. Penney, "Re-Examining Machiavelli: A Three-Dimensional Model of Machiavellianism in the Workplace," *Journal of Applied Social Psychology*, August 2010, pp. 1868-1896; W. Amelia, "Anatomy of a Classic: Machiavelli's Daring Gift," *Wall Street Journal*, August 30–31, 2008, p. W10; R. G. Vleeming, "Machiavellianism: A Preliminary Review," *Psychological Reports*, February 1979, pp. 295–310; and S. A. Snook, "Love and Fear and the Modern Boss," *Harvard Business Review*, January 2008, pp. 16–17.

57. See J. Brockner, *Self-Esteem at Work: Research, Theory, and Practice* (Lexington, MA: Lexington Books, 1988), chapters 1–4; and N. Branden, *Self-Esteem at Work* (San Francisco: Jossey-Bass, 1 998).

58. "Social Studies," *Bloomberg BusinessWeek*, June 14–20, 2010, pp. 72–73.

59. See M. Snyder, *Public Appearances/Private Realities: The Psychology of Self-Monitoring* (New York: W. H. Freeman, 1987); and D. V. Day, D. J. Schleicher, A. L. Unckless, and N. J. Hiller, "Self-Monitoring Personality at Work: A Meta-Analytic Investigation of Construct Validity," *Journal of Applied Psychology*, April 2002, pp. 390–401.

60. Snyder, *Public Appearances/Private Realities*; and J. M. Jenkins, "Self-Monitoring and Turnover: The Impact of Personality on Intent to Leave," *Journal of Organizational Behavior*, January 1993, pp. 83–90.

61. M. Kilduff and D. V. Day, "Do Chameleons Get Ahead? The Effects of Self-Monitoring on Managerial Careers," *Academy of Management Journal*, August 1994, pp. 1047–1060; and A. Mehra, M. Kilduff, and D. J. Brass, "The Social Networks of High and Low Self-Monitors: Implications for Workplace Performance," *Administrative Science Quarterly*, March 2001, pp. 121–146.

62. N. Kogan and M. A. Wallach, "Group Risk Taking as a Function of Members' Anxiety and Defensiveness," *Journal of Personality*, March 1967, pp. 50–63; and J. M. Howell and C. A. Higgins, "Champions of Technological Innovation," *Administrative Science Quarterly*, June 1990, pp. 317–341.

63. data points box based on E. Pofeldt, "Take This Job—and Love It," *Cnn.money.com*, June 2012, p. 42; J. Yang and P. Trap, "Older Workers' Job Satisfaction," *USA Today*, June 28, 2012, p. 1B; J. Yang and P. Trap, "What Is the Longest College Students Can Go Without Using Digital Technology?" *USA Today*, June 26, 2012, p. 1B; J. Clifton, "CEOs: Bet Your Stock on a Great Workplace," [thechairmansblog.gallup.com], May 21, 2012; J. Yang and K. Gelles, "Loyalty Gap Widens," *USA Today*, May 16, 2012, p. 1B; J. Yang and P. Trap, "Is A Sense of Humor Important in the Workplace?" *USA Today*, April 18, 2012, p. 1B; J. Yang and P. Trap, "Are Students' Ways of Communicating Too Casual for the Recruiting Process?" *USA Today*, March 29, 2012, p. 1B; J. J. Deal, "Five Millennial Myths," *Strategy+Business Online*, February 28, 2012; J. Yang and V. Bravo, "Does Being Courteous to Co-Workers Affect Career Prospects?" *USA Today*, December 20, 2011, p. 1B; A. R. Carey and A. Gonzalez, "What Is Inappropriate in the Workplace?" *USA Today*, August 5, 2011, p. 1A; and J. Yang and K. Gelles, "What Co-Worker Behaviors Annoy You the Most?" *USA Today*, June 15, 2011, p. 1B.

64. M. Friedman and R. H. Rosenman, *Type A Behavior and Your Heart* (New York: Alfred A. Knopf, 1974).

65. S. K. Parker and C. G. Collins, "Taking Stock: Integrating and Differentiating Multiple Proactive Behaviors," *Journal of Management*, May 2010, pp. 633–662; J. D. Kammeyer-Mueller and C. R. Wanberg, "Unwrapping the Organizational Entry Process: Disentangling Multiple Antecedents and Their Pathways to Adjustment," *Journal of Applied Psychology*, October 2003, pp. 779–794; S. E. Seibert, M. L. Kraimer, and J. M. Crant, "What Do Proactive People Do? A Longitudinal Model Linking Proactive Personality and Career Success," *Personnel Psychology*, Winter 2001, pp. 845–874; J. M. Crant, "Proactive Behavior in Organizations," *Journal of Management*, vol. 26, no. 3, 2000, pp. 435–462; J. M. Crant and T. S. Bateman, "Charismatic Leadership Viewed from Above: The Impact of Proactive Personality," *Journal of Organizational Behavior*, February 2000, pp. 63–75; S. E. Seibert, J. M. Crant, and M. L. Kraimer, "Proactive Personality and Career Success," *Journal of Applied Psychology*, June 1999, pp. 416–427; R. C. Becherer and J. G. Maurer, "The Proactive Personality Disposition and Entrepreneurial Behavior Among Small Company Presidents," *Journal of Small Business Management*, January 1999, pp. 28–36; and T. S. Bateman and J. M. Crant, "The Proactive Component of Organizational Behavior: A Measure and Correlates," *Journal of Organizational Behavior*, March 1993, pp. 103–118.

66. "Resilience Key to Keeping Your Job, Accenture Research Finds," *Accenture.com*, March 5, 2010; J. D. Margolis and P. G. Stoltz, "How to Bounce Back from Adversity," *Harvard Business Review*, January–February, 2010, pp. 86–92; and A. Ollier-Malaterre, "Contributions of Work-Life Resilience Initiatives to the Individual/Organization Relationship," *Human Relations*, January 2010, pp. 41–62.

67. J. B. Avey, F. Luthans, R. M. Smith, and N. F. Palmer, "Impact of Positive Psychological Capital on Employee Well-Being Over Time," *Journal of Occupational Health Psychology*, January 2010, pp. 17–28; and J. B. Avey, F. Luthans, and S. M. Jensen, "Psychological Capital: A Positive Resource for Combating Employee Stress and Turnover," *Human Resource Management*, September–October 2009, pp. 677–693.

68. See, for instance, G. W. M. Ip and M. H. Bond, "Culture, Values, and the Spontaneous Self-Concept," *Asian Journal of Psychology*, vol. 1, 1995, pp. 30–36; J. E. Williams, J. L. Saiz, D. L. FormyDuval, M. L. Munick, E. E. Fogle, A. Adom, A. Haque, F. Neto, and J. Yu, "Cross-Cultural Variation in the Importance of Psychological Characteristics: A Seven-Year Country Study," *International Journal of Psychology*, October 1995, pp. 529–550; V. Benet and N. G. Walker, "The Big Seven Factor Model of Personality Description: Evidence for Its Cross-Cultural Generalizability in a Spanish Sample," *Journal of Personality and Social Psychology*, October 1995, pp. 701–718; R. R. McCrae and P. T. Costa Jr., "Personality Trait Structure as a Human Universal," *American Psychologist*, 1997, pp. 509–516; and M. J. Schmit, J. A. Kihm, and C. Robie, "Development of a Global Measure of Personality," *Personnel Psychology*, Spring 2000, pp. 153–193.

69. J. F. Salgado, "The Five Factor Model of Personality and Job Performance in the European Community," *Journal of Applied Psychology*, February 1997, pp. 30–43. Note: This study covered the original 15-nation European community and did not include the countries that have joined since.

70. J. Zaslow, "Happiness Inc.," *Wall Street Journal*, March 18–19, 2006, p. P1+.

71. N. P. Rothbard and S. L. Wilk, "Waking Up on the Right or Wrong Side of the Bed: Start-of-Workday Mood, Work Events, Employee Affect, and Performance," *Academy of Management Journal,* October 2011, pp. 959-980.

72. N. H. Frijda, "Moods, Emotion Episodes, and Emotions," in M. Lewis and J. M. Havilland (eds.), *Handbook of Emotions* (New York: Guilford Press, 1993), pp. 381-403.

73. T-Y. Kim, D. M. Cable, S-P. Kim, and J. Wang, "Emotional Competence and Work Performance: The Mediating Effect of Proactivity and the Moderating Effect of Job Autonomy," *Journal of Organizational Behavior,* October 2009, pp. 983-1000; J. M. Diefendorff and G. J. Greguras, "Contextualizing Emotional Display Rules: Examining the Roles of Targets and Discrete Emotions in Shaping Display Rule Perceptions," *Journal of Management,* August 2009, pp. 880-898; J. Gooty, M. Gavin, and N. M. Ashkanasy, "Emotions Research in OB: The Challenges That Lie Ahead," *Journal of Organizational Behavior,* August 2009, pp. 833-838; N. M. Ashkanasy and C. S. Daus, "Emotion in the Workplace: The New Challenge for Managers," *Academy of Management Executive,* February 2002, pp. 76-86; and N. M. Ashkanasy, C. E. J. Hartel, and C. S. Daus, "Diversity and Emotions: The New Frontiers in Organizational Behavior Research," *Journal of Management,* vol. 28, no. 3, 2002, pp. 307-338.

74. H. M. Weiss and R. Cropanzano, "Affective Events Theory," in B. M. Staw and L. L. Cummings, *Research in Organizational Behavior,* vol. 18 (Greenwich, CT: JAI Press, 1996), pp. 20-22.

75. "Critical Skills for Workforce 2020," *T&D,* September 2011, p. 19.

76. This section is based on D. Goleman, *Emotional Intelligence* (New York: Bantam, 1995); M. Davies, L. Stankov, and R. D. Roberts, "Emotional Intelligence: In Search of an Elusive Construct," *Journal of Personality and Social Psychology,* October 1998, pp. 989-1015; D. Goleman, *Working With Emotional Intelligence* (New York: Bantam, 1999); R. Bar-On and J. D. A. Parker, eds. *The Handbook of Emotional Intelligence: Theory, Development, Assessment, and Application at Home, School, and in the Workplace* (San Francisco: Jossey-Bass, 2000); and P. J. Jordan, N. M. Ashkanasy, and C. E. J. Hartel, "Emotional Intelligence as a Moderator of Emotional and Behavioral Reactions to Job Insecurity," *Academy of Management Review,* July 2002, pp. 361-372.

77. F. Walter, M. S. Cole, and R. H. Humphrey, "Emotional Intelligence? Sine Qua Non of Leadership or Folderol?, *Academy of Management Perspective,* February 2011, pp. 45-59.

78. E. J. O'Boyle, Jr., R. H. Humphrey, J. M. Pollack, T. H. Hawver, and P. A. Story, "The Relation Between Emotional Intelligence and Job Performance: A Meta-Analysis," *Journal of Organizational Behavior Online,* June 2010; R. D. Shaffer and M. A. Shaffer, "Emotional Intelligence Abilities, Personality, and Workplace Performance," *Academy of Management Best Conference Paper—HR,* August 2005; K. S. Law, C. Wong, and L. J. Song, "The Construct and Criterion Validity of Emotional Intelligence and Its Potential Utility for Management Studies," *Journal of Applied Psychology,* August 2004, pp. 483-496; D. L. Van Rooy and C. Viswesvaran, "Emotional Intelligence: A Meta-Analytic Investigation of Predictive Validity and Nomological Net," *Journal of Vocational Behavior,* August 2004, pp. 71-95; P. J. Jordan, N. M. Ashkanasy, and C. E. J. Härtel, "The Case for Emotional Intelligence in Organizational Research," *Academy of Management Review,* April 2003,

pp. 195-197; H. A. Elfenbein and N. Ambady, "Predicting Workplace Outcomes from the Ability to Eavesdrop on Feelings," *Journal of Applied Psychology,* October 2002, pp. 963-971; and C. Cherniss, "The Business Case for Emotional Intelligence," Consortium for Research on Emotional Intelligence in Organizations [www.eiconsortium.org], 1999.

79. F. J. Landy, "Some Historical and Scientific Issues Related to Research on Emotional Intelligence," *Journal of Organizational Behavior,* June 2005, pp. 411-424; E. A. Locke, "Why Emotional Intelligence Is an Invalid Concept," *Journal of Organizational Behavior,* June 2005, pp. 425-431; J. M. Conte, "A Review and Critique of Emotional Intelligence Measures," *Journal of Organizational Behavior,* June 2005, pp. 433-440; T. Becker, "Is Emotional Intelligence a Viable Concept?" *Academy of Management Review,* April 2003, pp. 192-195; and M. Davies, L. Stankov, and R. D. Roberts, "Emotional Intelligence: In Search of an Elusive Construct," *Journal of Personality and Social Psychology,* October 1998, pp. 989-1015.

80. G. Kranz, "Organizations Look to Get Personal in '07," *Workforce Management* [www.workforce.com], June 19, 2007.

81. J. L. Holland, *Making Vocational Choices: A Theory of Vocational Personalities and Work Environments* (Odessa, FL: Psychological Assessment Resources, 1997).

82. A. O'Connell, "Smile, Don't Bark in Tough Times," *Harvard Business Review,* November 2009, p. 27; and G. A. Van Kleef et al., "Searing Sentiment or Cold Calculation? The Effects of Leader Emotional Displays on Team Performance Depend on Follower Epistemic Motivation," *Academy of Management Journal,* June 2009, pp. 562-580.

83. Copyright © 2012 by Matt Davis, Cambridge University. Reprinted with permission.

84. See, for instance, M. J. Martinko (ed.), *Attribution Theory: An Organizational Perspective* (Delray Beach, FL: St. Lucie Press, 1995); and H. H. Kelley, "Attribution in Social Interaction," in E. Jones et al. (eds.), *Attribution: Perceiving the Causes of Behavior* (Morristown, NJ: General Learning Press, 1972).

85. See A. G. Miller and T. Lawson, "The Effect of an Informational Option on the Fundamental Attribution Error," *Personality and Social Psychology Bulletin,* June 1989, pp. 194-204.

86. See, for instance, G. R. Semin, "A Gloss on Attribution Theory," *British Journal of Social and Clinical Psychology,* November 1980, pp. 291-330; and M. W. Morris and K. Peng, "Culture and Cause: American and Chinese Attributions for Social and Physical Events," *Journal of Personality and Social Psychology,* December 1994, pp. 949-971.

87. S. Nam, "Cultural and Managerial Attributions for Group Performance," unpublished doctoral dissertation; University of Oregon. Cited in R. M. Steers, S. J. Bischoff, and L. H. Higgins, "Cross-Cultural Management Research," *Journal of Management Inquiry,* December 1992, pp. 325-326.

88. See, for example, S. T. Fiske, "Social Cognition and Social Perception," *Annual Review of Psychology,* 1993, pp. 155-194; G. N. Powell and Y. Kido, "Managerial Stereotypes in a Global Economy: A Comparative Study of Japanese and American Business Students' Perspectives," *Psychological Reports,* February 1994, pp. 219-226; and J. L. Hilton and W. von Hippel, "Stereotypes," in J. T. Spence, J. M. Darley, and D. J. Foss (eds.), *Annual Review of Psychology,* vol. 47 (Palo Alto, CA: Annual Reviews Inc., 1996), pp. 237-271.

89. P. White, "Baseball Elders Teach Lessons of the Game," *USA Today,* April 14, 2009, p. 1C+.

90. B. F. Skinner, *Contingencies of Reinforcement* (East Norwalk, CT: Appleton-Century-Crofts, 1971).

91. A. Applebaum, "Linear Thinking," *Fast Company,* December 2004, p. 35.

92. "The Mindset List for the Class of 2016" [www.beloit.edu/mindset/2016], August 31, 2012.

93. "Most Common Gen Y Job Titles Today," *T&D,* April 2012, p. 23; and P. Ketter, "Value Proposition? Oh, Yes!" *T&D,* November 2011, p. 10.

94. S. A. Hewlett, L. Sherbin, and K. Sumberg, "How Gen Y & Boomers Will Reshape Your Agenda," *Harvard Business Review,* July–August 2009, pp. 71–76; B. Frankel, "Boomers and Millennials: So Different, Yet So Similar," *Diversity Inc.,* July–August 2009, pp. 20–27; and S. Armour, "Generation Y: They've Arrived at Work with a New Attitude," *USA Today,* November 6, 2005, pp. 1B+.

95. N. Ramachandran, "New Paths at Work," *US News & World Report,* March 20, 2006, p. 47.

96. D. Sacks, "Scenes from the Culture Clash," *Fast Company,* January/February 2006, p. 75.

97. S. Armour, "Generation Y: They've Arrived at Work with a New Attitude," p. 2B.

98. J. C. Meister and K. Willyerd, "Mentoring Millennials," *Harvard Business Review,* May 2010, pp. 68–72; P. Trunk, "Motivating Gen Ys in a Downturn," *BusinessWeek Online,* June 9, 2009; S. Armour, "Generation Y: They've Arrived at Work with a New Attitude"; B. Moses, "The Challenges of Managing Gen Y," *The Globe and Mail,* March 11, 2005, p. C1; and C. A. Martin, *Managing Generation Y,* (Amherst, MA: HRD Press, 2001).

99. C. M. Pearson and C. L. Porath, "On the Nature, Consequences, and Remedies of Workplace Incivility: No Time for Nice? Think Again," *Academy of Management Executive,* February 2005, pp. 7–18.

100. J. Robison, "Be Nice: It's Good for Business," *Gallup Brain* [brain.gallup.com], August 12, 2004.

101. D. E. Gibson and R. R. Callister, "Anger in Organizations: Review and Integration," *Journal of Management,* January 2010, pp. 66–93; M. S. Hershcovis and J. Barling, "Towards a Multi-Foci Approach to Workplace Aggression: A Meta-Analytic Review of Outcomes from Different Perpetrators," *Journal of Organizational Behavior,* January 2010, pp. 24–44; S. D. Sidle, "Workplace Incivility: How Should Employees and Managers Respond?" *Academy of Management Perspectives,* November 2009, pp. 88–89; T. G. Reio, Jr. and R. Ghosh, "Antecedents and Outcomes of Workplace Incivility: Implications for Human Resource Development Research and Practice," *Human Resource Development Quarterly,* Fall 2009, pp. 237–264; Y. Vardi and E. Weitz, *Misbehavior in Organizations,* (Mahwah, NJ: Lawrence Erlbaum Associates, 2004), pp. 246–247.

102. M. Conlin, "Are People in Your Office Acting Oddly?" *BusinessWeek*, April 13, 2009, p. 54; and J. Hoffman, "Working Hard to Look Busy," *New York Times Online,* January 25, 2009.

103. "Unprofessional Dress Can Be a Career-Killer," *Springfield, Missouri, News-Leader,* January 13, 2009, p. 4C.

104. R. Karlgaard, "Which CEOs Have the Most Fun? *Forbes. com,* February 8, 2012, p. 57; M. Moskowitz and R. Levering, "The 100 Best Companies To Work For," *Fortune,* February 6, 2012, pp. 117+; R. Karlgaard, "Jim Goodnight King of Analytics," *Forbes,* August 22, 2011, p. 28; D. Bracken, "SAS Again Tops Fortune List of Best Places to Work," www.newsobserver.com, January 20, 2011; D. A. Kaplan, "THE Best Company to Work For," *Fortune,* February 8, 2010, pp. 56-64; R. Leung, "Working the Good Life," [www.cbsnews.com/2100-18560_162-550102.html], February 11, 2009; and J. Schu, "Even in Hard Times, SAS Keeps Its Culture Intact," *Workforce,* October 2001, p. 21.

105. K. J. O'Hara, "Measuring Sticks," *Smart Business Atlanta,* May 2010, pp. 14–18; "Working in an Ideal World," *T&D,* December 2009, p. 21; D. Smith, "Surviving a Down Economy With an Upbeat Attitude," *T&D,* November 2009, pp. 16–17; G. Mijuk, "Tough Times for Temp Agencies Likely to Prompt Consolidation," *Wall Street Journal,* March 17, 2009, p. B7; M. Laff, "Gen Y Proves Loyalty in Economic Downturn," *T&D,* December 2008, p. 18; and S. Berfield, "Bridging the Generation Gap," *BusinessWeek,* September 17, 2007, pp. 60–61.

CHAPTER 16

1. M. Lopresti, "Elimination by Twitter," *USA Today,* July 26, 2012, p. 1C; K. Paulson, "College Athlete Tweet Ban? Free Speech Sacks That Idea," *USA Today,* April 16, 2012, p. 9A; L. East, "Les Miles' Tweets Entertain CWS Fans," theadvocate.com/sports; July 12, 2012; P. Thamel, "Tracking Twitter, Raising Red Flags," *New York Times Online,* March 30, 2012; L. Dugan, "Twitter To Surpass 500 Million Registered Users on Wednesday," www.mediabistro.com, February 21, 2012; C. Ho, "Companies Tracking College Athletes' Tweets, Facebook Posts Go After Local Universities," *Washington Post Online,* October 16, 2011; D. Rovell, "Coaches Ban of Twitter Proves College Sports Isn't About Education," *CNBC Sports Business Online,* August 8, 2011; Staff of Corporate Executive Board, "Corporate Confidential: How Twitter Changes Everything," *BusinessWeek Online,* September 4, 2009; S. Johnson, "How Twitter Will Change the Way We Live," *Time,* June 15, 2009, pp. 30–37; J. Swartz, "A World That's All a-Twitter," *USA Today,* May 26, 2009, pp. 1B+; and K. Whiteside, "College Coaches Are Chirping About Twitter!" *USA Today,* April 29, 2009, pp. 1C+.

2. P. G. Clampitt, *Communicating for Managerial Effectiveness* 5th ed. (Thousand Oaks, CA: Sage Publications, 2009); T. Dixon, *Communication, Organization, and Performance* (Norwood, NJ: Ablex Publishing Corporation, 1996), p. 281; and L. E. Penley, E. R. Alexander, I. Edward Jernigan, and C. I. Henwood, "Communication Abilities of Managers: The Relationship to Performance," *Journal of Management*, March 1991, pp. 57–76.

3. S. Carey, "Southwest Grounds Pilot After Obscene Radio Rant," *Wall Street Journal,* June 23, 2011, p. B1; and "Southwest Pilot Grounded After Radio Rant," [www.wctv.tv], June 23, 2011.

4. C. O. Kursh, "The Benefits of Poor Communication," *Psychoanalytic Review*, Summer–Fall 1971, pp. 189–208.

5. "Irene Lewis, CEO of SAIT Polytechnic, To Receive IABC's 2012 EXCEL Award," www.iabc.com/awards, July 29, 2012.

6. W. G. Scott and T. R. Mitchell, *Organization Theory: A Structural and Behavioral Analysis* (Homewood, IL: Richard D. Irwin, 1976).

7. D. K. Berlo, *The Process of Communication* (New York: Holt, Rinehart & Winston, 1960), pp. 30–32.

8. G. Zoroya, "Commander's Letter Tackles Morale," *USA Today,* October 16, 2009, p. 1A+.

9. Clampitt, *Communicating for Managerial Effectiveness.*

10. A. Semnani-Azad and W. L. Adair, "Reading the Body Language in International Negotiations," *Strategy+Business Online,* September 16, 2011; S. Smith, "But What Are You

Really Saying?" *Realsimple.com,* December 2010, pp. 195+; J. Cloud, "Strike a Pose," *Time,* November 29, 2010, p. 61; L. Talley, "Body Language: Read It or Weep," *HR Magazine,* July 2010, pp. 64–65; Interview with A. Pentland, "The Impact of Unconscious Communication," *Gallup Management Journal Online,* September 3, 2009; D. Tannen, "Every Move You Make," *O Magazine,* August 2006, pp. 175–176; A. Warfield, "Do You Speak Body Language?" *Training & Development,* April 2001, pp. 60–61; D. Zielinski, "Body Language Myths," *Presentations,* April 2001, pp. 36–42; and "Visual Cues Speak Loudly in Workplace," *Springfield, Missouri, News-Leader,* January 21, 2001, p. 8B.

11. J. Levine, "Conversations on Culture," *DMI News & Views,* June 2012, p. 31; "Keeping It Creative," *Fast Company,* June 2012, pp. 22–24; E. Florian, "Tony Hsieh," *Fortune,* April 30, 2012, p. 19; M. Stettner, "Zappos Chief Treasures the Company's Culture," *Investors Business Daily,* April 30, 2012, p. A07; R. E. Silverman, "Firms Share Spaces, Ideas," *Wall Street Journal,* March 21, 2012, p. B8; T. Hsieh and R. Ten Pas, *Delivering Happiness: A Path to Profits, Passion, and Purpose* (Writers of the Round Table Press), 2012; and B. Stone, "What Starts Up in Vegas Stays in Vegas," *Bloomberg BusinessWeek,* February 6, 2012, pp. 37–39.

12. "Employee E-Mail Blunders," *Training,* September 2009, p. 8.

13. A. Williams, "At Meetings, It's Mind Your BlackBerry or Mind Your Manners," *New York Times Online,* June 22, 2009.

14. "They're Not Getting It," *Training,* September 2008, p. 8.

15. J. Yarow, "107,000,000,000,0000," articles.businessinsider.com, January 14, 2011; P. Korkki, "Swimming, or Just Wading, in Technology," *New York Times Online,* October 25, 2009; S. Shellenbarger, "A Day Without E-Mail Is Like…," *Wall Street Journal,* October 11, 2007, pp. D1+; M. Kessler, "Fridays Go from Casual to E-Mail-Free," *USA Today,* October 5, 2007, p. 1A; D. Beizer, "E-Mail is Dead," *Fast Company,* July–August 2007, p. 46; O. Malik, "Why E-Mail Is Bankrupt," *Business 2.0,* July 2007, p. 46; and D. Brady, "*!#?@ the E-Mail. Can We Talk?" *BusinessWeek,* December 4, 2006, p. 109.

16. Berlo, *The Process of Communication,* p. 103.

17. R. Buckman, "Why the Chinese Hate to Use Voice Mail," *Wall Street Journal,* December 1, 2005, p. B1+.

18. A. Mehrabian, "Communication Without Words," *Psychology Today,* September 1968, pp. 53–55.

19. L. Haggerman, "Strong, Efficient Leadership Minimizes Employee Problems," *Springfield, Missouri, Business Journal,* December 9–15, 2002, p. 23.

20. N. Bendapudi and V. Bendapudi, "How to Use Language That Employees Get," *Harvard Business Review,* September 2009, p. 24.

21. See, for instance, S. P. Robbins and P. L. Hunsaker, *Training in Interpersonal Skills,* 5th ed. (Upper Saddle River, NJ: Prentice Hall, 2009); M. Young and J. E. Post, "Managing to Communicate, Communicating to Manage: How Leading Companies Communicate with Employees," *Organizational Dynamics,* Summer 1993, pp. 31–43; J. A. DeVito, *The Interpersonal Communication Book,* 6th ed. (New York: HarperCollins, 1992); and A. G. Athos and J. J. Gabarro, *Interpersonal Behavior* (Upper Saddle River, NJ: Prentice Hall, 1978).

22. D. Beucke, "Aviva Fires Everyone: Great Moments in Employee Motivation," [www.businessweek.com], April 26, 2012.

23. K. O'Sullivan, "Escaping the Executive Bubble," *CFO,* January–February 2010, pp. 27–30.

24. O. Thomas, "Best-Kept Secrets of the World's Best Companies: The Three Minute Huddle," *Business 2.0,* April 2006, p. 94.

25. J. S. Lublin, "The 'Open Inbox,'" *Wall Street Journal,* October 10, 2005, pp. B1+.

26. Cited in "Shut Up and Listen," *Money,* November 2005, p. 27.

27. See, for instance, J. Smerd, "Gossip's Toll on the Workplace," *Workforce Management Online,* March 2010; D. L. Wheeler, "Going After Gossip," *Workforce Management Online,* July 2009; D. Sagario and L. Ballard, "Workplace Gossip Can Threaten Your Office," *Springfield News-Leader,* September 26, 2005, p. 5B; A. Bruzzese, "What to Do About Toxic Gossip," *USA Today* [www.usatoday.com], March 14, 2001; N. B. Kurland and L. H. Pelled, "Passing the Word: Toward a Model of Gossip and Power in the Workplace," *Academy of Management Review,* April 2000, pp. 428–438; N. DiFonzo, P. Bordia, and R. L. Rosnow, "Reining in Rumors," *Organizational Dynamics,* Summer 1994, pp. 47–62; M. Noon and R. Delbridge, "News from Behind My Hand: Gossip in Organizations," *Organization Studies,* vol. 14, no. 1, 1993, pp. 23–26; and J. G. March and G. Sevon, "Gossip, Information and Decision Making," in J. G. March (ed.), *Decisions and Organizations* (Oxford: Blackwell, 1988), pp. 429–442.

28. "Secrets of Top Performers: How Companies with Highly Effective Employee Communication Differentiate Themselves, 2007/2008 Communication ROI Study™," Towers Watson, Washington, DC.

29. Gensler, "The U.S. Workplace Survey, 2008" [www.gensler.com], July 11, 2010.

30. Ibid., p. 11.

31. C. C. Sullivan and B. Horwitz-Bennett, "High-Performance Workplaces," *Building Design + Construction,* January 2010, pp. 22–26.

32. J. B. Stryker, "In Open Workplaces, Traffic and Head Count Matter," *Harvard Business Review,* December 2009, p. 24.

33. K. D. Elsbach and M. G. Pratt, "The Physical Environment in Organizations," in *The Academy of Management Annals,* vol. 1, 2007, J. P. Walsh and A. P. Brief (eds.), pp. 181–114.

34. S. Shellenbarger, "Indecent Exposure: The Downsides of Working in a Glass Office," *Wall Street Journal,* January 4, 2012, p. D1+.

35. J. B. Stryker, "In Open Workplaces, Traffic and Head Count Matter;" and K. D. Elsbach and M. G. Pratt, "The Physical Environment in Organizations."

36. S. E. Needleman, "Office Personal Space Is Crowded Out," *Wall Street Journal,* December 7, 2009, p. B7.

37. These examples taken from A. Dizik, "Chefs Solve a Modern Kitchen Crisis: Recipe Clutter," *Wall Street Journal,* June 30, 2011, p. D1+; T. Henneman, "At Lockheed Martin, Social Networking Fills Key Workforce Needs While Improving Efficiency and Lowering Costs," *Workforce Management Online,* March 2010; S. Kirsner, "Being There," *Fast Company,* January–February 2006, pp. 90–91; R. Breeden, "More Employees Are Using the Web at Work," *Wall Street Journal,* May 10, 2005, p. B4; C. Woodward, "Some Offices Opt for Cellphones Only," *USA Today,* January 25, 2005, p. 1B; and J. Rohwer, "Today, Tokyo. Tomorrow, the World," *Fortune,* September 18, 2000, pp. 140–152.

38. G. Colvin, "Brave New Work: The Office of Tomorrow," *Fortune,* January 16, 2012, pp. 49+.

39. J. Karaian, "Where Wireless Works," *CFO,* May 2003, pp. 81–83.

40. S. Srivastava, "Doing More on the Go," *Wall Street Journal*, June 12, 2007, p. B3.

41. B. White, "Firms Take a Cue from YouTube," *Wall Street Journal*, January 2, 2007, p. B3.

42. K. Hafner, "For the Well Connected, All the World's an Office," *New York Times*, March 30, 2000, pp. D1+.

43. S. Luh, "Pulse Lunches at Asian Citibanks Feed Workers' Morale, Lower Job Turnover," *Wall Street Journal*, May 22, 2001, p. B11.

44. S. Shellenbager, "Backlash Against E-Mail Builds," *Wall Street Journal*, April 29, 2010, p. D6.

45. H. Green, "The Water Cooler Is Now on the Web," *BusinessWeek*, October 1, 2007, pp. 78–79.

46. The Associated Press, "Whole Foods Chief Apologizes for Posts," *New York Times Online*, July 18, 2007; E. White, J. S. Lublin, and D. Kesmodel, "Executives Get the Blogging Bug," *Wall Street Journal*, July 13, 2007, pp. B1+; C. Alldred, "U.K. Libel Case Slows E-Mail Delivery," *Business Insurance*, August 4, 1997, pp. 51–53; and T. Lewin, "Chevron Settles Sexual Harassment Charges," *New York Times Online*, February 22, 1995.

47. J. Eckberg, "E-Mail: Messages Are Evidence," *Cincinnati Enquirer* [www.enquirer.com], July 27, 2004.

48. M. Scott, "Worker E-Mail and Blog Misuse Seen as Growing Risk for Companies," *Workforce Management* [www.workforce.com], July 20, 2007.

49. K. Byron, "Carrying Too Heavy a Load? The Communication and Miscommunication of Emotion by E-Mail," *Academy of Management Review*, April 2008, pp. 309–327.

50. J. Marquez, "Virtual Work Spaces Ease Collaboration, Debate Among Scattered Employees," *Workforce Management*, May 22, 2006, p. 38; and M. Conlin, "E-Mail Is So Five Minutes Ago," *BusinessWeek*, November 28, 2005, pp. 111–112.

51. H. Green, "The Water Cooler Is Now on the Web"; E. Frauenheim, "Starbucks Employees Carve Out Own 'Space,'" *Workforce Management*, October 22, 2007, p. 32; and S. H. Wildstrom, "Harnessing Social Networks," *BusinessWeek*, April 23, 2007, p. 20.

52. J. Scanlon, "Woman of Substance," *Wired*, July 2002, p. 27.

53. H. Dolezalek, "Collaborating in Cyberspace," *Training*, April 2003, p. 33.

54. B. A. Gutek, M. Groth, and B. Cherry, "Achieving Service Success Through Relationship and Enhanced Encounters," *Academy of Management Executive*, November 2002, pp. 132–144.

55. data points box based on "What's Your Social IQ?" *CFO*, May 2012, p. 12; J. Yang and V. Bravo, "Average Office Space Per Worker," *USA Today*, February 27, 2012, p. 1B; "Technology," *HR Magazine*, HR Trendbook 2011, p. 70; L. Kwoh, "When Face Time Counts," *Wall Street Journal*, April 25, 2012, p. B8; A. R. Carey and P. Trap, "When North American Workers Use Mobile Devices To Work Outside the Office," *USA Today*, September 28, 2011, p. 1A; J. Yang and K. Gelles, "Do You Have A Negative View of Workers With A Messy Desk?" *USA Today*, September 14, 2011, p. 1B; J. Yang and K. O'Callaghan, "What Would You Say To Your Boss If There Were No Consequences?" *USA Today*, August 9, 2011, p. 1B; "Common Workplace Distraction By Activity," *T&D*, July 2011, p. 23; T. Neeley and P. Leonardi, "Effective Managers Say the Same Thing Twice (Or More)," *Harvard Business Review*, May 2011, p. 38; A. Smith, "E-Mail Training

Needed to Avoid Cyber Battles," [www.shrm.org/legal_issues], May 6, 2011; and "Smart Women, Dumb E-mails," *Women's Health*, January/February 2011, p. 118.

56. R. C. Ford and C. P. Heaton, "Lessons from Hospitality That Can Serve Anyone," *Organizational Dynamics*, Summer 2001, pp. 30–47.

57. M. J. Bitner, B. H. Booms, and L. A. Mohr, "Critical Service Encounters: The Employee's Viewpoint," *Journal of Marketing*, October 1994, pp. 95–106.

58. S. D. Pugh, J. Dietz, J. W. Wiley, and S. M. Brooks, "Driving Service Effectiveness Through Employee-Customer Linkages," *Academy of Management Executive*, November 2002, pp. 73–84.

59. J. Ewing, "Nokia: Bring on the Employee Rants," *BusinessWeek*, June 22, 2009, p. 50.

60. J. V. Thill and C. L. Bovee, *Excellence in Business Communication*, 9th ed. (Upper Saddle River, NJ: Prentice Hall, 2011), pp. 24–25.

61. Ibid.

62. Ibid.

63. Ibid.

64. Ibid.

65. M. Villano, "The Online Divide Between Work and Play," *New York Times Online*, April 26, 2009.

66. J. Fortt and M. V. Copeland, "The Great Debate," *Fortune*, May 3, 2010, p. 32.

67. M. V. Rafter, "Too Much Email on the Menu? Here Are Five Tips to Curb Company Consumption," *Workforce Management Online*, April 24, 2012; M.V. Rafter, "If Tim Fry Has His Way, He'll Eradicate Email for Good," *Workforce Management Online*, April 24, 2012; M. A. Field, "Turning Off Email, Turning Up Productivity," *Workforce Management Online*, February 29, 2012; "Internet 2011 in Numbers," royalpingdom.com, January 17, 2012; "Should Workplaces Curtail Email?" *New York Times Online*, December 7, 2011; W. Powers, "The Phony 'Zero Email' Alarm," *New York Times Online*, December 6, 2011; L. Suarez, "What We Would Miss," *New York Times Online*, December 5, 2011; P. Duncan, "Break Bad Habits," *New York Times Online*, December 5, 2011; N. Carr, "Put the Cost Back in Communication," *New York Times Online*, December 5, 2011; P. Allen, "One of the Biggest Information Technology Companies In the World To Abolish E-mails," [www.dailymail.com], November 30, 2011; and R. Z. Arndt, "25th Anniversary of Listserv," *Fastcompany.com*, June 2011, p. 32.

68. B. Levisohn and E. Gibson, "An Unwelcome Delivery," *BusinessWeek*, May 4, 2009, p. 15; S. Clifford, "Video Prank at Domino's Taints Brand," *New York Times Online*, April 16, 2009; B. Horovitz, "Domino's Nightmare Holds Lessons for Marketers," *USA Today*, April 16, 2009, p. 3B; and E. Bryson York, "Employee Misconduct and Internet Video Create PR Disaster for Domino's Pizza," *Workforce Management Online*, April 15, 2009.

CHAPTER 17

1. "2012 Update from the CEO," investor.google.com/corporate, August 1, 2012; S. Martin, "Welcome to Perksville, USA," *USA Today*, July 5, 2012, pp. 1A+; C. Kelly, "O.K., Google, Take a Deep Breath," *New York Times Online*, April 28, 2012; A. Lashinsky, "The *Fortune* Interview: Larry Page, *Fortune*, February 6, 2012, pp. 98-99; L. Petrecca, "Tech Companies Top List of 'Great Workplaces'," *USA Today*, October 31, 2011, p. 7B; C. C. Miller and J. Wortham, "Silicon Valley Hiring Perks:

Meals, iPads, and a Cubicle for Spot," *New York Times Online,* March 25, 2011; J. Light, "Google Is No. 1 on List of Desired Employers," *Wall Street Journal,* March 21, 2011, p. B8; C. C. Miller and M. Helft, "Google Shake-Up Is Effort to Revive Start-Up Spark," *New York Times Online,* January 20, 2011; C. C. Miller, "Google Grows and Works to Retain Nimble Minds," *New York Times Online,* November 28, 2010; and A. Efrati and P-Wing Tam, "Google Battles to Keep Talent," *Wall Street Journal,* November 11, 2010, pp. B1+.

2. G. A. Fowler, "In the Search for a Hot Job Title, Enter the Ninja," *Wall Street Journal,* April 7, 2010, pp. A1+.

3. A. Carmeli, B. Ben-Hador, D. A. Waldman, and D. E. Rupp, "How Leaders Cultivate Social Capital and Nurture Employee Vigor: Implications for Job Performance," *Journal of Applied Psychology,* November 2009, pp. 1533–1561.

4. R. M. Steers, R. T. Mowday, and D. L. Shapiro, "The Future of Work Motivation Theory," *Academy of Management Review,* July 2004, pp. 379–387.

5. C. Fritz, C. Fu Lam, and G. M. Spreitzer, "It's the Little Things That Matter: An Examination of Knowledge Workers' Energy Management," *Academy of Management Perspectives,* August 2011, pp. 28-39; A. Carmeli, B. Ben-Hador, D. A. Waldman, and D. E. Rupp, "How Leaders Cultivate Social Capital and Nurture Employee Vigor: Implications for Job Performance," *Journal of Applied Psychology,* November 2009, pp. 1553–1561; and N. Ellemers, D. De Gilder, and S. A. Haslam, "Motivating Individuals and Groups at Work: A Social Identity Perspective on Leadership and Group Performance," *Academy of Management Review,* July 2004, pp. 459–478.

6. J. Krueger and E. Killham, "At Work, Feeling Good Matters," *Gallup Management Journal* [http://gmj.gallup.com], December 8, 2005; "Gallup Study: Engaged Employees Inspire Company Innovation" from *Gallup Business Journal.*

7. M. Meece, "Using the Human Touch to Solve Workplace Problems," *New York Times Online,* April 3, 2008.

8. A. Maslow, *Motivation and Personality* (New York: McGraw-Hill, 1954); A. Maslow, D. C. Stephens, and G. Heil, *Maslow on Management* (New York: John Wiley & Sons, 1998); M. L. Ambrose and C. T. Kulik, "Old Friends, New Faces: Motivation Research in the 1990s," *Journal of Management,* vol. 25, no. 3, 1999, pp. 231–292; and "Dialogue," *Academy of Management Review,* October 2000, pp. 696–701.

9. See, for example, D. T. Hall and K. E. Nongaim, "An Examination of Maslow's Need Hierarchy in an Organizational Setting," *Organizational Behavior and Human Performance,* February 1968, pp. 12–35; E. E. Lawler III and J. L. Suttle, "A Causal Correlational Test of the Need Hierarchy Concept," *Organizational Behavior and Human Performance,* April 1972, pp. 265–287; R. M. Creech, "Employee Motivation," *Management Quarterly,* Summer 1995, pp. 33–39; J. Rowan, "Maslow Amended," *Journal of Humanistic Psychology,* Winter 1998, pp. 81–92; J. Rowan, "Ascent and Descent in Maslow's Theory," *Journal of Humanistic Psychology,* Summer 1999, pp. 125–133; and M. L. Ambrose and C. T. Kulik, "Old Friends, New Faces: Motivation Research in the 1990s."

10. E. McGirt, "Intel Risks It All…Again," *Fast Company,* November 2009, pp. 88+.

11. D. McGregor, *The Human Side of Enterprise* (New York: McGraw-Hill, 1960). For an updated description of Theories X and Y, see an annotated edition with commentary of *The Human Side of Enterprise* (McGraw-Hill, 2006); and G. Heil, W. Bennis, and D. C. Stephens, *Douglas McGregor, Revisited: Managing the Human Side of Enterprise* (New York: Wiley, 2000).

12. J. M. O'Brien, "The Next Intel," *Wired,* July 2002, pp. 100–107.

13. F. Herzberg, B. Mausner, and B. Snyderman, *The Motivation to Work* (New York: John Wiley, 1959); F. Herzberg, *The Managerial Choice: To Be Effective or to Be Human,* rev. ed. (Salt Lake City, Olympus, 1982); R. M. Creech, "Employee Motivation"; and M. L. Ambrose and C. T. Kulik, "Old Friends, New Faces: Motivation Research in the 1990s."

14. D. C. McClelland, *The Achieving Society* (New York: Van Nostrand Reinhold, 1961); J. W. Atkinson and J. O. Raynor, *Motivation and Achievement* (Washington, DC: Winston, 1974); D. C. McClelland, *Power: The Inner Experience* (New York: Irvington, 1975); and M. J. Stahl, *Managerial and Technical Motivation: Assessing Needs for Achievement, Power, and Affiliation* (New York: Praeger, 1986).

15. McClelland, *The Achieving Society.*

16. McClelland, *Power;* D. C. McClelland and D. H. Burnham, "Power Is the Great Motivator," *Harvard Business Review,* March–April 1976, pp. 100–110.

17. D. Miron and D. C. McClelland, "The Impact of Achievement Motivation Training on Small Businesses," *California Management Review,* Summer 1979, pp. 13–28.

18. "McClelland: An Advocate of Power," *International Management,* July 1975, pp. 27–29.

19. R. M. Steers, R. T. Mowday, and D. L. Shapiro, "The Future of Work Motivation Theory"; E. A. Locke and G. P. Latham, "What Should We Do About Motivation Theory? Six Recommendations for the Twenty-First Century," *Academy of Management Review,* July 2004, pp. 388–403; and M. L. Ambrose and C. T. Kulik, "Old Friends, New Faces: Motivation Research in the 1990s."

20. A. Barrett, "Cracking the Whip at Wyeth," *BusinessWeek,* February 6, 2006, pp. 70–71.

21. G. P. Latham and E. A. Locke, "Science and Ethics: What Should Count as Evidence Against the Use of Goal Setting?" *Academy of Management Perspective,* August 2009, pp. 88–91; M. L. Ambrose and C. T. Kulik, "Old Friends, New Faces: Motivation Research in the 1990s."

22. J. C. Naylor and D. R. Ilgen, "Goal Setting: A Theoretical Analysis of a Motivational Technique," in B. M. Staw and L. L. Cummings (eds.), *Research in Organizational Behavior,* vol. 6 (Greenwich, CT: JAI Press, 1984), pp. 95–140; A. R. Pell, "Energize Your People," *Managers Magazine,* December 1992, pp. 28–29; E. A. Locke, "Facts and Fallacies about Goal Theory: Reply to Deci," *Psychological Science,* January 1993, pp. 63–64; M. E. Tubbs, "Commitment as a Moderator of the Goal-Performance Relation: A Case for Clearer Construct Definition," *Journal of Applied Psychology,* February 1993, pp. 86–97; M. P. Collingwood, "Why Don't You Use the Research?" *Management Decision,* May 1993, pp. 48–54; M. E. Tubbs, D. M. Boehne, and J. S. Dahl, "Expectancy, Valence, and Motivational Force Functions in Goal-Setting Research: An Empirical Test," *Journal of Applied Psychology,* June 1993, pp. 361–373; E. A. Locke, "Motivation through Conscious Goal Setting," *Applied and Preventive Psychology,* vol. 5, 1996, pp. 117–124; M. L. Ambrose and C. T. Kulik, "Old Friends, New Faces: Motivation Research in the 1990s; E. A. Locke and G. P. Latham, "Building a Practically Useful Theory of Goal Setting and Task Motivation:

A 35-Year Odyssey," *American Psychologist,* September 2002, pp. 705–717; Y. Fried and L. H. Slowik, "Enriching Goal-Setting Theory with Time: An Integrated Approach," *Academy of Management Review,* July 2004, pp. 404–422; and G. P. Latham, "The Motivational Benefits of Goal-Setting," *Academy of Management Executive,* November 2004, pp. 126–129.

23. J. B. Miner, *Theories of Organizational Behavior* (Hinsdale, IL: Dryden Press, 1980), p. 65.

24. Leader Who Made a Difference box based on D. A. Kaplan, "The Best Company to Work For," *Fortune,* February 8, 2010, pp. 56–64; and S. Cooperman, "Goodnight High," *Forbes,* May 5, 2008, pp. 46–48.

25. J. A. Wagner III, "Participation's Effects on Performance and Satisfaction: A Reconsideration of Research and Evidence," *Academy of Management Review,* April 1994, pp. 312–330; J. George-Falvey, "Effects of Task Complexity and Learning Stage on the Relationship between Participation in Goal Setting and Task Performance," *Academy of Management Proceedings* on Disk, 1996; T. D. Ludwig and E. S. Geller, "Assigned versus Participative Goal Setting and Response Generalization: Managing Injury Control among Professional Pizza Deliverers," *Journal of Applied Psychology,* April 1997, pp. 253–261; and S. G. Harkins and M. D. Lowe, "The Effects of Self-Set Goals on Task Performance," *Journal of Applied Social Psychology,* January 2000, pp. 1–40.

26. J. M. Ivancevich and J. T. McMahon, "The Effects of Goal Setting, External Feedback, and Self-Generated Feedback on Outcome Variables: A Field Experiment," *Academy of Management Journal,* June 1982, pp. 359–372; and E. A. Locke, "Motivation through Conscious Goal Setting."

27. J. R. Hollenbeck, C. R. Williams, and H. J. Klein, "An Empirical Examination of the Antecedents of Commitment to Difficult Goals," *Journal of Applied Psychology,* February 1989, pp. 18–23; see also J. C. Wofford, V. L. Goodwin, and S. Premack, "Meta-Analysis of the Antecedents of Personal Goal Level and of the Antecedents and Consequences of Goal Commitment," *Journal of Management,* September 1992, pp. 595–615; Tubbs, "Commitment as a Moderator of the Goal-Performance Relation"; J. W. Smither, M. London, and R. R. Reilly, "Does Performance Improve Following Multisource Feedback? A Theoretical Model, Meta-Analysis, and Review of Empirical Findings," *Personnel Psychology,* Spring 2005, pp. 171–203.

28. Y. Gong, J-C. Huang, and J-L. Farh, "Employee Learning Orientation, Transformational Leadership, and Employee Creativity: The Mediating Role of Employee Self-Efficacy," *Academy of Management Journal,* August 2009, pp. 765–778; M. E. Gist, "Self-Efficacy: Implications for Organizational Behavior and Human Resource Management," *Academy of Management Review,* July 1987, pp. 472–485; and A. Bandura, *Self-Efficacy: The Exercise of Control* (New York: Freeman, 1997).

29. E. A. Locke, E. Frederick, C. Lee, and P. Bobko, "Effect of Self-Efficacy, Goals, and Task Strategies on Task Performance," *Journal of Applied Psychology,* May 1984, pp. 241–251; M. E. Gist and T. R. Mitchell, "Self-Efficacy: A Theoretical Analysis of Its Determinants and Malleability," *Academy of Management Review,* April 1992, pp. 183–211; A. D. Stajkovic and F. Luthans, "Self-Efficacy and Work-Related Performance: A Meta-Analysis," *Psychological Bulletin,* September 1998, pp. 240–261; and A. Bandura, "Cultivate Self-Efficacy for Personal and Organizational Effectiveness,"

in E. Locke (ed.), *Handbook of Principles of Organizational Behavior* (Malden, MA: Blackwell, 2004), pp. 120–136.

30. A. Bandura and D. Cervone, "Differential Engagement in Self-Reactive Influences in Cognitively-Based Motivation," *Organizational Behavior and Human Decision Processes,* August 1986, pp. 92–113; and R. Ilies and T. A. Judge, "Goal Regulation Across Time: The Effects of Feedback and Affect," *Journal of Applied Psychology,* May 2005, pp. 453–467.

31. See J. C. Anderson and C. A. O'Reilly, "Effects of an Organizational Control System on Managerial Satisfaction and Performance," *Human Relations,* June 1981, pp. 491–501; and J. P. Meyer, B. Schacht-Cole, and I. R. Gellatly, "An Examination of the Cognitive Mechanisms by Which Assigned Goals Affect Task Performance and Reactions to Performance," *Journal of Applied Social Psychology* vol. 18, no. 5, 1988, pp. 390–408.

32. K. Maher and K. Hudson, "Wal-Mart to Sweeten Bonus Plans for Staff," *Wall Street Journal,* March 22, 2007, p. A11; and Reuters, "Wal-Mart Workers to Get New Bonus Plan," *CNNMoney.com,* March 22, 2007.

33. B. F. Skinner, *Science and Human Behavior* (New York: Free Press, 1953); and Skinner, *Beyond Freedom and Dignity* (New York: Knopf, 1972).

34. The same data, for instance, can be interpreted in either goal-setting or reinforcement terms, as shown in E. A. Locke, "Latham vs. Komaki: A Tale of Two Paradigms," *Journal of Applied Psychology,* February 1980, pp. 16–23. Also, see M. O. Ambrose and C. T. Kulik, "Old Friends, New Faces: Motivation Research in the 1990s."

35. J. Katz, "Cozy Up to Customers," *Industry Week,* February 2010, p. 16.

36. See, for example, A. M. Grant and S. K. Parker, "Redesigning Work Design Theories: The Rise of Relational and Proactive Perspectives," in *The Academy of Management Annals,* J. P. Walsh and A. P. Brief (eds.), 2009, pp. 317–375; R. W. Griffin, "Toward an Integrated Theory of Task Design," in L. L. Cummings and B. M. Staw (eds.), *Research in Organizational Behavior,* vol. 9 (Greenwich, CT: JAI Press, 1987), pp. 79–120; and M. Campion, "Interdisciplinary Approaches to Job Design: A Constructive Replication with Extensions," *Journal of Applied Psychology,* August 1988, pp. 467–481.

37. N. Tasler, "Help Your Best People Do a Better Job," *BusinessWeek Online,* March 26, 2010; S. Caudron, "The De-Jobbing of America," *Industry Week,* September 5, 1994, pp. 31–36; W. Bridges, "The End of the Job," *Fortune,* September 19, 1994, pp. 62–74; and K. H. Hammonds, K. Kelly, and K. Thurston, "Rethinking Work," *BusinessWeek,* October 12, 1994, pp. 75–87.

38. M. A. Campion and C. L. McClelland, "Follow-Up and Extension of the Interdisciplinary Costs and Benefits of Enlarged Jobs," *Journal of Applied Psychology,* June 1993, pp. 339–351; and M. L. Ambrose and C. T. Kulik, "Old Friends, New Faces: Motivation Research in the 1990s."

39. See, for example, J. R. Hackman and G. R. Oldham, *Work Redesign* (Reading, MA: Addison-Wesley, 1980); Miner, *Theories of Organizational Behavior,* pp. 231–266; R. W. Griffin, "Effects of Work Redesign on Employee Perceptions, Attitudes, and Behaviors: A Long-Term Investigation," *Academy of Management Journal,* June 1991, pp. 425–435; J. L. Cotton, *Employee Involvement* (Newbury Park, CA: Sage, 1993), pp. 141–172; and M. L. Ambrose and C. T. Kulik, "Old Friends, New Faces: Motivation Research in the 1990s."

40. J. R. Hackman and G. R. Oldham, "Development of the Job Diagnostic Survey," *Journal of Applied Psychology*, April 1975, pp. 159–170; and J. R. Hackman and G. R. Oldham, "Motivation through the Design of Work: Test of a Theory," *Organizational Behavior and Human Performance*, August 1976, pp. 250–279.

41. J. R. Hackman, "Work Design," in J. R. Hackman and J. L. Suttle (eds.), *Improving Life at Work* (Glenview, IL: Scott, Foresman, 1977), p. 129; and M. L. Ambrose and C. T. Kulik, "Old Friends, New Faces: Motivation Research in the 1990s."

42. D. J. Holman, C. M. Axtell, C. A. Sprigg, P. Totterdell, and T. D. Wall, "The Mediating Role of Job Characteristics in Job Redesign Interventions: A Serendipitous Quasi-Experiment," *Journal of Organizational Behavior*, January 2010, pp. 84–105.

43. J. L. Pierce, I. Jussila, and A. Cummings, "Psychological Ownership Within the Job Design Context: Revision of the Job Characteristics Model," *Journal of Organizational Behavior*, May 2009, pp. 477–496.

44. A. M. Grant and S. K. Parker, "Redesigning Work Design Theories: The Rise of Relational and Proactive Perspectives."

45. J. Camps and R. Luna-Arocas, "High Involvement Work Practices and Firm Performance," *The International Journal of Human Resource Management*, May 2009, pp. 1056–1077; M. M. Butts, R. J. Vandenberg, D. M. DeJoy, B. S. Schaffer, and M. G. Wilson, "Individual Reactions to High Involvement Work Practices: Investigating the Role of Empowerment and Perceived Organizational Support," *Journal of Occupational Health Psychology*, April 2009, pp. 122–136; P. Boxall and K. Macky, "Research and Theory on High-Performance Work Systems: Progressing the High-Involvement Stream," *Human Resource Management Journal*, vol. 19, no. 1, 2009, pp. 3–23; R. D. Mohr and C. Zoghi, "High-Involvement Work Design and Job Satisfaction," *Industrial and Labor Relations Review*, April 2008, pp. 275–296; and C. D. Zatzick and R. D. Iverson, "High-Involvement Management and Workforce Reduction: Competitive Advantage or Disadvantage?" *Academy of Management Journal*, October 2006, pp. 999–1015.

46. J. S. Adams, "Inequity in Social Exchanges," in L. Berkowitz (ed.), *Advances in Experimental Social Psychology*, vol. 2 (New York: Academic Press, 1965), pp. 267–300; M. L. Ambrose and C. T. Kulik, "Old Friends, New Faces: Motivation Research in the 1990s"; and T. Menon and L. Thompson, "Envy at Work," *Harvard Business Review*, April 2010, pp. 74–79.

47. See, for example, P. S. Goodman and A. Friedman, "An Examination of Adams' Theory of Inequity," *Administrative Science Quarterly*, September 1971, pp. 271–288; M. R. Carrell, "A Longitudinal Field Assessment of Employee Perceptions of Equitable Treatment," *Organizational Behavior and Human Performance*, February 1978, pp. 108–118; E. Walster, G. W. Walster, and W. G. Scott, *Equity: Theory and Research* (Boston: Allyn & Bacon, 1978); R. G. Lord and J. A. Hohenfeld, "Longitudinal Field Assessment of Equity Effects on the Performance of Major League Baseball Players," *Journal of Applied Psychology*, February 1979, pp. 19–26; J. E. Dittrich and M. R. Carrell, "Organizational Equity Perceptions, Employee Job Satisfaction, and Departmental Absence and Turnover Rates," *Organizational Behavior and Human Performance*, August 1979, pp. 29–40; and J. Greenberg, "Cognitive Reevaluation of Outcomes in Response to Underpayment Inequity," *Academy of Management Journal*, March 1989, pp. 174–184.

48. P. S. Goodman, "An Examination of Referents Used in the Evaluation of Pay," *Organizational Behavior and Human Performance*, October 1974, pp. 170–195; S. Ronen, "Equity Perception in Multiple Comparisons: A Field Study," *Human Relations*, April 1986, pp. 333–346; R. W. Scholl, E. A. Cooper, and J. F. McKenna, "Referent Selection in Determining Equity Perception: Differential Effects on Behavioral and Attitudinal Outcomes," *Personnel Psychology*, Spring 1987, pp. 113–127; and C. T. Kulik and M. L. Ambrose, "Personal and Situational Determinants of Referent Choice," *Academy of Management Review*, April 1992, pp. 212–237.

49. See, for example, R. C. Dailey and D. J. Kirk, "Distributive and Procedural Justice as Antecedents of Job Dissatisfaction and Intent to Turnover," *Human Relations*, March 1992, pp. 305–316; D. B. McFarlin and P. D. Sweeney, "Distributive and Procedural Justice as Predictors of Satisfaction with Personal and Organizational Outcomes," *Academy of Management Journal*, August 1992, pp. 626–637; M. A. Konovsky, "Understanding Procedural Justice and Its Impact on Business Organizations," *Journal of Management*, vol. 26, no. 3, 2000, pp. 489–511; J. A. Colquitt, "Does the Justice of One Interact With the Justice of Many? Reactions to Procedural Justice in Teams," *Journal of Applied Psychology*, August 2004, pp. 633–646; J. Brockner, "Why It's So Hard to be Fair," *Harvard Business Review*, March 2006, pp. 122–129; and B. M. Wiesenfeld, W. B. Swann, Jr., J. Brockner, and C. A. Bartel, "Is More Fairness Always Preferred: Self-Esteem Moderates Reactions to Procedural Justice," *Academy of Management Journal*, October 2007, pp. 1235–1253.

50. V. H. Vroom, *Work and Motivation* (New York: John Wiley, 1964).

51. See, for example, H. G. Heneman III and D. P. Schwab, "Evaluation of Research on Expectancy Theory Prediction of Employee Performance," *Psychological Bulletin*, July 1972, pp. 1–9; and L. Reinharth and M. Wahba, "Expectancy Theory as a Predictor of Work Motivation, Effort Expenditure, and Job Performance," *Academy of Management Journal*, September 1975, pp. 502–537.

52. See, for example, V. H. Vroom, "Organizational Choice: A Study of Pre- and Postdecision Processes," *Organizational Behavior and Human Performance*, April 1966, pp. 212–225; L. W. Porter and E. E. Lawler III, *Managerial Attitudes and Performance* (Homewood, IL: Richard D. Irwin, 1968); W. Van Eerde and H. Thierry, "Vroom's Expectancy Models and Work-Related Criteria: A Meta-Analysis," *Journal of Applied Psychology*, October 1996, pp. 575–586; and M. L. Ambrose and C. T. Kulik, "Old Friends, New Faces: Motivation Research in the 1990s."

53. See, for instance, M. Siegall, "The Simplistic Five: An Integrative Framework for Teaching Motivation," *The Organizational Behavior Teaching Review*, vol. 12, no. 4, 1987–1988, pp. 141–43.

54. I. Mount, "Building a Community—and Staff Loyalty," *CNNMoney.com*, June 5, 2009.

55. J. M. O'Brien, "Zappos Know How to Kick It," *Fortune*, February 2, 2009, pp. 54–60.

56. T. Barber, "Inspire Your Employees Now," *Bloomberg BusinessWeek Online*, May 18, 2010; D. Mattioli, "CEOs Welcome Recovery to Look After Staff," *Wall Street Journal*, April 5, 2010, p. B5; J. Sullivan, "How Do We Keep People Motivated Following Layoffs?" *Workforce Management Online*, March 2010; S. Crabtree, "How to Bolster Employees'

Confidence," *The Gallup Management Journal Online,* February 25, 2010; S. E. Needleman, "Business Owners Try to Motivate Employees," *Wall Street Journal,* January 14, 2010, p. B5; H. Mintzberg, "Rebuilding Companies as Communities," *Harvard Business Review,* July–August 2009, pp. 140–143; and R. Luss, "Engaging Employees Through Periods of Layoffs," *Towers Watson* [www.towerswatson.com], March 3, 2009.

57. J. W. Miller and D. Kesmodel, "Drinking on the Job Comes to a Head at Carlsberg," *Wall Street Journal,* April 10–11, 2010, pp. A1+; and Associated Press, "Carlsberg Workers Balk At Loss of On-the-Job Beer," *Wall Street Journal,* April 9, 2010, p. B2.

58. data points box based on K. Tyler, "Undeserved Promotions," *HR Magazine,* June 2012, p. 79; R. R. Hastings, "Survey Suggests Room for Improvement in Employee Recognition," www.shrm.org, April 13, 2012; S. Castellano, "The Trust Differentiator," *T&D,* March 2012, p. 20; R. Huggins and K. Gelles, "How Do Americans Think Rewards in the Workplace Are Distributed Today vs. Five Years Ago?" *USA Today,* January 10, 2012, p. 1A; S. Miller, "Salary Increases to Stay Consistent in 2012, with Focus on Variable Pay," www.shrm.org, September 6, 2011; C. Jones and R. Yu, "Incentive Travel Bounces Back," *USA Today,* September 6, 2011, p. 3B; J. Yang and P. Trap, "Does Your Manager Acknowledge and Appreciate You At Work?" *USA Today,* March 24, 2011, p. 1B; and A. R. Carey and K. Gelles, "Which of These Is Most Important About Your Job?" *USA Today,* January 31, 2011, p. 1A.

59. N. J. Adler with A. Gundersen, *International Dimensions of Organizational Behavior,* 5th ed. (Cincinnati, OH: South-Western College Pub., 2008).

60. G. Hofstede, "Motivation, Leadership and Organization: Do American Theories Apply Abroad?" *Organizational Dynamics,* Summer 1980, p. 55.

61. Ibid.

62. J. K. Giacobbe-Miller, D. J. Miller, and V. I. Victorov, "A Comparison of Russian and U.S. Pay Allocation Decisions, Distributive Justice Judgments and Productivity under Different Payment Conditions," *Personnel Psychology,* Spring 1998, pp. 137–163.

63. S. L. Mueller and L. D. Clarke, "Political-Economic Context and Sensitivity to Equity: Differences between the United States and the Transition Economies of Central and Eastern Europe," *Academy of Management Journal,* June 1998, pp. 319–329.

64. S. D. Sidle, "Building a Committed Global Workforce: Does What Employees Want Depend on Culture?" *Academy of Management Perspective,* February 2009, pp. 79–80; and G. A. Gelade, P. Dobson, and K. Auer, "Individualism, Masculinity, and the Sources of Organizational Commitment," *Journal of Cross-Cultural Psychology,* vol. 39, no. 5, 2008, pp. 599–617.

65. P. Brotherton, "Employee Loyalty Slipping Worldwide; Respect, Work-Life Balance Are Top Engagers," *T&D,* February 2012, p. 24.

66. I. Harpaz, "The Importance of Work Goals: An International Perspective," *Journal of International Business Studies,* First Quarter 1990, pp. 75–93.

67. G. E. Popp, H. J. Davis, and T. T. Herbert, "An International Study of Intrinsic Motivation Composition," *Management International Review,* January 1986, pp. 28–35.

68. R. W. Brislin, R. MacNab, R. Worthley, F. Kabigting Jr., and B. Zukis, "Evolving Perceptions of Japanese Workplace Motivation: An Employee-Manager Comparison,"

International Journal of Cross-Cultural Management, April 2005, pp. 87–104.

69. J. T. Marquez, "Tailor-Made Careers," *Workforce Management Online,* January 2010.

70. J. R. Billings and D. L. Sharpe, "Factors Influencing Flextime Usage Among Employed Married Women," *Consumer Interests Annual,* 1999, pp. 89–94; and I. Harpaz, "The Importance of Work Goals: An International Perspective," *Journal of International Business Studies,* First Quarter 1990, pp. 75–93.

71. N. Ramachandran, "New Paths At Work," *US News & World Report,* March 20, 2006, p. 47; S. Armour, "Generation Y: They've Arrived at Work With a New Attitude," *USA Today,* November 6, 2005, pp. B1+; and R. Kanfer and P. L. Ackerman, "Aging, Adult Development, and Work Motivation," *Academy of Management Review,* July 2004, pp. 440–458.

72. T. D. Golden and J. F. Veiga, "The Impact of Extent of Telecommuting on Job Satisfaction: Resolving Inconsistent Findings," *Journal of Management,* April 2005, pp. 301–318.

73. See, for instance, M. Alpert, "The Care and Feeding of Engineers," *Fortune,* September 21, 1992, pp. 86–95; G. Poole, "How to Manage Your Nerds," *Forbes ASAP,* December 1994, pp. 132–136; T. J. Allen and R. Katz, "Managing Technical Professionals and Organizations: Improving and Sustaining the Performance of Organizations, Project Teams, and Individual Contributors," *Sloan Management Review,* Summer 2002, pp. S4–S5; and S. R. Barley and G. Kunda, "Contracting: A New Form of Professional Practice," *Academy of Management Perspectives,* February 2006, pp. 45–66.

74. J. P. Broschak and A. Davis-Blake, "Mixing Standard Work and Nonstandard Deals: The Consequences of Heterogeneity in Employment Arrangements," *Academy of Management Journal,* April 2006, pp. 371–393; M. L. Kraimer, S. J. Wayne, R. C. Liden, and R. T. Sparrowe, "The Role of Job Security in Understanding the Relationship Between Employees' Perceptions of Temporary Workers and Employees' Performance," *Journal of Applied Psychology,* March 2005, pp. 389–398; and C. E. Connelly and D. G. Gallagher, "Emerging Trends in Contingent Work Research," *Journal of Management,* November 2004, pp. 959–983.

75. C. Haddad, "FedEx: Gaining on the Ground," *BusinessWeek,* December 16, 2002, pp. 126–128; and L. Landro, "To Get Doctors to Do Better, Health Plans Try Cash Bonuses," *Wall Street Journal,* September 17, 2004, pp. A1+.

76. K. E. Culp, "Playing Field Widens for Stack's Great Game," *Springfield, Missouri, News-Leader,* January 9, 2005, pp. 1A+.

77. K. Berman and J. Knight, "What Your Employees Don't Know Will Hurt You," *Wall Street Journal,* February 27, 2012, p. R4; J. Case, "The Open-Book Revolution," *Inc.,* June 1995, pp. 26–50; J. P. Schuster, J. Carpenter, and M. P. Kane, *The Power of Open-Book Management* (New York: John Wiley, 1996); J. Case, "Opening the Books," *Harvard Business Review,* March–April 1997, pp. 118–127; and D. Drickhamer, "Open Books to Elevate Performance," *Industry Week,* November 2002, p. 16.

78. J. Ruhlman and C. Siegman, "Boosting Engagement While Cutting Costs," *The Gallup Management Journal Online,* June 18, 2009.

79. D. McCann, "No Employee Left Behind," *CFO,* April 2012, p. 29.

80. P. Lencioni, "The No-Cost Way to Motivate," *BusinessWeek,* October 5, 2009, p. 84; and F. Luthans and A. D. Stajkovic,

"Provide Recognition for Performance Improvement," in E. A. Locke (ed.), *Principles of Organizational Behavior* (Oxford, England: Blackwell, 2000), pp. 166–180.

81. C. Huff, "Recognition That Resonates," *Workforce Management Online*, April 1, 2008.

82. D. Drickhamer, "Best Plant Winners: Nichols Foods Ltd.," *Industry Week*, October 1, 2001, pp. 17–19.

83. A. Bryant, "A Wall of Honor That's Built by Your Colleagues," *New York Times Online*, June 30, 2012.

84. M. Littman, "Best Bosses Tell All," *Working Woman*, October 2000, p. 54; and Hoover's Online [www.hoovers.com], June 20, 2003.

85. E. White, "Praise From Peers Goes a Long Way," *Wall Street Journal*, December 19, 2005, p. B3.

86. Ibid.

87. K. J. Dunham, "Amid Sinking Workplace Morale, Employers Turn to Recognition," *Wall Street Journal*, November 19, 2002, p. B8.

88. Cited in S. Caudron, "The Top 20 Ways to Motivate Employees," *Industry Week*, April 3, 1995, pp. 15–16. See also B. Nelson, "Try Praise," *Inc.*, September 1996, p. 115; and J. Wiscombe, "Rewards Get Results," *Workforce*, April 2002, pp. 42–48.

89. R. Flandez, "Vegetable Gardens Help Morale Grow," *Wall Street Journal Online*, August 18, 2009; "Pay Raise Alternatives = Motivated Employees," *Training*, July/August 2009, p. 11; D. Koeppel, "Strange Brew: Beer and Office Democracy," *CNNMoney.com*, June 9, 2009; and B. Brim and T. Simon, "Strengths on the Factory Floor," *The Gallup Management Journal Online*, March 10, 2009.

90. V. M. Barret, "Fight the Jerks," *Forbes*, July 2, 2007, pp. 52–54.

91. E. White, "The Best vs. the Rest," *Wall Street Journal*, January 30, 2006, pp. B1+.

92. R. K. Abbott, "Performance-Based Flex: A Tool for Managing Total Compensation Costs," *Compensation and Benefits Review*, March–April 1993, pp. 18–21; J. R. Schuster and P. K. Zingheim, "The New Variable Pay: Key Design Issues," *Compensation and Benefits Review*, March–April 1993, pp. 27–34; C. R. Williams and L. P. Livingstone, "Another Look at the Relationship between Performance and Voluntary Turnover," *Academy of Management Journal*, April 1994, pp. 269–298; A. M. Dickinson and K. L. Gillette, "A Comparison of the Effects of Two Individual Monetary Incentive Systems on Productivity: Piece Rate Pay versus Base Pay Plus Incentives," *Journal of Organizational Behavior Management*, Spring 1994, pp. 3–82; and C. B. Cadsby, F. Song, and F. Tapon, "Sorting and Incentive Effects of Pay for Performance: An Experimental Investigation," *Academy of Management Journal*, April 2007, pp. 387–405.

93. S. Miller, "Salary Increases to Stay Consistent in 2012, with Focus on Variable Pay."

94. "More Than 20 Percent of Japanese Firms Use Pay Systems Based on Performance," *Manpower Argus*, May 1998, p. 7; and E. Beauchesne, "Pay Bonuses Improve Productivity, Study Shows," *Vancouver Sun*, September 13, 2002, p. D5.

95. H. Rheem, "Performance Management Programs," *Harvard Business Review*, September–October 1996, pp. 8–9; G. Sprinkle, "The Effect of Incentive Contracts on Learning and Performance," *Accounting Review*, July 2000, pp. 299–326; and "Do Incentive Awards Work?" *HRFocus*, October 2000, pp. 1–3.

96. R. D. Banker, S. Y. Lee, G. Potter, and D. Srinivasan, "Contextual Analysis of Performance Impacts on Outcome-Based Incentive Compensation," *Academy of Management Journal*, August 1996, pp. 920–948.

97. B. S. Frey and M. Osterloh, "Stop Typing Pay to Performance," *Harvard Business Review*, January-February 2012, pp. 51-52.

98. T. Reason, "Why Bonus Plans Fail," *CFO*, January 2003, p. 53; and "Has Pay For Performance Had Its Day?" *The McKinsey Quarterly*, no. 4, 2002, accessed on Forbes Web site [www.forbes.com].

99. M. Spector and D. Mattioli, "Bonuses Sought for Kodak Brass," *Wall Street Journal*, July 12, 2012, p. B3; and M. J. De La Merced, "Eastman Kodak Files for Bankruptcy," *New York Times Online*, January 19, 2012.

100. "Patagonia CEO & President Casey Sheahan Talks Business, Conservation & Compassion," offyonder.com, February 13, 2012; T. Henneman, "Patagonia Fills Payroll with People Who Are Passionate," www.workforce.com, November 4, 2011; M. Hanel, "Surf's Up at Patagonia," *Bloomberg BusinessWeek*, September 5–September 11, 2011, pp. 88-89; J. Wang, "Patagonia, From the Ground Up," *Entrepreneur*, June 2010, pp. 26-32; and J. Laabs, "Mixing Business with Pleasure," *Workforce*, March 2000, pp. 80–85.

101. S. Miller, "Study: Flexible Schedule Reduce Conflict, Lower Turnover," www.shrm.org, April 13, 2011; K. M. Butler, "We Can ROWE Our Way to a Better Work Environment," *EBN. BenefitNews.com*, April 1, 2011, p. 8; P. Moen, E. L. Kelly, and R. Hill, "Does Enhancing Work-Time Control and Flexibility Reduce Turnover? A Naturally Occurring Experiment," *Social Problems*, February 2011, pp. 69–98; M. Conlin, "Is Optimism a Competitive Advantage?" *BusinessWeek*, August 24 & 31, 2009, pp. 52–53; "New ROLE," *Training*, June 2009, p. 4; C. Ressler and J. Thompson, *Why Work Sucks and How to Fix It* (New York: Penguin Group, 2008); J. Marquez, "Changing A Company's Culture, Not Just Its Schedules, Pays Off," *Workforce Management Online*, November 17, 2008; S. Brown, "Results Should Matter, Not Just Working Late," *USA Today*, June 16, 2008, p. 4B; and J. Thottam, "Reworking Work," *Time*, July 25, 2005, pp. 50–55.

CHAPTER 18

1. D. Archer and A. Cameron, "Collaborative Leadership," [www.trainingjournal.com], June 2012, pp. 35–38; J. Katzenbach, "The Steve Jobs Way," *Strategy+Business Online*, April 23, 2012; W. Isaacson, "The Real Leadership Lessons of Steve Jobs," *Harvard Business Review*, April 2012, pp. 93–102; R. Williams, "Why Steve Jobs Was Not A Leader," [www.psychologytoday.com], April 7, 2012; R. Foroohar, "The Leadership Lessons of Steve Jobs," business.time.com, February 16, 2012; R. Foroohar, "What Would Steve Do?" www.time.com, February 27, 2012; F. E. Allen, "Steve Jobs Broke Every Leadership Rule. Don't Try It," www.forbes.com, August 27, 2011; J. Nocera, "What Makes Steve Jobs Great," *New York Times Online*, August 26, 2011; A. Sharma and D. Grant, "The Stagecraft of Steve Jobs," *Strategy+Business Online*, June 10, 2011; and A. Lashinsky, "How Apple Works: Inside the World's Biggest Startup," tech.fortune.com, May 9, 2011.

2. Most leadership research has focused on the actions and responsibilities of managers and extrapolated the results to leaders and leadership in general.

3. "Study: Long Finger Equals Success," *Springfield, Missouri, News-Leader*, January 13, 2009, p. 4B.

4. See R. L. Schaumberg and F. J. Flynn, "Uneasy Lies the Head That Wears the Crown: The Link Between Guilt Proneness

and Leadership," *Journal of Personality and Social Psychology,* August 2012, pp. 327–342; D. S. Derue, J. D. Nahrgang, N. Wellman, and S. E. Humphrey, "Trait and Behavioral Theories of Leadership: An Integration and Meta-Analytic Test of Their Relative Validity," *Personnel Psychology,* Spring 2011, pp. 7–52; T. A. Judge, J. E. Bono, R. Ilies, and M. W. Gerhardt, "Personality and Leadership: A Qualitative and Quantitative Review," *Journal of Applied Psychology,* August 2002, pp. 765–780; and S. A. Kirkpatrick and E. A. Locke, "Leadership: Do Traits Matter?" *Academy of Management Executive,* May 1991, pp. 48–60.

5. "Ensemble Acting in Business," *New York Times Online,* June 7, 2009; and J. M. O'Brien, "Ousted Seagate CEO Provocative to the End," *CNNMoney.com,* January 13, 2009.

6. D. S. Derue, J. D. Nahrgang, N. Wellman, and S. E. Humphrey, "Trait and Behavioral Theories of Leadership: An Integration and Meta-Analytic Test of Their Relative Validity."

7. K. Lewin and R. Lippitt, "An Experimental Approach to the Study of Autocracy and Democracy: A Preliminary Note," *Sociometry,* vol. 1, 1938, pp. 292–300; K. Lewin, "Field Theory and Experiment in Social Psychology: Concepts and Methods," *American Journal of Sociology,* vol. 44, 1939, pp. 868–896; K. Lewin, L. Lippitt, and R. K. White, "Patterns of Aggressive Behavior in Experimentally Created Social Climates," *Journal of Social Psychology,* vol. 10, 1939, pp. 271–301; and L. Lippitt, "An Experimental Study of the Effect of Democratic and Authoritarian Group Atmospheres," *University of Iowa Studies in Child Welfare,* vol. 16, 1940, pp. 43–95.

8. B. M. Bass, *Stogdill's Handbook of Leadership* (New York: Free Press, 1981), pp. 289–299.

9. R. M. Stogdill and A. E. Coons (eds.), *Leader Behavior: Its Description and Measurement,* Research Monograph no. 88 (Columbus: Ohio State University, Bureau of Business Research, 1951). For an updated literature review of Ohio State research, see S. Kerr, C. A. Schriesheim, C. J. Murphy, and R. M. Stogdill, "Toward a Contingency Theory of Leadership Based upon the Consideration and Initiating Structure Literature," *Organizational Behavior and Human Performance,* August 1974, pp. 62–82; and B. M. Fisher, "Consideration and Initiating Structure and Their Relationships with Leader Effectiveness: A Meta-Analysis," in F. Hoy (ed.), *Proceedings* of the 48th Annual Academy of Management Conference, Anaheim, California, 1988, pp. 201–205.

10. R. Kahn and D. Katz, "Leadership Practices in Relation to Productivity and Morale," in D. Cartwright and A. Zander (eds.), *Group Dynamics: Research and Theory,* 2d ed. (Elmsford, NY: Row, Paterson, 1960).

11. R. R. Blake and J. S. Mouton, *The Managerial Grid III* (Houston: Gulf Publishing, 1984).

12. L. L. Larson, J. G. Hunt, and R. N. Osborn, "The Great Hi-Hi Leader Behavior Myth: A Lesson from Occam's Razor," *Academy of Management Journal,* December 1976, pp. 628–641; and P. C. Nystrom, "Managers and the Hi-Hi Leader Myth," *Academy of Management Journal,* June 1978, pp. 325–331.

13. W. G. Bennis, "The Seven Ages of the Leader," *Harvard Business Review,* January 2004, p. 52.

14. F. E. Fiedler, *A Theory of Leadership Effectiveness* (New York: McGraw-Hill, 1967).

15. R. Ayman, M. M. Chemers, and F. Fiedler, "The Contingency Model of Leadership Effectiveness: Its Levels of Analysis," *Leadership Quarterly,* Summer 1995, pp. 147–167; C. A. Schriesheim, B. J. Tepper, and L. A. Tetrault, "Least Preferred Coworker Score, Situational Control, and Leadership Effectiveness: A Meta-Analysis of Contingency Model Performance Predictions," *Journal of Applied Psychology,* August 1994, pp. 561–573; and L. H. Peters, D. D. Hartke, and J. T. Pholmann, "Fiedler's Contingency Theory of Leadership: An Application of the Meta-Analysis Procedures of Schmidt and Hunter," *Psychological Bulletin,* March 1985, pp. 274–285.

16. See E. H. Schein, *Organizational Psychology,* 3rd ed. (Upper Saddle River, NJ: Prentice Hall, 1980), pp. 116–117; and B. Kabanoff, "A Critique of Leader Match and Its Implications for Leadership Research," *Personnel Psychology,* Winter 1981, pp. 749–764.

17. P. Hersey and K. Blanchard, "So You Want to Know Your Leadership Style?" *Training and Development Journal,* February 1974, pp. 1–15; and P. Hersey and K. H. Blanchard, *Management of Organizational Behavior: Leading Human Resources,* 8th ed. (Englewood Cliffs, NJ: Prentice Hall, 2001).

18. See, for instance, E. G. Ralph, "Developing Managers' Effectiveness: A Model with Potential," *Journal of Management Inquiry,* June 2004, pp. 152–163; C. L. Graeff, "Evolution of Situational Leadership Theory: A Critical Review," *Leadership Quarterly,* vol. 8, no. 2, 1997, pp. 153–170; and C. F. Fernandez and R. P. Vecchio, "Situational Leadership Theory Revisited: A Test of an Across-Jobs Perspective," *Leadership Quarterly,* vol. 8, no. 1, 1997, pp. 67–84.

19. R. J. House, "A Path-Goal Theory of Leader Effectiveness," *Administrative Science Quarterly,* September 1971, pp. 321–338; R. J. House and T. R. Mitchell, "Path-Goal Theory of Leadership," *Journal of Contemporary Business,* Autumn 1974, p. 86; and R. J. House, "Path-Goal Theory of Leadership: Lessons, Legacy, and a Reformulated Theory," *Leadership Quarterly,* Fall 1996, pp. 323–352.

20. M. L. Dixon and L. K. Hart, "The Impact of Path-Goal Leadership Styles on Work Group Effectiveness and Turnover Intention," *Journal of Managerial Issues,* Spring 2010, pp. 52–69; J. C. Wofford and L. Z. Liska, "Path-Goal Theories of Leadership: A Meta-Analysis," *Journal of Management,* Winter 1993, pp. 857–876; and A. Sagie and M. Koslowsky, "Organizational Attitudes and Behaviors as a Function of Participation in Strategic and Tactical Change Decisions: An Application of Path-Goal Theory," *Journal of Organizational Behavior,* January 1994, pp. 37–47.

21. R. M. Dienesch and R. C. Liden, "Leader–Member Exchange Model of Leadership: A Critique and Further Development," *Academy of Management Review,* July 1986, pp. 618–634; G. B. Graen and M. Uhl-Bien, "Relationship-Based Approach to Leadership: Development of Leader–Member Exchange (LMX) Theory of Leadership Over 25 Years: Applying a Multi-Domain Perspective," *Leadership Quarterly,* Summer 1995, pp. 219–247; R. C. Liden, R. T. Sparrowe, and S. J. Wayne, "Leader–Member Exchange Theory: The Past and Potential for the Future," in G. R. Ferris (ed.), *Research in Personnel and Human Resource Management,* vol. 15 (Greenwich, CT: JAI Press, 1997), pp. 47–119; and C. P. Schriesheim, S. L. Castro, X. Zhou, and F. J. Yammarino, "The Folly of Theorizing 'A' but Testing 'B': A Selective Level-of-Analysis Review of the Field and a Detailed Leader–Member Exchange Illustration," *Leadership Quarterly,* Winter 2001, pp. 515–551.

22. R. C. Liden and G. Graen, "Generalizability of the Vertical Dyad Linkage Model of Leadership," *Academy of*

Management Journal, September 1980, pp. 451–465; R. C. Liden, S. J. Wayne, and D. Stilwell, "A Longitudinal Study of the Early Development of Leader–Member Exchanges," *Journal of Applied Psychology,* August 1993, pp. 662–674; S. J. Wayne, L. J. Shore, W. H. Bommer, and L. E. Tetrick, "The Role of Fair Treatment and Rewards in Perceptions of Organizational Support and Leader–Member Exchange," *Journal of Applied Psychology,* June 2002, pp. 590–598; and S. S. Masterson, K. Lewis, and B. M. Goldman, "Integrating Justice and Social Exchange: The Differing Effects of Fair Procedures and Treatment on Work Relationships," *Academy of Management Journal,* August 2000, pp. 738–748.

23. D. Duchon, S. G. Green, and T. D. Taber, "Vertical Dyad Linkage: A Longitudinal Assessment of Antecedents, Measures, and Consequences," *Journal of Applied Psychology,* February 1986, pp. 56–60; R. C. Liden, S. J. Wayne, and D. Stilwell, "A Longitudinal Study of the Early Development of Leader–Member Exchanges"; M. Uhl-Bien, "Relationship Development as a Key Ingredient for Leadership Development," in S. E. Murphy and R. E. Riggio (eds.), *Future of Leadership Development* (Mahwah, NJ: Lawrence Erlbaum, 2003), pp. 129–147; R. Vecchio and D. M. Brazil, "Leadership and Sex-Similarity: A Comparison in a Military Setting," *Personnel Psychology,* vol. 60, 2007, pp. 303–335; and V. L. Goodwin, W. M. Bowler, and J. L. Whittington, "A Social Network Perspective on LMX Relationships: Accounting for the Instrumental Value of Leader and Follower Networks," *Journal of Management,* August 2009, pp. 954–980.

24. See, for instance, C. R. Gerstner and D. V. Day, "Meta-analytic Review of Leader–Member Exchange Theory: Correlates and Construct Issues," *Journal of Applied Psychology,* December 1997, pp. 827–844; R. Ilies, J. D. Nahrgang, and F. P. Morgerson, "Leader–Member Exchange and Citizenship Behaviors: A Meta-analysis," *Journal of Applied Psychology,* January 2007, pp. 269–277; Z. Chen, W. Lam, and J. A. Zhong, "Leader–Member Exchange and Member Performance: A New Look at Individual-Level Negative Feedback-Seeking Behavior and Team-Level Empowerment Culture," *Journal of Applied Psychology,* January 2007, pp. 202–212; and Z. Zhang, M. Wang, and J. Shi, "Leader-Follower Congruence in Proactive Personality and Work Outcomes: The Mediating Role of Leader-Member Exchange," *Academy of Management Journal,* February 2012, pp. 111–130.

25. Leader Who Made a Difference box based on D. Roberts, "Dynamic Duos," *Fortune,* June 11, 2012, pp. 24-25; R. Sidel, "Banga to Be MasterCard's Protector," *Wall Street Journal,* May 29–30, 2010, pp. B1+; A. Saha-Bubna and M. Jarzemsky, "MasterCard President Is Named CEO," *Wall Street Journal,* April 13, 2010, p. C3; "Why Banga Quit Citi," *Euromoney,* July 2009, p. 41; and E. Wilson, "Banga Demolishes Citi's Asia-Pac Silos," *Euromoney,* May 2009, p. 49.

26. B. M. Bass and R. E. Riggio, *Transformational Leadership,* 2d ed. (Mahwah, NJ: Lawrence Erlbaum Associates, Inc., 2006), p. 3.

27. B. M. Bass, "Leadership: Good, Better, Best," *Organizational Dynamics,* Winter 1985, pp. 26–40; and J. Seltzer and B. M. Bass, "Transformational Leadership: Beyond Initiation and Consideration," *Journal of Management,* December 1990, pp. 693–703.

28. B. J. Avolio and B. M. Bass, "Transformational Leadership, Charisma, and Beyond." Working paper, School of Management, State University of New York, Binghamton, 1985, p. 14.

29. B. J. Hoffman, B. H. Bynum, R. F. Piccolo, and A. W. Sutton, "Person-Organization Value Congruence: How Transformational Leaders Influence Work Group Effectiveness," *Academy of Management Journal,* August 2011, pp. 779–796; G. Wang, In-Sue Oh, S. H. Courtright, and A. E. Colbert, "Transformational Leadership and Performance Across Criteria and Levels: A Meta-Analytic Review of 25 Years of Research," *Group & Organization Management,* 36, no. 2, 2011, pp. 223–270; M. Tims, A. B. Bakker, and D. Xanthopoulou, "Do Transformational Leaders Enhance Their Followers' Daily Work Engagement?" *The Leadership Quarterly,* February 2011, pp. 121–131; S. J. Peterson and F. O. Walumba, "CEO Positive Psychological Traits, Transformational Leadership, and Firm Performance in High-Technology Start-up and Established Firms," *Journal of Management,* April 2009, pp. 348–368; R. S. Rubin, D. C. Munz, and W. H. Bommer, "Leading from Within: The Effects of Emotion Recognition and Personality on Transformational Leadership Behavior," *Academy of Management Journal,* October 2005, pp. 845–858; T. A. Judge and J. E. Bono, "Five-Factor Model of Personality and Transformational Leadership," *Journal of Applied Psychology,* October 2000, pp. 751–765; B. M. Bass and B. J. Avolio, "Developing Transformational Leadership: 1992 and Beyond," *Journal of European Industrial Training,* January 1990, p. 23; and J. J. Hater and B. M. Bass, "Supervisors' Evaluation and Subordinates' Perceptions of Transformational and Transactional Leadership," *Journal of Applied Psychology,* November 1988, pp. 695–702.

30. Y. Ling, Z. Simsek, M. H. Lubatkin, and J. F. Veiga, "Transformational Leadership's Role in Promoting Corporate Entrepreneurship: Examining the CEO-TMT Interface," *Academy of Management Journal,* June 2008, pp. 557–576; A. E. Colbert, A. L. Kristof-Brown, B. H. Bradley, and M. R. Barrick, "CEO Transformational Leadership: The Role of Goal Importance Congruence in Top Management Teams," *Academy of Management Journal,* February 2008, pp. 81–96; R. F. Piccolo and J. A. Colquitt, "Transformational Leadership and Job Behaviors: The Mediating Role of Core Job Characteristics," *Academy of Management Journal,* April 2006, pp. 327–340; O. Epitropaki and R. Martin, "From Ideal to Real: A Longitudinal Study of the Role of Implicit Leadership Theories on Leader–Member Exchanges and Employee Outcomes," *Journal of Applied Psychology,* July 2005, pp. 659–676; J. E. Bono and T. A. Judge, "Self-Concordance at Work: Toward Understanding the Motivational Effects of Transformational Leaders," *Academy of Management Journal,* October 2003, pp. 554–571; T. Dvir, D. Eden, B. J. Avolio, and B. Shamir, "Impact of Transformational Leadership on Follower Development and Performance: A Field Experiment," *Academy of Management Journal,* August 2002, pp. 735–744; N. Sivasubramaniam, W. D. Murry, B. J. Avolio, and D. I. Jung, "A Longitudinal Model of the Effects of Team Leadership and Group Potency on Group Performance," *Group and Organization Management,* March 2002, pp. 66–96; J. M. Howell and B. J. Avolio, "Transformational Leadership, Transactional Leadership, Locus of Control, and Support for Innovation: Key Predictors of Consolidated-Business-Unit Performance," *Journal of Applied Psychology,* December 1993, pp. 891–911; R. T. Keller, "Transformational Leadership and the Performance of Research and Development Project Groups,"

Journal of Management, September 1992, pp. 489–501; and Bass and Avolio, "Developing Transformational Leadership."

31. F. Vogelstein, "Mighty Amazon," *Fortune,* May 26, 2003, pp. 60–74.

32. F. Walter and H. Bruch, "An Affective Events Model of Charismatic Leadership Behavior: A Review, Theoretical Integration, and Research Agenda," *Journal of Management,* December 2009, pp. 1428-1452; A. Pentland, "We Can Measure the Power of Charisma," *Harvard Business Review,* January–February 2010, pp. 34–35; J. M. Crant and T. S. Bateman, "Charismatic Leadership Viewed From Above: The Impact of Proactive Personality," *Journal of Organizational Behavior*, February 2000, pp. 63–75; G. Yukl and J. M. Howell, "Organizational and Contextual Influences on the Emergence and Effectiveness of Charismatic Leadership," *Leadership Quarterly*, Summer 1999, pp. 257–283; and J. A. Conger and R. N. Kanungo, "Behavioral Dimensions of Charismatic Leadership," in J. A. Conger, R. N. Kanungo and Associates, *Charismatic Leadership* (San Francisco: Jossey-Bass, 1988), pp. 78–97.

33. J. A. Conger and R. N. Kanungo, *Charismatic Leadership in Organizations* (Thousand Oaks, CA: Sage, 1998).

34. F. Walter and H. Bruch, "An Affective Events Model of Charismatic Leadership Behavior: A Review, Theoretical Investigation, and Research Agenda," *Journal of Management,* December 2009, pp. 1428–1452; K. S. Groves, "Linking Leader Skills, Follower Attitudes, and Contextual Variables via An Integrated Model of Charismatic Leadership," *Journal of Management,* April 2005, pp. 255–277; J. J. Sosik, " The Role of Personal Values in the Charismatic Leadership of Corporate Managers: A Model and Preliminary Field Study," *Leadership Quarterly,* April 2005, pp. 221–244; A. H. B. deHoogh, D. N. den Hartog, P. L. Koopman, H. Thierry, P. T. van den Berg, J. G. van der Weide, and C. P. M. Wilderom, "Leader Motives, Charismatic Leadership, and Subordinates' Work Attitudes in the Profit and Voluntary Sector," *Leadership Quarterly,* February 2005, pp. 17–38; J. M. Howell and B. Shamir, "The Role of Followers in the Charismatic Leadership Process: Relationships and Their Consequences," *Academy of Management Review,* January 2005, pp. 96–112; J. Paul, D. L. Costley, J. P. Howell, P. W. Dorfman, and D. Trafimow, "The Effects of Charismatic Leadership on Followers' Self-Concept Accessibility," *Journal of Applied Social Psychology,* September 2001, pp. 1821–1844; J. A. Conger, R. N. Kanungo, and S. T. Menon, "Charismatic Leadership and Follower Effects," *Journal of Organizational Behavior,* vol. 21, 2000, pp. 747–767; R. W. Rowden, "The Relationship Between Charismatic Leadership Behaviors and Organizational Commitment," *Leadership & Organization Development Journal,* January 2000, pp. 30–35; G. P. Shea and C. M. Howell, "Charismatic Leadership and Task Feedback: A Laboratory Study of Their Effects on Self-Efficacy," *Leadership Quarterly*, Fall 1999, pp. 375–396; S. A. Kirkpatrick and E. A. Locke, "Direct and Indirect Effects of Three Core Charismatic Leadership Components on Performance and Attitudes," *Journal of Applied Psychology,* February 1996, pp. 36–51; D. A. Waldman, B. M. Bass, and F. J. Yammarino, "Adding to Contingent-Reward Behavior: The Augmenting Effect of Charismatic Leadership," *Group & Organization Studies*, December 1990, pp. 381–394; and R. J. House, J. Woycke, and E. M. Fodor, "Charismatic and Noncharismatic Leaders: Differences in Behavior and Effectiveness," in Conger and Kanungo, *Charismatic Leadership*, pp. 103–104.

35. B. R. Agle, N. J. Nagarajan, J. A. Sonnenfeld, and D. Srinivasan, "Does CEO Charisma Matter? An Empirical Analysis of the Relationships Among Organizational Performance, Environmental Uncertainty, and Top Management Team Perceptions of CEO Charisma," *Academy of Management Journal,* February 2006, pp. 161–174.

36. J. Antonakis, M. Fenley, and S. Liechti, "Can Charisma Be Taught? Tests of Two Interventions," *Academy of Management Learning & Education,* September 2011, pp. 374-396; R. Birchfield, "Creating Charismatic Leaders," *Management*, June 2000, pp. 30–31; S. Caudron, "Growing Charisma," *Industry Week*, May 4, 1998, pp. 54–55; and J. A. Conger and R. N. Kanungo, "Training Charismatic Leadership: A Risky and Critical Task," in Conger and Kanungo, *Charismatic Leadership*, pp. 309–323.

37. J. G. Hunt, K. B. Boal, and G. E. Dodge, "The Effects of Visionary and Crisis-Responsive Charisma on Followers: An Experimental Examination," *Leadership Quarterly*, Fall 1999, pp. 423–448; R. J. House and R. N. Aditya, "The Social Scientific Study of Leadership: Quo Vadis?" *Journal of Management*, vol. 23, no. 3, 1997, pp. 316–323; and R. J. House, "A 1976 Theory of Charismatic Leadership."

38. This definition is based on M. Sashkin, "The Visionary Leader," in Conger and Kanungo et al., *Charismatic Leadership*, pp. 124–125; B. Nanus, *Visionary Leadership* (New York: Free Press, 1992), p. 8; N. H. Snyder and M. Graves, "Leadership and Vision," *Business Horizons*, January–February 1994, p. 1; and J. R. Lucas, "Anatomy of a Vision Statement," *Management Review,* February 1998, pp. 22–26.

39. Nanus, *Visionary Leadership*, p. 8.

40. S. Caminiti, "What Team Leaders Need to Know," *Fortune*, February 20, 1995, pp. 93–100.

41. data points box based on D. Meinert, "Executive Briefing," *HRMagazine,* May 2012, p. 18; J. Yang and S. Ward, "Is Involvement in Office Politics Necessary To Get Ahead?" *USA Today,* May 2, 2012, p. 1B; "The Simple List," *Realsimple.com,* October 2011, p. 10; J. Yang and P. Trap, "I'm Concerned Most About My Manager," *USA Today,* April 25, 2011, p. 1B; J. Yang and A. Gonzalez, "Bossy Bosses," *USA Today,* November 3, 2010, p. 1B.

42. Ibid., p. 93.

43. Ibid., p. 100.

44. S. B. Sitkin and J. R. Hackman, "Developing Team Leadership: An Interview with Coach Mike Krzyzewski," *Academy of Management Learning and Education,* September 2011, pp. 494–501; and N. Steckler and N. Fondas, "Building Team Leader Effectiveness: A Diagnostic Tool," *Organizational Dynamics*, Winter 1995, p. 20.

45. R. S. Wellins, W. C. Byham, and G. R. Dixon, *Inside Teams* (San Francisco: Jossey-Bass, 1994), p. 318.

46. Steckler and Fondas, "Building Team Leader Effectiveness," p. 21.

47. G. Colvin, "The FedEx Edge," *Fortune,* April 3, 2006, pp. 77–84.

48. See J. R. P. French Jr. and B. Raven, "The Bases of Social Power," in D. Cartwright and A. F. Zander (eds.), *Group Dynamics: Research and Theory* (New York: Harper & Row, 1960), pp. 607–623; P. M. Podsakoff and C. A. Schriesheim, "Field Studies of French and Raven's Bases of Power: Critique, Reanalysis, and Suggestions for Future Research," *Psychological Bulletin,* May 1985, pp. 387–411; R. K. Shukla, "Influence of Power Bases in Organizational Decision Making: A Contingency Model,"

Decision Sciences, July 1982, pp. 450–470; D. E. Frost and A. J. Stahelski, "The Systematic Measurement of French and Raven's Bases of Social Power in Workgroups," *Journal of Applied Social Psychology*, April 1988, pp. 375–389; and T. R. Hinkin and C. A. Schriesheim, "Development and Application of New Scales to Measure the French and Raven (1959) Bases of Social Power," *Journal of Applied Psychology*, August 1989, pp. 561–567.

49. C. Leahey, "Building Trust Inside Your Company," *Fortune*, March 19, 2012, p. 35.

50. J. M. Kouzes and B. Z. Posner, *Credibility: How Leaders Gain and Lose It, and Why People Demand It* (San Francisco: Jossey-Bass, 1993), p. 14.

51. Based on F. D. Schoorman, R. C. Mayer, and J. H. Davis, "An Integrative Model of Organizational Trust: Past, Present, and Future," *Academy of Management Review*, April 2007, pp. 344–354; G. M. Spreitzer and A. K. Mishra, "Giving Up Control Without Losing Control," *Group & Organization Management*, June 1999, pp. 155–187; R. C. Mayer, J. H. Davis, and F. D. Schoorman, "An Integrative Model of Organizational Trust," *Academy of Management Review*, July 1995, p. 712; and L. T. Hosmer, "Trust: The Connecting Link between Organizational Theory and Philosophical Ethics," *Academy of Management Review*, April 1995, p. 393.

52. P. L. Schindler and C. C. Thomas, "The Structure of Interpersonal Trust in the Workplace," *Psychological Reports*, October 1993, pp. 563–573.

53. H. H. Tan and C. S. F. Tan, "Toward the Differentiation of Trust in Supervisor and Trust in Organization," *Genetic, Social, and General Psychology Monographs*, May 2000, pp. 241–260.

54. H. H. Brower, S. W. Lester, M. A. Korsgaard, and B. R. Dineen, "A Closer Look at Trust Between Managers and Subordinates: Understanding the Effects of Both Trusting and Being Trusted on Subordinate Outcomes," *Journal of Management*, April 2009, pp. 327–347; R. C. Mayer and M. B. Gavin, "Trust in Management and Performance: Who Minds the Shop While the Employees Watch the Boss?" *Academy of Management Journal*, October 2005, pp. 874–888; and K. T. Dirks and D. L. Ferrin, "Trust in Leadership: Meta-Analytic Findings and Implications for Research and Practice," *Journal of Applied Psychology*, August 2002, pp. 611–628.

55. See, for example, Dirks and Ferrin, "Trust in Leadership: Meta-Analytic Findings and Implications for Research and Practice"; J. K. Butler Jr., "Toward Understanding and Measuring Conditions of Trust: Evolution of a Conditions of Trust Inventory," *Journal of Management*, September 1991, pp. 643–663; and F. Bartolome, "Nobody Trusts the Boss Completely—Now What?" *Harvard Business Review*, March–April 1989, pp. 135–142.

56. P. H. Kim, K. T. Dirks, and C. D. Cooper, "The Repair of Trust: A Dynamic Bilateral Perspective and Multilevel Conceptualization," *Academy of Management Review*, July 2009, pp. 401–422; R. Zemke, "The Confidence Crisis," *Training*, June 2004, pp. 22–30; J. A. Byrne, "Restoring Trust in Corporate America," *BusinessWeek*, June 24, 2002, pp. 30–35; S. Armour, "Employees' New Motto: Trust No One," *USA Today*, February 5, 2002, p. 1B; J. Scott, "Once Bitten, Twice Shy: A World of Eroding Trust," *New York Times*, April 21, 2002, p. WK5; J. Brockner, P. A. Siegel, J. P. Daly, T. Tyler, and C. Martin, "When Trust Matters: The Moderating Effect of Outcome Favorability," *Administrative Science Quarterly*, September 1997, p. 558; and J. Brockner, P. A. Siegel, J. P.

Daly, T. Tyler, and C. Martin, "When Trust Matters: The Moderating Effect of Outcome Favorability," *Administrative Science Quarterly*, September 1997, p. 558.

57. "Weathering the Storm: A Study of Employee Attitudes and Opinions," *WorkUSA 2002 Study*, Watson Wyatt [www.watsonwyatt.com].

58. T. Vinas, "DuPont: Safety Starts at the Top," *Industry Week*, July 2002, p. 55.

59. A. Srivastava, K. M. Bartol, and E. A. Locke, "Empowering Leadership in Management Teams: Effects on Knowledge Sharing, Efficacy, and Performance," *Academy of Management Journal*, December 2006, pp. 1239–1251; P. K. Mills and G. R. Ungson, "Reassessing the Limits of Structural Empowerment: Organizational Constitution and Trust as Controls," *Academy of Management Review*, January 2003, pp. 143–153; W. A. Rudolph and M. Sashkin, "Can Organizational Empowerment Work in Multinational Settings?" *Academy of Management Executive*, February 2002, pp. 102–115; C. Gomez and B. Rosen, "The Leader–Member Link Between Managerial Trust and Employee Empowerment," *Group & Organization Management*, March 2001, pp. 53–69; C. Robert and T. M. Probst, "Empowerment and Continuous Improvement in the United States, Mexico, Poland, and India," *Journal of Applied Psychology*, October 2000, pp. 643–658; R. C. Herrenkohl, G. T. Judson, and J. A. Heffner, "Defining and Measuring Employee Empowerment," *Journal of Applied Behavioral Science*, September 1999, p. 373; R. C. Ford and M. D. Fottler, "Empowerment: A Matter of Degree," *Academy of Management Executive*, August 1995, pp. 21–31; and W. A. Rudolph, "Navigating the Journey to Empowerment," *Organizational Dynamics*, Spring 1995, pp. 19–32.

60. T. A. Stewart, "Just Think: No Permission Needed," *Fortune*, January 8, 2001, pp. 190–192.

61. M. Elliott, "Who Needs Charisma?" *Time*, July 20, 2009, pp. 35–38.

62. F. W. Swierczek, "Leadership and Culture: Comparing Asian Managers," *Leadership & Organization Development Journal*, December 1991, pp. 3–10.

63. House, "Leadership in the Twenty-First Century," p. 443; M. F. Peterson and J. G. Hunt, "International Perspectives on International Leadership," *Leadership Quarterly*, Fall 1997, pp. 203–231; and J. R. Schermerhorn and M. H. Bond, "Cross-Cultural Leadership in Collectivism and High Power Distance Settings," *Leadership & Organization Development Journal*, vol. 18, issue 4/5, 1997, pp. 187–193.

64. R. J. House, P. J. Hanges, S. A. Ruiz-Quintanilla, P. W. Dorfman, and Associates, "Culture Specific and Cross-Culturally Generalizable Implicit Leadership Theories: Are the Attributes of Charismatic/Transformational Leadership Universally Endorsed?" *Leadership Quarterly*, Summer 1999, pp. 219–256; and D. E. Carl and M. Javidan, "Universality of Charismatic Leadership: A Multi-Nation Study," paper presented at the National Academy of Management Conference, Washington, DC, August 2001.

65. D. E. Carl and M. Javidan, "Universality of Charismatic Leadership, p. 29.

66. See, for instance, R. Lofthouse, "Herding the Cats," *EuroBusiness*, February 2001, pp. 64–65; and M. Delahoussaye, "Leadership in the 21st Century," *Training*, September 2001, pp. 60–72.

67. See, for example, D. S. DeRue and N. Wellman, "Developing Leaders via Experience: The Role of Developmental Challenge, Learning Organization, and Feedback Availability,"

Journal of Applied Psychology, July 2009, pp. 859–875;
A. A. Vicere, "Executive Education: The Leading Edge," *Organizational Dynamics,* Autumn 1996, pp. 67–81; J. Barling, T. Weber, and E. K. Kelloway, "Effects of Transformational Leadership Training on Attitudinal and Financial Outcomes: A Field Experiment," *Journal of Applied Psychology,* December 1996, pp. 827–832; and D. V. Day, "Leadership Development: A Review in Context," *Leadership Quarterly,* Winter 2000, pp. 581–613.

68. K. Y. Chan and F. Drasgow, "Toward a Theory of Individual Differences and Leadership: Understanding the Motivation to Lead," *Journal of Applied Psychology,* June 2001, pp. 481–498.

69. M. Sashkin, "The Visionary Leader," in J. A. Conger, R. N. Kanungo and Associates (eds.), *Charismatic Leadership* (San Francisco: Jossey-Bass, 1988), p. 150.

70. S. Kerr and J. M. Jermier, "Substitutes for Leadership: Their Meaning and Measurement," *Organizational Behavior and Human Performance*, December 1978, pp. 375–403; J. P. Howell, P. W. Dorfman, and S. Kerr, "Leadership and Substitutes for Leadership," *Journal of Applied Behavioral Science* 22, No. 1 (1986), pp. 29–46; J. P. Howell, D. E. Bowen, P. W. Dorfman, S. Kerr, and P. M. Podsakoff, "Substitutes for Leadership: Effective Alternatives to Ineffective Leadership," *Organizational Dynamics*, Summer 1990, pp. 21–38; and P. M. Podsakoff, B. P. Niehoff, S. B. MacKenzie, and M. L. Williams, "Do Substitutes for Leadership Really Substitute for Leadership? An Empirical Examination of Kerr and Jermier's Situational Leadership Model," *Organizational Behavior and Human Decision Processes*, February 1993, pp. 1–44.

71. S. Adams, "The World's Best Companies for Leadership," *Forbes.com,* May 2, 2012; J. R. Hagerty and J. S. Lublin, "3M Taps 33-Year Veteran and Operating Chief as CEO," *Wall Street Journal,* February 9, 2012, p. B3; R. M. Murphy, "How Do Great Companies Groom Talent?" [management.fortune.cnn.com], November 3, 2011; J. R. Hagerty and B. Tita, "3M Works on Succession Plan," *Wall Street Journal,* December 21, 2010, p. B2; A. Bernasek, "World's Most Admired Companies," *Fortune,* March 22, 2010, pp. 121+; "Selected Results from Best Companies for Leadership Survey," *Bloomberg BusinessWeek Online,* February 16, 2010; J. Kerr and R. Albright, "Finding and Cultivating Finishers," *Leadership Excellence,* July 2009, p. 20; D. Jones, "3M CEO Emphasizes Importance of Leaders," *USA Today,* May 18, 2009, p. 4B; G. Colvin, "World's Most Admired Companies 2009," *Fortune,* March 16, 2009, pp. 75+; and M. C. Mankins and R. Steele, "Turning Great Strategy into Great Performance," *Harvard Business Review,* July–August 2005, pp. 64–72.

72. Bharat Vaid, "Book Review: Maverick!" *Global Management Review,* August 2011, pp. 96–97; R. Spitzer, "Take Responsibility: How the Best Organizations in the World Survive in a Down Economy and Thrive When Times Are Good," *The Journal for Quality & Participation,* October 2010, p. 16; M. Skapinker, "The American Global Dream," *Foreign Policy,* September/October 2010, pp. 157–159; J. Krohe, Jr., "If You Love Your People, Set Them Free," *Conference Board Review,* Summer 2010, pp. 28–37; L. M. Fisher, "Ricardo Semler Won't Take Control," *Strategy and Business,* Winter 2005 pp. 78–88; R. Semler, *Maverick: The Success Story Behind the World's Most Unusual Workplace* (New York: Grand Central Publishing, 2005); R. Semler, *The Seven-Day Weekend: Changing the Way Work Works* (New York: Penguin Group, 2004); A. J. Vogl, "The Anti-CEO," *Across the Board,* May/June 2004, pp. 30–36; G. Colvin, "The Anti-Control Freak," *Fortune,* November 26, 2001, p. 22; and R. Semler, "Managing Without Managers," *Harvard Business Review,* September/October 1989, pp. 76–84.

APPENDIX—MANAGING ENTREPRENEURIAL VENTURES

1. R. Schmidt and P. O'Connor, "Def Jam's Founder Out-Lobbies Big Banks," *Bloomberg BusinessWeek,* June 28, 2010, pp. 21–22; R. A. Smith, "From Phat to Skinny," *Wall Street Journal,* May 1, 2010, p. W7; J. Dean, "The Endless Flow of Russell Simmons," *Entrepreneur,* September 2009, pp. 24–28; S. Page, "Top 25 Influential People," *USA Today,* September 4, 2007, p. A10; S. Berfield, "Hip-Hop Nation," *BusinessWeek,* June 13, 2005, p. 12; R. Kurtz, "Russell Simmons, Rush Communications," *Inc.,* April 2004, p. 137; J. Reingold, "Rush Hour," *Fast Company,* November 2003, pp. 68–80; S. Berfield, "The CEO of Hip Hop," *BusinessWeek,* October 27, 2003, pp. 90–98; J. L. Roberts, "Beyond Definition," *Newsweek,* July 28, 2003, pp. 40–43; and C. Dugas, "Hip-Hop Legend Far Surpassed Financial Goals," *USA Today,* May 15, 2003, p. 6B.

2. P. Burrows, "Ringing Off the Hook in China," *BusinessWeek,* June 9, 2003, pp. 80–82.

3. J. W. Carland, F. Hoy, W. R. Boulton, and J. C. Carland, "Differentiating Entrepreneurs from Small Business Owners: A Conceptualization," *Academy of Management Review,* vol. 9, no. 2, 1984, pp. 354–359.

4. J. McDowell, "Small Business Continues to Drive U.S. Economy," Office of Advocacy, U.S. Small Business Administration [www.sba.gov/advo/press], October 3, 2005.

5. P. Almeida and B. Kogut, "The Exploration of Technological Diversity and Geographic Localization in Innovation: Start-Up Firms in the Semiconductor Industry," *Small Business Economics,* vol. 9, no. 1, 1997, pp. 21–31.

6. R. J. Arend, "Emergence of Entrepreneurs Following Exogenous Technological Change," *Strategic Management Journal,* vol. 20, no. 1, 1999, pp. 31–47.

7. U.S. Small Business Administration Office of Advocacy, "Frequently Asked Questions," *Small Business Administration* [www.sba.gov], April 16. 2007.

8. "The Small Business Economy: A Report to the President," U.S. Small Business Administration, Office of Advocacy [www.sba.gov/advo/].

9. Press release, "Where Do Jobs Come From? New Analysis of Job Gains and Losses from the Office of Advocacy," U.S. Small Business Administration, Office of Advocacy [www.sba.gov/advo/].

10. N. Bosma, J. Levie et al., "Global Entrepreneurship Monitor: 2009 Executive Report" [www.gemconsortium.org], pp. 5–8.

11. W. Royal, "Real Expectations," *Industry Week,* September 4, 2000, pp. 31–34.

12. "Creating a Sustainable Business Among South Africa's Poor One Bite at a Time," *Knowledge @ Wharton* [http://knowledge.wharton.upenn.edu], July 13, 2006.

13. T. Purdum, "25 Growing Companies," *Industry Week,* November 20, 2000, p. 82.

14. C. Sandlund, "Trust Is a Must," *Entrepreneur,* October 2002, pp. 70–75.

15. B. I. Koerner, "Cereal in the Bowl, Not on the Floor," *New York Times Online* [www.nytimes.com], June 18, 2006.

16. "Facts for Features," *U.S. Census Bureau Newsroom*, January 3, 2006; and M. Arndt, "Zimmer: Growing Older Gracefully," *BusinessWeek*, June 9, 2003, pp. 82–84.

17. G. B. Knight, "How Wall Street Whiz Found a Niche Selling Books on the Internet," *Wall Street Journal*, May 15, 1996, pp. A1+.

18. N. F. Krueger, Jr., "The Cognitive Infrastructure of Opportunity Emergence," *Entrepreneurship Theory and Practice*, Spring 2000, p. 6.

19. D. P. Forbes, "Managerial Determinants of Decision Speed in New Ventures," *Strategic Management Journal*, April 2005, pp. 355–366.

20. P. Drucker, *Innovation and Entrepreneurship* (New York: Harper & Row, 1985).

21. G. Bounds, "Hybrids Fuel Agency's Fast Ride," *Wall Street Journal*, July 11, 2006, pp. B1+.

22. B. Bergstein, The Associated Press, "RSA Security Finds Future in Threat of Identity Theft," *Springfield News-Leader*, August 22, 2005, p. 5B.

23. B. McClean, "This Entrepreneur Is Changing Underwear," *Fortune*, September 18, 2000, p. 60.

24. S. Schubert, "The Ultimate Music Buff," *Business 2.0*, March 2006, p. 64.

25. Latest figures on registered users from Hoover's Online [www.hoovers.com], July 13, 2008; and A. Cohen, "eBay's Bid to Conquer All," *Time*, February 5, 2001, pp. 48–51.

26. S. McFarland, "Cambodia's Internet Service Is in Kids' Hands," *Wall Street Journal*, May 15, 2000, p. A9A.

27. Information on Whole Foods Market from Hoovers Online [www.hoovers.com], July 13, 2008.

28. D. Fahmy, "Making Necessities Stylish and Getting a Higher Price," *New York Times Online* [www.nytimes.com], March 9, 2006.

29. A. Eisenberg, "What's Next: New Fabrics Can Keep Wearers Healthy and Smelling Good," *New York Times*, February 3, 2000, pp. D1+.

30. A. Morse, "An Entrepreneur Finds Tokyo Shares Her Passion for Bagels," *Wall Street Journal*, October 18, 2005, pp. B1+.

31. S. Greco, "The Start-Up Years," *Inc. 500*, October 21, 1997, p. 57.

32. T. Stevens, "Master of His Universe," *Industry Week*, January 15, 2001, pp. 76–80; and R. Grover, "Back from a Black Hole," *BusinessWeek*, May 29, 2000, p. 186.

33. E. Neuborne, "Hey, Good-Looking," *BusinessWeek*, May 29, 2000, p. 192.

34. A. Barrett, B. Turek, and C. Faivre d'Arcier, "Bottoms Up—and Profits, Too," *BusinessWeek*, September 12, 2005, pp. 80–82; and C. Hajim, "Growth in Surprising Places," *Fortune*, September 5, 2005, bonus section.

35. J. Hovey, "25 Growing Companies," *Industry Week*, November 20, 2000, p. 66.

36. "Best Employer," *Working Woman*, May 1999, p. 54.

37. R. L. Heneman, J. W. Tansky, and S. J. Camp, "Human Resource Management Practices in Small and Medium-Sized Enterprises: Unanswered Questions and Future Research Perspectives," *Entrepreneurship Theory and Practice*, vol. 25, no. 1, pp. 11–26.

38. Based on G. Fuchsberg, "Small Firms Struggle with Latest Management Trends," *Wall Street Journal*, August 26, 1993, p. B2; M. Barrier, "Reengineering Your Company," *Nation's Business*, February 1994, pp. 16–22; J. Weiss, "Reengineering the Small Business," *Small Business Reports*, May 1994, pp. 37–43; and K. D. Godsey, "Back on Track," *Success*, May 1997, pp. 52–54.

39. S. Stecklow, "StubHub's Ticket to Ride," *Wall Street Journal*, January 17, 2006, pp. B1+.

40. G. N. Chandler, C. Keller, and D. W. Lyon, "Unraveling the Determinants and Consequences of an Innovation-Supportive Organizational Culture," *Entrepreneurship Theory and Practice*, Fall 2000, pp. 59–76.

41. Ibid.

42. P. Gogoi, "Pregnant with Possibility," *BusinessWeek*, December 26, 2005, p. 50.

43. Information from company's Web site [www.sapient.com], July 7, 2003; and S. Herrera, "People Power," *Forbes*, November 2, 1998, p. 212.

44. "Saluting the Global Awards Recipients of Arthur Andersen's Best Practices Awards 2000," *Fortune Online* [www.fortune.com], January 16, 2001.

45. T. Purdum, "Winning with Empowerment," *Industry Week*, October 16, 2000, pp. 109–110.

46. Company financial information from Hoover's Online [www.hoovers.com], July 13, 2006; and P. Strozniak, "Rescue Operation," *Industry Week*, October 16, 2000, pp. 103–104.

47. M. Depree, *Leadership Jazz* (New York: Dell, 1993).

48. J. C. Collins and J. I. Porras, *Built to Last: Successful Habits of Visionary Companies* (New York: Harper-Business, 1994).

49. P. Strozniak, "Teams at Work," *Industry Week*, September 18, 2000, pp. 47–50.

50. Ibid.

51. T. Siegel Bernard, "Scooter's Popularity Offers A Chance for Growth," *Wall Street Journal*, September 20, 2005, p. B3.

52. J. Bailey, "Growth Needs a Plan or Only Losses May Build," *Wall Street Journal*, October 29, 2002, p. B9; and L. Beresford, "Growing Up," *Entrepreneur*, July 1995, pp. 124–128.

53. R. D. Hof, "EBay's Rhine Gold," *BusinessWeek*, April 3, 2006, pp. 44–45.

54. J. Summer, "More, Please!" *Business Finance*, July 2000, pp. 57–61.

55. T. Stevens, "Pedal Pushers," *Industry Week*, July 17, 2000, pp. 46–52.

56. P. Lorange and R. T. Nelson, "How to Recognize—and Avoid—Organizational Decline," *Sloan Management Review*, Spring 1987, pp. 41–48.

57. S. D. Chowdhury and J. R. Lange, "Crisis, Decline, and Turnaround: A Test of Competing Hypotheses for Short-Term Performance Improvement in Small Firms," *Journal of Small Business Management*, October 1993, pp. 8–17.

58. C. Farrell, "How to Survive a Downturn," *BusinessWeek*, April 28, 1997, pp. ENT4–ENT6.

59. R. W. Pricer and A. C. Johnson, "The Accuracy of Valuation Methods in Predicting the Selling Price of Small Firms," *Journal of Small Business Management*, October 1997, pp. 24–35.

60. J. Bailey, "Selling the Firm and Letting Go of the Dream," *Wall Street Journal*, December 10, 2002, p. B6; P. Hernan, "Finding the Exit," *Industry Week*, July 17, 2000, pp. 55–61; D. Rodkin, "For Sale by Owner," *Entrepreneur*, January 1998, pp. 148–53; A. Livingston, "Avoiding Pitfalls When Selling a Business," *Nation's Business*, July 1998, pp. 25–26; and G. Gibbs Marullo, "Selling Your Business: A Preview of the Process," *Nation's Business*, August 1998, pp. 25–26.

61. K. Stringer, "Time Out," *Wall Street Journal*, March 27, 2002, p. R14; T. Stevens, "Striking a Balance," *Industry Week*, November 20, 2000, pp. 26–36; and S. Caudron, "Fit to Lead," *Industry Week*, July 17, 2000, pp. 63–68.

Name Index

Organization Index

Timken, 312

T-Mobile, 389, 389n44

Tom's Of Maine, 58

TOMS Shoes, 154, 154n101

Torrefazione It, 68

TOTAL, SA, 134

Towers Watson, 5, 5n5, 5n6, 382, 382n13, 490, 490n28

Toyota, 49n23, 236, 324, 382

Training, 394E13-8, 429n39, 484n12, 484n14, 525n89, 532n101

Transnational or Borderless Organization, 82, 82n48

Tsingtao Brewery, 191–192, 191n13

Turner Industries Group LLC, 114, 114n77

Twitter, 15, 15n38, 15n39, 257, 478, 478n1, 479

Tyson Foods, 59

U

UBS AG, 142, 142n58, 267

Ulsan plant, Hyundai Motor, 229

UN Global Compact, 140, 140n52

Under Armour (UA), 211–212

Unilever, 40, 81, 246, 295, 295n8

UniRush, 565

Unisys, 398, 411

Unite, 382, 382n14

United Airlines, 227, 298

United Nations, 140–141

United Parcel Service (UPS), 131, 133, 133n24, 134, 201, 201n47, 322, 368, 368n56, 408, 408n124, 488

United Plastics Group, 83, 83n52

United Technologies Corporation (UTC), 142

United Way, 6

Unity, 492, 492n37

Univenture Inc., 568

Universal Music Group, 565

University Hospital, Erlangen, Germany, 43

University of Arizona, 224

University of Cambridge, 536

University of Iowa, 537–538, 537n7, 538E18-2, 554

University of Michigan, 538E18-2, 539, 539n10, 554

U.S. Armed Forces, 457

U.S. Army, 388, 388n40

U.S. Bankruptcy Court (Southern District of New York), 154, 154n102

U.S. Bureau of Labor Statistics (BLS), 105, 105n24, 105n25, 398, 398n74, 411, 411n3, 411n4

U.S. Cellular, 502

U.S. Census Bureau, 7n15, 105–106, 105n21, 106n26, 110, 110n53, 111n55, 568n16

U.S. Coast Guard, 291

U.S. Congress, 307

U.S. Department of Defense, 187

U.S. Department of Education, 242, 242n12

U.S. Department of Justice, 140, 140n50

U.S. Department of Labor, 21, 112, 112E4-6, 112n57, 283, 283n52, 442

U.S. Equal Employment Opportunity Commission, 111, 399n85, 399n86

U.S. Federal Trade Commission, 246

U.S. Justice Department, 291

U.S. Military, 298, 332

U.S. National Institute of Occupational Safety and Health, 283

U.S. Navy Seals, 434

U.S. Postal Service (USPS), 192, 241–242, 242n9, 242n10

U.S. State Department, 104, 469

U.S. Small Business Administration, 566, 566n8

U.S. Small Business Administration's Office of Advocacy, 566, 566n7, 566n8, 566n9

U.S. Supreme Court, 383, 383n20, 400, 400n89

USA Today, 75n4, 105E4-3, 146n77, 240n2, 522n71, 564, 565

U.S.–Central America Free Trade Agreement (CAFTA), 78, 91

Uterqüe, 261

UTStarcom, 565

V

Valeo Klimasystemme GmbH, 321, 321n46

Verizon, 191, 191n11, 375, 400

Visa, 172–173, 264–266, 264n1

Volkswagen AG, 194n21, 398, 311, 311n10

Volkswagen Sweden, 194

Volvo, 299, 428

Volvo Construction Equipment, 298

Vurv Technology, 507

VZ-LIFE, 400, 400n97

W

W. L. Gore & Associates, 51, 51n27, 54, 380, 428

Wachovia, 148

Walgreen, 112, 112n58, 254

Wall Street, 46

Wall Street Journal, 2n1, 11n25, 113n73, 116, 116n82, 143n61, 154n101, 199n38, 267n6, 342, 373, 400, 400n90

Wall Street Journal Online, 128n1

Walmart, 16, 16n44, 16n45, 81, 81m47, 95, 132, 132n12, 224, 240, 240n3, 241, 245, 248, 249–250, 250, 254, 254n38, 279, 314, 314n21, 315–316, 346, 512, 512n32

Walt Disney Company, 279, 279n30

Waste Management, 555

Watson Wyatt, 367, 367n48, 550n57

Watson Wyatt Worldwide, 5n5, 380n4, 450n14, 453n39

Wayfair.com, 525, 525n83

Weather Channel, 385, 385n22

Weber Shandwick, 502

Wellmark Blue Cross & Blue Shield, 201, 321, 321n51

Wellness Corporate Solutions, 193

Wells Fargo, 322

Wendy's, 313, 319

Western Electric Company Works, 32, 32n7

Western Kentucky, 479

Western Provident Association, 494

Whirlpool, 343

White Castle, 180–181, 180n39, 555

Whole Foods Market, 34, 34n11, 251, 494, 546, 570, 570n27

Wild Oats Markets, 494

William Wrigley Jr. Co., 495, 495n53

Wilson Sporting Goods, 333, 333n6

Winter Olympics, 62

Wipro Limited, 229–230, 229n29

Women's Health, 495n55

Workforce Management Online, 284E10-13

Working Woman, 579n36

World Bank Group, 80, 80n41, 80n42, 81, 91

World Business Council for Sustainable Development (2005), 16

World Cup Games, 281

World Economic Forum, 46, 46n11, 136

World Factbook, The, 25n35, 77n20, 85, 85n62, 105, 105n22, 105n23, 310n3, 382n10

World Health Organization, 437

World Trade Organization (WTO), 80, 80n34, 89, 91

WorldCom, 136, 154

WorldNow, 56, 56n43

Wormald Security, 321, 321n45

Wyeth research division, 508, 510n20

X

Xerox, 59, 244, 358, 363, 363n32, 429

Xerox Innovation Group, 202

Y

Yahoo!, 2, 43, 343, 343n30, 378–380, 465

Yamaha Corporation of America, 402, 402n116

Yankee Candle, 555

YouTube, 15, 15n39, 67

Yum Brands Inc., 93, 525, 525n86

Z

Zappos.com, 65–66, 65n66, 313, 452, 452n24, 484, 484n11, 520n55

Zara, 261–262, 261n44

Zimbabwe, 84, 84n54

Zimmer Holdings, 568–569, 568n16

Zippo Manufacturing, 48

Zynga, 2–4, 2n1, 6

Glindex

social, 147

social responsibility issues facing, 567–568

Entrepreneurship   *The process of starting new businesses, generally in response to opportunities,* 565

context of, 565–568

defined, 565

global, 566

growth of, 583–585, 585EA–5

importance of, 565–566

process of, 566–567

Environment. *See also* external environment

assessment of, 294–298

competitive advantage and, 568–570

dynamic, 48

global, 76–79

organizational strategies for today's, 253–254

political, 83–84

stable, 48

Environmental complexity   *The number of components in an organization's environment and the extent of the organization's knowledge about those components,* 48–49

Environmentalism, 133–134

Environmental scanning   *Screening information to detect emerging trends,* 230, 294–296

competitor intelligence and, 295

global scanning and, 295–296

Environmental uncertainty   *The degree of change and complexity in an organization's environment,* 48–50, 49E2–3, 344

Equal employment opportunity laws, 117, 117E4–8

Equal opportunity, 116–117

Equity, 516

Equity theory   *The theory that an employee compares his or her job's input-outcomes ratio with that of relevant others and then corrects any inequity,* 515–517, 516E17–7, 521

Escalation of commitment   *An increased commitment to a previous decision despite evidence it may have been wrong,* 167

Esteem needs   *A person's needs for internal factors such as self-respect, autonomy, and achievement, and external factors such as status, recognition, and attention,* 507

Ethical behavior

encouraging, 141–146

factors for determining, 136–139, 137E5–3

of managers, 136–141

Ethical communication   *Communication that includes all relevant information, is true in every sense, and is not deceptive in any way,* 497

Ethical dilemmas, 142–144, 144E5–8

Ethical leadership, 146, 147E5–9

Ethics   *Principles, values, and beliefs that define what is right and wrong behavior,* 136

codes of, 142–144, 143E5–7

entrepreneurs, issues facing, 567–568

international, 139–141

social responsibilities and, 146–148

training on, 145

Ethnicity   *Social traits (such as cultural background or allegiance) that are shared by a human population,* 110

Ethnocentric attitude   *The parochialistic belief that the best work approaches and practices are those of the home country,* 75

Euro   *A single common European currency,* 77

European Commission, 77

European Union (EU)   *A union of 27 European nations created as a unified economic and trade entity,* 76–77, 76E3–1

problems in, 77

Euro zone, 77

Events   *End points that represent the completion of major activities in a PERT network,* 301, 302EPCM–8

Evidence-based management (EBMgt)   *The systematic use of the best available evidence to improve management practice,* 168–169

Excellence in Communication Leadership (EXCEL) Award, 481

Executive summary, 574

Expectancy, 517

Expectancy theory   *The theory that an individual tends to act in a certain way based on the expectation that the act will be followed by a given outcome and on the attractiveness of that outcome to the individual,* 517–518, 517E17–8

Expected value, 172, 172E6–8

Expenses, 299

Expert power   *Power that's based on expertise, special skills, or knowledge,* 548

Exporting   *Making products domestically and selling them abroad,* 82, 82E3–3

External analysis, 242–243

External boundaries, 359

External collaboration, 364–365, 364E12–5

External environment   *Those factors and forces outside the organization that affect its performance,* 44–50, 44E2–2

challenges of, 44–50

components of, 44, 44E2–2

constraints of, 44–50

demographic environment and, 46–47

economic environment and, 45–46

employment and, 47–48

environmental uncertainty and, 48–50, 49E2–3

managers, effect on, 47–50

stakeholders, relationships with, 50

External forces for change, 188, 188E7–1

External locus of control, 457–458

External relationships, 515

External support, 431–432

Extinction, 468

Extraversion, 456, 457

F

Face-to-face communication, 485, 491, 496

Factor-driven economies, 566

Family-friendly benefits   *Benefits that accommodate employees' needs for work-life balance,* 400

Feasibility of entrepreneurial ventures, 571–573

competitors and, 573

evaluation of ideas and, 571–573

financing and, 573

Feasibility region, 305

Feasibility study   *An analysis of the various aspects of a proposed entrepreneurial venture designed to determine its feasibility,* 572, 572EA–2

Feedback   *The degree to which carrying out work activities required by a job results in the individual's obtaining direct and clear information about his or her performance effectiveness,* 273, 482, 485–486, 514–515

Feedback control   *Control that takes place after a work activity is done,* 275E10–9, 276

Feedforward control   *Control that takes place before a work activity is done,* 275, 275E10–9

Feelings, 456

Fiedler contingency model   *A leadership theory proposing that effective group performance depends on the proper match between a leader's style and the degree to which the situation allows the leader to control and influence,* 540–541, 541E18–3

Filtering   *The deliberate manipulation of information to make it appear more favorable to the receiver,* 484

Financial-based pressures, 282

Financial controls, 276–277, 277E10–10

Financial data, 575

Financial reporting, 286

Financing of entrepreneurial ventures, 573

First-line managers   *Managers at the lowest level of management who manage the work of nonmanagerial employees,* 6E1–1, 7

First mover   *An organization that's first to bring a product innovation to the market or to use a new process innovation,* 255, 255E9–6

Five forces model for competitive advantage, 249

Fixed costs, 303

Flexibility, 306, 316–317, 365–367, 414, 522–523

strategic, 252–253, 253E9–5

Flexible work hours   *A scheduling system in which employees are required to work a specific number of hours a week but are free to vary those hours within certain limits,* 367

Flextime   *A scheduling system in which employees are required to work a specific number of hours a week but are free to vary those hours within certain limits,* 367

Focused work, 491

Focus strategy, 250

Follower, 543

Forecasting, 296–298

effectiveness of, 296–298

qualitative, 296, 297EPCM–1

quantitative, 296, 297EPCM–1

techniques for, 296, 297EPCM–1

Forecasts   *Predictions of outcomes,* 296, 297EPCM–1. *See also* forecasting

Foreign Corrupt Practices Act (FCPA), 140

Foreign subsidiary   *Directly investing in a foreign country by setting up a separate and independent production facility or office,* 82, 82E3–3

Formal communication   *Communication that takes place within prescribed organizational work arrangements,* 488

Formality, 482

Formalization   *How standardized an organization's jobs are and the extent to which employee behavior is guided by rules and procedures,* 332, 341–342

Formal planning. *See* plans/planning

Formal planning department   *A group of planning specialists whose sole responsibility is helping to write organizational plans,* 228

Formal status, 423

Formal work groups, 418, 418E14–1

Organizational performance   *The accumulated results of all the organization's work activities*
defined, 271
managerial controls for, 271–273
measuring of, 271–273
workforce diversity management and, 103–104
Organizational processes   *The ways that organizational work is done,* 315–316, 315EMOM–2
Organizational stories, 55–56
Organizational strategies. *See also* strategies
customer service strategies and, 254
e-business strategies and, 253–254
innovation strategies and, 254–255
organizational design and, 343
strategic management process and, 242
for today's environment, 253–254
Organizational structure   *The formal arrangement of jobs within an organization,* 199, 332. *See also* structure
centralization and, 332, 339–341, 340E11–7
chain of command and, 332, 334–339
decentralization and, 332, 339–341, 340E11–7
departmentalization and, 332, 334
formalization and, 332, 341–342
issues of, 575–580
organizational design and, 578
organizational design of, 332–342
span of control and, 332, 339, 339E11–6, 342
work specialization and, 332, 333–334, 333E11–2
Organization for Economic Cooperation and Development (OECD)   *An international economic organization that helps its 30 member countries achieve sustainable economic growth and employment,* 80–81
Organizing   *Arranging and structuring work to accomplish the organization's goals,* 9, 9E1–4, 332, 332E11–1
Oriental culture, 196
Orientation   *Introducing a new employee to his or her job and the organization,* 393
of employees, 392–393
future, 88
humane, 87
of organization, 393
performance, 88
sexual, 113–114
work unit, 393
Overconfidence bias, 175

P

Parochialism   *Viewing the world solely through your own perspectives, leading to an inability to recognize differences between people,* 75
Participating leadership style, 542
Participative leader, 543
Path-goal theory   *A leadership theory that says the leader's job is to assist followers in attaining their goals and to provide direction or support needed to ensure that their goals are compatible with the goals of the group or organization,* 542–544, 543E18–4
Patient Protection and Affordable Care Act (PPACA), 383
Pay-for-performance programs   *Variable compensation plans that pay employees on the basis of some performance measure,* 525–526

Payoff matrix, 172, 172E6–9
Pension plan costs for employees, 403
People. *See* employees
Perceived organizational support   *Employees' general belief that their organization values their contribution and cares about their well-being,* 452
Perception   *A process by which we give meaning to our environment by organizing and interpreting sensory impressions,* 456, 463, 463–466
attribution theory and, 464–465, 465E15–6
factors influencing, 463, 464E15–5
judgment and, 465
managerial implications and, 466
organizational behaviors and, 463–466
Perceptual changes, 570
Performance   *The end result of an activity,* 268E10–3, 271. *See also* employee performance; organizational performance
actual, 268–270, 268E10–3
appraisal methods for, 395, 396E13–10
feedback on, 273
planning and, 221
reviews of, 144–145
standard, 269–270
Performance management system   *Establishes performance standards used to evaluate employee performance,* 395
Performance orientation, 88
Performance planning programs, 200
Performance-reward, 517
Performing stage   *The fourth stage of group development when the group is fully functional and works on group task,* 418–419, 419E14–2
Persistence, 506
Personal achievement, 5
Personal bias, 114–116
Personal interaction on Internet, 495
Personality   *The unique combination of emotional, thought, and behavioral patterns that affect how a person reacts to situations and interacts with others,* 420–421, 455–463
Big Five Model of, 457
cultural, 459–460
dominant, 459
emotional intelligence and, 460–461
emotions and, 460–461
of entrepreneurs, 580–581
insights on, 457–459
managerial implications and, 462–463, 462E15–4
MBTI® assessment of, 456–457
proactive, 458–459, 581
Type A, 459
Type B, 459
Personality-job fit, Holland's, 462, 462E15–4
Personality traits. *See* personality
Personal life choices, 586–587
PERT network   *A flowchart diagram showing the sequence of activities needed to complete a project and the time or cost associated with each,* 301–303, 302EPCM–7, 302EPCM–8, 303EPCM–9
Physical attractiveness, 114
Physiological needs   *A person's needs for food, drink, shelter, sexual satisfaction, and other physical needs,* 507

Plan   *Documents that outline how goals are going to be met,* 221, 223E8–1. *See also* managerial planning; planning
directional, 223, 223E8–1
long-term, 223, 223E8–1
operational, 223, 223E8–1
recovery, 228
short-term, 223, 223E8–1
single-use, 223E8–1, 224
specific, 223, 223E8–1
standing, 223E8–1, 224–225
strategic, 223, 223E8–1
Planned economy   *An economic system in which economic decisions are planned by a central government,* 84
Planning   *Management function that involves setting goals, establishing strategies for achieving those goals, and developing plans to integrate and coordinate activities,* 9, 9E1–4, 220. *See also* managerial planning; plans
approaches to, 228
contemporary issues in, 229–230
contingency, 227–228, 307
controlling and, link between, 267, 267E10–1
control techniques and, 306–308, 306EPCM–13
defined, 220
developing, 227–228
for entrepreneurial growth, 583–584
foundations of, 218–230
goals and, 221–224
human resource, 387
performance and, 221
for quality, 320
startup and, 568–575
types of, 222–224, 223E8–1
Policy   *A guideline for making decisions,* 170
Political environment, 83–84
Polycentric attitude   *The view that the managers in the host country know the best work approaches and practices for running their business,* 75
Position power   *One of Fiedler's situational contingencies that describes the degree of influence a leader has over activities such as hiring, firing, discipline, promotions, and salary increases,* 540
Post-Millennials, 46, 47
Potential stress, 198
Power, 509, 540, 548–549. *See also* specific types of
Power distance, 87
Prejudice   *A preconceived belief, opinion, or judgment toward a person or a group of people,* 114
Principles of management   *Fundamental rules of management that could be applied in all organizational situations and taught in schools,* 30, 30EMH–3
Proactive personality   *People who identify opportunities, show initiative, take action, and persevere until meaningful change occurs,* 458–459, 581
Proactive perspective of work design   *An approach to job design in which employees take the initiative to change how their work is performed,* 515
Problem   *An obstacle that makes it difficult to achieve a desired goal or purpose,* 162
decision-making and identification of, 162–163

Problem-solving team   *A team from the same department or functional area that's involved in efforts to improve work activities or to solve specific problems,* 429

Procedural justice   *Perceived fairness of the process used to determine the distribution of rewards,* 516

Procedure   *A series of sequential steps used to respond to a well-structured problem,* 170

Process conflict   *Conflict over how work gets done,* 426

Process development, 255

Process need, 569

Process production   *The production of items in continuous processes,* 344, 344E11–9

Production. *See also* productivity
   capacity of, 304–305, 305EPCM–11
   mass, 344, 344E11–9
   process, 344, 344E11–9
   unit, 344, 344E11–9

Production-oriented leaders, 539

Productivity   *The amount of goods or services produced divided by the inputs needed to generate that output,* 272. *See also* production
   job satisfaction, 451
   operations management of, 311–312
   organizational, 272

Products
   country of ownership origin for, 74–75
   radical development of, 566
   replenishment rates for, 315

Professionals, motivation of, 523

Programmed decision   *A repetitive decision that can be handled by a routine approach,* 170, 171E6–7

Project   *A one-time-only set of activities that has a definite beginning and ending point in time,* 306, 306EPCM–13, 358

Project management   *The task of getting a projects activities done on time, within budget, and according to specifications,* 306–307, 306EPCM–13

Project structure   *An organizational structure in which employees continuously work on projects,* 358

Protective mechanisms, 145–146

Psychological capital, 90E3–6

"Pulse lunches," 494

Punishment, 468

Q

Qualitative forecasting   *Forecasting that uses the judgment and opinions of knowledgeable individuals to predict outcomes,* 296, 297EPCM–1

Quality   *The ability of a product or service to reliably do what it's supposed to do and to satisfy customer expectations,* 320
   as competitive advantage, 248
   controlling for, 320–321
   of fill, 390
   goals for, 321–322
   initiatives for, 319–321
   leading for, 320
   organizing for, 320
   planning for, 320

Quantitative approach   *The use of quantitative techniques to improve decision making,* 33–34

Quantitative forecasting   *Forecasting that applies a set of mathematical rules to a series of past data to predict outcome,* 296, 297EPCM–1

Question marks, 247

R

Race   *The biological heritage (including skin color and associated traits) that people use to identify themselves,* 110

Radical product development, 566

Radio-frequency identification (RFID), 278

Randomness bias, 175

Range of variation   *The acceptable parameters of variance between actual performance and the standard,* 269, 269E10–1

Rational decision making   *Describes choices that are logical and consistent and maximize value,* 166–167

Readiness   *The extent to which people have the ability and willingness to accomplish a specific task,* 541–542

"Ready-fire-aim" culture, 57

Real goals   *Goals that an organization actually pursues, as defined by the actions of its members,* 222

Realistic job preview (RJP)   *A preview of a job that provides both positive and negative information about the job and the company,* 390–391

Recovery plans, 228

Recruitment   *Locating, identifying, and attracting capable applicants,* 388
   of employees, 388, 388E13–4, 579

Redesigning, 515

Referent power   *Power that arises because of a person's desirable resources or personal traits,* 548

Referents   *The persons, systems, or selves against which individuals compare themselves to assess equity,* 516, 516E17–7

Refreezing, 189

Regional trading alliances
   African Union, 79
   Association of Southeast Asian Nations, 78–79, 79E3–2
   Central America Free Trade Agreement, 78
   East African Community, 79
   European Union, 76–77, 76E3–1
   Free Trade Area of the Americas, 78
   in global environment, 76–79
   North American Free Trade Agreement, 77–78
   South Asian Association for Regional Cooperation, 79

Regret matrix, 173, 173E6–10

Reinforcement processes, 468

Reinforcement theory   *The theory that behavior is a function of its consequences,* 512–513, 525

Reinforcers   *Consequences immediately following a behavior, which increase the probability that the behavior will be repeated,* 512

Reinvention of self, 413

Relational perspective of work design   *An approach to job design that focuses on how people's tasks and jobs are increasingly based on social relationships,* 515

Relationship conflict   *Conflict based on interpersonal relationships,* 426

Relationship oriented leaders, 540–541

Relevant skills, 430

Reliability of employee selection, 390

Religion, 112–113

Renewal strategy   *A corporate strategy designed to address declining performance,* 246–247

Representation bias, 175

Resilience   *An individual's ability to overcome challenges and turn them into opportunities,* 458

Resistance to change
   of employees, 194
   management of, 194–196
   reduction techniques for, 195–196, 196E7–5
   sources of, 195
   types of, 195

Resource   *An organization's assets that are used to develop, manufacture, and deliver products to its customers,* 243, 299

Resource allocation, 299–305
   breakeven analysis and, 303–304, 304EPCM–10
   budget/budgeting and, 299–300
   linear programming and, 304–306, 305EPCM–12
   scheduling and, 300–303

Responsibility   *The obligation or expectation to perform any assigned duties,* 337. *See also* social responsibility
   of chain of command, 334, 337–338
   of managers, 7–13

Restraining forces, 189

Retention of employees, 395–397, 579

Retention processes, 467

Retrenchment strategy, 246–247

Revenues, 299

Reverse engineering, 295

Reward attractiveness, 517

Reward power   *The power a leader has to give positive rewards,* 548

Reward programs, 524–526

Risk   *A situation in which the decision maker is able to estimate the likelihood of certain outcomes,* 172, 172E6–8

"Risk-control freak," 57

Risk-taking, 412, 458–459

Role   *Behavior patterns expected of someone occupying a given position in a social unit,* 420

Role ambiguity   *When role expectations are not clearly understood,* 199

Role conflicts   *Work expectations that are hard to satisfy,* 199, 421

Role demands, 199

Role overload   *Having more work to accomplish than time permits,* 199

Rolling forecasts, 298

Rule   *An explicit statement that tells managers what can or cannot be done,* 170

S

Sadness, 461

Safety needs   *A person's needs for security and protection from physical and emotional harm,* 507

Sarbanes-Oxley Act, 147, 286

Satisfaction *vs.* dissatisfaction, 509, 509E17–3

Satisfice   *Accept solutions that are "good enough,"* 167

Scanability, 482

Scenario   *A consistent view of what the future is likely to be,* 307–308

Scheduling *Detailing what activities have to be done, the order in which they are to be completed, who is to do each, and when they are to be completed,* 300–303
Gantt chart for, 300–301, 300EPCM–5
load charts for, 301, 301EPCM–6
PERT network for, 301–303, 302EPCM–7, 302EPCM–8, 303EPCM–9

Scientific management *An approach that involves using the scientific method to find the "one best way" for a job to be done,* 27EMH–1, 28–29, 29EMH–2

S corporation *A specialized type of corporation that has the regular characteristics of a C corporation but is unique in that the owners are taxed as a partnership as long as certain criteria are met,* 576, 577EA–4

Security, 369, 494
Segmentation, 402

Selection *Screening job applicants to ensure that the most appropriate candidates are hired,* 142, 389–391, 389E13–6

Selective perception bias, 175

Self-actualization needs *A person's need to become what he or she is capable of becoming,* 507

Self-awareness, 461

Self-efficacy *An individual's belief that he or she is capable of performing a task,* 511, 512E17–5

Self-esteem *An individual's degree of like or dislike for himself or herself,* 458

Self-managed work team *A type of work team that operates without a manager and is responsible for a complete work process or segment,* 429

Self-management, 461

Self-monitoring *A personality trait that measures the ability to adjust behavior to external situational factors,* 458

Self-motivation, 461

Self-serving bias *The tendency for individuals to attribute their own successes to internal factors while putting the blame for failures on external factors,* 175, 465

Selling leadership style, 542
Sensing, 456

Service organizations *Organizations that produce nonphysical products in the form of services,* 310

Service profit chain *The service sequence from employees to customers to profit,* 285

Sexual harassment *Any unwanted action or activity of a sexual nature that explicitly or implicitly affects an individual's employment, performance, or work environment,* 398–400

Sexual orientation, 113–114
Shades of green, 134

Shaping behavior *The process of guiding learning in graduated steps using reinforcement or lack of reinforcement,* 468

Shift managers, 6

Short-term plans *Plans covering one year or less,* 223, 223E8–1

"Sick" days, 451
Silent employees, 414
Simple organizational design, 345, 345E11–10

Simple structure *An organizational design with low departmentalization, wide spans of control, centralized authority, and little formalization,* 345, 345E11–10

Single-use plan *A one-time plan specifically designed to meet the needs of a unique situation,* 223E8–1, 224

Situational approach. *See* contingency approach

Situational leadership theory (SLT) *A leadership contingency theory that focuses on followers' readiness,* 541–542

Six Sigma *A quality program designed to reduce defects and help lower costs, save time, and improve customer satisfaction,* 321–322

Skill-based pay *A pay system that rewards employees for the job skills they can demonstrate,* 397

Skill variety *The degree to which a job requires a variety of activities so that an employee can use a number of different skills and talents,* 514

Slack time *The amount of time an individual activity can be delayed without delaying the whole project,* 301

Small business *An organization that is independently owned, operated, and financed; has fewer than 100 employees; doesn't necessarily engage in any new or innovative practices; and has relatively little impact on its industry,* 565

Social capital, 90E3–6
Social changes, 148

Social entrepreneur *An individual or organization who seeks out opportunities to improve society by using practical, innovative, and sustainable approaches,* 147–148

Social entrepreneurship, 147–148

Socialization *The process that helps employees adapt to the organization's culture,* 54, 54E2–8, 491

Social learning theory *A theory of learning that says people can learn through observation and direct experience,* 467–468

Social loafing *The tendency for individuals to expend less effort when working collectively than when working individually,* 423, 433

Socially responsible investing (SRI), 133

Social media *Forms of electronic communication through which users create online communities to share ideas, information, personal messages, and other content,* 15–16

Social needs *A person's needs for affection, belongingness, acceptance, and friendship,* 507

Social Networking Online Protection Act (SNOPA), 383

Social network structure *The patterns of informal connections among individuals within a group,* 434

Social obligation *When a firm engages in social actions because of its obligation to meet certain economic and legal responsibilities,* 130–132

Social responsibility *A business's intention, beyond its legal and economic obligations, to do the right things and act in ways that are good for society,* 131, 132E5–1
concept of, 130
defined, 130–133
entrepreneurs, issues facing, 567–568
ethics and, 146–148
lapses in, 146–147, 147E5–9
of organizations, 132–133, 132E5–1
social changes and, 148

social entrepreneurship and, 147–148
social obligations and, 130–132
social responsiveness and, 130–132

Social responsiveness *When a firm engages in social actions in response to some popular social need,* 130–132

Social screening *Applying social criteria (screens) to investment decisions,* 133

Social skills, 461

Socioeconomic view *The view that management's social responsibility goes beyond making profits to include protecting and improving society's welfare,* 114, 131

Sole proprietorship *A form of legal organization in which the owner maintains sole and complete control over the business and is personally liable for business debts,* 576, 577EA–4

South Asian Association for Regional Cooperation (SAARC), 79

Span of control *The number of employees a manager can efficiently and effectively manage,* 332, 339, 339E11–6, 342

"Special treatment," 113

Specific plans *Plans that are clearly defined and leave no room for interpretation,* 223, 223E8–1

Spirituality, 59–60

Stability strategy *A corporate strategy in which an organization continues to do what it is currently doing,* 246

Stable environment, 48

Staff authority *Positions with some authority that have been created to support, assist, and advise those holding line authority,* 337, 337E11–5

Stakeholders *Any constituencies in the organization's environment that are affected by an organization's decisions and actions,* 50, 50E2–4
external environment, relationship with, 50
going green, approaches to, 134–135
organizational, 50, 50E2–4

Standard performance, 269–270

Standing plans *Ongoing plans that provide guidance for activities performed repeatedly,* 223E8–1, 224–225

Stars, 247
Startups, 566. *See also* entrepreneurial venture
controlling issues in, 583–587
leading issues in, 580–583
organizing issues in, 575–580
planning issues and, 569–575

Stated goals *Official statements of what an organization says, and what it wants its various stakeholders to believe, its goals are,* 222

Status *A prestige grading, position, or rank within a group,* 422–423, 433. *See also* specific types of

Stereotyping *Judging a person based on a perception of a group to which that person belongs,* 115, 465

Stimulation
change and, 579–580
innovation and, 202–206
nurturing and, 203

STOP (Safety Training Observation Program), 551

Storming stage *The second stage of group development, characterized by intragroup conflict,* 418–419, 419E14–2

Total quality management (TQM) *A philosophy of management that is driven by continuous improvement and responsiveness to customer needs and expectations,* 34, 34MH–6, 206

Town hall meeting *Informal public meetings where information can be relayed, issues can be discussed, or just as a way to bring employees together to celebrate accomplishments,* 488

Toxic assets, 45

Traditional goal-setting *An approach to setting goals in which top managers set goals that then flow down through the organization and become subgoals for each organizational area,* 224, 225E8–2

Traditional view of conflict *The view that all conflict is bad and must be avoided,* 425

Transactional leaders *Leaders who lead primarily by using social exchanges (or transactions),* 545

Transformational leaders *Leaders who stimulate and inspire (transform) followers to achieve extraordinary outcomes,* 545

Transnational organization *An MNC in which artificial geographical barriers are eliminated,* 81–82

Trust *The belief in the integrity, character, and ability of a leader,* 549–550, 550E18–6

Turn-around strategy, 247

Turnover *The voluntary and involuntary permanent withdrawal from an organization,* 449

Two-factor theory *The motivation theory that intrinsic factors are related to job satisfaction and motivation, whereas extrinsic factors are associated with job dissatisfaction,* 508–509, 509E17–2, 509E17–3

Two Sigma, 321

Type A personality *People who have a chronic sense of urgency and an excessive competitive drive,* 199, 459

Type B personality *People who are relaxed and easygoing and accept change easily,* 199, 459

U

Uncertainty *A situation in which a decision maker has neither certainty nor reasonable probability estimates available,* 87, 172–173, 172E6–9, 172E6–10

avoiding, 87

Unexpected opportunities, 569

Unfreezing, 189

Unified commitment, 431

UN Global Compact, 140–141, 141E5–6

U.S. population characteristics, 104–107, 105E4–3

Unit production *The production of items in units or small batches,* 344, 344E11–9

Unity of command *The management principle that each person should report to only one manager,* 334, 338

Universality of management *The reality that management is needed in all types and sizes of organizations, at all organizational levels, in all organizational areas, and in organizations no matter where located,* 17, 17E1–9

University of Iowa studies on leadership behavior theories, 537 539

University of Michigan studies, 539

Unprecedented rate, 106

Unstructured problems *Problems that are new or unusual and for which information is ambiguous or incomplete,* 170–171, 171E6–7

Upward communication *Communication that flows upward from employees to managers,* 488

Upward flow, 488

V

Valence, 517

Validity of employee selection, 390

Value *The performance characteristics, features, and attributes, and any other aspects of goods and services for which customers are willing to give up resources,* 137, 313

Value chain *The entire series of organizational work activities that add value at each step from raw materials to finished product,* 313, 315EMOM–2

Value chain management *The process of managing the sequence of activities and information along the entire value chain,* 313, 315EMOM–2, 317EMOM–3. *See also* value chain strategy

benefits of, 314

concepts of, 312–313

defined, 312–313, 313–314

goal of, 313–314

importance of, 312–313

obstacles to, 317–318, 317EMOM–3

requirements for, 314, 315EMOM–2

using operations management, 314–318

Value chain strategy, 314–317

attitudes and, 317

collaboration and, 314–315

coordination and, 314–315

employee/human resources and, 316–317

leadership and, 316

organizational culture and, 317

organizational processes and, 315–316

technology investment and, 315

Values-based management *The organization's values guide employees in the way they do their jobs,* 139

Variable cost (VC), 303

Variable pay *A pay system in which an individual's compensation is contingent on performance,* 397

Venture capitalists *External equity financing provided by professionally managed pools of investor money,* 574, 574EA–3

Verbal intonation *An emphasis given to words or phrases that conveys meaning,* 484

Vertical integration, 245

Vertical job expansion, 515

Vice-based pressures, 282

Virtual organization *An organization that consists of a small core of full-time employees and outside specialists temporarily hired as needed to work on projects,* 359

Virtual team *A type of work team that uses technology to link physically dispersed members in order to achieve a common goal,* 430

Viruses, 278

Vision, 546

Visionary leadership *The ability to create and articulate a realistic, credible, and attractive vision of the future that improves upon the present situation,* 546

"Vision-creation," 552

Volunteering by employees, 148

W

"War stories," 363

Weaknesses *Activities the organization does not do well or resources it needs but does not possess,* 52, 54E2–7, 242E9–1, 243, 345, 345E11–10

Webcams, 369

Web-conferencing, 366

Weight and diversity, 114

Wellness programs, 201

Well-written goals, 226, 226E8–4

Wheel network, 489

Whistle-blower *Individuals who raise ethical concerns or issues to others,* 147

White-water rapids metaphor, 189–190

Wireless capabilities, 493

Work arrangements, 365–367

Work councils *Groups of nominated or elected employees who must be consulted when management makes decisions involving personnel,* 385

Work design, 515. *See also* organizational design

Workforce. *See* workplace

Workforce diversity *The ways in which people in an organization are different from and similar to one another,* 98–120, 101, 101E4–1, 102E4–2, 522–523. *See also* Diversity

benefits of, 102, 102E4–2

changing trends in, 104–107, 105E4–3, 107E4–4

defined, 100–102

evolution of, timeline for, 100, 101E4–1

initiatives for, 117–120

legal aspect of, 117–118, 117E4–8

management of, 102–104

challenges in, 114–116

commitment to, 118

organizational performance and, 103–104

people management and, 102–103

strategic benefits of, 104

types of, 107–114, 108E4–5

Work groups. *See also* groups

formal, 418, 418E14–1

informal, 418

performance/satisfaction model for, 420–427, 420E14–3

Working from home, 365–366

Work-life balance, 400–402

Workplace

behavioral management in, 470

contingent, 368–369

design of, 490–491

employee concerns in, 281–282, 283E10–12

independent, 368

misbehavior in, 452

privacy in, 281–282

romances in, 400

violence in, 282–285, 284E10–13

Workplace misbehavior *Any intentional employee behavior that is potentially damaging to the organization or to individuals within the organization,* 449

Workplace spirituality *A culture where organizational values promote a sense of purpose through meaningful work that takes place in the context of community,* 59

Work specialization *Dividing work activities into separate job tasks,* 332, 333–334, 333E11–2

Work teams *Groups whose members work intensely on a specific, common goal using their positive synergy, individual and mutual accountability, and complementary skills,* 428E14–9, 429. *See also* specific types of
characteristics of effective, 430–432, 430E14–10
defined, 428–429
groups, turning into, 428–432, 428E14–9
leading, 583
types of, 429–430

Work unit orientation, 393

World Bank Group *A group of five closely associated institutions that provides financial and technical assistance to developing countries,* 80–81

World-oriented view, 75–76

World Trade Organization (WTO) *A global organization of 153 countries that deals with the rules of trade among nations,* 80

Wraparound mortgages, 45